EXECUTIVE OFFICE OF THE PRESIDENT
OFFICE OF MANAGEMENT AND BUDGET

NORTH AMERICAN INDUSTRY CLASSIFICATION SYSTEM

United States, 1997

Dedication

The Office of Management and Budget (OMB) is indebted to the many individuals and organizations whose vision, insights, and energies have made NAICS United States a reality.

This NAICS United States manual is dedicated to the memory of **William C. Bennett, Jr.,** *of the Bureau of Labor Statistics who chaired the Business and Personal Services Subcommittee until his death.*

This product is the result of collaboration and a partnership between Bernan Press and the Department of Commerce's National Technical Information Service (NTIS). Users of the product are advised that subsequent updates, additions and notifications of alteration with answers to frequently asked questions can be found on the site http://www.ntis.gov/naics as listed on each page of the publication. Additional copies may be conveniently ordered from Bernan Press, NTIS, or through most major book outlets.

Bernan Press is an imprint of Bernan Associates, a division of The Kraus Organization Limited

Published 1998
Printed in the United States of America

01 00 99 98   4 3 2

Bernan Press
4611-F Assembly Drive
Lanham, MD 20706-4391
(800) 274-4447
e-mail: info@bernan.com

National Technical Information Service
5285 Port Royal Road
Springfield, VA 22161
(800) 553-6847
e-mail: info@ntis.fedworld.gov

This official product is released as available in these formats:

Hardcover ISBN 0-89059-097-4   (NTIS Order Number: PB98-127293)
Softcover ISBN 0-89059-098-2   (NTIS Order Number: PB98-136187)
CD-ROM version ISBN 0-934213-55-0   (NTIS Order Number: PB98-502024)

Foreword

The contents of this volume mark an important landmark in the history of the statistical offices that made its creation possible. The Instituto Nacional de Estadística, Geografía e Informática (INEGI) of Mexico, Statistics Canada, and the United States Office of Management and Budget, through its Economic Classification Policy Committee, have jointly developed a system of classification of economic activities that will make the industrial statistics produced in the three countries comparable. The new North American Industry Classification System (NAICS) is scheduled to go into effect for reference year 1997 in Canada and the United States, and 1998 in Mexico. It was developed to provide a consistent framework for the collection, analysis and dissemination of industrial statistics used by government policy analysts, by academics and researchers, by the business community, and by the public.

Classifications serve as a lens through which to view the data they classify. NAICS is the first industry classification system that was developed in accordance with a single principle of aggregation, the principle that producing units that use similar production processes should be grouped together. NAICS also reflects, in a much more explicit way, the enormous changes in technology and in the growth and diversification of services that have marked recent decades. Though NAICS differs from other industry classification systems, statistics compiled on NAICS are comparable with statistics compiled according to the latest revision of the United Nations' International Standard Industrial Classification (ISIC, Revision 3) for some sixty high level groupings.

The actual classification reveals only the tip of the work carried out by dedicated staff from INEGI, Statistics Canada, and U.S. statistical agencies. It is through their efforts, painstaking analysis, and spirit of accommodation that NAICS has emerged as a harmonized international classification of economic activities.

Ivan P. Fellegi
Statistics Canada

Carlos M. Jarque
Instituto Nacional de
Estadística, Geografía e
Informática, Mexico

Katherine K. Wallman
United States Office of
Management and Budget

Preface

Statistics Canada, Mexico's Instituto Nacional de Estadística, Geografía e Informática (INEGI), and the Economic Classification Policy Committee (ECPC) of the United States, acting on behalf of the Office of Management and Budget, have created a common classification system to replace the existing classification of each country, the Standard Industrial Classification (1980) of Canada, the Mexican Classification of Activities and Products (1994), and the Standard Industrial Classification (1987) of the United States.

The North American Industry Classification System (NAICS) is unique among industry classifications in that it is constructed within a single conceptual framework. Economic units that have similar production processes are classified in the same industry, and the lines drawn between industries demarcate, to the extent practicable, differences in production processes. This supply-based, or production-oriented, economic concept was adopted for NAICS because an industry classification system is a framework for collecting and publishing information on both inputs and outputs, for statistical uses that require that inputs and outputs be used together and be classified consistently. Examples of such uses include measuring productivity, unit labor costs, and the capital intensity of production, estimating employment-output relationships, constructing input-output tables, and other uses that imply the analysis of production relationships in the economy. The classification concept for NAICS will produce data that facilitate such analyses.

In the design of NAICS, attention was given to developing production-oriented classifications for (a) new and emerging industries, (b) service industries in general, and (c) industries engaged in the production of advanced technologies. These special emphases are embodied in the particular features of NAICS, discussed below. These same areas of special emphasis account for many of the differences between the structure of NAICS and the structures of industry classification systems in use elsewhere. NAICS provides enhanced industry comparability among the three NAFTA trading partners, while also increasing compatibility with the two-digit level of the International Standard Industrial Classification (ISIC Rev.3) of the United Nations.

NAICS divides the economy into twenty sectors. Industries within these sectors are grouped according to the production criterion. Though the goods/services distinction is not explicitly reflected in the structure of NAICS, five sectors are largely goods-producing and fifteen are entirely services-producing industries.

A new feature of NAICS is the creation of an Information sector that groups industries that primarily create and disseminate a product subject to copyright. The NAICS Information sector brings together those activities that transform information into a commodity that is produced and distributed, and activities that provide the means for distributing those products, other than through traditional wholesale-retail distribution channels. A few of the new and important industries in this sector include: software publishing; database and directory publishing; satellite telecommunications; paging, cellular and other wireless telecommunications; and on-line information and other information services. Also included in the Information sector are newspaper, book, and periodical publishing (formerly included in manufacturing); motion picture and sound recording industries; libraries; and other information services.

Another feature of NAICS is a sector for Professional, Scientific and Technical Services, which comprises establishments engaged in activities where human capital is the major input. The industries within this sector are each defined by the expertise and training of the service provider. The sector includes such industries as offices of lawyers; engineering services; architectural services; advertising agencies; and interior design services. Thirty-five NAICS industries comprise this sector, many of which are now recognized for the first time.

A new sector for Arts, Entertainment and Recreation greatly expands the number of industries providing services in these three areas.

Another new sector, Health Care and Social Assistance, recognizes the merging of the boundaries of health care and social assistance. The industries in this new sector are arranged in an order that reflects the range and extent of health care and social assistance provided. Some new industries are family planning centers, out-patient mental health and substance abuse centers, and continuing into community care facilities for the elderly.

In the Manufacturing sector, an important new subsector, Computer and Electronic Product Manufacturing, brings together industries producing electronic products and their components. The manufacture of computers, communications equipment, and semiconductors, for example, are grouped into the same subsector because of the inherent technological similarities of their production processes, and the likelihood that these technologies will continue to converge in the future. An important change is that reproduction of packaged software is placed in this sector, rather than in the services sector, because the reproduction of packaged software is a manufacturing process, and the product moves through the wholesale and retail distribution systems like any other manufactured product. NAICS acknowledges the importance of these electronic industries, their rapid growth over the past several years and the likelihood that these industries will, in the future, become even more important in the economies of the three North American countries.

This NAICS structure reflects the levels at which data comparability was agreed upon by the three statistical agencies. The boundaries of all the sectors of NAICS have been delineated. In most sectors, NAICS provides for compatibility at the industry (five-digit) level. However, for real estate; utilities; finance and insurance; and for three of the four subsectors in other services (except public administration), three-country compatibility will occur either at the industry group (four-digit) or subsector (three-digit) levels. For these sectors, differences in the economies of the three countries prevent full compatibility at the NAICS industry level. For retail trade, wholesale trade, construction, and public administration, the three countries' statistical agencies have agreed, at this time, only on the boundaries of the sector (two-digit level). Below the agreed upon level of compatibility, each country may add additional detailed industries, as necessary to meet national needs, provided that this additional detail aggregates to the NAICS level.

The new classification will be adopted by Canada in their annual surveys of economic statistics for reference year 1997 and by Mexico and the United States in their economic censuses for reference years 1998 and 1997, respectively.

Acknowledgments

The development of the North American Industry Classification System (NAICS) was an immense undertaking requiring the time, energy, creativity, and cooperation of numerous people and organizations throughout the three countries. The work that has been accomplished is a testament to the individual and collective willingness of many persons and organizations both inside and outside government to contribute to the development of NAICS. Within the United States, NAICS was developed under the guidance of the Office of Management and Budget by the Economic Classification Policy Committee (ECPC). Members of the ECPC were **Jack E. Triplett,** (former Chair) and **John R. Kort,** Bureau of Economic Analysis, U.S. Department of Commerce; **Charles A. Waite** (retired), **Thomas L. Mesenbourg,** and **Carole A. Ambler** (current Chair) Bureau of the Census, U.S. Department of Commerce; **Thomas J. Plewes** (retired), **Brian MacDonald** (retired), and **George S. Werking,** Bureau of Labor Statistics, U.S. Department of Labor; and ex officio, **Paul Bugg**, Office of Management and Budget.

The ECPC established seven U.S. interagency subcommittees to work with their counterparts in Canada and Mexico to develop the structure of NAICS. Twenty U.S. government agencies provided staff for these subcommittees. Their contributions were invaluable. The agencies which generously made their staff available to support this process were as follows: Bureau of the Census; Bureau of Economic Analysis; Bureau of Labor Statistics; Bureau of Mines; Bureau of Transportation Statistics; Economic Research Service; Energy Information Administration; Federal Communications Commission; Federal Emergency Management Agency; Federal Reserve Board; Health Care Financing Administration; International Trade Administration; International Trade Commission; Internal Revenue Service; National Agricultural Statistics Service; National Forest Service; National Marine Fisheries Service; National Science Foundation; Social Security Administration; U.S. Fish and Wildlife Service; and U.S. Geological Survey.

The ECPC established two additional committees to coordinate the work of the NAICS Development Subcommittees and to implement ECPC recommendations following the development of the NAICS structure.

NAICS Development Subcommittees:

Agriculture, Forestry, and Fishing—**Douglas G. Kleweno,** Chair, National Agricultural Statistics Service

Construction—**Frank A. Szumilo** (retired), Chair, Bureau of Economic Analysis

Manufacturing and Mining—**Michael J. Zampogna,** Chair, Bureau of the Census

Distribution Networks—**Dennis L. Shoemaker,** Chair, Bureau of the Census

Finance, Insurance, and Real Estate—**Sidney O. Marcus III,** Chair, Bureau of the Census; **Helen S. Tice,** Co-Chair, Bureau of Economic Analysis

Business and Personal Services—**William C. Bennett, Jr.,** (deceased), Chair, Bureau of Labor Statistics; **Jack B. Moody,** Chair, Bureau of the Census

Health, Social Assistance, and Public Administration—**Mary Anne Phillips,** Chair, Bureau of Labor Statistics

The U.S. Coordinating Committee coordinated the U.S. effort internally and with Canada and Mexico. In addition to the Bureau of the Census, the Bureau of Economic Analysis, and the Bureau of Labor Statistics, membership included the Internal Revenue Service and the Social Security Administration. After the NAICS structure, hierarchy, and industries were established, the ECPC formed an Administrative Subcommittee from the Coordinating Committee and added a representative from the Bureau of Transportation Statistics. The Administrative Subcommittee was responsible for implementing the ECPC's recommendations and completing and preparing the manual and other materials.

Coordinating Committee/Administrative Subcommittee:

Carole A. Ambler (Coordinating Committee Chair), **William G. Bostic, Jr.,** (Administrative Subcommittee Chair), and **Bruce M. Goldhirsch,** Bureau of the Census

Ned G. Howenstine, Frank A. Szumilo (retired), and **Paula C. Young,** Bureau of Economic Analysis

William C. Bennett, Jr., (deceased), **Brian MacDonald** (retired), and **John B. Murphy,** Bureau of Labor Statistics

Susan C. Hostetter (retired), **David E. Jordan,** and **Laura R. Rosage,** Internal Revenue Service

Linda M. Dill, Social Security Administration

Dana M. Larkin, U.S. Department of Transportation Volpe Center, representing the Bureau of Transportation Statistics

Contents

EXPLANATION OF SYMBOLS

NAICS users may obtain current information about the placement of new types of business activities within the 1997 NAICS structure, the directory of Federal Government agencies that use NAICS for statistical and nonstatistical purposes, and Frequently Asked Questions by accessing the National Technical Information Service's NAICS web address ⟨**http://www.ntis.gov/naics**⟩ found at the bottom of each page.

In Part I, Titles and Descriptions

Symbol	Explanation
US	United States industry only.
CAN	United States and Canadian industries are comparable.
[Blank]	[No superscript symbol] Canadian, Mexican, and United States industries are comparable.

In Appendix A

Symbol	Explanation
US	United States industry only.
CAN	United States and Canadian industries are comparable.
[Blank]	Canadian, Mexican, and United States industries are comparable.

Introduction

Background

In 1937, the Central Statistical Board established an Interdepartmental Committee on Industrial Classification "to develop a plan of classification of various types of statistical data by industries and to promote the general adoption of such classification as the standard classification of the Federal Government.[1]" The List of Industries for manufacturing was first available in 1938, with the List of Industries for nonmanufacturing following in 1939. These Lists of Industries became the first Standard Industrial Classification (SIC) for the United States.

The SIC was developed for use in the classification of establishments by type of activity in which they are primarily engaged; for purposes of facilitating the collection, tabulation, presentation, and analysis of data relating to establishments; and for promoting uniformity and comparability in the presentation of statistical data collected by various agencies of the United States Government, State agencies, trade associations, and private research organizations. The SIC covered the entire field of economic activities by defining industries in accordance with the composition and structure of the economy.

Since the inception of the SIC in the 1930s, the system has been periodically revised to reflect the economy's changing industrial composition and organization. The last revision of the SIC was in 1987.

Rapid changes in both the U.S. and world economies brought the SIC under increasing criticism. In 1991, an International Conference on the Classification of Economic Activities was convened in Williamsburg, Virginia, to provide a forum for responding to such criticism and to explore new approaches to classifying economic activity. In July 1992, the Office of Management and Budget (OMB) established the Economic Classification Policy Committee (ECPC) and charged it with a "fresh slate" examination of economic classifications for statistical purposes. The ECPC prepared a number of issue papers regarding classification, consulted with outside users, and ultimately joined with Mexico's Instituto Nacional de Estadística, Geografía e Informática (INEGI) and Statistics Canada to develop the North American Industry Classification System (NAICS), which replaces the 1987 U.S. SIC and the classification systems of Canada (1980 SIC) and Mexico (1994 Mexican Classification of Activities and Products (CMAP)).

Purpose of NAICS

NAICS is an industry classification system that groups establishments into industries based on the activities in which they are primarily engaged. It is a comprehensive system covering the entire field of economic activities, producing and nonproducing. There are 20 sectors in NAICS and 1,170 industries in NAICS United States.

NAICS was developed by Mexico's INEGI, Statistics Canada, and the U.S. ECPC (the latter acting on behalf of OMB) to provide common industry definitions for Canada, Mexico, and the United States that will facilitate economic analyses of the economies of the three North American countries. The statistical agencies in the three countries produce information on inputs and outputs,

---

[1]Pearce, Esther, *History of the Standard Industrial Classification,* Executive Office of the President, Office of Statistical Standards, U.S. Bureau of the Budget, Washington, DC, July 1957 (mimeograph).

http://www.ntis.gov/naics

industrial performance, productivity, unit labor costs, and employment. NAICS, which is based on a production-oriented concept, ensures maximum usefulness of industrial statistics for these and similar purposes.

NAICS United States will be used by U.S. statistical agencies to: facilitate the collection, tabulation, presentation, and analysis of data relating to establishments, and to provide uniformity and comparability in the presentation of statistical data describing the U.S. economy. NAICS United States is designed for statistical purposes. Although the classification also may be used for various administrative, regulatory and taxation purposes, the requirements of government agencies that use it for nonstatistical purposes played no role in its development.

Development of NAICS

The U.S. ECPC established by OMB in 1992 was chaired by the Bureau of Economic Analysis, U.S. Department of Commerce, with representatives from the Bureau of the Census, U.S. Department of Commerce, and the Bureau of Labor Statistics, U.S. Department of Labor. The ECPC was asked to examine economic classifications for statistical purposes and to determine the desirability of developing a new industry classification system for the United States based on a single economic concept. On March 31, 1993, OMB published a **Federal Register** Notice (58FR16990-17004) announcing the intention to revise the SIC for 1997, the establishment of the ECPC, and the process for revising the SIC.

The ECPC established seven subcommittees composed of senior economists, statisticians, and classification specialists representing 20 of the Federal agencies that use the SIC for statistical programs. Those subcommittees, which were Agriculture, Forestry, and Fishing; Manufacturing and Mining; Construction; Distribution Networks (retail trade, wholesale trade, and transportation, communications, and utilities); Finance, Insurance, and Real Estate; Business and Personal Services; and Health, Social Assistance, and Public Administration, were responsible for developing the proposed structure of NAICS in cooperation with representatives from INEGI and Statistics Canada. The ECPC also established the U.S. Coordinating Committee that was responsible for coordinating the work of the U.S. subcommittees and the work with INEGI and Statistics Canada.

In July 1994, the OMB announced plans to develop a new industry classification system in cooperation with Mexico's INEGI and Statistics Canada. The new system—NAICS—replaces the current U.S. SIC. The concepts of the new system and the principles upon which NAICS was to be developed were announced in a July 26, 1994 **Federal Register** (59FR38092-38096) notice and were as follows:

1. NAICS will be erected on a production-oriented or supply-based conceptual framework. This means that producing units that use identical or similar production processes will be grouped together in NAICS.

2. The system will give special attention to developing production-oriented classifications for (a) new and emerging industries, (b) service industries in general, and (c) industries engaged in the production of advanced technologies.

3. Time series continuity will be maintained to the extent possible. However, changes in the economy and proposals from data users must be considered. In addition, adjustments will be required for sectors where the United States, Canada, and Mexico have incompatible industry classification definitions in order to produce a common industry system for all three North American countries.

4. The system will strive for compatibility with the two-digit level of the International Standard Industrial Classification of All Economic Activities (ISIC, Rev. 3) of the United Nations.

http://www.ntis.gov/naics

The structure of NAICS was developed in a series of meetings among the three countries. Public proposals for individual industries from all three countries were considered for acceptance if the proposed industry was based on the production-oriented concept of the system. In the United States, public comments also were solicited as groups of subsectors of NAICS were completed and agreed upon by the three countries. The ECPC published the proposed industries for those subsectors in a series of five successive **Federal Register** notices, in 1995 and 1996, asking for comments from interested data users.

Conceptual Framework

NAICS is erected on a production-oriented or supply-based conceptual framework in that establishments are grouped into industries according to similarity in the processes used to produce goods or services. A production-oriented industry classification system ensures that statistical agencies in the three countries can produce information on inputs and outputs, industrial performance, productivity, unit labor costs, employment, and other statistics and structural changes occurring in each of the three economies.

When an industry is defined on a production-oriented concept, producing units within the industry's boundaries share a basic production process; they use closely similar technology. In the language of economics, producing units within an industry share the same production functions; producing units in different industries have different production functions. The boundaries between industries thus demarcate, in principle, differences in production processes and production technologies.

The reasoning behind the three countries' decision to base NAICS on a production-oriented concept is summarized as follows: An industry is a grouping of economic activities. Though it inevitably groups the products of the economic activities that are included in the industry definition, it is not solely a grouping of products; put another way, an industry groups producing units. Accordingly, an industry classification system provides a framework for collecting data on inputs and outputs together.

The uses of economic data that require that data on inputs and outputs be used together and be collected on the same basis, include production analyses, productivity measurement, and studying input usage and input intensities. The North American statistical agencies developed NAICS using a production-oriented concept as the framework for two reasons: an industry classification system groups producing units, not products or services; and groupings of producing units permit the collection of data on inputs and outputs on a comparable basis, which is required for production-oriented analysis, but do not facilitate a comprehensive collection of data on the total output of any particular product or service, which is required for market-oriented analysis. Thus, the efficient organizing concept of an industry classification system is production-oriented rather than market-oriented.

Structure of NAICS

The structure of NAICS is hierarchical, much like that of the 1987 SIC. The first two digits of the structure designate the NAICS sectors that represent general categories of economic activities. NAICS classifies all economic activities into 20 sectors. The NAICS sectors, their two-digit codes, and the distinguishing activities of each are:

11 Agriculture, Forestry, Fishing and Hunting—Activities of this sector are growing crops, raising animals, harvesting timber, and harvesting fish and other animals from farms, ranches, or the animals' natural habitats.

http://www.ntis.gov/naics

21 Mining—Activities of this sector are extracting naturally occurring mineral solids, such as coal and ore; liquid minerals, such as crude petroleum; and gases, such as natural gas; and beneficiating (e.g., crushing, screening, washing, and flotation) and other preparation at the mine site, or as part of mining activity.

22 Utilities—Activities of this sector are generating, transmitting, and/or distributing electricity, gas, steam, and water and removing sewage through a permanent infrastructure of lines, mains, and pipe.

23 Construction—Activities of this sector are erecting buildings and other structures (including additions); heavy construction other than buildings; and alterations, reconstruction, installation, and maintenance and repairs.

31-33 Manufacturing—Activities of this sector are the mechanical, physical, or chemical transformation of material, substances, or components into new products.

41-43 Wholesale Trade—Activities of this sector are selling or arranging for the purchase or sale of goods for resale; capital or durable nonconsumer goods; and raw and intermediate materials and supplies used in production, and providing services incidental to the sale of the merchandise.

44-46 Retail Trade—Activities of this sector are retailing merchandise generally in small quantities to the general public and providing services incidental to the sale of the merchandise.

48-49 Transportation and Warehousing—Activities of this sector are providing transportation of passengers and cargo, warehousing and storing goods, scenic and sightseeing transportation, and supporting these activities.

51 Information—Activities of this sector are distributing information and cultural products, providing the means to transmit or distribute these products as data or communications, and processing data.

52 Finance and Insurance—Activities of this sector involve the creation, liquidation, or change in ownership of financial assets (financial transactions) and/or facilitating financial transactions.

53 Real Estate and Rental and Leasing—Activities of this sector are renting, leasing, or otherwise allowing the use of tangible or intangible assets (except copyrighted works), and providing related services.

54 Professional, Scientific, and Technical Services—Activities of this sector are performing professional, scientific, and technical services for the operations of other organizations.

55 Management of Companies and Enterprises—Activities of this sector are the holding of securities of companies and enterprises, for the purpose of owning controlling interest or influencing their management decision, or administering, overseeing, and managing other establishments of the same company or enterprise and normally undertaking the strategic or organizational planning and decisionmaking of the company or enterprise.

http://www.ntis.gov/naics

56 Administrative and Support and Waste Management and Remediation Services—Activities of this sector are performing routine support activities for the day-to-day operations of other organizations.

61 Educational Services—Activities of this sector are providing instruction and training in a wide variety of subjects.

62 Health Care and Social Assistance—Activities of this sector are providing health care and social assistance for individuals.

71 Arts, Entertainment, and Recreation—Activities of this sector are operating or providing services to meet varied cultural, entertainment, and recreational interests of their patrons.

72 Accommodation and Food Services—Activities of this sector are providing customers with lodging and/or preparing meals, snacks, and beverages for immediate consumption.

81 Other Services (except Public Administration)—Activities of this sector are providing services not elsewhere specified, including repairs, religious activities, grantmaking, advocacy, laundry, personal care, death care, and other personal services.

91-93 Public Administration—Activities of this sector are administration, management, and oversight of public programs by Federal, State, and local governments.

NAICS uses a six-digit coding system to identify particular industries and their placement in this hierarchical structure of the classification system. The first two digits of the code designate the sector, the third designates the subsector, the fourth digit designates the industry group, the fifth digit designates the NAICS industry, and the sixth digit designates the national industry. A zero as the sixth digit generally indicates that the NAICS industry and the U.S. industry are the same.

The subsectors, industry groups, and NAICS industries, in accord with the conceptual principle of NAICS, are production-oriented combinations of establishments. However, the production distinctions become more narrowly defined as one moves down the hierarchy.

NAICS agreements permit each country to designate detailed industries, below the level of a NAICS industry, to meet national needs. The United States has such industry detail in many places in the new classification system to recognize large, important U.S. industries that cannot be recognized in the other countries because of size, specialization, or organization of the industry.

Typically the level at which comparable data will be available for Canada, Mexico, and the United States is the five-digit NAICS industry; for some sectors (or subsectors or industry groups) however, the three countries agreed upon the boundaries at a higher level of detail rather than the detailed industry structure (five-digit). Agreement was reached at the sector level for construction; wholesale trade; retail trade; and public administration and at the subsector level for finance; personal and laundry services; religious, grantmaking, civic, and professional and similar organizations; and waste management and remediation services. For insurance and real estate, the three countries agreed on comparability at the industry group level.

Differences in the economies of the three countries or time constraints necessitated these modifications. For each of these sectors, except wholesale trade and public administration, Canada and the United States have agreed upon an industry structure and hierarchy to ensure comparability of statistics between those two countries. Canada and the United States also have established the same national detail (six-digit) industries where possible, adopting the same codes to describe

http://www.ntis.gov/naics

comparable industries. For this reason, the numbers of the U.S. industries may not be consecutive. In a few cases, it was necessary for the United States to use all of the numbers available to establish its six-digit detail so that the same six-digit codes do not represent comparable industries in the U.S. and Canada. In Appendix A, a "CAN" notation in the first column indicates comparability between the two countries. In Part I, Titles and Descriptions, a superscript or "CAN" at the end of an industry title indicates the same thing. A blank in the first column or no superscript indicates comparability among the three countries.

NAICS with U.S. detail will be known as NAICS United States (denoted by "US" in Appendix A and a superscript "US" at the end of the title in Part I) while Canada and Mexico will produce six-digit detail and will publish that detail as NAICS Canada and NAICS (SCIAN in Spanish) Mexico.

Definition of an Establishment

NAICS is a classification system for establishments. The establishment as a statistical unit is defined as the smallest operating entity for which records provide information on the cost of resources — materials, labor, and capital — employed to produce the units of output. The output may be sold to other establishments and receipts or sales recorded, or the output may be provided without explicit charge, that is, the good or service may be "sold" within the company itself.

The establishment, in NAICS United States, is generally a single physical location, where business is conducted or where services or industrial operations are performed (for example, a factory, mill, store, hotel, movie theater, mine, farm, airline terminal, sales office, warehouse, or central administrative office). There are cases where records identify distinct and separate economic activities performed at a single physical location (e.g., shops in a hotel). These retailing activities, operated out of the same physical location as the hotel, are identified as separate establishments and classified in retail trade while the hotel is classified in accommodations. In such cases, each activity is treated as a separate establishment provided: (1) no one industry description in the classification includes such combined activities; (2) separate reports can be prepared on the number of employees, their wages and salaries, sales or receipts, and expenses; and (3) employment and output are significant for both activities.

Exceptions to the single location exist for physically dispersed operations, such as construction, transportation, and communication. For these activities the individual sites, projects, fields, networks, lines, or systems of such dispersed activities are not normally considered to be establishments. The establishment is represented by those relatively permanent main or branch offices, terminals, stations, and so forth, that are either (1) directly responsible for supervising such activities, or (2) the base from which personnel operate to carry out these activities.

Although an establishment may be identical with the enterprise (company), the two terms should not be confused. An enterprise (company) may consist of more than one establishment. Such multiunit enterprises may have establishments in more than one industry in NAICS. If such enterprises have a separate establishment primarily engaged in providing headquarters services, these establishments are classified in NAICS Sector 55, Management of Companies and Enterprises.

Although all establishments have output, they may or may not have receipts. In large enterprises it is not unusual for establishments to exist that solely serve other establishments of the same enterprise (auxiliary establishments). In such cases, these units often do not collect receipts from the establishments they serve. This type of support (captive) activity is found throughout the economy and involves goods producing activities as well as services.

In the 1987 SIC, auxiliary service establishments, defined as establishments primarily engaged in performing management or support services for other establishments of the same enterprise, were classified to industries based on the industry classification of the establishments they serviced—not the primary activity. However, captive goods producing establishments, defined as operating establishments, were classified based on what they did, not whom they served. This traditional treatment of auxiliary units implied that captive services producing establishments should be treated differently from captive goods producing units.

NAICS changes this traditional classification of auxiliary establishments. NAICS is based on the economic principle that establishments should be grouped together based on their production processes and does not distinguish between captive services and goods establishments. Those units that carry out support activities for the enterprise to which they belong are classified, to the extent feasible, according to the NAICS code related to their own activity and, if possible, to that of the enterprise they support. This means that warehouses that provide storage facilities for their own enterprise will be classified as a warehouse and not as an automobile assembly plant (if that is the primary unit they serve).

Determining an Establishment's Industry Classification

An establishment is classified to an industry when its primary activity meets the definition for that industry. Because establishments may perform more than one activity, it is necessary to determine procedures for identifying the primary activity of the establishment.

In most cases, if an establishment is engaged in more than one activity, the industry code is assigned based on the establishment's principal product or group of products produced or distributed, or services rendered. Ideally, the principal product or service should be determined by its relative share of current production costs and capital investment at the establishment. In practice, however, it is often necessary to use other variables such as revenue, shipments, or employment as proxies for measuring significance.

There are two types of combined activities that are given special attention in NAICS. They are vertical integration and joint production. These combined activities have an economic basis and occur in both goods-producing and services-producing sectors. In some cases, there are efficiencies to be gained from combining certain activities in the same establishment. Some of these combinations occur so commonly or frequently that their combination can be treated as a third activity in its own right and explicitly classified in a specific industry.

One approach to classifying these activities would be to use the primary activity rule, that is, whichever activity is largest. However, the fundamental principle of NAICS is that establishments that employ the same production process should be classified in the same industry. If the premise that the combined activities correspond to a distinct third activity is accepted, then using the primary activity rule would place establishments performing the same combination of activities in different industries, thereby violating the production principle of NAICS. A second reason for NAICS recognizing combined activities is to improve the stability of establishment classification, both over time and among the various agencies that implement the classification. An establishment should remain classified in the same industry unless its production process changes, and different agencies should code the same establishment or type of establishment in the same way. A consistent treatment of establishments with combined activities is more likely if they are classified to a single industry.

Vertical integration involves consecutive stages of fabrication or production processes in which the output of one step is the input of the next. In general, establishments will be classified based on the final process in a vertically integrated production environment, unless specifically identified as classified in another industry. For example, paper may be produced either by establishments that first produce pulp and then consume that pulp to produce paper or by those establishments

http://www.ntis.gov/naics

producing paper from purchased pulp. NAICS specifically specifies that both of these types of paper-producing processes should be classified in 32212, Paper Mills, the industry, or the final step in paper manufacturing, rather than in NAICS 32211, Pulp Mills. In other cases, NAICS specifies that vertically integrated establishments be classified in the industry representing the first stage of the manufacturing process. For example, steel mills that make steel and also perform other activities such as producing steel castings are classified in NAICS 33111, Iron and Steel Mills and Ferroalloy Manufacturing, the first stage of the manufacturing process.

The joint production of goods or services represents the second type of combined activities. For example, automobile dealers both sell and repair autos; automotive parts dealers may both sell parts and repair automobiles; and musical instrument stores may both sell and rent instruments. In the manufacturing sector, establishments may make two different products such as women's dresses and women's suits, activities that are classified in two different NAICS United States detailed industries. In general, receipts/sales and revenue data are used as a proxy to determine primary activity for these establishments. The assumption is that the activity generating the most receipts is also the activity using the most resources and most indicative of the production process.

In some cases, however, these combined activities have been assigned to a specific NAICS industry. Most of these activities involve either the sale and repair of goods or the sale and rental of goods in the same establishment. For example, establishments that both sell automobile parts and repair automobiles are classified in NAICS 44131, Automotive Parts and Accessories Stores, and those music stores that both sell and rent musical instruments are classified in NAICS 45114, Musical Instrument and Supplies Stores. In other cases, specific industries have been identified for these combined activities, such as 44711, Gasoline Stations with Convenience Stores.

Classfication rules related to the agreement to permit individual country detail at the six-digit level for NAICS sometimes results in less comparable NAICS industries at the five-digit level and above. For example in NAICS, the assignment of the industry code is at the most detailed level of the classification (the six-digit U.S. detail code), except for agriculture. That is, if the value of an establishment's production consists of 30 percent from computers, 30 percent from computer storage devices, and 40 percent from semiconductors and related devices, it will be classified in U.S. detail industry 334413, Semiconductor and Related Device Manufacturing, that will be aggregated to NAICS 33441, Semiconductor and Other Electronic Component Manufacturing, the level at which comparable information is shown for all three countries. If the classification for the above example were at the five-digit NAICS level, that establishment would be classified in NAICS 33411, Computer and Peripheral Equipment Manufacturing. There would then be more comparable information at the NAICS level, but it would be impossible to classify this establishment to a U.S. detail six-digit industry.

In agriculture, however, NAICS coding will be at the five-digit NAICS level. This is possible because of the identification in NAICS of combination farms. Therefore, the above situation does not occur.

Comparison of NAICS to the International Standard Industrial Classification (ISIC)

Recognizing the need for international comparability of economic statistics, the United Nations (UN) first adopted an International Standard Industrial Classification (ISIC) system in 1948. Revisions to the ISIC structure and codes were adopted by the UN's Statistical Commission in 1958, 1968, and 1989.[2]

---

[2]*International Standard Industrial Classification of all Economic Activities,* Statistical Papers, Series M., No. 4, Department of International Economic and Social Affairs, Statistical Office, United Nations, New York, 1958, *International Standard Industrial Classification of All Economic Activities,* Statistical Papers, Series M., No. 4, Rev. 2, Department of International Economic and Social Affairs, Statistical Office, United Nations, New York, 1968. *International Standard*

Similar to NAICS, ISIC was designed primarily to provide classifications for grouping establishments (rather than enterprises or firms), and the primary focus for the ISIC classification system is the kind of activity in which establishments or other statistical entities are engaged. The main criteria employed in delineating divisions and groups (the two- and three-digit categories, respectively) of ISIC are: (a) the character of the goods and services produced, (b) the uses to which the goods and services are put; and (c) the inputs, the process, and the technology of production.

The third classification criterion of the ISIC is the conceptual foundation of NAICS, and thus, NAICS is aligned more closely with ISIC than was the 1987 SIC system. However, there are differences between the NAICS and ISIC classification schemes. Most important, perhaps, is the single (production process) conceptual framework of NAICS. As noted elsewhere, this is unique among industry classifications. Distinctions also were made during ISIC's development with regard to (1) select characteristics of goods and services produced; (2) the range of kinds of activity frequently carried out under the same ownership or control; (3) differences between enterprises in scale, organization of activities, capital requirements, and finance; and (4) the pattern of categories at various levels of classification in national classifications.

The ISIC groups economic activity into 17 broad Sections, 60 Divisions, 159 Groups, and 292 Classes. In the coding system, Sections are distinguished by the letters A through Q and the Divisions, Groups, and Classes are identified as the two-digit, three-digit, and four-digit groupings, respectively. NAICS United States groups economic activity into 20 sectors, 96 subsectors, 311 industry groups, 459 NAICS industries (for which there is comparability among all three countries), and 1,170 U.S. industries corresponding to the two-digit, three-digit, four-digit, and five-digit levels in the coding system. In some cases, the NAICS U.S. industry codes include a sixth-digit to identify an economic type unique to the United States, but within the general NAICS structure.

In the development of NAICS industries, the statistical agencies of the three countries strove to create industries that did not cross ISIC two-digit boundaries. A detailed concordance among NAICS United States and ISIC, Revision 3 will be conducted and the results of that concordance published on the Census Bureau NAICS Internet web site (**http://www.census.gov/naics**).

Industrial Classification of All Economic Activities, Statistical Papers, Series M., No. 4., Rev. 3, Department of International Economic and Social Affairs, Statistical Office, United Nations, New York, 1990.

http://www.ntis.gov/naics

Why the NAICS Was Needed

The United States has enjoyed the advantages of a Standard Industrial Classification (SIC) system for some 60 years, but structural changes in national and global economics and the desire for a consistent classification criterion created the need to move forward to a new classification taxonomy, the North American Industry Classification System (NAICS).

A good industrial classification system is essential to understanding the economy. An understanding of the structure and functioning of the economy is heavily dependent on the way in which economic information is classified and presented. Which industries are growing; which declining? Where are the job opportunities of the future? Which industries compete most successfully in world markets? The search for answers to critically important questions such as these requires consistent definitions of the industries being examined; that is, it requires an industry classification system.

To be fully useful, the classifications must group business activities according to a consistent system designed to illuminate key aspects of the economic structure. In the NAICS structure, business establishments producing the same or similar products by similar production methods are placed in the same industry. Related industries are grouped together in higher levels of classification, building up to 20 major economic sectors. Using these consistent industry definitions, information from many sources can be used to construct a coherent picture of each industry.

Recognition of these principles led the U.S. Government some 60 years ago to establish a U.S. Standard Industrial Classification (SIC) so that statistical information gathered by different Government agencies could be presented using a common set of industry definitions. The SIC also has been widely adopted by State governments, trade associations, private research organizations, and others who gather and publish economic information. Over the years the United States, using the SIC, has developed a very complete set of industrial statistics, so that information on production, employment, wages, prices, productivity, capital investment, and research and development spending is readily available on an industry-by-industry basis.

The U.S. industrial classification needed comprehensive revision. Since its inception the SIC has undergone a number of periodic revisions to incorporate the emergence of new industries and the decline of existing industries. The change from the SIC to the NAICS is considerably more sweeping than past revisions. Why was such a major revision necessary?

The service-producing sector has grown far more important. In 1940, 47 percent of private nonfarm employment was in the goods-producing sectors (manufacturing, mining, and construction) and as recently as 1970 the proportion was still 40 percent. The manufacturing sector in particular, with its sensitivity to the business cycle, its prominence in international trade, and its traditional leadership in terms of technological innovation and productivity gains, long has been viewed as of special importance for economic analysis. So it is not surprising that the goods-producing sectors traditionally have received careful attention in industry classification and that the classifications have in general been more detailed than has been the case for service-producing industries.

By 1990, however, goods production accounted for only 27 percent of private nonfarm employment. The greatly increased importance of service-producing industries gave urgency to the need for better understanding of the role they play in the economy, including their employment patterns, their productivity trends, and their export potential. The NAICS provides for substantially revamped and much more detailed service industry classifications. Of the 358 new industries identified in the NAICS, 250 are service-producing industries. Nine new sectors pertain to service-producing groups of industries.

As service industry data based on the new NAICS classifications become available, a clearer picture of each individual service industry will emerge. Traditionally, the service sector often has been viewed as the low-wage, low-tech part of the economy. With respect to many service-producing industries, this is a serious misconception.

http://www.ntis.gov/naics

New NAICS Service Sectors
Information Real Estate and Rental and Leasing Professional, Scientific, and Technical Services Administrative and Support, Waste Management and Remediation Services Educational Services Health Care and Social Assistance Arts, Entertainment, and Recreation Accommodation and Food Services Other Services

Communication services, to take only one example, have undergone revolutionary changes in technology and in patterns of service delivery. Changes such as these often imply strong productivity gains, falling prices, a well-paid, highly-skilled work force, and a strong competitive position in the international economy. However, the detailed information needed to fully analyze these relationships has been lacking. The more detailed and more up-to-date industry classifications in the NAICS will form the basis for developing a more complete statistical picture of modern service industries.

New industries have emerged. Factors such as the rapid pace of technological innovation, the push for international competitiveness, the need to control costs, and the changing shopping preferences of consumers have combined to produce enormous changes in the structure of the U.S. economy. Despite its periodic revisions, the SIC code no longer reflected the structure of our Nation's economy. Closely associated industries that had emerged over the years since the inception of the SIC were classified in different divisions. The problems were not new, but had been only partially addressed in previous SIC revisions. And, with the accelerating pace of technological change, the problems were more serious.

One prominent example of structural problems with the SIC was the placement of computer manufacturing in an industry group titled "Industrial and Commercial Machinery and Computer Equipment," while electronic components such as semiconductors fell into a different group titled "Electronic and Other Electrical Equipment." Production of "prepackaged" computer software, though it clearly had become a manufacturing process, was classified under business services.

Another area of concern was the way in which wholesale and retail trade are defined in the SIC. The classifications were not designed to accommodate office supply discount stores (classified as wholesale although they sell to both businesses and consumers), warehouse shopping clubs, and other new ways of selling. A further example was the lack of suitable classifications for new ways of delivering health services, such as health maintenance organizations (HMOs). These are only a few examples of the difficulty of fitting the current industrial structure into a classification structure originally designed to describe a far different economy. If the United States was to have an industrial classification system truly useful for describing today's economy, major changes from the SIC were required.

Canada, Mexico, and the United States needed a common classification system. In 1993, these North American countries joined together in the North American Free Trade Agreement (NAFTA), under which tariffs and other barriers to trade within North America are being eliminated. Though cross-national flows of goods, services, and capital investment would have continued to grow, the creation of NAFTA has accelerated these trends.

Canada has long been the United States' most important trading partner. In 1997 Mexico surpassed Japan as the second largest export market for U.S. goods. The need to compare economic

http://www.ntis.gov/naics

performance in the three North American countries has taken on a new importance. An industry-by-industry view of comparative trends in wages, prices, productivity, and other economic variables is crucial to identifying new trade and investment opportunities as well as to understanding the problems that more vigorous international competition creates for some industries. Such industry-by-industry analysis up to now has been impeded by differences in industry definitions among the three countries. As NAICS comes into use in all three countries a much clearer picture of economic relationships within North America will emerge.

Industry classifications will continue to need periodic revision. Even as NAICS is being implemented, new industries and new production techniques continue to emerge. The NAICS process has been designed to adapt to this need. The three sponsoring countries will join in reviewing and updating the NAICS codes on a regular 5-year cycle rather than the less regular cycle that characterized the SIC.

Implementing the NAICS

NAICS will be implemented by Federal statistical agencies over a period of several years beginning with the release early in 1999 of the first data from the 1997 Economic Census. The size and complexity of U.S. economic statistics programs makes gradual implementation a necessity. A general description of the implementation process is provided below. Individuals wanting more detailed current information should check the NAICS web site maintained by the Bureau of the Census ⟨**www.census.gov/naics**⟩.

The 1997 Economic Census. The 1997 Economic Census will provide the first comprehensive look at the economy according to NAICS. During 1998 the Bureau of the Census is collecting and tabulating data pertaining to 1997 from more than five million U.S. businesses. The information collected will enable the Bureau to classify each of these businesses according to both the SIC and the NAICS. An *Advance Report*, to be released early in 1999, will provide national estimates of employment, payroll, and receipts at the NAICS subsector and industry group levels. Additional NAICS-based reports will follow during 1999. Early in the year 2000 the Bureau plans to release detailed tables showing information on both a NAICS and an SIC basis, thus providing information needed to link data from the two classification systems. (See "Bridging from the SIC to NAICS" on the next page for more detail.)

Bureau of the Census economic surveys. In 1998, the Bureau of the Census is beginning to implement the NAICS in its annual industry surveys. The 1998 *Annual Survey of Manufactures* and the 1998 *County Business Patterns* will be published on a NAICS basis. Other annual programs, including surveys of services, transportation, communications, and retail trade will move to a NAICS basis for calendar year 1999. Data in these surveys will be collected for both 1998 and 1999 to provide annual time series consistent with the Economic Census data for 1997.

Implementation of NAICS goes beyond questions of data collection and publication through existing survey programs. The identification of new economic sectors in NAICS will require the Bureau to restructure its survey program. Emphasis in this restructuring will be given to developing data series that will help improve the quality of gross domestic product estimates. Improved coverage of service-producing industries, including a proposed annual survey of the new information sector, is high on the agenda.

With respect to the *Census Bureau's population censuses and surveys,* an adapted version of the NAICS will be used in the decennial census for 2000 and subsequent surveys.

The *Bureau of Economic Analysis* will convert its surveys of foreign direct investment as they are conducted and data published over the period 1997 through 2002. The benchmark input-output accounts derived from the 1997 Economic Census will be on a NAICS basis, with publication scheduled for 2002. Gross product originating by industry also is scheduled for publication in 2002. Major data series from the *Bureau of Labor Statistics* will be converted to a NAICS basis over a period extending to 2004.

Beginning January 1, 1999, the *Internal Revenue Service* will change the industry codes in taxpayer instructions to reflect the NAICS.

Bridging from the SIC to the NAICS

Data for more than two-thirds of all 4-digit SICs will be derivable from the NAICS system, either because the industry definition has not changed or because the new industries are subdivisions of old SIC industries and can be recombined. For the remaining industries, however, there will be breaks in time series, and the broad sectors, like manufacturing and retailing, that we use to describe our economy in everyday conversation will lose some of their historical comparability.

The problem of data comparability across time was recognized early in the development of NAICS, but the Economic Classification Policy Committee (ECPC) nonetheless chose to start with a "fresh slate." The Committee concluded a July 1993 issue paper by stating:

> . . .it is unproductive to collect and maintain time series data that have questionable value. Thus, it may be preferable to accept a onetime break in historical continuity if the benefits of conversion to a new classification structure are apparent and accepted by users.[3]

In conducting the 1997 Economic Census, the Bureau of the Census is collecting the information necessary to classify establishments on both a NAICS and an SIC basis. Thus, it will be possible to publish data tables showing the same data on both the old and the new basis. The *Advance Report* to be published early in 1999 will contain national level data for NAICS sectors, subsectors, and industry groups and for SIC divisions, major groups, and industry groups. A *Comparative Statistics Report*, scheduled for January 2000, will show information on employment, payroll, receipts, and number of establishments on an SIC basis. A further report, the *Bridge Between NAICS and SIC Report*, scheduled for March 2000 will show data on a 6-digit NAICS by 4-digit SIC basis and correspondingly on a 4-digit SIC by 6-digit NAICS basis. These bridge tables will provide the link needed to compare data between the two systems.

The 1997 bridge tables will be published only at the national level. Comparative statistics, simply showing data on each basis, will be published at the State level. Sub-State data will be published only on the NAICS basis.

The nature of these bridge tables can be illustrated with tables showing the bridge constructed between the 1972 and 1987 SIC classifications. The first of the tables below shows how 1987 data for SIC 3571, Electronic Computers would be distributed among the classifications used in the 1972 SIC. The second table shows how 1987 data classified on the former (1972) SIC was distributed among the new (1987) classifications.

---

[3]U.S. Economic Policy Classification Committee Issue Paper Number 5 "The Impact of Classification Revisions on Time Series," July 1993.

Bridge Table: (Distribution of 1987 SIC-based Industries Among 1972 SIC-based Industries)

Industry	Estab-lish-ments	Employees (1,000)	Payroll (million$)	Value of shipments (millions$)
New 3571, Electronic Computers	974	151.9	4,953.0	33,626.5
Old 3573, Electronic Computing Equipment (pt.)	969	151.9	4,954.2	33,591.9
Old 3662, Radio and Television Commun. Equip. (pt.)	4	(D)	(D)	(D)
All Other	1	(D)	(D)	(D)
New 3572, Computer Storage Devices	106	43.3	1,442.6	6,394.8
Old 3573, Electronic Computing Equipment (pt.)	106	43.3	1,442.6	6,394.8
New 3575, Computer Terminals	121	15.0	441.7	1,799.0
Old 3573, Electronic Computing Equipment (pt.)	115	(D)	(D)	(D)
Old 3661, Telephone and Telegraph Apparatus (pt.)	6	(D)	(D)	(D)
New 3577, Computer Peripheral Equipment, n.e.c.	549	76.2	2,625.4	13,965.5
Old 3573, Electronic Computing Equipment (pt.)	549	76.2	2,625.4	13,965.5

Bridge Table: (Distribution of 1972 SIC-based Industries Among 1987 SIC-based Industries)

Industry	Estab-lish-ments	Employees (1,000)	Payroll (million$)	Value of shipments (million$)
Old 3573, Electronic Computing Equipment	1,852	310.7	10,119.4	59,195.4
New 3571, Electronic Computers (pt.)	969	151.5	4,945.2	33,591.9
New 3572, Computer Storage Devices	106	43.3	1,442.6	6,394.8
New 3575, Computer Terminals (pt.)	115	(D)	(D)	(D)
New 3577, Computer Peripheral Equipment, n.e.c.	549	76.2	2,625.4	13,965.5
New 3661, Telephone and Telegraph Apparatus (pt.)	39	(D)	(D)	(D)
New 3696, Magnetic & Optical Recording Media (pt.)	67	15.5	401.4	1,755.4
Nonmanufacturing	7	2.1	61.0	240.2

Note that in these tables some detail, indicated by (D), has been suppressed because publication might enable information about individual businesses to be identified. Similar suppressions will be necessary in some of the 1997 bridge tables.

Business Advantages in Using the NAICS

The North American Industry Classification System will be used by many governmental organizations to classify economic and demographic information. However, these organizations are not the only groups to benefit from the use of the NAICS. Businesses will also gain an advantage from knowledge of the NAICS code. Firstly, it is required on many governmental documents. Also, a familiarity with the system can help businesses gain access to many different types of important information relating to specific industries, from the overall economic health of a sector to the

http://www.ntis.gov/naics

performance of an individual U.S. industry. The NAICS code, as has been mentioned, is a more comprehensive classification system than the SIC code it replaces, and therefore will be capable of providing more detailed and accurate information.

Many different departments, offices, and bureaus within the government require a classification number on applications, forms and other submissions. Knowledge of the NAICS, which will replace the SIC to become the standard industrial classification system, will be important in the completion of grant requests, tax returns, and other forms that are gathered along industry lines. Misunderstanding the NAICS code may result in a classification error, with economic and regulatory implications for business.

In addition, knowledge of the NAICS code can help locate information pertaining to a particular type of business activity. Industrial information in many sources will largely be presented using the NAICS. Data on current and projected employment, capital expenditures by industry and value of shipments will be organized by NAICS, allowing for inter-industrial comparisons to be made. Cross-references located in the NAICS manual make comparing related industries uncomplicated, giving a complete picture of the environment in which an enterprise operates, from suppliers to consumers. For example, an auto repair service will be able to review the economic performance of its industry and also be able to review the performance of related industries, like Auto Retailing, Auto Part Retailing, and Auto Manufacturing.

NAICS represents an important step in the collection and analysis of statistical information, but it is also of use to the business world itself. The classifications make understanding the economic environment easier for all concerned. Business will be able to paint a much clearer picture of their own industry and use that picture to boost performance, making NAICS as important to business as it is to those organizations that collect information on industry.

NAICS United States Structure

Sector	Name	Sub-sectors	Industry groups	NAICS 5-digit industries	U.S. 6-digit industries	Total U.S. industries	New industries
11	Agriculture, Forestry, Fishing and Hunting	5	19	42	32	64	20
21	Mining	3	5	10	28	29	-
22	Utilities	1	3	6	6	10	6
23	Construction	3	14	28	-	28	3
31-33	Manufacturing	21	84	184	408	474	79
42	Wholesale Trade	2	18	69	-	69	-
44-45	Retail Trade	12	27	61	18	72	17
48-49	Transportation and Warehousing	11	29	42	25	57	28
51	Information	4	9	28	12	34	20
52	Finance and Insurance	5	11	32	15	42	23
53	Real Estate and Rental and Leasing	3	8	19	9	24	15
54	Professional, Scientific, and Technical Services	1	9	35	17	47	28
55	Management of Companies and Enterprises	1	1	1	3	3	1
56	Administrative and Support and Waste Management and Remediation Services	2	11	29	23	43	29
61	Educational Services	1	7	12	7	17	12
62	Health Care and Social Assistance	4	18	30	16	39	27
71	Arts, Entertainment, and Recreation	3	9	23	3	25	19
72	Accommodation and Food Services	2	7	11	7	15	10
81	Other Services (except Public Administration)	4	14	30	30	49	19
92	Public Administration	8	8	29	-	29	2
	Total	96	311	721	659	1170	358

Frequently Asked Questions About Economic Classifications

1. What is the purpose of an industry classification system?

   - An industry classification system facilitates the collection, tabulation, presentation, and analysis of data relating to establishments and ensures that data about the U.S. economy published by U.S. statistical agencies are uniform and comparable. NAICS ensures that such data are uniform and comparable among the North American countries.

2. What is an establishment?

   - An establishment is generally a single, physical location at which economic activity occurs (e.g., store, factory, farm, etc.). An enterprise, on the other hand, may consist of more than one location performing the same or different types of economic activities. Each establishment of that enterprise is assigned a NAICS code.

3. In which industry is my company classified?

   - NAICS is an establishment classification system, not a company classification system. To determine in which industry each establishment of your company is classified, you should first identify the primary activity of each establishment and then go to the alphabetic list of activities in the NAICS United States Manual. Find that activity in the alphabetic index, turn to the industry description of the specified code, read the definition of the industry as printed in the description, and determine if that description fits the activities of your establishment.
   or
   - Contact the Census Bureau by telephone at 1-888-75NAICS or by E-mail at naics@census.gov (do not include any capital letters in the address). Describe the activity of the establishment for which you need a NAICS code and you will receive a reply.

4. How are NAICS codes assigned?

   - NAICS codes are assigned to each establishment of an enterprise based on the primary activity of that establishment. When a company applies for an Employer Identification Number (EIN), information about the type of activity in which that business is engaged is requested in order to assign a NAICS code. In addition, statistical agencies such as the Census Bureau and the Bureau of Labor Statistics assign NAICS codes based on information reported to them.

5. How do I apply for a NAICS code?

   - As explained above, NAICS codes are assigned based on the primary activity of the business establishment. You may contact the Census Bureau (see question 3) to determine your NAICS code.

6. Have the Small Business Administration's size standards been updated to reflect the NAICS codes?

   - You should contact the Office of Size Standards of the Small Business Administration, 409 Third Street S.W., Washington, DC 20416 for this information. They can be reached at 202-205-6618.

7. How do the NAICS codes affect the Environmental Protection Agency's regulations?

   - You should contact the Environmental Protection Agency at 202-260-3071 for answers to those questions.

http://www.ntis.gov/naics

8. When will NAICS codes be used in Federal Procurement regulations?

   • You should contact the U.S. General Services Administration at 202-401-1529.
   For answers to other NAICS questions, you may visit the Census Bureau NAICS web site
   at http://www.census.gov/naics

9. What are NAICS' principal advantages as compared to the SIC ?

   • Relevancy. NAICS is more relevant to today's economy. It identifies over 350 new industries and nine new service industry sectors.
   • Consistency. NAICS uses a consistent classification principle. Businesses that use similar
   production processes are grouped together.
   • Comparability. NAICS will be used by the United States, Canada, and Mexico to produce
   comparable data.
   • Adaptability. NAICS will be reviewed every 5 years, so classifications can keep pace with
   the changing economy.

10. How can comparability with previous economic data be achieved?

   • Full comparability will not always be possible; in any major revision, some time series
   continuity will inevitably be lost. However, data for more than two-thirds of all 4-digit SICs
   will be derivable from the NAICS system, either because the industry definition has not
   changed or because the new NAICS industries are subdivisions of SIC industries and can
   be recombined. National and State level data from the 1997 Economic Census will be
   published on both the SIC and the NAICS basis, and this will assist in making estimates
   where precise comparisons are not possible.

11. How frequently will NAICS be updated?

   • The NAICS structure will be reviewed every 5 years.

12. Will U.S. international trade data be available on a NAICS basis?

   • Data on international trade in goods necessarily are collected on a commodity basis, whereas
   NAICS (and SIC) data are on an establishment basis. However, it has proved possible to
   combine the commodity data into categories approximating the groups of products produced
   by establishments within an SIC category, so that export and import data on an SIC basis
   could be published. It should be possible to develop similar approximations for the NAICS
   categories. Foreign trade import/export data are scheduled to be converted to a NAICS basis
   in 1998.

13. For some uses, market-based, rather than production-based, statistical classifications are more
   useful. Will NAICS be able to provide these?

   • The Economic Classification Policy Committee is committed to developing a demand-based
   product classification system, beginning in the near future, and focusing on service-producing
   industries for the 2002 Economic Census. A complete system should be available for the
   2007 Economic Census.

14. For some sectors, such as construction, agreement among the three North American countries
   was reached only at the broad sector level. Are discussions aimed at reaching more detailed
   agreement continuing?

   • Yes. It is hoped that agreement will be reached by the time of the 2002 Economic Census
   with respect to construction and wholesale trade.

Directory of Selected Federal Government Agencies

Government agencies that were involved in the development of the NAICS are listed below. In addition, Government agencies that will use the NAICS in the collection and dissemination of data are also listed.

U.S. Economic Classification Policy Committee (ECPC)

Office of Management and Budget
Statistical Policy Branch
New Executive Office Building
Washington, DC 20503
direct (202) 395-3093
fax (202) 395-7245
http://www.whitehouse.gov/WH/EOP/OMB/html/ombhome.html

Bureau of Economic Analysis (Department of Commerce)
Regional Economic Analysis Division
1441 L Street, NW
Washington, DC 20230
(202) 606-9900
fax (202) 606-5321
http://www.bea.doc.gov/

Bureau of Labor Statistics (Department of Labor)
2 Massachusetts Avenue, NE
Washington, DC 20210
http://www.bls.gov

Employment Projections
Industry Employment Projections
Industry Output and Employment—Historical and Projected
(202) 606-5700
fax (202) 606-5745
http://www.bls.gov/empcon02.htm

Employment and Unemployment Statistics
Occupational and Employment Statistics
(202) 606-6569
fax (202) 606-6645
oesinfo@bls.gov
http://www.bls.gov/oes_con.htm

http://www.ntis.gov/naics

Productivity and Technology
Industry Productivity and Technology Studies
fax (202) 606-5664

Manufacturing   **Non-manufacturing**
For SIC codes 20-31   For SIC codes 32-39
direct (202) 606-5641   direct (202) 606-5624   direct (202) 606-5633

Bureau of the Census (Department of Commerce)
Federal Center
Suitland, Maryland 20233
http://www.census.gov/epcd/www/naics.html

Services Division
direct (301) 457-2668
fax (301) 457-1343

Participating Agencies

Department of Agriculture
http://www.usda.gov

National Agriculture Statistics Service
fax (202) 720-8738

Commodity Survey Secretary
1400 Independence Avenue, SW
Washington, DC 20250
direct (202) 720-4028
Agriculture Data and Classification Structure

Commodities Secretary
437 Iverson Mall
Washington, DC 20233
direct (301) 763-8576
Census of Agriculture Data

Economic Research Service
fax (202) 694-5757

1800 M Street, NW
Washington, DC 20036-5831
direct (202) 694-5395

http://www.ntis.gov/naics

Forest Service
   fax (202) 205-1087

   Research and Development Economist
   PO Box 96090
   Washington, DC 20090-6090
   (202) 205-1052
   Forestry Data

Department of Commerce
International Trade Administration
   Office of Trade and Economic Analysis
   14th Street and Constitution Avenue, NW
   Washington, DC 20230
   (202) 482-5145
   fax (202) 482-4614
   http://www.ita.doc.gov

Department of Energy
Energy Information Administration
   National Energy Information Center—General Information
   1000 Independence Avenue, SW
   Washington, DC 20585-0001
   (202) 586-8800
   fax (202) 586-0721
   infoctr@eia.doe.gov
   http://www.eia.doc.gov

Department of the Interior
U.S. Geological Survey
   Geological Division
   Mineral Information Team
   988 National Center
   Reston, VA 22092
   (703) 648-6410
   fax (703) 648-4995
   http://www.usgs.gov

Department of Labor
Occupational Safety and Health Administration (OSHA)
   Office of Statistics
   200 Constitution Avenue, NW
   Washington, DC 20210
   (202) 606-5900
   fax (202) 219-5161

http://www.ntis.gov/naics

Department of Transportation
Bureau of Transportation Statistics
Transportation Studies
400 7th Street, SW
Washington, DC 20590
(202) 366-3282
fax (202)366-3640
http://www.bts.gov

Department of the Treasury
Internal Revenue Service
Statistics of Income Division
1111 Constitution Avenue, NW
Washington, DC 20224-0002
(202) 874-0700
fax (202) 874-0964
http://www.irs.ustreas.gov

Environmental Protection Agency
401 M Street, SW
Washington, DC MC 6101
http://www.epa.gov

Office of Administration and Resource Management
Information Resource Management
(202) 260-4465
fax (202) 260-5419
http://www.epa.gov/irmpoli8

Environmental Data Registry
(202) 260-3017
http://www.epa.gov/edr/

Federal Reserve Board
Industrial Production
20th and C Streets, NW
Washington, DC 20551
(202) 452-3197
http://www.bog.frb.fed.us/

General Services Administration
Governmentwide Information Systems
Federal Procurement Data Center
7th and D Streets, SW, Room 5652
Washington, DC 20407
(202) 401-1529
fax (202) 401-1546
http://www.fpds.gsa.gov/fpds/fpds.htm

http://www.ntis.gov/naics

International Trade Commission

500 E Street, SW
Washington, DC 20436
http://www.usitc.gov

Office of Economics
(202) 205-3277
fax (202) 205-2340

Office of Industries
(202) 205-3296
fax (202) 205-3161

Office of Information Services
Statistical and Editorial Services Division
General Information
(202) 205-2513
fax (202) 205-2024

Small Business Administration

409 3rd Street, SW
Washington, DC 20416
http://www.sba.gov

Advocacy
Office of Economic Research
(202) 205-6975
fax (202) 205-6928

Government Contracting
Size Standards Staff
(202) 205-6618
fax (202) 205-6390

http://www.ntis.gov/naics

Part I

Titles and Descriptions
of Industries

Sector 11—Agriculture, Forestry, Fishing and Hunting

The Sector as a Whole

The Agriculture, Forestry, Fishing and Hunting sector comprises establishments primarily engaged in growing crops, raising animals, harvesting timber, and harvesting fish and other animals from a farm, ranch, or their natural habitats.

The establishments in this sector are often described as farms, ranches, dairies, greenhouses, nurseries, orchards, or hatcheries. A farm may consist of a single tract of land or a number of separate tracts which may be held under different tenures. For example, one tract may be owned by the farm operator and another rented. It may be operated by the operator alone or with the assistance of members of the household or hired employees, or it may be operated by a partnership, corporation, or other type of organization. When a landowner has one or more tenants, renters, croppers, or managers, the land operated by each is considered a farm.

The sector distinguishes two basic activities: agricultural production and agricultural support activities. Agricultural production includes establishments performing the complete farm or ranch operation, such as farm owner-operators, tenant farm operators, and sharecroppers. Agricultural support activities include establishments that perform one or more activities associated with farm operation, such as soil preparation, planting, harvesting, and management, on a contract or fee basis.

Excluded from the Agriculture, Forestry, Hunting and Fishing sector are establishments primarily engaged in agricultural research and establishments primarily engaged in administering programs for regulating and conserving land, mineral, wildlife, and forest use. These establishments are classified in Industry 54171, Research and Development in the Physical, Engineering, and Life Sciences; and Industry 92412, Administration of Conservation Programs, respectively.

111 Crop Production

Industries in the Crop Production subsector grow crops mainly for food and fiber. The subsector comprises establishments, such as farms, orchards, groves, greenhouses, and nurseries, primarily engaged in growing crops, plants, vines, or trees and their seeds.

The industries in this subsector are grouped by similarity of production activity, including biological and physiological characteristics and economic requirements, the length of growing season, degree of crop rotation, extent of input specialization, labor requirements, and capital demands. The production process is typically completed when the raw product or commodity grown reaches the "farm gate" for market, that is, at the point of first sale or price determination.

Establishments are classified to the crop production subsector when crop production (i.e., value of crops for market) accounts for one-half or more of the establishment's total agricultural production. Within the subsector, establishments are classified to a specific industry when a product or industry family of products (i.e., oilseed and grain farming, vegetable and melon farming, fruit and tree nut farming) account for one-half or more of the establishment's agricultural production. Establishments with one-half or more crop production with no one product or family of products of an industry accounting for one-half of the establishment's agricultural production are treated as general combination crop farming and are classified in Industry 11199, All Other Crop Farming.

---

http://www.ntis.gov/naics

Industries in the Crop Production subsector include establishments that own, operate, and manage and those that operate and manage. Those that manage only are classified in Subsector 115, Support Activities for Agriculture and Forestry.

1111 Oilseed and Grain Farming

This industry group comprises establishments primarily engaged in (1) growing oilseed and/or grain crops and/or (2) producing oilseed and grain seeds. These crops have an annual life cycle and are typically grown in open fields.

11111 Soybean Farming
See industry description for 111110 below.

111110 Soybean Farming

This industry comprises establishments primarily engaged in growing soybeans and/or producing soybean seeds.

Cross-References.

Establishments engaged in growing soybeans in combination with grain(s) with the soybeans or grain(s) not accounting for one-half of the establishment's agricultural production (value of crops for market) are classified in U.S. Industry 111191, Oilseed and Grain Combination Farming.

11112 Oilseed (except Soybean) Farming
See industry description for 111120 below.

111120 Oilseed (except Soybean) Farming

This industry comprises establishments primarily engaged in growing fibrous oilseed producing plants and/or producing oilseed seeds, such as sunflower, safflower, flax, rape, canola, and sesame.

Cross-References. Establishments primarily engaged in—

- Growing soybeans—are classified in Industry 111110, Soybean Farming; and

- Growing oilseed(s) in combination with grain(s) with no one oilseed (or family of oilseeds) or grain(s) (or family of grains) accounting for one-half of the establishment's agricultural production (value of crops for market)—are classified in U.S. Industry 111191, Oilseed and Grain Combination Farming.

11113 Dry Pea and Bean Farming
See industry description for 111130 below.

111130 Dry Pea and Bean Farming

This industry comprises establishments primarily engaged in growing dried peas, beans, and/or lentils.

US—United States industry only. CAN—United States and Canadian industries are comparable. When neither US nor CAN appears, Canadian, Mexican, and United States industries are comparable.

http://www.ntis.gov/naics

Cross-References.

Establishments primarily engaged in growing fresh green beans and peas are classified in U.S. Industry 111219, Other Vegetable (except Potato) and Melon Farming.

11114 Wheat Farming
See industry description for 111140 below.

111140 Wheat Farming

This industry comprises establishments primarily engaged in growing wheat and/or producing wheat seeds.

Cross-References.

Establishments growing wheat in combination with oilseed(s) with the wheat or oilseed(s) not accounting for one-half of the establishment's agricultural production (value of crops for market) are classified in U.S. Industry 111191, Oilseed and Grain Combination Farming.

11115 Corn Farming
See industry description for 111150 below.

111150 Corn Farming

This industry comprises establishments primarily engaged in growing corn (except sweet corn) and/or producing corn seeds.

Cross-References. Establishments primarily engaged in—

- Growing sweet corn—are classified in U.S. Industry 111219, Other Vegetable (except Potato) and Melon Farming; and

- Growing corn in combination with oilseed(s) with the corn or oilseed(s) not accounting for one-half of the establishment's production (value of crops for market)—are classified in U.S. Industry 111191, Oilseed and Grain Combination Farming.

11116 Rice Farming
See industry description for 111160 below.

111160 Rice Farming

This industry comprises establishments primarily engaged in growing rice (except wild rice) and/or producing rice seeds.

US—United States industry only. CAN—United States and Canadian industries are comparable. When neither US nor CAN appears, Canadian, Mexican, and United States industries are comparable.

Cross-References. Establishments primarily engaged in—

- Growing wild rice—are classified in U.S. Industry 111199, All Other Grain Farming; and

- Engaged in growing rice in combination with oilseed(s) with the rice or oilseed(s) not accounting for one-half of the establishment's agricultural production (value of crops for market)—are classified in U.S. Industry 111191, Oilseed and Grain Combination Farming.

11119 Other Grain Farming

This industry comprises establishments primarily engaged in (1) growing grain(s) and/or producing grain seeds (except wheat, corn, and rice) or (2) growing a combination of grain(s) and oilseed(s) with no one grain (or family of grains) or oilseed (or family of oilseeds) accounting for one-half of the establishment's agriculture production (value of crops for market). Combination grain(s) and oilseed(s) establishments may produce oilseed(s) and grain(s) seeds and/or grow oilseed(s) and grain(s).

Illustrative Examples:

Barley farming	Rye farming
Milo farming	Sorghum farming
Oat farming	Wild rice farming
Oilseed and grain combination farming	

Cross-References. Establishments primarily engaged in—

- Growing wheat—are classified in U.S. Industry 11114, Wheat Farming;

- Growing corn (except sweet corn)—are classified in U.S. Industry 11115, Corn Farming;

- Growing sweet corn—are classified in U.S. Industry 11121, Vegetable and Melon Farming; and

- Growing rice (except wild rice)—are classified in U.S. Industry 11116, Rice Farming.

111191 Oilseed and Grain Combination Farming[US]

This U.S. industry comprises establishments engaged in growing a combination of oilseed(s) and grain(s) with no one oilseed (or family of oilseeds) or grain (or family of grains) accounting for one-half of the establishment's agricultural production (value of crops for market). These establishments may produce oilseed(s) and grain(s) seeds and/or grow oilseed(s) and grain(s).

Cross-References.

Establishments engaged in growing one grain (or family of grains) or oilseed (or family of oilseeds) accounting for one-half of the establishment's agriculture production (value of crops for market) are classified in Industry Group 1111, Oilseed and Grain Farming accordingly by the prominent grain(s) or oilseed(s) grown.

US—United States industry only. CAN—United States and Canadian industries are comparable. When neither US nor CAN appears, Canadian, Mexican, and United States industries are comparable.

111199 All Other Grain Farming[US]

This U.S. industry comprises establishments primarily engaged in growing grains and/or producing grain(s) seeds (except wheat, corn, rice, and oilseed(s) and grain(s) combinations).

Illustrative Examples:

Barley farming	Sorghum farming
Oat farming	Wild rice farming
Rye farming	

Cross-References. Establishments primarily engaged in—

- Growing wheat—are classified in Industry 111140, Wheat Farming;

- Growing corn—are classified in Industry 111150, Corn Farming;

- Growing rice (except wild rice)—are classified in Industry 111160, Rice Farming;

- Growing sweet corn—are classified in U.S. Industry 111219, Other Vegetable (except Potato) and Melon Farming; and

- Growing a combination of grain(s) and oilseed(s) with no one grain (or family of grains) or oilseed (or family of oilseeds) accounting for one-half of the establishment's agricultural production (value of crops for market)—are classified in U.S. Industry 111191, Oilseed and Grain Combination Farming.

1112 Vegetable and Melon Farming

This industry group comprises establishments primarily engaged in growing root and tuber crops (except sugar beets and peanuts) or edible plants and/or producing root and tuber or edible plant seeds. The crops included in this group have an annual growth cycle and are grown in open fields. Climate and cultural practices limit producing areas but often permit the growing of a combination of crops in a year.

11121 Vegetable and Melon Farming

This industry comprises establishments primarily engaged in one or more of the following: (1) growing vegetable and/or melon crops; (2) producing vegetable and melon seeds; and (3) growing vegetable and/or melon bedding plants.

Cross-References. Establishments primarily engaged in—

- Growing sugar beets—are classified in Industry 11199, All Other Crop Farming;

- Growing vegetables and melons under glass or protective cover—are classified in Industry 11141, Food Crops Grown Under Cover;

- Growing dry peas and beans—are classified in Industry 11113, Dry Pea and Bean Farming;

- Growing corn (except sweet corn)—are classified in Industry 11115, Corn Farming;

US—United States industry only. CAN—United States and Canadian industries are comparable. When neither US nor CAN appears, Canadian, Mexican, and United States industries are comparable.

http://www.ntis.gov/naics

- Canning, pickling, and/or drying (artificially) vegetables—are classified in Industry 31142, Fruit and Vegetable Canning, Pickling and Drying; and

- Growing fruit on trees and other fruit-bearing plants (except melons)—are classified in Industry Group 1113, Fruit and Tree Nut Farming.

111211 Potato Farming[CAN]

This U.S. industry comprises establishments primarily engaged in growing potatoes and/or producing seed potatoes (except sweet potatoes).

Cross-References. Establishments primarily engaged in—

- Growing sweet potatoes, cassava, and yams—are classified in U.S. Industry 111219, Other Vegetable (except Potato) and Melon Farming; and

- Canning or drying potatoes—are classified in Industry 31142, Fruit and Vegetable Canning, Pickling and Drying.

111219 Other Vegetable (except Potato) and Melon Farming[CAN]

This U.S. industry comprises establishments primarily engaged in one or more of the following: (1) growing melons and/or vegetables (except potatoes; dry peas; dry beans; field, silage, or seed corn; and sugar beets); (2) producing vegetable and/or melon seeds; and (3) growing vegetable and/or melon bedding plants.

Illustrative Examples:

Carrot farming	Squash farming
Green bean farming	Sweet potato farming
Melon farming (e.g., cantaloupe, casaba, honeydew, watermelon)	Tomato farming
	Vegetable (except potato) and melon farming
Pepper farming (e.g., bell, chili, green, red, sweet peppers)	Watermelon farming

Cross-References. Establishments primarily engaged in—

- Growing potatoes—are classified in U.S. Industry 111211, Potato Farming;

- Growing sugar beets—are classified in U.S. Industry 111991, Sugar Beet Farming;

- Growing vegetables and melons under glass or protective cover—are classified in U.S. Industry 111419, Other Food Crops Grown Under Cover;

- Growing dry peas and beans—are classified in Industry 111130, Dry Pea and Bean Farming;

- Growing corn (except sweet corn)—are classified in Industry 111150, Corn Farming;

- Canning, pickling, and/or drying (artificially) vegetables—are classified in Industry 31142, Fruit and Vegetable Canning, Pickling and Drying; and

---

US—United States industry only. CAN—United States and Canadian industries are comparable. When neither US nor CAN appears, Canadian, Mexican, and United States industries are comparable.

- Growing fruit on trees and other fruit-bearing plants (except melons)—are classified in Industry Group 1113, Fruit and Tree Nut Farming.

1113 Fruit and Tree Nut Farming

This industry group comprises establishments primarily engaged in growing fruit and/or tree nut crops. The crops included in this industry group are generally not grown from seeds and have a perennial life cycle.

11131 Orange Groves
    See industry description for 111310 below.

111310 Orange Groves

This industry comprises establishments primarily engaged in growing oranges.

11132 Citrus (except Orange) Groves
    See industry description for 111320 below.

111320 Citrus (except Orange) Groves

This industry comprises establishments primarily engaged in growing citrus fruits (except oranges).

Illustrative Examples:

Citrus groves (except oranges)	Mandarin groves
Grapefruit groves	Tangelo groves
Lemon groves	Tangerine groves

Cross-References.

Establishments primarily engaged in growing oranges are classified in Industry 111310, Orange Groves.

11133 Noncitrus Fruit and Tree Nut Farming

This industry comprises establishments primarily engaged in one or more of the following: (1) growing noncitrus fruits (e.g., apples, grapes, berries, peaches); (2) growing tree nuts (e.g., pecans, almonds, pistachios); or (3) growing a combination of fruit(s) and tree nut(s) with no one fruit (or family of fruit) or family of tree nuts accounting for one-half of the establishment's agriculture production (value of crops for market).

Cross-References. Establishments primarily engaged in—

- Harvesting berries or nuts from native and noncultivated plants—are classified in Industry 11321, Forest Nurseries and Gathering of Forest Products; and

---

US—United States industry only. CAN—United States and Canadian industries are comparable. When neither US nor CAN appears, Canadian, Mexican, and United States industries are comparable.

- Canning and/or drying (artificially) fruit—are classified in Industry 31142, Fruit and Vegetable Canning, Pickling and Drying.

111331 Apple Orchards[US]

This U.S. industry comprises establishments primarily engaged in growing apples.

Cross-References.

Establishments engaged in growing apples in combination with tree nut(s) with the apples or family of tree nuts not accounting for one-half of the establishment's agriculture production (i.e., value of crops for market) are classified in U.S. Industry 111336, Fruit and Tree Nut Combination Farming.

111332 Grape Vineyards[US]

This U.S. industry comprises establishments primarily engaged in growing grapes and/or growing grapes to sun dry into raisins.

Cross-References. Establishments primarily engaged in—

- Drying grapes artificially—are classified in U.S. Industry 311423, Dried and Dehydrated Food Manufacturing; and

- Growing grapes in combination with tree nut(s) with the grapes or family of tree nuts not accounting for one-half of the establishment's agriculture production (i.e., value of crops for market)—are classified in U.S. Industry 111336, Fruit and Tree Nut Combination Farming.

111333 Strawberry Farming[US]

This U.S. industry comprises establishments primarily engaged in growing strawberries.

Cross-References.

Establishments engaged in growing strawberries in combination with tree nut(s) with the strawberries or family of tree nuts not accounting for one-half of the establishment's agriculture production (i.e., value of crops for market) are classified in U.S. Industry 111336, Fruit and Tree Nut Combination Farming.

111334 Berry (except Strawberry) Farming[US]

This U.S. industry comprises establishments primarily engaged in growing berries.

Illustrative Examples:

Berry (except strawberries) farming	Cranberry farming
Blackberry farming	Currant farming
Blueberry farming	Raspberry farming

Cross-References. Establishments primarily engaged in—

- Growing strawberries—are classified in U.S. Industry 111333, Strawberry Farming;

- Harvesting berries from native and noncultivated bushes or vines—are classified in Industry 113210, Forest Nurseries and Gathering of Forest Products; and

- Growing berries in combination with tree nut(s) with the berries or family of tree nuts not accounting for one-half of the establishment's agriculture production (i.e., value of crops for market)—are classified in U.S. Industry 111336, Fruit and Tree Nut Combination Farming.

111335 Tree Nut Farming^{US}

This U.S. industry comprises establishments primarily engaged in growing tree nuts.

Illustrative Examples:

Almond farming	Pistachio farming
Filbert farming	Tree nut farming
Macadamia farming	Walnut farming
Pecan farming	

Cross-References. Establishments primarily engaged in—

- Growing coconut and coffee—are classified in U.S. Industry 111339, Other Noncitrus Fruit Farming; and

- Growing tree nut(s) in combination with fruit(s) with no one fruit (or family of fruit or of tree nuts) accounting for one-half of the establishment's agriculture production (i.e., value of crops for market)—are classified in U.S. Industry 111336, Fruit and Tree Nut Combination Farming.

111336 Fruit and Tree Nut Combination Farming^{US}

This U.S. industry comprises establishments primarily engaged in growing a combination of fruit(s) and tree nut(s) with no one fruit (or family of fruit) or family of tree nuts accounting for one-half of the establishment's agriculture production (i.e., value of crops for market).

Cross-References.

Establishments engaged in growing fruit(s) or the family of tree nut(s) accounting for one-half of the establishment's agriculture production (i.e., value of crops for market) are classified in Industry Group 1113, Fruit and Tree Nut Farming accordingly by the prominent fruit(s) or tree nut(s) grown.

111339 Other Noncitrus Fruit Farming^{US}

This U.S. industry comprises establishments primarily engaged in growing noncitrus fruits (except apples, grapes, berries, and fruit(s) and tree nut(s) combinations).

US—United States industry only. CAN—United States and Canadian industries are comparable. When neither US nor CAN appears, Canadian, Mexican, and United States industries are comparable.

http://www.ntis.gov/naics

Illustrative Examples:

Apricot farming	Fig farming
Banana farming	Noncitrus fruit farming
Cherry farming	Peach farming
Coffee farming	Pineapple farming
Date farming	Prune farming

Cross-References. Establishments primarily engaged in—

- Growing apples—are classified in U.S. Industry 111331, Apple Orchards;

- Growing grapes including sun drying of grapes into raisins—are classified in U.S. Industry 111332, Grape Vineyards;

- Growing strawberries—are classified in U.S. Industry 111333, Strawberry Farming;

- Growing berries (except strawberries)—are classified in U.S. Industry 111334, Berry (except Strawberry) Farming;

- Drying fruit artificially—are classified in U.S. Industry 311423, Dried and Dehydrated Food Manufacturing; and

- Growing noncitrus fruit(s) in combination with tree nut(s) with no one fruit (or family of fruits) or family of tree nuts accounting for one-half of the establishment's agriculture production (i.e., value of crops for market)—are classified in U.S. Industry 111336, Fruit and Tree Nut Combination Farming.

1114 Greenhouse, Nursery, and Floriculture Production

This industry group comprises establishments primarily engaged in growing crops of any kind under cover and/or growing nursery stock and flowers. "Under cover" is generally defined as greenhouses, cold frames, cloth houses, and lath houses. The crops grown are removed at various stages of maturity and have annual and perennial life cycles. The nursery stock includes short rotation woody crops that have growth cycles of 10 years or less.

11141 Food Crops Grown Under Cover

This industry comprises establishments primarily engaged in growing food crops (e.g., fruits, melons, tomatoes) under glass or protective cover.

Cross-References.

Establishments primarily engaged in growing vegetable and melon bedding plants are classified in Industry 11121, Vegetable and Melon Farming.

111411 Mushroom Production[CAN]

This U.S. industry comprises establishments primarily engaged in growing mushrooms under cover in mines underground, or in other controlled environments.

US—United States industry only. CAN—United States and Canadian industries are comparable. When neither US nor CAN appears, Canadian, Mexican, and United States industries are comparable.

111419 Other Food Crops Grown Under Cover^{CAN}

This U.S. industry comprises establishments primarily engaged in growing food crops (except mushrooms) under glass or protective cover.

Illustrative Examples:

Alfalfa sprout farming, grown under cover   Melon farming, grown under cover
Fruit farming, grown under cover   Vegetable farming, grown under cover
Hydroponic crop farming

Cross-References.

Establishments primarily engaged in growing mushrooms under cover are classified in U.S. Industry 111411, Mushroom Production.

11142 Nursery and Floriculture Production

This industry comprises establishments primarily engaged in (1) growing nursery and floriculture products (e.g., nursery stock, shrubbery, cut flowers, flower seeds, foliage plants) under cover or in open fields and/or (2) growing short rotation woody trees with a growing and harvesting cycle of 10 years or less for pulp or tree stock (e.g., cut Christmas trees, cottonwoods).

Cross-References. Establishments primarily engaged in—

- Growing vegetable and melon bedding plants—are classified in Industry 11121, Vegetable and Melon Farming;

- Operating timber tracts (i.e., growing cycle greater than 10 years)—are classified in Industry 11311, Timber Tract Operations; and

- Retailing nursery, tree stock, and floriculture products primarily purchased from others— are classified in Industry 44422, Nursery and Garden Centers.

111421 Nursery and Tree Production^{CAN}

This U.S. industry comprises establishments primarily engaged in (1) growing nursery products, nursery stock, shrubbery, bulbs, fruit stock, sod, and so forth, under cover or in open fields and/ or (2) growing short rotation woody trees with a growth and harvest cycle of 10 years or less for pulp or tree stock.

Cross-References. Establishments primarily engaged in—

- Growing vegetable and melon bedding plants—are classified in Industry 11121, Vegetable and Melon Farming;

- Operating timber tracts (i.e., growing cycle greater than 10 years)—are classified in Industry 113110, Timber Tract Operations; and

---

US—United States industry only. CAN—United States and Canadian industries are comparable. When neither US nor CAN appears, Canadian, Mexican, and United States industries are comparable.

http://www.ntis.gov/naics

• Retailing nursery, tree stock, and floriculture products primarily purchased from others—are classified in Industry 444220, Nursery and Garden Centers.

111422 Floriculture Production^{CAN}

This U.S. industry comprises establishments primarily engaged in growing and/or producing floriculture products (e.g., cut flowers and roses, cut cultivated greens, potted flowering and foliage plants, and flower seeds) under cover and in open fields.

Cross-References.

Establishments primarily engaged in retailing floriculture products primarily purchased from others are classified in Industry 444220, Nursery and Garden Centers.

1119 Other Crop Farming

This industry group comprises establishments primarily engaged in (1) growing crops (except oilseed and/or grain; vegetable and/or melon; fruit and tree nut; and greenhouse, nursery, and/or floriculture products). These establishments grow crops, such as tobacco, cotton, sugarcane, hay, sugar beets, peanuts, agave, herbs and spices, and hay and grass seeds; or (2) growing a combination of crops (except a combination of oilseed(s) and grain(s) and a combination of fruit(s) and tree nut(s)).

11191 Tobacco Farming
See industry description for 111910 below.

111910 Tobacco Farming

This industry comprises establishments primarily engaged in growing tobacco.

11192 Cotton Farming
See industry description for 111920 below.

111920 Cotton Farming

This industry comprises establishments primarily engaged in growing cotton.

Cross-References.

Establishments primarily engaged in ginning cotton are classified in U.S. Industry 115111, Cotton Ginning.

11193 Sugarcane Farming
See industry description for 111930 below.

111930 Sugarcane Farming

This industry comprises establishments primarily engaged in growing sugarcane.

US—United States industry only. CAN—United States and Canadian industries are comparable. When neither US nor CAN appears, Canadian, Mexican, and United States industries are comparable.

11194 Hay Farming

See industry description for 111940 below.

111940 Hay Farming

This industry comprises establishments primarily engaged in growing hay, alfalfa, clover, and/or mixed hay.

Cross-References. Establishments primarily engaged in—

- Growing grain hay—are classified in Industry Group 1111, Oilseed and Grain Farming; and

- Growing grass and hay seeds—are classified in U.S. Industry 111998, All Other Miscellaneous Crop Farming.

11199 All Other Crop Farming

This industry comprises establishments primarily engaged in (1) growing crops (except oilseeds and/or grains; vegetables and/or melons; fruits and/or tree nuts; greenhouse, nursery and/or floriculture products; tobacco; cotton; sugarcane; or hay) or (2) growing a combination of crops (except a combination of oilseed(s) and grain(s); and a combination of fruit(s) and tree nut(s)) with no one crop or family of crops accounting for one-half of the establishment's agricultural production (i.e., value of crops for market).

Illustrative Examples:

Agave farming	Hay seed farming
Algae farming	Maple sap gathering
General combination crop farming (except oilseed and grain; vegetables and melons; fruit and nut combinations)	Peanut farming
	Spice farming
	Sugar beet farming
Grass seed farming	Tea farming

Cross-References. Establishments primarily engaged in—

- Growing oilseeds and/or wheat, corn, rice, or other grains—are classified in Industry Group 1111, Oilseed and Grain Farming;

- Growing vegetables and/or melons—are classified in Industry Group 1112, Vegetable and Melon Farming;

- Growing fruits and/or tree nuts—are classified in Industry Group 1113, Fruit and Tree Nut Farming;

- Growing greenhouse, nursery, and/or floriculture products—are classified in Industry Group 1114, Greenhouse, Nursery, and Floriculture Production;

- Growing tobacco—are classified in Industry 11191, Tobacco Farming;

- Growing cotton—are classified in Industry 11192, Cotton Farming;

US—United States industry only. CAN—United States and Canadian industries are comparable. When neither US nor CAN appears, Canadian, Mexican, and United States industries are comparable.

- Growing sugarcane—are classified in Industry 11193, Sugarcane Farming; and

- Growing hay—are classified in Industry 11194, Hay Farming.

111991 Sugar Beet Farming^{US}

This U.S. industry comprises establishments primarily engaged in growing sugar beets.

Cross-Referencesc.

Establishments primarily engaged in growing beets (except sugar beets) are classified in U.S. Industry 111219, Other Vegetable (except Potato) and Melon Farming.

111992 Peanut Farming^{US}

This U.S. industry comprises establishments primarily engaged in growing peanuts.

111998 All Other Miscellaneous Crop Farming^{US}

This U.S. industry comprises establishments primarily engaged in one of the following: (1) growing crops (except oilseeds and/or grains; vegetables and/or melons; fruits and/or tree nuts; greenhouse, nursery and/or floriculture products; tobacco; cotton; sugarcane; hay; sugar beets; or peanuts); (2) growing a combination of crops (except a combination of oilseed(s) and grain(s); and a combination of fruit(s) and tree nut(s)) with no one crop or family of crop(s) accounting for one-half of the establishment's agricultural production (i.e., value of crops for market); or (3) gathering tea or maple sap.

Illustrative Examples:

Agave farming	Grass seed farming
Algae farming	Hay seed farming
General combination crop farming (except	Hop farming
oilseed and grain; vegetables and melons;	Mint farming
fruit and tree nut combinations)	Spice farming

Cross-References. Establishment primarily engaged in—

- Growing oilseeds and/or wheat, corn, rice, or other grains—are classified in Industry Group 1111, Oilseed and Grain Farming;

- Growing vegetables and/or melons—are classified in Industry Group 1112, Vegetable and Melon Farming;

- Growing fruits and/or tree nuts—are classified in Industry Group 1113, Fruit and Tree Nut Farming;

- Growing greenhouse, nursery and/or floriculture products—are classified in Industry Group 1114, Greenhouse, Nursery, and Floriculture Production;

US—United States industry only. CAN—United States and Canadian industries are comparable. When neither US nor CAN appears, Canadian, Mexican, and United States industries are comparable.

- Growing tobacco—are classified in Industry 111910, Tobacco Farming;

- Growing cotton—are classified in Industry 111920, Cotton Farming;

- Growing sugarcane—are classified in Industry 111930, Sugarcane Farming;

- Growing hay—are classified in Industry 111940, Hay Farming;

- Growing sugar beets—are classified in U.S. Industry 111991, Sugar Beet Farming; and

- Growing peanuts—are classified in U.S. Industry 111992, Peanut Farming.

112 Animal Production

Industries in the Animal Production subsector raise or fatten animals for the sale of animals or animal products. The subsector comprises establishments, such as ranches, farms, and feedlots primarily engaged in keeping, grazing, breeding, or feeding animals. These animals are kept for the products they produce or for eventual sale. The animals are generally raised in various environments, from total confinement or captivity to feeding on an open range pasture.

The industries in this subsector are grouped by important factors, such as suitable grazing or pasture land, specialized buildings, type of equipment, and the amount and types of labor required. Establishments are classified to the Animal Production subsector when animal production (i.e., value of animals for market) accounts for one-half or more of the establishment's total agricultural production. Establishments with one-half or more animal production with no one animal product or family of animal products of an industry accounting for one-half of the establishment's agricultural production are treated as combination animal farming classified to Industry 11299, All Other Animal Production.

1121 Cattle Ranching and Farming

This industry group comprises establishments primarily engaged in raising cattle, milking dairy cattle, or feeding cattle for fattening.

11211 Beef Cattle Ranching and Farming, including Feedlots

This industry comprises establishments primarily engaged in raising cattle (including cattle for dairy herd replacements), or feeding cattle for fattening.

Cross-References. Establishments primarily engaged in—

- Milking dairy cattle—are classified in Industry 11212, Dairy Cattle and Milk Production; and

- Operating stockyards for transportation and not buying, selling, or auctioning livestock—are classified in Industry 48899, Other Support Activities for Transportation.

112111 Beef Cattle Ranching and Farming[US]

This U.S. industry comprises establishments primarily engaged in raising cattle (including cattle for dairy herd replacements).

US—United States industry only. CAN—United States and Canadian industries are comparable. When neither US nor CAN appears, Canadian, Mexican, and United States industries are comparable.

Cross-References.

Establishments primarily engaged in milking dairy cattle are classified in Industry 112120, Dairy Cattle and Milk Production.

112112 Cattle Feedlots[US]

This U.S. industry comprises establishments primarily engaged in feeding cattle for fattening.

Cross-References.

Establishments primarily engaged in operating stockyards for transportation and not buying, selling, or auctioning livestock are classified in U.S. Industry 488999, All Other Support Activities for Transportation.

11212 Dairy Cattle and Milk Production
See industry description for 112120 below.

112120 Dairy Cattle and Milk Production

This industry comprises establishments primarily engaged in milking dairy cattle.

Cross-References. Establishment primarily engaged in—

- Raising dairy herd replacements—are classified in U.S. Industry 112111, Beef Cattle Ranching and Farming; and

- Milking goats—are classified in Industry 112420, Goat Farming.

11213 Dual-Purpose Cattle Ranching and Farming
See industry description for 112130 below.

112130 Dual-Purpose Cattle Ranching and Farming

This industry comprises establishments primarily engaged in raising cattle for both milking and meat production.

Cross-References. Establishments primarily engaged in—

- Milking dairy cattle—are classified in Industry 11212, Dairy Cattle and Milk Production;

- Raising cattle or feeding cattle for fattening—are classified in Industry 11211, Beef Cattle Ranching and Farming, including Feedlots; and

- Operating stockyards for transportation and not buying, selling, or auctioning livestock— are classified in U.S. Industry 48899, All Other Support Activities for Transportation.

1122 Hog and Pig Farming

US—United States industry only. CAN—United States and Canadian industries are comparable. When neither US nor CAN appears, Canadian, Mexican, and United States industries are comparable.

11221 Hog and Pig Farming
See industry description for 112210 below.

112210 Hog and Pig Farming

This industry comprises establishments primarily engaged in raising hogs and pigs. These establishments may include farming activities, such as breeding, farrowing, and the raising of weanling pigs, feeder pigs, or market size hogs.

Cross-References.

Establishments primarily engaged in operating stockyards for transportation and not buying, selling, or auctioning livestock are classified in U.S. Industry 488999, All Other Support Activities for Transportation.

1123 Poultry and Egg Production

This industry group comprises establishments primarily engaged in breeding, hatching, and raising poultry for meat or egg production.

11231 Chicken Egg Production
See industry description for 112310 below.

112310 Chicken Egg Production

This industry comprises establishments primarily engaged in raising chickens for egg production. The eggs produced may be for use as table eggs or hatching eggs.

Cross-References.

Establishments primarily engaged in raising chickens for the production of meat are classified in Industry 112320, Broilers and Other Meat Type Chicken Production.

11232 Broilers and Other Meat Type Chicken Production
See industry description for 112320 below.

112320 Broilers and Other Meat Type Chicken Production

This industry comprises establishments primarily engaged in raising broilers, fryers, roasters, and other meat type chickens.

Cross-References.

Establishments primarily engaged in raising chickens for egg production are classified in Industry 112310, Chicken Egg Production.

US—United States industry only. CAN—United States and Canadian industries are comparable. When neither US nor CAN appears, Canadian, Mexican, and United States industries are comparable.

11233 Turkey Production
See industry description for 112330 below.

112330 Turkey Production

This industry comprises establishments primarily engaged in raising turkeys for meat or egg production.

11234 Poultry Hatcheries
See industry description for 112340 below.

112340 Poultry Hatcheries

This industry comprises establishments primarily engaged in hatching poultry of any kind.

11239 Other Poultry Production
See industry description for 112390 below.

112390 Other Poultry Production

This industry comprises establishments primarily engaged in raising poultry (except chickens for meat or egg production and turkeys).

Illustrative Examples:

Duck production	Ostrich production
Emu production	Pheasant production
Geese production	Quail production

Cross-References. Establishments primarily engaged in—

- Raising aviary birds, such as parakeets, canaries, and love birds,—are classified in Industry 112990, All Other Animal Production;

- Raising chickens for egg production—are classified in Industry 112310, Chicken Egg Production;

- Raising broilers and other meat type chickens—are classified in Industry 112320, Broilers and Other Meat Type Chicken Production;

- Raising turkeys—are classified in Industry 112330, Turkey Production; and

- Raising swans, peacocks, flamingos or other ''adornment birds''—are classified in Industry 112990, All Other Animal Production.

1124 Sheep and Goat Farming

This industry group comprises establishments primarily engaged in raising sheep, lambs, and goats, or feeding lambs for fattening.

US—United States industry only. CAN—United States and Canadian industries are comparable. When neither US nor CAN appears, Canadian, Mexican, and United States industries are comparable.

11241 Sheep Farming

See industry description for 112410 below.

112410 Sheep Farming

This industry comprises establishments primarily engaged in raising sheep and lambs, or feeding lambs for fattening. The sheep or lambs may be raised for sale or wool production.

Cross-References.

Establishments primarily engaged in operating stockyards for transportation and not buying, selling, or auctioning livestock are classified in U.S. Industry 488999, All Other Support Activities for Transportation.

11242 Goat Farming

See industry description for 112420 below.

112420 Goat Farming

This industry comprises establishments primarily engaged in raising goats.

1125 Animal Aquaculture

11251 Animal Aquaculture

This industry comprises establishments primarily engaged in the farm raising of finfish, shellfish, or any other kind of animal aquaculture. These establishments use some form of intervention in the rearing process to enhance production, such as holding in captivity, regular stocking, feeding, and protecting from predators.

Cross-References.

Establishments primarily engaged in the catching or taking of fish and other aquatic animals from their natural habitat are classified in Industry 11411, Fishing.

112511 Finfish Farming and Fish Hatcheries[US]

This U.S. industry comprises establishments primarily engaged in (1) farm raising finfish (e.g., catfish, trout, goldfish, tropical fish, minnows) and/or (2) hatching fish of any kind.

Cross-References.

Establishments primarily engaged in the catching or taking of finfish from their natural habitat are classified in U.S. Industry 114111, Finfish Fishing.

US—United States industry only. CAN—United States and Canadian industries are comparable. When neither US nor CAN appears, Canadian, Mexican, and United States industries are comparable.

http://www.ntis.gov/naics

112512 Shellfish Farming[US]

This U.S. industry comprises establishments primarily engaged in farm raising shellfish (e.g., crayfish, shrimp, oysters, clams, mollusks).

Cross-References.

Establishments primarily engaged in the catching or taking of shellfish from their natural habitat are classified in U.S. Industry 114112, Shellfish Fishing.

112519 Other Animal Aquaculture[US]

This U.S. industry comprises establishments primarily engaged in farm raising animal aquaculture (except finfish and shellfish). Alligator, frog, or turtle production is included in this industry.

Cross-References. Establishments primarily engaged in—

- Miscellaneous fishing activities, such as catching or taking of terrapins, turtles, and frogs in their natural habitat,—are classified in U.S. Industry 114119, Other Marine Fishing;

- Farm raising finfish—are classified in U.S. Industry 112511, Finfish Farming and Fish Hatcheries; and

- Farm raising shellfish—are classified in U.S. Industry 112512, Shellfish Farming.

1129 Other Animal Production

This industry group comprises establishments primarily engaged in raising animals and insects (except cattle, hogs and pigs, poultry, sheep and goats, animal aquaculture) for sale or product production. These establishments are primarily engaged in raising one of the following: bees, horses and other equines, rabbits and other fur-bearing animals, and so forth, and producing products, such as honey and other bee products. Establishments primarily engaged in raising a combination of animals with no one animal or family of animals accounting for one-half of the establishment's agricultural production (i.e., value of animals for market) are included in this industry group.

11291 Apiculture
See industry description for 112910 below.

112910 Apiculture

This industry comprises establishments primarily engaged in raising bees. These establishments may collect and gather honey; and/or sell queen bees, packages of bees, royal jelly, bees' wax, propolis, venom, and/or other bee products.

US—United States industry only. CAN—United States and Canadian industries are comparable. When neither US nor CAN appears, Canadian, Mexican, and United States industries are comparable.

11292 Horses and Other Equine Production
See industry description for 112920 below.

112920 Horses and Other Equine Production

This industry comprises establishments primarily engaged in raising horses, mules, donkeys, and other equines.

Cross-References.

- Establishments primarily engaged in equine boarding are classified in Industry 115210, Support Activities for Animal Production; and

- Equine owners entering horses in racing or other spectator sporting events are classified in U.S. Industry 711219, Other Spectator Sports.

11293 Fur-Bearing Animal and Rabbit Production
See industry description for 112930 below.

112930 Fur-Bearing Animal and Rabbit Production

This industry comprises establishments primarily engaged in raising fur-bearing animals including rabbits. These animals may be raised for sale or for their pelt production.

Cross-References.

Establishments primarily engaged in the trapping or hunting of wild fur-bearing animals are classified in Industry 114210, Hunting and Trapping.

11299 All Other Animal Production
See industry description for 112990 below.

112990 All Other Animal Production

This industry comprises establishments primarily engaged in: (1) raising animals (except cattle, hogs and pigs, poultry, sheep and goats, animal aquaculture, apiculture, horses and other equines, and fur-bearing animals including rabbits) or (2) raising a combination of animals, with no one animal or family of animals accounting for one-half of the establishment's agricultural production (i.e., value of animals for market) are included in this industry.

Illustrative Examples:

Bird production (e.g., canaries, parakeets, parrots)	Deer production
Combination animal farming (except dairy, poultry)	Laboratory animal production (e.g., rats, mice, guinea pigs)
Companion animals production (e.g., cats, dogs)	Llama production
	Worm production

US—United States industry only. CAN—United States and Canadian industries are comparable. When neither US nor CAN appears, Canadian, Mexican, and United States industries are comparable.

http://www.ntis.gov/naics

Cross-References. Establishments primarily engaged in—

- Raising cattle, dairy cattle or feeding cattle for fattening—are classified in Industry Group 1121, Cattle Ranching and Farming;

- Raising hogs and pigs—are classified in Industry Group 1122, Hog and Pig Farming; Raising poultry and raising poultry for egg production—are classified in Industry

- Group 1123, Poultry and Egg Production;

- Raising sheep and goats—are classified in Industry Group 1124, Sheep and Goat Farming;

- Raising animal aquaculture—are classified in Industry Group 1125, Animal Aquaculture;

- Raising bees—are classified in Industry 112910, Apiculture;

- Raising horses and other equines—are classified in Industry 112920, Horses and Other Equine Production; and

- Raising fur-bearing animals including rabbits—are classified in Industry 112930, Fur-Bearing Animals and Rabbit Production.

113 Forestry and Logging

Industries in the Forestry and Logging subsector grow and harvest timber on a long production cycle (i.e., of 10 years or more). Long production cycles use different production processes than short production cycles, which require more horticultural interventions prior to harvest, resulting in processes more similar to those found in the Crop Production subsector. Consequently, Christmas tree production and other production involving production cycles of less than 10 years, are classified in the Crop Production subsector.

Industries in this subsector specialize in different stages of the production cycle. Reforestation requires production of seedlings in specialized nurseries. Timber production requires natural forest or suitable areas of land that are available for a long duration. The maturation time for timber depends upon the species of tree, the climatic conditions of the region, and the intended purpose of the timber. The harvesting of timber (except when done on an extremely small scale) requires specialized machinery unique to the industry. Establishments gathering forest products, such as gums, barks, balsam needles, rhizomes, fibers, Spanish moss, and ginseng and truffles, are also included in this subsector.

1131 Timber Tract Operations

11311 Timber Tract Operations
See industry description for 113110 below.

113110 Timber Tract Operations

This industry comprises establishments primarily engaged in the operation of timber tracts for the purpose of selling standing timber.

US—United States industry only. CAN—United States and Canadian industries are comparable. When neither US nor CAN appears, Canadian, Mexican, and United States industries are comparable.

Cross-References. Establishments primarily engaged in—

- Acting as lessors of land with trees as real estate property—are classified in Industry 53119, Lessors of Other Real Estate Property;

- Growing short rotation woody trees (i.e., growing and harvesting cycle is 10 years or less)—are classified in U.S. Industry 111421, Nursery and Tree Production; and

- Cutting timber—are classified in Industry 113310, Logging.

1132 Forest Nurseries and Gathering of Forest Products

11321 Forest Nurseries and Gathering of Forest Products
See industry description for 113210 below.

113210 Forest Nurseries and Gathering of Forest Products

This industry comprises establishments primarily engaged in (1) growing trees for reforestation and/or (2) gathering forest products, such as gums, barks, balsam needles, rhizomes, fibers, Spanish moss, ginseng, and truffles.

Cross-References. Establishments primarily engaged in—

- Gathering tea and maple sap—are classified in U.S. Industry 111998, All Other Miscellaneous Crop Farming; and

- Processing maple syrup into other products—are classified in Industry 31199, All Other Food Manufacturing.

1133 Logging

11331 Logging
See industry description for 113310 below.

113310 Logging

This industry comprises establishments primarily engaged in one or more of the following: (1) cutting timber; (2) cutting and transporting timber; and (3) producing wood chips in the field.

Cross-References.

Establishments primarily engaged in trucking timber are classified in Industry 484220, Specialized Freight (except Used Goods) Trucking, Local.

114 Fishing, Hunting and Trapping

Industries in the Fishing, Hunting, and Trapping subsector harvest fish and other wild animals from their natural habitats and are dependent upon a continued supply of the natural resource. The

US—United States industry only. CAN—United States and Canadian industries are comparable. When neither US nor CAN appears, Canadian, Mexican, and United States industries are comparable.

harvesting of fish is the predominant economic activity of this subsector and it usually requires specialized vessels that, by the nature of their size, configuration and equipment, are not suitable for any other type of production, such as transportation.

Hunting and trapping activities utilize a wide variety of production processes and are classified in the same subsector as fishing because the availability of resources and the constraints imposed, such as conservation requirements and proper habitat maintenance, are similar.

1141 Fishing

11411 Fishing

This industry comprises establishments primarily engaged in the commercial catching or taking of finfish, shellfish, or miscellaneous marine products from a natural habitat, such as the catching of bluefish, eels, salmon, tuna, clams, crabs, lobsters, mussels, oysters, shrimp, frogs, sea urchins, and turtles.

Cross-References. Establishments primarily engaged in—

- Farm raising finfish, shellfish or other marine animals—are classified in Industry 11251, Animal Aquaculture; and

- Gathering and processing (known as "floating factory ships") seafood into canned seafood products—are classified in Industry 31171, Seafood Product Preparation and Packaging.

114111 Finfish Fishing[US]

This U.S. industry comprises establishments primarily engaged in the commercial catching or taking of finfish (e.g., bluefish, salmon, trout, tuna) from their natural habitat.

Cross-References. Establishments primarily engaged in—

- Farm raising finfish—are classified in U.S. Industry 112511, Finfish Farming and Fish Hatcheries; and

- Gathering and processing (known as "floating factory ships") seafood into canned seafood products—are classified in U.S. Industry 311711, Seafood Canning.

114112 Shellfish Fishing[US]

This U.S. industry comprises establishments primarily engaged in the commercial catching or taking of shellfish (e.g., clams, crabs, lobsters, mussels, oysters, sea urchins, shrimp) from their natural habitat.

Cross-References.

Establishments primarily engaged in farm raising shellfish—are classified in U.S. Industry 112512, Shellfish Farming.

US—United States industry only. CAN—United States and Canadian industries are comparable. When neither US nor CAN appears, Canadian, Mexican, and United States industries are comparable.

114119 Other Marine Fishing[US]

This U.S. industry comprises establishments primarily engaged in the commercial catching or taking of marine animals (except finfish and shellfish).

Cross-References. Establishments primarily engaged in—

- Raising animal aquaculture (except finfish and shellfish)—are classified in U.S. Industry 112519, Other Animal Aquaculture;

- The commercial catching or taking of finfish from their natural habitat—are classified in U.S. Industry 114111, Finfish Fishing; and

- The commercial catching or taking of shellfish from their natural habitat—are classified in U.S. Industry 114112, Shellfish Fishing.

1142 Hunting and Trapping

11421 Hunting and Trapping
See industry description for 114210 below.

114210 Hunting and Trapping

This industry comprises establishments primarily engaged in one or more of the following: (1) commercial hunting and trapping; (2) operating commercial game preserves, such as game retreats; and (3) operating hunting preserves.

Cross-References. Establishments primarily engaged in—

- Operating nature preserves—are classified in Industry 712190, Nature Parks and Other Similar Institutions; and

- Farm raising rabbits and other fur-bearing animals—are classified in Industry 112930, Fur-Bearing Animal and Rabbit Production.

115 Support Activities for Agriculture and Forestry

Industries in the Support Activities for Agriculture and Forestry subsector provide support services that are an essential part of agricultural and forestry production. These support activities may be performed by the agriculture or forestry producing establishment or conducted independently as an alternative source of inputs required for the production process for a given crop, animal, or forestry industry. Establishments that primarily perform these activities independent of the agriculture or forestry producing establishment are in this subsector.

1151 Support Activities for Crop Production

11511 Support Activities for Crop Production

This industry comprises establishments primarily engaged in providing support activities for growing crops.

US—United States industry only. CAN—United States and Canadian industries are comparable. When neither US nor CAN appears, Canadian, Mexican, and United States industries are comparable.

Illustrative Examples:

Aerial dusting or spraying (i.e., using
  specialized or dedicated aircraft)
Cotton ginning
Cultivating services

Farm management services
Planting crops
Vineyard cultivation services

Cross-References. Establishments primarily engaged in—

- Performing crop production that are generally known as farms, orchards, groves, or vineyards (including sharecroppers and tenant farms),—are classified in the appropriate crop industry within Subsector 111, Crop Production;

- Providing support activities for forestry—are classified in Industry 11531, Support Activities for Forestry;

- Landscaping and horticultural services, such as lawn and maintenance care and ornamental shrub and tree services,—are classified in Industry 56173, Landscaping Services;

- Land clearing, land leveling, and earth moving for terracing, ponds, and irrigation—are classified in Industry 23499, All Other Heavy Construction;

- Artificially drying and dehydrating fruits and vegetables—are classified in Industry 31142, Fruit and Vegetable Canning, Pickling and Drying;

- Stemming and redrying tobacco—are classified in Industry 31221, Tobacco Stemming and Redrying;

- Providing water for irrigation—are classified in Industry 22131, Water Supply and Irrigation Systems; and

- Buying farm products, such as fruits or vegetables, for resale to other wholesalers or retailers, and preparing them for market or further processing—are classified in Industry 42248, Fresh Fruit and Vegetable Wholesalers.

115111 Cotton Ginning[US]

This U.S. industry comprises establishments primarily engaged in ginning cotton.

115112 Soil Preparation, Planting, and Cultivating[US]

This U.S. industry comprises establishments primarily engaged in performing a soil preparation activity or crop production service, such as plowing, fertilizing, seed bed preparation, planting, cultivating, and crop protecting services.

Cross-References. Establishments primarily engaged in—

- Land clearing, land leveling, and earth moving for terracing, ponds, and irrigation—are classified in Industry 234990, All Other Heavy Construction; and

---

US—United States industry only. CAN—United States and Canadian industries are comparable.
When neither US nor CAN appears, Canadian, Mexican, and United States industries are comparable.

- Providing water for irrigation—are classified in Industry 221310, Water Supply and Irrigation Systems.

115113 Crop Harvesting, Primarily by Machine[US]

This U.S. industry comprises establishments primarily engaged in mechanical harvesting, picking, and combining of crops, and related activities. The machinery used is provided by the servicing establishment.

Cross-References. Establishments primarily engaged in—

- Providing personnel for manual harvesting—are classified in U.S. Industry 115115, Farm Labor Contractors and Crew Leaders; and

- Providing farm management services (i.e., a contract or fee basis) and arranging or contracting crop mechanical or manual harvesting operations for the farm(s) it manages—are classified in U.S. Industry 115116, Farm Management Services.

115114 Postharvest Crop Activities (except Cotton Ginning)[US]

This U.S. industry comprises establishments primarily engaged in performing services on crops, subsequent to their harvest, with the intent of preparing them for market or further processing. These establishments provide postharvest activities, such as crop cleaning, sun drying, shelling, fumigating, curing, sorting, grading, packing, and cooling.

Cross-References. Establishments primarily engaged in—

- Ginning cotton—are classified in U.S. Industry 115111, Cotton Ginning;

- Artificially drying and dehydrating fruits and vegetables—are classified in U.S. Industry 311423, Dried and Dehydrated Food Manufacturing;

- Stemming and redrying tobacco—are classified in Industry 312210, Tobacco Stemming and Redrying;

- Buying farm products for resale to other wholesalers or retailers and preparing them for market or further processing—are classified in Industry 422480, Fresh Fruit and Vegetable Wholesalers; and

- Providing farm management services (i.e., a contract or fee basis) and arranging or contracting postharvesting crop activities for the farm(s) it manages—are classified in U.S. Industry 115116, Farm Management Services.

115115 Farm Labor Contractors and Crew Leaders[US]

This U.S. industry comprises establishments primarily engaged in supplying labor for agricultural production or harvesting.

US—United States industry only. CAN—United States and Canadian industries are comparable. When neither US nor CAN appears, Canadian, Mexican, and United States industries are comparable.

Cross-References. Establishments primarily engaged in—

- Providing machine harvesting—are classified in U.S. Industry 115113, Crop Harvesting, Primarily by Machine; and

- Providing farm management services (i.e., a contract or fee basis) and arranging or contracting farm labor for the farm(s) it manages—are classified in U.S. Industry 115116, Farm Management Services.

115116 Farm Management Services[US]

This U.S. industry comprises establishments primarily engaged in providing farm management services on a contract or fee basis usually to citrus groves, orchards, or vineyards. These establishments always provide management and may arrange or contract for the partial or the complete operations of the farm establishment(s) it manages. Operational activities may include cultivating, harvesting, and/or other specialized agricultural support activities.

Cross-References.

Establishments primarily engaged in crop production that are generally known as farms, orchards, groves, or vineyards (including share croppers and tenant farms), are classified in the appropriate crop industry within Subsector 111, Crop Production.

1152 Support Activities for Animal Production

11521 Support Activities for Animal Production
See industry description for 115210 below.

115210 Support Activities for Animal Production

This industry comprises establishments primarily engaged in performing support activities related to raising livestock (e.g., cattle, goats, hogs, horses, poultry, sheep). These establishments may perform one or more of the following: (1) breeding services for animals, including companion animals (e.g., cats, dogs, pet birds); (2) pedigree record services; (3) boarding horses; (4) dairy herd improvement activities; (5) livestock spraying; and (6) sheep dipping and shearing.

1153 Support Activities for Forestry

11531 Support Activities for Forestry
See industry description for 115310 below.

115310 Support Activities for Forestry

This industry comprises establishments primarily engaged in performing particular support activities related to timber production, wood technology, forestry economics and marketing, and forest

US—United States industry only. CAN—United States and Canadian industries are comparable. When neither US nor CAN appears, Canadian, Mexican, and United States industries are comparable.

protection. These establishments may provide support activities for forestry, such as estimating timber, forest firefighting, forest pest control, and consulting on wood attributes and reforestation.

Cross-References.

Establishments primarily engaged in the public administration and conservation of forest lands are classified in Industry 924120, Administration of Conservation Programs.

Sector 21—Mining

The Sector as a Whole

The Mining sector comprises establishments that extract naturally occurring mineral solids, such as coal and ores; liquid minerals, such as crude petroleum; and gases, such as natural gas. The term mining is used in the broad sense to include quarrying, well operations, beneficiating (e.g., crushing, screening, washing, and flotation), and other preparation customarily performed at the mine site, or as a part of mining activity.

The Mining sector distinguishes two basic activities: mine operation and mining support activities. Mine operation includes establishments operating mines, quarries, or oil and gas wells on their own account or for others on a contract or fee basis. Mining support activities include establishments that perform exploration (except geophysical surveying) and/or other mining services on a contract or fee basis.

Establishments in the Mining sector are grouped and classified according to the natural resource mined or to be mined. Industries include establishments that develop the mine site, extract the natural resources, and /or those that beneficiate (i.e., prepare) the mineral mined. Beneficiation is the process whereby the extracted material is reduced to particles that can be separated into mineral and waste, the former suitable for further processing or direct use. The operations that take place in beneficiation are primarily mechanical, such as grinding, washing, magnetic separation, and centrifugal separation. In contrast, manufacturing operations primarily use chemical and electro-chemical processes, such as electrolysis and distillation. However some treatments, such as heat treatments, take place in both the beneficiation and the manufacturing (i.e., smelting/refining) stages. The range of preparation activities varies by mineral and the purity of any given ore deposit. While some minerals, such as petroleum and natural gas, require little or no preparation, others are washed and screened, while yet others, such as gold and silver, can be transformed into bullion before leaving the mine site.

Mining, beneficiating, and manufacturing activities often occur in a single location. Separate receipts will be collected for these activities whenever possible. When receipts cannot be broken out between mining and manufacturing, establishments that mine or quarry nonmetallic minerals, beneficiate the nonmetallic minerals into more finished manufactured products are classified based on the primary activity of the establishment. A mine that manufactures a small amount of finished products will be classified in Sector 21, Mining. An establishment that mines whose primary output is a more finished manufactured product will be classified in Sector 31-33, Manufacturing.

211 Oil and Gas Extraction

Industries in the Oil and Gas Extraction subsector operate and/or develop oil and gas field properties. Such activities may include exploration for crude petroleum and natural gas; drilling, completing, and equipping wells; operating separators, emulsion breakers, desilting equipment, and field gathering lines for crude petroleum; and all other activities in the preparation of oil and gas up to the point of shipment from the producing property. This subsector includes the production of crude petroleum, the mining and extraction of oil from oil shale and oil sands, and the production of natural gas and recovery of hydrocarbon liquids.

US—United States industry only. CAN—United States and Canadian industries are comparable. When neither US nor CAN appears, Canadian, Mexican, and United States industries are comparable.

Establishments in this subsector include those that operate oil and gas wells on their own account or for others on a contract or fee basis. Establishments primarily engaged in providing support services, on a fee or contract basis, required for the drilling or operation of oil and gas wells (except geophysical surveying and mapping) are classified in Subsector 213, Support Activities for Mining.

2111 Oil and Gas Extraction

21111 Oil and Gas Extraction

This industry comprises establishments primarily engaged in operating and/or developing oil and gas field properties and establishments primarily engaged in recovering liquid hydrocarbons from oil and gas field gases. Such activities may include exploration for crude petroleum and natural gas; drilling, completing, and equipping wells; operation of separators, emulsion breakers, desilting equipment, and field gathering lines for crude petroleum; and all other activities in the preparation of oil and gas up to the point of shipment from the producing property. This industry includes the production of crude petroleum, the mining and extraction of oil from oil shale and oil sands, the production of natural gas and the recovery of hydrocarbon liquids from oil and gas field gases. Establishments in this industry operate oil and gas wells on their own account or for others on a contract or fee basis.

Cross-References. Establishments primarily engaged in—

- Performing oil field services for operators on a contract or fee basis—are classified in Industry 21311, Support Activities for Mining;

- Manufacturing acyclic and cyclic aromatic hydrocarbons from refined petroleum or liquid hydrocarbons—are classified in Industry 32511, Petrochemical Manufacturing;

- Refining crude petroleum into refined petroleum and liquid hydrocarbons—are classified in Industry 32411, Petroleum Refineries; and

- Recovering helium from natural gas—are classified in Industry 32512, Industrial Gas Manufacturing.

211111 Crude Petroleum and Natural Gas Extraction[US]

This U.S. industry comprises establishments primarily engaged in (1) the exploration, development and/or the production of petroleum or natural gas from wells in which the hydrocarbons will initially flow or can be produced using normal pumping techniques, or (2) the production of crude petroleum from surface shales or tar sands or from reservoirs in which the hydrocarbons are semisolids. Establishments in this industry operate oil and gas wells on their own account or for others on a contract or fee basis.

Cross-References. Establishments primarily engaged in—

- Performing oil field services for operators on a contract or fee basis—are classified in Industry 21311, Support Activities for Mining;

US—United States industry only. CAN—United States and Canadian industries are comparable. When neither US nor CAN appears, Canadian, Mexican, and United States industries are comparable.

- Refining crude petroleum into refined petroleum and liquid hydrocarbons—are classified in Industry 324110, Petroleum Refineries; and

- Recovering helium from natural gas—are classified in Industry 325120, Industrial Gas Manufacturing.

211112 Natural Gas Liquid Extraction[US]

This U.S. industry comprises establishments primarily engaged in the recovery of liquid hydrocarbons from oil and gas field gases. Establishments primarily engaged in sulfur recovery from natural gas are included in this industry.

Cross-References. Establishments primarily engaged in—

- Manufacturing acyclic and cyclic aromatic hydrocarbons from refined petroleum or converting refined petroleum into liquid hydrocarbons (petrochemicals) and/or recovering liquid hydrocarbons—are classified in Industry 325110, Petrochemical Manufacturing;

- Refining crude petroleum into refined petroleum and liquid hydrocarbons—are classified in Industry 324110, Petroleum Refineries; and

- Recovering helium from natural gas—are classified in Industry 325120, Industrial Gas Manufacturing.

212 Mining (except Oil and Gas)

Industries in the Mining (except Oil and Gas) subsector primarily engage in mining, mine site development, and beneficiating (i.e, preparing) metallic minerals and nonmetallic minerals, including coal. The term ''mining'' is used in the broad sense to include ore extraction, quarrying, and beneficiating (e.g., crushing, screening, washing, sizing, concentrating, and flotation), customarily done at the mine site.

Beneficiation is the process whereby the extracted material is reduced to particles which can be separated into mineral and waste, the former suitable for further processing or direct use. The operations that take place in beneficiation are primarily mechanical, such as grinding, washing, magnetic separation, centrifugal separation, and so on. In contrast, manufacturing operations primarily use chemical and electrochemical processes, such as electrolysis, distillation, and so on. However some treatments, such as heat treatments, take place in both stages: the beneficiation and the manufacturing (i.e., smelting/refining) stages. The range of preparation activities varies by mineral and the purity of any given ore deposit. While some minerals, such as petroleum and natural gas, require little or no preparation, others are washed and screened, while yet others, such as gold and silver, can be transformed into bullion before leaving the mine site.

Establishments in the Mining (except Oil and Gas) subsector include those that have complete responsibility for operating mines and quarries (except oil and gas wells) and those that operate mines and quarries (except oil and gas wells) for others on a contract or fee basis. Establishments

---

US—United States industry only. CAN—United States and Canadian industries are comparable. When neither US nor CAN appears, Canadian, Mexican, and United States industries are comparable.

primarily engaged in providing support services, on a contract or fee basis, required for the mining and quarrying of minerals are classified in Subsector 213, Support Activities for Mining.

2121 Coal Mining

21211 Coal Mining

This industry comprises establishments primarily engaged in one or more of the following: (1) mining bituminous coal, anthracite, and lignite by underground mining, auger mining, strip mining, culm bank mining, and other surface mining; (2) developing coal mine sites; and (3) beneficiating (i.e, preparing) coal (e.g., cleaning, washing, screening, and sizing coal).

Cross-References. Establishments primarily engaged in—

* Manufacturing code oven products in coke oven establishments—are classified in Industry 32419, Other Petroleum and Coal Products Manufacturing; and

* Manufacturing coal products in steel mills—are classified in Industry 33111, Iron and Steel Mills and Ferroalloy Manufacturing.

212111 Bituminous Coal and Lignite Surface Mining[US]

This U.S. industry comprises establishments primarily engaged in one or more of the following: (1) surface mining or development of bituminous coal and lignite; (2) developing bituminous coal and lignite surface mine sites; and (3) beneficiating bituminous coal (e.g., cleaning, washing, screening, and sizing coal) whether mined on surface or underground.

Cross-References. Establishments primarily engaged in—

* Manufacturing coke oven products in coke oven establishments—are classified in U.S. Industry 324199, All Other Petroleum and Coal Products Manufacturing;

* Underground mining of bituminous coal—are classified in U.S. Industry 212112, Bituminous Coal Underground Mining; and

* Mining and/or beneficiating anthracite coal—are classified in U.S. Industry 212113, Anthracite Mining.

212112 Bituminous Coal Underground Mining[US]

This U.S. industry comprises establishments primarily engaged in one or more of the following: (1) the underground mining of bituminous coal; (2) developing bituminous coal underground mine sites; and (3) the underground mining and beneficiating bituminous coal (e.g, cleaning, washing, screening, and sizing coal).

Cross-References. Establishments primarily engaged in—

* Manufacturing coke oven products in coke oven establishments—are classified in U.S. Industry 324199, All Other Petroleum and Coal Products Manufacturing;

US—United States industry only. CAN—United States and Canadian industries are comparable. When neither US nor CAN appears, Canadian, Mexican, and United States industries are comparable.

- Surface mining and/or beneficiating of bituminous coal or lignite—are classified in U.S. Industry 212111, Bituminous Coal and Lignite Surface Mining; and

- Mining and/or beneficiating anthracite coal—are classified in U.S. Industry 212113, Anthracite Mining.

212113 Anthracite Mining[US]

This U.S. industry comprises establishments primarily engaged in one or more of the following: (1) mining anthracite coal; (2) developing anthracite coal mining sites; and (3) beneficiating anthracite coal (e.g., cleaning, washing, screening, and sizing coal).

Cross-References. Establishments primarily engaged in—

- Manufacturing coke oven products in coke oven establishments—are classified in U.S. Industry 324199, All Other Petroleum and Coal Products Manufacturing;

- Surface mining and/or beneficiating bituminous coal or lignite—are classified in U.S. Industry 212111, Bituminous Coal and Lignite Surface Mining; and

- Underground mining of bituminous coal—are classified in U.S. Industry 212112, Bituminous Coal Underground Mining.

2122 Metal Ore Mining

This industry group comprises establishments primarily engaged in developing mine sites or mining metallic minerals, and establishments primarily engaged in ore dressing and beneficiating (i.e., preparing) operations, such as crushing, grinding, washing, drying, sintering, concentrating, calcining, and leaching. Beneficiating may be performed at mills operated in conjunction with the mines served or at mills, such as custom mills, operated separately.

21221 Iron Ore Mining
See industry description for 212210 below.

212210 Iron Ore Mining

This industry comprises establishments primarily engaged in (1) developing mine sites, mining, and/or beneficiating (i.e., preparing) iron ores and manganiferous ores valued chiefly for their iron content and/or (2) producing sinter iron ore (except iron ore produced in iron and steel mills) and other iron ore agglomerates.

Cross-References.

Establishments primarily engaged in manufacturing pig iron ore are classified in U.S. Industry 331111, Iron and Steel Mills.

US—United States industry only. CAN—United States and Canadian industries are comparable. When neither US nor CAN appears, Canadian, Mexican, and United States industries are comparable.

21222 Gold Ore and Silver Ore Mining

This industry comprises establishments primarily engaged in developing the mine site, mining, and/or beneficiating (i.e., preparing) ores valued chiefly for their gold and or silver content. Establishments primarily engaged in the transformation of the gold and silver into bullion or dore bar in combination with mining activities are included in this industry.

Cross-References.

Establishments primarily engaged in manufacturing gold or silver bullion or dore bar without mining are classified in Industry 33141, Nonferrous Metal (except Aluminum) Smelting and Refining.

212221 Gold Ore Mining[US]

This U.S. industry comprises establishments primarily engaged in developing the mine site, mining, and/or beneficiating (i.e., preparing) ores valued chiefly for their gold content. Establishments primarily engaged in transformation of the gold into bullion or dore bar in combination with mining activities are included in this industry.

Cross-References.

Establishments primarily engaged in manufacturing gold bullion or dore bar without mining are classified in U.S. Industry 331419, Primary Smelting and Refining of Nonferrous Metal (except Copper and Aluminum).

212222 Silver Ore Mining[US]

This U.S. industry comprises establishments primarily engaged in developing the mine site, mining, and/or beneficiating (i.e, preparing) ores valued chiefly for their silver content. Establishments primarily engaged in transformation of the silver into bullion or dore bar in combination with mining activities are included in this industry.

Cross-References.

Establishments primarily engaged in manufacturing silver bullion or dore bar without mining are classified in U.S. Industry 331419, Primary Smelting and Refining of Nonferrous Metal (except Copper and Aluminum).

21223 Copper, Nickel, Lead, and Zinc Mining

This industry comprises establishments primarily engaged in developing the mine site, mining, and/or beneficiating (i.e., preparing) ores valued chiefly for their copper, nickel, lead, or zinc content. Beneficiating includes the transformation of ores into concentrates.

US—United States industry only. CAN—United States and Canadian industries are comparable. When neither US nor CAN appears, Canadian, Mexican, and United States industries are comparable.

Cross-References. Establishments primarily engaged in—

- Refining copper concentrates—are classified in Industry 33141, Nonferrous Metal (except Aluminum) Smelting and Refining; and

- Developing the mine site, mining, and/or beneficiating iron and manganiferous ores valued for their iron content—are classified in Industry 21221, Iron Ore Mining.

212231 Lead Ore and Zinc Ore Mining^{CAN}

This U.S. industry comprises establishments primarily engaged in developing the mine site, mining, and/or beneficiating (i.e., preparing) lead ores, zinc ores, or lead-zinc ores.

212234 Copper Ore and Nickel Ore Mining^{US}

This U.S. industry comprises establishments primarily engaged in (1) developing the mine site, mining, and/or beneficiating (i.e, preparing) copper and/or nickel ores, and (2) recovering copper concentrates by the precipitation, leaching, or electrowinning of copper ore.

Cross-References.

Establishments primarily engaged in refining copper concentrates are classified in U.S. Industry 331411, Primary Smelting and Refining of Copper.

21229 Other Metal Ore Mining

This industry comprises establishments primarily engaged in developing the mine site, mining, and/or beneficiating (i.e., preparing) metal ores (except iron and manganiferous ores valued for their iron content, gold ore, silver ore, copper, nickel, lead, and zinc ore).

Illustrative Examples:

Antimony ores mining and/or beneficiating	Tantalum ores mining and/or beneficiating
Columbite ores mining and/or beneficiating	Tungsten ores mining and/or beneficiating
Ilmenite ores mining and/or beneficiating	Uranium-radium-vanadium ores mining and/or
Molybdenum ores mining and/or beneficiating	beneficiating

Cross-References. Establishments primarily engaged in—

- Developing the mine site, mining, and/or beneficiating iron and manganiferous ores valued chiefly for their iron content—are classified in Industry 21221, Iron Ore Mining;

- Developing the mine site, mining, and/or beneficiating ores valued chiefly for their gold or silver content—are classified in Industry 21222, Gold Ore and Silver Ore Mining;

- Developing the mine site, mining, and/or beneficiating ores valued chiefly for their copper, nickel, lead, or zinc content—are classified in Industry 21223, Copper, Nickel, Lead, and Zinc Mining; and

---

US—United States industry only. CAN—United States and Canadian industries are comparable. When neither US nor CAN appears, Canadian, Mexican, and United States industries are comparable.

http://www.ntis.gov/naics

- Enriching uranium—are classified in Industry 32518, Other Basic Inorganic Chemical Manufacturing.

212291 Uranium-Radium-Vanadium Ore Mining[US]

This U.S. industry comprises establishments primarily engaged in developing the mine site, mining, and/or beneficiating (i.e., preparing) uranium-radium-vanadium ores.

Cross-References.

Establishments primarily engaged in enriching uranium are classified in U.S. Industry 325188, All Other Basic Inorganic Chemical Manufacturing.

212299 All Other Metal Ore Mining[US]

This U.S. industry comprises establishments primarily engaged in developing the mine site, mining, and/or beneficiating (i.e., preparing) metal ores (except iron and manganiferous ores valued for their iron content, gold ore, silver ore, copper, nickel, lead, zinc, and uranium-radium-vanadium ore).

Illustrative Examples:

Antimony ores mining and/or beneficiating
Columbite ores mining and/or beneficiating
Ilmenite ores mining and/or beneficiating
Molybdenum ores mining and/or beneficiating

Rare-earth metal ores mining and/or beneficiating
Tantalum ores mining and/or beneficiating
Tungsten ores mining and/or beneficiating

Cross-References. Establishments primarily engaged in—

- Developing the mine site, mining, and/or beneficiating iron and manganiferous ores valued for their iron content—are classified in Industry 212210, Iron Ore Mining;

- Developing the mine site, mining, and/or beneficiating ores valued chiefly for their gold or silver content—are classified in Industry 21222, Gold Ore and Silver Ore Mining;

- Developing the mine site, mining, and/or beneficiating ores valued chiefly for their copper, nickel, lead, or zinc content—are classified in Industry 21223, Copper, Nickel, Lead, and Zinc Mining; and

- Developing the mine site, mining, and/or beneficiating uranium-radium-vanadium ores— are classified in U.S. Industry 212291, Uranium-Radium-Vanadium Ore Mining.

2123 Nonmetallic Mineral Mining and Quarrying

This industry group comprises establishments primarily engaged in developing mine sites, or in mining or quarrying nonmetallic minerals (except fuels). Also included are certain well and brine operations, and preparation plants primarily engaged in beneficiating (e.g., crushing, grinding, washing, and concentrating) nonmetallic minerals.

US—United States industry only. CAN—United States and Canadian industries are comparable. When neither US nor CAN appears, Canadian, Mexican, and United States industries are comparable.

Beneficiation is the process whereby the extracted material is reduced to particles which can be separated into mineral and waste, the former suitable for further processing or direct use. The operations that take place in beneficiation are primarily mechanical, such as grinding, washing, magnetic separation, and centrifugal separation. In contrast, manufacturing operations primarily use chemical and electrochemical processes, such as electrolysis and distillation. However some treatments, such as heat treatments, take place in both the beneficiation and the manufacturing (i.e., smelting/refining) stages. The range of preparation activities varies by mineral and the purity of any given ore deposit. While some minerals, such as petroleum and natural gas, require little or no preparation, others are washed and screened, while yet others, such as gold and silver, can be transformed into bullion before leaving the mine site.

21231 Stone Mining and Quarrying

This industry comprises (1) establishments primarily engaged in developing the mine site, mining or quarrying dimension stone (i.e., rough blocks and/or slabs of stone), or mining and quarrying crushed and broken stone and/or (2) preparation plants primarily engaged in beneficiating stone (e.g., crushing, grinding, washing, screening, pulverizing, and sizing).

Cross-References. Establishments primarily engaged in—

- Producing lime—are classified in Industry 32741, Lime Manufacturing; and

- Quarrying and dressing dimension stone—are classified Industry 32799, All Other Nonmetallic Mineral Product Manufacturing.

212311 Dimension Stone Mining and Quarrying[US]

This U.S. industry comprises establishments primarily engaged in developing the mine site and/ or mining or quarrying dimension stone (i.e., rough blocks and/or slabs of stone).

Cross-References.

Establishments primarily engaged in dressing dimension stone and manufacturing stone products are classified in U.S. Industry 327991, Cut Stone and Stone Product Manufacturing.

212312 Crushed and Broken Limestone Mining and Quarrying[US]

This U.S. industry comprises (1) establishments primarily engaged in developing the mine site, mining or quarrying crushed and broken limestone (including related rocks, such as dolomite, cement rock, marl, travertine, and calcareous tufa), and (2) preparation plants primarily engaged in beneficiating limestone (e.g., grinding or pulverizing).

Cross-References. Establishments primarily engaged in—

- Producing lime—are classified in Industry 327410, Lime Manufacturing; and

- Mining or quarrying bituminous limestone—are classified U.S. Industry 212319, Other Crushed and Broken Stone Mining and Quarrying.

US—United States industry only. CAN—United States and Canadian industries are comparable. When neither US nor CAN appears, Canadian, Mexican, and United States industries are comparable.

212313 Crushed and Broken Granite Mining and Quarrying[US]

This U.S. industry comprises (1) establishments primarily engaged in developing the mine site, and/or mining or quarrying crushed and broken granite (including related rocks, such as gneiss, syenite, and diorite) and (2) preparation plants primarily engaged in beneficiating granite (e.g. grinding or pulverizing).

212319 Other Crushed and Broken Stone Mining and Quarrying[US]

This U.S. industry comprises (1) establishments primarily engaged in developing the mine site and/or mining or quarrying crushed and broken stone (except limestone and granite), (2) preparation plants primarily engaged in beneficiating (e.g., grinding and pulverizing) stone (except limestone and granite), and (3) establishments primarily engaged in mining or quarrying bituminous limestone and bituminous sandstone.

Illustrative Examples:

Bituminous limestone mining and/or beneficiating	Marble crushed and broken stone mining and/or beneficiating
Bituminous sandstone mining and/or beneficiating	Sandstone crushed and broken stone mining and/or beneficiating

Cross-References. Establishments primarily engaged in—

- Mining or quarrying crushed and broken limestone—are classified in U.S. Industry 212312, Crushed and Broken Limestone Mining and Quarrying; and

- Mining or quarrying crushed and broken granite—are classified in U.S. Industry 212313, Crushed and Broken Granite Mining and Quarrying.

21232 Sand, Gravel, Clay, and Ceramic and Refractory Minerals Mining and Quarrying

This industry comprises (1) establishments primarily engaged in developing the mine site and/ or mining, quarrying, dredging for sand and gravel, or mining clay, (e.g., china clay, paper clay and slip clay) and (2) preparation plants primarily engaged in beneficiating (e.g., washing, screening, and grinding) sand and gravel, clay, and ceramic and refractory minerals.

Cross-References Establishments primarily engaged in—

- Calcining, dead burning, or otherwise processing (i.e., beyond basic preparation) clay or refractory minerals—are classified in Industry 32799, All Other Nonmetallic Mineral Product Manufacturing;

- Shaping, molding, baking, burning, or hardening nonclay ceramics, clay and nonclay refractories, and structural clay products—are classified in Industry 32712, Clay Building Material and Refractories Manufacturing; and

---

US—United States industry only. CAN—United States and Canadian industries are comparable. When neither US nor CAN appears, Canadian, Mexican, and United States industries are comparable.

- Shaping, molding, glazing, and firing pottery, ceramics, and plumbing fixtures—are classi-fied in Industry 32711, Pottery, Ceramics and Plumbing Fixture Manufacturing.

212321 Construction Sand and Gravel Mining[US]

This U.S. industry comprises establishments primarily engaged in one or more of the following: (1) operating commercial grade (i.e., construction) sand and gravel pits; (2) dredging for commercial grade sand and gravel; and (3) washing, screening, or otherwise preparing commercial grade sand and gravel.

Cross-References.

Establishments primarily engaged in mining industrial grade sand are classified in U.S. Industry 212322, Industrial Sand Mining.

212322 Industrial Sand Mining[US]

This U.S. industry comprises establishments primarily engaged in one or more of the following: (1) operating industrial grade sand pits; (2) dredging for industrial grade sand; and (3) washing, screening, or otherwise preparing industrial grade sand.

Cross-References.

Establishments primarily engaged in mining commercial (i.e., construction) grade gravel are classified in U.S. Industry 212321, Construction Sand and Gravel Mining.

212324 Kaolin and Ball Clay Mining[US]

This U.S. industry comprises (1) establishments primarily engaged in developing the mine site and/or mining kaolin or ball clay (e.g., china clay, paper clay, and slip clay) and (2) establishments primarily engaged in beneficiating (i.e., preparing) kaolin or ball clay.

Cross-References.

Establishments primarily engaged in calcining, dead burning, or otherwise processing (i.e., beyond basic preparation) kaolin and ball clay are classified in U.S. Industry 327992, Ground or Treated Mineral and Earth Manufacturing.

212325 Clay and Ceramic and Refractory Minerals Mining[US]

This U.S. industry comprises establishments primarily engaged in one or more of the following: (1) mining clay (except kaolin and ball), ceramic, or refractory minerals; (2) developing the mine site for clay, ceramic, or refractory minerals; and (3) beneficiating (i.e., preparing) clay (except kaolin and ball), ceramic, or refractory minerals.

US—United States industry only. CAN—United States and Canadian industries are comparable. When neither US nor CAN appears, Canadian, Mexican, and United States industries are comparable.

http://www.ntis.gov/naics

Illustrative Examples:

Bentonite mining and/or beneficiating
Common clay mining and/or beneficiating
Feldspar mining and/or beneficiating
Fire clay mining and/or beneficiating
Fuller's earth mining and/or beneficiating

Magnesite mining and/or beneficiating
Nepheline syenite mining and/or beneficiating
Shale (except oil shale) mining and/or
 beneficiating

Cross-References. Establishments primarily engaged in—

* Shaping, molding, baking, burning, or hardening clay and nonclay refractories, and structural clay products—are classified in Industry 32712, Clay Building Material and Refractories Manufacturing;

* Developing the mine site, mining, and/or beneficiating kaolin or ball clay—are classified in U.S. Industry 212324, Kaolin and Ball Clay Mining; and

* Shaping, molding, glazing, and firing pottery, ceramics, and plumbing fixtures—are classified in Industry 32711, Pottery, Ceramics and Plumbing Fixture Manufacturing.

21239 Other Nonmetallic Mineral Mining and Quarrying

This industry comprises establishments primarily engaged in developing the mine site, mining, and/or milling or otherwise beneficiating (i.e., preparing) nonmetallic minerals (except coal, stone, sand, gravel, clay, ceramic, and refractory minerals).

Illustrative Examples:

Barite mining and/or beneficiating
Borate, natural, mining and/or beneficiating
Peat mining and/or beneficiating

Phosphate rock mining and/or beneficiating
Potash mining and/or beneficiating
Rock salt mining and/or beneficiating

Cross-References. Establishments primarily engaged in—

* Mining or quarrying dimension stone—are classified in Industry 21231, Stone Mining and Quarrying;

* Mining or quarrying sand, gravel, clay and ceramic and refractory minerals—are classified in Industry 21232, Sand, Gravel, Clay, and Ceramic and Refractory Minerals Mining and Quarrying;

* Calcining, dead burning, or otherwise processing (i.e., beyond basic preparation) minerals, such as talc, mica, feldspar, barite, and soapstone,—are classified in Industry 32799, All Other Nonmetallic Mineral Product Manufacturing;

* Manufacturing boron compounds and potassium salts—are classified in Industry 32518, Other Basic Inorganic Chemical Manufacturing;

* Manufacturing table salt—are classified in Industry 31194, Seasoning and Dressing Manufacturing;

US—United States industry only. CAN—United States and Canadian industries are comparable.
When neither US nor CAN appears, Canadian, Mexican, and United States industries are comparable.

- Manufacturing salt (except table salt)—are classified in Industry 32599, All Other Chemical Product and Preparation Manufacturing; and

- Manufacturing phosphoric acid, superphosphates, or other phosphatic fertilizer materials—are classified in Industry 32531, Fertilizer Manufacturing

212391 Potash, Soda, and Borate Mineral Mining[US]

This U.S. industry comprises establishments primarily engaged in developing the mine site, mining and/or milling, or otherwise beneficiating (i.e., preparing) natural potassium, sodium, or boron compounds. Drylake brine operations are included in this industry, as well as establishments engaged in producing the specified minerals from underground and open pit mines.

Cross-References. Establishments primarily engaged in—

- Manufacturing boron compounds and potassium salts—are classified in U.S. Industry 325188, All Other Basic Inorganic Chemical Manufacturing;

- Manufacturing sodium carbonate—are classified in U.S. Industry 325181, Alkalies and Chlorine Manufacturing; and

- Manufacturing table salt—are classified in U.S. Industry 311942, Spice and Extract Manufacturing.

212392 Phosphate Rock Mining[US]

This U.S. industry comprises establishments primarily engaged in developing the mine site, mining, milling, and/or drying or otherwise beneficiating (i.e., preparing) phosphate rock.

Cross-References.

Establishments primarily engaged in manufacturing phosphoric acid, superphosphates, or other phosphatic fertilizer materials are classified in U.S. Industry 325312, Phosphatic Fertilizer Manufacturing.

212393 Other Chemical and Fertilizer Mineral Mining[US]

This U.S. industry comprises establishments primarily engaged in developing the mine site, mining, milling, and/or drying or otherwise beneficiating (i.e., preparing) chemical or fertilizer mineral raw materials (except potash, soda, boron, and phosphate rock).

Illustrative Examples:

Barite mining and/or beneficiating   Rock salt mining and/or beneficiating

---

US—United States industry only. CAN—United States and Canadian industries are comparable. When neither US nor CAN appears, Canadian, Mexican, and United States industries are comparable.

Celestite mining and/or beneficiating   Sulfur mining and/or beneficiating
Fluorspar mining and/or beneficiating

Cross-References. Establishment primarily engaged in—

- Mining and/or milling or otherwise beneficiating natural potassium, sodium, or boron compounds—are classified in U.S. Industry 212391, Potash, Soda, and Borate Mineral Mining;

- Manufacturing industrial salt—are classified in U.S. Industry 325998, All Other Miscellaneous Chemical Product and Preparation Manufacturing;

- Mining, milling, drying, and/or sintering or otherwise beneficiating phosphate rock—are classified in U.S. Industry 212392, Phosphate Rock Mining; and

- Manufacturing table salt—are classified in U.S. Industry 311942, Spice and Extract Manufacturing.

212399 All Other Nonmetallic Mineral Mining[US]

This U.S. industry comprises establishments primarily engaged in developing the mine site, mining and/or milling or otherwise beneficiating (i.e., preparing) nonmetallic minerals (except stone, sand, gravel, clay, ceramic, refractory minerals, chemical and fertilizer minerals).

Illustrative Examples:

Gypsum mining and/or beneficiating   Soapstone mining and/or beneficiating
Mica mining and/or beneficiating   Talc mining and/or beneficiating
Pyrophyllite mining and/or beneficiating

Cross-References. Establishments primarily engaged in—

- Mining or quarrying dimension stone—are classified in Industry 21231, Stone Mining and Quarrying;

- Mining, quarrying, or beneficiating sand, gravel, clay, and ceramic and refractory minerals—are classified in Industry 21232, Sand, Gravel, Clay, and Ceramic and Refractory Minerals Mining and Quarrying;

- Mining, quarrying or beneficiating natural potash, soda, and borate—are classified in U.S. Industry 212391, Potash, Soda, and Borate Mineral Mining; and

- Mining and/or milling or otherwise beneficiating phosphate rock—are classified in U.S. Industry 212392, Phosphate Rock Mining.

213 Support Activities for Mining

Industries in the Support Activities for Mining subsector group establishments primarily providing support services, on a fee or contract basis, required for the mining and quarrying of minerals and

---

US—United States industry only. CAN—United States and Canadian industries are comparable. When neither US nor CAN appears, Canadian, Mexican, and United States industries are comparable.

for the extraction of oil and gas. Establishments performing exploration (except geophysical survey-ing and mapping) for minerals, on a contract or fee basis, are included in this subsector. Exploration includes traditional prospecting methods, such as taking core samples and making geological observations at prospective sites.

The activities performed on a fee or contract basis by establishments in the Support Activities for Mining subsector are also often performed in-house by mining operators. These activities include: taking core samples, making geological observations at prospective sites, and such oil and gas operations as spudding in, drilling in, redrilling, directional drilling, excavating slush pits and cellars; grading and building foundations at well locations; well surveying; running, cutting, and pulling casings, tubes and rods; cementing wells; shooting wells; perforating well casings; acidizing and chemically treating wells; and cleaning out, bailing, and swabbing wells.

2131 Support Activities for Mining

21311 Support Activities for Mining

This industry comprises establishments primarily engaged in providing support services, on a fee or contract basis, required for the mining and quarrying of minerals and for the extraction of oil and gas. Drilling, taking core samples, and making geological observations at prospective sites (except geophysical surveying and mapping) for minerals, on a fee or contract basis, is included in this industry.

Cross-References. Establishments primarily engaged in—

- Performing geophysical surveying services for minerals (i.e., coal, metal ores, oil and gas, and nonmetallic minerals) on a contract or fee basis—are classified in Industry 54136, Geophysical Surveying and Mapping Services;

- Mining, quarrying, and/or beneficiating on a contract or fee basis—are classified in Subsec-tor 212, Mining (except Oil and Gas) based on the mineral mined; and

- Operating oil and gas field properties on a contract or fee basis—are classified in Subsector 211, Oil and Gas Extraction based on the activity.

213111 Drilling Oil and Gas Wells[CAN]

This U.S. industry comprises establishments primarily engaged in drilling oil and gas wells for others on a contract or fee basis. This industry includes contractors that specialize in spudding in, drilling in, redrilling, and directional drilling.

Cross-References. Establishments primarily engaged in—

- Performing exploration (except geophysical surveying and mapping) services for oil and gas on a contract or fee basis—are classified in U.S. Industry 213112, Support Activities for Oil and Gas Operations; and

- Performing geophysical surveying and mapping services for oil and gas on a contract or fee basis—are classified in Industry 541360, Geophysical Surveying and Mapping Services.

US—United States industry only. CAN—United States and Canadian industries are comparable. When neither US nor CAN appears, Canadian, Mexican, and United States industries are comparable.

213112 Support Activities for Oil and Gas Operations[US]

This U.S. industry comprises establishments primarily engaged in performing oil and gas field services (except contract drilling) for others, on a contract or fee basis. Services included are exploration (except geophysical surveying and mapping); excavating slush pits and cellars; grading and building foundations at well locations; well surveying; running, cutting, and pulling casings, tubes, and rods; cementing wells; shooting wells; perforating well casings; acidizing and chemically treating wells; and cleaning out, bailing, and swabbing wells.

Cross-References. Establishments primarily engaged in—

- Contract drilling for oil and gas—are classified in U.S. Industry 213111, Drilling Oil and Gas Wells;

- Operating oil and gas field properties on a contract or fee basis—are classified in Subsector 211, Oil and Gas Extraction, based on the activity; and

- Performing geophysical surveying and mapping services for oil and gas on a contract or fee basis—are classified in Industry 541360, Geophysical Surveying and Mapping Services.

213113 Support Activities for Coal Mining[US]

This U.S. industry comprises establishments primarily engaged in providing support services, on a fee or contract basis, required for coal mining. Exploration for coal is included in this industry. Exploration includes traditional prospecting methods, such as taking core samples and making geological observations at prospective sites.

Cross-References. Establishments primarily engaged in—

- Performing geophysical surveying services for coal on a contract or fee basis—are classified in Industry 541360, Geophysical Surveying and Mapping Services; and

- Operating coal mines or quarries on a contract or fee basis—are classified in Industry Group 2121, Coal Mining, based on the type of coal mined.

213114 Support Activities for Metal Mining[US]

This U.S. industry comprises establishments primarily engaged in providing support services, on a fee or contract basis, required for the mining and quarrying of metallic minerals and for the extraction of metal ores. Exploration for minerals is included in this industry. Exploration (except geophysical surveying and mapping services) includes traditional prospecting methods, such as taking core samples and making geological observations at prospective sites.

Cross-References. Establishments primarily engaged in—

- Performing geophysical surveying services for metallic minerals on a contract or fee basis— are classified in Industry 541360, Geophysical Surveying and Mapping Services; and

---

US—United States industry only. CAN—United States and Canadian industries are comparable. When neither US nor CAN appears, Canadian, Mexican, and United States industries are comparable.

- Operating metallic mineral mines or quarries on a contract or fee basis—are classified in Industry Group 2122, Metal Ore Mining, based on the type of ore mined.

213115 Support Activities for Nonmetallic Minerals (except Fuels)^{US}

This U.S. industry comprises establishments primarily engaged in providing support services, on a fee or contract basis, required for the mining and quarrying of nonmetallic minerals and for the extraction of nonmetallic minerals. Exploration for minerals is included in this industry. Exploration (except geophysical surveying and mapping services) includes traditional prospecting methods, such as taking core samples and making geological observations at prospective sites.

Cross-References. Establishments primarily engaged in—

- Performing geophysical survey services for nonmetallic minerals on a contract or fee basis—are classified in Industry 541360, Geophysical Surveying and Mapping Services; and

- Operating nonmetallic mineral mines or quarries on a contract or fee basis—are classified in Industry Group 2123, Nonmetallic Mineral Mining and Quarrying, based on the type of mineral mined or quarried.

US—United States industry only. CAN—United States and Canadian industries are comparable. When neither US nor CAN appears, Canadian, Mexican, and United States industries are comparable.

http://www.ntis.gov/naics

Sector 22—Utilities

The Sector as a Whole

The Utilities sector comprises establishments engaged in the provision of the following utility services: electric power, natural gas, steam supply, water supply, and sewage removal. Within this sector, the specific activities associated with the utility services provided vary by utility: electric power includes generation, transmission, and distribution; natural gas includes distribution; steam supply includes provision and/or distribution; water supply includes treatment and distribution; and sewage removal includes collection, treatment, and disposal of waste through sewer systems and sewage treatment facilities.

Excluded from this sector are establishments primarily engaged in waste management services classified in Subsector 562, Waste Management and Remediation Services. These establishments also collect, treat, and dispose of waste materials; however, they do not use sewer systems or sewage treatment facilities.

221 Utilities

Industries in the Utilities subsector provide electric power, natural gas, steam supply, water supply, and sewage removal through a permanent infrastructure of lines, mains, and pipes. Establishments are grouped together based on the utility service provided and the particular system or facilities required to perform the service.

2211 Electric Power Generation, Transmission and Distribution[CAN]

This industry group comprises establishments primarily engaged in generating, transmitting, and/or distributing electric power. Establishments in this industry group may perform one or more of the following activities: (1) operate generation facilities that produce electric energy; (2) operate transmission systems that convey the electricity from the generation facility to the distribution system; and (3) operate distribution systems that convey electric power received from the generation facility or the transmission system to the final consumer.

22111 Electric Power Generation[CAN]

This industry comprises establishments primarily engaged in operating electric power generation facilities. These facilities convert other forms of energy, such as water power (i.e., hydroelectric), fossil fuels, nuclear power, and solar power, into electrical energy. The establishments in this industry produce electric energy and provide electricity to transmission systems or to electric power distribution systems.

Cross-References.

Establishments primarily engaged in operating trash incinerators that also generate electricity are classified in Industry 56221, Waste Treatment and Disposal.

US—United States industry only. CAN—United States and Canadian industries are comparable. When neither US nor CAN appears, Canadian, Mexican, and United States industries are comparable.

221111 Hydroelectric Power Generation^{CAN}

This U.S. industry comprises establishments primarily engaged in operating hydroelectric power generation facilities. These facilities use water power to drive a turbine and produce electric energy. The electric energy produced in these establishment is provided to electric power transmission systems or to electric power distribution systems.

221112 Fossil Fuel Electric Power Generation^{CAN}

This U.S. industry comprises establishments primarily engaged in operating fossil fuel powered electric power generation facilities. These facilities use fossil fuels, such as coal, oil, or gas, in internal combustion or combustion turbine conventional steam process to produce electric energy. The electric energy produced in these establishments are provided to electric power transmission systems or to electric power distribution systems.

221113 Nuclear Electric Power Generation^{CAN}

This U.S. industry comprises establishments primarily engaged in operating nuclear electric power generation facilities. These facilities use nuclear power to produce electric energy. The electric energy produced in these establishments are provided to electric power transmission systems or to electric power distribution systems.

221119 Other Electric Power Generation^{CAN}

This U.S. industry comprises establishments primarily engaged in operating electric power generation facilities (except hydroelectric, fossil fuel, nuclear). These facilities convert other forms of energy, such as solar, wind, or tidal power, into electrical energy. The electric energy produced in these establishment is provided to electric power transmission systems or to electric power distribution systems.

Cross-References. Establishments primarily engaged in—

- Operating trash disposal incinerators that also generate electricity—are classified in U.S. Industry 562213, Solid Waste Combustors and Incinerators;

- Operating hydroelectric power generation facilities—are classified in U.S. Industry 221111, Hydroelectric Power Generation;

- Operating fossil fuel powered electric power generation facilities—are classified in U.S. Industry 221112, Fossil Fuel Electric Power Generation; and

- Operating nuclear electric power generation facilities—are classified in U.S. Industry 221113, Nuclear Electric Power Generation.

22112 Electric Power Transmission, Control, and Distribution^{CAN}

This industry comprises establishments primarily engaged in operating electric power transmission systems, controlling (i.e., regulating voltages) the transmission of electricity, and/or distributing

---

US—United States industry only. CAN—United States and Canadian industries are comparable. When neither US nor CAN appears, Canadian, Mexican, and United States industries are comparable.

electricity. The transmission system includes lines and transformer stations. These establishments arrange, facilitate, or coordinate the transmission of electricity from the generating source to the distribution centers, other electric utilities, or final consumers. The distribution system consists of lines, poles, meters, and wiring that deliver the electricity to final consumers.

Cross-References.

Establishments primarily engaged in generating electric energy are classified in Industry 22111, Electric Power Generation.

221121 Electric Bulk Power Transmission and Control[CAN]

This U.S. industry comprises establishments primarily engaged in operating electric power transmission systems and/or controlling (i.e., regulatory voltage) the transmission of electricity from the generating source to distribution centers or other electric utilities. The transmission system includes lines and transformer stations.

Cross-References. Establishments primarily engaged in—

- Generating electric energy—are classified in Industry 22111, Electric Power Generation; and

- Distributing electricity to final consumers—are classified in U.S. Industry 221122, Electric Power Distribution.

221122 Electric Power Distribution[CAN]

This U.S. industry comprises electric power establishments primarily engaged in (1) operating electric power distribution systems (i.e., consisting of lines, poles, meters, and wiring) or (2) operating as electric power brokers or agents that arrange the sale of electricity via power distribution systems operated by others.

Cross-References. Establishments primarily engaged in—

- Generating electric energy—are classified in Industry 22111, Electric Power Generation; and

- Transmitting electricity between generating sources or distribution centers—are classified in U.S. Industry 221121, Electric Bulk Power Transmission and Control.

2212 Natural Gas Distribution[CAN]

22121 Natural Gas Distribution[CAN]
See industry description for 221210 below.

221210 Natural Gas Distribution[CAN]

This industry comprises: (1) establishments primarily engaged in operating gas distribution systems (e.g., mains, meters); (2) establishments known as gas marketers that buy gas from the well and sell it to a distribution system; (3) establishments known as gas brokers or agents that

---

US—United States industry only. CAN—United States and Canadian industries are comparable. When neither US nor CAN appears, Canadian, Mexican, and United States industries are comparable.

arrange the sale of gas over gas distribution systems operated by others; and (4) establishments primarily engaged in transmitting and distributing gas to final consumers.

Cross-References. Establishments primarily engaged in—

- Pipeline transportation of natural gas from process plants to local distribution systems— are classified in Industry 486210, Pipeline Transportation of Natural Gas; and

- Retailing liquified petroleum (LP) gas via direct selling—are classified in U.S. Industry 454312, Liquefied Petroleum Gas (Bottled Gas) Dealers.

2213 Water, Sewage and Other Systems[CAN]

22131 Water Supply and Irrigation Systems[CAN]
See industry description for 221310 below.

221310 Water Supply and Irrigation Systems[CAN]

This industry comprises establishments primarily engaged in operating water treatment plants and/or operating water supply systems. The water supply system may include pumping stations, aqueducts, and/or distribution mains. The water may be used for drinking, irrigation, or other uses.

22132 Sewage Treatment Facilities[CAN]
See industry description for 221320 below.

221320 Sewage Treatment Facilities[CAN]

This industry comprises establishments primarily engaged in operating sewer systems or sewage treatment facilities that collect, treat, and dispose of waste.

Cross-References. Establishments primarily engaged in—

- Operating waste treatment or disposal facilities (except sewer systems or sewage treatment facilities)—are classified in Industry 56221, Waste Treatment and Disposal;

- Pumping (i.e., cleaning) septic tanks and cesspools—are classified in U.S. Industry 562991, Septic Tank and Related Services; and

- Cleaning and rodding sewers and catch basins—are classified in U.S. Industry 562998, All Other Miscellaneous Waste Management Services.

22133 Steam and Air-Conditioning Supply[CAN]
See industry description for 221330 below.

221330 Steam and Air-Conditioning Supply[CAN]

This industry comprises establishments primarily engaged in providing steam, heated air, or cooled air. The steam distribution may be through mains.

US—United States industry only. CAN—United States and Canadian industries are comparable. When neither US nor CAN appears, Canadian, Mexican, and United States industries are comparable.

Sector 23—Construction

The Sector as a Whole

The Construction sector comprises establishments primarily engaged in the construction of buildings and other structures, heavy construction (except buildings), additions, alterations, reconstruction, installation, and maintenance and repairs. Establishments engaged in demolition or wrecking of buildings and other structures, clearing of building sites, and sale of materials from demolished structures are also included. This sector also includes those establishments engaged in blasting, test drilling, landfill, leveling, earthmoving, excavating, land drainage, and other land preparation. The industries within this sector have been defined on the basis of their unique production processes. As with all industries, the production processes are distinguished by their use of specialized human resources and specialized physical capital. Construction activities are generally administered or managed at a relatively fixed place of business, but the actual construction work is performed at one or more different project sites.

This sector is divided into three subsectors of construction activities: (1) building construction and land subdivision and land development; (2) heavy construction (except buildings), such as highways, power plants, and pipelines; and (3) construction activity by special trade contractors.

Establishments classified in Subsector 233, Building, Developing, and General Contracting and Subsector 234, Heavy Construction, usually assume responsibility for an entire construction project, and may subcontract some or all of the actual construction work. Operative builders who build on their own account for sale, and land subdividers and land developers, who engage in subdividing real property into lots for sale, are included in Subsector 233, Building, Developing, and General Contracting. (Special trade contractors are included in Subsector 234, Heavy Construction, if they are engaged in activities primarily relating to heavy construction, such as grading for highways.) Establishments included in these subsectors operate as general contractors, design-builders, engineer-constructors, joint-venture contractors, and turnkey construction contractors. Establishments identified as construction management firms are also included.

Establishments classified in Subsector 235, Special Trade Contractors, are primarily engaged in specialized construction activities, such as plumbing, painting, and electrical work, and work for builders and general contractors under subcontract or directly for project owners. Establishments engaged in demolition or wrecking of buildings and other structures, dismantling of machinery, excavating, shoring and underpinning, anchored earth retention activities, foundation drilling, and grading for buildings are also included in this subsector.

''Force account'' construction is construction work performed by an establishment primarily engaged in some business other than construction, for its own account and use, and by employees of the establishment. This activity is not included in this industry sector unless the construction work performed is the primary activity of a separate establishment of the enterprise.

The installation of prefabricated building equipment and materials, such as elevators and revolving doors, is classified in the Construction sector. Installation work incidental to sales by employees of a manufacturing or retail establishment is classified as an activity of those establishments.

233 Building, Developing, and General Contracting[US]

Industries in the Building, Developing, and General Contracting subsector comprises establishments primarily responsible for the entire construction (i.e., new work, additions, alterations, and

---

US—United States industry only. CAN—United States and Canadian industries are comparable. When neither US nor CAN appears, Canadian, Mexican, and United States industries are comparable.

http://www.ntis.gov/naics

repair) of building projects. Builders, developers, and general contractors, as well as land subdividers and land developers are included in this subsector. Establishments identified as construction management firms for building projects are also included. The construction work may be for others and performed by custom builders, general contractors, design builders, engineer-constructors, joint-venture contractors, and turnkey contractors, or may be on their own account for sale and performed by speculative or operative builders.

2331 Land Subdivision and Land Development[US]

23311 Land Subdivision and Land Development[US]
See industry description for 233110 below.

233110 Land Subdivision and Land Development[US]

This industry comprises establishments primarily engaged in subdividing real property into lots and/or developing building lots for sale.

Cross-References.

Establishments primarily engaged in constructing buildings on lots they subdivide or develop are classified in Industry Group 2332, Residential Building Construction, or Industry Group 2333, Nonresidential Building Construction, based on the type of construction project.

2332 Residential Building Construction[US]

23321 Single Family Housing Construction[US]
See industry description for 233210 below.

233210 Single Family Housing Construction[US]

This industry comprises establishments primarily responsible for the entire construction (i.e., new work, additions, alterations, and repairs) of single family residential housing units (e.g., single family detached houses, town houses, or row houses where each housing unit is separated by a ground-to-roof wall and where no housing units are constructed above or below). This industry includes establishments responsible for additions and alterations to mobile homes and on-site assembly of modular and prefabricated houses. Establishments identified as single family construction management firms are also included in this industry. Establishments in this industry may perform work for others or on their own account for sale as speculative or operative builders. Kinds of establishments include single family housing custom builders, general contractors, design builders, engineer-constructors, joint-venture contractors, and turnkey contractors.

Cross-References. Establishments primarily engaged in—

- Performing mobile home site setup and tie-down work—are classified in Industry 235990, All Other Special Trade Contractors; and

---

US—United States industry only. CAN—United States and Canadian industries are comparable. When neither US nor CAN appears, Canadian, Mexican, and United States industries are comparable.

- Performing specialized construction work on single family housing units generally on a subcontract basis—are classified in Subsector 235, Special Trade Contractors.

23322 Multifamily Housing Construction[US]
See industry description for 233220 below.

233220 Multifamily Housing Construction[US]

This industry comprises establishments primarily responsible for the entire construction (i.e., new work, additions, alterations, and repairs) of multifamily residential housing units (e.g., highrise, garden, and town house apartments where each unit is not separated by a ground-to-roof wall). The units may be constructed for sale as condominiums or cooperatives, or for rental as apartments. Establishments identified as multifamily construction management firms are also included in this industry. Establishments in this industry may perform work for others or on their own account for sale as speculative or operative builders. Kinds of establishments include multifamily housing general contractors, design builders, engineer-constructors, joint-venture contractors, and turnkey contractors.

Cross-References. Establishments primarily engaged in—

- Performing specialized construction work on multifamily housing units generally on a subcontract basis—are classified in Subsector 235, Special Trade Contractors; and

- Developing, constructing, and operating residential buildings on their own account for investment purposes—are classified in Industry 531110, Lessors of Residential Buildings and Dwellings.

2333 Nonresidential Building Construction[US]

23331 Manufacturing and Industrial Building Construction[US]
See industry description for 233310 below.

233310 Manufacturing and Industrial Building Construction[US]

This industry comprises establishments primarily responsible for the entire construction (i.e., new work, additions, alterations, and repairs) of manufacturing and industrial buildings (e.g., plants, mills, factories). Establishments identified as manufacturing and industrial building construction management firms are also included in this industry. Kinds of establishments include manufacturing and industrial building general contractors, design builders, engineer-constructors, joint-venture contractors, and turnkey contractors.

Cross-References. Establishments primarily engaged in—

- Constructing commercial and institutional buildings—are classified in Industry 233320, Commercial and Institutional Building Construction;

US—United States industry only. CAN—United States and Canadian industries are comparable. When neither US nor CAN appears, Canadian, Mexican, and United States industries are comparable.

- Constructing heavy, nonbuilding industrial structures—are classified in Industry 234930, Industrial Nonbuilding Structure Construction; and

- Performing specialized construction work on manufacturing and industrial buildings generally on a subcontract basis—are classified in Subsector 235, Special Trade Contractors.

23332 Commercial and Institutional Building Construction[US]

See industry description for 233320 below.

233320 Commercial and Institutional Building Construction[US]

This industry comprises establishments primarily responsible for the entire construction (i.e., new work, additions, alterations, and repairs) of commercial and institutional buildings (e.g., stores, schools, hospitals office buildings, public warehouses). Establishments identified as commercial and institutional building construction management firms are also included in this industry. Kinds of establishments include commercial and institutional building general contractors, design builders, engineer-constructors, joint-venture contractors, and turnkey contractors.

Illustrative Examples:

Administration building construction	Hotel construction
Amusement building construction	Municipal building construction
Bank building construction	Office building construction
Casino construction	Prison construction
Church, synagogue, mosque, temple, and related building construction	Public warehouse construction
	Restaurant construction
Cinema construction	School building construction
Farm building construction	Service station construction
Hospital construction	Shopping center or mall construction

Cross-References. Establishments primarily engaged in—

- Performing specialized construction work on commercial and institutional buildings generally on a subcontract basis—are classified in Subsector 235, Special Trade Contractors; and

- Constructing manufacturing and industrial buildings—are classified in Industry 233310, Manufacturing and Industrial Building Construction.

234 Heavy Construction[US]

Industries in the Heavy Construction subsector group establishments that engage in the construction of heavy engineering and industrial projects (except buildings), for example, highways, power plants, and pipelines. The construction work performed may include new work, reconstruction, or repairs. Establishments identified as heavy construction management firms are also included. Establishments in this subsector usually assume responsibility for entire nonbuilding projects but may subcontract some or all of the actual construction work. Special trade contractors are included in this group if they are engaged in activities primarily related to heavy construction, for example,

---

US—United States industry only. CAN—United States and Canadian industries are comparable. When neither US nor CAN appears, Canadian, Mexican, and United States industries are comparable.

grading for highways. Kinds of establishments include heavy construction general contractors, design builders, engineer-constructors, and joint-venture contractors.

2341 Highway, Street, Bridge, and Tunnel Construction[US]

23411 Highway and Street Construction[US]
See industry description for 234110 below.

234110 Highway and Street Construction[US]

This industry comprises: (1) establishments primarily responsible for the entire construction (i.e., new work, reconstruction, or repairs) of highways (except elevated), streets, roads, or airport runways; (2) establishments identified as highway and street construction management firms; and (3) establishments identified as special trade contractors engaged in performing subcontract work primarily related to highway and street construction (e.g., grading for highways, installing guardrails, public sidewalk construction). Establishments in this industry may subcontract some or all of the actual construction work. Kinds of establishments include highway and street general contractors, design builders, engineer-constructors, and joint-venture contractors.

Cross-References. Establishments primarily engaged in—

- Constructing elevated highways—are classified in Industry 234120, Bridge and Tunnel Construction;

- Constructing private driveways and private sidewalks—are classified in Industry 235710, Concrete Contractors; and

- Traffic lane painting—are classified in Industry 235210, Painting and Wall Covering Contractors.

23412 Bridge and Tunnel Construction[US]
See industry description for 234120 below.

234120 Bridge and Tunnel Construction[US]

This industry comprises: (1) establishments primarily responsible for the entire construction (i.e., new work, reconstruction, or repairs) of bridges, viaducts, elevated highways, and tunnels; (2) establishments identified as bridge and tunnel construction management firms; and (3) establishments identified as special trade contractors primarily engaged in performing subcontract work related to bridge and tunnel construction. Establishments in this industry may subcontract some or all of the actual construction work. Kinds of establishments include bridge and tunnel general contractors, design builders, engineer-constructors, and joint-venture contractors.

Cross-References.

- Establishments primarily engaged in and responsible for entire subway construction projects as general contractors, design-builders, engineer-constructors, or joint-venture contractors are classified in Industry 234990, All Other Heavy Construction; and

----

US—United States industry only. CAN—United States and Canadian industries are comparable. When neither US nor CAN appears, Canadian, Mexican, and United States industries are comparable.

- Establishments primarily engaged in bridge painting are classified in Industry 235210, Painting and Wall Covering Contractors.

2349 Other Heavy Construction^{US}

This industry group comprises establishments primarily engaged in heavy nonbuilding construction (except highway, street, bridge, and tunnel construction).

23491 Water, Sewer, and Pipeline Construction^{US}
See industry description for 234910 below.

234910 Water, Sewer, and Pipeline Construction^{US}

This industry comprises: (1) establishments primarily responsible for the entire construction (i.e., new work, reconstruction, rehabilitation, or repairs) of water mains, sewers, drains, gas mains, natural gas pumping stations, and gas and oil pipelines; (2) establishments identified as water, sewer, and pipeline construction management firms; and (3) establishments identified as special trade contractors engaged in activities primarily related to water, sewer, and pipeline construction. Establishments in this industry may subcontract some or all of the actual construction work. Kinds of establishments include water, sewer, and pipeline general contractors, design builders, engineer-constructors, and joint-venture contractors.

Cross-References.

Establishments primarily engaged in the construction of water and sewer treatment plants are classified in Industry 234990, All Other Heavy Construction.

23492 Power and Communication Transmission Line Construction^{US}
See industry description for 234920 below.

234920 Power and Communication Transmission Line Construction^{US}

This industry comprises: (1) establishments primarily responsible for the entire construction (i.e., new work, reconstruction, or repairs) of electric power and communication transmission lines and towers, radio and television transmitting/receiving towers, cable laying, and cable television lines; (2) establishments identified as power and communication transmission line construction management firms; and (3) establishments identified as special trade contractors engaged in activities primarily related to power and communication transmission line construction. Establishments in this industry may subcontract some or all of the actual construction work. Kinds of establishments include power and communication transmission line general contractors, design builders, engineer-constructors, and joint-venture contractors.

Cross-References.

- Establishments primarily engaged in performing electrical work within buildings are classified in Industry 235310, Electrical Contractors; and

---

US—United States industry only. CAN—United States and Canadian industries are comparable. When neither US nor CAN appears, Canadian, Mexican, and United States industries are comparable.

- Installation and maintenance of power and communication transmission lines performed by broadcasting and telecommunications companies are classified in Subsector 513, Broadcasting and Telecommunications.

23493 Industrial Nonbuilding Structure Construction[US]
See industry description for 234930 below.

234930 Industrial Nonbuilding Structure Construction[US]

This industry comprises: (1) establishments primarily responsible for the entire construction (i.e., new work, reconstruction, or repairs) of heavy industrial nonbuilding structures, such as chemical complexes or facilities, cement plants, petroleum refineries, industrial incinerators, ovens, kilns, power plants (except hydroelectric plants), and nuclear reactor containment structures; (2) establishments identified as industrial nonbuilding construction management firms; and (3) establishments identified as special trade contractors engaged in activities primarily related to industrial nonbuilding construction. Establishments in this industry may subcontract some or all of the actual construction work. Kinds of establishments include industrial nonbuilding general contractors, design builders, engineer-constructors, and joint-venture contractors.

Cross-References. Establishments primarily engaged in—

- Constructing manufacturing and industrial buildings—are classified in Industry 233310, Manufacturing and Industrial Building Construction; and

- Constructing hydroelectric plants—are classified in Industry 234990, All Other Heavy Construction.

23499 All Other Heavy Construction[US]
See industry description for 234990 below.

234990 All Other Heavy Construction[US]

This industry comprises: (1) establishments primarily responsible for the entire construction (i.e., new work, reconstruction, or repairs) of heavy nonbuilding construction projects (except highway, street, bridge, tunnel, water lines, sewer lines, pipelines, power and communication transmission lines, and industrial nonbuilding structures); (2) establishments identified as all other heavy construction management firms; (3) establishments primarily engaged in construction equipment rental with an operator; and (4) establishments identified as special trade contractors engaged in activities related primarily to all other heavy construction. Typical projects constructed by establishments in this industry include athletic fields, dams, dikes, docks, drainage projects, golf courses, harbors, parks, reservoirs, canals, sewage treatment plants, water treatment plants, hydroelectric plants, subways, and other mass transit projects. Establishments in this industry may subcontract some or all of the actual construction work. Kinds of establishments include heavy construction general contractors, design builders, engineer-constructors, and joint-venture contractors.

US—United States industry only. CAN—United States and Canadian industries are comparable. When neither US nor CAN appears, Canadian, Mexican, and United States industries are comparable.

Cross-References. Establishments primarily engaged in—

- Constructing highways (except elevated) and streets—are classified in Industry 234110, Highway and Street Construction;

- Constructing bridges via ducts, elevated highways, and tunnels—are classified in Industry 234120, Bridge and Tunnel Construction;

- Constructing water mains, sewers, and pipelines—are classified in Industry 234910, Water, Sewer, and Pipeline Construction;

- Constructing communication transmission lines—are classified in Industry 234920, Power and Communication Transmission Line Construction;

- Constructing industrial nonbuilding structures—are classified in Industry 234930, Industrial Nonbuilding Structure Construction; and

- Heavy equipment rental without an operator—are classified in U.S. Industry 532412, Construction, Mining and Forestry Machinery and Equipment Rental and Leasing.

235 Special Trade Contractors[US]

Industries in the Special Trade Contractors subsector engage in specialized construction activities, such as plumbing, painting, and electrical work. Those establishments that engage in activities primarily related to heavy construction, such as grading for highways, are classified in Subsector 234, Heavy Construction. The activities of this subsector may be subcontracted from builders or general contractors or it may be performed directly for project owners. The construction work performed may include new work, additions, alterations, or maintenance and repairs. Special trade contractors usually perform most of their work at the job site, although they may have shops where they perform prefabrication and other work.

2351 Plumbing, Heating, and Air-Conditioning Contractors[US]

23511 Plumbing, Heating, and Air-Conditioning Contractors[US]
See industry description for 235110 below.

235110 Plumbing, Heating, and Air-Conditioning Contractors[US]

This industry comprises establishments primarily engaged in one or more of the following: (1) installing plumbing, heating, and air-conditioning equipment; (2) servicing plumbing, heating, and air-conditioning equipment; and (3) the combined activity of selling and installing plumbing, heating, and air-conditioning equipment. The plumbing, heating, and air-conditioning work performed includes new work, additions, alterations, and maintenance and repairs. The activities performed by these establishments range from duct fabrication and installation at the site to installation of refrigeration equipment, installation of sprinkler systems, and installation of environmental controls.

2352 Painting and Wall Covering Contractors[US]

23521 Painting and Wall Covering Contractors[US]

See industry description for 235210 below.

235210 Painting and Wall Covering Contractors[US]

This industry comprises establishments primarily engaged in interior or exterior painting and interior wall covering. The painting and wall covering work performed includes new work, additions, alterations, and maintenance and repairs. Activities performed by these establishments range from bridge, ship, and traffic lane painting to paint and wall covering removal.

Cross-References. Establishments primarily engaged in—

- Roof painting—are classified in Industry 235610, Roofing, Siding, and Sheet Metal Contractors; and

- Installing wood paneling—are classified in Industry 235510, Carpentry Contractors.

2353 Electrical Contractors[US]

23531 Electrical Contractors[US]

See industry description for 235310 below.

235310 Electrical Contractors[US]

This industry comprises establishments primarily engaged in one or more of the following: (1) performing electrical work at the site (e.g., installing wiring); (2) servicing electrical equipment at the site; and (3) the combined activity of selling and installing electrical equipment. The electrical work performed includes new work, additions, alterations, and maintenance and repairs.

Illustrative Examples:

Computer cable construction contractors
Electrical construction contractors
Electrical repair construction contractors
Fiber optic cable construction contractors

Lighting system construction contractors
Telecommunication equipment construction
contractors

Cross-References. Establishments primarily engaged in—

- Constructing power and communication transmission lines—are classified in Industry 234920, Power and Communication Transmission Line Construction; and

- Installing burglar and fire alarms—are classified in U.S. Industry 561621, Security Systems Services (except Locksmiths).

2354 Masonry, Drywall, Insulation, and Tile Contractors[US]

US—United States industry only. CAN—United States and Canadian industries are comparable. When neither US nor CAN appears, Canadian, Mexican, and United States industries are comparable.

23541 Masonry and Stone Contractors^{US}
See industry description for 235410 below.

235410 Masonry and Stone Contractors^{US}

This industry comprises establishments primarily engaged in masonry work, stone setting, and other stone work. The masonry work, stone setting, and other stone work performed includes new work, additions, alterations, and maintenance and repairs. Activities performed by establishments in this industry range from the construction of foundations made of block, stone, or brick to glass block laying; exterior marble, granite and slate work; and tuck pointing.

Cross-References.

Establishments primarily engaged in installing concrete parking areas, foundations, retaining walls, and private driveways and walks are classified in Industry 235710, Concrete Contractors.

23542 Drywall, Plastering, Acoustical, and Insulation Contractors^{US}
See industry description for 235420 below.

235420 Drywall, Plastering, Acoustical, and Insulation Contractors^{US}

This industry comprises establishments primarily engaged in drywall, plaster work, acoustical, and building insulation work. The drywall, plaster work, acoustical, and insulation work performed includes new work, additions, alterations, and maintenance and repairs. Plaster work includes applying plain or ornamental plaster, including installation of lathing to receive plaster.

Illustrative Examples:

Acoustical paneling construction contractors	Plastering (i.e., plain or ornamental)
Ceiling construction contractors	construction contractors
Drywall construction contractors	Soundproofing construction contractors

Cross-References.

Establishments primarily engaged in insulating pipes and boilers are classified in Industry 235990, All Other Special Trade Contractors.

23543 Tile, Marble, Terrazzo, and Mosaic Contractors^{US}
See industry description for 235430 below.

235430 Tile, Marble, Terrazzo, and Mosaic Contractors^{US}

This industry comprises establishments primarily engaged in (1) setting and installing ceramic tile, marble (interior only), terrazzo, and mosaic and/or (2) mixing marble particles and cement to make terrazzo at the job site. The tile, marble, terrazzo, and mosaic work performed includes new work, additions, alterations, and maintenance and repairs.

US—United States industry only. CAN—United States and Canadian industries are comparable. When neither US nor CAN appears, Canadian, Mexican, and United States industries are comparable.

Cross-References. Establishments primarily engaged in—

- Manufacturing precast terrazzo products—are classified in Industry 327390, Other Concrete Product Manufacturing; and

- Exterior marble work—are classified in Industry 235410, Masonry and Stone Contractors.

2355 Carpentry and Floor Contractors[US]

23551 Carpentry Contractors[US]
See industry description for 235510 below.

235510 Carpentry Contractors[US]

This industry comprises establishments primarily engaged in framing, carpentry, and finishing work. The carpentry work performed includes new work, additions, alterations, and maintenance and repairs. Activities performed by establishments in this industry range from the installation of doors and windows to paneling, steel framing work, and ship joinery.

Cross-References.

Establishments primarily engaged in building custom kitchen cabinets in a shop are classified in Industry 337110, Wood Kitchen Cabinet and Countertop Manufacturing.

23552 Floor Laying and Other Floor Contractors[US]
See industry description for 235520 below.

235520 Floor Laying and Other Floor Contractors[US]

This industry comprises establishments primarily engaged in the installation of resilient floor tile, carpeting, linoleum, and wood or resilient flooring. The floor laying and other floor work performed includes new work, additions, alterations, and maintenance and repairs.

Cross-References.

- Establishments primarily engaged in installing stone or ceramic floor tile are classified in Industry 235430, Tile, Marble, Terrazzo, and Mosaic Contractors;

- Establishments primarily engaged in laying concrete flooring are classified in Industry 235710, Concrete Contractors; and

- Stores selling and installing carpet and other flooring products as retail establishments are classified in Sector 44-45, Retail Trade.

2356 Roofing, Siding, and Sheet Metal Contractors[US]

US—United States industry only. CAN—United States and Canadian industries are comparable. When neither US nor CAN appears, Canadian, Mexican, and United States industries are comparable.

23561 Roofing, Siding, and Sheet Metal Contractors^{US}
See industry description for 235610 below.

235610 Roofing, Siding, and Sheet Metal Contractors^{US}

This industry comprises establishments primarily engaged in the installation of roofing, siding, sheet metal work, and roof drainage-related work, such as downspouts and gutters. Activities performed by these establishments also include treating roofs (i.e., by spraying, painting, or coating), copper smithing, tin smithing, installing skylights, installing metal ceilings, flashing, duct work, and capping. The roofing, siding, and sheet metal work performed includes new work, additions, alterations, and maintenance and repairs.

2357 Concrete Contractors^{US}

23571 Concrete Contractors^{US}
See industry description for 235710 below.

235710 Concrete Contractors^{US}

This industry comprises establishments primarily engaged in the use of concrete and asphalt to produce parking areas, building foundations, structures, and retaining walls, and in the use of all materials to produce patios, private driveways, and private walks. Activities performed by these establishments include grout and shotcrete work. The concrete work performed includes new work, additions, alterations, and maintenance and repairs.

Cross-References. Establishments primarily engaged in—

- Constructing or paving streets, highways, and public sidewalks—are classified in Industry 234110, Highway and Street Construction; and

- Constructing swimming pools—are classified in Industry 235990, All Other Special Trade Contractors.

2358 Water Well Drilling Contractors^{US}

23581 Water Well Drilling Contractors^{US}
See industry description for 235810 below.

235810 Water Well Drilling Contractors^{US}

This industry comprises establishments primarily engaged in drilling, tapping, and capping of water wells, and geothermal drilling. The water well drilling work performed includes new work, servicing, and maintenance and repairs.

Cross-References.

Establishments primarily engaged in drilling oil and gas field water intake wells are classified in Industry 21311, Support Activities for Mining.

US—United States industry only. CAN—United States and Canadian industries are comparable. When neither US nor CAN appears, Canadian, Mexican, and United States industries are comparable.

2359 Other Special Trade Contractors[US]

This industry group comprises establishments primarily engaged in specialized construction activities (except plumbing, painting, electrical, masonry, drywall, insulation, tile, carpentry, flooring work, roofing, siding, sheet metal, concrete, and water well drilling).

23591 Structural Steel Erection Contractors[US]
See industry description for 235910 below.

235910 Structural Steel Erection Contractors[US]

This industry comprises establishments primarily engaged in one or more of the following: (1) erecting metal, structural steel, and similar products of prestressed or precast concrete to produce structural elements, building exteriors, and elevator fronts; (2) setting rods, bars, rebar, mesh, and cages, to reinforce poured-in-place concrete; and (3) erecting cooling towers and metal storage tanks. The structural steel erection work performed includes new work, additions, alterations, reconstruction, and maintenance and repairs.

Cross-References.

Establishments primarily engaged in structural work for nonbuilding projects are classified in Subsector 234, Heavy Construction.

23592 Glass and Glazing Contractors[US]
See industry description for 235920 below.

235920 Glass and Glazing Contractors[US]

This industry comprises establishments primarily engaged in installing glass (i.e., glazing work) and/or tinting glass. The glass work performed includes new work, additions, alterations, and maintenance and repairs.

Cross-References.

Establishments primarily engaged in the replacement, repair, and/or tinting of automotive glass are classified in U.S. Industry 811122, Automotive Glass Replacement Shops.

23593 Excavation Contractors[US]
See industry description for 235930 below.

235930 Excavation Contractors[US]

This industry comprises establishments primarily engaged in preparing land for building construction. Activities performed by these establishments are drilling shafts, foundation digging, foundation drilling, and grading. The excavation work performed includes new work, additions, alterations, and repairs.

US—United States industry only. CAN—United States and Canadian industries are comparable. When neither US nor CAN appears, Canadian, Mexican, and United States industries are comparable.

Cross-References. Establishments primarily engaged in—

- Concrete work—are classified in Industry 235710, Concrete Contractors;

- Trenching, earthmoving and land clearing not related to building construction—are classified in Subsector 234, Heavy Construction; or in Sector 21, Mining; and

- Earth retention or shoring—are classified in Industry 235990, All Other Special Trade Contractors.

23594 Wrecking and Demolition Contractors[US]
See industry description for 235940 below.

235940 Wrecking and Demolition Contractors[US]

This industry comprises establishments primarily engaged in the wrecking and demolition of buildings and other structures, including underground tank removal and the dismantling of steel oil tanks, except those for hazardous materials. The establishments engaged in wrecking and demolition work may or may not sell materials derived from demolishing operations.

Cross-References. Establishments primarily engaged in—

- Demolition of tanks in oil fields—are classified in U.S. Industry 213112, Support Activities for Oil and Gas Operations; and

- Environmental remediation work, such as the removal of underground steel tanks for hazardous materials,—are classified in Industry 562910, Remediation Services.

23595 Building Equipment and Other Machinery Installation Contractors[US]
See industry description for 235950 below.

235950 Building Equipment and Other Machinery Installation Contractors[US]

This industry comprises establishments primarily engaged in one or more of the following: (1) the installation or dismantling of building equipment, machinery or other industrial equipment (except plumbing, heating, air conditioning or electrical equipment); (2) machine rigging; and (3) millwriting. Types of equipment installed include automated and revolving doors, conveyor systems, dumbwaiters, dust collecting equipment, elevators, small incinerators, pneumatic tubes systems, and built-in vacuum cleaning systems. The building equipment and other machinery installation work performed includes new work, additions, alterations, and maintenance and repairs.

Cross-References. Establishments primarily engaged in—

- Installing plumbing, heating, or air-conditioning equipment—are classified in Industry 235110, Plumbing, Heating, and Air-Conditioning Contractors;

- Installing electrical equipment—are classified in Industry 235310, Electrical Contractors;

US—United States industry only. CAN—United States and Canadian industries are comparable. When neither US nor CAN appears, Canadian, Mexican, and United States industries are comparable.

- Constructing of industrial incinerator, furnace, and oven structures—are classified in Industry 234930, Industrial Nonbuilding Structure Construction; and

- Manufacturing of industrial equipment with incidental installation—are classified in Sector 31-33, Manufacturing.

23599 All Other Special Trade Contractors[US]
See industry description for 235990 below.

235990 All Other Special Trade Contractors[US]

This industry comprises establishments primarily engaged in specialized construction work, (except plumbing, painting, electrical, masonry, drywall, insulation, tile, carpentry, flooring, roofing, siding, sheet metal work, concrete work, glass and glazing, structural steel erection, excavation, wrecking and demolition, and building equipment installation work). Activities undertaken by these establishments include constructing swimming pools and fences, house moving, waterproofing, dewatering, dampproofing, fireproofing, and sandblasting; installing antennas, artificial turf, awnings, countertops, fire escapes, forms for poured concrete, gasoline pumps, lightning conductors, ornamental metal, shoring systems, and signs (on buildings); and specialized activities, such as bathtub refinishing, coating and glazing of concrete surfaces, gas leakage detection, insulation of pipes and boilers, mobile home site setup and tie-down, posthole digging, radon remediation, scaffolding work, and on-site welding. The other special trade work performed includes new work, additions, alterations, and maintenance and repairs.

Cross-References. Establishments primarily engaged in—

- Installing plumbing, heating, and air-conditioning equipment—are classified in Industry 235110, Plumbing, Heating, and Air-Conditioning Contractors;

- Painting and interior wall covering—are classified in Industry 235210, Painting and Wall Covering Contractors;

- Installing electrical equipment—are classified in Industry 235310, Electrical Contractors;

- Masonry work, drywall work, insulation work, and tile work—are classified in Industry Group 2354, Masonry, Drywall, Insulation, and Tile Contractors;

- Carpentry work—are classified in Industry 235510, Carpentry Contractors;

- Installing flooring—are classified in Industry 235520, Floor Laying and Other Floor Contractors;

- Installing roofing, siding, and sheet metal—are classified in Industry 235610, Roofing, Siding, and Sheet Metal Contractors;

- The use of concrete and asphalt in their work—are classified in Industry 235710, Concrete Contractors;

- Erecting structural steel—are classified in Industry 235910, Structural Steel Erection Contractors;

US—United States industry only. CAN—United States and Canadian industries are comparable. When neither US nor CAN appears, Canadian, Mexican, and United States industries are comparable.

- Installing or tinting glass—are classified in Industry 235920, Glass and Glazing Contractors;

- Preparing land for building construction—are classified in Industry 235930, Excavation Contractors;

- Wrecking and demolitions—are classified in Industry 235940, Wrecking and Demolition Contractors;

- Environmental remediation work, such as asbestos abatement,—are classified in Industry 562910, Remediation Services;

- Installing or dismantling building equipment, machinery, and other industrial equipment— are classified in Industry 235950, Building Equipment and Other Machinery Installation Contractors;

- Equipment rental without an operator—are classified in U.S. Industry 532412, Construction, Mining, and Forestry Machinery and Equipment Rental and Leasing; and

- Construction equipment rental with an operator—are classified in Industry 234990, All Other Heavy Construction.

US—United States industry only. CAN—United States and Canadian industries are comparable. When neither US nor CAN appears, Canadian, Mexican, and United States industries are comparable.

http://www.ntis.gov/naics

Sector 31-33—Manufacturing

The Sector as a Whole

The Manufacturing sector comprises establishments engaged in the mechanical, physical, or chemical transformation of materials, substances, or components into new products. The assembling of component parts of manufactured products is considered manufacturing, except in cases where the activity is appropriately classified in Sector 23, Construction.

Establishments in the Manufacturing sector are often described as plants, factories, or mills and characteristically use power-driven machines and materials-handling equipment. However, establishments that transform materials or substances into new products by hand or in the worker's home and those engaged in selling to the general public products made on the same premises from which they are sold, such as bakeries, candy stores, and custom tailors, may also be included in this sector. Manufacturing establishments may process materials or may contract with other establishments to process their materials for them. Both types of establishments are included in manufacturing.

The materials, substances, or components transformed by manufacturing establishments are raw materials that are products of agriculture, forestry, fishing, mining, or quarrying as well as products of other manufacturing establishments. The materials used may be purchased directly from producers, obtained through customary trade channels, or secured without recourse to the market by transferring the product from one establishment to another, under the same ownership.

The new product of a manufacturing establishment may be finished in the sense that it is ready for utilization or consumption, or it may be semifinished to become an input for an establishment engaged in further manufacturing. For example, the product of the alumina refinery is the input used in the primary production of aluminum; primary aluminum is the input to an aluminum wire drawing plant; and aluminum wire is the input for a fabricated wire product manufacturing establishment.

The subsectors in the Manufacturing sector generally reflect distinct production processes related to material inputs, production equipment, and employee skills. In the machinery area, where assembling is a key activity, parts and accessories for manufactured products are classified in the industry of the finished manufactured item when they are made for separate sale. For example, a replacement refrigerator door would be classified with refrigerators and an attachment for a piece of metal working machinery would be classified with metal working machinery. However, components, input from other manufacturing establishments, are classified based on the production function of the component manufacturer. For example, electronic components are classified in Subsector 334, Computer and Electronic Product Manufacturing and stampings are classified in Subsector 332, Fabricated Metal Product Manufacturing.

Manufacturing establishments often perform one or more activities that are classified outside the Manufacturing sector of NAICS. For instance, almost all manufacturing has some captive research and development or administrative operations, such as accounting, payroll, or management. These captive services are treated the same as captive manufacturing activities. When the services are provided by separate establishments, they are classified to the NAICS sector where such services are primary, not in manufacturing.

The boundaries of manufacturing and the other sectors of the classification system can be somewhat blurry. The establishments in the manufacturing sector are engaged in the transformation

US—United States industry only. CAN—United States and Canadian industries are comparable. When neither US nor CAN appears, Canadian, Mexican, and United States industries are comparable.

http://www.ntis.gov/naics

of materials into new products. Their output is a new product. However, the definition of what constitutes a new product can be somewhat subjective. As clarification, the following activities are considered manufacturing in NAICS:

Milk bottling and pasteurizing;

Water bottling and processing;

Fresh fish packaging (oyster shucking, fish filleting);

Apparel jobbing (assigning of materials to contract factories or shops for fabrication or other contract operations) as well as contracting on materials owned by others;

Printing and related activities;

Ready-mixed concrete production;

Leather converting;

Grinding of lenses to prescription;

Wood preserving;

Electroplating, plating, metal heat treating, and polishing for the trade;

Lapidary work for the trade;

Fabricating signs and advertising displays;

Rebuilding or remanufacturing machinery (i.e., automotive parts)

Ship repair and renovation;

Machine shops; and

Tire retreading.

Conversely, there are activities that are sometimes considered manufacturing, but which for NAICS are classified in another sector (i.e., not classified as manufacturing). They include:

1. Logging, classified in Sector 11, Agriculture, Forestry, Fishing and Hunting is considered a harvesting operation;

2. The beneficiating of ores and other minerals, classified in Sector 21, Mining, is considered part of the activity of mining;

3. The construction of structures and fabricating operations performed at the site of construction by contractors, is classified in Sector 23, Construction;

4. Establishments engaged in breaking of bulk and redistribution in smaller lots, including packaging, repackaging, or bottling products, such as liquors or chemicals; the customized assembly of computers; sorting of scrap; mixing paints to customer order; and cutting metals to customer order, classified in Sector 42, Wholesale Trade or Sector 44-45, Retail Trade, produce a modified version of the same product, not a new product; and

5. Publishing and the combined activity of publishing and printing, classified in Sector 51, Information, perform the transformation of information into a product where as the value of the product to the consumer lies in the information content, not in the format in which it is distributed (i.e., the book or software diskette).

311 Food Manufacturing

Industries in the Food Manufacturing subsector transform livestock and agricultural products into products for intermediate or final consumption. The industry groups are distinguished by the raw materials (generally of animal or vegetable origin) processed into food products.

The food products manufactured in these establishments are typically sold to wholesalers or retailers for distribution to consumers, but establishments primarily engaged in retailing bakery and candy products made on the premises not for immediate consumption are included.

US—United States industry only. CAN—United States and Canadian industries are comparable. When neither US nor CAN appears, Canadian, Mexican, and United States industries are comparable.

Establishments primarily engaged in manufacturing beverages are classified in Subsector 312, Beverage and Tobacco Product Manufacturing.

3111 Animal Food Manufacturing

31111 Animal Food Manufacturing

This industry comprises establishments primarily engaged in manufacturing food and feed for animals from ingredients, such as grains, oilseed mill products, and meat products.

Cross-References. Establishments primarily engaged in—

- Slaughtering animals for feed—are classified in Industry 31161, Animal Slaughtering and Processing; and

- Manufacturing vitamins and minerals for animals—are classified in Industry 32541, Pharmaceutical and Medicine Manufacturing.

311111 Dog and Cat Food Manufacturing[CAN]

This U.S. industry comprises establishments primarily engaged in manufacturing dog and cat food from ingredients, such as grains, oilseed mill products, and meat products.

Cross-References. Establishments primarily engaged in—

- Manufacturing food for animals (except dog and cat)—are classified in U.S. Industry 311119, Other Animal Food Manufacturing;

- Slaughtering animals for feed—are classified in Industry 31161, Animal Slaughtering and Processing; and

- Manufacturing vitamins and minerals for dogs and cats—are classified in Industry 32541, Pharmaceutical and Medicine Manufacturing.

311119 Other Animal Food Manufacturing[CAN]

This U.S. industry comprises establishments primarily engaged in manufacturing animal food (except dog and cat) from ingredients, such as grains, oilseed mill products, and meat products.

Cross-References. Establishments primarily engaged in—

- Manufacturing dog and cat foods—are classified in U.S. Industry 311111, Dog and Cat Food Manufacturing;

- Slaughtering animals for feed—are classified in Industry 31161, Animal Slaughtering and Processing; and

---

US—United States industry only. CAN—United States and Canadian industries are comparable. When neither US nor CAN appears, Canadian, Mexican, and United States industries are comparable.

- Manufacturing vitamins and minerals for animals—are classified in Industry 32541, Pharmaceutical and Medicine Manufacturing.

3112 Grain and Oilseed Milling

31121 Flour Milling and Malt Manufacturing

This industry comprises establishments primarily engaged in one or more of the following: (1) milling flour or meal from grains or vegetables; (2) preparing flour mixes or doughs from flour milled in the same establishment; (3) milling, cleaning, and polishing rice; and (4) manufacturing malt from barley, rye, or other grains.

Cross-References. Establishments primarily engaged in—

- Preparing breakfast cereals from flour milled in the same establishment—are classified in Industry 31123, Breakfast Cereal Manufacturing;

- Crushing soybeans or wet milling corn and vegetables—are classified in Industry 31122, Starch and Vegetable Fats and Oils Manufacturing;

- Manufacturing prepared flour mixes or doughs from flour ground elsewhere—are classified in Industry 31182, Cookie, Cracker, and Pasta Manufacturing;

- Brewing malt beverages—are classified in Industry 31212, Breweries;

- Mixing purchased dried and dehydrated ingredients with purchased rice—are classified in Industry 31199, All Other Food Manufacturing;

- Drying and/or dehydrating ingredients and packaging them with purchased rice—are classified in Industry 31142, Fruit and Vegetable Canning, Pickling and Drying; and

- Manufacturing malt extract and syrups—are classified in Industry 31194, Seasoning and Dressing Manufacturing.

311211 Flour Milling[CAN]

This U.S. industry comprises establishments primarily engaged in (1) milling flour or meal from grains (except rice) or vegetables and/or (2) milling flour and preparing flour mixes or doughs.

Cross-References. Establishments primarily engaged in—

- Preparing breakfast cereals from flour milled in the same establishment—are classified in Industry 311230, Breakfast Cereal Manufacturing;

- Manufacturing prepared flour mixes or doughs from flour ground elsewhere—are classified in U.S. Industry 311822, Flour Mixes and Dough Manufacturing from Purchased Flour;

- Milling rice or cleaning and polishing rice—are classified in U.S. Industry 311212, Rice Milling;

US—United States industry only. CAN—United States and Canadian industries are comparable. When neither US nor CAN appears, Canadian, Mexican, and United States industries are comparable.

http://www.ntis.gov/naics

- Wet milling corn and vegetables—are classified in U.S. Industry, 311221, Wet Corn Milling; and

- Crushing soybean and extracting soybean oil—are classified in U.S. Industry 311222, Soybean Processing.

311212 Rice Milling[US]

This U.S. industry comprises establishments primarily engaged in one of the following: (1) milling rice; (2) cleaning and polishing rice; or (3) milling, cleaning, and polishing rice. The establishments in this industry may package the rice they mill with other ingredients.

Cross-References. Establishments primarily engaged in—

- Drying and/or dehydrating ingredients and packaging them with purchased rice—are classified in U.S. Industry 311423, Dried and Dehydrated Food Manufacturing; and

- Mixing purchased dried and/or dehydrated ingredients with purchased rice—are classified in U.S. Industry 311999, All Other Miscellaneous Food Manufacturing.

311213 Malt Manufacturing[US]

This U.S. industry comprises establishments primarily engaged in manufacturing malt from barley, rye, or other grains.

Cross-References. Establishments primarily engaged in—

- Brewing malt beverages—are classified in Industry 312120, Breweries; and

- Manufacturing malt extract and syrups—are classified in U.S. Industry 311942, Spice and Extract Manufacturing.

31122 Starch and Vegetable Fats and Oils Manufacturing

This industry comprises establishments primarily engaged in one or more of the following: (1) wet milling corn and vegetables; (2) crushing oilseeds and tree nuts; (3) refining and/or blending vegetable oils; (4) manufacturing shortening and margarine; and (5) blending purchased animal fats with vegetable fats.

Cross-References. Establishments primarily engaged in—

- Manufacturing table syrups from corn syrup and starch base dessert powders—are classified in Industry 31199, All Other Food Manufacturing;

- Reducing maple sap to maple syrup—are classified in Industry 11199, All Other Crop Farming;

- Milling flour or meal from grains and vegetables—are classified in Industry 31121, Flour Milling and Malt Manufacturing;

US—United States industry only. CAN—United States and Canadian industries are comparable. When neither US nor CAN appears, Canadian, Mexican, and United States industries are comparable.

- Wet milling corn to produce nonpotable ethyl alcohol—are classified in Industry 32519, Other Basic Organic Chemical Manufacturing;

- Rendering or refining animal fats and oils—are classified in Industry 31161, Animal Slaughtering and Processing; and

- Manufacturing laundry starches—are classified in Industry 32561, Soap and Cleaning Compound Manufacturing.

311221 Wet Corn Milling[CAN]

This U.S. industry comprises establishments primarily engaged in wet milling corn and other vegetables (except to make ethyl alcohol). Examples of products made in these establishments are corn sweeteners, such as glucose, dextrose, and fructose; corn oil; and starches (except laundry).

Cross-References. Establishments primarily engaged in—

- Refining and/or blending corn oil from purchased oils—are classified in U.S. Industry 311225, Fats and Oils Refining and Blending;

- Manufacturing sweetening syrups from corn syrup and starch base dessert powders—are classified in U.S. Industry 311999, All Other Miscellaneous Food Manufacturing;

- Reducing maple sap to maple syrup—are classified in U.S. Industry 111998, All Other Miscellaneous Crop Farming;

- Milling corn—are classified in U.S. Industry 311211, Flour Milling;

- Wet milling corn to produce nonpotable ethyl alcohol—are classified in U.S. Industry 325193, Ethyl Alcohol Manufacturing; and

- Manufacturing laundry starches—are classified in U.S. Industry 325612, Polish and Other Sanitation Good Manufacturing.

311222 Soybean Processing[US]

This U.S. industry comprises establishments engaged in crushing soybeans. Examples of products produced in these establishments are soybean oil, soybean cake and meal, and soybean protein isolates and concentrates.

Cross-References. Establishments primarily engaged in—

- Refining and/or blending soybean oil from purchased oil—are classified in U.S. Industry 311225, Fats and Oils Refining and Blending;

- Wet milling corn and other vegetables—are classified in U.S. Industry 311221, Wet Corn Milling; and

- Crushing oilseeds (except soybeans) and tree nuts—are classified in U.S. Industry 311223, Other Oilseed Processing.

US—United States industry only. CAN—United States and Canadian industries are comparable. When neither US nor CAN appears, Canadian, Mexican, and United States industries are comparable.

311223 Other Oilseed Processing[US]

This U.S. industry comprises establishments engaged in crushing oilseeds (except soybeans) and tree nuts, such as cottonseeds, linseeds, peanuts, and sunflower seeds.

Cross-References. Establishments primarily engaged in—

- Wet milling corn and other vegetables—are classified in U.S. Industry 311221, Wet Corn Milling;

- Crushing soybeans—are classified in U.S. Industry 311222, Soybean Processing; and

- Refining and/or blending vegetable, oilseed, and tree nut oils from purchased oils—are classified in U.S. Industry 311225, Fats and Oils Refining and Blending.

311225 Fats and Oils Refining and Blending[CAN]

This U.S. industry comprises establishments primarily engaged in one or more of the following: (1) manufacturing shortening and margarine from purchased fats and oils; (2) refining and/or blending vegetable, oilseed, and tree nut oils from purchased oils; and (3) blending purchased animal fats with purchased vegetable fats.

Cross-References. Establishments primarily engaged in—

- Refining and/or blending soybean oil in soybean crushing mills—are classified in U.S. Industry 311222, Soybean Processing;

- Refining and/or blending corn oil made by wet corn milling—are classified in U.S. Industry 311221, Wet Corn Milling;

- Refining and/or blending oilseeds (except soybeans) and tree nuts in crushing mills—are classified in U.S. Industry 311223, Other Oilseed Processing; and

- Rendering or refining animal fats and oils—are classified in Industry 31161, Animal Slaughtering and Processing.

31123 Breakfast Cereal Manufacturing
See industry description for 311230 below.

311230 Breakfast Cereal Manufacturing

This industry comprises establishments primarily engaged in manufacturing breakfast cereal foods.

Cross-References. Establishments primarily engaged in—

- Manufacturing nonchocolate-coated granola bars and other types of breakfast bars—are classified in Industry 311340, Nonchocolate Confectionery Manufacturing;

US—United States industry only. CAN—United States and Canadian industries are comparable. When neither US nor CAN appears, Canadian, Mexican, and United States industries are comparable.

http://www.ntis.gov/naics

- Manufacturing chocolate-coated granola bars from purchased chocolate—are classified in Industry 311330, Confectionery Manufacturing from Purchased Chocolate;

- Manufacturing chocolate-coated granola bars from cacao beans—are classified in Industry 311320, Chocolate and Confectionery Manufacturing from Cacao Beans; and

- Manufacturing coffee substitutes from grain—are classified in Industry 311920, Coffee and Tea Manufacturing.

3113 Sugar and Confectionery Product Manufacturing

This industry group comprises (1) establishments that process agricultural inputs, such as sugarcane, beet, and cacao, to give rise to a new product (sugar or chocolate) and (2) those that begin with sugar and chocolate and process these further.

31131 Sugar Manufacturing

This industry comprises establishments primarily engaged in manufacturing raw sugar, liquid sugar, and refined sugar from sugarcane, raw cane sugar and sugarbeets.

Cross-References. Establishments primarily engaged in—

- Manufacturing corn sweeteners by wet milling corn—are classified in Industry 31122, Starch and Vegetable Fats and Oils Manufacturing;

- Manufacturing table syrups from corn syrup and starch base dessert powders—are classified in Industry 31199, All Other Food Manufacturing;

- Reducing maple sap to maple syrup—are classified in Industry 11199, All Other Crop Farming; and

- Manufacturing synthetic sweeteners (i.e., sweetening agents), such as saccharin and sugar substitutes (i.e., synthetic sweetener blended with other ingredients),—are classified in Subsector 325, Chemical Manufacturing.

311311 Sugarcane Mills[US]

This U.S. industry comprises establishments primarily engaged in processing sugarcane.

Cross-References. Establishments primarily engaged in—

- Manufacturing refined cane sugar from raw cane sugar—are classified in U.S. Industry 311312, Cane Sugar Refining;

- Manufacturing beet sugar—are classified in U.S. Industry 311313, Beet Sugar Manufacturing;

- Manufacturing corn sweetener by wet milling corn—are classified in U.S. Industry 311221, Wet Corn Milling;

US—United States industry only. CAN—United States and Canadian industries are comparable. When neither US nor CAN appears, Canadian, Mexican, and United States industries are comparable.

- Manufacturing table syrups from corn syrup—are classified in U.S. Industry 311999, All Other Miscellaneous Food Manufacturing; and

- Manufacturing synthetic sweeteners (i.e., sweetening agents), such as saccharin and sugar substitutes (i.e., synthetic sweetener blended with other ingredients),—are classified in Subsector 325, Chemical Manufacturing.

311312 Cane Sugar Refining^{US}

This U.S. industry comprises establishments primarily engaged in refining cane sugar from raw cane sugar.

Cross-References. Establishments primarily engaged in—

- Processing and refining sugarcane—are classified in U.S. Industry 311311, Sugarcane Mills;

- Manufacturing beet sugar—are classified in U.S. Industry 311313, Beet Sugar Manufacturing;

- Manufacturing corn sweetener by wet milling corn—are classified in U.S. Industry 311221, Wet Corn Milling;

- Reducing maple sap to maple syrup—are classified in U.S. Industry 111998, All Other Miscellaneous Crop Farming;

- Manufacturing table syrups from corn syrup—are classified in U.S. Industry 311999, All Other Miscellaneous Food Manufacturing; and

- Manufacturing synthetic sweeteners (i.e., sweetening agents), such as saccharin and sugar substitutes (i.e., synthetic sweetener blended with other ingredients),—are classified in Subsector 325, Chemical Manufacturing.

311313 Beet Sugar Manufacturing^{US}

This U.S. industry comprises establishments primarily engaged in manufacturing refined beet sugar from sugarbeets.

Cross-References. Establishments primarily engaged in—

- Manufacturing raw cane sugar and/or refined cane sugar from sugarcane—are classified in U.S. Industry 311311, Sugarcane Mills;

- Manufacturing refined cane sugar from raw cane sugar—are classified in U.S. Industry 311312, Cane Sugar Refining;

- Manufacturing corn sweeteners by wet milling corn—are classified in U.S. Industry 311221, Wet Corn Milling;

- Manufacturing table syrups from corn syrup—are classified in U.S. Industry 311999, All Other Miscellaneous Food Manufacturing;

US—United States industry only. CAN—United States and Canadian industries are comparable. When neither US nor CAN appears, Canadian, Mexican, and United States industries are comparable.

- Reducing maple sap to maple syrup—are classified in U.S. Industry 111998, All Other Miscellaneous Crop Farming; and

- Manufacturing synthetic sweeteners (i.e., sweetening agents), such as saccharin and sugar substitutes (i.e., synthetic sweetener blended with other ingredients),—are classified in Subsector 325, Chemical Manufacturing.

31132 Chocolate and Confectionery Manufacturing from Cacao Beans
See industry description for 311320 below.

311320 Chocolate and Confectionery Manufacturing from Cacao Beans

This industry comprises establishments primarily engaged in shelling, roasting, and grinding cacao beans and making chocolate cacao products and chocolate confectioneries.

Cross-References. Establishments primarily engaged in—

- Manufacturing, not for immediate consumption, chocolate confectioneries from chocolate made elsewhere—are classified in Industry 311330, Confectionery Manufacturing from Purchased Chocolate;

- Manufacturing, not for immediate consumption, nonchocolate candies—are classified in Industry 311340, Nonchocolate Confectionery Manufacturing;

- Preparing and selling confectioneries for immediate consumption—are classified in U.S. Industry 722213, Snack and Nonalcoholic Beverage Bars; and

- Retailing confectioneries not for immediate consumption made elsewhere are classified in U.S. Industry 445292, Confectionery and Nut Stores.

31133 Confectionery Manufacturing from Purchased Chocolate
See industry description for 311330 below.

311330 Confectionery Manufacturing from Purchased Chocolate

This industry comprises establishments primarily engaged in manufacturing chocolate confectioneries from chocolate produced elsewhere. Included in this industry are establishments primarily engaged in retailing chocolate confectionery products not for immediate consumption made on the premises from chocolate made elsewhere.

Cross-References. Establishments primarily engaged in—

- Manufacturing chocolate confectioneries from cacao beans—are classified in Industry 311320, Chocolate and Confectionery Manufacturing from Cacao Beans;

- Manufacturing nonchocolate confectioneries—are classified in Industry 311340, Nonchocolate Confectionery Manufacturing;

US—United States industry only. CAN—United States and Canadian industries are comparable. When neither US nor CAN appears, Canadian, Mexican, and United States industries are comparable.

- Retailing confectioneries not for immediate consumption made elsewhere—are classified in U.S. Industry 445292, Confectionery and Nut Stores; and

- Preparing and selling confectioneries for immediate consumption—are classified in U.S. Industry 722213, Snack and Nonalcoholic Beverage Bars

31134 Nonchocolate Confectionery Manufacturing
See industry description for 311340 below.

311340 Nonchocolate Confectionery Manufacturing

This industry comprises establishments primarily engaged in manufacturing nonchocolate confectioneries. Included in this industry are establishments primary engaged in retailing nonchocolate confectionery products not for immediate consumption made on the premises.

Cross-References. Establishments primarily engaged in—

- Manufacturing chocolate confectioneries from cacao beans—are classified in Industry 311320, Chocolate and Confectionery Manufacturing from Cacao Beans;

- Manufacturing chocolate confectioneries from chocolate made elsewhere—are classified in Industry 311330, Confectionery Manufacturing from Purchased Chocolate;

- Retailing confectioneries not for immediate consumption made elsewhere—are classified in U.S. Industry 445292, Confectionery and Nut Stores;

- Preparing and selling confectioneries for immediate consumption—are classified in U.S. Industry 722213, Snack and Nonalcoholic Beverage Bars; and

- Roasting, salting, drying, cooking, or canning nuts and seeds—are classified in U.S. Industry 311911, Roasted Nuts and Peanut Butter Manufacturing.

3114 Fruit and Vegetable Preserving and Specialty Food Manufacturing

This industry group includes (1) establishments that freeze food and (2) those that use preservation processes, such as pickling, canning, and dehydrating. Both types begin their production process with inputs of vegetable or animal origin.

31141 Frozen Food Manufacturing

This industry comprises establishments primarily engaged in manufacturing frozen fruit, frozen juices, frozen vegetables, and frozen specialty foods (except seafood), such as frozen dinners, entrees, and side dishes; frozen pizza; frozen whipped toppings; and frozen waffles, pancakes, and french toast.

Cross-References. Establishments primarily engaged in—

- Manufacturing frozen dairy specialties—are classified in Industry 31152, Ice Cream and Frozen Dessert Manufacturing;

US—United States industry only. CAN—United States and Canadian industries are comparable. When neither US nor CAN appears, Canadian, Mexican, and United States industries are comparable.

- Manufacturing frozen bakery products—are classified in Industry 31181, Bread and Bakery Product Manufacturing;

- Manufacturing frozen seafood products—are classified in Industry 31171, Seafood Product Preparation and Packaging; and

- Manufacturing frozen meat products—are classified in Industry 31161, Animal Slaughtering and Processing.

311411 Frozen Fruit, Juice, and Vegetable Manufacturing[US]

This U.S. industry comprises establishments primarily engaged in manufacturing frozen fruits; frozen vegetables; and frozen fruit juices, − Nades, drinks, cocktail mixes and concentrates.

Cross-References.

Establishments primarily engaged in manufacturing frozen specialty foods are classified in U.S. Industry 311412, Frozen Specialty Food Manufacturing.

311412 Frozen Specialty Food Manufacturing[US]

This U.S. industry comprises establishments primarily engaged in manufacturing frozen specialty foods (except seafood), such as frozen dinners, entrees, and side dishes; frozen pizza; frozen whipped topping; and frozen waffles, pancakes, and french toast.

Cross-References. Establishments primarily engaged in—

- Manufacturing frozen dairy specialties—are classified in Industry 311520, Ice Cream and Frozen Dessert Manufacturing;

- Manufacturing frozen bakery products—are classified in U.S. Industry 311813, Frozen Cakes, Pies, and Other Pastries Manufacturing;

- Manufacturing frozen fruits, frozen fruit juices, and frozen vegetables—are classified in U.S. Industry 311411, Frozen Fruit, Juice, and Vegetable Manufacturing;

- Manufacturing frozen meat products—are classified in Industry 31161, Animal Slaughtering and Processing; and

- Manufacturing frozen seafood products—are classified in U.S. Industry 311712, Fresh and Frozen Seafood Processing.

31142 Fruit and Vegetable Canning, Pickling, and Drying

This industry comprises establishments primarily engaged in manufacturing canned, pickled, and dried fruits, vegetables, and specialty foods. Establishments in this industry may package the dried or dehydrated ingredients they make with other purchased ingredients. Examples of products made by these establishments are canned juices; canned baby foods; canned soups (except seafood);

US—United States industry only. CAN—United States and Canadian industries are comparable. When neither US nor CAN appears, Canadian, Mexican, and United States industries are comparable.

canned dry beans; canned tomato-based sauces, such as catsup, salsa, chili, spaghetti, barbeque, and tomato paste, pickles, relishes, jams and jellies, dried soup mixes and bullions, and sauerkraut.

Cross-References. Establishments primarily engaged in—

- Manufacturing canned dairy products—are classified in Industry 31151, Dairy Product (except Frozen) Manufacturing;

- Manufacturing canned seafood soups and seafood products—are classified in Industry 31171, Seafood Product Preparation and Packaging;

- Manufacturing canned meat products—are classified in Industry 31161, Animal Slaughtering and Processing;

- Milling rice and packaging it with other ingredients or manufacturing vegetable flours and meals—are classified in Industry 31121, Flour Milling and Malt Manufacturing;

- Manufacturing dry pasta and packaging it with other ingredients—are classified in Industry 31182, Cookie, Cracker, and Pasta Manufacturing;

- Mixing purchased dried and/or dehydrated potatoes, rice, and pasta and packaging them with other purchased ingredients; mixing purchased dried and/or dehydrated ingredients for soup mixes and bouillon; and manufacturing canned puddings—are classified in Industry 31199, All Other Food Manufacturing;

- Manufacturing dry salad dressing and dry sauce mixes—are classified in Industry 31194, Seasoning and Dressing Manufacturing; and

- Manufacturing canned fruit and vegetable drinks, cocktails, and −Nades—are classified in Industry 31211, Soft Drink and Ice Manufacturing.

311421 Fruit and Vegetable Canning^{US}

This U.S. industry comprises establishments primarily engaged in manufacturing canned, pickled, and brined fruits and vegetables. Examples of products made in these establishments are canned juices; canned jams and jellies; canned tomato-based sauces, such as catsup, salsa, chili, spaghetti, barbeque, and tomato paste; pickles, relishes, and sauerkraut.

Cross-References. Establishments primarily engaged in—

- Manufacturing canned baby foods, canned soups (except seafood), and canned specialty foods (except seafood)—are classified in U.S. Industry 311422, Specialty Canning;

- Manufacturing canned seafood soups and canned seafood products—are classified in U.S. Industry 311711, Seafood Canning;

- Manufacturing canned meat products—are classified in Industry 31161, Animal Slaughtering and Processing; and

- Manufacturing canned fruit and canned vegetable drinks, "ades", and cocktails—are classified in U.S. Industry 312111, Soft Drink Manufacturing.

US—United States industry only. CAN—United States and Canadian industries are comparable. When neither US nor CAN appears, Canadian, Mexican, and United States industries are comparable.

311422 Specialty Canning^{US}

This U.S. industry comprises establishments primarily engaged in manufacturing canned specialty foods. Examples of products made in these establishments are canned baby food, canned baked beans, canned soups (except seafood), canned spaghetti, and other canned nationality foods.

Cross-References. Establishments primarily engaged in—

- Manufacturing canned dairy products—are classified in U.S. Industry 311514, Dry, Condensed, and Evaporated Dairy Product Manufacturing;

- Manufacturing canned fruits, canned vegetables, and canned juices—are classified in U.S. Industry 311421, Fruit and Vegetable Canning;

- Manufacturing canned seafood soups and canned seafood products—are classified in U.S. Industry 311711, Seafood Canning;

- Manufacturing canned meat products—are classified in Industry 31161, Animal Slaughtering and Processing; and

- Manufacturing canned puddings—are classified in U.S. Industry 311999, All Other Miscellaneous Food Manufacturing.

311423 Dried and Dehydrated Food Manufacturing^{US}

This U.S. industry comprises establishments primarily engaged in (1) drying (including freeze-dried) and/or dehydrating fruits, vegetables, and soup mixes and bouillon and/or (2) drying and/or dehydrating ingredients and packaging them with other purchased ingredients, such as rice and dry pasta.

Cross-References. Establishments primarily engaged in—

- Milling rice and packaging it with other ingredients—are classified in U.S. Industry 311212, Rice Milling;

- Manufacturing dry pasta and packaging it with other ingredients—are classified in U.S. Industry 311823, Dry Pasta Manufacturing;

- Manufacturing vegetable flours and meals—are classified in U.S. Industry 311211, Flour Milling;

- Mixing purchased dried and/or dehydrated potatoes, rice, and dry pasta, and packaging them with other purchased ingredients, and mixing purchased dried and/or dehydrated ingredients for soup mixes and bouillon—are classified in U.S. Industry 311999, All Other Miscellaneous Food Manufacturing; and

- Manufacturing dry salad dressing and dry sauce mixes—are classified in U.S. Industry 311942, Spice and Extract Manufacturing.

US—United States industry only. CAN—United States and Canadian industries are comparable. When neither US nor CAN appears, Canadian, Mexican, and United States industries are comparable.

3115 Dairy Product Manufacturing

This industry group comprises establishments that manufacture dairy products from raw milk, processed milk, and dairy substitutes.

31151 Dairy Product (except Frozen) Manufacturing

This industry comprises establishments primarily engaged in one or more of the following: (1) manufacturing dairy products (except frozen) from raw milk and/or processed milk products; (2) manufacturing dairy substitutes (except frozen) from soybeans and other nondairy substances; and (3) manufacturing dry, condensed, concentrated, and evaporated dairy and dairy substitute products.

Cross-References. Establishments primarily engaged in—

- Manufacturing cheese-based salad dressings—are classified in Industry 31194, Seasoning and Dressing Manufacturing;

- Manufacturing margarine or margarine-butter blends—are classified in Industry 31122, Starch and Vegetable Fats and Oils Manufacturing;

- Manufacturing frozen whipped toppings—are classified in Industry 31141, Frozen Food Manufacturing; and

- Manufacturing ice cream, frozen yogurt, and other frozen dairy desserts—are classified in Industry 31152, Ice Cream and Frozen Dessert Manufacturing.

311511 Fluid Milk Manufacturing[CAN]

This U.S. industry comprises establishments primarily engaged in (1) manufacturing processed milk products, such as pasteurized milk or cream and sour cream and/or (2) manufacturing fluid milk dairy substitutes from soybeans and other nondairy substances.

Cross-References. Establishments primarily engaged in—

- Manufacturing dry mix whipped toppings, canned milk, and ultra high temperature milk—are classified in U.S. Industry 311514, Dry, Condensed, and Evaporated Dairy Product Manufacturing;

- Manufacturing frozen whipped toppings—are classified in U.S. Industry 311412, Frozen Specialty Food Manufacturing; and

- Manufacturing ice cream and frozen yogurt and other frozen desserts—are classified in Industry 311520, Ice Cream and Frozen Dessert Manufacturing.

311512 Creamery Butter Manufacturing[US]

This U.S. industry comprises establishments primarily engaged in manufacturing creamery butter from milk and/or processed milk products.

US—United States industry only. CAN—United States and Canadian industries are comparable. When neither US nor CAN appears, Canadian, Mexican, and United States industries are comparable.

http://www.ntis.gov/naics

Cross-References.

Establishments primarily engaged in manufacturing margarine or margarine-butter blends are classified in U.S. Industry 311225, Fats and Oils Refining and Blending.

311513 Cheese Manufacturing[US]

This U.S. industry comprises establishments primarily engaged in (1) manufacturing cheese products (except cottage cheese) from raw milk and/or processed milk products and/or (2) manufacturing cheese substitutes from soybean and other nondairy substances.

Cross-References. Establishments primarily engaged in—

- Manufacturing cheese-based salad dressings—are classified in U.S. Industry 311941, Mayonnaise, Dressing, and Other Prepared Sauce Manufacturing; and

- Manufacturing cottage cheese—are classified in U.S. Industry 311511, Fluid Milk Manufacturing.

311514 Dry, Condensed, and Evaporated Dairy Product Manufacturing[US]

This U.S. industry comprises establishments primarily engaged in manufacturing dry, condensed, and evaporated milk and dairy substitute products.

Cross-References. Establishments primarily engaged in—

- Manufacturing fluid milk products—are classified in U.S. Industry 311511, Fluid Milk Manufacturing;

- Manufacturing creamery butter—are classified in U.S. Industry 311512, Creamery Butter Manufacturing; and

- Manufacturing cheese products—are classified in U.S. Industry 311513, Cheese Manufacturing.

31152 Ice Cream and Frozen Dessert Manufacturing
See industry description for 311520 below.

311520 Ice Cream and Frozen Dessert Manufacturing

This industry comprises establishments primarily engaged in manufacturing ice cream, frozen yogurts, frozen ices, sherbets, frozen tofu, and other frozen desserts (except bakery products).

Cross-References. Establishments primarily engaged in—

- Manufacturing frozen bakery products—are classified in U.S. Industry 311813, Frozen Cakes, Pies, and Other Pastries Manufacturing; and

---

US—United States industry only. CAN—United States and Canadian industries are comparable. When neither US nor CAN appears, Canadian, Mexican, and United States industries are comparable.

- Manufacturing ice cream and ice milk mixes—are classified in U.S. Industry 311514, Dry, Condensed, and Evaporated Dairy Product Manufacturing.

3116 Animal Slaughtering and Processing

31161 Animal Slaughtering and Processing

This industry comprises establishments primarily engaged in one or more of the following: (1) slaughtering animals; (2) preparing processed meats and meat byproducts; and (3) rendering and/ or refining animal fat, bones, and meat scraps. This industry includes establishments primarily engaged in assembly cutting and packing of meats (i.e., boxed meats) from purchased carcasses.

Cross-References. Establishments primarily engaged in—

- Manufacturing canned meat for baby food—are classified in Industry 31142, Fruit and Vegetable Canning, Pickling and Drying;

- Manufacturing meat-based animal feeds from carcasses—are classified in Industry 31111, Animal Food Manufacturing;

- Blending purchased animal fats with vegetable fats—are classified in Industry 31122, Starch and Vegetable Fats and Oils Manufacturing;

- Manufacturing canned and frozen specialty foods containing meat, such as nationality foods (e.g., enchiladas, pizza, egg rolls) and frozen dinners,—are classified in Industry Group 3114, Fruit and Vegetable Preserving and Specialty Food Manufacturing;

- Drying, freezing, or breaking eggs—are classified in Industry 31199, All Other Food Manufacturing; and

- Cutting meat (except box meat)—are classified in Industry 42247, Meat and Meat Product Wholesalers.

311611 Animal (except Poultry) Slaughtering^{CAN}

This U.S. industry comprises establishments primarily engaged in slaughtering animals (except poultry and small game). Establishments that slaughter and prepare meats are included in this industry.

Cross-References. Establishments primarily engaged in—

- Processing meat and meat byproducts (except poultry and small game) from purchased meats—are classified in U.S. Industry 311612, Meat Processed from Carcasses;

- Slaughtering and/or processing poultry and small game—are classified in U.S. Industry 311615, Poultry Processing;

- Rendering lard and other animal fats and oils, animal fat, bones, and meat scraps—are classified in U.S. Industry 3116133, Rendering and Meat By-product Processing; and

---

- Manufacturing canned and frozen specialty foods containing meat, such as nationality foods (e.g., enchiladas, egg rolls, pizza) and frozen dinners,—are classified in Industry Group 3114, Fruit and Vegetable Preserving and Specialty Food Manufacturing.

311612 Meat Processed from Carcasses[US]

This U.S. industry comprises establishments primarily engaged in processing or preserving meat and meat byproducts (except poultry and small game) from purchased meats. This industry includes establishments primarily engaged in assembly cutting and packing of meats (i.e., boxed meats) from purchased meats.

Cross-References. Establishments primarily engaged in—

- Slaughtering animals (except poultry and small game)—are classified in U.S. Industry 311611, Animal (except Poultry) Slaughtering;

- Slaughtering poultry and small game—are classified in U.S. Industry 311615, Poultry Processing;

- Rendering animal fat, bones, and meat scraps—are classified in U.S. Industry 311613, Rendering and Meat By-product Processing;

- Manufacturing canned meats for baby food—are classified in U.S. Industry 311422, Specialty Canning;

- Manufacturing meat-based animal feeds from carcasses—are classified in Industry 31111, Animal Food Manufacturing;

- Manufacturing canned and frozen specialty foods containing meat, such as nationality foods (e.g., enchiladas, egg rolls, pizza) and frozen dinners,—are classified in Industry Group 3114, Fruit and Vegetable Preserving and Specialty Food Manufacturing; and

- Cutting meat (except boxed meat)—are classified in U.S. Industry 422470, Meat and Meat Product Wholesalers.

311613 Rendering and Meat Byproduct Processing[US]

This U.S. industry comprises establishments primarily engaged in rendering animal fat, bones, and meat scraps.

Cross-References.

Establishments primarily engaged in blending purchased animal fats with vegetable fats are classified in U.S. Industry 311225, Fats and Oils Refining and Blending.

311615 Poultry Processing[CAN]

This U.S. industry comprises establishments primarily engaged in (1) slaughtering poultry and small game and/or (2) preparing processed poultry and small game meat and meat byproducts.

US—United States industry only. CAN—United States and Canadian industries are comparable. When neither US nor CAN appears, Canadian, Mexican, and United States industries are comparable.

Cross-References. Establishments primarily engaged in—

- Slaughtering animals (except poultry and small game) and/or preparing meats—are classified in U.S. Industry 311611, Animal (except Poultry) Slaughtering;

- Preparing meat and meat byproducts (except poultry and small game) from purchased meats—are classified in U.S. Industry 311612, Meat Processed from Carcasses;

- Rendering animal fat, bones, and meat scraps—are classified in U.S. Industry 311613, Rendering and Meat By-product Processing;

- Canning poultry and small game for baby food—are classified in U.S. Industry 311422, Specialty Canning;

- Producing meat-based animal feeds from carcasses—are classified in Industry 31111, Animal Food Manufacturing;

- Manufacturing canned and frozen meat products, such as nationality foods (e.g., enchiladas, egg rolls, pizza) and frozen dinners,—are classified in Industry Group 3114, Fruit and Vegetable Preserving and Specialty Food Manufacturing; and

- Drying, freezing, and breaking eggs—are classified in U.S. Industry 311999, All Other Miscellaneous Food Manufacturing.

3117 Seafood Product Preparation and Packaging

31171 Seafood Product Preparation and Packaging

This industry comprises establishments primarily engaged in one or more of the following: (1) canning seafood (including soup); (2) smoking, salting, and drying seafoods; (3) eviscerating fresh fish by removing heads, fins, scales, bones, and entrails; (4) shucking and packing fresh shellfish; (5) processing marine fats and oils; and (6) freezing seafood. Establishments known as "floating factory ships" that are engaged in the gathering and processing of seafood into canned seafood products are included in this industry.

311711 Seafood Canning[US]

This U.S. industry comprises establishments primarily engaged in (1) canning seafood (including soup) and marine fats and oils and/or (2) smoking, salting, and drying seafoods. Establishments known as "floating factory ships" that are engaged in the gathering and processing of seafood into canned seafood products are included in this industry.

Cross-References.

Establishments primarily engaged in preparing fresh and frozen seafood and marine fats and oils are classified in U.S. Industry 311712, Fresh and Frozen Seafood Processing.

US—United States industry only. CAN—United States and Canadian industries are comparable. When neither US nor CAN appears, Canadian, Mexican, and United States industries are comparable.

http://www.ntis.gov/naics

311712 Fresh and Frozen Seafood Processing[US]

This U.S. industry comprises establishments primarily engaged in one or more of the following: (1) eviscerating fresh fish by removing heads, fins, scales, bones, and entrails; (2) shucking and packing fresh shellfish; (3) manufacturing frozen seafood; and (4) processing fresh and frozen marine fats and oils.

Cross-References.

Establishments primarily engaged in canning and curing seafood are classified in U.S. Industry 311711, Seafood Canning.

3118 Bakeries and Tortilla Manufacturing

31181 Bread and Bakery Product Manufacturing

This industry comprises establishments primarily engaged in manufacturing fresh and frozen bread and other bakery products.

Cross-References. Establishments primarily engaged in—

- Manufacturing cookies and crackers—are classified in Industry 31182, Cookie, Cracker, and Pasta Manufacturing;

- Preparing and selling bakery products (e.g., cookies, pretzels) for immediate consumption— are classified in Industry 72221, Limited-Service Eating Places;

- Retailing bakery products not for immediate consumption made elsewhere—are classified in Industry 44529, Other Specialty Food Stores; and

- Manufacturing pretzels (except soft)—are classified in Industry 31191, Snack Food Manufacturing.

311811 Retail Bakeries[CAN]

This U.S. industry comprises establishments primarily engaged in retailing bread and other bakery products not for immediate consumption made on the premises from flour, not from prepared dough.

Cross-References. Establishments primarily engaged in—

- Retailing bakery products not for immediate consumption made elsewhere—are classified in U.S. Industry 445291, Baked Goods Stores;

- Preparing and selling bakery products (e.g.,cookies, pretzels) for immediate consumption— are classified in U.S. Industry 722213, Snack and Nonalcoholic Beverage Bars;

- Manufacturing fresh or frozen breads and other fresh bakery (except cookies and crackers) products—are classified in U.S. Industry 311812, Commercial Bakeries; and

---

US—United States industry only. CAN—United States and Canadian industries are comparable. When neither US nor CAN appears, Canadian, Mexican, and United States industries are comparable.

- Manufacturing cookies and crackers—are classified in U.S. Industry 311821, Cookie and Cracker Manufacturing.

311812 Commercial Bakeries[US]

This U.S. industry comprises establishments primarily engaged in manufacturing fresh and frozen bread and bread-type rolls and other fresh bakery (except cookies and crackers) products.

Cross-References. Establishments primarily engaged in—

- Retailing bread and other bakery products not for immediate consumption made on the premises from flour, not from prepared dough—are classified in U.S. Industry 311811, Retail Bakeries;

- Manufacturing frozen bakery products (except bread)—are classified in U.S. Industry 311813, Frozen Cakes, Pies, and Other Pastries Manufacturing;

- Preparing and selling bakery products (e.g., cookies, pretzels) for immediate consumption— are classified in U.S. Industry 722213, Snack and Nonalcoholic Beverage Bars;

- Retailing bakery products not for immediate consumption made elsewhere—are classified in U.S. Industry 445291, Baked Goods Stores;

- Manufacturing cookies and crackers—are classified in U.S. Industry 311821, Cookie and Cracker Manufacturing; and

- Manufacturing pretzels (except soft)—are classified in U.S. Industry 311919, Other Snack Food Manufacturing.

311813 Frozen Cakes, Pies, and Other Pastries Manufacturing[US]

This U.S. industry comprises establishments primarily engaged in manufacturing frozen bakery products (except bread), such as cakes, pies, and doughnuts.

Cross-References. Establishments primarily engaged in—

- Manufacturing frozen breads   are classified in U.S. Industry 311812, Commercial Bakeries;

- Retailing bakery products not for immediate consumption made on the premises from flour, not from prepared dough—are classified in U.S. Industry 311811, Retail Bakeries;

- Preparing and selling bakery products (e.g., cookies, pretzels) for immediate consumption— are classified in U.S. Industry 722213, Snack and Nonalcoholic Beverage Bars;

- Manufacturing cookies and crackers—are classified in U.S. Industry 311821, Cookie and Cracker Manufacturing; and

- Retailing bakery products not for immediate consumption made elsewhere—are classified in U.S. Industry 445291, Baked Goods Stores.

US—United States industry only. CAN—United States and Canadian industries are comparable. When neither US nor CAN appears, Canadian, Mexican, and United States industries are comparable.

31182 Cookie, Cracker, and Pasta Manufacturing

This industry comprises establishments primarily engaged in one of the following: (1) manufacturing cookies and crackers; (2) preparing flour and dough mixes and dough from flour ground elsewhere; and (3) manufacturing dry pasta. The establishments in this industry may package the dry pasta they manufacture with other ingredients.

Cross-References. Establishments primarily engaged in—

- Preparing and selling bakery products (eg., cookies, pretzels) for immediate consumption— are classified in Industry 72221, Limited-Service Eating Places;

- Retailing bakery products not for immediate consumption made elsewhere—are classified in Industry 44529, Other Specialty Food Stores;

- Manufacturing bakery products (e.g., bread, cookies, pies)—are classified in Industry 31181, Bread and Bakery Product Manufacturing;

- Milling flour and preparing flour mixes or doughs—are classified in Industry 31121, Flour Milling and Malt Manufacturing;

- Manufacturing canned pasta specialties—are classified in Industry 31142, Fruit and Vegetable Canning, Pickling and Drying;

- Manufacturing fresh pasta—are classified in Industry 31199, All Other Food Manufacturing;

- Manufacturing pretzels (except soft)—are classified in Industry 31191, Snack Food Manufacturing;

- Mixing purchased dried and/or dehydrated ingredients with purchased dry pasta—are classified in Industry 31199, All Other Food Manufacturing; and

- Drying and/or dehydrating ingredients and packaging them with purchased dry pasta—are classified in Industry 31142, Fruit and Vegetable Canning, Pickling and Drying.

311821 Cookie and Cracker Manufacturing[CAN]

This U.S. industry comprises establishments primarily engaged in manufacturing cookies, crackers, and other products, such as ice cream cones.

Cross-References. Establishments primarily engaged in—

- Preparing and selling bakery products (e.g., cookies, pretzels) for immediate consumption— are classified in U.S. Industry 722213, Snack and Nonalcoholic Beverage Bars;

- Retailing bakery products not for immediate consumption made elsewhere—are classified in U.S. Industry 445291, Baked Goods Stores;

- Manufacturing bakery products (e.g., breads, cookies, pies)—are classified in Industry 31181, Bread and Bakery Product Manufacturing; and

---

US—United States industry only. CAN—United States and Canadian industries are comparable. When neither US nor CAN appears, Canadian, Mexican, and United States industries are comparable.

- Manufacturing pretzels (except soft)—are classified in U.S. Industry 311919, Other Snack Food Manufacturing.

311822 Flour Mixes and Dough Manufacturing from Purchased Flour^{CAN}

This U.S. industry comprises establishments primarily engaged in manufacturing prepared flour mixes or dough mixes from flour ground elsewhere.

Cross-References.

Establishments primarily engaged in milling flour and preparing flour mixes or doughs are classified in U.S. Industry 311211, Flour Milling.

311823 Dry Pasta Manufacturing^{CAN}

This U.S. industry comprises establishments primarily engaged in manufacturing dry pasta. The establishments in this industry may package the dry pasta they manufacture with other ingredients.

Cross-References. Establishments primarily engaged in—

- Manufacturing fresh pasta—are classified in U.S. Industry 311991, Perishable Prepared Food Manufacturing;

- Manufacturing pasta specialties—are classified in Industry Group 3114, Fruit and Vegetable Preserving and Specialty Food Manufacturing;

- Mixing purchased dried and/or dehydrated ingredients with purchased dry pasta—are classified in U.S. Industry 311999, All Other Miscellaneous Food Manufacturing; and

- Drying and/or dehydrating ingredients packaged with purchased dry pasta—are classified in U.S. Industry 311423, Dried and Dehydrated Food Manufacturing.

31183 Tortilla Manufacturing
See industry description for 311830 below.

311830 Tortilla Manufacturing

This industry comprises establishments primarily engaged in manufacturing tortillas.

Cross-References. Establishments primarily engaged in—

- Manufacturing canned nationality foods using tortillas—are classified in U.S. Industry 311422, Specialty Canning;

- Manufacturing frozen nationality foods using tortillas—are classified in U.S. Industry 311412, Frozen Specialty Food Manufacturing; and

- Manufacturing tortilla chips—are classified in U.S. Industry 311919, Other Snack Food Manufacturing.

US—United States industry only. CAN—United States and Canadian industries are comparable. When neither US nor CAN appears, Canadian, Mexican, and United States industries are comparable.

3119 Other Food Manufacturing

This industry group comprises establishments primarily engaged in manufacturing food (except animal food; grain and oilseed milling; sugar and confectionery products; preserved fruit, vegetable, and specialty foods; dairy products; meat products; seafood products; and bakeries and tortillas). The industry group includes industries with different productive processes, such as snack food manufacturing; coffee and tea manufacturing; concentrate, syrup, condiment, and spice manufacturing; and, in general, an entire range of other miscellaneous food product manufacturing.

31191 Snack Food Manufacturing

This industry comprises establishments primarily engaged in one or more of the following: (1) salting, roasting, drying, cooking, or canning nuts; (2) processing grains or seeds into snacks; (3) manufacturing peanut butter; and (4) manufacturing potato chips, corn chips, popped popcorn, pretzels (except soft), pork rinds, and similar snacks.

Cross-References. Establishments primarily engaged in—

- Manufacturing crackers—are classified in Industry 31182, Cookie, Cracker, and Pasta Manufacturing;

- Manufacturing unpopped popcorn—are classified in Industry 31199, All Other Food Manufacturing;

- Manufacturing chocolate or candy-coated nuts and candy-covered popcorn—are classified in Industry Group 3113, Sugar and Confectionery Product Manufacturing; and

- Manufacturing soft pretzels—are classified in Industry 31181, Bread and Bakery Product Manufacturing.

311911 Roasted Nuts and Peanut Butter Manufacturing[CAN]

This U.S. industry comprises establishments primarily engaged in one or more of the following: (1) salting, roasting, drying, cooking, or canning nuts; (2) processing grains or seeds into snacks; and (3) manufacturing peanut butter.

Cross-References.

Establishments primarily engaged in manufacturing chocolate or candy-coated nuts and candy-covered popcorn are classified in Industry Group 3113, Sugar and Confectionery Product Manufacturing.

311919 Other Snack Food Manufacturing[CAN]

This U.S. industry comprises establishments primarily engaged in manufacturing snack foods (except roasted nuts and peanut butter).

US—United States industry only. CAN—United States and Canadian industries are comparable. When neither US nor CAN appears, Canadian, Mexican, and United States industries are comparable.

Illustrative Examples:

Corn chips and related corn snacks
  manufacturing
Popped popcorn (except candy-covered)
  manufacturing

Pork rinds manufacturing
Potato chips manufacturing
Pretzels (except soft) manufacturing
Tortilla chips manufacturing

Cross-References. Establishments primarily engaged in—

- Manufacturing cookies and crackers—are classified in U.S. Industry 311821, Cookie and Cracker Manufacturing;

- Manufacturing candy covered popcorn and nonchocolate granola bars—are classified in Industry 311340, Nonchocolate Confectionery Manufacturing;

- Salting, roasting, drying, cooking, or canning nuts and seeds—are classified in U.S. Industry 311911, Roasted Nuts and Peanut Butter Manufacturing;

- Manufacturing unpopped popcorn—are classified in U.S. Industry 311999, All Other Miscellaneous Food Manufacturing; and

- Manufacturing soft pretzels—are classified in U.S. Industry 311812, Commercial Bakeries.

31192 Coffee and Tea Manufacturing
See industry description for 311920 below.

311920 Coffee and Tea Manufacturing

This industry comprises establishments primarily engaged in one or more of the following: (1) roasting coffee; (2) manufacturing coffee and tea concentrates (including instant and freeze-dried); (3) blending tea; (4) manufacturing herbal tea; and (5) manufacturing coffee extracts, flavorings, and syrups.

Cross-References.

Establishments primarily engaged in bottling and canning ice tea are classified in U.S. Industry 312111, Soft Drink Manufacturing.

31193 Flavoring Syrup and Concentrate Manufacturing
See industry description for 311930 below.

311930 Flavoring Syrup and Concentrate Manufacturing

This industry comprises establishments primarily engaged in manufacturing flavoring syrup drink concentrates and related products for soda fountain use or for the manufacture of soft drinks.

Cross-References. Establishments primarily engaged in—

- Manufacturing chocolate syrup—are classified in Industry 311320, Chocolate and Confectionery Manufacturing from Cacao Beans;

US—United States industry only. CAN—United States and Canadian industries are comparable. When neither US nor CAN appears, Canadian, Mexican, and United States industries are comparable.

- Manufacturing flavoring extracts (except coffee and meat) and natural food colorings—are classified in U.S. Industry 311942, Spice and Extract Manufacturing;

- Manufacturing coffee extracts—are classified in Industry 311920, Coffee and Tea Manufacturing;

- Manufacturing meat extracts—are classified in Industry 31161, Animal Slaughtering and Processing;

- Manufacturing powdered drink mixes (except coffee, tea, chocolate, or milk-based) and table syrup from corn syrup—are classified in U.S. Industry 311999, All Other Miscellaneous Food Manufacturing;

- Reducing maple sap to maple syrup—are classified in U.S. Industry 111998, All Other Miscellaneous Crop Farming; and

- Manufacturing natural nonfood colorings—are classified in U.S. Industry 325199, All Other Basic Organic Chemical Manufacturing.

31194 Seasoning and Dressing Manufacturing

This industry comprises establishments primarily engaged in one or more of the following: (1) manufacturing dressings and sauces, such as mayonnaise, salad dressing, vinegar, mustard, horseradish, soy sauce, tarter sauce, Worcestershire sauce, and other prepared sauces (except tomato-based and gravies); (2) manufacturing spices, table salt, seasoning, and flavoring extracts (except coffee and meat), and natural food colorings; and (3) manufacturing dry mix food preparations, such as salad dressing mixes, gravy and sauce mixes, frosting mixes, and other dry mix preparations.

Cross-References. Establishments primarily engaged in—

- Manufacturing catsup and other tomato-based sauces—are classified in Industry 31142, Fruit and Vegetable Canning, Pickling and Drying;

- Mixing purchased dried and/or dehydrated potato, rice, and pasta and packaging them with other purchased ingredients, and manufacturing prepared frosting—are classified in Industry 31199, All Other Food Manufacturing;

- Drying and/or dehydrating ingredients for dry soup mixes and bouillon—are classified in Industry 31142, Fruit and Vegetable Canning, Pickling and Drying;

- Mixing purchased dried and/or dehydrated ingredients for dry soup mixes and bouillon—are classified in Industry 31199, All Other Food Manufacturing;

- Manufacturing industrial salts—are classified in Industry 32599, Other Chemical Product and Preparation Manufacturing;

- Manufacturing flavoring syrups (except coffee)—are classified in Industry 31193, Flavoring Syrup and Concentrate Manufacturing;

- Manufacturing synthetic food colorings—are classified in Industry 32513, Synthetic Dye and Pigment Manufacturing;

- Manufacturing natural organic colorings for nonfood uses—are classified in Industry 32519, Other Basic Organic Chemical Manufacturing;

- Manufacturing coffee extracts—are classified in Industry 31192, Coffee and Tea Manufacturing;

- Manufacturing meat extracts—are classified in Industry 31161, Animal Slaughtering and Processing; and

- Manufacturing gravies—are classified in Industry 31199, All Other Food Manufacturing.

311941 Mayonnaise, Dressing, and Other Prepared Sauce Manufacturing[US]

This U.S. industry comprises establishments primarily engaged in manufacturing mayonnaise, salad dressing, vinegar, mustard, horseradish, soy sauce, tarter sauce, Worcestershire sauce, and other prepared sauces (except tomato-based and gravy).

Cross-References. Establishments primarily engaged in—

- Manufacturing catsup and similar tomato-based sauces—are classified in U.S. Industry 311421, Fruit and Vegetable Canning;

- Manufacturing dry salad dressing and dry sauce mixes—are classified in U.S. Industry 311942, Spice and Extract Manufacturing; and

- Manufacturing gravies—are classified in U.S. Industry 311999, All Other Miscellaneous Food Manufacturing.

311942 Spice and Extract Manufacturing[US]

This U.S. industry comprises establishments primarily engaged in (1) manufacturing spices, table salt, seasonings, flavoring extracts (except coffee and meat), and natural food colorings and/or (2) manufacturing dry mix food preparations, such as salad dressing mixes, gravy and sauce mixes, frosting mixes, and other dry mix preparations.

Cross-References. Establishments primarily engaged in—

- Manufacturing catsup and other tomato-based sauces—are classified in U.S. Industry 311421, Fruit and Vegetable Canning;

- Manufacturing mayonnaise, dressings, and prepared nontomato-based sauces—are classified in U.S. Industry 311941, Mayonnaise, Dressing, and Other Prepared Sauce Manufacturing;

- Manufacturing industrial salts—are classified in U.S. Industry 325998, All Other Miscellaneous Chemical Product and Preparation Manufacturing;

- Drying and/or dehydrating ingredients for dry soup mixes and bouillon—are classified in U.S. Industry 311423, Dried and Dehydrated Food Manufacturing;

- Mixing purchased dried and/or dehydrated ingredients for dry soup mixes and bouillon—are classified in U.S. Industry 311999, All Other Miscellaneous Food Manufacturing;

- Manufacturing flavoring syrups—are classified in Industry 311930, Flavoring Syrup and Concentrate Manufacturing;

- Manufacturing dried and dehydrated potato, rice, or dry pasta packaged with other ingredients, and prepared frostings—are classified in U.S. Industry 311999, All Other Miscellaneous Food Manufacturing;

- Manufacturing coffee extracts—are classified in Industry 311920, Coffee and Tea Manufacturing;

- Manufacturing meat extracts—are classified in Industry 31161, Animal Slaughtering and Processing;

- Manufacturing synthetic food colorings—are classified in U.S. Industry 325132, Synthetic Organic Dye and Pigment Manufacturing; and

- Manufacturing natural organic colorings for nonfood uses—are classified in U.S. Industry 325199, All Other Basic Organic Chemical Manufacturing.

31199 All Other Food Manufacturing

This industry comprises establishments primarily engaged in manufacturing food (except animal food; grain and oilseed milling; sugar and confectionery products; preserved fruits, vegetables, and specialties; dairy products; meat products; seafood products; bakeries and tortillas; snack foods; coffee and tea; flavoring syrups and concentrates; seasonings; and dressings). Included in this industry are establishments primarily engaged in mixing purchased dried and/or dehydrated ingredients including those mixing purchased dried and/or dehydrated ingredients for soup mixes and bouillon.

Illustrative Examples:

Baking powder manufacturing	Honey processing
Cut or peeled fresh vegetables manufacturing	Popcorn (except popped) manufacturing
Dessert puddings manufacturing	Powdered drink mixes (except chocolate,
Egg substitutes manufacturing	coffee, tea, or milk based) manufacturing
Fresh pasta manufacturing	Sweetening syrups (except pure maple)
Fresh pizza manufacturing	manufacturing

Cross-References. Establishments primarily engaged in—

- Manufacturing animal foods—are classified in Industry Group 3111, Animal Food Manufacturing;

- Milling grain and oilseed—are classified in Industry Group 3112, Grain and Oilseed Milling;

- Manufacturing sugar and confectionery products—are classified in Industry Group 3113, Sugar and Confectionery Product Manufacturing;

US—United States industry only. CAN—United States and Canadian industries are comparable. When neither US nor CAN appears, Canadian, Mexican, and United States industries are comparable.

- Preserving fruit, vegetables, and specialty foods—are classified in Industry Group 3114, Fruit and Vegetable Preserving and Specialty Food Manufacturing;

- Manufacturing dairy products—are classified in Industry Group 3115, Dairy Product Manufacturing;

- Manufacturing meat products—are classified in Industry Group 3116, Animal Slaughtering and Processing;

- Manufacturing seafood products—are classified in Industry Group 3117, Seafood Product Preparation and Packaging;

- Manufacturing bakery and tortilla products—are classified in Industry Group 3118, Bakeries and Tortilla Manufacturing;

- Manufacturing snack foods—are classified in Industry 31191, Snack Food Manufacturing;

- Manufacturing coffee and tea—are classified in Industry 31192, Coffee and Tea Manufacturing;

- Manufacturing flavoring syrups and concentrates—are classified in Industry 31193, Flavoring Syrup and Concentrate Manufacturing;

- Manufacturing seasonings and dressings—are classified in Industry 31194, Seasoning and Dressing Manufacturing;

- Milling rice and packaging it with other ingredients—are classified in Industry 31121, Flour Milling and Malt Manufacturing;

- Manufacturing dry pasta and packaging it with other ingredients—are classified in Industry 31182, Cookie, Cracker, and Pasta Manufacturing; and

- Drying and/or dehydrating ingredients and packaging them with other purchased ingredients—are classified in Industry 31142, Fruit and Vegetable Canning, Pickling and Drying.

311991 Perishable Prepared Food Manufacturing[US]

This U.S. industry comprises establishments primarily engaged in manufacturing perishable prepared foods, such as salads, sandwiches, prepared meals, fresh pizza, fresh pasta, and peeled or cut vegetables.

311999 All Other Miscellaneous Food Manufacturing[US]

This U.S. industry comprises establishments primarily engaged in manufacturing food (except animal food; grain and oilseed milling; sugar and confectionery products; preserved fruits, vegetables, and specialties; dairy products; meat products; seafood products; bakeries and tortillas; snack foods; coffee and tea; flavoring syrups and concentrates; seasonings and dressings; and perishable prepared food). Included in this industry are establishments primarily engaged in mixing purchased dried and/or dehydrated ingredients including those mixing purchased dried and/or dehydrated ingredients for soup mixes and bouillon.

US—United States industry only. CAN—United States and Canadian industries are comparable. When neither US nor CAN appears, Canadian, Mexican, and United States industries are comparable.

Illustrative Examples:

Baking powder manufacturing
Cake frosting manufacturing
Dessert puddings manufacturing
Egg substitutes manufacturing
Gelatin dessert preparations manufacturing
Honey processing

Popcorn (except popped) manufacturing
Powdered drink mixes (except chocolate, coffee, tea, or milk based) manufacturing
Sweetening syrups (except pure maple) manufacturing
Yeast manufacturing

Cross-References. Establishments primarily engaged in—

- Manufacturing animal foods—are classified in Industry Group 3111, Animal Food Manufacturing;

- Milling grain and oilseed—are classified in Industry Group 3112, Grain and Oilseed Milling;

- Manufacturing sugar and confectionery products—are classified in Industry Group 3113, Sugar and Confectionery Product Manufacturing;

- Preserving fruit, vegetable, and specialty foods—are classified in Industry Group 3114, Fruit and Vegetable Preserving and Specialty Food Manufacturing;

- Manufacturing dairy products—are classified in Industry Group 3115, Dairy Product Manufacturing;

- Manufacturing meat products—are classified in Industry Group 3116, Meat Product Manufacturing;

- Manufacturing seafood products—are classified in Industry Group 3117, Seafood Product Preparation and Packaging;

- Manufacturing bakery and tortilla products—are classified in Industry Group 3118, Bakeries and Tortilla Manufacturing;

- Manufacturing snack foods—are classified in Industry 31191, Snack Food Manufacturing;

- Manufacturing coffee and tea—are classified in Industry 31192, Coffee and Tea Manufacturing;

- Manufacturing flavoring syrups and concentrates—are classified in Industry 31193, Flavoring Syrup and Concentrate Manufacturing;

- Manufacturing seasonings and dressings—are classified in Industry 31194, Seasoning and Dressing Manufacturing;

- Manufacturing perishable prepared foods—are classified in U.S. Industry 311991, Perishable Prepared Food Manufacturing;

- Milling rice and packaging it with other ingredients—are classified in U.S. Industry 311212, Rice Milling;

- Manufacturing dry pasta and packaging it with ingredients—are classified in U.S. Industry 311823, Dry Pasta Manufacturing; and

---

US—United States industry only. CAN—United States and Canadian industries are comparable. When neither US nor CAN appears, Canadian, Mexican, and United States industries are comparable.

http://www.ntis.gov/naics

- Drying and/or dehydrating ingredients and packaging them with other purchased ingredients—are classified in U.S. Industry 311423, Dried and Dehydrated Food Manufacturing.

312 Beverage and Tobacco Product Manufacturing

Industries in the Beverage and Tobacco Product Manufacturing subsector manufacture beverages and tobacco products. The industry group, Beverage Manufacturing, includes three types of establishments: (1) those that manufacture nonalcoholic beverages; (2) those that manufacture alcoholic beverages through the fermentation process; and (3) those that produce distilled alcoholic beverages. Ice manufacturing, while not a beverage, is included with nonalcoholic beverage manufacturing because it uses the same production process as water purification.

In the case of activities related to the manufacture of beverages, the structure follows the defined productive processes. Brandy, a distilled beverage, was not placed under distillery product manufacturing, but rather under the NAICS class for winery product manufacturing since the productive process used in the manufacturing of alcoholic grape-based beverages produces both wines (fermented beverage) and brandies (distilled beverage).

The industry group, Tobacco Manufacturing, includes two types of establishments: (1) those engaged in redrying and stemming tobacco and (2) those that manufacture tobacco products, such as cigarettes and cigars.

3121 Beverage Manufacturing

31211 Soft Drink and Ice Manufacturing

This industry comprises establishments primarily engaged in one or more of the following: (1) manufacturing soft drinks; (2) manufacturing ice; and (3) purifying and bottling water.

Cross-References. Establishments primarily engaged in—

- Canning fruit and vegetable juices—are classified in Industry 31142, Fruit and Vegetable Canning, Pickling and Drying;

- Manufacturing soft drink bases—are classified in Industry 31193, Flavoring Syrup and Concentrate Manufacturing;

- Manufacturing nonalcoholic cider—are classified in Industry 31199, All Other Food Manufacturing;

- Manufacturing dry ice—are classified in Industry 32512, Industrial Gas Manufacturing;

- Manufacturing milk-based drinks—are classified in Industry 31151, Dairy Product (except Frozen) Manufacturing;

- Manufacturing nonalcoholic beers—are classified in Industry 31212, Breweries;

- Manufacturing nonalcoholic wines—are classified in Industry 31213, Wineries; and

- Bottling purchased purified water—are classified in Industry 42249, Other Grocery and Related Products Wholesalers.

312111 Soft Drink Manufacturing[US]

This U.S. industry comprises establishments primarily engaged in manufacturing soft drinks and artificially carbonated waters.

Cross-References. Establishments primarily engaged in—

- Canning fruit and vegetable juices—are classified in U.S. Industry 311421, Fruit and Vegetable Canning;

- Manufacturing fruit syrups for flavoring—are classified in Industry 31193, Flavoring Syrup and Concentrate Manufacturing;

- Manufacturing nonalcoholic cider—are classified in U.S. Industry 311999, All Other Miscellaneous Food Manufacturing;

- Purifying and bottling water (except artificially carbonated and flavored water)—are classified in U.S. Industry 312112, Bottled Water Manufacturing;

- Manufacturing milk-based drinks—are classified in U.S. Industry 311511, Fluid Milk Manufacturing;

- Manufacturing nonalcoholic beers—are classified in Industry 312120, Breweries; and

- Manufacturing nonalcoholic wines—are classified in Industry 312130, Wineries.

312112 Bottled Water Manufacturing[US]

This U.S. industry comprises establishments primarily engaged in purifying and bottling water (including naturally carbonated).

Cross-References. Establishments primarily engaged in—

- Manufacturing artificially carbonated waters—are classified in U.S. Industry 312111, Soft Drink Manufacturing; and

- Bottling purchased purified water—are classified in Industry 422490, Other Grocery and Related Products Wholesalers.

312113 Ice Manufacturing[US]

This U.S. industry comprises establishments primarily engaged in manufacturing ice.

Cross-References.

Establishments primarily engaged in manufacturing dry ice are classified in Industry 325120, Industrial Gas Manufacturing.

US—United States industry only. CAN—United States and Canadian industries are comparable. When neither US nor CAN appears, Canadian, Mexican, and United States industries are comparable.

http://www.ntis.gov/naics

31212 Breweries
See industry description for 312120 below.

312120 Breweries

This industry comprises establishments primarily engaged in brewing beer, ale, malt liquors, and nonalcoholic beer.

Cross-References. Establishments primarily engaged in—

- Bottling purchased malt beverages—are classified in Industry 422810, Beer and Ale Wholesalers; and

- Manufacturing malt—are classified in U.S. Industry 311213, Malt Manufacturing.

31213 Wineries
See industry description for 312130 below.

312130 Wineries

This industry comprises establishments primarily engaged in one or more of the following: (1) growing grapes and manufacturing wine and brandies; (2) manufacturing wine and brandies from grapes and other fruits grown elsewhere; and (3) blending wines and brandies.

Cross-References.

Establishments primarily engaged in bottling wines made elsewhere are classified in Industry 422820, Wine and Distilled Alcoholic Beverage Wholesalers.

31214 Distilleries
See industry description for 312140 below.

312140 Distilleries

This industry comprises establishments primarily engaged in one or more of the following: (1) distilling potable liquors (except brandies); (2) distilling and blending liquors; and (3) blending and mixing liquors and other ingredients.

Cross-References. Establishments primarily engaged in—

- Manufacturing nonpotable ethyl alcohol—are classified in U.S. Industry 325193, Ethyl Alcohol Manufacturing;

US—United States industry only. CAN—United States and Canadian industries are comparable. When neither US nor CAN appears, Canadian, Mexican, and United States industries are comparable.

- Bottling liquors made elsewhere—are classified in Industry 422820, Wine and Distilled Alcoholic Beverage Wholesalers; and

- Manufacturing brandies—are classified in Industry 312130, Wineries.

3122 Tobacco Manufacturing

31221 Tobacco Stemming and Redrying
See industry description for 312210 below.

312210 Tobacco Stemming and Redrying

This industry comprises establishments primarily engaged in the stemming and redrying of tobacco.

Cross-References. Establishments primarily engaged in—

- Reconstituting tobacco—are classified in U.S. Industry 312229, Other Tobacco Product Manufacturing; and

- Selling leaf tobacco as merchant wholesalers, agents, or brokers, and that also engage in stemming tobacco—are classified in Industry 422940, Tobacco and Tobacco Product Wholesalers.

31222 Tobacco Product Manufacturing

This industry comprises establishments primarily engaged in manufacturing cigarettes, cigars, smoking and chewing tobacco, and reconstituted tobacco.

Cross-References.

Establishments primarily engaged in stemming and redrying tobacco are classified in Industry 31221, Tobacco Stemming and Redrying.

312221 Cigarette Manufacturing[US]

This U.S. industry comprises establishments primarily engaged in manufacturing cigarettes.

Cross-References.

Establishments primarily engaged in manufacturing cigars, smoking tobacco, chewing tobacco, and reconstituted tobacco are classified in U.S. Industry 312229, Other Tobacco Product Manufacturing.

312229 Other Tobacco Product Manufacturing[US]

This U.S. industry comprises establishments primarily engaged in manufacturing tobacco products (except cigarettes).

US—United States industry only. CAN—United States and Canadian industries are comparable. When neither US nor CAN appears, Canadian, Mexican, and United States industries are comparable.

Illustrative Examples:

Chewing tobacco manufacturing	Prepared pipe tobacco manufacturing
Cigar manufacturing	Snuff manufacturing
Reconstituting tobacco	

Cross-References. Establishments primarily engaged in—

- Manufacturing cigarettes—are classified in U.S. Industry 312221, Cigarette Manufacturing; and

- Stemming and redrying tobacco—are classified in Industry 312210, Tobacco Stemming and Redrying.

313 Textile Mills

Industries in the Textile Mills subsector group establishments that transform a basic fiber (natural or synthetic) into a product, such as yarn or fabric, that is further manufactured into usable items, such as apparel, sheets towels, and textile bags for individual or industrial consumption. The further manufacturing may be performed in the same establishment and classified in this subsector, or it may be performed at a separate establishment and be classified elsewhere in manufacturing.

The main processes in this subsector include preparation and spinning of fiber, knitting or weaving of fabric, and the finishing of the textile. The NAICS structure follows and captures this process flow. Major industries in this flow, such as preparation of fibers, weaving of fabric, knitting of fabric, and fiber and fabric finishing, are uniquely identified. Texturizing, throwing, twisting, and winding of yarn contains aspects of both fiber preparation and fiber finishing and is classified with preparation of fibers rather than with finishing of fiber.

NAICS separates the manufacturing of primary textiles and the manufacturing of textile products (except apparel) when the textile product is produced from purchased primary textiles, such as fabric. The manufacturing of textile products (except apparel) from purchased fabric is classified in Subsector 314, Textile Product Mills, and apparel from purchased fabric is classified in Subsector 315, Apparel Manufacturing.

Excluded from this subsector are establishments that weave or knit fabric and make garments. These establishments are included in Subsector 315, Apparel Manufacturing.

3131 Fiber, Yarn, and Thread Mills

31311 Fiber, Yarn, and Thread Mills

This industry comprises establishments primarily engaged in one or more of the following: (1) spinning yarn; (2) manufacturing thread of any fiber; (3) texturizing, throwing, twisting, and winding purchased yarn or manmade fiber filaments; and (4) producing hemp yarn and further processing into rope or bags.

Cross-References.

Establishments primarily engaged in manufacturing artificial and synthetic fibers and filaments and texturizing these filaments are classified in Industry 32522, Artificial and Synthetic Fibers and Filaments Manufacturing.

US—United States industry only. CAN—United States and Canadian industries are comparable. When neither US nor CAN appears, Canadian, Mexican, and United States industries are comparable.

http://www.ntis.gov/naics

313111 Yarn Spinning Mills[US]

This U.S. industry comprises establishments primarily engaged in spinning yarn from any fiber and/or producing hemp yarn and further processing into rope or bags.

313112 Yarn Texturizing, Throwing, and Twisting Mills[US]

This U.S. industry comprises establishments primarily engaged in texturizing, throwing, twisting, spooling, or winding purchased yarns or manmade fiber filaments.

Cross-References.

Establishments primarily engaged in manufacturing artificial and synthetic fiber and filament and texturizing these fibers and filaments are classified in Industry 32522, Artificial and Synthetic Fibers and Filament Manufacturing.

313113 Thread Mills[US]

This U.S. industry comprises establishments primarily engaged in manufacturing thread (e.g., sewing, hand-knitting, crochet) of all fibers.

3132 Fabric Mills

31321 Broadwoven Fabric Mills
See industry description for 313210 below.

313210 Broadwoven Fabric Mills

This industry comprises establishments primarily engaged in weaving broadwoven fabrics and felts (except tire fabrics and rugs). Establishments in this industry may weave only, weave and finish, or weave, finish, and further fabricate fabric products.

Cross-References. Establishments primarily engaged in—

- Weaving widths specifically constructed for cutting to narrow widths—are classified in U.S. Industry 313221, Narrow Fabric Mills;

- Weaving or tufting carpet and rugs—are classified in Industry 314110, Carpet and Rug Mills; and

- Making tire cord and fabrics—are classified in Industry 31499, All Other Textile Product Mills.

31322 Narrow Fabric Mills and Schiffli Machine Embroidery

This industry comprises establishments primarily engaged in one or more of the following: (1) weaving or braiding narrow fabrics; (2) manufacturing Schiffli machine embroideries; and (3) making fabric-covered elastic yarn and thread.

US—United States industry only. CAN—United States and Canadian industries are comparable. When neither US nor CAN appears, Canadian, Mexican, and United States industries are comparable.

313221 Narrow Fabric Mills[US]

This U.S. industry comprises establishments primarily engaged in (1) weaving or braiding narrow fabrics in their final form or initially made in wider widths that are specially constructed for narrower widths and/or (2) making fabric-covered elastic yarn and thread. Establishments in this industry may weave only; weave and finish; or weave, finish, and further fabricate fabric products.

313222 Schiffli Machine Embroidery[US]

This U.S. industry comprises establishments primarily engaged in manufacturing Schiffli machine embroideries.

31323 Nonwoven Fabric Mills
See industry description for 313230 below.

313230 Nonwoven Fabric Mills

This industry comprises establishments primarily engaged in manufacturing nonwoven fabrics and felts. Processes used include bonding and/or interlocking fibers by mechanical, chemical, thermal, or solvent means, or by combinations thereof.

31324 Knit Fabric Mills

This industry comprises establishments primarily engaged in one of the following: (1) knitting weft (i.e., circular) and warp (i.e., flat) fabric; (2) knitting and finishing weft and warp fabric; (3) manufacturing lace; or (4) manufacturing, dyeing, and finishing lace and lace goods. Establishments in this industry may knit only; knit and finish; or knit, finish, and further fabricate fabric products (except apparel).

Cross-References.

Establishments primarily engaged in knitting aparel as classified in Industry Group 3151, Apparel Knitting Mills.

313241 Weft Knit Fabric Mills[US]

This U.S. industry comprises establishments primarily engaged in knitting weft (i.e., circular) fabric or knitting and finishing weft fabric. Establishments in this industry may knit only; knit and finish; or knit, finish, and further fabricate fabric products (except apparel).

Cross-References.

Establishments primarily engaged in knitting aparel as classified in Industry Group 3151, Apparel Knitting Mills.

US—United States industry only. CAN—United States and Canadian industries are comparable. When neither US nor CAN appears, Canadian, Mexican, and United States industries are comparable.

http://www.ntis.gov/naics

313249 Other Knit Fabric and Lace Mills[US]

This U.S. industry comprises establishments primarily engaged in one of the following: (1) knitting warp (i.e., flat) fabric; (2) knitting and finishing warp fabric; (3) manufacturing lace; or (4) manufacturing, dyeing, or finishing lace and lace goods. Establishments in this industry may knit only; knit and finish; or knit, finish, and further fabricate fabric products (except apparel).

Cross-References.

Establishments primarily engaged in knitting aparel as classified in Industry Group 3151, Apparel Knitting Mills.

3133 Textile and Fabric Finishing and Fabric Coating Mills

31331 Textile and Fabric Finishing Mills

This industry comprises (1) establishments primarily engaged in finishing of textiles, fabrics, and apparel, and (2) establishments of converters who buy fabric goods in the grey, have them finished on contract, and sell at wholesale. Finishing operations include: bleaching, dyeing, printing (e.g., roller, screen, flock, plisse), stonewashing, and other mechanical finishing, such as preshrinking, shrinking, sponging, calendering, mercerizing, and napping; as well as cleaning, scouring, and the preparation of natural fibers and raw stock.

Cross-References. Establishments primarily engaged in—

- Coating or impregnating fabrics—are classified in Industry 31332, Fabric Coating Mills;

- Knitting or knitting and finishing fabric—are classified in Industry 31324, Knit Fabric Mills;

- Manufacturing and finishing apparel—are classified in Subsector 315, Apparel Manufacturing;

- Weaving and finishing fabrics—are classified in Industry Group 3132, Fabric Mills;

- Manufacturing and finishing rugs and carpets—are classified in Industry 31411, Carpet and Rug Mills; and

- Printing on apparel—are classified in Industry 32311, Printing.

313311 Broadwoven Fabric Finishing Mills[US]

This U.S. industry comprises (1) establishments primarily engaged in finishing broadwoven fabrics and (2) establishments of converters who buy broadwoven fabrics in the grey, have them finished on contract, and sell at wholesale. Finishing operations include bleaching, dyeing, printing (roller, screen, flock, plisse), and other mechanical finishing, such as preshrinking, shrinking, sponging, calendering, mercerizing and napping.

US—United States industry only. CAN—United States and Canadian industries are comparable. When neither US nor CAN appears, Canadian, Mexican, and United States industries are comparable.

Cross-References. Establishments primarily engaged in—

- Coating or impregnating fabrics—are classified in Industry 313320, Fabric Coating Mills; and

- Weaving and finishing broadwoven fabrics—are classified in Industry 313210, Broadwoven Fabric Mills.

313312 Textile and Fabric Finishing (except Broadwoven Fabric) Mills[US]

This U.S. industry comprises (1) establishments primarily engaged in dyeing, bleaching, printing, and other finishing of textiles, apparel, and fabrics (except broadwoven) and (2) establishments of converters who buy fabrics (except broadwoven) in the grey, have them finished on contract, and sell at wholesale. Finishing operations include bleaching, dyeing, printing (e.g., roller, screen, flock, plisse), stonewashing, and other mechanical finishing, such as preshrinking, shrinking, sponging, calendering, mercerizing and napping; as well as cleaning, scouring, and the preparation of natural fibers and raw stock.

Cross-References. Establishments primarily engaged in—

- Knitting and finishing fabric—are classified in Industry 31324, Knit Fabric Mills;

- Finishing broadwoven fabric—are classified in U.S. Industry 313311, Broadwoven Fabric Finishing Mills;

- Weaving and finishing narrow woven fabric—are classified in U.S. Industry 313221, Narrow Fabric Mills;

- Manufacturing and finishing apparel—are classified in Subsector 315, Apparel Manufacturing;

- Coating or impregnating fabrics—are classified in Industry 313320, Fabric Coating Mills; and

- Printing on apparel—are classified in Industry 32311, Printing.

31332 Fabric Coating Mills
See industry description for 313320 below.

313320 Fabric Coating Mills

This industry comprises establishments primarily engaged in coating, laminating, varnishing, waxing, and rubberizing textiles and apparel.

Cross-References.

Establishments primarily engaged in dyeing and finishing textiles are classified in Industry 31331, Textile and Fabric Finishing Mills.

US—United States industry only. CAN—United States and Canadian industries are comparable. When neither US nor CAN appears, Canadian, Mexican, and United States industries are comparable.

314 Textile Product Mills

Industries in the Textile Product Mills subsector group establishments that made textile products (except apparel). With a few exceptions, processes used in these industries are generally cut and sew (i.e., purchasing fabric and cutting and sewing to make nonapparel textile products, such as sheets and towels).

3141 Textile Furnishings Mills

31411 Carpet and Rug Mills
     See industry description for 314110 below.

314110 Carpet and Rug Mills

This industry comprises establishments primarily engaged in (1) manufacturing woven, tufted, and other carpets and rugs, such as art squares, floor mattings, needlepunch carpeting, and door mats and mattings, from textile materials or from twisted paper, grasses, reeds, sisal, jute, or rags and/or (2) finishing carpets and rugs.

31412 Curtain and Linen Mills

This industry comprises establishments primarily engaged in manufacturing household textile products, such as curtains, draperies, linens, bedspreads, sheets, tablecloths, towels, and shower curtains, from purchased materials.

Cross-References. Establishments primarily engaged in—

- Weaving fabrics—are classified in Industry 31321, Broadwoven Fabric Mills;

- Manufacturing lace curtains on lace machines—are classified in Industry 31324, Knit Fabric Mills;

- Manufacturing textile blanket, wardrobe, and laundry bags—are classified in Industry 31491, Textile Bag and Canvas Mills; and

- Manufacturing mops—are classified in Industry 33999, All Other Miscellaneous Manufacturing.

314121 Curtain and Drapery Mills[US]

This U.S. industry comprises establishments primarily engaged in manufacturing window curtains and draperies from purchased fabrics or sheet goods. The curtains and draperies may be made on a stock or custom basis for sale to individual retail customers.

Cross-References.

Establishments primarily engaged in manufacturing lace curtains on lace machines are classified in Industry 313249, Other Knit Fabric and Lace Mills.

US—United States industry only. CAN—United States and Canadian industries are comparable. When neither US nor CAN appears, Canadian, Mexican, and United States industries are comparable.

314129 Other Household Textile Product Mills[US]

This U.S. industry comprises establishments primarily engaged in manufacturing household textile products (except window curtains and draperies), such as bedspreads, sheets, tablecloths, towels, and shower curtains, from purchased materials.

Cross-References. Establishments primarily engaged in

- Weaving fabrics—are classified in Industry 313210, Broadwoven Fabric Mills;

- Manufacturing blanket, laundry, and wardrobe bags—are classified in U.S. Industry 314911, Textile Bag Mills;

- Manufacturing mops—are classified in U.S. Industry 339994, Broom, Brush, and Mop Manufacturing; and

- Manufacturing window curtains and draperies—are classified in U.S. Industry 314121, Curtain and Drapery Mills.

3149 Other Textile Product Mills

This industry group comprises establishments primarily engaged in making textile products, (except carpets and rugs, curtains and draperies, and other household textile products) from purchased materials.

31491 Textile Bag and Canvas Mills

This industry comprises establishments primarily engaged in manufacturing textile bags, awnings, tents, and related products from purchased textile fabrics.

Cross-References. Establishments primarily engaged in—

- Manufacturing plastic bags—are classified in Industry 32611, Unsupported Plastics Film, Sheet, and Bag Manufacturing;

- Manufacturing canvas blinds and shades—are classified in Industry 33792, Blind and Shade Manufacturing;

- Manufacturing luggage—are classified in Industry 31699, Other Leather and Allied Product Manufacturing; and

- Manufacturing women's handbags and purses of leather or other material (except precious metal)—are classified in Industry 31699, Other Leather and Allied Product Manufacturing.

314911 Textile Bag Mills[US]

This U.S. industry comprises establishments primarily engaged in manufacturing bags from purchased textile fabrics or yarns.

US—United States industry only. CAN—United States and Canadian industries are comparable. When neither US nor CAN appears, Canadian, Mexican, and United States industries are comparable.

Illustrative Examples:

Canvas bags manufacturing
Laundry bags made from purchased woven or
knitted materials
Seed bags made from purchased woven or
knitted materials

Textile bags made from purchased woven or
knitted materials

Cross-References. Establishments primarily engaged in—

- Manufacturing plastics bags—are classified in U.S. Industry 326111, Unsupported Plastics Bag Manufacturing;

- Manufacturing luggage—are classified in U.S. Industry 316991, Luggage Manufacturing; and

- Manufacturing women's handbags and purses of leather or other material, except precious metal—are classified in U.S. Industry 316992, Women's Handbag and Purse Manufacturing.

314912 Canvas and Related Product Mills[US]

This U.S. industry comprises establishments primarily engaged in manufacturing canvas and canvas-like products, such as awnings, sails, tarpaulins, and tents, from purchased fabrics.

Cross-References. Establishments primarily engaged in—

- Manufacturing canvas blinds and shades—are classified in Industry 337920, Blind and Shade Manufacturing; and

- Manufacturing canvas bags—are classified in U.S. Industry 314911, Textile Bag Mills.

31499 All Other Textile Product Mills

This industry comprises establishments primarily engaged in manufacturing nonapparel textile products (except carpet, rugs, curtains, linens, bags, and canvas products) from purchased materials.

Illustrative Examples:

Batts and batting (except nonwoven fabrics)
manufacturing
Carpet cutting and binding
Diapers (except disposable) made from
purchased fabric
Dust cloths made from purchased fabric
Embroidering on textile products (except apparel)
for the trade

Fishing nets made from purchased materials
Sleeping bags manufacturing
Textile fire hoses made from purchased
materials
Weatherstripping made from purchased
textiles

Cross-References. Establishments primarily engaged in—

- Manufacturing yarns and thread—are classified in Industry 31311, Fiber, Yarn, and Thread Mills;

US—United States industry only. CAN—United States and Canadian industries are comparable.
When neither US nor CAN appears, Canadian, Mexican, and United States industries are comparable.

- Manufacturing carpets and rugs—are classified in Industry 31411, Carpet and Rug Mills;

- Manufacturing apparel—are classified in Subsector 315, Apparel Manufacturing;

- Manufacturing curtains and linens—are classified in Industry 31412, Curtain and Linen Mills; and

- Manufacturing textile bags and canvas products—are classified in Industry 31491, Textile Bag and Canvas Mills.

314991 Rope, Cordage, and Twine Mills[US]

This U.S. industry comprises establishments primarily engaged in manufacturing rope, cable, cordage, twine, and related products from all materials (e.g., abaca, sisal, henequen, hemp, cotton, paper, jute, flax, manmade fibers including glass).

Cross-References.

Establishments primarily engaged in manufacturing yarns and filaments are classified in U.S. Industry 313111, Yarn Spinning Mills.

314992 Tire Cord and Tire Fabric Mills[US]

This U.S. industry comprises establishments primarily engaged in manufacturing cord and fabric of polyester, rayon, cotton, glass, steel, or other materials for use in reinforcing rubber tires, industrial belting, and similar uses.

314999 All Other Miscellaneous Textile Product Mills[US]

This U.S. industry comprises establishments primarily engaged in manufacturing textile products (except carpets and rugs; curtains and linens; textile bags and canvas products; rope, cordage, and twine; and tire cords and tire fabrics) from purchased materials.

Illustrative Examples:

Batts and batting (except nonwoven fabrics) manufacturing
Carpet cutting and binding
Diapers (except disposable) made from purchased fabric
Dust cloths made from purchased fabric

Embroidering on textile products (except apparel) for the trade
Sleeping bags manufacturing
Textile fire hose made from purchased materials

Cross-References. Establishments primarily engaged in—

- Manufacturing yarns and thread—are classified in Industry 31311, Fiber, Yarn, and Thread Mills;

- Manufacturing carpets and rugs—are classified in Industry 314110, Carpet and Rug Mills;

- Manufacturing curtains and linens—are classified in Industry 31412, Curtain and Linen Mills;

- Manufacturing textile bags and canvas products—are classified in Industry 31491, Textile Bag and Canvas Mills;

- Manufacturing rope, cordage, and twine—are classified in U.S. Industry 314991, Rope, Cordage, and Twine Mills; and

- Manufacturing tire cords and tire fabrics—are classified in U.S. Industry 314992, Tire Cord and Tire Fabric Mills.

315 Apparel Manufacturing

Industries in the Apparel Manufacturing subsector group establishments with two distinct manufacturing processes: (1) cut and sew (i.e., purchasing fabric and cutting and sewing to make a garment) and (2) the manufacture of garments in establishments that first knit fabric and then cut and sew the fabric into a garment. The Apparel Manufacturing subsector includes a diverse range of establishments manufacturing full lines of ready-to-wear apparel and custom apparel: apparel contractors, performing cutting or sewing operations on materials owned by others; jobbers performing entrepreneurial functions involved in apparel manufacture; and tailors, manufacturing custom garments for individual clients are all included. Knitting, when done alone, is classified in the Textile Mills subsector, but when knitting is combined with the production of complete garments, the activity is classified in Apparel Manufacturing.

3151 Apparel Knitting Mills

This industry group comprises establishments primarily engaged in knitting apparel or knitting fabric and then manufacturing apparel. This industry group includes jobbers performing entrepreneurial functions involved in knitting apparel and accessories. Knitting fabric, without manufacturing apparel, is classified in Subsector 313, Textile Mills.

31511 Hosiery and Sock Mills

This industry comprises establishments primarily engaged in knitting or knitting and finishing hosiery and socks.

Cross-References. Establishments primarily engaged in—

- Manufacturing orthopedic hosiery—are classified in Industry 33911, Medical Equipment and Supplies Manufacturing;

- Manufacturing slipper socks from purchased socks—are classified in Industry 31621, Footwear Manufacturing; and

- Finishing apparel products only—are classified in Industry 31331, Textile and Fabric Finishing Mills.

US—United States industry only. CAN—United States and Canadian industries are comparable. When neither US nor CAN appears, Canadian, Mexican, and United States industries are comparable.

315111 Sheer Hosiery Mills[US]

This U.S. industry comprises establishments primarily engaged in knitting or knitting and finishing women's, misses', and girls' full-length and knee-length sheer hosiery (except socks).

Cross-References. Establishments primarily engaged in—

- Knitting or knitting and finishing socks—are classified in U.S. Industry 315119, Other Hosiery and Sock Mills;

- Fnishing apparel products only—are classified in U.S. Industry 313312, Textile and Fabric Finishing (except Broadwoven Fabric) Mills; and

- Manufacturing orthopedic hosiery—are classified in U.S. Industry 339113, Surgical Appliance and Supplies Manufacturing.

315119 Other Hosiery and Sock Mills[US]

This U.S. industry comprises establishments primarily engaged in knitting or knitting and finishing hosiery (except women's, misses', and girls' sheer hosiery).

Cross-References. Establishments primarily engaged in—

- Knitting or knitting and finishing women's, misses', and girls' full-length and knee-length sheer hosiery—are classified in U.S. Industry 315111, Sheer Hosiery Mills;

- Manufacturing orthopedic hosiery—are classified in U.S. Industry 339113, Surgical Appliance and Supplies Manufacturing;

- Fnishing apparel products only—are classified in U.S. Industry 313312, Textile and Fabric Finishing (except Broadwoven Fabric) Mills; and

- Manufacturing slipper socks from purchased socks—are classified in U.S. Industry 316212, House Slipper Manufacturing.

31519 Other Apparel Knitting Mills

This industry comprises establishments primarily engaged in one of the following: (1) knitting underwear, outerwear, and/or nightwear; (2) knitting fabric and manufacturing underwear, outerwear, and/or nightwear; or (3) knitting, manufacturing, and finishing knit underwear, outerwear, and/or nightwear.

Cross-References. Establishments primarily engaged in—

- Manufacturing outerwear, underwear, and nightwear from purchased fabric—are classified in Industry Group 3152, Cut and Sew Apparel Manufacturing; and

- Finishing apparel products only—are classified in Industry 31331, Textile and Fabric Finishing Mills.

US—United States industry only. CAN—United States and Canadian industries are comparable. When neither US nor CAN appears, Canadian, Mexican, and United States industries are comparable.

315191 Outerwear Knitting Mills[US]

This U.S. industry comprises establishments primarily engaged in one or more of the following: (1) knitting outerwear; (2) knitting fabric and manufacturing outerwear; and (3) knitting, manufacturing, and finishing knit outerwear. Examples of products made in knit outerwear mills are shirts, shorts, sweat suits, sweaters, gloves, and pants.

Cross-References. Establishments primarily engaged in—

- Manufacturing outerwear from purchased fabric—are classified in Industry Group 3152, Cut and Sew Apparel Manufacturing;

- Finishing apparel products only—are classified in U.S. Industry 313312, Textile and Fabric Finishing (except Broadwoven Fabric) Mills; and

- Knitting underwear and nightwear, knitting fabric and manufacturing underwear and nightwear, or knitting, manufacturing, and finishing knit underwear and nightwear—are classified in U.S. Industry 315192, Underwear and Nightwear Knitting Mills.

315192 Underwear and Nightwear Knitting Mills[US]

This U.S. industry comprises establishments primarily engaged in one of the following: (1) knitting underwear and nightwear; (2) knitting fabric and manufacturing underwear and nightwear; or (3) knitting, manufacturing, and finishing knit underwear and nightwear. Examples of products produced in underwear and nightwear knitting mills are briefs, underwear T-shirts, pajamas, nightshirts, foundation garments, and panties.

Cross-References. Establishments primarily engaged in—

- Manufacturing underwear and nightwear from purchased fabric—are classified in Industry Group 3152, Cut and Sew Apparel Manufacturing; and

- Finishing apparel products only—are classified in U.S. Industry 313312, Textile and Fabric Finishing (except Broadwoven Fabric) Mills.

3152 Cut and Sew Apparel Manufacturing

This industry group comprises establishments primarily engaged in manufacturing cut and sew apparel from woven fabric or purchased knit fabric. Included in this industry group is a diverse range of establishments manufacturing full lines of ready-to-wear apparel and custom apparel: apparel contractors, performing cutting or sewing operations on materials owned by others; jobbers performing entrepreneurial functions involved in apparel manufacture; and tailors, manufacturing custom garments for individual clients. Establishments weaving or knitting fabric, without manufacturing apparel, are classified in Subsector 313, Textile Mills.

31521 Cut and Sew Apparel Contractors[CAN]

This industry comprises establishments commonly referred to as contractors primarily engaged in (1) cutting materials owned by others for apparel and accessories and/or (2) sewing materials owned by others for apparel and accessories.

US—United States industry only. CAN—United States and Canadian industries are comparable. When neither US nor CAN appears, Canadian, Mexican, and United States industries are comparable.

Cross-References. Establishments primarily engaged in—

- Manufacturing men's and boys' apparel from purchased fabric—are classified in Industry 31522, Men's and Boys' Cut and Sew Apparel Manufacturing;

- Manufacturing women's and girls' apparel from purchased fabric—are classified in Industry 31523, Women's and Girls' Cut and Sew Apparel Manufacturing;

- Manufacturing infants' apparel and all other cut and sew apparel from purchased fabric—are classified in Industry 31529, Other Cut and Sew Apparel Manufacturing; and

- Manufacturing apparel accessories from purchased fabric—are classified in Industry 31599, Apparel Accessories and Other Apparel Manufacturing.

315211 Men's and Boys' Cut and Sew Apparel Contractors[US]

This U.S. industry comprises establishments commonly referred to as contractors primarily engaged in (1) cutting materials owned by others for men's and boys' apparel and/or (2) sewing materials owned by others for men's and boys' apparel.

Cross-References. Establishments primarily engaged in—

- Manufacturing men's and boys' apparel from purchased fabric—are classified in Industry 31522, Men's and Boys' Cut and Sew Apparel Manufacturing;

- Manufacturing infants' apparel from purchased fabric—are classified in U.S. Industry 315291, Infants' Cut and Sew Apparel Manufacturing; and

- Manufacturing men's and boys' apparel accessories from purchased fabric—are classified in Industry 31599, Apparel Accessories and Other Apparel Manufacturing.

315212 Women's, Girls', and Infants' Cut and Sew Apparel Contractors[US]

This U.S. industry comprises establishments commonly referred to as contractors primarily engaged in (1) cutting materials owned by others for women's, girls', and infants' apparel and accessories and/or (2) sewing materials owned by others for women's, girls', and infants' apparel and accessories.

Cross-References. Establishments primarily engaged in—

- Manufacturing women's and girls' apparel from purchased fabric—are classified in Industry 31523, Women's and Girls' Cut and Sew Apparel Manufacturing;

- Manufacturing infants' apparel from purchased fabric—are classified in U.S. Industry 315291, Infants' Cut and Sew Apparel Manufacturing; and

- Manufacturing women's, girls', and infants' apparel accessories from purchased fabric— are classified in Industry 31599, Apparel Accessories and Other Apparel Manufacturing.

US—United States industry only. CAN—United States and Canadian industries are comparable. When neither US nor CAN appears, Canadian, Mexican, and United States industries are comparable.

31522 Men's and Boys' Cut and Sew Apparel Manufacturing[CAN]

This industry comprises establishments primarily engaged in manufacturing men's and boys' cut and sew apparel from purchased fabric. Men's and boys' clothing jobbers, who perform entrepreneurial functions involved in apparel manufacture, including buying raw materials, designing and preparing samples, arranging for apparel to be made from their materials, and marketing finished apparel, are included.

Cross-References. Establishments primarily engaged in—

- Cutting and/or sewing materials owned by others for men's and boys' apparel—are classified in Industry 31521, Cut and Sew Apparel Contractors;

- Knitting men's and boys' apparel or knitting fabric and manufacturing men's and boys' apparel—are classified in Industry Group 3151, Apparel Knitting Mills; and

- Manufacturing fur or leather apparel and team athletic uniforms—are classified in Industry 31529, Other Cut and Sew Apparel Manufacturing.

315221 Men's and Boys' Cut and Sew Underwear and Nightwear Manufacturing[CAN]

This U.S. industry comprises establishments primarily engaged in manufacturing men's and boys' underwear and nightwear from purchased fabric. Men's and boys' underwear and nightwear jobbers, who perform entrepreneurial functions involved in apparel manufacture, including buying raw materials, designing and preparing samples, arranging for apparel to be made from their materials, and marketing finished apparel, are included. Examples of products made by these establishments are briefs, bathrobes, underwear T-shirts and shorts, nightshirts, and pajamas.

Cross-References. Establishments primarily engaged in—

- Knitting men's and boys' underwear and nightwear and/or knitting and manufacturing men's and boys' underwear and nightwear—are classified in U.S. Industry 315192, Underwear and Nightwear Knitting Mills; and

- Cutting and/or sewing materials owned by others for men's and boys' underwear and nightwear—are classified in U.S. Industry 315211, Men's and Boys' Cut and Sew Apparel Contractors.

315222 Men's and Boys' Cut and Sew Suit, Coat, and Overcoat Manufacturing[CAN]

This U.S. industry comprises establishments primarily engaged in manufacturing men's and boys' suits, overcoats, sport coats, tuxedoes, dress uniforms, and other tailored apparel (except fur and leather) from purchased fabric. Men's and boys' suit, coat, and overcoat jobbers, who perform entrepreneurial functions involved in apparel manufacture, including buying raw materials, designing and preparing samples, arranging for apparel to be made from their materials, and marketing finished apparel, are included.

US—United States industry only. CAN—United States and Canadian industries are comparable. When neither US nor CAN appears, Canadian, Mexican, and United States industries are comparable.

Cross-References. Establishments primarily engaged in—

- Manufacturing men's and boys' nontailored coats and jackets such as down coats and windbreakers made from purchased fabric—are classified in U.S. Industry 315228, Men's and Boys' Cut and Sew Other Outerwear Manufacturing;

- Manufacturing fur and leather apparel—are classified in U.S. Industry 315292, Fur and Leather Apparel Manufacturing;

- Manufacturing men's and boys' washable service apparel from purchased fabric—are classified in U.S. Industry 315225, Men's and Boys' Cut and Sew Work Clothing Manufacturing;

- Manufacturing men's and boys' team athletic uniforms from purchased fabric—are classified in U.S. Industry 315299, All Other Cut and Sew Apparel Manufacturing; and

- Cutting and/or sewing materials owned by others for men's and boys' suits, coats, and overcoats—are classified in U.S. Industry 315211, Men's and Boys' Cut and Sew Apparel Contractors.

315223 Men's and Boys' Cut and Sew Shirt (except Work Shirt) Manufacturing[US]

This U.S. industry comprises establishments primarily engaged in manufacturing men's and boys' outerwear shirts from purchased fabric. Men's and boys' shirt (except work shirt) jobbers, who perform entrepreneurial functions involved in apparel manufacture, including buying raw materials, designing and preparing samples, arranging for apparel to be made from their materials, and marketing finished apparel, are included. Unisex outerwear shirts, such as T-shirts and sweatshirts that are sized without specific reference to gender (i.e., adult S, M, L, XL) are included in this industry.

Cross-References. Establishments primarily engaged in—

- Manufacturing men's and boys' work shirts from purchased fabric—are classified in U.S. Industry 315225, Men's and Boys' Cut and Sew Work Clothing Manufacturing;

- Manufacturing men's and boys' underwear T-shirts and underwear tank tops from purchased fabric—are classified in U.S. Industry 315221, Men's and Boys' Cut and Sew Underwear and Nightwear Manufacturing;

- Cutting and/or sewing materials owned by others for men's and boys' shirts—are classified in U.S. Industry 315211, Men's and Boys' Cut and Sew Apparel Contractors; and

- Knitting men's and boys' outerwear shirts or knitting fabric and manufacturing men's and boys' outerwear shirts—are classified in U.S. Industry 315191, Outerwear Knitting Mills.

315224 Men's and Boys' Cut and Sew Trouser, Slack, and Jean Manufacturing[US]

This U.S. industry comprises establishments primarily engaged in manufacturing men's and boys' jeans, dungarees, and other separate trousers and slacks (except work pants) from purchased

---

US—United States industry only. CAN—United States and Canadian industries are comparable. When neither US nor CAN appears, Canadian, Mexican, and United States industries are comparable.

fabric. Men's and boys' trouser, slack, and jean jobbers, who perform entrepreneurial functions involved in apparel manufacture, including buying raw materials, designing and preparing samples, arranging for apparel to be made from their materials, and marketing finished apparel, are included.

Cross-References. Establishments primarily engaged in—

- Manufacturing men's and boys' work pants from purchased fabric—are classified in U.S. Industry 315225, Men's and Boys' Cut and Sew Work Clothing Manufacturing;

- Manufacturing fur and leather apparel—are classified in U.S. Industry 315292, Fur and Leather Apparel Manufacturing;

- Manufacturing men's and boys' sweatpants and shorts from purchased fabric—are classified in U.S. Industry 315228, Men's and Boys' Cut and Sew Other Outerwear Manufacturing; and

- Cutting and/or sewing materials owned by others for men's and boys' separate trousers, slacks, and jeans—are classified in U.S. Industry 315211, Men's and Boys' Cut and Sew Apparel Contractors.

315225 Men's and Boys' Cut and Sew Work Clothing Manufacturing[US]

This U.S. industry comprises establishments primarily engaged in manufacturing men's and boys' work shirts, work pants (excluding jeans and dungarees), other work clothing, and washable service apparel from purchased fabric. Men's and boys' work clothing jobbers, who perform entrepreneurial functions involved in apparel manufacture, including buying raw materials, designing and preparing samples, arranging for apparel to be made from their materials, and marketing finished apparel, are included. Examples of products made by these establishments are washable service apparel, laboratory coats, work shirts, work pants (except jeans and dungarees), and hospital apparel.

Cross-References. Establishments primarily engaged in—

- Manufacturing men's and boys' separate trousers, slacks, and pants, including jeans and dungarees from purchased fabric—are classified in U.S. Industry 315224, Men's and Boys' Cut and Sew Trouser, Slack, and Jean Manufacturing; and

- Cutting and/or sewing materials owned by others for men's and boys' work clothing—are classified in U.S. Industry 315211, Men's and Boys' Cut and Sew Apparel Contractors.

315228 Men's and Boys' Cut and Sew Other Outerwear Manufacturing[US]

This U.S. industry comprises establishments primarily engaged in manufacturing men's and boys' cut and sew outerwear from purchased fabric (except underwear, nightwear, shirts, suits, overcoats and tailored coats, separate trousers and slacks, and work clothing). Men's and boys' other outerwear jobbers, who perform entrepreneurial functions involved in apparel manufacture, including buying raw materials, designing and preparing samples, arranging for apparel to be made from their materials, and marketing finished apparel, are included. Unisex sweatpants and similar garments that are sized without specific reference to gender (i.e., adult S, M, L, XL) are also included in this industry. Examples of products made by these establishments are athletic clothing (except athletic uniforms), bathing suits, down coats, outerwear shorts, windbreakers and jackets, and jogging suits.

Cross-References. Establishments primarily engaged in—

- Manufacturing men's and boys' athletic uniforms from purchased fabric—are classified in U.S. Industry 315299, All Other Cut and Sew Apparel Manufacturing;

- Manufacturing leather and fur apparel—are classified in U.S. Industry 315292, Fur and Leather Apparel Manufacturing;

- Knitting men's and boys' apparel or knitting fabric and manufacturing men's and boys' apparel—are classified in Industry Group 3151, Apparel Knitting Mills;

- Cutting and/or sewing materials owned by others for men's and boys' apparel—are classified in U.S. Industry 315211, Men's and Boys' Cut and Sew Apparel Contractors;

- Manufacturing men's and boys' underwear and nightwear from purchased fabric—are classified in U.S. Industry 315221, Men's and Boys' Cut and Sew Underwear and Nightwear Manufacturing;

- Manufacturing men's and boys' tailored suits, coats, and overcoats from purchased fabric— are classified in U.S. Industry 315222, Men's and Boys' Cut and Sew Suit, Coat and Overcoat Manufacturing;

- Manufacturing men's and boys' outerwear shirts (except work shirts) from purchased fabric—are classified in U.S. Industry 315223, Men's and Boys' Cut and Sew Shirt (except Work Shirt) Manufacturing;

- Manufacturing men's and boys' separate pants, trousers, and slacks from purchased fabric— are classified in U.S. Industry 315224, Men's and Boys' Cut and Sew Trouser, Slack, and Jean Manufacturing; and

- Manufacturing men's and boys' work clothing from purchased fabric—are classified in U.S. Industry 315225, Men's and Boys' Cut and Sew Work Clothing Manufacturing.

31523 Women's and Girls' Cut and Sew Apparel Manufacturing[CAN]

This industry comprises establishments primarily engaged in manufacturing women's and girls' apparel from purchased fabric. Women's and girls' clothing jobbers, who perform entrepreneurial functions involved in apparel manufacture, including buying raw materials, designing and preparing samples, arranging for apparel to be made from their materials, and marketing finished apparel, are included.

Cross-References. Establishments primarily engaged in—

- Knitting women's and girls' apparel or knitting fabric and manufacturing women's and girls' apparel—are classified in Industry Group 3151, Apparel Knitting Mills;

US—United States industry only. CAN—United States and Canadian industries are comparable. When neither US nor CAN appears, Canadian, Mexican, and United States industries are comparable.

- Manufacturing unisex outerwear garments, such as T-shirts, sweatshirts, and sweatpants that are sized without reference to specific gender (i.e., adult S, M, L, XL),—are classified in Industry 31522, Men's and Boys' Cut and Sew Apparel Manufacturing;

- Cutting and/or sewing materials owned by others for women's and girls' apparel—are classified in Industry 31521, Cut and Sew Apparel Contractors; and

- Manufacturing fur or leather apparel and team athletic uniforms—are classified in Industry 31529, Other Cut and Sew Apparel Manufacturing.

315231 Women's and Girls' Cut and Sew Lingerie, Loungewear, and Nightwear Manufacturing[CAN]

This U.S. industry comprises establishments primarily engaged in manufacturing women's and girls' bras, girdles, and other underwear; lingerie; loungewear; and nightwear from purchased fabric. Women's and girls' lingerie, loungewear, and nightwear jobbers, who perform entrepreneurial functions involved in apparel manufacture, including buying raw materials, designing and preparing samples, arranging for apparel to be made from their materials, and marketing finished apparel, are included. Examples of products made by these establishments are bathrobes, foundation garments, nightgowns, pajamas, panties, and slips.

Cross-References. Establishments primarily engaged in—

- Knitting women's and girls' underwear, nightwear, and lingerie or knitting fabric and manufacturing women's and girls' underwear, nightwear, and lingerie—are classified in U.S. Industry 315192, Underwear and Nightwear Knitting Mills; and

- Cutting and/or sewing materials owned by others for women's and girls' underwear, nightwear, and lingerie—are classified in U.S. Industry 315212, Women's, Girls', and Infants' Cut and Sew Apparel Contractors.

315232 Women's and Girls' Cut and Sew Blouse and Shirt Manufacturing[CAN]

This U.S. industry comprises establishments primarily engaged in manufacturing women's and girls' blouses and shirts from purchased fabric. Women's and girls' blouse and shirt jobbers, who perform entrepreneurial functions involved in apparel manufacture, including buying raw materials, designing and preparing samples, arranging for apparel to be made from their materials, and marketing finished apparel, are included.

Cross-References. Establishments primarily engaged in—

- Knitting women's and girls' blouses, shirts, and tops or knitting fabric and manufacturing women's and girls' blouses, shirts, and tops—are classified in U.S. Industry 315191, Outerwear Knitting Mills;

- Manufacturing unisex outerwear shirts, such as T-shirts and sweatshirts that are sized without specific reference to gender (i.e., adult S, M, L, XL),—are classified in U.S. Industry 315223, Men's and Boys' Cut and Sew Shirt (except Work Shirt) Manufacturing; and

- Cutting and/or sewing materials owned by others for women's and girls' shirts and blouses—are classified in U.S. Industry 315212, Women's, Girls', and Infants' Cut and Sew Apparel Contractors.

315233 Women's and Girls' Cut and Sew Dress Manufacturing[CAN]

This U.S. industry comprises establishments primarily engaged in manufacturing women's and girls' dresses from purchased fabric. Women's and girls' dress jobbers, who perform entrepreneurial functions involved in apparel manufacture, including buying raw materials, designing and preparing samples, arranging for apparel to be made from their materials, and marketing finished apparel, are included.

Cross-References. Establishments primarily engaged in—

- Knitting women's and girls' dresses or knitting fabric and manufacturing women's and girls' dresses—are classified in U.S. Industry 315191, Outerwear Knitting Mills; and

- Cutting and/or sewing materials owned by others for women's and girls' dresses—are classified in U.S. Industry 315212, Women's, Girls', and Infants' Cut and Sew Apparel Contractors.

315234 Women's and Girls' Cut and Sew Suit, Coat, Tailored Jacket, and Skirt Manufacturing[CAN]

This U.S. industry comprises establishments primarily engaged in manufacturing women's and girls' suits, pantsuits, skirts, tailored jackets, vests, raincoats, and other tailored coats, (except fur and leather coats) from purchased fabric. Women's and girls' suit, coat, tailored jacket, and skirt jobbers, who perform entrepreneurial functions involved in apparel manufacture, including buying raw materials, designing and preparing samples, arranging for apparel to be made from their materials, and marketing finished apparel, are included.

Cross-References. Establishments primarily engaged in—

- Manufacturing women's and girls' team athletic uniforms from purchased fabric—are classified in U.S. Industry 315299, All Other Cut and Sew Apparel Manufacturing;

- Manufacturing women's and girls' separate slacks, jeans, pants, and nontailored coats and jackets, such as down coats and windbreakers from purchased fabric,—are classified in U.S. Industry 315239, Women's and Girls' Cut and Sew Other Outerwear Manufacturing;

- Manufacturing fur and leather apparel—are classified in U.S. Industry 315292, Fur and Leather Apparel Manufacturing;

- Knitting women's and girls' tailored skirts, suits, vests, and coats or knitting fabric and manufacturing women's and girls' tailored skirts, suits, vests, and coats—are classified in U.S. Industry 315191, Outerwear Knitting Mills; and

- Cutting and/or sewing materials owned by others for women's and girls' suits, coats, tailored jackets, and skirts—are classified in U.S. Industry 315212, Women's, Girls', and Infants' Cut and Sew Apparel Contractors.

US—United States industry only. CAN—United States and Canadian industries are comparable. When neither US nor CAN appears, Canadian, Mexican, and United States industries are comparable.

315239 Women's and Girls' Cut and Sew Other Outerwear Manufacturing[CAN]

This U.S. industry comprises establishments primarily engaged in manufacturing women's and girls' cut and sew apparel from purchased fabric (except underwear, lingerie, nightwear, blouses, shirts, dresses, suits, tailored coats, tailored jackets, and skirts). Women's and girls' other outerwear clothing jobbers, who perform entrepreneurial functions involved in apparel manufacture, including buying raw materials, designing and preparing samples, arranging for apparel to be made from their materials, and marketing finished apparel, are included. Examples of products made by these establishments are bathing suits, down coats, sweaters, jogging suits, outerwear pants and shorts, and windbreakers.

Cross-References. Establishments primarily engaged in—

- Manufacturing women's and girls' team athletic uniforms from purchased fabric—are classified in U.S. Industry 315299, All Other Cut and Sew Apparel Manufacturing;

- Knitting women's and girls' apparel or knitting fabric and manufacturing women's and girls' apparel—are classified in U.S. Industry 315191, Outerwear Knitting Mills;

- Manufacturing women's and girls' fur and leather apparel—are classified in U.S. Industry 315292, Fur and Leather Apparel Manufacturing;

- Cutting and/or sewing materials owned by others for women's and girls' apparel—are classified in U.S. Industry 315212, Women's, Girls', and Infants' Cut and Sew Apparel Contractors;

- Manufacturing women's and girls' lingerie, loungewear, and nightwear from purchased fabric—are classified in U.S. Industry 315231, Women's and Girls' Cut and Sew Lingerie, Loungewear, and Nightwear Manufacturing;

- Manufacturing women's and girls' blouses and outerwear shirts from purchased fabric—are classified in U.S. Industry 315232, Women's and Girls' Cut and Sew Blouse and Shirt Manufacturing;

- Manufacturing unisex sweatpants and similar outerwear garments that are sized without specific reference to gender (i.e., adult S, M, L, XL)—are classified in U.S. Industry 315228, Men's and Boys' Cut and Sew Other Outerwear Manufacturing;

- Manufacturing women's and girls' dresses from purchased fabric—are classified in U.S. Industry 315233, Women's and Girls' Cut and Sew Dress Manufacturing; and

- Manufacturing women's and girls' suits, skirts, and tailored coats and jackets from purchased fabric—are classified in U.S. Industry 315234, Women's and Girls' Cut and Sew Suit, Coat, Tailored Jacket, and Skirt Manufacturing.

31529 Other Cut and Sew Apparel Manufacturing[CAN]

This industry comprises establishments primarily engaged in manufacturing cut and sew apparel from purchased fabric (except men's, boys', women's, and girls' apparel). This industry includes

US—United States industry only. CAN—United States and Canadian industries are comparable. When neither US nor CAN appears, Canadian, Mexican, and United States industries are comparable.

establishments manufacturing apparel, such as fur apparel, leather apparel, infants' apparel, costumes, and clerical vestments.

Cross-References. Establishments primarily engaged in—

- Manufacturing men's and boys' apparel from purchased fabric—are classified in Industry 31522, Men's and Boys' Cut and Sew Apparel Manufacturing;

- Manufacturing women's and girls' apparel from purchased fabric—are classified in Industry 31523, Women's and Girls' Cut and Sew Apparel Manufacturing;

- Knitting apparel or knitting fabric and manufacturing apparel—are classified in Industry Group 3151, Apparel Knitting Mills;

- Cutting and/or sewing materials owned by others for apparel—are classified in Industry 31521, Cut and Sew Apparel Contractors;

- Manufacturing fur and leather mittens and gloves—are classified in Industry 31599, Apparel Accessories and Other Apparel Manufacturing; and

- Dyeing and dressing furs—are classified in Industry 31611, Leather and Hide Tanning and Finishing.

315291 Infants' Cut and Sew Apparel Manufacturing[CAN]

This U.S. industry comprises establishments primarily engaged in manufacturing infants' dresses, blouses, shirts, and all other infants' wear from purchased fabric. Infants' clothing jobbers, who perform entrepreneurial functions involved in apparel manufacture, including buying raw materials, designing and preparing samples, arranging for apparel to be made from their materials, and marketing finished apparel, are included. For the purposes of classification, the term "infants' apparel" includes apparel for young children of an age not exceeding 24 months.

Cross-References. Establishments primarily engaged in—

- Knitting infants' apparel or knitting fabric and manufacturing infants' apparel—are classified in U.S. Industry 315191, Outerwear Knitting Mills; and

- Cutting and/or sewing materials owned by others for infants' apparel—are classified in U.S. Industry 315212, Women's, Girls', and Infants' Cut and Sew Apparel Contractors.

315292 Fur and Leather Apparel Manufacturing[CAN]

This U.S. industry comprises establishments primarily engaged in manufacturing cut and sew fur and leather apparel, and sheep-lined clothing. Fur and leather apparel jobbers, who perform entrepreneurial functions involved in apparel manufacture, including buying raw materials, designing and preparing samples, arranging for apparel to be made from their materials, and marketing finished apparel, are included.

US—United States industry only. CAN—United States and Canadian industries are comparable. When neither US nor CAN appears, Canadian, Mexican, and United States industries are comparable.

http://www.ntis.gov/naics

Cross-References. Establishments primarily engaged in—

- Cutting and/or sewing materials owned by others for apparel—are classified in Industry 31521, Cut and Sew Apparel Contractors;

- Dyeing and dressing furs—are classified in Industry 316110, Leather and Hide Tanning and Finishing; and

- Manufacturing fur and leather mittens and gloves—are classified in U.S. Industry 315992, Glove and Mitten Manufacturing.

315299 All Other Cut and Sew Apparel Manufacturing[CAN]

This U.S. industry comprises establishments primarily engaged in manufacturing cut and sew apparel form purchased fabric (except cut and sew apparel contractors; men's and boys' cut and sew underwear, nightwear, suits, coats, shirts, trousers, work clothing, and other outerwear; women's and girls' lingerie, blouses, shirts, dresses, suits, coats, and other outerwear; infants' apparel; and fur and leather apparel). Clothing jobbers for these products, who perform entrepreneurial functions involved in apparel manufacture, including buying raw materials, designing and preparing samples, arranging for apparel to be made from their materials, and marketing finished apparel, are included. Examples of products made by these establishments are team athletic uniforms, band uniforms, academic caps and gowns, clerical vestments, and costumes.

Cross-References. Establishments primarily engaged in—

- Cutting and/or sewing materials owned by others for apparel—are classified in Industry 31521, Cut and Sew Apparel Contractors;

- Knitting apparel or knitting fabric and manufacturing apparel—are classified in Industry Group 3151, Apparel Knitting Mills;

- Manufacturing men's and boys' underwear and nightwear from purchased fabric—are classified in U.S. Industry 315221, Men's and Boys' Cut and Sew Underwear and Nightwear Manufacturing;

- Manufacturing men's and boys' suits, coats, and overcoats from purchased fabric—are classified in U.S. Industry 315222, Men's and Boys' Cut and Sew Suit, Coat and Overcoat Manufacturing;

- Manufacturing men's and boys' shirts (except work shirts) from purchased fabric—are classified in U.S. Industry 315223, Men's and Boys' Cut and Sew Shirt (except Work Shirt) Manufacturing;

- Manufacturing men's and boys' pants, slacks, trousers, and jeans from purchased fabric—are classified in U.S. Industry 315224, Men's and Boys' Cut and Sew Trouser, Slack, and Jean Manufacturing;

- Manufacturing men's and boys' work clothing from purchased fabric—are classified in U.S. Industry 315225, Men's and Boys' Cut and Sew Work Clothing Manufacturing;

US—United States industry only. CAN—United States and Canadian industries are comparable. When neither US nor CAN appears, Canadian, Mexican, and United States industries are comparable.

- Manufacturing other men's and boys' outerwear from purchased fabric—are classified in U.S. Industry 315228, Men's and Boys' Cut and Sew Other Outerwear Manufacturing;

- Manufacturing women's and girls' lingerie and nightwear from purchased fabric—are classified in U.S. Industry 315231, Women's and Girls' Cut and Sew Lingerie, Loungewear, and Nightwear Manufacturing;

- Manufacturing women's and girls' blouses and shirts from purchased fabric—are classified in U.S. Industry 315232, Women's and Girls' Cut and Sew Blouse and Shirt Manufacturing;

- Manufacturing women's and girls' dresses from purchased fabric—are classified in U.S. Industry 315233, Women's and Girls' Cut and Sew Dress Manufacturing;

- Manufacturing women's and girls' suits, tailored coats and jackets, and skirts from purchased fabric—are classified in U.S. Industry 315234, Women's and Girls' Cut and Sew Suit, Coat, Tailored Jacket, and Skirt Manufacturing;

- Manufacturing other women's and girls' outerwear from purchased fabric—are classified in U.S. Industry 315239, Women's and Girls' Cut and Sew Other Outerwear Manufacturing;

- Manufacturing infants' apparel from purchased fabric—are classified in U.S. Industry 315291, Infants' Cut and Sew Apparel Manufacturing; and

- Manufacturing fur and leather apparel—are classified in U.S. Industry 315292, Fur and Leather Apparel Manufacturing.

3159 Apparel Accessories and Other Apparel Manufacturing

This industry group comprises establishments primarily engaged in manufacturing apparel accessories and other apparel (except apparel knitting mills, apparel contractors, men's and boys' cut and sew apparel, women's and girls' cut and sew apparel, infants' cut and sew apparel, fur and leather apparel, and all other cut and sew apparel). This industry group includes jobbers performing entrepreneurial functions involved in manufacturing apparel accessories.

31599 Apparel Accessories and Other Apparel Manufacturing

This industry comprises establishments primarily engaged in manufacturing apparel and accessories (except apparel knitting mills, cut and sew apparel contractors, men's and boys' cut and sew apparel, women's and girls' cut and sew apparel, and other cut and sew apparel). Jobbers, who perform entrepreneurial functions involved in apparel accessories manufacture, including buying raw materials, designing and preparing samples, arranging for apparel accessories to be made from their materials, and marketing finished apparel accessories, are included. Examples of products made by these establishments are belts, caps, gloves (except medical, sporting, safety), hats, and neckties.

Cross-References. Establishments primarily engaged in—

- Cutting and/or sewing materials owned by others for apparel accessories—are classified in Industry 31521, Cut and Sew Apparel Contractors;

US—United States industry only. CAN—United States and Canadian industries are comparable. When neither US nor CAN appears, Canadian, Mexican, and United States industries are comparable.

- Manufacturing paper hats and caps—are classified in Industry 32229, Other Converted Paper Product Manufacturing;

- Manufacturing plastics or rubber hats and caps (except bathing caps)—are classified in Subsector 326, Plastics and Rubber Products Manufacturing;

- Manufacturing athletic gloves, such as boxing gloves, baseball gloves, golf gloves, batting gloves, and racquetball gloves,—are classified in Industry 33992, Sporting and Athletic Goods Manufacturing;

- Manufacturing metal fabric, metal mesh, or rubber gloves—are classified in Industry 33911, Medical Equipment and Supplies Manufacturing;

- Knitting apparel, mittens, gloves, hats, and caps or knitting fabric and manufacturing apparel, mittens, gloves, hats, and caps—are classified in Industry Group 3151, Apparel Knitting Mills;

- Cutting and/or sewing materials owned by others for apparel—are classified in Industry 31521, Cut and Sew Apparel Contractors;

- Manufacturing men's and boys' underwear and outerwear from purchased fabric—are classified in Industry 31522, Men's and Boys' Cut and Sew Apparel Manufacturing;

- Manufacturing women's and girls' underwear and outerwear from purchased fabric—are classified in Industry 31523, Women's and Girls' Cut and Sew Apparel Manufacturing; and

- Manufacturing other apparel from purchased fabric and manufacturing fur and leather apparel, hats, and caps—are classified in Industry 31529, Other Cut and Sew Apparel Manufacturing.

315991 Hat, Cap, and Millinery Manufacturing[US]

This U.S. industry comprises establishments primarily engaged in manufacturing cut and sew hats, caps, millinery, and hat bodies form purchased fabric. Jobbers, who perform entrepreneurial functions involved in hat, cap, and millinery manufacture, including buying raw materials, designing and preparing samples, arranging for hats, caps, and millinery to be made from their materials, and marketing finished hats, caps, and millinery, are included.

Cross-References. Establishments primarily engaged in—

- Cutting and/or sewing materials owned by others for hats, caps, and millinery—are classified in Industry 31521, Cut and Sew Apparel Contractors;

- Manufacturing paper hats and caps—are classified in U.S. Industry 322299, All Other Converted Paper Product Manufacturing;

- Manufacturing plastics or rubber hats and caps (except bathing caps)—are classified in Subsector 326, Plastics and Rubber Products Manufacturing; and

- Manufacturing fur and leather hats and caps—are classified in U.S. Industry 315292, Fur and Leather Apparel Manufacturing.

US—United States industry only. CAN—United States and Canadian industries are comparable. When neither US nor CAN appears, Canadian, Mexican, and United States industries are comparable.

315992 Glove and Mitten Manufacturing[US]

This U.S. industry comprises establishments primarily engaged in manufacturing cut and sew gloves (except rubber, metal, and athletic gloves) and mittens from purchased fabric, fur, leather, or from combinations of fabric, fur, or leather. Jobbers, who perform entrepreneurial functions involved in glove and mitten manufacture, including buying raw materials, designing and preparing samples, arranging for gloves and mittens to be made from their materials, and marketing finished gloves and mittens, are included.

Cross-References. Establishments primarily engaged in—

- Cutting and/or sewing materials owned by others for gloves and mittens—are classified in Industry 31521, Cut and Sew Apparel Contractors;

- Knitting mittens and gloves or knitting fabric and manufacturing mittens and gloves—are classified in U.S. Industry 315191, Outerwear Knitting Mills;

- Manufacturing athletic gloves, such as boxing gloves, baseball gloves, golf gloves, batting gloves, and racquetball gloves—are classified in Industry 339920, Sporting and Athletic Goods Manufacturing; and

- Manufacturing metal fabric, metal mesh, or rubber gloves—are classified in U.S. Industry 339113, Surgical Appliance and Supplies Manufacturing.

315993 Men's and Boys' Neckwear Manufacturing[US]

This U.S. industry comprises establishments primarily engaged in manufacturing men's and boys' cut and sew neckties, scarves, and mufflers from purchased fabric, leather, or from combinations of leather and fabric. Men's and boys' neckwear jobbers, who perform entrepreneurial functions involved in neckwear manufacture, including buying raw materials, designing and preparing samples, arranging for neckwear to be made from their materials, and marketing finished neckwear, are included.

Cross-References.

Establishments primarily engaged in cutting and/or sewing materials owned by others for men's and boys' neckwear are classified in U.S. Industry 315211, Men's and Boys' Cut and Sew Apparel Contractors.

315999 Other Apparel Accessories and Other Apparel Manufacturing[US]

This U.S. industry comprises establishments primarily engaged in manufacturing apparel and apparel accessories (except apparel knitting mills; cut and sew apparel contractors; cut and sew apparel; hats and caps; mittens and gloves; and men's and boys' neckwear). Jobbers for these products, who perform entrepreneurial functions involved in other apparel and accessory manufacture, including buying raw materials, designing and preparing samples, arranging for other apparel

---

US—United States industry only. CAN—United States and Canadian industries are comparable. When neither US nor CAN appears, Canadian, Mexican, and United States industries are comparable.

and accessories to be made from their materials, and marketing finished other apparel and accessories, are included. Examples of products made by these establishments are apparel trimmings and findings, belts, women's scarves, suspenders, and waterproof outerwear.

Cross-References. Establishments primarily engaged in—

- Knitting apparel or knitting fabric and manufacturing apparel—are classified in Industry Group 3151, Apparel Knitting Mills;

- Cutting and/or sewing materials owned by others for apparel—are classified in Industry 31521, Cut and Sew Apparel Contractors;

- Manufacturing men's and boys' cut and sew underwear and outerwear from purchased fabric—are classified in Industry 31522, Men's and Boys' Cut and Sew Apparel Manufacturing;

- Manufacturing women's and girls' cut and sew underwear and outerwear from purchased fabric—are classified in Industry 31523, Women's and Girls' Cut and Sew Apparel Manufacturing;

- Manufacturing infants' cut and sew apparel from purchased fabric—are classified in U.S. Industry 315291, Infants' Cut and Sew Apparel Manufacturing;

- Manufacturing fur and leather apparel—are classified in U.S. Industry 315292, Fur and Leather Apparel Manufacturing;

- Manufacturing hats, caps, and millinery—are classified in U.S. Industry 315991, Hat, Cap, and Millinery Manufacturing;

- Manufacturing gloves and mittens—are classified in U.S. Industry 315992, Glove and Mitten Manufacturing; and

- Manufacturing men's and boys' neckwear—are classified in U.S. Industry 315993, Men's and Boys' Neckwear Manufacturing.

316 Leather and Allied Product Manufacturing

Establishments in the Leather and Allied Product Manufacturing subsector transform hides into leather by tanning or curing and fabricating the leather into products for final consumption. It also includes the manufacture of similar products from other materials, including products (except apparel) made from ''leather substitutes,'' such as rubber, plastics, or textiles. Rubber footwear, textile luggage, and plastics purses or wallets are examples of ''leather substitute'' products included in this group. The products made from leather substitutes are included in this subsector because they are made in similar ways leather products are made (e.g., luggage). They are made in the same establishments, so it is not practical to separate them.

US—United States industry only. CAN—United States and Canadian industries are comparable. When neither US nor CAN appears, Canadian, Mexican, and United States industries are comparable.

http://www.ntis.gov/naics

The inclusion of leather making in this subsector is partly because leather tanning is a relatively small industry that has few close neighbors as a production process, partly because leather is an input to some of the other products classified in this subsector and partly for historical reasons.

3161 Leather and Hide Tanning and Finishing

31611 Leather and Hide Tanning and Finishing
See industry description for 316110 below

316110 Leather and Hide Tanning and Finishing

This industry comprises establishments primarily engaged in one or more of the following: (1) tanning, currying, and finishing hides and skins; (2) having others process hides and skins on a contract basis; and (3) dyeing or dressing furs.

3162 Footwear Manufacturing

31621 Footwear Manufacturing

This industry comprises establishments primarily engaged in manufacturing footwear (except orthopedic extension footwear).

Cross-References.

Establishments primarily engaged in manufacturing orthopedic extension footwear are classified in Industry 33911, Medical Equipment and Supplies Manufacturing.

316211 Rubber and Plastics Footwear Manufacturing[US]

This U.S. industry comprises establishments primarily engaged in manufacturing rubber and plastics footwear with vulcanized rubber or plastics soles, molded or cemented to rubber, plastics, or fabric uppers, and rubber and plastics protective footwear.

Cross-References. Establishments primarily engaged in—

- Manufacturing house slippers with fabric uppers and rubber or plastics soles—are classified in U.S. Industry 316212, House Slipper Manufacturing;

- Manufacturing men's footwear (except athletic) with leather or vinyl uppers, regardless of sole material—are classified in U.S. Industry 316213, Men's Footwear (except Athletic) Manufacturing;

- Manufacturing women's footwear (except athletic) with leather or vinyl uppers, regardless of sole material—are classified in U.S. Industry 316214, Women's Footwear (except Athletic) Manufacturing; and

---

US—United States industry only. CAN—United States and Canadian industries are comparable. When neither US nor CAN appears, Canadian, Mexican, and United States industries are comparable.

- Manufacturing youths' children's and infants' footwear and athletic footwear with leather or vinyl uppers, regardless of sole material—are classified in U.S. Industry 316219, Other Footwear Manufacturing.

316212 House Slipper Manufacturing[US]

This U.S. industry comprises establishments primarily engaged in manufacturing house slippers and slipper socks, regardless of material.

316213 Men's Footwear (except Athletic) Manufacturing[US]

This U.S. industry comprises establishments primarily engaged in manufacturing men's footwear designed primarily for dress, street, and work. This industry includes men's shoes with rubber or plastics soles and leather or vinyl uppers.

Cross-References. Establishments primarily engaged in—

- Manufacturing men's footwear with fabric uppers and rubber or plastics soles—are classified in U.S. Industry 316211, Rubber and Plastics Footwear Manufacturing;

- Manufacturing orthopedic extension footwear—are classified in U.S. Industry 339113, Surgical Appliance and Supplies Manufacturing; and

- Manufacturing men's leather or vinyl upper athletic footwear and youths' and boys' footwear—are classified in U.S. Industry 316219, Other Footwear Manufacturing.

316214 Women's Footwear (except Athletic) Manufacturing[US]

This U.S. industry comprises establishments primarily engaged in manufacturing women's footwear designed for dress, street, and work. This industry includes women's shoes with rubber or plastics soles and leather or vinyl uppers.

Cross-References. Establishments primarily engaged in—

- Manufacturing women's footwear with fabric uppers and rubber or plastics soles and rubber or plastics sandals—are classified in U.S. Industry 316211, Rubber and Plastics Footwear Manufacturing;

- Manufacturing orthopedic extension footwear—are classified in U.S. Industry 339113, Surgical Appliance and Supplies Manufacturing; and

- Manufacturing women's leather or vinyl upper athletic footwear and youths' and girls' footwear—are classified in U.S. Industry 316219, Other Footwear Manufacturing.

316219 Other Footwear Manufacturing[US]

This U.S. industry comprises establishments primarily engaged in manufacturing other footwear (except rubber and plastics footwear; house slippers; men's footwear (except athletic); and women's footwear (except athletic)).

US—United States industry only. CAN—United States and Canadian industries are comparable. When neither US nor CAN appears, Canadian, Mexican, and United States industries are comparable.

Illustrative Examples:

Athletic shoes (except rubber-soled, fabric upper) manufacturing

Ballet slippers manufacturing

Children's shoes (except plastics and rubber footwear and orthopedic extension shoes) manufacturing

Cleated athletic shoes manufacturing

Infants' shoes (except plastics and rubber footwear) manufacturing

Cross-References. Establishments primarily engaged in—

- Manufacturing rubber and plastics footwear with fabric uppers—are classified in U.S. Industry 316211, Rubber and Plastics Footwear Manufacturing;

- Manufacturing house slippers—are classified in U.S. Industry 316212, House Slipper Manufacturing;

- Manufacturing men's footwear (except athletic)—are classified in U.S. Industry 316213, Men's Footwear (except Athletic) Manufacturing;

- Manufacturing orthopedic extension footwear—are classified in Industry 339113, Surgical Appliance and Supplies Manufacturing; and

- Manufacturing women's footwear (except athletic)—are classified in U.S. Industry 316214, Women's Footwear (except Athletic) Manufacturing.

3169 Other Leather and Allied Product Manufacturing

31699 Other Leather and Allied Product Manufacturing

This industry comprises establishments primarily engaged in manufacturing leather products (except footwear and apparel) from purchased leather or leather substitutes (e.g., fabric, plastics).

Illustrative Examples:

Billfolds, all materials, manufacturing

Boot and shoe cut stock and findings, leather, manufacturing

Dog furnishings (e.g., collars, leashes, harnesses, muzzles), manufacturing

Luggage, all materials, manufacturing

Purses, women's, all materials (except metal), manufacturing

Shoe soles, leather, manufacturing

Toilet kits and cases (except metal) manufacturing

Watchbands (except metal) manufacturing

Welders' jackets, leggings, and sleeves, leather, manufacturing

Cross-References. Establishments primarily engaged in—

- Manufacturing leather apparel—are classified in Industry 31529, Other Cut and Sew Apparel Manufacturing;

US—United States industry only. CAN—United States and Canadian industries are comparable. When neither US nor CAN appears, Canadian, Mexican, and United States industries are comparable.

- Manufacturing leather gloves, mittens, belts, and apparel accessories—are classified in Industry 31599, Apparel Accessories and Other Apparel Manufacturing;

- Manufacturing footwear—are classified in Industry 31621, Footwear Manufacturing;

- Manufacturing nonleather soles—are classified elsewhere based on the primary input material;

- Manufacturing small articles made of metal carried on or about the person made of metal—are classified in Industry 33991, Jewelry and Silverware Manufacturing; and

- Manufacturing leather gaskets—are classified in Industry 33999, All Other Miscellaneous Manufacturing.

316991 Luggage Manufacturing[US]

This U.S. industry comprises establishments primarily engaged in manufacturing luggage of any material.

316992 Women's Handbag and Purse Manufacturing[US]

This U.S. industry comprises establishments primarily engaged in manufacturing women's handbags and purses of any material (except precious metal).

Cross-References.

Establishments primarily engaged in manufacturing precious metal handbags and purses are classified in U.S. Industry 339911, Jewelry (except Costume) Manufacturing.

316993 Personal Leather Good (except Women's Handbag and Purse) Manufacturing[US]

This U.S. industry comprises establishments primarily engaged in manufacturing personal leather goods (i.e., small articles of any material (except metal) normally carried on or about the person or in a handbag). Examples of personal leather goods made by these establishments are billfolds, coin purses, key cases, toilet kits, and watchbands (except metal).

Cross-References.   Establishments primarily engaged in—

- Manufacturing personal goods of precious metal—are classified in U.S. Industry 339911, Jewelry (except Costume) Manufacturing; and

- Manufacturing personal goods of metal (except precious)—are classified in U.S. Industry 339914, Costume Jewelry and Novelty Manufacturing.

316999 All Other Leather Good Manufacturing[US]

This U.S. industry comprises establishments primarily engaged in manufacturing leather goods (except footwear, luggage, handbags, purses, and personal leather goods).

US—United States industry only. CAN—United States and Canadian industries are comparable. When neither US nor CAN appears, Canadian, Mexican, and United States industries are comparable.

Illustrative Examples:

> Boot and shoe cut stock and findings, leather, manufacturing
> Dog furnishings (e.g., collars, leashes, harnesses, muzzles) manufacturing
> Leather belting for machinery (e.g., flat, solid, twisted, built-up) manufacturing

> Shoe soles, leather, manufacturing
> Welders' jackets, leggings, and sleeves, leather, manufacturing

Cross-References. Establishments primarily engaged in—

- Manufacturing leather gloves or mittens—are classified in U.S. Industry 315992, Glove and Mitten Manufacturing;

- Manufacturing leather apparel belts—are classified in U.S. Industry 315999, Other Apparel Accessories and Other Apparel Manufacturing;

- Manufacturing footwear—are classified in Industry 31621, Footwear Manufacturing;

- Manufacturing luggage of any material—are classified in U.S. Industry 316991, Luggage Manufacturing;

- Manufacturing handbags and purses—are classified in U.S. Industry 316992, Women's Handbag and Purse Manufacturing;

- Manufacturing personal leather goods, such as wallets and key cases, of all materials (except metal)—are classified in U.S. Industry 316993, Personal Leather Good (except Women's Handbag and Purse) Manufacturing;

- Manufacturing nonleather soles—are classified elsewhere based on the primary input material;

- Manufacturing leather apparel—are classified in U.S. Industry 315292, Fur and Leather Apparel Manufacturing; and

- Manufacturing leather gaskets—are classified in U.S. Industry 339991, Gasket, Packing, and Sealing Device Manufacturing.

321 Wood Product Manufacturing

Industries in the Wood Product Manufacturing subsector manufacture wood products, such as lumber, plywood, veneers, wood containers, wood flooring, wood trusses, manufactured homes (i.e., mobile home), and prefabricated wood buildings. The production processes of the Wood Product Manufacturing subsector include sawing, planing, shaping, laminating, and assembling of wood products starting from logs that are cut into bolts, or lumber that then may be further cut, or shaped by lathes or other shaping tools. The lumber or other transformed wood shapes may also be subsequently planed or smoothed, and assembled into finished products, such as wood containers.

The Wood Product Manufacturing subsector includes establishments that make wood products from logs and bolts that are sawed and shaped, and establishments that purchase sawed lumber

---

US—United States industry only. CAN—United States and Canadian industries are comparable. When neither US nor CAN appears, Canadian, Mexican, and United States industries are comparable.

and make wood products. With the exception of sawmills and wood preservation establishments, the establishments are grouped into industries mainly based on the specific products manufacutured.

3211 Sawmills and Wood Preservation

This industry group comprises establishments whose primary production process begins with logs or bolts that are transformed into boards, dimension lumber, beams, timbers, poles, ties, shingles, shakes, siding, and wood chips. Establishments that cut and treat round wood and/or treat wood products made in other establishments to prevent rotting by impregnation with creosote or other chemical compounds are also included in this industry group.

32111 Sawmills and Wood Preservation

This industry comprises establishments primarily engaged in one or more of the following: (1) sawing dimension lumber, boards, beams, timber, poles, ties, shingles, shakes, siding, and wood chips from logs or bolts; (2) sawing round wood poles, pilings, and posts and treating them with preservatives; and (3) treating wood sawed, planed, or shaped in other establishments with creosote or other preservatives to prevent decay and to protect against fire and insects. Sawmills may plane the rough lumber that they make with a planing machine to achieve smoothness and uniformity of size.

Cross-References. Establishments primarily engaged in—

- Operating portable chipper mills in the field—are classified in Industry 11331, Logging;

- Manufacturing wood products (except round wood poles, pilings, and posts) and treating them with preservatives—are classified elsewhere in Subsector 321, Wood Product Manufacturing, based on the related production process;

- Manufacturing veneer from logs and bolts or manufacturing engineered lumber and structural members other than solid wood—are classified in Industry 32121, Veneer, Plywood, and Engineered Wood Product Manufacturing; and

- Planing purchased lumber or manufacturing cut stock or dimension stock (i.e., shapes) from logs or bolts—are classified in Industry 32191, Millwork.

321113 Sawmills[US]

This U.S. industry comprises establishments primarily engaged in sawing dimension lumber, boards, beams, timbers, poles, ties, shingles, shakes, siding, and wood chips from logs or bolts. Sawmills may plane the rough lumber that they make with a planing machine to achieve smoothness and uniformity of size.

Cross-References. Establishments primarily engaged in—

- Planing purchased lumber or manufacturing cut stock or dimension stock (i.e., shapes) from logs or bolts—are classified in Industry 32191, Millwork;

US—United States industry only. CAN—United States and Canadian industries are comparable. When neither US nor CAN appears, Canadian, Mexican, and United States industries are comparable.

- Manufacturing veneer from logs or bolts—are classified in Industry 32121, Veneer, Plywood, and Engineered Wood Product Manufacturing; and

- Operating portable chipper mills in the field—are classified in Industry 113310, Logging.

321114 Wood Preservation[CAN]

This U.S. industry comprises establishments primarily engaged in (1) treating wood sawed, planed, or shaped in other establishments with creosote or other preservatives, such as chromated copper arsenate, to prevent decay and to protect against fire and insects and/or (2) sawing round wood poles, pilings, and posts and treating them with preservatives.

Cross-References.

Establishments primarily engaged in manufacturing wood products (except round wood poles, pilings, and posts) and treating them with preservatives are classified elsewhere in Subsector 321, Wood Product Manufacturing, based on the related production process.

3212 Veneer, Plywood, and Engineered Wood Product Manufacturing

32121 Veneer, Plywood, and Engineered Wood Product Manufacturing

This industry comprises establishments primarily engaged in one or more of the following: (1) manufacturing veneer and/or plywood; (2) manufacturing engineered wood members; and (3) manufacturing reconstituted wood products. This industry includes manufacturing plywood from veneer made in the same establishment or from veneer made in other establishments, and manufacturing plywood faced with nonwood materials, such as plastics or metal.

Illustrative Examples:

Fabricated structural wood members manufacturing	Particleboard manufacturing
Laminated structural wood members manufacturing	Plywood manufacturing
Medium density fiberboard (MDF) manufacturing	Reconstituted wood sheets and boards manufacturing
Oriented strandboard (OSB) manufacturing	Roof trusses, wood, manufacturing
	Veneer mills
	Waferboard manufacturing

Cross-References. Establishments primarily engaged in—

- Manufacturing veneer and further processing that veneer into wood containers or wood container parts in the same establishment—are classified in Industry 32192, Wood Container and Pallet Manufacturing;

- Manufacturing prefabricated wood buildings or wood sections, and panels for buildings—are classified in Industry 32199, All Other Wood Product Manufacturing; and

---

US—United States industry only. CAN—United States and Canadian industries are comparable. When neither US nor CAN appears, Canadian, Mexican, and United States industries are comparable.

- Manufacturing solid wood structural members, such as dimension lumber and timber from logs or bolts in sawmills—are classified in Industry 32111, Sawmills and Wood Preservation.

321211 Hardwood Veneer and Plywood Manufacturing[CAN]

This U.S. industry comprises establishments primarily engaged in manufacturing hardwood veneer and/or hardwood plywood.

Cross-References. Establishments primarily engaged in—

- Manufacturing veneer and further processing that veneer into wood containers or wood container parts—are classified in Industry 321920, Wood Container and Pallet Manufacturing;

- Manufacturing softwood veneer and softwood plywood—are classified in U.S. Industry 321212, Softwood Veneer and Plywood Manufacturing; and

- Manufacturing reconstituted wood sheets and boards—are classified in U.S. Industry 321219, Reconstituted Wood Product Manufacturing.

321212 Softwood Veneer and Plywood Manufacturing[CAN]

This U.S. industry comprises establishments primarily engaged in manufacturing softwood veneer and/or softwood plywood.

Cross-References. Establishments primarily engaged in—

- Manufacturing veneer and further processing that veneer into wood containers or wood container parts—are classified in Industry 321920, Wood Container and Pallet Manufacturing;

- Manufacturing hardwood veneer and hardwood plywood—are classified in U.S. Industry 321211, Hardwood Veneer and Plywood Manufacturing; and

- Manufacturing reconstituted wood sheets and boards—are classified in U.S. Industry 321219, Reconstituted Wood Product Manufacturing.

321213 Engineered Wood Member (except Truss) Manufacturing[US]

This U.S. industry comprises establishments primarily engaged in manufacturing fabricated or laminated wood arches and/or other fabricated or laminated wood structural members.

Illustrative Examples:

Finger joint lumber manufacturing	Parallel strand lumber manufacturing
I-joists, wood, fabricating	Timbers, structural, glue laminated or
Laminated veneer lumber (LVL)	pre-engineered wood, manufacturing
manufacturing	

US—United States industry only. CAN—United States and Canadian industries are comparable. When neither US nor CAN appears, Canadian, Mexican, and United States industries are comparable.

Cross-References. Establishments primarily engaged in—

- Manufacturing prefabricated wood buildings, or wood sections, and panels for buildings—are classified in U.S. Industry 321992, Prefabricated Wood Building Manufacturing;

- Manufacturing wood trusses—are classified in U.S. Industry 321214, Truss Manufacturing; and

- Manufacturing solid wood structural members, such as dimension lumber and timber from logs or bolts,—are classified in U.S. Industry 321113, Sawmills.

321214 Truss Manufacturing[US]

This U.S. industry comprises establishments primarily engaged in manufacturing laminated or fabricated wood roof and floor trusses.

Cross-References.

Establishments primarily engaged in manufacturing wood I-joists are classified in U.S. Industry 321213, Engineered Wood Member (except Truss) Manufacturing.

321219 Reconstituted Wood Product Manufacturing[US]

This U.S. industry comprises establishments primarily engaged in manufacturing reconstituted wood sheets and boards.

Illustrative Examples:

Medium density fiberboard (MDF)
  manufacturing
Oriented strandboard (OSB) manufacturing
Particleboard manufacturing

Reconstituted wood sheets and boards
  manufacturing
Waferboard manufacturing

Cross-References. Establishments primarily engaged in—

- Manufacturing softwood plywood—are classified in U.S. Industry 321212, Softwood Veneer and Plywood Manufacturing; and

- Manufacturing hardwood plywood—are classified in U.S. Industry 321211, Hardwood Veneer and Plywood Manufacturing.

3219 Other Wood Product Manufacturing

This industry group comprises establishments primarily engaged in manufacturing wood products (except establishments operating sawmills and wood preservation facilities; and establishments manufacturing veneer, plywood, or engineered wood products).

US—United States industry only. CAN—United States and Canadian industries are comparable. When neither US nor CAN appears, Canadian, Mexican, and United States industries are comparable.

32191 Millwork

This industry comprises establishments primarily engaged in manufacturing hardwood and softwood cut stock and dimension stock (i.e., shapes); wood windows and wood doors; and other millwork including wood flooring. Dimension stock or cut stock is defined as lumber and worked wood products cut or shaped to specialized sizes. These establishments generally use woodworking machinery, such as jointers, planers, lathes, and routers to shape wood.

Cross-References. Establishments primarily engaged in—

- Manufacturing dimension lumber, boards, beams, timbers, poles, ties, shingles, shakes, siding, and wood chips from logs and bolts—are classified in Industry 32111, Sawmills and Wood Preservation;

- Fabricating millwork at the construction site—are classified in Sector 23, Construction; and

- Manufacturing wood furniture frames and finished wood furniture parts—are classified in Industry 33721, Office Furniture (including Fixtures) Manufacturing.

321911 Wood Window and Door Manufacturing[CAN]

This U.S. industry comprises establishments primarily engaged in manufacturing window and door units, sash, window and door frames, and doors from wood or wood clad with metal or plastics.

Cross-References.

Establishments primarily engaged in fabricating wood windows or wood doors at the construction site are classified in Sector 23, Construction.

321912 Cut Stock, Resawing Lumber, and Planing[US]

This U.S. industry comprises establishments primarily engaged in one or more of the following: (1) manufacturing dimension lumber from purchased lumber; (2) manufacturing dimension stock (i.e., shapes) or cut stock; (3) resawing the output of sawmills; and (4) planing purchased lumber. These establishments generally use woodworking machinery, such as jointers, planers, lathes, and routers to shape wood.

Cross-References. Establishments primarily engaged in—

- Manufacturing dimension lumber, boards, beams, timbers, poles, ties, shingles, shakes, siding, and wood chips from logs or bolts—are classified in U.S. Industry 321113, Sawmills;

- Manufacturing wood stairwork, wood molding, wood trim, and other millwork—are classified in U.S. Industry 321918, Other Millwork (including Flooring); and

- Manufacturing wood furniture frames and finished wood furniture parts—are classified in U.S. Industry 337215, Showcase, Partition, Shelving, and Locker Manufacturing.

US—United States industry only. CAN—United States and Canadian industries are comparable. When neither US nor CAN appears, Canadian, Mexican, and United States industries are comparable.

321918 Other Millwork (including Flooring)[US]

This U.S. industry comprises establishments primarily engaged in manufacturing millwork (except wood windows, wood doors, and cut stock).

Illustrative Examples:

Clear and finger joint wood moldings manufacturing

Decorative wood moldings (e.g., base, chair rail, crown, shoe) manufacturing

Ornamental woodwork (e.g., cornices, mantel) manufacturing

Planing mills, millwork

Stairwork (e.g., panel posts, railings, stairs, showcases), wood, manufacturing

Wood flooring manufacturing

Wood shutters manufacturing

Cross-References. Establishments primarily engaged in—

- Manufacturing wood windows and doors—are classified in U.S. Industry 321911, Wood Window and Door Manufacturing; and

- Manufacturing cut stock, resawing lumber, and/or planing purchased lumber—are classified in U.S. Industry 321912, Cut Stock, Resawing Lumber, and Planing.

32192 Wood Container and Pallet Manufacturing
See industry description for 321920 below

321920 Wood Container and Pallet Manufacturing

This industry comprises establishments primarily engaged in manufacturing wood pallets, wood box shook, wood boxes, other wood containers, and wood parts for pallets and containers.

Cross-References.

Establishments primarily engaged in manufacturing wood burial caskets are classified in U.S. Industry 339995, Burial Casket Manufacturing.

32199 All Other Wood Product Manufacturing

This industry comprises establishments primarily engaged in manufacturing wood products (except establishments operating sawmills and wood preservation facilities; and establishments manufacturing veneer, plywood, engineered wood products, millwork, wood containers, or pallets).

Illustrative Examples:

Mobile home manufacturing

Panels, prefabricated wood building, manufacturing

Prefabricated wood buildings

Sections, prefabricated wood building, manufacturing

Wood dowels manufacuturing

Wood handles (e.g., broom, handtool, mop), manufacturing

US—United States industry only. CAN—United States and Canadian industries are comparable. When neither US nor CAN appears, Canadian, Mexican, and United States industries are comparable.

Cross-References. Establishments primarily engaged in—

- Operating sawmills or preserving wood—are classified in Industry 32111, Sawmills and Wood Preservation;

- Manufacturing veneer, plywood, and engineered wood products—are classified in Industry 32121, Veneer, Plywood, and Engineered Wood Product Manufacturing;

- Manufacturing millwork—are classified in Industry 32191, Millwork;

- Manufacturing wood containers, pallets, and wood container parts—are classified in Industry 32192, Wood Container and Pallet Manufacturing;

- Manufacturing travel trailers with self-contained facilities for storage of water and waste— are classified in Industry 33621, Motor Vehicle Body and Trailer Manufacturing; and

- Fabricating of wood buildings or wood sections and panels for buildings at the construction site—are classified in Sector 23, Construction.

321991 Manufactured Home (Mobile Home) Manufacturing[CAN]

This U.S. industry comprises establishments primarily engaged in making manufactured homes (i.e., mobile homes) and nonresidential mobile buildings. Manufactured homes are designed to accept permanent water, sewer, and utility connections and although equipped with wheels, they are not intended for regular highway movement.

Cross-References. Establishments primarily engaged in—

- Manufacturing prefabricated wood buildings not equipped with wheels—are classified in U.S. Industry 321992, Prefabricated Wood Building Manufacturing; and

- Manufacturing travel trailers with self-contained facilities for storage of water and waste— are classified in U.S. Industry 336214, Travel Trailer and Camper Manufacturing.

321992 Prefabricated Wood Building Manufacturing[CAN]

This U.S. industry comprises establishments primarily engaged in manufacturing prefabricated wood buildings and wood sections and panels for prefabricated wood buildings.

Cross-References. Establishments primarily engaged in—

- Fabricating wood buildings or wood sections and panels for buildings at the construction site—are classified in Sector 23, Construction; and

- Making manufactured homes (i.e., mobile homes)—are classified in U.S. Industry 321991, Manufactured Home (Mobile Home) Manufacturing.

321999 All Other Miscellaneous Wood Product Manufacturing[CAN]

This U.S. industry comprises establishments primarily engaged in manufacturing wood products (except establishments operating sawmills and preservation facilities; establishments manufacturing

---

US—United States industry only. CAN—United States and Canadian industries are comparable. When neither US nor CAN appears, Canadian, Mexican, and United States industries are comparable.

veneer, engineered wood products, millwork, wood containers, pallets, and wood container parts; and establishments making manufactured homes (i.e., mobile homes) and prefabricated buildings and components).

Illustrative Examples:

Cork products (except gaskets) manufacturing

Kiln drying lumber

Shoe trees manufacturing

Wood dowels manufacturing

Wood extension ladders manufacturing

Wood handles (e.g., broom, handtool, mop), manufacturing

Wood kitchenware manufacturing

Wood stepladders manufacturing

Wood toilet seats manufacturing

Wood toothpicks manufacturing

Cross-References. Establishments primarily engaged in—

- Operating sawmills and preserving wood—are classified in Industry 32111, Sawmills and Wood Preservation;

- Manufacturing veneer and engineered wood products—are classified in Industry 32121, Veneer, Plywood, and Engineered Wood Product Manufacturing;

- Manufacturing millwork—are classified in Industry 32191, Millwork;

- Manufacturing boxes, box shook, wood containers, pallets, and wood parts for containers— are classified in Industry 321920, Wood Container and Pallet Manufacturing;

- Making manufactured homes (i.e., mobile homes)—are classified in U.S. Industry 321991, Manufactured Home (Mobile Home) Manufacturing; and

- Manufacturing prefabricated wood buildings or wood sections and panels for buildings— are classified in U.S. Industry 321992, Prefabricated Wood Building Manufacturing.

322 Paper Manufacturing

Industries in the Paper Manufacturing subsector make pulp, paper, or converted paper products. The manufacturing of these products is grouped together because they constitute a series of vertically connected processes. More than one is often carried out in a single establishment. There are essentially three activities. The manufacturing of pulp involves separating the cellulose fibers from other impurities in wood or used paper. The manufacturing of paper involves matting these fibers into a sheet. Converted paper products are made from paper and other materials by various cutting and shaping techniques and includes coating and laminating activities.

The Paper Manufacturing subsector is subdivided into two industry groups, the first for the manufacturing of pulp and paper and the second for the manufacturing of converted paper products. Paper making is treated as the core activity of the subsector. Therefore, any establishment that makes paper (including paperboard), either alone or in combination with pulp manufacturing or paper converting, is classified as a paper or paperboard mill. Establishments that make pulp without making paper are classified as pulp mills. Pulp mills, paper mills and paperboard mills comprise the first industry group.

Establishments that make products from purchased paper and other materials make up the second industry group, Converted Paper Product Manufacturing. This general activity is then subdivided based, for the most part, on process distinctions. Paperboard container manufacturing uses corrugating, cutting, and shaping machinery to form paperboard into containers. Paper bag and coated and treated paper manufacturing establishments cut and coat paper and foil. Stationery product manufacturing establishments make a variety of paper products used for writing, filing, and similar applications. Other converted paper product manufacturing includes, in particular, the conversion of sanitary paper stock into such things as tissue paper and disposable diapers.

An important process used in the Paper Bag and Coated and Treated Paper Manufacturing industry is lamination, often combined with coating. Lamination and coating makes a composite material with improved properties of strength, impermeability, and so on. The laminated materials may be paper, metal foil, or plastics film. While paper is often one of the components, it is not always. Lamination of plastics film to plastics film is classified in the NAICS Subsector 326, Plastics and Rubber Products Manufacturing, because establishments that do this often first make the film.

The same situation holds with respect to bags. The manufacturing of bags from plastics only, whether or not laminated, is classified in Subsector 326, Plastics and Rubber Products Manufacturing, but all other bag manufacturing is classified in this subsector.

Excluded from this subsector are photosensitive papers. These papers are chemically treated and are classified in Industry 32599, All Other Chemical Product and Preparation Manufacturing.

3221 Pulp, Paper, and Paperboard Mills

This industry group comprises establishments primarily engaged in manufacturing pulp, paper, or paperboard.

32211 Pulp Mills
See industry description for 322110 below.

322110 Pulp Mills

This industry comprises establishments primarily engaged in manufacturing pulp without manufacturing paper or paperboard. The pulp is made by separating the cellulose fibers from the other impurities in wood or other materials, such as used or recycled rags, linters, scrap paper, and straw.

Cross-References. Establishments primarily engaged in—

- Manufacturing both pulp and paper—are classified in Industry 32212, Paper Mills; and

- Manufacturing both pulp and paperboard—are classified in Industry 322130, Paperboard Mills.

32212 Paper Mills

This industry comprises establishments primarily engaged in manufacturing paper from pulp. These establishments may manufacture or purchase pulp. In addition, the establishments may

---

US—United States industry only. CAN—United States and Canadian industries are comparable. When neither US nor CAN appears, Canadian, Mexican, and United States industries are comparable.

convert the paper they make. The activity of making paper classifies an establishment into this industry regardless of the output.

Cross-References. Establishments primarily engaged in—

- Manufacturing pulp without manufacturing paper—are classified in Industry 32211, Pulp Mills;

- Manufacturing paperboard—are classified in Industry 32213, Paperboard Mills;

- Converting paper without manufacturing paper—are classified in Industry Group 3222, Converted Paper Product Manufacturing; and

- Manufacturing photographic sensitized paper—are classified in Industry 32599, All Other Chemical Product and Preparation Manufacturing.

322121 Paper (except Newsprint) Mills[CAN]

This U.S. industry comprises establishments primarily engaged in manufacturing paper (except newsprint and uncoated groundwood paper) from pulp. These establishments may manufacture or purchase pulp. In addition, the establishments may also convert the paper they make.

Cross-References. Establishments primarily engaged in—

- Manufacturing newsprint and uncoated groundwood paper—are classified in U.S. Industry 322122, Newsprint Mills;

- Converting paper without manufacturing paper—are classified in Industry Group 3222, Converted Paper Product Manufacturing;

- Manufacturing paperboard—are classified in Industry 322130, Paperboard Mills;

- Manufacturing pulp without manufacturing paper—are classified in Industry 322110, Pulp Mills; and

- Manufacturing photographic sensitized paper from purchased paper—are classified in U.S. Industry 325992, Photographic Film, Paper, Plate, and Chemical Manufacturing.

322122 Newsprint Mills[CAN]

This U.S. industry comprises establishments primarily engaged in manufacturing newsprint and uncoated groundwood paper from pulp. These establishments may manufacture or purchase pulp. In addition, the establishments may also convert the paper they make.

Cross-References. Establishments primarily engaged in—

- Manufacturing paper (except newsprint and uncoated groundwood)—are classified in U.S. Industry 322121, Paper (except Newsprint) Mills;

- Converting paper without manufacturing paper—are classified in Industry Group 3222, Converted Paper Product Manufacturing;

• Manufacturing paperboard—are classified in Industry 322130, Paperboard Mills; and

• Manufacturing pulp without manufacturing paper—are classified in Industry 322110, Pulp Mills.

32213 Paperboard Mills

See industry description for 322130 below.

322130 Paperboard Mills

This industry comprises establishments primarily engaged in manufacturing paperboard from pulp. These establishments may manufacture or purchase pulp. In addition, the establishments may also convert the paperboard they make.

Cross-References. Establishments primarily engaged in—

• Manufacturing pulp without manufacturing paperboard—are classified in Industry 322110, Pulp Mills;

• Converting paperboard without manufacturing paperboard—are classified in Industry Group 3222, Converted Paper Product Manufacturing; and

• Manufacturing insulation board and other reconstituted wood fiberboard—are classified in U.S. Industry 321219, Reconstituted Wood Product Manufacturing.

3222 Converted Paper Product Manufacturing

This industry group comprises establishments primarily engaged in converting paper or paperboard without manufacturing paper or paperboard.

32221 Paperboard Container Manufacturing

This industry comprises establishments primarily engaged in converting paperboard into containers without manufacturing paperboard. These establishments use corrugating, cutting, and shaping machinery to form paperboard into containers. Products made by these establishments include boxes; corrugated sheets, pads, and pallets; paper dishes; and fiber drums and reels.

Cross-References. Establishments primarily engaged in—

• Manufacturing similar items of plastics materials—are classified in Industry Group 3261, Plastics Product Manufacturing;

• Manufacturing paperboard and converting paperboard into containers—are classified in Industry 32213, Paperboard Mills;

• Manufacturing egg cartons, food trays, and other food containers from molded pulp—are classified in Industry 32229, Other Converted Paper Product Manufacturing;

• Manufacturing paper and converting paper into containers—are classified in Industry 32212, Paper Mills; and

---

US—United States industry only. CAN—United States and Canadian industries are comparable. When neither US nor CAN appears, Canadian, Mexican, and United States industries are comparable.

- Manufacturing paperbags without manufacturing paper—are classified in Industry 32222, Paper Bag and Coated and Treated Paper Manufacturing.

322211 Corrugated and Solid Fiber Box Manufacturing[CAN]

This U.S. industry comprises establishments primarily engaged in laminating purchased paper or paperboard into corrugated or solid fiber boxes and related products, such as pads, partitions, pallets, and corrugated paper without manufacturing paperboard. These boxes are generally used for shipping.

Cross-References. Establishments primarily engaged in—

- Manufacturing setup paperboard boxes (except corrugated or laminated solid fiber boxes)—are classified in U.S. Industry 322213, Setup Paperboard Box Manufacturing;

- Manufacturing folding paperboard boxes (except corrugated or laminated solid fiber boxes)—are classified in U.S. Industry 322212, Folding Paperboard Box Manufacturing; and

- Manufacturing paperboard and converting paperboard into boxes—are classified in Industry 322130, Paperboard Mills.

322212 Folding Paperboard Box Manufacturing[CAN]

This U.S. industry comprises establishments primarily engaged in converting paperboard (except corrugated) into folding paperboard boxes without manufacturing paper and paperboard.

Cross-References. Establishments primarily engaged in—

- Manufacturing setup paperboard boxes (except corrugated)—are classified in U.S. Industry 322213, Setup Paperboard Box Manufacturing;

- Manufacturing corrugated and solid fiber boxes—are classified in U.S. Industry 322211, Corrugated and Solid Fiber Box Manufacturing;

- Manufacturing paperboard and converting paperboard into containers—are classified in Industry 322130, Paperboard Mills;

- Manufacturing paper and converting paper into containers—are classified in Industry 32212, Paper Mills;

- Manufacturing milk cartons—are classified in U.S. Industry 322215, Nonfolding Sanitary Food Container Manufacturing; and

- Manufacturing paper bags—are classified in Industry 32222, Paper Bag and Coated and Treated Paper Manufacturing.

322213 Setup Paperboard Box Manufacturing[US]

This U.S. industry comprises establishments primarily engaged in converting paperboard into setup paperboard boxes (i.e., rigid-sided boxes not shipped flat) without manufacturing paperboard.

US—United States industry only. CAN—United States and Canadian industries are comparable. When neither US nor CAN appears, Canadian, Mexican, and United States industries are comparable.

Cross-References. Establishments primarily engaged in—

- Manufacturing folding paperboard boxes (except corrugated)—are classified in U.S. Industry 322212, Folding Paperboard Box Manufacturing;

- Manufacturing corrugated and solid fiber boxes—are classified in U.S. Industry 322211, Corrugated and Solid Fiber Box Manufacturing; and

- Manufacturing paperboard and converting paperboard into containers—arc classified in Industry 322130, Paperboard Mills.

322214 Fiber Can, Tube, Drum, and Similar Products Manufacturing[US]

This U.S. industry comprises establishments primarily engaged in converting paperboard into fiber cans, tubes, drums, and similar products without manufacturing paperboard.

Cross-References.

Establishments engaged in manufacturing paperboard and converting paperboard into containers are classified in Industry 322130, Paperboard Mills.

322215 Nonfolding Sanitary Food Container Manufacturing[US]

This U.S. industry comprises establishments primarily engaged in converting sanitary foodboard into food containers (except folding).

Cross-References. Establishments primarily engaged in—

- Manufacturing sanitary food containers of solely plastics materials—are classified in Industry Group 3261, Plastics Product Manufacturing;

- Manufacturing egg cartons, food trays, and other food containers from molded pulp—are classified in U.S. Industry 322299, All Other Converted Paper Product Manufacturing; and

- Manufacturing folding sanitary cartons—are classified in U.S. Industry 322212, Folding Paperboard Box Manufacturing.

32222 Paper Bag and Coated and Treated Paper Manufacturing

This industry comprises establishments primarily engaged in one or more of the following: (1) cutting and coating paper and paperboard; (2) cutting and laminating paper and paperboard and other flexible materials (except plastics film to plastics film); (3) manufacturing bags or multiwall bags or sacks of paper, metal foil, coated paper, or laminates or coated combinations of paper and foil with plastics film; (4) manufacturing laminated aluminum and other converted metal foils from purchased foils; and (5) surface coating paper or paperboard.

Cross-References. Establishments primarily engaged in—

- Manufacturing paper from pulp—are classified in Industry 32212, Paper Mills;

- Manufacturing photographic sensitized paper—are classified in Industry 32599, All Other Chemical Product and Preparation Manufacturing;

US—United States industry only. CAN—United States and Canadian industries are comparable. When neither US nor CAN appears, Canadian, Mexican, and United States industries are comparable.

- Manufacturing textile bags—are classified in Industry 31491, Textile Bag and Canvas Mills;

- Manufacturing single and multiwall plastics bags or plastics laminated bags—are classified in Industry 32611, Unsupported Plastics Film, Sheet, and Bag Manufacturing;

- Making aluminum and aluminum foil—are classified in Industry 33131, Alumina and Aluminum Production and Processing; and

- Cutting purchased aluminum foil into smaller lengths and widths—are classified in Industry 33299, All Other Fabricated Metal Product Manufacturing.

322221 Coated and Laminated Packaging Paper and Plastics Film Manufacturing[US]

This U.S. industry comprises establishments primarily engaged in performing one or more of the following activities associated with the manufacturing of packaging materials: (1) cutting and coating paper; and (2) cutting and laminating paper with other flexible materials (except plastics to plastics or foil to paper laminates). The products made in this industry are made from purchased sheet materials and may be printed in the same establishment.

Cross-References. Establishments primarily engaged in—

- Manufacturing coated or laminated paper for nonpackaging purposes—are classified in U.S. Industry 322222, Coated and Laminated Paper Manufacturing;

- Manufacturing unsupported plastics film—are classified in U.S. Industry 326113, Unsupported Plastics Film and Sheet (except Packaging) Manufacturing;

- Manufacturing laminated aluminum foil for flexible packaging uses—are classified in U.S. Industry 322225, Laminated Aluminum Foil Manufacturing for Flexible Packaging Uses;

- Making aluminum and aluminum foil—are classified in Industry 33131, Alumina and Aluminum Production and Processing;

- Cutting purchased aluminum foil into smaller lengths and widths—are classified in U.S. Industry 332999, All Other Miscellaneous Fabricated Metal Product Manufacturing; and

- Manufacturing paper from pulp—are classified in Industry 32212, Paper Mills.

322222 Coated and Laminated Paper Manufacturing[US]

This U.S. industry comprises establishments primarily engaged in performing one or more of the following activities associated with making products designed for purposes other than packaging: (1) cutting and coating paper; (2) cutting and laminating paper and other flexible materials (except plastics film to plastics film); and (3) manufacturing converted aluminum and other metal foils for nonpackaging uses from purchased foils. The products made in this industry are made from purchased sheet materials and may be printed in the same establishment.

US—United States industry only. CAN—United States and Canadian industries are comparable. When neither US nor CAN appears, Canadian, Mexican, and United States industries are comparable.

Illustrative Examples:

Book paper made by coating purchased paper
Gift wrap paper (except laminated foil) made from purchased paper
Gummed paper products (e.g., labels sheets, tapes) made from purchased paper

Tapes, gummed (e.g., cellophane, masking, pressure sensitive) made from purchased paper or other structures
Wallpaper made from purchased papers or other materials

Cross-References. Establishments primarily engaged in—

- Manufacturing coated and laminated paper for packaging uses—are classified in U.S. Industry 322221, Coated and Laminated Packaging Paper and Plastics Film Manufacturing;

- Manufacturing photographic sensitized paper—are classified in U.S. Industry 325992, Photographic Film, Paper, Plate, and Chemical Manufacturing;

- Making aluminum and aluminum foil—are classified in Industry 33131, Alumina and Aluminum Production and Processing;

- Cutting purchased aluminum foil into smaller lengths and widths—are classified in U.S. Industry 332999, All Other Miscellaneous Fabricated Metal Product Manufacturing; and

- Manufacturing laminated aluminum foil for flexible packaging uses—are classified in U.S. Industry 322225, Laminated Aluminum Foil Manufacturing for Flexible Packaging Uses.

322223 Plastics, Foil, and Coated Paper Bag Manufacturing[US]

This U.S. industry comprises establishments primarily engaged in manufacturing bags of coated paper, of metal foil, or of laminated or coated combinations of plastics, foil, and paper, whether or not printed.

Cross-References. Establishments primarily engaged in—

- Manufacturing uncoated paper bags and multiwall bags and sacks—are classified in U.S. Industry 322224, Uncoated Paper and Multiwall Bag Manufacturing;

- Manufacturing textile bags—are classified in U.S. Industry 314911, Textile Bag Mills; and

- Manufacturing single and multiwall plastics bags—are classified in U.S. Industry 326111, Unsupported Plastics Bag Manufacturing.

322224 Uncoated Paper and Multiwall Bag Manufacturing[US]

This U.S. industry comprises establishments primarily engaged in manufacturing uncoated paper bags or multiwall bags and sacks.

Cross-References. Establishments primarily engaged in—

- Manufacturing single wall and multiwall bags from plastics unsupported film—are classified in U.S. Industry 326111, Unsupported Plastics Bag Manufacturing;

US—United States industry only. CAN—United States and Canadian industries are comparable. When neither US nor CAN appears, Canadian, Mexican, and United States industries are comparable.

- Manufacturing bags of coated paper, of metal foil, or of laminated or coated combinations of plastics, foil, and paper bags—are classified in U.S. Industry 322223, Plastics, Foil, and Coated Paper Bag Manufacturing; and

- Manufacturing textile bags—are classified in U.S. Industry 314911, Textile Bag Mills.

322225 Laminated Aluminum Foil Manufacturing for Flexible Packaging Uses[US]

This U.S. industry comprises establishments primarily engaged in laminating aluminum and other metal foil into products with flexible packaging uses or gift wrap and other packaging wrap applications.

Cross-References. Establishments primarily engaged in—

- Manufacturing plain aluminum foil—are classified in U.S. Industry 331315, Aluminum Sheet, Plate, and Foil Manufacturing;

- Manufacturing laminated aluminum bags and liners—are classified in U.S. Industry 322223, Plastics, Foil, and Coated Paper Bag Manufacturing;

- Manufacturing converted aluminum and other metal foils for nonpackaging uses from purchased foils—are classified in U.S. Industry 322222, Coated and Laminated Paper Manufacturing; and

- Manufacturing cookware, dinnerware, and other semirigid metal containers—are classified in U.S. Industry 332999, All Other Miscellaneous Fabricated Metal Product Manufacturing.

322226 Surface-Coated Paperboard Manufacturing[US]

This U.S. industry comprises establishments primarily engaged in laminating, lining, or surface coating purchased paperboard to make other paperboard products.

32223 Stationery Product Manufacturing

This industry comprises establishments primarily engaged in converting paper or paperboard into products used for writing, filing, art work, and similar applications.

Illustrative Examples:

Die-cut paper products for office use made from purchased paper or paperboard
Envelopes (i.e., mailing, stationery) made from any material
Tapes (e.g., adding machines, calculator, cash register) made from purchased paper

Stationery made from purchased paper
Tablets (e.g., memo, note, writing) made from purchased paper

Cross-References.

Establishments primarily engaged in manufacturing die-cut paper and paperboard products other than office supplies are classified in U.S. Industry 322299, All Other Converted Paper Product Manufacturing.

US—United States industry only. CAN—United States and Canadian industries are comparable. When neither US nor CAN appears, Canadian, Mexican, and United States industries are comparable.

322231 Die-Cut Paper and Paperboard Office Supplies Manufacturing[US]

This U.S. industry comprises establishments primarily engaged in converting paper rollstock or paperboard into die-cut paper or paperboard office supplies. For the purpose of this industry, office supplies are defined as office products, such as filing folders, index cards, rolls for adding machines, file separators and dividers, tabulating cards, and other paper and paperboard office supplies.

Cross-References. Establishments primarily engaged in—

- Manufacturing die-cut paper and paperboard products (except office supplies)—are classified in U.S. Industry 322299, All Other Converted Paper Product Manufacturing; and

- Manufacturing paper and paperboard products used for writing and similar applications (e.g., looseleaf fillers, notebooks, pads, stationery, tablets)—are classified in U.S. Industry 322233, Stationery, Tablet, and Related Product Manufacturing.

322232 Envelope Manufacturing[US]

This U.S. industry comprises establishments primarily engaged in manufacturing envelopes for mailing or stationery of any material including combinations.

Cross-References.

Establishments primarily engaged in manufacturing stationery are classified in U.S. Industry 322233, Stationery, Tablet, and Related Product Manufacturing.

322233 Stationery, Tablet, and Related Product Manufacturing[US]

This U.S. industry comprises establishments primarily engaged in converting paper and paperboard into products used for writing and similar applications (e.g., looseleaf fillers, notebooks, pads, stationery, tablets).

Cross-References. Establishments primarily engaged in—

- Manufacturing envelopes—are classified in U.S. Industry 322232, Envelope Manufacturing; and

- Manufacturing die-cut paper and paperboard office supplies—are classified in U.S. Industry 322231, Die-Cut Paper and Paperboard Office Supplies Manufacturing.

32229 Other Converted Paper Product Manufacturing

This industry comprises establishments primarily engaged in (1) converting paper and paperboard into products (except containers, bags, coated and treated paper and paperboard, and stationery products), or (2) converting pulp into pulp products, such as disposable diapers, or molded pulp egg cartons, food trays, and dishes. Processes used include laminating or lining purchased paper or paperboard.

US—United States industry only. CAN—United States and Canadian industries are comparable. When neither US nor CAN appears, Canadian, Mexican, and United States industries are comparable.

Illustrative Examples:

Crepe paper made from purchased paper
Die-cut paper products (except for office use)
  made from purchased paper or paperboard
Molded pulp products (e.g., egg cartons, food
  containers, food trays) manufacturing

Paper novelties made from purchased paper
Sanitary products made from purchased
  sanitary paper stock

Cross-References. Establishments primarily engaged in—

- Manufacturing pulp from wood or from other materials—are classified in Industry 32211, Pulp Mills;

- Manufacturing paper from pulp or making pulp and manufacturing paper—are classified in Industry 32212, Paper Mills;

- Manufacturing paperboard from pulp or making pulp and manufacturing paperboard—are classified in Industry 32213, Paperboard Mills;

- Manufacturing paperboard containers—are classified in Industry 32221, Paperboard Container Manufacturing;

- Manufacturing bags of coated, laminated, or uncoated paper, of metal foil, or combinations thereof—are classified in Industry 32222, Paper Bag and Coated and Treated Paper Manufacturing; and

- Manufacturing stationery and other related office supplies—are classified in Industry 32223, Stationery Product Manufacturing.

322291 Sanitary Paper Product Manufacturing[CAN]

This U.S. industry comprises establishments primarily engaged in converting purchased sanitary paper stock or wadding into sanitary paper products, such as facial tissues and handkerchiefs, table napkins, toilet paper, towels, disposable diapers, sanitary napkins, and tampons.

322299 All Other Converted Paper Product Manufacturing[CAN]

This U.S. industry comprises establishments primarily engaged in converting paper or paperboard into products (except containers, bags, coated and treated paper, stationery products, and sanitary paper products) or converting pulp into pulp products, such as egg cartons, food trays, and other food containers from molded pulp.

Illustrative Examples:

Crepe paper made from purchased paper
Die-cut paper products (except for office use)
  made from purchased paper or paperboard

Molded pulp products (e.g., egg cartons, food
  containers, food trays) manufacturing
Paper novelties made from purchased paper

US—United States industry only. CAN—United States and Canadian industries are comparable. When neither US nor CAN appears, Canadian, Mexican, and United States industries are comparable.

http://www.ntis.gov/naics

Cross-References. Establishments primarily engaged in—

- Manufacturing pulp from wood or from other materials—are classified in Industry 322110, Pulp Mills;

- Manufacturing paper from pulp or making pulp and manufacturing paper—are classified in Industry 32212, Paper Mills;

- Manufacturing paperboard from pulp or making pulp and manufacturing paperboard—are classified in Industry 322130, Paperboard Mills;

- Manufacturing paperboard containers—are classified in Industry 32221, Paperboard Container Manufacturing;

- Manufacturing bags of coated, laminated, or uncoated paper, of metal foil, or combinations thereof—are classified in Industry 32222, Paper Bag and Coated and Treated Paper Manufacturing; and

- Manufacturing stationery and other related office supplies—are classified in Industry 32223, Stationery Product Manufacturing.

323 Printing and Related Support Activities

Industries in the Printing and Related Support Activities subsector print products, such as newspapers, books, periodicals, business forms, greeting cards, and other materials, and perform support activities, such as bookbinding, platemaking services, and data imaging. The support activities included here are an integral part of the printing industry, and a product (a printing plate, a bound book, or a computer disk or file) that is an integral part of the printing industry is almost always provided by these operations.

Processes used in printing include a variety of methods used to transfer an image from a plate, screen, or computer file to some medium, such as paper, plastics, metal, textile articles, or wood. The most prominent of these methods is to transfer the image from a plate or screen to the medium (lithographic, gravure, screen, and flexographic printing). A rapidly growing new technology uses a computer file to directly ''drive'' the printing mechanism to create the image and new electrostatic and other types of equipment (digital or nonimpact printing).

In contrast to many other classification systems that locate publishing of printed materials in manufacturing, NAICS classifies the publishing of printed products in Subsector 511, Publishing Industries. Though printing and publishing are often carried out by the same enterprise (a newspaper, for example), it is less and less the case that these distinct activities are carried out in the same establishment. When publishing and printing are done in the same establishment, the establishment is classified in Sector 51, Information, in the appropriate NAICS industry even if the receipts for printing exceed those for publishing.

This subsector includes printing on clothing because the production process for that activity is printing, not clothing manufacturing. For instance, the printing of T-shirts is included in this subsector. In contrast, printing on fabric (or grey goods) is not included. This activity is part of

---

US—United States industry only. CAN—United States and Canadian industries are comparable. When neither US nor CAN appears, Canadian, Mexican, and United States industries are comparable.

the process of finishing the fabric and is included in the NAICS Textile Mills subsector in Industry 31331, Textile and Fabric Finishing Mills.

3231 Printing and Related Support Activities

32311 Printing

This industry comprises establishments primarily engaged in printing on apparel and textile products, paper, metal, glass, plastics, and other materials, except fabric (grey goods). The printing processes employed include, but are not limited to, lithographic, gravure, screen, flexographic, digital, and letterpress. Establishments in this industry do not manufacture the stock that they print but may perform postprinting activities, such as bending, cutting, or laminating the materials they print, and mailing.

Cross-References. Establishments primarily engaged in—

- Providing photocopying service on nondigital photocopy equipment without performing traditional printing activities—are classified in Industry 56143, Business Service Centers;

- Printing on grey goods—are classified in Industry 31331, Textile and Fabric Finishing Mills;

- Printing and publishing, known as publishers,—are classified in Subsector 511, Publishing Industries; and

- Performing prepress or postpress services without performing traditional printing activities—are classified in Industry 32312, Support Services for Printing.

323110 Commercial Lithographic Printing[US]

This U.S. industry comprises establishments primarily engaged in lithographic (i.e., offset) printing without publishing (except books, grey goods, and manifold business forms). This industry includes establishments engaged in lithographic printing on purchased stock materials, such as stationery, letterhead, invitations, labels, and similar items, on a job order basis.

Cross-References. Establishments primarily engaged in—

- Quick printing—are classified in U.S. Industry 323114, Quick Printing;

- Printing on grey goods—are classified in Industry 31331, Textile and Fabric Finishing Mills;

- Printing books and pamphlets—are classified in U.S. Industry 323117, Books Printing;

- Printing manifold business forms including checkbooks—are classified in U.S. Industry 323116, Manifold Business Forms Printing;

- Manufacturing printed stationery, invitations, labels, and similar items—are classified in Subsector 322, Paper Manufacturing; and

- Printing and publishing, known as publishers,—are classified in Subsector 511, Publishing Industries.

US—United States industry only. CAN—United States and Canadian industries are comparable. When neither US nor CAN appears, Canadian, Mexican, and United States industries are comparable.

323111 Commercial Gravure Printing[US]

This U.S. industry comprises establishments primarily engaged in gravure printing without publishing (except books, grey goods, and manifold business forms). This industry includes establishments engaged in gravure printing on purchased stock materials, such as stationery, letterhead, invitations, labels, and similar items, on a job order basis.

Cross-References. Establishments primarily engaged in—

- Printing on grey goods—are classified in Industry 31331, Textile and Fabric Finishing Mills;

- Printing books and pamphlets—are classified in U.S. Industry 323117, Book Printing;

- Printing manifold business forms including checkbooks—are classified in U.S. Industry 323116, Manifold Business Form Printing;

- Manufacturing printed stationery, invitations, labels, and similar items—are classified in Subsector 322, Paper Manufacturing; and

- Printing and publishing, known as publishers,—are classified in Subsector 511, Publishing Industries.

323112 Commercial Flexographic Printing[US]

This U.S. industry comprises establishments primarily engaged in flexographic printing without publishing (except books, grey goods, and manifold business forms). This industry includes establishments engaged in flexographic printing on purchased stock materials, such as stationery, invitations, labels, and similar items, on a job order basis.

Cross-References. Establishments primarily engaged in—

- Printing on grey goods—are classified in Industry 31331, Textile and Fabric Finishing Mills;

- Printing books and pamphlets—are classified in U.S. Industry 323117, Books Printing;

- Printing manifold business forms including checkbooks—are classified in U.S. Industry 323116, Manifold Business Forms Printing;

- Manufacturing printed stationery, invitations, labels, and similar items—are classified elsewhere in Subsector 322, Manufacturing; and

- Printing and publishing, known as publishers,—are classified in Subsector 511, Publishing Industries.

323113 Commercial Screen Printing[CAN]

This U.S. industry comprises establishments primarily engaged in screen printing without publishing (except books, grey goods, and manifold business forms). This industry includes establishments engaged in screen printing on purchased stock materials, such as stationery, invitations, labels, and similar items, on a job order basis. Establishments primarily engaged in printing on apparel and textile products, such as T-shirts, caps, jackets, towels, and napkins, are included in this industry.

US—United States industry only. CAN—United States and Canadian industries are comparable. When neither US nor CAN appears, Canadian, Mexican, and United States industries are comparable.

Cross-References. Establishments primarily engaged in—

- Printing on grey goods—are classified in Industry 31331, Textile and Fabric Finishing Mills;

- Printing books and pamphlets—are classified in U.S. Industry 323117, Books Printing;

- Printing manifold business forms including checkbooks—are classified in U.S. Industry 323116, Manifold Business Forms Printing;

- Manufacturing printed stationery, invitations, labels, and similar items—are classified in Subsector 322, Paper Manufacturing; and

- Printing and publishing, known as publishers,—are classified in Subsector 511, Publishing Industries.

323114 Quick Printing[CAN]

This U.S. industry comprises establishments primarily engaged in traditional printing activities, such as short-run offset printing or prepress services, in combination with providing document photocopying service. Prepress services include receiving documents in electronic format and directly duplicating from the electronic file and formatting, colorizing, and otherwise modifying the original document to improve presentation. These establishments, known as quick printers, generally provide short-run printing and copying with fast turnaround times.

Cross-References. Establishments primarily engaged in—

- Providing photocopying service on nondigital photocopy equipment without performing traditional printing activities—are classified in U.S. Industry 561439, Other Business Service Centers (including Copy Shops);

- Printing on lithographic equipment known as commercial lithographic printers—are classified in U.S. Industry 323110, Commercial Lithographic Printing; and

- Digital printing on graphical material—are classified in U.S. Industry 323115, Digital Printing.

323115 Digital Printing[CAN]

This U.S. industry comprises establishments primarily engaged in printing graphical materials using digital printing equipment. Establishments known as digital printers typically provide sophisticated prepress services including using scanners to input images and computers to manipulate and format the graphic images prior to printing.

Cross-References.

Establishments primarily engaged in printing with "up front" computer files on conventional-type printing equipment are classified based on the type of printing equipment (e.g., lithographic, flexographic, screen) being used.

US—United States industry only. CAN—United States and Canadian industries are comparable. When neither US nor CAN appears, Canadian, Mexican, and United States industries are comparable.

http://www.ntis.gov/naics

323116 Manifold Business Forms Printing^{CAN}

This U.S. industry comprises establishments primarily engaged in printing special forms, including checkbooks, for use in the operation of a business. The forms may be in single and multiple sets, including carbonized, interleaved with carbon, or otherwise processed for multiple reproduction.

Cross-References.

Establishments primarily engaged in manufacturing single layered continuous computer paper and similar products are classified in U.S. Industry 322231, Die-Cut Paper and Paperboard Office Supplies Manufacturing.

323117 Books Printing^{US}

This U.S. industry comprises establishments primarily engaged in printing or printing and binding books and pamphlets without publishing.

Cross-References. Establishments primarily engaged in—

- Printing and publishing, known as book publishers,—are classified in Subsector 511, Publishing Industries; and

- Binding books without printing in the same establishment—are classified in U.S. Industry 323121, Tradebinding and Related Work.

323118 Blankbook, Looseleaf Binders, and Devices Manufacturing^{US}

This U.S. industry comprises establishments primarily engaged in manufacturing blankbooks, looseleaf devices, and binders. Establishments in this industry may print or print and bind.

Cross-References. Establishments primarily engaged in—

- Checkbook printing—are classified in U.S. Industry 323116, Manifold Business Form Printing; and

- Binding books without printing in the same establishment—are classified in U.S. Industry 323121, Tradebinding and Related Work.

323119 Other Commercial Printing^{US}

This U.S. industry comprises establishments primarily engaged in commercial printing (except lithographic, gravure, screen, or flexographic printing) without publishing (except books, grey goods, and manifold business forms). Printing processes included in this industry are letterpress printing and engraving printing. This industry includes establishments engaged in commercial printing on purchased stock materials, such as stationery, invitations, labels, and similar items, on a job order basis.

US—United States industry only. CAN—United States and Canadian industries are comparable. When neither US nor CAN appears, Canadian, Mexican, and United States industries are comparable.

Cross-References. Establishments primarily engaged in—

- Lithographic, gravure, screen, or flexographic printing on purchased stock materials (except books, grey goods, and manifold business forms)—are classified in Industry 32311, Printing, by printing process employed;

- Printing on grey goods—are classified in Industry 31331, Textile and Fabric Finishing Mills;

- Quick printing—are classified in U.S. Industry 323114, Quick Printing;

- Digital printing on graphical materials—are classified in U.S. Industry 323115, Digital Printing;

- Printing books and pamphlets—are classified in U.S. Industry 323117, Books Printing;

- Printing manifold business forms including checkbooks—are classified in U.S. Industry 323116, Manifold Business Forms Printing;

- Manufacturing printed stationery, invitations, labels, and similar items—are classified in Subsector 322, Paper Manufacturing; and

- Printing and publishing, known as book publishers,—are classified in Subsector 511, Publishing Industries.

32312 Support Activities for Printing

This industry comprises establishments primarily engaged in performing prepress (e.g., platemaking, typesetting) and postpress services (e.g., book binding) in support of printing activities.

Cross-References. Establishments primarily engaged in—

- Engraving of the type done on metal—are classified in Industry 33281, Coating, Engraving, Heat Treating, and Allied Activities;

- Manufacturing photosensitive plates for printing—are classified in Industry 32599, All Other Chemical Product and Preparation Manufacturing;

- Manufacturing blank plates for printing—are classified in Industry 33329, Other Industrial Machinery Manufacturing; and

- Printing books or printing and binding books—are classified in Industry 32311, Printing.

323121 Tradebinding and Related Work[US]

This U.S. industry comprises establishments primarily engaged in one or more of the following: (1) tradebinding; (2) sample mounting; and (3) postpress services (e.g., book or paper bronzing, die-cutting, edging, embossing, folding, gilding, gluing, indexing).

Cross-References.

Establishments primarily engaged in printing books or printing and binding books are classified in U.S. Industry 323117, Books Printing.

US—United States industry only. CAN—United States and Canadian industries are comparable. When neither US nor CAN appears, Canadian, Mexican, and United States industries are comparable.

323122 Prepress Services[US]

This U.S. industry comprises (1) establishments primarily engaged in prepress services, such as imagesetting or typesetting, for printers and (2) establishments primarily engaged in preparing film or plates for printing purposes.

Cross-References. Establishments primarily engaged in—

- Engraving of the type done on metal—are classified in U.S. Industry 332812, Metal Coating, Engraving (except jewelry and silverware), and Allied Services to Manufacturers;

- Manufacturing blank plates (except photosensitive plates) for printing—are classified in U.S. Industry 333293, Printing Machinery and Equipment Manufacturing; and

- Manufacturing photosensitive plates for printing—are classified in U.S. Industry 325992, Photographic Film, Paper, Plate, and Chemical Manufacturing.

324 Petroleum and Coal Products Manufacturing

The Petroleum and Coal Products Manufacturing subsector is based on the transformation of crude petroleum and coal into usable products. The dominant process is petroleum refining that involves the separation of crude petroleum into component products through such techniques as cracking and distillation.

In addition, this subsector includes establishments that primarily further process refined petroleum and coal products and produce products, such as asphalt coatings and petroleum lubricating oils. However, establishments that manufacture petrochemicals from refined petroleum are classified in Industry 32511, Petrochemical Manufacturing.

3241 Petroleum and Coal Products Manufacturing

32411 Petroleum Refineries
See industry description for 324110 below.

324110 Petroleum Refineries

This industry comprises establishments primarily engaged in refining crude petroleum into refined petroleum. Petroleum refining involves one or more of the following activities: (1) fractionation; (2) straight distillation of crude oil; and (3) cracking.

Cross-References. Establishments primarily engaged in—

- Manufacturing asphalt paving, roofing, and saturated materials from refined petroleum— are classified in Industry 32412, Asphalt Paving, Roofing, and Saturated Materials Manufacturing;

- Manufacturing paper mats and felts and saturating them with asphalt or tar into rolls and sheets—are classified in U.S. Industry 322121, Paper (except Newsprint) Mills;

US—United States industry only. CAN—United States and Canadian industries are comparable. When neither US nor CAN appears, Canadian, Mexican, and United States industries are comparable.

- Blending or compounding refined petroleum to make lubricating oils and greases and/or re-refining used petroleum lubricating oils—are classified in U.S. Industry 324191, Petroleum Lubricating Oil and Grease Manufacturing;

- Manufacturing synthetic lubricating oils and greases—are classified in U.S. Industry 325998, All Other Miscellaneous Chemical Product and Preparation Manufacturing;

- Recovering natural gasoline and/or liquid hydrocarbons from oil and gas field gases—are classified in Industry 21111, Oil and Gas Extraction;

- Manufacturing acyclic and cyclic aromatic hydrocarbons (i.e., petrochemicals) from refined petroleum or liquid hydrocarbons—are classified in Industry 325110, Petrochemical Manufacturing;

- Manufacturing cyclic and acyclic chemicals (except petrochemicals)—are classified in Industry 32519, Other Basic Organic Chemical Manufacturing;

- Manufacturing coke oven products in steel mills—are classified in U.S. Industry 331111, Iron and Steel Mills; and

- Manufacturing coke oven products in coke oven establishments—are classified in U.S. Industry, 324199, All Other Petroleum and Coal Products Manufacturing.

32412 Asphalt Paving, Roofing, and Saturated Materials Manufacturing

This industry comprises establishments primarily engaged in (1) manufacturing asphalt and tar paving mixtures and blocks and roofing cements and coatings from purchased asphaltic materials and/or (2) saturating purchased mats and felts with asphalt or tar from purchased asphaltic materials.

Cross-References. Establishments primarily engaged in—

- Refining crude petroleum and manufacturing asphalt and tar paving, roofing, and saturated materials—are classified in Industry 324110, Petroleum Refineries; and

- Manufacturing paper mats and felts and saturating them with asphalt or tar—are classified in Industry 32212, Paper Mills.

324121 Asphalt Paving Mixture and Block Manufacturing[CAN]

This U.S. industry comprises establishments primarily engaged in manufacturing asphalt and tar paving mixtures and blocks from purchased asphaltic materials.

Cross-References.

Establishments primarily engaged in refining crude petroleum and manufacturing asphalt and tar paving mixtures and blocks are classified in Industry 324110, Petroleum Refineries.

324122 Asphalt Shingle and Coating Materials Manufacturing[CAN]

This U.S. industry comprises establishments primarily engaged in (1) saturating purchased mats and felts with asphalt or tar from purchased asphaltic materials and (2) manufacturing asphalt and tar and roofing cements and coatings from purchased asphaltic materials.

US—United States industry only. CAN—United States and Canadian industries are comparable. When neither US nor CAN appears, Canadian, Mexican, and United States industries are comparable.

Cross-References. Establishments primarily engaged in—

- Refining crude petroleum and saturating purchased mats and felts with asphalt or tar into rolls and sheets and/or refining crude petroleum and manufacturing asphalt and tar roofing cements and coatings—are classified in Industry 324110, Petroleum Refineries; and

- Manufacturing paper mats and felts and saturating them with asphalt or tar into rolls and sheets—are classified in U.S. Industry 322121, Paper (except Newsprint) Mills.

32419 Other Petroleum and Coal Products Manufacturing

This industry comprises establishments primarily engaged in manufacturing petroleum products (except asphalt paving, roofing and saturated materials) from refined petroleum or coal products made in coke ovens not integrated with a steel mill.

Illustrative Examples:

Coke oven products (e.g., coke, gases, tars) made in coke oven establishments
Petroleum brake fluids made from refined petroleum
Petroleum briquettes made from refined petroleum

Petroleum jelly made from refined petroleum
Petroleum lubricating oils and greases made from refined petroleum
Petroleum waxes made from refined petroleum
Re-refined used petroleum lubricating oils

Cross-References. Establishments primarily engaged in—

- Manufacturing petroleum products by refining crude petroleum—are classified in Industry 32411, Petroleum Refineries;

- Manufacturing asphalt and tar paving, roofing, and saturated materials from refined petroleum—are classified in Industry 32412, Asphalt Paving, Roofing, and Saturated Materials Manufacturing;

- Manufacturing coke oven products in steel mills—are classified in Industry 33111, Iron and Steel Mills and Ferroalloy Manufacturing;

- Manufacturing acyclic and cyclic aromatic hydrocarbons (i.e., petrochemicals) from refined petroleum or liquid hydrocarbons—are classified in Industry 32511, Petrochemical Manufacturing;

- Manufacturing cyclic and acyclic organic chemicals (except petrochemicals)—are classified in Industry 32519, Other Basic Organic Chemical Manufacturing; and

- Manufacturing synthetic lubricating oils and greases—are classified in Industry 32599, All Other Chemical Product and Preparation Manufacturing.

324191 Petroleum Lubricating Oil and Grease Manufacturing[US]

This U.S. industry comprises establishments primarily engaged in blending or compounding refined petroleum to make lubricating oils and greases and/or re-refining used petroleum lubricating oils.

US—United States industry only. CAN—United States and Canadian industries are comparable. When neither US nor CAN appears, Canadian, Mexican, and United States industries are comparable.

Cross-References. Establishments primarily engaged in—

- Refining crude petroleum and manufacturing lubricating oils and greases—are classified in Industry 324110, Petroleum Refineries; and

- Manufacturing synthetic lubricating oils and greases—are classified in U.S. Industry 325998, All Other Miscellaneous Chemical Product and Preparation Manufacturing.

324199 All Other Petroleum and Coal Products Manufacturing[US]

This U.S. industry comprises establishments primarily engaged in manufacturing petroleum products (except asphalt paving, roofing, and saturated materials and lubricating oils and greases) from refined petroleum and coal products made in coke ovens not integrated with a steel mill.

Illustrative Examples:

Coke oven products (e.g., coke, gases, tars) made in coke oven establishments
Petroleum briquettes made from refined petroleum

Petroleum jelly made from refined petroleum
Petroleum waxes made from refined petroleum

Cross-References. Establishments primarily engaged in—

- Manufacturing petroleum products by refining crude petroleum—are classified in Industry 324110, Petroleum Refining;

- Manufacturing asphalt paving and roofing materials from refined petroleum—are classified in Industry 32412, Asphalt Paving, Roofing, and Saturated Materials Manufacturing;

- Blending and compounding petroleum lubricating oils and greases and/or re-refining used petroleum lubrication oils and greases are classified in U.S. Industry 324191, Petroleum Lubricating Oil and Grease Manufacturing;

- Manufacturing coke oven products in steel mills—are classified in U.S. Industry 331111, Iron and Steel Mills;

- Manufacturing acyclic and cyclic aromatic hydrocarbons (i.e., petrochemicals) from refined petroleum or liquid hydrocarbons—are classified in Industry 325110, Petrochemical Manufacturing; and

- Manufacturing cyclic and acyclic organic chemicals (except petrochemicals)—are classified in Industry 32519, Other Basic Organic Chemical Manufacturing.

325 Chemical Manufacturing

The Chemical Manufacturing subsector is based on the transformation of organic and inorganic raw materials by a chemical process and the formulation of products. This subsector distinguishes the production of basic chemicals that comprise the first industry group from the production of intermediate and end products produced by further processing of basic chemicals that make up the remaining industry groups.

US—United States industry only. CAN—United States and Canadian industries are comparable. When neither US nor CAN appears, Canadian, Mexican, and United States industries are comparable.

http://www.ntis.gov/naics

This subsector does not include all industries transforming raw materials by a chemical process. It is common for some chemical processing to occur during mining operations. These beneficiating operations, such as copper concentrating, are classified in Sector 21, Mining. Furthermore, the refining of crude petroleum is included in Subsector 324, Petroleum and Coal Products Manufacturing. In addition, the manufacturing of aluminum oxide is included in Subsector 331, Primary Metal Manufacturing; and beverage distilleries are classified in Subsector 312, Beverage and Tobacco Product Manufacturing. As in the case of these two activities, the grouping of industries into subsectors may take into account the association of the activities performed with other activities in the subsector.

3251 Basic Chemical Manufacturing

This industry group comprises establishments primarily engaged in manufacturing chemicals using basic processes, such as thermal cracking and distillation. Chemicals manufactured in this industry group are usually separate chemical elements or separate chemically-defined compounds.

32511 Petrochemical Manufacturing
See industry description for 325110 below.

325110 Petrochemical Manufacturing

This industry comprises establishments primarily engaged in (1) manufacturing acyclic (i.e., aliphatic) hydrocarbons such as ethylene, propylene, and butylene made from refined petroleum or liquid hydrocarbon and/or (2) manufacturing cyclic aromatic hydrocarbons such as benzene, toluene, styrene, xylene, ethyl benzene, and cumene made from refined petroleum or liquid hydrocarbons.

Cross-References. Establishments primarily engaged in—

- Manufacturing petrochemicals by refining crude petroleum—are classified in Industry 324110, Petroleum Refineries;

- Manufacturing acetylene—are classified in Industry 325120, Industrial Gas Manufacturing;

- Manufacturing basic organic chemicals (except petrochemicals)—are classified in Industry 325190, Other Basic Organic Chemical Manufacturing; and

- Recovering liquid hydrocarbons from oil and gas field gases—are classified in Industry 211110, Oil and Gas Extraction.

32512 Industrial Gas Manufacturing
See industry description for 325120 below.

325120 Industrial Gas Manufacturing

This industry comprises establishments primarily engaged in manufacturing industrial organic and inorganic gases in compressed, liquid, and solid forms.

US—United States industry only. CAN—United States and Canadian industries are comparable. When neither US nor CAN appears, Canadian, Mexican, and United States industries are comparable.

http://www.ntis.gov/naics

Cross-References. Establishments primarily engaged in—

- Manufacturing chlorine gas—are classified in U.S. Industry 325181, Alkalies and Chlorine Manufacturing; and

- Manufacturing ethane and butane gases made from refined petroleum or liquid hydrocarbons—are classified in Industry 325110, Petrochemical Manufacturing.

32513 Synthetic Dye and Pigment Manufacturing

This industry comprises establishments primarily engaged in manufacturing synthetic organic and inorganic dyes and pigments, such as lakes and toners (except electrostatic and photographic).

Cross-References. Establishments primarily engaged in—

- Manufacturing wood byproducts used as dying materials—are classified in Industry 32519, Other Basic Organic Chemical Manufacturing;

- Manufacturing carbon, bone, and lamp black—are classified in Industry 32518, Other Basic Inorganic Chemical Manufacturing;

- Manufacturing electrostatic and photographic toners—are classified in Industry 32599, All Other Chemical Product Manufacturing;

- Manufacturing natural food colorings—are classified in Industry 31193, Flavoring Syrup and Concentrate Manufacturing; and

- Manufacturing natural organic colorings for nonfood uses—are classified in Industry 32519, Other Basic Organic Chemical Manufacturing.

325131 Inorganic Dye and Pigment Manufacturing[US]

This U.S. industry comprises establishments primarily engaged in manufacturing inorganic dyes and pigments.

Cross-References. Establishments primarily engaged in—

- Manufacturing wood byproducts used as dyeing materials—are classified in U.S. Industry 325191, Gum and Wood Chemical Manufacturing;

- Manufacturing organic synthetic dyes and pigments—are classified in U.S. Industry 325132, Organic Dye and Pigment Manufacturing;

- Manufacturing carbon, bone, and lamp black—are classified in U.S. Industry 325182, Carbon Black Manufacturing; and

- Manufacturing natural food colorings—are classified in Industry 311930, Flavoring Syrup and Concentrate Manufacturing.

US—United States industry only. CAN—United States and Canadian industries are comparable. When neither US nor CAN appears, Canadian, Mexican, and United States industries are comparable.

325132 Synthetic Organic Dye and Pigment Manufacturing[US]

This U.S. industry comprises establishments primarily engaged in manufacturing synthetic organic dyes and pigments, such as lakes and toners (except electrostatic and photographic).

Cross-References. Establishments primarily engaged in—

- Manufacturing wood byproducts used as dyeing materials—are classified in U.S. Industry 325191, Gum and Wood Chemical Manufacturing;

- Manufacturing inorganic dyes and pigments—are classified in U.S. Industry 325131, Inorganic Dye and Pigment Manufacturing;

- Manufacturing electrostatic and photographic toners—are classified in U.S. Industry 325992, Photographic Film, Paper, Plate, and Chemical Manufacturing;

- Manufacturing natural food colorings—are classified in Industry 311930, Flavoring Syrup and Concentrate Manufacturing; and

- Manufacturing natural organic colorings for nonfood uses (except wood byproducts)—are classified in U.S. Industry 325199, All Other Basic Organic Chemical Manufacturing.

32518 Other Basic Inorganic Chemical Manufacturing

This industry comprises establishments primarily engaged in manufacturing basic inorganic chemicals (except industrial gases and synthetic dyes and pigments).

Illustrative Examples:

Alkalies manufacturing	Hydrochloric acid manufacturing
Aluminum compounds, not specified elsewhere by process, manufacturing	Potassium inorganic compounds, not specified elsewhere by process, manufacturing
Carbides (e.g., baron, calcium, silium, tungsten) manufacturing	Radioactive isotopes manufacturing
Carbon black manufacturing	Sulfides and sulfites manufacturing
Chlorine manufacturing	Sulfuric acid manufacturing

Cross-References. Establishments primarily engaged in—

- Manufacturing industrial gases—are classified in Industry 32512, Industrial Gas Manufacturing;

- Manufacturing inorganic dyes and pigments—are classified in Industry 32513, Dye and Pigment Manufacturing;

- Manufacturing household bleaches—are classified in Industry 32561, Soap and Cleaning Compound Manufacturing;

- Mining and/or beneficiating alkalies—are classified in Industry 21239, Other Nonmetallic Mineral Mining and Quarrying;

US—United States industry only. CAN—United States and Canadian industries are comparable. When neither US nor CAN appears, Canadian, Mexican, and United States industries are comparable.

- Manufacturing chlorine preparations (e.g., for swimming pools)—are classified in Industry 32599, All Other Chemical Product and Preparation Manufacturing;

- Manufacturing nitrogenous and phosphoric fertilizers and fertilizer materials—are classified in Industry 32531, Fertilizer Manufacturing;

- Manufacturing aluminum oxide (alumina)—are classified in Industry 33131, Alumina and Aluminum Production and Processing;

- Manufacturing inorganic insecticidal, herbicidal, fungicidal and pesticidal preparations—are classified in Industry 32532, Pesticide and Other Agricultural Chemical Manufacturing; and

- Manufacturing photographic chemicals—are classified in Industry 32599, All Other Chemical Product Manufacturing.

325181 Alkalies and Chlorine Manufacturing[CAN]

This U.S. industry comprises establishments primarily engaged in manufacturing chlorine, sodium hydroxide (i.e., caustic soda), and other alkalies often using an electrolysis process.

Cross-References. Establishments primarily engaged in—

- Mining and beneficiating alkalies—are classified in U.S. Industry 212391, Potash, Soda, and Borate Mineral Mining;

- Manufacturing chlorine preparations (e.g., for swimming pools)—are classified in U.S. Industry 325998, All Other Miscellaneous Chemical Product and Preparation Manufacturing;

- Manufacturing industrial bleaches—are classified in U.S. Industry 325188, All Other Basic Inorganic Chemical Manufacturing; and

- Manufacturing household bleaches—are classified in U.S. Industry 325611, Soap and Other Detergent Manufacturing.

325182 Carbon Black Manufacturing[US]

This U.S. industry comprises establishments primarily engaged in manufacturing carbon black, bone black, and lamp black.

Cross-References.

Establishments primarily engaged in manufacturing pigments are classified in Industry 32513, Synthetic Dye and Pigment Manufacturing.

325188 All Other Basic Inorganic Chemical Manufacturing[US]

This U.S. industry comprises establishments primarily engaged in manufacturing basic inorganic chemicals (except industrial gases, inorganic dyes and pigments, alkalies and chlorine, and carbon black).

US—United States industry only. CAN—United States and Canadian industries are comparable. When neither US nor CAN appears, Canadian, Mexican, and United States industries are comparable.

Illustrative Examples:

Aluminum compounds, not specified elsewhere by process, manufacturing

Carbides (e.g., baron, calcium, silicon, tungsten) manufacturing

Fluorine manufacturing

Hydrochloric acid manufacturing

Potassium inorganic compounds, not specified elsewhere by process, manufacturing

Sodium inorganic compounds, not specified elsewhere by process, manufacturing

Sulfides and sulfites manufacturing

Sulfuric acid manufacturing

Cross-References. Establishments primarily engaged in—

- Manufacturing industrial gases—are classified in Industry 325120, Industrial Gas Manufacturing;

- Manufacturing inorganic dyes and pigments—are classified in U.S. Industry 325131, Inorganic Dye and Pigment Manufacturing;

- Manufacturing alkalies and chlorine—are classified in U.S. Industry 325181, Alkalies and Chlorine Manufacturing;

- Manufacturing carbon black—are classified in U.S. Industry 325182, Carbon Black Manufacturing;

- Manufacturing household bleaches—are classified in U.S. Industry 325612, Polish and Other Sanitation Good Manufacturing;

- Manufacturing nitrogenous and phosphoric fertilizers and fertilizer material—are classified in Industry 32531, Fertilizer Manufacturing;

- Manufacturing aluminum oxide (i.e., alumina)—are classified in U.S. Industry 331311, Alumina Refining;

- Manufacturing inorganic insecticidal, herbicidal, fungicidal, and pesticidal preparations—are classified in Industry 325320, Pesticide and Other Agriculture Chemical Manufacturing; and

- Manufacturing photographic chemicals—are classified in U.S. Industry 325992, Photographic Film, Paper, Plate, and Chemical Manufacturing.

32519 Other Basic Organic Chemical Manufacturing

This industry comprises establishments primarily engaged in manufacturing basic organic chemicals (except petrochemicals, industrial gases, and synthetic dyes and pigments).

Illustrative Examples:

Carbon organic compounds, not specified elsewhere by process, manufacturing

Cyclic intermediates made from refined petroleum or natural gas

Enzyme proteins (i.e., basic synthetic chemicals) (except pharmaceutical use) manufacturing

Fatty acids (e.g., margaric, oleic, stearic) manufacturing

Gum and wood chemicals manufacturing

Organo-inorganic compound manufacturing

Plasticizers (i.e., basic synthetic chemical) manufacturing

Silicone (except resins) manufacturing

Synthetic sweeteners (i.e., sweetening agents) manufacturing

US—United States industry only. CAN—United States and Canadian industries are comparable. When neither US nor CAN appears, Canadian, Mexican, and United States industries are comparable.

Cross-References. Establishments primarily engaged in—

- Manufacturing petrochemicals from refined petroleum or liquid hydrocarbons—are classified in Industry 32511, Petrochemical Manufacturing;

- Manufacturing petrochemicals by refining crude petroleum—are classified in Industry 32411, Petroleum Refineries;

- Manufacturing organic industrial gases—are classified in Industry 32512, Industrial Gas Manufacturing;

- Manufacturing synthetic organic dyes and pigments—are classified in Industry 32513, Synthetic Dye and Pigment Manufacturing;

- Manufacturing natural glycerin—are classified in Industry 32561, Soap and Cleaning Compound Manufacturing;

- Manufacturing activated charcoal—are classified in Industry 32599, All Other Chemical Product and Preparation Manufacturing;

- Manufacturing organic insecticidal, herbicidal, fungicidal, and pesticidal preparations—are classified in Industry 32532, Pesticide and Other Agriculture Chemical Manufacturing;

- Manufacturing elastomers—are classified in Industry 32521, Resin and Synthetic Rubber Manufacturing;

- Manufacturing urea—are classified in Industry 32531, Fertilizer Manufacturing;

- Manufacturing coal tar crudes in integrated steel mills with coke ovens—are classified in Industry 33111, Iron and Steel Mills and Ferroalloy Manufacturing;

- Manufacturing coal tar crudes in coke ovens not intergrated with steel mills and fuel briquettes from refined petroleum—are classified in Industry 32419, Other Petroleum and Coal Products Manufacturing; and

- Manufacturing natural food colorings—are classified in Industry 31194, Seasoning and Dressing Manufacturing.

325191 Gum and Wood Chemical Manufacturing[US]

This U.S. industry comprises establishments primarily engaged in (1) distilling wood or gum into products, such as tall oil and wood distillates, and (2) manufacturing wood or gum chemicals, such as naval stores, natural tanning materials, charcoal briquettes, and charcoal (except activated).

Cross-References. Establishments primarily engaged in—

- Manufacturing activated charcoal—are classified in U.S. Industry 325998, All Other Miscellaneous Chemical Product and Preparation Manufacturing; and

- Manufacturing fuel briquettes from refined petroleum—are classified in U.S. Industry 324199, All Other Petroleum and Coal Products Manufacturing.

US—United States industry only. CAN—United States and Canadian industries are comparable. When neither US nor CAN appears, Canadian, Mexican, and United States industries are comparable.

325192 Cyclic Crude and Intermediate Manufacturing[US]

This U.S. industry comprises establishments primarily engaged in (1) distilling coal tars and/ or (2) manufacturing cyclic crudes or, cyclic intermediates (i.e., hydrocarbons, except aromatic petrochemicals) from refined petroleum or natural gas.

Cross-References. Establishments primarily engaged in—

- Manufacturing cyclic chemicals (except aromatic and intermediates)—are classified in U.S. Industry 325199, All Other Basic Organic Chemical Manufacturing;

- Manufacturing aromatic petrochemicals from refined petroleum or natural gas—are classified in Industry 325110, Petrochemical Manufacturing;

- Manufacturing aromatic petrochemicals by refining crude petroleum—are classified in Industry 324110, Petroleum Refineries;

- Distilling wood products—are classified in U.S. Industry 325191, Gum and Wood Chemical Manufacturing;

- Manufacturing coal tar crudes in steel mills with coke ovens—are classified in U.S. Industry 331111, Iron and Steel Mills; and

- Manufacturing coal tar crudes in coke oven establishments and fuel briquettes from refined petroleum—are classified in U.S. Industry 324199, All Other Petroleum and Coal Products Manufacturing.

325193 Ethyl Alcohol Manufacturing[US]

This U.S. industry comprises establishments primarily engaged in manufacturing nonpotable ethyl alcohol.

Cross-References. Establishments primarily engaged in—

- Distilling liquors (except brandy)—are classified in Industry 312140, Distilleries; and

- Manufacturing brandies—are classified in Industry 312130, Wineries.

325199 All Other Basic Organic Chemical Manufacturing[US]

This U.S. industry comprises establishments primarily engaged in manufacturing basic organic chemical products (except aromatic petrochemicals, industrial gases, synthetic organic dyes and pigments, gum and wood chemicals, cyclic crudes and intermediates, and ethyl alcohol).

US—United States industry only. CAN—United States and Canadian industries are comparable. When neither US nor CAN appears, Canadian, Mexican, and United States industries are comparable.

Illustrative Examples:

Calcium organic compounds, not specified elsewhere by process, manufacturing

Carbon organic compounds, not specified elsewhere by process, manufacturing

Enzyme proteins (i.e., basic synthetic chemicals) (except pharmaceutical use) manufacturing

Fatty acids (e.g., margaric, oleic, stearic) manufacturing

Organo-inorganic compound manufacturing

Plasticizers (i.e., basic synthetic chemical) manufacturing

Silicone (except resins) manufacturing

Synthetic sweeteners (i.e., sweetening agents) manufacturing

Cross-References. Establishments primarily engaged in—

- Manufacturing aromatic petrochemicals from refined petroleum or natural gas—are classified in Industry 325110, Petrochemical Manufacturing;

- Manufacturing aromatic petrochemicals by refining crude petroleum—are classified in Industry 324110, Petroleum Refineries;

- Manufacturing organic industrial gases—are classified in Industry 325120, Industrial Gas Manufacturing;

- Manufacturing synthetic organic dyes and pigments—are classified in U.S. Industry 325132, Synthetic Organic Dye and Pigment Manufacturing;

- Manufacturing ethyl alcohol—are classified in U.S. Industry 325193, Ethyl Alcohol Manufacturing;

- Manufacturing organic insecticidal, herbicidal, fungicidal, and pesticidal preparations—are classified in Industry 325320, Pesticide and Other Agriculture Chemical Manufacturing;

- Manufacturing elastomers—are classified in Industry 325210, Resin and Synthetic Rubber Manufacturing;

- Manufacturing urea—are classified in U.S. Industry 325311, Nitrogenous Fertilizer Manufacturing;

- Manufacturing natural glycerin—are classified in U.S. Industry 325611, Soap and Other Detergent Manufacturing; and

- Manufacturing natural food colorings—are classified in U.S. Industry 311942, Spice and Extract Manufacturing.

3252 Resin, Synthetic Rubber, and Artificial Synthetic Fibers and Filaments Manufacturing

32521 Resin and Synthetic Rubber Manufacturing

This industry comprises establishments primarily engaged in one or more of the following: (1) manufacturing synthetic resins, plastics materials, and nonvulcanizable elastomers and mixing and

US—United States industry only. CAN—United States and Canadian industries are comparable. When neither US nor CAN appears, Canadian, Mexican, and United States industries are comparable.

blending resins on a custom basis; (2) manufacturing noncustomized synthetic resins; and (3) manufacturing synthetic rubber.

Cross-References. Establishments primarily engaged in—

- Manufacturing plastics resins and converting resins into plastics products—are classified in Industry Group 3261, Plastics Product Manufacturing;

- Processing natural, synthetic, or reclaimed rubber into intermediate or final products—are classified in Industry Group 3262, Rubber Product Manufacturing;

- Custom compounding resins made elsewhere—are classified in Industry 32599, All Other Chemical Product and Preparation Manufacturing; and

- Manufacturing resin adhesives—are classified in Industry 32552, Adhesive Manufacturing.

325211 Plastics Material and Resin Manufacturing[US]

This U.S. industry comprises establishments primarily engaged in (1) manufacturing resins, plastics materials, and nonvulcanizable thermoplastic elastomers and mixing and blending resins on a custom basis and/or (2) manufacturing noncustomized synthetic resins.

Cross-References. Establishments primarily engaged in—

- Manufacturing plastics resins and converting the resins into plastics products—are classified in 3261, Plastics Product Manufacturing;

- Custom compounding resins made elsewhere—are classified in U.S. Industry 325991, Custom Compounding of Purchased Resin; and

- Manufacturing plastics adhesives—are classified in Industry 325520, Adhesive Manufacturing.

325212 Synthetic Rubber Manufacturing[US]

This U.S. industry consists of establishments primarily engaged in manufacturing synthetic rubber.

Cross-References. Establishments primarily engaged in—

- Processing natural, synthetic, or reclaimed rubber into intermediate or final products (except adhesives)—are classified in Industry Group 3262, Rubber Product Manufacturing; and

- Manufacturing rubber adhesives—are classified Industry 325520, Adhesive Manufacturing.

32522 Artificial and Synthetic Fibers and Filaments Manufacturing[US]

This industry comprises establishments primarily engaged in (1) manufacturing cellulosic (i.e., rayon and acetate) and noncellulosic (i.e., nylon, polyolefin, and polyester) fibers and filaments in

---

US—United States industry only. CAN—United States and Canadian industries are comparable. When neither US nor CAN appears, Canadian, Mexican, and United States industries are comparable.

the form of monofilament, filament yarn, staple, or tow or (2) manufacturing and texturing cellulosic and noncellulosic fibers and filaments.

Cross-References. Establishments primarily engaged in—

- Texturizing cellulosic and noncellulosic fiber and filament made elsewhere—are classified in Industry 31311, Fiber, Yarn, and Thread Mills; and

- Manufacturing textile glass fibers—are classified in Industry 32721, Glass and Glass Product Manufacturing.

325221 Cellulosic Organic Fiber Manufacturing[US]

This U.S. industry comprises establishments primarily engaged in (1) manufacturing cellulosic (i.e., rayon and acetate) fibers and filaments in the form of monofilament, filament yarn, staple, or tow or (2) manufacturing and texturizing cellulosic fibers and filaments.

Cross-References. Establishments primarily engaged in—

- Texturizing cellulosic fibers and filaments made elsewhere—are classified in U.S. Industry 313112, Yarn Texturing, Throwing, and Twisting Mills; and

- Manufacturing noncellulosic fibers and filaments—are classified in U.S. Industry 325222, Noncellulosic Organic Fiber Manufacturing.

325222 Noncellulosic Organic Fiber Manufacturing[US]

This U.S. industry consists of establishments primarily engaged in (1) manufacturing noncellulosic (i.e., nylon, polyolefin, and polyester) fibers and filaments in the form of monofilament, filament yarn, staple, or tow or (2) manufacturing and texturizing noncellulosic fibers and filaments.

Cross-References. Establishments primarily engaged in—

- Texturizing noncellulosic fibers—are classified in U.S. Industry 313112, Yarn Texturing, Throwing, and Twisting Mills;

- Manufacturing cellulose fibers—are classified in U.S. Industry 325221, Cellulosic Organic Fiber Manufacturing; and

- Manufacturing textile glass fibers—are classified in U.S. Industry 327212, Other Pressed and Blown Glass and Glassware Manufacturing.

3253 Pesticide, Fertilizer, and Other Agricultural Chemical Manufacturing

32531 Fertilizer Manufacturing

This industry comprises establishments primarily engaged in one or more of the following: (1) manufacturing nitrogenous or phosphatic fertilizer materials; (2) manufacturing fertilizers from

---

US—United States industry only. CAN—United States and Canadian industries are comparable. When neither US nor CAN appears, Canadian, Mexican, and United States industries are comparable.

sewage or animal waste; (3) manufacturing nitrogenous or phosphatic materials and mixing with other ingredients into fertilizers; and (4) mixing ingredients made elsewhere into fertilizers.

325311 Nitrogenous Fertilizer Manufacturing[US]

This U.S. industry comprises establishments primarily engaged in one or more of the following: (1) manufacturing nitrogenous fertilizer materials and mixing ingredients into fertilizers; (2) manufacturing fertilizers from sewage or animal waste; and (3) manufacturing nitrogenous materials and mixing them into fertilizers.

Cross-References.

Establishments primarily engaged in mixing ingredients made elsewhere into nitrogenous fertilizers are classified in U.S. Industry 325314, Fertilizer (Mixing Only) Manufacturing.

325312 Phosphatic Fertilizer Manufacturing[US]

This U.S. industry comprises establishments primarily engaged in (1) manufacturing phosphatic fertilizer materials or (2) manufacturing phosphatic materials and mixing them into fertilizers.

Cross-References.

Establishments primarily engaged in mixing ingredients made elsewhere into phosphatic fertilizers are classified in U.S. Industry 325314, Fertilizer (Mixing Only) Manufacturing.

325314 Fertilizer (Mixing Only) Manufacturing[CAN]

This U.S. industry comprises establishments primarily engaged in mixing ingredients made elsewhere into fertilizers.

Cross-References. Establishments primarily engaged in—

- Manufacturing nitrogenous fertilizer materials or fertilizer materials from sewage or animal waste and mixing these ingredients into nitrogenous fertilizers—are classified in U.S. Industry 325311, Nitrogenous Fertilizer Manufacturing; and

- Manufacturing phosphatic fertilizer materials and mixing ingredients into fertilizers—are classified in U.S. Industry 325312, Phosphatic Fertilizer Manufacturing.

32532 Pesticide and Other Agricultural Chemical Manufacturing
See industry description for 325320 below.

325320 Pesticide and Other Agricultural Chemical Manufacturing

This industry comprises establishments primarily engaged in the formulation and preparation of agricultural and household pest control chemicals (except fertilizers).

US—United States industry only. CAN—United States and Canadian industries are comparable. When neither US nor CAN appears, Canadian, Mexican, and United States industries are comparable.

Cross-References. Establishments primarily engaged in—

- Manufacturing basic chemicals requiring further processing before use as agriculture chemicals—are classified in Industry Group 3251, Basic Chemical Manufacturing;

- Manufacturing fertilizers—are classified in Industry 325310, Fertilizer Manufacturing; and

- Manufacturing agricultural lime products—are classified in Industry 327410, Lime Manufacturing.

3254 Pharmaceutical and Medicine Manufacturing

32541 Pharmaceutical and Medicine Manufacturing

This industry comprises establishments primarily engaged in one or more of the following: (1) manufacturing biological and medicinal products; (2) processing (i.e., grading, grinding, and milling) botanical drugs and herbs; (3) isolating active medicinal principals from botanical drugs and herbs; and (4) manufacturing pharmaceutical products intended for internal and external consumption in such forms as ampoules, tablets, capsules, vials, ointments, powders, solutions, and suspensions.

325411 Medicinal and Botanical Manufacturing[US]

This U.S. industry comprises establishments primarily engaged in (1) manufacturing uncompounded medicinal chemicals and their derivatives (i.e., generally for use by pharmaceutical preparation manufacturers) and/or (2) grading, grinding, and milling uncompounded botanicals.

Cross-References. Establishments primarily engaged in—

- Manufacturing packaged compounded medicinals and botanicals—are classified in U.S. Industry 325412, Pharmaceutical Preparation Manufacturing; and

- Manufacturing vaccines, toxoids, blood fractions, and culture media of plant or animal origin (except for diagnostic use)—are classified in U.S. Industry 325414, Biological Product (except Diagnostic) Manufacturing.

325412 Pharmaceutical Preparation Manufacturing[US]

This U.S. industry comprises establishments primarily engaged in manufacturing in-vivo diagnostic substances and pharmaceutical preparations (except biological) intended for internal and external consumption in dose forms, such as ampoules, tablets, capsules, vials, ointments, powders, solutions, and suspensions.

Cross-References. Establishments primarily engaged in—

- Manufacturing uncompounded medicinal chemicals and their derivatives—are classified in U.S. Industry 325411, Medicinal and Botanical Manufacturing;

- Manufacturing in-vitro diagnostic substances—are classified in U.S. Industry 325413; In-Vitro Diagnostic Substance Manufacturing; and

---

US—United States industry only. CAN—United States and Canadian industries are comparable. When neither US nor CAN appears, Canadian, Mexican, and United States industries are comparable.

http://www.ntis.gov/naics

- Manufacturing vaccines, toxoids, blood fractions, and culture media of plant or animal origin (except for diagnostic use)—are classified in U.S. Industry 325414, Biological Product (except Diagnostic) Manufacturing.

325413 In-Vitro Diagnostic Substance Manufacturing[US]

This U.S. industry comprises establishments primarily engaged in manufacturing in-vitro (i.e., not taken internally) diagnostic substances, such as chemical, biological, or radioactive substances. The substances are used for diagnostic tests that are performed in test tubes, petri dishes, machines, and other diagnostic test-type devices.

Cross-References.

Establishments primarily engaged in manufacturing in-vivo diagnostic substances are classified in U.S. Industry 325412, Pharmaceutical Preparation Manufacturing.

325414 Biological Product (except Diagnostic) Manufacturing[US]

This U.S. industry comprises establishments primarily engaged in manufacturing vaccines, toxoids, blood fractions, and culture media of plant or animal origin (except diagnostic).

Cross-References. Establishments primarily engaged in—

- Manufacturing in-vitro diagnostic substances—are classified in U.S. Industry 325413, In-Vitro Diagnostic Substance Manufacturing; and

- Manufacturing pharmaceutical preparations, (except biological and in-vivo diagnostic substances)—are classified in U.S. Industry 325412, Pharmaceutical Preparation Manufacturing.

3255 Paint, Coating, and Adhesive Manufacturing

32551 Paint and Coating Manufacturing
See industry description for 325510 below.

325510 Paint and Coating Manufacturing

This industry comprises establishments primarily engaged in (1) mixing pigments, solvents, and binders into paints and other coatings, such as stains, varnishes, lacquers, enamels, shellacs, and water repellant coatings for concrete and masonry, and/or (2) manufacturing allied paint products, such as putties, paint and varnish removers, paint brush cleaners, and frit.

Cross-References. Establishments primarily engaged in—

- Manufacturing creosote—are classified in Industry 32519, Other Basic Organic Chemical Manufacturing;

US—United States industry only. CAN—United States and Canadian industries are comparable. When neither US nor CAN appears, Canadian, Mexican, and United States industries are comparable.

- Manufacturing caulking compounds and sealants—are classified in Industry 325520, Adhesive Manufacturing;

- Manufacturing artists' paints—are classified in U.S. Industry 339942, Lead Pencil and Art Good Manufacturing; and

- Manufacturing turpentine—are classified in U.S. Industry 325191, Gum and Wood Chemical Manufacturing.

32552 Adhesive Manufacturing

See industry description for 325520 below.

325520 Adhesive Manufacturing

This industry comprises establishments primarily engaged in manufacturing adhesives, glues, and caulking compounds.

Cross-References. Establishments primarily engaged in—

- Manufacturing asphalt and tar roofing cements from purchased asphaltic materials—are classified in Industry 324122, Asphalt Shingle and Coating Materials Manufacturing; and

- Manufacturing gypsum based caulking compounds—are classified in Industry 327420, Gypsum and Gypsum Product Manufacturing.

3256 Soap, Cleaning Compound, and Toilet Preparation Manufacturing

32561 Soap and Cleaning Compound Manufacturing

This industry comprises establishments primarily engaged in manufacturing and packaging soap and other cleaning compounds, surface active agents, and textile and leather finishing agents used to reduce tension or speed the drying process.

Cross-References. Establishments primarily engaged in—

- Manufacturing synthetic glycerin—are classified in Industry 32519, Other Basic Organic Chemical Manufacturing;

- Manufacturing industrial bleaches—are classified in Industry 32518 Other Basic Inorganic Chemical Manufacturing; and

- Manufacturing shampoos and shaving preparations—are classified in Industry 32562, Toilet Preparation Manufacturing.

325611 Soap and Other Detergent Manufacturing[US]

This U.S. industry comprises establishments primarily engaged in manufacturing and packaging soaps and other detergents, such as laundry detergents; dishwashing detergents; toothpaste gels, and tooth powders; and natural glycerin.

US—United States industry only. CAN—United States and Canadian industries are comparable. When neither US nor CAN appears, Canadian, Mexican, and United States industries are comparable.

Cross-References. Establishments primarily engaged in—

- Manufacturing synthetic glycerin—are classified in U.S. Industry 325199, All Other Basic Organic Chemical Manufacturing; and

- Manufacturing shampoos and shaving preparations—are classified in Industry 325620, Toilet Preparation Manufacturing.

325612 Polish and Other Sanitation Good Manufacturing[US]

This U.S. industry comprises establishments primarily engaged in manufacturing and packaging polishes and specialty cleaning preparations.

Cross-References.

Establishments primarily engaged in manufacturing chlorine dioxide (i.e., industrial bleaching agent) are classified in U.S. Industry 325188, All Other Basic Inorganic Chemical Manufacturing.

325613 Surface Active Agent Manufacturing[US]

This U.S. industry comprises establishments primarily engaged in (1) manufacturing bulk surface active agents for use as wetting agents, emulsifiers, and penetrants, and/or (2) manufacturing textiles and leather finishing agents used to reduce tension or speed the drying process.

32562 Toilet Preparation Manufacturing
See industry description for 325620 below.

325620 Toilet Preparation Manufacturing

This industry comprises establishments primarily engaged in preparing, blending, compounding, and packaging toilet preparations, such as perfumes, shaving preparations, hair preparations, face creams, lotions (including sunscreens), and other cosmetic preparations.

Cross-References.

Establishments primarily engaged in manufacturing toothpaste are classified in U.S. Industry 325611, Soap and Other Detergent Manufacturing.

3259 Other Chemical Product and Preparation Manufacturing

This industry group comprises establishments primarily engaged in manufacturing chemical products (except basic chemicals; resins, synthetic rubber, cellulosic and noncellulosic fibers and filaments; pesticides, fertilizers, and other agricultural chemicals; pharmaceuticals and medicines; paints, coatings, and adhesives; soaps and cleaning compounds; and toilet preparations).

US—United States industry only. CAN—United States and Canadian industries are comparable. When neither US nor CAN appears, Canadian, Mexican, and United States industries are comparable.

32591 Printing Ink Manufacturing
See industry description for 325910 below.

325910 Printing Ink Manufacturing

This industry comprises establishments primarily engaged in manufacturing printing and inkjet inks and inkjet cartridges.

Cross-References. Establishments primarily engaged in—

- Recycling inkjet cartridges—are classified in U.S. Industry 811212, Computer and Office Machine Repair and Maintenance;

- Manufacturing writing, drawing, and stamping ink—are classified in U.S. Industry 325998, All Other Miscellaneous Chemical Product and Preparation Manufacturing;

- Manufacturing toners and toner cartridges for photocopiers, fax machines, computer printers and similar office machines—are classified in U.S. Industry 325992, Photographic Film, Paper, Plate, and Chemical Manufacturing; and

- Manufacturing inkjet cartridges—are classified in U.S. Industry 334119, Other Computer Peripheral Equipment Manufacturing.

32592 Explosives Manufacturing
See industry description for 325920 below.

325920 Explosives Manufacturing

This industry comprises establishments primarily engaged in manufacturing explosives.

Cross-References. Establishments primarily engaged in—

- Manufacturing ammunition, ammunition detonators, and percussion caps—are classified in U.S. Industry 332992, Small Arms Ammunition Manufacturing; and

- Manufacturing pyrotechnics—are classified in U.S. Industry 325998, All Other Miscellaneous Chemical Product and Preparation Manufacturing.

32599 All Other Chemical Product and Preparation Manufacturing

This industry comprises establishments primarily engaged in manufacturing chemical products (except basic chemicals, resins, and synthetic rubber; cellulosic and noncellulosic fibers and filaments; pesticides, fertilizers, and other agricultural chemicals; pharmaceuticals and medicines; paints, coatings, and adhesives; and soaps, cleaning compounds, and toilet preparations; printing inks; and explosives).

US—United States industry only. CAN—United States and Canadian industries are comparable. When neither US nor CAN appears, Canadian, Mexican, and United States industries are comparable.

Illustrative Examples:

Activated carbon and charcoal manufacturing
Antifreeze preparations manufacturing
Custom compounding (i.e., blending and
  mixing) of purchased plastics resins
Industrial salt manufacturing
Matches and matchbook manufacturing
Photographic chemicals manufacturing
Pyrotechnics (e.g., flares, flashlight bombs,
  signals) manufacturing

Sugar substitutes (i.e., synthetic sweeteners
  blended with other ingredients) made from
  purchased synthetic sweetners
Swimming pool chemical preparations
  manufacturing
Writing inks and fluids manufacturing

Cross-References. Establishments primarily engaged in—

- Manufacturing basic chemicals—are classified in Industry Group 3251, Basic Chemical Manufacturing;

- Manufacturing resins, synthetic rubber, and artificial synthetic fibers and filaments—are classified in Industry Group 3252, Resin, Synthetic Rubber, and Artificial and Synthetic Fibers and Filaments Manufacturing;

- Manufacturing pesticides, fertilizers, and other agricultural chemicals—are classified in Industry Group 3253, Pesticide, Fertilizer, and Other Agriculture Chemical Manufacturing;

- Manufacturing pharmaceuticals and medicine including medicinal vegetable gelatin (i.e., agar-agar)—are classified in Industry Group 3254, Pharmaceutical and Medicine Manufacturing;

- Manufacturing paints, coatings, and adhesives—are classified in Industry Group 3255, Paint, Coating, and Adhesive Manufacturing;

- Manufacturing soaps and cleaning compounds—are classified in Industry Group 3256, Soap, Cleaning Compound, and Toilet Preparation Manufacturing;

- Manufacturing printing and inkjet inks—are classified in Industry 32591, Printing Ink Manufacturing;

- Manufacturing explosives—are classified in Industry 32592, Explosives Manufacturing;

- Manufacturing photographic toner cartridges—are classified in Industry 33331, Commercial and Service Industry Machinery Manufacturing;

- Manufacturing computer printer toner cartridges—are classified in Industry 33411, Computer and Peripheral Equipment Manufacturing;

- Manufacturing facsimile toner cartridges—are classified in Industry 33429, Other Communications Equipment Manufacturing;

- Manufacturing photographic paper stock (i.e., unsensitized) and paper mats, mounts, easels, and folders for photographic use—are classified in Subsector 322, Paper Manufacturing;

- Manufacturing dessert gelatins—are classified in Industry 31199, All Other Miscellaneous Food Manufacturing; and

---

US—United States industry only. CAN—United States and Canadian industries are comparable.
When neither US nor CAN appears, Canadian, Mexican, and United States industries are comparable.

- Manufacturing medicinal gelatins—are classified in Industry 32541, Pharmaceutical and Medicine Manufacturing.

325991 Custom Compounding of Purchased Resins[CAN]

This industry comprises establishments primarily engaged in (1) custom mixing and blending plastics resins made elsewhere or (2) reformulating plastics resins from recycled plastics products.

Cross-References.

Establishments primarily engaged in manufacturing synthetic resins and custom mixing and blending resins are classified in U.S. Industry 325211, Plastics Material and Resin Manufacturing.

325992 Photographic Film, Paper, Plate, and Chemical Manufacturing[US]

This U.S. industry comprises establishments primarily engaged in manufacturing sensitized film, sensitized paper, sensitized cloth, sensitized plates, toners (i.e., for photocopiers, laser printers, and similar electrostatic printing devices), toner cartridges, and photographic chemicals.

Cross-References.

Establishments primarily engaged in manufacturing photographic paper stock (i.e., unsensitized) and paper mats, mounts, easels, and folders for photographic use—are classified in Subsector 322, Paper Manufacturing.

325998 All Other Miscellaneous Chemical Product and Preparation Manufacturing[US]

This U.S. industry comprises establishments primarily engaged in manufacturing chemical products (except basic chemicals, resins, synthetic rubber; cellulosic and noncellulosic fiber and filaments; pesticides, fertilizers, and other agricultural chemicals; pharmaceuticals and medicines; paints, coatings and adhesives; soap, cleaning compounds, and toilet preparations; printing inks; explosives; custom compounding of purchased resins; and photographic films, papers, plates, and chemicals).

Illustrative Examples:

Activated carbon and charcoal manufacturing
Antifreeze preparations manufacturing
Industrial salt manufacturing
Lighter fluids (e.g., charcoal, cigarette)
Matches and matchbook manufacturing
Pyrotechnics (e.g., flares, flashlight bombs, signals) manufacturing
Sugar substitutes (i.e., synthetic sweetners blended with other ingredients) made from purchased synthetic sweetners
Swimming pool chemical preparations manufacturing
Writing inks manufacturing

US—United States industry only. CAN—United States and Canadian industries are comparable. When neither US nor CAN appears, Canadian, Mexican, and United States industries are comparable.

Cross-References. Establishments primarily engaged in—

- Manufacturing basic chemicals—are classified in Industry Group 3251, Basic Chemical Manufacturing;

- Manufacturing resins, synthetic rubber, and artificial synthetic fibers and filaments—are classified in Industry Group 3252, Resin, Synthetic Rubber, and Artificial and Synthetic Fibers and Filaments Manufacturing;

- Manufacturing pesticides, fertilizers, and other agricultural chemicals—are classified in Industry Group 3253, Pesticide, Fertilizer, and Other Agriculture Chemical Manufacturing;

- Manufacturing pharmaceuticals and medicines including medicinal vegetable gelatin (i.e., agar-agar))—are classified in Industry Group 3254, Pharmaceutical and Medicine Manufacturing;

- Manufacturing paints, coatings, and adhesives—are classified in Industry Group 3255, Paint, Coating, and Adhesive Manufacturing;

- Manufacturing soaps and cleaning compounds—are classified in Industry Group 3256, Soap, Cleaning Compound, and Toilet Preparation Manufacturing;

- Manufacturing printing and inkjet inks—are classified in Industry 325910, Printing Ink Manufacturing;

- Manufacturing explosives—are classified in Industry 325920, Explosives Manufacturing;

- Custom compounding purchased plastics resins—are classified in U.S. Industry 325991, Custom Compounding of Purchased Resin;

- Manufacturing photographic films, papers, plates, and chemicals—are classified in U.S. Industry 325992, Photographic Film, Paper, Plate, and Chemical Manufacturing; and

- Manufacturing dessert gelatin—are classified in U.S. Industry 311999, All Other Miscellaneous Food Manufacturing.

326 Plastics and Rubber Products Manufacturing

Industries in the Plastics and Rubber Products Manufacturing subsector make goods by processing plastics materials and raw rubber. The core technology employed by establishments in this subsector is that of plastics or rubber product production. Plastics and rubber are combined in the same subsector because plastics are increasingly being used as a substitute for rubber; however the subsector is generally restricted to the production of products made of just one material, either solely plastics or rubber.

Many manufacturing activities use plastics or rubber, for example the manufacture of footwear, or furniture. Typically, the production process of these products involves more than one material. In these cases, technologies that allow disparate materials to be formed and combined are of central importance in describing the manufacturing activity. In NAICS, such activities (the footwear and furniture manufacturing) are not classified in the Plastics and Rubber Products Manufacturing subsector because the core technologies for these activities are diverse and involve multiple materials.

US—United States industry only. CAN—United States and Canadian industries are comparable. When neither US nor CAN appears, Canadian, Mexican, and United States industries are comparable.

Within the Plastics and Rubber Products Manufacturing subsector, a distinction is made between plastics and rubber products at the industry group level, although it is not a rigid distinction, as can be seen from the definition of Industry 32622, Rubber and Plastics Hose and Belting Manufacturing. As materials technology progresses, plastics are increasingly being used as a substitute for rubber; and eventually, the distinction may disappear as a basis for establishment classification.

In keeping with the core technology focus of plastics, lamination of plastics film to plastics film as well as the production of bags from plastics only is classified in this subsector. Lamination and bag production involving plastics and materials other than plastics are classified in the NAICS Subsector 322, Paper Manufacturing.

3261 Plastics Product Manufacturing

This industry group comprises establishments primarily engaged in processing new or spent (i.e., recycled) plastics resins into intermediate or final products, using such processes as compression molding; extrusion molding; injection molding; blow molding; and casting. Within most of these industries, the production process is such that a wide variety of products can be made.

32611 Unsupported Plastics Film, Sheet, and Bag Manufacturing

This industry comprises establishments primarily engaged in (1) converting plastics resins into unsupported plastics film and sheet and/or (2) forming, coating or laminating plastics film and sheet into plastics bags.

Cross-References. Establishments primarily engaged in—

- Laminating plastics sheet (except for packaging)—are classified in Industry 32613, Laminated Plastics Plate, Sheet, and Shapes Manufacturing;

- Manufacturing plastics blister and bubble packaging—are classified in Industry 32619, Other Plastics Product Manufacturing; and

- Coating or laminating combinations of plastics, foils and paper (except plastics film to plastics film) into film, sheet or bags—are classified in Industry 32222, Paper Bag and Coated and Treated Paper Manufacturing.

326111 Unsupported Plastics Bag Manufacturing[CAN]

This U.S. industry comprises establishments primarily engaged in (1) converting plastics resins into plastics bags or (2) forming, coating or laminating plastics film and sheet into single wall or multiwall plastics bags. Establishments in this industry may print on the bags they manufacture.

Cross-References. Establishments primarily engaged in—

- Manufacturing laminated or coated combinations of plastics, foils and paper (except plastics film to plastics film) materials into single wall bags—are classified in U.S. Industry 322223, Plastics, Foil, and Coated Paper Bag Manufacturing; and

---

US—United States industry only. CAN—United States and Canadian industries are comparable. When neither US nor CAN appears, Canadian, Mexican, and United States industries are comparable.

- Manufacturing laminated or coated combinations of plastics, foils and paper (except plastics film to plastics film) into multiwalled bags—are classified in U.S. Industry 322224, Uncoated Paper and Multiwall Bag Manufacturing.

326112 Unsupported Plastics Packaging Film and Sheet Manufacturing[US]

This U.S. industry comprises establishments primarily engaged in converting plastics resins into plastics packaging (flexible) film and packaging sheet.

Cross-References. Establishments primarily engaged in—

- Converting plastics resins into plastics film and unlaminated sheet (except packaging)—are classified in U.S. Industry 326113, Unsupported Plastics Film and Sheet (except Packaging) Manufacturing;

- Laminating or coating packaging combinations of plastics, foils and paper (except plastics film to plastics film) film and sheet—are classified in U.S. Industry 322221, Coated and Laminated Packaging Paper and Plastics Film Manufacturing;

- Laminating or coating combinations of plastics, foils, and paper (except plastics film to plastics film) nonpackaging film and sheet—are classified in U.S. Industry 322222, Coated and Laminated Paper Manufacturing;

- Laminating plastics sheet (except for packaging)—are classified in Industry 326130, Laminated Plastics Plate, Sheet, and Shapes Manufacturing; and

- Manufacturing plastics bags—are classified in U.S. Industry 326111, Unsupported Plastics Bag Manufacturing.

326113 Unsupported Plastics Film and Sheet (except Packaging) Manufacturing[US]

This U.S. industry comprises establishments primarily engaged in converting plastics resins into plastics film and unlaminated sheet (except packaging).

Cross-References. Establishments primarily engaged in—

- Converting plastics resins into plastics packaging film and unlaminated packaging sheet—are classified in U.S. Industry 326112, Unsupported Plastics Packaging Film and Sheet Manufacturing;

- Laminating plastics sheet (except for packaging)—are classified in Industry 326130, Laminated Plastics Plate, Sheet, and Shapes Manufacturing;

- Laminating or coating a combination of plastics, foils, and paper (except plastics film to plastics film) nonpackaging film and sheet—are classified in U.S. Industry 322222, Coated and Laminated Paper Manufacturing; and

- Manufacturing plastics bags—are classified in U.S. Industry 326111, Unsupported Plastics Bag Manufacturing.

US—United States industry only. CAN—United States and Canadian industries are comparable. When neither US nor CAN appears, Canadian, Mexican, and United States industries are comparable.

32612 Plastics Pipe, Pipe Fitting, and Unsupported Profile Shape Manufacturing

This industry comprises establishments primarily engaged in manufacturing plastics pipes and pipe fittings, and plastics profile shapes such as rod, tube, and sausage casings.

Cross References. Establishments primarily engaged in—

- Manufacturing plastics hose—are classified in Industry 32622, Rubber and Plastics Hoses and Belting Manufacturing;

- Manufacturing noncurrent carrying plastics conduit—are classified in Industry 33593, Wiring Device Manufacturing;

- Manufacturing plastics plumbing fixtures—are classified in Industry 32619, Other Plastics Product Manufacturing; and

- Manufacturing plastics film, plastics unlaminated sheet, and plastics bags—are classified in Industry 32611, Unsupported Plastics Film, Sheet, and Bag Manufacturing.

326121 Unsupported Plastics Profile Shapes Manufacturing[CAN]

This U.S. industry comprises establishments primarily engaged in converting plastics resins into nonrigid plastics profile shapes (except film, sheet and bags), such as rod, tube, and sausage casings.

Cross-References. Establishments primarily engaged in—

- Manufacturing plastics film, plastics unlaminated sheet, and plastics bags—are classified in Industry 32611, Unsupported Plastics Film, Sheet, and Bag Manufacturing; and

- Manufacturing plastics hoses—are classified in Industry 326220, Rubber and Plastics Hoses and Belting Manufacturing.

326122 Plastics Pipe and Pipe Fitting Manufacturing[CAN]

This U.S. industry comprises establishments primarily engaged in converting plastics resins into rigid plastics pipes and pipe fittings.

Cross-References. Establishments primarily engaged in—

- Manufacturing plastics hose—are classified in Industry 326220, Rubber and Plastics Hoses and Belting Manufacturing;

- Manufacturing noncurrent-carrying plastics conduit—are classified in U.S. Industry 335932, Noncurrent-Carrying Wiring Device Manufacturing; and

- Manufacturing plastics plumbing fixtures—are classified in U.S. Industry 326191, Plastics Plumbing Fixture Manufacturing.

US—United States industry only. CAN—United States and Canadian industries are comparable. When neither US nor CAN appears, Canadian, Mexican, and United States industries are comparable.

32613 Laminated Plastics Plate, Sheet, and Shape Manufacturing
See industry description for 326130 below.

326130 Laminated Plastics Plate, Sheet, and Shape Manufacturing

This industry comprises establishments primarily engaged in laminating plastics profile shapes such as plate, sheet (except packaging), and rod. The lamination process generally involves bonding or impregnating profiles with plastics resins and compressing them under heat.

Cross-References. Establishments primarily engaged in—

- Manufacturing plastics film, plastics unlaminated sheet, and plastics bags—are classified in Industry 32611, Unsupported Plastics Film, Sheet, and Bag Manufacturing;

- Coating or laminating nonplastics film, sheet, or bags with plastics—are classified in Industry 32222, Paper Bag and Coated and Treated Paper Manufacturing; and

- Manufacturing plastics bags—are classified in U.S. Industry 326111, Unsupported Plastics Bag Manufacturing.

32614 Polystyrene Foam Product Manufacturing
See industry description for 326140 below.

326140 Polystyrene Foam Product Manufacturing

This industry comprises establishments primarily engaged in manufacturing polystyrene foam products.

Cross-References.

Establishments primarily engaged in manufacturing plastics foam products (except polystyrene) are classified in Industry 326150, Urethane and Other Foam Product (except Polystyrene) Manufacturing.

32615 Urethane and Other Foam Product (except Polystyrene) Manufacturing
See industry description for 326150 below.

326150 Urethane and Other Foam Product (except Polystyrene) Manufacturing

This industry comprises establishments primarily engaged in manufacturing plastics foam products (except polystyrene).

Cross-References.

Establishments primarily engaged in manufacturing polystyrene foam products are classified in Industry 326140, Polystyrene Foam Product Manufacturing.

US—United States industry only. CAN—United States and Canadian industries are comparable. When neither US nor CAN appears, Canadian, Mexican, and United States industries are comparable.

32616 Plastics Bottle Manufacturing

See industry description for 32616 below.

326160 Plastics Bottle Manufacturing

This industry comprises establishments primarily engaged in manufacturing plastics bottles.

Cross-References.

Establishments primarily engaged in manufacturing plastics containers (except bottles) are classified in U.S. Industry 326199, All Other Plastics Product Manufacturing.

32619 Other Plastics Product Manufacturing

This industry comprises establishments primarily engaged in manufacturing resilient floor covering and other plastics products (except film, sheet, bags, profile shapes, pipes, pipe fittings, laminates, foam products, and bottles).

Illustrative Examples:

Inflatable plastics boats manufacturing
Plastics bowls and bowl covers manufacturing
Plastics cups (except foam) manufacturing
Plastics dinnerware (except foam) manufacturing
Plastics gloves manufacturing
Plastics hardware manufacturing

Plastics or fiberglass plumbing fixtures (e.g., toilets, shower stalls, urinals) manufacturing
Plastics siding manufacturing
Plastics trash containers manufacturing
Resilient floor coverings (e.g., sheet, tiles) manufacturing

Cross-References. Establishments primarily engaged in—

- Manufacturing plastics film, plastics unlaminated sheet, and plastics bags—are classified in Industry 32611, Unsupported Plastics Film, Sheet, and Bag Manufacturing;

- Manufacturing plastics pipes, pipe fittings and plastics profile shapes (except films, sheet, bags) are classified in Industry 32612, Plastic Pipe, Pipe Fitting, and Unsupported Profile Shapes Manufacturing;

- Laminating plastics profile shapes, such as plate, sheet and rod,—are classified in Industry 32613, Laminated Plastics Plate, Sheets and Shapes Manufacturing;

- Manufacturing polystyrene foam products—are classified in Industry 32614, Polystyrene Foam Product Manufacturing;

- Manufacturing foam products (except polystyrene)—are classified in Industry 32615 Urethane and Other Foam Product (except Polystyrene) Manufacturing;

- Manufacturing plastics bottles—are classified in Industry 32616, Plastics Bottle Manufacturing;

US—United States industry only. CAN—United States and Canadian industries are comparable. When neither US nor CAN appears, Canadian, Mexican, and United States industries are comparable.

- Manufacturing plastics furniture parts—are classified in Industry 33721, Office Furniture (including Fixtures) Manufacturing;

- Assembling plastics components into plumbing fixture fittings, such as faucets,—are classified in Industry 33291, Metal Valve Manufacturing; and

- Manufacturing rubber floor mats and rubber treads—are classified in Industry 32629, Office Rubber Product Manufacturing.

326191 Plastics Plumbing Fixture Manufacturing[CAN]

This U.S. industry comprises establishments primarily engaged in manufacturing plastics or fiberglass plumbing fixtures. Examples of products made by these establishments are plastics or fiberglass bathtubs, hot tubs, portable toilets, and shower stalls.

Cross-References. Establishments primarily engaged in—

- Assembling plastics components into plumbing fixture fittings, such as faucets,—are classified in U.S. Industry 332913, Plumbing Fixture Fitting and Trim Manufacturing; and

- Manufacturing plastics pipe and pipe fittings—are classified in U.S. Industry 326122, Plastics Pipe and Pipe Fitting Manufacturing.

326192 Resilient Floor Covering Manufacturing[US]

This U.S. industry comprises establishments primarily engaged in manufacturing resilient floor coverings for permanent installation.

Cross-References.

Establishments primarily engaged in manufacturing rubber floor mats and rubber treads are classified in U.S. Industry 326299, All Other Rubber Product Manufacturing.

326199 All Other Plastics Product Manufacturing[US]

This U.S. industry comprises establishments primarily engaged in manufacturing plastics products (except film, sheet, bags, profile shapes, pipes, pipe fittings, laminates, foam products, bottles, plumbing fixtures, and resilient floor coverings).

Illustrative Examples:

Inflatable plastics boats manufacturing
Plastics air mattreses manufacturing
Plastics bowls and bowl covers manufactring
Plastics clothes hangers manufacturing
Plastics cups (except foam) manufacturing
Plastics dinnerware (except foam)
  manufacturing

Plastics gloves manufacturing
Plastics hardware manufacturing
Plastics siding manufacturing
Plastics trash containers manufacturing

US—United States industry only. CAN—United States and Canadian industries are comparable. When neither US nor CAN appears, Canadian, Mexican, and United States industries are comparable.

Cross-References. Establishments primarily engaged in—

- Manufacturing plastics film, plastics unlaminated sheet, and plastics bags—are classified in Industry 32611 Unsupported Plastics Film, Sheet, and Bag Manufacturing;

- Manufacturing plastics pipes, pipe fittings, and plastics profile shapes (except film, sheet, bags)—are classified in Industry 32612, Plastics Pipe, Pipe Fittings, and Unsupported Plastics Profile Shapes Manufacturing;

- Manufacturing plastic pipes and pipe fittings—are classified in U.S. Industry 326122, Plastics Pipe and Pipe Fitting Manufacturing;

- Laminating plastics profile shapes, such as plate, sheet, and rod,—are classified in Industry 326130, Laminated Plastics Plate, Sheet, and Shapes Manufacturing;

- Manufacturing polystyrene foam products—are classified in Industry 326140, Polystyrene Foam Product Manufacturing;

- Manufacturing foam (except polystyrene) products—are classified in Industry 326150, Urethane and Other Foam Product (except Polystyrene) Manufacturing;

- Manufacturing plastics bottles—are classified in Industry 326160, Plastics Bottle Manufacturing;

- Manufacturing plastics furniture parts and components—are classified in U.S. Industry 337215, Showcase, Partition, Shelving, and Locker Manufacturing;

- Manufacturing plastics plumbing fixtures—are classified in U.S. Industry 326191, Plastics Plumbing Fixture Manufacturing;

- Manufacturing resilient floor coverings—are classified in U.S. Industry 326192, Resilient Floor Covering Manufacturing; and

- Assembling plastics components into plumbing fixtures fittings such as faucets—are classified in U.S. Industry 332913, Plumbing Fixture Fitting and Trim Manufacturing.

3262 Rubber Product Manufacturing

This industry group comprises establishments primarily engaged in processing natural, and synthetic or reclaimed rubber materials into intermediate or final products using processes such as vulcanizing, cementing, molding, extruding, and lathe-cutting.

32621 Tire Manufacturing

This industry comprises establishments primarily engaged in manufacturing tires and inner tubes from natural and synthetic rubber and retreading or rebuilding tires.

Cross-References. Establishments primarily engaged in—

- Repairing tires, such as plugging,—are classified in Industry 81119, Other Automotive Repair and Maintenance; and

- Retailing tires—are classified in the Industry 44132, Tire Dealers.

US—United States industry only. CAN—United States and Canadian industries are comparable. When neither US nor CAN appears, Canadian, Mexican, and United States industries are comparable.

326211 Tire Manufacturing (except Retreading)[US]

This U.S. industry comprises establishments primarily engaged in manufacturing tires and inner tubes from natural and synthetic rubber.

Cross-References.

Establishments primarily engaged in retreading or rebuilding tires are classified in U.S. Industry 326212, Tire Retreading.

326212 Tire Retreading[US]

This U.S. industry comprises establishments primarily engaged in retreading, or rebuilding tires.

Cross-References. Establishments primarily engaged in—

- Repairing tires, such as pluggings—are classified in U.S. Industry 811198, All Other Automotive Repair and Maintenance;

- Retailing tires—are classified in Industry 441320, Tire Dealers; and

- Manufacturing tires and inner tubes from natural and synthetic rubber—are classified in U.S. Industry 326211, Tire Manufacturing (except Retreading).

32622 Rubber and Plastics Hoses and Belting Manufacturing
See industry description for 326220 below.

326220 Rubber and Plastics Hoses and Belting Manufacturing

This industry comprises establishments primarily engaged in manufacturing rubber hose and/or plastics (reinforced) hose and belting from natural and synthetic rubber and/or plastics resins. Establishments manufacturing garden hoses from purchased hose are included in this industry.

Cross-References. Establishments primarily engaged in—

- Manufacturing rubber tubing—are classified in U.S. Industry 326299, All Other Rubber Product Manufacturing;

- Manufacturing plastics tubing—are classified in U.S. Industry 326121, Unsupported Plastics Profile Shapes Manufacturing; and

- Manufacturing fluid power hose assemblies—are classified in U.S. Industry 332912, Fluid Power Valve and Hose Fitting Manufacturing.

32629 Other Rubber Product Manufacturing

This industry comprises establishments primarily engaged in manufacturing rubber products (except tires, hoses, and belting) from natural and synthetic rubber.

US—United States industry only. CAN—United States and Canadian industries are comparable. When neither US nor CAN appears, Canadian, Mexican, and United States industries are comparable.

Illustrative Examples:

Birth control devices (e.g., diaphragms, prophylactics) manufacturing

Latex foam rubber manufacturing

Mechanical rubber goods (i.e., molded, extruded, lathe-cut) manufacturing

Reclaiming rubber from waste and scrap

Rubber balloons manufacturing

Rubberbands manufacturing

Rubber floor mats (e.g., door, bath) manufacturing

Rubber hair care products (e.g., combs, curlers) manufacturing

Rubber tubing (except extruded, lathe-cut, molded) manufacturing

Cross-References. Establishments primarily engaged in—

- Manufacturing tires and inner tubes—are classified in Industry 32621, Tire Manufacturing;

- Manufacturing rubber hoses and belting—are classified in Industry 32622, Rubber and Plastics Hoses and Belting Manufacturing;

- Rubberizing fabric—are classified in Industry 31332, Fabric Coating Mills;

- Manufacturing rubber gaskets, packing and sealing devices—are classified in Industry 33999, All Other Miscellaneous Manufacturing;

- Manufacturing rubber gloves—are classified in Industry 33911, Medical Equipment and Supplies Manufacturing;

- Manufacturing rubber clothing accessories (e.g., bathing caps)—are classified in Industry 31599, Apparel Accessories and Other Apparel Manufacturing; and

- Manufacturing rubber toys—are classified in Industry 33993, Doll, Toy, and Game Manufacturing.

326291 Rubber Product Manufacturing for Mechanical Use[US]

This U.S. industry comprises establishments primarily engaged in molding, extruding or lathe-cutting rubber to manufacture rubber goods (except tubing) for mechanical applications. Products of this industry are generally parts for motor vehicles, machinery, and equipment.

Cross-References.

Establishments primarily engaged in manufacturing rubber tubing from natural and synthetic rubber and manufacturing rubber products for mechanical applications using a process other than molding, extruding or lathe-cutting are classified in U.S. Industry 326299, All Other Rubber Product Manufacturing.

326299 All Other Rubber Product Manufacturing[US]

This U.S. industry comprises establishments primarily engaged in manufacturing rubber products (except tires; hoses and belting; and molded, extruded, and lathe-cut rubber goods for mechanical applications) from natural and synthetic rubber.

US—United States industry only. CAN—United States and Canadian industries are comparable. When neither US nor CAN appears, Canadian, Mexican, and United States industries are comparable.

http://www.ntis.gov/naics

Illustrative Examples:

Birth control devices (i.e., diaphrams, prophylactics) manufacturing

Inflatable rubber life rafts manufacturing

Latex foam rubber manufacturing

Reclaiming rubber from waste and scrap

Rubber balloons manufacturing

Rubberbands manufacturing

Rubber floor mats (e.g., door, bath) manufacturing

Rubber hair care products (e.g., combs, curlers) manufacturing

Rubber tubing (except extruded, lathe-cut, molded) manufacturing

Cross-References. Establishments primarily engaged in—

- Manufacturing tires and inner tubes and tire rebuilding—are classified in Industry 32621, Tire Manufacturing;

- Manufacturing rubber hoses and belting—are classified in Industry 326220, Rubber and Plastics Hoses and Belting Manufacturing;

- Molding, extruding, and lathe-cutting rubber to manufacture rubber goods (except tubing) for mechanical applications—are classified in Industry 326291, Rubber Product Manufacturing for Mechanical Use;

- Rubberizing fabrics—are classified in Industry 313320, Fabric Coating Mills;

- Manufacturing rubber gaskets, packing and sealing devices—are classified in U.S. Industry 339991, Gasket, Packing, and Sealing Device Manufacturing;

- Manufacturing rubber toys—are classified in Industry 33993, Doll, Toy, and Game Manufacturing;

- Manufacturing rubber gloves—are classified in U.S. Industry 339113, Surgical Appliance and Supplies Manufacturing; and

- Manufacturing rubber clothing accessories (e.g., bathing caps)—are classified in U.S. Industry 315999, Other Apparel Accessories and Other Apparel Manufacturing.

327 Nonmetallic Mineral Product Manufacturing

The Nonmetallic Mineral Product Manufacturing subsector transforms mined or quarried nonmetallic minerals, such as sand, gravel, stone, clay, and refractory materials, into products for intermediate or final consumption. Processes used include grinding, mixing, cutting, shaping, and honing. Heat often is used in the process and chemicals are frequently mixed to change the composition, purity, and chemical properties for the intended product. For example, glass is produced by heating silica sand to the melting point (sometimes combined with cullet or recycled glass) and then drawn, floated, or blow molded to the desired shape or thickness. Refractory materials are heated and then formed into bricks or other shapes for use in industrial applications.

The Nonmetallic Mineral Product Manufacturing subsector includes establishments that manufacture products, such as bricks, refractories, ceramic products, and glass and glass products, such as plate glass and containers. Also included are cement and concrete products, lime, gypsum and other nonmetallic mineral products including abrasive products, ceramic plumbing fixtures, statuary,

---

US—United States industry only. CAN—United States and Canadian industries are comparable. When neither US nor CAN appears, Canadian, Mexican, and United States industries are comparable.

cut stone products, and mineral wool. The products are used in a wide range of activities from construction and heavy and light manufacturing to articles for personal use.

Mining, beneficiating, and manufacturing activities often occur in a single location. Separate receipts will be collected for these activities whenever possible. When receipts cannot be broken out between mining and manufacturing, establishments that mine or quarry nonmetallic minerals, beneficiate the nonmetallic minerals and further process the nonmetallic minerals into a more finished manufactured product are classified based on the primary activity of the establishment. A mine that manufactures a small amount of finished products will be classified in Sector 21, Mining. An establishment that mines whose primary output is a more-finished manufactured product will be classified in the Manufacturing Sector.

Excluded from the Nonmetallic Mineral Product Manufacturing subsector are establishments that primarily beneficiate mined nonmetallic minerals. Beneficiation is the process whereby the extracted material is reduced to particles that can be separated into mineral and waste, the former suitable for further processing or direct use. Beneficiation establishments are included in Sector 21, Mining.

3271 Clay Product and Refractory Manufacturing

32711 Pottery, Ceramics, and Plumbing Fixture Manufacturing

This industry comprises establishments primarily engaged in shaping, molding, glazing, and firing pottery, ceramics, and plumbing fixtures made entirely or partly of clay or other ceramic materials.

Cross-References. Establishments primarily engaged in—

- Manufacturing ferrite microwave devices and electronic components—are classified in Subsector 334, Computer and Electronic Product Manufacturing;

- Manufacturing enameled iron and steel plumbing fixtures—are classified in Industry 33299, All Other Fabricated Metal Product Manufacturing;

- Manufacturing metal bathroom accessories—are classified in Subsector 332, Fabricated Metal Product Manufacturing;

- Manufacturing plastic bathroom accessories, cultured marble, and other plastic plumbing fixtures—are classified in Industry 32619, Other Plastics Product Manufacturing; and

- Manufacturing clay building materials, such as ceramic tile, bricks, and clay roofing tiles, and refractories—are classified in Industry 32712, Clay Building Material and Refractories Manufacturing.

327111 Vitreous China Plumbing Fixture and China and Earthenware Bathroom Accessories Manufacturing[US]

This U.S. industry comprises establishments primarily engaged in manufacturing vitreous china plumbing fixtures and china and earthenware bathroom accessories, such as faucet handles, towel bars, and soap dishes.

US—United States industry only. CAN—United States and Canadian industries are comparable. When neither US nor CAN appears, Canadian, Mexican, and United States industries are comparable.

Cross-References. Establishments primarily engaged in—

- Manufacturing enameled iron and steel plumbing fixtures—are classified in U.S. Industry 332998, Enameled Iron and Metal Sanitary Ware Manufacturing;

- Manufacturing metal bathroom accessories—are classified in Subsector 332, Fabricated Metal Product Manufacturing;

- Manufacturing plastic bathroom accessories—are classified in U.S. Industry 326199, All Other Plastics Product Manufacturing;

- Manufacturing cultured marble and other plastic plumbing fixtures—are classified in U.S. Industry 326191, Plastics Plumbing Fixture Manufacturing; and

- Manufacturing china and earthenware products (except bathroom fixtures and accessories)— are classified in U.S. Industry 327112, Vitreous China, Fine Earthenware, and Other Pottery Product Manufacturing.

327112 Vitreous China, Fine Earthenware, and Other Pottery Product Manufacturing[US]

This U.S. industry comprises establishments primarily engaged in manufacturing table and kitchen articles, art and ornamental items, and similar vitreous china, fine earthenware, stoneware, coarse earthenware, and pottery products.

Illustrative Examples:

Chemical stoneware (i.e., pottery products) manufacturing
Clay and ceramic statuary manufacturing
Cooking ware (e.g., stoneware, coarse earthenware, pottery) manufacturing
Earthenware table and kitchen articles, coarse, manufacturing

Florists' articles, red earthenware, manufacturing
Vases, pottery (e.g., china, earthenware, stoneware), manufacturing

Cross-References. Establishments primarily engaged in—

- Manufacturing vitreous china plumbing fixtures—are classified in U.S. Industry 327111, Vitreous China Plumbing Fixture and China and Earthenware Bathroom Accessories Manufacturing;

- Manufacturing porcelain and ceramic electrical products, such as insulators,—are classified in U.S. Industry 327113, Porcelain Electrical Supply Manufacturing; and

- Manufacturing clay building materials, such as ceramic tile, bricks, and clay roofing tiles, and refractories,—are classified in Industry 32712, Clay Building Material and Refractories Manufacturing.

US—United States industry only. CAN—United States and Canadian industries are comparable. When neither US nor CAN appears, Canadian, Mexican, and United States industries are comparable.

327113 Porcelain Electrical Supply Manufacturing^{US}

This U.S. industry comprises establishments primarily engaged in manufacturing porcelain electrical insulators, molded porcelain parts for electrical devices, ferrite or ceramic magnets, and electronic and electrical supplies from nonmetallic minerals, such as clay and ceramic materials.

Cross-References.

Establishments primarily engaged in manufacturing ferrite microwave devices and electronic components are classified in Subsector 334, Computer and Electronic Product Manufacturing.

32712 Clay Building Material and Refractories Manufacturing

This industry comprises establishments primarily engaged in shaping, molding, baking, burning, or hardening clay refractories, nonclay refractories, ceramic tile, structural clay tile, brick, and other structural clay building materials.

Cross-References. Establishments primarily engaged in—

- Manufacturing glass blocks—are classified in Industry 32721, Glass and Glass Product Manufacturing;

- Manufacturing concrete brick and block—are classified in Industry 32733, Concrete Pipe, Brick, and Block Manufacturing; and

- Manufacturing resilient flooring—are classified in Industry 32619, Other Plastics Product Manufacturing.

327121 Brick and Structural Clay Tile Manufacturing^{US}

This U.S. industry comprises establishments primarily engaged in manufacturing brick and structural clay tiles.

Cross-References. Establishments primarily engaged in—

- Manufacturing clay fire brick (i.e., refractories)—are classified in U.S. Industry 327124, Clay Refractory Manufacturing;

- Manufacturing nonclay fire brick (i.e., refractories)—are classified in U.S. Industry 327125, Nonclay Refractory Manufacturing;

- Manufacturing glass brick—are classified in Industry 32721, Glass and Glass Product Manufacturing;

- Manufacturing concrete bricks—are classified in U.S. Industry 327331, Concrete Block and Brick Manufacturing; and

- Manufacturing adobe bricks or clay roofing tiles—are classified in U.S. Industry 327123, Other Structural Clay Product Manufacturing.

327122 Ceramic Wall and Floor Tile Manufacturing[US]

This U.S. industry comprises establishments primarily engaged in manufacturing ceramic wall and floor tiles.

Cross-References. Establishments primarily engaged in—

- Manufacturing structural clay tiles—are classified in U.S. Industry 327121, Brick and Structural Clay Tile Manufacturing;

- Manufacturing clay drain tiles—are classified in U.S. Industry 327123, Other Structural Clay Product Manufacturing; and

- Manufacturing resilient flooring and asphalt floor tiles—are classified in U.S. Industry 326192, Resilient Floor Covering Manufacturing.

327123 Other Structural Clay Product Manufacturing[US]

This U.S. industry comprises establishments primarily engaged in manufacturing clay sewer pipe, drain tile, flue lining tile, architectural terra-cotta, and other structural clay products.

Cross-References. Establishments primarily engaged in—

- Manufacturing bricks and structural clay tiles—are classified in U.S. Industry 327121, Brick and Structural Clay Tile Manufacturing;

- Manufacturing ceramic floor and wall tiles—are classified in U.S. Industry 327122, Ceramic Wall and Floor Tile Manufacturing;

- Manufacturing clay refractories—are classified in U.S. Industry 327124, Clay Refractory Manufacturing; and

- Manufacturing nonclay refractories—are classified in U.S. Industry 327125, Nonclay Refractory Manufacturing.

327124 Clay Refractory Manufacturing[US]

This U.S. industry comprises establishments primarily engaged in manufacturing clay refractory, mortar, brick, block, tile, and fabricated clay refractories, such as melting pots. A refractory is a material that will retain its shape and chemical identity when subjected to high temperatures and is used in applications that require extreme resistance to heat, such as furnace linings.

Cross-References.

Establishments primarily engaged in manufacturing nonclay refractories are classified in U.S. Industry 327125, Nonclay Refractory Manufacturing.

327125 Nonclay Refractory Manufacturing[US]

This U.S. industry comprises establishments primarily engaged in manufacturing nonclay refractory, mortar, brick, block, tile, and fabricated nonclay refractories such as graphite, magnesite,

---

US—United States industry only. CAN—United States and Canadian industries are comparable. When neither US nor CAN appears, Canadian, Mexican, and United States industries are comparable.

silica, or alumina crucibles. A refractory is a material that will retain its shape and chemical identity when subjected to high temperatures and is used in applications that require extreme resistance to heat, such as furnace linings.

Cross-References.

Establishments primarily engaged in manufacturing clay refractories are classified in U.S. Industry 327124, Clay Refractory Manufacturing.

3272 Glass and Glass Product Manufacturing

32721 Glass and Glass Product Manufacturing

This industry comprises establishments primarily engaged in manufacturing glass and/or glass products. Establishments in this industry may manufacture glass and/or glass products by melting silica sand or cullet, or purchasing glass.

Cross-References. Establishments primarily engaged in—

- Manufacturing glass wool (i.e., fiberglass) insulation products—are classified in Industry 32799, All Other Nonmetallic Mineral Product Manufacturing;

- Manufacturing optical lenses (except ophthalmic), such as magnifying, photographic, and projection lenses,—are classified in Industry 33331, Commercial and Service Industry Machinery Manufacturing;

- Grinding ophthalmic (i.e., eyeglass) lenses for the trade—are classified in Industry 33911, Medical Equipment and Supplies Manufacturing; and

- Manufacturing fiber optic cable from purchased fiber optic strand— are classified in Industry 33592, Communication and Energy Wire and Cable Manufacturing.

327211 Flat Glass Manufacturing[US]

This U.S. industry comprises establishments primarily engaged in (1) manufacturing flat glass by melting silica sand or cullet or (2) manufacturing both flat glass and laminated glass by melting silica sand or cullet.

Cross-References.

Establishments primarily engaged in manufacturing laminated glass from purchased flat glass are classified in U.S. Industry 327215, Glass Product Manufacturing Made of Purchased Glass.

327212 Other Pressed and Blown Glass and Glassware Manufacturing[US]

This U.S. industry comprises establishments primarily engaged in manufacturing glass by melting silica sand or cullet and making pressed, blown, or shaped glass or glassware (except glass packaging containers).

US—United States industry only. CAN—United States and Canadian industries are comparable. When neither US nor CAN appears, Canadian, Mexican, and United States industries are comparable.

Cross-References. Establishments primarily engaged in—

- Manufacturing flat glass—are classified in U.S. Industry 327211, Flat Glass Manufacturing;

- Manufacturing glass packaging containers in glassmaking operations—are classified in U.S. Industry 327213, Glass Container Manufacturing;

- Manufacturing glass wool (i.e., fiberglass) insulation—are classified in U.S. Industry 327993, Mineral Wool Manufacturing;

- Manufacturing glassware from purchased glass—are classified in U.S. Industry 327215, Glass Product Manufacturing Made of Purchased Glass; and

- Manufacturing fiber optic cable—are classified in U.S. Industry 335921, Fiber Optic Cable Manufacturing.

327213 Glass Container Manufacturing[US]

This U.S. industry comprises establishments primarily engaged in manufacturing glass packaging containers.

327215 Glass Product Manufacturing Made Of Purchased Glass[CAN]

This U.S. industry comprises establishments primarily engaged in remelting, pressing, blowing, or shaping purchased glass.

Cross-References. Establishments primarily engaged in—

- Manufacturing optical lenses (except ophthalmic), such as magnifying, photographic and projection lenses,—are classified in U.S. Industry 333314, Optical Instrument and Lens Manufacturing;

- Manufacturing ophthalmic (i.e., eyeglass) lenses—are classified in U.S. Industry 339115, Ophthalmic Goods Manufacturing; and

- Manufacturing fiber optic cable from purchased fiber optic strand—are classified in U.S. Industry 335921, Fiber Optic Cable Manufacturing.

3273 Cement and Concrete Product Manufacturing

32731 Cement Manufacturing
See industry description for 327310 below.

327310 Cement Manufacturing

This industry comprises establishments primarily engaged in manufacturing portland, natural, masonry, pozzalanic, and other hydraulic cements. Cement manufacturing establishments may calcine earths or mine, quarry, manufacture, or purchase lime.

US—United States industry only. CAN—United States and Canadian industries are comparable. When neither US nor CAN appears, Canadian, Mexican, and United States industries are comparable.

Cross-References. Establishments primarily engaged in—

- Mining or quarrying limestone—are classified in U.S. Industry 212312, Crushed and Broken Limestone Mining and Quarrying;

- Manufacturing lime—are classified in Industry 327410, Lime Manufacturing;

- Manufacturing ready-mix concrete—are classified in Industry 327320, Ready-Mix Concrete Manufacturing; and

- Manufacturing dry mix concrete—are classified in U.S. Industry 327999, All Other Miscellaneous Nonmetallic Mineral Product Manufacturing.

32732 Ready-Mix Concrete Manufacturing
See industry description for 327320 below.

327320 Ready-Mix Concrete Manufacturing

This industry comprises establishments, such as batch plants or mix plants, primarily engaged in manufacturing concrete delivered to a purchaser in a plastic and unhardened state. Ready-mix concrete manufacturing establishments may mine, quarry, or purchase sand and gravel.

Cross-References. Establishments primarily engaged in—

- Operating sand or gravel pits—are classified in U.S. Industry 212321, Construction Sand and Gravel Mining; and

- Manufacturing dry mix concrete—are classified in U.S. Industry 327999, All Other Miscellaneous Nonmetallic Mineral Product Manufacturing.

32733 Concrete Pipe, Brick, and Block Manufacturing

This industry comprises establishments primarily engaged in manufacturing concrete pipe, brick, and block.

Cross-References.

Establishments primarily engaged in manufacturing concrete products (except brick, block, and pipe) are classified in Industry 32739, Other Concrete Product Manufacturing.

327331 Concrete Block and Brick Manufacturing[US]

This U.S. industry comprises establishments primarily engaged in manufacturing concrete block and brick.

327332 Concrete Pipe Manufacturing[US]

This U.S. industry comprises establishments primarily engaged in manufacturing concrete pipe.

32739 Other Concrete Product Manufacturing
See industry description for 327390 below.

327390 Other Concrete Product Manufacturing

This industry comprises establishments primarily engaged in manufacturing concrete products (except block, brick, and pipe).

Cross-References. Establishments primarily engaged in—

- Manufacturing concrete brick and block—are classified in U.S. Industry 327331, Concrete Block and Brick Manufacturing; and

- Manufacturing concrete pipe—are classified in U.S. Industry 327332, Concrete Pipe Manufacturing.

3274 Lime and Gypsum Product Manufacturing

32741 Lime Manufacturing
See industry description for 327410 below.

327410 Lime Manufacturing

This industry comprises establishments primarily engaged in manufacturing lime from calcitic limestone, dolomitic limestone, or other calcareous materials, such as coral, chalk, and shells. Lime manufacturing establishments may mine, quarry, collect, or purchase the sources of calcium carbonate.

Cross-References.

Establishments primarily engaged in manufacturing dolomite refractories are classified in U.S. Industry 327125, Nonclay Refractory Manufacturing.

32742 Gypsum Product Manufacturing
See industry description for 327420 below.

327420 Gypsum Product Manufacturing

This industry comprises establishments primarily engaged in manufacturing gypsum products such as wallboard, plaster, plasterboard, molding, ornamental moldings, statuary, and architectural plaster work. Gypsum product manufacturing establishments may mine, quarry, or purchase gypsum.

Cross-References.

Establishments primarily engaged in operating gypsum mines or quarries are classified in U.S. Industry 212399, All Other Nonmetallic Mineral Mining.

US—United States industry only. CAN—United States and Canadian industries are comparable. When neither US nor CAN appears, Canadian, Mexican, and United States industries are comparable.

3279 Other Nonmetallic Mineral Product Manufacturing

The Other Nonmetallic Mineral Product Manufacturing industry group comprises establishments manufacturing nonmetallic mineral products (except clay products, refractory products, glass products, cement and concrete products, lime, and gypsum products).

32791 Abrasive Product Manufacturing
See industry description for 327910 below.

327910 Abrasive Product Manufacturing

This industry comprises establishments primarily engaged in manufacturing abrasive grinding wheels of natural or synthetic materials, abrasive-coated products, and other abrasive products.

Illustrative Examples:

Aluminum oxide (fused) abrasives
  manufacturing
Buffing and polishing wheels, abrasive and
  nonabrasive, manufacturing

Diamond dressing wheels manufacturing
Sandpaper manufacturing
Silicon carbide abrasives manufacturing
Whetstones manufacturing

Cross-References. Establishments primarily engaged in—

- Mining and cutting grindstones, pulpstones, and whetstones—are classified in U.S. Industry 212399, All Other Nonmetallic Mineral Mining;

- Manufacturing plastic scouring pads—are classified in U.S. Industry 326199, All Other Plastics Product Manufacturing; and

- Manufacturing metallic scouring sponges and soap impregnated scouring pads—are classified in U.S. Industry 332999, All Other Miscellaneous Fabricated Metal Product Manufacturing.

32799 All Other Nonmetallic Mineral Product Manufacturing

This industry comprises establishments primarily engaged in manufacturing nonmetallic mineral products (except pottery, ceramics, and plumbing fixtures; clay building materials and refractories; glass and glass products; cement; ready-mix concrete; concrete products; lime; gypsum products; and abrasive products).

Cross-References. Establishments primarily engaged in—

- Manufacturing pottery, ceramics, and plumbing fixtures—are classified in Industry 32711, Pottery, Ceramics, and Plumbing Fixture Manufacturing;

- Mining or quarrying stone, earth, or other nonmetallic minerals—are classified in Industry Group 2123, Nonmetallic Mineral Mining and Quarrying;

US—United States industry only. CAN—United States and Canadian industries are comparable. When neither US nor CAN appears, Canadian, Mexican, and United States industries are comparable.

- Buying and selling semifinished monuments and tombstones with no work other than polishing, lettering, or shaping to custom order—are classified in Sector 42, Wholesale Trade or Sector 44-45, Retail Trade;

- Manufacturing clay building materials and refractories—are classified in Industry 32712, Clay Building Material and Refractories Manufacturing;

- Manufacturing glass and glass products—are classified in Industry 32721, Glass and Glass Product Manufacturing;

- Manufacturing cement—are classified in Industry 32731, Cement Manufacturing;

- Mixing and delivering ready-mix concrete—are classified in Industry 32732, Ready-Mix Concrete Manufacturing;

- Manufacturing concrete pipe, brick, and block—are classified in Industry 32733, Concrete Pipe, Brick, and Block Manufacturing;

- Manufacturing concrete products (except pipe, brick, and block)—are classified in Industry 32739, Other Concrete Product Manufacturing;

- Manufacturing lime—are classified in Industry 32741, Lime Manufacturing;

- Manufacturing gypsum products—are classified in Industry 32742, Gypsum Product Manufacturing;

- Manufacturing abrasive products—are classified in Industry 32791, Abrasive Product Manufacturing; and

- Manufacturing metallic scouring pads and steel wool—are classified in Industry 33299, All Other Fabricated Metal Product Manufacturing.

327991 Cut Stone and Stone Product Manufacturing[US]

This U.S. industry comprises establishments primarily engaged in cutting, shaping, and finishing granite, marble, limestone, slate, and other stone for building and miscellaneous uses. Stone product manufacturing establishments may mine, quarry, or purchase stone.

Cross-References. Establishments primarily engaged in—

- Mining or quarrying stone—are classified in Industry Group 2123, Nonmetallic Mineral Mining and Quarrying; and

- Buying and selling semifinished monuments and tombstones with no work other than polishing, lettering, or shaping to custom order—are classified in Sector 42, Wholesale Trade or Sector 44-45, Retail Trade.

327992 Ground or Treated Mineral and Earth Manufacturing[US]

This U.S. industry comprises establishments primarily engaged in calcining, dead burning, or otherwise processing beyond beneficiation, clays, ceramic and refractory minerals, barite, and miscellaneous nonmetallic minerals.

US—United States industry only. CAN—United States and Canadian industries are comparable. When neither US nor CAN appears, Canadian, Mexican, and United States industries are comparable.

Cross-References.

Establishments primarily engaged in crushing, grinding, pulverizing, washing, screening, sizing, or otherwise beneficiating mined clays, ceramics and refractory, and other miscellaneous nonmetallic minerals are classified in Industry Group 2123, Nonmetallic Mineral Mining and Quarrying.

327993 Mineral Wool Manufacturing[US]

This U.S. industry comprises establishments primarily engaged in manufacturing mineral wool and mineral wool (i.e. fiberglass) insulation products made of such siliceous materials as rock, slag, and glass or combinations thereof.

Cross-References.

Establishments primarily engaged in manufacturing metallic scouring pads and steel wool are classified in U.S. Industry 332999, All Other Miscellaneous Fabricated Metal Product Manufacturing.

327999 All Other Miscellaneous Nonmetallic Mineral Product Manufacturing[US]

This U.S. industry comprises establishments primarily engaged in manufacturing nonmetallic mineral products (except pottery, ceramics, and plumbing fixtures; clay building materials and refractories; glass and glass products; cement; ready-mix concrete; concrete products; lime; gypsum products; abrasive products; cut stone and stone products; ground and treated minerals and earth; and mineral wool).

Illustrative Examples:

Dry mix concrete manufacturing
Mica products manufacturing
Synthetic stones, for gem stones and industrial use, manufacturing

Stucco and stucco products manufacturing

Cross-References. Establishments primarily engaged in—

* Manufacturing pottery, ceramics, and plumbing fixtures—are classified in Industry 32711, Pottery, Ceramics, and Plumbing Fixture Manufacturing;

* Manufacturing clay building materials and refractories—are classified in Industry 32712, Clay Building Material and Refractories Manufacturing;

* Manufacturing glass and glass products—are classified in Industry 32721, Glass and Glass Product Manufacturing;

* Manufacturing cement—are classified in Industry 327310, Cement Manufacturing;

* Mixing and delivering ready-mix concrete—are classified in Industry 327320, Ready-Mix Concrete Manufacturing;

- Manufacturing concrete pipe, brick, and block—are classified in Industry 32733, Concrete Pipe, Brick, and Block Manufacturing;

- Manufacturing concrete products (except pipe, brick, and block)—are classified in Industry 327390, Other Concrete Product Manufacturing;

- Manufacturing lime—are classified in Industry 327410, Lime Manufacturing;

- Manufacturing gypsum products—are classified in Industry 327420, Gypsum Product Manufacturing;

- Manufacturing abrasives and abrasive products—are classified in Industry 327910, Abrasive Product Manufacturing;

- Manufacturing cut stone and stone products—are classified in U.S. Industry 327991, Cut Stone and Stone Product Manufacturing;

- Manufacturing ground and treated minerals and earth (i.e., not at the mine site)—are classified in U.S. Industry 327992, Ground or Treated Mineral and Earth Manufacturing; and

- Manufacturing mineral wool and fiberglass insulation products—are classified in U.S. Industry 327993, Mineral Wool Manufacturing.

331 Primary Metal Manufacturing

Industries in the Primary Metal Manufacturing subsector smelt and/or refine ferrous and nonferrous metals from ore, pig or scrap, using electrometallurgical and other process metallurgical techniques. Establishments in this subsector also manufacture metal alloys and superalloys by introducing other chemical elements to pure metals. The output of smelting and refining, usually in ingot form, is used in rolling, drawing, and extruding operations to make sheet, strip, bar, rod, or wire, and in molten form to make castings and other basic metal products.

Primary manufacturing of ferrous and nonferrous metals begins with ore or concentrate as the primary input. Establishments manufacturing primary metals from ore and/or concentrate remain classified in the primary smelting, primary refining, or iron and steel mill, industries regardless of the form of their output. Establishments primarily engaged in secondary smelting and/or secondary refining recover ferrous and nonferrous metals from scrap and/or dross. The output of the secondary smelting and/or secondary refining industries is limited to shapes, such as ingot or billet, that will be further processed. Recovery of metals from scrap often occurs in establishments that are primarily engaged in activities, such as rolling, drawing, extruding, or similar processes.

Excluded from the Primary Metal Manufacturing subsector are establishments primarily engaged in manufacturing ferrous and nonferrous forgings (except ferrous forgings made in steel mills) and stampings. Although forging, stamping, and casting are all methods used to make metal shapes, forging and stamping do not use molten metals and are included in Subsector 332, Fabricated Metal Product Manufacturing. Establishments primarily engaged in operating coke ovens are classified in Industry 32419, Other Petroleum and Coal Products Manufacturing.

3311 Iron and Steel Mills and Ferroalloy Manufacturing

33111 Iron and Steel Mills and Ferroalloy Manufacturing

This industry comprises establishments primarily engaged in one or more of the following: (1) direct reduction of iron ore; (2) manufacturing pig iron in molten or solid form; (3) converting pig

---

iron into steel; (4) manufacturing ferroalloys; (5) making steel; (6) making steel and manufacturing shapes (e.g., bar, plate, rod, sheet, strip, wire); and (7) making steel and forming pipe and tube.

Cross-References. Establishments primarily engaged in—

- Manufacturing nonferrous superalloys, such as cobalt or nickel-based superalloys,—are classified in Industry 33149, Nonferrous Metal (except Copper and Aluminum) Rolling, Drawing, Extruding, and Alloying; and

- Operating coke ovens—are classified in Industry 32419, Other Petroleum and Coal Products Manufacturing.

331111 Iron and Steel Mills[US]

This U.S. industry comprises establishments primarily engaged in one or more of the following: (1) direct reduction of iron ore; (2) manufacturing pig iron in molten or solid form; (3) converting pig iron into steel; (4) making steel; (5) making steel and manufacturing shapes (e.g., bar, plate, rod, sheet, strip, wire); and (6) making steel and forming tube and pipe.

Cross-References. Establishments primarily engaged in—

- Manufacturing ferroalloys (i.e., alloying elements used to improve, strengthen, or otherwise alter the characteristics of steel)—are classified in U.S. Industry 331112, Electrometallurgical Ferroalloy Product Manufacturing; and

- Operating coke ovens—are classified in U.S. Industry 324199, All Other Petroleum and Coal Products Manufacturing.

331112 Electrometallurgical Ferroalloy Product Manufacturing[US]

This U.S. industry comprises establishments primarily engaged in manufacturing electrometallurgical ferroalloys. Ferroalloys add critical elements, such as silicon and manganese for carbon steel and chromium, vanadium, tungsten, titanium, and molybdenum for low- and high-alloy metals. Ferroalloys include iron-rich alloys and more pure forms of elements added during the steel manufacturing process that alter or improve the characteristics of the metal being made.

Cross-References. Establishments primarily engaged in—

- Manufacturing electrometallurgical steel and iron-based superalloys—are classified in U.S. Industry 331111, Iron and Steel Mills; and

- Manufacturing nonferrous superalloys, such as cobalt or nickel-based superalloys,—are classified in U.S. Industry 331492, Secondary Smelting, Refining, and Alloying of Nonferrous Metal (except Copper and Aluminum).

3312 Steel Product Manufacturing from Purchased Steel

This industry group comprises establishments primarily engaged in manufacturing iron and steel tube and pipe, drawing steel wire, and rolling or drawing shapes from purchased iron or steel.

US—United States industry only. CAN—United States and Canadian industries are comparable. When neither US nor CAN appears, Canadian, Mexican, and United States industries are comparable.

33121 Iron and Steel Pipe and Tube Manufacturing from Purchased Steel
See industry description for 331210 below.

331210 Iron and Steel Pipe and Tube Manufacturing from Purchased Steel

This industry comprises establishments primarily engaged in manufacturing welded, riveted, or seamless pipe and tube from purchased iron or steel.

Cross-References.

Establishments primarily engaged in making steel and further processing the steel into steel pipe and tube are classified in U.S. Industry 331111, Iron and Steel Mills.

33122 Rolling and Drawing of Purchased Steel

This industry comprises establishments primarily engaged in rolling and/or drawing steel shapes, such as plate, sheet, strip, rod, and bar, from purchased steel.

Cross-References. Establishments primarily engaged in—

- Making steel and rolling and/or drawing steel—are classified in Industry 33111, Iron and Steel Mills and Ferroalloy Manufacturing; and

- Manufacturing wire products from purchased wire—are classified in Industry 33261, Spring and Wire Product Manufacturing.

331221 Rolled Steel Shape Manufacturing[CAN]

This U.S. industry comprises establishments primarily engaged in rolling or drawing shapes (except wire), such as plate, sheet, strip, rod, and bar, from purchased steel.

Cross-References. Establishments primarily engaged in—

- Making steel and rolling or drawing steel shapes—are classified in U.S. Industry 331111, Iron and Steel Mills; and

- Drawing wire from purchased steel—are classified in U.S. Industry 331222, Steel Wire Drawing.

331222 Steel Wire Drawing[CAN]

This U.S. industry comprises establishments primarily engaged in drawing wire from purchased steel.

Cross-References. Establishments primarily engaged in—

- Making steel and drawing steel wire—are classified in U.S. Industry 331111, Iron and Steel Mills; and

---

US—United States industry only. CAN—United States and Canadian industries are comparable. When neither US nor CAN appears, Canadian, Mexican, and United States industries are comparable.

- Manufacturing wire products, such as nails, spikes, and paper clips, from purchased steel wire—are classified in Industry 33261, Spring and Wire Product Manufacturing.

3313 Alumina and Aluminum Production and Processing

33131 Alumina and Aluminum Production and Processing

This industry comprises establishments primarily engaged in one or more of the following: (1) refining alumina; (2) making (i.e., the primary production) aluminum from alumina; (3) recovering aluminum from scrap or dross; (4) alloying purchased aluminum; and (5) manufacturing aluminum primary forms (e.g., bar, foil, pipe, plate, rod, sheet, tube, wire).

Cross-References. Establishments primarily engaged in—

- Manufacturing aluminum oxide abrasives and refractories—are classified in Subsector 327, Nonmetallic Mineral Product Manufacturing;

- Sorting and breaking up scrap aluminum metal without also smelting or refining—are classified in Sector 42, Wholesale Trade; and

- Operating facilities where commingled recyclable materials, such as paper, plastics, used beverage cans, and metals are sorted into distinct categories without also smelting or refining—are classified in Industry 56292, Materials Recovery Facilities.

331311 Alumina Refining[US]

This U.S. industry comprises establishments primarily engaged in refining alumina (i.e., aluminum oxide) generally from bauxite.

Cross-References. Establishments primarily engaged in—

- Manufacturing aluminum oxide abrasives and refractories—are classified in Subsector 327, Nonmetallic Mineral Product Manufacturing; and

- Making aluminum from alumina—are classified in U.S. Industry 331312, Primary Aluminum Production.

331312 Primary Aluminum Production[US]

This U.S. industry comprises establishments primarily engaged in (1) making aluminum from alumina and/or (2) making aluminum from alumina and rolling, drawing, extruding, or casting the aluminum they make into primary forms (e.g., bar, billet, ingot, plate, rod, sheet, strip). Establishments in this industry may make primary aluminum or aluminum-based alloys from alumina.

Cross-References. Establishments primarily engaged in—

- Refining alumina—are classified in U.S. Industry 331311, Alumina Refining; and

- Recovering aluminum from scrap or alloying purchased aluminum—are classified in U.S. Industry 331314, Secondary Smelting and Alloying of Aluminum.

US—United States industry only. CAN—United States and Canadian industries are comparable. When neither US nor CAN appears, Canadian, Mexican, and United States industries are comparable.

331314 Secondary Smelting and Alloying of Aluminum[US]

This U.S. industry comprises establishments primarily engaged in (1) recovering aluminum and aluminum alloys from scrap and/or dross (i.e., secondary smelting) and making billet or ingot (except by rolling) and/or (2) manufacturing alloys, powder, paste, or flake from purchased aluminum.

Cross-References. Establishments primarily engaged in—

- Making aluminum and/or aluminum alloys from alumina—are classified in U.S. Industry 331312, Primary Aluminum Production;

- Refining alumina—are classified in U.S. Industry 331311, Alumina Refining;

- Manufacturing aluminum sheet, plate, and foil from purchased aluminum or by recovering aluminum from scrap and flat rolling or continuous casting—are classified in U.S. Industry 331315, Aluminum Sheet, Plate, and Foil Manufacturing;

- Manufacturing aluminum extruded products from purchased aluminum or by recovering aluminum from scrap and extruding—are classified in U.S. Industry 331316, Aluminum Extruded Product Manufacturing;

- Manufacturing rolled ingot, billet from purchased aluminum or by recovering aluminum from scrap and rolling or drawing—are classified in U.S. Industry 331319, Other Aluminum Rolling and Drawing;

- Sorting and breaking up scrap metal without also smelting or refining—are classified in Industry 421930, Recyclable Material Wholesalers; and

- Operating facilities where commingled recyclable materials, such as paper, plastics, used beverage cans, and metals, are sorted into distinct categories without also smelting or refining—are classified in Industry 562920, Materials Recovery Facilities.

331315 Aluminum Sheet, Plate, and Foil Manufacturing[US]

This U.S. industry comprises establishments primarily engaged in (1) flat rolling or continuous casting sheet, plate, foil and welded tube from purchased aluminum and/or (2) recovering aluminum from scrap and flat rolling or continuous casting sheet, plate, foil, and welded tube in integrated mills.

Cross-References.

Establishments primarily engaged in making aluminum from alumina and flat rolling or continuous casting aluminum sheet, plate, foil, and welded tube are classified in U.S. Industry 331312, Primary Aluminum Production.

331316 Aluminum Extruded Product Manufacturing[US]

This U.S. industry comprises establishments primarily engaged in (1) extruding aluminum bar, pipe, and tube blooms or extruding or drawing tube from purchased aluminum; and/or (2) recovering aluminum from scrap and extruding bar, pipe, and tube blooms or drawing tube in integrated mills.

US—United States industry only. CAN—United States and Canadian industries are comparable. When neither US nor CAN appears, Canadian, Mexican, and United States industries are comparable.

http://www.ntis.gov/naics

Cross-References.

Establishments primarily engaged in making aluminum from alumina and extruding aluminum bar, pipe, tube or tube blooms are classified in U.S. Industry 331312, Primary Aluminum Production.

331319 Other Aluminum Rolling and Drawing[US]

This U.S. Industry comprises establishments primarily engaged in (1) rolling, drawing, or extruding shapes (except flat rolled sheet, plate, foil, and welded tube; extruded rod, bar, pipe, and tube blooms; and drawn or extruded tube) from purchased aluminum and/or (2) recovering aluminum from scrap and rolling, drawing or extruding shapes (except flat rolled sheet, plate, foil, and welded tube; extruded rod, bar, pipe, and tube blooms; and drawn or extruded tube) in integrated mills.

Cross-References. Establishments primarily engaged in—

- Flat rolling sheet, plate, foil, and welded tube from either purchased aluminum or by recovering aluminum from scrap and flat rolling or continuous casting—are classified in U.S. Industry 331315, Aluminum Sheet, Plate, and Foil Manufacturing;

- Extruding rod, bar, pipe, tube and tube blooms or drawing tube from purchased aluminum or by recovering aluminum from scrap and extruding—are classified in U.S. Industry 331316, Aluminum Extruded Product Manufacturing; and

- Making aluminum from alumina and making aluminum shapes—are classified in U.S. Industry 331312, Primary Aluminum Production.

3314 Nonferrous Metal (except Aluminum) Production and Processing

33141 Nonferrous Metal (except Aluminum) Smelting and Refining

This industry comprises establishments primarily engaged in (1) smelting ores into nonferrous metals and/or (2) the primary refining of nonferrous metals (except aluminum) using electrolytic or other processes.

Cross-References. Establishments primarily engaged in—

- Making aluminum from alumina or recovery of aluminum from scrap—are classified in Industry 33131, Alumina and Aluminum Production and Processing;

- Recovering copper or copper alloys from scrap or dross and/or alloying, rolling, drawing, and extruding purchased copper—are classified in Industry 33142, Copper Rolling, Drawing, Extruding, and Alloying;

- Recovering nonferrous metals (except copper and aluminum) from scrap and/or alloying, rolling, drawing, and extruding purchased nonferrous metals (except copper and aluminum)—are classified in Industry 33149, Nonferrous Metal (except Copper and Aluminum) Rolling, Drawing, Extruding, and Alloying;

US—United States industry only. CAN—United States and Canadian industries are comparable. When neither US nor CAN appears, Canadian, Mexican, and United States industries are comparable.

- Mining and making copper and other nonferrous concentrates (including gold and silver bullion) using processes, such as solvent extraction or electrowinning,—are classified in Industry Group 2122, Metal Ore Mining;

- Sorting and breaking up scrap metal without also smelting or refining—are classified in Sector 42, Wholesale Trade; and

- Operating facilities where commingled recyclable materials, such as paper, plastics, used beverage cans, and metals, are sorted into distinct categories without also smelting or refining—are classified in Industry 56292, Materials Recovery Facilities.

331411 Primary Smelting and Refining of Copper[US]

This U.S. industry comprises establishments primarily engaged in (1) smelting copper ore and/or (2) the primary refining of copper by electrolytic methods or other processes. Establishments in this industry make primary copper and copper-based alloys, such as brass and bronze, from ore or concentrates.

Cross-References. Establishments primarily engaged in—

- Recovering copper or copper alloys from scrap and making primary forms; and/or alloying purchased copper—are classified in U.S. Industry 331423, Secondary Smelting, Refining, and Alloying of Copper;

- Mining and making copper concentrates by processes, such as solvent extraction or electrowinning,—are classified in U.S. Industry 212234, Copper Ore and Nickel Ore Mining;

- Drawing copper wire (except mechanical) from purchased copper or recovering copper from scrap and drawing wire (except mechanical)—are classified in U.S. Industry 331422, Copper Wire (except Mechanical) Drawing; and

- Rolling, drawing, or extruding copper shapes (except communication and energy wire) from purchased copper or recovering copper from scrap and rolling, drawing, and extruding copper shapes—are classified in U.S. Industry 331421, Copper Rolling, Drawing, and Extruding.

331419 Primary Smelting and Refining of Nonferrous Metal (except Copper and Aluminum)[US]

This U.S. industry comprises establishments primarily engaged in (1) making (i.e., the primary production) nonferrous metals by smelting ore and/or (2) the primary refining of nonferrous metals by electrolytic methods or other processes.

Cross-References. Establishments primarily engaged in—

- Recovering nonferrous metals (except copper and aluminum) from scrap and making primary forms and/or alloying purchased nonferrous metals (except copper and aluminum)— are classified in U.S. Industry 331492, Secondary Smelting, Refining, and Alloying of Nonferrous Metal (except Copper and Aluminum);

US—United States industry only. CAN—United States and Canadian industries are comparable. When neither US nor CAN appears, Canadian, Mexican, and United States industries are comparable.

- Making aluminum from alumina—are classified in U.S. Industry 331312, Primary Aluminum Production;

- Primary smelting and primary refining of copper—are classified in U.S. Industry 331411, Primary Smelting and Refining of Copper;

- Mining and making copper and other nonferrous concentrates (including gold and silver bullion), by processes, such as solvent extraction or electrowinning,—are classified in Industry Group 2122, Metal Ore Mining; and

- Rolling, drawing, and/or extruding nonferrous metal shapes (except copper and aluminum) from purchased nonferrous metals (except copper and aluminum) or by recovering nonferrous metals (except copper and aluminum) and rolling, drawing, or extruding—are classified in U.S. Industry 331491, Nonferrous Metal (except Copper and Aluminum) Rolling, Drawing, and Extruding.

33142 Copper Rolling, Drawing, Extruding, and Alloying

This industry comprises establishments primarily engaged in one or more of the following: (1) recovering copper or copper alloys from scraps; (2) alloying purchased copper; (3) rolling, drawing, or extruding shapes, (e.g., bar, plate, sheet, strip, tube, and wire) from purchased copper; and (4) recovering copper or copper alloys from scrap and rolling drawing, or extruding shapes (e.g., bar, plate, sheet, strip, tube, and wire).

Cross-References. Establishments primarily engaged in—

- Smelting copper ore, primary copper refining, and/or rolling, drawing or extruding primary copper made in the same establishment—are classified in Industry 33141, Nonferrous Metal (except Aluminum) Smelting and Refining;

- Manufacturing wire products from purchased wire—are classified in Industry 33261, Spring and Wire Product Manufacturing;

- Insulating purchased copper wire—are classified in Industry 33592, Communication and Energy Wire and Cable Manufacturing;

- Sorting and breaking up scrap metal without also smelting or refining—are classified in Sector 42, Wholesale Trade;

- Operating facilities where commingled recyclable materials, such as paper, plastics, used beverage cans, and metals, are sorted into distinct categories without also smelting or refining—are classified in Industry 56292, Materials Recovery Facilities;

- Die-casting purchased copper—are classified in Industry 33152, Nonferrous Metal Foundries; and

- Recovering nonferrous metals (except copper and aluminum) from scrap, and/or rolling, drawing, extruding, or alloying purchased nonferrous metals (except copper and aluminum)—are classified in Industry 33149, Nonferrous Metal (except Copper and Aluminum) Rolling, Drawing, Extruding, and Alloying.

US—United States industry only. CAN—United States and Canadian industries are comparable. When neither US nor CAN appears, Canadian, Mexican, and United States industries are comparable.

http://www.ntis.gov/naics

331421 Copper Rolling, Drawing, and Extruding[US]

This U.S. industry comprises establishments primarily engaged in (1) rolling, drawing, and/or extruding shapes (e.g., bar, plate, sheet, strip, tube (except bare or insulated copper communication or energy wire) from purchased copper; and/or (2) recovering copper from scrap and rolling, drawing, and/or extruding shapes (e.g., bar, plate, sheet, strip,tube (except bare or insulated copper communication or energy wire in integrated mills.))

Cross-References. Establishments primarily engaged in—

- Recovering copper or copper alloys from scrap and making primary forms and/or alloying purchased copper—are classified in U.S. Industry 331423, Secondary Smelting, Refining, and Alloying of Copper;

- Drawing copper wire (except mechanical) from purchased copper or recovering copper from scrap and drawing copper wire (except mechanical)—are classified in U.S. Industry 331422, Copper Wire (except Mechanical) Drawing;

- Die-casting purchased copper—are classified in U.S. Industry 331522, Nonferrous (except Aluminum) Die-Casting Foundries;

- Making primary copper and rolling, drawing, and/or extruding copper shapes (e.g., bar, plate, rod, sheet, strip)—are classified in U.S. Industry 331411, Primary Smelting and Refining of Copper; and

- Rolling, drawing, or extruding shapes from purchased nonferrous metal (except copper and aluminum) or recovering nonferrous metals from scrap and rolling, drawing or extruding— are classified in U.S. Industry 331491, Nonferrous Metal (except Copper and Aluminum) Rolling, Drawing, and Extruding.

331422 Copper Wire (except Mechanical) Drawing[US]

This U.S. industry comprises establishments primarily engaged in drawing or drawing and insulating communication and energy wire and cable from purchased copper or in integrated secondary smelting and wire drawing plants.

Cross-References. Establishments primarily engaged in—

- Manufacturing copper mechanical wire from purchased copper or by recovering copper from scrap and drawing or extruding—are classified in U.S. Industry 331421, Copper Rolling, Drawing, and Extruding;

- Insulating purchased copper wire—are classified in U.S. Industry 335929, Other Communication and Energy Wire Manufacturing;

- Making primary copper and drawing copper wire—are classified in U.S. Industry 331411, Primary Smelting and Refining of Copper; and

- Manufacturing wire products from purchased copper wire—are classified in Industry 33261, Spring and Wire Product Manufacturing.

US—United States industry only. CAN—United States and Canadian industries are comparable. When neither US nor CAN appears, Canadian, Mexican, and United States industries are comparable.

331423 Secondary Smelting, Refining, and Alloying of Copper[US]

This U.S. industry comprises establishments primarily engaged in (1) recovering copper and copper alloys from scrap and/or (2) alloying purchased copper. Establishments in this industry make primary forms, such as ingot, wire bar, cake, and slab from copper or copper alloys, such as brass and bronze.

Cross-References. Establishments primarily engaged in—

- Sorting and breaking up scrap metal without also smelting or refining—are classified in Industry 421930, Recyclable Material Wholesalers;

- Operating facilities where commingled recyclable materials, such as paper, plastics, used beverage cans, and metals, are sorted into distinct categories without also smelting or refining—are classified in Industry 562920, Materials Recovery Facilities;

- Smelting copper ore and/or the primary refining of copper—are classified in U.S. Industry 331411, Primary Smelting and Refining of Copper;

- Recovering copper and copper alloys from scrap and rolling, drawing, or extruding shapes— are classified in U.S. Industry 331421, Copper Rolling, Drawing, and Extruding;

- Recovering copper and copper alloys from scrap and drawing wire (except mechanical)— are classified in U.S. Industry 331422, Copper Wire (except Mechanical) Drawing; and

- Recovering nonferrous metals (except copper, aluminum) from scrap and making primary forms and/or alloying purchased nonferrous metals (except copper and aluminum)—are classified in U.S. Industry 331492, Secondary Smelting, Refining, and Alloying of Nonferrous Metal (except Copper and Aluminum).

33149 Nonferrous Metal (except Copper and Aluminum) Rolling, Drawing, Extruding, and Alloying

This industry comprises establishments primarily engaged in one or more of the following: (1) recovering nonferrous metals (except copper and aluminum) and nonferrous metal alloys from scrap; (2) alloying purchased nonferrous metals (except copper and aluminum); (3) rolling, drawing, and extruding shapes from purchased nonferrous metals (except copper and aluminum); and (4) recovering nonferrous metals from scrap (except copper and aluminum) and rolling, drawing, or extruding shapes in integrated facilities.

Cross-References. Establishments primarily engaged in—

- Rolling, drawing, and/or extruding aluminum or secondary smelting and alloying of aluminum—are classified in Industry 33131, Alumina and Aluminum Production and Processing;

- Recovering copper and copper alloys from scrap, alloying purchased copper, rolling, drawing, or extruding shapes from purchased copper, and recovering copper or copper alloys from scrap and rolling, drawing, or extruding shapes in integrated mills—are classified in Industry 33142, Copper Rolling, Drawing, Extruding, and Alloying;

US—United States industry only. CAN—United States and Canadian industries are comparable. When neither US nor CAN appears, Canadian, Mexican, and United States industries are comparable.

- Insulating purchased nonferrous wire—are classified in Industry 33592, Communication and Energy Wire and Cable Manufacturing;

- Making primary nonferrous metals and rolling, drawing, or extruding nonferrous metal shapes—are classified in Industry 33141, Nonferrous Metal (except Aluminum) Smelting and Refining;

- Manufacturing products from purchased wire—are classified in Industry 33261, Spring and Wire Product Manufacturing;

- Sorting and breaking up scrap metal without also smelting or refining—are classified in Sector 42, Wholesale Trade; and

- Operating facilities where commingled recyclable materials, such as paper, plastics, used beverage cans, and metals, are sorted into distinct categories without also smelting or refining—are classified in Industry 56292, Materials Recovery Facilities.

331491 Nonferrous Metal (except Copper and Aluminum) Rolling, Drawing, and Extruding[US]

This U.S. industry comprises establishments primarily engaged in (1) rolling, drawing, or extruding shapes (e.g., bar, plate, sheet, strip, tube) from purchased nonferrous metals) and/or (2) recovering nonferrous metals from scrap and rolling, drawing, and/or extruding shapes (e.g., bar, plate, sheet, strip, tube) in integrated mills.

Cross-References. Establishments primarily engaged in—

- Rolling, drawing, and/or extruding shapes from purchased copper or recovering copper from scrap and rolling, drawing, or extruding shapes—are classified in U.S. Industry 331421, Copper Rolling, Drawing, and Extruding;

- Recovering nonferrous metals (except copper and aluminum) from scrap and making primary forms and/or alloying purchased nonferrous metals—are classified in U.S. Industry 331492, Secondary Smelting, Refining, and Alloying of Nonferrous Metal (except Copper and Aluminum);

- Rolling, drawing, and/or extruding aluminum—are classified in Industry 33131, Alumina and Aluminum Production and Processing;

- Making primary nonferrous metals and rolling, drawing, or extruding nonferrous metal shapes—are classified in U.S. Industry 331419, Primary Smelting and Refining of Nonferrous Metal (except Copper and Aluminum); and

- Insulating purchased nonferrous wire—are classified in U.S. Industry 335929, Other Communication and Energy Wire Manufacturing.

331492 Secondary Smelting, Refining, and Alloying of Nonferrous Metal (except Copper and Aluminum)[US]

This U.S. industry comprises establishments primarily engaged in (1) alloying purchased nonferrous metals and/or (2) recovering nonferrous metals from scrap. Establishments in this industry

---

US—United States industry only. CAN—United States and Canadian industries are comparable. When neither US nor CAN appears, Canadian, Mexican, and United States industries are comparable.

make primary forms (e.g., bar, billet, bloom, cake, ingot, slab, slug, wire) using smelting or refining processes.

Cross-References. Establishments primarily engaged in—

- Recovering aluminum and aluminum alloys from scrap and/or alloying purchased aluminum—are classified in U.S. Industry 331314, Secondary Smelting and Alloying of Aluminum;

- Sorting and breaking up scrap metal without also smelting or refining—are classified in Industry 421930, Recyclable Material Wholesalers;

- Recovering nonferrous metals from scrap and rolling, drawing, or extruding shapes in integrated facilities—are classified in U.S. Industry 331491, Nonferrous Metal (except Copper and Aluminum) Rolling, Drawing, and Extruding;

- Operating facilities where commingled recyclable materials, such as paper, plastics, used beverage cans, and metals, are sorted into distinct categories without also smelting or refining—are classified in Industry 562920, Materials Recovery Facilities; and

- Recovering copper and copper alloys from scrap and making primary forms; and/or alloying purchased copper—are classified in U.S. Industry 331423, Secondary Smelting, Refining, and Alloying of Copper.

3315 Foundries

This industry group comprises establishments primarily engaged in pouring molten metal into molds or dies to form castings. Establishments making castings and further manufacturing, such as machining or assembling, a specific manufactured product are classified in the industry of the finished product. Foundries may perform operations, such as cleaning and deburring, on the castings they manufacture. More involved processes, such as tapping, threading, milling, or machining to tight tolerances, that transform castings into more finished products are classified elsewhere in the manufacturing sector based on the product being made.

Establishments in this industry group make castings from purchased metals or in integrated secondary smelting and casting facilities. When the production of primary metals is combined with making castings, the establishment is classified in 331 with the primary metal being made.

33151 Ferrous Metal Foundries

This industry comprises establishments primarily engaged in pouring molten iron and steel into molds of a desired shape to made castings. Establishments in this industry purchase iron and steel made in other establishments.

Cross-References.

Establishments primarily engaged in manufacturing iron or steel castings and further manufacturing them into finished products are classified based on the specific finished product.

US—United States industry only. CAN—United States and Canadian industries are comparable. When neither US nor CAN appears, Canadian, Mexican, and United States industries are comparable.

331511 Iron Foundries[CAN]

This U.S. industry comprises establishments primarily engaged in pouring molten pig iron or iron alloys into molds to manufacture castings, (e.g., cast iron man-hole covers, cast iron pipe, cast iron skillets). Establishments in this industry purchase iron made in other establishments.

Cross-References.

Establishments primarily engaged in manufacturing iron castings and further manufacturing them into finished products are classified based on the specific finished product.

331512 Steel Investment Foundries[US]

This U.S. industry comprises establishments primarily engaged in manufacturing steel investment castings. Investment molds are formed by covering a wax shape with a refractory slurry. After the refractory slurry hardens, the wax is melted, leaving a seamless mold. Investment molds provide highly detailed, consistent castings. Establishments in this industry purchase steel made in other establishments.

Cross-References. Establishments primarily engaged in—

- Manufacturing steel castings (except steel investment castings)—are classified in U.S. Industry 331513, Steel Foundries (except Investment); and

- Manufacturing steel investment castings and further manufacturing them into finished products—are classified based on the specific finished product.

331513 Steel Foundries (except Investment)[US]

This U.S. industry comprises establishments primarily engaged in manufacturing steel castings (except steel investment castings). Establishments in this industry purchase steel made in other establishments.

Cross-References. Establishments primarily engaged in—

- Manufacturing steel investment castings—are classified in U.S. Industry 331512, Steel Investment Foundries; and

- Manufacturing steel castings and further manufacturing them into finished products—are classified based on the specific finished product.

33152 Nonferrous Metal Foundries

This industry comprises establishments primarily engaged in pouring and/or introducing molten nonferrous metal, under high pressure, into metal molds or dies to manufacture castings. Establishments in this industry purchase nonferrous metals made in other establishments.

US—United States industry only. CAN—United States and Canadian industries are comparable. When neither US nor CAN appears, Canadian, Mexican, and United States industries are comparable.

Cross-References. Establishments primarily engaged in—

- Manufacturing iron or steel castings—are classified in Industry 33151, Ferrous Metal Foundries; and

- Manufacturing nonferrous metal castings and further manufacturing them into finished products—are classified based on the specific finished product.

331521 Aluminum Die-Casting Foundries[US]

This U.S. industry comprises establishments primarily engaged in introducing molten aluminum, under high pressure, into molds or dies to make aluminum die-castings. Establishments in this industry purchase aluminum made in other establishments.

Cross-References. Establishments primarily engaged in—

- Pouring molten aluminum into molds to manufacture aluminum castings—are classified in U.S. Industry 331524, Aluminum Foundries (except Die-Casting); and

- Manufacturing aluminum die-castings and further manufacturing them into finished products—are classified based on the specific finished product.

331522 Nonferrous (except Aluminum) Die-Casting Foundries[US]

This U.S. industry comprises establishments primarily engaged in introducing molten nonferrous metal (except aluminum), under high pressure, into molds to make nonferrous metal die-castings. Establishments in this industry purchase nonferrous metals made in other establishments.

Cross-References. Establishments primarily engaged in—

- Manufacturing aluminum die-castings—are classified in U.S. Industry 331521, Aluminum Die-Casting Foundries;

- Pouring molten aluminum into molds to manufacture aluminum castings—are classified in U.S. Industry 331524, Aluminum Foundries (except Die-Casting);

- Pouring molten copper into molds to manufacture copper castings—are classified in U.S. Industry 331525, Copper Foundries (except Die-Casting);

- Pouring molten nonferrous metal (except copper and aluminum) into molds to manufacture nonferrous (except copper and aluminum) castings—are classified in U.S. Industry 331528, Other Nonferrous Foundries (except Die-Casting); and

- Manufacturing nonferrous die-castings and further manufacturing them into finished products—are classified based on the specific finished product.

331524 Aluminum Foundries (except Die-Casting)[US]

This U.S. industry comprises establishments primarily engaged in pouring molten aluminum into molds to manufacture aluminum castings. Establishments in this industry purchase aluminum made in other establishments.

US—United States industry only. CAN—United States and Canadian industries are comparable. When neither US nor CAN appears, Canadian, Mexican, and United States industries are comparable.

Cross-References. Establishments primarily engaged in—

- Manufacturing aluminum die-castings—are classified in U.S. Industry 331521, Aluminum Die-Casting Foundries; and

- Manufacturing aluminum or aluminum alloy castings and further manufacturing them into finished products—are classified based on the specific finished product.

331525 Copper Foundries (except Die-Casting)[US]

This U.S. industry comprises establishments primarily engaged in pouring molten copper into molds to manufacture copper castings. Establishments in this industry purchase copper made in other establishments.

Cross-References. Establishments primarily engaged in—

- Manufacturing copper die-castings—are classified in U.S. Industry 331522, Nonferrous (except Aluminum) Die-Casting Foundries; and

- Manufacturing copper castings and further manufacturing them into finished products— are classified based on the specific finished product.

331528 Other Nonferrous Foundries (except Die-Casting)[US]

This U.S. industry comprises establishments primarily engaged in pouring molten nonferrous metals (except aluminum and copper) into molds to manufacture nonferrous castings (except aluminum die-castings, nonferrous (except aluminum) die-castings, aluminum castings, and copper castings). Establishments in this industry purchase nonferrous metals, such as nickel, lead, and zinc, made in other establishments.

Cross-References. Establishments primarily engaged in—

- Manufacturing aluminum die-castings—are classified in U.S. Industry 331521, Aluminum Die-Casting Foundries;

- Manufacturing nonferrous (except aluminum) die-castings—are classified in U.S. Industry 331522, Nonferrous (except Aluminum) Die-Casting Foundries;

- Pouring molten aluminum into molds to manufacture aluminum castings—are classified in U.S. Industry 331524, Aluminum Foundries (except Die-Casting);

- Manufacturing copper castings—are classified in U.S. Industry 331525, Copper Foundries (except Die-Casting); and

- Manufacturing nonferrous castings and further manufacturing them into finished products— are classified based on the specific finished product.

332 Fabricated Metal Product Manufacturing

Industries in the Fabricated Metal Product Manufacturing subsector transform metal into intermediate or end products, other than machinery, computers and electronics, and metal furniture or

---

US—United States industry only. CAN—United States and Canadian industries are comparable. When neither US nor CAN appears, Canadian, Mexican, and United States industries are comparable.

treating metals and metal formed products fabricated elsewhere. Important fabricated metal processes are forging, stamping, bending, forming, and machining, used to shape individual pieces of metal; and other processes, such as welding and assembling, used to join separate parts together. Establishments in this subsector may use one of these processes or a combination of these processes.

The NAICS structure for this subsector distinguishes the forging and stamping processes in a single industry. The remaining industries, in the subsector, group establishments based on similar combinations of processes used to make products.

The manufacturing performed in the Fabricated Metal Product Manufacturing subsector begins with manufactured metal shapes. The establishments in this sector further fabricate the purchased metal shapes into a product. For instance, the Spring and Wire Product Manufacturing industry starts with wire and fabricates such items.

Within manufacturing there are other establishments that make the same products made by this subsector; only these establishments begin production further back in the production process. These establishments have a more integrated operation. For instance, one establishment may manufacture steel, draw it into wire, and make wire products in the same establishment. Such operations are classified in the Primary Metal Manufacturing subsector.

3321 Forging and Stamping

33211 Forging and Stamping

This industry comprises establishments primarily engaged in one or more of the following: (1) manufacturing forgings from purchased metals; (2) manufacturing metal custom roll forming products; (3) manufacturing metal stamped and spun products (except automotive, cans, coins); and (4) manufacturing powder metallurgy products. Establishments making metal forgings, metal stampings, and metal spun products and further manufacturing (e.g., machining, assembling) a specific manufactured product are classified in the industry of the finished product. Metal forging, metal stamping, and metal spun products establishments may perform surface finishing operations, such as cleaning and deburring, on the products they manufacture.

Cross-References. Establishments primarily engaged in—

- Manufacturing metal forgings in integrated primary metal establishments—are classified in Subsector 331, Primary Metal Manufacturing;

- Stamping automotive stampings—are classified in Industry 33637, Motor Vehicle Metal Stamping;

- Manufacturing and installing rolled formed seamless gutters at construction sites—are classified in Industry 23561, Roofing, Siding, and Sheet Meal Contractors; and

- Stamping coins—are classified in Industry 33991, Jewelry and Silverware Manufacturing.

332111 Iron and Steel Forging[US]

This U.S. industry comprises establishments primarily engaged in manufacturing iron and steel forgings from purchased iron and steel by hammering mill shapes. Establishments making iron

---

US—United States industry only. CAN—United States and Canadian industries are comparable. When neither US nor CAN appears, Canadian, Mexican, and United States industries are comparable.

and steel forgings and further manufacturing (e.g., machining, assembling) a specific manufactured product are classified in the industry of the finished product. Iron and steel forging establishments may perform surface finishing operations, such as cleaning and deburring, on the forgings they manufacture.

Cross-References. Establishments primarily engaged in—

- Manufacturing iron and steel forgings in integrated iron and steel mills—are classified in U.S. Industry 331111, Iron and Steel Mills; and

- Manufacturing nonferrous forgings—are classified in U.S. Industry 332112, Nonferrous Forging.

332112 Nonferrous Forging^{US}

This U.S. industry comprises establishments primarily engaged in manufacturing nonferrous forgings from purchased nonferrous metals by hammering mill shapes. Establishments making nonferrous forgings and further manufacturing (e.g., machining, assembling) a specific manufactured product are classified in the industry of the finished product. Nonferrous forging establishments may perform surface finishing operations, such as cleaning and deburring, on the forgings they manufacture.

Cross-References. Establishments primarily engaged in—

- Manufacturing iron and steel forgings—are classified in U.S. Industry 332111, Iron and Steel Forging; and

- Manufacturing nonferrous forgings in integrated primary or secondary nonferrous metal production facilities—are classified in Subsector 331, Primary Metal Manufacturing.

332114 Custom Roll Forming^{US}

This U.S. industry comprises establishments primarily engaged in custom roll forming metal products by use of rotary motion of rolls with various contours to bend or shape the products.

Cross-References.

Establishments primarily engaged in manufacturing and installing rolled formed seamless gutters at construction sites are classified in Industry 235610, Roofing, Siding, and Sheet Metal Contractors.

332115 Crown and Closure Manufacturing^{US}

This U.S. industry comprises establishments primarily engaged in stamping metal crowns and closures, such as bottle caps and home canning lids and rings.

332116 Metal Stamping^{US}

This U.S. industry comprises establishments primarily engaged in manufacturing unfinished metal stampings and spinning unfinished metal products (except crowns, cans, closures, automotive,

---

US—United States industry only. CAN—United States and Canadian industries are comparable. When neither US nor CAN appears, Canadian, Mexican, and United States industries are comparable.

and coins). Establishments making metal stampings and metal spun products and further manufacturing (e.g., machining, assembling) a specific product are classified in the industry of the finished product. Metal stamping and metal spun products establishments may perform surface finishing operations, such as cleaning and deburring, on the products they manufacture.

Cross-References. Establishments primarily engaged in—

- Stamping automotive stampings—are classified in Industry 336370, Motor Vehicle Metal Stamping;

- Stamping metal crowns and closures—are classified in U.S. Industry 332115, Crown and Closure Manufacturing;

- Manufacturing metal cans—are classified in U.S. Industry 332431, Metal Can Manufacturing; and

- Stamping coins—are classified in U.S. Industry 339911, Jewelry (except Costume) Manufacturing.

332117 Powder Metallurgy Part Manufacturing^{US}

This U.S. industry comprises establishments primarily engaged in manufacturing powder metallurgy products by compacting them in a shaped die and sintering. Establishments in this industry generally make a wide range of parts on a job or order basis.

3322 Cutlery and Handtool Manufacturing

33221 Cutlery and Handtool Manufacturing

This industry comprises establishments primarily engaged in one or more of the following: (1) manufacturing nonprecious and precious plated metal cutlery and flatware; (2) manufacturing nonpowered hand and edge tools, (3) manufacturing nonpowered handsaws; (4) manufacturing saw blades, all types (including those for sawing machines); and (5) manufacturing metal kitchen utensils (except cutting-type) and pots and pans (except those manufactured by casting (e.g., cast iron skillets) or stamped without further fabrication).

Cross-References. Establishments primarily engaged in—

- Manufacturing precious (except precious plated) metal cutlery and flatware—are classified in Industry 33991, Jewelry and Silverware Manufacturing;

- Manufacturing electric razors and hair clippers for use on humans—are classified in Industry 33521, Small Electrical Appliance Manufacturing;

- Manufacturing power hedge shears and trimmers and electric hair clippers for use on animals—are classified in Industry 33311, Agricultural Implement Manufacturing;

- Manufacturing metal cutting dies, attachments, and accessories for machine tools—are classified in Industry 33351, Metalworking Machinery Manufacturing;

- Manufacturing handheld power-driven handtools—are classified in Industry 33399, All Other General Purpose Machinery Manufacturing; and

- Manufacturing finished cast iron kitchen utensils (i.e., cast iron skillets) and castings for kitchen utensils, pots, and pans—are classified in Industry Group 3315, Foundries.

332211 Cutlery and Flatware (except Precious) Manufacturing[US]

This U.S. industry comprises establishments primarily engaged in manufacturing nonprecious and precious plated metal cutlery and flatware.

Cross-References. Establishments primarily engaged in—

- Manufacturing precious (except precious plated) metal cutlery and flatware—are classified in U.S. Industry 339912, Silverware and Hollowware Manufacturing;

- Manufacturing electric razors and hair clippers for use on humans and housewares—are classified in U.S. Industry 335211, Electric Housewares and Household Fan Manufacturing;

- Manufacturing power hedge shears and trimmers and electric hair clippers for animal use— are classified in U.S. Industry 333112, Lawn and Garden Tractor and Home Lawn and Garden Equipment Manufacturing; and

- Manufacturing nonelectric hair clippers for use on animals—are classified in U.S. Industry 332212, Hand and Edge Tool Manufacturing.

332212 Hand and Edge Tool Manufacturing[US]

This industry comprises establishments primarily engaged in manufacturing nonpowered hand and edge tools (except saws).

Cross-References. Establishments primarily engaged in—

- Manufacturing saw blades and handsaws—are classified in U.S. Industry 332213, Saw Blade and Handsaw Manufacturing;

- Manufacturing metal cutting dies, attachments, and accessories for machine tools—are classified in Industry 33351, Metalworking Machinery Manufacturing;

- Manufacturing handheld power-driven handtools—are classified in U.S. Industry 333991, Power-Driven Handtool Manufacturing;

- Manufacturing electric razors and hair clippers for use on humans—are classified in U.S. Industry 335211, Electric Housewares and Household Fan Manufacturing;

- Manufacturing electric hair clippers for use on animals—are classified in U.S. Industry 333111, Farm Machinery and Equipment Manufacturing; and

- Manufacturing nonelectric household-type scissors and shears—are classified in U.S. Industry 332211, Cutlery and Flatware (except Precious) Manufacturing.

US—United States industry only. CAN—United States and Canadian industries are comparable. When neither US nor CAN appears, Canadian, Mexican, and United States industries are comparable.

332213 Saw Blade and Handsaw Manufacturing[US]

This U.S. industry comprises establishments primarily engaged in (1) manufacturing nonpowered handsaws and/or (2) manufacturing saw blades, all types (including those for power sawing machines).

Cross-References.

Establishments primarily engaged in manufacturing handheld powered saws are classified in U.S. Industry 333991, Power-Driven Handtool Manufacturing.

332214 Kitchen Utensil, Pot, and Pan Manufacturing[US]

This U.S. industry comprises establishments primarily engaged in manufacturing metal kitchen utensils (except cutting-type), pots, and pans (except those manufactured by casting (e.g., cast iron skillets) or stamped without further fabrication).

Cross-References. Establishments primarily engaged in—

- Manufacturing finished cast metal kitchen utensils or castings for kitchen utensils—are classified in Industry Group 3315, Foundries;

- Manufacturing stampings for kitchen utensils, pots, and pans—are classified in U.S. Industry 332116, Metal Stamping; and

- Manufacturing metal cutting-type kitchen utensils—are classified in U.S. Industry 332211, Cutlery and Flatware (except Precious) Manufacturing.

3323 Architectural and Structural Metals Manufacturing

33231 Plate Work and Fabricated Structural Product Manufacturing

This industry comprises establishments primarily engaged in manufacturing one or more of the following: (1) prefabricated metal buildings, panels and sections; (2) structural metal products; and (3) metal plate work products.

Cross-References. Establishments primarily engaged in—

- Making manufactured homes (i.e., mobile homes) and prefabricated wood buildings—are classified in Industry 32199, All Other Wood Product Manufacturing;

- Constructing buildings, bridges, and other heavy construction projects on site—are classified in Sector 23, Construction;

- Building ships, boats and barges—are classified in Industry 33661, Ship and Boat Building;

- Manufacturing power boilers and heat exchangers—are classified in Industry 33241, Power Boiler and Heat Exchanger Manufacturing;

US—United States industry only. CAN—United States and Canadian industries are comparable. When neither US nor CAN appears, Canadian, Mexican, and United States industries are comparable.

- Manufacturing heavy gauge tanks—are classified in Industry 33242, Metal Tank (Heavy Gauge) Manufacturing;

- Manufacturing metal plate cooling towers—are classified in Industry 33341, Ventilation, Heating, Air-Conditioning, and Commercial Refrigeration Equipment Manufacturing; and

- Manufacturing metal windows, doors and studs—are classified in Industry 33232, Ornamental and Architectural Metal Products Manufacturing.

332311 Prefabricated Metal Building and Component Manufacturing[CAN]

This U.S. industry comprises establishments primarily engaged in manufacturing prefabricated metal buildings, panels and sections.

Cross-References.   Establishments primarily engaged in—

- Making manufactured homes (i.e., mobile homes) and prefabricated wood buildings—are classified in Industry 32199, All Other Wood Product Manufacturing;

- Constructing prefabricated buildings on site—are classified in Industry Group 233, Building, Developing, and General Contracting; and

- Manufacturing metal windows and doors—are classified in U.S. Industry 332321, Metal Window and Door Manufacturing.

332312 Fabricated Structural Metal Manufacturing[US]

This U.S. industry comprises establishments primarily engaged in fabricating structural metal products, such as concrete reinforcing bars and fabricated bar joists.

Cross-References. Establishments primarily engaged in—

- Manufacturing metal windows and doors—are classified in U.S. Industry 332321, Metal Window and Door Manufacturing;

- Manufacturing metal studs—are classified in U.S. Industry 332322, Sheet Metal Work Manufacturing;

- Constructing buildings, bridges and other heavy construction projects on site—are classified in Sector 23, Construction;

- Building ships, boats and barges—are classified in Industry 33661, Ship and Boat Building; and

- Prefabricating metal buildings, panels and sections—are classified in U.S. Industry 332311, Prefabricated Metal Building and Component Manufacturing.

332313 Plate Work Manufacturing[US]

This industry comprises establishments primarily engaged in manufacturing fabricated metal plate work by cutting, punching, bending, shaping, and welding purchased metal plate.

US—United States industry only. CAN—United States and Canadian industries are comparable. When neither US nor CAN appears, Canadian, Mexican, and United States industries are comparable.

Cross-References. Establishments primarily engaged in—

- Manufacturing power boilers and heat exchangers—are classified in Industry 332410, Power Boiler and Heat Exchanger Manufacturing;

- Manufacturing heavy gauge tanks—are classified in Industry 332420, Metal Tank (Heavy Gauge) Manufacturing; and

- Manufacturing metal plate cooling towers—are classified in U.S. Industry 333415, Air-Conditioning and Warm Air Heating Equipment and Commercial and Industrial Refrigeration Equipment Manufacturing.

33232 Ornamental and Architectural Metal Products Manufacturing

This industry comprises establishments primarily engaged in manufacturing one or more of the following: (1) metal framed windows (i.e., typically using purchased glass) and metal doors; (2) sheet metal work; and (3) ornamental and architectural metal products.

Cross-References. Establishments primarily engaged in—

- Manufacturing metal covered (i.e., clad) wood windows and doors—are classified in Industry 32191, Millwork;

- Manufacturing bins, cans, vats, and light tanks of sheet metal—are classified in Industry 33243, Metal Can, Box, and Other Metal Container (Light Gauge) Manufacturing;

- Manufacturing prefabricated metal buildings, panels, and sections—are classified in Industry 33231, Plate Work and Fabricated Structural Product Manufacturing;

- Fabricating sheet metal work on site—are classified in Sector 23, Construction;

- Manufacturing metal stampings (except automotive, coins) and custom roll forming products—are classified in Industry 33211, Forging and Stamping;

- Manufacturing automotive stampings—are classified in Industry 33637, Motor Vechile Metal Stamping; and

- Stamping coins—are classified in Industry 33991, Jewelry and Silverware Manufacturing.

332321 Metal Window and Door Manufacturing[CAN]

This U.S. industry comprises establishments primarily engaged in manufacturing metal framed windows (i.e., typically using purchased glass) and metal doors. Examples of products made by these establishments are metal door frames; metal framed window and door screens; metal molding and trim (except automotive); and metal curtain walls.

Cross-References. Establishments primarily engaged in—

- Manufacturing wood or metal covered (i.e., clad) wood framed windows and doors—are classified in U.S. Industry 321911, Wood Window and Door Manufacturing; and

---

US—United States industry only. CAN—United States and Canadian industries are comparable. When neither US nor CAN appears, Canadian, Mexican, and United States industries are comparable.

- Manufacturing metal automotive molding and trim—are classified in Industry 336370, Motor Vehicle Metal Stamping.

332322 Sheet Metal Work Manufacturing[US]

This U.S. industry comprises establishments primarily engaged in manufacturing sheet metal work (except stampings).

Cross-References. Establishments primarily engaged in—

- Manufacturing sheet metal bins, vats and light tanks of sheet metal—are classified in U.S. Industry 332439, Other Metal Container Manufacturing;

- Manufacturing metal cans, lids, and ends—are classified in U.S. Industry 332431, Metal Can Manufacturing;

- Fabricating sheet metal work on site—are classified in Sector 23, Construction;

- Manufacturing metal stampings (except automotive, coins) and custom roll forming products—are classified in Industry 33211, Forging and Stamping;

- Manufacturing automotive stampings—are classified in Industry 336370, Motor Vehicle Metal Stamping; and

- Stamping coins—are classified in U.S. Industry 339911, Jewelry (except Costume) Manufacturing.

332323 Ornamental and Architectural Metal Work Manufacturing[US]

This U.S. industry comprises establishments primarily engaged in manufacturing ornamental and architectural metal work, such as staircases, metal open steel flooring, fire escapes, railings, and scaffolding.

Cross-References.

Establishments primarily engaged in manufacturing prefabricated metal buildings, panels, and sections are classified in U.S. Industry 332311, Prefabricated Metal Building and Component Manufacturing.

3324 Boiler, Tank, and Shipping Container Manufacturing

33241 Power Boiler and Heat Exchanger Manufacturing
See industry description for 332410 below.

332410 Power Boiler and Heat Exchanger Manufacturing

This industry comprises establishments primarily engaged in manufacturing power boilers and heat exchangers. Establishments in this industry may perform installation in addition to manufacturing power boilers and heat exchangers.

US—United States industry only. CAN—United States and Canadian industries are comparable. When neither US nor CAN appears, Canadian, Mexican, and United States industries are comparable.

Cross-References. Establishments primarily engaged in—

- Manufacturing heavy gauge metal tanks—are classified in Industry 332420, Metal Tank (Heavy Gauge) Manufacturing;

- Manufacturing stream or hot water low pressure heating boilers—are classified in U.S. Industry 333414, Heating Equipment (except Warm Air Furnaces) Manufacturing; and

- Installing power boilers and heat exchanges without manufacturing—are classified in Industry 235110, Plumbing, Heating, and Air-Conditioning Contractors.

33242 Metal Tank (Heavy Gauge) Manufacturing
See industry description for 332420 below.

332420 Metal Tank (Heavy Gauge) Manufacturing

This industry comprises establishments primarily engaged in cutting, forming, and joining heavy gauge metal to manufacture tanks, vessels, and other containers.

Cross-References. Establishments primarily engaged in—

- Manufacturing power boilers—are classified in Industry 332410, Power Boiler and Heat Exchanger Manufacturing;

- Manufacturing light gauge metal containers—are classified in Industry 33243, Metal Can, Box, and Other Metal Container (Light Gauge) Manufacturing; and

- Installing heavy gauge metal tanks without manufacturing—are classified in Sector 23, Construction.

33243 Metal Can, Box, and Other Metal Container (Light Gauge) Manufacturing

This industry comprises establishments primarily engaged in forming light gauge metal containers.

Cross-References. Establishments primarily engaged in—

- Manufacturing foil containers—are classified in Industry 33299, All Other Fabricated Metal Product Manufacturing;

- Reconditioning barrels and drums—are classified in Industry 81131, Commercial and Industrial Machinery and Equipment (except Automotive and Electronic) Repair and Maintenance; and

- Manufacturing heavy gauge metal containers—are classified in Industry 33242, Metal Tank (Heavy Gauge) Manufacturing.

332431 Metal Can Manufacturing[CAN]

This U.S. industry comprises establishments primarily engaged in manufacturing metal cans, lids, and ends.

US—United States industry only. CAN—United States and Canadian industries are comparable. When neither US nor CAN appears, Canadian, Mexican, and United States industries are comparable.

http://www.ntis.gov/naics

Cross-References. Establishments primarily engaged in—

- Manufacturing foil containers—are classified in U.S. Industry 332999, All Other Miscellaneous Fabricated Metal Product Manufacturing; and

- Manufacturing light gauge metal containers (except cans)—are classified in U.S. Industry 332439, Other Metal Container Manufacturing.

332439 Other Metal Container Manufacturing^{CAN}

This U.S. industry comprises establishments primarily engaged in manufacturing metal (light gauge) containers (except cans).

Illustrative Examples:

Light gauge metal bins manufacturing	Light gauge metal tool boxes manufacturing
Light gauge metal drums manufacturing	Light gauge metal vats manufacturing
Light gauge metal garbage cans manufacturing	Metal air cargo containers manufacturing
Light gauge metal lunch boxes manufacturing	Metal barrels manufacturing
Light gauge metal mailboxes manufacturing	Vacuum bottles and jugs manufacturing

Cross-References. Establishments primarily engaged in—

- Manufacturing foil containers—are classified in U.S. Industry 332999, All Other Miscellaneous Fabricated Metal Product Manufacturing;

- Manufacturing metal cans—are classified in U.S. Industry 332431, Metal Can Manufacturing;

- Reconditioning barrels and drums—are classified in Industry 811310, Commercial and Industrial Machinery and Equipment (except Automotive and Electronic) Repair and Maintenance; and

- Manufacturing heavy gauge metal containers—are classified in Industry 332420, Metal Tank (Heavy Gauge) Manufacturing.

3325 Hardware Manufacturing

33251 Hardware Manufacturing
See industry description for 332510 below.

332510 Hardware Manufacturing

This industry comprises establishments primarily engaged in manufacturing metal hardware, such as metal hinges, metal handles, keys, and locks (except coin-operated, time locks).

Cross-References. Establishments primarily engaged in—

- Manufacturing bolts, nuts, screws, rivets, washers, hose clamps, and turn buckles—are classified in U.S. Industry 332722, Bolt, Nut, Screw, Rivet, and Washer Manufacturing;

US—United States industry only. CAN—United States and Canadian industries are comparable. When neither US nor CAN appears, Canadian, Mexican, and United States industries are comparable.

- Manufacturing nails and spikes from wire drawn elsewhere—are classified in U.S. Industry 332618, Other Fabricated Wire Product Manufacturing;

- Manufacturing metal furniture parts (except hardware)—are classified in U.S. Industry 337215, Showcase, Partition, Shelving, and Locker Manufacturing;

- Drawing wire and manufacturing nails and spikes—are classified in Subsector 331, Primary Metal Manufacturing;

- Manufacturing pole line and transmission hardware—are classified in U.S. Industry 335932, Noncurrent-Carrying Wiring Device Manufacturing;

- Manufacturing coin-operated locking mechanisms—are classified in U.S. Industry 333311, Automatic Vending Machine Manufacturing;

- Manufacturing time locks—are classified in U.S. Industry 334518, Watch, Clock, and Part Manufacturing;

- Manufacturing fireplace fixtures and equipment, traps, handcuffs and leg irons, ladder jacks, and other like metal products—are classified in U.S. Industry 332999, All Other Miscellaneous Fabricated Metal Product Manufacturing;

- Manufacturing fire hose nozzles and couplings—are classified in U.S. Industry 332919, Other Metal Valve and Pipe Fitting Manufacturing; and

- Manufacturing luggage and utility racks—are classified in U.S. Industry 336399, All Other Motor Vehicle Parts Manufacturing.

3326 Spring and Wire Product Manufacturing

33261 Spring and Wire Product Manufacturing

This industry comprises establishments primarily engaged in (1) manufacturing steel springs by forming, such as cutting, bending, and heat winding metal rod or strip stock and/or (2) manufacturing wire springs and fabricated wire products from wire drawn elsewhere (except watch and clock springs).

Cross-References. Establishments primarily engaged in—

- Manufacturing watch and clock springs from purchased wire—are classified in Industry 33451, Navigational, Measuring, Electromedical, and Control Instruments Manufacturing;

- Drawing wire and manufacturing wire products—are classified in Subsector 331, Primary Metal Manufacturing; and

- Manufacturing nonferrous insulated wire from wire drawn elsewhere—are classified in Industry 33592, Communication and Energy Wire and Cable Manufacturing.

332611 Spring (Heavy Gauge) Manufacturing[CAN]

This U.S. industry comprises establishments primarily engaged in manufacturing heavy gauge springs by forming, such as cutting, bending, and heat winding rod or strip stock.

US—United States industry only. CAN—United States and Canadian industries are comparable. When neither US nor CAN appears, Canadian, Mexican, and United States industries are comparable.

Cross-References. Establishments primarily engaged in—

- Manufacturing light gauge springs from purchased wire or strip—are classified in U.S. Industry 332612, Spring (Light Gauge) Manufacturing; and

- Drawing wire and manufacturing wire spring—are classified in Subsector 331, Primary Metal Manufacturing.

332612 Spring (Light Gauge) Manufacturing[US]

This U.S. industry comprises establishments primarily engaged in manufacturing light gauge springs from purchased wire or strip.

Cross-References. Establishments primarily engaged in—

- Manufacturing watch and clock springs—are classified in U.S. Industry 334518, Watch, Clock, and Part Manufacturing;

- Manufacturing heavy gauge springs—are classified in U.S. Industry 332611, Spring (Heavy Gauge) Manufacturing; and

- Drawing wire and manufacturing wire spring—are classified in Subsector 331, Primary Metal Manufacturing.

332618 Other Fabricated Wire Product Manufacturing[US]

This industry comprises establishments primarily engaged in manufacturing fabricated wire products (except springs) made from purchased wire.

Illustrative Examples:

Barbed wire made from purchased wire
Chain link fencing and fence gates made from purchased wire
Metal baskets made from purchased wire
Nails, brads, and staples made from purchased wire

Noninsulated wire cable made from purchased wire
Paper clips made from purchased wire
Woven wire cloth made from purchased wire

Cross-References. Establishments primarily engaged in—

- Drawing wire and manufacturing wire products—are classified in Sector 331, Primary Metal Manufacturing;

- Manufacturing heavy gauge springs—are classified in U.S. Industry 332611, Spring (Heavy Gauge) Manufacturing;

- Manufacturing light gauge springs from purchased wire or strip—are classified in U.S. Industry 332612, Spring (Light Gauge) Manufacturing; and

---

US—United States industry only. CAN—United States and Canadian industries are comparable. When neither US nor CAN appears, Canadian, Mexican, and United States industries are comparable.

- Insulating nonferrous wire from wire drawn elsewhere—are classified in Industry 33592, Communication and Energy Wire and Cable Manufacturing.

3327 Machine Shops; Turned Product; and Screw, Nut, and Bolt Manufacturing

33271 Machine Shops
See industry description for 332710 below.

332710 Machine Shops

This industry comprises establishments known as machine shops primarily engaged in machining metal parts on a job or order basis. Generally machine shop jobs are low volume using machine tools, such as lathes (including computer numerically controlled); automatic screw machines; and machines for boring, grinding, and milling.

Cross-References. Establishments primarily engaged in—

- Repairing industrial machinery and equipment—are classified in Industry 81131, Commercial and Industrial Machinery and Equipment (except Automotive and Electronic) Repair and Maintenance; and

- Manufacturing parts (except on a job or order basis) for machinery and equipment—are generally classified in the same manufacturing industry that makes complete machinery and equipment.

33272 Turned Product and Screw, Nut, and Bolt Manufacturing

This industry comprises establishments primarily engaged in (1) machining precision turned products or (2) manufacturing metal bolts, nuts, screws, rivets, and other industrial fasteners. Included in this industry are establishments primarily engaged manufacturing parts for machinery and equipment on a customized basis.

Cross-References.

Establishments primarily engaged in manufacturing plastics fasteners are classified in Industry 32619, Other Plastics Product Manufacturing.

332721 Precision Turned Product Manufacturing[US]

This U.S. industry comprises establishments known as precision turned manufacturers primarily engaged in machining precision products of all materials on a job or order basis. Generally precision turned product jobs are large volume using machines, such as automatic screw machines, rotary transfer machines, computer numerically controlled (CNC) lathes, or turning centers.

Cross-References.

Establishments primarily engaged in manufacturing metal bolts, nuts, screws, rivets, washers, and other industrial fasteners on machines, such as headers, threaders, and nut forming machines, are classified in U.S. Industry 332722, Bolt, Nut, Screw, Rivet, and Washer Manufacturing.

US—United States industry only. CAN—United States and Canadian industries are comparable. When neither US nor CAN appears, Canadian, Mexican, and United States industries are comparable.

332722 Bolt, Nut, Screw, Rivet, and Washer Manufacturing[US]

This U.S. industry comprises establishments primarily engaged in manufacturing metal bolts, nuts, screws, rivets, and washers, and other industrial fasteners using machines, such as headers, threaders, and nut forming machines.

Cross-References. Establishments primarily engaged in—

- Manufacturing precision turned products—are classified in U.S. Industry 332721, Precision Turned Product Manufacturing; and

- Plastics fasteners—are classified in U.S. Industry 326199, All Other Plastics Product Manufacturing.

3328 Coating, Engraving, Heat Treating, and Allied Activities

33281 Coating, Engraving, Heat Treating, and Allied Activities

This industry comprises establishments primarily engaged in one or more of the following: (1) heat treating metals and metal products; (2) enameling, lacquering, varnishing metals and metal products; (3) hot dip galvanizing metals and metal products; (4) engraving, chasing, or etching metals and metal products (except jewelry; personal goods carried on or about the person, such as compacts and cigarette cases; precious metal products (except precious plated flatware and other plated ware); and printing plates); (5) powder coating metals and metal products; (6) electroplating, plating, anodizing, coloring, and finishing metals and metal products; and (7) providing other metal surfacing services for the trade. Establishments in this industry coat engravings and heat treat metals and metal formed products fabricated elsewhere.

Cross-References. Establishments primarily engaged in—

- Engraving, chasing or etching jewelry, metal personal goods, or precious (except precious plated) metal flatware and other plated ware—are classified in Industry 33991, Jewelry and Silverware Manufacturing;

- Engraving, chasing or etching printing plates—are classified in Industry 32312, Support Activities for Printing; and

- Both fabricating and coating, engraving, and heat treating metals and metal products—are classified in manufacturing according to the product made.

332811 Metal Heat Treating[US]

This U.S. industry comprises establishments primarily engaged in heat treating, such as annealing, tempering, and brazing, metals and metal products for the trade.

Cross-References.

Establishments primarily engaged in both fabricating and heat treating metal products are classified in the Manufacturing sector according to the product made.

US—United States industry only. CAN—United States and Canadian industries are comparable. When neither US nor CAN appears, Canadian, Mexican, and United States industries are comparable.

332812 Metal Coating, Engraving (except Jewelry and Silverware), and Allied Services to Manufacturers[US]

This U.S. industry comprises establishments primarily engaged in one or more of the following: (1) enameling, lacquering, and varnishing metals and metal products; (2) hot dip galvanizing metals and metal products; (3) engraving, chasing, or etching metals and metal products (except jewelry; personal goods carried on or about the person, such as compacts and cigarette cases; precious metal products (except precious plated flatware and other plated ware); and printing plates); (4) powder coating metals and metal products; and (5) providing other metal surfacing services for the trade.

Cross-References. Establishments primarily engaged in—

- Both fabricating and coating and engraving products—are classified in the Manufacturing sector according to the product made;

- Engraving, chasing or etching jewelry, metal personal goods, or precious metal products (except precious plated metal flatware and other plated ware)—are classified in Industry 33991, Jewelry and Silverware Manufacturing; and

- Engraving, chasing or etching printing plates—are classified in U.S. Industry 323122, Prepress Services.

332813 Electroplating, Plating, Polishing, Anodizing, and Coloring[US]

This U.S. industry comprises establishments primarily engaged in electroplating, plating, anodizing, coloring, buffing, polishing, cleaning, and sandblasting metals and metal products for the trade.

Cross-References.

Establishments primarily engaged in both fabricating and electroplating, plating, polishing, anodizing, and coloring products are classified in the Manufacturing sector according to the product made.

3329 Other Fabricated Metal Product Manufacturing

This industry group comprises establishments primarily engaged in manufacturing fabricated metal products (except forgings and stampings, cutlery and handtools, architectural and structural metals, boilers, tanks, shipping containers, hardware, spring and wire products, machine shop products, turned products, screws, and nuts and bolts).

33291 Metal Valve Manufacturing

This industry comprises establishments primarily engaged in manufacturing one or more of the following metal valves: (1) industrial valves; (2) fluid power valves and hose fittings; (3) plumbing fixture fittings and trim; and (4) other metal valves and pipe fittings.

US—United States industry only. CAN—United States and Canadian industries are comparable. When neither US nor CAN appears, Canadian, Mexican, and United States industries are comparable.

Cross-References. Establishments primarily engaged in—

- Manufacturing fluid power cylinder and pumps—are classified in Industry 33399, All Other General Purpose Machinery Manufacturing;

- Manufacturing intake and exhaust valves for internal combustion engines—are classified in Industry 33631, Motor Vehicle Gasoline Engine and Engine Parts Manufacturing;

- Manufacturing metal shower rods and metal couplings from purchased metal pipe—are classified in Industry 33299, All Other Fabricated Metal Product Manufacturing;

- Manufacturing plastics aerosol spray nozzles—are classified in Industry 32619, Other Plastics Product Manufacturing;

- Casting iron pipe fittings and couplings without machining—are classified in Industry 33151, Ferrous Metal Foundries; and

- Manufacturing plastics pipe fittings and couplings—are classified in Industry 32612, Plastics Pipe, Pipe Fitting, and Unsupported Profile Shape Manufacturing.

332911 Industrial Valve Manufacturing^{US}

This U.S. industry comprises establishments primarily engaged in manufacturing industrial valves and valves for water works and municipal water systems.

Illustrative Examples:

Complete fire hydrants manufacturing	Industrial-type plug valves manufacturing
Industrial-type ball valves manufacturing	Industrial-type solenoid valves (except fluid
Industrial-type butterfly valves manufacturing	power) manufacturing
Industrial-type check valves manufacturing	Industrial-type steam traps manufacturing
Industrial-type gate valves manufacturing	Valves for nuclear applications manufacturing
Industrial-type globe valves manufacturing	

Cross-References.   Establishments primarily engaged in—

- Manufacturing fluid power valves—are classified in U.S. Industry 332912, Fluid Power Valve and Hose Fitting Manufacturing; and

- Manufacturing plumbing and heating valves—are classified in U.S. Industry 332919, Other Metal Valve and Pipe Fitting Manufacturing.

332912 Fluid Power Valve and Hose Fitting Manufacturing^{US}

This U.S. industry comprises establishments primarily engaged in manufacturing fluid power valves and hose fittings.

US—United States industry only. CAN—United States and Canadian industries are comparable. When neither US nor CAN appears, Canadian, Mexican, and United States industries are comparable.

http://www.ntis.gov/naics

Illustrative Examples:

Fluid power aircraft subassemblies
Hose assemblies for fluid power systems
Hydraulic and pneumatic hose and tube
  fittings

Hydraulic and pneumatic valves

Cross-References. Establishments primarily engaged in—

- Manufacturing fluid power cylinders—are classified in U.S. Industry 333995, Fluid Power Cylinder and Actuator Manufacturing;

- Manufacturing fluid power pumps—are classified in U.S. Industry 333996, Fluid Power Pump and Motor Manufacturing;

- Manufacturing intake and exhaust valves for internal combustion engines—are classified in U.S. Industry 336311, Carburetor, Piston, Piston Ring, and Valve Manufacturing;

- Manufacturing industrial-type valves—are classified in U.S. Industry 332911, Industrial Valve Manufacturing; and

- Manufacturing plumbing and heating valves—are classified in U.S. Industry 332919, Other Metal Valve and Pipe Fitting Manufacturing.

332913 Plumbing Fixture Fitting and Trim Manufacturing[US]

This U.S. industry comprises establishments primarily engaged in manufacturing metal and plastics plumbing fixture fittings and trim, such as faucets, flush valves, and shower heads.

Cross-References. Establishments primarily engaged in—

- Manufacturing metal shower rods—are classified in U.S. Industry 332999, All Other Miscellaneous Fabricated Metal Product Manufacturing; and

- Manufacturing fire hose nozzles, lawn hose nozzles, water traps, and couplings—are classified in U.S. Industry 332919, Other Metal Valve and Pipe Fitting Manufacturing.

332919 Other Metal Valve and Pipe Fitting Manufacturing[US]

This U.S. industry comprises establishments primarily engaged in manufacturing metal valves (except industrial valves, fluid power valves, fluid power hose fittings, and plumbing fixture fittings and trim).

Illustrative Examples:

Aerosol valves manufacturing
Firefighting nozzles manufacturing
Lawn hose nozzles manufacturing
Lawn sprinklers manufacturing
Metal hose couplings (except fluid power)
  manufacturing

Metal pipe flanges and flange unions
  manufacturing
Plumbing and heating in-line valves (e.g.,
  check, cutoff, stop) manufacturing

US—United States industry only. CAN—United States and Canadian industries are comparable. When neither US nor CAN appears, Canadian, Mexican, and United States industries are comparable.

Cross-References. Establishments primarily engaged in—

- Manufacturing fluid power valves and hose fittings—are classified in U.S. Industry 332912, Fluid Power Valve and Hose Fitting Manufacturing;

- Manufacturing industrial valves—are classified in U.S. Industry 332911, Industrial Valve Manufacturing;

- Manufacturing plastics aerosol spray nozzles—are classified in U.S. Industry 326199, All Other Plastics Product Manufacturing;

- Casting iron pipe fittings and couplings without machining—are classified in U.S. Industry 331511, Iron Foundries;

- Manufacturing metal couplings from purchased metal pipe—are classified in U.S. Industry 332996, Fabricated Pipe and Pipe Fitting Manufacturing; and

- Manufacturing plastics pipe fittings and couplings—are classified in U.S. Industry 326122, Plastics Pipe and Pipe Fitting Manufacturing.

33299 All Other Fabricated Metal Product Manufacturing

This industry comprises establishments primarily engaged in manufacturing fabricated metal products (except forgings and stampings, cutlery and handtools, architectural and structural metal products, boilers, tanks, shipping containers, hardware, spring and wire products, machine shop products, turned products, screws, nuts and bolts, and metal valves).

Illustrative Examples:

Ammunition manufacturing	Foil container (except bags) manufacturing
Ball and roller bearing manufacturing	Industrial pattern manufacturing
Enameled iron and metal sanitary ware manufacturing	Metal safes manufacturing
	Portable metal ladder manufacturing
Fabricated pipe and pipe fittings made from purchased metal pipe	Small arms and other ordnance manufacturing
	Steel wool manufacturing

Cross-References. Establishments primarily engaged in—

- Manufacturing forging and stamping and powder metallurgy parts—are classified in Industry 33211, Forging and Stamping;

- Manufacturing cutlery and handtools—are classified in Industry 33221, Cutlery and Handtool Manufacturing;

- Manufacturing architectural and structural metals—are classified in Industry Group 3323, Architectural and Structural Metals Manufacturing;

- Manufacturing boilers, tanks, and shipping containers—are classified in Industry Group 3324, Boiler, Tank, and Shipping Container Manufacturing;

US—United States industry only. CAN—United States and Canadian industries are comparable. When neither US nor CAN appears, Canadian, Mexican, and United States industries are comparable.

- Manufacturing hardware and safe and vault locks—are classified in Industry 33251, Hardware Manufacturing;

- Manufacturing spring and wire products—are classified in Industry 33261, Spring and Wire Product Manufacturing;

- Manufacturing machine shop products, turned products, screws, and nuts and bolts—are classified in Industry Group 3327, Machine Shops; Turned Product; and Screw, Nut, and Bolt Manufacturing;

- Coating, engraving, heat treating and allied activities—are classified in Industry 33281, Coating, Engraving, Heat Treating, and Allied Activities;

- Manufacturing plain bearings—are classified in Industry 33361, Engine, Turbine, and Power Transmission Equipment Manufacturing;

- Manufacturing military tanks—are classified in Industry 33699, Other Transportation Equipment Manufacturing;

- Manufacturing guided missiles—are classified in Industry 33641, Aerospace Product and Parts Manufacturing;

- Manufacturing cast iron pipe and fittings—are classified in Industry 33151, Ferrous Metal Foundries;

- Manufacturing pipe system fittings (except cast iron couplings and couplings made from purchased pipe) and metal aerosol spray nozzles—are classified in Industry 33291, Metal Valve Manufacturing;

- Manufacturing welded and seamless steel pipes from purchased steel—are classified in Industry 33121, Iron and Steel Pipe and Tube Manufacturing from Purchased Steel;

- Manufacturing plastics plumbing fixtures and plastics portable chemical toilets—are classified in Industry 32619, Other Plastics Product Manufacturing;

- Manufacturing vitreous and semivitreous pottery sanitary ware—are classified in Industry 32711, Pottery, Ceramics, and Plumbing Fixture Manufacturing;

- Manufacturing blasting caps, detonating caps, and safety fuses—are classified in Industry 32592, Explosives Manufacturing;

- Manufacturing fireworks—are classified in Industry 32599, All Other Chemical Product and Preparation Manufacturing;

- Manufacturing metal furniture frames—are classified in Industry 33721, Office Furniture (including Fixtures) Manufacturing;

- Manufacturing nonprecious metal trophies—are classified in Industry 33991, Jewelry and Silverware Manufacturing;

- Manufacturing metal mechanically refrigerated drinking fountains—are classified in Industry 33341, Ventilation, Heating, Air-Conditioning, and Commercial Refrigeration Equipment Manufacturing;

US—United States industry only. CAN—United States and Canadian industries are comparable. When neither US nor CAN appears, Canadian, Mexican, and United States industries are comparable.

http://www.ntis.gov/naics

- Manufacturing metal foil bags—are classified in Industry 32222, Paper Bag and Coated and Treated Paper Manufacturing;

- Manufacturing aluminum foil—are classified in Industry 33131, Alumina and Aluminum Production and Processing;

- Manufacturing metal foil (except aluminum)—are classified in Industry Group 3314, Nonferrous Metal (except Aluminum) Production and Process; and

- Manufacturing metal burial vaults—are classified in Industry 33999, All Other Miscellaneous Manufacturing.

332991 Ball and Roller Bearing Manufacturing^{CAN}

This U.S. industry comprises establishments primarily engaged in manufacturing ball and roller bearings of all materials.

Cross-References.

Establishments primarily engaged in manufacturing plain bearings are classified in U.S. Industry 333613, Mechanical Power Transmission Equipment Manufacturing.

332992 Small Arms Ammunition Manufacturing^{US}

This U.S. industry comprises establishments primarily engaged in manufacturing small arms ammunition.

Cross-References. Establishments primarily engaged in—

- Manufacturing ammunition (except small arms)—are classified in U.S. Industry 332993, Ammunition (except Small Arms) Manufacturing;

- Manufacturing blasting and detonating caps and safety fuses—are classified in Industry 325920, Explosives Manufacturing; and

- Manufacturing fireworks—are classified in U.S. Industry 325998, All Other Miscellaneous Chemical Product and Preparation Manufacturing.

332993 Ammunition (except Small Arms) Manufacturing^{US}

This U.S. industry comprises establishments primarily engaged in manufacturing ammunition (except small arms). Examples of products made by these establishments are bombs, depth charges, rockets (except guided missiles), grenades, mines, and torpedoes.

Cross-References. Establishments primarily engaged in—

- Manufacturing small arms ammunition—are classified in U.S. Industry 332992, Small Arms Ammunition Manufacturing;

US—United States industry only. CAN—United States and Canadian industries are comparable. When neither US nor CAN appears, Canadian, Mexican, and United States industries are comparable.

- Manufacturing blasting and detonating caps and safety fuses—are classified in Industry 325920, Explosives Manufacturing;

- Manufacturing fireworks—are classified in U.S. Industry 325998, All Other Miscellaneous Chemical Product and Preparation Manufacturing; and

- Manufacturing guided missiles—are classified in U.S. Industry 336414, Guided Missile and Space Vehicle Manufacturing.

332994 Small Arms Manufacturing[US]

This U.S. industry comprises establishments primarily engaged in manufacturing small firearms that are carried and fired by the individual.

Cross-References.

Establishments primarily engaged in manufacturing firearms (except small) are classified in U.S. Industry 332995, Other Ordnance and Accessories Manufacturing.

332995 Other Ordnance and Accessories Manufacturing[US]

This U.S. industry comprises establishments primarily engaged in manufacturing ordnance (except small arms) and accessories.

Cross-References. Establishments primarily engaged in—

- Manufacturing small arms—are classified in U.S. Industry 332994, Small Arms Manufacturing;

- Manufacturing military tanks—are classified in U.S. Industry 336992, Military Armored Vehicle, Tank, and Tank Component Manufacturing; and

- Manufacturing guided missiles—are classified in U.S. Industry 336414, Guided Missile and Space Vehicle Manufacturing.

332996 Fabricated Pipe and Pipe Fitting Manufacturing[US]

This U.S. industry comprises establishments primarily engaged in fabricating (such as cutting, threading and bending) metal pipes and pipe fittings made from purchased metal pipe.

Cross-References. Establishments primarily engaged in—

- Manufacturing cast iron pipe and fittings—are classified in U.S. Industry 331511, Iron Foundries;

- Manufacturing pipe system fittings (except cast iron couplings)—are classified in U.S. Industry 332919, Other Metal Valve and Pipe Fitting Manufacturing; and

- Manufacturing welded and seamless steel pipes from purchased steel—are classified in Industry 331210, Iron and Steel Pipe and Tube Manufacturing from Purchased Steel.

332997 Industrial Pattern Manufacturing[US]

This U.S. industry comprises establishments primarily engaged in manufacturing industrial patterns.

332998 Enameled Iron and Metal Sanitary Ware Manufacturing[US]

This U.S. industry comprises establishments primarily engaged in manufacturing enameled iron and metal sanitary ware.

Cross-References. Establishments primarily engaged in—

- Manufacturing plastics plumbing fixtures—are classified in U.S. Industry 326191, Plastics Plumbing Fixture Manufacturing;

- Manufacturing vitreous and semivitreous pottery sanitary ware—are classified in U.S. Industry 327111, Vitreous China Plumbing Fixture and China and Earthenware Bathroom Accessories Manufacturing;

- Manufacturing plastics portable chemical toilets—are classified in U.S. Industry 326199, All Other Plastics Product Manufacturing; and

- Manufacturing metal mechanically refrigerated drinking fountains—are classified in U.S. Industry 333415, Air-Conditioning and Warm Air Heating Equipment and Commercial and Industrial Refrigeration Equipment Manufacturing.

332999 All Other Miscellaneous Fabricated Metal Product Manufacturing[US]

This U.S. industry comprises establishments primarily engaged in manufacturing fabricated metal products (except forgings and stampings, cutlery and handtools, architectural and structural metals, boilers, tanks, shipping containers, hardware, spring and wire products, machine shop products, turned products, screws, nuts and bolts, metal valves, ball and roller bearings, ammunition, small arms and other ordnances, fabricated pipes and pipe fittings, industrial patterns, and enameled iron and metal sanitary ware).

Illustrative Examples:

Foil containers (except bags) manufacturing
Metal hair curlers manufacturing
Metal ironing boards manufacturing
Metal pipe hangers and supports
 manufacturing
Metal pallets manufacturing

Metal safes manufacturing
Metal vaults (except burial) manufacturing
Permanent metallic magnets manufacturing
Portable metal ladders manufacturing
Steel wool manufacturing

Cross-References. Establishments primarily engaged in—

- Manufacturing forgings and stampings—are classified in Industry 33211, Forgings and Stampings;

US—United States industry only. CAN—United States and Canadian industries are comparable.
When neither US nor CAN appears, Canadian, Mexican, and United States industries are comparable.

- Manufacturing cutlery and handtools—are classified in Industry 33221, Cutlery and Hand-tool Manufacturing;

- Manufacturing architectural and structural metals—are classified in Industry Group 3323, Architectural and Structural Metals Manufacturing;

- Manufacturing boilers, tanks, and shipping containers—are classified in Industry Group 3324, Boiler, Tank, and Shipping Container Manufacturing;

- Manufacturing hardware and safe and vault locks—are classified in Industry 332510, Hardware Manufacturing;

- Manufacturing spring and wire products—are classified in Industry 33261, Spring and Wire Product Manufacturing;

- Manufacturing machine shop products, turned products, screws, and nut and bolt—are classified in Industry Group 3327, Machine Shops; Turned Product; and Screw Nut, and Bolt Manufacturing;

- Coating, engraving, heat treating and allied activities—are classified in Industry 33281, Coating, Engraving, Heat Treating, and Allied Activities;

- Manufacturing ball and roller bearings—are classified in U.S. Industry 332991, Ball and Roller Bearing Manufacturing;

- Manufacturing small arms ammunition—are classified in U.S. Industry 332992, Small Arms Ammunition Manufacturing;

- Manufacturing ammunition (except small arms)—are classified in U.S. Industry 332993, Ammunition (except Small Arms) Manufacturing;

- Manufacturing small firearms that are carried and fired by the individual—are classified in U.S. Industry 332994, Small Arms Manufacturing;

- Manufacturing ordnances (except small) and accessories—are classified in U.S. Industry 332995, Other Ordnance and Accessories Manufacturing;

- Manufacturing metal pipes and pipe fittings from metal pipe produced elsewhere—are classified in U.S. Industry 332996, Fabricated Pipe and Pipe Fitting Manufacturing;

- Manufacturing cast iron pipe and fittings—are classified in U.S. Industry 331511, Iron Foundries;

- Manufacturing welded and seamless steel pipes from purchased steel—are classified in Industry 331210, Iron and Steel Pipe and Tube Manufacturing form Purchased Steel;

- Manufacturing metal furniture frames—are classified in U.S. 337215, Showcase, Partition, Shelving, and Locker Manufacturing;

- Manufacturing powder metallurgy parts—are classified in U.S. Industry 332117, Powder Metallurgy Part Manufacturing;

- Manufacturing metal boxes—are classified in U.S. Industry 332439, Other Metal Container Manufacturing;

US—United States industry only. CAN—United States and Canadian industries are comparable. When neither US nor CAN appears, Canadian, Mexican, and United States industries are comparable.

- Manufacturing metal nozzles, hose couplings, and aerosol valves—are classified in U.S. Industry 332919, Other Metal Valve and Pipe Fitting Manufacturing;

- Manufacturing nonprecious metal trophies—are classified in U.S. Industry 339914, Costume Jewelry and Novelty Manufacturing;

- Manufacturing metal foil bags—are classified in U.S Industry 322223, Plastics, Foil, and Coated Paper Bag Manufacturing;

- Manufacturing aluminum foil—are classified in Industry 33131, Alumina and Aluminum Production and Processing;

- Manufacturing metal foil (except aluminum)—are classified in Industry Group 3314, Nonferrous Metal (except Aluminum) Production and Processing; and

- Manufacturing metal burial vaults—are classified in U.S. Industry 339995, Burial Casket Manufacturing.

333 Machinery Manufacturing

Industries in the Machinery Manufacturing subsector create end products that apply mechanical force, for example, the application of gears and levers, to perform work. Some important processes for the manufacture of machinery are forging, stamping, bending, forming, and machining that are used to shape individual pieces of metal. Processes, such as welding and assembling are used to join separate parts together. Although these processes are similar to those used in metal fabricating establishments, machinery manufacturing is different because it typically employs multiple metal forming processes in manufacturing the various parts of the machine. Moreover, complex assembly operations are an inherent part of the production process.

In general, design considerations are very important in machinery production. Establishments specialize in making machinery designed for particular applications. Thus, design is considered to be part of the production process for the purpose of implementing NAICS. The NAICS structure reflects this by defining industries and industry groups that make machinery for different applications. A broad distinction exists between machinery that is generally used in a variety of industrial applications (i.e., general purpose machinery) and machinery that is designed to be used in a particular industry (i.e., special purpose machinery). Three industry groups consist of special purpose machinery—Agricultural, Construction, and Mining Machinery Manufacturing; Industrial Machinery Manufacturing; and Commercial and Service Industry Machinery Manufacturing. The other industry groups make general-purpose machinery: Ventilation, Heating, Air Conditioning, and Commercial Refrigeration Equipment Manufacturing; Metalworking Machinery Manufacturing; Engine, Turbine, and Power Transmission Equipment Manufacturing; and Other General Purpose Machinery Manufacturing.

3331 Agriculture, Construction, and Mining Machinery Manufacturing

33311 Agricultural Implement Manufacturing

This industry comprises establishments primarily engaged in manufacturing farm machinery and equipment, powered mowing equipment and other powered home lawn and garden equipment.

US—United States industry only. CAN—United States and Canadian industries are comparable. When neither US nor CAN appears, Canadian, Mexican, and United States industries are comparable.

Illustrative Examples:

Combines (i.e., harvester-threshers) manufacturing

Cotton ginning machinery manufacturing

Farm tractors and attachments manufacturing

Farm-type fertilizing machinery manufacturing

Haying machines manufacturing

Milking machines manufacturing

Powered lawnmowers manufacturing

Planting machines, farm-type, manufacturing

Poultry brooders, feeders, and waterers manufacturing

Residential-type snowblowers and throwers manufacturing

Cross-References. Establishments primarily engaged in—

- Manufacturing agricultural handtools and nonpowered lawnmowers—are classified in Industry 33221, Cutlery and Handtool Manufacturing;

- Manufacturing farm conveyors—are classified in Industry 33392, Material Handling Equipment Manufacturing; and

- Manufacturing forestry machinery and equipment such as brush, limb and log chippers; log splitters; and equipment—are classified in Industry 33312, Construction Machinery Manufacturing.

333111 Farm Machinery and Equipment Manufacturing[US]

This U.S. industry comprises establishments primarily engaged in manufacturing agricultural and farm machinery and equipment, and other turf and grounds care equipment, including planting, harvesting, and grass mowing equipment (except lawn and garden-type).

Illustrative Examples:

Combines (i.e., harvester-threshers) manufacturing

Cotton ginning machinery manufacturing

Farm-type feed processing equipment manufacuturing

Farm-type fertilizing machinery manufacturing

Farm-type planting machines manufacturing

Farm-type plows manufacturing

Farm-type tractors and attachments manufacturing

Haying machines manufacturing

Milking machines manufacturing

Poultry brooders, feeders, and waterers manufacturing

Cross-References. Establishments primarily engaged in—

- Manufacturing farm conveyors—are classified in U.S. Industry 333922, Conveyor and Conveying Equipment Manufacturing;

- Manufacturing tractors and lawnmowers for home lawn and garden care—are classified in U.S. Industry 333112, Lawn and Garden Tractor and Home Lawn and Garden Equipment Manufacturing; and

- Manufacturing construction-type tractors—are classified in Industry 333120, Construction Machinery Manufacturing.

US—United States industry only. CAN—United States and Canadian industries are comparable. When neither US nor CAN appears, Canadian, Mexican, and United States industries are comparable.

http://www.ntis.gov/naics

333112 Lawn and Garden Tractor and Home Lawn and Garden Equipment Manufacturing[US]

This U.S. industry comprises establishments primarily engaged in manufacturing powered lawnmowers, lawn and garden tractors, and other home lawn and garden equipment, such as tillers, shredders, and yard vacuums and blowers.

Cross-References. Establishments primarily engaged in—

- Manufacturing commercial mowing and other turf and grounds care equipment—are classified in U.S. Industry 333111, Farm Machinery and Equipment Manufacturing; and

- Manufacturing nonpowered lawn and garden shears, edgers, pruners, and lawnmowers—are classified in Industry 33221, Cutlery and Handtool Manufacturing.

33312 Construction Machinery Manufacturing
See industry description for 333120 below.

333120 Construction Machinery Manufacturing

This industry comprises establishments primarily engaged in manufacturing construction machinery, surface mining machinery, and logging equipment.

Illustrative Examples:

Backhoes manufacturing
Bulldozers manufacturing
Construction and surface mining-type rock drill bits manufacturing
Construction-type tractors and attachments manufacturing
Off-highway trucks manufacturing

Pile-driving equipment manufacturing
Portable crushing, pulverizing, and screening machinery manufacturing
Powered post hole diggers manufacturing
Road graders manufacturing
Surface mining machinery (except drilling) manufacturing

Cross-References. Establishments primarily engaged in—

- Manufacturing drilling and underground mining machinery and equipment—are classified in Industry 33313, Mining and Oil and Gas Field Machinery Manufacturing;

- Manufacturing industrial plant overhead traveling cranes, hoists, truck-type cranes and hoists, winches, aerial work platforms, and automotive wrecker hoists—are classified in Industry 33392, Material Handling Equipment Manufacturing; and

- Manufacturing rail layers, ballast distributors and other railroad track-laying equipment—are classified in Industry 336510, Railroad Rolling Stock Manufacturing.

33313 Mining and Oil and Gas Field Machinery Manufacturing

This industry comprises establishments primarily engaged in manufacturing oil and gas field and underground mining machinery and equipment.

US—United States industry only. CAN—United States and Canadian industries are comparable. When neither US nor CAN appears, Canadian, Mexican, and United States industries are comparable.

http://www.ntis.gov/naics

Illustrative Examples:

Coal breakers, cutters, and pulverizers
manufacturing
Core drills, underground mining-type,
manufacturing
Mineral processing and beneficiating
machinery manufacturing
Mining cars manufacturing

Oil and gas field-type derricks manufacturing
Oil and gas field-type drilling machinery and
equipment (except offshore floating platforms)
manufacturing
Stationary rock crushing machinery
manufacturing
Water well drilling machinery manufacturing

Cross-References. Establishments primarily engaged in—

- Manufacturing offshore oil and gas well drilling and production floating platforms—are classified in Industry 33661, Ship and Boat Building;

- Manufacturing surface mining machinery and equipment—are classified in Industry 33312, Construction Machinery Manufacturing;

- Manufacturing coal and ore conveyors—are classified in Industry 33392, Material Handling Equipment Manufacturing;

- Manufacturing underground mining locomotives—are classified in Industry 33651, Railroad Rolling Stock Manufacturing; and

- Manufacturing pumps and pumping equipment—are classified in Industry 33391, Pump and Compressor Manufacturing.

333131 Mining Machinery and Equipment Manufacturing[US]

This U.S. industry comprises establishments primarily engaged in (1) manufacturing underground mining machinery and equipment, such as coal breakers, mining cars, core drills, coal cutters, rock drills and (2) manufacturing mineral beneficiating machinery and equipment used in surface or underground mines.

Cross-References. Establishments primarily engaged in—

- Manufacturing surface mining machinery and equipment—are classified in Industry 333120, Construction Machinery Manufacturing;

- Manufacturing well-drilling machinery—are classified in U.S. Industry 333132, Oil and Gas Field Machinery and Equipment Manufacturing;

- Manufacturing coal and ore conveyors—are classified in U.S. Industry 333922, Conveyor and Conveying Equipment Manufacturing; and

- Manufacturing underground mining locomotives—are classified in Industry 336510, Railroad Rolling Stock Manufacturing.

333132 Oil and Gas Field Machinery and Equipment Manufacturing[US]

This U.S. industry comprises establishments primarily engaged in (1) manufacturing oil and gas field machinery and equipment, such as oil and gas field drilling machinery and equipment; oil

---

and gas field production machinery and equipment; and oil and gas field derricks and (2) manufacturing water well drilling machinery.

Cross-References. Establishments primarily engaged in—

- Manufacturing offshore oil and gas well drilling and production floating platforms—are classified in U.S. Industry 336611, Ship Building and Repairing;

- Manufacturing underground mining drills—are classified in U.S. Industry 333131, Mining Machinery and Equipment Manufacturing; and

- Manufacturing pumps and pumping equipment—are classified in U.S. Industry 333911, Pump and Pumping Equipment Manufacturing.

3332 Industrial Machinery Manufacturing

33321 Sawmill and Woodworking Machinery Manufacturing
See industry description for 333210 below.

333210 Sawmill and Woodworking Machinery Manufacturing

This industry comprises establishments primarily engaged in manufacturing sawmill and woodworking machinery (except handheld), such as circular and band sawing equipment, planing machinery, and sanding machinery.

Cross-References. Establishments primarily engaged in—

- Manufacturing planes, axes, drawknives, and handsaws—are classified in Industry 33221, Cutlery and Handtool Manufacturing; and

- Manufacturing power-driven handtools—are classified in U.S. Industry 333991, Power-Driven Handtool Manufacturing.

33322 Plastics and Rubber Industry Machinery Manufacturing
See industry description for 333220 below.

333220 Plastics and Rubber Industry Machinery Manufacturing

This industry comprises establishments primarily engaged in manufacturing plastics and rubber products making machinery, such as plastics compression, extrusion and injection molding machinery and equipment, and tire building and recapping machinery and equipment.

Cross-References.

Establishments primarily engaged in manufacturing industrial metal molds for plastics and rubber products making machinery are classified in U.S. Industry 333511, Industrial Mold Manufacturing.

US—United States industry only. CAN—United States and Canadian industries are comparable. When neither US nor CAN appears, Canadian, Mexican, and United States industries are comparable.

http://www.ntis.gov/naics

33329 Other Industrial Machinery Manufacturing

This industry comprises establishments primarily engaged in manufacturing industrial machinery (except agricultural and farm-type, construction, mining, sawmill and woodworking, and plastics and rubber products making machinery).

Illustrative Examples:

Bakery ovens manufacturing
Chemical processing machinery and
   equipment manufacturing
Glass making machinery (e.g., blowing,
   forming, molding) manufacturing
Paper making machinery manufacturing
Petroleum refinery machinery manufacturing
Printing presses (except textile) manufacturing

Semiconductor making machinery
   manufacturing
Sewing machines (including household-type)
   manufacturing
Tannery machinery manufacturing
Textile making machinery (except sewing
   machines) manufacturing

Cross-References. Establishments primarily engaged in—

- Manufacturing agricultural and farm-type, construction, and mining machinery—are classified in Industry Group 3331, Agriculture, Construction, and Mining Machinery Manufacturing;

- Manufacturing sawmill and woodworking machinery—are classified in Industry 33321, Sawmill and Woodworking Machinery Manufacturing;

- Manufacturing plastics and rubber products making machinery—are classified in Industry 33322, Plastics and Rubber Industry Machinery Manufacturing;

- Manufacturing food and beverage packaging machinery—are classified in Industry 33399, All Other General Purpose Machinery Manufacturing;

- Manufacturing commercial and industrial refrigeration and freezer equipment—are classified in Industry 33341, Ventilation, Heating, Air-Conditioning, and Commercial Refrigeration Equipment Manufacturing;

- Manufacturing commercial-type cooking and food warming equipment, automotive maintenance equipment (except mechanics' handtools) and photocopiers—are classified in Industry 33331, Commercial and Service Industry Machinery Manufacturing; and

- Manufacturing mechanics' handtools—are classified in Industry 33221, Cutlery and Handtool Manufacturing.

333291 Paper Industry Machinery Manufacturing[CAN]

This U.S. industry comprises establishments primarily engaged in manufacturing paper industry machinery for making paper and paper products, such as pulp making machinery, paper and paperboard making machinery, and paper and paperboard converting machinery.

US—United States industry only. CAN—United States and Canadian industries are comparable. When neither US nor CAN appears, Canadian, Mexican, and United States industries are comparable.

Cross-References.

Establishments primarily engaged in manufacturing printing machinery are classified in U.S. Industry 333293, Printing Machinery and Equipment Manufacturing.

333292 Textile Machinery Manufacturing[US]

This U.S. industry comprises establishments primarily engaged in manufacturing textile machinery for making thread, yarn, and fiber.

Illustrative Examples:

Drawing machinery for textiles manufacturing
Extruding machinery for yarn manufacturing
Finishing machinery for textiles
  manufacturing
Knitting machinery manufacturing

Spinning machinery for textiles manufacturing
Texturizing machinery for textiles
  manufacturing
Weaving machinery manufacturing

Cross-References.

Establishments primarily engaged in manufacturing sewing machines are classified in U.S. Industry 333298, All Other Industrial Machinery Manufacturing.

333293 Printing Machinery and Equipment Manufacturing[US]

This U.S. industry comprises establishments primarily engaged in manufacturing printing and bookbinding machinery and equipment, such as printing presses, typesetting machinery, and bindery machinery.

Cross-References. Establishments primarily engaged in—

- Manufacturing textile printing machinery—are classified in U.S. Industry 333292, Textile Machinery Manufacturing; and

- Manufacturing photocopiers—are classified in U.S. Industry 333315, Photographic and Photocopying Equipment Manufacturing.

333294 Food Product Machinery Manufacturing[US]

This U.S. industry comprises establishments primarily engaged in manufacturing food and beverage manufacturing-type machinery and equipment, such as dairy product plant machinery and equipment (e.g., homogenizers, pasteurizers, ice cream freezers), bakery machinery and equipment (e.g., dough mixers, bake ovens, pastry rolling machines), meat and poultry processing and preparation machinery, and other commercial food products machinery (e.g., slicers, choppers, and mixers).

US—United States industry only. CAN—United States and Canadian industries are comparable. When neither US nor CAN appears, Canadian, Mexican, and United States industries are comparable.

Cross-References. Establishments primarily engaged in—

- Manufacturing food and beverage packaging machinery—are classified in U.S. Industry 333993, Packaging Machinery Manufacturing;

- Manufacturing commercial and industrial refrigeration and freezer equipment—are classified in U.S. Industry 333415, Air Conditioning and Warm Air Heating Equipment and Commercial and Industrial Refrigeration Equipment Manufacturing; and

- Manufacturing commercial-type cooking and food warming equipment—are classified in U.S. Industry 333319, Other Commercial and Service Industry Machinery Manufacturing.

333295 Semiconductor Machinery Manufacturing[US]

This U.S. industry comprises establishments primarily engaged in manufacturing wafer processing equipment, semiconductor assembly and packaging equipment, and other semiconductor making machinery.

Cross-References. Establishments primarily engaged in—

- Manufacturing printed circuit board manufacturing machinery—are classified in U.S. Industry 333298, All Other Industrial Machinery Manufacturing; and

- Manufacturing semiconductor testing instruments—are classified in U.S. Industry 334515, Instrument Manufacturing for Measuring and Testing Electricity and Electrical Signals.

333298 All Other Industrial Machinery Manufacturing[US]

This U.S. industry comprises establishments primarily engaged in manufacturing industrial machinery (except agricultural and farm-type, construction and mining machinery, sawmill and woodworking machinery, plastics and rubber making machinery, paper and paperboard making machinery, textile machinery, printing machinery and equipment, food manufacturing-type machinery, and semiconductor making machinery).

Illustrative Examples:

Chemical processing machinery and equipment manufacturing
Cigarette making machinery manufacturing
Circuit board making machinery manufacturing
Glass making machinery (e.g., blowing, forming, molding) manufacturing
Light bulb and tube (i.e., electric lamp) machinery manufacturing

Petroleum refining machinery manufacturing
Sewing machines (including household-type) manufacturing
Shoe making and repairing machinery manufacturing
Tannery machinery manufacturing
Wire and cable insulating machinery manufacturing

Cross-References. Establishments primarily engaged in—

- Manufacturing agricultural and farm-type, construction, and mining machinery—are classified in Industry Group 3331, Agriculture, Construction, and Mining Machinery Manufacturing;

- Manufacturing sawmill and woodworking machinery—are classified in Industry 333210, Sawmill and Woodworking Machinery Manufacturing;

- Manufacturing plastics and rubber products making machinery—are classified in Industry 333220, Plastics and Rubber Industry Machinery Manufacturing;

- Manufacturing paper and paperboard making machinery—are classified in U.S. Industry 333291, Paper Industry Machinery Manufacturing;

- Manufacturing textile machinery—are classified in U.S. Industry 333292, Textile Machinery Manufacturing;

- Manufacturing printing and bookbinding machinery and equipment—are classified in U.S. Industry 333293, Printing Machinery and Equipment Manufacturing;

- Manufacturing food and beverage manufacturing-type machinery—are classified in U.S. Industry 333294, Food Product Machinery Manufacturing;

- Manufacturing semiconductor making machinery—are classified in U.S. Industry 333295, Semiconductor Machinery Manufacturing;

- Manufacturing automotive maintenance equipment (except mechanics' handtools)—are classified in U.S. Industry 333319, Other Commercial and Service Industry Machinery Manufacturing; and

- Manufacturing mechanics' handtools—are classified in U.S. Industry 332212, Hand and Edge Tool Manufacturing.

3333 Commercial and Service Industry Machinery Manufacturing

33331 Commercial and Service Industry Machinery Manufacturing

This industry comprises establishments primarily engaged in manufacturing commercial and service machinery, such as automatic vending machinery, commercial laundry and dry-cleaning machinery, office machinery, photographic and photocopying machinery, optical instruments and machinery, automotive maintenance equipment (except mechanic's handtools), industrial vacuum cleaners, and commercial-type cooking equipment.

Cross-References. Establishments primarily engaged in—

- Manufacturing household-type appliances—are classified in Industry Group 3352, Household Appliance Manufacturing;

- Manufacturing computer and peripheral equipment (including point-of-sale terminals and funds transfer devices (ATMs))—are classified in Industry 33411, Computer and Peripheral Equipment Manufacturing;

- Manufacturing facsimile equipment—are classified in Industry 33421, Telephone Apparatus Manufacturing;

US—United States industry only. CAN—United States and Canadian industries are comparable. When neither US nor CAN appears, Canadian, Mexican, and United States industries are comparable.

- Manufacturing timeclocks, timestamps, and electron and proton microscopes—are classified in Industry 33451, Navigational, Measuring, Electromedical, and Control Instruments Manufacturing;

- Manufacturing pencil sharpeners and staplers—are classified in Industry 33994, Office Supplies (except Paper) Manufacturing;

- Manufacturing sensitized film, paper, cloth, and plates, and prepared photographic chemicals—are classified in Industry 32599, All Other Chemical Product and Preparation Manufacturing;

- Manufacturing ophthalmic focus lenses—are classified in Industry 33911, Medical Equipment and Supplies Manufacturing;

- Manufacturing television, video, and digital cameras—are classified in Subsector 334, Computer and Electronic Product Manufacturing;

- Manufacturing coin-operated arcade games—are classified in Industry 33999, All Other Miscellaneous Manufacturing;

- Manufacturing mechanics' handtools—are classified in Industry 33221, Cutlery and Handtool Manufacturing;

- Manufacturing molded plastics lens blanks—are classified in Industry 32619, Other Plastics Product Manufacturing; and

- Manufacturing molded glass lens blanks—are classified in Industry 32721, Glass and Glass Product Manufacturing.

333311 Automatic Vending Machine Manufacturing[US]

This U.S. industry comprises establishments primarily engaged in (1) manufacturing coin, token, currency or magnetic card operated vending machines and/or (2) manufacturing coin operated mechanism for machines, such as vending machines, lockers, and laundry machines.

Cross-References.

Establishments primarily engaged in manufacturing coin-operated arcade games are classified in U.S. Industry 339999, All Other Miscellaneous Manufacturing.

333312 Commercial Laundry, Drycleaning, and Pressing Machine Manufacturing[US]

This U.S. industry comprises establishments primarily engaged in manufacturing commercial and industrial laundry and drycleaning equipment and pressing machines.

Cross-References.

Establishments primarily engaged in manufacturing household-type laundry equipment are classified in U.S. Industry 335224, Household Laundry Equipment Manufacturing.

US—United States industry only. CAN—United States and Canadian industries are comparable. When neither US nor CAN appears, Canadian, Mexican, and United States industries are comparable.

333313 Office Machinery Manufacturing[US]

This U.S. industry comprises establishments primarily engaged in manufacturing office machinery (except computers and photocopying equipment), such as mailhandling machinery and equipment, calculators, typewriters, and dedicated word processing equipment.

Cross-References. Establishments primarily engaged in—

- Manufacturing computers and peripheral (including point-of-sale terminals and automatic teller machines (ATMs)) equipment—are classified in Industry 33411, Computer and Peripheral Equipment Manufacturing;

- Manufacturing photocopy equipment—are classified in U.S. Industry 333315, Photographic and Photocopying Equipment Manufacturing;

- Manufacturing facsimile equipment—are classified in Industry 334210, Telephone Apparatus Manufacturing;

- Manufacturing timeclocks and timestamps—are classified in U.S. Industry 334518, Watch, Clock, and Part Manufacturing; and

- Manufacturing pencil sharpeners, staplers, staple removers, hand paper punches, cutters, trimmers, and other hand office equipment—are classified in U.S. Industry 339942, Lead Pencil and Art Good Manufacturing.

333314 Optical Instrument and Lens Manufacturing[US]

This U.S. industry comprises establishments primarily engaged in one or more of the following: (1) manufacturing optical instruments and lens, such as binoculars, microscopes (except electron, proton), telescopes, prisms, and lenses (except ophthalmic); (2) coating or polishing lenses (except ophthalmic); and (3) mounting lenses (except ophthalmic).

Cross-References. Establishments primarily engaged in—

- Manufacturing ophthalmic focus lenses—are classified in U.S. Industry 339115, Ophthalmic Goods Manufacturing;

- Manufacturing electron and proton microscopes—are classified in U.S. Industry 334516, Analytical Laboratory Instrument Manufacturing;

- Manufacturing molded plastics lens blanks—are classified in U.S. Industry 326199, All Other Plastics Product Manufacturing; and

- Manufacturing molded glass lens blanks—are classified in U.S. Industry 327212, Other Pressed and Blown Glass and Glassware Manufacturing.

333315 Photographic and Photocopying Equipment Manufacturing[US]

This U.S. industry comprises establishments primarily engaged in manufacturing photographic and photocopying equipment, such as cameras (except television, video, digital projectors, film developing equipment, photocopying equipment, and microfilm equipment).

US—United States industry only. CAN—United States and Canadian industries are comparable. When neither US nor CAN appears, Canadian, Mexican, and United States industries are comparable.

Cross-References. Establishments primarily engaged in—

- Manufacturing sensitized film, paper, cloth, and plates, and prepared photographic chemicals—are classified in U.S. Industry 325992, Photographic Film, Paper, Plate, and Chemical Manufacturing;

- Manufacturing photographic lenses—are classified in U.S. Industry 333314, Optical Instrument and Lens Manufacturing; and

- Manufacturing television, video, and digital cameras—are classified in Subsector 334, Computer and Electronic Product Manufacturing.

333319 Other Commercial and Service Industry Machinery Manufacturing[US]

This U.S. industry comprises establishments primarily engaged in manufacturing commercial and service industry equipment (except automatic vending machines, commercial laundry, drycleaning and pressing machines, office machinery, optical instruments and lenses, and photographic and photocopying equipment).

Illustrative Examples:

Carnival and amusement park rides manufacturing
Carwashing machinery manufacturing
Commercial-type coffee makers and urns manufacturing
Commercial-type cooking equipment (i.e., fryers, microwave ovens, ovens, ranges) manufacturing
Industrial and commercial-type vacuum cleaners manufacturing

Mechanical carpet sweepers manufacturing
Motor vehicle alignment equipment manufacturing
Power washer cleaning equipment manufacturing
Teaching machines (e.g., flight simulators) manufacturing
Water treatment equipment manufacturing

Cross-References. Establishments primarily engaged in—

- Manufacturing automatic vending machines—are classified in U.S. Industry 333311, Automatic Vending Machine Manufacturing;

- Manufacturing commercial laundry drycleaning and pressing machines—are classified in U.S. Industry 333312, Commercial Laundry, Drycleaning, and Pressing Machine Manufacturing;

- Manufacturing office machinery—are classified in U.S. Industry 333313, Office Machinery Manufacturing;

- Manufacturing optical instruments and lenses—are classified in U.S. Industry 333314, Optical Instrument and Lens Manufacturing;

- Manufacturing photographic and photocopying equipment—are classified in U.S. Industry 333315, Photographic and Photocopying Equipment Manufacturing;

US—United States industry only. CAN—United States and Canadian industries are comparable. When neither US nor CAN appears, Canadian, Mexican, and United States industries are comparable.

http://www.ntis.gov/naics

- Manufacturing household-type appliances—are classified in Industry Group 3352, Household Appliance Manufacturing; and

- Manufacturing mechanics' handtools—are classified in U.S. Industry 332212, Hand and Edge Tool Manufacturing.

3334 Ventilation, Heating, Air-Conditioning, and Commercial Refrigeration Equipment Manufacturing

33341 Ventilation, Heating, Air-Conditioning, and Commercial Refrigeration Equipment Manufacturing

This industry comprises establishments primarily engaged in manufacturing ventilating, heating, air-conditioning, and commercial and industrial refrigeration and freezer equipment.

Illustrative Examples:

Air-conditioning and warm air heating
combination units manufacturing
Air-conditioner filters manufacturing
Attic fans manufacturing
Dust and fume collecting equipment
manufacturing
Gas fireplaces manufacturing
Heating boilers manufacturing

Industrial and commercial-type fans
manufacturing
Refrigerated counter and display cases
manufacturing
Refrigerated drinking fountains manufacturing
Space heaters (except portable electric)
manufacturing

Cross-References. Establishments primarily engaged in—

- Manufacturing household-type fans (except attic), portable electric space heaters, humidifiers, dehumidifiers, and air purification equipment—are classified in Industry 33521, Small Electrical Appliance Manufacturing;

- Manufacturing household-type appliances, such as cooking stoves, ranges, refrigerators, and freezers—are classified in Industry 33522, Major Appliance Manufacturing;

- Manufacturing commercial-type cooking equipment—are classified in Industry 33329, Other Industrial Machinery Manufacturing;

- Manufacturing industrial, power, and marine boilers—are classified in Industry 33241, Power Boiler and Heat Exchanger Manufacturing;

- Manufacturing industrial process furnaces and ovens—are classified in Industry 33399, All Other General Purpose Machinery Manufacturing; and

- Manufacturing motor vehicle air-conditioning systems and compressors—are classified in Industry 33639, Other Motor Vehicle Parts Manufacturing.

US—United States industry only. CAN—United States and Canadian industries are comparable. When neither US nor CAN appears, Canadian, Mexican, and United States industries are comparable.

http://www.ntis.gov/naics

333411 Air Purification Equipment Manufacturing^{US}

This U.S. industry comprises establishments primarily engaged in manufacturing stationary air purification equipment, such as industrial dust and fume collection equipment, electrostatic precipitation equipment, warm air furnace filters, air washers, and other dust collection equipment.

Cross-References. Establishments primarily engaged in—

- Manufacturing air-conditioning units (except motor vehicle)—are classified in U.S. Industry 333415, Air-Conditioning and Warm Air Heating Equipment and Commercial and Industrial Refrigeration Equipment Manufacturing;

- Manufacturing motor vehicle air-conditioning systems and compressors—are classified in U.S. Industry 336391, Motor Vehicle Air-Conditioning Manufacturing;

- Manufacturing household-type fans (except attic) and portable air purification equipment—are classified in U.S. Industry 335211, Electric Housewares and Household Fan Manufacturing; and

- Manufacturing industrial and commercial blowers, industrial and commercial exhaust and ventilating fans, and attic fans—are classified in U.S. Industry 333412, Industrial and Commercial Fan and Blower Manufacturing.

333412 Industrial and Commercial Fan and Blower Manufacturing^{US}

This U.S. industry comprises establishments primarily engaged in manufacturing attic fans and industrial and commercial fans and blowers, such as commercial exhaust fans and commercial ventilating fans.

Cross-References. Establishments primarily engaged in—

- Manufacturing air-conditioning units (except motor vehicle)—are classified in U.S. Industry 333415, Air-Conditioning and Warm Air Heating Equipment and Commercial and Industrial Refrigeration Equipment Manufacturing;

- Manufacturing motor vehicle air-conditioning systems and compressors—are classified in U.S. Industry 336391, Motor Vehicle Air-Conditioning Manufacturing;

- Manufacturing household-type fans (except attic) and portable air purification equipment—are classified in U.S. Industry 335211, Electric Housewares and Household Fan Manufacturing; and

- Manufacturing stationary air purification equipment—are classified in U.S. Industry 333411, Air Purification Equipment Manufacturing.

333414 Heating Equipment (except Warm Air Furnaces) Manufacturing^{US}

This U.S. industry comprises establishments primarily engaged in manufacturing heating equipment (except electric and warm air furnaces), such as heating boilers, heating stoves, floor and wall furnaces, and wall and baseboard heating units.

US—United States industry only. CAN—United States and Canadian industries are comparable. When neither US nor CAN appears, Canadian, Mexican, and United States industries are comparable.

Cross-References. Establishments primarily engaged in—

- Manufacturing warm air furnaces—are classified in U.S. Industry 333415, Air-Conditioning and Warm Air Heating Equipment and Commercial and Industrial Refrigeration Equipment Manufacturing;

- Manufacturing electric space heaters—are classified in U.S. Industry 335211, Electric Housewares and Household Fan Manufacturing;

- Manufacturing household-type cooking stoves and ranges—are classified in U.S. Industry 335221, Household Cooking Appliance Manufacturing;

- Manufacturing industrial, power, and marine boilers—are classified in Industry 332410, Power Boiler and Heat Exchanger Manufacturing;

- Manufacturing industrial process furnaces and ovens—are classified in U.S. Industry 333994, Industrial Process Furnace and Oven Manufacturing; and

- Manufacturing commercial-type cooking equipment—are classified in U.S. Industry 333319, Other Commercial and Service Industry Machinery Manufacturing.

333415 Air-Conditioning and Warm Air Heating Equipment and Commercial and Industrial Refrigeration Equipment Manufacturing[US]

This U.S. industry comprises establishments primarily engaged in (1) manufacturing air-conditioning (except motor vehicle) and warm air furnace equipment and/or (2) manufacturing commercial and industrial refrigeration and freezer equipment.

Illustrative Examples:

Air-conditioning and warm air heating
  combination units manufacturing
Air-conditioning compressors (except motor
  vehicle) manufacturing
Air-conditioning condensers and condensing
  units manufacturing
Dehumidifiers (except portable electric)
  manufacturing
Heat pumps manufacturing

Humidifying equipment (except portable)
  manufacturing
Refrigerated counter and display cases
  manufacturing
Refrigerated drinking fountains manufacturing
Soda fountain cooling and dispensing
  equipment manufacturing
Snow making machinery manufacturing

Cross-References. Establishments primarily engaged in—

- Manufacturing motor vehicle air-conditioning systems and compressors—are classified in U.S. Industry 336391, Motor Vehicle Air-Conditioning Manufacturing;

- Manufacturing household-type refrigerators and freezers—are classified in U.S. Industry 335222, Household Refrigerator and Home Freezer Manufacturing;

- Manufacturing portable electric space heaters, humidifiers, and dehumidifiers—are classified in U.S. Industry 335211, Electric Housewares and Household Fan Manufacturing;

US—United States industry only. CAN—United States and Canadian industries are comparable. When neither US nor CAN appears, Canadian, Mexican, and United States industries are comparable.

- Manufacturing heating boilers, heating stoves, floor and wall mount furnaces, and electric wall and baseboard heating units—are classified in U.S. Industry 333414, Heating Equipment (except Warm Air Furnaces) Manufacturing; and

- Manufacturing furnace air filters—are classified in U.S. Industry 333411, Air Purification Equipment Manufacturing,

3335 Metalworking Machinery Manufacturing

33351 Metalworking Machinery Manufacturing

This industry comprises establishments primarily engaged in manufacturing metalworking machinery, such as metal cutting and metal forming machine tools; cutting tools; and accessories for metalworking machinery; special dies, tools, jigs, and fixtures; industrial molds; rolling mill machinery; assembly machinery; coil handling, conversion, or straightening equipment; and wire drawing and fabricating machines.

Cross-References. Establishments primarily engaged in—

- Manufacturing handtools (except power-driven), cutting dies (except metal cutting), saw-blades, and handsaws—are classified in Industry 33221, Cutlery and Handtool Manufacturing;

- Manufacturing casting molds for heavy steel ingots—are classified in Industry 33151, Ferrous Metal Foundries; and

- Manufacturing power-driven handtools and welding and soldering equipment—are classified in Industry 33399, All Other General Purpose Machinery Manufacturing.

333511 Industrial Mold Manufacturing[CAN]

This U.S. industry comprises establishments primarily engaged in manufacturing industrial molds for casting metals or forming other materials, such as plastics, glass, or rubber.

Cross-References.

Establishments primarily engaged in manufacturing casting molds for steel ingots are classified in U.S. Industry 331511, Iron Foundries.

333512 Machine Tool (Metal Cutting Types) Manufacturing[US]

This U.S. industry comprises establishments primarily engaged in manufacturing metal cutting machine tools (except handtools).

Illustrative Examples:

Home workshop metal cutting machine tools (except handtools, welding equipment) manufacturing

Metalworking grinding machines manufacturing

Metalworking lathes manufacturing

US—United States industry only. CAN—United States and Canadian industries are comparable. When neither US nor CAN appears, Canadian, Mexican, and United States industries are comparable.

http://www.ntis.gov/naics

Metalworking boring machines manufacturing
Metalworking buffing and polishing machines manufacturing
Metalworking drilling machines manufacturing

Metalworking milling machines manufacturing

Cross-References. Establishments primarily engaged in—

- Manufacturing welding and soldering equipment—are classified in U.S. Industry 333992, Welding and Soldering Equipment Manufacturing;

- Manufacturing metal-forming machine tools—are classified in U.S. Industry 333513, Machine Tool (Metal Forming Types) Manufacturing;

- Manufacturing power-driven metal cutting handtools—are classified in U.S. Industry 333991, Power-Driven Handtool Manufacturing; and

- Manufacturing accessories and attachments for metal cutting machine tools—are classified in U.S. Industry 333515, Cutting Tool and Machine Tool Accessory Manufacturing.

333513 Machine Tool (Metal Forming Types) Manufacturing[US]

This U.S. industry comprises establishments primarily engaged in manufacturing metal forming machine tools (except handtools), such as punching, sheering, bending, forming, pressing, forging and die-casting machines.

Cross-References. Establishments primarily engaged in—

- Manufacturing welding and soldering equipment—are classified in U.S. Industry 333992, Welding and Soldering Equipment Manufacturing;

- Manufacturing metal-cutting machine tools—are classified in U.S. Industry 333512, Machine Tool (Metal Cutting Types) Manufacturing;

- Manufacturing power-driven handtools—are classified in U.S. Industry 333991, Power-Driven Handtool Manufacturing;

- Manufacturing rolling mill machinery and equipment—are classified in U.S. Industry 333516, Rolling Mill Machinery and Equipment Manufacturing; and

- Manufacturing accessories and attachments for metal forming machine tools—are classified in U.S. Industry 333515, Cutting Tool and Machine Tool Accessory Manufacturing.

333514 Special Die and Tool, Die Set, Jig, and Fixture Manufacturing[US]

This U.S. industry comprises establishments, known as tool and die shops, primarily engaged in manufacturing special tools and fixtures, such as cutting dies and jigs.

Cross-References. Establishments primarily engaged in—

- Manufacturing molds for die-casting and foundry casting; and metal molds for plaster working, rubber working, plastics working, and glass working machinery—are classified in U.S. Industry 333511, Industrial Mold Manufacturing;

- Manufacturing molds for heavy steel ingots—are classified in U.S. Industry 331511, Iron Foundries; and

- Manufacturing cutting dies for materials other than metal—are classified in U.S. Industry 332212, Hand and Edge Tool Manufacturing.

333515 Cutting Tool and Machine Tool Accessory Manufacturing[US]

This U.S. industry comprises establishments primarily engaged in manufacturing accessories and attachments for metal cutting and metal forming machine tools.

Illustrative Examples:

Knives and bits for metalworking lathes, planers, and shapers manufacturing
Measuring attachments (e.g., sine bars) for machine tool manufacturing

Metalworking drill bits
Taps and dies (i.e., machine tool accessories) manufacturing

Cross-References. Establishments primarily engaged in—

- Manufacturing accessories and attachments for cutting and forming machines (except metal cutting, metal forming machinery)—are classified in U.S. Industry 332212, Hand and Edge Tool Manufacturing; and

- Manufacturing saw blades and handsaws—are classified in U.S. Industry 332213, Saw Blade and Handsaw Manufacturing.

333516 Rolling Mill Machinery and Equipment Manufacturing[US]

This U.S. industry comprises establishments primarily engaged in manufacturing rolling mill machinery and equipment for metal production.

333518 Other Metalworking Machinery Manufacturing[US]

This U.S. industry comprises establishments primarily engaged in manufacturing metal working machinery (except industrial molds; metal cutting machine tools; metal forming machine tools; special dies and tools, die sets, jigs, and fixtures; cutting tools and machine tool accessories; and rolling mill machinery and equipment).

Illustrative Examples:

Assembly machines manufacturing
Cradle assemblies machinery (i.e., wire making equipment) manufacturing
Metalworking coil winding and cutting machinery machinery

Wiredrawing and fabricating machinery and equipment (except dies) manufacturing

---

US—United States industry only. CAN—United States and Canadian industries are comparable. When neither US nor CAN appears, Canadian, Mexican, and United States industries are comparable.

Cross-References. Establishments primarily engaged in—

- Manufacturing industrial molds—are classified in U.S. Industry 333511, Industrial Mold Manufacturing;

- Manufacturing metal cutting machinery—are classified in U.S. Industry 333512, Machine Tool (Metal Cutting Types) Manufacturing;

- Manufacturing metal forming machinery—are classified in U.S. Industry 333513, Machine Tool (Metal Forming Types) Manufacturing;

- Manufacturing special dies and tools, die sets, jigs, and fixtures—are classified in U.S. Industry 333514, Special Die and Tool, Die Set, Jig, and Fixture Manufacturing;

- Manufacturing cutting tools and machine tool accessories—are classified in U.S. Industry 333515, Cutting Tool and Machine Tool Accessory Manufacturing; and

- Manufacturing rolling mill machinery—are classified in U.S. Industry 333516, Rolling Mill Machinery and Equipment Manufacturing.

3336 Engine, Turbine, and Power Transmission Equipment Manufacturing

33361 Engine, Turbine, and Power Transmission Equipment Manufacturing

This industry comprises establishments primarily engaged in manufacturing turbines, power transmission equipment, and internal combustion engines (except automotive gasoline and aircraft).

Illustrative Examples:

Clutches and brakes (except electromagnetic industrial controls, motor vehicle) manufacturing
Diesel and semidiesel engines manufacturing
Electric outboard motors manufacturing
Plain bearings (except internal combustion engine) manufacturing
Plain bushings (except internal combustion engine) manufacturing

Power transmission pulleys manufacturing
Speed changers (i.e., power transmission equipment) manufacturing
Speed reducers (i.e. power transmission equipment) manufacturing
Turbine generator set units manufacturing
Universal joints (except aircraft, motor vehicle) manufacturing

Cross-References. Establishments primarily engaged in—

- Manufacturing motor vehicle power transmission equipment—are classified in Industry 33635, Motor Vehicle Transmission and Power Train Parts Manufacturing;

- Manufacturing aircraft engines and aircraft power transmission equipment—are classified in Industry 33641, Aerospace Product and Parts Manufacturing;

- Manufacturing ball and roller bearings—are classified in Industry 33299, All Other Fabricated Metal Product Manufacturing;

US—United States industry only. CAN—United States and Canadian industries are comparable. When neither US nor CAN appears, Canadian, Mexican, and United States industries are comparable.

- Manufacturing automotive engines (except diesel)—are classified in Industry 33631, Motor Vehicle Gasoline Engine and Engine Parts Manufacturing; and

- Manufacturing electric power transmission, electric power distribution equipment, generators, or prime mover generator sets (except turbines)—are classified in Industry 33531, Electrical Equipment Manufacturing.

333611 Turbine and Turbine Generator Set Units Manufacturing[CAN]

This U.S. industry comprises establishments primarily engaged in manufacturing turbines (except aircraft); and complete turbine generator set units, such as steam, hydraulic, gas, and wind.

Cross-References. Establishments primarily engaged in—

- Manufacturing aircraft turbines—are classified in U.S. Industry 336412, Aircraft Engine and Engine Parts Manufacturing; and

- Manufacturing generators or prime mover generator sets (except turbines)—are classified in U.S. Industry 335312, Motor and Generator Manufacturing.

333612 Speed Changer, Industrial High-Speed Drive, and Gear Manufacturing[US]

This U.S. industry comprises establishments primarily engaged in manufacturing gears, speed changers, and industrial high-speed drives (except hydrostatic).

Cross-References. Establishments primarily engaged in—

- Manufacturing motor vehicle power transmission equipment—are classified in Industry 336350, Motor Vehicle Transmission and Power Train Parts Manufacturing;

- Manufacturing aircraft power transmission equipment—are classified in U.S. Industry 336413, Other Aircraft Parts and Auxiliary Equipment Manufacturing; and

- Manufacturing industrial hydrostatic transmissions—are classified in U.S. Industry 333613, Mechanical Power Transmission Equipment Manufacturing.

333613 Mechanical Power Transmission Equipment Manufacturing[US]

This U.S. industry comprises establishments primarily engaged in manufacturing mechanical power transmission equipment (except motor vehicle and aircraft), such as plain bearings, brakes and clutches (except motor vehicle and electromagnetic industrial control), couplings, joints, and drive chains.

Cross-References. Establishments primarily engaged in—

- Manufacturing motor vehicle power transmission equipment—are classified in Industry 336350, Motor Vehicle Transmission and Power Train Parts Manufacturing;

- Manufacturing aircraft power transmission equipment—are classified in U.S. Industry 336413, Other Aircraft Parts and Auxiliary Equipment Manufacturing;

US—United States industry only. CAN—United States and Canadian industries are comparable. When neither US nor CAN appears, Canadian, Mexican, and United States industries are comparable.

- Manufacturing ball and roller bearings—are classified in U.S. Industry 332991, Ball and Roller Bearing Manufacturing; and

- Manufacturing gears, speed changers, and industrial high-speed drives (except hydrostatic)—are classified in U.S. Industry 333612, Speed Changer, Industrial High-Speed Drive, and Gear Manufacturing.

333618 Other Engine Equipment Manufacturing[US]

This U.S. industry comprises establishments primarily engaged in manufacturing internal combustion engines (except automotive gasoline and aircraft).

Cross-References. Establishments primarily engaged in—

- Manufacturing gasoline motor vehicle engines and motor vehicle transmissions—are classified in Industry Group 3363, Motor Vehicle Parts Manufacturing;

- Manufacturing gasoline aircraft engines and aircraft transmissions—are classified in Industry 33641, Aerospace Product and Parts Manufacturing;

- Manufacturing turbine and turbine generator sets units—are classified in U.S. Industry 333611, Turbine and Turbine Generator Set Units Manufacturing;

- Manufacturing speed changers and industrial high-speed drivers and gears—are classified in U.S. Industry 333612, Speed Changer, Industrial High-Speed Drive, and Gear Manufacturing; and

- Manufacturing mechanical power transmission equipment (except motor vehicle and aircraft)—are classified in U.S. Industry 333613, Mechanical Power Transmission Equipment Manufacturing.

3339 Other General Purpose Machinery Manufacturing

33391 Pump and Compressor Manufacturing

This industry comprises establishments primarily engaged in manufacturing pumps and compressors, such as general purpose air and gas compressors, nonagricultural spraying and dusting equipment, general purpose pumps and pumping equipment (except fluid power pumps and motors), and measuring and dispensing pumps.

Cross-References. Establishments primarily engaged in—

- Manufacturing fluid power pumps and motors and handheld pneumatic spray guns—are classified in Industry 33399, All Other General Purpose Machinery Manufacturing;

- Manufacturing agricultural spraying and dusting equipment—are classified in Industry 33311, Agricultural Implement Manufacturing;

- Manufacturing laboratory vacuum pumps—are classified in Industry 33911, Medical Equipment and Supplies Manufacturing;

US—United States industry only. CAN—United States and Canadian industries are comparable. When neither US nor CAN appears, Canadian, Mexican, and United States industries are comparable.

- Manufacturing pumps and air-conditioning systems and compressors for motor vehicles—are classified in Industry Group 3363, Motor Vehicle Parts Manufacturing; and

- Manufacturing air-conditioning systems and compressors (except motor vehicle)—are classified in Industry 33341, Ventilation, Heating, Air-Conditioning, and Commercial Refrigeration Equipment Manufacturing.

333911 Pump and Pumping Equipment Manufacturing[US]

This U.S. industry comprises establishments primarily engaged in manufacturing general purpose pumps and pumping equipment (except fluid power pumps and motors), such as reciprocating pumps, turbine pumps, centrifugal pumps, rotary pumps, diaphragm pumps, domestic water system pumps, oil well and oil field pumps and sump pumps.

Cross-References. Establishments primarily engaged in—

- Manufacturing fluid power pumps and motors—are classified in U.S. Industry 333996, Fluid Power Pump and Motor Manufacturing;

- Manufacturing measuring and dispensing pumps—are classified in U.S. Industry 333913, Measuring and Dispensing Pump Manufacturing;

- Manufacturing vacuum pumps (except laboratory)—are classified in U.S. Industry 333912, Air and Gas Compressor Manufacturing;

- Manufacturing laboratory vacuum pumps—are classified in U.S. Industry 339111, Laboratory Apparatus and Furniture Manufacturing; and

- Manufacturing fluid pumps for motor vehicles, such as oil pumps, water pumps, and power steering pumps,—are classified in Industry Group 3363, Motor Vehicle Parts Manufacturing.

333912 Air and Gas Compressor Manufacturing[US]

This U.S. industry comprises establishments primarily engaged in manufacturing general purpose air and gas compressors, such as reciprocating compressors, centrifugal compressors, vacuum pumps (except laboratory), and nonagricultural spraying and dusting compressors and spray gun units.

Cross-References. Establishments primarily engaged in—

- Manufacturing refrigeration and air-conditioning (except motor vehicle) systems and compressors—are classified in U.S. Industry 333415, Air-Conditioning and Warm Air Heating Equipment and Commercial and Industrial Refrigeration Equipment Manufacturing;

- Manufacturing motor vehicle air-conditioning systems and compressors—are classified in U.S. Industry 336391, Motor Vehicle Air-Conditioning Manufacturing;

- Manufacturing fluid power pumps and motors—are classified in U.S. Industry 333996, Fluid Power Pump and Motor Manufacturing;

- Manufacturing agricultural spraying and dusting equipment—are classified in U.S. Industry 333111, Farm Machinery and Equipment Manufacturing;

- Manufacturing laboratory vacuum pumps—are classified in U.S. Industry 339111, Laboratory Apparatus and Furniture Manufacturing; and

- Manufacturing handheld pneumatic spray guns—are classified in U.S. Industry 333991, Power-Driven Handtool Manufacturing

333913 Measuring and Dispensing Pump Manufacturing[US]

This U.S. industry comprises establishments primarily engaged in manufacturing measuring and dispensing pumps, such as gasoline pumps and lubricating oil measuring and dispensing pumps.

Cross-References.

Establishments primarily engaged in manufacturing pumps and pumping equipment for general industrial use are classified in U.S. Industry 333911, Pump and Pumping Equipment Manufacturing.

33392 Material Handling Equipment Manufacturing

This industry comprises establishments primarily engaged in manufacturing material handling equipment, such as elevators and moving stairs; conveyors and conveying equipment; overhead traveling cranes, hoists, and monorail systems; and industrial trucks, tractors, trailers, and stacker machinery.

Cross-References. Establishments primarily engaged in—

- Manufacturing motor vehicle-type trailers—are classified in Industry 33621, Motor Vehicle Body and Trailer Manufacturing;

- Manufacturing farm-type tractors—are classified in Industry 33311, Agricultural Implement Manufacturing;

- Manufacturing construction-type tractors and cranes—are classified in Industry 33312, Construction Machinery Manufacturing; and

- Manufacturing power transmission pulleys—are classified in Industry 33361, Engine, Turbine, and Power Transmission Equipment Manufacturing.

333921 Elevator and Moving Stairway Manufacturing[US]

This U.S. industry comprises establishments primarily engaged in manufacturing elevators and moving stairways.

Illustrative Examples:

Automobile lifts (i.e., garage-type, service station) manufacturing
Escalators manufacturing

Moving walkways manufacturing
Passenger and freight elevators manufacturing

US—United States industry only. CAN—United States and Canadian industries are comparable. When neither US nor CAN appears, Canadian, Mexican, and United States industries are comparable.

Cross-References.

Establishments primarily engaged in manufacturing commercial conveyor systems and equipment are classified in U.S. Industry 333922, Conveyor and Conveying Equipment Manufacturing.

333922 Conveyor and Conveying Equipment Manufacturing[US]

This U.S. industry comprises establishments primarily engaged in manufacturing conveyors and conveying equipment, such as gravity conveyors, trolley conveyors, tow conveyors, pneumatic tube conveyors, carousel conveyors, farm conveyors, and belt conveyors.

Cross-References. Establishments primarily engaged in—

- Manufacturing passenger or freight elevators, dumbwaiters, and moving stairways—are classified in U.S. Industry 333921, Elevator and Moving Stairway Manufacturing; and

- Manufacturing overhead traveling cranes and monorail systems—are classified in U.S. Industry 333923, Overhead Traveling Crane, Hoist, and Monorail System Manufacturing.

333923 Overhead Traveling Crane, Hoist, and Monorail System Manufacturing[US]

This U.S. industry comprises establishments primarily engaged in manufacturing overhead traveling cranes, hoists, and monorail systems.

Illustrative Examples:

Aerial work platforms manufacturing
Automobile wrecker (i.e., tow truck) hoists
  manufacturing
Block and tackle manufacturing

Metal pulleys (except power transmission)
  manufacturing
Winches manufacturing

Cross-References. Establishments primarily engaged in—

- Manufacturing construction-type cranes—are classified in Industry 333120, Construction Machinery Manufacturing;

- Manufacturing aircraft loading hoists—are classified in U.S. Industry 333924, Industrial Truck, Tractor, Trailer, and Stacker Machinery Manufacturing; and

- Manufacturing power transmission pulleys—are classified in U.S. Industry 333613, Mechanical Power Transmission Equipment Manufacturing.

333924 Industrial Truck, Tractor, Trailer, and Stacker Machinery Manufacturing[US]

This U.S. industry comprises establishments primarily engaged in manufacturing industrial trucks, tractors, trailers, and stackers (i.e., truck-type) such as forklifts, pallet loaders and unloaders, and portable loading docks.

US—United States industry only. CAN—United States and Canadian industries are comparable. When neither US nor CAN appears, Canadian, Mexican, and United States industries are comparable.

Cross-References. Establishments primarily engaged in—

- Manufacturing motor vehicle-type trailers—are classified in U.S. Industry 336212, Truck Trailer Manufacturing;

- Manufacturing farm-type tractors—are classified in U.S. Industry 333111, Farm Machinery and Equipment Manufacturing; and

- Manufacturing construction-type tractors—are classified in Industry 333120, Construction Machinery Manufacturing.

33399 All Other General Purpose Machinery Manufacturing

This industry comprises establishments primarily engaged in manufacturing general purpose machinery (except ventilation, heating, air-conditioning, and commercial refrigeration equipment; metal working machinery; engines, turbines, and power transmission equipment; pumps and compressors; and material handling equipment).

Illustrative Examples:

Automatic fire sprinkler systems manufacturing
Bridge and gate lifting machinery manufacturing
Fluid power cylinders manufacturing
Fluid power pumps manufacturing

Hydraulic and pneumatic jacks manufacturing
Industrial-type furnaces manufacturing
Packaging machinery manufacturing
Power-driven handtools manufacturing
Scales (except laboratory-type) manufacturing
Welding equipment manufacturing

Cross-References. Establishments primarily engaged in—

- Manufacturing ventilating, heating, air-conditioning (except motor vehicle), commercial refrigeration, and furnace filters—are classified in Industry 33341, Ventilation, Heating, Air-Conditioning, and Commercial Refrigeration Equipment Manufacturing;

- Manufacturing metalworking machinery—are classified in Industry Group 3335, Metalworking Machinery Manufacturing;

- Manufacturing engine, turbine and power transmission equipment—are classified in Industry Group 3336, Engine, Turbine, and Power Transmission Equipment Manufacturing;

- Manufacturing pumps and compressors—are classified in Industry 33391, Pump and Compressor Manufacturing;

- Manufacturing material handling equipment—are classified in Industry 33392, Material Handling Equipment Manufacturing;

- Manufacturing motor vehicle air-conditioning systems and compressors, engine filters, and pumps—are classified in Industry Group 3363, Motor Vehicle Parts Manufacturing;

- Manufacturing laboratory scales, balances, ovens, and furnaces—are classified in Industry 33911, Medical Equipment and Supplies Manufacturing;

US—United States industry only. CAN—United States and Canadian industries are comparable. When neither US nor CAN appears, Canadian, Mexican, and United States industries are comparable.

- Manufacturing metal cutting and metal forming machinery—are classified in Industry 33351, Metalworking Machinery Manufacturing;

- Manufacturing power driven heavy construction and mining hand operated tools, such as tampers and augers,—are classified in Industries 33312, Construction Machinery Manufacturing and 33313, Mining and Oil and Gas Field Machinery Manufacturing;

- Manufacturing bakery ovens and industrial kilns, such as cement, wood, and chemical,—are classified in Industry 33329, Other Industrial Machinery Manufacturing;

- Manufacturing mechanical jacks, handheld soldering irons, countersink bits, drill bits, router bits, milling cutters, and other machine tools for woodcutting—are classified in Industry 33221, Cutlery and Handtool Manufacturing;

- Manufacturing carnival amusement park equipment, automotive maintenance equipment, and coin-operated vending machines—are classified in Industry 33331, Commercial and Service Industry Machinery Manufacturing; and

- Manufacturing transformers for arc-welding—are classified in Industry 33531, Electrical Equipment Manufacturing.

333991 Power-Driven Handtool Manufacturing[US]

This U.S. industry comprises establishments primarily engaged in manufacturing power-driven (e.g., battery, corded, pneumatic) handtools, such as drills, screwguns, circular saws, chain saws, staplers, and nailers.

Cross-References. Establishments primarily engaged in—

- Manufacturing metal cutting-type and metal forming-type machines (including home workshop)—are classified in Industry 33351, Metalworking Machinery Manufacturing;

- Manufacturing countersink bits, drill bits, router bits, milling cutters, and other machine tools for woodcutting—are classified in U.S. Industry 332212, Hand and Edge Tool Manufacturing;

- Manufacturing power-driven heavy construction or mining hand operated tools, such as tampers, jackhammers, and augers, are classified in Industries 333120, Construction Machinery Manufacturing and 333130, Mining and Oil and Gas Field Machinery Manufacturing; and

- Manufacturing powered home lawn and garden equipment—are classified in U.S. Industry 333112, Lawn and Garden Tractor and Home Lawn and Garden Equipment Manufacturing.

333992 Welding and Soldering Equipment Manufacturing[US]

This U.S. industry comprises establishments primarily engaged in manufacturing welding and soldering equipment and accessories (except transformers), such as arc, resistance, gas, plasma, laser, electron beam, and ultrasonic welding equipment; welding electrodes; coated or cored welding wire; and soldering equipment (except handheld).

US—United States industry only. CAN—United States and Canadian industries are comparable. When neither US nor CAN appears, Canadian, Mexican, and United States industries are comparable.

http://www.ntis.gov/naics

Cross-References. Establishments primarily engaged in—

- Manufacturing handheld soldering irons—are classified in U.S. Industry 332212, Hand and Edge Tool Manufacturing; and

- Manufacturing transformers for arc-welding—are classified in U.S. Industry 335311, Power, Distribution, and Specialty Transformer Manufacturing.

333993 Packaging Machinery Manufacturing[US]

This U.S. industry comprises establishments primarily engaged in manufacturing packaging machinery, such as wrapping, bottling, canning, and labeling machinery.

333994 Industrial Process Furnace and Oven Manufacturing[US]

This U.S. Industry comprises establishments primarily engaged in manufacturing industrial process furnaces, ovens, induction and dielectric heating equipment, and kilns (except cement, chemical, wood).

Cross-References. Establishments primarily engaged in—

- Manufacturing bakery ovens—are classified in U.S. Industry 333294, Food Product Machinery Manufacturing;

- Manufacturing cement, wood, and chemical kilns—are classified in U.S. Industry 333298, All Other Industrial Machinery Manufacturing;

- Manufacturing cremating ovens—are classified in U.S. Industry 333999, All Other Miscellaneous General Purpose Machinery Manufacturing; and

- Manufacturing laboratory furnaces and ovens—are classified in U.S. Industry 339111, Laboratory Apparatus and Furniture Manufacturing.

333995 Fluid Power Cylinder and Actuator Manufacturing[US]

This U.S. industry comprises establishments primarily engaged in manufacturing fluid power (i.e., hydraulic and pneumatic) cylinders and actuators.

333996 Fluid Power Pump and Motor Manufacturing[US]

This U.S. industry comprises establishments primarily engaged in manufacturing fluid power (i.e., hydraulic and pneumatic) pumps and motors.

Cross-References. Establishments primarily engaged in—

- Manufacturing fluid pumps for motor vehicles, such as oil pumps, water pumps, and power steering pumps—are classified in Industry Group 3363, Motor Vehicle Parts Manufacturing;

- Manufacturing general purpose pumps (except fluid power)—are classified in U.S. Industry 333911, Pump and Pumping Equipment Manufacturing; and

---

US—United States industry only. CAN—United States and Canadian industries are comparable. When neither US nor CAN appears, Canadian, Mexican, and United States industries are comparable.

- Manufacturing air compressors—are classified in U.S. Industry 333912, Air and Gas Compressor Manufacturing.

333997 Scale and Balance (except Laboratory) Manufacturing[US]

This U.S. industry comprises establishments primarily engaged in manufacturing scales and balances (except laboratory).

Cross-References.

Establishments primarily engaged in manufacturing laboratory scales and balances are classified in U.S. Industry 339111, Laboratory Apparatus and Furniture Manufacturing.

333999 All Other Miscellaneous General Purpose Machinery Manufacturing[US]

This U.S. industry comprises establishments primarily engaged in manufacturing general purpose machinery (except ventilating, heating, air-conditioning, and commercial refrigeration equipment; metal working machinery; engines, turbines, and power transmission equipment; pumps and compressors; material handling equipment; power-driven handtools; welding and soldering equipment; packaging machinery; industrial process furnaces and ovens; fluid power cylinders and actuators; fluid power pumps and motors; and scales and balances).

Illustrative Examples:

Automatic fire sprinkler systems
  manufacturing
Baling machinery (e.g., paper, scrap metal)
  manufacturing
Bridge and gate lifting machinery
  manufacturing
Cremating ovens manufacturing

General purpose-type sieves and screening
  equipment manufacturing
Hydraulic and pneumatic jacks manufacturing
Industrial and general line filters (except
  internal combustion engine, warm air
  furnace) manufacturing
Industrial-type centrifuges manufacturing

Cross-References. Establishments primarily engaged in—

- Manufacturing ventilating, heating, air-conditioning (except motor vehicle), and commercial refrigeration—are classified in Industry 33341, Ventilation, Heating, Air-Conditioning, and Commercial Refrigeration Manufacturing;

- Manufacturing motor vehicle air-conditioning systems and compressors—are classified in U.S. Industry 336391, Motor Vehicle Air-Conditioning Manufacturing;

- Manufacturing metalworking machinery—are classified in Industry Group 3335, Metalworking Machinery Manufacturing;

- Manufacturing engine, turbine, and power transmission equipment—are classified in Industry Group 3336, Engine, Turbine, and Power Transmission Equipment Manufacturing;

- Manufacturing pumps and compressors—are classified in Industry 33391, Pump and Compressor Manufacturing;

US—United States industry only. CAN—United States and Canadian industries are comparable. When neither US nor CAN appears, Canadian, Mexican, and United States industries are comparable.

- Manufacturing material handling equipment—are classified in Industry 33392, Material Handling Equipment Manufacturing;

- Manufacturing power-driven handtools—are classified in U.S. Industry 333991, Power-Driven Handtool Manufacturing;

- Manufacturing welding and soldering equipment (except handheld soldering irons)—are classified in U.S. Industry 333992, Welding and Soldering Equipment Manufacturing;

- Manufacturing packaging machinery—are classified in U.S. Industry 333993, Packaging Machinery Manufacturing;

- Manufacturing bakery ovens and cement, wood, and chemical kilns—are classified in U.S. Industry 333298, All Other Industrial Machinery Manufacturing;

- Manufacturing industrial process furnaces and ovens (except bakery)—are classified in U.S. Industry 333994, Industrial Process Furnace and Oven Manufacturing;

- Manufacturing fluid power cylinders and actuators—are classified in U.S. Industry 333995, Fluid Power Cylinder and Actuator Manufacturing;

- Manufacturing fluid power pumps and motors—are classified in U.S. Industry 333996, Fluid Power Pump and Motor Manufacturing;

- Manufacturing scales and balances (except laboratory)—are classified in U.S. Industry 333997, Scale and Balance (except Laboratory) Manufacturing (except Laboratory);

- Manufacturing carnival and amusement park equipment, automotive maintenance equipment and coin-operated vending machines—are classified in Industry 33331, Commercial and Service Industry Machinery Manufacturing;

- Manufacturing motor vehicle engine filters and pumps—are classified in Industry Group 3363, Motor Vehicle Parts Manufacturing; and

- Manufacturing mechanical jacks—are classified in U.S. Industry 332212, Hand and Edge Tool Manufacturing.

334 Computer and Electronic Product Manufacturing

Industries in the Computer and Electronic Product Manufacturing subsector group establishments that manufacture computers, computer peripherals, communications equipment, and similar electronic products, and establishments that manufacture components for such products. The Computer and Electronic Product Manufacturing industries have been combined in the hierarchy of NAICS because of the economic significance they have attained. Their rapid growth suggests that they will become even more important to the economies of all three North American countries in the future, and in addition their manufacturing processes are fundamentally different from the manufacturing processes of other machinery and equipment. The design and use of integrated circuits and the application of highly specialized miniaturization technologies are common elements in the production technologies of the computer and electronic subsector. Convergence of technology motivates this NAICS subsector. Digitalization of sound recording, for example, causes both the medium (the compact disc) and the equipment to resemble the technologies for recording, storing,

US—United States industry only. CAN—United States and Canadian industries are comparable. When neither US nor CAN appears, Canadian, Mexican, and United States industries are comparable.

http://www.ntis.gov/naics

transmitting, and manipulating data. Communications technology and equipment have been converging with computer technology. When technologically-related components are in the same sector, it makes it easier to adjust the classification for future changes, without needing to redefine its basic structure. The creation of the Computer and Electronic Product Manufacturing subsector will assist in delineating new and emerging industries because the activities that will serve as the probable sources of new industries, such as computer manufacturing and communications equipment manufacturing, or computers and audio equipment are brought together. As new activities emerge, they are less likely therefore, to cross the subsector boundaries of the classification.

3341 Computer and Peripheral Equipment Manufacturing

33411 Computer and Peripheral Equipment Manufacturing

This industry comprises establishments primarily engaged in manufacturing and/or assembling electronic computers, such as mainframes, personal computers, workstations, laptops, and computer servers; and computer peripheral equipment, such as storage devices, printers, monitors, input/output devices and terminals. Computers can be analog, digital, or hybrid. Digital computers, the most common type, are devices that do all of the following: (1) store the processing program or programs and the data immediately necessary for the execution of the program; (2) can be freely programmed in accordance with the requirements of the user; (3) perform arithmetical computations specified by the user; and (4) execute, without human intervention, a processing program that requires the computer to modify its execution by logical decision during the processing run. Analog computers are capable of simulating mathematical models and comprise at least analog, control, and programming elements.

Cross-References. Establishments primarily engaged in—

- Manufacturing digital telecommunications switches, local area network and wide area network communications equipment, such as bridges, routers, and gateways,—are classified in Industry 33421, Telephone Apparatus Manufacturing;

- Manufacturing blank magnetic and optical recording media—are classified in Industry 33461, Manufacturing and Reproducing Magnetic and Optical Media;

- Manufacturing machinery or equipment that incorporate electronic computers for operation or control purposes and embedded control applications—are classified in the Manufacturing sector based on the classification of the complete machinery or equipment;

- Manufacturing external audio speakers for computer use—are classified in Industry 33431, Audio and Video Equipment Manufacturing;

- Manufacturing internal loaded printed circuit board devices, such as sound, video, controller, and network interface cards; internal and external computer modems; and semiconductor storage devices,—are classified in Industry 33441, Semiconductor and Other Electronic Component Manufacturing; and

- Manufacturing other parts, such as casings, stampings, cable sets, and switches, for computers, storage devices and other peripheral equipment,—are classified in the Manufacturing sector based on their associated production processes.

US—United States industry only. CAN—United States and Canadian industries are comparable. When neither US nor CAN appears, Canadian, Mexican, and United States industries are comparable.

334111 Electronic Computer Manufacturing[US]

This U.S. industry comprises establishments primarily engaged in manufacturing and/or assembling electronic computers, such as mainframes, personal computers, workstations, laptops, and computer servers. Computers can be analog, digital, or hybrid. Digital computers, the most common type, are devices that do all of the following: (1) store the processing program or programs and the data immediately necessary for the execution of the program; (2) can be freely programmed in accordance with the requirements of the user; (3) perform arithmetical computations specified by the user; and (4) execute, without human intervention, a processing program that requires the computer to modify its execution by logical decision during the processing run. Analog computers are capable of simulating mathematical models and contain at least analog, control, and programming elements. The manufacture of computers includes the assembly or integration of processors, coprocessors, memory, storage, and input/output devices into a user-programmable final product.

Cross-References. Establishments primarily engaged in—

- Manufacturing digital telecommunications switches, local area network and wide area network communication equipment, such as bridges, routers, and gateways,—are classified in Industry 334210, Telephone Apparatus Manufacturing;

- Manufacturing blank magnetic and optical recording media—are classified in U.S. Industry 334613, Magnetic and Optical Recording Media Manufacturing;

- Manufacturing machinery or equipment that incorporates electronic computers for operation or control purposes and embedded control applications—are classified in the Manufacturing sector based on the classification of the complete machinery or equipment;

- Manufacturing internal, loaded, printed circuit board devices, such as sound, video, controller, and network interface cards; internal and external computer modems; and solid state storage devices for computers,—are classified in Industry 33441, Semiconductor and Other Electronic Component Manufacturing; and

- Manufacturing other parts, such as casings, stampings, cable sets, and switches, for computers,—are classified in the Manufacturing sector based on their associated production processes.

334112 Computer Storage Device Manufacturing[US]

This U.S. industry comprises establishments primarily engaged in manufacturing computer storage devices that allow the storage and retrieval of data from a phase change, magnetic, optical, or magnetic/optical media. Examples of products made by these establishments are CD-ROM drives, floppy disk drives, hard disk drives, and tape storage and backup units.

Cross-References. Establishments primarily engaged in—

- Manufacturing blank magnetic and optical recording media—are classified in U.S. Industry 334613, Magnetic and Optical Recording Media Manufacturing;

US—United States industry only. CAN—United States and Canadian industries are comparable. When neither US nor CAN appears, Canadian, Mexican, and United States industries are comparable.

- Manufacturing semiconductor storage devices, such as memory chips,—are classified in U.S. Industry 334413, Semiconductor and Related Device Manufacturing;

- Manufacturing drive controller cards, internal or external to the storage device—are classified in U.S. Industry 334418, Printed Circuit Assembly (Electronic Assembly) Manufacturing; and

- Manufacturing other parts, such as casings, stampings, cable sets, and switches, for computer storage devices,—are classified in the Manufacturing sector based on their associated production processes.

334113 Computer Terminal Manufacturing[US]

This U.S. industry comprises establishments primarily engaged in manufacturing computer terminals. Computer terminals are input/output devices that connect with a central computer for processing.

Cross-References. Establishments primarily engaged in—

- Manufacturing point-of-sale terminals, funds transfer, automatic teller machines, and monitors—are classified in U.S. Industry 334119, Other Computer Peripheral Equipment Manufacturing;

- Manufacturing internal loaded printed circuit board devices, such as sound, video, controller, and network interface cards for computer terminals,—are classified in U.S. Industry 334418, Printed Circuit Assembly (Electronic Assembly) Manufacturing; and

- Manufacturing other parts, such as casings, stampings, cable sets, and switches, for computer terminals, —are classified in the Manufacturing sector based on their associated production processes.

334119 Other Computer Peripheral Equipment Manufacturing[US]

This U.S. industry comprises establishments primarily engaged in manufacturing computer peripheral equipment (except storage devices and computer terminals).

Illustrative Examples:

Automatic teller machines (ATM)
  manufacturing
Joystick devices manufacturing
Keyboards, computer peripheral equipment,
  manufacturing
Monitors, computer peripheral equipment,
  manufacturing

Mouse devices, computer peripheral
  equipment, manufacturing
Optical readers and scanners manufacturing
Plotters, computer, manufacturing
Point-of-sale terminals, manufacturing
Printers, computer, manufacturing

Cross-References. Establishments primarily engaged in—

- Manufacturing local area network and wide area network communications equipment, such as bridges, routers, and gateways,—are classified in Industry 334210, Telephone Apparatus Manufacturing;

US—United States industry only. CAN—United States and Canadian industries are comparable. When neither US nor CAN appears, Canadian, Mexican, and United States industries are comparable.

- Manufacturing computer storage devices—are classified in U.S. Industry 334112, Computer Storage Device Manufacturing;

- Manufacturing computer terminals—are classified in U.S. Industry 334113, Computer Terminal Manufacturing;

- Manufacturing external audio speakers for computer use—are classified in Industry 334310, Audio and Video Equipment Manufacturing;

- Manufacturing internal, loaded, printed circuit board devices, such as sound, video, controller, and network interface cards; and internal and external computer modems used as computer peripherals,—are classified in U.S. Industry 334418, Printed Circuit Assembly (Electronic Assembly) Manufacturing; and

- Manufacturing other parts, such as casings, stampings, cable sets, and switches, for computer peripheral equipment,—are classified in the Manufacturing sector based on their associated production processes.

3342 Communications Equipment Manufacturing

33421 Telephone Apparatus Manufacturing
See industry description for 334210 below.

334210 Telephone Apparatus Manufacturing

This industry comprises establishments primarily engaged in manufacturing wire telephone and data communications equipment. These products may be standalone or board-level components of a larger system. Examples of products made by these establishments are central office switching equipment, cordless telephones (except cellular), PBX equipment, telephones, telephone answering machines, and data communications equipment, such as bridges, routers, and gateways.

Cross-References. Establishments primarily engaged in—

- Manufacturing internal and external computer modems, fax/modems and electronic components used in telephone apparatus—are classified in Industry 33441, Semiconductor and Other Electronic Component Manufacturing; and

- Manufacturing cellular telephones—are classified in Industry 334220, Radio and Television Broadcasting and Wireless Communications Equipment Manufacturing.

33422 Radio and Television Broadcasting and Wireless Communications Equipment Manufacturing
See industry description for 334220 below.

334220 Radio and Television Broadcasting and Wireless Communications Equipment Manufacturing

This industry comprises establishments primarily engaged in manufacturing radio and television broadcast and wireless communications equipment. Examples of products made by these establishments are: transmitting and receiving antennas, cable television equipment, GPS equipment, pagers,

---

US—United States industry only. CAN—United States and Canadian industries are comparable. When neither US nor CAN appears, Canadian, Mexican, and United States industries are comparable.

cellular phones, mobile communications equipment, and radio and television studio and broadcasting equipment.

Cross-References. Establishments primarily engaged in—

- Manufacturing household-type audio and video equipment, such as televisions and radio sets,—are classified in Industry 334310, Audio and Video Equipment Manufacturing; and

- Manufacturing wired and nonwired intercommunications equipment (i.e., intercoms)—are classified in Industry 334290, Other Communications Equipment Manufacturing.

33429 Other Communications Equipment Manufacturing
See industry description for 334290 below.

334290 Other Communications Equipment Manufacturing

This industry comprises establishments primarily engaged in manufacturing communications equipment (except telephone apparatus, and radio and television broadcast, and wireless communications equipment).

Illustrative Examples:

Fire detection and alarm systems manufacturing
Intercom systems and equipment manufacturing

Signals (e.g., highway, pedestrian, railway, traffic) manufacturing

Cross-References. Establishments primarily engaged in—

- Manufacturing telephone apparatus—are classified in Industry 334210, Telephone Apparatus Manufacturing;

- Manufacturing radio and television broadcast and wireless communication equipment— are classified in Industry 334220, Radio and Television Broadcasting and Wireless Communications Equipment Manufacturing; and

- Manufacturing automobile audio and related equipment—are classified in Industry 334310, Audio and Video Equipment Manufacturing.

3343 Audio and Video Equipment Manufacturing

33431 Audio and Video Equipment Manufacturing
See industry description for 334310 below.

334310 Audio and Video Equipment Manufacturing

This industry comprises establishments primarily engaged in manufacturing electronic audio and video equipment for home entertainment, motor vehicle, public address and musical instrument

---

US—United States industry only. CAN—United States and Canadian industries are comparable. When neither US nor CAN appears, Canadian, Mexican, and United States industries are comparable.

amplifications. Examples of products made by these establishments are video cassette recorders, televisions, stereo equipment, speaker systems, household-type video cameras, jukeboxes, and amplifiers for musical instruments and public address systems.

Cross-References. Establishments primarily engaged in—

- Manufacturing telephone answering machines—are classified in Industry 334210, Telephone Apparatus Manufacturing;

- Manufacturing photographic (i.e., still and motion picture) equipment—are classified in U.S. Industry 333315, Photographic and Photocopying Equipment Manufacturing;

- Manufacturing phonograph needles and cartridges—are classified in Industry 33441, Semiconductor and Other Electronic Component Manufacturing;

- Manufacturing auto theft alarms—are classified in Industry 334290, Other Communications Equipment Manufacturing; and

- Manufacturing mobile radios, such as citizens band and FM transceivers for household or motor vehicle uses; studio and broadcast video cameras; and cable decoders and satellite television equipment,—are classified in Industry 334220, Radio and Television Broadcasting and Wireless Communications Equipment Manufacturing.

3344 Semiconductor and Other Electronic Component Manufacturing

33441 Semiconductor and Other Electronic Component Manufacturing

This industry comprises establishments primarily engaged in manufacturing semiconductors and other components for electronic applications. Examples of products made by these establishments are capacitors, resistors, microprocessors, bare and loaded printed circuit boards, electron tubes, electronic connectors, and computer modems.

Cross-References. Establishments primarily engaged in—

- Manufacturing X-ray tubes—are classified in Industry 33451, Navigational, Measuring, Electromedical, and Control Instruments Manufacturing;

- Manufacturing glass blanks for electron tubes—are classified in Industry 32721, Glass and Glass Product Manufacturing;

- Manufacturing telephone system components or modules—are classified in Industry 33421, Telephone Apparatus Manufacturing;

- Manufacturing finished products that incorporate loaded printed circuit boards—are classified in the Manufacturing sector based on the production process of making the final product;

- Manufacturing communications antennas—are classified in Industry 33422, Radio and Television Broadcasting and Wireless Communications Equipment Manufacturing; and

US—United States industry only. CAN—United States and Canadian industries are comparable. When neither US nor CAN appears, Canadian, Mexican, and United States industries are comparable.

- Manufacturing coils, switches, transformers, connectors, capacitors, rheostats, and similar devices for electrical applications—are classified in Subsector 335, Electrical Equipment, Appliance, and Component Manufacturing.

334411 Electron Tube Manufacturing[US]

This U.S. industry comprises establishments primarily engaged in manufacturing electron tubes and parts (except glass blanks). Examples of products made by these establishments are cathode ray tubes (i.e., picture tubes), klystron tubes, magnetron tubes, and traveling wave tubes.

Cross-References. Establishments primarily engaged in—

- Manufacturing X-ray tubes—are classified in U.S. Industry 334517, Irradiation Apparatus Manufacturing; and

- Manufacturing glass blanks for electron tubes—are classified in Industry 32721, Glass and Glass Product Manufacturing.

334412 Bare Printed Circuit Board Manufacturing[US]

This U.S. industry comprises establishments primarily engaged in manufacturing bare (i.e., rigid or flexible) printed circuit boards without mounted electronic components. These establishments print, perforate, plate, screen, etch, or photoprint interconnecting pathways for electric current on laminates.

Cross-References. Establishments primarily engaged in—

- Loading components onto printed circuit boards, or whose output is loaded printed circuit boards—are classified in U.S. Industry 334418, Printed Circuit Assembly (Electronic Assembly) Manufacturing; and

- Manufacturing printed circuit laminates—are classified in U.S. Industry 334419, Other Electronic Component Manufacturing.

334413 Semiconductor and Related Device Manufacturing[US]

This U.S. industry comprises establishments primarily engaged in manufacturing semiconductors and related solid state devices. Examples of products made by these establishments are integrated circuits, memory chips, microprocessors, diodes, transistors, solar cells and other optoelectronic devices.

334414 Electronic Capacitor Manufacturing[US]

This U.S. industry comprises establishments primarily engaged in manufacturing electronic fixed and variable capacitors and condensers.

US—United States industry only. CAN—United States and Canadian industries are comparable. When neither US nor CAN appears, Canadian, Mexican, and United States industries are comparable.

http://www.ntis.gov/naics

Cross-References.

Establishments primarily engaged in manufacturing electrical capacitors for power generation and distribution, heavy industrial equipment, induction heating and melting, and similar industrial applications are classified in U.S. Industry 335999, All Other Miscellaneous Electrical Equipment and Component Manufacturing.

334415 Electronic Resistor Manufacturing[US]

This U.S. industry comprises establishments primarily engaged in manufacturing electronic resistors, such as fixed and variable resistors, resistor networks, thermistors, and varistors.

Cross-References.

Establishments primarily engaged in manufacturing electronic rheostats are classified in U.S. Industry 334419, Other Electronic Component Manufacturing.

334416 Electronic Coil, Transformer, and Other Inductor Manufacturing[US]

This U.S. industry comprises establishments primarily engaged in manufacturing electronic inductors, such as coils and transformers.

Cross-References.

Establishments primarily engaged in manufacturing electrical transformers used in the generation, storage, transmission, transformation, distribution, and utilization of electrical energy are classified in U.S. Industry 335311, Power, Distribution, and Specialty Transformer Manufacturing.

334417 Electronic Connector Manufacturing[US]

This U.S. industry comprises establishments primarily engaged in manufacturing electronic connectors, such as coaxial, cylindrical, rack and panel, pin and sleeve, printed circuit and fiber optic.

Cross-References.

Establishments primarily engaged in manufacturing electrical connectors, such as plugs, bus bars, twist on wire connectors and terminals, are classified in U.S. Industry 335931, Current-Carrying Wiring Device Manufacturing.

334418 Printed Circuit Assembly (Electronic Assembly) Manufacturing[US]

This U.S. industry comprises establishments primarily engaged in loading components onto printed circuit boards or who manufacture and ship loaded printed circuit boards. Also known as printed circuit assemblies, electronics assemblies, or modules, these products are printed circuit boards that have some or all of the semiconductor and electronic components inserted or mounted and are inputs to a wide variety of electronic systems and devices.

US—United States industry only. CAN—United States and Canadian industries are comparable. When neither US nor CAN appears, Canadian, Mexican, and United States industries are comparable.

Cross-References. Establishments primarily engaged in—

- Manufacturing printed circuit laminates—are classified in U.S. Industry 334419, Other Electronic Component Manufacturing;

- Manufacturing bare printed circuit boards—are classified in U.S. Industry 334412, Bare Printed Circuit Board Manufacturing;

- Manufacturing telephone system components or modules—are classified in Industry 334210, Telephone Apparatus Manufacturing; and

- Manufacturing finished products that incorporate loaded printed circuit boards—are classified in the Manufacturing sector based on the production process of making the final product.

334419 Other Electronic Component Manufacturing^{US}

This U.S. industry comprises establishments primarily engaged in manufacturing electronic components (except electron tubes; bare printed circuit boards; semiconductors and related devices; electronic capacitors; electronic resistors; coils, transformers and other inductors; connectors; and loaded printed circuit boards).

Illustrative Examples:

Crystals and crystal assemblies, electronic, manufacturing
LCD (liquid crystal display) screen units manufacturing
Microwave components manufacturing

Piezolelectric devices manufacturing
Printed circuit laminates manufacturing
Switches for electronic applications manufacturing
Transducers (except pressure) manufacturing

Cross-References. Establishments primarily engaged in—

- Manufacturing electron tubes—are classified in U.S. Industry 334411, Electron Tube Manufacturing;

- Manufacturing bare printed circuit boards—are classified in U.S. Industry 334412, Bare Printed Circuit Board Manufacturing;

- Manufacturing semiconductors and related devices—are classified in U.S. Industry 334413, Semiconductor and Related Device Manufacturing;

- Manufacturing electronic capacitors—are classified in U.S. Industry 334414, Electronic Capacitor Manufacturing;

- Manufacturing electronic resistors—are classified in U.S. Industry 334415, Electronic Resistor Manufacturing;

- Manufacturing electronic inductors—are classified in U.S. Industry 334416, Electronic Coil, Transformer, and Other Inductor Manufacturing;

- Manufacturing electronic connectors—are classified in U.S. Industry 334417, Electronic Connector Manufacturing;

- Loading components onto printed circuit boards or whose output is loaded printed circuit boards—are classified in U.S. Industry 334418, Printed Circuit Assembly (Electronic Assembly) Manufacturing; and

- Manufacturing communications antennas—are classified in Industry 334220, Radio and Television Broadcasting and Wireless Communications Equipment Manufacturing.

3345 Navigational, Measuring, Electromedical, and Control Instruments Manufacturing

33451 Navigational, Measuring, Electromedical, and Control Instruments Manufacturing

This industry comprises establishments primarily engaged in manufacturing navigational, measuring, electromedical, and control instruments. Examples of products made by these establishments are aeronautical instruments, appliance regulators and controls (except switches), laboratory analytical instruments, navigation and guidance systems, and physical properties testing equipment.

Cross-References. Establishments primarily engaged in—

- Manufacturing global positioning system (GPS) equipment—are classified in Industry 33422, Radio and Television Broadcasting and Wireless Communications Equipment Manufacturing;

- Manufacturing motor control switches and relays (including timing relays)—are classified in Industry 33531, Electrical Equipment Manufacturing;

- Manufacturing switches for appliances—are classified in Industry 33593, Wiring Device Manufacturing;

- Manufacturing optical instruments—are classified in Industry 33331, Commercial and Service Industry Machinery Manufacturing;

- Manufacturing equipment for measuring and testing communications signals—are classified in Industry Group 3342, Communications Equipment Manufacturing;

- Manufacturing glass watch and clock crystals—are classified in Industry 32721, Glass and Glass Product Manufacturing;

- Manufacturing plastics watch and clock crystals—are classified in Industry 32619, Other Plastics Product Manufacturing; and

- Manufacturing medical thermometers and other nonelectrical medical apparatus—are classified in Industry Group 3391, Medical Equipment and Supplies Manufacturing.

334510 Electromedical and Electrotherapeutic Apparatus Manufacturing[US]

This U.S. industry comprises establishments primarily engaged in manufacturing electromedical and electrotherapeutic apparatus, such as magnetic resonance imaging equipment, medical ultrasound equipment, pacemakers, hearing aids, electrocardiographs, and electromedical endoscopic equipment.

US—United States industry only. CAN—United States and Canadian industries are comparable. When neither US nor CAN appears, Canadian, Mexican, and United States industries are comparable.

Cross-References. Establishments primarily engaged in—

- Manufacturing medical irradiation apparatus—are classified in U.S. Industry 334517, Irradiation Apparatus Manufacturing; and

- Manufacturing nonelectrical medical and therapeutic apparatus—are classified in Industry Group 3391, Medical Equipment and Supplies Manufacturing.

334511 Search, Detection, Navigation, Guidance, Aeronautical, and Nautical System and Instrument Manufacturing[US]

This U.S. industry comprises establishments primarily engaged in manufacturing search, detection, navigation, guidance, aeronautical, and nautical systems and instruments. Examples of products made by these establishments are aircraft instruments (except engine), flight recorders, navigational instruments and systems, radar systems and equipment, and sonar systems and equipment.

Cross-References. Establishments primarily engaged in—

- Manufacturing global positioning system (GPS) equipment—are classified in Industry 334220, Radio and Television Broadcasting and Wireless Communications Equipment Manufacturing; and

- Manufacturing aircraft engine instruments and meteorological systems and equipment—are classified in U.S. Industry 334519, Other Measuring and Controlling Device Manufacturing.

334512 Automatic Environmental Control Manufacturing for Residential, Commercial, and Appliance Use[US]

This U.S. industry comprises establishments primarily engaged in manufacturing automatic controls and regulators for applications, such as heating, air-conditioning, refrigeration and appliances.

Cross-References. Establishments primarily engaged in—

- Manufacturing industrial process controls—are classified in U.S. Industry 334513, Instruments and Related Products Manufacturing for Measuring, Displaying, and Controlling Industrial Process Variables;

- Manufacturing motor control switches and relays—are classified in U.S. Industry 335314, Relay and Industrial Control Manufacturing;

- Manufacturing switches for appliances—are classified in U.S. Industry 335931, Current-Carrying Wiring Device Manufacturing; and

- Manufacturing appliance timers—are classified in U.S. Industry 334518, Watch, Clock, and Part Manufacturing.

US—United States industry only. CAN—United States and Canadian industries are comparable. When neither US nor CAN appears, Canadian, Mexican, and United States industries are comparable.

http://www.ntis.gov/naics

334513 Instruments and Related Products Manufacturing for Measuring, Displaying, and Controlling Industrial Process Variables[US]

This U.S. industry comprises establishments primarily engaged in manufacturing instruments and related devices for measuring, displaying, indicating, recording, transmitting, and controlling industrial process variables. These instruments measure, display or control (monitor, analyze, and so forth) industrial process variables, such as temperature, humidity, pressure, vacuum, combustion, flow, level, viscosity, density, acidity, concentration, and rotation.

Cross-References. Establishments primarily engaged in—

- Manufacturing instruments for measuring or testing of electricity and electrical signals—are classified in U.S. Industry 334515, Instrument Manufacturing for Measuring and Testing Electricity and Electrical Signals;

- Manufacturing medical thermometers—are classified in U.S. Industry 339112, Surgical and Medical Instruments Manufacturing;

- Manufacturing glass hydrometers and thermometers for other nonmedical uses—are classified in U.S. Industry 334519, Other Measuring and Controlling Device Manufacturing;

- Manufacturing instruments and instrumentation systems for laboratory analysis of samples—are classified in U.S. Industry 334516, Analytical Laboratory Instrument Manufacturing; and

- Manufacturing optical alignment and display instruments, optical comparators, and optical test and inspection equipment—are classified in U.S. Industry 333314, Optical Instrument and Lens Manufacturing.

334514 Totalizing Fluid Meter and Counting Device Manufacturing[US]

This U.S. industry comprises establishments primarily engaged in manufacturing totalizing (i.e., registering) fluid meters and counting devices. Examples of products made by these establishments are gas consumption meters, water consumption meters, parking meters, taxi meters, motor vehicle gauges, and fare collection equipment.

Cross-References. Establishments primarily engaged in—

- Manufacturing integrating meters and counters for measuring the characteristics of electricity and electrical signals—are classified in U.S. Industry 334515, Instrument Manufacturing for Measuring and Testing Electricity and Electrical Signals; and

- Manufacturing instruments and devices that measure, display, or control (i.e., monitor or analyze) related industrial process variables—are classified in U.S. Industry 334513, Instruments and Related Products Manufacturing for Measuring, Displaying, and Controlling Industrial Process Variables.

US—United States industry only. CAN—United States and Canadian industries are comparable. When neither US nor CAN appears, Canadian, Mexican, and United States industries are comparable.

334515 Instrument Manufacturing for Measuring and Testing Electricity and Electrical Signals[US]

This U.S. industry comprises establishments primarily engaged in manufacturing instruments for measuring and testing the characteristics of electricity and electrical signals. Examples of products made by these establishments are circuit and continuity testers, volt meters, ohm meters, wattmeters, multimeters, and semiconductor test equipment.

Cross-References. Establishments primarily engaged in—

- Manufacturing electronic monitoring, evaluating, and other electronic support equipment for navigational, radar, and sonar systems—are classified in U.S. Industry 334511, Search, Detection, Navigation, Guidance, Aeronautical, and Nautical System and Instrument Manufacturing; and

- Manufacturing equipment for measuring and testing communications signals—are classified in Industry Group 3342, Communications Equipment Manufacturing.

334516 Analytical Laboratory Instrument Manufacturing[US]

This U.S. industry comprises establishments primarily engaged in manufacturing instruments and instrumentation systems for laboratory analysis of the chemical or physical composition or concentration of samples of solid, fluid, gaseous, or composite material.

Cross-References. Establishments primarily engaged in—

- Manufacturing instruments for monitoring and analyzing continuous samples from medical patients—are classified in U.S. Industry 334510, Electromedical and Electrotherapeutic Apparatus Manufacturing; and

- Manufacturing instruments and related devices that measure, display, or control (i.e., monitor or analyze) industrial process variables—are classified in U.S. Industry 334513, Instruments and Related Products Manufacturing for Measuring, Displaying, and Controlling Industrial Process Variables.

334517 Irradiation Apparatus Manufacturing[US]

This U.S. industry comprises establishments primarily engaged in manufacturing irradiation apparatus and tubes for applications, such as medical diagnostic, medical therapeutic, industrial, research and scientific evaluation. Irradiation can take the form of beta-rays, gamma-rays, X-rays, or other ionizing radiation.

334518 Watch, Clock, and Part Manufacturing[US]

This U.S. industry comprises establishments primarily engaged in manufacturing and/or assembling: clocks; watches; timing mechanisms for clockwork operated devices; time clocks; time and date recording devices; and clock and watch parts (except crystals), such as springs, jewels, and modules.

US—United States industry only. CAN—United States and Canadian industries are comparable. When neither US nor CAN appears, Canadian, Mexican, and United States industries are comparable.

http://www.ntis.gov/naics

Cross-References. Establishments primarily engaged in—

- Manufacturing glass watch and clock crystals—are classified in Industry 32721, Glass and Glass Product Manufacturing;

- Manufacturing plastics watch and clock crystals—are classified in U.S. Industry 326199, All Other Plastics Product Manufacturing; and

- Manufacturing timing relays—are classified in U.S. Industry 335314, Relay and Industrial Control Manufacturing.

334519 Other Measuring and Controlling Device Manufacturing[US]

This U.S. industry comprises establishments primarily engaged in manufacturing measuring and controlling devices (except search, detection, navigation, guidance, aeronautical, and nautical instruments and systems; automatic environmental controls for residential, commercial, and appliance use; instruments for measurement, display, and control of industrial process variables; totalizing fluid meters and counting devices; instruments for measuring and testing electricity and electrical signals; analytical laboratory instruments; watches, clocks, and parts; irradiation equipment; and electromedical and electrotherapeutic apparatus).

Illustrative Examples:

Aircraft engine instruments manufacturing
Automotive emissions testing equipment
  manufacturing
Meteorological instruments manufacturing
Physical properties testing and inspection
  equipment manufacturing

Polygraph machines manufacturing
Radiation detection and monitoring
  instruments manufacturing
Surveying instruments manufacturing
Thermometers liquid-in-glass and bimetal types
  (except medical), manufacturing

Cross-References. Establishments primarily engaged in—

- Manufacturing medical thermometers—are classified in U.S. Industry 339112, Surgical and Medical Instrument Manufacturing;

- Manufacturing search, detection, navigation, guidance, aeronautical, and nautical systems and instruments—are classified in U.S. Industry 334511, Search, Detection, Navigation, Guidance, Aeronautical, and Nautical System and Instrument Manufacturing;

- Manufacturing automatic controls and regulators for applications, such as heating, air-conditioning, refrigeration and appliances,—are classified in U.S. Industry 334512, Automatic Environmental Control Manufacturing for Residential, Commercial, and Appliance Use;

- Manufacturing instruments and related devices that measure, display, or control (i.e., monitor or analyze) industrial process variables—are classified in U.S. Industry 334513, Instruments and Related Products Manufacturing for Measuring, Displaying, and Controlling Industrial Process Variables;

US—United States industry only. CAN—United States and Canadian industries are comparable. When neither US nor CAN appears, Canadian, Mexican, and United States industries are comparable.

- Manufacturing totalizing (i.e., registering) fluid meters and counting devices, including motor vehicle gauges—are classified in U.S. Industry 334514, Totalizing Fluid Meter and Counting Device Manufacturing;

- Manufacturing instruments for measuring and testing the characteristics of electricity and electrical signals—are classified in U.S. Industry 334515, Instrument Manufacturing for Measuring and Testing Electricity and Electrical Signals;

- Manufacturing instruments for laboratory analysis of the physical composition or concentration of samples of solid, fluid, gaseous, or composite materials—are classified in U.S. Industry 334516, Analytical Laboratory Instrument Manufacturing;

- Manufacturing and/or assembling watches, clocks, or parts—are classified in U.S. Industry 334518, Watch, Clock, and Part Manufacturing;

- Manufacturing X-ray apparatus, tubes, or related irradiation apparatus—are classified in U.S. Industry 334517, Irradiation Apparatus Manufacturing; and

- Manufacturing electromedical and electrotherapeutic apparatus—are classified in U.S. Industry 334510, Electromedical and Electrotherapeutic Apparatus Manufacturing.

3346 Manufacturing and Reproducing Magnetic and Optical Media

33461 Manufacturing and Reproducing Magnetic and Optical Media

This industry comprises establishments primarily engaged in (1) manufacturing optical and magnetic media, such as blank audio tape, blank video tape, and blank diskettes and/or (2) mass duplicating (i.e., making copies) audio, video, software, and other data on magnetic, optical, and similar media.

Cross-References. Establishments primarily engaged in—

- Designing, developing, and publishing prepackaged software—are classified in Industry 51121, Software Publishers; and

- Audio, motion picture and/or video production and/or distribution—are classified in Subsector 512, Motion Picture and Sound Recording Industries.

334611 Software Reproducing^US

This U.S. industry comprises establishments primarily engaged in mass reproducing computer software. These establishments do not generally develop any software, they mass reproduce data and programs on magnetic media, such as diskettes, tapes, or cartridges. Establishments in this industry mass reproduce products, such as CD-ROMs and game cartridges.

Cross-References.

Establishments primarily engaged in designing, developing, and publishing prepackaged software are classified in Industry 511210, Software Publishers.

US—United States industry only. CAN—United States and Canadian industries are comparable. When neither US nor CAN appears, Canadian, Mexican, and United States industries are comparable.

http://www.ntis.gov/naics

334612 Prerecorded Compact Disc (except Software), Tape, and Record Reproducing^{US}

This U.S. industry comprises establishments primarily engaged in mass reproducing audio and video material on magnetic or optical media. Examples of products mass reproduced by these establishments are audio compact discs, prerecorded audio and video cassettes, and laser discs.

Cross-References. Establishments primarily engaged in—

- Designing, developing, and publishing prepackaged software—are classified in Industry 511210, Software Publishers;

- Audio, motion picuture and/or video production and/or distribution—are classified in Subsector 512, Motion Picture and Sound Recording Industries; and

- Manufacturing blank audio and video tape, blank diskettes, and blank optical discs—are classified in U.S. Industry 334613, Magnetic and Optical Recording Media Manufacturing.

334613 Magnetic and Optical Recording Media Manufacturing^{US}

This U.S. industry comprises establishments primarily engaged in manufacturing magnetic and optical recording media, such as blank magnetic tape, blank diskettes, blank optical discs, hard drive media, and blank magnetic tape cassettes.

Cross-References. Establishments primarily engaged in—

- Mass reproducing computer software—are classified in U.S. Industry 334611, Software Reproducing; and

- Mass reproducing audio and video material—are classified in U.S. Industry 334612, Prerecorded Compact Disc (Except Software), Tape, and Record Reproducing.

335 Electrical Equipment, Appliance, and Component Manufacturing

Industries in the Electrical Equipment, Appliance, and Component Manufacturing subsector manufacture products that generate, distribute and use electrical power. Electric Lighting Equipment Manufacturing establishments produce electric lamp bulbs, lighting fixtures, and parts. Household Appliance Manufacturing establishments make both small and major electrical appliances and parts. Electrical Equipment Manufacturing establishments make goods, such as electric motors, generators, transformers, and switchgear apparatus. Other Electrical Equipment and Component Manufacturing establishments make devices for storing electrical power (e.g., batteries), for transmitting electricity (e.g., insulated wire), and wiring devices (e.g., electrical outlets, fuse boxes, and light switches).

3351 Electric Lighting Equipment Manufacturing

33511 Electric Lamp Bulb and Part Manufacturing
See industry description for 335110 below.

335110 Electric Lamp Bulb and Part Manufacturing

This industry comprises establishments primarily engaged in manufacturing electric light bulbs and tubes, and parts and components (except glass blanks for electric light bulbs).

US—United States industry only. CAN—United States and Canadian industries are comparable. When neither US nor CAN appears, Canadian, Mexican, and United States industries are comparable.

Cross-References. Establishments primarily engaged in—

- Manufacturing glass blanks for electric light bulbs—are classified in U.S. Industry 327212, Other Pressed and Blown Glass and Glassware Manufacturing;

- Manufacturing vehicular lighting fixtures—are classified in U.S. Industry 336321, Vehicular Lighting Equipment Manufacturing;

- Manufacturing light emitting diodes (LEDs)—are classified in U.S. Industry 334413, Semiconductor and Related Device Manufacturing; and

- Manufacturing other lighting fixtures (except vehicular)—are classified in Industry 33512, Lighting Fixture Manufacturing.

33512 Lighting Fixture Manufacturing

This industry comprises establishments primarily engaged in manufacturing electric lighting fixtures (except vehicular), nonelectric lighting equipment, lamp shades (except glass and plastics) and lighting fixture components (except current-carrying wiring devices).

Cross-References. Establishments primarily engaged in—

- Manufacturing vehicular lighting fixtures—are classified in Industry 33632, Motor Vehicle Electrical and Electronic Equipment Manufacturing;

- Manufacturing electric light bulbs, tubes, and parts—are classified in Industry 33511, Electric Lamp Bulb and Part Manufacturing;

- Manufacturing current-carrying wiring devices for lighting fixtures—are classified in Industry 33593, Wiring Devices Manufacturing;

- Manufacturing ceiling fans or bath fans with integrated lighting fixtures—are classified in Industry 33521, Small Electrical Appliance Manufacturing;

- Manufacturing plastics lamp shades—are classified in Industry 32619, Other Plastics Product Manufacturing;

- Manufacturing glassware and glass parts for lighting fixtures—are classified in Industry 32721, Glass and Glass Product Manufacturing; and

- Manufacturing signaling devices that incorporate electric light bulbs, such as traffic and railway signals,—are classified in Industry 33429, Other Communications Equipment Manufacturing.

335121 Residential Electric Lighting Fixture Manufacturing[US]

This U.S. industry comprises establishments primarily engaged in manufacturing fixed or portable residential electric lighting fixtures and lamp shades of metal, paper, or textiles. Residential electric lighting fixtures include those for use both inside and outside the residence.

US—United States industry only. CAN—United States and Canadian industries are comparable. When neither US nor CAN appears, Canadian, Mexican, and United States industries are comparable.

Illustrative Examples:

Ceiling lighting fixtures, residential, manufacturing

Chandeliers, residential, manufacturing

Table lamps (i.e., lighting fixtures) manufacturing

Cross-References. Establishments primarily engaged in—

- Manufacturing glassware for residential lighting fixtures—are classified in Industry 32721, Glass and Glass Product Manufacturing;

- Manufacturing plastics lamp shades—are classified in U.S. Industry 326199, All Other Plastics Product Manufacturing;

- Manufacturing electric light bulbs, tubes, and parts—are classified in Industry 335110, Electric Lamp Bulb and Part Manufacturing;

- Manufacturing ceiling fans or bath fans with integrated lighting fixtures—are classified in U.S. Industry 335211, Electric Housewares and Household Fan Manufacturing;

- Manufacturing current-carrying wiring devices for lighting fixtures—are classified in U.S. Industry 335931, Current-Carrying Wiring Device Manufacturing;

- Manufacturing commercial, industrial, and institutional electric lighting fixtures—are classified in U.S. Industry 335122, Commercial, Industrial, and Institutional Electric Lighting Fixture Manufacturing; and

- Manufacturing other lighting fixtures, such as street lights, flashlights, and nonelectric lighting fixtures,—are classified in U.S. Industry 335129, Other Lighting Equipment Manufacturing.

335122 Commercial, Industrial, and Institutional Electric Lighting Fixture Manufacturing[US]

This U.S. industry comprises establishments primarily engaged in manufacturing commercial, industrial, and institutional electric lighting fixtures.

Cross-References. Establishments primarily engaged in—

- Manufacturing glassware for commercial, industrial, and institutional electric lighting fixtures—are classified in Industry 32721, Glass and Glass Product Manufacturing;

- Manufacturing residential electric lighting fixtures—are classified in U.S. Industry 335121, Residential Electric Lighting Fixture Manufacturing;

- Manufacturing current-carrying wiring devices for lighting fixtures—are classified in U.S. Industry 335931, Current-Carrying Wiring Device Manufacturing;

- Manufacturing vehicular lighting fixtures—are classified in U.S. Industry 336321, Vehicular Lighting Equipment Manufacturing;

US—United States industry only. CAN—United States and Canadian industries are comparable. When neither US nor CAN appears, Canadian, Mexican, and United States industries are comparable.

- Manufacturing electric light bulbs, tubes, and parts—are classified in Industry 335110, Electric Lamp Bulb and Part Manufacturing; and

- Manufacturing other lighting fixtures, such as street lights, flashlights, and nonelectric lighting equipment,—are classified in U.S. Industry 335129, Other Lighting Equipment Manufacturing

335129 Other Lighting Equipment Manufacturing[US]

This U.S. industry comprises establishments primarily engaged in manufacturing electric lighting fixtures (except residential, commercial, industrial, institutional, and vehicular electric lighting fixtures) and nonelectric lighting equipment.

Illustrative Examples:

Christmas tree lighting sets, electric, manufacturing
Fireplace logs, electric, manufacturing
Flashlights manufacturing
Insect lamps, electric, manufacturing

Lanterns (e.g., carbide, electric, gas, gasoline, kerosene) manufacturing
Spotlights (except vehicular) manufacturing
Street lighting fixtures (except traffic signals) manufacturing

Cross-References. Establishments primarily engaged in—

- Manufacturing glassware for lighting fixtures—are classified in Industry 32721, Glass and Glass Product Manufacturing;

- Manufacturing electric light bulbs, tubes, and parts—are classified in Industry 335110, Electric Lamp Bulb and Part Manufacturing;

- Manufacturing current-carrying wiring devices for lighting fixtures—are classified in U.S. Industry 335931, Current-Carrying Wiring Device Manufacturing;

- Manufacturing residential electric lighting fixtures—are classified in U.S. Industry 335121, Residential Electric Lighting Fixture Manufacturing;

- Manufacturing commercial, industrial, and institutional electric lighting fixtures—are classified in U.S. Industry 335122, Commercial, Industrial, and Institutional Electric Lighting Fixture Manufacturing;

- Manufacturing vehicular lighting fixtures—are classified in U.S. Industry 336321, Vehicular Lighting Equipment Manufacturing; and

- Manufacturing signaling devices that incorporate electric light bulbs, such as traffic and railway signals,—are classified in Industry 334290, Other Communications Equipment Manufacturing.

3352 Household Appliance Manufacturing

33521 Small Electrical Appliance Manufacturing

This industry comprises establishments primarily engaged in manufacturing small electric appliances and electric housewares, household-type fans, household-type vacuum cleaners, and other electric household-type floor care machines.

US—United States industry only. CAN—United States and Canadian industries are comparable. When neither US nor CAN appears, Canadian, Mexican, and United States industries are comparable.

http://www.ntis.gov/naics

Cross-References. Establishments primarily engaged in—

- Manufacturing room air-conditioners, attic fans, wall and baseboard heating units for permanent installation, and commercial ventilation and exhaust fans—are classified in Industry 33341, Ventilation, Heating, Air-Conditioning, and Commercial Refrigeration Equipment Manufacturing;

- Manufacturing commercial, industrial, and institutional vacuum cleaners, and mechanical carpet sweepers—are classified in Industry 33331, Commercial and Service Industry Machinery Manufacturing;

- Manufacturing major household-type appliances, such as washing machines, dryers, stoves, and hot water heaters,—are classified in Industry 33522, Major Appliance Manufacturing; and

- Installing central vacuum cleaning systems—are classified in Sector 23, Construction.

335211 Electric Housewares and Household Fan Manufacturing[US]

This U.S. industry comprises establishments primarily engaged in manufacturing small electric appliances and electric housewares for heating, cooking, and other purposes, and electric household-type fans (except attic fans).

Illustrative Examples:

Bath fans, residential, manufacturing	Portable electric space heaters manufacturing
Ceiling fans, residential, manufacturing	Portable hair dryers, electric, manufacturing
Curling irons, household-type electric, manufacturing	Portable humidifiers and dehumidifiers manufacturing
Electronic blankets manufacturing	Scissors, electric, manufacturing
Portable cooking appliances (except microwave, convection ovens), household-type electric, manufacturing	Ventilating and exhaust fans (except attic fans), household-type, manufacturing

Cross-References. Establishments primarily engaged in—

- Manufacturing attic fans—are classified in U.S. Industry 333412, Industrial and Commercial Fan and Blower Manufacturing;

- Manufacturing wall and baseboard heating units for permanent installation—are classified in U.S. Industry 333414, Heating Equipment (except Warm Air Furnaces) Manufacturing;

- Manufacturing room air-conditioners—are classified in U.S. Industry 333415, Air-Conditioning and Warm Air Heating Equipment and Commercial and Industrial Refrigeration Equipment Manufacturing; and

- Manufacturing microwave and convection ovens—are classified in U.S. Industry 335221, Household Cooking Appliance Manufacturing.

US—United States industry only. CAN—United States and Canadian industries are comparable. When neither US nor CAN appears, Canadian, Mexican, and United States industries are comparable.

335212 Household Vacuum Cleaner Manufacturing[US]

This U.S. industry comprises establishments primarily engaged in manufacturing electric vacuum cleaners, electric floor waxing machines, and other electric floor care machines typically for household use.

Cross-References. Establishments primarily engaged in—

- Manufacturing electric vacuum cleaners for commercial, industrial, and institutional uses, and mechanical carpet sweepers—are classified in U.S. Industry 333319, Other Commercial and Service Industry Machinery Manufacturing; and

- Installing central vacuum cleaning systems—are classified in Industry 235950, Building Equipment and Other Machinery Installation Contractors.

33522 Major Appliance Manufacturing

This industry comprises establishments primarily engaged in manufacturing household-type cooking appliances, household-type laundry equipment, household-type refrigerators, upright and chest freezers, and other electrical and nonelectrical major household-type appliances, such as dishwashers, water heaters, and garbage disposal units.

Cross-References. Establishments primarily engaged in—

- Manufacturing small electric appliances and electric housewares, such as hot plates, griddles, toasters, and electric irons,—are classified in Industry 33521, Small Electrical Appliance Manufacturing;

- Manufacturing commercial and industrial refrigerators and freezers—are classified in Industry 33341, Ventilation, Heating, Air-Conditioning, and Commercial Refrigeration Equipment Manufacturing;

- Manufacturing commercial-type cooking equipment and commercial-type laundry, dry-cleaning, and pressing equipment—are classified in Industry 33331, Commercial and Service Industry Machinery Manufacturing; and

- Manufacturing household-type sewing machines—are classified in Industry 33329, Other Industrial Machinery Manufacturing.

335221 Household Cooking Appliance Manufacturing[US]

This U.S. industry comprises establishments primarily engaged in manufacturing household-type electric and nonelectric cooking equipment (except small electric appliances and electric housewares).

Cross-References. Establishments primarily engaged in—

- Manufacturing small electric appliances and electric housewares used for cooking, such as electric skillets, electric hot plates, electric griddles, toasters, and percolators,—are classified in U.S. Industry 335211, Electric Housewares and Household Fan Manufacturing; and

---

US—United States industry only. CAN—United States and Canadian industries are comparable. When neither US nor CAN appears, Canadian, Mexican, and United States industries are comparable.

• Manufacturing commercial-type cooking equipment—are classified in U.S. Industry 333319, Other Commercial and Service Industry Machinery Manufacturing.

335222 Household Refrigerator and Home Freezer Manufacturing[US]

This U.S. industry comprises establishments primarily engaged in manufacturing household-type refrigerators and upright and chest freezers.

Cross-References.

Establishments primarily engaged in manufacturing commercial and industrial refrigeration equipment, such as refrigerators and freezers, are classified in U.S. Industry 333415, Air-Conditioning and Warm Air Heating Equipment and Commercial and Industrial Refrigeration Equipment Manufacturing.

335224 Household Laundry Equipment Manufacturing[US]

This U.S. industry comprises establishments primarily engaged in manufacturing household-type laundry equipment.

Cross-References. Establishments primarily engaged in—

• Manufacturing portable electric irons—are classified in U.S. Industry 335211, Electric Housewares and Household Fan Manufacturing; and

• Manufacturing commercial-type laundry and drycleaning equipment—are classified in U.S. Industry 333312, Commercial Laundry, Dry Cleaning, and Pressing Machine Manufacturing.

335228 Other Major Household Appliance Manufacturing[US]

This U.S. industry comprises establishments primarily engaged in manufacturing electric and nonelectric major household-type appliances (except cooking equipment, refrigerators, upright and chest freezers, and household-type laundry equipment).

Illustrative Examples:

Dishwashers, household-type, manufacturing
Garbage disposal units, household-type, manufacturing
Hot water heaters (including nonelectric), household-type, manufacturing

Trash and garbage compactors, household-type, manufacturing

Cross-References. Establishments primarily engaged in—

• Manufacturing household-type cooking equipment—are classified in U.S. Industry 335221, Household Cooking Appliance Manufacturing;

US—United States industry only. CAN—United States and Canadian industries are comparable. When neither US nor CAN appears, Canadian, Mexican, and United States industries are comparable.

- Manufacturing household-type sewing machines—are classified in U.S. Industry 333298, All Other Industrial Machinery Manufacturing;

- Manufacturing household-type refrigerators and upright and chest freezers—are classified in U.S. Industry 335222, Household Refrigerator and Home Freezer Manufacturing; and

- Manufacturing small electric appliances—are classified in U.S. Industry 335211, Electric Housewares and Household Fan Manufacturing.

3353 Electrical Equipment Manufacturing

33531 Electrical Equipment Manufacturing

This industry comprises establishments primarily engaged in manufacturing power, distribution, and specialty transformers; electric motors, generators, and motor generator sets; switchgear and switchboard apparatus; relays; and industrial controls.

Cross-References. Establishments primarily engaged in—

- Manufacturing turbine generator set units and electric outboard motors—are classified in Industry 33361, Engine, Turbine, and Power Transmission Equipment Manufacturing;

- Manufacturing electronic component-type transformers and switches—are classified in Industry 33441, Semiconductor and Other Electronic Component Manufacturing;

- Manufacturing environmental controls and industrial process control instruments—are classified in Industry 33451, Navigational, Measuring, Electromedical, and Control Instruments Manufacturing;

- Manufacturing switches for electrical circuits, such as pushbutton and snap switches,—are classified in Industry 33593, Wiring Device Manufacturing;

- Manufacturing complete for welding and soldering equipment—are classified in Industry 33399, All Other General Purpose Machinery Manufacturing; and

- Manufacturing starting motors and generators for internal combustion engines—are classified in Industry 33632, Motor Vehicle Electrical and Electronic Equipment Manufacturing.

335311 Power, Distribution, and Specialty Transformer Manufacturing[CAN]

This U.S. industry comprises establishments primarily engaged in manufacturing power, distribution, and specialty transformers (except electronic components). Industrial-type and consumer-type transformers in this industry vary (e.g., step up or step down) voltage but do not convert alternating to direct or direct to alternating current.

Illustrative Examples:

Distribution transformers, electric, manufacturing

Fluorescent ballasts (i.e., transformers) manufacturing

Substation transformers, electric power distribution, manufacturing

Transmission and distribution voltage regulators manufacturing

---

US—United States industry only. CAN—United States and Canadian industries are comparable. When neither US nor CAN appears, Canadian, Mexican, and United States industries are comparable.

Cross-References.

Establishments primarily engaged in manufacturing electronic component-type transformers are classified in U.S. Industry 334416, Electronic Coil, Transformers, and Other Inductor Manufacturing.

335312 Motor and Generator Manufacturing[CAN]

This U.S. industry comprises establishments primarily engaged in manufacturing electric motors (except internal combustion engine starting motors), power generators (except battery charging alternators for internal combustion engines), and motor generator sets (except turbine generator set units). This industry includes establishments rewinding armatures on a factory basis.

Cross-References. Establishments primarily engaged in—

- Manufacturing electric outboard motors—are classified in U.S. Industry 333618, Other Engine Equipment Manufacturing;

- Manufacturing gas, steam, or hydraulic turbine generator set units—are classified in U.S. Industry 333611, Turbine and Turbine Generator Set Units Manufacturing;

- Manufacturing starting motors and battery charging alternators for internal combustion engines—are classified in U.S. Industry 336322, Other Motor Vehicle Electrical and Electronic Equipment Manufacturing;

- Rewinding armatures, not on a factory basis,—are classified in Industry 811310, Commercial and Industrial Machinery and Equipment (except Automotive and Electronic) Repair and Maintenance; and

- Manufacturing complete welding and soldering equipment—are classified in U.S. Industry 333992, Welding and Soldering Equipment Manufacturing.

335313 Switchgear and Switchboard Apparatus Manufacturing[US]

This U.S. industry comprises establishments primarily engaged in manufacturing switchgear and switchboard apparatus.

Illustrative Examples:

Circuit breakers, power, manufacturing
Control panels, electric power distribution, manufacturing
Duct for electrical switchboard apparatus manufacturing

Fuses, electric, manufacturing
Power switching equipment manufacturing
Switches, electric power (except pushbutton, snap, solenoid, tumbler), manufacturing

Cross-References. Establishments primarily engaged in—

- Manufacturing relays—are classified in U.S. Industry 335314, Relay and Industrial Control Manufacturing;

US—United States industry only. CAN—United States and Canadian industries are comparable. When neither US nor CAN appears, Canadian, Mexican, and United States industries are comparable.

- Manufacturing switches for electronic applications—are classified in U.S. Industry 334419, Other Electronic Component Manufacturing; and

- Manufacturing snap, pushbutton, and similar switches for electrical circuits—are classified in U.S. Industry 335931, Current-Carrying Wiring Device Manufacturing.

335314 Relay and Industrial Control Manufacturing[US]

This U.S. industry comprises establishments primarily engaged in manufacturing relays, motor starters and controllers, and other industrial controls and control accessories.

Cross-References. Establishments primarily engaged in—

- Manufacturing environmental and appliance control equipment—are classified in U.S. Industry 334512, Automatic Environmental Control Manufacturing for Residential, Commercial, and Appliance Use; and

- Manufacturing instruments for controlling industrial process variables—are classified in U.S. Industry 334513, Instruments and Related Products Manufacturing for Measuring, Displaying, and Controlling Industrial Process Variables.

3359 Other Electrical Equipment and Component Manufacturing

This industry group comprises establishments manufacturing electrical equipment and components (except electric lighting equipment, household-type appliances, transformers, switchgear, relays, motors, and generators).

33591 Battery Manufacturing

This industry comprises establishments primarily engaged in manufacturing primary and storage batteries.

335911 Storage Battery Manufacturing[US]

This U.S. industry comprises establishments primarily engaged in manufacturing storage batteries.

Illustrative Examples:

Lead acid storage batteries manufacturing

Rechargeable nickel cadmium (NICAD) batteries manufacturing

Cross-References.

Establishments primarily engaged in manufacturing primary batteries are classified in U.S. Industry 335912, Primary Battery Manufacturing.

US—United States industry only. CAN—United States and Canadian industries are comparable. When neither US nor CAN appears, Canadian, Mexican, and United States industries are comparable.

http://www.ntis.gov/naics

335912 Primary Battery Manufacturing[US]

This U.S. industry comprises establishments primarily engaged in manufacturing wet or dry primary batteries.

Illustrative Examples:

Disposable flashlight batteries manufacturing
Dry cells, primary (e.g., AAA, AA, C, D, 9V), manufacturing

Lithium batteries, primary, manufacturing
Watch batteries manufacturing

Cross-References.

Establishments primarily engaged in manufacturing storage batteries are classified in U.S. Industry 335911, Storage Battery Manufacturing.

33592 Communication and Energy Wire and Cable Manufacturing

This industry comprises establishments insulating fiber-optic cable, and manufacturing insulated nonferrous wire and cable from nonferrous wire drawn in other establishments.

Cross-References. Establishments primarily engaged in—

- Drawing nonferrous wire—are classified in Subsector 331, Primary Metal Manufacturing;

- Manufacturing cable sets consisting of insulated wire and various connectors for electronic applications—are classified in Industry 33441, Semiconductor and Other Electronic Component Manufacturing;

- Manufacturing extension cords, appliance cords, and similar electrical cord sets from purchased, insulated wire or cable—are classified in Industry 33599, All Other Electrical Equipment and Component Manufacturing; and

- Manufacturing unsheathed fiber-optic materials—are classified in Industry 32721, Glass and Glass Product Manufacturing.

335921 Fiber Optic Cable Manufacturing[US]

This U.S. industry comprises establishments primarily engaged in manufacturing insulated fiber-optic cable from purchased fiber-optic strand.

Cross-References. Establishments primarily engaged in—

- Manufacturing unsheathed fiber-optic materials—are classified in Industry 32721, Glass and Glass Product Manufacturing; and

- Manufacturing insulated nonferrous wire and cable from purchased wire—are classified in U.S. Industry 335929, Other Communication and Energy Wire Manufacturing.

US—United States industry only. CAN—United States and Canadian industries are comparable. When neither US nor CAN appears, Canadian, Mexican, and United States industries are comparable.

http://www.ntis.gov/naics

335929 Other Communication and Energy Wire Manufacturing[US]

This U.S. industry comprises establishments primarily engaged in manufacturing insulated wire and cable of nonferrous metals from purchased wire.

Cross-References. Establishments primarily engaged in—

- Manufacturing cable sets consisting of insulated wire and various connectors for electronic applications—are classified in U.S. Industry 334419, Other Electronic Component Manufacturing;

- Manufacturing extension cords, appliance cords, and similar electrical cord sets from purchased insulated wire—are classified in U.S. Industry 335999, All Other Miscellaneous Electrical Equipment and Component Manufacturing;

- Drawing and insulating copper wire in the same establishment—are classified in U.S. Industry 331422, Copper Wire (except Mechanical) Drawing;

- Drawing and insulating aluminum wire in the same establishment—are classified in U.S. Industry 331319, Other Aluminum Rolling and Drawing; and

- Drawing nonferrous wire (except copper and aluminum)—are classified in U.S. Industry 331491, Nonferrous Metal (except Copper and Aluminum) Rolling, Drawing, and Extruding.

33593 Wiring Device Manufacturing

This industry comprises establishments primarily engaged in manufacturing current-carrying wiring devices and noncurrent-carrying wiring devices for wiring electrical circuits.

Cross-References. Establishments primarily engaged in—

- Manufacturing ceramic and glass insulators—are classified in Subsector 327, Nonmetallic Mineral Product Manufacturing; and

- Manufacturing electronic component-type connectors, sockets, and switches—are classified in Industry 33441, Semiconductor and Other Electronic Component Manufacturing.

335931 Current-Carrying Wiring Device Manufacturing[US]

This U.S. industry comprises establishments primarily engaged in manufacturing current-carrying wiring devices.

Illustrative Examples:

Bus bars, electrical conductors (except switchgear-type), manufacturing	Receptacles (i.e., outlets), electrical, manufacturing
GFCI (ground fault circuit interrupters) manufacturing	Switches for electrical wiring (e.g., pressure, pushbutton, snap, tumbler) manufacturing
Lamp holders manufacturing	
Lightning arrestors and coils manufacturing	

US—United States industry only. CAN—United States and Canadian industries are comparable. When neither US nor CAN appears, Canadian, Mexican, and United States industries are comparable.

Cross-References. Establishments primarily engaged in—

- Manufacturing electronic component-type connectors—are classified in U.S. Industry 334417, Electronic Connector Manufacturing;

- Manufacturing noncurrent-carrying wiring devices—are classified in U.S. Industry 335932, Noncurrent-Carrying Wiring Device Manufacturing; and

- Manufacturing electronic component-type sockets and switches—are classified in U.S. Industry 334419, Other Electronic Component Manufacturing.

335932 Noncurrent-Carrying Wiring Device Manufacturing[US]

This U.S. industry comprises establishments primarily engaged in manufacturing noncurrent-carrying wiring devices.

Illustrative Examples:

Boxes, electrical wiring (e.g., junction, outlet, switch), manufacturing
Conduits and fittings, electrical, manufacturing

Face plates (i.e., outlet or switch covers) manufacturing
Transmission pole and line hardware manufacturing

Cross-References. Establishments primarily engaged in—

- Manufacturing porcelain and ceramic insulators—are classified in U.S. Industry 327113, Porcelain Electrical Supply Manufacturing;

- Manufacturing current-carrying wiring devices—are classified in U.S. Industry 335931, Current-Carrying Wiring Device Manufacturing; and

- Manufacturing glass insulators—are classified in Industry 32721, Glass and Glass Product Manufacturing.

33599 All Other Electrical Equipment and Component Manufacturing

This industry comprises establishments primarily engaged in manufacturing electrical equipment (except electric lighting equipment, household-type appliances, transformers, motors, generators, switchgear, relays, industrial controls, batteries, communication and energy wire and cable, and wiring devices).

Illustrative Examples:

Carbon and graphite electrodes and brushes manufacturing
Extension cords made from purchased insulated wire

Surge suppressors manufacturing

US—United States industry only. CAN—United States and Canadian industries are comparable. When neither US nor CAN appears, Canadian, Mexican, and United States industries are comparable.

Cross-References. Establishments primarily engaged in—

- Manufacturing lighting equipment—are classified in Industry Group 3351, Electric Lighting Equipment Manufacturing;

- Manufacturing household-type appliances—are classified in Industry Group 3352, Household Appliance Manufacturing;

- Manufacturing transformers, motors, generators, switchgear, relays, and industrial controls—are classified in Industry 33531, Electrical Equipment Manufacturing;

- Manufacturing batteries—are classified in Industry 33591, Battery Manufacturing;

- Manufacturing communication and energy wire—are classified in Industry 33592, Communication and Energy Wire and Cable Manufacturing;

- Manufacturing current-carrying and noncurrent-carrying wiring devices—are classified in Industry 33593, Wiring Device Manufacturing;

- Manufacturing carbon or graphite gaskets—are classified in Industry 33999, All Other Miscellaneous Manufacturing;

- Manufacturing electronic component-type rectifiers, voltage regulating integrated circuits, power converting integrated circuits, electronic capacitors, electronic resistors, and similar devices—are classified in Industry 33441, Semiconductor and Other Electronic Component Manufacturing; and

- Manufacturing equipment incorporating lasers—are classified in various subsectors of manufacturing based on the associated production process of the finished equipment.

335991 Carbon and Graphite Product Manufacturing[US]

This U.S. industry comprises establishments primarily engaged in manufacturing carbon, graphite, and metal-graphite brushes and brush stock; carbon or graphite electrodes for thermal and electrolytic uses; carbon and graphite fibers; and other carbon, graphite, and metal-graphite products.

Cross-References.

Establishments primarily engaged in manufacturing carbon or graphite gaskets are classified in U.S. Industry 339991, Gasket, Packing, and Sealing Device Manufacturing.

335999 All Other Miscellaneous Electrical Equipment and Component Manufacturing[US]

This U.S. industry comprises establishments primarily engaged in manufacturing industrial and commercial electric apparatus and other equipment (except lighting equipment, household appliances, transformers, motors, generators, switchgear, relays, industrial controls, batteries, communication and energy wire and cable, wiring devices, and carbon and graphite products). This industry includes power converters (i.e., AC to DC and DC to AC), power supplies, surge suppressors, and similar equipment for industrial-type and consumer-type equipment.

US—United States industry only. CAN—United States and Canadian industries are comparable. When neither US nor CAN appears, Canadian, Mexican, and United States industries are comparable.

Illustrative Examples:

Appliance cords made from purchased
  insulated wire
Battery chargers, solid-state, manufacturing
Door opening and closing devices, electrical,
  manufacturing
Electric bells manufacturing

Extension cords made from purchased
  insulated wire
Inverters manufacturing
Surge suppressers manufacturing
Uninterruptible power supplies (UPS)
  manufacturing

Cross-References. Establishments primarily engaged in—

- Manufacturing lighting equipment—are classified in Industry Group 3351, Electric Lighting Equipment Manufacturing;

- Manufacturing household-type appliances—are classified in Industry Group 3352, Household Appliance Manufacturing;

- Manufacturing transformers, motors, generators, switchgear, relays, and industrial controls—are classified in Industry 33531, Electrical Equipment Manufacturing;

- Manufacturing primary and storage batteries—are classified in Industry 33591, Battery Manufacturing;

- Manufacturing communication and energy wire and cable from purchased wire—are classified in Industry 33592, Communication and Energy Wire and Cable Manufacturing;

- Manufacturing current-carrying and noncurrent-carrying wiring devices—are classified in Industry 33593, Wiring Device Manufacturing;

- Manufacturing electronic component-type rectifiers (except semiconductor)—are classified in U.S. Industry 334419, Other Electronic Component Manufacturing;

- Manufacturing semiconductor rectifiers, voltage regulating integrated circuits, power converting integrated circuits, and similar semiconductor devices—are classified in U.S. Industry 334413, Semiconductor and Related Device Manufacturing;

- Manufacturing electronic component-type capacitors and condensers—are classified in U.S. Industry 334414, Electronic Capacitor Manufacturing;

- Manufacturing carbon and graphite products—are classified in U.S. Industry 335991, Carbon and Graphite Product Manufacturing; and

- Manufacturing equipment incorporating lasers—are classified in various manufacturing subsectors based on the associated production process of the finished equipment.

336 Transportation Equipment Manufacturing

Industries in the Transportation Equipment Manufacturing subsector produce equipment for transporting people and goods. Transportation equipment is a type of machinery. An entire subsector is devoted to this activity because of the significance of its economic size in all three North American countries.

Establishments in this subsector utilize production processes similar to those of other machinery manufacturing establishments - bending, forming, welding, machining, and assembling metal or plastic parts into components and finished products. However, the assembly of components and subassemblies and their further assembly into finished vehicles tends to be a more common production process in this subsector than in the Machinery Manufacturing subsector.

NAICS has industry groups for the manufacture of equipment for each mode of transport—road, rail, air and water. Parts for motor vehicles warrant a separate industry group because of their importance and because parts manufacture requires less assembly, and the establishments that manufacture only parts are not as vertically integrated as those that make complete vehicles.

Land use motor vehicle equipment not designed for highway operation (e.g., agricultural equipment, construction equipment, and materials handling equipment) is classified in the appropriate NAICS subsector based on the type and use of the equipment.

3361 Motor Vehicle Manufacturing

33611 Automobile and Light Duty Motor Vehicle Manufacturing

This industry comprises establishments primarily engaged in (1) manufacturing complete automobile and light duty motor vehicles (i.e., body and chassis or unibody) or (2) manufacturing chassis only.

Cross-References.

Establishments primarily engaged in manufacturing car, truck, and bus bodies and assembling vehicles on a purchased chassis and manufacturing kit cars for highway use are classified in Industry 33621, Motor Vehicle Body and Trailer Manufacturing.

336111 Automobile Manufacturing[US]

This U.S. industry comprises establishments primarily engaged in (1) manufacturing complete automobiles (i.e., body and chassis or unibody) or (2) manufacturing automobile chassis only.

Cross-References.

Establishments primarily engaged in manufacturing car bodies and assembling vehicles on a purchased chassis and manufacturing kit cars for highway use are classified in U.S. Industry 336211, Motor Vehicle Body Manufacturing.

336112 Light Truck and Utility Vehicle Manufacturing[US]

This U.S. industry comprises establishments primarily engaged in (1) manufacturing complete light trucks and utility vehicles (i.e., body and chassis) or (2) manufacturing light truck and utility vehicle chassis only. Vehicles made include light duty vans, pick-up trucks, minivans, and sport utility vehicles.

US—United States industry only. CAN—United States and Canadian industries are comparable. When neither US nor CAN appears, Canadian, Mexican, and United States industries are comparable.

Cross-References.

Establishments primarily engaged in manufacturing truck and bus bodies and assembling vehicles on a purchased chassis are classified in U.S. Industry 336211, Motor Vehicle Body Manufacturing.

33612 Heavy Duty Truck Manufacturing
See industry description for 336120 below.

336120 Heavy Duty Truck Manufacturing

This industry comprises establishments primarily engaged in (1) manufacturing heavy duty truck chassis and assembling complete heavy duty trucks, buses, heavy duty motor homes, and other special purpose heavy duty motor vehicles for highway use or (2) manufacturing heavy duty truck chassis only.

Cross-References. Establishments primarily engaged in—

- Manufacturing truck and bus bodies and assembling vehicles on a purchased chassis—are classified in U.S. Industry 336211, Motor Vehicle Body Manufacturing;

- Manufacturing motor homes on purchased chassis—are classified in U.S. Industry 336213, Motor Home Manufacturing;

- Manufacturing vans, minivans, and light trucks—are classified in Industry 336112, Light Truck and Utility Vehicle Manufacturing;

- Manufacturing military armored vehicles—are classified in U.S. Industry 336992, Military Armored Vehicle, Tank, and Tank Component Manufacturing; and

- Manufacturing off highway construction equipment—are classified in Industry 333120, Construction Machinery Manufacturing.

3362 Motor Vehicle Body and Trailer Manufacturing

33621 Motor Vehicle Body and Trailer Manufacturing

This industry comprises establishments primarily engaged in (1) manufacturing motor vehicle bodies and cabs or (2) manufacturing truck, automobile and utility trailers, truck trailer chassis, detachable trailer bodies and detachable trailer chassis. The products made may be sold separately or may be assembled on purchased chassis and sold as complete vehicles.

Motor homes are units where the motor and the living quarters are contained in the same integrated unit, while travel trailers are designed to be towed by a motor unit, such as an automobile or a light truck.

Illustrative Examples:

Bodies and cabs, truck, manufacturing
Camper unit, slide-in, for pick-up trucks, manufacturing
Motor homes, self-contained, assembling on purchased chassis

Pickup canopies, caps, or covers manufacturing
Travel trailers, recreational, manufacturing
Semitrailer manufacturing

Cross-References. Establishments primarily engaged in—

- Making manufactured homes (i.e., mobile homes)—are classified in Industry 32199, All Other Wood Product Manufacturing;

- Customizing automotive vehicle and trailer interiors (i.e. van conversions) on an individual basis—are classified in Industry 81112, Automotive Body, Paint, Interior, and Glass Repair;

- Manufacturing light duty motor home chassis and assembling complete motor homes—are classified in Industry 33611, Automobile and Light Duty Motor Vehicle Manufacturing; and

- Manufacturing heavy duty truck chassis and assembling heavy duty trucks, buses, motor homes, and other special purpose heavy duty motor vehicles for highway use—are classified in Industry 33612, Heavy Duty Truck Manufacturing.

336211 Motor Vehicle Body Manufacturing^{CAN}

This U.S. industry comprises establishments primarily engaged in manufacturing truck and bus bodies and cabs and automobile bodies. The products made may be sold separately or may be assembled on purchased chassis and sold as complete vehicles.

Cross-References.

Establishments primarily engaged in manufacturing heavy duty chassis and assembling heavy duty trucks, buses, motor homes, and other special purpose heavy duty motor vehicles for highway use are classified in Industry 336120, Heavy Duty Truck Manufacturing.

336212 Truck Trailer Manufacturing^{CAN}

This U.S. industry comprises establishments primarily engaged in manufacturing truck trailers, truck trailer chassis, cargo container chassis, detachable trailer bodies, and detachable trailer chassis for sale separately.

Cross-References.

Establishments primarily engaged in manufacturing utility trailers, light-truck trailers, and travel trailers are classified in U.S. Industry 336214, Travel Trailer and Camper Manufacturing.

336213 Motor Home Manufacturing^{US}

This U.S. industry comprises establishments primarily engaged in (1) manufacturing motor homes on purchased chassis and/or (2) manufacturing conversion vans on an assembly line basis. Motor homes are units where the motor and the living quarters are integrated in the same unit.

Cross-References. Establishments primarily engaged in—

- Manufacturing light duty motor homes chassis and assembling complete motor homes— are classified in U.S. Industry 336112, Light Truck and Utility Vehicle Manufacturing;

US—United States industry only. CAN—United States and Canadian industries are comparable. When neither US nor CAN appears, Canadian, Mexican, and United States industries are comparable.

- Customizing automotive vehicle and trailer interiors (i.e. van conversions) on an individual basis—are classified in U.S. Industry 811121, Automotive Body, Paint, and Interior Repair and Maintenance; and

- Producing manufactured homes (i.e., mobile homes)—are classified in U.S. Industry 321991, Manufactured Home (Mobile Home) Manufacturing.

336214 Travel Trailer and Camper Manufacturing[US]

This U.S. industry comprises establishments primarily engaged in one or more of the following: (1) manufacturing travel trailers and campers designed to attach to motor vehicles; (2) manufacturing pickup coaches (i.e., campers) and caps (i.e., covers) for mounting on pickup trucks; and (3) manufacturing automobile, utility and light-truck trailers. Travel trailers do not have their own motor but are designed to be towed by a motor unit, such as an automobile or a light truck.

Illustrative Examples:

Automobile transporter trailers, single car, manufacturing
Camping trailers and chassis manufacturing
Horse trailers (except fifth wheel type) manufacturing

Travel trailers, recreational, manufacturing
Utility trailers manufacturing

Cross-References.

Establishments primarily engaged in making manufactured homes (i.e., mobile homes) designed to accept permanent water, sewer, and utility connections and equipped with wheels, but not intended for regular highway use, are classified in U.S. Industry 321991, Manufactured Home (Mobile Home) Manufacturing.

3363 Motor Vehicle Parts Manufacturing

33631 Motor Vehicle Gasoline Engine and Engine Parts Manufacturing

This industry comprises establishments primarily engaged in manufacturing and/or rebuilding motor vehicle gasoline engines, and engine parts, whether or not for vehicular use.

Illustrative Examples:

Carburetors, all types, manufacturing
Crankshaft assemblies, automotive and truck gasoline engine, manufacturing
Cylinder heads, automotive and truck gasoline engine, manufacturing
Fuel injection systems and parts, automotive and truck gasoline engine, manufacturing
Manifolds (i.e., intake and exhaust), automotive and truck gasoline engine, manufacturing

Pistons and piston rings manufacturing
Pumps (e.g., fuel, oil, water), mechanical automotive and truck gasoline engine (except power steering) manufacturing
Timing gears and chains, automotive and truck gasoline engine, manufacturing
Valves, engine, intake and exhaust, manufacturing

US—United States industry only. CAN—United States and Canadian industries are comparable. When neither US nor CAN appears, Canadian, Mexican, and United States industries are comparable.

Cross-References. Establishments primarily engaged in—

- Manufacturing wiring harnesses and other vehicular electrical and electronic equipment—are classified in Industry 33632, Motor Vehicle Electrical and Electronic Equipment Manufacturing;

- Manufacturing transmission and power train equipment—are classified in Industry 33635, Motor Vehicle Transmission and Power Train Parts Manufacturing;

- Manufacturing radiators—are classified in Industry 33639, Other Motor Vehicle Parts Manufacturing;

- Manufacturing steering and suspension components—are classified in Industry 33633, Motor Vehicle Steering and Suspension Components (except Spring) Manufacturing;

- Manufacturing parts for machine repair and equipment parts (except electric) on a job or shop basis—are classified in Industry 33271, Machine Shops;

- Manufacturing rubber and plastic belts and hoses without fittings—are classified in Industry 32622, Rubber and Plastics Hoses and Belting Manufacturing; and

- Manufacturing stationary and diesel engines—are classified in Industry 33361, Engine, Turbine, and Power Transmission Equipment Manufacturing.

336311 Carburetor, Piston, Piston Ring, and Valve Manufacturing[US]

This U.S. industry comprises establishments primarily engaged in manufacturing and/or rebuilding carburetors, pistons, piston rings, and engine intake and exhaust valves.

Cross-References.

Establishments primarily engaged in manufacturing parts for machine repair and equipment parts (except electric) on a job or shop basis are classified in Industry 332710, Machine Shops.

336312 Gasoline Engine and Engine Parts Manufacturing[US]

This U.S. industry comprises establishments primarily engaged in manufacturing and/or rebuilding gasoline motor vehicle engines and gasoline motor vehicle engine parts, excluding carburetors, pistons, piston rings, and valves.

Illustrative Examples:

Crankshaft assemblies, automotive and truck gasoline engine, manufacturing

Flywheels and ring gears, automotive and truck gasoline engine, manufacturing

Fuel injection systems and parts, automotive and truck gasoline engine, manufacturing

Manifolds (i.e., intake and exhaust), automotive and truck gasoline engine, manufacturing

Positive crankcase ventilation (PCV) valves, engine, manufacturing

Pumps (e.g., fuel, oil, water), mechanical, automotive and truck gasoline engine (except power steering), manufacturing

Timing gears and chains, automotive and truck gasoline engine, manufacturing

---

US—United States industry only. CAN—United States and Canadian industries are comparable. When neither US nor CAN appears, Canadian, Mexican, and United States industries are comparable.

http://www.ntis.gov/naics

Cross-References. Establishments primarily engaged in—

- Manufacturing carburetors, pistons, piston rings, and valves—are classified in U.S. Industry 336311, Carburetor, Piston, Piston Ring, and Valve Manufacturing;

- Manufacturing wiring harnesses and other vehicular electrical and electronic equipment— are classified in U.S. Industry 336322, Other Motor Vehicle Electrical and Electronic Equipment Manufacturing;

- Manufacturing transmission and power train equipment—are classified in Industry 336350, Motor Vehicle Transmission and Power Train Parts Manufacturing;

- Manufacturing radiators—are classified in U.S. Industry 336399, All Other Motor Vehicle Parts Manufacturing;

- Manufacturing steering and suspension components—are classified in Industry 336330, Motor Vehicle Steering and Suspension Components (except Spring) Manufacturing;

- Manufacturing rubber and plastic belts and hoses without fittings—are classified in Industry 326220, Rubber and Plastics Hoses and Belting Manufacturing; and

- Manufacturing stationary and diesel engines—are classified in U.S. Industry 333618, Other Engine Equipment Manufacturing.

33632 Motor Vehicle Electrical and Electronic Equipment Manufacturing

This industry comprises establishments primarily engaged in (1) manufacturing vehicular lighting and/or (2) manufacturing and/or rebuilding motor vehicle electrical and electronic equipment. The products made can be used for all types of transportation equipment (i.e., aircraft, automobiles, trains, ships).

Illustrative Examples:

Alternators and generators for internal combustion engines manufacturing
Automotive lighting fixtures manufacturing
Coils, ignition, internal combustion engines, manufacturing
Distributors for internal combustion engines manufacturing
Electrical ignition cable sets for internal combustion engines manufacturing
Generators for internal combustion engines manufacturing

Ignition wiring harness for internal combustion engines manufacturing
Instrument control panels (i.e., assembling purchased gauges), automotive, truck, and bus, manufacturing
Spark plugs for internal combustion engines manufacturing
Windshield washer pumps, automotive, truck, and bus, manufacturing

Cross-References. Establishments primarily engaged in—

- Manufacturing automotive lamps—are classified in Industry 33511, Electric Lamp Bulb and Part Manufacturing;

US—United States industry only. CAN—United States and Canadian industries are comparable. When neither US nor CAN appears, Canadian, Mexican, and United States industries are comparable.

- Manufacturing batteries—are classified in Industry 33591, Battery Manufacturing;

- Manufacturing electric motors for motor vehicles (including electric vehicles)—are classified in Industry 33531, Electrical Equipment Manufacturing;

- Manufacturing railway traffic control signals and passenger car alarms—are classified in Industry 33429, Other Communications Equipment Manufacturing; and

- Manufacturing car stereos—are classified in Industry 33431, Audio and Video Equipment Manufacturing.

336321 Vehicular Lighting Equipment Manufacturing[US]

This U.S. industry comprises establishments primarily engaged in manufacturing vehicular lighting fixtures.

Cross-References.

Establishments primarily engaged in manufacturing automotive lamps (i.e., bulbs) are classified in Industry 335110, Electric Lamp Bulb and Part Manufacturing.

336322 Other Motor Vehicle Electrical and Electronic Equipment Manufacturing[US]

This U.S. industry comprises establishments primarily engaged in manufacturing and/or rebuilding electrical and electronic equipment for motor vehicles and internal combustion engines.

Illustrative Examples:

Alternators and generators for internal
  combustion engines manufacturing
Coils, ignition, internal combustion engines, manufacturing
Distributors for internal combustion engines
  manufacturing
Electrical ignition cable sets for internal
  combustion engines manufacturing
Generators for internal combustion engines
  manufacturing

Ignition wiring harness for internal
  combustion engines manufacturing
Instrument control panel (i.e., assembling
  purchased gauges), automotive, truck, and
  bus, manufacturing
Spark plugs for internal combustion engines manufacturing
Windshield washer pumps, automotive, truck,
  and bus, manufacturing

Cross-References. Establishments primarily engaged in—

- Manufacturing vehicular lighting equipment—are classified in U.S. Industry 336321, Vehicular Lighting Equipment Manufacturing;

- Manufacturing automotive lamps—are classified in Industry 335110, Electric Lamp Bulb and Part Manufacturing;

- Manufacturing batteries—are classified in U.S. Industry 335911, Storage Battery Manufacturing;

US—United States industry only. CAN—United States and Canadian industries are comparable.
When neither US nor CAN appears, Canadian, Mexican, and United States industries are comparable.

- Manufacturing electric motors for electric vehicles—are classified in U.S. Industry 335312, Motor and Generator Manufacturing;

- Manufacturing railway traffic control signals and passenger car alarms—are classified in Industry 334290, Other Communications Equipment Manufacturing; and

- Manufacturing car stereos—are classified in Industry 334310, Audio and Video Equipment Manufacturing.

33633 Motor Vehicle Steering and Suspension Components (except Spring) Manufacturing

See industry description for 336330 below.

336330 Motor Vehicle Steering and Suspension Components (except Spring) Manufacturing

This industry comprises establishments primarily engaged in manufacturing and/or rebuilding motor vehicle steering mechanisms and suspension components (except springs).

Illustrative Examples:

Rack and pinion steering assemblies manufacturing
Shock absorbers, automotive, truck, and bus, manufacturing
Steering columns, automotive, truck, and bus, manufacturing

Steering wheels, automotive, truck, and bus, manufacturing
Struts, automotive, truck, and bus, manufacturing

Cross-References.

Establishments primarily engaged in manufacturing springs are classified in Industry 33261, Spring and Wire Product Manufacturing.

33634 Motor Vehicle Brake System Manufacturing

See industry description for 336340 below.

336340 Motor Vehicle Brake System Manufacturing

This industry comprises establishments primarily engaged in manufacturing and/or rebuilding motor vehicle brake systems and related components.

Illustrative Examples:

Brake cylinders, master and wheel, automotive, truck, and bus, manufacturing
Brake drums, automotive, truck, and bus, manufacturing
Brake hose assemblies manufacturing

Brake pads and shoes, automotive, truck, and bus, manufacturing
Calipers, brake, automotive, truck, and bus, manufacturing

US—United States industry only. CAN—United States and Canadian industries are comparable. When neither US nor CAN appears, Canadian, Mexican, and United States industries are comparable.

Cross-References.

Establishments primarily engaged in manufacturing rubber and plastics belts and hoses without fittings are classified in Industry 326220, Rubber and Plastics Hoses and Belting Manufacturing.

33635 Motor Vehicle Transmission and Power Train Parts Manufacturing
See industry description for 336350 below.

336350 Motor Vehicle Transmission and Power Train Parts Manufacturing

This industry comprises establishments primarily engaged in manufacturing and/or rebuilding motor vehicle transmission and power train parts.

Illustrative Examples:

Automatic transmissions, automotive, truck, and bus, manufacturing

Axle bearings, automotive, truck, and bus, manufacturing

Constant velocity joints, automotive, truck, and bus, manufacturing

Differential and rear axle assemblies, automotive, truck, and bus, manufacturing

Torque converters, automotive, truck, and bus, manufacturing

Universal joints, automotive, truck, and bus, manufacturing

33636 Motor Vehicle Seating and Interior Trim Manufacturing
See industry description for 336360 below.

336360 Motor Vehicle Seating and Interior Trim Manufacturing

This industry comprises establishments primarily engaged in manufacturing motor vehicle seating, seats, seat frames, seat belts, and interior trimmings.

Cross-References.

Establishments primarily engaged in manufacturing convertible tops for vehicles and those manufacturing air bags are classified in U.S. Industry 336399, All Other Motor Vehicle Parts Manufacturing.

33637 Motor Vehicle Metal Stamping
See industry description for 336370 below.

336370 Motor Vehicle Metal Stamping

This industry comprises establishments primarily engaged in manufacturing motor vehicle stampings, such as fenders, tops, body parts, trim, and molding.

US—United States industry only. CAN—United States and Canadian industries are comparable. When neither US nor CAN appears, Canadian, Mexican, and United States industries are comparable.

Cross-References. Establishments primarily engaged in—

- Manufacturing stampings and further processing the stampings—are classified according to the process of the specific product made; and

- Manufacturing stampings (except motor vehicle)—are classified in U.S. Industry 332116 Metal Stamping.

33639 Other Motor Vehicle Parts Manufacturing

This industry comprises establishments primarily engaged in manufacturing and/or rebuilding motor vehicle parts and accessories (except motor vehicle gasoline engines and engine parts, motor vehicle electrical and electronic equipment, motor vehicle steering and suspension components, motor vehicle brake systems, motor vehicle transmission and power train parts, motor vehicle seating and interior trim, and motor vehicle stampings).

Illustrative Examples:

Air bag assemblies manufacturing	Mufflers and resonators, motor vehicle, manufacturing
Air-conditioners, motor vehicle, manufacturing	Radiators and cores, manufacturing
Catalytic converters, engine exhaust, automotive, truck, and bus, manufacturing	Wheels (i.e., rims), automotive, truck, and bus, manufacturing

Cross-References. Establishments primarily engaged in—

- Manufacturing motor vehicle gasoline engines and engine parts—are classified in Industry 33631, Motor Vehicle Gasoline Engine and Engine Parts Manufacturing;

- Manufacturing motor vehicle electrical and electronic equipment—are classified in Industry 33632, Motor Vehicle Electrical and Electronic Equipment Manufacturing;

- Manufacturing motor vehicle steering and suspension components—are classified in Industry 33633, Motor Vehicle Steering and Suspension Components (except Spring) Manufacturing;

- Manufacturing motor vehicle brake systems—are classified in Industry 33634, Motor Vehicle Brake System Manufacturing;

- Manufacturing motor vehicle transmission and power train parts—are classified in Industry 33635, Motor Vehicle Transmission and Power Train Parts Manufacturing;

- Manufacturing motor vehicle seating and interior trim—are classified in Industry 33636, Motor Vehicle Seating and Interior Trim Manufacturing;

- Manufacturing motor vehicle stampings—are classified in Industry 33637, Motor Vehicle Metal Stamping; and

- Manufacturing air-conditioning systems and compressors (except motor vehicle air-conditioning systems)—are classified in Industry 33341, Ventilation, Heating, Air-Conditioning, and Commercial Refrigeration Equipment Manufacturing.

US—United States industry only. CAN—United States and Canadian industries are comparable. When neither US nor CAN appears, Canadian, Mexican, and United States industries are comparable.

336391 Motor Vehicle Air-Conditioning Manufacturing[US]

This U.S. industry comprises establishments primarily engaged in manufacturing air conditioning systems and compressors for motor vehicles, such as automobiles, trucks, buses, aircraft, farm machinery, construction machinery, and other related vehicles.

Cross-References.

Establishments primarily engaged in manufacturing air-conditioning systems and compressors (except motor vehicle air-conditioning systems) are classified in U.S. Industry 333415, Air-Conditioning and Warm Air Heating Equipment and Commercial and Industrial Refrigeration Equipment Manufacturing.

336399 All Other Motor Vehicle Parts Manufacturing[US]

This U.S. industry comprises establishments primarily engaged in manufacturing and/or rebuilding motor vehicle parts and accessories (except motor vehicle gasoline engines and engine parts, motor vehicle electrical and electronic equipment, motor vehicle steering and suspension components, motor vehicle brake systems, motor vehicle transmission and power train parts, motor vehicle seating and interior trim, motor vehicle stampings, and motor vehicle air-conditioning systems and compressors).

Illustrative Examples:

Air bag assemblies manufacturing
Air-filters, automotive, truck, and bus, manufacturing
Catalytic converters, engine exhaust, automotive, truck, and bus, manufacturing

Mufflers and resonators, motor vehicle, manufacturing
Radiators and cores, manufacturing
Wheels (i.e., rims), automotive, truck, and bus, manufacturing

Cross-References. Establishments primarily engaged in—

- Manufacturing motor vehicle gasoline engines and engine parts —are classified in Industry 33631, Motor Vehicle Gasoline Engine and Engine Parts Manufacturing;

- Manufacturing motor vehicle electrical and electronic equipment—are classified in Industry 33632, Motor Vehicle Electrical and Electronic Equipment Manufacturing;

- Manufacturing motor vehicle steering and suspension components—are classified in Industry 336330, Motor Vehicle Steering and Suspension Components (except Spring) Manufacturing;

- Manufacturing motor vehicle brake systems—are classified in Industry 336340, Motor Vehicle Brake System Manufacturing;

- Manufacturing motor vehicle transmission and power train parts—are classified in Industry 336350, Motor Vehicle Transmission and Power Train Parts Manufacturing;

US—United States industry only. CAN—United States and Canadian industries are comparable. When neither US nor CAN appears, Canadian, Mexican, and United States industries are comparable.

http://www.ntis.gov/naics

- Manufacturing motor vehicle seating and interior trim—are classified in Industry 336360, Motor Vehicle Seating and Interior Trim Manufacturing;

- Manufacturing motor vehicle stampings—are classified in Industry 336370, Motor Vehicle Metal Stamping; and

- Manufacturing motor vehicle air-conditioning systems and compressors—are classified in U.S. Industry 336391, Motor Vehicle Air-Conditioning Manufacturing.

3364 Aerospace Product and Parts Manufacturing

33641 Aerospace Product and Parts Manufacturing

This industry comprises establishments primarily engaged in one or more of the following: (1) manufacturing complete aircraft, missiles, or space vehicles; (2) manufacturing aerospace engines, propulsion units, auxiliary equipment or parts; (3) developing and making prototypes of aerospace products; (4) aircraft conversion (i.e., major modifications to systems); and (5) complete aircraft or propulsion systems overhaul and rebuilding (i.e., periodic restoration of aircraft to original design specifications).

Cross-References.
- Establishments primarily engaged in manufacturing space satellites are classified in Industry 33422, Radio and Television Broadcasting and Wireless Communications Equipment Manufacturing;

- Establishments primarily engaged in the repair of aircraft or aircraft engines (except overhauling, conversion, and rebuilding) are classified in Industry 48819, Other Support Activities for Air Transportation;

- Research and development establishments primarily engaged in aerospace R&D (except prototype production) are classified in Industry 54171, Research and Development in the Physical, Engineering, and Life Sciences;

- Establishments primarily engaged in manufacturing aircraft engine intake and exhaust valves, pistons, or engine filters are classified in Industry 33631, Motor Vehicle Gasoline Engine and Engine Parts Manufacturing;

- Establishments primarily engaged in manufacturing of aircraft seating are classified in Industry 33636, Motor Vehicle Seating and Interior Trim Manufacturing;

- Establishments primarily engaged in manufacturing aeronautical, navigational, and guidance systems and instruments are classified in Industry 33451, Navigational, Measuring, Electromedical, and Control Instruments Manufacturing;

- Establishment primarily engaged in manufacturing aircraft engine electrical (aeronautical electrical) equipment or aircraft lighting fixtures are classified in Industry 33632, Motor Vehicle Electrical and Electronic Equipment Manufacturing; and

- Establishments primarily engaged in manufacturing of aircraft fluid power subassemblies are classified in Industry 33291, Metal Valve Manufacturing.

US—United States industry only. CAN—United States and Canadian industries are comparable. When neither US nor CAN appears, Canadian, Mexican, and United States industries are comparable.

336411 Aircraft Manufacturing[US]

This U.S. industry comprises establishments primarily engaged in one or more of the following: (1) manufacturing or assembling complete aircraft; (2) developing and making aircraft prototypes; (3) aircraft conversion (i.e., major modifications to systems); and (4) complete aircraft overhaul and rebuilding (i.e., periodic restoration of aircraft to original design specifications).

Cross-References.

- Establishments primarily engaged in manufacturing guided missiles and space vehicles are classified in U.S. Industry 336414, Guided Missile and Space Vehicle Manufacturing;

- Establishments primarily engaged in the repair of aircraft (except overhauling, conversion, and rebuilding) are classified in Industry 488190, Other Support Activities for Air Transportation; and

- Research and development establishments primarily engaged in aircraft R&D (except prototype production) are classified in Industry 541710, Research and Development in the Physical, Engineering, and Life Sciences.

336412 Aircraft Engine and Engine Parts Manufacturing[US]

This U.S. industry comprises establishments primarily engaged in one or more of the following: (1) manufacturing aircraft engines and engine parts; (2) developing and making prototypes of aircraft engines and engine parts; (3) aircraft propulsion system conversion (i.e., major modifications to systems); and (4) aircraft propulsion systems overhaul and rebuilding (i.e., periodic restoration of aircraft propulsion system to original design specifications).

Cross-References.

- Establishments primarily engaged in manufacturing guided missile and space vehicle propulsion units and parts are classified in U.S. Industry 336415, Guided Missile and Space Vehicle Propulsion Unit and Propulsion Unit Parts Manufacturing;

- Establishments primarily engaged in manufacturing aircraft intake and exhaust valves and pistons are classified in U.S. Industry 336311, Carburetor, Piston, Piston Ring, and Valve Manufacturing;

- Establishments primarily engaged in manufacturing aircraft internal combustion engine filters are classified in U.S. Industry 336312, Gasoline Engine and Engine Parts Manufacturing;

- Establishments primarily engaged in the repair of aircraft engines (except overhauling, conversion, and rebuilding) are classified in Industry 488190, Other Support Activities for Air Transportation;

- Research and development establishments primarily engaged in aircraft engine and engine parts R&D (except prototype production) are classified in Industry 541710, Research and Development in the Physical, Engineering, and Life Sciences; and

---

US—United States industry only. CAN—United States and Canadian industries are comparable. When neither US nor CAN appears, Canadian, Mexican, and United States industries are comparable.

- Establishments primarily engaged in manufacturing aeronautical instruments are classified in U.S. Industry 334511, Search, Detection, Navigation, Guidance, Aeronautical, and Nautical System and Instrument Manufacturing.

336413 Other Aircraft Parts and Auxiliary Equipment Manufacturing[US]

This U.S. industry comprises establishment primarily engaged in (1) manufacturing aircraft parts or auxiliary equipment (except engines and aircraft fluid power subassemblies) and/or (2) developing and making prototypes of aircraft parts and auxiliary equipment. Auxiliary equipment includes such items as crop dusting apparatus, armament racks, inflight refueling equipment, and external fuel tanks.

Cross-References.

- Establishments primarily engaged in manufacturing aircraft engines and engine parts are classified in U.S. Industry 336412, Aircraft Engine and Engine Parts Manufacturing;

- Establishments primarily engaged in manufacturing aeronautical instruments are classified in U.S. Industry 334511, Search, Detection, Navigation, Guidance, Aeronautical, and Nautical System and Instrument Manufacturing;

- Establishments primarily engaged in manufacturing aircraft lighting fixtures are classified in U.S. Industry 336321, Vehicular Lighting Equipment Manufacturing;

- Establishments primarily engaged in manufacturing aircraft engine electrical (aeronautical electrical) equipment are classified in U.S. Industry 336322, Other Motor Vehicle Electrical and Electronic Equipment Manufacturing;

- Establishments primarily engaged in manufacturing guided missile and space vehicle parts and auxiliary equipment are classified in U.S. Industry 336419, Other Guided Missile and Space Vehicle Parts and Auxiliary Equipment Manufacturing;

- Establishments primarily engaged in manufacturing of aircraft fluid power subassemblies are classified in U.S. Industry 332912, Fluid Power Valve and Hose Fitting Manufacturing;

- Establishments primarily engaged in manufacturing of aircraft seating are classified in Industry 336360, Motor Vehicle Seating and Interior Trim Manufacturing; and

- Research and development establishments primarily engaged in aircraft parts and auxiliary equipment R&D (except prototype production) are classified in Industry 541710, Research and Development in the Physical, Engineering, and Life Sciences.

336414 Guided Missile and Space Vehicle Manufacturing[US]

This U.S. industry comprises establishments primarily engaged in (1) manufacturing complete guided missiles and space vehicles and/or (2) developing and making prototypes of guided missile or space vehicles.

US—United States industry only. CAN—United States and Canadian industries are comparable. When neither US nor CAN appears, Canadian, Mexican, and United States industries are comparable.

Cross-References.

- Establishments primarily engaged in manufacturing space satellites are classified in Industry 334220, Radio and Television Broadcasting and Wireless Communications Equipment Manufacturing; and

- Research and development establishments primarily engaged in guided missile and space vehicle R&D (except prototype production) are classified in Industry 541710, Research and Development in the Physical, Engineering, and Life Sciences.

336415 Guided Missile and Space Vehicle Propulsion Unit and Propulsion Unit Parts Manufacturing[US]

This U.S. industry comprises establishments primarily engaged in (1) manufacturing guided missile and/or space vehicle propulsion units and propulsion unit parts and/or (2) developing and making prototypes of guided missile and space vehicle propulsion units and propulsion unit parts.

Cross-References.

Research and development establishments primarily engaged in guided missile and space propulsion unit and propulsion unit parts R&D (except prototype production) are classified in Industry 541710, Research and Development in the Physical, Engineering, and Life Sciences.

336419 Other Guided Missile and Space Vehicle Parts and Auxiliary Equipment Manufacturing[US]

This U.S. Industry comprises establishments primarily engaged in (1) manufacturing guided missile and space vehicle parts and auxiliary equipment (except guided missile and space vehicle propulsion units and propulsion unit parts) and/or (2) developing and making prototypes of guided missile and space vehicle parts and auxiliary equipment.

Cross-References.

- Establishments primarily engaged in manufacturing navigational and guidance systems are classified in U.S. Industry 334511, Search, Detection, Navigation, Guidance, Aeronautical, and Nautical System and Instrument Manufacturing;

- Establishments primarily engaged in manufacturing guided missile and space vehicle propulsion units and propulsion unit parts are classified in U.S. Industry 336415, Guided Missile and Space Vehicle Propulsion Unit and Propulsion Unit Parts Manufacturing; and

- Research and development establishments primarily engaged in guided missile and space vehicle parts and auxiliary equipment R&D (except prototype production) are classified in

---

US—United States industry only. CAN—United States and Canadian industries are comparable. When neither US nor CAN appears, Canadian, Mexican, and United States industries are comparable.

http://www.ntis.gov/naics

Industry 541710, Research and Development in the Physical, Engineering, and Life Sciences.

3365 Railroad Rolling Stock Manufacturing

33651 Railroad Rolling Stock Manufacturing
See industry description for 336510 below.

336510 Railroad Rolling Stock Manufacturing

This industry comprises establishments primarily engaged in one or more of the following: (1) manufacturing and/or rebuilding locomotives, locomotive frames and parts; (2) manufacturing railroad, street, and rapid transit cars and car equipment for operation on rails for freight and passenger service; and (3) manufacturing rail layers, ballast distributors, rail tamping equipment and other railway track maintenance equipment.

Cross-References.

- Establishments primarily engaged in manufacturing mining rail cars are classified in U.S. Industry 333131, Mining Machinery and Equipment Manufacturing;

- Establishments primarily engaged in manufacturing locomotive fuel lubricating or cooling medium pumps are classified in U.S. Industry 333911, Pump and Pumping Equipment Manufacturing;

- Repair establishments of railroad and local transit companies primarily engaged in repairing railroad and transit cars are classified in Industry 488210, Support Activities for Rail Transportation; and

- Establishments not owned by railroad or local transit companies primarily engaged in repairing railroad cars and locomotive engines are classified in Industry 811310, Commercial and Industrial Machinery and Equipment (except Automotive and Electronic) Repair and Maintenance.

3366 Ship and Boat Building

33661 Ship and Boat Building

This industry comprises establishments primarily engaged in operating shipyards or boat yards (i.e., ship or boat manufacturing facilities). Shipyards are fixed facilities with drydocks and fabrication equipment capable of building a ship, defined as watercraft typically suitable or intended for other than personal or recreational use. Boats are defined as watercraft typically suitable or intended for personal use. Activities of shipyards include the construction of ships, their repair, conversion and alteration, the production of prefabricated ship and barge sections, and specialized services, such as ship scaling.

US—United States industry only. CAN—United States and Canadian industries are comparable. When neither US nor CAN appears, Canadian, Mexican, and United States industries are comparable.

Illustrative Examples:

Barge building

Boat yards (i.e., boat manufacturing facilities)

Cargo ship building

Drilling and production platforms, floating, oil and gas, building

Passenger ship building

Rowboats manufacturing

Cross-References. Establishments primarily engaged in—

- Manufacturing rubber boats—are classified in Industry 32629, Other Rubber Product Manufacturing;

- Manufacturing nonrigid (i.e., inflatable) plastics boats—are classified in Industry 32619, Other Plastics Product Manufacturing;

- Fabricating structural assemblies or components for ships, or subcontractors engaged in ship painting, joinery, carpentry work, and electrical wiring installation,—are classified based on the production process used; and

- Ship repairs performed in floating drydocks—are classified in Industry 48839, Other Support Activities for Water Transportation.

336611 Ship Building and Repairing[CAN]

This U.S. industry comprises establishments primarily engaged in operating a shipyard. Shipyards are fixed facilities with drydocks and fabrication equipment capable of building a ship, defined as watercraft typically suitable or intended for other than personal or recreational use. Activities of shipyards include the construction of ships, their repair, conversion and alteration, the production of prefabricated ship and barge sections, and specialized services, such as ship scaling.

Illustrative Examples:

Barge building

Cargo ship building

Drilling and production platforms, floating, oil and gas, building

Passenger ship building

Submarine building

Cross-References. Establishments primarily engaged in—

- Fabricating structural assemblies or components for ships, or subcontractors engaged in ship painting, joinery, carpentry work, and electrical wiring installation—are classified based on the production process used; and

- Ship repairs performed in floating drydocks—are classified in Industry 488390, Other Support Activities for Water Transportation.

US—United States industry only. CAN—United States and Canadian industries are comparable. When neither US nor CAN appears, Canadian, Mexican, and United States industries are comparable.

336612 Boat Building[CAN]

This U.S. industry comprises establishments primarily engaged in building boats. Boats are defined as watercraft not built in shipyards and typically of the type suitable or intended for personal use.

Illustrative Examples:

Dinghy (except inflatable rubber) manufacturing	Rowboats manufacturing
Motorboats, inboard or outboard, building	Sailboat building, not done in shipyards
	Yacht building, not done in shipyards

Cross-References. Establishments primarily engaged in—

- Ship building or ship repairs performed in a shipyard—are classified in U.S. Industry 336611, Ship Building and Repairing;

- Manufacturing rubber boats and life rafts—are classified in U.S. Industry 326299, All Other Rubber Product Manufacturing; and

- Manufacturing nonrigid (i.e., inflatable) plastics boats—are classified in U.S. Industry 326199, All Other Plastics Product Manufacturing.

3369 Other Transportation Equipment Manufacturing

This industry group comprises establishments primarily engaged in manufacturing transportation equipment (except motor vehicles and parts, aerospace products and parts, railroad rolling stock, ship building, and boat manufacturing).

33699 Other Transportation Equipment Manufacturing

This industry comprises establishments primarily engaged in manufacturing motorcycles, bicycles, metal tricycles, complete military armored vehicles, tanks, self-propelled weapons, vehicles pulled by draft animals, and other transportation equipment (except motor vehicles, boats, ships, railroad rolling stock, and aerospace products), including parts thereof.

Cross-References. Establishments primarily engaged in—

- Manufacturing ships and boats—are classified in Industry 33661, Ship and Boat Building;

- Manufacturing aerospace products and parts—are classified in Industry 33641, Aerospace Product and Parts Manufacturing;

- Manufacturing motor vehicle parts—are classified in Industry Group 3363, Motor Vehicle Parts Manufacturing;

- Manufacturing children's vehicles (except bicycles and metal tricycles)—are classified in Industry 33993, Doll, Toy, and Game Manufacturing; and

---

US—United States industry only. CAN—United States and Canadian industries are comparable. When neither US nor CAN appears, Canadian, Mexican, and United States industries are comparable.

http://www.ntis.gov/naics

- Manufacturing railroad rolling stock—are classified in Industry 33651, Railroad Rolling Stock Manufacturing; and

- Manufacturing motor vehicles—are classified in Industry Group 3361, Motor Vehicle Manufacturing.

336991 Motorcycle, Bicycle, and Parts Manufacturing[US]

This U.S. industry comprises establishments primarily engaged in manufacturing motorcycles, bicycles, tricycles and similar equipment, and parts.

Cross-References. Establishments primarily engaged in—

- Manufacturing children's vehicles (except bicycles and metal tricycles)—are classified in U.S. Industry 339932, Game, Toy, and Children's Vehicle Manufacturing; and

- Manufacturing golf carts and other similar personnel carriers—are classified in U.S. Industry 336999, All Other Transportation Equipment Manufacturing.

336992 Military Armored Vehicle, Tank, and Tank Component Manufacturing[US]

This U.S. industry comprises establishments primarily engaged in manufacturing complete military armored vehicles, combat tanks, specialized components for combat tanks, and self-propelled weapons.

Cross-References.

Establishments primarily engaged in manufacturing nonarmored military universal carriers are classified in U.S. Industry 336112, Light Truck and Utility Vehicle Manufacturing.

336999 All Other Transportation Equipment Manufacturing[US]

This U.S. industry comprises establishments primarily engaged in manufacturing transportation equipment (except motor vehicles, motor vehicle parts, boats, ships, railroad rolling stock, aerospace products, motorcycles, bicycles, armored vehicles and tanks).

Illustrative Examples:

All-terrain vehicles (ATVs), wheeled or tracked, manufacturing
Animal-drawn vehicles and parts manufacturing
Gocarts (except children's) manufacturing

Golf carts and similar motorized passenger carriers manufacturing
Race cars manufacturing
Snowmobiles and parts manufacturing

Cross-References. Establishments primarily engaged in—

- Manufacturing motorcycles, bicycles and parts—are classified in U.S. Industry 336991, Motorcycle, Bicycle, and Parts Manufacturing;

US—United States industry only. CAN—United States and Canadian industries are comparable. When neither US nor CAN appears, Canadian, Mexican, and United States industries are comparable.

- Manufacturing military armored vehicles, tanks, and tank components—are classified in U.S. Industry 336992, Military Armored Vehicle, Tank, and Tank Component Manufacturing;

- Manufacturing ships and boats—are classified in Industry 33661, Ship and Boat Building;

- Manufacturing aerospace products and parts—are classified in Industry 33641, Aerospace Product and Parts Manufacturing;

- Manufacturing motor vehicle parts—are classified in Industry Group 3363, Motor Vehicle Parts Manufacturing;

- Manufacturing railroad rolling stock—are classified in Industry 336510, Railroad Rolling Stock Manufacturing; and

- Manufacturing motor vehicles—are classified in Industry Group 3361, Motor Vehicle Manufacturing.

337 Furniture and Related Product Manufacturing

Industries in the Furniture and Related Product Manufacturing subsector make furniture and related articles, such as mattresses, window blinds, cabinets, and fixtures. The processes used in the manufacture of furniture include the cutting, bending, molding, laminating, and assembly of such materials as wood, metal, glass, plastics, and rattan. However, the production process for furniture is not solely bending metal, cutting and shaping wood, or extruding and molding plastics. Design and fashion trends play an important part in the production of furniture. The integrated design of the article for both esthetic and functional qualities is also a major part of the process of manufacturing furniture. Design services may be performed by the furniture establishment's work force or may be purchased from industrial designers.

Furniture may be made of any material, but the most common ones used in North America are metal and wood. Furniture manufacturing establishments may specialize in making articles primarily from one material. Some of the equipment required to make a wooden table, for example, is different from that used to make a metal one. However, furniture is usually made from several materials. A wooden table might have metal brackets, and a wooden chair a fabric or plastics seat. Therefore, in NAICS, furniture initially is classified based on the type of furniture (application for which it is designed) rather than the material used. For example, an upholstered sofa is treated as household furniture, although it may also be used in hotels or offices.

When classifying furniture according to the component material from which it is made, furniture made from more than one material is classified based on the material used in the frame, or if there is no frame, the predominant component material. Upholstered household furniture (excluding kitchen and dining room chairs with upholstered seats) is classified without regard to the frame material. Kitchen or dining room chairs with upholstered seats are classified according to the frame material.

Furniture may be made on a stock or custom basis and may be shipped assembled or unassembled (i.e., knockdown). The manufacture of furniture parts and frames is included in this subsector.

Some of the processes used in furniture manufacturing are similar to processes that are used in other segments of manufacturing. For example, cutting and assembly occurs in the production of wood trusses that are classified in Subsector 321, Wood Product Manufacturing. However, the

---

US—United States industry only. CAN—United States and Canadian industries are comparable. When neither US nor CAN appears, Canadian, Mexican, and United States industries are comparable.

multiple processes that distinguish wood furniture manufacturing from wood product manufacturing warrant inclusion of wooden furniture manufacturing in the Furniture and Related Product Manufacturing subsector. Metal furniture manufacturing uses techniques that are also employed in the manufacturing of roll-formed products classified in Subsector 332, Fabricated Metal Product Manufacturing. The molding process for plastics furniture is similar to the molding of other plastics products. However, plastics furniture producing establishments tend to specialize in furniture.

NAICS attempts to keep furniture manufacturing together, but there are two notable exceptions: seating for transportation equipment and laboratory and hospital furniture. These exceptions are related to that fact that some of the aspects of the production process for these products, primarily the design, are highly integrated with that of other manufactured goods, namely motor vehicles and health equipment.

3371 Household and Institutional Furniture and Kitchen Cabinet Manufacturing

This industry group comprises establishments manufacturing household-type furniture, such as living room, kitchen and bedroom furniture and institutional (i.e., public building) furniture, such as furniture for schools, theaters, and churches.

33711 Wood Kitchen Cabinet and Countertop Manufacturing
See industry description for 337110 below.

337110 Wood Kitchen Cabinet and Countertop Manufacturing

This industry comprises establishments primarily engaged in manufacturing wood or plastics laminated on wood kitchen cabinets, bathroom vanities, and countertops (except freestanding). The cabinets and counters may be made on a stock or custom basis.

Cross-References. Establishments primarily engaged in—

- Manufacturing metal kitchen and bathroom cabinets (except freestanding)—are classified in U.S. Industry 337124, Metal Household Furniture Manufacturing;

- Manufacturing plastics countertops—are classified in U.S. Industry 326199, All Other Plastics Product Manufacturing;

- Manufacturing stone countertops—are classified in U.S. Industry 327991, Cut Stone and Stone Product Manufacturing; and

- Manufacturing wood or plastics laminated on wood countertops (except kitchen and bathroom)—are classified in U.S. Industry 337215, Showcase, Partition, Shelving, and Locker Manufacturing.

33712 Household and Institutional Furniture Manufacturing

This industry comprises establishments primarily engaged in manufacturing household-type and public building furniture (i.e., library, school, theater, and church furniture). The furniture may be made on a stock or custom basis and may be assembled or unassembled (i.e., knockdown).

US—United States industry only. CAN—United States and Canadian industries are comparable. When neither US nor CAN appears, Canadian, Mexican, and United States industries are comparable.

Cross-References. Establishments primarily engaged in—

- Manufacturing laboratory and hospital furniture—are classified in Industry 33911, Medical Equipment and Supplies Manufacturing;

- Manufacturing wood or plastics laminated on wood kitchen cabinets, bathroom vanities, and countertops (except freestanding)—are classified in Industry 33711, Wood Kitchen Cabinet and Countertop Manufacturing;

- Manufacturing office-type furniture and/or office or store fixtures—are classified in Industry 33721, Office Furniture (including Fixtures) Manufacturing; and

- Repairing or refinishing furniture—are classified in Industry 81142, Reupholstery and Furniture Repair.

337121 Upholstered Household Furniture Manufacturing^{CAN}

This U.S. industry comprises establishments primarily engaged in manufacturing upholstered household-type furniture. The furniture may be made on a stock or custom basis.

Cross-References. Establishments primarily engaged in—

- Reupholstering furniture or upholstering frames to individual order—are classified in Industry 811420, Reupholstery and Furniture Repair;

- Wood kitchen and dining room chairs with upholstered seats or backs—are classified in U. S. Industry 337122, Nonupholstered Wood Household Furniture Manufacturing;

- Metal kitchen and dining room chairs with upholstered seats or backs—are classified in U.S. Industry 337124, Metal Household Furniture Manufacturing; and

- Kitchen and dining room chairs (except wood and metal) with upholstered seats or backs—are classified in U.S. Industry 337125, Household Furniture (except Wood and Metal) Manufacturing.

337122 Nonupholstered Wood Household Furniture Manufacturing^{US}

This U.S. industry comprises establishments primarily engaged in manufacturing nonupholstered wood household-type furniture and freestanding cabinets (except television, radio, and sewing machine cabinets). The furniture may be made on a stock or custom basis and may be assembled or unassembled (i.e., knockdown).

Cross-References. Establishments primarily engaged in—

- Manufacturing reed, rattan, plastics and similar furniture—are classified in U.S. Industry 337125, Household Furniture (except Wood and Metal) Manufacturing;

- Manufacturing wood or plastics laminated on wood kitchen cabinets, bathroom vanities, and countertops (except freestanding)—are classified in Industry 337110, Wood Kitchen Cabinet and Countertop Manufacturing;

US—United States industry only. CAN—United States and Canadian industries are comparable. When neither US nor CAN appears, Canadian, Mexican, and United States industries are comparable.

- Manufacturing wood television, stereo, loudspeaker, and sewing machine cabinets (i.e., housings)—are classified in U.S. Industry 337129, Wood Television, Radio, and Sewing Machine Cabinet Manufacturing; and

- Repairing or refinishing furniture—are classified in Industry 811420, Reupholstery and Furniture Repair.

337124 Metal Household Furniture Manufacturing[US]

This U.S. industry comprises establishments primarily engaged in manufacturing metal household-type furniture and freestanding cabinets. The furniture may be made on a stock or custom basis and may be assembled or unassembled (i.e., knockdown).

Cross-References.

Establishments primarily engaged in manufacturing metal laboratory and hospital furniture including beds are classified in Industry 33911, Medical Equipment and Supplies Manufacturing.

337125 Household Furniture (except Wood and Metal) Manufacturing[US]

This U.S. industry comprises establishments primarily engaged in manufacturing household-type furniture of materials other than wood or metal, such as plastics, reed, rattan, wicker, and fiberglass. The furniture may be made on a stock or custom basis and may be assembled or unassembled (i.e., knockdown).

Cross-References. Establishments primarily engaged in—

- Manufacturing concrete, ceramic, or stone furniture—are classified in Subsector 327, Nonmetallic Mineral Product Manufacturing, according to the materials used;

- Manufacturing upholstered household-type furniture—are classified in U.S. Industry 337121, Upholstered Household Furniture Manufacturing;

- Manufacturing metal household-type furniture—are classified in U.S. Industry 337124, Metal Household Furniture Manufacturing; and

- Manufacturing nonupholstered wood household-type furniture—are classified in U.S. Industry 337122, Nonupholstered Wood Household Furniture Manufacturing.

337127 Institutional Furniture Manufacturing[CAN]

This U.S. industry comprises establishments primarily engaged in manufacturing institutional-type furniture (e.g., library, school, theater, and church furniture). The furniture may be made on a stock or custom basis and may be assembled or unassembled (i.e., knockdown).

Cross-References. Establishments primarily engaged in—

- Manufacturing laboratory and hospital furniture—are classified in Industry 33911, Medical Equipment and Supplies Manufacturing;

US—United States industry only. CAN—United States and Canadian industries are comparable. When neither US nor CAN appears, Canadian, Mexican, and United States industries are comparable.

http://www.ntis.gov/naics

- Manufacturing wood kitchen cabinets, wood bathroom vanities, and countertops designed for permanent installation—are classified in Industry 337110, Wood Kitchen Cabinet and Countertop Manufacturing;

- Manufacturing office-type furniture and/or office or store fixtures—are classified in Industry 33721, Office Furniture (including Fixtures) Manufacturing; and

- Repairing or refinishing furniture—are classified in Industry 811420, Reupholstery and Furniture Repair.

337129 Wood Television, Radio, and Sewing Machine Cabinet Manufacturing[US]

This industry comprises establishments primarily engaged in manufacturing wood cabinets used as housings by television, stereo, loudspeaker, and sewing machine manufacturers.

Cross-References. Establishments primarily engaged in—

- Manufacturing plastics housings used by television, stereo, loudspeaker, and sewing machine manufacturers—are classified in U.S. Industry 326199, All Other Plastics Product Manufacturing;

- Manufacturing metal housings used by television, stereo, loudspeaker, and sewing machine manufacturers—are classified in U.S. Industry 332322, Sheet Metal Work Manufacturing;

- Manufacturing freestanding wood household-type cabinets (e.g., entertainment centers, stands) for consumer electronics—are classified in U.S. Industry 337122, Nonupholstered Wood Household Furniture Manufacturing;

- Manufacturing freestanding metal household-type cabinets (e.g., entertainment centers, stands) for consumer electronics—are classified in U.S. Industry 337124, Metal Household Furniture Manufacturing; and

- Manufacturing freestanding household-type cabinets (e.g., entertainment centers, stands)(except wood and metal) for consumer electronics—are classified in U.S. Industry 337125, Household Furniture (except Wood and Metal) Manufacturing.

3372 Office Furniture (including Fixtures) Manufacturing

33721 Office Furniture (including Fixtures) Manufacturing

This industry comprises establishments primarily engaged in manufacturing office furniture and/ or office and store fixtures. The furniture may be made on a stock or custom basis and may be assembled or unassembled (i.e., knockdown).

Cross-References. Establishments primarily engaged in—

- Manufacturing millwork on a factory basis—are classified in Industry 32191, Millwork;

- Manufacturing household-type and institutional-type furniture—are classified in Industry 33712, Household and Institutional Furniture Manufacturing;

US—United States industry only. CAN—United States and Canadian industries are comparable. When neither US nor CAN appears, Canadian, Mexican, and United States industries are comparable.

- Manufacturing refrigerated cabinets, showcases, and display cases—are classified in Industry 33341, Ventilation, Heating, Air-Conditioning, and Commercial Refrigeration Equipment Manufacturing; and

- Manufacturing metal safes and vaults—are classified in Industry 33299, All Other Fabricated Metal Product Manufacturing.

337211 Wood Office Furniture Manufacturing^{US}

This U.S. industry comprises establishments primarily engaged in manufacturing wood office-type furniture. The furniture may be made on a stock or custom basis and may be assembled or unassembled (i.e., knockdown).

337212 Custom Architectural Woodwork and Millwork Manufacturing^{US}

This U.S. industry comprises establishments primarily engaged in manufacturing custom designed interiors consisting of architectural woodwork and fixtures utilizing wood, wood products, and plastics laminates. All of the industry output is made to individual order on a job shop basis and requires skilled craftsmen as a labor input. A job might include custom manufacturing of display fixtures, gondolas, wall shelving units, entrance and window architectural detail, sales and reception counters, wall paneling, and matching furniture.

Cross-References. Establishments primarily engaged in—

- Manufacturing millwork on a factory basis—are classified in U.S. Industry 321918, Other Millwork (including Flooring);

- Manufacturing wood office-type furniture on a stock or custom basis—are classified in U.S. Industry 337211, Wood Office Furniture Manufacturing; and

- Manufacturing wood office-type furniture and store fixtures on a stock basis—are classified in U.S. Industry 337215, Showcase, Partition, Shelving, and Locker Manufacturing.

337214 Office Furniture (except Wood) Manufacturing^{CAN}

This U.S. industry comprises establishments primarily engaged in manufacturing nonwood office-type furniture. The furniture may be made on a stock or custom basis and may be assembled or unassembled (i.e., knockdown).

337215 Showcase, Partition, Shelving, and Locker Manufacturing^{CAN}

This U.S. industry comprises establishments primarily engaged in manufacturing wood and nonwood office and store fixtures, shelving, lockers, frames, partitions, and related fabricated products of wood and nonwood materials, including plastics laminated fixture tops. The products are made on a stock basis and may be assembled or unassembled (i.e., knockdown). Establishments exclusively making furniture parts (e.g., frames) are included in this industry.

US—United States industry only. CAN—United States and Canadian industries are comparable. When neither US nor CAN appears, Canadian, Mexican, and United States industries are comparable.

http://www.ntis.gov/naics

Cross-References. Establishments primarily engaged in—

- Manufacturing refrigerated cabinets, showcases, and display cases—are classified in U.S. Industry 333415, Air-Conditioning and Warm Air Heating Equipment and Commercial and Industrial Refrigeration Equipment Manufacturing;

- Manufacturing metal safes and vaults—are classified in U.S. Industry 332999, All Other Miscellaneous Fabricated Metal Product Manufacturing; and

- Manufacturing wood or plastics laminated kitchen and bathroom countertops—are classified in Industry 337110, Wood Kitchen Cabinet and Countertop Manufacturing.

3379 Other Furniture Related Product Manufacturing

This industry group comprises establishments manufacturing furniture related products, such as mattresses, blinds, and shades.

33791 Mattress Manufacturing
See industry description for 337910 below.

337910 Mattress Manufacturing

This industry comprises establishments primarily engaged in manufacturing innerspring, box spring, and noninnerspring mattresses, including mattresses for waterbeds.

Cross-References. Establishments primarily engaged in—

- Manufacturing individual wire springs—are classified in Industry 33261, Spring and Wire Product Manufacturing; and

- Manufacturing inflatable mattresses—are classified in Subsector 326, Plastics and Rubber Products Manufacturing.

33792 Blind and Shade Manufacturing
See industry description for 337920 below.

337920 Blind and Shade Manufacturing

This industry comprises establishments primarily engaged in manufacturing one or more of the following: venetian blinds, other window blinds, shades; curtain and drapery rods, poles; and/or curtain and drapery fixtures. The blinds, and shades may be made on a stock or custom basis and may be made of any material.

Cross-References. Establishments primarily engaged in—

- Manufacturing canvas awnings—are classified in U.S. Industry 314912, Canvas and Related Product Mills; and

---

US—United States industry only. CAN—United States and Canadian industries are comparable. When neither US nor CAN appears, Canadian, Mexican, and United States industries are comparable.

- Manufacturing curtains and draperies—are classified in U.S. Industry 314121, Curtain and Drapery Mills.

339 Miscellaneous Manufacturing

Industries in the Miscellaneous Manufacturing subsector make a wide range of products that cannot readily be classified in specific NAICS subsectors in manufacturing. Processes used by these establishments vary significantly, both among and within industries. For example, a variety of manufacturing processes are used in manufacturing sporting and athletic goods that include products, such as tennis racquets and golf balls. The processes for these products differ from each other, and the processes differ significantly from the fabrication processes used in making dolls or toys, the melting and shaping of precious metals to make jewelry, and the bending, forming, and assembly used in making medical products.

The industries in this subsector are defined by what is made rather than how it is made. Although individual establishments might be appropriately classified elsewhere in the NAICS structure, for historical continuity, these product-based industries were maintained. In most cases, no one process or material predominates for an industry.

Establishments in this subsector manufacture products as diverse as medical equipment and supplies, jewelry, sporting goods, toys, and office supplies.

3391 Medical Equipment and Supplies Manufacturing

33911 Medical Equipment and Supplies Manufacturing

This industry comprises establishments primarily engaged in manufacturing medical equipment and supplies. Examples of products made by these establishments are laboratory apparatus and furniture, surgical and medical instruments, surgical appliances and supplies, dental equipment and supplies, orthodontic goods, dentures, and orthodontic appliances.

Cross-References. Establishments primarily engaged in—

- Manufacturing laboratory instruments, X-ray apparatus, electromedical apparatus (including electronic hearing aids), and thermometers (except medical)—are classified in Industry 33451, Navigational, Measuring, Electromedical, and Control Instruments Manufacturing;

- Manufacturing molded glass lens blanks—are classified in Industry 32721, Glass and Glass Product Manufacturing;

- Manufacturing molded plastics lens blanks—are classified in Industry 32619, Other Plastics Product Manufacturing;

- Retailing and grinding prescription eyeglasses—are classified in Industry 44613, Optical Goods Stores; and

- Manufacturing sporting goods helmets and protective equipment—are classified in Industry, 33992 Sporting and Athletic Goods Manufacturing.

US—United States industry only. CAN—United States and Canadian industries are comparable. When neither US nor CAN appears, Canadian, Mexican, and United States industries are comparable.

339111 Laboratory Apparatus and Furniture Manufacturing[US]

This U.S. industry comprises establishments primarily engaged in manufacturing laboratory apparatus and laboratory and hospital furniture (except dental). Examples of products made by these establishments are hospital beds, operating room tables, laboratory balances and scales, furnaces, ovens, centrifuges, cabinets, cases, benches, tables, and stools.

Cross-References. Establishments primarily engaged in—

- Manufacturing dental laboratory apparatus and furniture—are classified in U.S. Industry 339114, Dental Equipment and Supplies Manufacturing; and

- Manufacturing laboratory instruments—are classified in U.S. Industry 334516, Analytical Laboratory Instrument Manufacturing.

339112 Surgical and Medical Instrument Manufacturing[US]

This U.S. industry comprises establishments primarily engaged in manufacturing medical, surgical, ophthalmic, and veterinary instruments and apparatus (except electrotherapeutic, electromedical and irradiation apparatus). Examples of products made by these establishments are syringes, hypodermic needles, anesthesia apparatus, blood transfusion equipment, catheters, surgical clamps, and medical thermometers.

Cross-References. Establishments primarily engaged in—

- Manufacturing electromedical and electrotherapeutic apparatus—are classified in U.S. Industry 334510, Electromedical and Electrotherapeutic Apparatus Manufacturing;

- Manufacturing irradiation apparatus—are classified in U.S. Industry 334517, Irradiation Apparatus Manufacturing;

- Manufacturing surgical and orthopedic appliances—are classified in U.S. Industry 339113 Surgical Appliance and Supplies Manufacturing;

- Manufacturing dental equipment, dental supplies, dental laboratory apparatus, and dental laboratory furniture—are classified in U.S. Industry 339114, Dental Equipment and Supplies Manufacturing;

- Manufacturing laboratory apparatus and laboratory and hospital furniture (except dental)—are classified in U.S. Industry 339111, Laboratory Apparatus and Furniture Manufacturing; and

- Manufacturing thermometers (except medical)—are classified in U.S. Industry 334519, Other Measuring and Controlling Device Manufacturing.

339113 Surgical Appliance and Supplies Manufacturing[US]

This U.S. industry comprises establishments primarily engaged in manufacturing surgical appliances and supplies. Examples of products made by these establishments are orthopedic devices,

---

US—United States industry only. CAN—United States and Canadian industries are comparable. When neither US nor CAN appears, Canadian, Mexican, and United States industries are comparable.

prosthetic appliances, surgical dressings, crutches, surgical sutures, and personal industrial safety devices (except protective eyeware).

Cross-References. Establishments primarily engaged in—

- Manufacturing dental equipment, dental supplies, dental laboratory apparatus, and dental laboratory furniture—are classified in U.S. Industry 339114, Dental Equipment and Supplies Manufacturing;

- Manufacturing laboratory apparatus and laboratory and hospital furniture (except dental)—are classified in U.S. Industry 339111, Laboratory Apparatus and Furniture Manufacturing;

- Manufacturing electronic hearing aids—are classified in U.S. Industry 334510, Electromedical and Electrotherapeutic Apparatus Manufacturing;

- Manufacturing industrial protective eyeware—are classified in U.S. Industry 339115, Ophthalmic Goods Manufacturing; and

- Manufacturing sporting goods helmets and protective equipment—are classified in Industry 339920, Sporting and Athletic Goods Manufacturing.

339114 Dental Equipment and Supplies Manufacturing[US]

This U.S. industry comprises establishments primarily engaged in manufacturing dental equipment and supplies used by dental laboratories and offices of dentists, such as dental chairs, dental instrument delivery systems, dental hand instruments, and dental impression material.

Cross-References. Establishments primarily engaged in—

- Manufacturing dentures, crowns, bridges, and orthodontic appliances customized for individual application—are classified in U.S. Industry 339116, Dental Laboratories; and

- Manufacturing laboratory apparatus and laboratory and hospital furniture (except dental)—are classified in U.S. Industry 339111, Laboratory Apparatus and Furniture Manufacturing.

339115 Ophthalmic Goods Manufacturing[US]

This U.S. industry comprises establishments primarily engaged in manufacturing ophthalmic goods. Examples of products made by these establishments are prescription eyeglasses (except manufactured in a retail setting), contact lenses, sunglasses, eyeglass frames, and reading glasses made to standard powers.

Cross-References. Establishments primarily engaged in—

- Manufacturing molded glass lens blanks—are classified in U.S. Industry 327212, Other Pressed and Blown Glass and Glassware Manufacturing;

- Manufacturing molded plastics lens blanks—are classified in U.S. Industry 326199, All Other Plastics Product Manufacturing; and

---

US—United States industry only. CAN—United States and Canadian industries are comparable. When neither US nor CAN appears, Canadian, Mexican, and United States industries are comparable.

- Retailing and grinding prescription eyeglasses—are classified in Industry 446130, Optical Goods Stores.

339116 Dental Laboratories[US]

This U.S. industry comprises establishments primarily engaged in manufacturing dentures, crowns, bridges, and orthodontic appliances customized for individual application.

Cross-References.

Establishments primarily engaged in manufacturing dental equipment and supplies are classified in U.S. Industry 339114, Dental Equipment and Supplies Manufacturing.

3399 Other Miscellaneous Manufacturing

33991 Jewelry and Silverware Manufacturing

This industry comprises establishments primarily engaged in one or more of the following: (1) manufacturing, engraving, chasing, or etching jewelry; (2) manufacturing metal personal goods (i.e., small articles carried on or about the person, such as compacts or cigarette cases); (3) manufacturing, engraving, chasing, or etching precious metal solid, precious metal clad, or pewter cutlery and flatware; (4) manufacturing, engraving, chasing, or etching personal metal goods (i.e., small articles carried on or about the person, such as compacts or cigarette cases); (5) stamping coins; (6) manufacturing unassembled jewelry parts and stock shop products, such as sheet, wire, and tubing; (7) cutting, slabbing, tumbling, carving, engraving, polishing, or faceting precious or semiprecious stones and gems; (8) recutting, repolishing, and setting gem stones; and (9) drilling, sawing, and peeling cultured and costume pearls.

Cross-References. Establishments primarily engaged in—

- Manufacturing nonprecious and precious plated metal cutlery and flatware—are classified in Industry 33221, Cutlery and Handtool Manufacturing;

- Manufacturing nonprecious plated ware (except cutlery, flatware)—are classified in Industry 33299, All Other Fabricated Metal Product Manufacturing;

- Engraving, chasing, or etching nonprecious and precious plated metal flatware and other plated ware and plated jewelry—are classified in Industry 33281, Coating, Engraving, Heat Treating, and Allied Activities;

- Manufacturing synthetic stones or gem stones—are classified in Industry 32799, All Other Nonmetallic Mineral Product Manufacturing; and

- Manufacturing personal goods (except metal) carried on or about the person, such as compacts and cigarette cases,—are classified in Industry 31699, Other Leather and Allied Product Manufacturing.

US—United States industry only. CAN—United States and Canadian industries are comparable. When neither US nor CAN appears, Canadian, Mexican, and United States industries are comparable.

339911 Jewelry (except Costume) Manufacturing[US]

This U.S. industry comprises establishments primarily engaged in one or more of the following: (1) manufacturing, engraving, chasing, or etching precious metal solid or precious metal clad jewelry; (2) manufacturing, engraving, chasing, or etching personal goods (i.e., small articles carried on or about the person, such as compacts or cigarette cases) made of precious solid or clad metal; and (3) stamping coins.

Cross-References. Establishments primarily engaged in—

- Manufacturing, engraving, chasing, or etching costume jewelry and nonprecious metal personal goods—are classified in U.S. Industry 339914, Costume Jewelry and Novelty Manufacturing;

- Manufacturing jewelers' materials or performing lapidary work—are classified in U.S. Industry 339913, Jewelers' Material and Lapidary Work Manufacturing; and

- Plating jewelry—are classified in U.S. Industry 332813, Electroplating, Plating, Polishing, Anodizing and Coloring.

339912 Silverware and Hollowware Manufacturing[US]

This U.S. industry comprises establishments primarily engaged in manufacturing, engraving, chasing, or etching precious metal solid, precious metal clad, or pewter flatware and other plated ware.

Cross-References. Establishments primarily engaged in—

- Manufacturing nonprecious and precious plated metal cutlery and flatware—are classified in U.S. Industry 332211, Cutlery and Flatware (except Precious) Manufacturing;

- Manufacturing nonprecious metal plated ware (except cutlery and flatware)—are classified in U.S. Industry 332999, All Other Miscellaneous Fabricated Metal Product Manufacturing;

- Engraving, chasing, or etching nonprecious and precious plated metal cutlery, flatware and other plated ware—are classified in U.S. Industry 332812, Metal Coating, Engraving (except Jewelry and Silverware), and Allied Services to Manufactures; and

- Manufacturing, engraving, chasing, or etching precious (except precious plated) metal jewelry and personal goods—are classified in U.S. Industry 339911, Jewelry (excluding Costume) Manufacturing.

339913 Jewelers' Material and Lapidary Work Manufacturing[US]

This U.S. industry comprises establishments primarily engaged in one or more of the following: (1) manufacturing unassembled jewelry parts and stock shop products, such as sheet, wire, and tubing; (2) cutting, slabbing, tumbling, carving, engraving, polishing or faceting precious or semiprecious stones and gems; (3) recutting, repolishing, and setting gem stones; and (4) drilling, sawing, and peeling cultured pearls.

US—United States industry only. CAN—United States and Canadian industries are comparable. When neither US nor CAN appears, Canadian, Mexican, and United States industries are comparable.

http://www.ntis.gov/naics

Cross-References. Establishments primarily engaged in—

- Manufacturing synthetic stones—are classified in Industry U.S. 327999, All Other Miscellaneous Nonmetallic Mineral Product Manufacturing; and

- Manufacturing costume pearls—are classified in U.S. Industry 339914, Costume Jewelry and Novelty Manufacturing.

339914 Costume Jewelry and Novelty Manufacturing[US]

This U.S. industry comprises establishments primarily engaged in (1) manufacturing, engraving, chasing, and etching costume jewelry; and/or (2) manufacturing, engraving, chasing, or etching nonprecious metal personal goods (i.e., small articles carried on or about the person, such as compacts or cigarette cases). This industry includes establishments primarily engaged in manufacturing precious plated jewelry and precious plated personal goods.

Cross-References. Establishments primarily engaged in—

- Manufacturing, engraving, chasing, or etching precious (except precious plated) metal jewelry and novelties—are classified in U.S. Industry 339911, Jewelry (excluding Costume) Manufacturing;

- Manufacturing personal goods (except metal) carried on or about the person, such as compacts and cigarette cases,—are classified in U.S. Industry 316993, Personal Leather Goods (except Women's Handbag and Purse) Manufacturing; and

- Manufacturing synthetic stones—are classified in U.S. Industry 327999, All Other Miscellaneous Nonmetallic Mineral Product Manufacturing.

33992 Sporting and Athletic Goods Manufacturing
See industry description for 339920 below.

339920 Sporting and Athletic Goods Manufacturing

This industry comprises establishments primarily engaged in manufacturing sporting and athletic goods (except apparel and footwear).

Cross-References. Establishments primarily engaged in—

- Manufacturing athletic apparel—are classified in Subsector 315, Apparel Manufacturing;

- Manufacturing athletic footwear—are classified in U.S. Industry 316219, Other Footwear Manufacturing; and

- Manufacturing small arms and small arms ammunition—are classified in Industry 33299, All Other Fabricated Metal Product Manufacturing.

US—United States industry only. CAN—United States and Canadian industries are comparable. When neither US nor CAN appears, Canadian, Mexican, and United States industries are comparable.

33993 Doll, Toy, and Game Manufacturing

This industry comprises establishments primarily engaged in manufacturing dolls, toys, and games, such as complete dolls, doll parts, doll clothes, action figures, toys, games (including electronic), hobby kits, and children's vehicles (except metal bicycles and tricycles).

Cross-References. Establishments primarily engaged in—

- Manufacturing bicycles and metal tricycles—are classified in Industry 33699, Other Transportation Equipment Manufacturing;

- Manufacturing sporting and athletic goods—are classified in Industry 33992, Sporting and Athletic Goods Manufacturing;

- Manufacturing coin-operated game machines—are classified in Industry 33999, All Other Miscellaneous Manufacturing; and

- Manufacturing electronic video game cartridges and reproducing video game software—are classified in Industry 33461, Manufacturing and Reproducing Magnetic and Optical Media.

339931 Doll and Stuffed Toy Manufacturing[US]

This U.S. industry comprises establishments primarily engaged in manufacturing complete dolls, doll parts, and doll clothes, action figures, and stuffed toys.

Cross-References.

Establishments primarily engaged in manufacturing toys (except stuffed) are classified in U.S. Industry 339932, Game, Toy, and Children's Vehicle Manufacturing.

339932 Game, Toy, and Children's Vehicle Manufacturing[US]

This U.S. industry comprises establishments primarily engaged in manufacturing games (including electronic), toys, and children's vehicles (except bicycles and metal tricycles).

Cross-References. Establishments primarily engaged in—

- Manufacturing dolls and stuffed toys—are classified in U.S. Industry 339931, Doll and Stuffed Toy Manufacturing;

- Manufacturing metal tricycles and bicycles—are classified in U.S. Industry 336991, Motorcycle, Bicycle, and Parts Manufacturing;

- Manufacturing sporting and athletic goods—are classified in Industry 339920, Sporting and Athletic Goods Manufacturing;

- Manufacturing coin-operated game machines—are classified in U.S. Industry 339999, All Other Miscellaneous Manufacturing; and

US—United States industry only. CAN—United States and Canadian industries are comparable. When neither US nor CAN appears, Canadian, Mexican, and United States industries are comparable.

- Mass reproducing electronic video game cartridges—are classified in U.S. Industry 334611, Software Reproducing.

33994 Office Supplies (except Paper) Manufacturing

This industry comprises establishments primarily engaged in manufacturing office supplies. Examples of products made by these establishments are pens, pencils, felt tip markers, crayons, chalk, pencil sharpeners, staplers, hand operated stamps, modeling clay, and inked ribbons.

Cross-References. Establishments primarily engaged in—

- Manufacturing writing, drawing, and india inks—are classified in Industry 32599, All Other Chemical Product and Preparation Manufacturing;

- Manufacturing drafting tables and boards—are classified in Industry 33712, Household and Institutional Furniture Manufacturing;

- Manufacturing rubber erasers—are classified in Industry 32629, Other Rubber Product Manufacturing;

- Manufacturing paper office supplies—are classified in Subsector 322, Paper Manufacturing;

- Manufacturing manifold business forms, blankbooks, and looseleaf binders—are classified in Industry 32311, Printing; and

- Manufacturing inkjet cartridges—are classified in Industry 32591, Printing Ink Manufacturing.

339941 Pen and Mechanical Pencil Manufacturing[US]

This U.S. industry comprises establishments primarily engaged in manufacturing pens, ballpoint pen refills and cartridges, mechanical pencils, and felt tipped markers.

Cross-References. Establishments primarily engaged in—

- Manufacturing nonmechanical pencils and pencil leads—are classified in U.S. Industry 339942, Lead Pencil and Art Good Manufacturing;

- Manufacturing writing, drawing, and india inks—are classified in U.S. Industry 325998, All Other Miscellaneous Chemical Product and Preparation Manufacturing; and

- Manufacturing rubber erasers—are classified in U.S. Industry 326299, All Other Rubber Product Manufacturing.

339942 Lead Pencil and Art Good Manufacturing[US]

This U.S. industry comprises establishments primarily engaged in manufacturing nonmechanical pencils, and art goods. Examples of products made by these establishments are pencil leads, crayons, chalk, framed blackboards, pencil sharpeners, staplers, artists' palettes and paints, and modeling clay.

US—United States industry only. CAN—United States and Canadian industries are comparable. When neither US nor CAN appears, Canadian, Mexican, and United States industries are comparable.

Cross-References. Establishments primarily engaged in—

- Manufacturing mechanical pencils—are classified in U.S. Industry 339941, Pen and Mechanical Pencil Manufacturing;

- Manufacturing writing, drawing, and india inks—are classified in U.S. Industry 325998, All Other Miscellaneous Chemical Product and Preparation Manufacturing;

- Manufacturing rubber erasers—are classified in U.S. Industry 326299, All Other Rubber Product Manufacturing;

- Manufacturing paper office supplies—are classified in Subsector 322, Paper Manufacturing;

- Printing manifold business forms and manufacturing blankbooks and looseleaf binders and devices—are classified in Industry 32311, Printing; and

- Manufacturing drafting tables and boards—are classified in U.S. Industry 337127, Institutional Furniture Manufacturing.

339943 Marking Device Manufacturing[US]

This U.S. industry comprises establishments primarily engaged in manufacturing marking devices, such as hand operated stamps, embossing stamps, stamp pads, and stencils.

Cross-References.

Establishments primarily engaged in manufacturing felt tipped markers are classified in U.S. Industry 339941, Pen and Mechanical Pencil Manufacturing.

339944 Carbon Paper and Inked Ribbon Manufacturing[US]

This U.S. industry comprises establishments primarily engaged in manufacturing carbon paper and inked ribbons.

Cross-References.

Establishments primarily engaged in manufacturing inkjet cartridges are classified in Industry 325910, Printing Ink Manufacturing.

33995 Sign Manufacturing
See industry description for 39950 below.

339950 Sign Manufacturing

This industry comprises establishments primarily engaged in manufacturing signs and related displays of all materials (except printing paper and paperboard signs, notices, displays).

US—United States industry only. CAN—United States and Canadian industries are comparable. When neither US nor CAN appears, Canadian, Mexican, and United States industries are comparable.

Cross-References. Establishments primarily engaged in—

- Printing advertising specialties or printing paper and paperboard signs, notices, and displays—are classified in Industry 32311, Printing;

- Manufacturing and printing advertising specialties—are classified in the manufacturing sector according to products manufactured;

- Manufacturing die-cut paperboard displays—are classified in U.S. Industry 322299, All Other Converted Paper Product Manufacturing; and

- Sign lettering and painting—are classified in Industry 541890, Other Services Related to Advertising.

33999 All Other Miscellaneous Manufacturing.

This industry comprises establishments primarily engaged in miscellaneous manufacturing (except medical equipment and supplies, jewelry and flatware, sporting and athletic goods, dolls, toys, games, office supplies (except paper), and signs).

Illustrative Examples:

Artificial Christmas trees manufacturing
Burial caskets and cases manufacturing
Candles manufacturing
Coin-operated amusement machines (except jukebox) manufacturing
Fasteners, buttons, needles, and pins (except precious metals or precious and semiprecious stones and gems) manufacturing

Floor and dust mops manufacturing
Gasket, packing, and sealing devices manufacturing
Musical instruments (except toy) manufacturing
Portable fire extinguishers manufacturing
Umbrellas manufacturing

Cross-References. Establishments primarily engaged in—

- Manufacturing medical equipment and supplies—are classified in Industry Group 3391; Medical Equipment and Supplies Manufacturing

- Manufacturing jewelry and flatware—are classified in Industry 33991, Jewelry and Silverware Manufacturing;

- Manufacturing sporting and athletic goods—are classified in Industry 33992, Sporting and Athletic Goods Manufacturing;

- Manufacturing dolls, toys, and games—are classified in Industry 33993, Doll, Toy, and Game Manufacturing;

- Manufacturing office supplies (except paper)—are classified in Industry 39994, Office Supplies (except Paper) Manufacturing;

- Manufacturing signs—are classified in Industry 33995, Sign Manufacturing;

US—United States industry only. CAN—United States and Canadian industries are comparable. When neither US nor CAN appears, Canadian, Mexican, and United States industries are comparable.

http://www.ntis.gov/naics

- Manufacturing concrete burial vaults—are classified in Industry 32739, Other Concrete Product Manufacturing;

- Manufacturing Christmas tree glass ornaments and glass lamp shades—are classified in Industry 32721, Glass and Glass Product Manufacturing;

- Manufacturing Christmas tree lighting sets—are classified in Industry 33512, Lighting Fixture Manufacturing;

- Manufacturing beauty and barber chairs—are classified in Industry 33712, Household and Institutional Furniture Manufacturing;

- Manufacturing burnt wood articles—are classified in Industry 32199, All Other Wood Product Manufacturing;

- Dressing and bleaching furs—are classified in Industry 31611, Leather and Hide Tanning and Finishing;

- Manufacturing paper, textile, and metal lamp shades—are classified in Industry 33512, Lighting Fixture Manufacturing;

- Manufacturing plastics lamp shades—are classified in Industry 32619, Other Plastics Product Manufacturing;

- Manufacturing matches—are classified in Industry 32599, All Other Chemical Product and Preparation Manufacturing;

- Manufacturing metal products, such as metal combs and hair curlers,—are classified in Industry 33299, All Other Fabricated Metal Product Manufacturing;

- Manufacturing plastics products, such as plastics combs and hair curlers,—are classified in Industry 32619, Other Plastics Product Manufacturing; and

- Manufacturing electric hair clippers for use on humans—are classified in Industry 33521, Small Electrical Appliance Manufacturing.

339991 Gasket, Packing, and Sealing Device Manufacturing[US]

This industry comprises establishments primarily engaged in manufacturing gaskets, packing, and sealing devices of all materials.

339992 Musical Instrument Manufacturing[US]

This U.S. industry comprises establishments primarily engaged in manufacturing musical instruments (except toys).

Cross-References.

Establishments primarily engaged in manufacturing toy musical instruments are classified in U.S. Industry 339932, Game, Toy, and Children's Vehicle Manufacturing.

US—United States industry only. CAN—United States and Canadian industries are comparable. When neither US nor CAN appears, Canadian, Mexican, and United States industries are comparable.

339993 Fastener, Button, Needle, and Pin Manufacturing[US]

This U.S. industry comprises establishments primarily engaged in manufacturing fasteners, buttons, needles, pins, and buckles (except precious metals or precious and semiprecious stones and gems).

Cross-References. Establishments primarily engaged in—

- Manufacturing buttons, pins, and buckles made of precious metals or precious and semiprecious stones and gems—are classified in U.S. Industry 339911, Jewelry (except Costume) Manufacturing;

- Manufacturing hypodermic and suture needles—are classified in U.S. Industry 339112, Surgical and Medical Instrument Manufacturing; and

- Manufacturing phonograph and styli needles—are classified in U.S. Industry 334419, Other Electronic Component Manufacturing.

339994 Broom, Brush, and Mop Manufacturing[US]

This U.S. industry comprises establishments primarily engaged in manufacturing brooms, mops, and brushes.

339995 Burial Casket Manufacturing[US]

This U.S. industry comprises establishments primarily engaged in manufacturing burial caskets, cases, and vaults (except concrete).

Cross-References.

Establishments primarily engaged in manufacturing concrete burial vaults are classified in Industry 327390, Other Concrete Product Manufacturing.

339999 All Other Miscellaneous Manufacturing[US]

This U.S. industry comprises establishments primarily engaged in miscellaneous manufacturing (except medical equipment and supplies, jewelry and flatware, sporting and athletic goods, dolls, toys, games, office supplies (except paper), musical instruments, fasteners, buttons, needles, pins, brooms, brushes, mops, and burial caskets).

Illustrative Examples:

Artificial Christmas trees manufacturing
Candles manufacturing
Christmas tree ornaments (except glass and electric) manufacturing
Cigarette lighters (except precious metal) manufacturing
Coin-operated amusement machines (except jukebox) manufacturing
Hair pieces (e.g., wigs, toupees, wiglets) manufacturing
Portable fire extinguishers manufacturing
Potpourri manufacturing
Tobacco pipes manufacturing
Umbrellas manufacturing

US—United States industry only. CAN—United States and Canadian industries are comparable. When neither US nor CAN appears, Canadian, Mexican, and United States industries are comparable.

Cross-References. Establishments primarily engaged in—

- Manufacturing medical equipment and supplies—are classified in Industry Group 3391, Medical Equipment and Supplies Manufacturing;

- Manufacturing jewelry and flatware—are classified in Industry 33991, Jewelry and Silverware Manufacturing;

- Manufacturing sporting and athletic goods—are classified in Industry 339920, Sporting and Athletic Goods Manufacturing;

- Manufacturing dolls, toys, and games—are classified in Industry 33993, Doll, Toy, and Game Manufacturing;

- Manufacturing office supplies (except paper)—are classified in Industry 39994, Office Supplies (except Paper) Manufacturing;

- Manufacturing signs—are classified in Industry 33995, Sign Manufacturing;

- Manufacturing gasket, packing, and sealing devices—are classified in U.S. Industry 339991, Gasket, Packing, and Sealing Device Manufacturing;

- Manufacturing musical instruments—are classified in U.S. Industry 339992, Musical Instrument Manufacturing;

- Manufacturing fasteners, buttons, needles, and pins—are classified in U.S. Industry 339993, Fastener, Button, Needle, and Pin Manufacturing;

- Manufacturing brooms, brushes, and mops—are classified in U.S. Industry 339994, Broom, Brush, and Mop Manufacturing;

- Manufacturing burial caskets—are classified in U.S. Industry 339995, Burial Casket Manufacturing;

- Manufacturing Christmas tree glass ornaments and glass lamp shades—are classified in U.S. Industry 327215, Glass Product Manufacturing Made of Purchased Glass;

- Manufacturing Christmas tree lighting sets—are classified in U.S. Industry 335129, Other Lighting Equipment Manufacturing;

- Manufacturing beauty and barber chairs—are classified in U.S. Industry 337127, Institutional Furniture Manufacturing;

- Manufacturing burnt wood articles—are classified in U.S. Industry 321999, All Other Miscellaneous Wood Product Manufacturing;

- Dressing and bleaching furs—are classified in Industry 316110, Leather and Hide Tanning and Finishing;

- Manufacturing paper, textile, and metal lamp shades—are classified in U.S. Industry 335121, Residential Electric Lighting Fixture Manufacturing;

US—United States industry only. CAN—United States and Canadian industries are comparable. When neither US nor CAN appears, Canadian, Mexican, and United States industries are comparable.

http://www.ntis.gov/naics

- Manufacturing plastics lamp shades—are classified in U.S. Industry 326199, All Other Plastics Product Manufacturing;

- Manufacturing matches—are classified in U.S. Industry 325998, All Other Miscellaneous Chemical Product and Preparation Manufacturing;

- Manufacturing metal products, such as metal combs and hair curlers,—are classified in U.S. Industry 332999, All Other Miscellaneous Fabricated Metal Product Manufacturing;

- Manufacturing plastics products, such as plastics combs and hair curlers,—are classified in U.S. Industry 326199, All Other Plastics Product Manufacturing; and

- Manufacturing electric hair clippers for use on humans—are classified in U.S. Industry 335211, Electric Housewares and Household Fan Manufacturing.

US—United States industry only. CAN—United States and Canadian industries are comparable. When neither US nor CAN appears, Canadian, Mexican, and United States industries are comparable.

http://www.ntis.gov/naics

Sector 42—Wholesale Trade

The Sector as a Whole

The Wholesale Trade sector comprises establishments engaged in wholesaling merchandise, generally without transformation, and rendering services incidental to the sale of merchandise.

The wholesaling process is an intermediate step in the distribution of merchandise. Wholesalers are organized to sell or arrange the purchase or sale of (a) goods for resale (i.e., goods sold to other wholesalers or retailers), (b) capital or durable nonconsumer goods, and (c) raw and intermediate materials and supplies used in production.

Wholesalers sell merchandise to other businesses and normally operate from a warehouse or office. These warehouses and offices are characterized by having little or no display of merchandise. In addition, neither the design nor the location of the premises is intended to solicit walk-in traffic. Wholesalers do not normally use advertising directed to the general public. Customers are generally reached initially via telephone, in-person marketing, or by specialized advertising that may include Internet and other electronic means. Follow-up orders are either vendor-initiated or client-initiated, generally based on previous sales, and typically exhibit strong ties between sellers and buyers. In fact, transactions are often conducted between wholesalers and clients that have long-standing business relationships.

This sector comprises two main types of wholesalers: those that sell goods on their own account and those that arrange sales and purchases for others for a commission or fee.

(1) Establishments that sell goods on their own account are known as wholesale merchants, distributors, jobbers, drop shippers, import/export merchants, and sales branches. These establishments typically maintain their own warehouse, where they receive and handle goods for their customers. Goods are generally sold without transformation, but may include integral functions, such as sorting, packaging, labeling, and other marketing services.

(2) Establishments arranging for the purchase or sale of goods owned by others or purchasing goods on a commission basis are known as agents and brokers, commission merchants, import/export agents and brokers, auction companies, and manufacturers' representatives. These establishments operate from offices and generally do not own or handle the goods they sell.

Some wholesale establishments may be connected with a single manufacturer and promote and sell the particular manufacturers' products to a wide range of other wholesalers or retailers. Other wholesalers may be connected to a retail chain or a limited number of retail chains and only provide a variety of products needed by that particular retail operation(s). These wholesalers may obtain the products from a wide range of manufacturers. Still other wholesalers may not take title to the goods, but act as agents and brokers for a commission.

Although, in general, wholesaling normally denotes sales in large volumes, durable nonconsumer goods may be sold in single units. Sales of capital or durable nonconsumer goods used in the production of goods and services, such as farm machinery, medium and heavy duty trucks, and industrial machinery, are always included in wholesale trade.

421 Wholesale Trade, Durable Goods[US]

Industries in the Wholesale Trade, Durable Goods subsector sell or arrange the purchase or sale of capital or durable goods to other businesses. Durable goods are new or used items generally

---

US—United States industry only. CAN—United States and Canadian industries are comparable. When neither US nor CAN appears, Canadian, Mexican, and United States industries are comparable.

http://www.ntis.gov/naics

with a normal life expectancy of three years or more. Durable goods wholesale trade establishments are engaged in wholesaling products, such as motor vehicles, furniture, construction materials, machinery and equipment (including household-type appliances), metals and minerals (except petroleum), sporting goods, toys and hobby goods, recyclable materials, and parts.

The detailed industries within the subsector are organized in the classification structure based on the products sold. Within an industry, the types of establishments may vary, including wholesale merchants and/or agents and brokers.

4211 Motor Vehicle and Motor Vehicle Parts and Supplies Wholesalers[US]

This industry group comprises establishments primarily engaged in wholesaling automobiles and other motor vehicles, motor vehicle supplies, tires, and new and used parts.

42111 Automobile and Other Motor Vehicle Wholesalers[US]
See industry description for 421110 below.

421110 Automobile and Other Motor Vehicle Wholesalers[US]

This industry comprises establishments primarily engaged in wholesaling new and used passenger automobiles, trucks, trailers, and other motor vehicles, such as motorcycles, motor homes, and snowmobiles.

42112 Motor Vehicle Supplies and New Parts Wholesalers[US]
See industry description for 421120 below.

421120 Motor Vehicle Supplies and New Parts Wholesalers[US]

This industry comprises establishments primarily engaged in wholesaling motor vehicle supplies, accessories, tools, and equipment; and new motor vehicle parts (except new tires and tubes).

Cross-References. Establishments primarily engaged in—

- Wholesaling new and/or used tires and tubes—are classified in Industry 421130, Tire and Tube Wholesalers;

- Wholesaling automotive chemicals (except lubricating oils and greases)—are classified in Industry 422690, Other Chemical and Allied Products Wholesalers;

- Wholesaling lubricating oils and greases—are classified in Industry 422720, Petroleum and Petroleum Products Wholesalers (except Bulk Stations and Terminals); and

- Wholesaling used motor vehicle parts—are classified in Industry 421140, Motor Vehicle Parts (Used) Wholesalers.

US—United States industry only. CAN—United States and Canadian industries are comparable. When neither US nor CAN appears, Canadian, Mexican, and United States industries are comparable.

42113 Tire and Tube Wholesalers[US]

See industry description for 421130 below.

421130 Tire and Tube Wholesalers[US]

This industry comprises establishments primarily engaged in wholesaling new and/or used tires and tubes for passenger and commercial vehicles.

42114 Motor Vehicle Parts (Used) Wholesalers[US]

See industry description for 421140 below.

421140 Motor Vehicle Parts (Used) Wholesalers[US]

This industry comprises establishments primarily engaged in wholesaling used motor vehicle parts (except used tires and tubes) and establishments primarily engaged in dismantling motor vehicles for the purpose of selling the parts.

Cross-References. Establishments primarily engaged in—

- Dismantling motor vehicles for the purpose of selling scrap—are classified in Industry 421930, Recyclable Material Wholesalers; and

- Wholesaling new and/or used tires and tubes—are classified in Industry 421130, Tire and Tube Wholesalers.

4212 Furniture and Home Furnishing Wholesalers[US]

42121 Furniture Wholesalers[US]

See industry description for 421210 below.

421210 Furniture Wholesalers[US]

This industry comprises establishments primarily engaged in wholesaling furniture (except hospital beds, medical furniture, and drafting tables).

Illustrative Examples:

Household-type furniture wholesaling	Outdoor furniture wholesaling
Mattresses wholesaling	Public building furniture wholesaling
Office furniture wholesaling	Religious furniture wholesaling

Cross-References. Establishments primarily engaged in—

- Wholesaling partitions, shelving, lockers, and store fixtures—are classified in Industry 421440, Other Commercial Equipment Wholesalers;

- Wholesaling hospital beds and medical furniture—are classified in Industry 421450, Medical, Dental, and Hospital Equipment and Supplies Wholesalers; and

---

US—United States industry only. CAN—United States and Canadian industries are comparable. When neither US nor CAN appears, Canadian, Mexican, and United States industries are comparable.

http://www.ntis.gov/naics

- Wholesaling drafting tables—are classified in Industry 421490, Other Professional Equipment and Supplies Wholesalers.

42122 Home Furnishing Wholesalers[US]
See industry description for 421220 below.

421220 Home Furnishing Wholesalers[US]

This industry comprises establishments primarily engaged in wholesaling home furnishings and/or housewares.

Illustrative Examples:

Carpets wholesaling	Glassware wholesaling
Chinaware wholesaling	Household-type cooking utensils wholesaling
Curtains wholesaling	Lamps wholesaling
Draperies wholesaling	Linens (e.g., bath, bed, table) wholesaling
Floor coverings wholesaling	Window blinds and shades wholesaling

Cross-References. Establishments primarily engaged in—

- Wholesaling electrical household-type goods—are classified in Industry 421620, Electrical Appliance, Television, and Radio Set Wholesalers; and

- Wholesaling precious metal flatware—are classified in Industry 421940, Jewelry, Watch, Precious Stone, and Precious Metal Wholesalers.

4213 Lumber and Other Construction Materials Wholesalers[US]

42131 Lumber, Plywood, Millwork, and Wood Panel Wholesalers[US]
See industry description for 421310 below.

421310 Lumber, Plywood, Millwork, and Wood Panel Wholesalers[US]

This industry comprises establishments primarily engaged in wholesaling lumber; plywood; reconstituted wood fiber products; wood fencing; doors and windows and their frames (all materials); wood roofing and siding; and/or other wood or metal millwork.

Cross-References.

Establishments primarily engaged in wholesaling timber and timber products, such as railroad ties, logs, firewood, and pulpwood, are classified in Industry 421990, Other Miscellaneous Durable Goods Wholesalers.

US—United States industry only. CAN—United States and Canadian industries are comparable. When neither US nor CAN appears, Canadian, Mexican, and United States industries are comparable.

42132 Brick, Stone, and Related Construction Material Wholesalers^{US}

See industry description for 421320 below.

421320 Brick, Stone, and Related Construction Material Wholesalers^{US}

This industry comprises establishments primarily engaged in wholesaling stone, cement, lime, construction sand, and gravel; brick; asphalt and concrete mixtures; and/or concrete, stone, and structural clay products.

Cross-References. Establishments primarily engaged in—

- Wholesaling refractory brick and other refractory products—are classified in Industry 421840, Industrial Supplies Wholesalers; and

- Selling ready-mixed concrete—are classified in Industry 327320, Ready-Mix Concrete Manufacturing.

42133 Roofing, Siding, and Insulation Material Wholesalers^{US}

See industry description for 421330 below.

421330 Roofing, Siding, and Insulation Material Wholesalers^{US}

This industry comprises establishments primarily engaged in wholesaling nonwood roofing and nonwood siding and insulation materials.

Cross-References.

Establishments primarily engaged in wholesaling wood roofing and wood siding are classified in Industry 421310, Lumber, Plywood, Millwork, and Wood Panel Wholesalers.

42139 Other Construction Material Wholesalers^{US}

See industry description for 421390 below.

421390 Other Construction Material Wholesalers^{US}

This industry comprises (1) establishments primarily engaged in wholesaling manufactured homes (i.e., mobile homes) and/or prefabricated buildings and (2) establishments primarily engaged in wholesaling construction materials (except lumber, plywood, millwood, wood panel, brick, stone, roofing, siding, and insulation material).

Illustrative Examples:

Flat glass wholesaling
Ornamental ironwork wholesaling
Plate glass wholesaling
Prefabricated buildings (except wood) wholesaling

Wire fencing and fencing accessories wholesaling

US—United States industry only. CAN—United States and Canadian industries are comparable. When neither US nor CAN appears, Canadian, Mexican, and United States industries are comparable.

http://www.ntis.gov/naics

Cross-References. Establishments primarily engaged in—

- Wholesaling products of the primary metals industries—are classified in Industry 421510, Metal Service Centers and Offices;

- Wholesaling lumber; plywood; reconstituted wood fiber products; wood fencing; doors, windows, and their frames; wood roofing and wood siding; and other wood or metal millwork—are classified in Industry 421310, Lumber, Plywood, Millwork, and Wood Panel Wholesalers;

- Wholesaling stone, cement, lime, construction sand and gravel; brick; asphalt and concrete mixtures (except ready-mix concrete); and/or concrete, stone, and structural clay products— are classified in Industry 421320, Brick, Stone, and Related Construction Material Wholesalers;

- Wholesaling nonwood roofing and nonwood siding and insulation materials—are classified in Industry 421330, Roofing, Siding, and Insulation Material Wholesalers; and

- Selling ready-mix concrete—are classified in Industry 327320, Ready-Mix Concrete Manufacturing.

4214 Professional and Commercial Equipment and Supplies Wholesalers[US]

This industry group comprises establishments primarily engaged in wholesaling photographic equipment and supplies; office, computer, and computer peripheral equipment; and medical, dental, hospital, ophthalmic, and other commercial and professional equipment and supplies.

42141 Photographic Equipment and Supplies Wholesalers[US]
See industry description for 421410 below.

421410 Photographic Equipment and Supplies Wholesalers[US]

This industry comprises establishments primarily engaged in wholesaling photographic equipment and supplies (except office equipment).

Illustrative Examples:

Photofinishing equipment wholesaling
Photographic camera equipment and supplies
  wholesaling
Photographic film wholesaling

Television cameras wholesaling
Video cameras (except household-type)
  wholesaling

Cross-References. Establishments primarily engaged in—

- Wholesaling household-type video cameras—are classified in Industry 421620, Electrical Appliance, Television, and Radio Set Wholesalers; and

- Wholesaling office equipment, such as photocopy and microfilm equipment,—are classified in Industry 421420, Office Equipment Wholesalers.

US—United States industry only. CAN—United States and Canadian industries are comparable. When neither US nor CAN appears, Canadian, Mexican, and United States industries are comparable.

42142 Office Equipment WholesalersUS

See industry description for 421420 below.

421420 Office Equipment WholesalersUS

This industry comprises establishments primarily engaged in wholesaling office machines and related equipment (except computers and computer peripheral equipment).

Illustrative Examples:

Accounting machines wholesaling
Calculator and calculating machines
  wholesaling
Cash registers wholesaling
Copying machines wholesaling

Mailing machines wholesaling
Microfilm equipment and supplies
  wholesaling
Security safes wholesaling

Cross-References. Establishments primarily engaged in—

- Wholesaling office furniture—are classified in Industry 421210, Furniture Wholesalers;

- Wholesaling computers and computer peripheral equipment—are classified in Industry 421430, Computer and Computer Peripheral Equipment and Software Wholesalers; and

- Wholesaling office supplies—are classified in Industry 422120, Stationery and Office Supplies Wholesalers.

42143 Computer and Computer Peripheral Equipment and Software WholesalersUS

See industry description for 421430 below.

421430 Computer and Computer Peripheral Equipment and Software WholesalersUS

This industry comprises establishments primarily engaged in wholesaling computers, computer peripheral equipment, loaded computer boards, and/or computer software.

Cross-References. Establishments primarily engaged in—

- Wholesaling modems and other electronic communications equipment—are classified in Industry 421690, Other Electronic Parts and Equipment Wholesalers; and

- Selling, planning, and designing computer systems that integrate computer hardware, software, and communication technologies—are classified in U.S. Industry 541512, Computer Systems Design Services.

US—United States industry only. CAN—United States and Canadian industries are comparable. When neither US nor CAN appears, Canadian, Mexican, and United States industries are comparable.

http://www.ntis.gov/naics

42144 Other Commercial Equipment Wholesalers[US]
See industry description for 421440 below.

421440 Other Commercial Equipment Wholesalers[US]

This industry comprises establishments primarily engaged in wholesaling commercial and related machines and equipment (except photographic equipment and supplies; office equipment; and computers and computer peripheral equipment and software) generally used in restaurants and stores.

Illustrative Examples:

Balances and scales (except laboratory) wholesaling
Coin-operated merchandising machines wholesaling
Commercial chinaware wholesaling
Commercial cooking equipment wholesaling

Commercial shelving wholesaling
Electrical signs wholesaling
Partitions wholesaling
Store fixtures (except refrigerated) wholesaling

Cross-References. Establishments primarily engaged in—

- Wholesaling photographic equipment and supplies—are classified in Industry 421410, Photographic Equipment and Supplies Wholesalers;

- Wholesaling office machines and related equipment—are classified in Industry 421420, Office Equipment Wholesalers;

- Wholesaling computers, computer peripheral equipment, and computer software—are classified in Industry 421430, Computer and Computer Peripheral Equipment and Software Wholesalers;

- Wholesaling laboratory scales and balances—are classified in Industry 421490, Other Professional Equipment and Supplies Wholesalers; and

- Wholesaling refrigerated store fixtures—are classified in Industry 421740, Refrigeration Equipment and Supplies Wholesalers.

42145 Medical, Dental, and Hospital Equipment and Supplies Wholesalers[US]
See industry description for 421450 below.

421450 Medical, Dental, and Hospital Equipment and Supplies Wholesalers[US]

This industry comprises establishments primarily engaged in wholesaling medical professional equipment, instruments, and supplies (except ophthalmic equipment, instruments and goods used by ophthalmologists, optometrists, and opticians).

US—United States industry only. CAN—United States and Canadian industries are comparable. When neither US nor CAN appears, Canadian, Mexican, and United States industries are comparable.

Illustrative Examples:

Dental equipment and supplies wholesaling
Electromedical equipment wholesaling
Hospital beds wholesaling
Hospital furniture wholesaling
Medical and dental X ray machines
  wholesaling

Medical dressings wholesaling
Patient monitoring equipment wholesaling
Prosthetic appliance and supplies wholesaling
Surgical instrument and apparatus wholesaling

Cross-References.

Establishments primarily engaged in wholesaling professional equipment, instruments and/or goods sold, prescribed, or used by ophthalmologists, optometrists, and opticians are classified in Industry 421460, Ophthalmic Goods Wholesalers.

42146 Ophthalmic Goods Wholesalers[US]
See industry description for 421460 below.

421460 Ophthalmic Goods Wholesalers[US]

This industry comprises establishments primarily engaged in wholesaling professional equipment, instruments, and/or goods sold, prescribed, or used by ophthalmologists, optometrists, and opticians.

Illustrative Examples:

Binoculars wholesaling
Ophthalmic frames wholesaling
Ophthalmic lenses wholesaling

Optometric equipment and supplies
  wholesaling
Sunglasses wholesaling

42149 Other Professional Equipment and Supplies Wholesalers[US]
See industry description for 421490 below.

421490 Other Professional Equipment and Supplies Wholesalers[US]

This industry comprises establishments primarily engaged in wholesaling professional equipment and supplies (except ophthalmic goods and medical, dental, and hospital equipment and supplies).

Illustrative Examples:

Church supplies (except silverware, plated ware)
  wholesaling
Drafting tables and instruments wholesaling
Laboratory equipment (except medical,
  dental) wholesaling

School equipment and supplies (except books,
  furniture) wholesaling
Scientific instruments wholesaling
Surveying equipment and supplies
  wholesaling

US—United States industry only. CAN—United States and Canadian industries are comparable. When neither US nor CAN appears, Canadian, Mexican, and United States industries are comparable.

Cross-References. Establishments primarily engaged in—

- Wholesaling professional equipment, instruments, and/or goods sold, prescribed, or used by ophthalmologists, optometrists, and opticians, such as ophthalmic frames and lenses, and sunglasses,—are classified in Industry 421460, Ophthalmic Goods Wholesalers;

- Wholesaling medical professional equipment, instruments, and supplies used by medical and dental practitioners (except ophthalmic equipment, instruments, and goods used by ophthalmologists, optometrists, and opticians) and medical facilities—are classified in Industry 421450, Medical, Dental, and Hospital Equipment and Supplies Wholesalers;

- Wholesaling silverware and plated flatware—are classified in Industry 421940, Jewelry, Watch, Precious Stone, and Precious Metal Wholesalers;

- Wholesaling books—are classified in Industry 422920, Book, Periodical, and Newspaper Wholesalers; and

- Wholesaling school furniture—are classified in Industry 421210, Furniture Wholesalers.

4215 Metal and Mineral (except Petroleum) Wholesalers^{US}

42151 Metal Service Centers and Offices^{US}
See industry description for 421510 below.

421510 Metal Service Centers and Offices^{US}

This industry comprises establishments primarily engaged in wholesaling products of the primary metals industries. Service centers maintain inventory and may perform functions, such as sawing, shearing, bending, leveling, cleaning, or edging, on a custom basis as part of sales transactions. Sales offices are usually affiliated or owned by a particular manufacturer and take orders but have no inventory.

Illustrative Examples:

Cast iron pipe wholesaling	Metal rods wholesaling
Metal bars (except precious) wholesaling	Metal sheets wholesaling
Metal ingots (except precious) wholesaling	Metal spikes wholesaling
Metal pipe wholesaling	Nails wholesaling
Metal plates wholesaling	Noninsulated wire wholesaling

Cross-References. Establishments primarily engaged in—

- Wholesaling gold, silver, and platinum—are classified in Industry 421940, Jewelry, Watch, Precious Stone, and Precious Metal Wholesalers;

- Wholesaling automotive, industrial, and other recyclable metal scrap—are classified in Industry 421930, Recyclable Material Wholesalers; and

- Wholesaling insulated wire—are classified in Industry 421610, Electrical Apparatus and Equipment, Wiring Supplies, and Construction Material Wholesalers.

US—United States industry only. CAN—United States and Canadian industries are comparable. When neither US nor CAN appears, Canadian, Mexican, and United States industries are comparable.

42152 Coal and Other Mineral and Ore Wholesalers[US]
See industry description for 421520 below.

421520 Coal and Other Mineral and Ore Wholesalers[US]

This industry comprises establishments primarily engaged in wholesaling coal, coke, metal ores, and/or nonmetallic minerals (except precious and semiprecious stones and minerals used in construction, such as sand and gravel).

Cross-References. Establishments primarily engaged in—

- Wholesaling nonmetallic minerals used in construction, such as sand and gravel,—are classified in Industry 421320, Brick, Stone, and Related Construction Material Wholesalers;

- Wholesaling crude petroleum—are classified in Industry Group 4227, Petroleum and Petroleum Products Wholesalers; and

- Wholesaling precious and semiprecious stones and metals—are classified in Industry 421940, Jewelry, Watch, Precious Stone, and Precious Metal Wholesalers.

4216 Electrical Goods Wholesalers[US]

42161 Electrical Apparatus and Equipment, Wiring Supplies, and Construction Material Wholesalers[US]
See industry description for 421610 below.

421610 Electrical Apparatus and Equipment, Wiring Supplies, and Construction Material Wholesalers[US]

This industry comprises establishments primarily engaged in wholesaling electrical construction materials; wiring supplies; electric light fixtures; light bulbs; and/or electrical power equipment for the generation, transmission, distribution, or control of electric energy.

42162 Electrical Appliance, Television, and Radio Set Wholesalers[US]
See industry description for 421620 below.

421620 Electrical Appliance, Television, and Radio Set Wholesalers[US]

This industry comprises establishments primarily engaged in wholesaling household-type electrical appliances, room air-conditioners, gas clothes dryers, and/or household-type audio or video equipment.

Illustrative Examples:

Electric water heaters wholesaling
Household-type radios (including automotive) wholesaling
Household-type refrigerators wholesaling
Household-type sewing machines wholesaling
Household-type video cameras wholesaling
Television sets wholesaling

US—United States industry only. CAN—United States and Canadian industries are comparable. When neither US nor CAN appears, Canadian, Mexican, and United States industries are comparable.

http://www.ntis.gov/naics

Cross-References. Establishments primarily engaged in—

- Wholesaling gas household-type appliances (except gas clothes dryers)—are classified in Industry 421720, Plumbing and Heating Equipment and Supplies (Hydronics) Wholesalers; and

- Wholesaling nonhousehold-type video cameras—are classified in Industry 421410, Photographic Equipment and Supplies Wholesalers.

42169 Other Electronic Parts and Equipment Wholesalers[US]
See industry description for 421690 below.

421690 Other Electronic Parts and Equipment Wholesalers[US]

This industry comprises establishments primarily engaged in wholesaling electronic parts and equipment (except electrical apparatus and equipment, wiring supplies and construction material; and electrical appliances, television and radio sets).

Illustrative Examples:

Blank audio tapes wholesaling	Radar equipment wholesaling
Blank diskettes wholesaling	Telegraph equipment wholesaling
Blank video tapes wholesaling	Telephone equipment wholesaling
Broadcasting equipment wholesaling	Unloaded computer boards wholesaling
Communications equipment wholesaling	

Cross-References. Establishments primarily engaged in—

- Wholesaling household-type electrical appliances, televisions, and radio sets—are classified in Industry 421620, Electrical Appliance, Television, and Radio Set Wholesalers;

- Wholesaling computers, computer peripheral equipment, and loaded computer boards—are classified in Industry 421430, Computer and Computer Peripheral Equipment and Software Wholesalers; and

- Wholesaling electrical construction materials, wiring supplies, electric light fixtures, light bulbs; and/or electrical power equipment for generation, transmission, distribution, or control of electric energy—are classified in Industry 421610, Electrical Apparatus and Equipment, Wiring Supplies, and Construction Material Wholesalers.

4217 Hardware, and Plumbing and Heating Equipment and Supplies Wholesalers[US]

42171 Hardware Wholesalers[US]
See industry description for 421710 below.

421710 Hardware Wholesalers[US]

This industry comprises establishments primarily engaged in wholesaling hardware, knives, or handtools.

US—United States industry only. CAN—United States and Canadian industries are comparable. When neither US nor CAN appears, Canadian, Mexican, and United States industries are comparable.

Illustrative Examples:

Brads wholesaling	Knives (except disposable plastics)
Cutlery wholesaling	wholesaling
Fasteners (e.g., bolts, nuts, rivets, screws)	Power handtools (e.g., drills, saws, sanders)
wholesaling	wholesaling
Handtools (except motor vehicle, machinists'	Staples wholesaling
precision) wholesaling	Tacks wholesaling

Cross-References. Establishments primarily engaged in—

- Wholesaling nails, noninsulated wire, and screening—are classified in Industry 421510, Metal Service Centers and Offices;

- Wholesaling motor vehicle handtools and equipment—are classified in Industry 421120, Motor Vehicle Supplies and New Parts Wholesalers;

- Wholesaling machinists' precision handtools—are classified in Industry 421830, Industrial Machinery and Equipment Wholesalers; and

- Wholesaling disposable plastics knives and eating utensils—are classified in Industry 422130, Industrial and Personal Service Paper Wholesalers.

42172 Plumbing and Heating Equipment and Supplies (Hydronics) Wholesalers[US]
See industry description for 421720 below.

421720 Plumbing and Heating Equipment and Supplies (Hydronics) Wholesalers[US]

This industry comprises establishments primarily engaged in wholesaling plumbing equipment, hydronic heating equipment, household-type gas appliances (except gas clothes dryers), and/or supplies.

Cross-References. Establishments primarily engaged in—

- Selling and installing plumbing, heating and air conditioning equipment—are classified in Industry 235110, Plumbing, Heating, and Air-Conditioning Contractors;

- Wholesaling warm air heating and air-conditioning equipment—are classified in Industry 421730, Warm Air Heating and Air-Conditioning Equipment and Supplies Wholesalers; and

- Wholesaling household-type electrical appliances, room air conditioners, gas clothes dryers, and/or household-type audio or video equipment—are classified in Industry 421620, Electrical Appliance, Television, and Radio Set Wholesalers.

42173 Warm Air Heating and Air-Conditioning Equipment and Supplies Wholesalers[US]
See industry description for 421730 below.

US—United States industry only. CAN—United States and Canadian industries are comparable. When neither US nor CAN appears, Canadian, Mexican, and United States industries are comparable.

421730 Warm Air Heating and Air-Conditioning Equipment and Supplies WholesalersUS

This industry comprises establishments primarily engaged in wholesaling warm air heating and air-conditioning equipment and supplies.

Illustrative Examples:

Air pollution control equipment and supplies wholesaling

Air-conditioning equipment (except room units) wholesaling

Automotive air-conditioners wholesaling

Nonportable electric baseboard heaters wholesaling

Warm-air central heating equipment wholesaling

Cross-References. Establishments primarily engaged in—

- Wholesaling household-type electrical appliances and room air-conditioners—are classified in Industry 421620, Electrical Appliance, Television, and Radio Set Wholesalers;

- Wholesaling hydronic heating equipment—are classified in Industry 421720, Plumbing and Heating Equipment and Supplies (Hydronics) Wholesalers; and

- Selling and installing warm air heating and air-conditioning equipment—are classified in Industry 235110, Plumbing, Heating, and Air-Conditioning Contractors.

42174 Refrigeration Equipment and Supplies WholesalersUS
See industry description for 421740 below.

421740 Refrigeration Equipment and Supplies WholesalersUS

This industry comprises establishments primarily engaged in wholesaling refrigeration equipment (except household-type refrigerators, freezers, and air-conditioners).

Illustrative Examples:

Cold storage machinery wholesaling

Commercial refrigerators wholesaling

Refrigerated display cases wholesaling

Water coolers wholesaling

Cross-References. Establishments primarily engaged in—

- Wholesaling household-type refrigerators, freezers, and room air-conditioners—are classified in Industry 421620, Electrical Appliance, Television, and Radio Set Wholesalers; and

- Wholesaling air-conditioning equipment (except room units)—are classified Industry 421730, Warm Air Heating and Air Conditioning Equipment and Supplies Wholesalers.

4218 Machinery, Equipment, and Supplies WholesalersUS

This industry group comprises establishments primarily engaged in wholesaling construction, mining, farm, garden, industrial, service establishment, and transportation machinery, equipment and supplies.

US—United States industry only. CAN—United States and Canadian industries are comparable. When neither US nor CAN appears, Canadian, Mexican, and United States industries are comparable.

http://www.ntis.gov/naics

42181 Construction and Mining (except Oil Well) Machinery and Equipment Wholesalers[US]

See industry description for 421810 below.

421810 Construction and Mining (except Oil Well) Machinery and Equipment Wholesalers[US]

This industry comprises establishments primarily engaged in wholesaling specialized machinery, equipment, and related parts generally used in construction, mining (except oil well) and logging activities.

Illustrative Examples:

Excavating machinery and equipment
wholesaling
Forestry machinery and equipment
wholesaling

Mining cranes wholesaling
Road construction and maintenance machinery
wholesaling
Scaffolding wholesaling

Cross-References.

Establishments primarily engaged in wholesaling oil well machinery and equipment are classified in Industry 421830, Industrial Machinery and Equipment Wholesalers.

42182 Farm and Garden Machinery and Equipment Wholesalers[US]

See industry description for 421820 below.

421820 Farm and Garden Machinery and Equipment Wholesalers[US]

This industry comprises establishments primarily engaged in wholesaling specialized machinery, equipment, and related parts generally used in agricultural, farm, and lawn and garden activities.

Illustrative Examples:

Animal feeders wholesaling
Harvesting machinery and equipment
wholesaling
Lawnmowers wholesaling

Milking machinery and equipment
wholesaling
Planting machinery and equipment
wholesaling

42183 Industrial Machinery and Equipment Wholesalers[US]

See industry description for 421830 below.

421830 Industrial Machinery and Equipment Wholesalers[US]

This industry comprises establishments primarily engaged in wholesaling specialized machinery, equipment, and related parts generally used in manufacturing, oil well, and warehousing activities.

US—United States industry only. CAN—United States and Canadian industries are comparable. When neither US nor CAN appears, Canadian, Mexican, and United States industries are comparable.

http://www.ntis.gov/naics

Illustrative Examples:

Fluid power transmission equipment
wholesaling

Food-processing machinery and equipment
wholesaling

Materials handling machinery and equipment
wholesaling

Metalworking machinery and equipment
wholesaling

Oil well machinery and equipment
wholesaling

Cross-References. Establishments primarily engaged in—

- Wholesaling specialized machinery, equipment, and related parts generally used in construction, mining (except oil well), and logging activities—are classified in Industry 421810, Construction and Mining (except Oil Well) Machinery and Equipment Wholesalers; and

- Wholesaling supplies used in machinery and equipment generally used in manufacturing, oil well, and warehousing activities—are classified in Industry 421840, Industrial Supplies Wholesalers.

42184 Industrial Supplies Wholesalers[US]

See industry description for 421840 below.

421840 Industrial Supplies Wholesalers[US]

This industry comprises establishments primarily engaged in wholesaling supplies used in machinery and equipment generally used in manufacturing, oil well, and warehousing activities.

Illustrative Examples:

Industrial containers wholesaling
Industrial diamonds wholesaling
Printing inks wholesaling
Refractory materials (e.g., brick, blocks, shapes)
wholesaling

Welding supplies (except welding gases)
wholesaling

Cross-References. Establishments primarily engaged in—

- Wholesaling hydraulic and pneumatic (fluid-power) pumps, motors, pistons, and valves—are classified in Industry 421830, Industrial Machinery and Equipment Wholesalers; and

- Wholesaling welding gases—are classified in Industry 422690, Other Chemical and Allied Products Wholesalers.

42185 Service Establishment Equipment and Supplies Wholesalers[US]

See industry description for 421850 below.

421850 Service Establishment Equipment and Supplies Wholesalers[US]

This industry comprises establishments primarily engaged in wholesaling specialized equipment and supplies of the type used by service establishments (except specialized equipment and supplies

US—United States industry only. CAN—United States and Canadian industries are comparable. When neither US nor CAN appears, Canadian, Mexican, and United States industries are comparable.

http://www.ntis.gov/naics

used in offices, stores, hotels, restaurants, schools, health and medical facilities, photographic facilities, as well as specialized equipment used in transportation and construction activities).

Illustrative Examples:

Amusement park equipment wholesaling
Beauty parlor equipment and supplies
  wholesaling
Car wash equipment and supplies wholesaling
Drycleaning equipment and supplies
  wholesaling

Janitorial equipment and supplies wholesaling
Undertakers' equipment and supplies
  wholesaling
Upholsterers' equipment and supplies (except
  fabrics) wholesaling

Cross-References. Establishments primarily engaged in—

- Wholesaling janitorial and automotive chemicals—are classified in Industry 422690, Other Chemical and Allied Products Wholesalers; and

- Wholesaling piece goods, fabrics, yarns, thread and other notions—are classified in Industry 422310, Piece Goods, Notions, and Other Dry Goods Wholesalers.

42186 Transportation Equipment and Supplies (except Motor Vehicle) Wholesalers[US]

See industry description for 421860 below.

421860 Transportation Equipment and Supplies (except Motor Vehicle) Wholesalers[US]

This industry comprises establishments primarily engaged in wholesaling transportation equipment and supplies (except marine pleasure craft and motor vehicles).

Illustrative Examples:

Aircraft wholesaling
Motorized passenger golf carts wholesaling

Railroad cars wholesaling
Ships wholesaling

Cross-References. Establishments primarily engaged in—

- Wholesaling motor vehicles and motor vehicle parts—are classified in Industry Group 4211, Motor Vehicle and Motor Vehicle Parts and Supplies Wholesalers; and

- Wholesaling marine pleasure craft—are classified in Industry 421910, Sporting and Recreational Goods and Supplies Wholesalers.

4219 Miscellaneous Durable Goods Wholesalers[US]

This industry group comprises establishments primarily engaged in wholesaling sporting, recreational, toy, hobby, and jewelry goods and supplies, and precious stones and metals.

US—United States industry only. CAN—United States and Canadian industries are comparable. When neither US nor CAN appears, Canadian, Mexican, and United States industries are comparable.

http://www.ntis.gov/naics

42191 Sporting and Recreational Goods and Supplies Wholesalers[US]
See industry description for 421910 below.

421910 Sporting and Recreational Goods and Supplies Wholesalers[US]

This industry comprises establishments primarily engaged in wholesaling sporting goods and accessories; billiard and pool supplies; sporting firearms and ammunition; and/or marine pleasure craft, equipment, and supplies.

Cross-References. Establishments primarily engaged in—

- Wholesaling motor vehicles and trailers—are classified in Industry 421110, Automobile and Other Motor Vehicle Wholesalers;

- Wholesaling motorized passenger golf carts—are classified in Industry 421860, Transportation Equipment and Supplies (except Motor Vehicle) Wholesalers;

- Wholesaling athletic apparel—are classified in Industry Group 4223, Apparel, Piece Goods, and Notions Wholesalers; and

- Wholesaling athletic footwear—are classified in Industry 422340, Footwear Wholesalers.

42192 Toy and Hobby Goods and Supplies Wholesalers[US]
See industry description for 421920 below.

421920 Toy and Hobby Goods and Supplies Wholesalers[US]

This industry comprises establishments primarily engaged in wholesaling games, toys, fireworks, playing cards, hobby goods and supplies, and/or related goods.

42193 Recyclable Material Wholesalers[US]
See industry description for 421930 below.

421930 Recyclable Material Wholesalers[US]

This industry comprises establishments primarily engaged in wholesaling scrap from automotive, industrial, and other recyclable materials. Included in this industry are auto wreckers primarily engaged in dismantling motor vehicles for the purpose of wholesaling scrap.

Cross-References. Establishments primarily engaged in—

- Dismantling motor vehicles for the purpose of selling used parts—are classified in Industry 421140, Motor Vehicle Parts (Used) Wholesalers; and

- Operating facilities for separating and sorting recyclable materials—are classified in Industry 562920, Materials Recovery Facilities.

US—United States industry only. CAN—United States and Canadian industries are comparable. When neither US nor CAN appears, Canadian, Mexican, and United States industries are comparable.

42194 Jewelry, Watch, Precious Stone, and Precious Metal Wholesalers^{US}

See industry description for 421940 below.

421940 Jewelry, Watch, Precious Stone, and Precious Metal Wholesalers^{US}

This industry comprises establishments primarily engaged in wholesaling jewelry, precious and semiprecious stones, precious metals and metal flatware, costume jewelry, watches, clocks, silverware, and/or jewelers' findings.

Cross-References. Establishments primarily engaged in—

- Wholesaling precious metal ores or concentrates—are classified in Industry 421520, Coal and Other Mineral and Ore Wholesalers; and

- Wholesaling nonprecious flatware—are classified in Industry 421220, Home Furnishing Wholesalers.

42199 Other Miscellaneous Durable Goods Wholesalers^{US}

See industry description for 421990 below.

421990 Other Miscellaneous Durable Goods Wholesalers^{US}

This industry comprises establishments primarily engaged in wholesaling durable goods (except motor vehicle and motor vehicle parts and supplies; furniture and home furnishings; lumber and other construction materials; professional and commercial equipment and supplies; metals and minerals (except petroleum); electrical goods; hardware, and plumbing and heating equipment and supplies; machinery, equipment and supplies; sporting and recreational goods and supplies; toy and hobby goods and supplies; recyclable materials; and jewelry, watches, precious stones and precious metals).

Illustrative Examples:

Musical instruments wholesaling
Phonograph records wholesaling
Prerecorded audio and video cassettes
  wholesaling
Prerecorded audio and video tapes and discs
  wholesaling

Prerecorded compact discs (CDs) wholesaling
Timber and timber products (except lumber)
  wholesaling

Cross-References. Establishments primarily engaged in—

- Wholesaling automobiles and other motor vehicles, motor vehicle supplies, tires, and new and used parts—are classified in Industry Group 4211, Motor Vehicle and Motor Vehicle Parts and Supplies Wholesalers;

- Wholesaling furniture and home furnishings—are classified in Industry Group 4212, Furniture and Home Furnishing Wholesalers;

US—United States industry only. CAN—United States and Canadian industries are comparable. When neither US nor CAN appears, Canadian, Mexican, and United States industries are comparable.

http://www.ntis.gov/naics

- Wholesaling lumber, plywood, millwork, wood panels, brick, stone, roofing, siding, and other nonelectrical construction materials—are classified in Industry Group 4213, Lumber and Other Construction Materials Wholesalers;

- Wholesaling photographic; office; computer and computer peripheral; medical, dental, hospital, ophthalmic; and other commercial and professional equipment and supplies—are classified in Industry Group 4214, Professional and Commercial Equipment and Supplies Wholesalers;

- Wholesaling coal and other minerals and ores and semifinished metal products—are classified in Industry Group 4215, Metal and Mineral (except Petroleum) Wholesalers;

- Wholesaling electrical goods—are classified in Industry Group 4216, Electrical Goods Wholesalers;

- Wholesaling hardware, and plumbing, heating, air conditioning, and refrigeration equipment and supplies—are classified in Industry Group 4217, Hardware, and Plumbing and Heating Equipment and Supplies Wholesalers;

- Wholesaling construction, mining, farm, garden, industrial, service establishment, and transportation machinery, equipment and supplies—are classified in Industry Group 4218, Machinery, Equipment, and Supplies Wholesalers;

- Wholesaling sporting goods and accessories; billiard and pool supplies; sporting firearms and ammunition; and/or marine pleasure craft, equipment, and supplies—are classified in Industry 421910, Sporting and Recreational Goods and Supplies Wholesalers;

- Wholesaling toys, fireworks, playing cards, hobby goods and supplies and/or related goods—are classified in Industry 421920, Toy and Hobby Goods and Supplies Wholesalers;

- Wholesaling automotive, industrial, and other recyclable materials—are classified in Industry 421930, Recyclable Material Wholesalers; and

- Wholesaling jewelry, precious and semiprecious stones, precious metals and metal flatware, costume jewelry, watches, clocks, silverware, and/or jewelers' findings—are classified in Industry 421940, Jewelry, Watch, Precious Stone, and Precious Metal Wholesalers.

422 Wholesale Trade, Nondurable Goods[US]

Industries in the Wholesale Trade, Nondurable Goods subsector sell or arrange the purchase or sale of nondurable goods to other businesses. Nondurable goods are items generally with a normal life expectancy of less than three years. Nondurable goods wholesale trade establishments are engaged in wholesaling products, such as paper and paper products, chemicals and chemical products, drugs, textiles and textile products, apparel, footwear, groceries, farm products, petroleum and petroleum products, alcoholic beverages, books, magazines, newspapers, flowers and nursery stock, and tobacco products.

US—United States industry only. CAN—United States and Canadian industries are comparable. When neither US nor CAN appears, Canadian, Mexican, and United States industries are comparable.

The detailed industries within the subsector are organized in the classification structure based on the products sold. Within an industry, the types of establishments may vary, including wholesale merchants and/or agents and brokers.

4221 Paper and Paper Product Wholesalers[US]

42211 Printing and Writing Paper Wholesalers[US]
See industry description for 422110 below.

422110 Printing and Writing Paper Wholesalers[US]

This industry comprises establishments primarily engaged in wholesaling bulk printing and/or writing paper generally on rolls for further processing.

Illustrative Examples:

Bulk envelope paper wholesaling
Bulk groundwood paper wholesaling

Bulk paper (e.g., fine, printing, writing)
  wholesaling

Cross-References.

Establishments primarily engaged in wholesaling stationery are classified in Industry 422120, Stationery and Office Supplies Wholesalers.

42212 Stationery and Office Supplies Wholesalers[US]
See industry description for 422120 below.

422120 Stationery and Office Supplies Wholesalers[US]

This industry comprises establishments primarily engaged in wholesaling stationery, office supplies and/or gift wrap.

Illustrative Examples:

Computer paper supplies wholesaling
Envelopes wholesaling
File cards and folders wholesaling
Greeting cards wholesaling
Pencils wholesaling

Photocopy supplies wholesaling
Social stationery wholesaling
Typewriter paper wholesaling
Writing pens wholesaling

Cross-References.

Establishments primarily engaged in wholesaling bulk printing and/or writing paper are classified in Industry 422110, Printing and Writing Paper Wholesalers.

US—United States industry only. CAN—United States and Canadian industries are comparable. When neither US nor CAN appears, Canadian, Mexican, and United States industries are comparable.

42213 Industrial and Personal Service Paper Wholesalers[US]
See industry description for 422130 below.

422130 Industrial and Personal Service Paper Wholesalers[US]

This industry comprises establishments primarily engaged in wholesaling wrapping and other coarse paper, paperboard, converted paper (except stationery and office supplies), and/or related disposable plastics products.

Illustrative Examples:

Disposable plastics eating utensils wholesaling
Paper and disposable plastics dishes
  wholesaling
Paper and disposable plastics shipping
  supplies wholesaling
Paper bags wholesaling

Paper napkins wholesaling
Paperboard and disposable plastics boxes
  wholesaling
Plastics bags wholesaling
Sanitary paper products wholesaling

Cross-References.

Establishments primarily engaged in stationery, office supplies, and/or gift wrap are classified in Industry 422120, Stationery and Office Supplies Wholesalers.

4222 Drugs and Druggists' Sundries Wholesalers[US]

42221 Drugs and Druggists' Sundries Wholesalers[US]
See industry description for 422210 below.

422210 Drugs and Druggists' Sundries Wholesalers[US]

This industry comprises establishments primarily engaged in wholesaling biological and medical products; botanical drugs and herbs; and pharmaceutical products intended for internal and external consumption in such forms as ampoules, tablets, capsules, vials, ointments, powders, solutions, and suspensions.

Illustrative Examples:

Antibiotics wholesaling
Blood derivatives wholesaling
Botanicals wholesaling
Cosmetics wholesaling

Endocrine substances wholesaling
In vitro- and in-vivo diagnostics wholesaling
Vaccines wholesaling
Vitamins wholesaling

US—United States industry only. CAN—United States and Canadian industries are comparable. When neither US nor CAN appears, Canadian, Mexican, and United States industries are comparable.

Cross-References.

Establishments primarily engaged in wholesaling surgical, dental, and hospital equipment are classified in Industry 421450, Medical, Dental, and Hospital Equipment and Supplies Wholesalers.

4223 Apparel, Piece Goods, and Notions Wholesalers^{US}

42231 Piece Goods, Notions, and Other Dry Goods Wholesalers^{US}
See industry description for 422310 below.

422310 Piece Goods, Notions, and Other Dry Goods Wholesalers^{US}

This industry comprises establishments primarily engaged in wholesaling piece goods, fabrics, yarns, thread and other notions, and/or hair accessories.

Cross-References.

Establishments primarily engaged as converters who buy fabric goods in the grey, have them finished on a contract basis, and sell at wholesale are classified in Industry 31331, Textile and Fabric Finishing Mills.

42232 Men's and Boys' Clothing and Furnishings Wholesalers^{US}
See industry description for 422320 below.

422320 Men's and Boys' Clothing and Furnishings Wholesalers^{US}

This industry comprises establishments primarily engaged in wholesaling men's and/or boys' clothing and furnishings.

Illustrative Examples:

Men's and boys' hosiery wholesaling	Men's and boys' suits wholesaling
Men's and boys' nightwear wholesaling	Men's and boys' underwear wholesaling
Men's and boys' sportswear wholesaling	Men's and boys' work clothing wholesaling

Cross-References.

Establishments primarily engaged in wholesaling unisex clothing and men's fur clothing are classified in Industry 422330, Women's, Children's, and Infants' Clothing and Accessories Wholesalers.

42233 Women's, Children's, and Infants' Clothing and Accessories Wholesalers^{US}
See industry description for 422330 below.

422330 Women's, Children's, and Infants' Clothing and Accessories Wholesalers^{US}

This industry comprises establishments primarily engaged in wholesaling (1) women's, children's, infants', and/or unisex clothing and accessories and/or (2) fur clothing.

US—United States industry only. CAN—United States and Canadian industries are comparable. When neither US nor CAN appears, Canadian, Mexican, and United States industries are comparable.

http://www.ntis.gov/naics

Illustrative Examples:

Dresses wholesaling
Fur clothing wholesaling
Lingerie wholesaling

Millinery wholesaling
Women's, children's, and infants' hosiery
  wholesaling

42234 Footwear Wholesalers[US]
See industry description for 422340 below.

422340 Footwear Wholesalers[US]

This industry comprises establishments primarily engaged in wholesaling footwear (including athletic) of leather, rubber, and other materials.

4224 Grocery and Related Product Wholesalers[US]

42241 General Line Grocery Wholesalers[US]
See industry description for 422410 below.

422410 General Line Grocery Wholesalers[US]

This industry comprises establishments primarily engaged in wholesaling a general line (wide range) of groceries.

Cross-References.

Establishments primarily engaged in wholesaling a specialized line of groceries are classified according to the product sold.

42242 Packaged Frozen Food Wholesalers[US]
See industry description for 422420 below.

422420 Packaged Frozen Food Wholesalers[US]

This industry comprises establishments primarily engaged in wholesaling packaged frozen foods (except dairy products).

Illustrative Examples:

Frozen bakery products wholesaling
Frozen juices wholesaling
Frozen vegetables wholesaling

Packaged frozen fish wholesaling
Packaged frozen meats wholesaling
Packaged frozen poultry wholesaling

Cross-References.

Establishments primarily engaged in wholesaling frozen dairy products are classified in Industry 422430, Dairy Product (except Dried or Canned) Wholesalers.

US—United States industry only. CAN—United States and Canadian industries are comparable. When neither US nor CAN appears, Canadian, Mexican, and United States industries are comparable.

42243 Dairy Product (except Dried or Canned) Wholesalers^{US}

See industry description for 422430 below.

422430 Dairy Product (except Dried or Canned) Wholesalers^{US}

This industry comprises establishments primarily engaged in wholesaling dairy products (except dried or canned).

Illustrative Examples:

Butter wholesaling	Fluid milk (except canned) wholesaling
Cheese wholesaling	Ice cream and ices wholesaling
Cream wholesaling	Yogurt wholesaling

Cross-References. Establishments primarily engaged in—

- Wholesaling dried or canned dairy products and dairy substitutes—are classified in Industry 422490, Other Grocery and Related Products Wholesalers; and

- Pasteurizing and bottling milk—are classified in U.S. Industry 311511, Fluid Milk Manufacturing.

42244 Poultry and Poultry Product Wholesalers^{US}

See industry description for 422440 below.

422440 Poultry and Poultry Product Wholesalers^{US}

This industry comprises establishments primarily engaged in wholesaling poultry and/or poultry products (except canned and packaged frozen).

Cross-References. Establishments primarily engaged in—

- Wholesaling packaged frozen poultry—are classified in Industry 422420, Packaged Frozen Food Wholesalers;

- Wholesaling canned poultry—are classified in Industry 422490, Other Grocery and Related Products Wholesalers; and

- Slaughtering and dressing poultry—are classified in U.S. Industry 311615, Poultry Processing.

42245 Confectionery Wholesalers^{US}

See industry description for 422450 below.

422450 Confectionery Wholesalers^{US}

This industry comprises establishments primarily engaged in wholesaling confectioneries; salted or roasted nuts; popcorn; potato, corn, and similar chips; and/or fountain fruits and syrups.

US—United States industry only. CAN—United States and Canadian industries are comparable. When neither US nor CAN appears, Canadian, Mexican, and United States industries are comparable.

http://www.ntis.gov/naics

Cross-References. Establishments primarily engaged in—

- Wholesaling frozen pretzels—are classified in Industry 422420, Packaged Frozen Food Wholesalers; and

- Wholesaling pretzels (except frozen)—are classified in Industry 422490, Other Grocery and Related Products Wholesalers.

42246 Fish and Seafood Wholesalers[US]
See industry description for 422460 below.

422460 Fish and Seafood Wholesalers[US]

This industry comprises establishments primarily engaged in wholesaling fish and seafood (except canned or packaged frozen).

Cross-References. Establishments primarily engaged in—

- Wholesaling packaged frozen fish and seafood—are classified in Industry 422420, Packaged Frozen Food Wholesalers;

- Wholesaling canned fish and seafood—are classified in Industry 422490, Other Grocery and Related Products Wholesalers; and

- Canning, smoking, salting, drying, or freezing seafood and shucking and packing fresh shellfish—are classified in Industry 31171, Seafood Product Preparation and Packaging.

42247 Meat and Meat Product Wholesalers[US]
See industry description for 422470 below.

422470 Meat and Meat Product Wholesalers[US]

This industry comprises establishments primarily engaged in wholesaling meats and meat products (except canned and packaged frozen) and/or lard.

Cross-References. Establishments primarily engaged in—

- Wholesaling packaged frozen meats—are classified in Industry 422420, Packaged Frozen Food Wholesalers;

- Wholesaling canned meats—are classified in Industry 422490, Other Grocery and Related Products Wholesalers; and

- Preparing boxed beef—are classified in U.S. Industry 311612, Meat Processed from Carcasses.

42248 Fresh Fruit and Vegetable Wholesalers[US]
See industry description for 422480 below.

422480 Fresh Fruit and Vegetable Wholesalers[US]

This industry comprises establishments primarily engaged in wholesaling fresh fruits and vegetables.

US—United States industry only. CAN—United States and Canadian industries are comparable. When neither US nor CAN appears, Canadian, Mexican, and United States industries are comparable.

42249 Other Grocery and Related Products Wholesalers[US]

See industry description for 422490 below.

422490 Other Grocery and Related Products Wholesalers[US]

This industry comprises establishments primarily engaged in wholesaling groceries and related products (except a general line of groceries; packaged frozen food; dairy products (except dried and canned); poultry products (except canned); confectioneries; fish and seafood (except canned); meat products (except canned); and fresh fruits and vegetables). Included in this industry are establishments primarily engaged in bottling and wholesaling spring and mineral waters processed by others.

Illustrative Examples:

Bakery products (except frozen) wholesaling	Canned seafood wholesaling
Canned fish wholesaling	Canned vegetables wholesaling
Canned fruits wholesaling	Dried milk wholesaling
Canned meats wholesaling	Soft drinks wholesaling
Canned milk wholesaling	

Cross-References. Establishments primarily engaged in—

- Wholesaling grains, field beans, livestock, and other farm product raw materials—are classified in Industry Group 4225, Farm Product Raw Material Wholesalers;

- Wholesaling beer, wine, and distilled alcoholic beverages—are classified in Industry Group 4228, Beer, Wine, and Distilled Alcoholic Beverage Wholesalers;

- Bottling soft drinks—are classified in Industry 31211, Soft Drink and Ice Manufacturing;

- Wholesaling a general line of groceries—are classified in Industry 422410, General Line Grocery Wholesalers;

- Wholesaling packaged frozen foods (except dairy)—are classified in Industry 422420, Packaged Frozen Food Wholesalers;

- Wholesaling dairy products—are classified in Industry 422430, Dairy Products (except Dried or Canned) Wholesalers;

- Wholesaling poultry and poultry products (except canned and packaged frozen)—are classified in Industry 422440, Poultry and Poultry Product Wholesalers;

- Wholesaling confectioneries; salted or roasted nuts; popcorn; potato, corn, and similar chips; and/or fountain fruits and syrups—are classified in Industry 422450, Confectionery Wholesalers;

- Wholesaling fish and seafoods (except canned and packaged frozen)—are classified in Industry 422460, Fish and Seafood Wholesalers;

- Wholesaling meats (except canned and packaged frozen)—are classified in Industry 422470, Meat and Meat Product Wholesalers;

US—United States industry only. CAN—United States and Canadian industries are comparable. When neither US nor CAN appears, Canadian, Mexican, and United States industries are comparable.

- Wholesaling fresh fruits and vegetables—are classified in Industry 422480, Fresh Fruit and Vegetable Wholesalers; and

- Roasting coffee—are classified in Industry 311920, Coffee and Tea Manufacturing.

4225 Farm Product Raw Material Wholesalers[US]

This industry group comprises establishments primarily engaged in wholesaling agricultural products (except raw milk, live poultry, and fresh fruit and vegetables), such as grains, field beans, livestock, and other farm product raw materials (excluding seeds).

42251 Grain and Field Bean Wholesalers[US]
See industry description for 422510 below.

422510 Grain and Field Bean Wholesalers[US]

This industry comprises establishments primarily engaged in wholesaling grains, such as corn, wheat, oats, barley, and unpolished rice; dry beans; and soybeans and other inedible beans. Included in this industry are establishments primarily engaged in operating country or terminal grain elevators primarily for the purpose of wholesaling.

Cross-References. Establishments primarily engaged in—

- Wholesaling field and garden seeds—are classified in Industry 422910, Farm Supplies Wholesalers; and

- Operating grain elevators for storage only—are classified in Industry 493130, Farm Product Warehousing and Storage.

42252 Livestock Wholesalers[US]
See industry description for 422520 below.

422520 Livestock Wholesalers[US]

This industry comprises establishments primarily engaged in wholesaling livestock (except horses and mules).

Illustrative Examples:

Cattle wholesaling   Hogs wholesaling
Goats wholesaling   Sheep wholesaling

Cross-References.

Establishments primarily engaged in wholesaling horses and mules are classified in Industry 422590, Other Farm Product Raw Material Wholesalers.

US—United States industry only. CAN—United States and Canadian industries are comparable. When neither US nor CAN appears, Canadian, Mexican, and United States industries are comparable.

42259 Other Farm Product Raw Material Wholesalers^{US}

See industry description for 422590 below.

422590 Other Farm Product Raw Material Wholesalers^{US}

This industry comprises establishments primarily engaged in wholesaling farm products (except grain and field beans, livestock, raw milk, live poultry, and fresh fruits and vegetables).

Illustrative Examples:

Chicks wholesaling	Mules wholesaling
Hides wholesaling	Raw cotton wholesaling
Horses wholesaling	Raw pelts wholesaling
Leaf tobacco wholesaling	

Cross-References. Establishments primarily engaged in—

- Wholesaling raw milk—are classified in Industry 422430, Dairy Product (except Dried or Canned) Wholesalers;

- Wholesaling live poultry (except chicks)—are classified in Industry 422440, Poultry and Poultry Product Wholesalers;

- Wholesaling grain, dry beans, and soybeans and other inedible beans—are classified in Industry 422510, Grain and Field Bean Wholesalers;

- Wholesaling livestock (except horses and mules), such as cattle, hogs, sheep, and goats,— are classified in Industry 422520, Livestock Wholesalers; and

- Wholesaling fresh fruits and vegetables—are classified in Industry 422480, Fresh Fruit and Vegetable Wholesalers.

4226 Chemical and Allied Products Wholesalers^{US}

This industry group comprises establishments primarily engaged in wholesaling chemicals; plastics materials and basic forms and shapes; and allied products.

42261 Plastics Materials and Basic Forms and Shapes Wholesalers^{US}

See industry description for 422610 below.

422610 Plastics Materials and Basic Forms and Shapes Wholesalers^{US}

This industry comprises establishments primarily engaged in wholesaling plastics materials and resins, and unsupported plastics film, sheet, sheeting, rod, tube, and other basic forms and shapes.

US—United States industry only. CAN—United States and Canadian industries are comparable. When neither US nor CAN appears, Canadian, Mexican, and United States industries are comparable.

42269 Other Chemical and Allied Products Wholesalers[US]

See industry description for 422690 below.

422690 Other Chemical and Allied Products Wholesalers[US]

This industry comprises establishments primarily engaged in wholesaling chemicals and allied products (except agricultural and medicinal chemicals, paints and varnishes, fireworks, and plastics materials and basic forms and shapes).

Illustrative Examples:

Acids wholesaling
Automotive chemicals (except lubricating oils and greases) wholesaling
Dyestuffs wholesaling
Explosives (except ammunition and fireworks) wholesaling

Industrial chemicals wholesaling
Industrial salts wholesaling
Rosins wholesaling
Turpentine wholesaling

Cross-References. Establishments primarily engaged in—

- Wholesaling ammunition—are classified in Industry Group 4219, Miscellaneous Durable Goods Wholesalers;

- Wholesaling biological and medical products; botanical drugs and herbs; and pharmaceutical products intended for internal and external consumption in such forms as ampoules, tablets, capsules, vials, ointments, powders, solutions, and suspensions—are classified in Industry 422210, Drugs and Druggists' Sundries Wholesalers;

- Wholesaling farm supplies, such as animal feeds, fertilizers, agricultural chemicals, pesticides, seeds and plant bulbs,—are classified in Industry 422910, Farm Supplies Wholesalers;

- Wholesaling paints, and varnishes and similar coatings, pigments, wallpaper, and supplies, such as paint brushes and rollers,—are classified in Industry 422950, Paint, Varnish and Supplies Wholesalers;

- Wholesaling lubricating oils and greases—are classified in Industry 422720, Petroleum and Petroleum Products Wholesalers (except Bulk Stations and Terminals);

- Wholesaling fireworks—are classified in Industry 421920, Toy and Hobby Goods and Supplies Wholesalers; and

- Wholesaling plastics materials and resins, and unsupported plastics film, sheet, sheeting, rod, tube, and other basic forms and shapes—are classified in Industry 422610, Plastics Materials and Basic Forms and Shapes Wholesalers.

4227 Petroleum and Petroleum Products Wholesalers[US]

42271 Petroleum Bulk Stations and Terminals[US]

See industry description for 422710 below.

422710 Petroleum Bulk Stations and Terminals[US]

This industry comprises establishments with bulk liquid storage facilities primarily engaged in wholesaling crude petroleum and petroleum products, including liquefied petroleum gas.

US—United States industry only. CAN—United States and Canadian industries are comparable. When neither US nor CAN appears, Canadian, Mexican, and United States industries are comparable.

Cross-References.

Establishments primarily engaged in bulk storage of petroleum are classified in Industry 493190, Other Warehousing and Storage.

42272 Petroleum and Petroleum Products Wholesalers (except Bulk Stations and Terminals)[US]
See industry description for 422720 below.

422720 Petroleum and Petroleum Products Wholesalers (except Bulk Stations and Terminals)[US]

This industry comprises establishments primarily engaged in wholesaling petroleum and petroleum products (except from bulk liquid storage facilities).

Illustrative Examples:

Bottled liquid petroleum gas wholesaling
Fuel oil wholesaling (except bulk stations, terminals)
Gasoline wholesaling (except bulk stations, terminals)

Lubricating oil and grease wholesaling (except bulk stations, terminals)

Cross-References.

Establishments primarily engaged in wholesaling crude petroleum and petroleum products from bulk liquid storage facilities are classified in Industry 422710, Petroleum Bulk Stations and Terminals.

4228 Beer, Wine, and Distilled Alcoholic Beverage Wholesalers[US]

42281 Beer and Ale Wholesalers[US]
See industry description for 422810 below.

422810 Beer and Ale Wholesalers[US]

This industry comprises establishments primarily engaged in wholesaling beer, ale, porter, and other fermented malt beverages.

42282 Wine and Distilled Alcoholic Beverage Wholesalers[US]
See industry description for 422820 below.

422820 Wine and Distilled Alcoholic Beverage Wholesalers[US]

This industry comprises establishments primarily engaged in wholesaling wine, distilled alcoholic beverages, and/or neutral spirits and ethyl alcohol used in blended wines and distilled liquors.

US—United States industry only. CAN—United States and Canadian industries are comparable. When neither US nor CAN appears, Canadian, Mexican, and United States industries are comparable.

4229 Miscellaneous Nondurable Goods Wholesalers^{US}

This industry group comprises establishments primarily engaged in wholesaling nondurable goods, such as farm supplies; books, periodicals and newspapers; flowers; nursery stock; paints; varnishes; tobacco and tobacco products; and other miscellaneous nondurable goods, such as cut Christmas trees and pet supplies.

42291 Farm Supplies Wholesalers^{US}
See industry description for 422910 below.

422910 Farm Supplies Wholesalers^{US}

This industry comprises establishments primarily engaged in wholesaling farm supplies, such as animal feeds, fertilizers, agricultural chemicals, pesticides, plant seeds, and plant bulbs.

Cross-References. Establishments primarily engaged in—

- Wholesaling pet food—are classified in Industry 422490, Other Grocery and Related Products Wholesalers;

- Wholesaling grains—are classified in Industry 422510, Grain and Field Bean Wholesalers;

- Wholesaling pet supplies—are classified in Industry 422990, Other Miscellaneous Nondurable Goods Wholesalers; and

- Wholesaling nursery stock (except seeds and plant bulbs)—are classified in Industry 422930, Flower, Nursery Stock and Florists' Supplies Wholesalers.

42292 Book, Periodical, and Newspaper Wholesalers^{US}
See industry description for 422920 below.

422920 Book, Periodical, and Newspaper Wholesalers^{US}

This industry comprises establishments primarily engaged in wholesaling books, periodicals, and newspapers.

42293 Flower, Nursery Stock, and Florists' Supplies Wholesalers^{US}
See industry description for 422930 below.

422930 Flower, Nursery Stock, and Florists' Supplies Wholesalers^{US}

This industry comprises establishments primarily engaged in wholesaling flowers, florists' supplies, and/or nursery stock (except seeds and plant bulbs).

Cross-References. Establishments primarily engaged in—

- Wholesaling cut Christmas trees—are classified in Industry 422990, Other Miscellaneous Nondurable Goods Wholesalers; and

---

US—United States industry only. CAN—United States and Canadian industries are comparable. When neither US nor CAN appears, Canadian, Mexican, and United States industries are comparable.

• Wholesaling plant seeds and plant bulbs—are classified in Industry 422910, Farm Supplies Wholesalers.

42294 Tobacco and Tobacco Product Wholesalers[US]

See industry description for 422940 below.

422940 Tobacco and Tobacco Product Wholesalers[US]

This industry comprises establishments primarily engaged in wholesaling tobacco products, such as cigarettes, snuff, cigars, and pipe tobacco.

Cross-References.

Establishments primarily engaged in wholesaling leaf tobacco are classified in Industry 422590, Other Farm Product Raw Material Wholesalers.

42295 Paint, Varnish, and Supplies Wholesalers[US]

See industry description for 422950 below.

422950 Paint, Varnish, and Supplies Wholesalers[US]

This industry comprises establishments primarily engaged in wholesaling paints, varnishes, and similar coatings; pigments; wallpaper; and supplies, such as paint brushes and rollers.

Cross-References.

Establishments primarily engaged in wholesaling artists' paints are classified in Industry 422990, Other Miscellaneous Nondurable Goods Wholesalers.

42299 Other Miscellaneous Nondurable Goods Wholesalers[US]

See industry description for 422990 below.

422990 Other Miscellaneous Nondurable Goods Wholesalers[US]

This industry comprises establishments primarily engaged in wholesaling nondurable goods (except printing and writing paper; stationery and office supplies; industrial and personal service paper; drugs and druggists' sundries; apparel, piece goods, and notions; grocery and related products; farm product raw materials; chemical and allied products; petroleum and petroleum products; beer, wine, and distilled alcoholic beverages; farm supplies; books, periodicals and newspapers; flower, nursery stock and florists' supplies; tobacco and tobacco products; and paint, varnishes, wallpaper, and supplies).

Illustrative Examples:

Artists' supplies wholesaling
Burlap wholesaling
Christmas trees wholesaling
Pet supplies (except pet food) wholesaling

Statuary goods (except religious) wholesaling
Textile bags wholesaling
Yarn wholesaling

Cross-References. Establishments primarily engaged in—

- Wholesaling advertising specialties—are classified in Industry 541870, Advertising Material Distribution Services;

- Wholesaling farm supplies—are classified in Industry 422910, Farm Supplies Wholesalers;

- Wholesaling books, periodicals, and newspapers—are classified in Industry 422920, Book, Periodical, and Newspaper Wholesalers;

- Wholesaling flowers, nursery stock, and florists' supplies—are classified in Industry 422930, Flower, Nursery Stock, and Florists' Supplies Wholesalers;

- Wholesaling tobacco and its products—are classified in Industry 422940, Tobacco and Tobacco Product Wholesalers;

- Wholesaling paints, varnishes, and similar coatings; pigments; wallpaper; and supplies— are classified in Industry 422950, Paint, Varnish, and Supplies Wholesalers;

- Wholesaling bulk printing and/or writing paper—are classified in Industry 422110, Printing and Writing Paper Wholesalers;

- Wholesaling stationery, office supplies, and/or gift wrap—are classified in Industry 422120, Stationery and Office Supplies Wholesalers;

- Wholesaling wrapping and other coarse paper, paperboard, converted paper (except stationery and office supplies), and related disposable plastics products—are classified in Industry 422130, Industrial and Personal Service Paper Wholesalers;

- Wholesaling biological and medical products; botanical drugs and herbs; and pharmaceutical products intended for internal and external consumption—are classified in Industry 422210, Drugs and Druggists' Sundries Wholesalers;

- Wholesaling clothing and accessories, footwear, piece goods, yard goods, notions, and/or hair accessories—are classified in Industry Group 4223, Apparel, Piece Goods, and Notions Wholesalers;

- Wholesaling meat, poultry, seafood, confectioneries, fruits and vegetables; and other groceries—are related products are classified in Industry Group 4224, Grocery and Related Product Wholesalers;

- Wholesaling grains, field beans, livestock, and other farm product raw materials—are classified in Industry Group 4225, Farm Product Raw Material Wholesalers;

- Wholesaling chemicals; plastics materials and basic forms and shapes; and allied products— are classified in Industry Group 4226, Chemical and Allied Products Wholesalers;

- Wholesaling petroleum and petroleum products—are classified in Industry Group 4227, Petroleum and Petroleum Products Wholesalers;

- Wholesaling beer, ale, wine, and distilled alcoholic beverages—are classified Industry Group 4228, Beer, Wine, and Distilled Alcoholic Beverage Wholesalers;

US—United States industry only. CAN—United States and Canadian industries are comparable. When neither US nor CAN appears, Canadian, Mexican, and United States industries are comparable.

- Wholesaling pet foods—are classified in Industry 422490, Other Grocery and Related Products Wholesalers; and

- Wholesaling religious statuaries—are classified in Industry 421990, Other Miscellaneous Durable Goods Wholesalers.

Sector 44-45—Retail Trade

The Sector as a Whole

The Retail Trade sector comprises establishments engaged in retailing merchandise, generally without transformation, and rendering services incidental to the sale of merchandise.

The retailing process is the final step in the distribution of merchandise; retailers are, therefore, organized to sell merchandise in small quantities to the general public. This sector comprises two main types of retailers: store and nonstore retailers.

1. Store retailers operate fixed point-of-sale locations, located and designed to attract a high volume of walk-in customers. In general, retail stores have extensive displays of merchandise and use mass-media advertising to attract customers. They typically sell merchandise to the general public for personal or household consumption, but some also serve business and institutional clients. These include establishments, such as office supply stores, computer and software stores, building materials dealers, plumbing supply stores, and electrical supply stores. Catalog showrooms, gasoline services stations, automotive dealers, and mobile home dealers are treated as store retailers.

   In addition to retailing merchandise, some types of store retailers are also engaged in the provision of after-sales services, such as repair and installation. For example, new automobile dealers, electronic and appliance stores, and musical instrument and supply stores often provide repair services. As a general rule, establishments engaged in retailing merchandise and providing after-sales services are classified in this sector.

   The first eleven subsectors of retail trade are store retailers. The establishments are grouped into industries and industry groups typically based on one or more of the following criteria:

   (a) The merchandise line or lines carried by the store; for example, specialty stores are distinguished from general-line stores.

   (b) The usual trade designation of the establishments. This criterion applies in cases where a store type is well recognized by the industry and the public, but difficult to define strictly in terms of commodity lines carried; for example, pharmacies, hardware stores, and department stores.

   (c) Capital requirements in terms of display equipment; for example, food stores have equipment requirements not found in other retail industries.

   (d) Human resource requirements in terms of expertise; for example, the staff of an automobile dealer requires knowledge in financing, registering, and licensing issues that are not necessary in other retail industries.

2. Nonstore retailers, like store retailers, are organized to serve the general public, but their retailing methods differ. The establishments of this subsector reach customers and market merchandise with methods, such as the broadcasting of "infomercials," the broadcasting and publishing of direct-response advertising, the publishing of paper and electronic catalogs, door-to-door solicitation, in-home demonstration, selling from portable stalls (street vendors, except

---

US—United States industry only. CAN—United States and Canadian industries are comparable. When neither US nor CAN appears, Canadian, Mexican, and United States industries are comparable.

http://www.ntis.gov/naics

food), and distribution through vending machines. Establishments engaged in the direct sale (nonstore) of products, such as home heating oil dealers and home delivery newspaper routes.

The buying of goods for resale is a characteristic of retail trade establishments that particularly distinguishes them from establishments in the agriculture, manufacturing, and construction industries. For example, farms that sell their products at or from the point of production are not classified in retail, but rather in agriculture. Similarly, establishments that both manufacture and sell their products to the general public are not classified in retail, but rather in manufacturing. However, establishments that engage in processing activities incidental to retailing are classified in retail. This includes establishments, such as optical goods stores that do in-store grinding of lenses, and meat and seafood markets.

Wholesalers also engage in the buying of goods for resale, but they are not usually organized to serve the general public. They typically operate from a warehouse or office and neither the design nor the location of these premises is intended to solicit a high volume of walk-in traffic. Wholesalers supply institutional, industrial, wholesale, and retail clients; their operations are, therefore, generally organized to purchase, sell, and deliver merchandise in larger quantities. However, dealers of durable nonconsumer goods, such as farm machinery and heavy duty trucks, are included in wholesale trade even if they often sell these products in single units.

441 Motor Vehicle and Parts Dealers[CAN]

Industries in the Motor Vehicle and Parts Dealers subsector retail motor vehicle and parts merchandise from fixed point-of-sale locations. Establishments in this subsector typically operate from a showroom and/or an open lot where the vehicles are on display. The display of vehicles and the related parts require little by way of display equipment. The personnel generally include both the sales and sales support staff familiar with the requirements for registering and financing a vehicle as well as a staff of parts experts and mechanics trained to provide repair and maintenance services for the vehicles. Specific industries have been included in this subsector to identify the type of vehicle being retailed.

Sales of capital or durable nonconsumer goods, such as medium and heavy-duty trucks, are always included in wholesale trade. These goods are virtually never sold through retail methods.

4411 Automobile Dealers[CAN]

This industry group comprises establishments primarily engaged in retailing new and used automobiles and light trucks, such as sport utility vehicles, and passenger and cargo vans.

44111 New Car Dealers[CAN]
See industry description for 441110 below.

441110 New Car Dealers[CAN]

This industry comprises establishments primarily engaged in retailing new automobiles and light trucks, such as sport utility vehicles, and passenger and cargo vans, or retailing these new vehicles in combination with activities, such as repair services, retailing used cars, and selling replacement parts and accessories.

US—United States industry only. CAN—United States and Canadian industries are comparable. When neither US nor CAN appears, Canadian, Mexican, and United States industries are comparable.

Illustrative Examples:

> Automobile dealers, new only, or new and used
>
> Light utility truck dealers, new only, or new and used

Cross-References. Establishments primarily engaged in—

- Retailing used automobiles and light trucks without retailing new automobiles and light trucks—are classified in Industry 441120, Used Car Dealers.

- Providing automotive repair services without retailing new automotive vehicles—are classified in Industry Group 8111, Automotive Repair and Maintenance.

44112 Used Car Dealers[CAN]
See industry description for 441120 below.

441120 Used Car Dealers[CAN]

This industry comprises establishments primarily engaged in retailing used automobiles and light trucks, such as sport utility vehicles, and passenger and cargo vans.

Illustrative Examples:

> Antique auto dealers
> Automobile dealers, used only
>
> Light truck dealers, used only

Cross-References.

Establishments primarily engaged in retailing new automobiles and light trucks are classified in Industry 441110, New Car Dealers.

4412 Other Motor Vehicle Dealers[CAN]

This industry group comprises establishments primarily engaged in retailing new and used vehicles (except automobiles, light trucks, such as sport utility vehicles, and passenger and cargo vans).

44121 Recreational Vehicle Dealers[CAN]
See industry description for 441210 below.

441210 Recreational Vehicle Dealers[CAN]

This industry comprises establishments primarily engaged in retailing new and/or used recreational vehicles commonly referred to as RVs or retailing these new vehicles in combination with activities, such as repair services and selling replacement parts and accessories.

US—United States industry only. CAN—United States and Canadian industries are comparable. When neither US nor CAN appears, Canadian, Mexican, and United States industries are comparable.

http://www.ntis.gov/naics

Illustrative Examples:

Motor home dealers
Recreational vehicle (RV) dealers

Recreational vehicle parts and accessories stores
Travel trailer dealers

Cross-References. Establishments primarily engaged in—

- Retailing new or used boat trailers and utility trailers—are classified in Industry 44122, Motorcycle, Boat, and Other Motor Vehicle Dealers; and

- Retailing manufactured homes (i.e., mobile homes), parts, and equipment—are classified in Industry 453930, Manufactured (Mobile) Home Dealers.

44122 Motorcycle, Boat, and Other Motor Vehicle Dealers[CAN]

This industry comprises establishments primarily engaged in retailing new and used motorcycles, boats, and other vehicles (except automobiles, light trucks, and recreational vehicles), or retailing these new vehicles in combination with activities, such as repair services and selling replacement parts and accessories.

Illustrative Examples:

Aircraft dealers
All-terrain vehicle (ATV) dealers
Boat dealers, new and used

Motorcycle dealers
Utility trailer dealers

Cross-References. Establishments primarily engaged in—

- Retailing new nonmotorized bicycles, surfboards, or wind sail boards—are classified in Industry 45111, Sporting Goods Stores;

- Retailing used nonmotorized bicycles, surfboards, or wind sail boards—are classified in Industry 45331, Used Merchandise Stores;

- Retailing new or used automobiles and light trucks —are classified in Industry Group 4411, Automotive Dealers;

- Retailing new or used recreational vehicles, such as travel trailers,—are classified in Industry 44121, Recreational Vehicle Dealers;

- Providing repair services for vehicles without retailing new vehicles—are classified in the appropriate industry for the repair services; and

- Retailing fuel and marine supplies at a marina—are classified in Industry 71393, Marinas

441221 Motorcycle Dealers[US]

This U.S. industry comprises establishments primarily engaged in retailing new and/or used motorcycles, motor scooters, motor bikes, mopeds, off-road all-terrain vehicles, and personal

US—United States industry only. CAN—United States and Canadian industries are comparable. When neither US nor CAN appears, Canadian, Mexican, and United States industries are comparable.

watercraft, or retailing these new vehicles in combination with repair services and selling replacement parts and accessories.

Illustrative Examples:

All-terrain vehicle (ATV) dealers   Motorcycle parts and accessories dealers
Moped dealers   Personal watercraft dealers
Motorcycle dealers

Cross-References. Establishments primarily engaged in—

- Providing motorcycle repair services without retailing new motorcycles—are classified in Industry 811490, Other Personal and Household Goods Repair and Maintenance;

- Retailing new nonmotorized bicycles—are classified in Industry 451110, Sporting Goods Stores;

- Retailing used nonmotorized bicycles—are classified in Industry 453310, Used Merchandise Stores; and

- Retailing new or used boats—are classified in U.S. Industry 441222, Boat Dealers.

441222 Boat Dealers[US]

This U.S. industry comprises establishments primarily engaged in (1) retailing new and/or used boats or retailing new boats in combination with activities, such as repair services and selling replacement parts and accessories, and/or (2) retailing new and/or used outboard motors, boat trailers, marine supplies, parts, and accessories.

Illustrative Examples:

Boat dealers (e.g., powerboats, rowboats,   Marine supply dealers
    sailboats)   Outboard motor dealers

Cross-References. Establishments primarily engaged in—

- Retailing new surfboards or wind sail boards—are classified in Industry 451110, Sporting Goods Stores;

- Retailing used surfboards or wind sail boards—are classified in Industry 453310, Used Merchandise Stores;

- Providing boat repair services without retailing new boats—are classified in Industry 811490, Other Personal or Household Goods Repair and Maintenance;

- Retailing new or used personal watercraft—are classified in U.S. Industry 441221, Motorcycle Dealers; and

- Operating docking and/or storage facilities for pleasure craft owners—are classified in Industry 713930, Marinas.

US—United States industry only. CAN—United States and Canadian industries are comparable. When neither US nor CAN appears, Canadian, Mexican, and United States industries are comparable.

441229 All Other Motor Vehicle Dealers[US]

This U.S. industry comprises establishments primarily engaged in retailing new and/or used utility trailers and vehicles (except automobiles, light trucks, recreational vehicles, motorcycles, boats, motor scooters, motorbikes, off-road all-terrain vehicles, and personal watercraft) or retailing these new vehicles in combination with activities, such as repair services and selling replacement parts and accessories.

Illustrative Examples:

Aircraft dealers   Snowmobile dealers
Powered golf cart dealers   Utility trailer dealers

Cross-References. Establishments primarily engaged in—

- Retailing new automobiles and light trucks—are classified in Industry 441110, New Car Dealers;

- Retailing used automobiles and light trucks—are classified in Industry 441120, Used Car Dealers;

- Retailing new or used recreational vehicles, such as travel trailers,—are classified in Industry 441210, Recreational Vehicle Dealers;

- Retailing new or used motorcycles, motor scooters, motorbikes, off-road all-terrain vehicles, and personal watercraft—are classified in U.S. Industry 441221, Motorcycle Dealers;

- Retailing new or used boats, outboard motors, boat trailers, and marine supplies—are classified in U.S. Industry 441222, Boat Dealers; and

- Providing vehicle repair services without retailing new vehicles—are classified in the appropriate industry for the repair services.

4413 Automotive Parts, Accessories, and Tire Stores[CAN]

44131 Automotive Parts and Accessories Stores[CAN]
See industry description for 441310 below.

441310 Automotive Parts and Accessories Stores[CAN]

This industry comprises one or more of the following: (1) establishments known as automotive supply stores primarily engaged in retailing new, used, and/or rebuilt automotive parts and accessories; (2) automotive supply stores that are primarily engaged in both retailing automotive parts and accessories and repairing automobiles; and (3) establishments primarily engaged in retailing and installing automotive accessories.

Illustrative Examples:

Automotive parts and supply stores   Truck cap stores
Automotive stereo stores   Used automotive parts stores
Speed shops

US—United States industry only. CAN—United States and Canadian industries are comparable. When neither US nor CAN appears, Canadian, Mexican, and United States industries are comparable.

Cross-References. Establishments primarily engaged in—

- Retailing automotive parts and accessories via electronic home shopping, mail-order, or direct sale—are classified in Subsector 454, Nonstore Retailers;

- Retailing new or used tires—are classified in Industry 441320, Tire Dealers; and

- Repairing and replacing automotive parts, such as transmissions, mufflers, brake linings, and glass (except establishments known as automotive supply stores),—are classified in Industry 81111, Automotive Mechanical and Electrical Repair and Maintenance.

44132 Tire Dealers[CAN]
See industry description for 441320 below.

441320 Tire Dealers[CAN]

This industry comprises establishments primarily engaged in retailing new and/or used tires and tubes or retailing new tires in combination with automotive repair services.

Cross-References. Establishments primarily engaged in –

- Retailing tires via electronic home shopping, mail-order, or direct sale—are classified in Subsector 454, Nonstore Retailers; and

- Providing automotive repair services without retailing new tires—are classified in U.S. Industry 811198, All Other Automotive Repair and Maintenance.

442 Furniture and Home Furnishings Stores[CAN]

Industries in the Furniture and Home Furnishings Stores subsector retail new furniture and home furnishings merchandise from fixed point-of-sale locations. Establishments in this subsector usually operate from showrooms and have substantial areas for the presentation of their products. Many offer interior decorating services in addition to the sale of products.

4421 Furniture Stores[CAN]

44211 Furniture Stores[CAN]
See industry description for 442110 below.

442110 Furniture Stores[CAN]

This industry comprises establishments primarily engaged in retailing new furniture, such as household furniture (e.g., baby furniture box springs and mattresses) and outdoor furniture; office furniture (except those sold in combination with office supplies and equipment); and/or furniture sold in combination with major appliances, home electronics, home furnishings, and/or floor covering.

US—United States industry only. CAN—United States and Canadian industries are comparable. When neither US nor CAN appears, Canadian, Mexican, and United States industries are comparable.

Cross-References. Establishments primarily engaged in—

- Retailing furniture via electronic home shopping, mail-order, or direct sale—are classified in Subsector 454, Nonstore Retailers;

- Retailing used furniture—are classified in Industry 453310, Used Merchandise Stores;

- Retailing custom furniture made on premises—are classified in Subsector 337, Furniture and Related Product Manufacturing; and

- Retailing new office furniture and a range of new office equipment and supplies—are classified in Industry 453210, Office Supplies and Stationery Stores.

4422 Home Furnishings Stores^{CAN}

This industry group comprises establishments primarily engaged in retailing new home furnishings (except furniture).

44221 Floor Covering Stores^{CAN}
See industry descriptions for 442210 below.

442210 Floor Covering Stores^{CAN}

This industry comprises establishments primarily engaged in retailing new floor coverings, such as rugs and carpets, vinyl floor coverings, and floor tile (except ceramic or wood only); or retailing new floor coverings in combination with installation and repair services.

Cross-References. Establishments primarily engaged in—

- Retailing floor coverings via electronic home shopping, mail-order, or direct sale—are classified in Subsector 454, Nonstore Retailers;

- Installing floor coverings without retailing new floor coverings—are classified in Industry 235520, Floor Laying and Other Floor Contractors;

- Retailing ceramic floor tile or wood floor coverings only—are classified in Industry 444190, Other Building Material Dealers; and

- Retailing used rugs and carpets—are classified in Industry 453310, Used Merchandise Stores.

44229 Other Home Furnishings Stores^{CAN}

This industry comprises establishments primarily engaged in retailing new home furnishings (except furniture and floor coverings).

Illustrative Examples:

Bath shops	Kitchenware stores
Chinaware stores	Window treatment stores
Glassware stores	

US—United States industry only. CAN—United States and Canadian industries are comparable. When neither US nor CAN appears, Canadian, Mexican, and United States industries are comparable.

Cross-References. Establishments primarily engaged in—

- Retailing home furnishings via electronic home shopping, mail-order, or direct sale—are classified in Subsector 454, Nonstore Retailers;

- Retailing custom curtains and draperies made on premises—are classified in Industry 31412, Curtain and Linen Mills;

- Retailing new mirrored glass, lighting fixtures, and new ceramic floor tile or wood floor coverings only—are classified in Industry 44419, Other Building Material Dealers;

- Retailing new furniture—are classified in Industry 44211, Furniture Stores;

- Retailing new floor coverings (except ceramic or wood only)—are classified in Industry 44221, Floor Covering Stores; and

- Retailing used home furnishings—are classified in Industry 45331, Used Merchandise Stores.

442291 Window Treatment Stores[CAN]

This U.S. industry comprises establishments primarily engaged in retailing new window treatments, such as curtains, drapes, blinds, and shades.

Cross-References. Establishments primarily engaged in—

- Retailing window treatments via electronic home shopping, mail-order, or direct sale—are classified in Subsector 454, Nonstore Retailers; and

- Retailing custom curtains and draperies made on premises—are classified in U.S. Industry 314121, Curtain and Drapery Mills.

442299 All Other Home Furnishings Stores[US]

This U.S. industry comprises establishments primarily engaged in retailing new home furnishings (except floor coverings, furniture, and window treatments).

Illustrative Examples:

Bath shops	Kitchenware stores
Chinaware stores	Linen stores
Electric lamp shops	Picture frame stores
Glassware stores	Wood-burning stove stores
Houseware stores	

Cross-References. Establishments primarily engaged in—

- Selling home furnishings via electronic home shopping, mail-order, or direct sale—are classified in Subsector 454, Nonstore Retailers;

US—United States industry only. CAN—United States and Canadian industries are comparable. When neither US nor CAN appears, Canadian, Mexican, and United States industries are comparable.

- Retailing new mirrored glass lighting fixtures—are classified in Industry 444190, Other Building Material Dealers;

- Retailing new furniture—are classified in Industry 442110, Furniture Stores;

- Retailing new floor coverings—are classified in Industry 442210, Floor Covering Stores;

- Retailing new window treatments—are classified in U.S. Industry 442291, Window Treatment Stores; and

- Retailing used home furnishings—are classified in Industry 453310, Used Merchandise Stores.

443 Electronics and Appliance Stores[CAN]

Industries in the Electronics and Appliance Stores subsector retail new electronics and appliance merchandise from point-of-sale locations. Establishments in this subsector often operate from locations that have special provisions for floor displays requiring special electrical capacity to accommodate the proper demonstration of the products. The staff includes sales personnel knowledgeable in the characteristics and warranties of the line of goods retailed and may also include trained repair persons to handle the maintenance and repair of the electronic equipment and appliances. The classifications within this subsector are made principally on the type of product and knowledge required to operate each type of store.

4431 Electronics and Appliance Stores[CAN]

This industry group comprises establishments primarily engaged in retailing the following new products: household-type appliances, cameras, computers, and other electronic goods.

44311 Appliance, Television, and Other Electronics Stores[CAN]

This industry comprises establishments primarily engaged in retailing one of the following: (1) retailing an array of new household-type appliances and consumer-type electronic products, such as radios, televisions, and computers; (2) specializing in retailing a single line of new consumer-type electronic products (except computers); and (3) retailing these new products in combination with repair services.

Illustrative Examples:

Appliance stores
Consumer electronics stores

Radio and television stores

Cross-References. Establishments primarily engaged in—

- Retailing new electronic products via electronic home shopping, mail-order, or direct sale—are classified in Subsector 454, Nonstore Retailers;

- Retailing new computers, computer peripherals, and prepackaged computer software without retailing other consumer-type electronic products or office equipment, office furniture, and

---

US—United States industry only. CAN—United States and Canadian industries are comparable. When neither US nor CAN appears, Canadian, Mexican, and United States industries are comparable.

office supplies; or retailing these products in combination with repair services—are classified in Industry 44312, Computer and Software Stores;

- Retailing new computers, computer peripherals, and prepackaged software in combination with retailing new office equipment, office furniture, and office supplies—are classified in Industry 45321, Office Supplies and Stationery Stores;

- Retailing new sewing machines in combination with selling new sewing supplies, fabrics, patterns, yarns, and other needlework accessories—are classified in Industry 45113, Sewing, Needlework, and Piece Goods Stores;

- Retailing new electronic toys—are classified in Industry 45112, Hobby, Toy, and Game Stores;

- Providing television or other electronic products repair services without retailing new televisions or electronic products—are classified in Industry 81121, Electronic and Precision Equipment Repair and Maintenance;

- Providing appliance repair services without retailing new appliances—are classified in Industry 81141, Home and Garden Equipment and Appliance Repair and Maintenance;

- Retailing used appliance and electronic products—are classified in Industry 45331, Used Merchandise Stores;

- Retailing new still and motion picture cameras—are classified in Industry 44313, Camera and Photographic Supplies Stores; and

- Retailing automotive electronic sound systems—are classified in Industry 44131, Automotive Parts and Accessories Stores.

443111 Household Appliance Stores[US]

This U.S. industry comprises establishments known as appliance stores primarily engaged in retailing an array of new household appliances, such as refrigerators, dishwashers, ovens, irons, coffeemakers, hair dryers, electric razors, room air-conditioners, microwave ovens, sewing machines, and vacuum cleaners, or retailing new appliances in combination with appliance repair services.

Cross-References. Establishments primarily engaged in—

- Retailing household appliances via electronic home shopping, mail-order, or direct sale—are classified in Subsector 454, Nonstore Retailers;

- Retailing new sewing machines in combination with selling new sewing supplies, fabrics, patterns, yarns, and other needlework accessories—are classified in Industry 451130, Sewing, Needlework, and Piece Goods Stores;

- Providing appliance repair services without retailing new appliances—are classified in U.S. Industry 811412, Appliance Repair and Maintenance; and

- Retailing used appliances—are classified in Industry 453310, Used Merchandise Stores.

US—United States industry only. CAN—United States and Canadian industries are comparable. When neither US nor CAN appears, Canadian, Mexican, and United States industries are comparable.

443112 Radio, Television, and Other Electronics Stores[US]

This U.S. industry comprises: (1) establishments known as consumer electronics stores primarily engaged in retailing a general line of new consumer-type electronic products; (2) establishments specializing in retailing a single line of consumer-type electronic products (except computers); or (3) establishments primarily engaged in retailing these new electronic products in combination with repair services.

Illustrative Examples:

Consumer electronic stores	Stereo stores (except automotive)
Radio and television stores	Telephone stores (including cellular)

Cross-References. Establishments primarily engaged in—

- Retailing electronic goods via electronic home shopping, mail-order, or direct sale—are classified in Subsector 454, Nonstore Retailers;

- Retailing automotive electronic sound systems—are classified in Industry 441310, Automotive Parts and Accessories Stores;

- Retailing new computers, computer peripherals, and prepackaged computer software without retailing other consumer-type electronic products or office equipment, office furniture and office supplies; or retailing these new computer products in combination with repair services—are classified in Industry 443120, Computer and Software Stores;

- Retailing new computers, computer peripherals, and prepackaged software in combination with retailing new office equipment, office furniture, and office supplies—are classified in Industry 453210, Office Supplies and Stationery Stores;

- Retailing new still and motion picture cameras—are classified in Industry 443130, Camera and Photographic Supplies Stores;

- Providing television or other electronic equipment repair services without retailing new televisions or electronic products—are classified in Industry 81121, Electronic and Precision Equipment Repair and Maintenance;

- Retailing new electronic toys—are classified in Industry 451120, Hobby, Toy, and Game Stores; and

- Retailing used electronics—are classified in Industry 453310, Used Merchandise Stores.

44312 Computer and Software Stores[CAN]
See industry description for 443120 below.

443120 Computer and Software Stores[CAN]

This industry comprises establishments primarily engaged in retailing new computers, computer peripherals, and prepackaged computer software without retailing other consumer-type electronic

---

US—United States industry only. CAN—United States and Canadian industries are comparable. When neither US nor CAN appears, Canadian, Mexican, and United States industries are comparable.

http://www.ntis.gov/naics

products or office equipment, office furniture and office supplies; or retailing these new products in combination with repair and support services.

Cross-References. Establishments primarily engaged in—

- Retailing computers and software via electronic home shopping, mail-order, or direct sale—are classified in Subsector 454, Nonstore Retailers;

- Retailing new electronic toys, such as video games and handheld electronic games,—are classified in Industry 451120, Hobby, Toy, and Game Stores;

- Providing computer repair services without retailing new computers—are classified in U.S. Industry 811212, Computer and Office Machine Repair and Maintenance;

- Retailing new computers, computer peripherals, and prepackaged software in combination with retailing new office equipment, office furniture, and office supplies—are classified in Industry 453210, Office Supplies and Stationery Stores;

- Retailing a general line of new electronic products or specializing in retailing a single line of consumer-type electronic products (except computers)—are classified in U.S. Industry 443112, Radio, Television, and Other Electronics Stores; and

- Retailing used computers, computer software, video games, and handheld electronic games—classified in Industry 453310, Used Merchandise Stores.

44313 Camera and Photographic Supplies Stores[CAN]
See industry description for 443130 below.

443130 Camera and Photographic Supplies Stores[CAN]

This industry comprises establishments primarily engaged in either retailing new cameras, photographic equipment, and photographic supplies or retailing new cameras and photographic equipment in combination with activities, such as repair services and film developing.

Cross-References. Establishments primarily engaged in—

- Retailing camera and photographic supplies via electronic home shopping, mail-order, or direct sale—are classified in Subsector 454, Nonstore Retailers;

- Retailing new video cameras—are classified in U.S. Industry 443112, Radio, Television, and Other Electronics Stores;

- One-hour film developing without retailing a range of new photographic equipment and supplies—are classified in U.S. Industry 812922, One-Hour Photofinishing;

- Providing repair services for photographic equipment without retailing new photographic equipment—are classified in U.S. Industry 811211, Consumer Electronics Repair and Maintenance;

US—United States industry only. CAN—United States and Canadian industries are comparable. When neither US nor CAN appears, Canadian, Mexican, and United States industries are comparable.

- Developing film and/or producing photographic prints, slides, and enlargements (except one-hour photofinishing labs)—are classified in U.S. Industry 812921, Photofinishing Laboratories (except One-Hour); and

- Retailing used cameras and photographic equipment—are classified in Industry 453310, Used Merchandise Stores.

444 Building Material and Garden Equipment and Supplies Dealers^{CAN}

Industries in the Building Material and Garden Equipment and Supplies Dealers subsector retail new building material and garden equipment and supplies merchandise from fixed point-of-sale locations. Establishments in this subsector have display equipment designed to handle lumber and related products and garden equipment and supplies that may be kept either indoors or outdoors under covered areas. The staff is usually knowledgeable in the use of the specific products being retailed in the construction, repair, and maintenance of the home and associated grounds.

4441 Building Material and Supplies Dealers^{CAN}

This industry group comprises establishments primarily engaged in retailing new building materials and supplies.

44411 Home Centers^{CAN}
See industry description for 444110 below.

444110 Home Centers^{CAN}

This industry comprises establishments known as home centers primarily engaged in retailing a general line of new home repair and improvement materials and supplies, such as lumber, plumbing goods, electrical goods, tools, housewares, hardware, and lawn and garden supplies, with no one merchandise line predominating. The merchandise lines are normally arranged in separate departments.

44412 Paint and Wallpaper Stores^{CAN}
See industry description for 444120 below.

444120 Paint and Wallpaper Stores^{CAN}

This industry comprises establishments known as paint and wallpaper stores primarily engaged in retailing paint, wallpaper, and related supplies.

44413 Hardware Stores^{CAN}
See industry description for 444130 below.

444130 Hardware Stores^{CAN}

This industry comprises establishments known as hardware stores primarily engaged in retailing a general line of new hardware items, such as tools and builders' hardware.

US—United States industry only. CAN—United States and Canadian industries are comparable. When neither US nor CAN appears, Canadian, Mexican, and United States industries are comparable.

Cross-References. Establishments primarily engaged in—

- Retailing hardware items via electronic home shopping, mail order, or direct sale—are classified in Subsector 454, Nonstore Retailers;

- Retailing a general line of home repair and improvement materials and supplies known as home centers—are classified in Industry 444110, Home Centers; and

- Retailing used hardware items—are classified in Industry 453310, Used Merchandise Stores.

44419 Other Building Material Dealers^{CAN}
See industry description for 444190 below.

444190 Other Building Material Dealers^{CAN}

This industry comprises establishments (except those known as home centers, paint and wallpaper stores, and hardware stores) primarily engaged in retailing specialized lines of new building materials, such as lumber, fencing, glass, doors, plumbing fixtures and supplies, electrical supplies, prefabricated buildings and kits, and kitchen and bath cabinets and countertops to be installed.

Illustrative Examples:

Electrical supply stores	Kitchen cabinet (except custom) stores
Fencing dealers	Lumber retailing yards
Floor covering stores, wood or ceramic tile only	Plumbing supply stores
Glass stores	Prefabricated building dealers

Cross-References. Establishments primarily engaged in—

- Retailing building materials via electronic home shopping, mail-order, or direct sale—are classified in Subsector 454, Nonstore Retailers;

- Retailing used building materials—are classified in Industry 453310, Used Merchandise Stores;

- Providing carpentry/installation services for products—are classified in Industry 235510, Carpentry Contractors;

- Installing plumbing fixtures and supplies—are classified in Industry 235110, Plumbing, Heating, and Air-Conditioning Contractors;

- Installing electrical supplies, such as lighting fixtures and ceiling fans,—are classified in Industry 235310, Electrical Contractors; and

- Making custom furniture (e.g. kitchen cabinets)—are classified in Subsector 337, Furniture and Related Product Manufacturing.

- Retailing a general line of new hardware items, known as hardware stores,—are classified in Industry 444130, Hardware Stores;

US—United States industry only. CAN—United States and Canadian industries are comparable. When neither US nor CAN appears, Canadian, Mexican, and United States industries are comparable.

- Retailing paint and wallpaper, known as paint and wallpaper stores,—are classified in Industry 444120, Paint and Wallpaper Stores; and

- Retailing a general line of home repair and improvement materials and supplies, known as home centers,—are classified in Industry 444110, Home Centers.

4442 Lawn and Garden Equipment and Supplies Stores[CAN]

This industry group comprises establishments primarily engaged in retailing new lawn and garden equipment and supplies.

44421 Outdoor Power Equipment Stores[CAN]
See industry description for 444210 below.

444210 Outdoor Power Equipment Stores[CAN]

This industry comprises establishments primarily engaged in retailing new outdoor power equipment or retailing new outdoor power equipment in combination with activities, such as repair services and selling replacement parts.

Cross-References. Establishments primarily engaged in—

- Retailing outdoor power equipment via electronic home shopping, mail-order, or direct sale—are classified in Subsector 454, Nonstore Retailers;

- Providing outdoor power equipment repair services without retailing new outdoor power equipment—are classified in U.S. Industry 811411, Home and Garden Equipment Repair and Maintenance; and

- Retailing used outdoor power equipment—are classified in Industry 453310, Used Merchandise Stores.

44422 Nursery and Garden Centers[CAN]
See industry description for 444220 below.

444220 Nursery and Garden Centers[CAN]

This industry comprises establishments primarily engaged in retailing nursery and garden products, such as trees, shrubs, plants, seeds, bulbs, and sod, that are predominantly grown elsewhere. These establishments may sell a limited amount of a product they grow themselves.

Cross-References. Establishments primarily engaged in—

- Retailing nursery and garden products via electronic home shopping, mail-order, or direct sale—are classified in Subsector 454, Nonstore Retailers;

- Providing landscaping services—are classified in Industry 561730, Landscaping Services; and

---

US—United States industry only. CAN—United States and Canadian industries are comparable. When neither US nor CAN appears, Canadian, Mexican, and United States industries are comparable.

- Growing and retailing nursery stock—are classified in U.S. Industry 111421, Nursery and Tree Production.

445 Food and Beverage Stores^{CAN}

Industries in the Food and Beverage Stores subsector usually retail food and beverage merchandise from fixed point-of-sale locations. Establishments in this subsector have special equipment (e.g., freezers, refrigerated display cases, refrigerators) for displaying food and beverage goods. They have staff trained in the processing of food products to guarantee the proper storage and sanitary conditions required by regulatory authority.

4451 Grocery Stores^{CAN}

This industry group comprises establishments primarily engaged in retailing a general line of food products.

44511 Supermarkets and Other Grocery (except Convenience) Stores^{CAN}
See industry description for 445110 below.

445110 Supermarkets and Other Grocery (except Convenience) Stores^{CAN}

This industry comprises establishments generally known as supermarkets and grocery stores primarily engaged in retailing a general line of food, such as canned and frozen foods; fresh fruits and vegetables; and fresh and prepared meats, fish, and poultry. Included in this industry are delicatessen-type establishments primarily engaged in retailing a general line of food.

Cross-References. Establishments primarily engaged in—

- Retailing automotive fuels in combination with a convenience store or food mart—are classified in Industry 447110, Gasoline Stations with Convenience Stores;

- Retailing a limited line of goods, known as convenience stores or food marts (except those with fuel pumps),—are classified in Industry 445120, Convenience Stores;

- Retailing frozen food and freezer plans via direct sales to residential customers—are classified in Industry 454390, Other Direct Selling Establishments;

- Providing food services in delicatessen-type establishments—are classified in U.S. Industry 722211, Limited-Service Restaurants; and

- Retailing fresh meat in delicatessen-type establishments—are classified in Industry 445210, Meat Markets.

44512 Convenience Stores^{CAN}
See industry description for 445120 below.

445120 Convenience Stores^{CAN}

This industry comprises establishments known as convenience stores or food marts (except those with fuel pumps) primarily engaged in retailing a limited line of goods that generally includes milk, bread, soda, and snacks.

US—United States industry only. CAN—United States and Canadian industries are comparable. When neither US nor CAN appears, Canadian, Mexican, and United States industries are comparable.

http://www.ntis.gov/naics

Cross-References. Establishments primarily engaged in—

- Retailing a general line of food, known as supermarkets and grocery stores,—are classified in Industry 445110, Supermarkets and Other Grocery (except Convenience) Stores; and

- Retailing automotive fuels in combination with a convenience store or food mart—are classified in Industry 447110, Gasoline Stations with Convenience Stores.

4452 Specialty Food Stores^{CAN}

This industry group comprises establishments primarily engaged in retailing specialized lines of food.

44521 Meat Markets^{CAN}
See industry description for 445210 below.

445210 Meat Markets^{CAN}

This industry comprises establishments primarily engaged in retailing fresh, frozen, or cured meats and poultry. Delicatessen-type establishments primarily engaged in retailing fresh meat are included in this industry.

Illustrative Examples:

Baked ham stores   Meat markets
Butcher shops   Poultry dealers
Frozen meat shops

Cross-References. Establishments primarily engaged in—

- Retailing meat and poultry via electronic home shopping, mail-order, or direct sale—are classified in Subsector 454, Nonstore Retailers;

- Retailing a general line of food, known as supermarkets and grocery stores,—are classified in Industry 445110, Supermarkets and Other Grocery (except Convenience) Stores; and

- Providing food services in delicatessen-type establishments—are classified in U.S. Industry 722211, Limited-Service Restaurants.

44522 Fish and Seafood Markets^{CAN}
See industry description for 445220 below.

445220 Fish and Seafood Markets^{CAN}

This industry comprises establishments primarily engaged in retailing fresh, frozen, or cured fish and seafood products.

US—United States industry only. CAN—United States and Canadian industries are comparable. When neither US nor CAN appears, Canadian, Mexican, and United States industries are comparable.

Cross-References.

Establishments primarily engaged in retailing fish and seafood products via electronic home shopping, mail-order, or direct sale are classified in Subsector 454, Nonstore Retailers.

44523 Fruit and Vegetable Markets^{CAN}

See industry descriptions for 445230 below.

445230 Fruit and Vegetable Markets^{CAN}

This industry comprises establishments primarily engaged in retailing fresh fruits and vegetables.

Cross-References. Establishments primarily engaged in—

- Retailing fruits and vegetables via electronic home shopping, mail-order, or direct sale—are classified in Subsector 454, Nonstore Retailers; and

- Growing and selling vegetables and/or fruits at roadside stands—are classified in Subsector 111, Crop Production.

44529 Other Specialty Food Stores^{CAN}

This industry comprises establishments primarily engaged in retailing specialty foods (except meat, fish, seafood, and fruits and vegetables) not for immediate consumption and not made on premises.

Illustrative Examples:

Bakery stores (except immediate consumption)	Dairy product stores
Coffee and tea (i.e., packaged) stores	Gourmet food stores
Confectionery (i.e., packaged) stores	Nut (i.e., packaged) stores

Cross-References. Establishments primarily engaged in—

- Retailing specialty foods via electronic home shopping, mail-order, or direct sale—are classified in Subsector 454, Nonstore Retailers;

- Retailing baked goods made on the premises, but not for immediate consumption—are classified in Industry 31181, Bread and Bakery Product Manufacturing;

- Retailing fresh, frozen, or cured meats and poultry—are classified in Industry 44521, Meat Markets;

- Retailing fresh, frozen, or cured fish and seafood products—are classified in Industry 44522, Fish and Seafood Markets;

- Retailing fresh fruits and vegetables—are classified in Industry 44523, Fruit and Vegetable Markets;

US—United States industry only. CAN—United States and Canadian industries are comparable. When neither US nor CAN appears, Canadian, Mexican, and United States industries are comparable.

- Retailing candy and confectionery products not for immediate consumption and not made on premises—are classified in Industry Group 3113, Sugar and Confectionery Product Manufacturing; and

- Selling snack foods (e.g., doughnuts, bagels, ice cream, popcorn) for immediate consumption—are classified in Subsector 722, Food Services and Drinking Places.

445291 Baked Goods Stores^{CAN}

This U.S. industry comprises establishments primarily engaged in retailing baked goods not for immediate consumption and not made on the premises.

Cross-References. Establishments primarily engaged in—

- Retailing baked goods via electronic home shopping, mail-order, or direct sale—are classified in Subsector 454, Nonstore Retailers;

- Selling snack foods (e.g., doughnuts, bagels, ice cream, popcorn) for immediate consumption—are classified in U.S. Industry 722213, Snack and Nonalcoholic Beverage Bars; and

- Retailing baked goods made on the premises but not for immediate consumption—are classified in Industry 311811, Retail Bakeries.

445292 Confectionery and Nut Stores^{CAN}

This U.S. industry comprises establishments primarily engaged in retailing candy and other confections, nuts, and popcorn not for immediate consumption and not made on the premises.

Cross-References. Establishments primarily engaged in—

- Retailing confectionery goods and nuts via electronic home shopping, mail-order, or direct sale—are classified in Subsector 454, Nonstore Retailers;

- Retailing confectionery goods and nuts made on premises and not packaged for immediate consumption—are classified in Industry Group 3113, Sugar and Confectionery Product Manufacturing;

- Selling snack foods (e.g., doughnuts, bagels, ice cream, popcorn) for immediate consumption—are classified in U.S. Industry 722213, Snack and Nonalcoholic Beverage Bars; and

- Retailing baked goods made on the premises but not for immediate consumption—are classified in Industry 311811, Retail Bakeries.

445299 All Other Specialty Food Stores^{CAN}

This U.S. industry comprises establishments primarily engaged in retailing miscellaneous specialty foods (except meat, fish, seafood, fruit and vegetables, confections, nuts, popcorn, and baked goods) not for immediate consumption and not made on the premises.

US—United States industry only. CAN—United States and Canadian industries are comparable. When neither US nor CAN appears, Canadian, Mexican, and United States industries are comparable.

Illustrative Examples:

Coffee and tea (i.e., packaged) stores
Dairy product stores
Gourmet food stores

Soft drink (i.e. bottled) stores
Spice stores
Water (i.e., bottled) stores

Cross-References. Establishments primarily engaged in—

- Retailing specialty foods via electronic home shopping, mail-order, or direct sale—are classified in Subsector 454, Nonstore Retailers;

- Selling snack foods (e.g., doughnuts, bagels, ice cream, popcorn) for immediate consumption—are classified in U.S. Industry 722213, Snack and Nonalcoholic Beverage Bars;

- Retailing fresh, frozen, or cured meats and poultry—are classified in Industry 445210, Meat Markets;

- Retailing fresh, frozen, or cured fish and seafood products—are classified in Industry 445220, Fish and Seafood Markets;

- Retailing fresh fruits and vegetables—are classified in Industry 445230, Fruit and Vegetable Markets;

- Retailing candy and other confections, nuts, and popcorn not for immediate consumption and not made on the premises—are classified in U.S. Industry 445292, Confectionery and Nut Stores; and

- Retailing baked goods not for immediate consumption and not made on the premises—are classified in U.S. Industry 445291, Baked Goods Stores.

4453 Beer, Wine, and Liquor Stores[CAN]

44531 Beer, Wine, and Liquor Stores[CAN]
See industry description for 445310 below.

445310 Beer, Wine, and Liquor Stores[CAN]

This industry comprises establishments primarily engaged in retailing packaged alcoholic beverages, such as ale, beer, wine, and liquor.

Cross-References.

Establishments primarily engaged in retailing packaged liquor in combination with providing prepared drinks for immediate consumption on the premises are classified in Industry 722410, Drinking Places (Alcoholic Beverages).

446 Health and Personal Care Stores[CAN]

Industries in the Health and Personal Care Stores subsector retail health and personal care merchandise from fixed point-of-sale locations. Establishments in this subsector are characterized

---

US—United States industry only. CAN—United States and Canadian industries are comparable. When neither US nor CAN appears, Canadian, Mexican, and United States industries are comparable.

principally by the products they retail, and some health and personal care stores may have specialized staff trained in dealing with the products. Staff may include pharmacists, opticians, and other professionals engaged in retailing, advising customers, and/or fitting the product sold to the customer's needs.

4461 Health and Personal Care Stores[CAN]

This industry group comprises establishments primarily engaged in retailing health and personal care products.

44611 Pharmacies and Drug Stores[CAN]
See industry descriptions for 446110 below.

446110 Pharmacies and Drug Stores[CAN]

This industry comprises establishments known as pharmacies and drug stores engaged in retailing prescription or nonprescription drugs and medicines.

Cross-References. Establishments primarily engaged in—

- Retailing food supplement products, such as vitamins, nutrition supplements, and body enhancing supplements,—are classified in U.S. Industry 446191, Food (Health) Supplement Stores; and

- Retailing prescription and nonprescription drugs via electronic home shopping, mail-order, or direct sale—are classified in Subsector 454, Nonstore Retailers.

44612 Cosmetics, Beauty Supplies, and Perfume Stores[CAN]
See industry descriptions for 446120 below.

446120 Cosmetics, Beauty Supplies, and Perfume Stores[CAN]

This industry comprises establishments known as a cosmetic or perfume stores or beauty supply shops primarily engaged in retailing cosmetics, perfumes, toiletries, and personal grooming products.

Cross-References. Establishments primarily engaged in—

- Providing beauty parlor services—are classified in U.S. Industry 812112, Beauty Salons; and

- Retailing perfumes, cosmetics, and beauty supplies via electronic home shopping, mail-order, or direct sale—are classified in Subsector 454, Nonstore Retailers.

44613 Optical Goods Stores[CAN]
See industry descriptions for 446130 below.

446130 Optical Goods Stores[CAN]

This industry comprises establishments primarily engaged in one or more of the following: (1) retailing and fitting prescription eyeglasses and contact lenses; (2) retailing prescription eyeglasses

---

US—United States industry only. CAN—United States and Canadian industries are comparable. When neither US nor CAN appears, Canadian, Mexican, and United States industries are comparable.

in combination with the grinding of lenses to order on the premises; and (3) selling nonprescription eyeglasses.

Cross-References. Establishments primarily engaged in—

- Grinding lenses without retailing lenses—are classified in U.S. Industry 339115, Ophthalmic Goods Manufacturing;

- The private or group practice of optometry, even though glasses and contact lenses are sold at these establishments—are classified Industry 621320, Offices of Optometrists; and

- Retailing eyeglasses and contact lenses via mail-order—are classified in Industry 454110, Electronic Shopping and Mail-Order Houses.

44619 Other Health and Personal Care Stores^{CAN}

This industry comprises establishments primarily engaged in retailing health and personal care items (except drugs, medicines, optical goods, perfumes, cosmetics, and beauty supplies).

Illustrative Examples:

Convalescent supply stores	Prosthetic stores
Food (i.e., health) supplement stores	Sick room supply stores
Hearing aid stores	

Cross-References. Establishments primarily engaged in—

- Retailing health and personal care items via electronic home shopping, mail-order, or direct sale—are classified in Subsector 454, Nonstore Retailers;

- Retailing orthopedic shoes—are classified in Industry 44821, Shoe Stores;

- Retailing orthopedic and prosthetic appliances that are made on premises—are classified in Industry 33911, Medical Equipment and Supplies Manufacturing;

- Retailing prescription and nonprescription drugs and medicines—are classified in Industry 44611, Pharmacies and Drug Stores;

- Retailing eyeglasses and contact lenses—are classified in Industry 44613, Optical Goods Stores;

- Retailing perfumes, cosmetics, and beauty supplies—are classified in Industry 44612, Cosmetics, Beauty Supplies, and Perfume Stores; and

- Retailing naturally organic foods, such as fruits and vegetables, dairy products, and cereals and grains,—are classified in Subsector 445, Food and Beverage Stores.

446191 Food (Health) Supplement Stores^{CAN}

This U.S. industry comprises establishments primarily engaged in retailing food supplement products, such as vitamins, nutrition supplements, and body enhancing supplements.

US—United States industry only. CAN—United States and Canadian industries are comparable. When neither US nor CAN appears, Canadian, Mexican, and United States industries are comparable.

Cross-References. Establishments primarily engaged in—

- Retailing food supplement products via electronic home shopping, mail-order, or direct sale—are classified in Subsector 454, Nonstore Retailers;

- Retailing prescription and nonprescription drugs and medicines—are classified in Industry 446110, Pharmacies and Drug Stores; and

- Retailing naturally organic foods, such as fruits and vegetables, dairy products, and cereals and grains,—are classified in Subsector 445, Food and Beverage Stores.

446199 All Other Health and Personal Care Stores[CAN]

This U.S. industry comprises establishments primarily engaged in retailing specialized lines of health and personal care merchandise (except drugs, medicines, optical goods, cosmetics, beauty supplies, perfume, and food supplement products).

Illustrative Examples:

Convalescent supply stores   Prosthetic stores
Hearing aid stores   Sick room supply stores

Cross-References. Establishments primarily engaged in—

- Retailing specialized health and personal care merchandise via electronic home shopping, mail-order, or direct sale—are classified in Subsector 454, Nonstore Retailers;

- Retailing food supplement products—are classified in U.S. Industry 446191, Food (Health) Supplement Stores;

- Retailing prescription or nonprescription drugs and medicines—are classified in Industry 446110, Pharmacies and Drug Stores;

- Retailing eyeglasses and contact lenses—are classified in Industry 446130, Optical Goods Stores;

- Retailing perfumes, cosmetics, and beauty supplies—are classified in Industry 446120, Cosmetics, Beauty Supplies, and Perfume Stores;

- Retailing orthopedic shoes—are classified in Industry 448210, Shoe Stores; and

- Retailing orthopedic and prosthetic appliances that are made on premises—are classified in U.S. Industry 339113, Surgical Appliance and Supplies Manufacturing.

447 Gasoline Stations[CAN]

Industries in the Gasoline Stations subsector group establishments retailing automotive fuels (e.g., gasoline, diesel fuel, gasohol) and automotive oils and retailing these products in combination

---

US—United States industry only. CAN—United States and Canadian industries are comparable. When neither US nor CAN appears, Canadian, Mexican, and United States industries are comparable.

with convenience store items. These establishments have specialized equipment for the storage and dispensing of automotive fuels.

4471 Gasoline Stations^{CAN}

44711 Gasoline Stations with Convenience Stores^{CAN}
See industry descriptions for 447110 below.

447110 Gasoline Stations with Convenience Stores^{CAN}

This industry comprises establishments engaged in retailing automotive fuels (e.g., diesel fuel, gasohol, gasoline) in combination with convenience store or food mart items. These establishments can either be in a convenience store (i.e., food mart) setting or a gasoline station setting. These establishments may also provide automotive repair services.

Cross-References. Establishments primarily engaged in—

- Retailing automotive fuels without a convenience store—are classified in Industry 447190, Other Gasoline Stations; and

- Retailing a limited line of goods, known as convenience stores or food marts (except those with fuel pumps),—are classified in Industry 445120, Convenience Stores.

44719 Other Gasoline Stations^{CAN}
See industry descriptions for 447190 below.

447190 Other Gasoline Stations^{CAN}

This industry comprises establishments known as gasoline stations (except those with convenience stores) primarily engaged in one of the following: (1) retailing automotive fuels (e.g., diesel fuel, gasohol, gasoline) or (2) retailing these fuels in combination with activities, such as repair services, selling automotive oils, replacement parts, and accessories, and/or with restaurants.

Illustrative Examples:

Gasoline stations without convenience stores   Truck stops
Marine service stations

Cross-References. Establishments primarily engaged in—

- Repairing motor vehicles without retailing automotive fuels—are classified in Industry 81111, Automotive Mechanical and Electrical Repair and Maintenance; and

- Retailing automotive fuels in combination with a convenience store or food mart—are classified in Industry 447110, Gasoline Stations with Convenience Stores.

US—United States industry only. CAN—United States and Canadian industries are comparable. When neither US nor CAN appears, Canadian, Mexican, and United States industries are comparable.

448 Clothing and Clothing Accessories Stores[CAN]

Industries in the Clothing and Clothing Accessories Stores subsector retailing new clothing and clothing accessories merchandise from fixed point-of-sale locations. Establishments in this subsector have similar display equipment and staff that is knowledgeable regarding fashion trends and the proper match of styles, colors, and combinations of clothing and accessories to the characteristics and tastes of the customer.

4481 Clothing Stores[CAN]

This industry group comprises establishments primarily engaged in retailing new clothing.

44811 Men's Clothing Stores[CAN]
See industry descriptions for 448110 below.

448110 Men's Clothing Stores[CAN]

This industry comprises establishments primarily engaged in retailing a general line of new men's and boys' clothing. These establishments may provide basic alterations, such as hemming, taking in or letting out seams, or lengthening or shortening sleeves.

Cross-References. Establishments primarily engaged in—

- Retailing men's and boys' clothing via electronic home shopping, mail-order, or direct sale—are classified in Subsector 454, Nonstore Retailers;

- Retailing custom men's clothing made on the premises—are classified in Industry Group 3152, Cut and Sew Apparel Manufacturing;

- Retailing new men's and boys' accessories—are classified in Industry 448150, Clothing Accessories Stores;

- Retailing specialized new apparel, such as raincoats, leather coats, fur apparel, and swimwear,—are classified in Industry 448190, Other Clothing Stores;

- Retailing new clothing for all genders and age groups—are classified in Industry 448140, Family Clothing Stores;

- Retailing secondhand clothes—are classified in Industry 453310, Used Merchandise Stores; and

- Providing clothing alterations and repair—are classified in Industry 811490, Other Personal and Household Goods Repair and Maintenance.

44812 Women's Clothing Stores[CAN]
See industry description for 448120 below.

448120 Women's Clothing Stores[CAN]

This industry comprises establishments primarily engaged in retailing a general line of new women's, misses' and juniors' clothing, including maternity wear. These establishments may

---

US—United States industry only. CAN—United States and Canadian industries are comparable. When neither US nor CAN appears, Canadian, Mexican, and United States industries are comparable.

provide basic alterations, such as hemming, taking in or letting out seams, or lengthening or shortening sleeves.

Cross-References. Establishments primarily engaged in—

- Retailing women's clothing via electronic home shopping, mail-order, or direct sale—are classified in Subsector 454, Nonstore Retailers;

- Retailing custom women's clothing made on premises—are classified in Industry Group 3152, Cut and Sew Apparel Manufacturing;

- Retailing new women's accessories—are classified in Industry 448150, Clothing Accessories Stores;

- Retailing new clothing for all genders and age groups—are classified in Industry 448140, Family Clothing Stores;

- Retailing specialized new apparel, such as bridal gowns, raincoats, leather coats, fur apparel, and swimwear,—are classified in Industry 448190, Other Clothing Stores;

- Retailing secondhand clothes—are classified in Industry 453310, Used Merchandise Stores; and

- Providing clothing alterations and repair—are classified in Industry 811490, Other Personal and Household Goods Repair and Maintenance.

44813 Children's and Infants' Clothing Stores[CAN]

See industry description for 448130 below.

448130 Children's and Infants' Clothing Stores[CAN]

This industry comprises establishments primarily engaged in retailing a general line of new children's and infants' clothing. These establishments may provide basic alterations, such as hemming, taking in or letting out seams, or lengthening or shortening sleeves.

Cross-References. Establishments primarily engaged in—

- Retailing children's and infants' clothing via electronic home shopping, mail-order, or direct sale—are classified in Subsector 454, Nonstore Retailers;

- Retailing new children's and infants' accessories—are classified in Industry 448150, Clothing Accessories Stores;

- Retailing new clothing for all genders or age groups—are classified in Industry 448140, Family Clothing Stores;

- Retailing secondhand clothes—are classified in Industry 453310, Used Merchandise Stores; and

- Providing clothing alterations and repair—are classified in Industry 811490, Other Personal and Household Goods Repair and Maintenance.

US—United States industry only. CAN—United States and Canadian industries are comparable. When neither US nor CAN appears, Canadian, Mexican, and United States industries are comparable.

44814 Family Clothing Stores[CAN]

See industry description for 448140 below.

448140 Family Clothing Stores[CAN]

This industry comprises establishments primarily engaged in retailing a general line of new clothing for men, women, and children, without specializing in sales for an individual gender or age group. These establishments may provide basic alterations, such as hemming, taking in or letting out seams, or lengthening or shortening sleeves.

Cross-References. Establishments primarily engaged in—

- Retailing clothing for all genders via electronic home shopping, mail-order, or direct sale— are classified in Subsector 454, Nonstore Retailers;

- Retailing new men's and boys' clothing—are classified in Industry 448110, Men's Clothing Stores;

- Retailing new children's and infants' clothing—are classified in Industry 448130, Children's and Infants' Clothing Stores;

- Retailing new women's, misses', and juniors' clothing—are classified in Industry 448120, Women's Clothing Stores;

- Retailing specialized new apparel, such as raincoats, bridal gowns, leather coats, fur apparel, and swimwear,—are classified in Industry 448190, Other Clothing Stores;

- Retailing secondhand clothes—are classified in Industry 453310, Used Merchandise Stores; and

- Providing clothing alterations and repair—are classified in Industry 811490, Other Personal and Household Goods Repair and Maintenance.

44815 Clothing Accessories Stores[CAN]

See industry descriptions for 448150 below.

448150 Clothing Accessories Stores[CAN]

This industry comprises establishments primarily engaged in retailing single or combination lines of new clothing accessories, such as hats and caps, costume jewelry, gloves, handbags, ties, wigs, toupees, and belts.

Illustrative Examples:

Costume jewelry stores   Wig and hairpiece stores
Neckwear stores

Cross-References. Establishments primarily engaged in—

- Retailing specialized lines of clothing via electronic home shopping, mail-order, or direct sale—are classified in Subsector 454, Nonstore Retailers;

US—United States industry only. CAN—United States and Canadian industries are comparable. When neither US nor CAN appears, Canadian, Mexican, and United States industries are comparable.

- Retailing precious jewelry and watches—are classified in Industry 448310, Jewelry Stores;

- Retailing used clothing accessories—are classified in Industry 453310, Used Merchandise Stores;

- Retailing luggage, briefcases, trunks, or these products in combination with a general line of leather items (except leather apparel), known as luggage and leather goods stores,—are classified in Industry 448320, Luggage and Leather Goods Stores; and

- Retailing leather apparel—are classified in Industry 448190, Other Clothing Stores.

44819 Other Clothing Stores[CAN]

See industry description for 448190 below.

448190 Other Clothing Stores[CAN]

This industry comprises establishments primarily engaged in retailing specialized lines of new clothing (except general lines of men's, women's, children's, infants', and family clothing). These establishments may provide basic alterations, such as hemming, taking in or letting out seams, or lengthening or shortening sleeves.

Illustrative Examples:

Bridal gown (except custom) shops	Lingerie stores
Fur apparel stores	Swimwear stores
Hosiery stores	Uniform (except athletic) stores
Leather coat stores	

Cross-References. Establishments primarily engaged in—

- Retailing specialized apparel via electronic home shopping, mail-order, or direct sale—are classified in Subsector 454, Nonstore Retailers;

- Retailing custom apparel and accessories made on the premises—are classified in Subsector 315, Apparel Manufacturing;

- Retailing new women's, misses', and juniors' clothing, including maternity wear—are classified in Industry 448120, Women's Clothing Stores;

- Retailing new men's and boys' clothing—are classified in Industry 448110, Men's Clothing Stores;

- Retailing new children's and infants' clothing—are classified in Industry 448130, Children's and Infants' Clothing Stores;

- Retailing new clothing for all genders or age groups—are classified in Industry 448140, Family Clothing Stores;

- Retailing athletic uniforms—are classified in Industry 451110, Sporting Goods Stores;

- Retailing secondhand clothes—are classified in Industry 453310, Used Merchandise Stores;

US—United States industry only. CAN—United States and Canadian industries are comparable. When neither US nor CAN appears, Canadian, Mexican, and United States industries are comparable.

http://www.ntis.gov/naics

- Retailing luggage, briefcases, trunks, or these products in combination with a general line of leather items (except leather apparel), known as luggage and leather good stores,—are classified in Industry 448320, Luggage and Leather Goods Stores; and

- Providing clothing alterations and repair—are classified in Industry 811490, Other Personal Household Goods Repair and Maintenance.

4482 Shoe Stores^{CAN}

44821 Shoe Stores^{CAN}
See industry description for 448210 below.

448210 Shoe Stores^{CAN}

This industry comprises establishments primarily engaged in retailing all types of new footwear (except hosiery and specialty sports footwear, such as golf shoes, bowling shoes, and spiked shoes). Establishments primarily engaged in retailing new tennis shoes or sneakers are included in this industry.

Cross-References. Establishments primarily engaged in—

- Retailing footwear via electronic home shopping, mail-order, or direct sale—are classified in Subsector 454, Nonstore Retailers;

- Retailing hosiery—are classified in Industry 448190, Other Clothing Stores;

- Retailing new specialty sports footwear (e.g., bowling shoes, golf shoes, spiked shoes)— are classified in Industry 451110, Sporting Goods Stores; and

- Retailing used footwear—are classified in Industry 453310, Used Merchandise Stores.

4483 Jewelry, Luggage, and Leather Goods Stores^{CAN}

This industry group comprises establishments primarily engaged in retailing new jewelry (except costume jewelry); new silver and plated silverware; new watches and clocks; and new luggage with or without a general line of new leather goods and accessories, such as hats, gloves, handbags, ties, and belts.

44831 Jewelry Stores^{CAN}
See industry descriptions for 448310 below.

448310 Jewelry Stores^{CAN}

This industry comprises establishments primarily engaged in retailing one or more of the following items: (1) new jewelry (except costume jewelry); (2) new sterling and plated silverware; and (3) new watches and clocks. Also included are establishments retailing these new products in combination with lapidary work and/or repair services.

US—United States industry only. CAN—United States and Canadian industries are comparable. When neither US nor CAN appears, Canadian, Mexican, and United States industries are comparable.

Cross-References. Establishments primarily engaged in—

- Retailing new costume jewelry—are classified in Industry 448150, Clothing Accessories Stores;

- Retailing jewelry via electronic home shopping, mail order, or direct sale—are classified in Subsector 454, Nonstore Retailers;

- Retailing antiques or used jewelry, silverware, and watches and clocks—are classified in Industry 453310, Used Merchandise Stores;

- Providing jewelry or watch and clock repair without retailing new jewelry or watches and clocks—are classified in Industry 811490, Other Personal and Household Goods Repair and Maintenance; and

- Cutting and setting gem stones—are classified in U.S. Industry 339913, Jewelers' Material and Lapidary Work Manufacturing.

44832 Luggage and Leather Goods Stores[CAN]

See industry descriptions for 448320 below.

448320 Luggage and Leather Goods Stores[CAN]

This industry comprises establishments known as luggage and leather goods stores primarily engaged in retailing new luggage, briefcases, trunks, or these new products in combination with a general line of leather items (except leather apparel), such as belts, gloves, and handbags.

Cross-References. Establishments primarily engaged in—

- Retailing luggage and leather goods via electronic home shopping, mail-order, or direct sale—are classified in Subsector 454, Nonstore Retailers;

- Retailing used luggage and leather goods—are classified in Industry 453310, Used Merchandise Stores;

- Retailing single or combination lines of new clothing accessories (e.g., gloves, handbags, or leather belts)—are classified in Industry 448150, Clothing Accessories Stores; and

- Retailing new leather coats are classified in Industry 448190, Other Clothing Stores.

451 Sporting Goods, Hobby, Book, and Music Stores[CAN]

Industries in the Sporting Goods, Hobby, Book, and Music Stores subsector are engaged in retailing and providing expertise on use of sporting equipment or other specific leisure activities, such as needlework and musical instruments. Book stores are also included in this subsector.

4511 Sporting Goods, Hobby, and Musical Instrument Stores[CAN]

This industry group comprises establishments primarily engaged in retailing new sporting goods, games and toys, and musical instruments.

US—United States industry only. CAN—United States and Canadian industries are comparable. When neither US nor CAN appears, Canadian, Mexican, and United States industries are comparable.

45111 Sporting Goods Stores[CAN]

See industry description for 451110 below.

451110 Sporting Goods Stores[CAN]

This industry comprises establishments primarily engaged in retailing new sporting goods, such as bicycles and bicycle parts; camping equipment; exercise and fitness equipment; athletic uniforms; specialty sports footwear; and sporting goods, equipment, and accessories.

Illustrative Examples:

Athletic uniform supply stores
Bicycle (except motorized) shops
Bowling equipment and supply stores
Diving equipment stores
Exercise equipment stores
Fishing supply stores

Golf pro shops
Saddlery stores
Sporting goods (e.g., scuba, skiing, outdoor) stores
Sporting gun shops

Cross-References. Establishments primarily engaged in—

- Retailing sporting goods via electronic home shopping, mail order, or direct sale—are classified in Subsector 454, Nonstore Retailers;

- Retailing new or used campers (pickup coaches) and camping trailers—are classified in Industry 441210, Recreational Vehicle Dealers;

- Retailing new or used snowmobiles, motorized bicycles, and motorized golf carts—are classified in Industry 44122, Motorcycle, Boat, and Other Motor Vehicle Dealers;

- Retailing new shoes (except specialty sports footwear, such as golf shoes, bowling shoes, and spiked shoes)—are classified in Industry 448210, Shoe Stores;

- Repairing or servicing sporting goods, without retailing new sporting goods—are classified in Industry 811490, Other Personal and Household Goods Repair and Maintenance; and

- Retailing used sporting goods and used bicycles—are classified in Industry 453310, Used Merchandise Stores.

45112 Hobby, Toy, and Game Stores[CAN]

See industry description for 451120 below.

451120 Hobby, Toy, and Game Stores[CAN]

This industry comprises establishments primarily engaged in retailing new toys, games, and hobby and craft supplies (except needlecraft).

Cross-References. Establishments primarily engaged in—

- Retailing toys, games, and hobby and craft supplies via electronic home shopping, mail-order, or direct sale—are classified in Subsector 454, Nonstore Retailers;

- Retailing artists' supplies or collectors' items, such as coins, stamps, autographs, and cards,— are classified in U.S. Industry 453998, All Other Miscellaneous Store Retailers (except Tobacco Stores);

- Retailing new computer software (e.g., game software)—are classified in Industry 443120, Computer and Software Stores;

- Retailing used toys, games, and hobby supplies—are classified in Industry 453310, Used Merchandise Stores; and

- Retailing new sewing supplies, fabrics, and needlework accessories—are classified in Industry 451130, Sewing, Needlework, and Piece Goods Stores.

45113 Sewing, Needlework, and Piece Goods Stores[CAN]
See industry description for 451130 below.

451130 Sewing, Needlework, and Piece Goods Stores[CAN]

This industry comprises establishments primarily engaged in retailing new sewing supplies, fabrics, patterns, yarns, and other needlework accessories or retailing these products in combination with selling new sewing machines.

Illustrative Examples:

Fabric shops
Needlecraft sewing supply stores

Sewing supply stores
Upholstery materials stores

Cross-References. Establishments primarily engaged in—

- Retailing sewing supplies via electronic home shopping, mail-order, or direct sale—are classified in Subsector 454, Nonstore Retailers;

- Retailing new sewing machines only and in combination with retailing other new appliances—are classified in U.S. Industry 443111, Household Appliance Stores; and

- Retailing used sewing, needlework, and piece goods—are classified in Industry 453310, Used Merchandise Stores.

45114 Musical Instrument and Supplies Stores[CAN]
See industry description for 451140 below.

451140 Musical Instrument and Supplies Stores[CAN]

This industry comprises establishments primarily engaged in retailing new musical instruments, sheet music, and related supplies; or retailing these new products in combination with musical instrument repair, rental, or music instruction.

US—United States industry only. CAN—United States and Canadian industries are comparable. When neither US nor CAN appears, Canadian, Mexican, and United States industries are comparable.

Illustrative Examples:

Music instrument stores	Sheet music stores
Piano stores	

Cross-References. Establishments primarily engaged in—

- Retailing musical instruments, sheet music, and related supplies via electronic home shopping, mail-order, or direct sale—are classified in Subsector 454, Nonstore Retailers;

- Retailing new musical recordings—are classified in Industry 451220, Prerecorded Tape, Compact Disc, and Record Stores; and

- Retailing used musical instruments, sheet music, and related supplies—are classified in Industry 453310, Used Merchandise Stores.

4512 Book, Periodical, and Music Stores^{CAN}

This industry group comprises establishments primarily engaged in retailing new books, newspapers, magazines, and prerecorded audio and video media.

45121 Book Stores and News Dealers^{CAN}

This industry comprises establishments primarily engaged in retailing new books, newspapers, magazines, and other periodicals.

Cross-References. Establishments primarily engaged in—

- Retailing newspapers, magazines, and other periodicals via electronic home shopping, mail-order, or direct sale—are classified in Subsector 454, Nonstore Retailers;

- Home delivery of newspapers—are classified in Industry 45439, Other Direct Selling Establishments; and

- Retailing used books, newspapers, magazines, and other periodicals—are classified in Industry 45331, Used Merchandise Stores.

451211 Book Stores^{US}

This U.S. industry comprises establishments primarily engaged in retailing new books.

Cross-References. Establishments primarily engaged in—

- Retailing books via electronic home shopping, mail-order, or direct sale—are classified in Subsector 454, Nonstore Retailers; and

- Retailing used books—are classified in Industry 453310, Used Merchandise Stores.

US—United States industry only. CAN—United States and Canadian industries are comparable. When neither US nor CAN appears, Canadian, Mexican, and United States industries are comparable.

http://www.ntis.gov/naics

451212 News Dealers and Newsstands[US]

This U.S. industry comprises establishments primarily engaged in retailing current newspapers, magazines, and other periodicals.

Cross-References. Establishments primarily engaged in—

- Home delivery of newspapers—are classified in Industry 454390, Other Direct Selling Establishments;

- Retailing newspapers and periodicals by mail-order—are classified in Industry 454110, Electronic Shopping and Mail-Order Houses; and

- Retailing used newspapers, magazines, and other periodicals—are classified in Industry 453310, Used Merchandise Stores.

45122 Prerecorded Tape, Compact Disc, and Record Stores[CAN]

See industry description for 451220 below.

451220 Prerecorded Tape, Compact Disc, and Record Stores[CAN]

This industry comprises establishments primarily engaged in retailing new prerecorded audio and video tapes, compact discs (CDs), and phonograph records.

Cross-References. Establishments primarily engaged in—

- Retailing new computer software—are classified in Industry 443120, Computer and Software Stores;

- Retailing prerecorded tapes, compact discs, and records by mail-order—are classified in Industry 454110, Electronic Shopping and Mail-Order Houses;

- Retailing used phonograph records and prerecorded audio and video tapes and discs—are classified in Industry 453310, Used Merchandise Stores; and

- Retailing new audio sound equipment (except automotive)—are classified in U.S. Industry 443112, Radio, Television, and Other Electronics Stores.

452 General Merchandise Stores[CAN]

Industries in the General Merchandise Stores subsector retail new general merchandise from fixed point-of-sale locations. Establishments in this subsector are unique in that they have the equipment and staff capable of retailing a large variety of goods from a single location. This

---

US—United States industry only. CAN—United States and Canadian industries are comparable. When neither US nor CAN appears, Canadian, Mexican, and United States industries are comparable.

includes a variety of display equipment and staff trained to provide information on many lines of products.

4521 Department Stores[CAN]

45211 Department Stores[CAN]
See industry description for 452110 below.

452110 Department Stores[CAN]

This industry comprises establishments known as department stores primarily engaged in retailing a wide range of the following new products with no one merchandise line predominating: apparel, furniture, appliances and home furnishings; and selected additional items, such as paint, hardware, toiletries, cosmetics, photographic equipment, jewelry, toys, and sporting goods. Merchandise lines are normally arranged in separate departments.

Cross-References. Establishments primarily engaged in—

- Retailing prepackaged grocery items in combination with general lines of merchandise with no one merchandise line predominating—are classified in Industry 452910, Warehouse Clubs and Superstores;

- Retailing general lines of merchandise via electronic home shopping, mail-order, or direct sale—are classified in Subsector 454, Nonstore Retailers; and

- Retailing used merchandise—are classified in Industry 453310, Used Merchandise Stores.

4529 Other General Merchandise Stores[CAN]

This industry group comprises establishments primarily engaged in retailing new goods in general merchandise stores (except department stores).

45291 Warehouse Clubs and Superstores[CAN]
See industry description for 452910 below.

452910 Warehouse Clubs and Superstores[CAN]

This industry comprises establishments known as warehouse clubs, superstores or supercenters primarily engaged in retailing a general line of groceries in combination with general lines of new merchandise, such as apparel, furniture, and appliances.

Cross-References. Establishments primarily engaged in—

- Retailing general lines of merchandise via electronic home shopping, mail-order, or direct sale—are classified in Subsector 454, Nonstore Retailers;

US—United States industry only. CAN—United States and Canadian industries are comparable. When neither US nor CAN appears, Canadian, Mexican, and United States industries are comparable.

- Retailing a general line of food, generally known as supermarkets and grocery stores,—are classified in Industry 445110, Supermarkets and Other Grocery (except Convenience) Stores;

- Retailing general lines of new merchandise with little grocery item sales—are classified in Industry 452990, All Other General Merchandise Stores;

- Retailing new merchandise in department stores—are classified in Industry 452110, Department Stores; and

- Retailing used merchandise—are classified in Industry 453310, Used Merchandise Stores.

45299 All Other General Merchandise Stores^{CAN}
See industry description for 452990 below.

452990 All Other General Merchandise Stores^{CAN}

This industry comprises establishments primarily engaged in retailing new goods in general merchandise stores (except department stores, warehouse clubs, superstores, and supercenters). These establishments retail a general line of new merchandise, such as apparel, automotive parts, dry goods, hardware, groceries, housewares or home furnishings, and other lines in limited amounts, with none of the lines predominating.

Illustrative Examples:

Dollar stores
General merchandise catalog showrooms (except catalog mail-order)
General stores
General merchandise trading posts
Home and auto supply stores
Variety stores

Cross-References. Establishments primarily engaged in—

- Retailing general lines of merchandise via electronic home shopping, mail-order, or direct sale—are classified in Subsector 454, Nonstore Retailers;

- Retailing automotive parts—are classified in Industry 441310, Automotive Parts and Accessories Stores;

- Retailing merchandise in department stores—are classified in Industry 452110, Department Stores;

- Retailing merchandise in warehouse clubs, superstores, or supercenters—are classified in Industry 452910, Warehouse Clubs and Superstores;

- Retailing merchandise in catalogue showrooms of mail-order houses—are classified in Industry 454110, Electronic Shopping and Mail-Order Houses;

- Retailing a general line of new hardware items, known as hardware stores,—are classified in Industry 444130, Hardware Stores;

US—United States industry only. CAN—United States and Canadian industries are comparable. When neither US nor CAN appears, Canadian, Mexican, and United States industries are comparable.

- Retailing a general line of new home repair and improvement materials and supplies, known as home centers,—are classified in Industry 444110, Home Centers; and

- Retailing used merchandise—are classified in Industry 453310, Used Merchandise Stores.

453 Miscellaneous Store Retailers^{CAN}

Industries in the Miscellaneous Store Retailers subsector retail merchandise from fixed point-of-sale locations (except new or used motor vehicles and parts; new furniture and house furnishings; new appliances and electronic products; new building materials; and garden equipment and supplies; food and beverages; health and personal care goods; gasoline; new clothing and accessories; and new sporting goods, hobby goods, books, and music). Establishments in this subsector include stores with unique characteristics like florists, used merchandise stores, and pet and pet supply stores as well as other store retailers.

4531 Florists^{CAN}

45311 Florists^{CAN}
See industry description for 453110 below.

453110 Florists^{CAN}

This industry comprises establishments known as florists primarily engaged in retailing cut flowers, floral arrangements, and potted plants purchased from others. These establishments usually prepare the arrangements they sell.

Cross-References. Establishments primarily engaged in—

- Retailing flowers or nursery stock grown on premises—are classified in Industry 11142, Nursery and Floriculture Production;

- Retailing trees, shrubs, plants, seeds, bulbs, and sod grown elsewhere—are classified in Industry 444220, Nursery and Garden Centers; and

- Retailing flowers via electronic home shopping, mail-order, or direct sale—are classified in Subsector 454, Nonstore Retailers.

4532 Office Supplies, Stationery, and Gift Stores^{CAN}

45321 Office Supplies and Stationery Stores^{CAN}
See industry description for 453210 below.

453210 Office Supplies and Stationery Stores^{CAN}

This industry comprises establishments primarily engaged in one or more of the following: (1) retailing new stationery, school supplies, and office supplies; (2) selling a combination of new office equipment, furniture, and supplies; and (3) selling new office equipment, furniture, and supplies in combination with selling new computers.

US—United States industry only. CAN—United States and Canadian industries are comparable. When neither US nor CAN appears, Canadian, Mexican, and United States industries are comparable.

Cross-References. Establishments primarily engaged in—

- Retailing stationery, school supplies, and office supplies via electronic shopping, mail-order, or direct sale—are classified in Subsector 454, Nonstore Retailers;

- Retailing greeting cards—are classified in Industry 453220, Gift, Novelty, and Souvenir Stores;

- Retailing new typewriters—are classified in U.S. Industry 443112, Radio, Television, and Other Electronics Stores;

- Retailing new computers without retailing other consumer-type electronic products or office equipment, furniture, and supplies—are classified in Industry 443120, Computer and Software Stores;

- Printing business forms—are classified in Industry 32311, Printing;

- Retailing new office furniture—are classified in Industry 442110, Furniture Stores; and

- Retailing used office supplies—are classified in Industry 453310, Used Merchandise Stores.

45322 Gift, Novelty, and Souvenir Stores[CAN]
See industry description for 453220 below.

453220 Gift, Novelty, and Souvenir Stores[CAN]

This industry comprises establishments primarily engaged in retailing new gifts, novelty merchandise, souvenirs, greeting cards, seasonal and holiday decorations, and curios.

Illustrative Examples:

Balloon shops	Greeting card shops
Christmas stores	Novelty shops
Curio shops	Souvenir shops
Gift shops	

Cross-References. Establishments primarily engaged in—

- Retailing gifts and novelties via electronic home shopping, mail-order, or direct sale—are classified in Subsector 454, Nonstore Retailers;

- Retailing stationery—are classified in Industry 453210, Office Supplies and Stationery Stores; and

---

US—United States industry only. CAN—United States and Canadian industries are comparable. When neither US nor CAN appears, Canadian, Mexican, and United States industries are comparable.

- Retailing used curios and novelties—are classified in Industry 453310, Used Merchandise Stores.

4533 Used Merchandise Stores^{CAN}

45331 Used Merchandise Stores^{CAN}
See industry description for 453310 below.

453310 Used Merchandise Stores^{CAN}

This industry comprises establishments primarily engaged in retailing used merchandise, antiques, and secondhand goods (except motor vehicles, such as automobiles, RVs, motorcycles, and boats; motor vehicle parts; tires; and mobile homes).

Illustrative Examples:

Antique shops
Used book stores
Used clothing stores

Used household-type appliance stores
Used merchandise thrift shops
Used sporting goods stores

Cross-References. Establishments primarily engaged in—

- Retailing used merchandise via electronic home shopping, mail-order, or direct sale—are classified in Subsector 454, Nonstore Retailers;

- Operating pawnshops—are classified in U.S. Industry 522298, All Other Nondepository Credit Intermediation;

- Retailing used automobiles—are classified in Industry 441120, Used Car Dealers;

- Retailing used automobile parts (except tires and tubes)—are classified in Industry 441310, Automotive Parts and Accessories Stores;

- Retailing used tires—are classified in Industry 441320, Tire Dealers;

- Retailing used mobile homes—are classified in Industry 453930, Manufactured (Mobile) Home Dealers;

- Retailing used motorcycles—are classified in U.S. Industry 441221, Motorcycle Dealers;

- Retailing used recreational vehicles—are classified in Industry 441210, Recreation Vehicle Dealers;

- Retailing used boats—are classified in U.S. Industry 441222, Boat Dealers;

- Retailing used aircraft, snowmobiles, and utility trailers—are classified in U.S. Industry 441229, All Other Motor Vehicle Dealers; and

- Retailing a general line of used merchandise on an auction basis (not for others)—are classified in U.S. Industry 453998, All Other Miscellaneous Store Retailers (except Tobacco Stores).

US—United States industry only. CAN—United States and Canadian industries are comparable. When neither US nor CAN appears, Canadian, Mexican, and United States industries are comparable.

4539 Other Miscellaneous Store Retailers[CAN]

This industry group comprises establishments primarily engaged in retailing new miscellaneous specialty store merchandise (except motor vehicle and parts dealers; furniture and home furnishings stores; consumer-type electronics and appliance stores; building material and garden equipment and supplies dealers; food and beverage stores; health and personal care stores; gasoline stations; clothing and clothing accessories stores; sporting goods, hobby, book, and music stores; general merchandise stores; florists; office supplies, stationery, and gift stores; and used merchandise stores).

45391 Pet and Pet Supplies Stores[CAN]
See industry descriptions for 453910 below.

453910 Pet and Pet Supplies Stores[CAN]

This industry comprises establishments primarily engaged in retailing pets, pet foods, and pet supplies.

Cross References. Establishments primarily engaged in—

- Retailing pets, pet foods, and pet supplies via electronic home shopping, mail-order, or direct sale—are classified in Subsector 454, Nonstore Retailers;

- Providing pet grooming and boarding services—are classified in Industry 812910, Pet Care (except Veterinary) Services; and

- Providing veterinary services—are classified in Industry 541940, Veterinary Services.

45392 Art Dealers[CAN]
See industry descriptions for 453920 below.

453920 Art Dealers[CAN]

This industry comprises establishments primarily engaged in retailing original and limited edition art works. Included in this industry are establishments primarily engaged in displaying works of art for retail sale in art galleries.

Cross-References. Establishments primarily engaged in—

- Retailing original and limited edition art works via electronic home shopping, mail-order, or direct sale—are classified in Subsector 454, Nonstore Retailers;

- Retailing art reproductions (except limited editions)—are classified in U.S. Industry 442299, All Other Home Furnishings Stores;

- Retailing artists' supplies—are classified in U.S. Industry 453998, All Other Miscellaneous Store Retailers (except Tobacco Stores); and

- Displaying works of art not for retail sale in art galleries—are classified in Industry 712110, Museums.

US—United States industry only. CAN—United States and Canadian industries are comparable. When neither US nor CAN appears, Canadian, Mexican, and United States industries are comparable.

45393 Manufactured (Mobile) Home Dealers^{CAN}

See industry description for 453930 below.

453930 Manufactured (Mobile) Home Dealers^{CAN}

This industry comprises establishments primarily engaged in retailing new and/or used manufactured homes (i.e., mobile homes), parts, and equipment.

Cross-References. Establishments primarily engaged in—

- Retailing new or used motor homes, campers, and travel trailers—are classified in Industry 441210, Recreational Vehicle Dealers; and

- Retailing prefabricated buildings and kits without construction—are classified in Industry 444190, Other Building Material Dealers.

45399 All Other Miscellaneous Store Retailers^{CAN}

This industry comprises establishments primarily engaged in retailing specialized lines of merchandise (except motor vehicle and parts dealers; furniture and home furnishings stores; electronic and appliance stores; building material and garden equipment and supplies dealers; food and beverage stores; health and personal care stores; gasoline stations; clothing and clothing accessories stores; sporting goods, hobby, book, and music stores; general merchandise stores; florists; office supplies, stationery and gift stores; used merchandise stores; pet and pet supplies; art dealers; and manufactured home (i.e., mobile home) dealers). This industry also includes establishments primarily engaged in retailing a general line of new and used merchandise on an auction basis.

Illustrative Examples:

Art supply stores
Cemetery (e.g., markers, headstones, vaults)
  memorial dealers
Cigar stores
Swimming pool supply stores, new

Tobacco stores

Cross-References. Establishments primarily engaged in—

- Retailing merchandise via electronic home shopping, mail-order, or direct sale—are classified in Subsector 454, Nonstore Retailers;

- Auctioning on the location of others as independent auctioneers—are classified in Industry 56199, All Other Support Services;

- Retailing pets and pet supplies—are classified in Industry 45391, Pet and Pet Supplies Stores;

- Retailing original and limited edition art works—are classified in Industry 45392, Art Dealers;

US—United States industry only. CAN—United States and Canadian industries are comparable. When neither US nor CAN appears, Canadian, Mexican, and United States industries are comparable.

- Retailing manufactured homes (i.e., mobile homes)—are classified in Industry 45393, Manufactured (Mobile) Home Dealers;

- Retailing new books—are classified in Industry 45121, Book Stores and News Dealers;

- Retailing new jewelry (except costume jewelry)—are classified in Industry 44831, Jewelry Stores;

- Retailing new costume jewelry—are classified in Industry 44815, Clothing Accessories Stores; and

- Retailing used merchandise (except automobiles, RVs, mobile homes, motorcycles, boats, motor vehicle parts, and tires)—are classified in Industry 453310, Used Merchandise Stores.

453991 Tobacco Stores[US]

This U.S. industry comprises establishments primarily engaged in retailing cigarettes, cigars, tobacco, pipes, and other smokers' supplies.

Illustrative Examples:

Cigar stores
Cigarette stands (i.e., permanent)

Smokers' supply stores
Tobacco stores

Cross-References.

Establishments primarily engaged in retailing tobacco products and supplies via electronic home shopping, mail-order, or direct sale are classified in Subsector 454, Nonstore Retailers.

453998 All Other Miscellaneous Store Retailers (except Tobacco Stores)[US]

This U.S. industry comprises establishments primarily engaged in retailing specialized lines of merchandise (except motor vehicle and parts dealers; furniture and home furnishings stores; electronic and appliance stores; building material and garden equipment and supplies dealers; food and beverage stores; health and personal care stores; gasoline stations; clothing and clothing accessories stores; sporting goods, hobby, book and music stores; general merchandise stores; florists; office supplies, stationery and gift stores; used merchandise stores; pet and pet supplies stores; art dealers; manufactured home (i.e., mobile homes) dealers; and tobacco stores). This industry also includes establishments primarily engaged in retailing a general line of new and used merchandise on an auction basis.

Illustrative Examples:

Art supply stores
Candle shops
Cemetery memorial (e.g., headstones, markers, vaults) dealers
Collectors' items (e.g., autograph, coin, card, stamp) shops
Fireworks shops (permanent location)

Flower shops, artificial or dried
General merchandise auction houses
Home security equipment stores
Hot tub stores
Swimming pool supply stores
Trophy (e.g., awards and plaques) shops

US—United States industry only. CAN—United States and Canadian industries are comparable. When neither US nor CAN appears, Canadian, Mexican, and United States industries are comparable.

Cross-References. Establishments primarily engaged in—

- Retailing specialized lines of merchandise via electronic home shopping, mail-order, of direct sale—are classified in Subsector 454, Nonstore Retailers;

- Auctioning (i.e., on the location of others as independent auctioneers)—arc classified in Industry 561990, All Other Support Services;

- Retailing pets and pet supplies—are classified in Industry 453910, Pet and Pet Supplies Stores;

- Retailing original and limited edition art works—are classified in Industry 453920, Art Dealers;

- Retailing manufactured homes (i.e., mobile homes)—are classified in Industry 453930, Manufactured (Mobile) Home Dealers;

- Retailing cigarettes, cigars, tobacco, pipes, and other smokers' supplies—are classified in U.S. Industry 453991, Tobacco Stores;

- Retailing antiques—are classified in Industry 453310, Used Merchandise Stores;

- Retailing new books—are classified in U.S. Industry 451211, Book Stores;

- Retailing new jewelry (except costume jewelry)—are classified in Industry 448310, Jewelry Stores; and

- Retailing new costume jewelry—are classified in Industry 448150, Clothing Accessories Stores.

454 Nonstore Retailers[CAN]

Industries in the Nonstore Retailers subsector retail merchandise using methods, such as the broadcasting of infomercials, the broadcasting and publishing of direct-response advertising, the publishing of paper and electronic catalogues, door-to-door solicitation, in-home demonstration, selling from portable stalls and distribution through vending machines. Establishments in this subsector include mail-order houses, vending machine operators, home delivery sales, door-to-door sales, party plan sales, electronic shopping, and sales through portable stalls (e.g., street vendors, except food). Establishments engaged in the direct sale (i.e., nonstore) of products, such as home heating oil dealers, newspaper delivery are included in this subsector.

4541 Electronic Shopping and Mail-Order Houses[CAN]

45411 Electronic Shopping and Mail-Order Houses[CAN]
See industry description for 454110 below.

454110 Electronic Shopping and Mail-Order Houses[CAN]

This industry comprises establishments primarily engaged in retailing all types of merchandise by means of mail or by electronic media, such as interactive television or computer. Included in

---

US—United States industry only. CAN—United States and Canadian industries are comparable. When neither US nor CAN appears, Canadian, Mexican, and United States industries are comparable.

this industry are establishments primarily engaged in retailing from catalogue showrooms of mail-order houses.

Illustrative Examples:

Catalog (i.e., order-taking) office of mail-order houses

Collectors' items, mail-order houses

Computer software, mail-order houses

Home shopping television orders

Mail-order book clubs (not publishing)

Mail-order houses

Cross-References.

Establishments primarily engaged in providing telemarketing (e.g., telephone marketing) services for others are classified in U.S. Industry 561422, Telemarketing Bureaus.

4542 Vending Machine Operators^{CAN}

45421 Vending Machine Operators^{CAN}
See industry description for 454210 below.

454210 Vending Machine Operators^{CAN}

This industry comprises establishments primarily engaged in retailing merchandise through vending machines that they service.

Cross-References. Establishments primarily engaged in—

- Selling insurance policies through vending machines—are classified in Subsector 524, Insurance Carriers and Related Activities;

- Supplying and servicing coin-operated photobooths, restrooms, and lockers—are classified in Industry 812990, All Other Personal Services; and

- Supplying and servicing coin-operated amusement and gambling devices in places of business operated by others—are classified in Subsector 713, Amusement, Gambling, and Recreation Industries.

4543 Direct Selling Establishments^{CAN}

This industry group comprises establishments primarily engaged in nonstore retailing (except electronic, mail-order, or vending machine sales). These establishments typically go to the customers' location rather than the customer coming to them (e.g., door-to-door sales, home parties). Examples of establishments in this industry are home delivery newspaper routes; home delivery of heating oil, liquefied petroleum (LP) gas, and other fuels; locker meat provisioners; frozen food and freezer plan providers; coffee break services providers; and bottled water or water softener services.

US—United States industry only. CAN—United States and Canadian industries are comparable. When neither US nor CAN appears, Canadian, Mexican, and United States industries are comparable.

45431 Fuel Dealers^{CAN}

This industry comprises establishments primarily engaged in retailing heating oil, liquefied petroleum (LP) gas, and other fuels via direct selling.

Cross-References. Establishments primarily engaged in—

- Providing oil burner repair services—are classified in Industry 81141, Home and Garden Equipment and Appliance Repair and Maintenance; and

- Installing oil burners—are classified in Industry 23511, Plumbing, Heating, and Air-Conditioning Contractors.

454311 Heating Oil Dealers^{US}

This U.S. industry comprises establishments primarily engaged in retailing heating oil via direct selling.

Cross-References. Establishments primarily engaged in—

- Providing oil burner repair services—are classified in U.S. Industry 811411, Home and Garden Equipment Repair and Maintenance; and

- Installing oil burners—are classified in Industry 235110, Plumbing, Heating, and Air-Conditioning Contractors.

454312 Liquefied Petroleum Gas (Bottled Gas) Dealers^{US}

This U.S. industry comprises establishments primarily engaged in retailing liquefied petroleum (LP) gas via direct selling.

454319 Other Fuel Dealers^{US}

This U.S. industry comprises establishments primarily engaged in retailing fuels (except liquefied petroleum gas and heating oil) via direct selling.

45439 Other Direct Selling Establishments^{CAN}
See industry description for 454390 below.

454390 Other Direct Selling Establishments^{CAN}

This industry comprises establishments primarily engaged in retailing merchandise (except food for immediate consumption and fuel) via direct sale to the customer by means, such as in-house sales (i.e., party plan merchandising), truck or wagon sales, and portable stalls (i.e., street vendors).

US—United States industry only. CAN—United States and Canadian industries are comparable. When neither US nor CAN appears, Canadian, Mexican, and United States industries are comparable.

Illustrative Examples:

Direct selling bottled water providers
Direct selling coffee-break service providers
Direct selling frozen food and freezer plan
  providers

Direct selling home delivery newspaper routes
Direct selling party plan merchandisers
Direct selling locker meat provisioners

Cross-References. Establishments primarily engaged in—

- Preparing and selling meals and snacks for immediate consumption from motorized vehicles or nonmotorized carts catering a route—are classified in Industry 722330, Mobile Food Services;

- Retailing heating oil via direct sale—are classified in U.S. Industry 454311, Heating Oil Dealers;

- Retailing liquefied petroleum (LP) gas via direct sale—are classified in U.S. Industry 454312, Liquefied Petroleum Gas (Bottled Gas) Dealers; and

- Retailing other fuels, such as coal or wood, via direct sale—are classified in U.S. Industry 454319, Other Fuel Dealers.

Sector 48-49—Transportation and Warehousing

The Sector as a Whole

The Transportation and Warehousing sector includes industries providing transportation of passengers and cargo, warehousing and storage for goods, scenic and sightseeing transportation, and support activities related to modes of transportation. Establishments in these industries use transportation equipment or transportation related facilities as a productive asset. The type of equipment depends on the mode of transportation. The modes of transportation are air, rail, water, road, and pipeline.

The Transportation and Warehousing sector distinguishes three basic types of activities: subsectors for each mode of transportation, a subsector for warehousing and storage, and a subsector for establishments providing support activities for transportation. In addition, there are subsectors for establishments that provide passenger transportation for scenic and sightseeing purposes, postal services, and courier services.

A separate subsector for support activities is established in the sector because, first, support activities for transportation are inherently multimodal, such as freight transportation arrangement, or have multimodal aspects. Secondly, there are production process similarities among the support activity industries.

One of the support activities identified in the support activity subsector is the routine repair and maintenance of transportation equipment (e.g., aircraft at an airport, railroad rolling stock at a railroad terminal, or ships at a harbor or port facility). Such establishments do not perform complete overhauling or rebuilding of transportation equipment (i.e., periodic restoration of transportation equipment to original design specifications) or transportation equipment conversion (i.e., major modification to systems). An establishment that primarily performs factory (or shipyard) overhauls, rebuilding, or conversions of aircraft, railroad rolling stock, or a ship is classified in Subsector 336, Transportation Equipment Manufacturing according to the type of equipment.

Many of the establishments in this sector often operate on networks, with physical facilities, labor forces, and equipment spread over an extensive geographic area.

Warehousing establishments in this sector are distinguished from merchant wholesaling in that the warehouse establishments do not sell the goods.

Excluded from this sector are establishments primarily engaged in providing travel agent services that support transportation and other establishments, such as hotels, businesses, and government agencies. These establishments are classified in Sector 56, Administrative and Support, Waste Management, and Remediation Services. Also, establishments primarily engaged in providing rental and leasing of transportation equipment without operator are classified in Subsector 532, Rental and Leasing Services.

481 Air Transportation

Industries in the Air Transportation subsector provide air transportation of passengers and/or cargo using aircraft, such as airplanes and helicopters. The subsector distinguishes scheduled from nonscheduled air transportation. Scheduled air carriers fly regular routes on regular schedules and operate even if flights are only partially loaded. Nonscheduled carriers often operate during nonpeak time slots at busy airports. These establishments have more flexibility with respect to choice of

US—United States industry only. CAN—United States and Canadian industries are comparable. When neither US nor CAN appears, Canadian, Mexican, and United States industries are comparable.

http://www.ntis.gov/naics

airport, hours of operation, load factors, and similar operational characteristics. Nonscheduled carriers provide chartered air transportation of passengers, cargo, or specialty flying services. Specialty flying services establishments use general purpose aircraft to provide a variety of specialized flying services.

Scenic and sightseeing air transportation and air courier services are not included in this subsector but are included in Subsector 487, Scenic and Sightseeing Transportation and in Subsector 492, Couriers and Messengers. Although these activities may use aircraft, they are different from the activities included in air transportation. Air sightseeing does not usually involve place-to-place transportation; the passenger's flight (e.g., balloon ride, aerial sightseeing) typically starts and ends at the same location. Courier services (individual package or cargo delivery) includes more than air transportation; road transportation is usually required to deliver the cargo to the intended recipient.

4811 Scheduled Air Transportation

48111 Scheduled Air Transportation

This industry comprises establishments primarily engaged in providing air transportation of passengers and/or cargo over regular routes and on regular schedules. Establishments in this industry operate flights even if partially loaded. Establishments primarily engaged in providing scheduled air transportation of mail on a contract basis are included in this industry.

Illustrative Examples:

Air commuter carriers, scheduled	Scheduled air passenger carriers
Scheduled air cargo carriers (except air couriers)	Scheduled helicopter passenger carriers

Cross-References. Establishments primarily engaged in—

- Providing air courier services—are classified in Industry 49211, Couriers;

- Providing air transportation of passengers, cargo, or specialty flying services with no regular routes and regular schedules—are classified in Industry 48121, Nonscheduled Air Transportation; and

- Providing helicopter rides for scenic and sightseeing transportation—are classified in Industry 48799, Scenic and Sightseeing Transportation, Other.

481111 Scheduled Passenger Air Transportation[US]

This U.S. industry comprises establishments primarily engaged in providing air transportation of passengers or passengers and freight over regular routes and on regular schedules. Establishments in this industry operate flights even if partially loaded. Scheduled air passenger carriers including commuter and helicopter carriers (except scenic and sightseeing) are included in this industry.

US—United States industry only. CAN—United States and Canadian industries are comparable. When neither US nor CAN appears, Canadian, Mexican, and United States industries are comparable.

Cross-References. Establishments primarily engaged in—

- Providing air transportation of passengers or passengers and cargo with no regular routes and regular schedules—are classified in U.S. Industry 481211; Nonscheduled Chartered Passenger Air Transportation;

- Providing helicopter rides for scenic and sightseeing transportation—are classified in Industry 487990, Scenic and Sightseeing Transportation, Other; and

- Providing air transportation of cargo (without transporting passengers) over regular routes and on regular schedules—are classified in U.S. Industry 481112, Scheduled Freight Air Transportation.

481112 Scheduled Freight Air Transportation[US]

This U.S. industry comprises establishments primarily engaged in providing air transportation of cargo without transporting passengers over regular routes and on regular schedules. Establishments in this industry operate flights even if partially loaded. Establishments primarily engaged in providing scheduled air transportation of mail on a contract basis are included in this industry.

Cross-References. Establishments primarily engaged in—

- Providing air courier services—are classified in Industry 492110, Couriers;

- Providing air transportation of cargo with no regular routes and regular schedules   are classified in U.S. Industry 481212, Nonscheduled Chartered Freight Air Transportation; and

- Providing air transportation of passengers or passengers and cargo over regular routes and on regular schedules—are classified in U.S. Industry 481112, Scheduled Passenger Air Transportation.

4812 Nonscheduled Air Transportation

48121 Nonscheduled Air Transportation

This industry comprises establishments primarily engaged in (1) providing air transportation of passengers and/or cargo with no regular routes and regular schedules or (2) providing specialty flying services with no regular routes and regular schedules using general purpose aircraft. These establishments have more flexibility with respect to choice of airports, hours of operation, load factors, and similar operational characteristics.

Illustrative Examples:

Air taxi services
Aircraft charter services
Nonscheduled air freight
 transportation services

Nonscheduled air passenger
 transportation services

US—United States industry only. CAN—United States and Canadian industries are comparable. When neither US nor CAN appears, Canadian, Mexican, and United States industries are comparable.

Cross-References. Establishments primarily engaged in—

- Crop dusting using specialized aircraft—are classified in Industry 11511, Support Activities for Crop Production;

- Fighting forest fires using specialized water bombers—are classified in Industry 11531, Support Activities for Forestry;

- Providing air transportation of passengers and/or cargo over regular routes and on regular schedules—are classified in Industry 48111, Scheduled Air Transportation;

- Providing specialized air sightseeing services—are classified in Industry 48799, Scenic and Sightseeing Transportation, Other;

- Aerial gathering of geophysical data—are classified in Industry 54136, Geophysical Surveying and Mapping Services;

- Providing aerial and/or other surveying and mapping services—are classified in Industry 54137, Surveying and Mapping (except Geophysical) Services;

- Providing air ambulance services using specialized equipment—are classified in Industry 62191, Ambulance Services;

- Operating specialized flying schools, including all training for commercial pilots—are classified in Industry 61151, Technical and Trade Schools;

- Operating recreation aviation clubs—are classified in Industry 71399, All Other Amusement and Recreation Industries;

- Operating advocacy aviation clubs—are classified in U.S. Industry 81331, Social Advocacy Organizations; and

- Providing air courier services—are classified in Industry 49211, Couriers.

481211 Nonscheduled Chartered Passenger Air Transportation[US]

This U.S. industry comprises establishments primarily engaged in providing air transportation of passengers or passengers and cargo with no regular routes and regular schedules.

Cross-References. Establishments primarily engaged in—

- Providing specialty air transportation or flying services with no regular routes and regular schedules using general purpose aircraft—are classified in U.S. Industry 481219, Other Nonscheduled Air Transportation;

- Providing specialized air sightseeing services—are classified in Industry 487990, Scenic and Sightseeing Transportation, Other;

- Providing air transportation of passengers or passengers and cargo over regular routes and on regular schedules—are classified in U.S. Industry 481111, Scheduled Passenger Air Transportation; and

- Providing air transportation of cargo (without transporting passengers) with no regular routes and schedules—are classified in U.S. Industry 481212, Nonscheduled Chartered Freight Air Transportation.

481212 Nonscheduled Chartered Freight Air Transportation[US]

This U.S. industry comprises establishments primarily engaged in providing air transportation of cargo without transporting passengers with no regular routes and regular schedules.

Cross-References. Establishments primarily engaged in—

- Providing specialty air transportation or flying services with no regular routes and regular schedules using general purpose aircraft—are classified in U.S. Industry 481219, Other Nonscheduled Air Transportation;

- Providing air courier services—are classified in Industry 492110, Couriers;

- Providing air transportation of cargo without transporting passengers over regular routes and on regular schedules—are classified in U.S. Industry 481112, Scheduled Freight Air Transportation; and

- Providing air transportation of cargo and passengers with no regular routes and schedules— are classified in U.S. Industry 481211, Nonscheduled Chartered Passenger Air Transportation.

481219 Other Nonscheduled Air Transportation[US]

This U.S. industry comprises establishments primarily engaged in providing air transportation with no regular routes and regular schedules (except nonscheduled chartered passenger and/or cargo air transportation). These establishments provide a variety of specialty air transportation or flying services based on individual customer needs using general purpose aircraft.

Illustrative Examples:

Aircraft charter services (i.e., general purpose aircraft used for a variety of specialty air and flying services)

Aviation clubs providing a variety of air transportation activities to the general public

Cross-References. Establishments primarily engaged in—

- Providing air transportation of passengers or passengers and cargo with no regular routes and regular schedules—are classified in U.S. Industry 481211, Nonscheduled Chartered Passenger Air Transportation;

- Providing air transportation of cargo without transporting passengers with no regular routes and regular schedules—are classified in U.S. Industry 481212, Nonscheduled Chartered Freight Air Transportation;

US—United States industry only. CAN—United States and Canadian industries are comparable. When neither US nor CAN appears, Canadian, Mexican, and United States industries are comparable.

- Crop dusting using specialized aircraft—are classified in U.S. Industry 115112, Soil Preparation, Planting, and Cultivating;

- Fighting forest fires using specialized water bombers—are classified in Industry 115310, Support Activities for Forestry;

- Providing specialized air sightseeing services—are classified in Industry 487990, Scenic and Sightseeing Transportation, Other;

- Operating specialized flying schools, including all training for commercial pilots—are classified in U.S. Industry 611512, Flight Training;

- Providing specialized air ambulance services using specialized equipment—are classified in U.S. Industry 621999, All Other Miscellaneous Ambulatory Health Care Services;

- Operating recreation aviation clubs—are classified in Industry 713990, All Other Amusement and Recreation Industries;

- Operating advocacy aviation clubs—are classified in U.S. Industry 813319, Other Social Advocacy Organizations;

- Aerial gathering of geophysical data for surveying and mapping—are classified in Industry 541360, Geophysical Surveying and Mapping Services; and

- Providing aerial and/or other surveying and mapping services—are classified in Industry 541370, Surveying and Mapping (except Geophysical) Services.

482 Rail Transportation

Industries in the Rail Transportation subsector provide rail transportation of passengers and/or cargo using railroad rolling stock. The railroads in this subsector primarily either operate on networks, with physical facilities, labor force, and equipment spread over an extensive geographic area, or operate over a short distance on a local rail line.

Scenic and sightseeing rail transportation and street railroads, commuter rail, and rapid transit are not included in this subsector but are included in Subsector 487, Scenic and Sightseeing Transportation, and Subsector 485, Transit and Ground Passenger Transportation, respectively. Although these activities use railroad rolling stock, they are different from the activities included in rail transportation. Sightseeing and scenic railroads do not usually involve place-to-place transportation; the passenger's trip typically starts and ends at the same location. Commuter railroads operate in a manner more consistent with local and urban transit and are often part of integrated transit systems.

4821 Rail Transportation

48211 Rail Transportation

This industry comprises establishments primarily engaged in operating railroads (except street railroads, commuter rail, urban rapid transit, and scenic and sightseeing trains). Line-haul railroads and short line railroads are included in this industry.

US—United States industry only. CAN—United States and Canadian industries are comparable. When neither US nor CAN appears, Canadian, Mexican, and United States industries are comparable.

Cross-References. Establishments primarily engaged in—

- Operating street railroads, commuter rail, and urban rapid transit systems—are classified in Industry Group 4851, Urban Transit Systems;

- Operating scenic and sightseeing trains—are classified in Industry 48711, Scenic and Sightseeing Transportation, Land; and

- Operating switching and terminal facilities as separate establishments—are classified in Industry 48821, Support Activities for Rail Transportation.

482111 Line-Haul Railroads[US]

This U.S. industry comprises establishments known as line-haul railroads primarily engaged in operating railroads for the transport of passengers and/or cargo over a long distance within a rail network. These establishments provide for the intercity movement of trains between the terminals and stations on main and branch lines of a line-haul rail network (except for local switching services).

Cross-References. Establishments primarily engaged in—

- Operating switching and terminal facilities as separate establishments—are classified in Industry 488210, Support Activities for Rail Transportation;

- Operating railroads over a short distance on local rail lines—are classified in U.S. Industry 482112, Short Line Railroads; and

- Operating commuter rail systems—are classified in U.S. Industry 485112, Commuter Rail Systems.

482112 Short Line Railroads[CAN]

This U.S. industry comprises establishments known as short line railroads primarily engaged in operating railroads for the transport of cargo over a short distance on local rail lines not part of a rail network.

Cross-References. Establishments primarily engaged in—

- Operating street railroads, commuter rail, and urban rapid transit systems—are classified in Industry Group 4851, Urban Transit Systems;

- Operating scenic and sightseeing trains—are classified in Industry 487110, Scenic and Sightseeing Transportation, Land;

- Operating switching and terminal facilities as separate establishments—are classified in Industry 488210, Support Activities for Rail Transportation; and

- Operating railroads for the transport of passengers and/or cargo over a long distance—are classified in U.S. Industry 482111, Line-Haul Railroads.

US—United States industry only. CAN—United States and Canadian industries are comparable. When neither US nor CAN appears, Canadian, Mexican, and United States industries are comparable.

483 Water Transportation

Industries in the Water Transportation subsector provide water transportation of passengers and cargo using watercraft, such as ships, barges, and boats.

The subsector is composed of two industry groups: (1) one for deep sea, coastal, and Great Lakes; and (2) one for inland water transportation. This split typically reflects the difference in equipment used.

Scenic and sightseeing water transportation services are not included in this subsector but are included in Subsector 487, Scenic and Sightseeing Transportation. Although these activities use watercraft, they are different from the activities included in water transportation. Water sightseeing does not usually involve place-to-place transportation; the passenger's trip starts and ends at the same location.

4831 Deep Sea, Coastal, and Great Lakes Water Transportation

48311 Deep Sea, Coastal, and Great Lakes Water Transportation

This industry comprises establishments primarily engaged in providing deep sea, coastal, Great Lakes, and St. Lawrence Seaway water transportation. Marine transportation establishments using the facilities of the St. Lawrence Seaway Authority Commission are considered to be using the Great Lakes Water Transportation System.

Cross-References. Establishments primarily engaged in—

- Providing inland water transportation on lakes, rivers, or intracoastal waterways (except on the Great Lakes System)—are classified in Industry 48321, Inland Water Transportation;

- Providing scenic and sightseeing water transportation, such as harbor cruises,—are classified in Industry 48721, Scenic and Sightseeing Transportation, Water; and

- Operating floating casinos (i.e., gambling cruises, riverboat gambling casinos)—are classified in Industry 71321, Casinos (except Casino Hotels).

483111 Deep Sea Freight Transportation[US]

This U.S. industry comprises establishments primarily engaged in providing deep sea transportation of cargo to or from foreign ports.

Cross-References.

Establishments primarily engaged in providing deep sea transportation of cargo to and from domestic ports are classified in U.S. Industry 483113, Coastal and Great Lakes Freight Transportation.

483112 Deep Sea Passenger Transportation[US]

This U.S. industry comprises establishments primarily engaged in providing deep sea transportation of passengers to or from foreign ports.

US—United States industry only. CAN—United States and Canadian industries are comparable. When neither US nor CAN appears, Canadian, Mexican, and United States industries are comparable.

Cross-References. Establishments primarily engaged in—

- Providing deep sea transportation of passengers to and from domestic ports—are classified in U.S. Industry 483114, Coastal and Great Lakes Passenger Transportation; and

- Operating floating casinos (i.e., gambling cruises)—are classified in Industry 713210, Casinos (except Casino Hotels).

483113 Coastal and Great Lakes Freight Transportation[US]

This U.S. industry comprises establishments primarily engaged in providing water transportation of cargo in coastal waters, on the Great Lakes System, or deep seas between ports of the United States, Puerto Rico, and United States island possessions or protectorates. Marine transportation establishments using the facilities of the St. Lawrence Seaway Authority Commission are considered to be using the Great Lakes Water Transportation System. Establishments primarily engaged in providing coastal and/or Great Lakes barge transportation services are included in this industry.

Cross-References. Establishments primarily engaged in—

- Providing deep sea transportation of cargo to or from foreign ports—are classified in U.S. Industry 483111, Deep Sea Freight Transportation; and

- Providing inland water transportation of cargo on lakes, rivers, or intracoastal waterways (except on the Great Lakes System)—are classified in U.S. Industry 483211, Inland Water Freight Transportation.

483114 Coastal and Great Lakes Passenger Transportation[US]

This U.S. industry comprises establishments primarily engaged in providing water transportation of passengers in coastal waters, the Great Lakes System, or deep seas between ports of the United States, Puerto Rico, and United States island possessions and protectorates. Marine transportation establishments using the facilities of the St. Lawrence Seaway Authority Commission are considered to be using the Great Lakes Water Transportation System.

Cross-References. Establishments primarily engaged in—

- Providing inland water transportation of passengers on lakes, rivers or intracoastal waterways (except on the Great Lakes System)—are classified in U.S. Industry 483212, Inland Water Passenger Transportation;

- Providing scenic and sightseeing water transportation, such as harbor cruises,—are classified in Industry 487210, Scenic and Sightseeing Transportation, Water; and

- Operating floating casinos (i.e., gambling cruises)—are classified in Industry 713210, Casinos (except Casino Hotels).

4832 Inland Water Transportation

48321 Inland Water Transportation

This industry comprises establishments primarily engaged in providing inland water transportation of passengers and/or cargo on lakes, rivers, or intracoastal waterways (except on the Great Lakes System).

US—United States industry only. CAN—United States and Canadian industries are comparable. When neither US nor CAN appears, Canadian, Mexican, and United States industries are comparable.

Cross-References. Establishments primarily engaged in—

- Providing water transportation in deep sea, coastal, or on the Great Lakes System—are classified in Industry Group 4831, Deep Sea, Coastal and Great Lakes Water Transportation;

- Providing scenic and sightseeing water transportation, such as harbor cruises,—are classified in Industry 48721, Scenic and Sightseeing Transportation, Water; and

- Operating floating casinos (i.e., gambling cruises, riverboat gambling casinos)—are classified in Industry 71321, Casinos (except Casino Hotels).

483211 Inland Water Freight Transportation[US]

This U.S. industry comprises establishments primarily engaged in providing inland water transportation of cargo on lakes, rivers, or intracoastal waterways (except on the Great Lakes System).

Cross-References. Establishments primarily engaged in—

- Providing deep sea transportation of cargo to and from foreign ports—are classified in U.S. Industry 483111, Deep Sea Freight Transportation; and

- Providing water transportation of cargo in coastal waters or on the Great Lakes System— are classified in U.S. Industry 483113, Coastal and Great Lakes Freight Transportation.

483212 Inland Water Passenger Transportation[US]

This U.S. industry comprises establishments primarily engaged in providing inland water transportation of passengers on lakes, rivers, or intracoastal waterways (except on the Great Lakes System).

Cross-References. Establishments primarily engaged in—

- Providing deep sea transportation of passengers to and from foreign ports—are classified in U.S. Industry 483112, Deep Sea Passenger Transportation;

- Operating cruise ships or ferries in coastal waters or on the Great Lakes System—are classified in U.S. Industry 483114, Coastal and Great Lakes Passenger Transportation; and

- Providing scenic and sightseeing water transportation, such as harbor cruises,—are classified in Industry 487210, Scenic and Sightseeing Transportation, Water.

484 Truck Transportation

Industries in the Truck Transportation subsector provide over-the-road transportation of cargo using motor vehicles, such as trucks and tractor trailers. The subsector is subdivided into general freight trucking and specialized freight trucking. This distinction reflects differences in equipment used, type of load carried, scheduling, terminal, and other networking services. General freight transportation establishments handle a wide variety of general commodities, generally palletized, and transported in a container or van trailer. Specialized freight transportation is the transportation of cargo that, because of size, weight, shape, or other inherent characteristics require specialized equipment for transportation.

US—United States industry only. CAN—United States and Canadian industries are comparable. When neither US nor CAN appears, Canadian, Mexican, and United States industries are comparable.

Each of these industry groups is further subdivided based on distance traveled. Local trucking establishments primarily carry goods within a single metropolitan area and its adjacent nonurban areas. Long distance trucking establishments carry goods between metropolitan areas.

The Specialized Freight Trucking industry group includes a separate industry for Used Household and Office Goods Moving. The household and office goods movers are separated because of the substantial network of establishments that has developed to deal with local and long-distance moving and the associated storage. In this area, the same establishment provides both local and long-distance services, while other specialized freight establishments generally limit their services to either local or long-distance hauling.

4841 General Freight Trucking

This industry group comprises establishments primarily engaged in providing general freight trucking. General freight establishments handle a wide variety of commodities, generally palletized, and transported in a container or van trailer. The establishments of this industry group provide a combination of the following network activities: local pickup, local sorting and terminal operations, line-haul, destination sorting and terminal operations, and local delivery.

48411 General Freight Trucking, Local
See industry description for 484110 below.

484110 General Freight Trucking, Local

This industry comprises establishments primarily engaged in providing local general freight trucking. General freight establishments handle a wide variety of commodities, generally palletized and transported in a container or van trailer. Local general freight trucking establishments usually provide trucking within a metropolitan area which may cross state lines. Generally the trips are same-day return.

Cross-References. Establishments primarily engaged in—

- Operating independent trucking terminals—are classified in Industry 488490, Other Support Activities for Road Transportation; and

- Providing general freight long-distance trucking including all North American international travel—are classified in Industry 48412, General Freight Trucking, Long-Distance.

48412 General Freight Trucking, Long-Distance

This industry comprises establishments primarily engaged in providing long-distance general freight trucking. General freight establishments handle a wide variety of commodities, generally palletized and transported in a container or van trailer. Long-distance general freight trucking establishments usually provide trucking between metropolitan areas which may cross North American country borders. Included in this industry are establishments operating as truckload (TL) or less than truckload (LTL) carriers.

US—United States industry only. CAN—United States and Canadian industries are comparable. When neither US nor CAN appears, Canadian, Mexican, and United States industries are comparable.

Cross-References. Establishments primarily engaged in—

- Providing courier services—are classified in Industry 49211, Couriers;

- Providing warehousing services of general freight—are classified in Industry 49311, General Warehousing and Storage;

- Providing specialized freight trucking—are classified in Industry Group 4842, Specialized Freight Trucking;

- Operating independent trucking terminals—are classified in Industry 48849, Other Support Activities for Road Transportation; and

- Providing local general freight trucking services—are classified in Industry 48411, General Freight Trucking, Local.

484121 General Freight Trucking, Long-Distance, Truckload[CAN]

This U.S. industry comprises establishments primarily engaged in providing long-distance general freight truckload (TL) trucking. These long-distance general freight truckload carrier establishments provide full truck movement of freight from origin to destination. The shipment of freight on a truck is characterized as a full single load not combined with other shipments.

Cross-References. Establishments primarily engaged in—

- Providing general freight long-distance, less than truckload trucking—are classified in U.S. Industry 484122, General Freight Trucking, Long-Distance, Less Than Truckload;

- Providing specialized freight trucking—are classified in Industry Group 4842, Specialized Freight Trucking;

- Operating independent trucking terminals—are classified in Industry 488490, Other Support Activities for Road Transportation; and

- Providing local general freight trucking services—are classified in Industry 484110, General Freight Trucking, Local.

484122 General Freight Trucking, Long-Distance, Less Than Truckload[CAN]

This U.S. industry comprises establishments primarily engaged in providing long-distance, general freight, less than truckload (LTL) trucking. LTL carriage is characterized as multiple shipments combined onto a single truck for multiple deliveries within a network. These establishments are generally characterized by the following network activities: local pickup, local sorting and terminal operations, line-haul, destination sorting and terminal operations, and local delivery.

Cross-References. Establishments primarily engaged in—

- Providing courier services—are classified in Industry 492110, Couriers;

- Providing warehousing services of general freight—are classified in Industry 493110, General Warehousing and Storage;

US—United States industry only. CAN—United States and Canadian industries are comparable. When neither US nor CAN appears, Canadian, Mexican, and United States industries are comparable.

- Providing specialized freight trucking—are classified in Industry Group 4842, Specialized Freight Trucking;

- Operating independent trucking terminals—are classified in Industry 488490, Other Support Activities for Road Transportation;

- Providing general freight long-distance truckload trucking—are classified in U.S. Industry 484121, General Freight Trucking, Long-Distance, Truckload; and

- Providing local general freight trucking services—are classified in Industry 484110, General Freight Trucking, Local.

4842 Specialized Freight Trucking

This industry group comprises establishments primarily engaged in providing local or long-distance specialized freight trucking. The establishments of this industry are primarily engaged in the transportation of freight which, because of size, weight, shape, or other inherent characteristics, requires specialized equipment, such as flatbeds, tankers, or refrigerated trailers. This industry includes the transportation of used household, institutional, and commercial furniture and equipment.

48421 Used Household and Office Goods Moving
See industry description for 484210 below.

484210 Used Household and Office Goods Moving

This industry comprises establishments primarily engaged in providing local or long-distance trucking of used household, used institutional, or used commercial furniture and equipment. Incidental packing and storage activities are often provided by these establishments.

48422 Specialized Freight (except Used Goods) Trucking, Local
See industry description for 484220 below.

484220 Specialized Freight (except Used Goods) Trucking, Local

This industry comprises establishments primarily engaged in providing local, specialized trucking. Local trucking establishments provide trucking within a metropolitan area that may cross state lines. Generally the trips are same-day return.

Illustrative Examples:

Local agricultural products trucking
Local boat hauling
Local bulk liquids trucking

Local dump trucking (e.g., gravel, sand, top-soil)
Local livestock trucking

Cross-References. Establishments primarily engaged in—

- Providing long-distance specialized freight (except used goods) trucking including all North American international travel—are classified in Industry 48423, Specialized Freight (except Used Goods) Trucking, Long-Distance;

US—United States industry only. CAN—United States and Canadian industries are comparable. When neither US nor CAN appears, Canadian, Mexican, and United States industries are comparable.

http://www.ntis.gov/naics

- Providing local general freight trucking—are classified in U.S. Industry 484110, General Freight Trucking, Local;

- Providing trucking of used household and office goods—are classified in Industry 484210, Used Household and Office Goods Moving; and

- Providing waste collection—are classified in Industry Group 5621, Waste Collection.

48423 Specialized Freight (except Used Goods) Trucking, Long-Distance
See industry description for 484230 below.

484230 Specialized Freight (except Used Goods) Trucking, Long-Distance

This industry comprises establishments primarily engaged in providing long-distance specialized trucking. These establishments provide trucking between metropolitan areas that may cross North American country borders.

Illustrative Examples:

Long-distance automobile carrier trucking   Long-distance bulk liquid trucking
Long-distance hazardous material trucking   Long-distance refrigerated product trucking

Cross-References. Establishments primarily engaged in—

- Providing local specialized freight trucking (except used goods)—are classified in Industry 484220, Specialized Freight (except Used Goods) Trucking, Local;

- Providing long-distance general freight trucking including all North American international travel—are classified in Industry 48412, General Freight Trucking, Long-Distance; and

- Providing trucking of used household and office goods—are classified in Industry 484210, Used Household and Office Goods Moving.

485 Transit and Ground Passenger Transportation

Industries in the Transit and Ground Passenger Transportation subsector include a variety of passenger transportation activities, such as urban transit systems; chartered bus, school bus, and interurban bus transportation; and taxis. These activities are distinguished based primarily on such production process factors as vehicle types, routes, and schedules.

In this subsector, the principal splits identify scheduled transportation as separate from nonscheduled transportation. The scheduled transportation industry groups are Urban Transit Systems, Interurban and Rural Bus Transportation, and School and Employee Bus Transportation. The nonscheduled industry groups are the Charter Bus Industry and Taxi and Limousine Service. The Other Transit and Ground Passenger Transportation Industry group includes both scheduled and nonscheduled transportation.

US—United States industry only. CAN—United States and Canadian industries are comparable. When neither US nor CAN appears, Canadian, Mexican, and United States industries are comparable.

Scenic and sightseeing ground transportation services are not included in this subsector but are included in Subsector 487, Scenic and Sightseeing Transportation. Sightseeing does not usually involve place-to-place transportation; the passenger's trip starts and ends at the same location.

4851 Urban Transit Systems

48511 Urban Transit Systems

This industry comprises establishments primarily engaged in operating local and suburban passenger transit systems over regular routes and on regular schedules within a metropolitan area and its adjacent nonurban areas. Such transportation systems involve the use of one or more modes of transport including light rail, commuter rail, subways, streetcars, as well as buses and other motor vehicles.

Cross-References. Establishments primarily engaged in—

- Operating local and suburban passenger transit systems using only one mode of transportation—are classified according to the mode of transport;

- Providing scenic and sightseeing transportation—are classified in Industry 48711, Scenic and Sightseeing Transportation, Land;

- Providing support services to transit and ground transportation—are classified in Industry Group 4884, Support Activities for Road Transportation; and

- Providing interurban and rural bus transportation—are classified in Industry 48521, Interurban and Rural Bus Transportation.

485111 Mixed Mode Transit Systems[US]

This U.S. industry comprises establishments primarily engaged in operating local and suburban ground passenger transit systems using more than one mode of transport over regular routes and on regular schedules within a metropolitan area and its adjacent nonurban areas.

Cross-References. Establishments primarily engaged in—

- Operating local and suburban passenger transit systems using only one mode of transportation—are classified according to the mode of transport; and

- Providing support services to transit and ground passenger transportation—are classified in Industry Group 4884, Support Activities for Road Transportation.

485112 Commuter Rail Systems[US]

This U.S. industry comprises establishments primarily engaged in operating local and suburban commuter rail systems over regular routes and on a regular schedule within a metropolitan area and its adjacent nonurban areas. Commuter rail is usually characterized by reduced fares, multiple ride, and commutation tickets and mostly used by passengers during the morning and evening peak periods.

US—United States industry only. CAN—United States and Canadian industries are comparable. When neither US nor CAN appears, Canadian, Mexican, and United States industries are comparable.

Cross-References. Establishments primarily engaged in—

- Operating local and suburban mass passenger transit systems using both commuter rail and another mode of transport—are classified in U.S. Industry 485111, Mixed Mode Transit Systems;

- Operating a subway system—are classified in U.S. Industry 485119, Other Urban Transit Systems; and

- Providing scenic and sightseeing transportation on land—are classified in Industry 487110, Scenic and Sightseeing Transportation, Land.

485113 Bus and Other Motor Vehicle Transit Systems[US]

This U.S. industry comprises establishments primarily engaged in operating local and suburban passenger transportation systems using buses or other motor vehicles over regular routes and on regular schedules within a metropolitan area and its adjacent nonurban areas.

Cross-References. Establishments primarily engaged in—

- Operating local and suburban passenger transportation systems using both a bus or other motor vehicle and another mode of transport—are classified in U.S. Industry 485111, Mixed Mode Transit Systems;

- Providing interurban and rural bus transportation—are classified in Industry 485210, Interurban and Rural Bus Transportation; and

- Providing scenic and sightseeing transportation using buses or other motor vehicles—are classified in Industry 487110, Scenic and Sightseeing Transportation, Land.

485119 Other Urban Transit Systems[US]

This U.S. industry comprises establishments primarily engaged in operating local and suburban ground passenger transit systems (except mixed mode transit systems, commuter rail systems, and buses and other motor vehicles) over regular routes and on regular schedules within a metropolitan area and its adjacent nonurban areas.

Illustrative Examples:

Commuter cable car systems (i.e., stand-alone)	Light rail systems (i.e., stand-alone)
Commuter tramway systems (i.e., stand-alone)	Monorail transit systems (i.e., stand-alone)
Commuter trolley systems (i.e., stand-alone)	

Cross-References. Establishment primarily engaged in—

- Operating local and suburban ground passenger transit systems using more than one mode of transport—are classified in U.S. Industry 485111, Mixed Mode Transit Systems;

- Providing local and suburban passenger transportation using commuter rail systems—are classified in U.S. Industry 485112, Commuter Rail Systems; and

---

US—United States industry only. CAN—United States and Canadian industries are comparable. When neither US nor CAN appears, Canadian, Mexican, and United States industries are comparable.

- Operating local and suburban bus transit systems—are classified in U.S. Industry 485113, Bus and Other Motor Vehicle Transit Systems.

4852 Interurban and Rural Bus Transportation

48521 Interurban and Rural Bus Transportation
See industry description for 485210 below.

485210 Interurban and Rural Bus Transportation

This industry comprises establishments primarily engaged in providing bus passenger transportation over regular routes and on regular schedules, principally outside a single metropolitan area and its adjacent nonurban areas.

Cross-References. Establishments primarily engaged in—

- Providing scenic and sightseeing transportation using buses—are classified in Industry 487110, Scenic and Sightseeing Transportation, Land;

- Providing buses for charter—are classified in Industry 485510, Charter Bus Industry;

- Operating local and suburban bus transit systems—are classified in U.S. Industry 485113, Bus and Other Motor Vehicle Transit Systems; and

- Operating independent bus terminals—are classified in Industry 488490, Other Support Activities for Road Transportation.

4853 Taxi and Limousine Service

48531 Taxi Service
See industry description for 485310 below.

485310 Taxi Service

This industry comprises establishments primarily engaged in providing passenger transportation by automobile or van, not operated over regular routes and on regular schedules. Establishments of taxicab owner/operator, taxicab fleet operators, or taxicab organizations are included in this industry.

Cross-References. Establishments primarily engaged in—

- Providing special needs transportation services (except to and from school or work) for the infirm, elderly, or handicapped—are classified in U.S. Industry 485991, Special Needs Transportation;

- Providing limousine services—are classified in Industry 485320, Limousine Service; and

- Providing scheduled shuttle services between hotels, airports, or other destination points— are classified in U.S. Industry 485999, All Other Transit and Ground Passenger Transportation.

US—United States industry only. CAN—United States and Canadian industries are comparable. When neither US nor CAN appears, Canadian, Mexican, and United States industries are comparable.

48532 Limousine Service
See industry description for 485320 below.

485320 Limousine Service

This industry comprises establishments primarily engaged in providing an array of specialty and luxury passenger transportation services via limousine or luxury sedans generally on a reserved basis. These establishments do not operate over regular routes and on regular schedules.

Cross-References. Establishments primarily engaged in—

- Providing taxi services—are classified in Industry 485310, Taxi Service; and

- Providing scheduled shuttle services between hotels, airports, or other destination points— are classified in U.S. Industry 485999, All Other Transit and Ground Passenger Transportation.

4854 School and Employee Bus Transportation

48541 School and Employee Bus Transportation
See industry description for 485410 below.

485410 School and Employee Bus Transportation

This industry comprises establishments primarily engaged in providing buses and other motor vehicles to transport pupils to and from school or employees to and from work.

Cross-References. Establishments primarily engaged in—

- Operating local and suburban bus transit systems—are classified in U.S. Industry, 485113 Bus and Other Motor Vehicle Transit Systems;

- Providing interurban and rural bus transportation—are classified in Industry 485210, Interurban and Rural Bus Transportation; and

- Providing buses for charter—are classified in Industry 485510, Charter Bus Industry.

4855 Charter Bus Industry

48551 Charter Bus Industry
See industry description for 485510 below.

485510 Charter Bus Industry

This industry comprises establishments primarily engaged in providing buses for charter. These establishments provide bus services to meet customers' road transportation needs and generally do not operate over fixed routes and on regular schedules.

US—United States industry only. CAN—United States and Canadian industries are comparable. When neither US nor CAN appears, Canadian, Mexican, and United States industries are comparable.

Cross-References. Establishments primarily engaged in—

- Providing scenic and local sightseeing transportation using buses—are classified in Industry 487110, Scenic and Sightseeing Transportation, Land, and

- Providing interurban and rural bus transportation—are classified in Industry 485210, Interurban and Rural Bus Transportation

4859 Other Transit and Ground Passenger Transportation

48599 Other Transit and Ground Passenger Transportation

This industry comprises establishments primarily engaged in providing other transit and ground passenger transportation (except urban transit systems, interurban and rural bus transportation, taxi services, school and employee bus transportation, charter bus services, and limousine services (except shuttle services)). Shuttle services (except employee bus) and special needs transportation services are included in this industry. Shuttle services establishments generally travel within a metropolitan area and its adjacent nonurban areas on regular routes, on regular schedules and provide services between hotels, airports, or other destination points. Special needs transportation establishments provide passenger transportation to the infirm, elderly, or handicapped. These establishments may use specially equipped vehicles to provide passenger transportation.

Cross-References. Establishments primarily engaged in—

- Providing school or employee bus transportation for the infirm, elderly, or handicapped—are classified in Industry 48541, School and Employee Bus Transportation;

- Providing ambulance services for emergency and medical purposes—are classified in Industry 62191, Ambulance Services;

- Operating urban transit systems—are classified in Industry Group 4851, Urban Transit Systems;

- Providing interurban and rural bus transportation—are classified in Industry 48521, Interurban and Rural Bus Transportation;

- Providing taxi services and/or limousine services (except shuttle services)—are classified in Industry Group 4853; Taxi and Limousine Service; and

- Providing buses for charter—are classified in Industry 48551, Charter Bus Industry.

485991 Special Needs Transportation[US]

This U.S. industry comprises establishments primarily engaged in providing special needs transportation (except to and from school or work) to the infirm, elderly, or handicapped. These establishments may use specially equipped vehicles to provide passenger transportation.

Cross-References. Establishments primarily engaged in—

- Providing school or employee bus transportation for the infirm, elderly, or handicapped—are classified in Industry 485410, School and Employee Bus Transportation; and

---

US—United States industry only. CAN—United States and Canadian industries are comparable. When neither US nor CAN appears, Canadian, Mexican, and United States industries are comparable.

- Providing ambulance services for emergency and medical purposes—are classified in Industry 62191, Ambulance Services.

485999 All Other Transit and Ground Passenger Transportation[US]

This U.S. industry comprises establishments primarily engaged in providing ground passenger transportation (except urban transit systems; interurban and rural bus transportation, taxi and/or limousine services (except shuttle services), school and employee bus transportation, charter bus services, and special needs transportation). Establishments primarily engaged in operating shuttle services and vanpools are included in this industry. Shuttle services establishments generally provide travel on regular routes and on regular schedules between hotels, airports, or other destination points.

Cross-References. Establishments primarily engaged in—

- Providing urban transit systems—are classified in Industry Group 4851, Urban Transit Systems;
- Providing interurban and rural bus transportation—are classified in Industry 485210, Interurban and Rural Bus Transportation;
- Providing taxi and/or limousine services (except shuttle services)—are classified in Industry Group 4853, Taxi and Limousine Service;
- Providing school and employee bus transportation (including for the infirm, elderly, or handicapped)—are classified in Industry 485410, School and Employee Bus Transportation;
- Providing buses for charter—are classified in Industry 485510, Charter Bus Industry;
- Providing special needs transportation (except to and from school or work) for the infirm, elderly, or handicapped—are classified in Industry 485991, Special Needs Transportation; and
- Providing ambulance services for emergency and medical purposes—are classified in Industry 621910, Ambulance Services.

486 Pipeline Transportation

Industries in the Pipeline Transportation subsector use transmission pipelines to transport products, such as crude oil, natural gas, refined petroleum products, and slurry. Industries are identified based on the products transported (i.e., pipeline transportation of crude oil, natural gas, refined petroleum products, and other products).

The Pipeline Transportation of Natural Gas industry includes the storage of natural gas because the storage is usually done by the pipeline establishment and because a pipeline is inherently a network in which all the nodes are interdependent.

4861 Pipeline Transportation of Crude Oil

48611 Pipeline Transportation of Crude Oil
See industry description for 486110 below.

486110 Pipeline Transportation of Crude Oil

This industry comprises establishments primarily engaged in the pipeline transportation of crude oil.

US—United States industry only. CAN—United States and Canadian industries are comparable. When neither US nor CAN appears, Canadian, Mexican, and United States industries are comparable.

Cross-References. Establishments primarily engaged in—

- Providing the pipeline transportation of natural gas—are classified in Industry 486210, Pipeline Transportation of Natural Gas; and

- Providing the pipeline transportation of refined petroleum products—are classified in Industry 486910, Pipeline Transportation of Refined Petroleum Products.

4862 Pipeline Transportation of Natural Gas

48621 Pipeline Transportation of Natural Gas
See industry description for 486210 below.

486210 Pipeline Transportation of Natural Gas

This industry comprises establishments primarily engaged in the pipeline transportation of natural gas from processing plants to local distribution systems.

Cross-References.

Establishments primarily engaged in providing natural gas to the end consumer are classified in Industry 221210, Natural Gas Distribution.

4869 Other Pipeline Transportation

This industry group comprises establishments primarily engaged in the pipeline transportation of products (except crude oil and natural gas).

48691 Pipeline Transportation of Refined Petroleum Products
See industry description for 486910 below.

486910 Pipeline Transportation of Refined Petroleum Products

This industry comprises establishments primarily engaged in the pipeline transportation of refined petroleum products.

48699 All Other Pipeline Transportation
See industry description for 486990 below.

486990 All Other Pipeline Transportation

This industry comprises establishments primarily engaged in the pipeline transportation of products except crude oil, natural gas, and refined petroleum products.

Cross-References. Establishments primarily engaged in—

- Providing pipeline transportation of crude oil—are classified in Industry 486110, Pipeline Transportation of Crude Oil;

US—United States industry only. CAN—United States and Canadian industries are comparable. When neither US nor CAN appears, Canadian, Mexican, and United States industries are comparable.

http://www.ntis.gov/naics

- Providing pipeline transportation of natural gas—are classified in Industry 486210, Pipeline Transportation of Natural Gas;

- Providing pipeline transportation of refined petroleum products—are classified in Industry 486910, Pipeline Transportation of Refined Petroleum Products; and

- Providing pipeline transportation of water—are classified in Industry 221310, Water Supply and Irrigation Systems.

487 Scenic and Sightseeing Transportation

Industries in the Scenic and Sightseeing Transportation subsector utilize transportation equipment to provide recreation and entertainment. These activities have a production process distinct from passenger transportation carried out for the purpose of other types of for-hire transportation. This process does not emphasize efficient transportation; in fact, such activities often use obsolete vehicles, such as steam trains, to provide some extra ambience. The activity is local in nature, usually involving a same-day return to the point of departure.

The Scenic and Sightseeing Transportation subsector is separated into three industries based on the mode: land, water, and other.

Activities that are recreational in nature and involve participation by the customer, such as white-water rafting, are generally excluded from this subsector, unless they impose an impact on part of the transportation system. Charter boat fishing, for example, is included in the Scenic and Sightseeing Transportation, Water industry.

4871 Scenic and Sightseeing Transportation, Land

48711 Scenic and Sightseeing Transportation, Land
See industry description for 487110 below.

487110 Scenic and Sightseeing Transportation, Land

This industry comprises establishments primarily engaged in providing scenic and sightseeing transportation on land, such as sightseeing buses and trolleys, steam train excursions, and horse-drawn sightseeing rides. The services provided are usually local and involve same-day return to place of origin.

Cross-References. Establishments primarily engaged in—

- Operating aerial trams or aerial cable cars—are classified in Industry 487990, Scenic and Sightseeing Transportation, Other;

- Providing sporting services, such as pack trains,—are classified in Industry 713990, All Other Recreation and Amusement Industries;

- Providing intercity and rural bus transportation—are classified in Industry 485210, Inter-urban and Rural Bus Transportation;

- Providing buses for charter—are classified in Industry 485510, Charter Bus Industry;

US—United States industry only. CAN—United States and Canadian industries are comparable. When neither US nor CAN appears, Canadian, Mexican, and United States industries are comparable.

- Operating local and suburban passenger transit systems—are classified in Industry 48511, Urban Transit Systems; and

- Providing passenger travel arrangements and tours—are classified in Industry Group 5615, Travel Arrangement and Reservation Services.

4872 Scenic and Sightseeing Transportation, Water

48721 Scenic and Sightseeing Transportation, Water
See industry description for 487210 below.

487210 Scenic and Sightseeing Transportation, Water

This industry comprises establishments primarily engaged in providing scenic and sightseeing transportation on water. The services provided are usually local and involve same-day return to place of origin.

Illustrative Examples:

Airboat (i.e., swamp buggy) operation
Charter fishing boat services
Dinner cruises

Excursion boat operation
Harbor sightseeing tours

Cross-References. Establishments primarily engaged in—

- Providing recreation services, such as fishing guides, white-water rafting, parasailing, and water skiing—are classified in Industry 713990, All Other Amusement and Recreation Industries;

- Providing water taxi services—are classified in Industry 48321, Inland Water Transportation;

- Providing water transportation of passengers—are classified in Subsector 483, Water Transportation;

- Operating floating casinos (i.e., gambling cruises or riverboat casinos)—are classified in Industry 713210, Casinos (except Casino Hotels); and

- Providing boat rental without operators—are classified in U.S. Industry 532292, Recreational Goods Rental.

4879 Scenic and Sightseeing Transportation, Other

48799 Scenic and Sightseeing Transportation, Other
See industry description for 487990 below.

487990 Scenic and Sightseeing Transportation, Other

This industry comprises establishments primarily engaged in providing scenic and sightseeing transportation (except on land and water). The services provided are usually local and involve same-day return to place of departure.

US—United States industry only. CAN—United States and Canadian industries are comparable. When neither US nor CAN appears, Canadian, Mexican, and United States industries are comparable.

http://www.ntis.gov/naics

Illustrative Examples:

Aerial tramways, scenic and sightseeing
operation
Aerial cablecars, scenic and sightseeing
operation
Glider excursions

Helicopter rides, scenic and sightseeing
operation
Hot air balloon rides, scenic and sightseeing
operation

Cross-References. Establishments primarily engaged in—

- Providing recreational activities, such as hang gliding,—are classified in Industry 713990, All Other Amusement and Recreation Industries; and

- Providing scheduled or nonscheduled air transportation of passengers or specialty flying services—are classified in Subsector 481, Air Transportation.

488 Support Activities for Transportation

Industries in the Support Activities for Transportation subsector provide services which support transportation. These services may be provided to transportation carrier establishments or to the general public. This subsector includes a wide array of establishments, including air traffic control services, marine cargo handling, and motor vehicle towing.

The Support Activities for Transportation subsector includes services to transportation but is separated by type of mode serviced. The Support Activities for Rail Transportation industry includes services to the rail industry (e.g., railroad switching and terminal establishments).

Ship repair and maintenance not done in a shipyard are included in Other Support Activities for Water Transportation. An example would be a floating drydock services in a harbor.

Excluded from this subsector are establishments primarily engaged in providing factory conversion and overhaul of transportation equipment, which are classified in Subsector 336, Transportation Equipment Manufacturing. Also, establishments primarily engaged in providing rental and leasing of transportation equipment without operator are classified in Subsector 532, Rental and Leasing Services.

4881 Support Activities for Air Transportation

This industry group comprises establishments primarily engaged in providing services to the air transportation industry. These services include airport operation, servicing, repairing (except factory conversion and overhaul of aircraft), maintaining and storing aircraft, and ferrying aircraft.

48811 Airport Operations

This industry comprises establishments primarily engaged in (1) operating international, national, or civil airports or public flying field or (2) supporting airport operations (except special food services contractors), such as rental of hangar space, air traffic control services, baggage handling services, and cargo handling services.

US—United States industry only. CAN—United States and Canadian industries are comparable. When neither US nor CAN appears, Canadian, Mexican, and United States industries are comparable.

Cross-References. Establishments primarily engaged in—

- Providing factory conversion, overhaul, and rebuilding of aircraft—are classified in Industry 33641, Aerospace Product and Parts Manufacturing;

- Wholesaling fuel at airports—are classified in Industry 42272, Petroleum and Petroleum Products Wholesalers (except Bulk Stations and Terminals),

- Providing airport janitorial services—are classified in Industry 56172, Janitorial Services; and

- Providing food services at airports on a contractual arrangement (i.e., food service contractors)—are classified in Industry 72231, Food Service Contractors.

488111 Air Traffic Control[CAN]

This U.S. industry comprises establishments primarily engaged in providing air traffic control services to regulate the flow of air traffic.

488119 Other Airport Operations [CAN]

This U.S. industry comprises establishments primarily engaged in (1) operating international, national, or civil airports, or public flying field or (2) supporting airport operations, such as rental of hangar space, and providing baggage handling and/or cargo handling services.

Cross-References. Establishments primarily engaged in—

- Providing air traffic control services—are classified in U.S. Industry 488111, Air Traffic Control;

- Providing factory conversion, overhaul, and rebuilding of aircraft—are classified in Industry 33641, Aerospace Product and Parts Manufacturing;

- Wholesaling fuel at airports—are classified in Industry 422720, Petroleum and Petroleum Products Wholesalers (except Bulk Stations and Terminals);

- Providing airport janitorial services—are classified in Industry 561720, Janitorial Services; and

- Providing food services at airports on a contractual arrangement—are classified in Industry 722310, Food Service Contractors.

48819 Other Support Activities for Air Transportation
See industry description for 488190 below.

488190 Other Support Activities for Air Transportation

This industry comprises establishments primarily engaged in providing specialized services for air transportation (except air traffic control and other airport operations).

US—United States industry only. CAN—United States and Canadian industries are comparable. When neither US nor CAN appears, Canadian, Mexican, and United States industries are comparable.

Illustrative Examples:

Aircraft services	Aircraft testing services
Aircraft maintenance and repair services (except factory conversions, overhauls, rebuilding)	

Cross-References. Establishments primarily engaged in—

- Wholesaling fuel at airports—are classified in Industry 422720, Petroleum and Petroleum Products Wholesalers (except Bulk Stations and Terminals);

- Providing aircraft janitorial services—are classified in Industry 561720, Janitorial Services;

- Providing air traffic control services—are classified in U.S. Industry 488111, Air Traffic Control;

- Providing airport operations (except air traffic control)—are classified in U.S. Industry 488119, Other Airport Operations (except Air Traffic Control);

- Providing factory conversion, overhaul, and rebuilding of aircraft—are classified in Industry 33641, Aerospace Product and Parts Manufacturing; and

- Providing food services to airlines on a contractual arrangement—are classified in Industry 722310, Food Service Contractors.

4882 Support Activities for Rail Transportation

48821 Support Activities for Rail Transportation
See industry description for 488210 below.

488210 Support Activities for Rail Transportation

This industry comprises establishments primarily engaged in providing specialized services for railroad transportation including servicing, routine repairing (except factory conversion, overhaul or rebuilding of rolling stock), and maintaining rail cars; loading and unloading rail cars; and operating independent terminals.

Cross-References. Establishments primarily engaged in—

- Providing railroad car rental—are classified in U.S. Industry 532411, Commercial Air, Rail, and Water Transportation Equipment Rental and Leasing;

- Factory conversion, overhaul, or rebuilding of railroad rolling stock—are classified in Industry 336510, Railroad Rolling Stock Manufacturing;

- Providing rail car janitorial services—are classified in Industry 561720, Janitorial Services; and

---

US—United States industry only. CAN—United States and Canadian industries are comparable. When neither US nor CAN appears, Canadian, Mexican, and United States industries are comparable.

- Providing dredging services—are classified in Industry 234990, All Other Heavy Construction.

4883 Support Activities for Water Transportation

48831 Port and Harbor Operations
See industry description for 488310 below.

488310 Port and Harbor Operations

This industry comprises establishments primarily engaged in operating ports, harbors (including docking and pier facilities), or canals.

Cross-References. Establishments primarily engaged in—

- Providing stevedoring and other marine cargo handling services—are classified in Industry 488320, Marine Cargo Handling;

- Providing navigational services to shipping—are classified in Industry 488330, Navigational Services to Shipping; and

- Operating docking and/or storage facilities and commonly known as marinas—are classified in Industry 713930, Marinas.

48832 Marine Cargo Handling
See industry description for 488320 below.

488320 Marine Cargo Handling

This industry comprises establishments primarily engaged in providing stevedoring and other marine cargo handling services (except warehousing).

Cross-References. Establishments primarily engaged in—

- Preparing freight for transportation—are classified in U.S. Industry 488991, Packing and Crating;

- Operating general merchandise, refrigerated, or other warehousing and storage facilities—are classified in Subsector 493, Warehousing and Storage; and

- Operating docking and pier facilities—are classified in Industry 488310, Port and Harbor Operations.

48833 Navigational Services to Shipping
See industry description for 488330 below.

488330 Navigational Services to Shipping

This industry comprises establishments primarily engaged in providing navigational services to shipping. Marine salvage establishments are included in this industry.

US—United States industry only. CAN—United States and Canadian industries are comparable. When neither US nor CAN appears, Canadian, Mexican, and United States industries are comparable.

Illustrative Examples:

Docking and undocking marine vessel services
Marine vessel traffic reporting services

Piloting services, water transportation
Tugboat services, harbor operation

Cross-References. Establishments primarily engaged in—

- Providing water transportation of barges (except coastal or Great Lake barge transportation services)—are classified in U.S. Industry 483211, Inland Water Freight Transportation; and

- Providing coastal and/or Great Lakes barge transportation services—are classified in U.S. Industry 483113, Coastal and Great Lakes Freight Transportation.

48839 Other Support Activities for Water Transportation
See industry description for 488390 below.

488390 Other Support Activities for Water Transportation

This industry comprises establishments primarily engaged in providing services to water transportation (except port and harbor operations; marine cargo handling services; and navigational services to shipping).

Illustrative Examples:

Floating drydocks (i.e., maintenance and
  routine repairs for ships and boats)

Marine cargo checkers and surveyors
Ship scaling services

Cross-References. Establishments primarily engaged in—

- Ship painting—are classified in Industry 235210, Painting and Wall Covering Contractors;

- Providing ship janitorial services—are classified in Industry 561720, Janitorial Services;

- Operating port, harbor, or canal facilities—are classified in Industry 488310, Port and Harbor Operations;

- Providing stevedoring and other marine cargo handling services—are classified in Industry 488320, Marine Cargo Handling;

- Providing navigational services to shipping—are classified in Industry 488330, Navigational Services to Shipping; and

- Providing ship overhauling or repairs in a shipyard—are classified in U.S. Industry 336611, Ship Building and Repairing.

4884 Support Activities for Road Transportation

48841 Motor Vehicle Towing
See industry description for 488410 below.

488410 Motor Vehicle Towing

This industry comprises establishments primarily engaged in towing light or heavy motor vehicles, both local and long distance. These establishments may provide incidental services, such as storage and emergency road repair services.

US—United States industry only. CAN—United States and Canadian industries are comparable. When neither US nor CAN appears, Canadian, Mexican, and United States industries are comparable.

Cross-References. Establishments primarily engaged in—

- Operating gasoline stations—are classified in Industry Group 4471, Gasoline Stations;

- Providing automotive repair and maintenance—are classified in Industry Group 8111, Automotive Repair and Maintenance, and

- Both retailing automotive parts and accessories, and repairing automobiles and known as automotive supply stores—are classified Industry 441310, Automotive Parts and Accessories Stores.

48849 Other Support Activities for Road Transportation
See industry description for 488490 below.

488490 Other Support Activities for Road Transportation

This industry comprises establishments primarily engaged in providing services (except motor vehicle towing) to road network users.

Illustrative Examples:

Bridge, tunnel, and highway operations	Pilot car services (i.e., wide load warning services)
Driving services (e.g., automobile, truck delivery)	Truck or weighing station operations

Cross-References. Establishments primarily engaged in—

- Providing automotive repair and maintenance—are classified in Industry Group 8111, Automotive Repair and Maintenance;

- Providing towing services to motor vehicles—are classified in Industry 488410, Motor Vehicle Towing;

- Providing a network for busing in combination with providing terminal services—are classified in Industry 485210, Interurban and Rural Bus Transportation; and

- Providing a network for trucking in combination with providing terminal services—are classified in Subsector 484, Truck Transportation.

4885 Freight Transportation Arrangement

48851 Freight Transportation Arrangement
See industry description for 488510 below.

488510 Freight Transportation Arrangement

This industry comprises establishments primarily engaged in arranging transportation of freight between shippers and carriers. These establishments are usually known as freight forwarders, marine

US—United States industry only. CAN—United States and Canadian industries are comparable. When neither US nor CAN appears, Canadian, Mexican, and United States industries are comparable.

shipping agents, or customs brokers and offer a combination of services spanning transportation modes.

Cross-References.

Establishments primarily engaged in tariff and freight rate consulting services are classified in U.S. Industry 541614, Process, Physical Distribution, and Logistics Consulting Services.

4889 Other Support Activities for Transportation

48899 Other Support Activities for Transportation

This industry comprises establishments primarily engaged in providing support activities to transportation (except for air transportation; rail transportation; water transportation; road transportation; and freight transportation arrangement).

Illustrative Examples:

Arrangement of vanpools or carpools
Independent pipeline terminal facilities

Stockyards (i.e., not for fattening or selling livestock)

Cross-References. Establishments primarily engaged in—

* Providing support activities for air transportation—are classified in Industry Group 4881, Support Activities for Air Transportation;

* Providing support activities for rail transportation—are classified in Industry Group 4882, Support Activities for Rail Transportation;

* Providing support activities for water transportation—are classified in Industry Group 4883, Support Activities for Water Transportation;

* Providing support activities for road transportation—are classified in Industry Group 4884, Support Activities for Road Transportation;

* Arranging transportation of freight between shippers and carriers—are classified in Industry 48851, Freight Transportation Arrangement;

* Providing tariff and freight rate consulting services—are classified in Industry 54161, Management Consulting Services;

* Operating stockyards for fattening livestock—are classified in Subsector 112, Animal Production; and

* Providing packaging and labeling services—are classified in Industry 56191, Packaging and Labeling Services.

488991 Packing and Crating[US]

This U.S. industry comprises establishments primarily engaged in packing, crating, and otherwise preparing goods for transportation.

US—United States industry only. CAN—United States and Canadian industries are comparable. When neither US nor CAN appears, Canadian, Mexican, and United States industries are comparable.

Cross-References.

Establishments primarily engaged in providing packaging and labeling services are classified in Industry 561910, Packaging and Labeling Services.

488999 All Other Support Activities for Transportation[US]

This U.S. industry comprises establishments primarily engaged in providing support activities to transportation (except for air transportation; rail transportation; water transportation; road transportation; freight transportation arrangement; and packing and crating).

Illustrative Examples:

Arrangement of vanpools or carpools
Independent pipeline terminal facilities

Stockyards (i.e., not for fattening or selling livestock)

Cross-References. Establishments primarily engaged in—

- Operating stockyards for fattening livestock—are classified in Subsector 112, Animal Production;

- Providing tariff and freight rate consulting services—are classified in U.S. Industry 541614, Process, Physical Distribution, and Logistics Consulting Services;

- Providing packing and crating services for transportation—are classified in U.S. Industry 488991, Packing and Crating;

- Providing support activities for air transportation—are classified in Industry Group 4881, Support Activities for Air Transportation;

- Providing support activities for rail transportation—are classified in Industry 488210, Support Activities for Rail Transportation;

- Providing support activities for water transportation—are classified in Industry Group 4883, Support Activities for Water Transportation;

- Providing support activities for road transportation—are classified in Industry Group 4884, Support Activities for Road Transportation; and

- Arranging transportation of freight between shippers and carriers —are classified in Industry 488510, Freight Transportation Arrangement.

491 Postal Service

The Postal Service subsector includes the activities of the National Post Office and its subcontractors in delivering letters and small parcels, normally without pick-up at the senders' location. These articles can be described as those that can be handled by one person without using special equipment. This allows the collection, pick-up, and delivery operations to be done with limited labor costs

---

US—United States industry only. CAN—United States and Canadian industries are comparable. When neither US nor CAN appears, Canadian, Mexican, and United States industries are comparable.

and minimal equipment. Sorting and transportation activities, where necessary, are generally mechanized. The restriction to small parcels distinguishes these establishments from those in the transportation industries.

The traditional activity of the National Postal Service is described in this subsector. Subcontractors include rural Post Offices on contract to the Postal Service.

Bulk transportation of mail on contract to the Postal Service is not included here, because it is usually done by transportation establishments that carry other customers' cargo as well.

4911 Postal Service

49111 Postal Service

See industry description for 491110 below.

491110 Postal Service

This industry comprises establishments primarily engaged in operating the National Postal Service. Establishments primarily engaged in performing one or more postal service, such as sorting, routing, and/or delivery, on a contract basis (except the bulk transportation of mail) are included in this industry.

Cross-References. Establishments primarily engaged in—

- Providing bulk transportation of mail on a contract basis to and from postal service establishments—are classified in Industry Group 4841, General Freight Trucking;

- Providing courier services—are classified in Industry 492110, Couriers;

- Providing mailbox services along with other business services—are classified in U.S. Industry 561431, Private Mail Centers; and

- Providing local messenger and delivery services—are classified in Industry 492210, Local Messengers and Local Delivery.

492 Couriers and Messengers

Industries in the Couriers and Messengers subsector provide intercity and/or local delivery of parcels. These articles can be described as those that may be handled by one person without using special equipment. This allows the collection, pick-up, and delivery operations to be done with limited labor costs and minimal equipment. Sorting and transportation activities, where necessary, are generally mechanized. The restriction to small parcels partly distinguishes these establishments from those in the transportation industries. The complete network of courier services establishments also distinguishes these transportation services from local messenger and delivery establishments in this subsector. This includes the establishments that perform intercity transportation as well as

---

US—United States industry only. CAN—United States and Canadian industries are comparable. When neither US nor CAN appears, Canadian, Mexican, and United States industries are comparable.

establishments that, under contract to them, perform local pick-up and delivery. Messengers, which usually deliver within a metropolitan or single urban area, may use bicycle, foot, small truck, or van.

4921 Couriers

49211 Couriers
See industry description for 492110 below.

492110 Couriers

This industry comprises establishments primarily engaged in providing air, surface, or combined courier delivery services of parcels generally between metropolitan areas or urban centers. The establishments of this industry form a network including courier local pick-up and delivery to serve their customers' needs.

Cross-References. Establishments primarily engaged in—

- Providing messenger and delivery services within a metropolitan area or within an urban center—are classified in Industry 492210, Local Messengers and Local Delivery; and

- Providing the truck transportation of palletized general freight—are classified in Industry Group 4841, General Freight Trucking.

4922 Local Messengers and Local Delivery

49221 Local Messengers and Local Delivery
See industry description for 492210 below.

492210 Local Messengers and Local Delivery

This industry comprises establishments primarily engaged in providing local messenger and delivery services of small items within a single metropolitan or within an urban center. These establishments generally provide point-to-point pickup and delivery and do not operate as part of an intercity courier network.

Illustrative Examples:

Alcoholic beverages delivery services
Grocery delivery services (i.e., independent service from grocery store)
Letters, documents, or small parcel local delivery services

Restaurant meals delivery services (i.e., independent service from restaurant)

Cross-References. Establishments primarily engaged in—

- Providing local letter and parcel delivery services as part of an intercity courier network—are classified in Industry 492110, Couriers;

US—United States industry only. CAN—United States and Canadian industries are comparable. When neither US nor CAN appears, Canadian, Mexican, and United States industries are comparable.

- Operating the National Postal Service or providing postal services on a contract basis (except the bulk transportation of mail)—are classified in Industry 491110, Postal Service; and

- Providing the bulk transportation of mail on a contract basis to and from Postal Service establishments—are classified in Industry Group 4841, General Freight Trucking.

493 Warehousing and Storage

Industries in the Warehousing and Storage subsector are primarily engaged in operating warehousing and storage facilities for general merchandise, refrigerated goods, and other warehouse products. These establishments provide facilities to store goods. They do not sell the goods they handle. These establishments take responsibility for storing the goods and keeping them secure. They may also provide a range of services, often referred to as logistics services, related to the distribution of goods. Logistics services can include labeling, breaking bulk, inventory control and management, light assembly, order entry and fulfillment, packaging, pick and pack, price marking and ticketing, and transportation arrangement. However, establishments in this industry group always provide warehousing or storage services in addition to any logistic services. Furthermore, the warehousing or storage of goods must be more than incidental to the performance of services, such as price marking.

Bonded warehousing and storage services and warehouses located in free trade zones are included in the industries of this subsector.

4931 Warehousing and Storage

49311 General Warehousing and Storage
See industry description for 493110 below.

493110 General Warehousing and Storage

This industry comprises establishments primarily engaged in operating merchandise warehousing and storage facilities. These establishments generally handle goods in containers, such as boxes, barrels, and/or drums, using equipment, such as forklifts, pallets, and racks. They are not specialized in handling bulk products of any particular type, size, or quantity of goods or products.

Cross-References. Establishments primarily engaged in—

- Renting or leasing space for self storage—are classified in Industry 531130, Lessors of Miniwarehouses and Self-Storage Units; and

- Selling in combination with handling and/or distributing goods to other wholesale or retail establishments—are classified in Sector 42, Wholesale Trade.

49312 Refrigerated Warehousing and Storage
See industry description for 493120 below.

493120 Refrigerated Warehousing and Storage

This industry comprises establishments primarily engaged in operating refrigerated warehousing and storage facilities. Establishments primarily engaged in the storage of furs for the trade are

---

US—United States industry only. CAN—United States and Canadian industries are comparable. When neither US nor CAN appears, Canadian, Mexican, and United States industries are comparable.

included in this industry. The services provided by these establishments include blast freezing, tempering, and modified atmosphere storage services.

Cross-References.

Establishments primarily engaged in storing furs (except for the trade) and garments are classified in Industry 812320, Drycleaning and Laundry Services (except Coin-Operated).

49313 Farm Product Warehousing and Storage
See industry description for 493130 below.

493130 Farm Product Warehousing and Storage

This industry comprises establishments primarily engaged in operating bulk farm product warehousing and storage facilities (except refrigerated). Grain elevators primarily engaged in storage are included in this industry.

Cross-References. Establishments primarily engaged in—

- Operating refrigerated warehousing and storage facilities—are classified in Industry 493120, Refrigerated Warehousing and Storage; and

- Storing grains and field beans (i.e., grain elevators) as an incidental activity to sales—are classified in Industry 42251, Grain and Field Bean Wholesalers.

49319 Other Warehousing and Storage
See industry description for 493190 below.

493190 Other Warehousing and Storage

This industry comprises establishments primarily engaged in operating warehousing and storage facilities (except general merchandise, refrigerated, and farm product warehousing and storage).

Illustrative Examples:

Bulk petroleum storage
Lumber storage terminals

Whiskey warehousing

Cross-References. Establishments primarily engaged in—

- Renting or leasing space for self storage—are classified in Industry 531130, Lessors of Miniwarehouses and Self-Storage Units;

- Storing hazardous materials for treatment and disposal—are classified in U.S. Industry 562211, Hazardous Waste Treatment and Disposal;

- Operating general warehousing and storage facilities—are classified in Industry 493110, General Warehousing and Storage;

- Operating refrigerated warehousing and storage facilities—are classified in Industry 493120, Refrigerated Warehousing and Storage; and

- Operating farm product warehousing and storage facilities—are classified in Industry 493130, Farm Product Warehousing and Storage.

Sector 51—Information

The Sector as a Whole

The Information sector comprises establishments engaged in the following processes: (a) producing and distributing information and cultural products, (b) providing the means to transmit or distribute these products as well as data or communications, and (c) processing data.

The main components of this sector are the publishing industries, including software publishing, the motion picture and sound recording industries, the broadcasting and telecommunications industries, and the information services and data processing industries.

The expressions "information age" and "global information economy" are used with considerable frequency today. The general idea of an "information economy" includes both the notion of industries primarily producing, processing, and distributing information, as well as the idea that every industry is using available information and information technology to reorganize and make themselves more productive.

For the purpose of developing NAICS, it is the transformation of information into a commodity that is produced and distributed by a number of growing industries that is at issue. The Information sector groups three types of establishments: (1) those engaged in producing and distributing information and cultural products; (2) those that provide the means to transmit or distribute these products as well as data or communications; and (3) those that process data. Cultural products are those that directly express attitudes, opinions, ideas, values, and artistic creativity; provide entertainment; or offer information and analysis concerning the past and present. Included in this definition are popular, mass-produced, products as well as cultural products that normally have a more limited audience, such as poetry books, literary magazines, or classical records. These activities were formerly classified throughout the existing national classifications. Traditional publishing is in manufacturing; broadcasting in communications; software production in business services; film production in amusement services; and so forth.

The unique characteristics of information and cultural products, and of the processes involved in their production and distribution, distinguish the Information sector from the goods-producing and service-producing sectors. Some of these characteristics are:

1. Unlike traditional goods, an "information or cultural product," such as a newspaper on-line or television program, does not necessarily have tangible qualities, nor is it necessarily associated with a particular form. A movie can be shown at a movie theater, on a television broadcast, through video-on-demand or rented at a local video store. A sound recording can be aired on radio, embedded in multimedia products, or sold at a record store.

2. Unlike traditional services, the delivery of these products does not require direct contact between the supplier and the consumer.

3. The value of these products to the consumer lies in their informational, educational, cultural, or entertainment content, not in the format in which they are distributed. Most of these products are protected from unlawful reproduction by copyright laws.

4. The intangible property aspect of information and cultural products makes the processes involved in their production and distribution very different from goods and services. Only those possessing the rights to these works are authorized to reproduce, alter, improve, and

---

US—United States industry only. CAN—United States and Canadian industries are comparable. When neither US nor CAN appears, Canadian, Mexican, and United States industries are comparable.

distribute them. Acquiring and using these rights often involves significant costs. In addition, technology is revolutionizing the distribution of these products. It is possible to distribute them in a physical form, via broadcast, or on-line.

5. Distributors of information and cultural products can easily add value to the products they distribute. For instance, broadcasters add advertising not contained in the original product. This capacity means that unlike traditional distributors, they derive revenue not from sale of the distributed product to the final consumer, but from those who pay for the privilege of adding information to the original product. Similarly, a database publisher can acquire the rights to thousands of previously published newspaper and periodical articles and add new value by providing search and software and organizing the information in a way that facilitates research and retrieval. These products often command a much higher price than the original information.

The distribution modes for information commodities may either eliminate the necessity for traditional manufacture, or reverse the conventional order of manufacture-distribute: A newspaper distributed on-line, for example, can be printed locally or by the final consumer. Similarly, it is anticipated that packaged software, which today is mainly bought through the traditional retail channels, will soon be available mainly on-line. The NAICS Information sector is designed to make such economic changes transparent as they occur, or to facilitate designing surveys that will monitor the new phenomena and provide data to analyze the changes.

Many of the industries in the NAICS Information sector are engaged in producing products protected by copyright law, or in distributing them (other than distribution by traditional wholesale and retail methods). Examples are traditional publishing industries, software and database publishing industries, and film and sound industries. Broadcasting and telecommunications industries and information providers and processors are also included in the Information sector, because their technologies are so closely linked to other industries in the Information sector.

511 Publishing Industries

Industries in the Publishing Industries subsector group establishments engaged in the publishing of newspapers, magazines, other periodicals, and books, as well as database and software publishing. In general, these establishments, which are known as publishers, issue copies of works for which they usually possess copyright. Works may be in one or more formats including traditional print form, CD-ROM, or on-line. Publishers may publish works originally created by others for which they have obtained the rights and/or works that they have created in-house. Software publishing is included here because the activity, creation of a copyrighted product and bringing it to market, is equivalent to the creation process for other types of intellectual products.

In NAICS, publishing, the reporting, writing, editing, and other processes that are required to create an edition of a newspaper, is treated as a major economic activity in its own right, rather than as a subsidiary activity to a manufacturing activity, printing. Thus, publishing is classified in the Information sector; whereas, printing remains in the NAICS Manufacturing sector. In part, the NAICS classification reflects the fact that publishing increasingly takes place in establishments that are physically separate from the associated printing establishments. More crucially, the NAICS classification of book and newspaper publishing is intended to portray their roles in a modern economy, in which they do not resemble manufacturing activities.

US—United States industry only. CAN—United States and Canadian industries are comparable. When neither US nor CAN appears, Canadian, Mexican, and United States industries are comparable.

Music publishers are not included in the Publishing Industries subsector, but are included in the Motion Picture and Sound Recording Industries subsector. Reproduction of prepackaged software is treated in NAICS as a manufacturing activity; on line distribution of software products is in the Information sector, and custom design of software to client specifications is included in the Professional, Scientific, and Technical Services sector. These distinctions arise because of the different ways that software is created, reproduced, and distributed.

The Information sector does not include products, such as manifold business forms. Information is not the essential component of these items. Establishments producing these items are included in Subsector 323, Printing and Related Support Activities.

5111 Newspaper, Periodical, Book, and Database Publishers

This industry group comprises establishments primarily engaged in publishing newspapers, magazines, other periodicals, books, databases, and other works, such as calendars, greeting cards, and maps. These works are characterized by the intellectual creativity required in their development and are usually protected by copyright. Publishers distribute or arrange for the distribution of these works.

Publishing establishments may create the works in-house, contract for, purchase, or compile works that were originally created by others. These works may be published in one or more formats, such as print and/or electronic form, including on-line. Establishments in this industry may print, reproduce, or offer direct access to the works themselves or may arrange with others to carry out such functions.

Establishments that both print and publish may fill excess capacity with commercial or job printing. However, the publishing activity is still considered to be the primary activity of these establishments.

51111 Newspaper Publishers
See industry description for 511110 below.

511110 Newspaper Publishers

This industry comprises establishments known as newspaper publishers. Establishments in this industry carry out operations necessary for producing and distributing newspapers, including gathering news; writing news columns, feature stories, and editorials; and selling and preparing advertisements. These establishments may publish newspapers in print or electronic form.

Cross-References.

- Establishments primarily engaged in printing newspapers without publishing are classified in Industry 32311, Printing;

- Establishments, such as trade associations, schools and universities, and social welfare organizations that publish newsletters for distribution to their membership, but that are not commonly known as newspaper publishers, are classified according to their primary activity designation;

US—United States industry only. CAN—United States and Canadian industries are comparable. When neither US nor CAN appears, Canadian, Mexican, and United States industries are comparable.

- Establishments primarily engaged in supplying the news media with information, such as news, reports, and pictures, are classified in Industry 514110, News Syndicates; and

- Establishments of independent representatives primarily engaged in selling advertising space are classified in Industry 541840, Media Representatives.

51112 Periodical Publishers

See industry description for 511120 below.

511120 Periodical Publishers

This industry comprises establishments known as magazine or periodical publishers. These establishments carry out the operations necessary for producing and distributing magazines and other periodicals, such as gathering, writing, and editing articles, and selling and preparing advertisements. These establishments may publish magazines and other periodicals in print or electronic form.

Illustrative Examples:

Comic book publishers   Radio and television guide publishers
Magazine publishers   Scholarly journal publishers
Newsletter publishers   Trade journal publishers

Cross-References.

- Establishments primarily engaged in printing periodicals without publishing are classified in Industry 32311, Printing;

- Establishments, such as trade associations, schools and universities, and social welfare organizations, that publish magazines and periodicals for distribution to their membership, but that are not commonly known as periodical publishers, are classified according to their primary activity designation;

- Establishments primarily engaged in publishing databases and directories are classified in Industry 511140, Database and Directory Publishers; and

- Establishments of independent representatives primarily engaged in selling advertising space are classified in Industry 541840, Media Representatives.

51113 Book Publishers

See industry description for 511130 below.

511130 Book Publishers

This industry comprises establishments known as book publishers. Establishments in this industry carry out design, editing, and marketing activities necessary for producing and distributing books. These establishments may publish books in print, electronic, or audio form.

US—United States industry only. CAN—United States and Canadian industries are comparable. When neither US nor CAN appears, Canadian, Mexican, and United States industries are comparable.

Illustrative Examples:

Book publishers	School textbook publishers
Encyclopedia publishers	Technical manual publishers
Religious book publishers	Travel guide book publishers

Cross-References.

- Establishments primarily engaged in printing books without publishing are classified in Industry 32311, Printing;

- Establishments known as music publishers are classified in Industry 512230, Music Publishers;

- Establishments, such as trade associations, schools and universities, and social welfare organizations, that publish books for distribution to their membership, that are not commonly known as book publishers, are classified according to their primary activity designation; and

- Book clubs primarily engaged in direct sales activities without publishing are classified in Industry 454390, Other Direct Selling Establishments.

51114 Database and Directory Publishers
See industry description for 511140 below.

511140 Database and Directory Publishers

This industry comprises establishments primarily engaged in publishing compilations and collections of information or facts that are logically organized to facilitate their use. These collections may be published in print or electronic form. Electronic versions may be provided directly to customers by the establishment or offered through on-line services or third-party vendors.

Illustrative Examples:

Business directory publishers	Mailing list publishers
Database and directory publishers	Telephone directory publishers

Cross-References. Establishments primarily engaged in—

- Printing without publishing databases and directories—are classified in Industry 32311, Printing;

- Publishing encyclopedias—are classified in Industry 511130, Book Publishers;

- Direct access to databases developed by others—are classified in U.S. Industry 514191, On-Line Information Services; and

- Publishing computer software—are classified in Industry 511210, Software Publishers.

US—United States industry only. CAN—United States and Canadian industries are comparable. When neither US nor CAN appears, Canadian, Mexican, and United States industries are comparable.

51119 Other Publishers

This industry comprises establishments known as publishers (except newspaper, magazine, book, directory, database, and music publishers). These establishments may publish works in print or electronic form.

Illustrative Examples:

Art print publishers   Greeting card publishers
Atlas publishers   Map publishers
Calendar publishers

Cross-References.

- Establishments known as newspaper publishers are classified in Industry 51111, Newspaper Publishers;

- Establishments known as magazine and other periodical publishers are classified in Industry 51112, Periodical Publishers;

- Establishments known as book publishers are classified in Industry 51113, Book Publishers;

- Establishments primarily engaged in directory and database publishing are classified in Industry 51114, Database and Directory Publishers;

- Establishments known as music publishers are classified in Industry 51223, Music Publishers; and

- Establishments primarily engaged in manufacturing manifold business forms are classified in Industry 32311, Printing.

511191 Greeting Card Publishers[US]

This U.S. industry comprises establishments primarily engaged in publishing greeting cards.

Cross-References.

Establishments primarily engaged in printing greeting cards without publishing are classified in Industry 32311, Printing.

511199 All Other Publishers[US]

This U.S. industry comprises establishments generally known as publishers (except newspaper, magazine, book, directory, database, music, and greeting card publishers). These establishment may publish works in print or electronic form.

Illustrative Examples:

Art print publishers   Map publishers
Atlas publishers   Street map guide publishers
Calendar publishers

US—United States industry only. CAN—United States and Canadian industries are comparable. When neither US nor CAN appears, Canadian, Mexican, and United States industries are comparable.

Cross-References.

- Establishments known as newspaper publishers are classified in Industry 511110, Newspaper Publishers;

- Establishments known as magazine or other periodical publishers are classified in Industry 511120, Magazine Publishers;

- Establishments known as book publishers are classified in Industry 511130, Book Publishers;

- Establishments primarily engaged in directory and database publishing are classified Industry 511140, Database and Directory Publishers;

- Establishments primarily engaged in greeting card publishing are classified in U.S. Industry 511191, Greeting Card Publishers;

- Establishments known as music publishers are classified in Industry 512230, Music Publishers;

- Establishments primarily engaged in manufacturing manifold business forms are classified in U.S. Industry 323116, Manifold Business Forms Printing; and

- Establishments primarily engaged in manufacturing day schedulers are classified in U.S. Industry 323118, Blankbooks, Looseleaf Binders and Devices Manufacturing.

5112 Software Publishers

51121 Software Publishers
See industry description for 511210 below.

511210 Software Publishers

This industry comprises establishments primarily engaged in computer software publishing or publishing and reproduction. Establishments in this industry carry out operations necessary for producing and distributing computer software, such as designing, providing documentation, assisting in installation, and providing support services to software purchasers. These establishments may design, develop, and publish, or publish only.

Cross-References. Establishments primarily engaged in—

- Reselling packaged software—are classified in Sector 42, Wholesale Trade or Sector 44-45, Retail Trade;

- Designing software to meet the needs of specific users—are classified in U.S. Industry 541511, Custom Computer Programming Services; and

- Mass duplication of software—are classified in U.S. Industry 334611, Software Reproducing.

US—United States industry only. CAN—United States and Canadian industries are comparable.
When neither US nor CAN appears, Canadian, Mexican, and United States industries are comparable.

http://www.ntis.gov/naics

512 Motion Picture and Sound Recording Industries

Industries in the Motion Picture and Sound Recording Industries subsector group establishments involved in the production and distribution of motion pictures and sound recordings. While producers and distributors of motion pictures and sound recordings issue works for sale as traditional publishers do, the processes are sufficiently different to warrant placing establishments engaged in these activities in a separate subsector. Production is typically a complex process that involves several distinct types of establishments that are engaged in activities, such as contracting with performers, creating the film or sound content, and providing technical postproduction services. Film distribution is often to exhibitors, such as theaters and broadcasters, rather than through the wholesale and retail distribution chain. When the product is in a mass-produced form, NAICS treats production and distribution as the major economic activity as it does in the Publishing Industries subsector, rather than as a subsidiary activity to the manufacture of such products.

This subsector does not include establishments primarily engaged in the wholesale distribution of video cassettes and sound recordings, such as compact discs and audio tapes; these establishments are included in the Wholesale Trade sector. Reproduction of video cassettes and sound recordings that is carried out separately from establishments engaged in production and distribution is treated in NAICS as a manufacturing activity.

5121 Motion Picture and Video Industries

This industry group comprises establishments primarily engaged in the production and/or distribution of motion pictures, videos, television programs, or commercials; in the exhibition of motion pictures; or in the provision of postproduction and related services.

51211 Motion Picture and Video Production
See industry description for 512110 below.

512110 Motion Picture and Video Production

This industry comprises establishments primarily engaged in producing, or producing and distributing motion pictures, videos, television programs, or television and video commercials.

Cross-References. Establishments primarily engaged in—

- Producing motion pictures and videos on contract as independent producers—are classified in Industry 711510, Independent Artists, Writers, and Performers;

- Providing teleproduction and other postproduction services—are classified in U.S. Industry 512191, Teleproduction and Other Postproduction Services;

- Providing video taping of weddings, special events, and/or business inventories—are classified in Industry 54192, Photographic Services;

- Providing motion picture laboratory services—are classified in U.S. Industry 512199, Other Motion Picture and Video Industries;

US—United States industry only. CAN—United States and Canadian industries are comparable. When neither US nor CAN appears, Canadian, Mexican, and United States industries are comparable.

- Providing mass duplication and packaging of video tapes—are classified in U.S. Industry 334612, Prerecorded Compact Disc (except Software), Tape, and Record Reproducing; and

- Acquiring distribution rights and distributing motion pictures and videos—are classified in Industry 512120, Motion Picture and Video Distribution.

51212 Motion Picture and Video Distribution
See industry description for 512120 below.

512120 Motion Picture and Video Distribution

This industry comprises establishments primarily engaged in acquiring distribution rights and distributing film and video productions to motion picture theaters, television networks and stations, and exhibitors.

Cross-References. Establishments primarily engaged in—

- Producing and distributing motion pictures and videos—are classified in Industry 512110, Motion Picture and Video Production;

- Wholesaling video cassette tapes and discs—are classified in Industry 421690, Other Electronic Parts and Equipment Wholesalers;

- Providing mass duplication and packaging of video tapes—are classified in U.S. Industry 334612, Prerecorded Compact Disc (except Software), Tape, and Record Reproducing;

- Providing motion picture footage (via film libraries) to producers—are classified in U.S. Industry 512199, Other Motion Picture and Video Industries;

- Renting video tapes and discs to the general public—are classified in Industry 532230, Video Tape and Disc Rental; and

- Selling video cassettes and discs to the general public—are classified in Industry 451220, Prerecorded Tape, Compact Disc and Record Stores.

51213 Motion Picture and Video Exhibition

This industry comprises establishments primarily engaged in operating motion picture theaters and/or exhibiting motion pictures or videos at film festivals, and so forth.

512131 Motion Picture Theaters (except Drive-Ins)[US]

This U.S. industry comprises establishments primarily engaged in operating motion picture theaters (except drive-ins) and/or exhibiting motion pictures or videos at film festivals, and so forth.

512132 Drive-In Motion Picture Theaters[US]

This U.S. industry comprises establishments primarily engaged in operating drive-in motion picture theaters.

US—United States industry only. CAN—United States and Canadian industries are comparable. When neither US nor CAN appears, Canadian, Mexican, and United States industries are comparable.

51219 Postproduction Services and Other Motion Picture and Video Industries

This industry comprises establishments primarily engaged in providing postproduction services and other services to the motion picture industry, including specialized motion picture or video postproduction services, such as editing, film/tape transfers, subtitling, credits, closed captioning, and computer-produced graphics, animation and special effects, as well as developing and processing motion picture film.

Illustrative Examples:

Motion picture film laboratories   Stock footage film libraries
Postproduction facilities   Teleproduction services

Cross-References. Establishments primarily engaged in—

- Mass duplicating video tapes and film—are classified in Industry 33461, Manufacturing and Reproducing Magnetic and Optical Media;

- Providing audio services for film, television, and video productions—are classified in Industry 51224, Sound Recording Studios;

- Renting wardrobes and costumes for motion picture production—are classified in Industry 53222, Formal Wear and Costume Rental;

- Renting studio equipment—are classified in Industry 53249, Other Commercial and Industrial Machinery and Equipment Rental and Leasing; and

- Casting actors and actresses with production companies—are classified in Industry 56131, Employment Placement Agencies.

512191 Teleproduction and Other Postproduction Services[US]

This U.S. industry comprises establishments primarily engaged in providing specialized motion picture or video postproduction services, such as editing, film/tape transfers, subtitling, credits, closed captioning, and animation and special effects.

Cross-References. Establishments primarily engaged in—

- Mass duplicating video tapes and film—are classified in Industry 33461, Manufacturing and Reproducing Magnetic and Optical Media;

- Developing and processing motion picture film—are classified in U.S. Industry 512199, Other Motion Picture and Video Industries;

- Providing audio services for film, television, and video productions—are classified in Industry 512240, Sound Recording Studios; and

- Acquiring distribution rights and distributing film and video productions to motion picture theaters, television networks and stations, and exhibitors—are classified in Industry 512120, Motion Picture and Video Distribution.

US—United States industry only. CAN—United States and Canadian industries are comparable. When neither US nor CAN appears, Canadian, Mexican, and United States industries are comparable.

512199 Other Motion Picture and Video Industries[US]

This U.S. industry comprises establishments primarily engaged in providing motion picture and video services (except motion picture and video production, distribution, exhibition, and teleproduction and other postproduction services).

Illustrative Examples:

Motion picture film laboratories   Stock footage film libraries

Cross-References. Establishments primarily engaged in—

- Renting wardrobes and costumes for motion picture production—are classified in Industry 532220, Formal Wear and Costume Rental;

- Renting studio equipment—are classified in Industry 532490, Other Commercial and Industrial Machinery and Equipment Rental and Leasing;

- Casting actors and actresses with production companies—are classified in Industry 561310, Employment Placement Agencies;

- Motion picture and video production—are classified in Industry 512110, Motion Picture and Video Production;

- Motion picture and video distribution—are classified in Industry 512120, Motion Picture and Video Distribution;

- Teleproduction and other postproduction services—are classified in U.S. Industry 512191, Teleproduction and Other Postproduction Services; and

- Motion picture and video exhibition—are classified in Industry 51213, Motion Picture and Video Exhibition.

5122 Sound Recording Industries

This industry group comprises establishments primarily engaged in producing and distributing musical recordings, in publishing music, or in providing sound recording and related services.

51221 Record Production
See industry description for 512210 below.

512210 Record Production

This industry comprises establishments primarily engaged in record production (e.g., tapes, CDs). These establishments contract with artists and arrange and finance the production of original master recordings. Establishments in this industry hold the copyright to the master recording and derive most of their revenues from the sales, leasing, and licensing of master recordings. Establishments in this industry do not have their own duplication or distribution capabilities.

US—United States industry only. CAN—United States and Canadian industries are comparable. When neither US nor CAN appears, Canadian, Mexican, and United States industries are comparable.

Cross-References. Establishments primarily engaged in—

- Releasing, promoting, and distributing recordings—are classified in Industry 512220, Integrated Record Production/Distribution;

- Promoting and authorizing the use of musical works in various media—are classified in Industry 512230, Music Publishers;

- Mass duplication services—are classified in U.S. Industry 334612, Prerecorded Compact Disc (except Software), Tape, and Record Reproducing;

- Wholesaling music recordings—are classified in Industry 421690, Other Electronic Parts and Equipment Wholesalers;

- Managing the careers of artists—are classified in Industry 711410, Agents and Managers for Artists, Athletes, Entertainers and Other Public Figures;

- Providing facilities and technical expertise for recording musical performances—are classified in Industry 512240, Sound Recording Studios; and

- Producing albums on contract as independent producers—are classified in Industry 711510, Independent Artists, Writers, and Performers.

51222 Integrated Record Production/Distribution
See industry description for 512220 below.

512220 Integrated Record Production/Distribution

This industry comprises establishments primarily engaged in releasing, promoting, and distributing sound recordings. These establishments manufacture or arrange for the manufacture of recordings, such as audio tapes/cassettes and compact discs, and promote and distribute these products to wholesalers, retailers, or directly to the public. Establishments in this industry produce master recordings themselves, or obtain reproduction and distribution rights to master recordings produced by record production companies or other integrated record companies.

Cross-References. Establishments primarily engaged in—

- Contracting with musical artists, arranging for the production of master recordings, and marketing the reproduction rights—are classified in Industry 512210, Record Production;

- Providing facilities and technical expertise for recording musical performances—are classified in Industry 512240, Sound Recording Studios;

- Mass duplication of recorded products—are classified in U.S. Industry 334612, Prerecorded Compact Disc (except Software), Tape, and Record Reproducing;

- Wholesaling records, tapes, and compact discs without producing recordings—are classified in Sector 42, Wholesale Trade; and

- Retailing records, tapes, and compact discs without producing recordings—are classified in Sector 44-45, Retail Trade.

US—United States industry only. CAN—United States and Canadian industries are comparable. When neither US nor CAN appears, Canadian, Mexican, and United States industries are comparable.

51223 Music Publishers
See industry description for 512230 below.

512230 Music Publishers

This industry comprises establishments primarily engaged in acquiring and registering copyrights for musical compositions in accordance with law and promoting and authorizing the use of these compositions in recordings, radio, television, motion pictures, live performances, print, or other media. Establishments in this industry represent the interests of the songwriter or other owners of musical compositions to produce revenues from the use of such works, generally through licensing agreements. These establishments may own the copyright or act as administrator of the music copyrights on behalf of copyright owners.

Cross-References.

Establishments primarily engaged as independent songwriters who act as their own publishers are classified in Industry 711510, Independent Artists, Writers, and Performers.

51224 Sound Recording Studios
See industry description for 512240 below.

512240 Sound Recording Studios

This industry comprises establishments primarily engaged in providing the facilities and technical expertise for sound recording in a studio. Establishments in this industry may provide audio production or postproduction services for producing master recordings, and may provide audio services for film, television, and video productions.

Cross-References. Establishments primarily engaged in—

- Releasing, promoting, and distributing sound recordings—are classified in Industry 512220, Integrated Record Production/Distribution;

- Providing mass duplication of recorded products—are classified in U.S. Industry 334612, Prerecorded Compact Disc (except Software), Tape, and Record Reproducing; and

- Contracting with musical artists, arranging for the production of master recordings, and marketing the reproduction rights—are classified in Industry 512210, Record Production.

51229 Other Sound Recording Industries
See industry description for 512290 below.

512290 Other Sound Recording Industries

This industry comprises establishments primarily engaged in providing sound recording services (except record production, distribution, music publishing, and sound recording in a studio). Establishments in this industry provide services, such as the audio recording of meetings and conferences.

US—United States industry only. CAN—United States and Canadian industries are comparable. When neither US nor CAN appears, Canadian, Mexican, and United States industries are comparable.

http://www.ntis.gov/naics

Cross-References. Establishments primarily engaged in—

- Producing records, including contracting with musical artists, arranging and financing the production of master recordings, and marketing the reproduction rights—are classified in Industry 512210, Record Production;

- Releasing, promoting, and distributing sound recordings—are classified in Industry 512220, Integrated Record Production/Distribution;

- Promoting and authorizing the use of musical works in various media—are classified in Industry 512230, Music Publishers;

- Providing facilities and expertise for recording musical performance—are classified in Industry 512240, Sound Recording Studios;

- Providing mass duplication of recorded products—are classified in U.S. Industry 334612, Prerecorded Compact Disc (except Software), Tape, and Record Reproducing; and

- Organizing and promoting the presentation of performing arts productions—are classified in Industry Group 7113, Promoters of Performing Arts, Sports and Similar Events.

513 Broadcasting and Telecommunications

Industries in the Broadcasting and Telecommunications subsector include establishments providing point-to-point communications and the services related to that activity. The industry groups (Radio and Television Broadcasting, Cable Networks and Program Distribution, and Telecommunications) are based on differences in the methods of communication and in the nature of services provided. The Radio and Television Broadcasting industry group includes establishments that operate broadcasting studios and facilities for over the air or satellite delivery of radio and television programs of entertainment, news, talk, and the like. These establishments are often engaged in the production and purchase of programs and generating revenues from the sale of air time to advertisers and from donations, subsidies, and/or the sale of programs. The Cable Networks and Program Distribution industry group includes two types of establishments. Those in the Cable Networks industry operate studios and facilities for the broadcasting of programs that are typically narrowcast in nature (limited format, such as news, sports, education, and youth-oriented programming). The services of these establishments are typically sold on a subscription or fee basis. Delivery of the programs to customers is handled by other establishments, in the Cable and Other Program Distribution industry, that operate cable systems, direct-to-home satellite systems, or other similar systems. The Telecommunications industry group is primarily engaged in operating, maintaining, and/or providing access to facilities for the transmission of voice, data, text, sound, and full motion picture video between network termination points. A transmission facility may be based on a single technology or a combination of technologies. Establishments primarily engaged as independent contractors in the maintenance and installation of broadcasting and telecommunications systems are classified in Sector 23, Construction.

5131 Radio and Television Broadcasting

This industry group comprises establishments primarily engaged in operating broadcast studios and facilities for over-the-air or satellite delivery of radio and television programs. These establishments are often engaged in the production or purchase of programs or generate revenues from the sale of air time to advertisers, from donations and subsidies, or from the sale of programs.

US—United States industry only. CAN—United States and Canadian industries are comparable. When neither US nor CAN appears, Canadian, Mexican, and United States industries are comparable.

51311 Radio Broadcasting

This industry comprises establishments primarily engaged in broadcasting audio signals. These establishments operate radio broadcasting studios and facilities for the transmission of aural programming by radio to the public, to affiliates, or to subscribers. The radio programs may include entertainment, news, talk shows, business data, or religious services.

Cross-References.

Establishments primarily engaged in producing taped radio programming are classified in Industry 51229, Other Sound Recording Industries.

513111 Radio Networks[US]

This U.S. industry comprises establishments primarily engaged in assembling and transmitting aural programming to their affiliates or subscribers via over-the-air broadcasts, cable, or satellite. The programming covers a wide variety of material, such as news services, religious programming, weather, sports, or music.

Cross-References.

Establishments primarily engaged in producing taped radio programming are classified in Industry 512290, Other Sound Recording Industries.

513112 Radio Stations[US]

This U.S. industry comprises establishments primarily engaged in broadcasting aural programs by radio to the public. Programming may originate in their own studios, from an affiliated network, or from external sources.

51312 Television Broadcasting
See industry description for 513120 below.

513120 Television Broadcasting

This industry comprises establishments primarily engaged in broadcasting images together with sound. These establishments operate television broadcasting studios and facilities for the programming and transmission of programs to the public. These establishments also produce or transmit visual programming to affiliated broadcast television stations, which in turn broadcast the programs to the public on a predetermined schedule. Programming may originate in their own studios, from an affiliated network, or from external sources.

Cross-References. Establishments primarily engaged in—

- Producing taped television program materials—are classified in Industry 512110, Motion Picture and Video Production;

US—United States industry only. CAN—United States and Canadian industries are comparable. When neither US nor CAN appears, Canadian, Mexican, and United States industries are comparable.

- Furnishing cable and other pay television services—are classified in Industry 513220, Cable and Other Program Distribution; and

- Producing and broadcasting television programs for cable and satellite television systems—are classified in Industry 513210, Cable Networks.

5132 Cable Networks and Program Distribution

This industry group comprises establishments that primarily assemble program material and transmit television programs for cable and satellite systems, or that operate these systems.

51321 Cable Networks
See industry description for 513210 below.

513210 Cable Networks

This industry comprises establishments primarily engaged in operating studios and facilities for the broadcasting of programs on a subscription or fee basis. The broadcast programming is typically narrowcast in nature (e.g., limited format, such as news, sports, education, or youth-oriented). These establishments produce programming in their own facilities or acquire programming from external sources. The programming material is usually delivered to a third party, such as cable systems or direct-to-home satellite systems, for transmission to viewers.

Cross-References. Establishments primarily engaged in—

- Producing taped television program material—are classified in Industry 512110, Motion Picture and Video Production;

- Producing and transmitting television programs to affiliated stations—are classified in Industry 513120, Television Broadcasting;

- Furnishing cable and other pay television services—are classified in Industry 513220, Cable and Other Program Distribution; and

- Retailing merchandise by electronic media, such as television,—are classified in Industry 454110, Electronic Shopping and Mail-Order Houses.

51322 Cable and Other Program Distribution
See industry description for 513220 below.

513220 Cable and Other Program Distribution

This industry comprises establishments primarily engaged as third-party distribution systems for broadcast programming. The establishments of this industry deliver visual, aural, or textual programming received from cable networks, local television stations, or radio networks to consumers via cable or direct-to-home satellite systems on a subscription or fee basis. These establishments do not generally originate programming material.

US—United States industry only. CAN—United States and Canadian industries are comparable. When neither US nor CAN appears, Canadian, Mexican, and United States industries are comparable.

Cross-References. Establishments primarily engaged in—

- Producing and broadcasting television programs for cable and satellite television systems— are classified in Industry 513210, Cable Networks; and

- Maintenance and installation of cable systems as independent contractors—are classified in Sector 23, Construction.

5133 Telecommunications

This industry group comprises establishments primarily engaged in operating, maintaining or providing access to facilities for the transmission of voice, data, text, and full motion picture video between network termination points and telecommunications reselling. Transmission facilities may be based on a single technology or a combination of technologies.

51331 Wired Telecommunications Carriers
See industry description for 513310 below.

513310 Wired Telecommunications Carriers

This industry comprises establishments engaged in (1) operating and maintaining switching and transmission facilities to provide direct communications via landlines, microwave, or a combination of landlines and satellite linkups or (2) furnishing telegraph and other nonvocal communications using their own facilities.

Cross-References. Establishments primarily engaged in—

- Broadcasting scheduled television programs via cable or satellite facilities on a subscription or fee basis—are classified in Industry 513220, Cable and Other Program Distribution;

- Providing coin-operated pay telephones—are classified in Industry 812990, All Other Personal Services;

- Operating and maintaining wireless networks—are classified in Industry 51332, Wireless Telecommunications Carriers (except Satellite);

- Reselling telecommunications, without operating a network—are classified in Industry 513330, Telecommunications Resellers;

- Publishing telephone directories—are classified in Industry 511140, Database and Directory Publishers; and

- Maintaining and installing wired telecommunication systems as independent contractors— are classified in Sector 23, Construction.

51332 Wireless Telecommunications Carriers (except Satellite)

This industry comprises establishments primarily engaged in operating and maintaining switching and transmission facilities that provide direct communications via airwaves. Included in this industry

US—United States industry only. CAN—United States and Canadian industries are comparable. When neither US nor CAN appears, Canadian, Mexican, and United States industries are comparable.

http://www.ntis.gov/naics

are establishments providing wireless telecommunications network services, such as cellular telephone or paging services.

Cross-References.

Establishments primarily engaged in providing telephone answering services using pagers are classified in Industry 56142, Telephone Call Centers.

513321 Paging[US]

This U.S. industry comprises establishments primarily engaged in operating paging networks. The establishments of this industry may also supply and maintain equipment used to receive signals.

Cross-References.

Establishments primarily engaged in providing telephone answering services using pagers are classified in U.S. Industry 561421, Telephone Answering Services.

513322 Cellular and Other Wireless Telecommunications[US]

This U.S. industry comprises establishments primarily engaged in operating cellular telecommunications and other wireless telecommunications networks (except paging).

Cross-References.

Establishments primarily engaged in operating paging networks are classified in U.S. Industry 513321, Paging.

51333 Telecommunications Resellers
See industry description for 513330 below.

513330 Telecommunications Resellers

This industry comprises establishments primarily engaged in purchasing access and network capacity from owners and operators of the networks and reselling wired and wireless telecommunications services to businesses and households. Establishments in this industry resell telecommunications; they do not operate and maintain telecommunications switching and transmission facilities.

Cross-References. Establishments primarily engaged in—

- Operating and maintaining wired telecommunications networks—are classified in Industry 513310, Wired Telecommunications Carriers;

- Reselling satellite telecommunications services—are classified in Industry 513340, Satellite Telecommunications; and

- Operating and maintaining wireless telecommunications—are classified in Industry 51332, Wireless Telecommunications Carriers (except Satellite).

US—United States industry only. CAN—United States and Canadian industries are comparable. When neither US nor CAN appears, Canadian, Mexican, and United States industries are comparable.

51334 Satellite Telecommunications
See industry description for 513340 below.

513340 Satellite Telecommunications

This industry comprises establishments primarily engaged in providing point-to-point telecommunications services to other establishments in the telecommunications and broadcasting industries by forwarding and receiving communications signals via a system of satellites or reselling satellite telecommunications.

Cross-References.

Establishments primarily engaged in providing direct-to-home satellite television systems to individual households or consumers are classified in Industry 513220, Cable and Other Program Distribution.

51339 Other Telecommunications
See industry description for 513390 below.

513390 Other Telecommunications

This industry comprises establishments primarily engaged in (1) providing specialized telecommunications applications, such as satellite tracking, communications telemetry, and radar station operations or (2) providing satellite terminal stations and associated facilities operationally connected with one or more terrestrial communications systems and capable of transmitting telecommunications to or receiving telecommunications from satellite systems.

Cross-References. Establishments primarily engaged in—

- Providing satellite telecommunications—are classified in Industry 513340, Satellite Telecommunications; and

- Providing custom design, programming, or facilities management services for integrated computer and telecommunications systems or operations—are classified in Industry 54151, Computer Systems Design and Related Services.

514 Information Services and Data Processing Services

Industries in the Information Services and Data Processing Services subsector group establishments providing information, storing information, providing access to information, and processing information. The main components of the subsector are news syndicates, libraries, archives, online information service providers, and data processors.

5141 Information Services

This industry group comprises establishments primarily engaged in providing information, storing information, and/or providing access to information.

US—United States industry only. CAN—United States and Canadian industries are comparable. When neither US nor CAN appears, Canadian, Mexican, and United States industries are comparable.

http://www.ntis.gov/naics

51411 News Syndicates

See industry description for 514110 below.

514110 News Syndicates

This industry comprises establishments primarily engaged in supplying information, such as news reports, articles, pictures, and features, to the news media.

Cross-References.

Independent writers and journalists (including photojournalists) are classified in Industry 711510, Independent Artists, Writers, and Performers.

51412 Libraries and Archives

See industry description for 514120 below.

514120 Libraries and Archives

This industry comprises establishments primarily engaged in providing library or archive services. These establishments are engaged in maintaining collections of documents (e.g., books, journals, newspapers, and music) and facilitating the use of such documents (recorded information regardless of its physical form and characteristics) as are required to meet the informational, research, educational, or recreational needs of their user. These establishments may also acquire, research, store, preserve, and generally make accessible to the public historical documents, photographs, maps, audio material, audiovisual material, and other archival material of historical interest. All or portions of these collections may be accessible electronically.

Cross-References. Establishments primarily engaged in—

- Providing stock footage (via motion picture and video tape libraries) to the media, multimedia, and advertising industries—are classified in Industry 512199, Other Motion Picture and Video Industries; and

- Distributing film and video productions to motion picture theaters, television networks and stations, and exhibitors—are classified in Industry 512120, Motion Picture and Video Distribution.

51419 Other Information Services

This industry comprises establishments primarily engaged in providing information services (except news syndicates, libraries, and archives). Included in this industry are Internet service providers, on-line information access services, and telephone-based (i.e., toll call) information services. On-line information services establishments are engaged in the provision of direct access to computer-held information published by others via telecommunications networks. These establishments often provide electronic mail services, bulletin boards, browsers, and search routines.

Cross-References. Establishments primarily engaged in—

- Publishing or compiling and offer direct on-line access to information that they publish or compile—are classified in Subsector 511, Publishing Industries, according to activity;

- Supplying information to the news media—are classified in Industry 514110, News Syndicates; and

- Operating libraries and archives—are classified in Industry 514120, Libraries and Archives.

514191 On-Line Information Services[CAN]

This U.S. industry comprises Internet access providers, Internet service providers, and similar establishments primarily engaged in providing direct access through telecommunications networks to computer-held information compiled or published by others.

Illustrative Examples:

Information access services, on-line   Internet service providers
Internet access providers

Cross-References.

Establishments primarily engaged in publishing or compiling information and offering direct on line access to the information that they publish or compile are classified in Subsector 511, Publishing Industries, according to activity.

514199 All Other Information Services[CAN]

This U.S. industry comprises establishments primarily engaged in providing information services (except news syndicates, libraries, archives, and on-line information access). Activities performed by establishments in this industry include telephone-based information recordings and information search services on a contract basis.

Cross-References. Establishments primarily engaged in—

- Publishing or compiling and offer direct on-line access to information that they publish or compile—are classified in Subsector 511, Publishing Industries, according to activity;

- Supplying information to the news media—are classified in Industry 514110, News Syndicates;

- Operating libraries and archives—are classified in Industry 514120, Libraries and Archives; and

---

US—United States industry only. CAN—United States and Canadian industries are comparable. When neither US nor CAN appears, Canadian, Mexican, and United States industries are comparable.

- Providing on-line information services—are classified in U.S. Industry 514191, On-Line Information Services.

5142 Data Processing Services

51421 Data Processing Services
See industry description for 514210 below.

514210 Data Processing Services

This industry comprises establishments primarily engaged in providing electronic data processing services. These establishments may provide complete processing and preparation of reports from data supplied by customers; specialized services, such as automated data entry services; or may make data processing resources available to clients on an hourly or timesharing basis.

Illustrative Examples:

Computer input preparation services	Electronic data processing services
Computer time rental	Optical scanning services

Cross-References. Establishments primarily engaged in—

- Providing text processing and desktop publishing services—are classified in Industry 561410, Document Preparation Services;

- Providing on-site management and operation of a client's data-processing facilities—are classified in U.S. Industry 541513, Computer Facilities Management Services;

- Providing on-line access to information and services developed by others—are classified in U.S. Industry 514191, On-Line Information Services;

- Providing access to microcomputers and office equipment, as well as other office support services—are classified in Industry 56143, Business Service Centers;

- Processing financial transactions, such as credit card transactions,—are classified in Industry 522320, Financial Transactions Processing, Reserve, and Clearinghouse Activities; and

- Providing payroll processing services using data processing techniques—are classified in U.S. Industry 541214, Payroll Services.

US—United States industry only. CAN—United States and Canadian industries are comparable. When neither US nor CAN appears, Canadian, Mexican, and United States industries are comparable.

http://www.ntis.gov/naics

Sector 52—Finance and Insurance

The Sector as a Whole

The Finance and Insurance sector comprises establishments primarily engaged in financial transactions (transactions involving the creation, liquidation, or change in ownership of financial assets) and/or in facilitating financial transactions. Three principal types of activities are identified:

1. Raising funds by taking deposits and/or issuing securities and, in the process, incurring liabilities. Establishments engaged in this activity use raised funds to acquire financial assets by making loans and/or purchasing securities. Putting themselves at risk, they channel funds from lenders to borrowers and transform or repackage the funds with respect to maturity, scale and risk. This activity is known as financial intermediation.

2. Pooling of risk by underwriting insurance and annuities. Establishments engaged in this activity collect fees, insurance premiums, or annuity considerations; build up reserves; invest those reserves; and make contractual payments. Fees are based on the expected incidence of the insured risk and the expected return on investment.

3. Providing specialized services facilitating or supporting financial intermediation, insurance, and employee benefit programs.

In addition, monetary authorities charged with monetary control are included in this sector.

The subsectors, industry groups, and industries within the NAICS Finance and Insurance sector are defined on the basis of their unique production processes. As with all industries, the production processes are distinguished by their use of specialized human resources and specialized physical capital. In addition, the way in which these establishments acquire and allocate financial capital, their source of funds, and the use of those funds provides a third basis for distinguishing characteristics of the production process. For instance, the production process in raising funds through deposit-taking is different from the process of raising funds in bond or money markets. The process of making loans to individuals also requires different production processes than does the creation of investment pools or the underwriting of securities.

Most of the Finance and Insurance subsectors contain one or more industry groups of (1) intermediaries with similar patterns of raising and using funds and (2) establishments engaged in activities that facilitate, or are otherwise related to, that type of financial or insurance intermediation.

Industries within this sector are defined in terms of activities for which a production process can be specified, and many of these activities are not exclusive to a particular type of financial institution. To deal with the varied activities taking place within existing financial institutions, the approach is to split these institutions into components performing specialized services. This requires defining the units engaged in providing those services and developing procedures that allow for their delineation. These units are the equivalents for finance and insurance of the establishments defined for other industries.

The output of many financial services, as well as the inputs and the processes by which they are combined, cannot be observed at a single location and can only be defined at a higher level of the organizational structure of the enterprise. Additionally, a number of independent activities that represent separate and distinct production processes may take place at a single location

---

US—United States industry only. CAN—United States and Canadian industries are comparable. When neither US nor CAN appears, Canadian, Mexican, and United States industries are comparable.

http://www.ntis.gov/naics

belonging to a multilocation financial firm. Activities are more likely to be homogeneous with respect to production characteristics than are locations, at least in financial services. The classification defines activities broadly enough that it can be used both by those classifying by location and by those employing a more top-down approach to the delineation of the establishment.

Establishments engaged in activities that facilitate, or are otherwise related to, the various types of intermediation have been included in individual subsectors, rather than in a separate subsector dedicated to services alone because these services are performed by intermediaries as well as by specialist establishments and the extent to which the activity of the intermediaries can be separately identified is not clear.

The Finance and Insurance sector has been defined to encompass establishments primarily engaged in financial transactions; that is, transactions involving the creation, liquidation, or change in ownership of financial assets or in facilitating financial transactions. Financial industries are extensive users of electronic means for facilitating the verification of financial balances, authorizing transactions, transferring funds to and from transactors' accounts, notifying banks (or credit card issuers) of the individual transactions, and providing daily summaries. Since these transaction processing activities are integral to the production of finance and insurance services, establishments that principally provide a financial transaction processing service are classified to this sector, rather than to the data processing industry in the Information sector.

Legal entities that hold portfolios of assets on behalf of others are significant and data on them are required for a variety of purposes. Thus for NAICS, these funds, trusts, and other financial vehicles are the fifth subsector of the Finance and Insurance sector. These entities earn interest, dividends, and other property income, but have little or no employment and no revenue from the sale of services. Separate establishments and employees devoted to the management of funds are classified in Industry Group 5239, Other Financial Investment Activities.

521 Monetary Authorities – Central Bank

The Monetary Authorities – Central Bank subsector groups establishments that engage in performing central banking functions, such as issuing currency, managing the Nation's money supply and international reserves, holding deposits that represent the reserves of other banks and other central banks, and acting as fiscal agent for the central government.

5211 Monetary Authorities – Central Bank

52111 Monetary Authorities – Central Bank^{CAN}

See industry description for 521110 below.

521110 Monetary Authorities-Central Bank^{CAN}

This industry comprises establishments primarily engaged in performing central banking functions, such as issuing currency, managing the Nation's money supply and international reserves, holding deposits that represent the reserves of other banks and other central banks, and acting as fiscal agent for the central government.

US—United States industry only. CAN—United States and Canadian industries are comparable. When neither US nor CAN appears, Canadian, Mexican, and United States industries are comparable.

Cross-References.

Establishments of the Board of Governors of the Federal Reserve System are classified in Industry 921130, Public Finance Activities.

522 Credit Intermediation and Related Activities

Industries in the Credit Intermediation and Related Activities subsector group establishments that (1) lend funds raised from depositors; (2) lend funds raised from credit market borrowing; or (3) facilitate the lending of funds or issuance of credit by engaging in such activities as mortgage and loan brokerage, clearinghouse and reserve services, and check cashing services.

5221 Depository Credit Intermediation^{CAN}

This industry group comprises establishments primarily engaged in accepting deposits (or share deposits) and in lending funds from these deposits. Within this group, industries are defined on the basis of differences in the types of deposit liabilities assumed and in the nature of the credit extended.

52211 Commercial Banking^{CAN}
See industry description for 522110 below.

522110 Commercial Banking^{CAN}

This industry comprises establishments primarily engaged in accepting demand and other deposits and making commercial, industrial, and consumer loans. Commercial banks and branches of foreign banks are included in this industry.

Cross-References.

- Establishments primarily engaged in credit card banking are classified in Industry 522210, Credit Card Issuing;

- Establishments known as industrial banks and primarily engaged in accepting deposits are classified in Industry 522190, Other Depository Credit Intermediation; and

- Establishments of depository institutions primarily engaged in trust activities are classified in U.S. Industry 523991, Trust, Fiduciary, and Custody Activities.

52212 Savings Institutions^{US}
See industry description for 522120 below.

522120 Savings Institutions^{US}

This industry comprises establishments primarily engaged in accepting time deposits, making mortgage and real estate loans, and investing in high-grade securities. Savings and loan associations and savings banks are included in this industry.

US—United States industry only. CAN—United States and Canadian industries are comparable. When neither US nor CAN appears, Canadian, Mexican, and United States industries are comparable.

http://www.ntis.gov/naics

Cross-References.

Establishments primarily engaged in accepting demand and other deposits and making all types of loans are classified in Industry 522110, Commercial Banking.

52213 Credit Unions[CAN]

See industry description for 522130 below.

522130 Credit Unions[CAN]

This industry comprises establishments primarily engaged in accepting members' share deposits in cooperatives that are organized to offer consumer loans to their members.

52219 Other Depository Credit Intermediation[CAN]

See industry description for 522190 below.

522190 Other Depository Credit Intermediation[CAN]

This industry comprises establishments primarily engaged in accepting deposits and lending funds (except commercial banking, savings institutions, and credit unions). Establishments known as industrial banks or Morris Plans and primarily engaged in accepting deposits, and private banks (i.e., unincorporated banks) are included in this industry.

Cross-References.

- Establishments primarily engaged in accepting demand and other deposits and making all types of loans are classified in Industry 522110, Commercial Banking;

- Establishments primarily engaged in accepting time deposits are classified in Industry 522120, Savings Institutions;

- Establishments primarily engaged in accepting members' share deposits in cooperatives are classified in Industry 522130, Credit Unions; and

- Establishments known as industrial banks and Morris Plans and are primarily engaged in providing nondepository credit are classified in U.S. Industry 52229, All Other Nondepository Credit Intermediation.

5222 Nondepository Credit Intermediation[CAN]

This industry group comprises establishments, both public (government-sponsored enterprises) and private, primarily engaged in extending credit or lending funds raised by credit market borrowing, such as issuing commercial paper or other debt instruments or by borrowing from other financial intermediaries. Within this group, industries are defined on the basis of the type of credit being extended.

US—United States industry only. CAN—United States and Canadian industries are comparable. When neither US nor CAN appears, Canadian, Mexican, and United States industries are comparable.

52221 Credit Card Issuing^{CAN}
See industry description for 522210 below.

522210 Credit Card Issuing^{CAN}

This industry comprises establishments primarily engaged in providing credit by issuing credit cards. Credit card issuance provides the funds required to purchase goods and services in return for payment of the full balance or payments on an installment basis. Credit card banks are included in this industry.

Cross-References.

Establishments primarily engaged in issuing cards that contain a stored prepaid value are classified with the industry providing the service represented by the cards, such as transit fare cards, in Subsector 482, Rail Transportation, and long-distance telephone cards in Subsector 513, Broadcasting and Telecommunications, respectively.

52222 Sales Financing^{CAN}
See industry description for 522220 below.

522220 Sales Financing^{CAN}

This industry comprises establishments primarily engaged in sales financing or sales financing in combination with leasing. Sales financing establishments are primarily engaged in lending money for the purpose of providing collaterized goods through a contractual installment sales agreement, either directly from or through arrangements with dealers.

Cross-References.

Establishments not engaged in sales financing, but primarily engaged in providing leases for equipment and other assets are classified in Subsector 532, Rental and Leasing Services.

52229 Other Nondepository Credit Intermediation^{CAN}

This industry comprises establishments primarily engaged in making cash loans or extending credit through credit instruments (except credit cards and sales finance agreements).

Illustrative Examples:

Consumer finance companies (i.e., unsecured cash loans)	Mortgage companies
International trade financing	Secondary market financing

Cross-References.

- Establishments primarily engaged in providing credit sales by issuing credit cards are classified in Industry 52221, Credit Card Issuing;

US—United States industry only. CAN—United States and Canadian industries are comparable. When neither US nor CAN appears, Canadian, Mexican, and United States industries are comparable.

- Establishments primarily engaged in providing leases for equipment and other assets without sales financing are classified in Subsector 532, Rental and Leasing Services;

- Establishments primarily engaged in accepting deposits and lending funds from these deposits are classified in Industry Group 5221, Depository Credit Intermediation;

- Establishments primarily engaged in arranging loans for others on a commission or fee basis are classified Industry 52231, Mortgage and Nonmortgage Loan Brokers; and

- Establishments primarily engaged in guaranteeing international trade loans are classified in Industry 52412, Direct Insurance (except Life, Health, and Medical) Carriers.

522291 Consumer Lending^{CAN}

This U.S. industry comprises establishments primarily engaged in making unsecured cash loans to consumers.

Illustrative Examples:

Finance companies (i.e., unsecured cash loans)
Loan companies (i.e., consumer, personal, student, small)

Personal credit institutions (i.e., unsecured cash loans)
Student loans companies

Cross-References. Establishments primarily engaged in—

- Accepting deposits and lending funds from these deposits—are classified in Industry Group 5221, Depository Credit Intermediation; and

- Arranging loans for others on a commission or fee basis—are classified Industry 522310, Mortgage and Nonmortgage Loan Brokers.

522292 Real Estate Credit^{US}

This U.S. industry comprises establishments primarily engaged in lending funds with real estate as collateral.

Illustrative Examples:

Home equity credit lending
Mortgage banking (i.e., nondepository mortgage lending)

Mortgage companies

Cross-References. Establishments primarily engaged in—

- Servicing loans—are classified in Industry 522390, Other Activities Related to Credit Intermediation;

- Arranging loans for others on a commission or fee basis—are classified in Industry 522310, Mortgage and Nonmortgage Loan Brokers; and

---

- Accepting deposits and lending funds secured by real estate—are classified in Industry Group 5221, Depository Credit Intermediation.

522293 International Trade Financing^{US}

This U.S. industry comprises establishments primarily engaged in providing one or more of the following: (1) working capital funds to U.S. exporters; (2) lending funds to foreign buyers of U.S. goods; and (3) lending funds to domestic buyers of imported goods.

Illustrative Examples:

Agreement corporations (i.e., international trade financing)
Edge Act corporations (i.e., international trade financing)

Export-Import banks
Trade banks (i.e., international trade financing)

Cross-References. Establishments primarily engaged in—

- Guaranteeing international trade loans—are classified in U.S. Industry 524126, Direct Property and Casualty Insurance Carriers;

- Brokering international trade loans—are classified in Industry 522310, Mortgage and Non-mortgage Loan Brokers; and

- Accepting deposits and lending funds from these deposits—are classified in Industry Group 5221, Depository Credit Intermediation.

522294 Secondary Market Financing^{US}

This U.S. industry comprises establishments primarily engaged in buying, pooling, and repackaging loans for sale to others on the secondary market.

Illustrative Examples:

Federal Home Loan Mortgage Corporation (FHLMC)
Federal National Mortgage Association (FNMA)

Government National Mortgage Association (GNMA)
Student Loan Marketing Association (SLMA)

522298 All Other Nondepository Credit Intermediation^{US}

This U.S. industry comprises establishments primarily engaged in providing nondepository credit (except credit card issuing, sales financing, consumer lending, real estate credit, international trade financing, and secondary market financing). Examples of types of lending in this industry are: short-term inventory credit, agricultural lending (except real estate and sales financing) and consumer cash lending secured by personal property.

US—United States industry only. CAN—United States and Canadian industries are comparable. When neither US nor CAN appears, Canadian, Mexican, and United States industries are comparable.

Illustrative Examples:

Commodity Credit Corporation	Morris Plans (i.e., known as), nondepository
Factoring accounts receivable	Pawnshops
Industrial banks (i.e., known as), nondepository	

Cross-References.

- Establishments primarily engaged in providing credit sales funding are classified in Industry 522210, Credit Card Issuing;

- Establishments primarily engaged in sales financing or sales financing in combination with leasing are classified in Industry 522220, Sales Financing;

- Establishments primarily engaged in making unsecured cash loans to consumers are classified in U.S. Industry 522291, Consumer Lending;

- Establishments primarily engaged in lending funds with real estate as collateral are classified in U.S. Industry 522292, Real Estate Credit;

- Establishments primarily engaged in international trade financing are classified in U.S. Industry 522293, International Trade Financing;

- Establishments primarily engaged in buying, pooling, and repackaging loans for sale to others on the secondary market are classified in U.S. Industry 522294, Secondary Market Financing; and

- Establishments known as industrial banks or Morris Plans and are primarily engaged in accepting deposits are classified in Industry 522190, Other Depository Credit Intermediation.

5223 Activities Related to Credit Intermediation[CAN]

This industry group comprises establishments primarily engaged in facilitating credit intermediation by performing activities, such as arranging loans by bringing borrowers and lenders together and clearing checks and credit card transactions.

52231 Mortgage and Nonmortgage Loan Brokers[CAN]
See industry description for 522310 below.

522310 Mortgage and Nonmortgage Loan Brokers[CAN]

This industry comprises establishments primarily engaged in arranging loans by bringing borrowers and lenders together on a commission or fee basis.

Cross-References. Establishments primarily engaged in—

- Lending funds with real estate as collateral—are classified in U.S. Industry 522292, Real Estate Credit; and

---

US—United States industry only. CAN—United States and Canadian industries are comparable. When neither US nor CAN appears, Canadian, Mexican, and United States industries are comparable.

- Servicing loans—are classified in Industry 522390, Other Activities Related to Credit Intermediation.

52232 Financial Transactions Processing, Reserve, and Clearinghouse Activities[CAN]
See industry description for 522320 below.

522320 Financial Transactions Processing, Reserve, and Clearinghouse Activities[CAN]

This industry comprises establishments primarily engaged in providing one or more of the following: (1) financial transaction processing (except central banks); (2) reserve and liquidity services (except central banks); and (3) check or other financial instrument clearinghouse services (except central banks).

Illustrative Examples:

Automated clearinghouses, bank or check
 (except central banks)
Check clearing services (except central banks)

Credit card processing services
Electronic funds transfer services

Cross-References.

- Establishments primarily engaged in nonfinancial data and electronic transaction processing are classified in Industry Group 5142, Data Processing Services; and

- Establishments of the central bank primarily engaged in check clearing and other financial transaction processing are classified in Industry 521110, Monetary Authorities-Central Bank.

52239 Other Activities Related to Credit Intermediation[CAN]
See industry description for 522390 below.

522390 Other Activities Related to Credit Intermediation[CAN]

This industry comprises establishments primarily engaged in facilitating credit intermediation (except mortgage and loan brokerage; and financial transactions processing, reserve, and clearing house activities).

Illustrative Examples:

Loans servicing
Money order issuance services

Travelers' check issuance services

Cross-References. Establishments primarily engaged in—

- Arranging loans for others on a commission or fee basis—are classified in Industry 522310, Mortgage and Nonmortgage Loan Brokers;

US—United States industry only. CAN—United States and Canadian industries are comparable. When neither US nor CAN appears, Canadian, Mexican, and United States industries are comparable.

http://www.ntis.gov/naics

- Providing financial transactions processing, reserve, and clearinghouse activities—are classified in Industry 522320, Financial Transactions Processing, Reserve, and Clearinghouse Activities;

- Foreign currency exchange dealing—are classified in Industry 523130, Commodity Contracts Dealing; and

- Providing escrow services (except real estate)—are classified in U.S. Industry 523991, Trust, Fiduciary, and Custody Activities.

523 Securities, Commodity Contracts, and Other Financial Investments and Related Activities

Industries in the Securities, Commodity Contracts, and Other Financial Investments and Related Activities subsector group establishments that are primarily engaged in one of the following: (1) underwriting securities issues and/or making markets for securities and commodities; (2) acting as agents (i.e., brokers) between buyers and sellers of securities and commodities; (3) providing securities and commodity exchange services; and (4) providing other services, such as managing portfolios of assets; providing investment advice; and trust, fiduciary, and custody services.

5231 Securities and Commodity Contracts Intermediation and Brokerage

This industry group comprises establishments primarily engaged in putting capital at risk in the process of underwriting securities issues or in making markets for securities and commodities; and those acting as agents and/or brokers between buyers and sellers of securities and commodities, usually charging a commission.

52311 Investment Banking and Securities Dealing[CAN]
See industry description for 523110 below.

523110 Investment Banking and Securities Dealing[CAN]

This industry comprises establishments primarily engaged in underwriting, originating, and/or maintaining markets for issues of securities. Investment bankers act as principals (i.e., investors who buy or sell on their own account) in firm commitment transactions or act as agents in best effort and standby commitments. This industry also includes establishments acting as principals in buying or selling securities generally on a spread basis, such as securities dealers or stock option dealers.

Illustrative Examples:

Bond dealing (i.e., acting as a principal in dealing securities to investors)

Securities underwriting
Stock option dealing

Cross-References.

- Establishments primarily engaged in acting as agents (i.e., brokers) in buying or selling securities on a commission or transaction fee basis are classified in Industry 523120, Securities Brokerage; and

---

US—United States industry only. CAN—United States and Canadian industries are comparable. When neither US nor CAN appears, Canadian, Mexican, and United States industries are comparable.

- Investment clubs or individual investors primarily engaged in buying or selling financial contracts (e.g., securities) on their own account are classified in Industry 523910, Miscellaneous Intermediation.

52312 Securities Brokerage^{CAN}
See industry description for 523120 below.

523120 Securities Brokerage^{CAN}

This industry comprises establishments primarily engaged in acting as agents (i.e., brokers) between buyers and sellers in buying or selling securities on a commission or transaction fee basis.

Illustrative Examples:

Mutual fund agencies (i.e., brokerages)   Stock brokerages
Securities brokerages

Cross-References.

Establishments primarily engaged in investment banking and securities dealing (i.e., buying or selling securities on their own account) are classified in Industry 523110, Investment Banking and Securities Dealing.

52313 Commodity Contracts Dealing^{CAN}
See industry description for 523130 below.

523130 Commodity Contracts Dealing^{CAN}

This U.S. industry comprises establishments primarily engaged in acting as principals (i.e., investors who buy or sell for their own account) in buying or selling spot or futures commodity contracts or options, such as precious metals, foreign currency, oil, or agricultural products, generally on a spread basis.

Cross-References. Establishments primarily engaged in—

- Acting as agents (i.e., brokers) in buying or selling spot or future commodity contracts on a commission or transaction fee basis—are classified in Industry 523140, Commodity Contracts Brokerage; and

- Buying and selling physical commodities for resale to other than the general public—are classified in Subsector 421, Wholesale Trade, Durable Goods.

52314 Commodity Contracts Brokerage^{CAN}
See industry description for 523140 below.

523140 Commodity Contracts Brokerage^{CAN}

This industry comprises establishments primarily engaged in acting as agents (i.e., brokers) in buying or selling spot or future commodity contracts or options on a commission or transaction fee basis.

US—United States industry only. CAN—United States and Canadian industries are comparable. When neither US nor CAN appears, Canadian, Mexican, and United States industries are comparable.

Illustrative Examples:

Commodity contracts brokerages   Financial futures brokerages
Commodity futures brokerages

Cross-References. Establishments primarily engaged in—

- Acting as principals in buying or selling spot or futures commodity contracts generally on a spread basis—are classified in Industry 523130, Commodity Contracts Dealing; and

- Buying and selling physical commodities for resale to other than the general public—are classified in Sector 421, Wholesale Trade, Durable Goods.

5232 Securities and Commodity Exchanges

52321 Securities and Commodity Exchanges
See industry description for 523210 below.

523210 Securities and Commodity Exchanges

This industry comprises establishments primarily engaged in furnishing physical or electronic marketplaces for the purpose of facilitating the buying and selling of stocks, stock options, bonds, or commodity contracts.

Cross-References.

Establishments primarily engaged in investment banking, and securities dealing, securities brokering commodity contracts dealing, or commodity contracts brokering are classified in Industry Group 5231, Securities and Commodity Contracts Intermediation and Brokerage.

5239 Other Financial Investment Activities

This industry group comprises establishments primarily engaged in one of the following: (1) acting as principals in buying or selling financial contracts (except investment bankers, securityes dealers, and commodity contracts dealers); (2) acting as agents (i.e., brokers) (except securities brokerages and commodity contracts brokerages) in buying or selling financial contracts; or (3) providing other investment services (except securities and commodity exchanges), such as portfolio management; investment advice; and trust, fiduciary, and custody services.

52391 Miscellaneous Intermediation[CAN]
See industry description for 523910 below.

523910 Miscellaneous Intermediation[CAN]

This industry comprises establishments primarily engaged in acting as principals (except investment bankers, securities dealers, and commodity contracts dealers) in buying or selling of financial contracts generally on a spread basis. Principals are investors that buy or sell for their own account.

US—United States industry only. CAN—United States and Canadian industries are comparable. When neither US nor CAN appears, Canadian, Mexican, and United States industries are comparable.

Illustrative Examples:

Investment clubs

Mineral royalties or leases dealing (i.e., acting as a principal in dealing royalties or leases to investors)

Tax liens dealing (i.e., acting as a principal in dealing tax liens to investors)

Venture capital companies

Cross-References.

Establishments primarily engaged in investment banking, securities dealing, securities brokering, commodity contracts dealing, or commodity contracts brokering are classified in Industry Group 5231, Securities and Commodity Contracts Intermediation and Brokerage.

52392 Portfolio Management[CAN]
See industry description for 523920 below.

523920 Portfolio Management[CAN]

This industry comprises establishments primarily engaged in managing the portfolio assets (i.e., funds) of others on a fee or commission basis. Establishments in this industry have the authority to make investment decisions, and they derive fees based on the size and/or overall performance of the portfolio.

Illustrative Examples:

Managing trusts

Mutual fund managing

Pension fund managing

Portfolio fund managing

Cross-References.

Establishments primarily engaged in investment banking and securities dealing, commodity contracts dealing, or commodity contracts brokering are classified in Industry Group 5231, Securities and Commodity Contracts Intermediation and Brokerage.

52393 Investment Advice[CAN]
See industry description for 523930 below.

523930 Investment Advice[CAN]

This industry comprises establishments primarily engaged in providing customized investment advice to clients on a fee basis, but do not have the authority to execute trades. Primary activities performed by establishments in this industry are providing financial planning advice and investment counseling to meet the goals and needs of specific clients.

US—United States industry only. CAN—United States and Canadian industries are comparable. When neither US nor CAN appears, Canadian, Mexican, and United States industries are comparable.

Illustrative Examples:

Financial investment advice services, customized, fees paid by client

Financial planning services, customized, fees paid by client

Investment advisory services, customized, fees paid by client

Cross-References.

- Establishments providing investment advice in conjunction with their primary activity, such as portfolio management, or the sale of stocks, bonds, annuities, and real estate, are classified according to their primary activity; and

- Establishments known as publishers providing generalized investment information to subscribers are classified in Subsector 511, Publishing Industries.

52399 All Other Financial Investment Activities[CAN]

This industry comprises establishments primarily engaged in acting as agents or brokers (except securities brokerages and commodity contracts brokerages) in buying and selling financial contracts providing financial investment activities (except securities and commodity exchanges, portfolio management, and investment advice).

Illustrative Examples:

Bank trust offices

Escrow agencies (except real estate)

Fiduciary agencies (except real estate)

Stock quotation services

Cross-References. Establishments primarily engaged in—

- Investment banking and securities dealing, securities brokering commodity contracts dealing, or commodity contracts brokering—are classified in Industry Group 5231, Securities and Commodity Contracts Intermediation and Brokerage;

- Acting as principals (except investment bankers, securities dealers, and commodity contracts dealers) in buying or selling financial contracts (except securities or commodity contracts)—are classified in Industry 52391, Miscellaneous Intermediation;

- Furnishing physical or electronic marketplaces for the purpose of facilitating the buying and selling of securities and commodities—are classified in Industry 52321, Securities and Commodity Exchanges;

- Managing the portfolio assets (i.e., funds) of others—are classified in Industry 52392, Portfolio Management;

- Providing customized investment advice—are classified in Industry 52393, Investment Advice;

- Awarding grants from trust funds—are classified in Industry 81321, Grantmaking and Giving Services;

US—United States industry only. CAN—United States and Canadian industries are comparable. When neither US nor CAN appears, Canadian, Mexican, and United States industries are comparable.

- Performing real estate escrow or real estate fiduciary activities—are classified in Industry 53139, Other Activities Related to Real Estate; and

- Financial transactions processing, reserve, and clearinghouse activities—are classified in Industry 52232, Financial Transactions Processing, Reserve, and Clearinghouse Activities

523991 Trust, Fiduciary, and Custody Activities[US]

This U.S. industry comprises establishments primarily engaged in providing trust, fiduciary, and custody services to others, as instructed, on a fee or contract basis, such as bank trust offices and escrow agencies (except real estate).

Cross-References. Establishments primarily engaged in—

- Managing the portfolio assets (i.e., funds) of others—are classified in Industry 523920, Portfolio Management;

- Performing real estate escrow or real estate fiduciary activities—are classified in Industry 531390, All Other Activities Related to Real Estate; and

- Awarding grants from trust funds—are classified in Industry 81321, Grantmaking and Giving Services.

523999 Miscellaneous Financial Investment Activities[US]

This U.S. industry comprises establishments primarily engaged in acting as agents and/or brokers (except securities brokerages and commodity contracts brokerages) in buying or selling financial contracts and those providing financial investment services (except securities and commodity exchanges; portfolio management; investment advice; and trust, fiduciary, and custody services) on a fee or commission basis.

Illustrative Examples:

Exchange clearinghouses, commodities or securities	Gas lease brokers' offices
	Stock quotation services

Cross-References. Establishments primarily engaged in—

- Investment banking and securities dealing, commodity contracts dealing, or commodity contracts brokering—are classified in Industry Group 5231, Securities and Commodity Contracts Intermediation and Brokerage;

- Acting as principals (except investment bankers, securities dealers, and commodity contracts dealers) in buying or selling financial contracts—are classified in Industry 523910, Miscellaneous Intermediation;

- Furnishing physical or electrical marketplaces for the purpose of facilitating the buying and selling of securities and commodities—are classified in Industry 523210, Securities and Commodity Exchanges;

- Managing the portfolio assets (i.e., funds) of others—are classified in Industry 523920, Portfolio Management;

- Providing customized investment advice—are classified in Industry 523930, Investment Advice;

- Providing trust, fiduciary, and custody services to others—are classified in U.S. Industry 523991, Trust, Fiduciary, and Custody Activities; and

- Financial transactions processing, reserve, and clearinghouse activities—are classified in Industry 522320, Financial Transactions Processing, Reserve, and Clearinghouse Activities.

524 Insurance Carriers and Related Activities

Industries in the Insurance Carriers and Related Activities subsector group establishments that are primarily engaged in one of the following (1) underwriting (assuming the risk, assigning premiums, and so forth) annuities and insurance policies or (2) facilitating such underwriting by selling insurance policies, and by providing other insurance and employee-benefit related services.

5241 Insurance Carriers

This industry group comprises establishments primarily engaged in underwriting (assuming the risk, assigning premiums, and so forth) annuities and insurance policies and investing premiums to build up a portfolio of financial assets to be used against future claims. Direct insurance carriers are establishments that are primarily engaged in initially underwriting and assuming the risk of annuities and insurance policies. Reinsurance carriers are establishments that are primarily engaged in assuming all or part of the risk associated with an existing insurance policy (or set of policies) originally underwritten by another insurance carrier.

Industries are defined in terms of the type of risk being insured against, such as death, loss of employment because of age or disability, and property damage. Contributions and premiums are set on the basis of actuarial calculations of probable payouts based on risk factors from experience tables and expected investment returns on reserves.

52411 Direct Life, Health, and Medical Insurance Carriers[CAN]

This industry comprises establishments primarily engaged in initially underwriting (i.e., assuming the risk and assigning premiums) annuities and life insurance policies, disability income insurance policies, accidental death and dismemberment insurance policies, and health and medical insurance policies.

Cross-References.

- Establishments primarily engaged in reinsuring life insurance policies are classified in Industry 52413, Reinsurance Carriers;

- Legal entities (i.e., funds, plans, and/or programs) organized to provide insurance and employee benefits exclusively for the sponsor, firm, or its employees or members are classified in Industry Group 5251, Insurance and Employee Benefit Funds; and

---

US—United States industry only. CAN—United States and Canadian industries are comparable. When neither US nor CAN appears, Canadian, Mexican, and United States industries are comparable.

- HMO establishments providing health care services are classified in Industry 62149, Other Outpatient Care Centers.

524113 Direct Life Insurance Carriers[US]

This U.S. industry comprises establishments primarily engaged in initially underwriting (i.e., assuming the risk and assigning premiums) annuities and life insurance policies, disability income insurance policies, and accidental death and dismemberment insurance policies.

Cross-References.

- Establishments primarily engaged in reinsuring life insurance policies, disability income insurance policies, and accidental death and dismemberment insurance policies are classified in Industry 524130, Reinsurance Carriers; and

- Legal entities (i.e., funds, plans, and/or programs) organized to provide insurance and employee benefits exclusively for the sponsor, firm, or its employees or members are classified in Industry Group 5251, Insurance and Employee Benefit Funds.

524114 Direct Health and Medical Insurance Carriers[US]

This U.S. industry comprises establishments primarily engaged in initially underwriting (i.e., assuming the risk and assigning premiums) health and medical insurance policies . Group hospitalization plans and HMO establishments (except those providing health care services) that provide health and medical insurance policies without providing health care services are included in this industry.

Cross-References.

- HMO establishments that provide both health care services and underwrite health and medical insurance are classified in U.S. Industry 621491, HMO Medical Centers;

- Establishments primarily engaged in reinsuring health insurance policies are classified in Industry 524130, Reinsurance Carriers; and

- Legal entities (i.e., funds, plans, and/or programs) organized to provide health- and welfare-related employee benefits exclusively for the sponsor's employees or members are classified in Industry 525120, Health and Welfare Funds.

52412 Direct Insurance (except Life, Health, and Medical) Carriers[CAN]

This industry comprises establishments primarily engaged in initially underwriting (i.e., assuming the risk and assigning premiums) various types of insurance policies (except life, disability income, accidental death and dismemberment, and health and medical insurance policies).

US—United States industry only. CAN—United States and Canadian industries are comparable. When neither US nor CAN appears, Canadian, Mexican, and United States industries are comparable.

Illustrative Examples:

Automobile insurance carriers, direct
Bank deposit insurance carriers, direct
Mortgage guaranty insurance carriers, direct
Property and casualty insurance carriers, direct

Title insurance carriers, real estate, direct
Warranty insurance carriers (e.g., appliance, automobile, homeowners, product), direct

Cross-References.

- Establishments primarily engaged in reinsuring insurance policies are classified in Industry 524130, Reinsurance Carriers;

- Legal entities (i.e., funds, plans, and/or programs) organized to provide insurance and employee benefits exclusively for the sponsor, firm, or its employees or members are classified in Industry Group 5251, Insurance and Employee Benefit Funds; and

- Establishments primarily engaged in initially underwriting annuities and life insurance policies, disability income insurance policies, accidental death and dismemberment insurance policies, and health and medical insurance policies are classified in Industry 52411, Direct Life, Health, and Medical Insurance Carriers.

524126 Direct Property and Casualty Insurance Carriers[US]

This U.S. industry comprises establishments primarily engaged in initially underwriting (i.e., assuming the risk and assigning premiums) insurance policies that protect policyholders against losses that may occur as a result of property damage or liability.

Illustrative Examples:

Automobile insurance carriers, direct
Fidelity insurance carriers, direct
Homeowners insurance carriers, direct
Liability insurance carriers, direct

Malpractice insurance carriers, direct
Mortgage guaranty insurance carriers, direct
Surety insurance carriers, direct

Cross-References.

Establishments primarily engaged in reinsuring property and casualty insurance policies are classified in Industry 524130, Reinsurance Carriers.

524127 Direct Title Insurance Carriers[US]

This U.S. industry comprises establishments primarily engaged in initially underwriting (i.e., assuming the risk and assigning premiums) insurance policies to protect the owners of real estate or real estate creditors against loss sustained by reason of any title defect to real property.

Cross-References.

Establishments primarily engaged in reinsuring title insurance policies are classified in Industry 524130, Reinsurance Carriers.

US—United States industry only. CAN—United States and Canadian industries are comparable. When neither US nor CAN appears, Canadian, Mexican, and United States industries are comparable.

524128 Other Direct Insurance (except Life, Health, and Medical) Carriers[US]

This U.S. industry comprises establishments primarily engaged in initially underwriting (e.g., assuming the risk, assigning premiums) insurance policies (except life, disability income, accidental death and dismemberment, health and medical, property and casualty, and title insurance policies).

Illustrative Examples:

Bank deposit insurance carriers, direct
Deposit or share insurance carriers, direct
Product warranty insurance carriers, direct

Warranty insurance carriers (e.g., appliance, automobile, homeowners, product), direct

Cross-References. Establishments primarily engaged in—

- Reinsuring insurance policies—are classified in Industry 524130, Reinsurance Carriers;

- Initially underwriting annuities and life insurance policies, disability income insurance policies, and accidental death and dismemberment insurance policies—are classified in U.S. Industry 524113, Direct Life Insurance Carriers;

- Initially underwriting health and medical insurance policies—are classified in U.S. Industry 524114, Direct Health and Medical Insurance Carriers;

- Initially underwriting property and casualty insurance policies—are classified in U.S. Industry 524126, Direct Property and Casualty Insurance Carriers; and

- Initially underwriting title insurance policies—are classified in U.S. Industry 524127, Direct Title Insurance Carriers.

52413 Reinsurance Carriers[CAN]
See industry description for 524130 below.

524130 Reinsurance Carriers[CAN]

This industry comprises establishments primarily engaged in assuming all or part of the risk associated with existing insurance policies originally underwritten by other insurance carriers.

Cross-References. Establishments primarily engaged in—

- Initially underwriting annuities and life insurance policies, disability income insurance policies, accidental death and dismemberment insurance policies, and health and medical insurance policies—are classified in Industry 52411, Direct Life, Health, and Medical Insurance Carriers; and

- Initially underwriting various types of insurance policies (except life, disability income, accidental death and dismemberment, and health and medical insurance policies)—are classified in Industry 52412, Direct Insurance (except Life, Health, and Medical) Carriers.

US—United States industry only. CAN—United States and Canadian industries are comparable. When neither US nor CAN appears, Canadian, Mexican, and United States industries are comparable.

5242 Agencies, Brokerages, and Other Insurance Related Activities

This industry group comprises establishments primarily engaged in (1) acting as agents (i.e., brokers) in selling annuities and insurance policies or (2) providing other employee benefits and insurance related services, such as claims adjustment and third party administration.

52421 Insurance Agencies and Brokerages[CAN]
See industry description for 524210 below.

524210 Insurance Agencies and Brokerages[CAN]

This industry comprises establishments primarily engaged in acting as agents (i.e., brokers) in selling annuities and insurance policies.

Cross-References.

Establishments primarily engaged in underwriting annuities and insurance policies are classified in Industry Group 5241, Insurance Carriers.

52429 Other Insurance Related Activities[CAN]

This industry comprises establishments primarily engaged in providing services related to insurance (except insurance agencies and brokerages).

Illustrative Examples:

Claims adjusting   Insurance plan administrative services
Insurance adjusting

Cross-References. Establishments primarily engaged in—

- Managing the portfolio assets (i.e., funds) of others—are classified in Industry 52392, Portfolio Management;

- Acting as agents (i.e., brokers) in selling annuities and insurance policies—are classified in Industry 52421, Insurance Agencies and Brokerages; and

- Providing actuarial consulting services—are classified in Industry 54161, Management Consulting Services.

524291 Claims Adjusting[CAN]

This U.S. industry comprises establishments primarily engaged in investigating, appraising, and settling insurance claims.

US—United States industry only. CAN—United States and Canadian industries are comparable. When neither US nor CAN appears, Canadian, Mexican, and United States industries are comparable.

524292 Third Party Administration of Insurance and Pension Funds[US]

This U.S. industry comprises establishments primarily engaged in providing third party administration services of insurance and pension funds, such as claims processing and other administrative services to insurance carriers, employee-benefit plans, and self-insurance funds.

Cross-References. Establishments primarily engaged in—

- Managing the portfolio assets (i.e., funds) of others—are classified in Industry 523920, Portfolio Management; and

- Providing actuarial consulting services—are classified in U.S. Industry 541612, Human Resources Management and Executive Search Consulting Services.

524298 All Other Insurance Related Activities[US]

This U.S. industry comprises establishments primarily engaged in providing insurance services on a contract or fee basis (except insurance agencies and brokerages, claims adjusting, and third party administration). Insurance advisory services and insurance ratemaking services are included in this industry.

Cross-References. Establishments primarily engaged in—

- Providing actuarial consulting services—are classified in U.S. Industry 541612, Human Resources Management and Executive Search Consulting Services;

- Acting as agents (i.e., brokers) in selling annuities and insurance policies—are classified in Industry 524210, Insurance Agencies and Brokerages;

- Insurance claims adjusting—are classified in U.S. Industry 524291, Claims Adjusting; and

- Third party administration services of insurance and pension funds—are classified in U.S. Industry 524292, Third Party Administration of Insurance and Pension Funds.

525 Funds, Trusts, and Other Financial Vehicles[US]

Industries in the Funds, Trusts, and Other Financial Vehicles subsector are comprised of legal entities (i.e., funds, plans, and/or programs) organized to pool securities or other assets on behalf of shareholders or beneficiaries of employee benefit or other trust funds. The portfolios are customized to achieve specific investment characteristics, such as diversification, risk, rate of return, and price volatility. These entities earn interest, dividends, and other property income, but have little or no employment and no revenue from the sale of services. Establishments with employees devoted to the management of funds are classified in Industry Group 5239, Other Financial Investment Activities.

Establishments primarily engaged in holding the securities of (or other equity interests in) other firms are classified in Sector 55, Management of Companies and Enterprises.

US—United States industry only. CAN—United States and Canadian industries are comparable. When neither US nor CAN appears, Canadian, Mexican, and United States industries are comparable.

5251 Insurance and Employee Benefit Funds[US]

This industry group comprises legal entities (i.e., funds, plans, and/or programs) organized to provide insurance and employee benefits exclusively for the sponsor, firm, or its employees or members.

52511 Pension Funds[US]

See industry description for 525110 below.

525110 Pension Funds[US]

This industry comprises legal entities (i.e., funds, plans, and/or programs) organized to provide retirement income benefits exclusively for the sponsor's employees or members.

Illustrative Examples:

Employee benefit plans   Retirement plans
Pension funds and plans

Cross-References. Establishments primarily engaged in—

- Managing portfolios of pension funds—are classified in Industry 523920, Portfolio Management; and

- Initially underwriting annuities—are classified in U.S. Industry 524113, Direct Life Insurance Carriers.

52512 Health and Welfare Funds[US]

See industry description for 525120 below.

525120 Health and Welfare Funds[US]

This industry comprises legal entities (i.e., funds, plans, and/or programs) organized to provide medical, surgical, hospital, vacation, training, and other health- and welfare-related employee benefits exclusively for the sponsor's employees or members.

Cross-References. Establishments primarily engaged in—

- Managing portfolios of health and welfare funds—are classified in Industry 523920, Portfolio Management; and

- Third party claims administration of health and welfare plans—are classified in U.S. Industry 524292, Third Party Administration of Insurance and Pension Funds.

US—United States industry only. CAN—United States and Canadian industries are comparable. When neither US nor CAN appears, Canadian, Mexican, and United States industries are comparable.

52519 Other Insurance Funds[US]
See industry description for 525190 below.

525190 Other Insurance Funds[US]

This industry comprises legal entities (i.e., funds (except pension, and health- and welfare-related employee benefit funds)) organized to provide insurance exclusively for the sponsor, firm, or its employees or members. Self-insurance funds (except employee benefit funds) and workers' compensation insurance funds are included in this industry.

Cross-References.

- Legal entities (i.e., funds, plans, and/or programs) organized to provide retirement income benefits exclusively for the sponsor's employees or members are classified in Industry 525110, Pension Funds;

- Legal entities (i.e., funds, plans, and/or programs) organized to provide health- and welfare-related employee benefits exclusively for the sponsor's employees or members are classified in Industry 525120, Health and Welfare Related Funds;

- Establishments primarily engaged in managing portfolios of insurance funds are classified in Industry 523920, Portfolio Management;

- Establishments primarily engaged in third party claims administration of insurance, and other employee benefit funds are classified in U.S. Industry 524292, Third Party Administration of Insurance and Pension Funds; and

- Establishments primarily engaged in providing insurance on a fee or contract basis are classified in Industry Group 5241, Insurance Carriers.

5259 Other Investment Pools and Funds[US]

This industry group comprises legal entities (i.e., investment pools and/or funds) organized to pool securities or other assets (except insurance and employee-benefit funds) on behalf of shareholders, unitholders, or beneficiaries.

52591 Open-End Investment Funds[US]
See industry description for 525910 below.

525910 Open-End Investment Funds[US]

This industry comprises legal entities (i.e., open-end investment funds) organized to pool assets that consist of securities or other financial instruments. Shares in these pools are offered to the public in an initial offering with additional shares offered continuously and perpetually and redeemed at a specific price determined by the net asset value.

Illustrative Examples:

Investment funds, open-ended   Money market mutual funds, open-ended

---

US—United States industry only. CAN—United States and Canadian industries are comparable. When neither US nor CAN appears, Canadian, Mexican, and United States industries are comparable.

http://www.ntis.gov/naics

52592 Trusts, Estates, and Agency Accounts[US]
See industry description for 525920 below.

525920 Trusts, Estates, and Agency Accounts[US]

This industry comprises legal entities, trusts, estates, or agency accounts, administered on behalf of the beneficiaries under the terms of a trust agreement, will, or agency agreement.

Illustrative Examples:

Bankruptcy estates
Personal investment trusts
Private estates (i.e., administering on behalf of
  beneficiaries)

Testamentary trusts

Cross-References. Establishments primarily engaged in—

- Managing portfolios of trusts—are classified in Industry 523920, Portfolio Management;

- Administering personal estates—are classified in U.S. Industry 523991, Trust, Fiduciary, and Custody Services; and

- Operating businesses of trusts and bankruptcy estates—are classified according to the kind of business operated.

52593 Real Estate Investment Trusts[US]
See industry description for 525930 below.

525930 Real Estate Investment Trusts[US]

This industry comprises legal entities that are Real Estate Investment Trusts (REITs).

Cross-References.

- Legal entities of mortgage-backed investment funds that are not REITs are classified elsewhere in the Funds, Trusts, and Other Financial Vehicles subsector based on the types of funds; and

- Legal entities of investments in real estate that are not REITs are classified in Industry Group 5311, Lessors of Real Estate.

52599 Other Financial Vehicles[US]
See industry description for 525990 below.

525990 Other Financial Vehicles[US]

This industry comprises legal entities (i.e., funds (except insurance and employee benefit funds; open-end investment funds; trusts, estates, and agency accounts; and Real Estate Investment Trusts (REITs)).

US—United States industry only. CAN—United States and Canadian industries are comparable. When neither US nor CAN appears, Canadian, Mexican, and United States industries are comparable.

Illustrative Examples:

Closed-end investment funds (except REITs)
Collateralized Mortgage Obligations (CMOs)
Face-amount certificate funds
Real Estate Mortgage Investment Conduits
(REMICs)

Special purpose vehicles
Unit investment trust funds

Cross-References.

- Legal entities (i.e., funds, plans, and programs) that provide insurance and employee benefits exclusively for the sponsor, firm, or its employees or members are classified in Industry Group 5251, Insurance and Employee Benefit Funds;

- Legal entities (i.e., open-end investment funds) organized to pool assets that consist of securities or other financial instruments, where the pools are offered to the public in an initial offering with additional shares offered continuously and perpetually at a specific price determined by the net asset value, are classified in Industry 525910, Open-End Investment Funds;

- Legal entities (i.e., trusts, estates, or agency accounts) administered on behalf of the beneficiaries under the terms of a trust agreement, will, or agency agreement are classified in Industry 525920, Trusts, Estates, and Agency Accounts; and

- Legal entities that are Real Estate Investment Trusts (REITs) are classified in Industry 525930, Real Estate Investment Trusts.

US—United States industry only. CAN—United States and Canadian industries are comparable. When neither US nor CAN appears, Canadian, Mexican, and United States industries are comparable.

http://www.ntis.gov/naics

Sector 53—Real Estate and Rental and Leasing

The Sector as a Whole

The Real Estate and Rental and Leasing sector comprises establishments primarily engaged in renting, leasing, or otherwise allowing the use of tangible or intangible assets, and establishments providing related services. The major portion of this sector comprises establishments that rent, lease, or otherwise allow the use of their own assets by others. The assets may be tangible, as is the case of real estate and equipment, or intangible, as is the case with patents and trademarks.

This sector also includes establishments primarily engaged in managing real estate for others, selling, renting and/or buying real estate for others, and appraising real estate. These activities are closely related to this sector's main activity, and it was felt that from a production basis they would best be included here. In addition, a substantial proportion of property management is self- performed by lessors.

The main components of this sector are the real estate lessors industries; equipment lessors industries (including motor vehicles, computers, and consumer goods); and lessors of nonfinancial intangible assets (except copyrighted works).

Excluded from this sector are real estate investment trusts (REITS) and establishments primarily engaged in renting or leasing equipment with operators. REITS are classified in Subsector 525, Funds, Trusts, and Other Financial Vehicles because they are considered investment vehicles. Establishments renting or leasing equipment with operators are classified in various subsectors of NAICS depending on the nature of the services provided (e.g, transportation, construction, agriculture). These activities are excluded from this sector because the client is paying for the expertise and knowledge of the equipment operator, in addition to the rental of the equipment. In many cases, such as, the rental of heavy construction equipment, the operator is essential to operate the equipment.

531 Real Estate

Industries in the Real Estate subsector group establishments that are primarily engaged in renting or leasing real estate to others; managing real estate for others; selling, buying, or renting real estate for others; and providing other real estate related services, such as appraisal services.

Establishments primarily engaged in subdividing and developing unimproved real estate and constructing buildings for sale are classified in Subsector 233, Building, Developing, and General Contracting.

Real Estate Investment Trusts (REITS) are classified in Subsector 525, Funds, Trusts, and Other Financial Vehicles because they are considered investment vehicles.

5311 Lessors of Real Estate

53111 Lessors of Residential Buildings and Dwellings[CAN]
See industry description for 531110 below.

531110 Lessors of Residential Buildings and Dwellings[CAN]

This industry comprises establishments primarily engaged in acting as lessors of buildings used as residences or dwellings, such as single-family homes, apartment buildings, and town homes.

Included in this industry are owner-lessors and establishments renting real estate and then acting as lessors in subleasing it to others. The establishments in this industry may manage the property themselves or have another establishment manage it for them.

Cross-References.

Establishments primarily engaged in managing residential real estate for others are classified in U.S. Industry 531311, Residential Property Managers.

53112 Lessors of Nonresidential Buildings (except Miniwarehouses)[CAN]
See industry description for 531120 below.

531120 Lessors of Nonresidential Buildings (except Miniwarehouses)[CAN]

This industry comprises establishments primarily engaged in acting as lessors of buildings (except miniwarehouses and self-storage units) that are not used as residences or dwellings. Included in this industry are owner-lessors and establishments renting real estate and then acting as lessors in subleasing it to others. The establishments in this industry may manage the property themselves or have another establishment manage it for them.

Cross-References. Establishments primarily engaged in—

- Acting as lessors of buildings used as residences or dwellings—are classified in Industry 531110, Lessors of Residential Buildings and Dwellings;

- Renting or leasing space for self-storage—are classified in Industry 531130, Lessors of Miniwarehouses and Self-Storage Units;

- Managing nonresidential real estate for others—are classified in U.S. Industry 531312, Nonresidential Property Managers;

- Managing and operating arenas, stadiums, theaters, or other related facilities and promoting and organizing performing arts productions, sports events, and similar events at those facilities—are classified in Industry 711310, Promoters of Performing Arts, Sports, and Similar Events with Facilities; and

- Operating public and contract general merchandise warehousing and storage facilities— are classified in Industry 493110, General Warehousing and Storage.

53113 Lessors of Miniwarehouses and Self-Storage Units[CAN]
See industry description for 531130 below.

531130 Lessors of Miniwarehouses and Self-Storage Units[CAN]

This industry comprises establishments primarily engaged in renting or leasing space for self-storage. These establishments provide secure space (i.e., rooms, compartments, lockers, containers, or outdoor space) where clients can store and retrieve their goods.

Cross-References. Establishments primarily engaged in—

- Operating public and contract general merchandise warehousing and storage facilities— are classified in Industry 493110, General Warehousing and Storage; and

- Operating coin-operated lockers—are classified in Industry 812990, All Other Personal Services.

53119 Lessors of Other Real Estate Property[CAN]
See industry description for 531190 below.

531190 Lessors of Other Real Estate Property[CAN]

This industry comprises establishments primarily engaged in acting as lessors of real estate (except buildings), such as manufactured home (i.e., mobile home) sites, vacant lots, and grazing land.

Cross-References. Establishments primarily engaged in—

- Acting as lessors of buildings used as residences or dwellings including manufactured (mobile) homes on-site—are classified in Industry 531110, Lessors of Residential Buildings and Dwellings;

- Acting as lessors of buildings (except miniwarehouses and self-storage units) that are not used as residences or dwellings—are classified in Industry 531120, Lessors of Nonresidential Buildings (except Miniwarehouses); and

- Renting or leasing space for self-storage—are classified in Industry 531130, Lessors of Miniwarehouses and Self-Storage Units.

5312 Offices of Real Estate Agents and Brokers

53121 Offices of Real Estate Agents and Brokers
See industry description for 531210 below.

531210 Offices of Real Estate Agents and Brokers

This industry comprises establishments primarily engaged in acting as agents and/or brokers in one or more of the following: (1) selling real estate for others; (2) buying real estate for others; and (3) renting real estate for others.

5313 Activities Related to Real Estate

This industry group comprises establishments primarily engaged in providing real estate services (except lessors of real estate and offices of real estate agents and brokers). Included in this industry group are establishments primarily engaged in activities, such as, managing real estate for others and appraising real estate.

US—United States industry only. CAN—United States and Canadian industries are comparable. When neither US nor CAN appears, Canadian, Mexican, and United States industries are comparable.

http://www.ntis.gov/naics

53131 Real Estate Property Managers[CAN]

This industry comprises establishments primarily engaged in managing real property for others. Management includes ensuring that various activities associated with the overall operation of the property are performed, such as collecting rents, and overseeing other services (e.g., maintenance, security, trash removal.)

Cross-References.

- Establishments primarily engaged in acting as lessors of real estate are classified in Industry Group 5311, Lessors of Real Estate; and

- Establishments formed on behalf of individual condominium owners or homeowners are classified in Industry 81399, Other Similar Organizations (except Business, Professional, Labor, and Political Organizations).

531311 Residential Property Managers[US]

This U.S. industry comprises establishments primarily engaged in managing residential real estate for others.

Cross-References.

- Establishments primarily engaged in managing nonresidential real estate for others are classified in U.S. Industry 531312, Nonresidential Property Managers;

- Establishments primarily engaged in acting as lessors of buildings used as residences or dwellings are classified in Industry 531110, Lessors of Residential Buildings and Dwellings; and

- Establishments formed on behalf of individual residential condominium owners or homeowners are classified in Industry 81399, Other Similar Organizations (except Business, Professional, Labor, and Political Organizations).

531312 Nonresidential Property Managers[US]

This U.S. industry comprises establishments primarily engaged in managing nonresidential real estate for others.

Cross-References.

- Establishments primarily engaged in managing residential real estate for others are classified in U.S. Industry 531311, Residential Property Managers;

- Establishments primarily engaged in acting as lessors of buildings (except miniwarehouses and self storage units) that are not used as residences or dwellings are classified in Industry 531120, Lessors of Nonresidential Buildings (except Miniwarehouses);

- Establishments primarily engaged in renting or leasing space for self-storage are classified in Industry 531130, Lessors of Miniwarehouses and Self-Storage Units; and

---

US—United States industry only. CAN—United States and Canadian industries are comparable. When neither US nor CAN appears, Canadian, Mexican, and United States industries are comparable.

- Establishments formed on behalf of individual nonresidential condominium owner are classified in Industry 81399, Other Similar Organizations (except Business, Professional, Labor, and Political Organizations).

53132 Offices of Real Estate Appraisers[CAN]
See industry description for 531320 below.

531320 Offices of Real Estate Appraisers[CAN]

This industry comprises establishments primarily engaged in estimating the fair market value of real estate.

53139 Other Activities Related to Real Estate[CAN]

531390 Other Activities Related to Real Estate[CAN]

This industry comprises establishments primarily engaged in performing real estate related services (except lessors of real estate, offices of real estate agents and brokers, real estate property managers, and offices of real estate appraisers).

Illustrative Examples:

Real estate escrow agencies	Real estate listing services
Real estate fiduciaries' offices	

Cross-References. Establishments primarily engaged in—

- Acting as lessors of real estate—are classified in Industry Group 5311, Lessors of Real Estate;

- Selling, buying, and/or renting real estate for others—are classified in Industry 531210, Offices of Real Estate Agents and Brokers;

- Managing real estate for others—are classified in Industry 53131, Real Estate Property Managers;

- Estimating fair market value of real estate—are classified in Industry 531320, Offices of Real Estate Appraisers; and

- Researching public land records for ownership of titles and/or conveying real estate titles— are classified in U.S. Industry 541191, Title Abstract and Settlement Offices.

532 Rental and Leasing Services

Industries in the Rental and Leasing Services subsector include establishments that provide a wide array of tangible goods, such as automobiles, computers, consumer goods, and industrial machinery and equipment, to customers in return for a periodic rental or lease payment.

US—United States industry only. CAN—United States and Canadian industries are comparable. When neither US nor CAN appears, Canadian, Mexican, and United States industries are comparable.

The subsector includes two main types of establishments: (1) those that are engaged in renting consumer goods and equipment and (2) those that are engaged in leasing machinery and equipment of the kind often used for business operations. The first type typically operates from a retail-like or store-front facility and maintains inventories of goods that are rented for short periods of time. The latter type typically does not operate from retail-like locations or maintain inventories, and offers longer term leases. These establishments work directly with clients to enable them to acquire the use of equipment on a lease basis, or they work with equipment vendors or dealers to support the marketing of equipment to their customers under lease arrangements. Equipment lessors generally structure lease contracts to meet the specialized needs of their clients and use their remarketing expertise to find other users for previously leased equipment. Establishments that provide operating and capital (i.e., finance) leases are included in this subsector.

Establishments primarily engaged in leasing in combination with providing loans are classified in Sector 52, Finance and Insurance. Establishments primarily engaged in leasing real property are classified in Subsector 531, Real Estate. Those establishments primarily engaged in renting or leasing equipment with operators are classified in various subsectors of NAICS depending on the nature of the services provided (e.g., Transportation, Construction, Agriculture). These activities are excluded from this subsector since the client is paying for the expertise and knowledge of the equipment operator, in addition to the rental of the equipment. In many cases, such as the rental of heavy construction equipment, the operator is essential to operate the equipment. Likewise, since the provision of crop harvesting services includes both the equipment and operator, it is included in the agriculture subsector. The rental or leasing of copyrighted works is classified in Sector 51, Information, and the rental or leasing of assets, such as patents, trademarks, and/or licensing agreements is classified in Subsector 533, Lessors of Nonfinancial Intangible Assets (except Copyrighted Works).

5321 Automotive Equipment Rental and Leasing

This industry group comprises establishments primarily engaged in renting or leasing the following types of vehicles: passenger cars and trucks without drivers, and utility trailers. These establishments generally operate from a retail-like facility. Some establishments offer only short-term rental, others only longer term leases, and some provide both type of services.

53211 Passenger Car Rental and Leasing

This industry comprises establishments primarily engaged in renting or leasing passenger cars without drivers.

Cross-References. Establishments primarily engaged in—

- Renting or leasing passenger cars with drivers (e.g., limousines, hearses, taxis)—are classified in Industry Group 4853, Taxi and Limousine Service;

- Retailing passenger cars through sales or lease arrangements—are classified in Industry Group 4411, Automobile Dealers; and

- Leasing passenger cars in combination with providing loans to buyers of such vehicles—are classified in Sector 52, Finance and Insurance.

US—United States industry only. CAN—United States and Canadian industries are comparable. When neither US nor CAN appears, Canadian, Mexican, and United States industries are comparable.

532111 Passenger Car Rental[CAN]

This U.S. industry comprises establishments primarily engaged in renting passenger cars without drivers, generally for short periods of time.

Cross References. Establishments primarily engaged in—

- Leasing passenger cars without drivers, generally for long periods of time—are classified in U.S. Industry 532112, Passenger Car Leasing; and

- Renting or leasing passenger cars with drivers (e.g., limousines, hearses, taxis)—are classified in Industry Group 4853, Taxi and Limousine Service.

532112 Passenger Car Leasing[CAN]

This U.S. industry comprises establishments primarily engaged in leasing passenger cars without drivers, generally for long periods of time.

Cross-References. Establishments primarily engaged in—

- Renting passenger cars without drivers, generally for short periods of time—are classified in U.S. Industry 532111, Passenger Car Rental;

- Renting or leasing passenger cars with drivers (e.g., limousines, hearses, taxis)—are classified in Industry Group 4853, Taxi and Limousine Service;

- Retailing passenger cars through sales or lease arrangements—are classified in Industry Group 4411, Automobile Dealers; and

- Leasing passenger cars in combination with providing loans to buyers of such vehicles—are classified in Sector 52, Finance and Insurance.

53212 Truck, Utility Trailer, and RV (Recreational Vehicle) Rental and Leasing
See industry description for 532120 below.

532120 Truck, Utility Trailer, and RV (Recreational Vehicle) Rental and Leasing

This industry comprises establishments primarily engaged in renting or leasing, without drivers, one or more of the following: trucks, truck tractors or buses; semitrailers, utility trailers, or RVs (recreational vehicles).

Cross-References. Establishments primarily engaged in—

- Renting recreational goods, such as pleasure boats, canoes, motorcycles, mopeds, or bicycles,—are classified in Industry 53229, Other Consumer Goods Rental;

- Renting or leasing farm tractors, industrial equipment, and industrial trucks, such as forklifts and other materials handling equipment,—are classified in Industry 532490, Other Commercial and Industrial Machinery Equipment Rental and Leasing;

US—United States industry only. CAN—United States and Canadian industries are comparable. When neither US nor CAN appears, Canadian, Mexican, and United States industries are comparable.

- Renting or leasing mobile home sites—are classified in Industry 53119, Lessors of Other Real Estate Property;

- Retailing vehicles commonly referred to as RVs through sales or lease arrangements—are classified in Industry 44121, Recreational Vehicle Dealers; and

- Leasing trucks, utility trailers, and RVs in combination with providing loans to buyers of such vehicles—are classified in Sector 52, Finance and Insurance.

5322 Consumer Goods Rental

This industry group comprises establishments primarily engaged in renting personal and household-type goods. Establishments classified in this industry group generally provide short-term rental although in some instances, the goods may be leased for longer periods of time. These establishments often operate from a retail-like or store-front facility.

53221 Consumer Electronics and Appliances Rental
See industry description for 532210 below.

532210 Consumer Electronics and Appliances Rental

This industry comprises establishments primarily engaged in renting consumer electronics equipment and appliances, such as televisions, stereos, and refrigerators. Included in this industry are appliance rental centers.

Cross-References. Establishments primarily engaged in—

- Renting or leasing computers—are classified in Industry 532420, Office Machinery and Equipment Rental and Leasing; and

- Renting a range of consumer, commercial, and industrial equipment, such as lawn and garden equipment, home repair tools, and party and banquet equipment,—are classified in Industry 532310, General Rental Centers.

53222 Formal Wear and Costume Rental
See industry description for 532220 below.

532220 Formal Wear and Costume Rental

This industry comprises establishments primarily engaged in renting clothing, such as formal wear, costumes (e.g., theatrical), or other clothing (except laundered uniforms and work apparel).

Cross-References.

Establishments primarily engaged in laundering and supplying uniforms and other work apparel are classified in Industry 81233, Linen and Uniform Supply.

US—United States industry only. CAN—United States and Canadian industries are comparable. When neither US nor CAN appears, Canadian, Mexican, and United States industries are comparable.

53223 Video Tape and Disc Rental

See industry description for 532230 below.

532230 Video Tape and Disc Rental

This industry comprises establishments primarily engaged in renting prerecorded video tapes and discs for home electronic equipment.

Cross-References. Establishments primarily engaged in—

- Theatrical distribution of motion pictures and videos—are classified in Subsector 512, Motion Picture and Sound Recording Industries;

- Renting video recorders and players—are classified in Industry 532210, Consumer Electronics and Appliances Rental; and

- Retailing prerecorded video tapes and discs—are classified in Industry 451220, Prerecorded Tape, Compact Disc, and Record Stores.

53229 Other Consumer Goods Rental

This industry comprises establishments primarily engaged in renting consumer goods (except consumer electronics and appliances, formal wear and costumes, and prerecorded video tapes).

Illustrative Examples:

Furniture rental centers	Sporting goods rental
Party rental supply centers	

Cross-References. Establishments primarily engaged in—

- Renting consumer electronics and appliances—are classified in Industry 53221, Consumer Electronics and Appliances Rental;

- Renting formal wear and costumes—are classified in Industry 53222, Formal Wear and Costume Rental;

- Renting prerecorded video tapes—are classified in Industry 53223, Video Tape and Disc Rental;

- Renting a general line of products, such as lawn and garden equipment, home repair tools, and party and banquet equipment,—are classified in Industry 53231, General Rental Centers;

- Renting medical equipment (except home health equipment), such as electromedical and electrotherapeutic apparatus,—are classified in Industry 53249, Other Commercial and Industrial Machinery and Equipment Rental and Leasing;

- Providing home health care services and home health equipment—are classified in Industry 62161, Home Health Care Services; and

---

US—United States industry only. CAN—United States and Canadian industries are comparable. When neither US nor CAN appears, Canadian, Mexican, and United States industries are comparable.

http://www.ntis.gov/naics

- Retailing and renting musical instruments—are classified in Industry 45114, Musical Instrument and Supplies Stores.

532291 Home Health Equipment Rental[US]

This U.S. industry comprises establishments primarily engaged in renting home-type health and invalid equipment, such as wheel chairs, hospital beds, oxygen tanks, walkers, and crutches.

Cross-References. Establishments primarily engaged in—

- Renting medical equipment (except home health equipment), such as electromedical and electrotherapeutic apparatus,—are classified in Industry 532490, Other Commercial and Industrial Machinery and Equipment Rental and Leasing; and

- Providing home health care services and home health equipment—are classified in Industry 62161, Home Health Care Services.

532292 Recreational Goods Rental[US]

This U.S. industry comprises establishments primarily engaged in renting recreational goods, such as bicycles, canoes, motorcycles, skis, sailboats, beach chairs, and beach umbrellas.

532299 All Other Consumer Goods Rental[US]

This U.S. industry comprises establishments primarily engaged in renting consumer goods and products (except consumer electronics and appliances; formal wear and costumes; prerecorded video tapes and discs for home electronic equipment; home health furniture and equipment; and recreational goods). Included in this industry are furniture rental centers and party rental supply centers.

Cross-References. Establishments primarily engaged in—

- Renting consumer electronics and appliances—are classified in Industry 532210, Consumer Electronics and Appliances Rental;

- Renting formal wear and costumes—are classified in Industry 532220, Formal Wear and Costume Rental;

- Renting video tapes—are classified in Industry 532230, Video Tape and Disc Rental;

- Renting home health furniture and equipment—are classified in U.S. Industry 532291, Home Health Equipment Rental;

- Renting recreational goods—are classified in U.S. Industry 532292, Recreational Goods Rental;

- Retailing and renting musical instruments—are classified in Industry 451140, Musical Instrument and Supplies Stores; and

---

US—United States industry only. CAN—United States and Canadian industries are comparable. When neither US nor CAN appears, Canadian, Mexican, and United States industries are comparable.

- Renting a range of consumer, commercial, and industrial equipment, such as lawn and garden equipment, home repair tools, and party and banquet equipment,—are classified in Industry 532310, General Rental Centers.

5323 General Rental Centers

53231 General Rental Centers
See industry description for 532310 below.

532310 General Rental Centers

This industry comprises establishments primarily engaged in renting a range of consumer, commercial, and industrial equipment. Establishments in this industry typically operate from conveniently located facilities where they maintain inventories of goods and equipment that they rent for short periods of time. The type of equipment that establishments in this industry provide often includes, but is not limited to: audio-visual equipment, contractors and builders tools and equipment, home repair tools, lawn and garden equipment, moving equipment and supplies, and party and banquet equipment and supplies.

Cross-References. Establishments primarily engaged in—

- Renting trucks and trailers without drivers—are classified in Industry 532120, Truck, Utility Trailer, and RV (Recreational Vehicle) Rental and Leasing;

- Renting party and banquet equipment—are classified in Industry 53229, Other Consumer Goods Rental;

- Renting heavy construction equipment without operators—are classified in U.S. Industry 532412, Construction, Mining, and Forestry Machinery and Equipment Rental and Leasing; and

- Renting specialized types of commercial and industrial equipment, such as garden tractors or public address systems,—are classified in Industry 532490, Other Commercial and Industrial Machinery and Equipment Rental and Leasing.

5324 Commercial and Industrial Machinery and Equipment Rental and Leasing

This industry group comprises establishments primarily engaged in renting or leasing commercial-type and industrial-type machinery and equipment. The types of establishments included in this industry group are generally involved in providing capital or investment-type equipment that clients use in their business operations. These establishments typically cater to a business clientele and do not generally operate a retail-like or store-front facility.

53241 Construction, Transportation, Mining, and Forestry Machinery and Equipment Rental and Leasing

This industry comprises establishments primarily engaged in renting or leasing one or more of the following without operators: heavy construction, off-highway transportation, mining, and forestry

---

machinery and equipment. Establishments in this industry may rent or lease products, such as aircraft, railroad cars, steamships, tugboats, bulldozers, earthmoving equipment, well-drilling machinery and equipment, or cranes.

Cross-References. Establishments primarily engaged in—

- Renting or leasing automobiles or trucks without operators—are classified in Industry Group 5321, Automotive Equipment Rental and Leasing;

- Renting or leasing air, rail, highway, and water transportation equipment with operators— are classified in Sector 48-49, Transportation and Warehousing, based on their primary activity;

- Renting or leasing heavy construction equipment with operators—are classified in Industry 23499, All Other Heavy Construction;

- Renting or leasing heavy equipment for mining with operators—are classified in Industry 21311, Support Activities for Mining;

- Renting or leasing heavy equipment for forestry with operators—are classified in Industry Group 1153, Support Activities for Forestry; and

- Leasing heavy equipment in combination with providing loans to buyers of such equipment—are classified in Sector 52, Finance and Insurance.

532411 Commercial Air, Rail, and Water Transportation Equipment Rental and Leasing[US]

This U.S. industry comprises establishments primarily engaged in renting or leasing off-highway transportation equipment without operators, such as aircraft, railroad cars, steamships, or tugboats.

Cross-References. Establishments primarily engaged in—

- Renting or leasing air, rail, highway, and water transportation equipment with operators— are classified in Sector 48-49, Transportation and Warehousing, based on their primary activity;

- Renting pleasure boats—are classified in U.S. Industry 532292, Recreational Goods Rental; and

- Renting or leasing automobiles or trucks without drivers—are classified in Industry Group 5321, Automotive Equipment Rental and Leasing.

532412 Construction, Mining, and Forestry Machinery and Equipment Rental and Leasing[US]

This U.S. industry comprises establishments primarily engaged in renting or leasing heavy equipment without operators that may be used for construction, mining, or forestry, such as bulldozers, earthmoving equipment, well-drilling machinery and equipment, or cranes.

US—United States industry only. CAN—United States and Canadian industries are comparable. When neither US nor CAN appears, Canadian, Mexican, and United States industries are comparable.

Cross-References. Establishments primarily engaged in—

- Renting or leasing heavy construction equipment with operators—are classified in Industry 23499, All Other Heavy Construction;

- Renting or leasing heavy equipment for mining with operators—are classified in Industry 21311, Support Activities for Mining;

- Renting or leasing heavy equipment for forestry with operators—are classified in Industry Group 1153, Support Activities for Forestry; and

- Leasing heavy equipment in combination with providing loans to buyers of such equipment—are classified in Sector 52, Finance and Insurance.

53242 Office Machinery and Equipment Rental and Leasing
See industry description for 532420 below.

532420 Office Machinery and Equipment Rental and Leasing

This industry comprises establishments primarily engaged in renting or leasing office machinery and equipment, such as computers, office furniture, duplicating machines (i.e., copiers), or facsimile machines.

Cross-References. Establishments primarily engaged in—

- Renting or leasing residential furniture—are classified in Industry 53229, Other Consumer Goods Rental; and

- Leasing office machinery and equipment in combination with providing loans to buyers of such equipment—are classified in Sector 52, Finance and Insurance.

53249 Other Commercial and Industrial Machinery and Equipment Rental and Leasing
See industry description for 532490 below.

532490 Other Commercial and Industrial Machinery and Equipment Rental and Leasing

This industry comprises establishments primarily engaged in renting or leasing nonconsumer-type machinery and equipment (except heavy construction, transportation, mining, and forestry machinery and equipment without operators; and office machinery and equipment). Establishments in this industry rent or lease products, such as, manufacturing equipment; metalworking, telecommunications, motion picture, or theatrical machinery and equipment; institutional (i.e., public building) furniture, such as furniture for schools, theaters, or buildings; or agricultural equipment without operators.

Cross-References. Establishments primarily engaged in—

- Renting or leasing heavy equipment without operators—are classified in Industry 53241, Construction, Transportation, Mining, and Forestry Machinery and Equipment Rental and Leasing;

---

* Renting or leasing office machinery and equipment—are classified in Industry 532420, Office Machinery and Equipment Rental and Leasing;

* Renting or leasing agricultural machinery and equipment with operators—are classified in Subsector 115, Support Activities for Agriculture and Forestry;

* Renting home furniture or medical equipment for home use—are classified in Industry 53229, Other Consumer Goods Rental and Leasing; and

* Leasing nonconsumer machinery and equipment in combination with providing loans to buyers of such equipment—are classified in Sector 52, Finance and Insurance.

533 Lessors of Nonfinancial Intangible Assets (except Copyrighted Works)

Industries in the Lessors of Nonfinancial Intangible Assets (except Copyrighted Works) subsector include establishments that are primarily engaged in assigning rights to assets, such as patents, trademarks, brand names, and/or franchise agreements for which a royalty payment or licensing fee is paid to the asset holder. Establishments in this subsector own the patents, trademarks, and/ or franchise agreements that they allow others to use or reproduce for a fee and may or may not have created those assets.

Establishments that allow franchisees the use of the franchise name, contingent on the franchisee buying products or services from the franchisor, are classified elsewhere.

Excluded from this subsector are establishments primarily engaged in leasing real property and establishments primarily engaged in leasing tangible assets, such as automobiles, computers, consumer goods, and industrial machinery and equipment. These establishments are classified in Subsector 531, Real Estate and Subsector 532, Rental and Leasing Services, respectively.

5331 Lessors of Nonfinancial Intangible Assets (except Copyrighted Works)

53311 Lessors of Nonfinancial Intangible Assets (except Copyrighted Works)
See industry description for 533110 below.

533110 Lessors of Nonfinancial Intangible Assets (except Copyrighted Works)

This industry comprises establishments primarily engaged in assigning rights to assets, such as patents, trademarks, brand names, and/or franchise agreements for which a royalty payment or licensing fee is paid to the asset holder.

Cross-References.

* Establishments primarily engaged in producing, reproducing, and/or distributing copyrighted works are classified in Sector 51, Information;

* Independent artists, writers, and performers primarily engaged in creating copyrighted works are classified in Industry 711510, Independent Artists, Writers, and Performers;

* Establishments primarily engaged in leasing real property are classified in Subsector 531, Real Estate;

US—United States industry only. CAN—United States and Canadian industries are comparable. When neither US nor CAN appears, Canadian, Mexican, and United States industries are comparable.

- Establishments primarily engaged in leasing tangible assets, such as automobiles, computers, consumer goods, and industrial machinery and equipment, are classified in Subsector 532, Rental and Leasing Services; and

- Establishments that allow franchisees the use of the franchise name, contingent on the franchisee buying products or services from the franchisor are classified elsewhere.

Sector 54—Professional, Scientific, and Technical Services

The Sector as a Whole

The Professional, Scientific, and Technical Services sector comprises establishments that specialize in performing professional, scientific, and technical activities for others. These activities require a high degree of expertise and training. The establishments in this sector specialize according to expertise and provide these services to clients in a variety of industries and, in some cases, to households. Activities performed include: legal advice and representation; accounting, bookkeeping, and payroll services; architectural, engineering, and specialized design services; computer services; consulting services; research services; advertising services; photographic services; translation and interpretation services; veterinary services; and other professional, scientific, and technical services.

This sector excludes establishments primarily engaged in providing a range of day-to-day office administrative services, such as financial planning, billing and recordkeeping, personnel, and physical distribution and logistics. These establishments are classified in Sector 56, Administrative and Support and Waste Management and Remediation Services.

541 Professional, Scientific, and Technical Services

Industries in the Professional, Scientific, and Technical Services subsector group establishments engaged in processes where human capital is the major input. These establishments make available the knowledge and skills of their employees, often on an assignment basis, where an individual or team is responsible for the delivery of services to the client. The individual industries of this subsector are defined on the basis of the particular expertise and training of the services provider.

The distinguishing feature of the Professional, Scientific, and Technical Services subsector is the fact that most of the industries grouped in it have production processes that are almost wholly dependent on worker skills. In most of these industries, equipment and materials are not of major importance, unlike health care, for example, where "high tech" machines and materials are important collaborating inputs to labor skills in the production of health care. Thus, the establishments classified in this subsector sell expertise. Much of the expertise requires degrees, though not in every case.

5411 Legal Services

54111 Offices of Lawyers
See industry description for 541110 below.

541110 Offices of Lawyers

This industry comprises offices of legal practitioners known as lawyers or attorneys (i.e., counselors-at-law) primarily engaged in the practice of law. Establishments in this industry may provide expertise in a range or in specific areas of law, such as criminal law, corporate law, family and estate law, patent law, real estate law, or tax law.

US—United States industry only. CAN—United States and Canadian industries are comparable. When neither US nor CAN appears, Canadian, Mexican, and United States industries are comparable.

Cross-References.

Establishments of legal practitioners (except lawyers or attorneys) primarily engaged in providing specialized legal or paralegal services are classified in Industry 54119, Other Legal Services.

54112 Offices of Notaries
See industry description for 541120 below.

541120 Offices of Notaries

This industry comprises establishments (except offices of lawyers and attorneys) primarily engaged in drafting, approving, and executing legal documents, such as real estate transactions, wills, and contracts; and in receiving, indexing, and storing such documents.

Cross-References.

- Establishments of lawyers and attorneys primarily engaged in the practice of law are classified in Industry 541110, Offices of Lawyers; and

- Establishments of notaries public engaged in activities, such as administering oaths and taking affidavits and depositions, witnessing and certifying signatures on documents, but not empowered to draw and approve legal documents and contracts, are classified in U.S. Industry 541199, All Other Legal Services.

54119 Other Legal Services

This industry comprises establishments of legal practitioners (except lawyers and attorneys) primarily engaged in providing specialized legal or paralegal services.

Illustrative Examples:

Notary public services	Process serving services
Paralegal services	Real estate settlement offices
Patent agent services (i.e., patent filing and searching services)	Real estate title abstract companies

Cross-References.

- Establishments of lawyers and attorneys primarily engaged in the practice of law are classified in Industry 54111, Offices of Lawyers; and

- Establishments (except offices of lawyers, attorneys, and paralegals) primarily engaged in providing arbitration and conciliation services are classified in Industry 54199, All Other Professional, Scientific, and Technical Services.

541191 Title Abstract and Settlement Offices[US]

This U.S. industry comprises establishments (except offices of lawyers and attorneys) primarily engaged in one or more of the following activities: (1) researching public land records to gather

---

US—United States industry only. CAN—United States and Canadian industries are comparable. When neither US nor CAN appears, Canadian, Mexican, and United States industries are comparable.

http://www.ntis.gov/naics

information relating to real estate titles; (2) preparing documents necessary for the transfer of the title, financing, and settlement; (3) conducting final real estate settlements and closings; and (4) filing legal and other documents relating to the sale of real estate. Real estate settlement offices, title abstract companies, and title search companies are included in this industry.

Cross-References.

Establishments of lawyers and attorneys primarily engaged in the practice of law are classified in Industry 541110, Offices of Lawyers.

541199 All Other Legal Services[US]

This U.S. industry comprises establishments of legal practitioners (except offices of lawyers and attorneys, settlement offices, and title abstract offices). These establishments are primarily engaged in providing specialized legal or paralegal services.

Illustrative Examples:

Notary public services   Process serving services
Paralegal services
Patent agent services (i.e., patent filing and
  searching services)

Cross-References.

- Establishments of lawyers and attorneys primarily engaged in the practice of law are classified in Industry 541110, Offices of Lawyers;

- Establishments (except offices of lawyers and attorneys) primarily engaged in researching public land records for ownership or title; preparing documents necessary for the transfer of the title, financing, and settlement; conducting final real estate settlements and closings; and/or filing legal and other documents relating to the sale of real estate are classified in U.S. Industry 541191, Title Abstract and Settlement Offices; and

- Establishments (except offices of lawyers, attorneys, and paralegals) primarily engaged in providing arbitration and conciliation services are classified in Industry 541990, All Other Professional, Scientific, and Technical Services.

5412 Accounting, Tax Preparation, Bookkeeping, and Payroll Services

54121 Accounting, Tax Preparation, Bookkeeping, and Payroll Services

This industry comprises establishments primarily engaged in providing services, such as auditing of accounting records, designing accounting systems, preparing financial statements, developing budgets, preparing tax returns, processing payrolls, bookkeeping, and billing.

US—United States industry only. CAN—United States and Canadian industries are comparable. When neither US nor CAN appears, Canadian, Mexican, and United States industries are comparable.

Illustrative Examples:

Accountants' offices	Payroll processing services
Auditing services, (CPA)	Tax return preparation services
Bookkeeping services	

541211 Offices of Certified Public Accountants[US]

This U.S. industry comprises establishments of accountants that are certified to audit the accounting records of public and private organizations and to attest to compliance with generally accepted accounting practices. Offices of certified public accountants (CPAs) may provide one or more of the following accounting services: (1) auditing financial statements; (2) designing accounting systems; (3) preparing financial statements; (4) developing budgets; and (5) providing advice on matters related to accounting. These establishments may also provide related services, such as bookkeeping, tax return preparation, and payroll processing.

Cross-References. Establishments of non-CPAs engaged in—

- Providing tax return preparation services only—are classified in U.S. Industry 541213, Tax Preparation Services;

- Providing payroll processing services only—are classified in U.S. Industry 541214, Payroll Services; and

- Providing accounting, bookkeeping, and billing services—are classified in U.S. Industry 541219, Other Accounting Services.

541213 Tax Preparation Services[CAN]

This U.S. industry comprises establishments (except offices of CPAs) engaged in providing tax return preparation services without also providing accounting, bookkeeping, billing, or payroll processing services. Basic knowledge of tax law and filing requirements is required.

Cross-References.

- Establishments of CPAs are classified in U.S. Industry 541211, Offices of Certified Public Accountants;

- Establishments of non-CPAs providing payroll services along with tax return preparation services are classified in U.S. Industry 541214, Payroll Services;

- Establishments of non-CPAs providing accounting, bookkeeping, or billing services along with tax return preparation services are classified in U.S. Industry 541219, Other Accounting Services; and

- Establishments providing computer data processing services at their own facility for others are classified in Industry 514210, Data Processing Services.

US—United States industry only. CAN—United States and Canadian industries are comparable. When neither US nor CAN appears, Canadian, Mexican, and United States industries are comparable.

http://www.ntis.gov/naics

541214 Payroll Services[US]

This U.S. industry comprises establishments (except offices of CPAs) engaged in the following without also providing accounting, bookkeeping, or billing services: (1) collecting information on hours worked, pay rates, deductions, and other payroll related data from their clients and (2) using that information to generate paychecks, payroll reports, and tax filings. These establishments may use data processing and tabulating techniques as part of providing their services.

Cross-References.

- Establishments of CPAs are classified in U.S. Industry 541211, Offices of Certified Public Accountants;

- Establishments of non-CPAs providing tax return preparation services only are classified in U.S. Industry 541213, Tax Preparation Services; and

- Establishments of non-CPAs providing accounting, bookkeeping, or billing services along with payroll services are classified in U.S. Industry 541219, Other Accounting Services.

541219 Other Accounting Services[US]

This U.S. industry comprises establishments (except offices of CPAs) engaged in providing accounting services (except tax return preparation services only or payroll services only). These establishments may also provide tax return preparation or payroll services. Accountant (except CPA) offices, bookkeeper offices, and billing offices are included in this industry.

Cross-References.

- Establishments of CPAs are classified in U.S. Industry 541211, Offices of Certified Public Accountants;

- Establishments of non-CPAs engaged in providing tax return preparation services only are classified in U.S. Industry 541213, Tax Preparation Services; and

- Establishments of non-CPAs engaged in providing payroll services only are classified in U.S. Industry 541214, Payroll Services.

5413 Architectural, Engineering, and Related Services

54131 Architectural Services
See industry description for 541310 below.

541310 Architectural Services

This industry comprises establishments primarily engaged in planning and designing residential, institutional, leisure, commercial, and industrial buildings and structures by applying knowledge of design, construction procedures, zoning regulations, building codes, and building materials.

US—United States industry only. CAN—United States and Canadian industries are comparable. When neither US nor CAN appears, Canadian, Mexican, and United States industries are comparable.

http://www.ntis.gov/naics

Cross-References. Establishments primarily engaged in—

- Planning and designing the development of land areas are classified in Industry 541320, Landscape Architectural Services; and

- Both the design and construction of buildings, highways, or other structures or in managing construction projects are classified Sector 23, Construction, according to the type of project.

54132 Landscape Architectural Services
See industry description for 541320 below.

541320 Landscape Architectural Services

This industry comprises establishments primarily engaged in planning and designing the development of land areas for projects, such as parks and other recreational areas; airports; highways; hospitals; schools; land subdivisions; and commercial, industrial, and residential areas, by applying knowledge of land characteristics, location of buildings and structures, use of land areas, and design of landscape projects.

Illustrative Examples:

Garden planning services	Industrial land use planning services
Golf course or ski area design services	Landscape architects' offices
Horticultural or landscape consulting services	Landscape design services

Cross-References.

Establishments primarily engaged in providing landscape care and maintenance services and/or installing trees, shrubs, plants, lawns, or gardens along with the design of landscape plans are classified in Industry 561730, Landscaping Services.

54133 Engineering Services
See industry description for 541330 below.

541330 Engineering Services

This industry comprises establishments primarily engaged in applying physical laws and principles of engineering in the design, development, and utilization of machines, materials, instruments, structures, processes, and systems. The assignments undertaken by these establishments may involve any of the following activities: provision of advice, preparation of feasibility studies, preparation of preliminary and final plans and designs, provision of technical services during the construction or installation phase, inspection and evaluation of engineering projects, and related services.

Illustrative Examples:

Civil engineering services	Environmental engineering services
Construction engineering services	Mechanical engineering services
Engineers' offices	

US—United States industry only. CAN—United States and Canadian industries are comparable. When neither US nor CAN appears, Canadian, Mexican, and United States industries are comparable.

Cross-References. Establishments primarily engaged in—

- Planning and designing computer systems that integrate computer hardware, software, and communication technologies—are classified in U.S. Industry 541512, Computer Systems Design Services;

- Performing surveying and mapping services of the surface of the earth, including the sea floor,—are classified in Industry 541370, Surveying and Mapping (except Geophysical) Services;

- Gathering, interpreting, and mapping geophysical data—are classified in Industry 541360, Geophysical Surveying and Mapping Services;

- Creating and developing designs and specifications that optimize the use, value, and appearance of products—are classified in Industry 541420, Industrial Design Services;

- Providing advice and assistance to others on environmental issues, such as the control of environmental contamination from pollutants, toxic substances, and hazardous materials—are classified in Industry 541620, Environmental Consulting Services; and

- Both the design and construction of buildings, highways, and other structures or in managing construction projects are classified in Sector 23, Construction, according to the type of project.

54134 Drafting Services

See industry description for 541340 below.

541340 Drafting Services

This industry comprises establishments primarily engaged in drawing detailed layouts, plans, and illustrations of buildings, structures, systems, or components from engineering and architectural specifications.

54135 Building Inspection Services

See industry description for 541350 below.

541350 Building Inspection Services

This industry comprises establishments primarily engaged in providing building inspection services. These establishments typically evaluate all aspects of the building structure and component systems and prepare a report on the physical condition of the property, generally for buyers or others involved in real estate transactions. Building inspection bureaus and establishments providing home inspection services are included in this industry.

Cross-References. Establishments primarily engaged in—

- Inspecting buildings for termites and other pests—are classified in Industry 561710, Exterminating and Pest Control Services;

US—United States industry only. CAN—United States and Canadian industries are comparable. When neither US nor CAN appears, Canadian, Mexican, and United States industries are comparable.

- Inspecting buildings for hazardous materials—are classified in Industry 541620, Environmental Consulting Services; and

- Conducting inspections and enforcing public building codes and standards—are classified in Industry 925110, Administration of Housing Programs.

54136 Geophysical Surveying and Mapping Services

See industry description for 541360 below.

541360 Geophysical Surveying and Mapping Services

This industry comprises establishments primarily engaged in gathering, interpreting, and mapping geophysical data. Establishments in this industry often specialize in locating and measuring the extent of subsurface resources, such as oil, gas, and minerals, but they may also conduct surveys for engineering purposes. Establishments in this industry use a variety of surveying techniques depending on the purpose of the survey, including magnetic surveys, gravity surveys, seismic surveys, or electrical and electromagnetic surveys.

Cross-References.

Establishments primarily engaged in taking core samples, drilling test wells, or other mine development activities (except geophysical surveying and mapping) on a contract basis for others are classified in Industry 21311, Support Activities for Mining.

54137 Surveying and Mapping (except Geophysical) Services

See industry description for 541370 below.

541370 Surveying and Mapping (except Geophysical) Services

This industry comprises establishments primarily engaged in performing surveying and mapping services of the surface of the earth, including the sea floor. These services may include surveying and mapping of areas above or below the surface of the earth, such as the creation of view easements or segregating rights in parcels of land by creating underground utility easements.

Illustrative Examples:

Cadastral surveying services
Cartographic surveying services
Geodetic surveying services

Mapping (except geophysical) services
Topographic surveying services

Cross-References. Establishments primarily engaged in—

- Providing geophysical surveying and mapping services—are classified in Industry 541360, Geophysical Surveying and Mapping Services; and

- Publishing atlases and maps—are classified in U.S. Industry 511199, All Other Publishers.

US—United States industry only. CAN—United States and Canadian industries are comparable. When neither US nor CAN appears, Canadian, Mexican, and United States industries are comparable.

54138 Testing Laboratories
See industry description for 541380 below.

541380 Testing Laboratories

This industry comprises establishments primarily engaged in performing physical, chemical, and other analytical testing services, such as acoustics or vibration testing, assaying, biological testing (except medical and veterinary), calibration testing, electrical and electronic testing, geotechnical testing, mechanical testing, nondestructive testing, or thermal testing. The testing may occur in a laboratory or on-site.

Cross-References. Establishments primarily engaged in—

- Laboratory testing for the medical profession—are classified in Industry 62151, Medical and Diagnostic Laboratories;

- Veterinary testing services—are classified in Industry 541940, Veterinary Services; and

- Auto emissions testing—are classified in U.S. Industry 811198, All Other Automotive Repair and Maintenance.

5414 Specialized Design Services

This industry group comprises establishments providing specialized design services (except architectural, engineering, and computer systems design).

54141 Interior Design Services
See industry description for 541410 below.

541410 Interior Design Services

This industry comprises establishments primarily engaged in planning, designing, and administering projects in interior spaces to meet the physical and aesthetic needs of people using them, taking into consideration building codes, health and safety regulations, traffic patterns and floor planning, mechanical and electrical needs, and interior fittings and furniture. Interior designers and interior design consultants work in areas, such as hospitality design, health care design, institutional design, commercial and corporate design, and residential design. This industry also includes interior decorating consultants engaged exclusively in providing aesthetic services associated with interior spaces.

54142 Industrial Design Services
See industry description for 541420 below.

541420 Industrial Design Services

This industry comprises establishments primarily engaged in creating and developing designs and specifications that optimize the use, value, and appearance of their products. These services

---

US—United States industry only. CAN—United States and Canadian industries are comparable. When neither US nor CAN appears, Canadian, Mexican, and United States industries are comparable.

can include the determination of the materials, construction, mechanisms, shape, color, and surface finishes of the product, taking into consideration human characteristics and needs, safety, market appeal, and efficiency in production, distribution, use, and maintenance. Establishments providing automobile or furniture industrial design services or industrial design consulting services are included in this industry.

Cross-References. Establishments primarily engaged in—

- Applying physical laws and principles of engineering in the design, development, and utilization of machines, materials, instruments, structures, processes, and systems—are classified in Industry 541330, Engineering Services; and

- Designing clothing, shoes, or jewelry—are classified in Industry 541490, Other Specialized Design Services.

54143 Graphic Design Services
See industry description for 541430 below.

541430 Graphic Design Services

This industry comprises establishments primarily engaged in planning, designing, and managing the production of visual communication in order to convey specific messages or concepts, clarify complex information, or project visual identities. These services can include the design of printed materials, packaging, advertising, signage systems, and corporate identification (logos). This industry also includes commercial artists engaged exclusively in generating drawings and illustrations requiring technical accuracy or interpretative skills.

Illustrative Examples:

Commercial art studios	Graphic design consulting services
Corporate identification (i.e., logo) design services	Independent commercial or graphic artists
	Medical art or illustration services

Cross-References.

- Establishments primarily engaged in creating and/or placing public display advertising material are classified in Industry 541850, Display Advertising; and

- Independent artists primarily engaged in creating and selling visual artwork for noncommercial use and independent cartoonists are classified in Industry 711510, Independent Artists, Writers, and Performers.

54149 Other Specialized Design Services
See industry description for 541490 below.

541490 Other Specialized Design Services

This industry comprises establishments primarily engaged in providing professional design services (except architectural, landscape architecture, engineering, interior, industrial, graphic, and computer system design).

US—United States industry only. CAN—United States and Canadian industries are comparable. When neither US nor CAN appears, Canadian, Mexican, and United States industries are comparable.

Illustrative Examples:

Costume design services (except independent
   theatrical costume designers)
Fashion design services
Float design services

Fur design services
Jewelry design services
Shoe design services
Textile design services

Cross-References. Establishments primarily engaged in—

- Providing architectural design services—are classified in Industry 541310, Architectural Services;

- Providing landscape architecture design services—are classified in Industry 541320, Landscape Architectural Services;

- Providing engineering design services—are classified in Industry 541330, Engineering Services;

- Providing interior design services—are classified in Industry 541410, Interior Design Services;

- Providing industrial design services—are classified in Industry 541420, Industrial Design Services;

- Providing graphic design services—are classified in Industry 541430, Graphic Design Services;

- Providing computer systems design services—are classified in U.S. Industry 541512, Computer Systems Design Services; and

- Operating as independent theatrical designers—are classified in Industry 711510, Independent Artists, Writers, and Performers.

5415 Computer Systems Design and Related Services

See industry description for 54151 below.

54151 Computer Systems Design and Related Services

This industry comprises establishments primarily engaged in providing expertise in the field of information technologies through one or more of the following activities: (1) writing, modifying, testing, and supporting software to meet the needs of a particular customer; (2) planning and designing computer systems that integrate computer hardware, software, and communication technologies; (3) on-site management and operation of clients' computer systems and/or data processing facilities; and (4) other professional and technical computer-related advice and services.

Illustrative Examples:

Computer facilities management services
Computer hardware or software consulting
   services

Computer systems integration design services
Custom computer programming services
Software installation services

US—United States industry only. CAN—United States and Canadian industries are comparable. When neither US nor CAN appears, Canadian, Mexican, and United States industries are comparable.

http://www.ntis.gov/naics

Cross-References. Establishments primarily engaged in—

- Selling computer hardware or software products from retail-like locations and providing supporting services, such as customized assembly of personal computers,—are classified in Industry 44312, Computer and Software Stores;

- Wholesaling computer hardware or software products and providing supporting services, such as customized assembly of personal computers,—are classified in Industry 42143, Computer and Computer Peripheral Equipment and Software Wholesalers;

- Publishing packaged software—are classified in Industry 51121, Software Publishers; and

- Providing computer data processing services at their own facility for others—are classified in Industry 51421, Data Processing Services.

541511 Custom Computer Programming Services[US]

This U.S. industry comprises establishments primarily engaged in writing, modifying, testing, and supporting software to meet the needs of a particular customer.

Cross-References. Establishments primarily engaged in—

- Publishing packaged software—are classified in Industry 511210, Software Publishers; and

- Planning and designing computer systems that integrate computer hardware, software, and communication technologies, even though such establishments may provide custom software as an integral part of their services,—are classified in U.S. Industry 541512, Computer Systems Design Services.

541512 Computer Systems Design Services[US]

This U.S. industry comprises establishments primarily engaged in planning and designing computer systems that integrate computer hardware, software, and communication technologies. The hardware and software components of the system may be provided by this establishment or company as part of integrated services or may be provided by third parties or vendors. These establishments often install the system and train and support users of the system.

Illustrative Examples:

Computer systems integration design
  consulting services
Information management computer systems
  integration design services

Local area network (LAN) computer systems
  integration design services
Office automation computer systems
  integration design services

Cross-References. Establishments primarily engaged in—

- Selling computer hardware or software products and systems from retail-like locations, and providing supporting services, such as customized assembly of personal computers—are classified in Industry 443120, Computer and Software Stores; and

---

US—United States industry only. CAN—United States and Canadian industries are comparable. When neither US nor CAN appears, Canadian, Mexican, and United States industries are comparable.

- Wholesaling computer hardware or software products and providing supporting services, such as customized assembly of personal computers,—are classified in Industry 421430, Computer and Computer Peripheral Equipment and Software Wholesalers.

541513 Computer Facilities Management Services[US]

This U.S. industry comprises establishments primarily engaged in providing on-site management and operation of clients' computer systems and/or data processing facilities. Establishments providing computer systems or data processing facilities support services are included in this industry.

Cross-References.

Establishments primarily engaged in providing computer data processing services at their own facility for others are classified in Industry 514210, Data Processing Services.

541519 Other Computer Related Services[US]

This U.S. industry comprises establishments primarily engaged in providing computer related services (except custom programming, systems integration design, and facilities management services). Establishments providing computer disaster recovery services or software installation services are included in this industry.

Cross-References. Establishments primarily engaged in—

- Providing custom computer programming services—are classified in U.S. Industry 541511, Custom Computer Programming Services;

- Providing computer systems integration design services—are classified in U.S. Industry 541512, Computer Systems Design Services; and

- Providing computer systems and/or data processing facilities management services—are classified in U.S. Industry 541513, Computer Facilities Management Services.

5416 Management, Scientific, and Technical Consulting Services

54161 Management Consulting Services

This industry comprises establishments primarily engaged in providing advice and assistance to businesses and other organizations on management issues, such as strategic and organizational planning; financial planning and budgeting; marketing objectives and policies; human resource policies, practices, and planning; production scheduling; and control planning.

Illustrative Examples:

Actuarial, benefit, and compensation consulting services	Marketing consulting services
Administrative and general management consulting services	Process, physical distribution, and logistics consulting services
Human resources and executive search consulting services	

US—United States industry only. CAN—United States and Canadian industries are comparable. When neither US nor CAN appears, Canadian, Mexican, and United States industries are comparable.

http://www.ntis.gov/naics

Cross-References.

- Establishments primarily engaged in providing a range of day-to-day office administrative services, such as financial planning, billing and recordkeeping, personnel, and physical distribution and logistics, are classified in Industry 56111, Office Administrative Services;

- Establishments primarily engaged in administering, overseeing, and managing other establishments of the company or enterprise (except government establishments) are classified in Industry 55111, Management of Companies and Enterprises;

- Government establishments primarily engaged in administering, overseeing, and managing governmental programs are classified in Sector 92, Public Administration;

- Establishments primarily engaged in professional and management development training are classified in Industry 61143, Professional and Management Development Training;

- Establishments primarily engaged in listing employment vacancies and in selecting, referring, and placing applicants in employment are classified in Industry 56131, Employment Placement Agencies;

- Establishments primarily engaged in developing and implementing public relations plans are classified in Industry 54182, Public Relations Agencies;

- Establishments primarily engaged in developing and conducting marketing research or public opinion polling are classified in Industry 54191, Market Research and Public Opinion Polling;

- Establishments primarily engaged in planning and designing industrial processes and systems are classified in Industry 54133, Engineering Services;

- Establishments primarily engaged in planning and designing computer systems are classified in Industry 54151, Computer Systems Design and Related Services; and

- Establishments primarily engaged in providing financial investment advice services are classified in Industry 52393, Investment Advice.

541611 Administrative Management and General Management Consulting Services[CAN]

This U.S. industry comprises establishments primarily engaged in providing operating advice and assistance to businesses and other organizations on administrative management issues, such as financial planning and budgeting, equity and asset management, records management, office planning, strategic and organizational planning, site selection, new business startup, and business process improvement. This industry also includes establishments of general management consultants that provide a full range of administrative; human resource; marketing; process, physical distribution, and logistics; or other management consulting services to clients.

US—United States industry only. CAN—United States and Canadian industries are comparable. When neither US nor CAN appears, Canadian, Mexican, and United States industries are comparable.

Illustrative Examples:

Administrative management consulting services

Financial management (except investment advice) consulting services

General management consulting services

Site selection consulting services

Strategic planning consulting services

Cross-References.

- Establishments primarily engaged in providing a range of day-to-day office administrative services, such as financial planning, billing and recordkeeping, personnel, and physical distribution and logistics, are classified in Industry 561110, Office Administrative Services;

- Establishments primarily engaged in administering, overseeing, and managing other establishments of the company or enterprise (except government establishments) are classified in U.S. Industry 551114, Corporate, Subsidiary, and Regional Managing Offices;

- Government establishments primarily engaged in administering, overseeing, and managing governmental programs are classified in Sector 92, Public Administration; and

- Establishments primarily engaged in providing investment advice are classified in Industry 523930, Investment Advice.

541612 Human Resources and Executive Search Consulting Services[CAN]

This U.S. industry comprises establishments primarily engaged in providing advice and assistance to businesses and other organizations in one or more of the following areas: (1) human resource and personnel policies, practices, and procedures; (2) employee benefits planning, communication, and administration; (3) compensation systems planning; (4) wage and salary administration; and (5) executive search and recruitment.

Illustrative Examples:

Benefit or compensation consulting services

Employee assessment consulting services

Executive placement or search consulting services

Human resources consulting services

Personnel management consulting services

Cross-References. Establishments primarily engaged in—

- Professional and management development training—are classified in Industry 611430, Professional and Management Development Training; and

- Listing employment vacancies and in selecting, referring, and placing applicants in employment—are classified in Industry 561310, Employment Placement Agencies.

541613 Marketing Consulting Services[US]

This U.S. industry comprises establishments primarily engaged in providing operating advice and assistance to businesses and other organizations on marketing issues, such as developing

---

US—United States industry only. CAN—United States and Canadian industries are comparable. When neither US nor CAN appears, Canadian, Mexican, and United States industries are comparable.

marketing objectives and policies, sales forecasting, new product developing and pricing, licensing and franchise planning, and marketing planning and strategy.

Illustrative Examples:

Customer services management consulting services

Marketing management consulting services

New product development consulting services

Sales management consulting services

Cross-References. Establishment primarily engaged in—

- Developing and implementing public relations plans—are classified in Industry 541820, Public Relations Agencies; and

- Developing and conducting marketing research or public opinion polling—are classified in Industry 541910, Marketing Research and Public Opinion Polling.

541614 Process, Physical Distribution, and Logistics Consulting Services[US]

This U.S. industry comprises establishments primarily engaged in providing operating advice and assistance to businesses and other organizations in areas, such as: (1) manufacturing operations improvement; (2) productivity improvement; (3) production planning and control; (4) quality assurance and quality control; (5) inventory management; (6) distribution networks; (7) warehouse use, operations, and utilization; (8) transportation and shipment of goods and materials; and (9) materials management and handling.

Illustrative Examples:

Freight rate or tariff rate consulting services

Inventory planning and control management consulting services

Manufacturing management consulting services

Productivity improvement consulting services

Transportation management consulting services

Cross-References. Establishments primarily engaged in—

- Planning and designing industrial processes and systems—are classified in Industry 541330, Engineering Services; and

- Providing computer systems integration design services—are classified in U.S. Industry 541512, Computer Systems Design Services.

541618 Other Management Consulting Services[US]

This U.S. industry comprises establishments primarily engaged in providing management consulting services (except administrative and general management consulting; human resources consulting; marketing consulting; or process, physical distribution, and logistics consulting). Establishments providing telecommunications or utilities management consulting services are included in this industry.

US—United States industry only. CAN—United States and Canadian industries are comparable. When neither US nor CAN appears, Canadian, Mexican, and United States industries are comparable.

Cross-References. Establishments primarily engaged in—

- Providing administrative and general management consulting services—are classified in U.S. Industry 541611, Administrative Management and General Management Consulting Services;

- Providing human resources and executive search consulting services—are classified in U.S. Industry 541612, Human Resources and Executive Search Consulting Services;

- Providing marketing consulting services—are classified in U.S. Industry 541613, Marketing Consulting Services; and

- Providing process, physical distribution, and logistics consulting services—are classified in U.S. Industry 541614, Process, Physical Distribution, and Logistics Consulting Services.

54162 Environmental Consulting Services

See industry description for 541620 below.

541620 Environmental Consulting Services

This industry comprises establishments primarily engaged in providing advice and assistance to businesses and other organizations on environmental issues, such as the control of environmental contamination from pollutants, toxic substances, and hazardous materials. These establishments identify problems (e.g., inspect buildings for hazardous materials), measure and evaluate risks, and recommend solutions. They employ a multidisciplined staff of scientists, engineers, and other technicians with expertise in areas, such as air and water quality, asbestos contamination, remediation, and environmental law. Establishments providing sanitation or site remediation consulting services are included in this industry.

Cross-References. Establishments primarily engaged in—

- Environmental remediation—are classified in Industry 562910, Remediation Services; and

- Providing environmental engineering services—are classified in Industry 541330, Engineering Services.

54169 Other Scientific and Technical Consulting Services

See industry description for 541690 below.

541690 Other Scientific and Technical Consulting Services

This industry comprises establishments primarily engaged in providing advice and assistance to businesses and other organizations on scientific and technical issues (except environmental).

Illustrative Examples:

Agricultural consulting services	Motion picture consulting services
Biological consulting services	Physics consulting services
Chemical consulting services	Radio consulting services
Economic consulting services	Safety consulting services
Energy consulting services	Security consulting services

US—United States industry only. CAN—United States and Canadian industries are comparable. When neither US nor CAN appears, Canadian, Mexican, and United States industries are comparable.

Cross-References.

Establishments primarily engaged in environmental consulting are classified in Industry 541620, Environmental Consulting Services.

5417 Scientific Research and Development Services

This industry group comprises establishments engaged in conducting original investigation undertaken on a systematic basis to gain new knowledge (research) and/or the application of research findings or other scientific knowledge for the creation of new or significantly improved products or processes (experimental development). The industries within this industry group are defined on the basis of the domain of research; that is, on the scientific expertise of the establishment.

54171 Research and Development in the Physical, Engineering, and Life Sciences
See industry description for 541710 below.

541710 Research and Development in the Physical, Engineering, and Life Sciences

This industry comprises establishments primarily engaged in conducting research and experimental development in the physical, engineering, or life sciences, such as agriculture, electronics, environmental, biology, botany, biotechnology, computers, chemistry, food, fisheries, forests, geology, health, mathematics, medicine, oceanography, pharmacy, physics, veterinary, and other allied subjects.

Cross-References. Establishments primarily engaged in—

- Providing physical, chemical, or other analytical testing services (except medical or veterinary)—are classified in Industry 541380, Testing Laboratories;

- Providing medical laboratory testing for humans—are classified in U.S. Industry 621511, Medical Laboratories; and

- Providing veterinary testing services—are classified in Industry 541940, Veterinary Services.

54172 Research and Development in the Social Sciences and Humanities
See industry description for 541720 below.

541720 Research and Development in the Social Sciences and Humanities

This industry comprises establishments primarily engaged in conducting research and analyses in cognitive development, sociology, psychology, language, behavior, economic, and other social science and humanities research.

US—United States industry only. CAN—United States and Canadian industries are comparable. When neither US nor CAN appears, Canadian, Mexican, and United States industries are comparable.

Cross-References.

Establishments primarily engaged in marketing research are classified in Industry 541910, Marketing Research and Public Opinion Polling.

5418 Advertising and Related Services

54181 Advertising Agencies
See industry description for 541810 below.

541810 Advertising Agencies

This industry comprises establishments primarily engaged in creating advertising campaigns and placing such advertising in periodicals, newspapers, radio and television, or other media. These establishments are organized to provide a full range of services (i.e., through in-house capabilities or subcontracting), including advice, creative services, account management, production of advertising material, media planning, and buying (i.e., placing advertising).

Cross-References. Establishments primarily engaged in—

- Purchasing advertising space from media outlets and reselling it directly to advertising agencies or individual companies—are classified in Industry 541830, Media Buying Agencies;

- Conceptualizing and producing artwork or graphic designs without providing other advertising agency services—are classified in Industry 541430, Graphic Design Services;

- Creating direct mail advertising campaigns—are classified in Industry 541860, Direct Mail Advertising;

- Providing marketing consulting services—are classified in U.S. Industry 541613, Marketing Consulting Services; and

- Selling media time or space for media owners as independent representatives—are classified in Industry 541840, Media Representatives.

54182 Public Relations Agencies
See industry description for 541820 below.

541820 Public Relations Agencies

This industry comprises establishments primarily engaged in designing and implementing public relations campaigns. These campaigns are designed to promote the interests and image of their clients. Establishments providing lobbying, political consulting, or public relations consulting are included in this industry.

US—United States industry only. CAN—United States and Canadian industries are comparable. When neither US nor CAN appears, Canadian, Mexican, and United States industries are comparable.

http://www.ntis.gov/naics

54183 Media Buying Agencies

See industry description for 541830 below.

541830 Media Buying Agencies

This industry comprises establishments primarily engaged in purchasing advertising time or space from media outlets and reselling it to advertising agencies or individual companies directly.

Cross-References. Establishments primarily engaged in—

- Selling time and space to advertisers for media owners as independent representatives— are classified in Industry 541840, Media Representatives; and

- Creating advertising campaigns and placing such advertising in media—are classified in Industry 541810, Advertising Agencies.

54184 Media Representatives

See industry description for 541840 below.

541840 Media Representatives

This industry comprises establishments of independent representatives primarily engaged in selling media time or space for media owners.

Illustrative Examples:

Newspaper advertising representatives (i.e., independent of media owners)	Radio advertising representatives (i.e., independent of media owners)
Publishers' advertising representatives (i.e., independent of media owners)	Television advertising representatives (i.e., independent of media owners)

Cross-References. Establishments primarily engaged in—

- Purchasing advertising time or space from media outlets and reselling it directly to advertising agencies or individual companies—are classified in Industry 541830, Media Buying Agencies; and

- Creating advertising campaigns and placing such advertising in media—are classified in Industry 541810, Advertising Agencies.

54185 Display Advertising

See industry description for 541850 below.

541850 Display Advertising

This industry comprises establishments primarily engaged in creating and designing public display advertising, campaign materials, such as printed, painted, or electronic displays, and/or

---

US—United States industry only. CAN—United States and Canadian industries are comparable. When neither US nor CAN appears, Canadian, Mexican, and United States industries are comparable.

placing such displays on indoor or outdoor billboards and panels, or on or within transit vehicles or facilities, shopping malls, retail (in-store) displays, and other display structures or sites.

Cross-References. Establishments primarily engaged in—

- Providing sign lettering and painting services   are classified in Industry 541890 , Other Services Related to Advertising;

- Printing paper on paperboard signs—are classified in Industry 32311, Printing;

- Erecting display boards—are classified in Sector 23, Construction; and

- Manufacturing electrical, mechanical, or plate signs and point-of-sale advertising displays— are classified in Industry 339950, Sign Manufacturing.

54186 Direct Mail Advertising
See industry description for 541860 below.

541860 Direct Mail Advertising

This industry comprises establishments primarily engaged in (1) creating and designing advertising campaigns for the purpose of distributing advertising materials (e.g., coupons, flyers, samples) or specialties (e.g., key chains, magnets, pens with customized messages imprinted) by mail or other direct distribution; and/or (2) preparing advertising materials or specialties for mailing or other direct distribution. These establishments may also compile, maintain, sell, and rent mailing lists.

Cross-References. Establishments primarily engaged in—

- The direct distribution or delivery (e.g., door-to-door, windshield placement) of advertisements or samples—are classified in Industry 541870, Advertising Material Distribution Services;

- Distributing advertising specialties for clients who wish to use such materials for promotional purposes—are classified in Industry 541890, Other Services Related to Advertising;

- Creating advertising campaigns and placing such advertising in media—are classified in Industry 541810, Advertising Agencies; and

- Compiling and selling mailing lists without providing direct mail advertising services— are classified in Industry 511140, Database and Directory Publishing.

54187 Advertising Material Distribution Services
See industry description for 541870 below.

541870 Advertising Material Distribution Services

This industry comprises establishments primarily engaged in the direct distribution or delivery of advertisements (e.g., circulars, coupons, handbills) or samples. Establishments in this industry use methods, such as delivering advertisements or samples door-to-door, placing flyers or coupons on car windshields in parking lots, or handing out samples in retail stores.

Cross-References. Establishments primarily engaged in—

- Creating and designing advertising campaigns for the purpose of distributing advertising materials or samples through the mail or by other direct distribution—are classified in Industry 541860, Direct Mail Advertising;

- Publishing newspapers or operating television stations or on-line information services— are classified in Sector 51, Information; and

- Distributing advertising specialties (e.g., key chains, magnets, or pens with customized messages imprinted) to clients who wish to use such materials for promotional purposes— are classified in Industry 541890, Other Services Related to Advertising.

54189 Other Services Related to Advertising
See industry description for 541890 below.

541890 Other Services Related to Advertising

This industry comprises establishments primarily engaged in providing advertising services (except advertising agency services, public relations agency services, media buying agency services, media representative services, display advertising services, direct mail advertising services, advertising material distribution services, and marketing consulting services).

Illustrative Examples:

Advertising specialties (e.g., key chains, magnets, pens) distribution services (except direct mail)	Merchandise demonstration services
	Sign lettering and painting services
	Store window dressing or trimming services
Display lettering services	Welcoming services (i.e., advertising services)
Mannequin decorating services	

Cross-References. Establishments primarily engaged in—

- Creating advertising campaigns and placing such advertising in newspapers, television, or other media—are classified in Industry 541810, Advertising Agencies;

- Designing and implementing public relations campaigns—are classified in Industry 541820, Public Relations Agencies;

- Purchasing advertising time or space from media outlets and reselling it directly to advertising agencies or individual companies—are classified in Industry 541830, Media Buying Agencies;

- Selling media time or space for media owners as independent representatives—are classified in Industry 541840, Media Representatives;

US—United States industry only. CAN—United States and Canadian industries are comparable. When neither US nor CAN appears, Canadian, Mexican, and United States industries are comparable.

- Providing display advertising services (except aerial)—are classified in Industry 541850, Display Advertising;

- Providing direct distribution or delivery (e.g., door-to-door, windshield placement) of advertisements or samples—are classified in Industry 541870, Advertising Material Distribution Services;

- Providing direct mail advertising services—are classified in Industry 541860, Direct Mail Advertising;

- Publishing newspapers or operating television stations or on-line information services—are classified in Sector 51, Information; and

- Providing marketing consulting services—are classified in U.S. Industry 541613, Marketing Consulting Services.

5419 Other Professional, Scientific, and Technical Services

This industry group comprises establishments engaged in professional, scientific, and technical services (except legal services; accounting, tax preparation, bookkeeping, and related services; architectural, engineering, and related services; specialized design services; computer systems design and related services; management, scientific, and technical consulting services; scientific research and development services; and advertising and related services).

54191 Marketing Research and Public Opinion Polling

See industry description for 541910 below.

541910 Marketing Research and Public Opinion Polling

This industry comprises establishments primarily engaged in systematically gathering, recording, tabulating, and presenting marketing and public opinion data.

Illustrative Examples:

Broadcast media rating services	Political opinion polling services
Marketing analysis or research services	Statistical sampling services
Opinion research services	

Cross-References. Establishments primarily engaged in—

- Providing research and analysis in economics, sociology, and related fields—are classified in Industry 541720, Research and Development in the Social Sciences and Humanities; and

- Providing advice and counsel on marketing strategies—are classified in U.S. Industry 541613, Marketing Consulting Services.

54192 Photographic Services

This industry comprises establishments primarily engaged in providing still, video, or digital photography services. These establishments may specialize in a particular field of photography, such

US—United States industry only. CAN—United States and Canadian industries are comparable. When neither US nor CAN appears, Canadian, Mexican, and United States industries are comparable.

http://www.ntis.gov/naics

as commercial and industrial photography, portrait photography, and special events photography. Commercial or portrait photography studios are included in this industry.

Cross-References. Establishments primarily engaged in—

- Producing film and videotape for commercial exhibition or sale—are classified in Industry 51211, Motion Picture and Video Production;

- Developing still photographs—are classified in Industry 81292, Photofinishing;

- Developing motion picture film—are classified in Industry 51219, Postproduction and Other Motion Picture and Video Industries;

- Taking, developing, and selling artistic, news or other types of photographs on a freelance basis, such as photojournalists,—are classified in Industry 71151, Independent Artists, Writers, and Performers; and

- Supplying and servicing automatic photography machines in places of business operated by others—are classified in Industry 81299, All Other Personal Services.

541921 Photography Studios, Portrait[US]

This U.S. industry comprises establishments known as portrait studios primarily engaged in providing still, video, or digital portrait photography services.

Illustrative Examples:

Home photography services
Passport photography services
School photography services

Videotaping services for special events (e.g., weddings)

Cross-References. Establishments primarily engaged in—

- Producing film and videotape for commercial exhibition or sale—are classified in Industry 512110, Motion Picture and Video Production;

- Developing still photographs—are classified in Industry 81292, Photofinishing;

- Developing motion picture film—are classified in U.S. Industry 512199, Other Motion Picture and Video Industries;

- Taking, developing, and selling artistic, news or other types of photographs on a freelance basis, such as photojournalists,—are classified in Industry 711510, Independent Artists, Writers, and Performers; and

- Supplying and servicing automatic photography machines in places of business operated by others—are classified in Industry 812990, All Other Personal Services.

541922 Commercial Photography[US]

This U.S. industry comprises establishments primarily engaged in providing commercial photography services, generally for advertising agencies, publishers, and other business and industrial users.

US—United States industry only. CAN—United States and Canadian industries are comparable. When neither US nor CAN appears, Canadian, Mexican, and United States industries are comparable.

Cross-References. Establishments primarily engaged in—

- Producing film and videotape for commercial exhibition or sale—are classified in Industry 512110, Motion Picture and Video Production;

- Developing still photographs—are classified in Industry 81292, Photofinishing;

- Developing motion picture film—are classified in U.S. Industry 512199, Other Motion Picture and Video Industries;

- Taking, developing, and selling artistic, news, or other types of photographs on a freelance basis, such as photojournalists,—are classified in Industry 711510, Independent Artists, Writers, and Performers; and

- Supplying and servicing coin-operated photography machines in places of business operated by others—are classified in Industry 812990, All Other Personal Services.

54193 Translation and Interpretation Services
See industry description for 541930 below.

541930 Translation and Interpretation Services

This industry comprises establishments primarily engaged in translating written material and interpreting speech from one language to another and establishments primarily engaged in providing sign language services.

Cross-References. Establishments primarily engaged in—

- Providing transcription services—are classified in Industry 561410, Document Preparation Services;

- Providing real-time (i.e., simultaneous) closed captioning services for live television performances, at meetings and conferences—are classified in U.S. Industry 561492, Court Reporting and Stenotype Services;

- Providing film or tape closed captioning services—are classified in U.S. Industry 512191, Teleproduction and Other Postproduction Services; and

- Analyzing handwriting—are classified in Industry 541990, All Other Professional, Scientific, and Technical Services.

54194 Veterinary Services
See industry description for industry 541940 below.

541940 Veterinary Services

This industry comprises establishments of licensed veterinary practitioners primarily engaged in the practice of veterinary medicine, dentistry, or surgery for animals; and establishments primarily engaged in providing testing services for licensed veterinary practitioners.

US—United States industry only. CAN—United States and Canadian industries are comparable. When neither US nor CAN appears, Canadian, Mexican, and United States industries are comparable.

Illustrative Examples:

Animal hospitals	Veterinary clinics
Veterinarians' offices	Veterinary testing laboratories

Cross-References. Establishments primarily engaged in—

- Providing veterinary research and development services—are classified in Industry 541710, Research and Development in the Physical, Engineering, and Life Sciences;

- Providing nonveterinary pet care services, such as boarding or grooming pets,—are classified in Industry 812910, Pet Care (except Veterinary) Services;

- Providing animal breeding services or boarding horses—are classified in Industry 115210, Support Activities for Animal Production; and

- Transporting pets—are classified in U.S. Industry 485991, Special Needs Transportation.

54199 All Other Professional, Scientific, and Technical Services
See industry description for 541990 below.

541990 All Other Professional, Scientific, and Technical Services

This industry comprises establishments primarily engaged in the provision of professional, scientific, or technical services (except legal services; accounting, tax preparation, bookkeeping, and related services; architectural, engineering, and related services; specialized design services; computer systems design and related services; management, scientific, and technical consulting services; scientific research and development services; advertising and related services; market research and public opinion polling; photographic services; translation and interpretation services; and veterinary services).

Illustrative Examples:

Appraisal (except real estate) services	Marine surveyor (i.e., appraiser) services
Arbitration and conciliation services (except by lawyer, attorney, or paralegal offices)	Patent broker services (i.e., patent marketing services)
Commodity inspector services	Pipeline or power line inspection (i.e., visual)
Consumer credit counseling services	services
Handwriting analysis services	Weather forecasting services

Cross-References. Establishments primarily engaged in—

- Providing legal services—are classified in Industry Group 5411, Legal Services;

- Providing accounting, tax preparation, bookkeeping, and payroll services—are classified in Industry Group 5412, Accounting, Tax Preparation, Bookkeeping, and Payroll Services;

- Providing architectural, engineering, and related services—are classified in Industry Group 5413, Architectural, Engineering, and Related Services;

US—United States industry only. CAN—United States and Canadian industries are comparable. When neither US nor CAN appears, Canadian, Mexican, and United States industries are comparable.

http://www.ntis.gov/naics

- Providing specialized design services—are classified in Industry Group 5414, Specialized Design Services;

- Providing computer systems design and related services—are classified in Industry Group 5415, Computer Systems Design and Related Services;

- Providing management, scientific, and technical consulting services—are classified in Industry Group 5416, Management, Scientific, and Technical Consulting Services;

- Providing scientific research and development services—are classified in Industry Group 5417, Scientific Research and Development Services;

- Providing advertising and related services—are classified in Industry Group 5418, Advertising and Related Services;

- Providing marketing research and public opinion polling—are classified in Industry 541910, Marketing Research and Public Opinion Polling;

- Providing photographic services—are classified in Industry 54192, Photographic Services;

- Providing translation and interpretation services—are classified in Industry 541930, Translation and Interpretation Services;

- Providing veterinary services—are classified in Industry 541940, Veterinary Services; and

- Providing real estate appraisal services—are classified in Industry 531320, Offices of Real Estate Appraisers.

Sector 55—Management of Companies and Enterprises

The Sector as a Whole

The Management of Companies and Enterprises sector comprises (1) establishments that hold the securities of (or other equity interests in) companies and enterprises for the purpose of owning a controlling interest or influencing management decisions or (2) establishments (except government establishments) that administer, oversee, and manage establishments of the company or enterprise and that normally undertake the strategic or organizational planning and decisionmaking role of the company or enterprise. Establishments that administer, oversee, and manage may hold the securities of the company or enterprise.

Establishments in this sector perform essential activities that are often undertaken, in-house, by establishments in many sectors of the economy. By consolidating the performance of these activities of the enterprise at one establishment, economies of scale are achieved.

Government establishments primarily engaged in administering, overseeing, and managing governmental programs are classified in Sector 92, Public Administration. Establishments primarily engaged in providing a range of day-to-day office administrative services, such as financial planning, billing and recordkeeping, personnel, and physical distribution and logistics are classified in Industry 56111, Office Administrative Services.

551 Management of Companies and Enterprises

Industries in the Management of Companies and Enterprises subsector include three main types of establishments: (1) those that hold the securities of (or other equity interests in) companies and enterprises; (2) those (except government establishments) that administer, oversee, and manage other establishments of the company or enterprise but do not hold the securities of these establishments; and (3) those that both administer, oversee, and manage other establishments of the company or enterprise and hold the securities of (or other equity interests in) these establishments. Those establishments that administer, oversee, and manage normally undertake the strategic or organizational planning and decisionmaking role of the company or enterprise.

5511 Management of Companies and Enterprises

55111 Management of Companies and Enterprises

This industry comprises (1) establishments primarily engaged in holding the securities of (or other equity interests in) companies and enterprises for the purpose of owning a controlling interest or influencing the management decisions or (2) establishments (except government establishments) that administer, oversee, and manage other establishments of the company or enterprise and that normally undertake the strategic or organizational planning and decisionmaking role of the company or enterprise. Establishments that administer, oversee, and manage may hold the securities of the company or enterprise.

http://www.ntis.gov/naics

Cross-References.

- Establishments primarily engaged in holding the securities of companies or enterprises and operating these entities are classified according to the business operated;

- Establishments primarily engaged in holding the securities of depository banks and operating these entities are classified in Industry Group 5221, Depository Credit Intermediation;

- Establishments primarily engaged in providing a single service to other establishments of the company or enterprise, such as trucking, warehousing, research and development, and data processing are classified according to the service provided; and

- Government establishments primarily engaged in administering, overseeing, and managing governmental programs are classified in Sector 92, Public Administration.

551111 Offices of Bank Holding Companies[US]

This U.S. industry comprises legal entities known as bank holding companies primarily engaged in holding the securities of (or other equity interests in) companies and enterprises for the purpose of owning a controlling interest or influencing the management decisions of these firms. The holding companies in this industry do not administer, oversee, and manage other establishments of the company or enterprise whose securities they hold.

Cross-References. Establishments primarily engaged in—

- Holding the securities of (or other equity interests in) a company or enterprise and administering, overseeing, and managing establishments of the company or enterprise whose securities they hold—are classified in U.S. Industry 551114, Corporate, Subsidiary, and Regional Managing Offices; and

- Holding the securities of depository banks and operating these entities—are classified in Industry Group 5221, Depository Credit Intermediation.

551112 Offices of Other Holding Companies[US]

This U.S. industry comprises legal entities known as holding companies (except bank holding) primarily engaged in holding the securities of (or other equity interests in) companies and enterprises for the purpose of owning a controlling interest or influencing the management decisions of these firms. The holding companies in this industry do not administer, oversee, and manage other establishments of the company or enterprise whose securities they hold.

Cross-References. Establishments primarily engaged in—

- Holding the securities of (or other equity interests in) depository banks for the purpose of owning a controlling interest or influencing the management decisions of these firms—are classified in U.S. Industry 551111, Offices of Bank Holding Companies;

- Holding the securities of (or other equity interests in) a company or enterprise and administering, overseeing, and managing establishments of the company or enterprise whose securities they hold—are classified in U.S. Industry 551114, Corporate, Subsidiary, and Regional Managing Offices; and

---

US—United States industry only. CAN—United States and Canadian industries are comparable. When neither US nor CAN appears, Canadian, Mexican, and United States industries are comparable.

- Holding the securities of companies or enterprises and operating these entities—are classified according to the business operated.

551114 Corporate, Subsidiary, and Regional Managing Offices[CAN]

This U.S. industry comprises establishments (except government establishments) primarily engaged in administering, overseeing, and managing other establishments of the company or enterprise. These establishments normally undertake the strategic or organizational planning and decisionmaking role of the company or enterprise. Establishments in this industry may hold the securities of the company or enterprise.

Illustrative Examples:

Centralized administrative offices	Head offices
Corporate offices	Holding companies that manage
District and regional offices	Subsidiary management offices

Cross-References.

- Government establishments primarily engaged in administering, overseeing, and managing governmental programs are classified in Sector 92, Public Administration;

- Legal entities known as bank holding companies that do not administer, oversee, and manage other establishments of the companies or enterprises whose securities they hold are classified in U.S. Industry 551111, Offices of Bank Holding Companies; and

- Legal entities known as holding companies(except bank holding) that do not administer, oversee, and manage other establishments of the companies or enterprises whose securities they hold are classified in U.S. Industry 551112, Offices of Other Holding Companies

US—United States industry only. CAN—United States and Canadian industries are comparable. When neither US nor CAN appears, Canadian, Mexican, and United States industries are comparable.

http://www.ntis.gov/naics

Sector 56—Administrative and Support and Waste Management and Remediation Services

The Sector as a Whole

The Administrative and Support and Waste Management and Remediation Services sector comprises establishments performing routine support activities for the day-to-day operations of other organizations. These essential activities are often undertaken in-house by establishments in many sectors of the economy. The establishments in this sector specialize in one or more of these support activities and provide these services to clients in a variety of industries and, in some cases, to households. Activities performed include: office administration, hiring and placing of personnel, document preparation and similar clerical services, solicitation, collection, security and surveillance services, cleaning, and waste disposal services.

The administrative and management activities performed by establishments in this sector are typically on a contract or fee basis. These activities may also be performed by establishments that are part of the company or enterprise. However, establishments involved in administering, overseeing, and managing other establishments of the company or enterprise, are classified in Sector 55, Management of Companies and Enterprises. These establishments normally undertake the strategic and organizational planning and decisionmaking role of the company or enterprise. Government establishments engaged in administering, overseeing, and managing governmental programs are classified in Sector 92, Public Administration.

561 Administrative and Support Services

Industries in the Administrative and Support Services subsector group establishments engaged in activities that support the day-to-day operations of other organizations. The processes employed in this sector (e.g., general management, personnel administration, clerical activities, cleaning activities) are often integral parts of the activities of establishments found in all sectors of the economy. The establishments classified in this subsector have specialized in one or more of these activities and can, therefore, provide services to clients in a variety of industries and, in some cases, to households. The individual industries of this subsector are defined on the basis of the particular process that they are engaged in and the particular services they provide.

Many of the activities performed in this subsector are ongoing routine support functions that all businesses and organizations must do and that they have traditionally done for themselves. Recent trends, however, are to contract or purchase such services from businesses that specialize in such activities and can, therefore, provide the services more efficiently.

The industries in this subsector cannot be viewed as strictly "support." The Travel Arrangement and Reservation Services industry group, includes travel agents, tour operators, and providers of other travel arrangement services, such as hotel and restaurant reservations and arranging the purchase of tickets, serves many types of clients, including individual consumers. This group was placed in this subsector because the services are often of the "support" nature (e.g., travel arrangement) and businesses and other organizations are increasingly the ones purchasing such services.

The administrative and management activities performed by establishments in this sector are typically on a contract or fee basis. These activities may also be performed by establishments that

---

US—United States industry only. CAN—United States and Canadian industries are comparable. When neither US nor CAN appears, Canadian, Mexican, and United States industries are comparable.

are part of the company or enterprise. However, establishments involved in administering, overseeing, and managing other establishments of the company or enterprise, are classified in Sector 55, Management of Companies and Enterprises. These establishments normally undertake the strategic and organizational planning and decisionmaking role of the company or enterprise. Government establishments engaged in administering, overseeing and managing governmental programs are classified in Sector 92, Public Administration.

5611 Office Administrative Services

56111 Office Administrative Services
See industry description for 561110 below.

561110 Office Administrative Services

This industry comprises establishments primarily engaged in providing a range of day-to-day office administrative services, such as financial planning; billing and recordkeeping; personnel; and physical distribution and logistics. These establishments do not provide operating staff to carry out the complete operations of a business.

Cross-References. Establishments primarily engaged in—

- Holding the securities or financial assets of companies and enterprises for the purpose of controlling them and influencing their management decisions—are classified in U.S. Industry 551111, Offices of Bank Holding Companies or U.S. Industry 551112, Offices of Other Holding Companies;

- Administering, overseeing, and managing other establishments of the company or enterprise (except government establishments)—are classified in U.S. Industry 551114, Corporate, Subsidiary, and Regional Managing Offices;

- Government establishments primarily engaged in administering, overseeing, and managing governmental programs—are classified in Sector 92, Public Administration;

- Providing computer facilities management—are classified in U.S. Industry 541513, Computer Facilities Management Services;

- Providing construction management—are classified in Sector 23, Construction, by type of construction project managed;

- Providing farm management—are classified in U.S. Industry 115116, Farm Management Services;

- Managing real property for others—are classified in Industry 53131, Real Estate Property Managers;

- Providing food services management at institutional, governmental, commercial, or industrial locations—are classified in Industry 722310, Food Service Contractors;

- Providing management advice without day-to-day management—are classified in Industry 54161, Management Consulting Services;

- Providing both management and operating staff for the complete operation of a client's business, such as a hotel, restaurant, mine site, or hospital,—are classified according to the industry of the establishment operated; and

- Providing only one of the support services (e.g., accounting services) that establishments in this industry provide—are classified in the appropriate industry according to the service provided.

5612 Facilities Support Services

56121 Facilities Support Services
See industry description for 561210 below.

561210 Facilities Support Services

This industry comprises establishments primarily engaged in providing operating staff to perform a combination of support services within a client's facilities. Establishments in this industry typically provide a combination of services, such as janitorial; maintenance; trash disposal; guard and security; mail routing reception; laundry; and related services to support operations within facilities. These establishments provide operating staff to carry out these support activities; but, are not involved with or responsible for the core business or activities of the client. Establishments providing facilities (except computer and/or data processing) operation support services and establishments operating correctional facilities (i.e., jails) on a contract or fee basis are included in this industry.

Cross-References.

- Establishments primarily engaged in providing only one of the support services (e.g., janitorial services) that establishments in this industry provide are classified in the appropriate industry according to the service provided;

- Establishments primarily engaged in providing management and operating staff for the complete operation of a client's establishment, such as a hotel, restaurant, mine, or hospital, are classified according to the industry of the establishment operated;

- Establishments primarily engaged in providing on-site management and operation of a client's computer systems and/or data processing facilities are classified in U.S. Industry 541513, Computer Facilities Management Services; and

- Government correctional institutions are classified in Industry 922140, Correctional Institutions.

5613 Employment Services

56131 Employment Placement Agencies
See industry description for 561310 below.

561310 Employment Placement Agencies

This industry comprises establishments primarily engaged in listing employment vacancies and in referring or placing applicants for employment. The individuals referred or placed are not employees of the employment agencies.

US—United States industry only. CAN—United States and Canadian industries are comparable. When neither US nor CAN appears, Canadian, Mexican, and United States industries are comparable.

http://www.ntis.gov/naics

Illustrative Examples:

Babysitting bureaus (i.e., registries)
Casting agencies or bureaus (i.e., motion
  picture, theatrical, video)

Employment agencies
Employment registries
Model registries

Cross-References. Establishments primarily engaged in—

- Providing executive search consulting services—are classified in U.S. Industry 541612, Human Resources and Executive Search Consulting Services;

- Supplying their own employees for limited periods of time to supplement the working force of a client's business—are classified in Industry 561320, Temporary Help Services;

- Providing human resources and human resource management services to clients—are classified in Industry 561330, Employee Leasing Services; and

- Representing models, entertainers, athletes, and other public figures in the capacity as their agent or manager—are classified in Industry 711410, Agents and Managers for Artists, Athletes, Entertainers, and Other Public Figures.

56132 Temporary Help Services
See industry description for 561320 below.

561320 Temporary Help Services

This industry comprises establishments primarily engaged in supplying workers to clients' businesses for limited periods of time to supplement the working force of the client. The individuals provided are employees of the temporary help service establishment. However, these establishments do not provide direct supervision of their employees at the clients' work sites.

Illustrative Examples:

Help supply services
Labor (except farm) contractors (i.e.,
  personnel suppliers)
Manpower pools

Model supply services
Temporary employment or temporary staffing
  services

Cross-References. Establishments primarily engaged in—

- Providing human resources and human resource management services to clients—are classified in Industry 561330, Employee Leasing Services;

- Supplying farm labor—are classified in U.S. Industry 115115, Farm Labor Contractors and Crew Leaders;

- Providing operating staff to perform a combination of services to support operations within a client's facilities—are classified in Industry 561210, Facilities Support Services;

US—United States industry only. CAN—United States and Canadian industries are comparable.
When neither US nor CAN appears, Canadian, Mexican, and United States industries are comparable.

- Listing employment vacancies and in referring or placing applicants for employment—are classified in Industry 561310, Employment Placement Agencies; and

- Representing models, entertainers, athletes, and other public figures in the capacity as their agent or manager—are classified in Industry 711410, Agents and Managers for Artists, Athletes, Entertainers, and Other Public Figures.

56133 Employee Leasing Services

See industry description for 561330 below.

561330 Employee Leasing Services

This industry comprises establishments primarily engaged in providing human resources and human resource management services to staff client businesses. Establishments in this industry operate in a coemployment relationship with client businesses or organizations and are specialized in performing a wide range of human resource and personnel management duties, such as payroll accounting, payroll tax return preparation, benefits administration, recruiting, and managing labor relations. Employee leasing establishments typically acquire and lease back some or all of the employees of their clients and serve as the employer of the leased employees for payroll, benefits, and related purposes. Employee leasing establishments exercise varying degrees of decisionmaking relating to their human resource or personnel management role, but do not have management accountability for the work of their clients' operations with regard to strategic planning, output, or profitability. Professional employer organizations (PEO) and establishments providing labor or staff leasing services are included in this industry.

Cross-References. Establishments primarily engaged in—

- Supplying their own employees for limited periods of time to supplement the working force of a client's business—are classified in Industry 561320, Temporary Help Services; and

- Listing employment vacancies and in referring or placing applicants for employment—are classified in Industry 561310, Employment Placement Agencies.

5614 Business Support Services

This industry group comprises establishments engaged in performing activities that are ongoing routine, business support functions that businesses and organizations traditionally do for themselves.

56141 Document Preparation Services

See industry description for 561410 below.

561410 Document Preparation Services

This industry comprises establishments primarily engaged in one or more of the following: (1) letter or resume writing; (2) document editing or proofreading; (3) typing, word processing, or desktop publishing; and (4) stenographic (except court reporting or stenotype recording), transcription, and other secretarial services.

US—United States industry only. CAN—United States and Canadian industries are comparable. When neither US nor CAN appears, Canadian, Mexican, and United States industries are comparable.

Cross-References. Establishments primarily engaged in—

- Providing verbatim reporting and steno recording of live legal proceedings and transcribing subsequent recorded materials—are classified in U.S. Industry 561492, Court Reporting and Stenotype Services;

- Performing prepress and postpress services in support of printing activities—are classified in Industry 32312, Support Activities for Printing;

- Providing document translation services—are classified in Industry 541930, Translation and Interpretation Services;

- Photocopying, duplicating, and other document copying services, with or without a range of other office support services (except printing)—are classified in U.S. Industry 561439, Other Business Service Centers (including Copy Shops); and

- Providing document copying services in combination with printing services, with or without a range of other office support services, and establishments known as quick or digital printers—are classified in Industry 32311, Printing.

56142 Telephone Call Centers

This industry comprises (1) establishments primarily engaged in answering telephone calls and relaying messages to clients and (2) establishments primarily engaged in providing telemarketing services on a contract or fee basis for others, such as promoting clients' products or services by telephone; taking orders for clients by telephone; and soliciting contributions or providing information for clients by telephone. Telemarketing establishments never own the product or provide the service that they are representing and generally can originate and/or receive calls for others.

Cross-References. Establishments primarily engaged in—

- Providing paging and beeper transmission services—are classified in Industry 51332, Wireless Telecommunications Carriers (except Satellite);

- Organizing and conducting fundraising campaigns on a contract or fee basis, that may include telephone solicitation services—are classified in Industry 56149, Other Business Support Services; and

- Gathering, recording, tabulating, and presenting marketing and public opinion data, that may include telephone canvassing services—are classified in Industry 54191, Marketing Research and Public Opinion Polling.

561421 Telephone Answering Services[US]

This U.S. industry comprises establishments primarily engaged in answering telephone calls and relaying messages to clients.

Cross-References.

Establishments primarily engaged in providing paging or beeper transmission services are classified in Industry 51332, Wireless Telecommunications Carriers (except Satellite).

US—United States industry only. CAN—United States and Canadian industries are comparable. When neither US nor CAN appears, Canadian, Mexican, and United States industries are comparable.

561422 Telemarketing Bureaus[US]

This U.S. industry comprises establishments primarily engaged in providing telemarketing services on a contract or fee basis for others, such as: (1) promoting clients' products or services by telephone, (2) taking orders for clients by telephone, and (3) soliciting contributions or providing information for clients by telephone. These establishments never own the product or provide the services they are representing and generally can originate and/or receive calls for others.

Cross-References. Establishments primarily engaged in—

- Organizing and conducting fundraising campaigns on a contract or fee basis, that may include telephone solicitation services—are classified in U.S. Industry 561499, All Other Business Support Services; and

- Gathering, recording, tabulating, and presenting marketing and public opinion data, that may include telephone canvassing services—are classified in Industry 541910, Marketing Research and Public Opinion Polling.

56143 Business Service Centers

This industry comprises (1) establishments primarily engaged in providing mailbox rental and other postal and mailing services (except direct mail advertising); (2) establishments, generally known as copy centers or shops, primarily engaged in providing photocopying, duplicating, blueprinting, and other document copying services without also providing printing services (i.e., offset printing, quick printing, digital printing, prepress services); and (3) establishments that provide a range of office support services (except printing services), such as mailing services, document copying services, facsimile services, word processing services, on-site PC rental services, and office product sales.

Cross-References. Establishments primarily engaged in—

- Operating contract post offices—are classified in Industry 49111, Postal Service;

- Delivering letters and parcels—are classified in Subsector 492, Couriers and Messengers;

- Providing voice mailbox services—are classified in Industry 56142, Telephone Call Centers;

- Providing direct mail advertising services—are classified in Industry 54186, Direct Mail Advertising;

- Providing document copying services in combination with printing services, with or without a range of other office support services, and establishments known as quick or digital printers—are classified in Industry 32311, Printing; and

- Providing only one of the support services (e.g., word processing services) that establishments in this industry provide—are classified in the appropriate industry according to the service provided.

US—United States industry only. CAN—United States and Canadian industries are comparable. When neither US nor CAN appears, Canadian, Mexican, and United States industries are comparable.

http://www.ntis.gov/naics

561431 Private Mail Centers[US]

This U.S. industry comprises (1) establishments primarily engaged in providing mailbox rental and other postal and mailing (except direct mail advertising) services or (2) establishments engaged in providing these mailing services along with one or more other office support services, such as facsimile services, word processing services, on-site PC rental services, and office product sales.

Cross-References. Establishments primarily engaged in—

- Operating contract post offices—are classified in Industry 491110, Postal Service;

- Delivering letters and parcels—are classified in Subsector 492, Couriers and Messengers;

- Providing voice mailbox services—are classified in U.S. Industry 561421, Telephone Answering Services;

- Providing direct mail advertising services—are classified in Industry 541860, Direct Mail Advertising; and

- Providing only one of the support services (e.g., word processing services) that establishments in this industry provide—are classified in the appropriate industry according to the service provided.

561439 Other Business Service Centers (including Copy Shops)[US]

This U.S. industry comprises (1) establishments generally known as copy centers or shops primarily engaged in providing photocopying, duplicating, blueprinting, and other document copying services, without also providing printing services (e.g., offset printing, quick printing, digital printing, prepress services) and (2) establishments (except private mail centers) engaged in providing a range of office support services (except printing services), such as document copying services, facsimile services, word processing services, on-site PC rental services, and office product sales.

Cross-References.

- Establishments engaged in providing document copying services in combination with printing services, with or without a range of other office support services, and establishments known as quick or digital printers are classified in Industry 32311, Printing;

- Establishments engaged in providing mailbox rental and other postal and mailing services with or without one or more other office support services (except printing) are classified in U.S. Industry 561431, Private Mail Centers; and

- Establishments exclusively engaged in providing a single office support service (except document copying) to clients, but not the range of office support services that establishments in this industry may provide, are classified according to the service provided.

US—United States industry only. CAN—United States and Canadian industries are comparable. When neither US nor CAN appears, Canadian, Mexican, and United States industries are comparable.

56144 Collection Agencies

See industry description for 561440 below.

561440 Collection Agencies

This industry comprises establishments primarily engaged in collecting payments for claims and remitting payments collected to their clients.

Illustrative Examples:

Account or delinquent account collection services

Bill or debt collection services

Tax collection services on a contract or fee basis

Cross-References. Establishments primarily engaged in—

- Repossessing tangible assets—are classified in U.S. Industry 561491, Repossession Services; and

- Providing financing to others by factoring accounts receivables (i.e., assuming the risk of collection and credit losses)—are classified in U.S. Industry 522298, All Other Nondepository Credit Intermediation.

56145 Credit Bureaus

See industry description for 561450 below.

561450 Credit Bureaus

This industry comprises establishments primarily engaged in compiling information, such as credit and employment histories on individuals and credit histories on businesses, and providing the information to financial institutions, retailers, and others who have a need to evaluate the credit worthiness of these persons and businesses.

Illustrative Examples:

Credit agencies

Credit investigation services

Credit rating services

Credit reporting bureaus

56149 Other Business Support Services

This industry comprises establishments primarily engaged in providing business support services (except secretarial and other document preparation services; telephone answering or telemarketing services; private mail services or document copying services conducted as separate activities or in conjunction with other office support services; monetary debt collection services; and credit reporting services).

Illustrative Examples:

Address bar coding services

Bar code imprinting services

Court reporting services

Fundraising organization services on a
contract or fee basis

Mail presorting services

Real-time (i.e., simultaneous) closed
captioning of live television performances,
meetings, conferences

Repossession services

Cross-References. Establishments primarily engaged in—

- Providing secretarial and other document preparation services—are classified in Industry 56141, Document Preparation Services;

- Providing telephone answering or telemarketing services—are classified in Industry 56142, Telephone Call Centers;

- Providing private mail services; document copying services (except printing services); and/ or a range of office support services (except printing)—are classified in Industry 56143, Business Service Centers;

- Providing document copying services in combination with printing services, with or without a range of other office support services, and establishments known as quick or digital printers—are classified in Industry 32311, Printing;

- Providing monetary debt collection services—are classified in Industry 56144, Collection Agencies;

- Providing credit reporting services—are classified in Industry 56145, Credit Bureaus; and

- Providing film or tape captioning or subtitling services—are classified in Industry 51219, Postproduction and Other Motion Picture and Video Industries.

561491 Repossession Services[US]

This U.S. industry comprises establishments primarily engaged in repossessing tangible assets (e.g., automobiles, boats, equipment, planes, furniture, appliances) for the creditor as a result of delinquent debts.

Cross-References.

Establishments primarily engaged in providing monetary debt collection services are classified in Industry 561440, Collection Agencies.

561492 Court Reporting and Stenotype Services[US]

This U.S. industry comprises establishments primarily engaged in providing verbatim reporting and stenotype recording of live legal proceedings and transcribing subsequent recorded materials.

US—United States industry only. CAN—United States and Canadian industries are comparable. When neither US nor CAN appears, Canadian, Mexican, and United States industries are comparable.

Illustrative Examples:

Court reporting or stenotype recording services

Public stenography services

Real-time (i.e., simultaneous) closed captioning of live television performances of meetings, conferences

Cross-References. Establishments primarily engaged in—

- Providing stenotype recording of correspondence, reports, and other documents or in providing document transcription services—are classified in Industry 561410, Document Preparation Services; and

- Providing film or tape captioning or subtitling services—are classified in U.S. Industry 512191, Teleproduction and Other Postproduction Services.

561499 All Other Business Support Services[US]

This U.S. industry comprises establishments primarily engaged in providing business support services (except secretarial and other document preparation services; telephone answering and telemarketing services; private mail services or document copying services conducted as separate activities or in conjunction with other office support services; monetary debt collection services; credit reporting services; repossession services; and court reporting and stenotype recording services).

Illustrative Examples:

Address bar coding services

Bar code imprinting services

Fundraising organization services on a contract or fee basis

Mail presorting services

Cross-References. Establishments primarily engaged in—

- Providing secretarial and other document preparation services—are classified in Industry 561410, Document Preparation Services;

- Providing telephone answering or telemarketing services—are classified in Industry 56142, Telephone Call Centers;

- Providing private mail services, document copying services without printing services and/ or a range of office support services—are classified in Industry 56143, Business Service Centers;

- Providing document copying services in combination with printing services (with or without one or more other office support services) and establishments known as quick or digital printers—are classified in Industry 32311, Printing;

- Providing monetary debt collection services—are classified in Industry 561440, Collection Agencies;

US—United States industry only. CAN—United States and Canadian industries are comparable. When neither US nor CAN appears, Canadian, Mexican, and United States industries are comparable.

- Providing credit reporting services—are classified in Industry 561450, Credit Bureaus;

- Providing repossession services—are classified in U.S. Industry 561491, Repossession Services; and

- Providing court reporting and stenotype services—are classified in U.S. Industry 561492, Court Reporting and Stenotype Services.

5615 Travel Arrangement and Reservation Services

56151 Travel Agencies
See industry description for 561510 below.

561510 Travel Agencies

This industry comprises establishments primarily engaged in acting as agents in selling travel, tour, and accommodation services to the general public and commercial clients.

Cross-References. Establishments primarily engaged in—

- Arranging and assembling tours that they generally sell through travel agencies or on their own account—are classified in Industry 561520, Tour Operators;

- Providing guide services, such as archeological, museum, tourist, hunting, or fishing,—are classified in Industry 713990, All Other Amusement and Recreation Industries; and

- Providing reservation services (e.g., accommodations, entertainment events, travel)—are classified in U.S. Industry 561599, All Other Travel Arrangement and Reservation Services.

56152 Tour Operators
See industry description for 561520 below.

561520 Tour Operators

This industry comprises establishments primarily engaged in arranging and assembling tours. The tours are sold through travel agencies or tour operators. Travel or wholesale tour operators are included in this industry.

Cross-References. Establishments primarily engaged in—

- Acting as agents in selling travel, tour, and accommodation services to the general public and commercial clients—are classified in Industry 561510, Travel Agencies;

- Conducting scenic and sightseeing tours—are classified in Subsector 487, Scenic and Sightseeing Transportation; and

- Providing guide services, such as archeological, museum, tourist, hunting, or fishing,—are classified in Industry 713990, All Other Amusement and Recreation Industries.

US—United States industry only. CAN—United States and Canadian industries are comparable. When neither US nor CAN appears, Canadian, Mexican, and United States industries are comparable.

http://www.ntis.gov/naics

56159 Other Travel Arrangement and Reservation Services

This industry comprises establishments (except travel agencies and tour operators) primarily engaged in providing travel arrangement and reservation services.

Illustrative Examples:

Condominium time-share exchange services
Convention or visitors bureaus
Reservation (e.g., airline, car rental, hotel, restaurant) services
Road and travel services automobile clubs

Ticket (e.g., airline, bus, cruiseship, sports, theatrical) offices
Ticket (e.g., amusement, sports, theatrical) agencies

Cross-References.

- Establishments primarily engaged in arranging the rental of vacation properties are classified in Industry 53121, Offices of Real Estate Agents and Brokers;

- Travel agencies are classified in Industry 56151, Travel Agencies;

- Tour operators are classified in Industry 56152, Tour Operators;

- Automobile clubs (i.e., enthusiasts' clubs) (except road and travel services) are classified in Industry 81341, Civic and Social Organizations; and

- Establishments primarily engaged in organizing, promoting, and/or managing events, such as business and trade shows, conventions, conferences, and meetings (whether or not they manage and provide the staff to operate the facilities in which these events take place), are classified in Industry 56192, Convention and Trade Show Organizers.

561591 Convention and Visitors Bureaus[US]

This U.S. industry comprises establishments primarily engaged in marketing and promoting communities and facilities to businesses and leisure travelers through a range of activities, such as assisting organizations in locating meeting and convention sites; providing travel information on area attractions, lodging accommodations, restaurants; providing maps; and organizing group tours of local historical, recreational, and cultural attractions.

Cross-References.

Establishments primarily engaged in organizing, promoting, and/or managing events, such as business and trade shows, conventions, conferences, and meetings (whether or not they manage and provide the staff to operate the facilities in which these events take place), are classified in Industry 561920, Convention and Trade Show Organizers.

561599 All Other Travel Arrangement and Reservation Services[US]

This U.S. industry comprises establishments (except travel agencies, tour operators, and convention and visitors bureaus) primarily engaged in providing travel arrangement and reservation services.

US—United States industry only. CAN—United States and Canadian industries are comparable. When neither US nor CAN appears, Canadian, Mexican, and United States industries are comparable.

Illustrative Examples:

Condominium time-share exchange services
Reservation (e.g., airline, car rental, hotel, restaurant) services
Road and travel services automobile clubs

Ticket (e.g., airline, bus, cruiseship, sports, theatrical) offices
Ticket (e.g., amusement, sports, theatrical) agencies

Cross-References.

- Establishments primarily engaged in arranging the rental of vacation properties are classified in Industry 531210, Offices of Real Estate Agents and Brokers;

- Travel agencies are classified in Industry 561510, Travel Agencies;

- Tour operators are classified in Industry 561520, Tour Operators;

- Convention and visitors bureaus are classified in U.S. Industry 561591, Convention and Visitors Bureaus;

- Establishments primarily engaged in organizing, promoting, and/or managing events, such as business and trade shows, conventions, conferences, and meetings (whether or not they manage and provide the staff to operate the facilities in which these events take place), are classified in Industry 561920, Convention and Trade Show Organizers; and

- Automobile clubs (i.e., enthusiasts' clubs) (except road and travel services) are classified in Industry 813410, Civic and Social Organizations.

5616 Investigation and Security Services

56161 Investigation, Guard, and Armored Car Services

This industry comprises establishments primarily engaged in providing one or more of the following: (1) investigation and detective services; (2) guard and patrol services; and (3) picking up and delivering money, receipts, or other valuable items with personnel and equipment to protect such properties while in transit.

Illustrative Examples:

Armored car services
Bodyguard services
Polygraph services

Private detective services
Security guard services

Cross-References. Establishments primarily engaged in—

- Providing credit checks—are classified in Industry 56145, Credit Bureaus; and

- Selling, installing, monitoring, and maintaining security systems and devices (e.g., burglar and fire alarm systems)—are classified in Industry 56162, Security Systems Services.

US—United States industry only. CAN—United States and Canadian industries are comparable. When neither US nor CAN appears, Canadian, Mexican, and United States industries are comparable.

561611 Investigation Services^{CAN}

This U.S. industry comprises establishments primarily engaged in providing investigation and detective services.

Illustrative Examples:

Fingerprinting services   Private detective services
Polygraph services   Private investigative services

Cross-References.

Establishments primarily engaged in providing credit checks are classified in Industry 561450, Credit Bureaus.

561612 Security Guards and Patrol Services^{CAN}

This U.S. industry comprises establishments primarily engaged in providing guard and patrol services, such as bodyguard, guard dog, and parking security services.

Cross-References.

Establishments primarily engaged in selling, installing, monitoring, and maintaining security systems and devices, such as burglar and fire alarms and locking devices, are classified in Industry 56162, Security Systems Services.

561613 Armored Car Services^{CAN}

This U.S. industry comprises establishments primarily engaged in picking up and delivering money, receipts, or other valuable items. These establishments maintain personnel and equipment to protect such properties while in transit.

56162 Security Systems Services

This industry comprises establishments engaged in (1) selling security systems, such as burglar and fire alarms and locking devices, along with installation, repair, or monitoring services or (2) remote monitoring of electronic security alarm systems.

Cross-References. Establishments primarily engaged in—

- Selling security systems for buildings without installation, repair, or monitoring services— are classified in Sector 42, Wholesale Trade or Sector 44-45, Retail Trade;

- Retailing motor vehicle security systems with or without installation or repair services— are classified in Industry 44131, Automotive Parts and Accessories Stores; and

- Providing key duplication services—are classified in Industry 81149, Other Personal and Household Goods Repair and Maintenance.

US—United States industry only. CAN—United States and Canadian industries are comparable. When neither US nor CAN appears, Canadian, Mexican, and United States industries are comparable.

561621 Security Systems Services (except Locksmiths)^{CAN}

This U.S. industry comprises establishments primarily engaged in (1) selling security alarm systems, such as burglar and fire alarms, along with installation, repair, or monitoring services or (2) remote monitoring of electronic security alarm systems.

Cross-References. Establishments primarily engaged in—

- Selling security alarm systems for buildings, without installation, repair, or monitoring services,—are classified in Sector 42, Wholesale Trade or Sector 44-45, Retail Trade; and

- Retailing motor vehicle security systems with or without installation or repair services— are classified in Industry 441310, Automotive Parts and Accessories Stores.

561622 Locksmiths^{CAN}

This U.S. industry comprises establishments primarily engaged in (1) selling mechanical or electronic locking devices, safes, and security vaults, along with installation, repair, rebuilding, or adjusting services or (2) installing, repairing, rebuilding, and adjusting mechanical or electronic locking devices, safes, and security vaults.

Cross-References. Establishments primarily engaged in—

- Selling security systems, such as locking devices, safes, and vaults, without installation or maintenance services—are classified in Sector 42, Wholesale Trade or Sector 44-45, Retail Trade; and

- Providing key duplication services—are classified in Industry 811490, Other Personal and Household Goods Repair and Maintenance.

5617 Services to Buildings and Dwellings

56171 Exterminating and Pest Control Services
See industry description for 561710 below.

561710 Exterminating and Pest Control Services

This industry comprises establishments primarily engaged in exterminating and controlling birds, mosquitoes, rodents, termites, and other insects and pests (except for crop production and forestry production). Establishments providing fumigation services are included in this industry.

Cross-References.

Establishments primarily engaged in providing pest control for crop or forestry production are classified in Subsector 115, Support Activities for Agriculture and Forestry.

US—United States industry only. CAN—United States and Canadian industries are comparable. When neither US nor CAN appears, Canadian, Mexican, and United States industries are comparable.

56172 Janitorial Services
See industry description for 561720 below.

561720 Janitorial Services

This industry comprises establishments primarily engaged in cleaning building interiors, interiors of transportation equipment (e.g., aircraft, rail cars, ships), and/or windows.

Illustrative Examples:

Custodial services
Housekeeping (i.e., cleaning) services
Maid (i.e., cleaning) services

Service station cleaning and degreasing
  services
Washroom sanitation services

Cross-References. Establishments primarily engaged in—

- Cleaning building exteriors (except sandblasting and window cleaning) or chimneys—are classified in Industry 561790, Other Services to Buildings and Dwellings; and

- Sandblasting building exteriors—are classified in Industry 235990, All Other Special Trade Contractors.

56173 Landscaping Services
See industry description for 561730 below.

561730 Landscaping Services

This industry comprises (1) establishments primarily engaged in providing landscape care and maintenance services and/or installing trees, shrubs, plants, lawns, or gardens and (2) establishments primarily engaged in providing these services along with the design of landscape plans and/or the construction (i.e., installation) of walkways, retaining walls, decks, fences, ponds, and similar structures.

Cross-References. Establishments primarily engaged in—

- Installing artificial turf or in constructing (i.e., installing) walkways, retaining walls, decks, fences, ponds, or similar structures—are classified in Sector 23, Construction;

- Planning and designing the development of land areas for projects, such as parks and other recreational areas; airports; highways; hospitals; schools; land subdivisions; and commercial, industrial, and residential areas (without also installing trees, shrubs, plants, lawns/gardens, walkways, retaining walls, decks, and similar items or structures),—are classified in Industry 541320, Landscape Architectural Services; and

- Retailing landscaping materials and providing the installation and maintenance of these materials—are classified in Industry 444220, Nursery and Garden Centers.

US—United States industry only. CAN—United States and Canadian industries are comparable. When neither US nor CAN appears, Canadian, Mexican, and United States industries are comparable.

http://www.ntis.gov/naics

56174 Carpet and Upholstery Cleaning Services
See industry description for 561740 below.

561740 Carpet and Upholstery Cleaning Services

This industry comprises establishments primarily engaged in cleaning and dyeing used rugs, carpets, and upholstery.

Cross-References. Establishments primarily engaged in—

- Rug repair not associated with rug cleaning—are classified in Industry 811490, Other Personal and Household Goods Repair and Maintenance; and

- Reupholstering and repairing furniture—are classified in Industry 811420, Reupholstery and Furniture Repair.

56179 Other Services to Buildings and Dwellings
See industry description for 561790 below.

561790 Other Services to Buildings and Dwellings

This industry comprises establishments primarily engaged in providing services to buildings and dwellings (except exterminating and pest control; janitorial; landscaping care and maintenance; and carpet and upholstery cleaning).

Illustrative Examples:

Building exterior cleaning services (except sandblasting and window cleaning)
Chimney cleaning services
Drain or gutter cleaning services

Swimming pool cleaning and maintenance services
Ventilation duct cleaning services

Cross-References. Establishments primarily engaged in—

- Providing exterminating and pest control services—are classified in Industry 561710, Exterminating and Pest Control Services;

- Providing janitorial services—are classified in Industry 561720, Janitorial Services;

- Providing landscaping care and maintenance—are classified in Industry 561730, Landscaping Services;

- Providing carpet and upholstery cleaning services—are classified in Industry 561740, Carpet and Upholstery Cleaning Services; and

- Sandblasting building exteriors—are classified in Industry 235990, All Other Special Trade Contractors.

US—United States industry only. CAN—United States and Canadian industries are comparable. When neither US nor CAN appears, Canadian, Mexican, and United States industries are comparable.

5619 Other Support Services

This industry group comprises establishments primarily engaged in providing day-to-day business and other organizational support services (except office administrative services; facilities support services; employment services; business support services; travel arrangement and reservation services; security and investigation services; and services to buildings and dwellings).

56191 Packaging and Labeling Services
See industry description for 561910 below.

561910 Packaging and Labeling Services

This industry comprises establishments primarily engaged in packaging client owned materials. The services may include labeling and/or imprinting the package.

Illustrative Examples:

Apparel and textile folding and packaging services	Gift wrapping services
	Kit assembling and packaging services
Blister packaging services	Shrink-wrapping services

Cross-References. Establishments primarily engaged in—

- Processing clients' owned materials into a different product, such as mixing water and concentrate to produce soft drinks,—are classified in Sector 31-33, Manufacturing;

- Providing aerosol packaging services—are classified in U.S. Industry 325998, All Other Miscellaneous Chemical Product and Preparation Manufacturing;

- Providing packing and crating services incidental to transportation—are classified in U.S. Industry 488991, Packing and Crating;

- Providing warehousing services, as well as packaging or other logistics services—are classified in Industry Group 4931, Warehousing and Storage; and

- Providing packing and crating services for agricultural products—are classified in U.S. Industry 115114, Postharvest Crop Activities (except Cotton Ginning).

56192 Convention and Trade Show Organizers
See industry description for 561920 below.

561920 Convention and Trade Show Organizers

This industry comprises establishments primarily engaged in organizing, promoting, and/or managing events, such as business and trade shows, conventions, conferences, and meetings (whether or not they manage and provide the staff to operate the facilities in which these events take place).

US—United States industry only. CAN—United States and Canadian industries are comparable. When neither US nor CAN appears, Canadian, Mexican, and United States industries are comparable.

http://www.ntis.gov/naics

Cross-References.

Establishments primarily engaged in organizing, promoting, and/or managing live performing arts productions, sports events, and similar events, such as festivals (whether or not they manage and provide the staff to operate the facilities in which that these events take place), are classified in Industry Group 7113, Promoters of Performing Arts, Sports, and Similar Events.

56199 All Other Support Services
See industry description for 561990 below.

561990 All Other Support Services

This industry comprises establishments primarily engaged in providing day-to-day business and other organizational support services (except office administrative services, facilities support services, employment services, business support services, travel arrangement and reservation services, security and investigation services, services to buildings and other structures, packaging and labeling services, and convention and trade show organizing services).

Illustrative Examples:

Bartering services	Flagging (i.e., traffic control) services
Bottle exchanges	Float decorating services
Cloth cutting, bolting, or winding for the trade	Inventory taking services
Contract meter reading services	Lumber grading services
Diving services on a contract or fee basis	Water softening and conditioning services

Cross-References. Establishments primarily engaged in—

- Providing office administrative services—are classified in Industry 561110, Office Administrative Services;

- Providing facilities support services—are classified in Industry 561210, Facilities Support Services;

- Providing employment services—are classified in Industry Group 5613, Employment Services;

- Providing business support services—are classified in Industry Group 5614, Business Support Services;

- Providing travel arrangement and reservation services—are classified in Industry Group 5615, Travel Arrangement and Reservation Services;

- Providing security and investigation services—are classified in Industry Group 5616, Investigation and Security Services;

- Providing services to buildings and other structures—are classified in Industry Group 5617, Services to Buildings and Dwellings;

US—United States industry only. CAN—United States and Canadian industries are comparable. When neither US nor CAN appears, Canadian, Mexican, and United States industries are comparable.

- Providing packaging and labeling services—are classified in Industry 561910, Packaging and Labeling Services; and

- Organizing, promoting, and/or managing conferences, conventions, and trade shows (whether or not they manage and provide the staff to operate the facilities in which these events take place)—are classified in Industry 561920, Convention and Trade Show Organizers.

562 Waste Management and Remediation Services

Industries in the Waste Management and Remediation Services subsector group establishments engaged in the collection, treatment, and disposal of waste materials. This includes establishments engaged in local hauling of waste materials; operating materials recovery facilities (i.e., those that sort recyclable materials from the trash stream); providing remediation services (i.e., those that provide for the cleanup of contaminated buildings, mine sites, soil, or ground water); and providing septic pumping and other miscellaneous waste management services. There are three industry groups within the subsector that separate these activities into waste collection, waste treatment and disposal, and remediation and other waste management.

Excluded from this subsector are establishments primarily engaged in collecting, treating, and disposing waste through sewer systems or sewage treatment facilities that are classified in Industry 22132, Sewage Treatment Facilities and establishments primarily engaged in long-distance hauling of waste materials that are classified in Industry 48423, Specialized Freight (except Used Goods) Trucking, Long-Distance. Also, there are some activities that appear to be related to waste management, but that are not included in this subsector. For example, establishments primarily engaged in providing waste management consulting services are classified in Industry 54162, Environmental Consulting Services.

5621 Waste Collection[CAN]

56211 Waste Collection[CAN]

This industry comprises establishments primarily engaged in (1) collecting and/or hauling hazardous waste, nonhazardous waste, and/or recyclable materials within a local area and/or (2) operating hazardous or nonhazardous waste transfer stations. Hazardous waste collection establishments may be responsible for the identification, treatment, packaging, and labeling of wastes for the purposes of transport.

Cross-References. Establishments primarily engaged in—

- Long-distance trucking of waste—are classified in Industry 48423, Specialized Freight (except Used Goods) Trucking, Long-Distance;

- Operating facilities for separating and sorting recyclable materials from nonhazardous waste streams (i.e., garbage) and/or for sorting commingled recyclable materials, such as paper, plastics, and metal cans, into distinct categories—are classified in Industry 56292, Materials Recovery Facilities; and

---

US—United States industry only. CAN—United States and Canadian industries are comparable. When neither US nor CAN appears, Canadian, Mexican, and United States industries are comparable.

- Collecting and/or hauling in combination with disposal of waste materials—are classified in Industry 56221, Waste Treatment and Disposal.

562111 Solid Waste Collection[US]

This U.S. industry comprises establishments primarily engaged in one or more of the following: (1) collecting and/or hauling nonhazardous solid waste (i.e., garbage) within a local area; (2) operating nonhazardous solid waste transfer stations; and (3) collecting and/or hauling mixed recyclable materials within a local area.

Cross-References. Establishments primarily engaged in—

- Long-distance trucking of waste—are classified in Industry 484230, Specialized Freight (except Used Goods) Trucking, Long-Distance;

- Collecting and/or hauling in combination with disposal of nonhazardous waste materials— are classified in Industry 56221, Waste Treatment and Disposal;

- Collecting and/or hauling hazardous waste within a local area and/or operating hazardous waste transfer stations—are classified in U.S. Industry 562112, Hazardous Waste Collection;

- Collecting and removing debris, such as brush or rubble, within a local area—are classified in U.S. Industry 562119, Other Waste Collection; and

- Operating facilities for separating and sorting recyclable materials from nonhazardous waste streams (i.e., garbage) and/or for sorting commingled recyclable materials, such as paper, plastics, and metal cans, into distinct categories—are classified in Industry 562920, Materials Recovery Facilities.

562112 Hazardous Waste Collection[US]

This U.S. industry comprises establishments primarily engaged in collecting and/or hauling hazardous waste within a local area and/or operating hazardous waste transfer stations. Hazardous waste collection establishments may be responsible for the identification, treatment, packaging, and labeling of wastes for the purposes of transport.

Cross-References. Establishments primarily engaged in—

- Long-distance trucking of waste—are classified in Industry 484230, Specialized Freight (except Used Goods) Trucking, Long-Distance;

- Collecting and/or hauling in combination with disposal of hazardous waste materials—are classified in U.S. Industry 562211, Hazardous Waste Treatment and Disposal;

- Collecting and/or hauling nonhazardous solid waste (i.e., garbage) and/or recyclable materials within a local area and/or operating nonhazardous solid waste transfer stations—are classified in U.S. Industry 562111, Solid Waste Collection; and

- Collecting and removing debris, such as brush or rubble, within a local area—are classified in U.S. Industry 562119, Other Waste Collection.

US—United States industry only. CAN—United States and Canadian industries are comparable. When neither US nor CAN appears, Canadian, Mexican, and United States industries are comparable.

562119 Other Waste Collection[US]

This U.S. industry comprises establishments primarily engaged in collecting and/or hauling waste (except nonhazardous solid waste and hazardous waste) within a local area. Establishments engaged in brush or rubble removal services are included in this industry.

Cross-References. Establishments primarily engaged in—

- Long-distance trucking of waste—are classified in Industry 484230, Specialized Freight (except Used Goods) Trucking, Long-Distance;

- Collecting and/or hauling in combination with disposal of waste materials—are classified in Industry Group 5622, Waste Treatment and Disposal;

- Collecting and/or hauling nonhazardous solid waste (i.e., garbage) or mixed recyclable materials within a local area or operating nonhazardous solid waste transfer stations—are classified in U.S. Industry 562111, Solid Waste Collection;

- Collecting and/or hauling hazardous waste within a local area or operating hazardous waste transfer stations—are classified in U.S. Industry 562112, Hazardous Waste Collection; and

- Operating facilities for separating and sorting recyclable materials from nonhazardous waste streams (i.e., garbage) and/or for sorting commingled recyclable materials, such as paper, plastics, and metal cans, into distinct categories—are classified in Industry 562920, Materials Recovery Facilities.

5622 Waste Treatment and Disposal[CAN]

56221 Waste Treatment and Disposal[CAN]

This industry comprises establishments primarily engaged in (1) operating waste treatment or disposal facilities (except sewer systems or sewage treatment facilities) or (2) the combined activity of collecting and/or hauling of waste materials within a local area and operating waste treatment or disposal facilities. Waste combusters or incinerators (including those that may produce byproducts such as electricity), solid waste landfills, and compost dumps are included in this industry.

Cross-References. Establishments primarily engaged in—

- Collecting, treating, and disposing waste through sewer systems or sewage treatment facilities—are classified in Industry 22132, Sewage Treatment Facilities; and

- Manufacturing compost—are classified in Industry 32531, Fertilizer Manufacturing.

562211 Hazardous Waste Treatment and Disposal[US]

This U.S. industry comprises establishments primarily engaged in (1) operating treatment and/or disposal facilities for hazardous waste or (2) the combined activity of collecting and/or hauling of hazardous waste materials within a local area and operating treatment or disposal facilities for hazardous waste.

US—United States industry only. CAN—United States and Canadian industries are comparable. When neither US nor CAN appears, Canadian, Mexican, and United States industries are comparable.

Cross-References. Establishments primarily engaged in—

- Operating landfills for the disposal of nonhazardous solid waste—are classified in U.S. Industry 562212, Solid Waste Landfill;

- Operating combustors and incinerators for the disposal of nonhazardous solid waste—are classified in U.S. Industry 562213, Solid Waste Combustors and Incinerators;

- Collecting, treating, and disposing waste through sewer systems or sewage treatment facilities—are classified in Industry 221320, Sewage Treatment Facilities; and

- Operating nonhazardous waste treatment and disposal facilities (except landfills, combustors, incinerators, and sewer systems or sewage treatment facilities)—are classified in U.S. Industry 562219, Other Nonhazardous Waste Treatment and Disposal.

562212 Solid Waste Landfill[US]

This U.S. industry comprises establishments primarily engaged in (1) operating landfills for the disposal of nonhazardous solid waste or (2) the combined activity of collecting and/or hauling nonhazardous waste materials within a local area and operating landfills for the disposal of nonhazardous solid waste.

Cross-References. Establishments primarily engaged in—

- Operating treatment and/or disposal facilities for hazardous waste—are classified in U.S. Industry 562211, Hazardous Waste Treatment and Disposal;

- Operating combustors and incinerators for the disposal of nonhazardous solid waste—are classified in U.S. Industry 562213, Solid Waste Combustors and Incinerators;

- Collecting, treating, and disposing waste through sewer systems or sewage treatment facilities—are classified in Industry 221320, Sewage Treatment Facilities;

- Operating nonhazardous waste treatment and disposal facilities (except landfills, combustors, incinerators, and sewer systems or sewage treatment facilities)—are classified in U.S. Industry 562219, Other Nonhazardous Waste Treatment and Disposal; and

- Manufacturing compost—are classified in U.S. Industry 325314, Fertilizer (Mixing Only) Manufacturing.

562213 Solid Waste Combustors and Incinerators[US]

This U.S. industry comprises establishments primarily engaged in operating combustors and incinerators for the disposal of nonhazardous solid waste. These establishments may produce byproducts, such as electricity and steam.

Cross-References. Establishments primarily engaged in—

- Operating treatment and/or disposal facilities for hazardous waste—are classified in U.S. Industry 562211, Hazardous Waste Treatment and Disposal;

US—United States industry only. CAN—United States and Canadian industries are comparable. When neither US nor CAN appears, Canadian, Mexican, and United States industries are comparable.

- Operating landfills for the disposal of nonhazardous solid waste—are classified in U.S. Industry 562212, Solid Waste Landfill;

- Collecting, treating, and disposing waste through sewer systems or sewage treatment facilities—are classified in Industry 221320, Sewage Treatment Facilities; and

- Operating nonhazardous waste treatment and disposal facilities (except landfills, combustors, incinerators, and sewer systems or sewage treatment facilities)—are classified in U.S. Industry 562219, Other Nonhazardous Waste Treatment and Disposal.

562219 Other Nonhazardous Waste Treatment and Disposal^{US}

This U.S. industry comprises establishments primarily engaged in (1) operating nonhazardous waste treatment and disposal facilities (except landfills, combustors, incinerators and sewer systems or sewage treatment facilities) or (2) the combined activity of collecting and/or hauling of nonhazardous waste materials within a local area and operating waste treatment or disposal facilities (except landfills, combustors, incinerators and sewer systems, or sewage treatment facilities). Compost dumps are included in this industry.

Cross-References. Establishments primarily engaged in—

- Operating landfills for the disposal of nonhazardous solid waste—are classified in U.S. Industry 562212, Solid Waste Landfill;

- Operating combustors and incinerators for the disposal of nonhazardous solid waste—are classified in U.S. Industry 562213, Solid Waste Combustors and Incinerators;

- Collecting, treating, and disposing waste through sewer systems or sewage treatment facilities—are classified in Industry 221320, Sewage Treatment Facilities; and

- Manufacturing compost—are classified in U.S. Industry 325314, Fertilizer (Mixing Only) Manufacturing.

5629 Remediation and Other Waste Management Services^{CAN}

This industry group comprises establishments primarily engaged in remediation and other waste management services (except waste collection, waste treatment and disposal, and waste management consulting services).

56291 Remediation Services^{CAN}
See industry description for 562910 below.

562910 Remediation Services^{CAN}

This industry comprises establishments primarily engaged in one or more of the following: (1) remediation and cleanup of contaminated buildings, mine sites, soil, or ground water; (2) integrated mine reclamation activities, including demolition, soil remediation, waste water treatment, hazardous material removal, contouring land, and revegetation; and (3) asbestos, lead paint, and other toxic material abatement.

US—United States industry only. CAN—United States and Canadian industries are comparable. When neither US nor CAN appears, Canadian, Mexican, and United States industries are comparable.

http://www.ntis.gov/naics

Cross-References. Establishments primarily engaged in—

- Developing remedial action plans—are classified in Industry 541620, Environmental Consulting Services;

- Excavating soil—are classified in Industry 235930, Excavation Contractors;

- Individual activities as part of a reclamation or remediation project—are classified according to the primary activity;

- Building modifications to alleviate radon gas—are classified in Sector 23, Construction; and

- Collecting, treating, and disposing waste water through sewer systems or sewage treatment facilities—are classified in Industry 221320, Sewage Treatment Facilities.

56292 Materials Recovery Facilities[CAN]

See industry description for 562920 below.

562920 Materials Recovery Facilities[CAN]

This industry comprises establishments primarily engaged in (1) operating facilities for separating and sorting recyclable materials from nonhazardous waste streams (i.e., garbage) and/or (2) operating facilities where commingled recyclable materials, such as paper, plastics, used beverage cans, and metals, are sorted into distinct categories.

Cross-References.

Establishments primarily engaged in wholesaling automotive, industrial, and other recyclable materials are classified in Industry 421930, Recyclable Material Wholesalers.

56299 All Other Waste Management Services[CAN]

This industry comprises establishments primarily engaged in waste management services (except waste collection, waste treatment and disposal, remediation, operation of materials recovery facilities, and waste management consulting services).

Illustrative Examples:

Beach cleaning and maintenance services
Cesspool cleaning services
Portable toilet renting and/or servicing
Pumping (i.e., cleaning) cesspools, portable
 toilets, or septic tanks

Sewer cleaning and rodding services
Sewer or storm basin cleanout services

Cross-References. Establishments primarily engaged in—

- Collecting and/or hauling waste within a local area—are classified in Industry 56211, Waste Collection;

US—United States industry only. CAN—United States and Canadian industries are comparable. When neither US nor CAN appears, Canadian, Mexican, and United States industries are comparable.

- Long-distance trucking of waste—are classified in Industry 48423, Specialized Freight (except Used Goods) Trucking, Long-Distance;

- Operating treatment or disposal facilities (except sewer systems or sewage treatment facilities) for wastes—are classified in Industry 56221, Waste Treatment and Disposal;

- Collecting, treating, and disposing waste through sewer systems or sewage treatment facilities—are classified in Industry 22132, Sewage Treatment Facilities;

- Remediation and cleanup of contaminated buildings, mine sites, soil, or ground water—are classified in Industry 56291, Remediation Services;

- Operating facilities for separating and sorting recyclable materials from nonhazardous waste streams (i.e., garbage) or where commingled recyclable materials, such as paper, plastics, and metal cans,—are sorted into distinct categories are classified in Industry 56292, Materials Recovery Facilities;

- Installing septic tanks—are classified in Industry 23511, Plumbing, Heating, and Air-Conditioning Contractors; and

- Providing waste management consulting services, such as developing remedial action plans,—are classified in Industry 54162, Environmental Consulting Services.

562991 Septic Tank and Related Services[US]

This U.S. industry comprises establishments primarily engaged in (1) pumping (i.e., cleaning) septic tanks and cesspools and/or (2) renting and/or servicing portable toilets.

Cross-References. Establishments primarily engaged in—

- Installing septic tanks—are classified in Industry 235110, Plumbing, Heating, and Air-Conditioning Contractors; and

- Cleaning and rodding sewers and catch basins—are classified in U.S. Industry 562998, All Other Miscellaneous Waste Management Services.

562998 All Other Miscellaneous Waste Management Services[US]

This U.S. industry comprises establishments primarily engaged in providing waste management services (except waste collection, waste treatment and disposal, remediation, operation of materials recovery facilities, septic tank pumping and related services, and waste management consulting services).

Illustrative Examples:

Beach cleaning and maintenance services	Sewer or storm basin cleanout services
Catch basin cleaning services	Tank cleaning and disposal services,
Sewer cleaning and rodding services	commercial or industrial

US—United States industry only. CAN—United States and Canadian industries are comparable. When neither US nor CAN appears, Canadian, Mexican, and United States industries are comparable.

Cross-References. Establishments primarily engaged in—

- Collecting and/or hauling waste within a local area—are classified in Industry 56211, Waste Collection;

- Long-distance trucking of waste—are classified in Industry 484230, Specialized Freight (except Used Goods) Trucking, Long-Distance;

- Operating treatment or disposal facilities (except sewer systems or sewage treatment facilities) for wastes—are classified in Industry 56221 Waste Treatment and Disposal;

- Collecting, treating, and disposing waste through sewer systems or sewage treatment facilities—are classified in Industry 221320, Sewage Treatment Facilities;

- The remediation and cleanup of contaminated buildings, mine sites, soil, or ground water—are classified in Industry 562910, Remediation Services;

- Operating facilities for separating and sorting recyclable materials from nonhazardous waste streams (i.e., garbage) or for sorting commingled recyclable materials, such as paper, plastics, and metal cans, into distinct categories—are classified in Industry 562920, Materials Recovery Facilities;

- Pumping (i.e., cleaning) cesspools, portable toilets, and septic tanks or renting portable toilets—are classified in U.S. Industry 562991, Septic Tank and Related Services; and

- Providing waste management consulting services, such as developing remedial action plans,—are classified in Industry 541620, Environmental Consulting Services.

Sector 61—Educational Services

The Sector as a Whole

The Educational Services sector comprises establishments that provide instruction and training in a wide variety of subjects. This instruction and training is provided by specialized establishments, such as schools, colleges, universities, and training centers. These establishments may be privately owned and operated for profit or not for profit, or they may be publicly owned and operated. They may also offer food and accommodation services to their students.

Educational services are usually delivered by teachers or instructors that explain, tell, demonstrate, supervise, and direct learning. Instruction is imparted in diverse settings, such as educational institutions, the workplace, or the home through correspondence, television, or other means. It can be adapted to the particular needs of the students, for example sign language can replace verbal language for teaching students with hearing impairments. All industries in the sector share this commonality of process, namely, labor inputs of instructors with the requisite subject matter expertise and teaching ability.

611 Educational Services

Industries in the Educational Services subsector provide instruction and training in a wide variety of subjects. The instruction and training is provided by specialized establishments, such as schools, colleges, universities, and training centers.

The subsector is structured according to level and type of educational services. Elementary and secondary schools, junior colleges and colleges, universities, and professional schools correspond to a recognized series of formal levels of education designated by diplomas, associate degrees (including equivalent certificates), and degrees. The remaining industry groups are based more on the type of instruction or training offered and the levels are not always as formally defined. The establishments are often highly specialized, many offering instruction in a very limited subject matter, for example ski lessons or one specific computer software package. Within the sector, the level and types of training that are required of the instructors and teachers vary depending on the industry.

Establishments that manage schools and other educational establishments on a contractual basis are classified in this subsector if they both manage the operation and provide the operating staff. Such establishments are classified in the educational services subsector based on the type of facility managed and operated.

6111 Elementary and Secondary Schools

61111 Elementary and Secondary Schools[CAN]
See industry description for 611110 below.

611110 Elementary and Secondary Schools[CAN]

This industry comprises establishments primarily engaged in furnishing academic courses and associated course work that comprise a basic preparatory education. A basic preparatory education

---

US—United States industry only. CAN—United States and Canadian industries are comparable. When neither US nor CAN appears, Canadian, Mexican, and United States industries are comparable.

ordinarily constitutes kindergarten through 12th grade. This industry includes school boards and school districts.

Illustrative Examples:

Elementary schools
High schools
Kindergartens
Military academies, elementary or secondary

Parochial schools, elementary or secondary
Primary schools
Schools for the physically disabled,
　elementary or secondary

Cross-References.

- Establishments primarily engaged in providing preschool or prekindergarten education are classified in Industry 624410, Child Day Care Services; and

- Military academies, college level are classified in Industry 61131, Colleges, Universities, and Professional Schools.

6112 Junior Colleges

61121 Junior Colleges
See industry description for 611210 below.

611210 Junior Colleges

This industry comprises establishments primarily engaged in furnishing academic, or academic and technical, courses and granting associate degrees, certificates, or diplomas below the baccalaureate level. The requirement for admission to an associate or equivalent degree program is at least a high school diploma or equivalent general academic training.

6113 Colleges, Universities, and Professional Schools

61131 Colleges, Universities, and Professional Schools
See industry description for 611310 below.

611310 Colleges, Universities, and Professional Schools

This industry comprises establishments primarily engaged in furnishing academic courses and granting degrees at baccalaureate or graduate levels. The requirement for admission is at least a high school diploma or equivalent general academic training.

Illustrative Examples:

Colleges (except junior colleges)
Military academies, college level
Professional schools (e.g., business
　administration, dental, law, medical)

Theological seminaries offering baccalaureate or
　graduate degrees
Universities

US—United States industry only. CAN—United States and Canadian industries are comparable. When neither US nor CAN appears, Canadian, Mexican, and United States industries are comparable.

Cross-References.

Establishments primarily engaged in furnishing academic, or academic and technical, courses and granting associate degrees, certificates, or diplomas below the baccalaureate level are classified in Industry 611210, Junior Colleges.

6114 Business Schools and Computer and Management Training

61141 Business and Secretarial Schools
See industry description for 611410 below.

611410 Business and Secretarial Schools

This industry comprises establishments primarily engaged in offering courses in office procedures and secretarial and stenographic skills and may offer courses in basic office skills, such as word processing. In addition, these establishments may offer such classes as office machine operation, reception, communications, and other skills designed for individuals pursuing a clerical or secretarial career.

Cross-References. Establishments primarily engaged in—

- Offering computer training (except computer repair)—are classified in Industry 611420, Computer Training;

- Offering academic degrees (e.g., baccalaureate, graduate level) in business education—are classified in Industry 611310, Colleges, Universities, and Professional Schools; and

- Offering training in the maintenance and repair of computers—are classified in Industry 611519, Other Technical and Trade Schools.

61142 Computer Training
See industry description for 611420 below.

611420 Computer Training

This industry comprises establishments primarily engaged in conducting computer training (except computer repair), such as computer programming, software packages, computerized business systems, computer electronics technology, computer operations, and local area network management. Instruction may be provided at the establishment's facilities or at an off-site location, including the client's own facilities.

Cross-References. Establishments primarily engaged in—

- Offering training in the maintenance and repair of computers—are classified in Industry 61151, Technical and Trade Schools; and

- Computer retailing, wholesaling, or computer system designing that may also provide computer training—are classified in their appropriate industries.

US—United States industry only. CAN—United States and Canadian industries are comparable. When neither US nor CAN appears, Canadian, Mexican, and United States industries are comparable.

http://www.ntis.gov/naics

61143 Professional and Management Development Training

See industry description for 611430 below.

611430 Professional and Management Development Training

This industry comprises establishments primarily engaged in offering an array of short duration courses and seminars for management and professional development. Training for career development may be provided directly to individuals or through employers' training programs; and courses may be customized or modified to meet the special needs of customers. Instruction may be provided at the establishment's facilities or at an off-site location, including the client's own facilities.

Cross-References. Establishments primarily engaged in—

- Advising clients on human resource and training issues without providing the training—are classified in U.S. Industry 541612, Human Resources and Executive Search Consulting Services; and

- Offering academic degrees (e.g., baccalaureate, graduate level)—are classified in Industry 611310, Colleges, Universities and Professional Schools.

6115 Technical and Trade Schools

61151 Technical and Trade Schools

This industry comprises establishments primarily engaged in offering vocational and technical training in a variety of technical subjects and trades. The training often leads to job-specific certification.

Illustrative Examples:

Apprenticeship training programs	Graphic arts schools
Aviation and flight training instruction schools	Modeling schools
Computer repair training	Nursing schools (except academic)
Cosmetology schools	Real estate schools
Electronic equipment repair training	Truck driving schools

Cross-References. Establishments primarily engaged in—

- Offering courses in office procedures and secretarial and stenographic skills—are classified in Industry 61141, Business and Secretarial Schools;

- Offering computer training (except computer repair)—are classified in Industry 61142, Computer Training;

- Offering professional and management development training—are classified in Industry 61143, Professional and Management Development Training;

- Offering academic courses that may also offer technical and trade courses—are classified according to the type of school;

- Specialty air transportation services which may also provide flight training—are classified in Industry 48121, Nonscheduled Air Transportation; and

- Offering registered nursing training—are classified in Industry 61121, Junior Colleges or Industry 61131, Colleges, Universities and Professional Schools.

611511 Cosmetology and Barber Schools[US]

This U.S. industry comprises establishments primarily engaged in offering training in barbering, hair styling, or the cosmetic arts, such as makeup or skin care. These schools provide job-specific certification.

611512 Flight Training[US]

This U.S. industry comprises establishments primarily engaged in offering aviation and flight training. These establishments may offer vocational training, recreational training, or both.

Cross-References.

Establishments primarily engaged in specialty air transportation services which may also provide flight training are classified in U.S. Industry 481219, Other Nonscheduled Air Transportation.

611513 Apprenticeship Training[US]

This U.S. industry comprises establishments primarily engaged in offering apprenticeship training programs. These programs involve applied training as well as course work.

611519 Other Technical and Trade Schools[US]

This U.S. industry comprises establishments primarily engaged in offering job or career vocational or technical courses (except cosmetology and barber training, aviation and flight training, and apprenticeship training). The curriculums offered by these schools are highly structured and specialized and lead to job-specific certification.

Illustrative Examples:

Bartending schools	Modeling schools
Broadcasting schools	Real estate schools
Computer repair training	Truck driving schools
Graphic arts schools	

Cross-References. Establishments primarily engaged in—

- Offering courses in office procedures and secretarial and stenographic skills—are classified in Industry 611410, Business and Secretarial Schools;

- Offering computer training (except computer repair)—are classified in Industry 611420, Computer Training;

US—United States industry only. CAN—United States and Canadian industries are comparable. When neither US nor CAN appears, Canadian, Mexican, and United States industries are comparable.

- Offering professional and management development training—are classified in Industry 611430, Professional and Management Development Training;

- Offering registered nursing training with academic degrees (e.g., associate baccalaureate)—are classified in Industry 611210, Junior Colleges or Industry 611310, Colleges, Universities and Professional Schools;

- Offering aviation and flight training—are classified in U.S. Industry 611512, Flight Training;

- Offering cosmetology and barber training—are classified in U.S. Industry 611511, Cosmetology and Barber Schools;

- Offering academic courses that may also offer technical and trade courses—are classified according to the type of school; and

- Offering apprenticeship training programs—are classified in U.S. Industry 611513, Apprenticeship Training.

6116 Other Schools and Instruction

This industry group comprises establishments primarily engaged in offering or providing instruction (except academic schools, colleges, and universities; and business, computer, management, technical, or trade instruction).

61161 Fine Arts Schools
See industry description for 611610 below.

611610 Fine Arts Schools

This industry comprises establishments primarily engaged in offering instruction in the arts, including dance, art, drama, and music.

Illustrative Examples:

Art (except commercial and graphic) instruction
Dance instruction
Dance studios
Drama schools (except academic)
Fine arts schools (except academic)

Music instruction (e.g., piano, guitar)
Music schools (except academic)
Performing arts schools (except academic)
Photography schools (except commercial photography)

Cross-References.

- Establishments offering high school diplomas or academic degrees (i.e., even if they specialize in fine arts) are classified elsewhere in this subsector according to the type of school; and

- Establishments primarily engaged in offering courses in commercial and graphic arts and commercial photography are classified in U.S. Industry 611519, Other Technical and Trade Schools.

US—United States industry only. CAN—United States and Canadian industries are comparable. When neither US nor CAN appears, Canadian, Mexican, and United States industries are comparable.

61162 Sports and Recreation Instruction
See industry description for 611620 below.

611620 Sports and Recreation Instruction

This industry comprises establishments, such as camps and schools, primarily engaged in offering instruction in athletic activities to groups of individuals. Overnight and day sports instruction camps are included in this industry.

Illustrative Examples:

Camps, sports instruction
Cheerleading instruction
Gymnastics instruction
Martial arts instruction, camps or schools
Professional sports instructors (i.e., not
  participating in sporting events)

Riding instruction academies or schools
Sports (e.g., baseball, basketball, football, golf)
Swimming instruction

Cross-References.

- Establishments primarily engaged in operating overnight recreational camps that may offer some athletic instruction in addition to other activities are classified in U.S. Industry 721214, Recreation and Vacation Camps (except campgrounds);

- Establishments primarily engaged in operating sports and recreation establishments that also offer athletic instruction are classified in Sector 71, Arts, Entertainment, and Recreation;

- Independent (i.e., freelance) athletes engaged in providing sports instruction and participating in spectator sporting events are classified in U.S. Industry 711219, Other Spectator Sports; and

- Offering academic courses that may also offer athletic instruction are classified according to the type of school.

61163 Language Schools
See industry description for 611630 below.

611630 Language Schools

This industry comprises establishments primarily engaged in offering foreign language instruction (including sign language). These establishments are designed to offer language instruction ranging from conversational skills for personal enrichment to intensive training courses for career or educational opportunities.

Cross-References. Establishments primarily engaged in—

- Offering academic courses that may also offer language instruction—are classified according to type of school; and

US—United States industry only. CAN—United States and Canadian industries are comparable. When neither US nor CAN appears, Canadian, Mexican, and United States industries are comparable.

http://www.ntis.gov/naics

• Providing translation and interpretation services—are classified in Industry 541930, Translation and Interpretation Services.

61169 All Other Schools and Instruction

This industry comprises establishments primarily engaged in offering instruction (except business, computer, management, technical, trade, fine arts, athletic, and language instruction). Also excluded from this industry are academic schools, colleges, and universities.

Illustrative Examples:

Academic tutoring services
Automobile driving schools
Exam preparation services

Public speaking training
Speed reading instruction

Cross-References. Establishments primarily engaged in—

• Offering elementary and secondary school instruction—are classified in Industry 61111, Elementary and Secondary Schools;

• Offering junior college instruction—are classified in Industry 61121, Junior Colleges;

• Offering college, university, and professional school instruction with academic degrees (e.g., baccalaureate, graduate)—are classified in Industry 61131, Colleges, Universities and Professional Schools;

• Offering business, computer (except computer repair), and management training—are classified in Industry Group 6114, Business Schools and Computer and Management Training;

• Offering technical and trade school instruction (e.g., computer repair and maintenance)—are classified in Industry 61151, Technical and Trade Schools;

• Offering fine arts instruction—are classified in Industry 61161, Fine Arts Schools;

• Offering sports and recreation instruction—are classified in Industry 61162, Sports and Recreation Instruction; and

• Offering language instruction—are classified in Industry 61163, Language Schools.

611691 Exam Preparation and Tutoring[US]

This U.S. industry comprises establishments primarily engaged in offering preparation for standardized examinations and/or academic tutoring services.

Illustrative Examples:

Academic tutoring services
College board preparation centers

Learning centers offering remedial courses
Professional examination review instruction

611692 Automobile Driving Schools[US]

This U.S. industry comprises establishments primarily engaged in offering automobile driving instruction.

Cross-References.

Establishments primarily engaged in offering truck and bus driving instruction are classified in U.S. Industry 611519, Other Technical and Trade Schools.

611699 All Other Miscellaneous Schools and Instruction[US]

This U.S. industry comprises establishments primarily engaged in offering instruction (except business, computer, management, technical, trade, fine arts, athletic, language instruction, tutoring, and automobile driving instruction). Also excluded from this industry are academic schools, colleges, and universities.

Illustrative Examples:

Public speaking training   Survival training
Speed reading instruction

Cross-References. Establishments primarily engaged in—

- Offering elementary and secondary school instruction—are classified in Industry 611110, Elementary and Secondary Schools;

- Offering junior college instruction—are classified in Industry 611210, Junior Colleges;

- Offering college, university, and professional school instruction with academic degrees (e.g., baccalaureate, graduate)—are classified in Industry 611310, Colleges, Universities and Professional Schools;

- Offering business, computer (except computer repair), and management training—are classified in Industry Group 6114, Business Schools and Computer and Management Training;

- Offering technical and trade school instruction (e.g., computer repair and maintenance)—are classified in Industry 61151, Technical and Trade Schools;

- Offering fine arts instruction—are classified in Industry 611610, Fine Arts Schools;

- Offering sports and recreation instruction—are classified in Industry 611620, Sports and Recreation Instruction;

- Offering language instruction—are classified in Industry 611630, Language Schools;

- Offering exam preparation and tutoring services—are classified in U.S. Industry 611691, Exam Preparation and Tutoring; and

US—United States industry only. CAN—United States and Canadian industries are comparable. When neither US nor CAN appears, Canadian, Mexican, and United States industries are comparable.

- Offering automobile driving instruction—are classified in U.S. Industry 611692, Automobile Driving Schools.

6117 Educational Support Services

61171 Educational Support Services
See industry description for 611710 below.

611710 Educational Support Services

This industry comprises establishments primarily engaged in providing noninstructional services that support educational processes or systems.

Illustrative Examples:

Educational consultants   Educational testing services
Educational guidance counseling services   Student exchange programs
Educational testing evaluation services

Cross-References. Establishments primarily engaged in—

- Providing job training for the unemployed, underemployed, physically disabled, and persons who have a job market disadvantage because of lack of education or job skills—are classified in Industry 624310, Vocational Rehabilitation Services; and

- Conducting research and analyses in cognitive development—are classified in Industry 541720, Research and Development in the Social Sciences and Humanities.

Sector 62—Health Care and Social Assistance

The Sector as a Whole

The Health Care and Social Assistance sector comprises establishments providing health care and social assistance for individuals. The sector includes both health care and social assistance because it is sometimes difficult to distinguish between the boundaries of these two activities. The industries in this sector are arranged on a continuum starting with those establishments providing medical care exclusively, continuing with those providing health care and social assistance, and finally finishing with those providing only social assistance. The services provided by establishments in this sector are delivered by trained professionals. All industries in the sector share this commonality of process, namely, labor inputs of health practitioners or social workers with the requisite expertise. Many of the industries in the sector are defined based on the educational degree held by the practitioners included in the industry.

Excluded from this sector are aerobic classes in Subsector 713, Amusement, Gambling and Recreation Industries and nonmedical diet and weight reducing centers in Subsector 812, Personal and Laundry Services. Although these can be viewed as health services, these services are not typically delivered by health practitioners.

621 Ambulatory Health Care Services

Industries in the Ambulatory Health Care Services subsector provide health care services directly or indirectly to ambulatory patients and do not usually provide inpatient services. Health practitioners in this subsector provide outpatient services, with the facilities and equipment not usually being the most significant part of the production process.

6211 Offices of Physicians

62111 Offices of Physicians

This industry comprises establishments of health practitioners having the degree of M.D. (Doctor of medicine) or D.O. (Doctor of osteopathy) primarily engaged in the independent practice of general or specialized medicine (e.g., anesthesiology, oncology, ophthalmology, psychiatry) or surgery. These practitioners operate private or group practices in their own offices (e.g., centers, clinics) or in the facilities of others, such as hospitals or HMO medical centers.

Cross-References.

- Medical centers primarily engaged in providing emergency medical care for accident or trauma victims and ambulatory surgical centers primarily engaged in providing surgery on an outpatient basis are classified in Industry 62149, Other Outpatient Care Centers;

- Establishments of oral pathologists are classified in Industry 62121, Offices of Dentists; and

- Establishments of speech or voice pathologists are classified in Industry 62134, Offices of Physical, Occupational and Speech Therapists, and Audiologists.

US—United States industry only. CAN—United States and Canadian industries are comparable. When neither US nor CAN appears, Canadian, Mexican, and United States industries are comparable.

http://www.ntis.gov/naics

621111 Offices of Physicians (except Mental Health Specialists)[US]

This U.S. industry comprises establishments of health practitioners having the degree of M.D. (Doctor of medicine) or D.O. (Doctor of osteopathy) primarily engaged in the independent practice of general or specialized medicine (except psychiatry or psychoanalysis) or surgery. These practitioners operate private or group practices in their own offices (e.g., centers, clinics) or in the facilities of others, such as hospitals or HMO medical centers.

Cross-References.

- Establishments of physicians primarily engaged in the independent practice of psychiatry or psychoanalysis are classified in U.S. Industry 621112, Offices of Physicians, Mental Health Specialists;

- Freestanding medical centers primarily engaged in providing emergency medical care for accident or catastrophe victims and freestanding ambulatory surgical centers primarily engaged in providing surgery on an outpatient basis are classified in U.S. Industry 621493, Freestanding Ambulatory Surgical and Emergency Centers;

- Establishments of oral pathologists are classified in Industry 621210, Offices of Dentists; and

- Establishments of speech or voice pathologists are classified in Industry 621340, Offices of Physical, Occupational and Speech Therapists, and Audiologists.

621112 Offices of Physicians, Mental Health Specialists[US]

This U.S. industry comprises establishments of health practitioners having the degree of M.D. (Doctor of medicine) or D.O. (Doctor of osteopathy) primarily engaged in the independent practice of psychiatry or psychoanalysis. These practitioners operate private or group practices in their own offices (e.g., centers, clinics) or in the facilities of others, such as hospitals or HMO medical centers.

6212 Offices of Dentists

62121 Offices of Dentists
See industry description for 621210 below.

621210 Offices of Dentists

This industry comprises establishments of health practitioners having the degree of D.M.D. (Doctor of dental medicine), D.D.S. (Doctor of dental surgery), or D.D.Sc. (Doctor of dental science) primarily engaged in the independent practice of general or specialized dentistry or dental surgery. These practitioners operate private or group practices in their own offices (e.g., centers, clinics) or in the facilities of others, such as hospitals or HMO medical centers. They can provide either comprehensive preventive, cosmetic, or emergency care, or specialize in a single field of dentistry.

US—United States industry only. CAN—United States and Canadian industries are comparable. When neither US nor CAN appears, Canadian, Mexican, and United States industries are comparable.

Cross-References.

- Establishments known as dental laboratories primarily engaged in making dentures, artificial teeth, and orthodontic appliances to order for dentists are classified U.S. Industry 339116, Dental Laboratories; and

- Establishments of dental hygienists primarily engaged in cleaning teeth and gums or establishments of denturists primarily engaged in taking impressions for and fitting dentures are classified in U.S. Industry 621399, Offices of All Other Miscellaneous Health Practitioners.

6213 Offices of Other Health Practitioners

This industry group comprises establishments of independent health practitioners (except physicians and dentists).

62131 Offices of Chiropractors
See industry description for 621310 below.

621310 Offices of Chiropractors

This industry comprises establishments of health practitioners having the degree of D.C. (Doctor of chiropractic) primarily engaged in the independent practice of chiropractic. These practitioners provide diagnostic and therapeutic treatment of neuromusculoskeletal and related disorders through the manipulation and adjustment of the spinal column and extremities, and operate private or group practices in their own offices (e.g., centers, clinics) or in the facilities of others, such as hospitals or HMO medical centers.

62132 Offices of Optometrists
See industry description for 621320 below.

621320 Offices of Optometrists

This industry comprises establishments of health practitioners having the degree of O.D. (Doctor of optometry) primarily engaged in the independent practice of optometry. These practitioners provide eye examinations to determine visual acuity or the presence of vision problems and to prescribe eyeglasses, contact lenses, and eye exercises. They operate private or group practices in their own offices (e.g., centers, clinics) or in the facilities of others, such as hospitals or HMO medical centers, and may also provide the same service as opticians, such as selling and fitting prescription eyeglasses and contact lenses.

Cross-References. Establishments of—

- Opticians primarily engaged in selling and fitting prescription eyeglasses and contact lenses—are classified in Industry 446130, Optical Goods Stores; and

- Physicians primarily engaged in the independent practice of ophthalmology—are classified in U.S. Industry 621111, Offices of Physicians (except Mental Health Specialists).

US—United States industry only. CAN—United States and Canadian industries are comparable. When neither US nor CAN appears, Canadian, Mexican, and United States industries are comparable.

http://www.ntis.gov/naics

62133 Offices of Mental Health Practitioners (except Physicians)
See industry description for 621330 below.

621330 Offices of Mental Health Practitioners (except Physicians)

This industry comprises establishments of independent mental health practitioners (except physicians) primarily engaged in (1) the diagnosis and treatment of mental, emotional, and behavioral disorders and/or (2) the diagnosis and treatment of individual or group social dysfunction brought about by such causes as mental illness, alcohol and substance abuse, physical and emotional trauma, or stress. These practitioners operate private or group practices in their own offices (e.g., centers, clinics) or in the facilities of others, such as hospitals or HMO medical centers.

Cross-References.

Establishments of psychiatrists, psychoanalysts, and psychotherapists having the degree of M.D. (Doctor of medicine) or D.O. (Doctor of osteopathy) are classified in U.S. Industry 621112, Offices of Physicians, Mental Health Specialists.

62134 Offices of Physical, Occupational and Speech Therapists, and Audiologists
See industry description for 621340 below.

621340 Offices of Physical, Occupational and Speech Therapists, and Audiologists

This industry comprises establishments of independent health practitioners primarily engaged in one of the following: (1) administering medically prescribed physical therapy treatment for patients suffering from injuries or muscle, nerve, joint, and bone disease; (2) planning and administering educational, recreational, and social activities designed to help patients or individuals with disabilities, regain physical or mental functioning or to adapt to their disabilities; and (3) diagnosing and treating speech, language, or hearing problems. These practitioners operate private or group practices in their own offices (e.g., centers, clinics) or in the facilities of others, such as hospitals or HMO medical centers.

Illustrative Examples:

Audiologists' offices	Recreational (e.g., art, dance, music)
Industrial therapists' offices	therapists' offices

62139 Offices of All Other Health Practitioners

This industry comprises establishments of independent health practitioners (except physicians; dentists; chiropractors; optometrists; mental health specialists; physical, occupational, and speech therapists; and audiologists). These practitioners operate private or group practices in their own offices (e.g., centers, clinics) or in the facilities of others, such as hospitals or HMO medical centers.

US—United States industry only. CAN—United States and Canadian industries are comparable. When neither US nor CAN appears, Canadian, Mexican, and United States industries are comparable.

Illustrative Examples:

Acupuncturists' (except MDs or DOs) offices	Inhalation or respiratory therapists' offices
Dental hygienists' offices	Midwives' offices
Denturists' offices	Naturopaths' offices
Dieticians' offices	Podiatrists' offices
Homeopaths' offices	Registered or licensed practical nurses' offices

Cross-References. Establishments primarily engaged in—

- The independent practice of medicine (i.e., physicians)—are classified in Industry 62111, Offices of Physicians;

- The independent practice of dentistry—are classified in Industry 62121, Offices of Dentists;

- The independent practice of chiropractic—are classified in Industry 62131, Offices of Chiropractors;

- The independent practice of optometry—are classified in Industry 62132, Offices of Optometrists;

- The independent practice of mental health (except physicians)—are classified in Industry 62133, Offices of Mental Health Practitioners (except Physicians); and

- The independent practice of physical, occupational, and speech therapy and audiology—are classified in Industry 62134, Offices of Physical, Occupational and Speech Therapists, and Audiologists.

621391 Offices of Podiatrists[US]

This U.S. industry comprises establishments of health practitioners having the degree of D.P. (Doctor of podiatry) primarily engaged in the independent practice of podiatry. These practitioners diagnose and treat diseases and deformities of the foot and operate private or group practices in their own offices (e.g., centers, clinics) or in the facilities of others, such as hospitals or HMO medical centers.

621399 Offices of All Other Miscellaneous Health Practitioners[US]

This U.S. industry comprises establishments of independent health practitioners (except physicians; dentists; chiropractors; optometrists; mental health specialists; physical, occupational, and speech therapists; audiologists; and podiatrists). These practitioners operate private or group practices in their own offices (e.g., centers, clinics) or in the facilities of others, such as hospitals or HMO medical centers.

Illustrative Examples:

Acupuncturists' (except MDs or DOs) offices	Hypnotherapists' offices
Dental hygienists' offices	Inhalation or respiratory therapists' offices
Denturists' offices	Midwives' offices
Dieticians' offices	Naturopaths' offices
Homeopaths' offices	Registered or licensed practical nurses' offices

---

US—United States industry only. CAN—United States and Canadian industries are comparable. When neither US nor CAN appears, Canadian, Mexican, and United States industries are comparable.

http://www.ntis.gov/naics

Cross-References. Establishments primarily engaged in—

- The independent practice of medicine (i.e., physicians)—are classified in Industry 62111, Offices of Physicians;

- The independent practice of dentistry—are classified in Industry 621210, Offices of Dentists;

- The independent practice of chiropractic—are classified in Industry 621310, Offices of Chiropractors;

- The independent practice of optometry—are classified in Industry 621320, Offices of Optometrists;

- The independent practice of mental health (except physicians)—are classified in Industry 621330, Offices of Mental Health Practitioners (except Physicians);

- The independent practice of physical, occupational, and speech therapy, and audiology— are classified in Industry 621340, Offices of Physical, Occupational and Speech Therapists, and Audiologists; and

- The independent practice of podiatry—are classified in U.S. Industry 621391, Offices of Podiatrists.

6214 Outpatient Care Centers

62141 Family Planning Centers
See industry description for 621410 below.

621410 Family Planning Centers

This industry comprises establishments with medical staff primarily engaged in providing a range of family planning services on an outpatient basis, such as contraceptive services, genetic and prenatal counseling, voluntary sterilization, and therapeutic and medically indicated termination of pregnancy.

Illustrative Examples:

Birth control clinics
Childbirth preparation classes

Fertility clinics
Pregnancy counseling centers

62142 Outpatient Mental Health and Substance Abuse Centers
See industry description for 621420 below.

621420 Outpatient Mental Health and Substance Abuse Centers

This industry comprises establishments with medical staff primarily engaged in providing outpatient services related to the diagnosis and treatment of mental health disorders and alcohol and other substance abuse. These establishments generally treat patients who do not require inpatient

---

US—United States industry only. CAN—United States and Canadian industries are comparable. When neither US nor CAN appears, Canadian, Mexican, and United States industries are comparable.

treatment. They may provide a counseling staff and information regarding a wide range of mental health and substance abuse issues and/or refer patients to more extensive treatment programs, if necessary.

Illustrative Examples:

Outpatient alcoholism treatment centers and clinics (except hospitals)
Outpatient detoxification centers and clinics (except hospitals)
Outpatient drug addiction treatment centers and clinics (except hospitals)

Outpatient mental health centers and clinics (except hospitals)
Outpatient substance abuse treatment centers and clinics (except hospitals)

Cross-References.

- Establishments known and licensed as hospitals primarily engaged in the inpatient treatment of mental health and substance abuse illnesses with an emphasis on medical treatment and monitoring are classified in Industry 622210, Psychiatric and Substance Abuse Hospitals; and

- Establishments primarily engaged in the inpatient treatment of mental health and substance abuse illness with an emphasis on residential care and counseling rather than medical treatment are classified in Industry 623220, Residential Mental Health and Substance Abuse Facilities.

62149 Other Outpatient Care Centers

This industry comprises establishments with medical staff primarily engaged in providing general or specialized outpatient care (except family planning centers and outpatient mental health and substance abuse centers). Centers or clinics of health practitioners with different degrees from more than one industry practicing within the same establishment (i.e., Doctor of medicine and Doctor of dental medicine) are included in this industry.

Illustrative Examples:

Freestanding ambulatory surgical centers and clinics
Freestanding emergency medical centers and clinics
Health maintenance organization (HMO) medical centers and clinics

Dialysis centers and clinics
Outpatient biofeedback centers and clinics
Outpatient community health centers and clinics
Outpatient sleep disorder centers and clinics

Cross-References.

- Physician walk-in centers are classified in Industry 62111, Offices of Physicians;

- Centers and clinics of health practitioners from the same industry primarily engaged in the independent practice of their profession are classified in Industry 62111, Offices of Physicians; Industry 62121, Offices of Dentists; and Industry Group 6213, Offices of Other Health Practitioners;

US—United States industry only. CAN—United States and Canadian industries are comparable. When neither US nor CAN appears, Canadian, Mexican, and United States industries are comparable.

- Family planning centers are classified in Industry 62141, Family Planning Centers;

- Outpatient mental health and substance abuse centers are classified in Industry 62142, Outpatient Mental Health and Substance Abuse Centers;

- HMO establishments (except those providing health care services) primarily engaged in underwriting health and medical insurance policies are classified in Industry 52411, Direct Life, Health, and Medical Insurance Carriers; and

- Establishments known and licensed as hospitals that also perform ambulatory surgery and emergency room services are classified in Subsector 622, Hospitals.

621491 HMO Medical Centers[US]

This U.S. industry comprises establishments with physicians and other medical staff primarily engaged in providing a range of outpatient medical services to the health maintenance organization (HMO) subscribers with a focus generally on primary health care. These establishments are owned by the HMO. Included in this industry are HMO establishments that both provide health care services and underwrite health and medical insurance policies.

Cross-References.

- Health practitioners or health practitioner groups contracting to provide their services to subscribers of prepaid health plans are classified in Industry 62111, Offices of Physicians; Industry 621210, Offices of Dentists; and Industry Group 6213, Offices of Other Health Practitioners; and

- HMO establishments (except those providing health care services) primarily engaged in underwriting and administering health and medical insurance policies are classified in U.S. Industry 524114, Direct Health and Medical Insurance Carriers.

621492 Kidney Dialysis Centers[US]

This U.S. industry comprises establishments with medical staff primarily engaged in providing outpatient kidney or renal dialysis services.

621493 Freestanding Ambulatory Surgical and Emergency Centers[US]

This U.S. industry comprises establishments with physicians and other medical staff primarily engaged in (1) providing surgical services (e.g., orthoscopic and cataract surgery) on an outpatient basis or (2) providing emergency care services (e.g., setting broken bones, treating lacerations, or tending to patients suffering injuries as a result of accidents, trauma, or medical conditions necessitating immediate medical care) on an outpatient basis. Outpatient surgical establishments have specialized facilities, such as operating and recovery rooms, and specialized equipment, such as anesthetic or X-ray equipment.

US—United States industry only. CAN—United States and Canadian industries are comparable. When neither US nor CAN appears, Canadian, Mexican, and United States industries are comparable.

Illustrative Examples:

Freestanding ambulatory surgical centers and clinics

Freestanding emergency medical centers and clinics

Freestanding trauma centers (except hospitals)

Urgent medical care centers and clinics (except hospitals)

Cross-References.

- Physician walk-in centers are classified in U.S. Industry 621111, Offices of Physicians (except Mental Health Specialists); and

- Establishments known and licensed as hospitals that also perform ambulatory surgery and emergency room services are classified in Subsector 622, Hospitals.

621498 All Other Outpatient Care Centers[US]

This U.S. industry comprises establishments with medical staff primarily engaged in providing general or specialized outpatient care (except family planning centers, outpatient mental health and substance abuse centers, HMO medical centers, kidney dialysis centers, and freestanding ambulatory surgical and emergency centers). Centers or clinics of health practitioners with different degrees from more than one industry practicing within the same establishment (i.e., Doctor of medicine and Doctor of dental medicine) are included in this industry.

Illustrative Examples:

Outpatient biofeedback centers and clinics

Outpatient community health centers and clinics

Outpatient pain therapy centers and clinics

Outpatient sleep disorder centers and clinics

Cross-References.

- Physician walk in centers are classified in U.S. Industry 621111, Offices of Physicians (except Mental Health Specialists);

- Centers and clinics of health practitioners from the same industry primarily engaged in the independent practice of their profession are classified in Industry 62111, Offices of Physicians; Industry 621210, Offices of Dentists; and Industry Group 6213, Offices of Other Health Practitioners;

- Family planning centers are classified in Industry 621410, Family Planning Centers;

- Outpatient mental health and substance abuse centers are classified in Industry 621420, Outpatient Mental Health and Substance Abuse Centers;

- HMO medical centers are classified in U.S. Industry 621491, HMO Medical Centers;

- Dialysis centers are classified in U.S. Industry 621492, Kidney Dialysis Centers; and

---

US—United States industry only. CAN—United States and Canadian industries are comparable. When neither US nor CAN appears, Canadian, Mexican, and United States industries are comparable.

- Freestanding ambulatory surgical and emergency centers are classified in U.S. Industry 621493, Freestanding Ambulatory Surgical and Emergency Centers.

6215 Medical and Diagnostic Laboratories

62151 Medical and Diagnostic Laboratories

This industry comprises establishments known as medical and diagnostic laboratories primarily engaged in providing analytic or diagnostic services, including body fluid analysis and diagnostic imaging, generally to the medical profession or to the patient on referral from a health practitioner.

Illustrative Examples:

Diagnostic imaging centers	Medical pathology laboratories
Dental or medical X-ray laboratories	Medical testing laboratories
Medical forensic laboratories	

Cross-References.

Establishments, such as dental, optical, and orthopedic laboratories, primarily engaged in providing the following activities to the medical profession, respectively: making dentures, artificial teeth, and orthodontic appliances to prescription; grinding of lenses to prescription; and making orthopedic or prosthetic appliances to prescription are classified in Industry 33911, Medical Equipment and Supplies Manufacturing.

621511 Medical Laboratories[US]

This U.S. industry comprises establishments known as medical laboratories primarily engaged in providing analytic or diagnostic services, including body fluid analysis, generally to the medical profession or to the patient on referral from a health practitioner.

Illustrative Examples:

Blood analysis laboratories	Medical pathology laboratories
Medical bacteriological laboratories	Medical testing laboratories
Medical forensic laboratories	

Cross-References.

- Establishments known as dental laboratories primarily engaged in making dentures, artificial teeth, and orthodontic appliances to prescription are classified in U.S. Industry 339116, Dental Laboratories;

- Establishments known as optical laboratories primarily engaged in grinding of lenses to prescription are classified in U.S. Industry 339115, Ophthalmic Goods Manufacturing; and

---

US—United States industry only. CAN—United States and Canadian industries are comparable. When neither US nor CAN appears, Canadian, Mexican, and United States industries are comparable.

- Establishments known as orthopedic laboratories primarily engaged in making orthopedic or prosthetic appliances to prescription are classified in U.S. Industry 339113, Surgical Appliance and Supplies Manufacturing.

621512 Diagnostic Imaging Centers[US]

This U.S. industry comprises establishments known as diagnostic imaging centers primarily engaged in producing images of the patient generally on referral from a health practitioner.

Illustrative Examples:

Computer tomography (CT-scan) centers
Dental or medical X-ray laboratories
Magnetic resonance imaging (MRI) centers

Medical radiological laboratories
Ultrasound imaging centers

6216 Home Health Care Services

62161 Home Health Care Services

See industry description for 621610 below.

621610 Home Health Care Services

This industry comprises establishments primarily engaged in providing skilled nursing services in the home, along with a range of the following: personal care services; homemaker and companion services; physical therapy; medical social services; medications; medical equipment and supplies; counseling; 24-hour home care; occupation and vocational therapy; dietary and nutritional services; speech therapy; audiology; and high-tech care, such as intravenous therapy.

Illustrative Examples:

Home health care agencies
In-home hospice care services

Visiting nurse associations

Cross-References.

- In-home health services provided by establishments of health practitioners and others primarily engaged in the independent practice of their profession are classified in Industry 62111, Offices of Physicians; Industry 621210, Offices of Dentists; and Industry Group 6213, Offices of Other Health Practitioners; and U.S. Industry 621999, All Other Miscellaneous Ambulatory Health Care Services; and

- Establishments primarily engaged in renting or leasing products for home health care are classified in U.S. Industry 532291, Home Health Equipment Rental.

6219 Other Ambulatory Health Care Services

This industry group comprises establishments primarily engaged in providing ambulatory health care services (except offices of physicians, dentists, and other health practitioners; outpatient care centers; medical laboratories and diagnostic imaging centers; and home health care providers).

US—United States industry only. CAN—United States and Canadian industries are comparable. When neither US nor CAN appears, Canadian, Mexican, and United States industries are comparable.

62191 Ambulance Services
See industry description for 621910 below.

621910 Ambulance Services

This industry comprises establishments primarily engaged in providing transportation of patients by ground or air, along with medical care. These services are often provided during a medical emergency but are not restricted to emergencies. The vehicles are equipped with lifesaving equipment operated by medically trained personnel.

Cross-References.

Establishments primarily engaged in providing transportation of the disabled or elderly (without medical care) are classified in U.S. Industry 485991, Special Needs Transportation.

62199 All Other Ambulatory Health Care Services

This industry comprises establishments primarily engaged in providing ambulatory health care services (except office physicians, dentists, and other health practitioners; outpatient care centers; medical and diagnostic laboratories; home health care providers; and ambulances).

Illustrative Examples:

Blood or body organ banks
Blood donor stations
Health screening services (except by health practitioner offices)
Hearing testing services (except by audiologist offices)

Pacemaker monitoring services
Physical fitness evaluation services (except by health practitioner offices)
Smoking cessation programs

Cross-References.

- Establishments primarily engaged in the independent practice of medicine are classified in Industry 62111, Offices of Physicians;

- Establishments primarily engaged in the independent practice of dentistry are classified in Industry 62121, Offices of Dentists;

- Establishments primarily engaged in the independent practice of health care (except offices of physicians and dentists) are classified in Industry Group 6213, Offices of Other Health Practitioners;

- Establishments primarily engaged in providing general or specialized outpatient care services are classified in Industry Group 6214, Outpatient Care Centers;

- Establishments primarily engaged in providing home health care services are classified in Industry 62161, Home Health Care Services;

US—United States industry only. CAN—United States and Canadian industries are comparable. When neither US nor CAN appears, Canadian, Mexican, and United States industries are comparable.

http://www.ntis.gov/naics

- Establishments primarily engaged in transportation of patients by ground or air, along with medical care are classified in Industry 62191, Ambulance Services; and

- Establishments known as medical and diagnostic laboratories primarily engaged in providing analytic or diagnostic services are classified in Industry 62151, Medical and Diagnostic Laboratories.

621991 Blood and Organ Banks[US]

This U.S. industry comprises establishments primarily engaged in collecting, storing, and distributing blood and blood products and storing and distributing body organs.

621999 All Other Miscellaneous Ambulatory Health Care Services[US]

This U.S. industry comprises establishments primarily engaged in providing ambulatory health care services (except offices of physicians, dentists, and other health practitioners; outpatient care centers; medical and diagnostic laboratories; home health care providers; ambulances; and blood and organ banks).

Illustrative Examples:

Health screening services (except by offices of health practitioners)

Hearing testing services (except by offices of audiologists)

Pacemaker monitoring services

Physical fitness evaluation services (except by offices of health practitioners)

Smoking cessation programs

Cross-References.

- Establishments primarily engaged in the independent practice of medicine are classified in Industry 62111, Offices of Physicians;

- Establishments primarily engaged in the independent practice of dentistry are classified in Industry 621210, Offices of Dentists;

- Establishments primarily engaged in the independent practice of health care (except offices of physicians and dentists) are classified in Industry Group 6213, Offices of Other Health Practitioners;

- Establishments primarily engaged in providing general or specialized outpatient care services are classified in Industry Group 6214, Outpatient Care Centers;

- Establishments primarily engaged in providing home health care services are classified in Industry 621610, Home Health Care Services;

- Establishments primarily engaged in the transportation of patients by ground or air, along with medical care are classified in Industry 621910, Ambulance Services;

- Establishments known as medical and diagnostic laboratories primarily engaged in providing analytic or diagnostic services are classified in Industry 62151, Medical and Diagnostic Laboratories; and

- Blood and organ banks are classified in U.S. Industry 621991, Blood and Organ Banks.

---

622 Hospitals

Industries in the Hospitals subsector provide medical, diagnostic, and treatment services that include physician, nursing, and other health services to inpatients and the specialized accommodation services required by inpatients. Hospitals may also provide outpatient services as a secondary activity. Establishments in the Hospitals subsector provide inpatient health services, many of which can only be provided using the specialized facilities and equipment that form a significant and integral part of the production process.

6221 General Medical and Surgical Hospitals

62211 General Medical and Surgical Hospitals
See industry description for 622110 below.

622110 General Medical and Surgical Hospitals

This industry comprises establishments known and licensed as general medical and surgical hospitals primarily engaged in providing diagnostic and medical treatment (both surgical and nonsurgical) to inpatients with any of a wide variety of medical conditions. These establishments maintain inpatient beds and provide patients with food services that meet their nutritional requirements. These hospitals have an organized staff of physicians and other medical staff to provide patient care services. These establishments usually provide other services, such as outpatient services, anatomical pathology services, diagnostic X-ray services, clinical laboratory services, operating room services for a variety of procedures, and pharmacy services.

6222 Psychiatric and Substance Abuse Hospitals

62221 Psychiatric and Substance Abuse Hospitals
See industry description for 622210 below.

622210 Psychiatric and Substance Abuse Hospitals

This industry comprises establishments known and licensed as psychiatric and substance abuse hospitals primarily engaged in providing diagnostic, medical treatment, and monitoring services for inpatients who suffer from mental illness or substance abuse disorders. The treatment often requires an extended stay in the hospital. These establishments maintain inpatient beds and provide patients with food services that meet their nutritional requirements. They have an organized staff of physicians and other medical staff to provide patient care services. Psychiatric, psychological, and social work services are available at the facility. These hospitals usually provide other services, such as outpatient services, clinical laboratory services, diagnostic X-ray services, and electroencephalograph services.

Cross-References.

- Establishments primarily engaged in providing treatment of mental health and substance abuse illnesses on an exclusively outpatient basis are classified in Industry 621420, Outpatient Mental Health and Substance Abuse Centers;

US—United States industry only. CAN—United States and Canadian industries are comparable. When neither US nor CAN appears, Canadian, Mexican, and United States industries are comparable.

- Establishments referred to as hospitals but are primarily engaged in providing inpatient treatment of mental health and substance abuse illness with the emphasis on counseling rather than medical treatment are classified in Industry 623220, Residential Mental Health and Substance Abuse Facilities; and

- Establishments referred to as hospitals but are primarily engaged in providing residential care for persons diagnosed with mental retardation are classified in Industry 623210, Residential Mental Retardation Facilities.

6223 Specialty (except Psychiatric and Substance Abuse) Hospitals

62231 Specialty (except Psychiatric and Substance Abuse) Hospitals
See industry description for 622310 below.

622310 Specialty (except Psychiatric and Substance Abuse) Hospitals

This industry consists of establishments known and licensed as specialty hospitals primarily engaged in providing diagnostic and medical treatment to inpatients with a specific type of disease or medical condition (except psychiatric or substance abuse). Hospitals providing long-term care for the chronically ill and hospitals providing rehabilitation, restorative, and adjustive services to physically challenged or disabled people are included in this industry. These establishments maintain inpatient beds and provide patients with food services that meet their nutritional requirements. They have an organized staff of physicians and other medical staff to provide patient care services. These hospitals may provide other services, such as outpatient services, diagnostic X-ray services, clinical laboratory services, operating room services, physical therapy services, educational and vocational services, and psychological and social work services.

Cross-References.

- Establishments known and licensed as hospitals primarily engaged in providing diagnostic and therapeutic inpatient services for a variety of medical conditions, both surgical and nonsurgical, are classified in Industry 622110, General Medical and Surgical Hospitals; and

- Establishments known and licensed as hospitals primarily engaged in providing diagnostic and treatment services for inpatients with psychiatric or substance abuse illnesses are classified in Industry 622210, Psychiatric and Substance Abuse Hospitals.

- Establishments referred to as hospitals but are primarily engaged in providing inpatient nursing and rehabilitative services to persons requiring convalescence are classified in Industry 623110, Nursing Care Facilities;

- Establishments referred to as hospitals but are primarily engaged in providing residential care of persons diagnosed with mental retardation are classified in Industry 623210, Residential Mental Retardation Facilities; and

- Establishments referred to as hospitals but are primarily engaged in providing inpatient treatment for mental health and substance abuse illnesses with the emphasis on counseling

http://www.ntis.gov/naics

rather than medical treatment are classified in Industry 623220, Residential Mental Health and Substance Abuse Facilities.

623 Nursing and Residential Care Facilities

Industries in the Nursing and Residential Care Facilities subsector provide residential care combined with either nursing, supervisory, or other types of care as required by the residents. In this subsector, the facilities are a significant part of the production process and the care provided is a mix of health and social services with the health services being largely some level of nursing services.

6231 Nursing Care Facilities

62311 Nursing Care Facilities
See industry description for 623110 below.

623110 Nursing Care Facilities

This industry comprises establishments primarily engaged in providing inpatient nursing and rehabilitative services. The care is generally provided for an extended period of time to individuals requiring nursing care. These establishments have a permanent core staff of registered or licensed practical nurses who, along with other staff, provide nursing and continuous personal care services.

Illustrative Examples:

Convalescent homes or convalescent hospitals (except psychiatric)
Homes for the elderly with nursing care

Inpatient care hospices
Nursing homes
Rest homes with nursing care

Cross-References.

- Assisted-living facilities with on-site nursing care facilities are classified in U.S. Industry 623311, Continuing Care Retirement Communities; and

- Psychiatric convalescent homes are classified in Industry 623220, Residential Mental Health and Substance Abuse Facilities.

6232 Residential Mental Retardation, Mental Health and Substance Abuse Facilities

This industry group comprises establishments primarily engaged in providing residential care (but not licensed hospital care) to people with mental retardation, mental illness, or substance abuse problems.

US—United States industry only. CAN—United States and Canadian industries are comparable. When neither US nor CAN appears, Canadian, Mexican, and United States industries are comparable.

62321 Residential Mental Retardation Facilities

See industry description for 623210 below.

623210 Residential Mental Retardation Facilities

This industry comprises establishments (e.g., group homes, hospitals, intermediate care facilities) primarily engaged in providing residential care services for persons diagnosed with mental retardation. These facilities may provide some health care, though the focus is room, board, protective supervision, and counseling.

Cross-References.

- Establishments primarily engaged in providing inpatient treatment of mental health and substance abuse illnesses with an emphasis on counseling rather than medical treatment are classified in Industry 623220, Residential Mental Health and Substance Abuse Facilities;

- Establishments primarily engaged in providing treatment of mental health and substance abuse illnesses on an exclusively outpatient basis are classified in Industry 621420, Outpatient Mental Health and Substance Abuse Centers; and

- Establishments known and licensed as hospitals primarily engaged in providing inpatient treatment of mental health and substance abuse illnesses with an emphasis on medical treatment and monitoring are classified in Industry 622210, Psychiatric and Substance Abuse Hospitals.

62322 Residential Mental Health and Substance Abuse Facilities

See industry description for 623220 below.

623220 Residential Mental Health and Substance Abuse Facilities

This industry comprises establishments primarily engaged in providing residential care and treatment for patients with mental health and substance abuse illnesses. These establishments provide room, board, supervision, and counseling services. Although medical services may be available at these establishments, they are incidental to the counseling, mental rehabilitation, and support services offered. These establishments generally provide a wide range of social services in addition to counseling.

Illustrative Examples:

Alcoholism or drug addiction rehabilitation
  facilities (except licensed hospitals)
Mental health halfway houses

Psychiatric convalescent homes or hospitals
Residential group homes for the emotionally
  disturbed

Cross-References.

- Establishments primarily engaged in providing treatment of mental health and substance abuse illnesses on an exclusively outpatient basis are classified in Industry 621420, Outpatient Mental Health and Substance Abuse Centers;

US—United States industry only. CAN—United States and Canadian industries are comparable. When neither US nor CAN appears, Canadian, Mexican, and United States industries are comparable.

- Establishments primarily engaged in providing residential care for persons diagnosed with mental retardation are classified in Industry 623210, Residential Mental Retardation Facilities; and

- Establishments known and licensed as hospitals primarily engaged in providing inpatient treatment of mental health and substance abuse illnesses with an emphasis on medical treatment and monitoring are classified in Industry 622210, Psychiatric and Substance Abuse Hospitals.

6233 Community Care Facilities for the Elderly

62331 Community Care Facilities for the Elderly

This industry comprises establishments primarily engaged in providing residential and personal care services for (1) the elderly and other persons who are unable to fully care for themselves and/ or (2) the elderly and other persons who do not desire to live independently. The care typically includes room, board, supervision, and assistance in daily living, such as housekeeping services. In some instances these establishments provide skilled nursing care for residents in separate on-site facilities.

Illustrative Examples:

Assisted-living facilities   Homes for the elderly without nursing care
Continuing care retirement communities   Rest homes without nursing care

Cross-References.

- Establishments primarily engaged in providing inpatient nursing and rehabilitative services are classified in Industry 62311, Nursing Care Facilities; and

- Apartment or condominium complexes where people live independently in rented housing units are classified in Industry 53111, Lessors of Residential Buildings and Dwellings.

623311 Continuing Care Retirement Communities[US]

This U.S. industry comprises establishments primarily engaged in providing a range of residential and personal care services with on-site nursing care facilities for (1) the elderly and other persons who are unable to fully care for themselves and/or (2) the elderly and other persons who do not desire to live independently. Individuals live in a variety of residential settings with meals, housekeeping, social, leisure, and other services available to assist residents in daily living. Assisted-living facilities with on-site nursing care facilities are included in this industry.

Cross-References.

- Establishments primarily engaged in providing inpatient nursing and rehabilitative services are classified in Industry 623110, Nursing Care Facilities;

US—United States industry only. CAN—United States and Canadian industries are comparable. When neither US nor CAN appears, Canadian, Mexican, and United States industries are comparable.

- Assisted-living facilities without on-site nursing care facilities are classified in U.S. Industry 623312, Homes for the Elderly; and

- Apartment or condominium complexes where people live independently in rented housing units are classified in Industry 531110, Lessors of Residential Buildings and Dwellings.

623312 Homes for the Elderly[US]

This U.S. industry comprises establishments primarily engaged in providing residential and personal care services (i.e., without on-site nursing care facilities) for (1) the elderly or other persons who are unable to fully care for themselves and/or (2) the elderly or other persons who do not desire to live independently. The care typically includes room, board, supervision, and assistance in daily living, such as housekeeping services.

Illustrative Examples:

Assisted-living facilities without on-site
  nursing care facilities

Homes for the elderly without nursing care
Rest homes without nursing care

Cross-References.

- Assisted-living facilities with on-site nursing care facilities are classified in U.S. Industry 623311, Continuing Care Retirement Communities;

- Homes for the elderly with nursing care or rest homes with nursing care are classified in Industry 623110, Nursing Care Facilities; and

- Apartment or condominium complexes where people live independently in rented or owned housing units are classified in Industry 53111, Lessors of Residential Buildings and Dwellings.

6239 Other Residential Care Facilities

This industry group comprises establishments of residential care facilities (except residential mental retardation, mental health, and substance abuse facilities and community care facilities for the elderly).

62399 Other Residential Care Facilities
See industry description for 623990 below.

623990 Other Residential Care Facilities

This industry comprises establishments primarily engaged in providing residential care (except residential mental retardation facilities, residential health and substance abuse facilities, continuing care retirement communities, and homes for the elderly). These establishments also provide supervision and personal care services.

US—United States industry only. CAN—United States and Canadian industries are comparable. When neither US nor CAN appears, Canadian, Mexican, and United States industries are comparable.

Illustrative Examples:

Boot or disciplinary camps (except
  correctional) for delinquent youth
Child group foster homes
Delinquent youth halfway group homes
Group homes for the hearing or visually
  impaired
Group homes for the disabled without nursing
  care

Halfway group homes for delinquents or
  ex-offenders
Homes for unwed mothers
Orphanages

Cross-References.

- Residential mental retardation facilities are classified in Industry 623210, Residential Mental Retardation Facilities;

- Continuing care retirement communities are classified in U.S. Industry 623311, Continuing Care Retirement Communities;

- Residential mental health and substance abuse facilities are classified in 623220, Residential Mental Health and Substance Abuse Facilities;

- Homes for the elderly without nursing care are classified in U.S. Industry 623312, Homes for the Elderly;

- Establishments primarily engaged in providing inpatient nursing and rehabilitative services are classified in Industry 623110, Nursing Care Facilities;

- Establishments primarily engaged in providing temporary shelter are classified in U.S. Industry 624221, Temporary Shelters; and

- Correctional camps are classified in Industry 922140, Correctional Institutions.

624 Social Assistance

Industries in the Social Assistance subsector provide a wide variety of social assistance services directly to their clients. These services do not include residential or accommodation services, except on a short stay basis.

6241 Individual and Family Services

62411 Child and Youth Services
See industry description for 624110 below.

624110 Child and Youth Services

This industry comprises establishments primarily engaged in providing nonresidential social assistance services for children and youth. These establishments provide for the welfare of children in such areas as adoption and foster care, drug prevention, life skills training, and positive social development.

US—United States industry only. CAN—United States and Canadian industries are comparable. When neither US nor CAN appears, Canadian, Mexican, and United States industries are comparable.

http://www.ntis.gov/naics

Illustrative Examples:

Adoption agencies
Child guidance organizations
Foster care placement services

Youth centers (except recreational only)
Youth self-help organizations

Cross-References.

- Youth recreational centers are classified in Industry 713940, Fitness and Recreational Sports Centers;

- Youth recreational sports teams and leagues are classified in Industry 713990, All Other Amusement and Recreation Industries;

- Scouting organizations are classified in Industry 813410, Civic and Social Organizations; and

- Establishments primarily engaged in providing day care services for children are classified in Industry 624410, Child Day Care Services.

62412 Services for the Elderly and Persons with Disabilities
See industry description for 624120 below.

624120 Services for the Elderly and Persons with Disabilities

This industry comprises establishments primarily engaged in providing nonresidential social assistance services to improve the quality of life for the elderly, persons diagnosed with mental retardation, or persons with disabilities. These establishments provide for the welfare of these of individuals in such areas as day care, nonmedical home care or homemaker services, social activities, group support, and companionship

Cross-References. Establishments primarily engaged in—

- Providing job training for persons diagnosed with mental retardation or persons with disabilities—are classified in Industry 624310, Vocational Rehabilitation Services;

- Providing residential care for the elderly, persons diagnosed with mental retardation, or persons with disabilities—are classified in Subsector 633, Nursing and Residential Care Facilities; and

- Providing in-home health care services—are classified in Subsector 621, Ambulatory Health Care Services.

62419 Other Individual and Family Services
See industry description for 624190 below.

624190 Other Individual and Family Services

This industry comprises establishments primarily engaged in providing nonresidential individual and family social assistance services (except those specifically directed toward children, the elderly, persons diagnosed with mental retardation, or persons with disabilities).

US—United States industry only. CAN—United States and Canadian industries are comparable. When neither US nor CAN appears, Canadian, Mexican, and United States industries are comparable.

Illustrative Examples:

Community action services agencies

Crisis intervention centers

Family social services agencies

Family welfare services

Hotline centers

Marriage counseling services (except by offices of mental health practitioners)

Multipurpose social services centers

Self-help organizations (except for disabled persons, the elderly, persons diagnosed with mental retardation)

Suicide crisis centers

Telephone counseling services

Cross-References. Establishments primarily engaged in—

- Providing clinical psychological and psychiatric social counseling services—are classified in Industry 621330, Offices of Mental Health Practitioners (except Physicians);

- Providing child and youth social assistance services (except day care)—are classified in Industry 624110, Child and Youth Services;

- Providing child day care services—are classified in Industry 624410, Child Day Care Services;

- Providing social assistance services for the elderly, persons diagnosed with mental retardation, and persons with disabilities—are classified in Industry 624120, Services for the Elderly and Persons with Disabilities;

- Community action advocacy—are classified in U.S. Industry 813319, Other Social Advocacy Organizations; and

- Providing in-home health care services—are classified in Subsector 621, Ambulatory Health Care Services.

6242 Community Food and Housing, and Emergency and Other Relief Services

62421 Community Food Services
See industry description for 624210 below.

624210 Community Food Services

This industry comprises establishments primarily engaged in the collection, preparation, and delivery of food for the needy. Establishments in this industry may also distribute clothing and blankets to the poor. These establishments may prepare and deliver meals to persons who by reason of age, disability, or illness are unable to prepare meals for themselves; collect and distribute salvageable or donated food; or prepare and provide meals at fixed or mobile locations. Food banks, meal delivery programs, and soup kitchens are included in this industry.

62422 Community Housing Services

This industry comprises establishments primarily engaged in providing one or more of the following community housing services: (1) short term emergency shelter for victims of domestic

---

US—United States industry only. CAN—United States and Canadian industries are comparable. When neither US nor CAN appears, Canadian, Mexican, and United States industries are comparable.

violence, sexual assault, or child abuse; (2) temporary residential shelter for the homeless, runaway youths, and patients and families caught in medical crises; (3) transitional housing for low-income individuals and families; (4) volunteer construction or repair of low cost housing, in partnership with the homeowner who may assist in construction or repair work; and (5) repair of homes for elderly or disabled homeowners. These establishments may operate their own shelter; or may subsidize housing using existing homes, apartments, hotels, or motels; or may require a low-cost mortgage or work (sweat) equity.

Cross-References.

Central offices of government housing programs are classified in Industry 92511, Administration of Housing Programs.

624221 Temporary Shelters[US]

This U.S. industry comprises establishments primarily engaged in providing (1) short term emergency shelter for victims of domestic violence, sexual assault, or child abuse and/or (2) temporary residential shelter for homeless individuals or families, runaway youth, and patients and families caught in medical crises. These establishments may operate their own shelters or may subsidize housing using existing homes, apartments, hotels, or motels.

Cross-References.

Establishments primarily engaged in providing emergency shelter for victims of domestic or international disasters or conflicts are classified in Industry 624230, Emergency and Other Relief Services.

624229 Other Community Housing Services[US]

This U.S. industry comprises establishments primarily engaged in providing one or more of the following community housing services: (1) transitional housing to low-income individuals and families; (2) volunteer construction or repair of low-cost housing, in partnership with the homeowner who may assist in the construction or repair work; and (3) the repair of homes for elderly or disabled homeowners. These establishments may subsidize housing using existing homes, apartments, hotels, or motels or may require a low-cost mortgage or sweat equity. These establishments may also provide low-income families with furniture and household supplies.

Cross-References.

Central offices of government housing programs are classified in Industry 925110, Administration of Housing Programs.

US—United States industry only. CAN—United States and Canadian industries are comparable. When neither US nor CAN appears, Canadian, Mexican, and United States industries are comparable.

http://www.ntis.gov/naics

62423 Emergency and Other Relief Services
See industry description for 624230 below.

624230 Emergency and Other Relief Services

This industry comprises establishments primarily engaged in providing food, shelter, clothing, medical relief, resettlement, and counseling to victims of domestic or international disasters or conflicts (e.g., wars).

6243 Vocational Rehabilitation Services

62431 Vocational Rehabilitation Services
See industry description for 624310 below.

624310 Vocational Rehabilitation Services

This industry comprises (1) establishments primarily engaged in providing vocational rehabilitation or habilitation services, such as job counseling, job training, and work experience, to unemployed and underemployed persons, persons with disabilities, and persons who have a job market disadvantage because of lack of education, job skill, or experience and (2) establishments primarily engaged in providing training and employment to persons with disabilities. Vocational rehabilitation job training facilities (except schools) and sheltered workshops (i.e., work experience centers) are included in this industry.

Cross-References.

- Schools (except high schools) primarily engaged in providing vocational training are classified in Industry 61151, Technical and Trade Schools;

- Vocational high schools are classified in Industry 611110, Elementary and Secondary Schools; and

- Establishments primarily engaged in providing career and vocational counseling (except rehabilitative) are classified in Industry 611710, Educational Support Services.

6244 Child Day Care Services

62441 Child Day Care Services
See industry description for 624410 below.

624410 Child Day Care Services

This industry comprises establishments primarily engaged in providing day care of infants or children. These establishments generally care for preschool children, but may care for older children when they are not in school and may also offer prekindergarten educational programs.

US—United States industry only. CAN—United States and Canadian industries are comparable. When neither US nor CAN appears, Canadian, Mexican, and United States industries are comparable.

Illustrative Examples:

Child day care babysitting services

Child or infant day care centers

Nursery schools

Preschool centers

Cross-References.

Establishments primarily engaged in offering kindergarten educational programs are classified in Industry 611110, Elementary and Secondary Schools.

Sector 71—Arts, Entertainment, and Recreation

The Sector as a Whole

The Arts, Entertainment, and Recreation sector includes a wide range of establishments that operate facilities or provide services to meet varied cultural, entertainment, and recreational interests of their patrons. This sector comprises (1) establishments that are involved in producing, promoting, or participating in live performances, events, or exhibits intended for public viewing; (2) establishments that preserve and exhibit objects and sites of historical, cultural, or educational interest; and (3) establishments that operate facilities or provide services that enable patrons to participate in recreational activities or pursue amusement, hobby, and leisure time interests.

Some establishments that provide cultural, entertainment, or recreational facilities and services are classified in other sectors. Excluded from this sector are: (1) establishments that provide both accommodations and recreational facilities, such as hunting and fishing camps and resort and casino hotels are classified in Subsector 721, Accommodation; (2) restaurants and night clubs that provide live entertainment in addition to the sale of food and beverages are classified in Subsector 722, Food Services and Drinking Places; (3) motion picture theaters, libraries and archives, and publishers of newspapers, magazines, books, periodicals, and computer software are classified in Sector 51, Information; and (4) establishments using transportation equipment to provide recreational and entertainment services, such as those operating sightseeing buses, dinner cruises, or helicopter rides are classified in Subsector 487, Scenic and Sightseeing Transportation.

711 Performing Arts, Spectator Sports, and Related Industries

Industries in the Performing Arts, Spectator Sports, and Related Industries subsector group establishments that produce or organize and promote live presentations involving the performances of actors and actresses, singers, dancers, musical groups and artists, athletes, and other entertainers, including independent (i.e., freelance) entertainers and the establishments that manage their careers. The classification recognizes four basic processes: (1) producing (i.e., presenting) events; (2) organizing, managing, and/or promoting events; (3) managing and representing entertainers; and (4) providing the artistic, creative and technical skills necessary to the production of these live events. Also, this subsector contains four industries for performing arts companies. Each is defined on the basis of the particular skills of the entertainers involved in the presentations.

The industry structure for this subsector makes a clear distinction between performing arts companies and performing artists (i.e., independent or freelance). Although not unique to arts and entertainment, freelancing is a particularly important phenomenon in this Performing Arts, Spectator Sports, and Related Industries subsector. Distinguishing this activity from the production activity is a meaningful process differentiation. This approach, however, is difficult to implement in the case of musical groups (i.e., companies) and artists, especially pop groups. These establishments tend to be more loosely organized and it can be difficult to distinguish companies from freelancers. For this reason, NAICS includes one industry that covers both musical groups and musical artists.

This subsector contains two industries for Industry Group 7113, Promoters of Performing Arts, Sports, and Similar Events, one for those that operate facilities and another for those that do not. This is because there are significant differences in cost structures between those promoters that manage and provide the staff to operate facilities and those that do not. In addition to promoters

US—United States industry only. CAN—United States and Canadian industries are comparable. When neither US nor CAN appears, Canadian, Mexican, and United States industries are comparable.

http://www.ntis.gov/naics

without facilities other industries in this subsector include establishments that may operate without permanent facilities. These types of establishments include: performing arts companies, musical groups and artists, spectator sports, and independent (i.e., freelance) artists, writers, and performers.

Excluded from this subsector are nightclubs. Some nightclubs promote live entertainment on a regular basis and it can be argued that they could be classified in Industry Group 7113, Promoters of Performing Arts, Sports, and Similar Events with Facilities. However, since most of these establishments function as any other drinking place when they do not promote entertainment and because most of their revenue is derived from sale of food and beverages, they are classified in Subsector 722, Food Services and Drinking Places.

7111 Performing Arts Companies

This industry group comprises establishments primarily engaged in producing live presentations involving the performances of actors and actresses, singers, dancers, musical groups and artists, and other performing artists.

71111 Theater Companies and Dinner Theaters
See industry description for 711110 below.

711110 Theater Companies and Dinner Theaters

This industry comprises (1) companies, groups, or theaters primarily engaged in producing the following live theatrical presentations: musicals; operas; plays; and comedy, improvisational, mime, and puppet shows and (2) establishments, commonly known as dinner theaters, engaged in producing live theatrical productions and in providing food and beverages for consumption on the premises. Theater groups or companies may or may not operate their own theater or other facility for staging their shows.

Illustrative Examples:

Comedy troupes	Musical theater companies
Live theatrical production (except dance) theaters	Opera companies
	Theatrical stock or repertory companies

Cross-References.

- Establishments, such as nightclubs, primarily engaged in providing food and beverages for consumption on the premises and that also present live nontheatrical entertainment, are classified in Subsector 722, Food Services and Drinking Places;

- Establishments primarily engaged in organizing, managing, and/or promoting performing arts productions without producing their own shows are classified in Industry Group 7113, Promoters of Performing Arts, Sports, and Similar Events;

- Companies, groups, or theaters primarily engaged in producing all types of live theatrical dance presentations are classified in Industry 711120, Dance Companies;

US—United States industry only. CAN—United States and Canadian industries are comparable. When neither US nor CAN appears, Canadian, Mexican, and United States industries are comparable.

http://www.ntis.gov/naics

- Freelance producers and performing artists (except musicians and vocalists) primarily engaged in theatrical activities independent of a company or group are classified in Industry 711510, Independent Artists, Writers, and Performers; and

- Musicians and vocalists are classified in Industry 711130, Musical Groups and Artists.

71112 Dance Companies
See industry description for 711120 below.

711120 Dance Companies

This industry comprises companies, groups, or theaters primarily engaged in producing all types of live theatrical dance (e.g., ballet, contemporary dance, folk dance) presentations. Dance companies or groups may or may not operate their own theater or other facility for staging their shows.

Cross-References.

- Establishments, such as exotic dance clubs, primarily engaged in providing food and beverages for consumption on the premises and that also present live dance entertainment, are classified in Subsector 722, Food Services and Drinking Places;

- Establishments primarily engaged in organizing, promoting, and/or managing dance productions without producing their own shows are classified in Industry Group 7113, Promoters of Performing Arts, Sports, and Similar Events; and

- Freelance producers and dancers primarily engaged in theatrical activities independent of a company or group are classified in Industry 711510, Independent Artists, Writers, and Performers.

71113 Musical Groups and Artists
See industry description for 711130 below.

711130 Musical Groups and Artists

This industry comprises (1) groups primarily engaged in producing live musical entertainment (except theatrical musical or opera productions) and (2) independent (i.e., freelance) artists primarily engaged in providing live musical entertainment. Musical groups and artists may perform in front of a live audience or in a studio, and may or may not operate their own facilities for staging their shows.

Illustrative Examples:

Bands

Drum and bugle corps (i.e., drill teams)

Independent musicians or vocalists

Musical groups (except theatrical musical groups)

Orchestras

US—United States industry only. CAN—United States and Canadian industries are comparable. When neither US nor CAN appears, Canadian, Mexican, and United States industries are comparable.

Cross-References.

- Establishments primarily engaged in organizing, promoting, and/or managing concerts and other musical performances without producing their own shows are classified in Industry Group 7113, Promoters of Performing Arts, Sports, and Similar Events;

- Companies, groups, or theaters primarily engaged in producing theatrical musicals and opera productions are classified in Industry 711110, Theater Companies and Dinner Theaters; and

- Freelance producers (except musical groups and artists) primarily engaged in musical activities independent of a company or group are classified in Industry 711510, Independent Artists, Writers, and Performers.

71119 Other Performing Arts Companies
See industry description for 711190 below.

711190 Other Performing Arts Companies

This industry comprises companies or groups (except theater companies, dance companies, musical groups, and artists) primarily engaged in producing live theatrical presentations.

Illustrative Examples:

Carnival traveling shows   Ice skating companies
Circuses   Magic shows

Cross-References.

- Establishments, such as comedy clubs or nightclubs, primarily engaged in providing food and beverages for consumption on the premises and that also present live nontheatrical entertainment are classified in Subsector 722, Food Services and Drinking Places;

- Establishments primarily engaged in organizing, promoting, and/or managing ice skating shows, circuses, and other live performing arts presentations without producing their own shows are classified in Industry Group 7113, Promoters of Performing Arts, Sports, and Similar Events;

- Theater companies and groups (except dance) or dinner theaters engaged in producing musicals; plays; operas; and comedy, improvisational, mime, and puppet shows are classified in Industry 711110, Theater Companies and Dinner Theaters;

- Dance companies or groups are classified in Industry 711120, Dance Companies;

- Freelance producers and performing artists (except musicians and vocalists) are classified in Industry 711510, Independent Artists, Writers, and Performers; and

US—United States industry only. CAN—United States and Canadian industries are comparable. When neither US nor CAN appears, Canadian, Mexican, and United States industries are comparable.

- Musical groups and independent musicians and vocalists are classified in Industry 711130, Musical Groups and Artists.

7112 Spectator Sports

71121 Spectator Sports

This industry comprises (1) sports teams or clubs primarily participating in live sporting events before a paying audience; (2) establishments primarily engaged in operating racetracks; (3) independent athletes engaged in participating in live sporting or racing events before a paying audience; (4) owners of racing participants, such as cars, dogs, and horses, primarily engaged in entering them in racing events or other spectator sports events; and (5) establishments, such as sports trainers, primarily engaged in providing specialized services to support participants in sports events or competitions. The sports teams and clubs included in this industry may or may not operate their own arena, stadium, or other facility for presenting their games or other spectator sports events.

Cross-References.

- Establishments primarily engaged in promoting sporting events without participating in sporting events are classified in Industry Group 7113, Promoters of Performing Arts, Sports, and Similar Events;

- Establishments, such as youth league baseball teams, primarily engaged in participating in sporting events for recreational purposes without playing before a paying audience are classified in Industry 71399, All Other Amusement and Recreation Industries;

- Amateur, semiprofessional, or professional athletic associations or leagues are classified in Industry 81399, Other Similar Organizations (except Business, Professional, Labor, and Political Organizations);

- Establishments primarily engaged in representing or managing the careers of sports figures are classified in Industry 71141, Agents and Managers for Artists, Athletes, Entertainers, and Other Public Figures;

- Independent athletes engaged in providing sports instruction without participating in sporting events before a paying audience are classified in Industry 61162, Sports and Recreation Instruction;

- Independent athletes exclusively engaged in endorsing products or making speeches are classified in Industry 71151, Independent Artists, Writers, and Performers; and

- Establishments primarily engaged in raising horses, mules, donkeys, and other equines are classified in Industry 112920, Horse and Other Equine Production.

711211 Sports Teams and Clubs[CAN]

This U.S. industry comprises professional or semiprofessional sports teams or clubs primarily engaged in participating in live sporting events, such as baseball, basketball, football, hockey,

---

US—United States industry only. CAN—United States and Canadian industries are comparable. When neither US nor CAN appears, Canadian, Mexican, and United States industries are comparable.

soccer, and jai alai games, before a paying audience. These establishments may or may not operate their own arena, stadium, or other facility for presenting these events.

Cross-References.

- Establishments primarily engaged in promoting sporting events without participating in sporting events are classified in Industry Group 7113, Promoters of Performing Arts, Sports, and Similar Events;

- Establishments, such as youth league baseball teams, primarily engaged in participating in sporting events for recreational purposes without playing before a paying audience are classified in Industry 713990, All Other Amusement and Recreation Industries; and

- Amateur, semiprofessional, or professional athletic associations or leagues are classified in Industry 813990, Other Similar Organizations (except Business, Professional, Labor, and Political Organizations).

711212 Racetracks[US]

This U.S. industry comprises establishments primarily engaged in operating racetracks. These establishments may also present and /or promote the events, such as auto, dog, and horse races, held in these facilities.

Cross-References.

Owners of racing participants, such as cars, dogs, and horses, primarily engaged in entering them in racing events; trainers of racing participants; and independent athletes, such as jockeys and race car drivers, primarily engaged in participating in racing events are classified in U.S. Industry 711219, Other Spectator Sports.

711219 Other Spectator Sports[US]

This U.S. industry comprises (1) independent athletes, such as professional or semiprofessional golfers, boxers, and race car drivers, primarily engaged in participating in live sporting or racing events before a paying audience; (2) owners of racing participants, such as cars, dogs, and horses, primarily engaged in entering them in racing events or other spectator sports events; and (3) establishments, such as sports trainers, primarily engaged in providing specialized services required to support participants in sports events or competitions.

Cross-References.

- Establishments primarily engaged in operating racetracks are classified in U.S. Industry 711212, Racetracks;

- Establishments primarily engaged in representing or managing the careers of sports figures are classified in Industry 711410, Agents and Managers for Artists, Athletes, Entertainers, and Other Public Figures;

US—United States industry only. CAN—United States and Canadian industries are comparable. When neither US nor CAN appears, Canadian, Mexican, and United States industries are comparable.

- Independent athletes engaged in providing sports instruction without participating in sporting events before a paying audience are classified in Industry 611620, Sports and Recreation Instruction;

- Independent athletes exclusively engaged in endorsing products or making speeches are classified in Industry 711510, Independent Artists, Writers, and Performers; and

- Establishments primarily engaged in raising horses, mules, donkeys, and other equines are classified in Industry 112920, Horse and Other Equine Production.

7113 Promoters of Performing Arts, Sports, and Similar Events

71131 Promoters of Performing Arts, Sports, and Similar Events with Facilities
See industry description for 711310 below.

711310 Promoters of Performing Arts, Sports, and Similar Events with Facilities

This industry comprises establishments primarily engaged in (1) organizing, promoting, and/or managing live performing arts productions, sports events, and similar events, such as State fairs, county fairs, agricultural fairs, concerts, and festivals, held in facilities that they manage and operate and/or (2) managing and providing the staff to operate arenas, stadiums, theaters, or other related facilities for rent to other promoters.

Cross-References. Establishments primarily engaged in—

- Producing live performances and that may also promote the performances and/or operate the facilities where the performances take place—are classified in Industry Group 7111, Performing Arts Companies;

- Operating racetracks and that may also promote the events held in these facilities—are classified in U.S. Industry 711212, Race Tracks;

- Presenting sporting events and that may also promote these sporting events and/or operate the stadiums or arenas where the sporting events take place—are classified in U.S. Industry 711211, Sports Teams and Clubs;

- Organizing, promoting, and/or managing conventions, conferences, and trade shows and that may also operate the facilities where these events take place—are classified in Industry 561920, Convention and Trade Show Organizers;

- Organizing, promoting, and/or managing performing arts productions, sports events, and similar events in facilities managed and operated by others—are classified in Industry 711320 Promoters of Performing Arts, Sports, and Similar Events without Facilities; and

- Leasing stadiums, arenas, theaters, and other related facilities to others without operating the facilities—are classified in Industry 531120, Lessors of Nonresidential Buildings (except Miniwarehouses).

US—United States industry only. CAN—United States and Canadian industries are comparable. When neither US nor CAN appears, Canadian, Mexican, and United States industries are comparable.

http://www.ntis.gov/naics

71132 Promoters of Performing Arts, Sports, and Similar Events without Facilities

See industry description for 711320 below.

711320 Promoters of Performing Arts, Sports, and Similar Events without Facilities

This industry comprises promoters primarily engaged in organizing, promoting, and/or managing live performing arts productions, sports events, and similar events, such as state fairs, county fairs, agricultural fairs, concerts, and festivals, in facilities that are managed and operated by others. Theatrical (except motion picture) booking agencies are included in this industry.

Cross-References. Establishments primarily engaged in—

- Booking motion pictures or videos—are classified in U.S. Industry 512199, Other Motion Picture and Video Industries;

- Producing live performances and that may also promote the performances—are classified in Industry Group 7111, Performing Arts Companies;

- Operating racetracks and that may also promote the events held in these facilities—are classified in U.S. Industry 711212, Racetracks;

- Presenting sporting events and that may also promote these events—are classified in U.S. Industry 711211, Sports Teams and Clubs;

- Organizing, promoting, and/or managing conventions, conferences, and trade shows and that may also operate the facilities where these events take place—are classified in Industry 561920, Convention and Trade Show Organizers;

- Organizing, promoting, and/or managing performing arts, sports, and similar events in facilities they manage or operate—are classified in Industry 711310, Promoters of Performing Arts, Sports, and Similar Events with Facilities; and

- Operating amateur, semiprofessional, or professional athletic associations or leagues—are classified in Industry 813990, Other Similar Organizations (except Business, Professional, Labor, and Political Organizations).

7114 Agents and Managers for Artists, Athletes, Entertainers, and Other Public Figures

71141 Agents and Managers for Artists, Athletes, Entertainers, and Other Public Figures

See industry description for 711410 below.

711410 Agents and Managers for Artists, Athletes, Entertainers, and Other Public Figures

This industry comprises establishments of agents and managers primarily engaged in representing and/or managing creative and performing artists, sports figures, entertainers, and other public

US—United States industry only. CAN—United States and Canadian industries are comparable. When neither US nor CAN appears, Canadian, Mexican, and United States industries are comparable.

http://www.ntis.gov/naics

figures. The representation and management includes activities, such as representing clients in contract negotiations; managing or organizing client's financial affairs; and generally promoting the careers of their clients.

Illustrative Examples:

Celebrity agents or managers
Literary agents
Modeling agents

Sports figure agents or managers
Talent agents

Cross-References.

- Establishments primarily engaged in supplying models to clients are classified in Industry 561320, Temporary Help Services; and

- Establishments known as model registries primarily engaged in recruiting and placing models for clients are classified in Industry 561310, Employment Placement Agencies.

7115 Independent Artists, Writers, and Performers

71151 Independent Artists, Writers, and Performers
See industry description for 711510 below.

711510 Independent Artists, Writers, and Performers

This industry comprises independent (i.e., freelance) individuals primarily engaged in performing in artistic productions, in creating artistic and cultural works or productions, or in providing technical expertise necessary for these productions. This industry also includes athletes and other celebrities exclusively engaged in endorsing products and making speeches or public appearances for which they receive a fee.

Illustrative Examples:

Independent actors or actresses
Independent art restorers
Independent artists (except musical, commercial, or medical)
Independent cartoonists
Independent dancers

Independent journalists
Independent producers
Independent recording technicians
Independent speakers
Independent theatrical costume designers
Independent theatrical lighting technicians

Cross-References.

- Freelance musicians and vocalists are classified in Industry 711130, Musical Groups and Artists;

- Independent commercial artists and graphic designers are classified in Industry 541430, Graphic Design Services; and

- Artisans and craftspersons are classified in the Sector 31-33, Manufacturing.

US—United States industry only. CAN—United States and Canadian industries are comparable. When neither US nor CAN appears, Canadian, Mexican, and United States industries are comparable.

http://www.ntis.gov/naics

712 Museums, Historical Sites, and Similar Institutions

Industries in the Museums, Historical Sites, and Similar Institutions subsector engage in the preservation and exhibition of objects, sites, and natural wonders of historical, cultural, and/or educational value.

7121 Museums, Historical Sites, and Similar Institutions

71211 Museums
See industry description for 712110 below.

712110 Museums

This industry comprises establishments primarily engaged in the preservation and exhibition of objects of historical, cultural, and/or educational value.

Illustrative Examples:

Art galleries (except retail) or museums   Science or technology museums
Halls of fame   Wax museums
Planetariums

Cross-References.

Commercial art galleries primarily engaged in selling art objects are classified in Industry 453920, Art Dealers.

71212 Historical Sites
See industry description for 712120 below.

712120 Historical Sites

This industry comprises establishments primarily engaged in the preservation and exhibition of sites, buildings, forts, or communities that describe events or persons of particular historical interest. Archeological sites, battlefields, historical ships, and pioneer villages are included in this industry.

71213 Zoos and Botanical Gardens
See industry description for 712130 below.

712130 Zoos and Botanical Gardens

This industry comprises establishments primarily engaged in the preservation and exhibition of live plant and animal life displays.

Illustrative Examples:

Aquariums   Wild animal parks
Arboreta   Zoological gardens
Aviaries

71219 Nature Parks and Other Similar Institutions
See industry description for 712190 below.

712190 Nature Parks and Other Similar Institutions

This industry comprises establishments primarily engaged in the preservation and exhibition of natural areas or settings.

Illustrative Examples:

Bird or wildlife sanctuaries   Nature centers or preserves
Conservation areas   National parks
Natural wonder (e.g., cavern, waterfall) tourist
   attractions

Cross-References.

Establishments primarily engaged in operating commercial hunting or fishing preserves (e.g., game farms) are classified in Industry 114210, Hunting and Trapping.

713 Amusement, Gambling, and Recreation Industries

Industries in the Amusement, Gambling, and Recreation Industries subsector (1) operate facilities where patrons can primarily engage in sports, recreation, amusement, or gambling activities and/or (2) provide other amusement and recreation services, such as supplying and servicing amusement devices in places of business operated by others; operating sports teams, clubs, or leagues engaged in playing games for recreational purposes; and guiding tours without using transportation equipment.

This subsector does not cover all establishments providing recreational services. Other sectors of NAICS also provide recreational services. Providers of recreational services are often engaged in processes classified in other sectors of NAICS. For example, operators of resorts and hunting and fishing camps provide both accommodation and recreational facilities and services. These establishments are classified in Subsector 721, Accommodation, partly to reflect the significant costs associated with the provision of accommodation services and partly to ensure consistency with international standards. Likewise, establishments using transportation equipment to provide recreational and entertainment services, such as those operating sightseeing buses, dinner cruises, or helicopter rides, are classified in Subsector 48-49, Transportation and Warehousing.

The industry groups in this subsector highlight particular types of activities: amusement parks and arcades, gambling industries, and other amusement and recreation industries. The groups, however, are not all inclusive of the activity. The Gambling Industries industry group does not provide for full coverage of gambling activities. For example, casino hotels are classified in

Subsector 721, Accommodation; and horse and dog racing tracks are classified in Industry Group 7112, Spectator Sports.

7131 Amusement Parks and Arcades

This industry group comprises establishments primarily engaged in operating amusement parks and amusement arcades and parlors.

71311 Amusement and Theme Parks
See industry description for 713110 below.

713110 Amusement and Theme Parks

This industry comprises establishments, known as amusement or theme parks, primarily engaged in operating a variety of attractions, such as mechanical rides, water rides, games, shows, theme exhibits, refreshment stands, and picnic grounds. These establishments may lease space to others on a concession basis.

Cross-References. Establishments primarily engaged in—

- Operating mechanical or water rides on a concession basis in amusement parks, fairs, and carnivals or in operating a single attraction, such as a waterslide,—are classified in Industry 713990, All Other Amusement and Recreation Industries;

- Operating refreshment stands on a concession basis—are classified in Industry Group 7222, Limited-Service Eating Places;

- Supplying and servicing coin-operated amusement (except gambling) devices in other's facilities—are classified in Industry 713990, All Other Amusement and Recreation Industries;

- Supplying and servicing coin-operated gambling devices (e.g., slot machines) in places of business operated by others—are classified in Industry 713290, Other Gambling Industries; and

- Organizing, promoting, and/or managing events, such as carnivals and fairs, with or without facilities—are classified in Industry Group 7113, Promoters of Performing Arts, Sports, and Similar Events.

71312 Amusement Arcades
See industry description for 713120 below.

713120 Amusement Arcades

This industry comprises establishments primarily engaged in operating amusement (except gambling, billiard, or pool) arcades and parlors.

US—United States industry only. CAN—United States and Canadian industries are comparable. When neither US nor CAN appears, Canadian, Mexican, and United States industries are comparable.

Cross-References. Establishments primarily engaged in—

- Supplying and servicing coin-operated amusement (except gambling) devices in places of business operated by others or in operating billiard or pool parlors—are classified in Industry 713990, All Other Amusement and Recreation Industries;

- Operating bingo, off-track betting, or slot machine parlors or in supplying and servicing coin-operated gambling devices (e.g., slot machines or video gambling terminals) in places of business operated by others—are classified in Industry 713290, Other Gambling Industries;

- Operating casinos (except casino hotels)—are classified in Industry 713210, Casinos (except Casino Hotels); and

- Operating casino hotels—are classified in Industry 721120, Casino Hotels.

7132 Gambling Industries

This industry group comprises establishments (except casino hotels) primarily engaged in operating gambling facilities, such as casinos, bingo halls, and video gaming terminals, or in the provision of gambling services, such as lotteries and off-track betting. Casino hotels are classified in Industry 72112.

71321 Casinos (except Casino Hotels)
See industry description for 713210 below.

713210 Casinos (except Casino Hotels)

This industry comprises establishments primarily engaged in operating gambling facilities that offer table wagering games along with other gambling activities, such as slot machines and sports betting. These establishments often provide food and beverage services. Included in this industry are floating casinos (i.e., gambling cruises, riverboat casinos).

Cross-References. Establishments primarily engaged in—

- Operating bingo, off-track betting, or slot machine parlors or in supplying and servicing coin-operated gambling devices, such as slot machines and video gaming terminals in places of business operated by others, are classified in Industry 713290, Other Gambling Industries; and

- Operating casino hotels—are classified in Industry 721120, Casino Hotels.

71329 Other Gambling Industries
See industry description for 713290 below.

713290 Other Gambling Industries

This industry comprises establishments primarily engaged in operating gambling facilities (except casinos or casino hotels) or providing gambling services.

US—United States industry only. CAN—United States and Canadian industries are comparable. When neither US nor CAN appears, Canadian, Mexican, and United States industries are comparable.

Illustrative Examples:

Bingo, off-track betting, or slot machine parlors
Bookmakers
Card rooms (e.g., poker rooms)

Coin-operated gambling device concession operators (i.e., supplying and servicing in other's facilities)
Lottery ticket sales agents (except retail stores)

Cross-References. Establishments primarily engaged in—

- Operating casinos—are classified in Industry 713210, Casinos (except Casino Hotels);

- Operating casino hotels—are classified in Industry 721120, Casino Hotels;

- Operating facilities with coin-operated nongambling amusement devices—are classified in Industry 713120, Amusement Arcades;

- Supplying and servicing coin-operated nongambling amusement devices in places of business operated by others—are classified in Industry 713990, All Other Amusement and Recreation Industries; and

- Operating racetracks or presenting live racing or sporting events—are classified in Industry 71121, Spectator Sports.

7139 Other Amusement and Recreation Industries

71391 Golf Courses and Country Clubs
See industry description for 713910 below.

713910 Golf Courses and Country Clubs

This industry comprises (1) establishments primarily engaged in operating golf courses (except miniature) and (2) establishments primarily engaged in operating golf courses, along with dining facilities and other recreational facilities that are known as country clubs. These establishments often provide food and beverage services, equipment rental services, and golf instruction services.

Cross-References. Establishments primarily engaged in—

- Operating driving ranges and miniature golf courses—are classified in Industry 713990, All Other Amusement and Recreation Industries; and

- Operating resorts where golf facilities are combined with accommodations—are classified in Industry Group 7211, Traveler Accommodation.

71392 Skiing Facilities
See industry description for 713920 below.

713920 Skiing Facilities

This industry comprises establishments engaged in (1) operating downhill, cross-country, or related skiing areas and/or (2) operating equipment, such as ski lifts and tows. These establishments

---

US—United States industry only. CAN—United States and Canadian industries are comparable. When neither US nor CAN appears, Canadian, Mexican, and United States industries are comparable.

http://www.ntis.gov/naics

often provide food and beverage services, equipment rental services, and ski instruction services. Four season resorts without accommodations are included in this industry.

Cross-References.

Establishments primarily engaged in operating resorts where skiing facilities are combined with accommodations are classified in Industry Group 7211, Traveler Accommodation.

71393 Marinas
See industry description for 713930 below.

713930 Marinas

This industry comprises establishments, commonly known as marinas, engaged in operating docking and/or storage facilities for pleasure craft owners, with or without one or more related activities, such as retailing fuel and marine supplies; and repairing, maintaining, or renting pleasure boats.

Cross-References. Establishments primarily engaged in—

- Renting pleasure boats—are classified in U.S. Industry 532292, Recreational Goods Rental;

- Repairing pleasure boats—are classified in Industry 811490, Other Personal and Household Goods Repair and Maintenance;

- Retailing marine supplies—are classified in U.S. Industry 441222, Boat Dealers; and

- Retailing fuel for boats—are classified in Industry 447190, Other Gasoline Stations.

71394 Fitness and Recreational Sports Centers
See industry description for 713940 below.

713940 Fitness and Recreational Sports Centers

This industry comprises establishments primarily engaged in operating fitness and recreational sports facilities featuring exercise and other active physical fitness conditioning or recreational sports activities, such as swimming, skating, or racquet sports.

Illustrative Examples:

Aerobic dance or exercise centers	Ice or roller skating rinks
Gymnasiums	Physical fitness
Handball, racquetball, or tennis club facilities	Swimming or wave pools

Cross-References.

- Establishments primarily engaged in providing nonmedical services to assist clients in attaining or maintaining a desired weight are classified in U.S. Industry 812191, Diet and Weight Reducing Centers;

US—United States industry only. CAN—United States and Canadian industries are comparable. When neither US nor CAN appears, Canadian, Mexican, and United States industries are comparable.

- Establishments primarily engaged in operating health resorts and spas where recreational facilities are combined with accommodations are classified in Industry 721110, Hotels (except Casino Hotels) and Motels; and

- Recreational sports clubs (i.e., sports teams) not operating sports facilities are classified in Industry 713990, All Other Amusement and Recreation Industries.

71395 Bowling Centers

See industry description for 713950 below.

713950 Bowling Centers

This industry comprises establishments engaged in operating bowling centers. These establishments often provide food and beverage services.

71399 All Other Amusement and Recreation Industries

See industry description for 713990 below.

713990 All Other Amusement and Recreation Industries

This industry comprises establishments (except amusement parks and arcades; gambling industries; golf courses and country clubs; skiing facilities; marinas; fitness and recreational sports centers; and bowling centers) primarily engaged in providing recreational and amusement services.

Illustrative Examples:

Amusement ride or coin-operated nongambling amusement device concession operators (i.e., supplying or servicing in others facilities)	Dance halls
	Miniature golf courses
	Recreational day camps (except instructional)
	Recreational or youth sports teams and leagues
Archery or shooting ranges	Recreational sports clubs (i.e., sports teams) not
Billiard or pool parlors	operating facilities
Boating clubs (without marinas)	Riding stables

Cross-References.

- Establishments primarily engaged in operating amusement parks and arcades are classified in Industry Group 7131, Amusement Parks and Arcades;

- Establishments primarily engaged in operating gambling facilities (except casino hotels) or providing gambling services are classified in Industry Group 7132, Gambling Industries;

- Establishments primarily engaged in operating casino hotels are classified in Industry 721120, Casino Hotels;

- Establishments primarily engaged in operating golf courses (except miniature) and country clubs are classified in Industry 713910, Golf Courses and Country Clubs;

US—United States industry only. CAN—United States and Canadian industries are comparable. When neither US nor CAN appears, Canadian, Mexican, and United States industries are comparable.

- Establishments primarily engaged in operating skiing facilities without hotel accommodation are classified in Industry 713920, Skiing Facilities;

- Establishments primarily engaged in operating resorts where recreational facilities are combined with lodging are classified in Industry Group 7211, Traveler Accommodation;

- Establishments primarily engaged in operating marinas are classified in Industry 713930, Marinas;

- Establishments primarily engaged in operating fitness and recreational sports centers are classified in Industry 713940, Fitness and Recreational Sports Centers;

- Establishments primarily engaged in operating bowling centers are classified in Industry 713950, Bowling Centers;

- Establishments primarily engaged in operating instructional camps, such as sports camps, fine arts camps, and computer camps, are classified in Sector 61, Educational Services, based on the nature of instruction;

- Independent athletes engaged in participating in sporting events before a paying audience are classified in U.S. Industry 711219, Other Spectator Sports;

- Independent athletes engaged in providing sports instruction without participating in sporting events before a paying audience are classified in Industry 611620, Sports and Recreation Instruction;

- Independent athletes exclusively engaged in endorsing products or making speeches are classified in Industry 71151, Independent Artists, Writers, and Performers;

- Establishments primarily engaged in providing scenic and sightseeing transportation are classified in Subsector 487, Scenic and Sightseeing Transportation;

- Aviation clubs primarily engaged in providing specialty air and flying services are classified in U.S. Industry 481219, Other Nonscheduled Air Transportation;

- Aviation clubs primarily engaged in advocating social and political causes are classified in U.S. Industry 813319, Other Social Advocacy Organizations; and

- Amateur, semiprofessional, or professional athletic associations or leagues are classified in Industry 813990, Other Similar Organizations (except Business, Professional, Labor, and Political Organizations).

US—United States industry only. CAN—United States and Canadian industries are comparable. When neither US nor CAN appears, Canadian, Mexican, and United States industries are comparable.

http://www.ntis.gov/naics

Sector 72—Accommodation and Food Services

The Sector as a Whole

The Accommodation and Food Services sector comprises establishments providing customers with lodging and/or preparing meals, snacks, and beverages for immediate consumption. The sector includes both accommodation and food services establishments because the two activities are often combined at the same establishment.

Excluded from this sector are civic and social organizations; amusement and recreation parks; theaters; and other recreation or entertainment facilities providing food and beverage services.

721 Accommodation

Industries in the Accommodation subsector provide lodging or short-term accommodations for travelers, vacationers, and others. There is a wide range of establishments in these industries. Some provide lodging only; while others provide meals, laundry, and recreational facilities, as well as lodging. Lodging establishments are classified in this subsector even if the provision of complementary services generates more revenue. The type of complementary services provided vary from establishment to establishment.

The subsector is organized into three industry groups: (1) traveler accommodation, (2) recreational accommodation, and (3) rooming and boarding houses. The Traveler Accommodation industry group includes establishments that primarily provide traditional types of lodging services. This group includes hotels, motels, and bed and breakfast inns. In addition to lodging, these establishments may provide a range of other services to their guests. The RV (Recreational Vehicle) Parks and Recreational Camps industry group includes establishments that operate lodging facilities primarily designed to accommodate outdoor enthusiasts. Included are travel trailer campsites, recreation vehicle parks, and outdoor adventure retreats. The Rooming and Boarding Houses industry group includes establishments providing temporary or longer-term accommodations that for the period of occupancy may serve as a principal residence. Board (i.e., meals) may be provided but is not essential.

Establishments that manage short-stay accommodation establishments (e.g., hotels and motels) on a contractual basis are classified in this subsector if they both manage the operation and provide the operating staff. Such establishments are classified based on the type of facility managed and operated.

7211 Traveler Accommodation

72111 Hotels (except Casino Hotels) and Motels
See industry description for 721110 below.

721110 Hotels (except Casino Hotels) and Motels

This industry comprises establishments primarily engaged in providing short-term lodging in facilities known as hotels, motor hotels, resort hotels, and motels. The establishments in this industry

---

US—United States industry only. CAN—United States and Canadian industries are comparable. When neither US nor CAN appears, Canadian, Mexican, and United States industries are comparable.

http://www.ntis.gov/naics

may offer services, such as food and beverage services, recreational services, conference rooms and convention services, laundry services, parking, and other services.

Cross-References. Establishments primarily engaged in—

- Providing short-term lodging with a casino on the premises—are classified in Industry 721120, Casino Hotels; and

- Providing short-term lodging in facilities known as bed-and-breakfast inns, youth hostels, housekeeping cabins and cottages, and tourist homes—are classified in Industry 72119, Other Traveler Accommodation.

72112 Casino Hotels
See industry description for 721120 below.

721120 Casino Hotels

This industry comprises establishments primarily engaged in providing short-term lodging in hotel facilities with a casino on the premises. The casino on premises includes table wagering games and may include other gambling activities, such as slot machines and sports betting. These establishments generally offer a range of services and amenities, such as food and beverage services, entertainment, valet parking, swimming pools, and conference and convention facilities.

Cross-References. Establishments primarily engaged in—

- Providing short-term lodging in facilities known as hotels and motels that provide limited gambling activities, such as slot machines, without a casino on the premises—are classified in Industry 721110, Hotels (except Casino Hotels) and Motels; and

- Operating as stand-alone casinos—are classified in Industry 713210, Casinos (except Casino Hotels).

72119 Other Traveler Accommodation

This industry comprises establishments primarily engaged in providing short-term lodging (except hotels, motels, and casino hotels).

Illustrative Examples:

Bed-and-breakfast inns	Tourist homes
Guest houses	Youth hostels
Housekeeping cabins and cottages	

Cross-References. Establishments primarily engaged in—

- Providing short-term lodging in facilities known as hotels without a casino on the premises— are classified in Industry 72111, Hotels (except Casino Hotels) and Motels; and

---

US—United States industry only. CAN—United States and Canadian industries are comparable. When neither US nor CAN appears, Canadian, Mexican, and United States industries are comparable.

- Providing short-term lodging in facilities known as hotels with a casino on the premises—are classified in Industry 72112, Casino Hotels.

721191 Bed-and-Breakfast Inns[CAN]

This U.S. industry comprises establishments primarily engaged in providing short-term lodging in facilities known as bed-and-breakfast inns. These establishments provide short-term lodging in private homes or small buildings converted for this purpose. Bed-and-breakfast inns are characterized by a highly personalized service and inclusion of a full breakfast in a room rate.

721199 All Other Traveler Accommodation[US]

This U.S. industry comprises establishments primarily engaged in providing short-term lodging (except hotels, motels, casino hotels, and bed-and-breakfast inns).

Illustrative Examples:

Guest houses	Tourist homes
Housekeeping cabins and cottages	Youth hostels

Cross-References. Establishments primarily engaged in—

- Providing short-term lodging in facilities known as hotels without a casino on the premises—are classified in Industry 721110, Hotels (except Casino Hotels) and Motels;

- Providing short-term lodging in facilities known as hotels with a casino on the premises—are classified in Industry 721120, Casino Hotels; and

- Providing short-term lodging in establishments known as bed-and-breakfast inns—are classified in U.S. Industry 721191, Bed-and-Breakfast Inns.

7212 RV (Recreational Vehicle) Parks and Recreational Camps

72121 RV (Recreational Vehicle) Parks and Recreational Camps

This industry comprises establishments primarily engaged in operating recreational vehicle parks and campgrounds and recreational and vacation camps. These establishments cater to outdoor enthusiasts and are characterized by the type of accommodation and by the nature and the range of recreational facilities and activities provided to their clients.

Illustrative Examples:

Fishing and hunting camps	Travel trailer campsites
Outdoor adventure retreats	Vacation camps (except instructional, day)
Recreational vehicle parks	

US—United States industry only. CAN—United States and Canadian industries are comparable. When neither US nor CAN appears, Canadian, Mexican, and United States industries are comparable.

Cross-References. Establishments primarily engaged in—

- Operating recreational facilities without accommodations—are classified in Subsector 713, Amusement, Gambling and Recreation Industries;

- Operating instructional camps, such as sports camps, fine arts camps, and computer camps,— are classified in Sector 61, Educational Services, based on the nature of instruction;

- Operating children's day camps (except instructional)—are classified in Industry 71399, All Other Amusement and Recreation Industries; and

- Acting as lessors of residential mobile home sites (i.e., trailer parks)—are classified in Industry 53119, Lessors of Other Real Estate Property.

721211 RV (Recreational Vehicle) Parks and Campgrounds[CAN]

This U.S. industry comprises establishments primarily engaged in operating sites to accommodate campers and their equipment, including tents, tent trailers, travel trailers, and RVs (recreational vehicles). These establishments may provide access to facilities, such as washrooms, laundry rooms, recreation halls and playgrounds, stores, and snack bars.

Cross-References. Establishments primarily engaged in—

- Operating recreational facilities without accommodations—are classified in Subsector 713, Amusement, Gambling, and Recreation Industries; and

- Acting as lessors of residential mobile home sites (i.e., trailer parks)—are classified in Industry 531190, Lessors of Other Real Estate Property.

721214 Recreational and Vacation Camps (except Campgrounds)[US]

This U.S. industry comprises establishments primarily engaged in operating overnight recreational camps, such as children's camps, family vacation camps, hunting and fishing camps, and outdoor adventure retreats that offer trail riding, white-water rafting, hiking, and similar activities. These establishments provide accommodation facilities, such as cabins and fixed camp sites, and other amenities, such as food services, recreational facilities and equipment, and organized recreational activities.

Illustrative Examples:

Fishing camps	Vacation camps (except instructional, day)
Hunting camps	Wilderness camps
Outdoor adventure retreats	

Cross-References. Establishments primarily engaged in—

- Operating instructional camps, such as sports camps, fine arts camps, and computer camps,— are classified in the Sector 61, Educational Services, based on the nature of instruction; and

---

US—United States industry only. CAN—United States and Canadian industries are comparable. When neither US nor CAN appears, Canadian, Mexican, and United States industries are comparable.

• Operating children's day camps (except instructional)—are classified in Industry 713990, All Other Amusement and Recreation Industries.

7213 Rooming and Boarding Houses

72131 Rooming and Boarding Houses
See industry description for 721310 below.

721310 Rooming and Boarding Houses

This industry comprises establishments primarily engaged in operating rooming and boarding houses and similar facilities, such as fraternity houses, sorority houses, off-campus dormitories, residential clubs, and workers' camps. These establishments provide temporary or longer-term accommodations which, for the period of occupancy, may serve as a principal residence. These establishments also may provide complementary services, such as housekeeping, meals, and laundry services.

Illustrative Examples:

Dormitories (off campus)   Sorority houses
Fraternity houses   Workers' camps
Rooming houses

722 Food Services and Drinking Places

Industries in the Food Services and Drinking Places subsector prepare meals, snacks, and beverages to customer order for immediate on-premises and off-premises consumption. There is a wide range of establishments in these industries. Some provide food and drink only; while others provide various combinations of seating space, waiter/waitress services and incidental amenities, such as limited entertainment. The industries in the subsector are grouped based on the type and level of services provided. The industry groups are full-service restaurants; limited-service eating places; special food services, such as food service contractors, caterers, and mobile food services, and drinking places.

Food services and drink activities at hotels and motels; amusement parks, theaters, casinos, country clubs, and similar recreational facilities; and civic and social organizations are included in this subsector only if these services are provided by a separate establishment primarily engaged in providing food and beverage services.

Excluded from this subsector are establishments operating dinner cruises. These establishments are classified in Subsector 487, Scenic and Sightseeing Transportation because those establishments utilize transportation equipment to provide scenic recreational entertainment.

7221 Full-Service Restaurants

This industry group comprises establishments primarily engaged in providing food services to patrons who order and are served while seated (i.e., waiter/waitress service) and pay after eating.

US—United States industry only. CAN—United States and Canadian industries are comparable. When neither US nor CAN appears, Canadian, Mexican, and United States industries are comparable.

Establishments that provide these type of food services to patrons with any combination of other services, such as carryout services are classified in this industry.

72211 Full-Service Restaurants
See industry description for 722110 below.

722110 Full-Service Restaurants

This industry comprises establishments primarily engaged in providing food services to patrons who order and are served while seated (i.e. waiter/waitress service) and pay after eating. These establishments may provide this type of food services to patrons in combination with selling alcoholic beverages, providing takeout services, or presenting live nontheatrical entertainment.

Cross-References. Establishments primarily engaged in—

- Providing food services where patrons generally order or select items and pay before eating—are classified in U.S. Industry 722211, Limited-Service Restaurants;

- Selling a specialty snack or nonalcoholic beverage for consumption on or near the premises—are classified in U.S. Industry 722213, Snack and Nonalcoholic Beverage Bars;

- Preparing and serving alcoholic beverages known as bars, taverns, or nightclubs—are classified in Industry 722410, Drinking Places (Alcoholic Beverages); and

- Presenting live theatrical productions and providing food and beverages for consumption on the premises—are classified in Industry 711110, Theater Companies and Dinner Theaters.

7222 Limited-Service Eating Places

This industry group comprises establishments primarily engaged in providing food services where patrons generally order or select items and pay before eating. Most establishments do not have waiter/waitress service, but some provide limited service, such as cooking to order (i.e., per special request), bringing food to seated customers, or providing off-site delivery.

72221 Limited-Service Eating Places

This industry comprises establishments primarily engaged in (1) providing food services where patrons generally order or select items and pay before eating or (2) selling a specialty snack or nonalcoholic beverage for consumption on or near the premises. Food and drink may be consumed on the premises, taken out, or delivered to customers' location. Some establishments in this industry may provide these food services (except snack and nonalcoholic beverage bars) in combination with selling alcoholic beverages.

Illustrative Examples:

Cafeterias	Pizza delivery establishments
Fast-food restaurants	Snack bars (e.g., cookies, pretzels, popcorn)
Nonalcoholic beverage bars	Takeout eating places

US—United States industry only. CAN—United States and Canadian industries are comparable. When neither US nor CAN appears, Canadian, Mexican, and United States industries are comparable.

http://www.ntis.gov/naics

Cross-References. Establishments primarily engaged in—

- Providing food services to patrons who order and are served while seated and pay after eating in combination with providing takeout service—are classified in Industry 72211, Full-Service Restaurants;

- Retailing confectionery goods and nuts not packaged for immediate consumption—are classified in Industry 44529, Other Specialty Food Stores;

- Retailing baked goods (e.g., pretzels, doughnuts, cookies, and bagels) not baked on the premises and not for immediate consumption—are classified in Industry 44529, Other Specialty Food Stores;

- Retailing baked goods (e.g., doughnuts and bagels) and providing food services to patrons who order and are served while seated and pay after eating—are classified in Industry 72211, Full-Service Restaurants;

- Selling snacks and nonalcoholic beverages from mobile vehicles—are classified in Industry 72233, Mobile Food Services; and

- Preparing and serving alcoholic beverages, known as bars, taverns, or nightclubs,—are classified in Industry 72241, Drinking Places (Alcoholic Beverages).

722211 Limited-Service Restaurants[US]

This U.S. industry comprises establishments primarily engaged in providing food services (except snack and nonalcoholic beverage bars) where patrons generally order or select items and pay before eating. Food and drink may be consumed on premises, taken out, or delivered to customers' location. Some establishments in this industry may provide these food services in combination with selling alcoholic beverages.

Illustrative Examples:

Fast-food restaurants
Carryout sandwich shops
Takeout eating places
Limited-service pizza parlors

Pizza delivery shops
Delicatessen restaurants
Family restaurants, limited service

Cross-References. Establishments primarily engaged in—

- Preparing and serving meals for immediate consumption using cafeteria-style serving equipment that are known as cafeterias—are classified in U.S. Industry 722212, Cafeterias;

- Providing food services to patrons who order and are served while seated and they pay after eating—are classified in Industry 722110, Full-Service Restaurants;

- Selling a specialty snack (e.g., ice cream, frozen yogurt, candy, cookies) or nonalcoholic beverages, for consumption on or near the premises—are classified in U.S. Industry 722213, Snack and Nonalcoholic Beverage Bars;

US—United States industry only. CAN—United States and Canadian industries are comparable. When neither US nor CAN appears, Canadian, Mexican, and United States industries are comparable.

- Retailing confectionery goods and nuts not packaged for immediate consumption—are classified in U.S. Industry 445292, Confectionery and Nut Stores;

- Retailing baked goods (e.g., pretzels, doughnuts, cookies, and bagels) not baked on the premises and not for immediate consumption—are classified in U.S. Industry 445291, Baked Goods Stores;

- Preparing and serving alcoholic beverages known as bars, taverns, or nightclubs,—are classified in Industry 722410, Drinking Places (Alcoholic Beverages); and

- Selling baked goods, (e.g., doughnuts and bagels) and providing food services to patrons who order and are served while seated and pay after eating,—are classified in Industry 722110, Full-Service Restaurants.

722212 Cafeterias[US]

This U.S. industry comprises establishments, known as cafeterias, primarily engaged in preparing and serving meals for immediate consumption using cafeteria-style serving equipment, such as steam tables, a refrigerated area, and self-service nonalcoholic beverage dispensing equipment. Patrons select from food and drink items on display in a continuous cafeteria line.

Cross-References. Establishments primarily engaged in—

- Providing food services to patrons who order and are served while seated and pay after eating—are classified in Industry 722110, Full-Service Restaurants; and

- Providing food services where patrons generally order or select items and pay before eating—are classified in U.S. Industry 722211, Limited-Service Restaurants.

722213 Snack and Nonalcoholic Beverage Bars[US]

This U.S. industry comprises establishments primarily engaged in (1) preparing and/or serving a specialty snack, such as ice cream, frozen yogurt, cookies, or popcorn or (2) serving nonalcoholic beverages, such as coffee, juices, or sodas for consumption on or near the premises. These establishments may carry and sell a combination of snack, nonalcoholic beverage, and other related products (e.g., coffee beans, mugs, coffee makers) but generally promote and sell a unique snack or nonalcoholic beverage.

Illustrative Examples:

Beverage bars	Carryout service donut shops with on-premises
Carryout service bagel shops with on-premises	baking
baking	Carryout service pretzel shops with on-premises
Carryout service cookie shops with on-premises	baking
baking	Ice cream parlors

Cross-References. Establishment primarily engaged in—

- Selling one or more of the following food specialties: hamburgers, hot dogs, pizza, chicken, specialty cuisines—are classified in U.S. Industry 722211, Limited-Service Restaurants

---

US—United States industry only. CAN—United States and Canadian industries are comparable. When neither US nor CAN appears, Canadian, Mexican, and United States industries are comparable.

or Industry 722110, Full-Service Restaurants, based on type of food services provided to patrons;

- Preparing and serving snacks and nonalcoholic beverages from mobile vehicles—are classified in Industry 722330 Mobile Food Services;

- Retailing confectionery goods and nuts not packaged for immediate consumption—are classified in U.S. Industry 445292, Confectionery and Nut Stores;

- Retailing baked goods (e.g., pretzels, doughnuts, cookies, and bagels) not baked on the premises and not for immediate consumption,—are classified in U.S. Industry 445291, Baked Goods Stores; and

- Retailing baked goods (e.g., doughnuts and bagels) and providing food services to patrons who order and are served while seated and pay after eating—are classified in Industry 722110, Full-Service Restaurants.

7223 Special Food Services

This industry group comprises establishments primarily engaged in providing one of the following food services: (1) at the customers' location; (2) a location designated by the customer; or (3) from motorized vehicles or nonmotorized carts.

72231 Food Service Contractors
See industry description for 722310 below.

722310 Food Service Contractors

This industry comprises establishments primarily engaged in providing food services at institutional, governmental, commercial, or industrial locations of others based on contractual arrangements with these type of organizations for a specified period of time. The establishments of this industry provide food services for the convenience of the contracting organization or the contracting organization's customers. The contractual arrangement of these establishments with contracting organizations may vary from type of facility operated (e.g., cafeteria, restaurant, fast-food eating place), revenue sharing, cost structure, to providing personnel. Management staff is always provided by the food services contractor.

Illustrative Examples:

Airline food services contractors
Cafeteria food services contractors (i.e., at schools, hospitals, government offices)

Food concession contractors (i.e., at sporting, entertainment, convention facilities)

Cross-References. Establishments primarily engaged in—

- Providing food services on a single-event basis—are classified in Industry 722320, Caterers; and

---

US—United States industry only. CAN—United States and Canadian industries are comparable. When neither US nor CAN appears, Canadian, Mexican, and United States industries are comparable.

- Supplying and servicing food vending machines—are classified in Industry 454210, Vending Machine Operators.

72232 Caterers
See industry description for 722320 below.

722320 Caterers

This industry comprises establishments primarily engaged in providing single event-based food services. These establishments generally have equipment and vehicles to transport meals and snacks to events and/or prepare food at an off-premise site. Banquet halls with catering staff are included in this industry. Examples of events catered by establishments in this industry are graduation parties, wedding receptions, business or retirement luncheons, and trade shows.

Cross-References. Establishments primarily engaged in—

- Preparing and serving meals and snacks for immediate consumption from motorized vehicles or nonmotorized carts—are classified in Industry 722330, Mobile Caterers;

- Providing food services at institutional, governmental, commercial, or industrial locations of others or providing food services (e.g., airline contractors, industrial caterers) based on contractual arrangements for a specified period of time—are classified in Industry 722310, Food Service Contractors; and

- Renting facilities without their own catering staff—are classified in Industry 531120, Lessors of Nonresidential Buildings (except Miniwarehouses).

72233 Mobile Food Services
See industry description for 722330 below.

722330 Mobile Food Services

This industry comprises establishments primarily engaged in preparing and serving meals and snacks for immediate consumption from motorized vehicles or nonmotorized carts. The establishment is the central location from which the caterer route is serviced, not each vehicle, or cart. Included in this industry are establishments primarily engaged in providing food services from vehicles, such as hot dog cart, and ice cream truck.

Illustrative Examples:

Ice cream truck vendors	Mobile food carts
Mobile canteens	Mobile refreshment stands
Mobile food concession stands	Mobile snack stands

Cross-References. Establishments primarily engaged in—

- Providing food services where patrons generally order or select items and pay before eating—are classified in U.S. Industry 722211, Limited-Service Restaurants;

US—United States industry only. CAN—United States and Canadian industries are comparable. When neither US nor CAN appears, Canadian, Mexican, and United States industries are comparable.

- Selling unprepared foods, such as vegetables, melons, and nuts or fruit from carts—are classified in Industry 454390, Other Direct Selling Establishments;

- Selling and promoting specialty snacks (e.g.. ice cream, frozen yogurt, cookies, popcorn) or nonalcoholic beverages in nonmobile facilities for consumption on or near the premises,—are classified in U.S. Industry 722213, Snack and Nonalcoholic Beverage Bars;

- Selling food specialties, such as hamburgers, hot dogs, chicken, pizza, or specialty cuisines from nonmobile facilities,—are classified in U.S. Industry 722211, Limited-Service Restaurants or Industry 722110, Full-Service Restaurants based on type of food services provided to patrons; and

- Operating as street vendors (except food)—are classified in Industry 454390, Other Direct Selling Establishments.

7224 Drinking Places (Alcoholic Beverages)

This industry group comprises establishments primarily engaged in preparing and serving alcoholic beverages for immediate consumption.

72241 Drinking Places (Alcoholic Beverages)
See industry description for 722410 below.

722410 Drinking Places (Alcoholic Beverages)

This industry comprises establishments known as bars, taverns, nightclubs or drinking places primarily engaged in preparing and serving alcoholic beverages for immediate consumption. These establishments may also provide limited food services.

Cross-References. Establishments primarily engaged in—

- Preparing and serving alcoholic beverages (i.e., not known as bars or taverns) and providing food services to patrons who order and are served while seated and pay after eating—are classified in Industry 722110, Full-Service Restaurants

- Preparing and serving alcoholic beverages (i.e., known as bars or taverns) and providing food services to patrons who order and are served while seated and pay after eating—are classified in Industry 722211, Limited-Service Restaurants;

- Operating a civic or social association with a bar for their members—are classified in Industry 81341, Civic and Social Organizations;

- Retailing packaged alcoholic beverages not for immediate consumption on the premises—are classified in Industry 445310, Beer, Wine, and Liquor Stores; and

- Operating discotheques or dance clubs without selling alcoholic beverages—are classified in Industry 713990, All Other Amusement and Recreation Industries.

US—United States industry only. CAN—United States and Canadian industries are comparable. When neither US nor CAN appears, Canadian, Mexican, and United States industries are comparable.

http://www.ntis.gov/naics

Sector 81—Other Services (except Public Administration)

The Sector as a Whole

The Other Services (except Public Administration) sector comprises establishments engaged in providing services not specifically provided for elsewhere in the classification system. Establishments in this sector are primarily engaged in activities, such as equipment and machinery repairing, promoting or administering religious activities, grantmaking, advocacy, and providing drycleaning and laundry services, personal care services, death care services, pet care services, photofinishing services, temporary parking services, and dating services.

Private households that engage in employing workers on or about the premises in activities primarily concerned with the operation of the household are included in this sector.

Excluded from this sector are establishments primarily engaged in retailing new equipment and also performing repairs and general maintenance on equipment. These establishments are classified in Sector 44-45, Retail Trade.

811 Repair and Maintenance

Industries in the Repair and Maintenance subsector restore machinery, equipment, and other products to working order. These establishments also typically provide general or routine maintenance (i.e., servicing) on such products to ensure they work efficiently and to prevent breakdown and unnecessary repairs.

The NAICS structure for this subsector brings together most types of repair and maintenance establishments and categorizes them based on production processes (i.e., on the type of repair and maintenance activity performed, and the necessary skills, expertise, and processes that are found in different repair and maintenance establishments). This NAICS classification does not delineate between repair services provided to businesses versus those that serve households. Although some industries primarily serve either businesses or households, separation by class of customer is limited by the fact that many establishments serve both. Establishments repairing computers and consumer electronics products are two examples of such overlap.

The Repair and Maintenance subsector does not include all establishments that do repair and maintenance. For example, a substantial amount of repair is done by establishments that also manufacture machinery, equipment, and other goods. These establishments are included in the Manufacturing sector in NAICS. In addition, repair of transportation equipment is often provided by or based at transportation facilities, such as airports, seaports, and these activities are included in the Transportation and Warehousing sector. A particularly unique situation exists with repair of buildings. Plumbing, electrical installation and repair, painting and decorating, and other construction-related establishments are often involved in performing installation or other work on new construction as well as providing repair services on existing structures. While some specialize in repair, it is difficult to distinguish between the two types and all have been included in the Construction sector.

Excluded from this subsector are establishments primarily engaged in rebuilding or remanufacturing machinery and equipment. These are classified in Sector 31-33, Manufacturing. Also excluded are retail establishments that provide after-sale services and repair. These are classified in Sector 44-45, Retail Trade.

US—United States industry only. CAN—United States and Canadian industries are comparable. When neither US nor CAN appears, Canadian, Mexican, and United States industries are comparable.

http://www.ntis.gov/naics

8111 Automotive Repair and Maintenance

This industry group comprises establishments involved in providing repair and maintenance services for automotive vehicles, such as passenger cars, trucks, and vans, and all trailers. Establishments in this industry group employ mechanics with specialized technical skills to diagnose and repair the mechanical and electrical systems for automotive vehicles, repair automotive interiors, and paint or repair automotive exteriors.

81111 Automotive Mechanical and Electrical Repair and Maintenance

This industry comprises establishments primarily engaged in providing mechanical or electrical repair and maintenance services for automotive vehicles, such as passenger cars, trucks and vans, and all trailers. These establishments specialize in or may provide a wide range of these services.

Cross-References. Establishments primarily engaged in—

- Retailing automotive vehicles and automotive parts and accessories and also providing automotive repair services—are classified in Subsector 441, Motor Vehicle and Parts Dealers;

- Retailing motor fuels and also providing automotive vehicle repair services—are classified in Industry Group 4471, Gasoline Stations;

- Changing motor oil and lubricating the chassis of automotive vehicles—are classified in Industry 81119, Other Automotive Repair and Maintenance;

- Providing automotive vehicle air-conditioning repair—are classified in Industry 81119, Other Automotive Repair and Maintenance; and

- Motorcycle repair and maintenance services—are classified in Industry 81149, Other Personal and Household Goods Repair and Maintenance.

811111 General Automotive Repair[CAN]

This U.S. industry comprises establishments primarily engaged in providing (1) a wide range of mechanical and electrical repair and maintenance services for automotive vehicles, such as passenger cars, trucks, and vans, and all trailers or (2) engine repair and replacement.

Illustrative Examples:

Automotive engine repair and replacement shops

Automobile repair garages (except gasoline service stations)

General automotive repair shops

Cross-References. Establishments primarily engaged in—

- Retailing new automotive parts and accessories and also providing automotive repair services—are classified in Industry 441310, Automotive Parts and Accessories Stores;

US—United States industry only. CAN—United States and Canadian industries are comparable. When neither US nor CAN appears, Canadian, Mexican, and United States industries are comparable.

- Changing motor oil and lubricating the chassis of automotive vehicles—are classified in U.S. Industry 811191, Automotive Oil Change and Lubrication Shops;

- Replacing and repairing automotive vehicle exhaust systems—are classified in U.S. Industry 811112, Automotive Exhaust System Repair;

- Replacing and repairing automotive vehicle transmissions—are classified in U.S. Industry 811113, Automotive Transmission Repair;

- Retailing motor fuels and also providing automotive vehicle repair services—are classified in Industry Group 4471, Gasoline Stations;

- Retailing automobiles and light trucks for highway use and also providing automotive repair services—are classified in Industry Group 4411, Automobile Dealers; and

- Motorcycle repair and maintenance services—are classified in Industry 811490, Other Personal and Household Goods Repair and Maintenance.

811112 Automotive Exhaust System Repair[CAN]

This U.S. industry comprises establishments primarily engaged in replacing or repairing exhaust systems of automotive vehicles, such as passenger cars, trucks, and vans.

Illustrative Examples:

Automotive exhaust system replacement and repair shops

Automotive muffler replacement and repair shops

Cross-References.

Establishments primarily engaged in motorcycle repair and maintenance services are classified in Industry 811490, Other Personal and Household Goods Repair and Maintenance.

811113 Automotive Transmission Repair[US]

This U.S. industry comprises establishments primarily engaged in replacing or repairing transmissions of automotive vehicles, such as passenger cars, trucks, and vans.

Cross-References.

Establishments primarily engaged in motorcycle repair and maintenance services are classified in Industry 811490, Other Personal and Household Goods Repair and Maintenance.

811118 Other Automotive Mechanical and Electrical Repair and Maintenance[US]

This U.S. industry comprises establishments primarily engaged in providing specialized mechanical or electrical repair and maintenance services (except engine repair and replacement, exhaust systems repair, and transmission repair) for automotive vehicles, such as passenger cars, trucks, and vans, and all trailers.

US—United States industry only. CAN—United States and Canadian industries are comparable. When neither US nor CAN appears, Canadian, Mexican, and United States industries are comparable.

Illustrative Examples:

Automotive brake repair shops	Automotive radiator repair shops
Automotive electrical repair shops	Automotive tune up shops

Cross-References. Establishments primarily engaged in—

- Providing a wide range of mechanical and electrical automotive vehicle repair or specializing in engine repair or replacement—are classified in U.S. Industry 811111, General Automotive Repair;

- Replacing and repairing automotive vehicle exhaust systems—are classified in U.S. Industry 811112, Automotive Exhaust System Repair;

- Replacing and repairing automotive vehicle transmissions—are classified in U.S. Industry 811113, Automotive Transmission Repair;

- Providing automotive vehicle air-conditioning repair—are classified in U.S. Industry 811198, All Other Automotive Repair and Maintenance; and

- Motorcycle repair and maintenance services—are classified in Industry 811490, Other Personal and Household Goods Repair and Maintenance.

81112 Automotive Body, Paint, Interior, and Glass Repair

This industry comprises establishments primarily engaged in providing one or more of the following: (1) repairing or customizing automotive vehicles, such as passenger cars, trucks, and vans, and all trailer bodies and interiors; (2) painting automotive vehicle and trailer bodies; (3) replacing, repairing, and/or tinting automotive vehicle glass; and (4) customizing automobile, truck, and van interiors for the physically disabled or other customers with special requirements.

Illustrative Examples:

Automotive body shops	Automotive paint shops
Automotive glass shops	

Cross-References. Establishments primarily engaged in—

- Manufacturing automotive vehicles and trailers or customizing these vehicles on an assembly-line basis—are classified in Subsector 336, Transportation Equipment Manufacturing;

- Motorcycle repair and maintenance services—are classified in Industry 81149, Other Personal and Household Goods Repair and Maintenance.

811121 Automotive Body, Paint, and Interior Repair and Maintenance[CAN]

This U.S. industry comprises establishments primarily engaged in repairing or customizing automotive vehicles, such as passenger cars, trucks, and vans, and all trailer bodies and interiors; and/or painting automotive vehicles and trailer bodies.

US—United States industry only. CAN—United States and Canadian industries are comparable. When neither US nor CAN appears, Canadian, Mexican, and United States industries are comparable.

Illustrative Examples:

Automotive body shops
Automotive paint shops

Automotive upholstery shops

Cross-References. Establishments primarily engaged in

- Automotive glass replacement, repair and/or tinting—are classified in U.S. Industry 811122, Automotive Glass Replacement Shops;

- Manufacturing automotive vehicles and trailers or customizing these vehicles on an assembly-line basis—are classified in Subsector 336, Transportation Equipment Manufacturing; and

- Motorcycle repair and maintenance services—are classified in Industry 811490, Other Personal and Household Goods Repair and Maintenance.

811122 Automotive Glass Replacement Shops[CAN]

This U.S. industry comprises establishments primarily engaged in replacing, repairing, and/or tinting automotive vehicle, such as passenger car, truck, and van, glass.

Cross-References.

Establishments primarily engaged in motorcycle repair and maintenance service are classified in Industry 811490, Other Personal and Household Goods Repair and Maintenance.

81119 Other Automotive Repair and Maintenance

This industry comprises establishments primarily engaged in providing automotive repair and maintenance services (except mechanical and electrical repair and maintenance; transmission repair; and body, paint, interior, and glass repair) for automotive vehicles, such as passenger cars, trucks, and vans, and all trailers.

Illustrative Examples:

Automotive air-conditioning repair shops
Automotive oil change and lubrication shops
Automotive rustproofing and undercoating shops

Automotive tire repair shops
Car washes

Cross-References. Establishments primarily engaged in—

- Tire retreading or recapping—are classified in Industry 32621, Tire Manufacturing;

- Automotive vehicle mechanical and electrical repair and maintenance—are classified in Industry 81111, Automotive Mechanical and Electrical Repair and Maintenance;

- Automotive body, paint, interior, and glass repair—are classified in Industry 81112, Automotive Body, Paint, Interior, and Glass Repair; and

---

US—United States industry only. CAN—United States and Canadian industries are comparable. When neither US nor CAN appears, Canadian, Mexican, and United States industries are comparable.

- Motorcycle repair and maintenance services—are classified in Industry 81149, Other Personal and Household Goods Repair and Maintenance.

811191 Automotive Oil Change and Lubrication Shops[US]

This U.S. industry comprises establishments primarily engaged in changing motor oil and lubricating the chassis of automotive vehicles, such as passenger cars, trucks, and vans.

Cross-References.

Establishments primarily engaged in motorcycle repair and maintenance services are classified in Industry 811490, Other Personal and Household Goods Repair and Maintenance.

811192 Car Washes[CAN]

This U.S. industry comprises establishments primarily engaged in cleaning, washing, and/or waxing automotive vehicles, such as passenger cars, trucks, and vans, and trailers.

Illustrative Examples:

Automotive detail shops
Car washes

Mobile car and truck washes

811198 All Other Automotive Repair and Maintenance[US]

This U.S. industry comprises establishments primarily engaged in providing automotive repair and maintenance services (except mechanical and electrical repair and maintenance; body, paint, interior, and glass repair; motor oil change and lubrication; and car washing) for automotive vehicles, such as passenger cars, trucks, and vans, and all trailers.

Illustrative Examples:

Automotive air-conditioning repair shops
Automotive tire repair (except retreading) shops

Automotive rustproofing and undercoating shops

Cross-References. Establishments primarily engaged in—

- Tire retreading or recapping—are classified in Industry 32621, Tire Manufacturing;

- Providing a range of mechanical and electrical automotive vehicle repair or specializing in engine repair or replacement—are classified in U.S. Industry 811111, General Automotive Repair;

- Replacing and repairing automotive vehicle exhaust systems—are classified in U.S. Industry 811112, Automotive Exhaust System Repair;

- Replacing and repairing automotive vehicle transmissions—are classified in U.S. Industry 811113, Automotive Transmission Repair;

- Repairing or customizing automotive vehicle bodies and interiors—are classified in U.S. Industry 811121, Automotive Body, Paint, and Interior Repair and Maintenance;

- Replacing, repairing, and/or tinting automotive glass—are classified in U.S. Industry 811122, Automotive Glass Replacement Shops;

- Changing motor oil and lubricating the chassis of automotive vehicles—are classified in U.S. Industry 811191, Automotive Oil Change and Lubrication Shops;

- Cleaning, washing, and/or waxing automotive vehicles and trailers—are classified in U.S. Industry 811192, Car Washes;

- Motorcycle repair and maintenance services—are classified in Industry 811490, Other Personal and Household Goods Repair and Maintenance; and

- Retailing and installing audio equipment—are classified in Industry 441310, Automotive Parts and Accessories Stores.

8112 Electronic and Precision Equipment Repair and Maintenance

This industry group comprises establishments primarily engaged in repairing electronic equipment, such as computers and communications equipment, and highly specialized precision instruments. Establishments in this industry group typically have staff skilled in repairing items having complex, electronic components.

81121 Electronic and Precision Equipment Repair and Maintenance

This industry comprises establishments primarily engaged in repairing and maintaining one or more of the following: (1) consumer electronic equipment; (2) computers; (3) office machines; (4) communication equipment; and (5) other electronic and precision equipment and instruments, without retailing these products as new. Establishments in this industry repair items, such as microscopes, radar and sonar equipment, televisions, stereos, video recorders, computers, fax machines, photocopying machines, two-way radios and other communications equipment, scientific instruments, and medical equipment.

Cross-References. Establishments primarily engaged in—

- Installing or maintaining home security systems—are classified in Industry 56162, Security Systems Services;

- Retailing new radios, televisions, and other consumer electronics and also providing repair services—are classified in Industry 44311, Appliance, Television, and Other Electronics Stores;

- Retailing new computers and computer peripherals and also providing repair services—are classified in Industry 44312, Computer and Software Stores; and

- Rewinding armatures and rebuilding electric motors on a factory basis—are classified in Industry 33531, Electrical Equipment Manufacturing.

811211 Consumer Electronics Repair and Maintenance[US]

This U.S. industry comprises establishments primarily engaged in repairing and maintaining consumer electronics, such as televisions, stereos, speakers, video recorders, CD players, radios, and cameras, without retailing new consumer electronics.

Cross-References. Establishments primarily engaged in—

- Repairing computers and peripheral equipment—are classified in U.S. Industry 811212, Computer and Office Machine Repair and Maintenance;

- Installing or maintaining home security systems—are classified in U.S. Industry 561621, Security Systems Services (except Locksmiths);

- Retailing new radios, televisions, and other consumer electronics and also providing repair services—are classified in U.S. Industry 443112, Radio, Television, and Other Electronics Stores; and

- Repairing two-way radios—are classified in U.S. Industry 811213, Communication Equipment Repair and Maintenance.

811212 Computer and Office Machine Repair and Maintenance[US]

This U.S. industry comprises establishments primarily engaged in repairing and maintaining computers and office machines without retailing new computers and office machines, such as photocopying machines; and computer terminals, storage devices, printers; and CD-ROM drives.

Cross-References. Establishments primarily engaged in—

- Retailing new computers and computer peripherals and also providing repair services— are classified in Industry 443120, Computer and Software Stores; and

- Repairing and servicing fax machines—are classified in Industry 811213, Communication Equipment Repair and Maintenance.

811213 Communication Equipment Repair and Maintenance[US]

This U.S. industry comprises establishments primarily engaged in repairing and maintaining communications equipment without retailing new communication equipment, such as telephones, fax machines, communications transmission equipment, and two-way radios.

Cross-References. Establishments primarily engaged in—

- Retailing new telephones and also providing repair services—are classified in U.S. Industry 443112, Radio, Television, and Other Electronics Stores; and

- Repairing stereo and other consumer electronic equipment—are classified in U.S. Industry 811211, Consumer Electronics Repair and Maintenance.

US—United States industry only. CAN—United States and Canadian industries are comparable. When neither US nor CAN appears, Canadian, Mexican, and United States industries are comparable.

811219 Other Electronic and Precision Equipment Repair and Maintenance[US]

This U.S. industry comprises establishments primarily engaged in repairing and maintaining (without retailing) electronic and precision equipment (except consumer electronics, computers and office machines, and communications equipment). Establishments in this industry repair and maintain equipment, such as medical diagnostic imaging equipment, measuring and surveying instruments, laboratory instruments, and radar and sonar equipment.

Cross-References. Establishments primarily engaged in—

- Rewinding armatures and rebuilding electric motors on a factory basis—are classified in U.S. Industry 335312, Motor and Generator Manufacturing;

- Repairing stereo and other consumer electronic equipment—are classified in U.S. Industry 811211, Consumer Electronics Repair and Maintenance;

- Repairing computers and office machines—are classified in U.S. Industry 811212, Computer and Office Machine Repair and Maintenance; and

- Repairing communications equipment—are classified in U.S. Industry 811213, Communication Equipment Repair and Maintenance.

8113 Commercial and Industrial Machinery and Equipment (except Automotive and Electronic) Repair and Maintenance

81131 Commercial and Industrial Machinery and Equipment (except Automotive and Electronic) Repair and Maintenance
See industry description for 811310 below.

811310 Commercial and Industrial Machinery and Equipment (except Automotive and Electronic) Repair and Maintenance

This industry comprises establishments primarily engaged in the repair and maintenance of commercial and industrial machinery and equipment. Establishments in this industry either sharpen/ install commercial and industrial machinery blades and saws or provide welding (e.g., automotive, general) repair services; or repair agricultural and other heavy and industrial machinery and equipment (e.g., forklifts and other materials handling eqipment, machine tools, commercial refrigeration equipment, construction equipment, and mining machinery).

Cross-References. Establishments primarily engaged in—

- Automotive repair (except welding) and maintenance are—classified in Industry Group 8111, Automotive Repair and Maintenance;

- Repairing and maintaining electronic and precision equipment—are classified in Industry 81121, Electronic and Precision Equipment Repair and Maintenance;

- Repairing and servicing aircraft—are classified in Industry 488190, Other Support Activities for Air Transportation;

US—United States industry only. CAN—United States and Canadian industries are comparable. When neither US nor CAN appears, Canadian, Mexican, and United States industries are comparable.

- Converting, rebuilding, and overhauling aircraft—are classified in Industry 336410, Aerospace Product and Parts Manufacturing;

- Repairing and servicing railroad cars and engines—are classified in Industry 488210, Support Activities for Rail Transportation;

- Rebuilding or remanufacturing railroad engines and cars—are classified in Industry 336510, Railroad Rolling Stock Manufacturing;

- Repairing and overhauling ships at floating dry docks—are classified in Industry 4883, Support Activities for Water Transportation;

- Repairing and overhauling ships at shipyards—are classified in Industry 33661, Ship and Boat Building;

- Rewinding armatures or rebuilding electric motors on a factory basis—are classified in U.S. Industry 335312, Motor and Generator Manufacturing; and

- Repairing and maintaining home and garden equipment (e.g., sharpening or installing blades and saws)—are classified in Industry 81141, Home and Garden Equipment and Appliance Repair and Maintenance.

8114 Personal and Household Goods Repair and Maintenance

81141 Home and Garden Equipment and Appliance Repair and Maintenance

This industry comprises establishments primarily engaged in repairing and servicing home and garden equipment and/or household-type appliances without retailing new equipment or appliances. Establishments in this industry repair and maintain items, such as lawnmowers, edgers, snow- and leaf-blowers, washing machines, clothes dryers, and refrigerators.

Cross-References. Establishments primarily engaged in—

- Retailing outdoor power equipment and also providing repair services—are classified in Industry 44421, Outdoor Power Equipment Stores;

- Retailing an array of new appliances and also providing repair services—are classified in Industry 44311, Appliance, Television, and Other Electronics Stores;

- Repairing, servicing, or installing central heating and air-conditioning equipment—are classified in Subsector 23, Construction; and

- Repairing commercial refrigeration equipment—are classified in Industry 81131, Commercial and Industrial Machinery and Equipment (except Automotive and Electronic) Repair and Maintenance.

811411 Home and Garden Equipment Repair and Maintenance[CAN]

This U.S. industry comprises establishments primarily engaged in repairing and servicing home and garden equipment without retailing new home and garden equipment, such as lawnmowers, handheld power tools, edgers, snow- and leaf-blowers, and trimmers.

US—United States industry only. CAN—United States and Canadian industries are comparable. When neither US nor CAN appears, Canadian, Mexican, and United States industries are comparable.

Cross-References.

Establishments primarily engaged in retailing new outdoor power equipment and also providing repair services are classified in Industry 444210, Outdoor Power Equipment Stores.

811412 Appliance Repair and Maintenance[CAN]

This U.S. industry comprises establishments primarily engaged in repairing and servicing household appliances without retailing new appliances, such as refrigerators, stoves, washing machines, clothes dryers, and room air-conditioners.

Cross-References. Establishments primarily engaged in—

- Installing central heating and air-conditioning equipment—are classified in Industry 235110, Plumbing, Heating, and Air-Conditioning Contractors;

- Repairing commercial refrigeration equipment—are classified in Industry 811310, Commercial and Industrial Machinery and Equipment (except Automotive and Electronic) Repair and Maintenance; and

- Retailing an array of new appliances and also providing repair services—are classified in U.S. Industry 443111, Household Appliance Stores.

81142 Reupholstery and Furniture Repair
See industry description for 811420 below.

811420 Reupholstery and Furniture Repair

This industry comprises establishments primarily engaged in one or more of the following: (1) reupholstering furniture; (2) refinishing furniture; (3) repairing furniture; and (4) repairing and restoring furniture.

Cross-References. Establishments primarily engaged in—

- Automotive vehicle and trailer upholstery repair—are classified in U.S. Industry 811121, Automotive Body, Paint, and Interior Repair and Maintenance; and

- The restoration of museum pieces—are classified in Industry 711510, Independent Artists, Writers, and Performers.

81143 Footwear and Leather Goods Repair
See industry description for 811430 below.

811430 Footwear and Leather Goods Repair

This industry comprises establishments primarily engaged in repairing footwear and/or repairing other leather or leather-like goods without retailing new footwear and leather or leather-like goods, such as handbags and briefcases.

US—United States industry only. CAN—United States and Canadian industries are comparable. When neither US nor CAN appears, Canadian, Mexican, and United States industries are comparable.

http://www.ntis.gov/naics

Cross-References. Establishments primarily engaged in—

- Retailing new luggage and leather goods and also providing repair services—are classified in Industry 448320, Luggage and Leather Goods Stores;

- Shining shoes—are classified in Industry 812990, All Other Personal Services; and

- Repairing leather clothing—are classified in Industry 811490, Other Personal and Household Goods Repair and Maintenance.

81149 Other Personal and Household Goods Repair and Maintenance
See industry description for 811490 below.

811490 Other Personal and Household Goods Repair and Maintenance

This industry comprises establishments primarily engaged in repairing and servicing personal or household-type goods without retailing new personal and household-type goods (except home and garden equipment, appliances, furniture, and footwear and leather goods). Establishments in this industry repair items, such as garments; watches; jewelry; musical instruments; bicycles and motorcycles; motorboats, canoes, sailboats, and other recreational boats.

Cross-References. Establishments primarily engaged in—

- Repairing home and garden equipment—are classified in U.S. Industry 811411, Home and Garden Equipment Repair and Maintenance;

- Repairing appliances—are classified in U.S. Industry 811412, Appliance Repair and Maintenance;

- Reupholstering and repairing furniture—are classified in Industry 811420, Reupholstery and Furniture Repair;

- Repairing footwear and leather goods—are classified in Industry 811430, Footwear and Leather Goods Repair;

- Operating marinas and providing a range of other services including boat cleaning and repair—are classified in Industry 713930, Marinas; and

- Drycleaning garments—are classified in Industry Group 8123, Drycleaning and Laundry Services.

812 Personal and Laundry Services

Industries in the Personal and Laundry Services subsector group establishments that provide personal and laundry services to individuals, households, and businesses. Services performed include: personal care services; death care services; laundry and drycleaning services; and a wide range of other personal services, such as pet care (except veterinary) services, photofinishing services, temporary parking services, and dating services.

The Personal and Laundry Services subsector is by no means all-inclusive of the services that could be termed personal services (i.e., those provided to individuals rather than businesses). There

US—United States industry only. CAN—United States and Canadian industries are comparable. When neither US nor CAN appears, Canadian, Mexican, and United States industries are comparable.

are many other subsectors, as well as sectors, that provide services to persons. Establishments providing legal, accounting, tax preparation, architectural, portrait photography, and similar professional services are classified in Sector 54, Professional, Scientific, and Technical Services; those providing job placement, travel arrangement, home security, interior and exterior house cleaning, exterminating, lawn and garden care, and similar support services are classified in Sector 56, Administrative and Support, Waste Management and Remediation Services; those providing health and social services are classified in Sector 62, Health Care and Social Assistance; those providing amusement and recreation services are classified in Sector 71, Arts, Entertainment and Recreation; those providing educational instruction are classified in Sector 61, Educational Services; those providing repair services are classified in Subsector 811, Repair and Maintenance; and those providing spiritual, civic, and advocacy services are classified in Subsector 813, Religious, Grantmaking, Civic, Professional, and Similar Organizations.

8121 Personal Care Services[CAN]

This industry group comprises establishments, such as barber and beauty shops, that provide appearance care services to individual consumers.

81211 Hair, Nail, and Skin Care Services[CAN]

This industry comprises establishments primarily engaged in one or more of the following: (1) providing hair care services; (2) providing nail care services; and (3) providing facials or applying makeup (except permanent makeup).

Illustrative Examples:

Barber shops   Hair stylist shops
Beauty salons   Nail salons
Cosmetology salons

Cross-References. Establishments primarily engaged in—

- Offering training in barbering, hair styling, or the cosmetic arts—are classified in Industry 61151, Technical and Trade Schools;

- Providing massage, electrolysis (i.e., hair removal), permanent makeup, or tanning services—are classified in Industry 81219, Other Personal Care Services; and

- Providing medical skin care services (e.g., cosmetic surgery, dermatology)—are classified in Sector 62, Health Care and Social Assistance.

812111 Barber Shops[US]

This U.S. industry comprises establishments known as barber shops or men's hair stylist shops primarily engaged in cutting, trimming, and styling boys' and men's hair; and/or shaving and trimming men's beards.

US—United States industry only. CAN—United States and Canadian industries are comparable. When neither US nor CAN appears, Canadian, Mexican, and United States industries are comparable.

Cross-References. Establishments primarily engaged in—

- Offering training in barbering—are classified in U.S. Industry 611511, Cosmetology and Barber Schools; and

- Providing hair care services (except establishments known as barber shops or men's hair stylists)—are classified in U.S. Industry 812112, Beauty Salons.

812112 Beauty Salons[US]

This U.S. industry comprises establishments (except those known as barber shops or men's hair stylist shops) primarily engaged in one or more of the following: (1) cutting, trimming, shampooing, weaving, coloring, waving, or styling hair; (2) providing facials; and (3) applying makeup (except permanent makeup).

Illustrative Examples:

Beauty parlors or shops
Combined beauty and barber shops
Cosmetology salons or shops

Facial salons or shops
Hairdressing salons or shops
Unisex or women's hair stylist shops

Cross-References. Establishments primarily engaged in—

- Cutting, trimming, and styling men's and boys' hair (known as barber shops or men's hair stylist shops)—are classified in U.S. Industry 812111, Barber Shops;

- Offering training in hair styling or the cosmetic arts—are classified in U.S. Industry 611511, Cosmetology and Barber Schools;

- Providing nail care services—are classified in U.S. Industry 812113, Nail Salons;

- Providing massage, electrolysis (i.e., hair removal), permanent makeup, or tanning services—are classified in U.S. Industry 812199, All Other Personal Care Services; and

- Providing medical skin care services (e.g., cosmetic surgery, dermatology)—are classified in Sector 62, Health Care and Social Assistance.

812113 Nail Salons[US]

This U.S. industry comprises establishments primarily engaged in providing nail care services, such as manicures, pedicures, and nail extensions.

81219 Other Personal Care Services[CAN]

This industry comprises establishments primarily engaged in providing personal care services (except hair, nail, facial, or nonpermanent makeup services).

US—United States industry only. CAN—United States and Canadian industries are comparable. When neither US nor CAN appears, Canadian, Mexican, and United States industries are comparable.

Illustrative Examples:

Depilatory or electrolysis (i.e., hair removal) salons

Ear piercing services

Hair replacement (except by offices of physicians) or weaving services

Massage parlors

Nonmedical diet and weight reducing centers

Permanent makeup salons

Steam or turkish baths

Tanning salons

Tattoo parlors

Cross-References. Establishments primarily engaged in—

- Providing hair, nail, facial, or nonpermanent makeup services—are classified in Industry 81211, Hair, Nail, and Skin Care Services;

- Operating physical fitness facilities—are classified in Industry 71394, Fitness and Recreational Sports Centers;

- Operating health resorts and spas that provide lodging—are classified in Industry 72111, Hotels (except Casino Hotels) and Motels; and

- Providing medical or surgical hair replacement or weight reduction—are classified in Sector 62, Health Care and Social Assistance.

812191 Diet and Weight Reducing Centers[US]

This U.S. industry comprises establishments primarily engaged in providing nonmedical services to assist clients in attaining or maintaining a desired weight. The sale of weight reduction products, such as food supplements, may be an integral component of the program. These services typically include individual or group counseling, menu and exercise planning, and weight and body measurement monitoring.

Cross-References. Establishments primarily engaged in—

- Operating physical fitness facilities—are classified in Industry 713940, Fitness and Recreational Sports Centers;

- Operating health resorts and spas that provide lodging—are classified in Industry 721110, Hotels (except Casino Hotels) and Motels; and

- Providing medical or surgical weight reduction—are classified in Sector 62, Health Care and Social Assistance.

812199 Other Personal Care Services[US]

This U.S. industry comprises establishments primarily engaged in providing personal care services (except hair, nail, facial, nonpermanent makeup, or nonmedical diet and weight reducing services).

US—United States industry only. CAN—United States and Canadian industries are comparable. When neither US nor CAN appears, Canadian, Mexican, and United States industries are comparable.

Illustrative Examples:

Depilatory or electrolysis (i.e., hair removal) salons	Permanent makeup salons
Ear piercing services	Saunas
Hair replacement (except by offices of physicians) or weaving services	Steam or turkish baths
Massage parlors	Tanning salons
	Tattoo parlors

Cross-References. Establishments primarily engaged in—

- Cutting, trimming, and styling men's and boys' hair (known as barber shops or men's hair stylist shops)—are classified in U. S. Industry 812111, Barber Shops;

- Providing hair, facial, or nonpermanent makeup services (except establishments known as barber shops or men's hair stylist shops)—are classified in U.S. Industry 812112, Beauty Shops;

- Nail care services—are classified in U.S. Industry 812113, Nail Salons;

- Providing nonmedical diet and weight reducing services—are classified in U.S. Industry 812191, Diet and Weight Reducing Centers; and

- Providing medical or surgical hair replacement or weight reduction services—are classified in Sector 62, Health Care and Social Assistance.

8122 Death Care Services[CAN]

81221 Funeral Homes and Funeral Services[CAN]
See industry description for 812210 below.

812210 Funeral Homes and Funeral Services[CAN]

This industry comprises establishments primarily engaged in preparing the dead for burial or interment and conducting funerals (i.e., providing facilities for wakes, arranging transportation for the dead, selling caskets and related merchandise). Funeral homes combined with crematories are included in this industry.

Cross-References.

Establishments (except funeral homes) primarily engaged in cremating the dead are classified in Industry 812220, Cemeteries and Crematories.

81222 Cemeteries and Crematories[CAN]
See industry description for 812220 below.

812220 Cemeteries and Crematories[CAN]

This industry comprises establishments primarily engaged in operating sites or structures reserved for the interment of human or animal remains and/or cremating the dead.

US—United States industry only. CAN—United States and Canadian industries are comparable. When neither US nor CAN appears, Canadian, Mexican, and United States industries are comparable.

Illustrative Examples:

Cemetery associations (i.e., operators of cemeteries)	Mausoleums
	Memorial gardens (i.e., burial places)
Crematories (except combined with funeral homes)	Pet cemeteries

Cross-References.

Crematories combined with funeral homes are classified in Industry 812210, Funeral Homes and Funeral Services.

8123 Drycleaning and Laundry Services^{CAN}

81231 Coin-Operated Laundries and Drycleaners^{CAN}
See industry description for 812310 below.

812310 Coin-Operated Laundries and Drycleaners^{CAN}

This industry comprises (1) establishments primarily engaged in operating facilities with coin-operated or similar self-service laundry and drycleaning equipment for customer use on the premises and (2) establishments primarily engaged in supplying and servicing coin-operated or similar self-service laundry and drycleaning equipment for customer use in places of business operated by others, such as apartments and dormitories.

81232 Drycleaning and Laundry Services (except Coin-Operated)^{CAN}
See industry description for 812320 below.

812320 Drycleaning and Laundry Services (except Coin-Operated)^{CAN}

This industry comprises establishments primarily engaged in one or more of the following: (1) providing drycleaning services (except coin-operated); (2) providing laundering services (except linen and uniform supply or coin-operated); (3) providing dropoff and pickup sites for laundries and/or drycleaners; and (4) providing specialty cleaning services for specific types of garments and other textile items (except carpets and upholstery), such as fur, leather, or suede garments; wedding gowns; hats; draperies; and pillows. These establishments may provide all, a combination of, or none of the cleaning services on the premises.

Cross-References. Establishments primarily engaged in—

- Supplying laundered linens and uniforms on a rental or contract basis—are classified in Industry 81233, Linen and Uniform Supply;

- Operating coin-operated or similar self-service laundry or drycleaning facilities—are classified in Industry 812310, Coin-Operated Laundries and Drycleaners; and

- Cleaning used carpets and upholstery—are classified in Industry 561740, Carpet and Upholstery Cleaning Services.

81233 Linen and Uniform Supply^{CAN}

This industry comprises establishments primarily engaged in supplying, on a rental or contract basis, laundered items, such as uniforms, gowns and coats, table linens, bed linens, towels, clean room apparel, and treated mops or shop towels.

812331 Linen Supply^{US}

This U.S. industry comprises establishments primarily engaged in supplying, on a rental or contract basis, laundered items, such as table and bed linens; towels; diapers; and uniforms, gowns, or coats of the type used by doctors, nurses, barbers, beauticians, and waitresses.

Cross-References.

Establishments primarily engaged in supplying, on a rental or contract basis, laundered industrial work uniforms and related work clothing are classified in U.S. Industry 812332, Industrial Launderers.

812332 Industrial Launderers^{US}

This U.S. industry comprises establishments primarily engaged in supplying, on a rental or contract basis, laundered industrial work uniforms and related work clothing, such as protective apparel (flame and heat resistant) and clean room apparel; dust control items, such as treated mops, rugs, mats, dust tool covers, cloths, and shop or wiping towels.

Cross-References.

Establishments primarily engaged in supplying, on a rental or contract basis, laundered uniforms, gowns or coats of the type used by doctors, nurses, barbers, beauticians, and waitresses are classified in U.S. Industry 812331, Linen Supply.

8129 Other Personal Services^{CAN}

The industry group comprises establishments primarily engaged in providing personal services (except personal care services, death care services, or drycleaning and laundry services).

81291 Pet Care (except Veterinary) Services^{CAN}
See industry description for 812910 below.

812910 Pet Care (except Veterinary) Services^{CAN}

This industry comprises establishments primarily engaged in providing pet care services (except veterinary), such as boarding, grooming, sitting, and training pets.

US—United States industry only. CAN—United States and Canadian industries are comparable. When neither US nor CAN appears, Canadian, Mexican, and United States industries are comparable.

Cross-References. Establishments primarily engaged in—

- Practicing veterinary medicine—are classified in Industry 541940, Veterinary Services;

- Boarding horses—are classified in Industry 115210, Support Activities for Animal Production; and

- Transporting pets—are classified in U.S. Industry 485991, Special Needs Transportation.

81292 Photofinishing[CAN]

This industry comprises establishments primarily engaged in developing film and/or making photographic slides, prints, and enlargements.

Cross-References.

Establishments primarily engaged in processing motion picture film for the motion picture and television industries are classified in Industry 51219, Postproduction and Other Motion Picture and Video Industries.

812921 Photofinishing Laboratories (except One-Hour)[CAN]

This U.S. industry comprises establishments (except those known as "one-hour" photofinishing labs) primarily engaged in developing film and/or making photographic slides, prints, and enlargements.

Cross-References.

- Establishments primarily engaged in processing motion picture film for the motion picture and television industries are classified in U.S. Industry 512199, Other Motion Picture and Video Industries; and

- Establishments known as "one-hour" photofinishing labs are classified in U.S. Industry 812922, One-Hour Photofinishing.

812922 One-Hour Photofinishing[CAN]

This U.S. industry comprises establishments known as "one-hour" photofinishing labs primarily engaged in developing film and/or making photographic slides, prints, and enlargements on a short turnaround or while-you-wait basis.

Cross-References.

Photofinishing laboratories (except those known as "one-hour" photofinishing labs) are classified in U.S. Industry 812921, Photofinishing Laboratories (except One-Hour).

US—United States industry only. CAN—United States and Canadian industries are comparable. When neither US nor CAN appears, Canadian, Mexican, and United States industries are comparable.

81293 Parking Lots and Garages[CAN]
See industry description for 812930 below.

812930 Parking Lots and Garages[CAN]

This industry comprises establishments primarily engaged in providing parking space for motor vehicles, usually on an hourly, daily, or monthly basis and/or valet parking services.

Cross-References.

Establishments primarily engaged in providing extended or dead storage of motor vehicles are classified in Industry 493190, Other Warehousing and Storage .

81299 All Other Personal Services[CAN]
See industry description for 812990 below.

812990 All Other Personal Services[CAN]

This industry comprises establishments primarily engaged in providing personal services (except personal care services, death care services, drycleaning and laundry services, pet care services, photofinishing services, or parking space and/or valet parking services).

Illustrative Examples:

Bail bonding or bondsperson services
Coin-operated personal services machine (e.g., blood pressure, locker, photographic, scale, shoeshine) concession operators
Consumer buying services

Dating services
Shoeshine services
Social escort services
Wedding planning services

Cross-References. Establishments primarily engaged in—

- Providing personal care services—are classified in Industry Group 8121, Personal Care Services;

- Providing death care services—are classified in Industry Group 8122, Death Care Services;

- Providing drycleaning and laundry services—are classified in Industry Group 8123, Drycleaning and Laundry Services;

- Providing pet care (except veterinary) services—are classified in Industry 812910, Pet Care (except Veterinary) Services;

- Practicing veterinary medicine—are classified in Industry 541940, Veterinary Services;

- Providing photofinishing services—are classified in Industry 81292, Photofinishing; and

- Providing parking space for motor vehicles and/or valet parking services—are classified in Industry 812930, Parking Lots and Garages.

US—United States industry only. CAN—United States and Canadian industries are comparable. When neither US nor CAN appears, Canadian, Mexican, and United States industries are comparable.

813 Religious, Grantmaking, Civic, Professional, and Similar Organizations

Industries in the Religious, Grantmaking, Civic, Professional, and Similar Organizations subsector group establishments that organize and promote religious activities; support various causes through grantmaking; advocate various social and political causes; and promote and defend the interests of their members.

The industry groups within the subsector are defined in terms of their activities, such as establishments that provide funding for specific causes or for a variety of charitable causes; establishments that advocate and actively promote causes and beliefs for the public good; and establishments that have an active membership structure to promote causes and represent the interests of their members. Establishments in this subsector may publish newsletters, books, and periodicals, for distribution to their membership.

8131 Religious Organizations^{CAN}

81311 Religious Organizations^{CAN}
See industry description for 813110 below.

813110 Religious Organizations^{CAN}

This industry comprises (1) establishments primarily engaged in operating religious organizations, such as churches, religious temples, and monasteries and/or (2) establishments primarily engaged in administering an organized religion or promoting religious activities.

Illustrative Examples:

Churches	Shrines, religious
Monasteries (except schools)	Temples, religious
Mosques, religious	Synagogues

Cross-References.

- Schools, colleges, or universities operated by religious organizations are classified in Sector 61, Educational Services;

- Radio and television stations operated by religious organizations are classified in Subsector 513, Broadcasting and Telecommunications;

- Publishing houses operated by religious organizations are classified in Subsector 511, Publishing Industries;

- Establishments operated by religious organizations primarily engaged in health and social assistance for individuals are classified in Sector 62, Health Care and Social Assistance; and

---

US—United States industry only. CAN—United States and Canadian industries are comparable. When neither US nor CAN appears, Canadian, Mexican, and United States industries are comparable.

http://www.ntis.gov/naics

- Used merchandise stores operated by religious organizations are classified in Industry 453310, Used Merchandise Stores.

8132 Grantmaking and Giving Services[CAN]

81321 Grantmaking and Giving Services[CAN]

This industry comprises (1) establishment known as grantmaking foundations or charitable trusts and (2) establishments primarily engaged in raising funds for a wide range of social welfare activities, such as health, educational, scientific, and cultural activities.

Cross-References. Establishments primarily engaged in—

- Providing trust management services for others—are classified in Industry 52392, Portfolio Management;

- Organizing and conducting fundraising campaigns on a contract or fee basis—are classified in Industry 56149, Other Business Support Services;

- Providing telemarketing services for others—are classified in Industry 56142, Telephone Call Centers;

- Raising funds for political purposes—are classified in Industry 81394, Political Organizations;

- Advocating social causes or issues—are classified in Industry 81331, Social Advocacy Organizations; and

- Conducting health research—are classified in Industry 54171, Research and Development in the Physical, Engineering, and Life Sciences.

813211 Grantmaking Foundations[US]

This U.S. industry comprises establishments known as grantmaking foundations or charitable trusts. Establishments in this industry award grants from trust funds based on a competitive selection process or the preferences of the foundation managers and grantors; or fund a single entity, such as a museum or university.

Illustrative Examples:

Community foundations	Scholarship trusts
Corporate foundations, awarding grants	Philanthropic trusts
Grantmaking foundations	

Cross-References.

Establishments primarily engaged in providing trust management services for others are classified in Industry 523920, Portfolio Management.

US—United States industry only. CAN—United States and Canadian industries are comparable. When neither US nor CAN appears, Canadian, Mexican, and United States industries are comparable.

813212 Voluntary Health Organizations[US]

This U.S. industry comprises establishments primarily engaged in raising funds for health related research, such as disease (e.g., heart, cancer, diabetes) prevention, health education, and patient services.

Illustrative Examples:

Disease awareness fundraising organizations
Disease research (e.g., heart, cancer) fundraising organizations

Health research fundraising organizations
Voluntary health organizations

Cross-References.

- Establishments primarily engaged in raising funds for a wide range of social welfare activities, such as educational, scientific, cultural, and health, are classified in U.S. Industry 813219, Other Grantmaking and Giving Services;

- Establishments primarily engaged in organizing and conducting fundraising campaigns on a contract or fee basis are classified in U.S. Industry 561499, All Other Business Support Services;

- Establishments primarily engaged in providing telemarketing services for others are classified in U.S. Industry 561422, Telemarketing Bureaus;

- Establishments known as grantmaking foundations or charitable trusts are classified in U.S. Industry 813211, Grantmaking Foundations; and

- Establishments primarily engaged in conducting health research are classified in Industry 541710, Research and Development in the Physical, Engineering, and Life Sciences.

813219 Other Grantmaking and Giving Services[US]

This U.S. industry comprises establishments (except voluntary health organizations) primarily engaged in raising funds for a wide range of social welfare activities, such as educational, scientific, cultural, and health.

Illustrative Examples:

Community chests
Federated charities

United fund councils
United funds for colleges

Cross-References.

- Establishments primarily engaged in raising funds for health related research are classified in U.S. Industry 813212, Voluntary Health Organizations;

- Establishments known as grantmaking foundations or charitable trusts are classified in U.S. Industry 813211, Grantmaking Foundations;

US—United States industry only. CAN—United States and Canadian industries are comparable. When neither US nor CAN appears, Canadian, Mexican, and United States industries are comparable.

http://www.ntis.gov/naics

- Establishments primarily engaged in organizing and conducting fundraising campaigns on a contract or fee basis are classified in U.S. Industry 561499, All Other Business Support Services;

- Establishments primarily engaged in providing telemarketing services for others are classified in U.S. Industry 561422, Telemarketing Bureaus;

- Establishments primarily engaged in raising funds for political purposes are classified in Industry 813940, Political Organizations; and

- Establishments primarily engaged in advocating social causes or issues are classified in Industry 81331, Social Advocacy Organizations.

8133 Social Advocacy Organizations[CAN]

81331 Social Advocacy Organizations[CAN]

This industry comprises establishments primarily engaged in promoting a particular cause or working for the realization of a specific social or political goal to benefit a broad or specific constituency. These organizations may solicit contributions and offer memberships to support these goals.

Illustrative Examples:

Conservation advocacy organizations	Firearms advocacy organizations
Community action advocacy organizations	Human rights advocacy organizations
Environmental advocacy organizations	Wildlife preservation organizations

Cross-References. Establishments primarily engaged in—

- Promoting the civic and social interests of their members—are classified in Industry 81341, Civic and Social Organizations;

- Promoting the interests of the organized labor and union employees—are classified in Industry 81393, Labor Unions and Similar Labor Organizations; and

- Providing legal services for social advocacy organizations—are classified in Industry Group 5411, Legal Services.

813311 Human Rights Organizations[US]

This U.S. industry comprises establishments primarily engaged in promoting causes associated with human rights either for a broad or specific constituency. Establishments in this industry address issues, such as protecting and promoting the broad constitutional rights and civil liberties of individuals and those suffering from neglect, abuse, or exploitation; promoting the interests of specific groups, such as children, women, senior citizens, or persons with disabilities; improving relations between racial, ethnic, and cultural groups; and promoting voter education and registration. These organizations may solicit contributions and offer memberships to support these causes.

US—United States industry only. CAN—United States and Canadian industries are comparable. When neither US nor CAN appears, Canadian, Mexican, and United States industries are comparable.

Illustrative Examples:

Civil liberties organizations   Senior citizens' advocacy organizations
Human rights advocacy organizations   Veterans' rights organizations

Cross-References. Establishments primarily engaged in—

- Promoting the interests of organized labor and union employees—are classified in Industry 813930, Labor Unions and Similar Labor Organizations; and

- Providing legal services for human rights organizations—are classified in Industry Group 5411, Legal Services.

813312 Environment, Conservation and Wildlife Organizations[US]

This U.S. industry comprises establishments primarily engaged in promoting the preservation and protection of the environment and wildlife. Establishments in this industry address issues, such as clean air and water; global warming; conserving and developing natural resources, including land, plant, water, and energy resources; and protecting and preserving wildlife and endangered species. These organizations may solicit contributions and offer memberships to support these causes.

Illustrative Examples:

Animal rights organizations   Natural resource preservation organizations
Conservation advocacy organizations   Wildlife preservation organizations
Humane societies

Cross-References.

Establishments primarily engaged in providing legal services for environment, conservation, and wildlife organizations are classified in Industry Group 5411, Legal Services.

813319 Other Social Advocacy Organizations[US]

This U.S. industry comprises establishments primarily engaged in social advocacy (except human rights and environmental protection, conservation, and wildlife preservation). Establishments in this industry address issues, such as peace and international understanding; community action (excluding civic organizations); or advancing social causes, such as firearms safety, drunk driving prevention, drug abuse awareness. These organizations may solicit contributions and offer memberships to support these causes.

Illustrative Examples:

Community action advocacy organizations   Substance abuse prevention advocacy
Firearms advocacy organizations   organizations
Peace advocacy organizations   Taxpayers' advocacy organizations

---

Cross-References. Establishments primarily engaged in—

- Advocating human rights issues—are classified in U.S. Industry 813311, Human Rights Organizations;

- Promoting the preservation and protection of the environment and wildlife—are classified in U.S. Industry 813312, Environment, Conservation and Wildlife Organizations;

- Promoting the civic and social interests of their members—are classified in Industry 813410, Civic and Social Organizations;

- Providing legal services for social advocacy organizations—are classified in Industry Group 5411, Legal Services; and

- Providing community action services, such as community action services agencies,—are classified in Industry 624190, Other Individual and Family Services.

8134 Civic and Social Organizations[CAN]

81341 Civic and Social Organizations[CAN]
See industry description for 813410 below.

813410 Civic and Social Organizations[CAN]

This industry comprises establishments primarily engaged in promoting the civic and social interests of their members. Establishments in this industry may operate bars and restaurants for their members.

Illustrative Examples:

Alumni associations	Granges
Automobile clubs (except travel)	Parent-teacher associations
Booster clubs	Scouting organizations
Ethnic associations	Social clubs
Fraternal lodges	Veterans' membership organizations

Cross-References.

- Establishments of insurance offices operated by fraternal benefit organizations are classified in Subsector 524, Insurance Carriers and Related Activities;

- Establishments primarily engaged in operating residential fraternity and sorority houses are classified in Industry 721310, Rooming and Boarding Houses; and

- Establishments primarily engaged in providing travel arrangements and reservation services, such as automobile travel clubs or motor travel clubs are classified in U.S. Industry 561599, All Other Travel Arrangement and Reservation Services.

US—United States industry only. CAN—United States and Canadian industries are comparable. When neither US nor CAN appears, Canadian, Mexican, and United States industries are comparable.

8139 Business, Professional, Labor, Political, and Similar Organizations[CAN]

This industry group comprises establishments primarily engaged in promoting the interests of their members (except religious organizations, social advocacy organizations, and civic and social organizations). Examples of establishments in this industry are business associations, professional organizations, labor unions, and political organizations.

81391 Business Associations[CAN]
See industry description for 813910 below.

813910 Business Associations[CAN]

This industry comprises establishments primarily engaged in promoting the business interests of their members. These establishments may conduct research on new products and services; develop market statistics; sponsor quality and certification standards; lobby public officials; or publish newsletters, books, or periodicals for distribution to their members.

Illustrative Examples:

Chambers of commerce
Farm bureaus
Manufacturers' associations

Real estate boards
Trade associations

Cross-References.

- Establishments owned by their members but organized to perform a specific business function, such as common marketing of crops, joint advertising, or buying cooperatives, are classified according to their primary activity;

- Establishments primarily engaged in promoting the professional interests of their members and the profession as a whole are classified in Industry 813920, Professional Organizations;

- Establishments primarily engaged in promoting the interests of organized labor and union employees, such as trade unions, are classified in Industry 813930, Labor Unions and Similar Labor Organizations; and

- Establishments primarily engaged in lobbying public officials (i.e., lobbyists) are classified in Industry 541820, Public Relations Agencies.

81392 Professional Organizations[CAN]
See industry description for 813920 below.

813920 Professional Organizations[CAN]

This industry comprises establishments primarily engaged in promoting the professional interests of their members and the profession as a whole. These establishments may conduct research; develop statistics; sponsor quality and certification standards; lobby public officials; or publish newsletters, books, or periodicals, for distribution to their members.

US—United States industry only. CAN—United States and Canadian industries are comparable. When neither US nor CAN appears, Canadian, Mexican, and United States industries are comparable.

Illustrative Examples:

Bar associations	Learned societies
Dentists' associations	Peer review boards
Engineers' associations	Professional standards review boards
Health professionals' associations	Scientists' associations

Cross-References. Establishments primarily engaged in—

- Promoting the business interests of their members—are classified in Industry 813910, Business Associations; and

- Lobbying public officials (i.e., lobbyists)—are classified in Industry 541820, Public Relations Agencies.

81393 Labor Unions and Similar Labor Organizations[CAN]
See industry description for 813930 below.

813930 Labor Unions and Similar Labor Organizations[CAN]

This industry comprises establishments primarily engaged in promoting the interests of organized labor and union employees.

81394 Political Organizations[CAN]
See industry description for 813940 below.

813940 Political Organizations[CAN]

This industry comprises establishments primarily engaged in promoting the interests of national, state, or local political parties or candidates. Included are political groups organized to raise funds for a political party or individual candidates.

Illustrative Examples:

Campaign organizations, political	Political organizations or clubs
Political action committees (PACs)	Political parties
Political campaign organizations	

Cross-References. Establishments primarily engaged in—

- Organizing and conducting fundraising campaigns on a contract or fee basis—are classified in U.S. Industry 561499, All Other Business Support Services; and

- Providing telemarketing services for others—are classified in U.S. Industry 561422, Telemarketing Bureaus.

US—United States industry only. CAN—United States and Canadian industries are comparable. When neither US nor CAN appears, Canadian, Mexican, and United States industries are comparable.

http://www.ntis.gov/naics

81399 Other Similar Organizations (except Business, Professional, Labor, and Political Organizations)[CAN]

See industry description for 813990 below.

813990 Other Similar Organizations (except Business, Professional, Labor, and Political Organizations)[CAN]

This industry comprises establishments (except religious organizations, social advocacy organizations, civic and social organizations, business associations, professional organizations, labor unions, and political organizations) primarily engaged in promoting the interest of their members.

Illustrative Examples:

Athletic associations, regulatory or administrative	Cooperative owners' associations
	Property owners' associations
Condominium and homeowners' associations	Tenant associations (except advocacy)

Cross-References. Establishments of primarily engaged in—

- Operating religious organizations, such as churches, religious temples, and monasteries,—are classified in Industry 813110, Religious Organizations;

- Raising funds for a wide range of social welfare activities and establishments known as grantmaking foundations or charitable trusts—are classified in Industry 81321, Grantmaking and Giving Services;

- Advocating social causes or issues—are classified in Industry 81331, Social Advocacy Organizations;

- Promoting the civic and social interests of their members—are classified in Industry 813410, Civic and Social Organizations;

- Promoting the business interests of their members—are classified in Industry 813910, Business Associations;

- Promoting the professional interests of their members and the profession as a whole—are classified in Industry 813920, Professional Organizations;

- Promoting the interests of organized labor and union employees—are classified in Industry 813930, Labor Unions and Similar Labor Organizations;

- Promoting the interests of national, state, or local political parties or candidates—are classified in Industry 813940, Political Organizations; and

- Providing recreational and amusement services, such as recreational or youth sports teams and leagues,—are classified in Industry 713990, All Other Amusement and Recreation Industries.

814 Private Households

Industries in the Private Households subsector include private households that engage in employing workers on or about the premises in activities primarily concerned with the operation of the

---

US—United States industry only. CAN—United States and Canadian industries are comparable.
When neither US nor CAN appears, Canadian, Mexican, and United States industries are comparable.

household. These private households may employ individuals, such as cooks, maids, and butlers, and outside workers, such as gardeners, caretakers, and other maintenance workers.

8141 Private Households

81411 Private Households

See industry description for 814110 below.

814110 Private Households

This industry comprises private households primarily engaged in employing workers on or about the premises in activities primarily concerned with the operation of the household. These private households may employ individuals, such as cooks, maids, nannies, and butlers, and outside workers, such as gardeners, caretakers, and other maintenance workers.

US—United States industry only. CAN—United States and Canadian industries are comparable. When neither US nor CAN appears, Canadian, Mexican, and United States industries are comparable.

Sector 92—Public Administration

The Sector as a Whole

The Public Administration sector consists of establishments of federal, state, and local government agencies that administer, oversee, and manage public programs and have executive, legislative, or judicial authority over other institutions within a given area. These agencies also set policy, create laws, adjudicate civil and criminal legal cases, provide for public safety and for national defense. In general, government establishments in the Public Administration sector oversee governmental programs and activities that are not performed by private establishments. Establishments in this sector typically are engaged in the organization and financing of the production of public goods and services, most of which are provided for free or at prices that are not economically significant.

Government establishments also engage in a wide range of productive activities covering not only public goods and services but also individual goods and services similar to those produced in sectors typically identified with private-sector establishments. In general, ownership is not a criterion for classification in NAICS. Therefore, government establishments engaged in the production of private-sector-like goods and services should be classified in the same industry as private-sector establishments engaged in similar activities.

As a practical matter, it is difficult to identify separate establishment detail for many government agencies. To the extent that separate establishment records are available, the administration of governmental programs is classified in Sector 92, Public Administration, while the operation of that same governmental program is classified elsewhere in NAICS based on the activities performed. For example, the governmental administrative authority for an airport is classified in Industry 92612, Regulation and Administration of Transportation Programs, while operating the airport is classified in Industry 48811, Airport Operations. When separate records are not available to distinguish between the administration of a governmental program and the operation of it, the establishment is classified in Sector 92, Public Administration.

Examples of government-provided goods and services that are classified in sectors other than Public Administration include: schools, classified in Sector 61, Educational Services; hospitals, classified in Subsector 622, Hospitals; establishments operating transportation facilities, classified in Sector 48-49, Transportation and Warehousing; the operation of utilities, classified in Sector 22, Utilities; and the Government Printing Office, classified in Subsector 323, Printing and Related Support Activities.

921 Executive, Legislative, and Other General Government Support[US]

The Executive, Legislative, and Other General Government Support subsector groups offices of government executives, legislative bodies, public finance and general government support.

9211 Executive, Legislative, and Other General Government Support[US]

92111 Executive Offices[US]
See industry description for 921110 below.

921110 Executive Offices[US]

This industry comprises government establishments serving as offices of chief executives and their advisory committees and commissions. This industry includes offices of the president, governors, and mayors, in addition to executive advisory commissions.

US—United States industry only. CAN—United States and Canadian industries are comparable. When neither US nor CAN appears, Canadian, Mexican, and United States industries are comparable.

http://www.ntis.gov/naics

92112 Legislative Bodies[US]
See industry description for 921120 below.

921120 Legislative Bodies[US]

This industry comprises government establishments serving as legislative bodies and their advisory committees and commissions. Included in this industry are legislative bodies, such as Congress, state legislatures, and advisory and study legislative commissions.

92113 Public Finance Activities[US]
See industry description for 921130 below.

921130 Public Finance Activities[US]

This industry comprises government establishments primarily engaged in public finance, taxation and monetary policy. Included are financial administration activities, such as monetary policy; tax administration and collection; custody and disbursement of funds; debt and investment administration; auditing activities; and government employee retirement trust fund administration.

Cross-References. Government establishments primarily engaged in—

- Administering income maintenance programs—are classified in Industry 923130, Administration of Human Resource Programs (except Education, Public Health, and Veterans' Affairs Programs);

- Regulating insurance and banking institutions—are classified in Industry 926150, Regulation, Licensing, and Inspection of Miscellaneous Commercial Sectors; and

- Performing central banking functions, such as issuing currency and acting as the fiscal agent for the central government—are classified in Industry 521110, Monetary Authorities-Central Bank.

92114 Executive and Legislative Offices, Combined[US]
See industry description for 921140 below.

921140 Executive and Legislative Offices, Combined[US]

This industry comprises government establishments serving as councils and boards of commissioners or supervisors and such bodies where the chief executive (e.g., county executive or city mayor) is a member of the legislative body (e.g., county or city council) itself.

Cross-References. Government establishments primarily engaged in—

- Serving as offices of chief executives—are classified in Industry 921110, Executive Offices; and

- Serving as legislative bodies—are classified in Industry 921120, Legislative Bodies.

US—United States industry only. CAN—United States and Canadian industries are comparable. When neither US nor CAN appears, Canadian, Mexican, and United States industries are comparable.

92115 American Indian and Alaska Native Tribal Governments[US]

See industry description for 921150 below.

921150 American Indian and Alaska Native Tribal Governments[US]

This industry comprises American Indian and Alaska Native governing bodies. Establishments in this industry perform legislative, judicial, and administrative functions for their American Indian and Alaska Native lands. Included in this industry are American Indian and Alaska Native councils, courts, and law enforcement bodies.

Cross-References.

- Establishments primarily engaged in providing funding for American Indian and Alaska Native tribal programs through commercial activities, such as gaming, are classified in the industry of the commercial activity; and

- Government establishments providing public administration of American Indian and Alaska Native affairs are classified in Industry 923130, Administration of Human Resource Programs (except Education, Public Health, and Veterans' Affairs Programs).

92119 Other General Government Support[US]

See industry description for 921190 below.

921190 Other General Government Support[US]

This industry comprises government establishments primarily engaged in providing general support for government. Such support services include personnel services, election boards, and other general government support establishments that are not classified elsewhere in public administration.

Illustrative Examples:

Civil rights commissions,	Personnel offices, government
Civil service commissions,	Supply agencies, government
General services departments, government	

Cross-References.

- Government establishments primarily engaged in serving as offices of chief executives and their advisory committees and commissions are classified in Industry 921110, Executive Offices;

- Government establishments primarily engaged in serving as legislative bodies and their advisory committees and commissions are classified in Industry 921120, Legislative bodies;

- Government establishments primarily engaged in providing administration of public finance, tax collection, and monetary policy programs are classified in Industry 921130, Public Finance Activities;

US—United States industry only. CAN—United States and Canadian industries are comparable. When neither US nor CAN appears, Canadian, Mexican, and United States industries are comparable.

- Government establishments primarily engaged in serving as combined executive and legislative offices are classified in Industry 921140, Executive and Legislative Offices, Combined; and

- Establishments primarily engaged in serving as American Indian or Alaska Native tribal leadership are classified in Industry 921150, American Indian and Alaska Native Tribal Governments.

922 Justice, Public Order, and Safety Activities[US]

The Justice, Public Order, and Safety Activities subsector groups government establishments engaged in the administration of justice, public order, and safety programs.

9221 Justice, Public Order, and Safety Activities[US]

92211 Courts[US]
See industry description for 922110 below.

922110 Courts[US]

This industry comprises civilian courts of law (except Indian tribal and Alaska Native courts). Included in this industry are civilian courts, courts of law, and sheriffs' offices conducting court functions only.

Cross-References.

- Government establishments primarily engaged in operating military courts are classified in Industry 928110, National Security; and

- Establishments primarily engaged in operating Indian tribal or Alaska Native courts are classified in Industry 921150, American Indian and Alaska Native Tribal Governments.

92212 Police Protection[US]
See industry description for 922120 below.

922120 Police Protection[US]

This industry comprises government establishments primarily engaged in criminal and civil law enforcement, police, traffic safety, and other activities related to the enforcement of the law and preservation of order. Combined police and fire departments are included in this industry.

Cross-References.

- Government establishments primarily engaged in prosecution are classified in Industry 922130, Legal Counsel and Prosecution;

- Government establishments primarily engaged in collection of law enforcement statistics are classified in Industry 922190, Other Justice, Public Order, and Safety Activities;

US—United States industry only. CAN—United States and Canadian industries are comparable. When neither US nor CAN appears, Canadian, Mexican, and United States industries are comparable.

- Government establishments primarily engaged in providing police service for the military or National Guard are classified in Industry 928110, National Security;

- Government establishments primarily engaged in providing police service for tribal governments are classified in Industry 921150, American Indian and Alaska Native Tribal Governments;

- Government establishments primarily engaged in enforcing immigration laws are classified in Industry 928120, International Affairs;

- Sheriffs' offices conducting court functions only are classified in Industry 922110, Courts; and

- Private establishments primarily engaged in providing security and investigation services are classified in Industry 56161, Investigation, Guard, and Armored Car Services.

92213 Legal Counsel and Prosecution^{US}

See industry description for 922130 below.

922130 Legal Counsel and Prosecution^{US}

This industry comprises government establishments primarily engaged in providing legal counsel or prosecution services for the government.

Illustrative Examples:

Attorney generals' offices	Public defenders' offices
District attorneys' offices	Public prosecutors' offices

Cross-References.

Government establishments primarily engaged in collecting criminal justice statistics are classified in Industry 922190, Other Justice, Public Order, and Safety Activities.

92214 Correctional Institutions^{US}

See industry description for 922140 below.

922140 Correctional Institutions^{US}

This industry comprises government establishments primarily engaged in managing and operating correctional institutions. The facility is generally designed for the confinement, correction, and rehabilitation of adult and/or juvenile offenders sentenced by a court.

Illustrative Examples:

Correctional institutions, public administration	Penitentiaries, public administration
Detention centers, public administration	Prisons, public administration
Jails, public administration	

US—United States industry only. CAN—United States and Canadian industries are comparable. When neither US nor CAN appears, Canadian, Mexican, and United States industries are comparable.

http://www.ntis.gov/naics

Cross-References.

- Government establishments primarily engaged in operating half-way houses for ex-criminal offenders and delinquent youths are classified in Industry 623990, Other Residential Care Facilities; and

- Establishments primarily engaged in managing or operating correctional facilities owned by others are classified in Industry 561210, Facilities Support Services.

92215 Parole Offices and Probation Offices[US]

See industry description for 922150 below.

922150 Parole Offices and Probation Offices[US]

This industry comprises government establishments primarily engaged in judicially administering probation offices, parole offices and boards, and pardon boards.

Cross-References.

Government establishments primarily engaged in providing probation, parole, and pardon activities as an integral part of a central administrative corrections' office are classified in Industry 922140, Correctional Institutions.

92216 Fire Protection[US]

See industry description for 922160 below.

922160 Fire Protection[US]

This industry comprises government establishments primarily engaged in fire fighting and other related fire protection activities. Government establishments providing combined fire protection and ambulance or rescue services are classified in this industry.

Cross-References. Government establishments primarily engaged in—

- Forest fire fighting—are classified in Industry 115310, Support Activities for Forestry;

- Providing combined police and fire protection services—are classified in Industry 922120, Police Protection;

- Providing fire fighting services as a commercial activity—are classified in Industry 561990, All Other Support Services; and

- Providing ambulance services without fire protection service—are classified in Industry 621910, Ambulance Services.

US—United States industry only. CAN—United States and Canadian industries are comparable. When neither US nor CAN appears, Canadian, Mexican, and United States industries are comparable.

92219 Other Justice, Public Order, and Safety Activities[US]

See industry description for 922190 below.

922190 Other Justice, Public Order, and Safety Activities[US]

This industry comprises government establishments primarily engaged in public order and safety (except courts, police protection, legal counsel and prosecution, correctional institutions, parole offices, probation offices, pardon boards, and fire protection). These establishments include the general administration of public order and safety programs. Government establishments responsible for the collection of statistics on public safety are included in this industry.

Illustrative Examples:

Consumer product safety commissions, public administration

Disaster preparedness and management offices, government

Emergency planning and management offices, government

Public safety bureaus and statistics centers, government

Cross-References. Government establishments primarily engaged in—

- Serving as civilian courts of law (except Indian tribal and Alaska Native)—are classified in Industry 922110, Courts;

- Criminal and civil law enforcement, police, traffic safety and similar activities related to the enforcement of law—are classified in Industry 922120, Police Protection;

- Providing legal counsel to or prosecution services for their governments—are classified in Industry 922130, Legal Counsel and Prosecution;

- The confinement, correction, and rehabilitation of adult and juvenile offenders sentenced by a court—are classified in Industry 922140, Correctional Institutions;

- Judicially administering probation offices, parole offices and boards, and pardon boards— are classified in Industry 922150, Parole Offices and Probation Offices; and

- Fire fighting and other related fire protection activities—are classified in Industry 922160, Fire Protection.

923 Administration of Human Resource Programs[US]

The Administration of Human Resources Programs subsector groups government establishments primarily engaged in the administration of human resource programs.

9231 Administration of Human Resource Programs[US]

92311 Administration of Education Programs[US]

See industry description for 923110 below.

923110 Administration of Education Programs[US]

This industry comprises government establishments primarily engaged in the central coordination, planning, supervision and administration of funds, policies, intergovernmental activities, statistical

---

US—United States industry only. CAN—United States and Canadian industries are comparable. When neither US nor CAN appears, Canadian, Mexican, and United States industries are comparable.

reports and data collection, and centralized programs for educational administration. Government scholarship programs are included in this industry.

Illustrative Examples:

Education offices, nonoperating, public administration
Education statistics centers, government

State education departments
University regents or boards, government

Cross-References.

Schools and local school boards are classified in Subsector 611, Educational Services.

92312 Administration of Public Health Programs[US]
See industry description for 923120 below.

923120 Administration of Public Health Programs[US]

This industry comprises government establishments primarily engaged in the planning, administration, and coordination of public health programs and services, including environmental health activities, mental health, categorical health programs, health statistics, and immunization services. Government establishments primarily engaged in conducting public health-related inspections are included in this industry.

Illustrative Examples:

Communicable disease program administration, public administration
Coroners' offices, public administration
Health program administration, public administration

Mental health program administration, public administration
Public health program administration, nonoperating, public administration

Cross-References. Government establishments primarily engaged in—

- Operating hospitals (i.e., government or military)—are classified in Subsector 622, Hospitals;

- Providing health care in a clinical setting (i.e., military or government clinics)—are classified in Subsector 621, Ambulatory Health Care Services; and

- Inspecting food, plants, animals, and other agriculture products—are classified in Industry 926140, Regulation of Agricultural Marketing and Commodities.

US—United States industry only. CAN—United States and Canadian industries are comparable. When neither US nor CAN appears, Canadian, Mexican, and United States industries are comparable.

92313 Administration of Human Resource Programs (except Education, Public Health, and Veterans' Affairs Programs)US

See industry description for 923130 below.

923130 Administration of Human Resource Programs (except Education, Public Health, and Veterans' Affairs Programs)US

This industry comprises government establishments primarily engaged in the planning, administration, and coordination of programs for public assistance, social work, and welfare activities. The administration of Social Security, disability insurance, Medicare, unemployment insurance, and workers' compensation programs are included in this industry.

Cross-References. Government establishments primarily engaged in—

- Administering veterans' programs—are classified in Industry 923140, Administration of Veterans' Affairs;

- Operating state employment job service offices—are classified in Industry 561310, Employment Placement Agencies; and

- Operating programs for public assistance, social work, and welfare—are classified in Subsector 624, Social Assistance.

92314 Administration of Veterans' AffairsUS

See industry description for 923140 below.

923140 Administration of Veterans' AffairsUS

This industry comprises government establishments primarily engaged in the administration of programs of assistance, training, counseling, and other services to veterans and their dependents, heirs or survivors. Included in this industry are Veterans' Affairs offices that maintain liaison and coordinate activities with other service organizations and governmental agencies.

Cross-References.

- Government establishments operating veterans' hospitals are classified in Subsector 622, Hospitals;

- Establishments providing veterans' insurance are classified in Subsector 524, Insurance Carriers and Related Activities; and

- Establishments operating civic and social organizations for veterans are classified in Industry 813410, Civic and Social Organizations.

US—United States industry only. CAN—United States and Canadian industries are comparable. When neither US nor CAN appears, Canadian, Mexican, and United States industries are comparable.

924 Administration of Environmental Quality Programs[US]

The Administration of Environmental Quality Programs subsector groups government establishments primarily engaged in the administration of environmental quality.

9241 Administration of Environmental Quality Programs[US]

92411 Administration of Air and Water Resource and Solid Waste Management Programs[US]
See industry description for 924110 below.

924110 Administration of Air and Water Resource and Solid Waste Management Programs[US]

This industry comprises government establishments primarily engaged in one or more of the following: (1) the administration, regulation, and enforcement of air and water resource programs; (2) the administration and regulation of solid waste management programs; (3) the administration and regulation of water and air pollution control and prevention programs; (4) the administration and regulation of flood control programs; (5) the administration and regulation of drainage development and water resource consumption programs; (6) the administration and regulation of toxic waste removal and cleanup programs; and (7) coordination of these activities at intergovernmental levels.

Illustrative Examples:

Environmental protection program
   administration, public administration
Pollution control program administration,
   public administration
Waste management program (except sanitation
   districts), administration, public
   administration

Water control and quality program
   administration, public administration

Cross-References. Government establishments primarily engaged in—

• Operating water and irrigation systems—are classified in Industry 221310, Water Supply and Irrigation Systems;

• Administering sanitation districts—are classified in Industry 926130, Regulation and Administration of Communications, Electric, Gas, and Other Utilities;

• Operating sewage treatment facilities—are classified in Industry 221320, Sewage Treatment Facilities; and

• Providing waste collection, treatment, disposal, and/or remediation—are classified in Subsector 562, Waste Management and Remediation Services.

US—United States industry only. CAN—United States and Canadian industries are comparable. When neither US nor CAN appears, Canadian, Mexican, and United States industries are comparable.

92412 Administration of Conservation Programs^{US}
See industry description for 924120 below.

924120 Administration of Conservation Programs^{US}

This industry comprises government establishments primarily engaged in the administration, regulation, supervision and control of land use, including recreational areas; conservation and preservation of natural resources; erosion control; geological survey program administration; weather forecasting program administration; and the administration and protection of publicly and privately owned forest lands. Government establishments responsible for planning, management, regulation and conservation of game, fish, and wildlife populations, including wildlife management areas and field stations; and other administrative matters relating to the protection of fish, game, and wildlife are included in this industry.

Cross-References. Government establishments primarily engaged in—

- Operating parks—are classified in Industry 712190, Nature Parks and Other Similar Institutions;

- Operating forest property—are classified in Subsector 113, Forestry and Logging;

- Geophysical surveying and/or mapping—are classified in Industry 541360, Geophysical Surveying and Mapping Services;

- Surveying and/or mapping (except geophysical)—are classified in Industry 541370, Surveying and Mapping (except Geophysical) Services;

- Weather forecasting—are classified in Industry 541990, All Other Professional, Scientific and Technical Services;

- Operating fish and game preserves—are classified in Industry 712130, Zoos and Botanical Gardens; and

- Serving as urban planning commissions—are classified in Industry 925120, Administration of Urban Planning and Community and Rural Development.

925 Administration of Housing Programs, Urban Planning, and Community Development^{US}

The Administration of Housing Programs, Urban Planning, and Community Development subsector groups government establishments primarily engaged in the administration of housing, urban planning, and community development.

9251 Administration of Housing Programs, Urban Planning, and Community Development^{US}

92511 Administration of Housing Programs^{US}
See industry description for 925110 below.

925110 Administration of Housing Programs^{US}

This industry comprises government establishments primarily engaged in the administration and planning of housing programs.

US—United States industry only. CAN—United States and Canadian industries are comparable. When neither US nor CAN appears, Canadian, Mexican, and United States industries are comparable.

Cross-References. Government establishments primarily engaged in—

- Operating government rental housing—are classified in Subsector 531, Real Estate;

- Conducting building inspections and enforcing building codes and standards—are classified in Industry 926150, Regulation, Licensing, and Inspection of Miscellaneous Commercial Sectors; and

- Buying, pooling, and repackaging mortgages or home loans for sale to others on the secondary market—are classified in U.S. Industry 522294, Secondary Market Financing.

92512 Administration of Urban Planning and Community and Rural Development[US]

See industry description for 925120 below.

925120 Administration of Urban Planning and Community and Rural Development[US]

This industry comprises government establishments primarily engaged in the administration and planning of the development of urban and rural areas. Included in this industry are government zoning boards and commissions.

Illustrative Examples:

Land redevelopment agencies, government
  Regional planning and development program
  administration, public administration

Urban planning commissions, government
  Zoning boards and commissions, public
  administration

926 Administration of Economic Programs[US]

This subsector comprises government establishments primarily engaged in the administration of economic programs.

9261 Administration of Economic Programs[US]

92611 Administration of General Economic Programs[US]

See industry description for 926110 below.

926110 Administration of General Economic Programs[US]

This industry comprises government establishments primarily engaged in the administration, promotion and development of economic resources, including business, industry, and tourism. Included in this industry are government establishments responsible for the development of general statistical data and analyses and promotion of the general economic well-being of the governed area.

US—United States industry only. CAN—United States and Canadian industries are comparable. When neither US nor CAN appears, Canadian, Mexican, and United States industries are comparable.

http://www.ntis.gov/naics

Illustrative Examples:

Consumer protection offices, public
administration
Economic development agencies, government
General economics statistical agencies, public
administration

Small business development agencies, public
administration
Trade commissions, government

92612 Regulation and Administration of Transportation Programs[US]
See industry description for 926120 below.

926120 Regulation and Administration of Transportation Programs[US]

This industry comprises government establishments primarily engaged in the administration, regulation, licensing, planning, inspection, and investigation of transportation services and facilities. Included in this industry are government establishments responsible for motor vehicle and operator licensing, the Coast Guard (except the Coast Guard Academy), and parking authorities.

Cross-References. Government establishments primarily engaged in—

- Operating airports, railroads, depots, ports, toll roads and bridges, and other transportation facilities—are classified in Sector 48-49, Transportation and Warehousing;

- Operating parking lots and parking garages—are classified in Industry 812930, Parking Lots and Garages;

- Operating automobile safety inspection and emission testing facilities—are classified in Industry Group 8111, Automotive Repair and Maintenance;

- Building and/or maintaining roads and highways—are classified in Industry 234110, Highway and Street Construction;

- Providing air traffic control services—are classified in U.S. Industry 488111, Air Traffic Control; and

- Operating weigh stations—are classified in Industry 488490, Other Support Activities for Road Transportation.

92613 Regulation and Administration of Communications, Electric, Gas, and Other Utilities[US]
See industry description for 926130 below.

926130 Regulation and Administration of Communications, Electric, Gas, and Other Utilities[US]

This industry comprises government establishments primarily engaged in the administration, regulation, licensing and inspection of utilities, such as communications, electric power (including fossil, nuclear, solar, water, and wind), gas and water supply, and sewerage.

US—United States industry only. CAN—United States and Canadian industries are comparable. When neither US nor CAN appears, Canadian, Mexican, and United States industries are comparable.

http://www.ntis.gov/naics

Cross-References.

Government establishments primarily engaged in operating utilities are classified in Subsector 221, Utilities.

92614 Regulation of Agricultural Marketing and Commodities[US]

See industry description for 926140 below.

926140 Regulation of Agricultural Marketing and Commodities[US]

This industry comprises government establishments primarily engaged in the planning, administration, and coordination of agricultural programs for production, marketing, and utilization, including educational and promotional activities. Included in this industry are government establishments responsible for regulating and controlling the grading and inspection of food, plants, animals, and other agricultural products.

Cross-References. Government establishments primarily engaged in—

- Administering programs for developing economic data about agricultural and trade in agricultural products—are classified in Industry 926110, Administration of General Economic Programs;

- Administering programs for the conservation of natural resources—are classified in Industry Group 9241, Administration of Environmental Quality Programs; and

- Administering food stamp programs—are classified in Industry 923130, Administration Human Resource Programs (except Education, Public Health, and Veterans' Affairs Programs).

92615 Regulation, Licensing, and Inspection of Miscellaneous Commercial Sectors[US]

See industry description for 926150 below.

926150 Regulation, Licensing, and Inspection of Miscellaneous Commercial Sectors[US]

This industry comprises government establishments primarily engaged in the regulation, licensing, and inspection of commercial sectors, such as retail trade, professional occupations, manufacturing, mining, construction and services. Included in this industry are government establishments maintaining physical standards, regulating hazardous conditions not elsewhere classified, and enforcing alcoholic beverage control regulations.

US—United States industry only. CAN—United States and Canadian industries are comparable. When neither US nor CAN appears, Canadian, Mexican, and United States industries are comparable.

Illustrative Examples:

Alcoholic beverage control boards, public
administration
Banking regulatory agencies, public
administration
Building inspections, government
Insurance commissions, government
Labor management negotiations boards,
government

Licensing and permit issuance for professional
occupations, government
Licensing and permit issuance for business
operations, government
Securities regulation commissions, public
administration

Cross-References. Government establishments primarily engaged in—

- Regulating, administering, and inspecting transportation services and facilities—are classified in Industry 926120, Regulation and Administration of Transportation Programs; and

- Regulating, administering, and inspecting communications, electric, gas, and other utilities—are classified in Industry 926130, Regulation and Administration of Communications, Electric, Gas, and Other Utilities.

927 Space Research and Technology[US]

This subsector group comprises government establishments that conduct space research.

9271 Space Research and Technology[US]

92711 Space Research and Technology[US]
See industry description for 927110 below.

927110 Space Research and Technology[US]

This industry comprises government establishments primarily engaged in the administration and operations of space flights, space research, and space exploration. Included in this industry are government establishments operating space flight centers.

Cross-References.

- Private establishments primarily engaged in providing space freight transportation are classified in U.S. Industry 481212, Nonscheduled Chartered Freight Air Transportation;

- Government establishments primarily engaged in manufacturing aerospace vehicles and parts are classified in Industry 33641, Aerospace Product and Parts Manufacturing; and

- Government establishments primarily engaged in manufacturing space satellites are classified in Industry 334220, Radio and Television Broadcasting and Wireless Communications Equipment Manufacturing.

US—United States industry only. CAN—United States and Canadian industries are comparable.
When neither US nor CAN appears, Canadian, Mexican, and United States industries are comparable.

http://www.ntis.gov/naics

928 National Security and International Affairs^{US}

This subsector comprises government establishments primarily engaged in national security and international affairs.

9281 National Security and International Affairs^{US}

92811 National Security^{US}
See industry description for 928110 below.

928110 National Security^{US}

This industry comprises government establishments of the Armed Forces, including the National Guard, primarily engaged in national security and related activities.

Illustrative Examples:

Air Force
Army
Marine Corps
Military courts
Military police

Military training schools (except military
  service academies)
National Guard
Navy

Cross-References. Government establishments primarily engaged in—

- Operating military service academies—are classified in Industry 611310, Colleges, Universities, and Professional Schools; and

- Regulating and administering water transportation, such as the U.S. Coast Guard and the Merchant Marine,—are classified in Industry 926120, Regulation and Administration of Transportation Programs.

92812 International Affairs^{US}
See industry description for 928120 below.

928120 International Affairs^{US}

This industry comprises establishments of U.S. and foreign governments primarily engaged in international affairs and programs relating to other nations and peoples.

Cross-References.

- Private sector trade associations and councils are classified in Industry 813910, Business Associations; and

- Government establishments administering international trade, such as trade commissions and councils are classified in Industry 926110, Administration of General Economic Programs.

US—United States industry only. CAN—United States and Canadian industries are comparable. When neither US nor CAN appears, Canadian, Mexican, and United States industries are comparable.

Part II

Numerical List of Short Titles

Numerical List of Short Titles

Standard Short Titles for NAICS United States are shown below. They have been created for the use of those who find that space limitations preclude the use of the full title for the dissemination of data classified to NAICS. The adoptions of these titles is recommended in all cases when the full title cannot be used.

The standard short titles are limited to 45 spaces. If the official full title falls within 45 spaces it remains unchanged.

It should be noted that these short titles produced for NAICS United States may differ from the short titles produced for NAICS Canada and NAICS Mexico. It is recommended that the codes rather than the titles be used for comparison. There are only three codes that are used by both the United States and Canada where the content of the classes is different. Those are as follows:

NAICS United States	323119	Other Commercial Printing
NAICS Canada	323119	Other Printing
NAICS United States	332999	All Other Miscellaneous Fabricated Metal Product Manufacturing
NAICS Canada	332999	All Other Miscellaneous Fabricated Metal Product Manufacturing
NAICS United States	334512	Automatic Environmental Control Manufacturing for Residential, Commercial, and Appliance Use
NAICS Canada	334512	Measuring, Medical, and Controlling Devices Manufacturing

Note: For definitions of abbreviations and substitute words see page 765.

http://www.ntis.gov/naics

Code	Short title	Code	Short title
11	**AGRICULTURE, FORESTRY, FISHING & HUNTING**	1119	Other Crop Farming
		11191	Tobacco Farming
		11192	Cotton Farming
111	**Crop Production**	11193	Sugarcane Farming
1111	Oilseed & Grain Farming	11194	Hay Farming
11111	Soybean Farming	11199	All Other Crop Farming
11112	Oilseed (except Soybean) Farming	111991	Sugar Beet Farming
		111992	Peanut Farming
11113	Dry Pea & Bean Farming	111998	All Other Miscellaneous Crop Farming
11114	Wheat Farming		
11115	Corn Farming		
11116	Rice Farming	**112**	**Animal Production**
11119	Other Grain Farming		
111191	Oilseed & Grain Combination Farming	1121	Cattle Ranching & Farming
		11211	Beef Cattle Ranching & Farming & Feedlots
111199	All Other Grain Farming		
1112	Vegetable & Melon Farming	112111	Beef Cattle Ranching & Farming
11121	Vegetable & Melon Farming	112112	Cattle Feedlots
111211	Potato Farming	11212	Dairy Cattle & Milk Production
111219	Other Vegetable (exc Potato) & Melon Farming	11213	Dual Purpose Cattle Ranching & Farming
1113	Fruit & Tree Nut Farming	1122	Hog & Pig Farming
11131	Orange Groves	11221	Hog & Pig Farming
11132	Citrus (except Orange) Groves	1123	Poultry & Egg Production
11133	Noncitrus Fruit & Tree Nut Farming	11231	Chicken Egg Production
		11232	Broilers & Other Meat Type Chicken Production
111331	Apple Orchards		
111332	Grape Vineyards	11233	Turkey Production
111333	Strawberry Farming	11234	Poultry Hatcheries
111334	Berry (except Strawberry) Farming	11239	Other Poultry Production
		1124	Sheep and Goat Farming
111335	Tree Nut Farming	11241	Sheep Farming
111336	Fruit & Tree Nut Combination Farming	11242	Goat Farming
		1125	Animal Aquaculture
111339	Other Noncitrus Fruit Farming	11251	Animal Aquaculture
1114	Greenhouse, Nursery & Floriculture Production	112511	Finfish Farming & Fish Hatcheries
		112512	Shellfish Farming
11141	Food Crops Grown Under Cover	112519	Other Animal Aquaculture
111411	Mushroom Production	1129	Other Animal Production
111419	Other Food Crops Grown Under Cover	11291	Apiculture
		11292	Horse & Other Equine Production
11142	Nursery & Floriculture Production	11293	Fur-bearing Animal & Rabbit Prod
111421	Nursery & Tree Production	11299	All Other Animal Production
111422	Floriculture Production		

Note: For definitions of abbreviations and substitute words see page 765.

http://www.ntis.gov/naics

Code	Short title
113	**Forestry and Logging**
1131	Timber Tract Operations
11311	Timber Tract Operations
1132	Forest Nurseries & Gathering Forest Products
11321	Forest Nurseries & Gathering Forest Products
1133	Logging
11331	Logging
114	**Fishing, Hunting & Trapping**
1141	Fishing
11411	Fishing
114111	Finfish Fishing
114112	Shellfish Fishing
114119	Other Marine Fishing
1142	Hunting & Trapping
11421	Hunting & Trapping
115	**Agriculture & Forestry Support Activities**
1151	Crop Production Support Activities
11511	Crop Production Support Activities
115111	Cotton Ginning
115112	Soil Preparation, Planting, & Cultivating
115113	Crop Harvesting, Primarily by Machine
115114	Postharvest Crop Activities (exc Ginning)
115115	Farm Labor Contractors & Crew Leaders
115116	Farm Management Services
1152	Animal Production Support Activities
11521	Animal Production Support Activities
1153	Forestry Support Activities
11531	Forestry Support Activities

Code	Short title
21	**MINING**
211	**Oil & Gas Extraction**
2111	Oil & Gas Extraction
21111	Oil & Gas Extraction
211111	Crude Petroleum & Natural Gas Extraction
211112	Natural Gas Liquid Extraction
212	**Mining (except Oil & Gas)**
2121	Coal Mining
21211	Coal Mining
212111	Bituminous Coal & Lignite Surface Mining
212112	Bituminous Coal Underground Mining
212113	Anthracite Mining
2122	Metal Ore Mining
21221	Iron Ore Mining
21222	Gold Ore & Silver Ore Mining
212221	Gold Ore Mining
212222	Silver Ore Mining
21223	Copper, Nickel, Lead & Zinc Mining
212231	Lead Ore & Zinc Ore Mining
212234	Copper Ore & Nickel Ore Mining
21229	Other Metal Ore Mining
212291	Uranium-Radium-Vanadium Ore Mining
212299	All Other Metal Ore Mining
2123	Nonmetallic Mineral Mining & Quarrying
21231	Stone Mining & Quarrying
212311	Dimension Stone Mining & Quarrying
212312	Crushed & Broken Limestone Mining & Quarrying
212313	Crushed & Broken Granite Mining & Quarrying
212319	Oth Crushed & Broken Stone Mining & Quarrying
21232	Sand/Gravel/Clay/Refractory Minerals Mining

Note: For definitions of abbreviations and substitute words see page 765.

http://www.ntis.gov/naics

Code	Short title	Code	Short title
212321	Construction Sand & Gravel Mining	221122	Electric Power Distribution
212322	Industrial Sand Mining	2212	Natural Gas Distribution
212324	Kaolin & Ball Clay Mining	22121	Natural Gas Distribution
212325	Clay & Ceramic & Refractory Minerals Mining	2213	Water, Sewage & Other Systems
21239	Other Nonmetallic Mineral Mining & Quarrying	22131	Water Supply & Irrigation Systems
212391	Potash, Soda, & Borate Mineral Mining	22132	Sewage Treatment Facilities
212392	Phosphate Rock Mining	22133	Steam & Air-Conditioning Supply

23 CONSTRUCTION

Code	Short title	Code	Short title
212393	Other Chemical & Fertilizer Mineral Mining	**233**	**Building, Developing & General Contracting**
212399	All Other Nonmetallic Mineral Mining	2331	Land Subdivision & Land Development
		23311	Land Subdivision & Land Development
213	**Mining Support Activities**	2332	Residential Building Construction
2131	Mining Support Activities	23321	Single-Family Housing Construction
21311	Mining Support Activities		
213111	Drilling Oil & Gas Wells	23322	Multifamily Housing Construction
213112	Oil & Gas Operations Support Activities	2333	Nonresidential Building Construction
213113	Support Activities for Coal Mining	23331	Mfg & Industrial Building Construction
213114	Support Activities for Metal Mining	23332	Commercial & Institutional Bldg Construction
213115	Nonmetallic Minerals Support Activity (exc Fuels)	**234**	**Heavy Construction**

22 UTILITIES

Code	Short title	Code	Short title
221	**Utilities**	2341	Highway, Street, Bridge & Tunnel Construction
2211	Elec Pwr Generation, Transmsn & Distribution	23411	Highway & Street Construction
		23412	Bridge & Tunnel Construction
22111	Electric Power Generation	2349	Other Heavy Construction
221111	Hydroelectric Power Generation	23491	Water, Sewer & Pipeline Construction
221112	Fossil Fuel Electric Power Generation	23492	Pwr/Communication Transmsn Line Construction
221113	Nuclear Electric Power Generation	23493	Industrial Nonbuilding Structure Construction
221119	Other Electric Power Generation	23499	All Other Heavy Construction
22112	Electric Pwr Transmsn, Control & Distribution	**235**	**Special Trade Contractors**
221121	Electric Bulk Power Transmission & Control	2351	Plumbing, Heating & AC Contractor

Note: For definitions of abbreviations and substitute words see page 765.

Code	Short title	Code	Short title
23511	Plumbing, Heating & AC Contractor	311111	Dog & Cat Food Mfg
2352	Painting & Wall Covering Contractors	311119	Other Animal Food Mfg
		3112	Grain & Oilseed Milling
23521	Painting & Wall Covering Contractors	31121	Flour Milling & Malt Mfg
		311211	Flour Milling
2353	Electrical Contractors	311212	Rice Milling
23531	Electrical Contractors	311213	Malt Mfg
2354	Masonry/Drywall/Insulation/Tile Contractors	31122	Starch & Vegetable Fats & Oils Mfg
23541	Masonry & Stone Contractors	311221	Wet Corn Milling
23542	Drywall, Acoustical & Insulation Contractors	311222	Soybean Processing
		311223	Other Oilseed Processing
23543	Tile, Marble, Terrazzo & Mosaic Contractors	311225	Fats & Oils Refining & Blending
		31123	Breakfast Cereal Manufacturing
2355	Carpentry & Floor Contractors	3113	Sugar & Confectionery Product Mfg
23551	Carpentry Contractors	31131	Sugar Mfg
23552	Floor Laying & Other Floor Contractors	311311	Sugarcane Mills
		311312	Cane Sugar Refining
2356	Roofing, Siding, & Sheet Metal Contractors	311313	Beet Sugar Mfg
		31132	Choc & Confectionery Mfg from Cacao Beans
23561	Roofing, Siding & Sheet Metal Contractors	31133	Confectionery Mfg from Purchased Chocolate
2357	Concrete Contractors		
23571	Concrete Contractors	31134	Nonchocolate Confectionery Mfg
2358	Water Well Drilling Contractors	3114	Fruit & Veg Preserving & Specialty Food Mfg
23581	Water Well Drilling Contractors		
2359	Other Special Trade Contractors	31141	Frozen Food Mfg
23591	Structural Steel Erection Contractors	311411	Frozen Fruit, Juice & Vegetable Mfg
23592	Glass & Glazing Contractors	311412	Frozen Specialty Food Mfg
23593	Excavation Contractors	31142	Fruit & Veg Canning, Pickling & Drying
23594	Wrecking & Demolition Contractors		
		311421	Fruit & Vegetable Canning
23595	Bldg Equip & Oth Mach Installation Contractor	311422	Specialty Canning
		311423	Dried & Dehydrated Food Mfg
23599	All Other Special Trade Contractors	3115	Dairy Product Mfg
		31151	Dairy Product (exc Frozen) Mfg
		311511	Fluid Milk Mfg
31-33	**MANUFACTURING**	311512	Creamery Butter Mfg
		311513	Cheese Mfg
311	**Food Mfg**	311514	Dry/Condensed/Evaporated Dairy Product Mfg
3111	Animal Food Mfg		
31111	Animal Food Mfg	31152	Ice Cream & Frozen Dessert Mfg

Note: For definitions of abbreviations and substitute words see page 765.

http://www.ntis.gov/naics

Code	Short title
3116	Animal Slaughtering & Processing
31161	Animal Slaughtering & Processing
311611	Animal (except Poultry) Slaughtering
311612	Meat Processed From Carcasses
311613	Rendering & Meat Byproduct Processing
311615	Poultry Processing
3117	Seafood Product Preparation & Packaging
31171	Seafood Product Preparation & Packaging
311711	Seafood Canning
311712	Fresh & Frozen Seafood Processing
3118	Bakeries & Tortilla Mfg
31181	Bread & Bakery Product Mfg
311811	Retail Bakeries
311812	Commercial Bakeries
311813	Frozen Cakes, Pies & Other Pasteries Mfg
31182	Cookie, Cracker & Pasta Mfg
311821	Cookie & Cracker Mfg
311822	Flour Mixes & Dough Mfg from Purchased Flour
311823	Dry Pasta Mfg
31183	Tortilla Mfg
3119	Other Food Mfg
31191	Snack Food Mfg
311911	Roasted Nuts & Peanut Butter Mfg
311919	Other Snack Food Mfg
31192	Coffee & Tea Mfg
31193	Flavoring Syrup & Concentrate Mfg
31194	Seasoning & Dressing Mfg
311941	Mayonnaise, Dressing & Oth Prepared Sauce Mfg
311942	Spice & Extract Mfg
31199	All Other Food Mfg
311991	Perishable Prepared Food Mfg
311999	All Other Miscellaneous Food Mfg

Code	Short title
312	**Beverage & Tobacco Product Mfg**
3121	Beverage Mfg
31211	Soft Drink & Ice Mfg
312111	Soft Drink Mfg
312112	Bottled Water Mfg
312113	Ice Mfg
31212	Breweries
31213	Wineries
31214	Distilleries
3122	Tobacco Mfg
31221	Tobacco Stemming & Redrying
31222	Tobacco Product Mfg
312221	Cigarette Mfg
312229	Other Tobacco Product Mfg
313	**Textile Mills**
3131	Fiber, Yarn & Thread Mills
31311	Fiber, Yarn & Thread Mills
313111	Yarn Spinning Mills
313112	Yarn Texturing, Throwing & Twisting Mills
313113	Thread Mills
3132	Fabric Mills
31321	Broadwoven Fabric Mills
31322	Narrow Fabric Mills & Schiffli Mach Embroid
313221	Narrow Fabric Mills
313222	Schiffli Machine Embroidery
31323	Nonwoven Fabric Mills
31324	Knit Fabric Mills
313241	Weft Knit Fabric Mills
313249	Other Knit Fabric & Lace Mills
3133	Textile/Fabric Finishing/Fabric Coating Mills
31331	Textile & Fabric Finishing Mills
313311	Broadwoven Fabric Finishing Mills
313312	Textile/Fabric Finishing (exc Broadwoven) Mill
31332	Fabric Coating Mills
314	**Textile Product Mills**
3141	Textile Furnishings Mills
31411	Carpet & Rug Mills

Note: For definitions of abbreviations and substitute words see page 765.

Code	Short title	Code	Short title
31412	Curtain & Linen Mills	31523	Women's/Girls' Cut & Sew Apparel Mfg
314121	Curtain & Drapery Mills	315231	Women's/Girls' Cut & Sew Lingerie Mfg
314129	Other Household Textile Product Mills	315232	Women's/Girls' Cut & Sew Blouse Mfg
3149	Other Textile Product Mills	315233	Women's/Girls' Cut & Sew Dress Mfg
31491	Textile Bag & Canvas Mills		
314911	Textile Bag Mills	315234	Women's/Girls' Cut & Sew Suit/ Coat/Skirt Mfg
314912	Canvas & Related Product Mills		
31499	All Other Textile Product Mills	315239	Women's/Girls' Cut & Sew Other Outerwear Mfg
314991	Rope, Cordage & Twine Mills	31529	Other Cut & Sew Apparel Mfg
314992	Tire Cord & Tire Fabric Mills	315291	Infants' Cut & Sew Apparel Mfg
314999	All Other Miscellaneous Textile Product Mills	315292	Fur & Leather Apparel Mfg
		315299	All Other Cut & Sew Apparel Mfg
315	**Apparel Manufacturing**	3159	Apparel Accessories & Other Apparel Mfg
3151	Apparel Knitting Mills	31599	Apparel Accessories & Other Apparel Mfg
31511	Hosiery & Sock Mills		
315111	Sheer Hosiery Mills	315991	Hat, Cap & Millinery Mfg
315119	Other Hosiery & Sock Mills	315992	Glove & Mitten Mfg
31519	Other Apparel Knitting Mills	315993	Men's & Boys' Neckwear Mfg
315191	Outerwear Knitting Mills	315999	Other Apparel Accessories & Other Apparel Mfg
315192	Underwear & Nightwear Knitting Mills		
3152	Cut & Sew Apparel Mfg	**316**	**Leather & Allied Product Mfg**
31521	Cut & Sew Apparel Contractors	3161	Leather & Hide Tanning & Finishing
315211	Men's/Boys' Cut & Sew Apparel Contractors	31611	Leather & Hide Tanning & Finishing
315212	Women's/Girls'/Infants' Cut/Sew Apparel Contr	3162	Footwear Mfg
		31621	Footwear Mfg
31522	Men's/Boys' Cut & Sew Apparel Mfg	316211	Rubber & Plastics Footwear Mfg
		316212	House Slipper Mfg
315221	Men's/Boys' Cut & Sew Underwear/Nightwear Mfg	316213	Men's Footwear (exc Athletic) Mfg
315222	Men's/Boys' Cut & Sew Suit, Coat/Overcoat Mfg	316214	Women's Footwear (exc Athletic) Mfg
315223	Men's/Boys' Cut & Sew Shirt (exc Work) Mfg	316219	Other Footwear Mfg
315224	Men's/Boys' Cut & Sew Trouser/ Slack/Jean Mfg	3169	Other Leather & Allied Product Mfg
315225	Men's/Boys' Cut & Sew Work Clothing Mfg	31699	Other Leather & Allied Product Mfg
315228	Men's/Boys' Cut & Sew Oth Outerwear Mfg		

Note: For definitions of abbreviations and substitute words see page 765.

http://www.ntis.gov/naics

Code	Short title	Code	Short title
316991	Luggage Mfg	32221	Paperboard Container Mfg
316992	Women's Handbag & Purse Mfg	322211	Corrugated & Solid Fiber Box Mfg
316993	Personal Leather Good (exc Purse) Mfg	322212	Folding Paperboard Box Mfg
316999	All Other Leather Good Mfg	322213	Setup Paperboard Box Mfg
		322214	Fiber Can, Tube, Drum & Similar Products Mfg

321   Wood Product Mfg

Code	Short title	Code	Short title
3211	Sawmills & Wood Preservation	322215	Nonfolding Sanitary Food Container Mfg
32111	Sawmills & Wood Preservation		
321113	Sawmills	32222	Paper Bag & Coated & Treated Paper Mfg
321114	Wood Preservation		
3212	Veneer, Plywood & Engineered Wood Product Mfg	322221	Coated & Lamnd Pkg Paper & Plastics Film Mfg
32121	Veneer, Plywood & Engineered Wood Product Mfg	322222	Coated & Laminated Paper Mfg
		322223	Plastics, Foil, & Coated Paper Bag Mfg
321211	Hardwood Veneer & Plywood Mfg		
321212	Softwood Veneer & Plywood Mfg	322224	Uncoated Paper & Multiwall Bag Mfg
321213	Engineered Wood Member (exc Truss) Mfg	322225	Laminated Aluminum Foil Mfg for Flexible Pkg
321214	Truss Mfg		
321219	Reconstituted Wood Product Mfg	322226	Surface-Coated Paperboard Mfg
3219	Other Wood Product Mfg	32223	Stationery Product Mfg
32191	Millwork	322231	Die-Cut Paper & Paperboard Office Supply Mfg
321911	Wood Window & Door Mfg		
321912	Cut Stock, Resawing Lumber & Planing	322232	Envelope Mfg
		322233	Stationery, Tablet & Related Product Mfg
321918	Other Millwork (including Flooring)	32229	Other Converted Paper Product Mfg
32192	Wood Container & Pallet Mfg		
32199	All Other Wood Product Mfg	322291	Sanitary Paper Product Mfg
321991	Manufactured Home (Mobile Home) Mfg	322299	All Other Converted Paper Product Mfg
321992	Prefabricated Wood Building Mfg		

323   Printing & Related Support Activities

| 321999 | All Other Miscellaneous Wood Product Mfg | | |

Code	Short title	Code	Short title
		3231	Printing & Related Support Activities

322   Paper Mfg

Code	Short title	Code	Short title
3221	Pulp, Paper & Paperboard Mills	32311	Printing
32211	Pulp Mills	323110	Commercial Lithographic Printing
32212	Paper Mills	323111	Commercial Gravure Printing
322121	Paper (except Newsprint) Mills	323112	Commercial Flexographic Printing
322122	Newsprint Mills		
32213	Paperboard Mills	323113	Commercial Screen Printing
3222	Converted Paper Product Mfg	323114	Quick Printing

Note: For definitions of abbreviations and substitute words see page 765.

http://www.ntis.gov/naics

Code	Short title	Code	Short title
323115	Digital Printing	325193	Ethyl Alcohol Mfg
323116	Manifold Business Form Printing	325199	All Other Basic Organic Chemical Mfg
323117	Book Printing		
323118	Blankbook, Looseleaf Binder & Device Mfg	3252	Resin, Syn Rubber, Artf & Syn Fibers/Fil Mfg
323119	Other Commercial Printing	32521	Resin & Synthetic Rubber Mfg
32312	Printing Support Activities	325211	Plastics Material & Resins Mfg
323121	Tradebinding & Related Work	325212	Synthetic Rubber Mfg
323122	Prepress Services	32522	Artificial & Synthetic Fibers/ Filaments Mfg
324	**Petroleum & Coal Products Mfg**	325221	Cellulose Organic Fiber Mfg
		325222	Noncellulosic Organic Fiber Mfg
3241	Petroleum & Coal Products Mfg	3253	Pesticide, Fertilizer & Oth Ag Chemical Mfg
32411	Petroleum Refineries		
32412	Asphalt Paving, Roofing & Saturated Mat Mfg	32531	Fertilizer Mfg
		325311	Nitrogenous Fertilizer Mfg
324121	Asphalt Paving Mixture & Block Mfg	325312	Phosphatic Fertilizer Mfg
		325314	Fertilizer (Mixing Only) Mfg
324122	Asphalt Shingle & Coating Materials Mfg	32532	Pesticide & Other Agricultural Chemical Mfg
32419	Other Petroleum & Coal Products Mfg	3254	Pharmaceutical & Medicine Mfg
		32541	Pharmaceutical & Medicine Mfg
324191	Petroleum Lubricating Oil & Grease Mfg	325411	Medicinal & Botanical Mfg
		325412	Pharmaceutical Preparation Mfg
324199	All Other Petroleum & Coal Products Mfg	325413	In-Vitro Diagnostic Substance Mfg
		325414	Biological Product (exc Diagnostic) Mfg
325	**Chemical Mfg**	3255	Paint, Coating & Adhesive Mfg
3251	Basic Chemical Mfg	32551	Paint & Coating Mfg
32511	Petrochemical Mfg	32552	Adhesive Mfg
32512	Industrial Gas Mfg	3256	Soap, Cleaners & Toilet Preparation Mfg
32513	Synthetic Dye & Pigment Mfg		
325131	Inorganic Dye & Pigment Mfg	32561	Soap & Cleaning Compound Mfg
325132	Synthetic Organic Dye & Pigment Mfg	325611	Soap & Other Detergent Mfg
		325612	Polish & Other Sanitation Good Mfg
32518	Other Basic Inorganic Chemical Mfg		
		325613	Surface Active Agent Mfg
325181	Alkalies & Chlorine Mfg	32562	Toilet Preparation Mfg
325182	Carbon Black Mfg	3259	Other Chemical Product & Preparation Mfg
325188	All Other Basic Inorganic Chemical Mfg		
		32591	Printing Ink Mfg
32519	Other Basic Organic Chemical Mfg	32592	Explosives Mfg
		32599	All Other Chemical Product & Preparation Mfg
325191	Gum & Wood Chemical Mfg		
325192	Cyclic Crude & Intermediate Mfg		

Note: For definitions of abbreviations and substitute words see page 765.

http://www.ntis.gov/naics

Code	Short title
325991	Custom Compounding of Purchased Resin
325992	Photo Film, Paper, Plate & Chemical Mfg
325998	All Oth Misc Chemical Product & Prep Mfg

326 **Plastics & Rubber Products Mfg**

Code	Short title
3261	Plastics Product Mfg
32611	Unsupported Plastics Film, Sheet & Bag Mfg
326111	Unsupported Plastics Bag Mfg
326112	Unsupported Plastics Packaging Film/Sheet Mfg
326113	Unsupported Plastics Film/Sheet (exc Pkg) Mfg
32612	Plastics Pipe/Fitting/Unsupported Shapes Mfg
326121	Unsupported Plastics Profile Shape Mfg
326122	Plastics Pipe & Pipe Fitting Mfg
32613	Laminated Plastics Plate, Sheet & Shape Mfg
32614	Polystyrene Foam Product Mfg
32615	Foam Product (exc Polystyrene) Mfg
32616	Plastics Bottle Mfg
32619	Other Plastics Product Mfg
326191	Plastics Plumbing Fixture Mfg
326192	Resilient Floor Covering Mfg
326199	All Other Plastics Product Mfg
3262	Rubber Product Mfg
32621	Tire Mfg
326211	Tire Mfg (exc Retreading)
326212	Tire Retreading
32622	Rubber & Plastics Hoses & Belting Mfg
32629	Other Rubber Product Mfg
326291	Rubber Product Mfg for Mechanical Use
326299	All Other Rubber Product Mfg

327 **Nonmetallic Mineral Product Mfg**

Code	Short title
3271	Clay Product & Refractory Mfg

Code	Short title
32711	Pottery, Ceramics & Plumbing Fixture Mfg
327111	Vitreous Plumbing Fixtures/Access/Fitting Mfg
327112	Vitreous China & Other Pottery Product Mfg
327113	Porcelain Electrical Supply Mfg
32712	Clay Building Material & Refractories Mfg
327121	Brick & Structural Clay Tile Mfg
327122	Ceramic Wall & Floor Tile Mfg
327123	Other Structural Clay Product Mfg
327124	Clay Refractory Mfg
327125	Nonclay Refractory Mfg
3272	Glass & Glass Product Mfg
32721	Glass & Glass Product Mfg
327211	Flat Glass Mfg
327212	Other Pressed & Blown Glass & Glassware Mfg
327213	Glass Container Mfg
327215	Glass Product Mfg Made of Purchased Glass
3273	Cement & Concrete Product Mfg
32731	Cement Mfg
32732	Ready-Mix Concrete Mfg
32733	Concrete Pipe, Brick & Block Mfg
327331	Concrete Block & Brick Mfg
327332	Concrete Pipe Mfg
32739	Other Concrete Product Mfg
3274	Lime & Gypsum Product Mfg
32741	Lime Mfg
32742	Gypsum Product Mfg
3279	Other Nonmetallic Mineral Product Mfg
32791	Abrasive Product Mfg
32799	All Other Nonmetallic Mineral Product Mfg
327991	Cut Stone & Stone Product Mfg
327992	Ground or Treated Mineral & Earth Mfg
327993	Mineral Wool Mfg
327999	All Oth Misc Nonmetallic Mineral Product Mfg

Note: For definitions of abbreviations and substitute words see page 765.

Code	Short title	Code	Short title
331	**Primary Metal Mfg**	331423	Secondary Smelting/Refining/ Alloying of Copper
3311	Iron & Steel Mills & Ferroalloy Mfg	33149	Other Nonferrous Roll/Draw/ Extruding/ Alloying
33111	Iron & Steel Mills & Ferroalloy Mfg	331491	Other Nonferrous Metal Roll/ Draw/Extruding
331111	Iron & Steel Mills	331492	Oth Nonferrous Secondary Smelt/ Refine/Alloying
331112	Electrometallurgical Ferroalloy Product Mfg	3315	Foundries
3312	Steel Product Mfg from Purchased Steel	33151	Ferrous Metal Foundries
		331511	Iron Foundries
33121	Iron/Steel Pipe & Tube Mfg from Purch Steel	331512	Steel Investment Foundries
33122	Rolling & Drawing of Purchased Steel	331513	Steel Foundries (except Investment)
331221	Rolled Steel Shape Mfg	33152	Nonferrous Metal Foundries
331222	Steel Wire Drawing	331521	Aluminum Die-Casting Foundries
3313	Alumina & Aluminum Production & Processing	331522	Nonferrous (exc Alum) Die- Casting Foundries
33131	Alumina & Aluminum Production & Processing	331524	Aluminum Foundries (except Die-Casting)
331311	Alumina Refining	331525	Copper Foundries (except Die- Casting)
331312	Primary Aluminum Production		
331314	Secondary Smelting & Alloying of Aluminum	331528	Oth Nonferrous Foundries (except Die-Casting)
331315	Aluminum Sheet, Plate & Foil Mfg	**332**	**Fabricated Metal Product Mfg**
331316	Aluminum Extruded Product Mfg	3321	Forging & Stamping
331319	Other Aluminum Rolling & Drawing	33211	Forging & Stamping
		332111	Iron & Steel Forging
3314	Nonferrous (exc Alum) Production & Processing	332112	Nonferrous Forging
		332114	Custom Roll Forming
33141	Nonferrous (exc Aluminum) Smelting & Refining	332115	Crown & Closure Mfg
		332116	Metal Stamping
331411	Primary Smelting & Refining of Copper	332117	Powder Metallurgy Parts Mfg
		3322	Cutlery & Handtool Mfg
331419	Other Nonferrous Metal Prim Smelting/Refining	33221	Cutlery & Handtool Mfg
		332211	Cutlery & Flatware (exc Precious) Mfg
33142	Copper Rolling/Drawing/ Extruding & Alloying	332212	Hand & Edge Tool Mfg
331421	Copper Rolling, Drawing & Extruding	332213	Saw Blade & Handsaw Mfg
		332214	Kitchen Utensil, Pot & Pan Mfg
331422	Copper Wire (except Mechanical) Drawing	3323	Architectural & Structural Metals Mfg

Note: For definitions of abbreviations and substitute words see page 765.

http://www.ntis.gov/naics

Code	Short title	Code	Short title
33231	Plate Work & Fabricated Structural Prod Mfg	332813	Electropl/Plating/Polish/Anodize/ Coloring
332311	Prefab Metal Building & Component Mfg	3329	Other Fabricated Metal Product Mfg
332312	Fabricated Structural Metal Mfg	33291	Metal Valve Mfg
332313	Plate Work Mfg	332911	Industrial Valve Mfg
33232	Ornamental & Architectural Metal Prod Mfg	332912	Fluid Power Valve & Hose Fitting Mfg
332321	Metal Window & Door Mfg	332913	Plumbing Fixture Fitting & Trim Mfg
332322	Sheet Metal Work Mfg	332919	Other Metal Valve & Pipe Fitting Mfg
332323	Ornamental & Architectural Metal Work Mfg	33299	All Other Fabricated Metal Product Mfg
3324	Boiler, Tank & Shipping Container Mfg	332991	Ball & Roller Bearing Mfg
33241	Power Boiler & Heat Exchanger Mfg	332992	Small Arms Ammunition Mfg
33242	Metal Tank (Heavy Gauge) Mfg	332993	Ammunition (exc Small Arms) Mfg
33243	Light Gauge Metal Container Mfg	332994	Small Arms Mfg
332431	Metal Can Mfg	332995	Other Ordnance & Accessories Mfg
332439	Other Metal Container Mfg	332996	Fabricated Pipe & Pipe Fitting Mfg
3325	Hardware Mfg	332997	Industrial Pattern Mfg
33251	Hardware Mfg	332998	Enameled Iron & Metal Sanitary Ware Mfg
3326	Spring & Wire Product Mfg	332999	All Other Misc Fabricated Metal Product Mfg
33261	Spring & Wire Product Mfg		
332611	Spring (Heavy Gauge) Mfg	**333**	**Machinery Mfg**
332612	Spring (Light Gauge) Mfg		
332618	Other Fabricated Wire Product Mfg	3331	Ag, Construction & Mining Machinery Mfg
3327	Mach Shops, Turn Prod, Screw, Nut, Bolt Mfg	33311	Agricultural Implement Mfg
33271	Machine Shops	333111	Farm Machinery & Equipment Mfg
33272	Turned Product & Screw, Nut & Bolt Mfg	333112	Lawn & Garden Equipment Mfg
332721	Precision Turned Product Mfg	33312	Construction Machinery Mfg
332722	Bolt, Nut, Screw, Rivet & Washer Mfg	33313	Mining & Oil & Gas Field Machinery Mfg
3328	Coating/Engrave/Heat Treating & Oth Activity	333131	Mining Machinery & Equipment Mfg
33281	Coating/Engrave/Heat Treating & Oth Activity	333132	Oil & Gas Field Machinery & Equipment Mfg
332811	Metal Heat Treating		
332812	Metal Coating, Engraving, & Allied Services		

Note: For definitions of abbreviations and substitute words see page 765.

Code	Short title	Code	Short title
3332	Industrial Machinery Mfg	333513	Machine Tool (Metal Forming Types) Mfg
33321	Sawmill & Woodworking Machinery Mfg	333514	Special Die/Tool, Die Set, Jig & Fixture Mfg
33322	Plastics & Rubber Industry Machinery Mfg	333515	Cutting Tool & Machine Tool Accessory Mfg
33329	Other Industrial Machinery Mfg	333516	Rolling Mill Machinery & Equipment Mfg
333291	Paper Industry Machinery Mfg		
333292	Textile Machinery Mfg	333518	Other Metalworking Machinery Mfg
333293	Printing Machinery & Equipment Mfg	3336	Engine, Turbine & Power Transmsn Equip Mfg
333294	Food Product Machinery Mfg	33361	Engine, Turbine & Power Transmsn Equip Mfg
333295	Semiconductor Machinery Mfg		
333298	All Other Industrial Machinery Mfg	333611	Turbine & Turbine Generator Set Unit Mfg
3333	Commercial & Service Industry Machinery Mfg	333612	Spd Changer, Ind High-Speed Drive & Gear Mfg
33331	Commercial & Service Industry Machinery Mfg	333613	Mechanical Power Transmission Equipment Mfg
333311	Automatic Vending Machine Mfg	333618	Other Engine Equipment Mfg
333312	Commercial Laundry, Dryclean & Press Mach Mfg	3339	Other General Purpose Machinery Mfg
333313	Office Machinery Mfg	33391	Pump & Compressor Mfg
333314	Optical Instrument & Lens Mfg	333911	Pump & Pumping Equipment Mfg
333315	Photographic & Photocopying Equipment Mfg	333912	Air & Gas Compressor Mfg
333319	Oth Commercial/Service Industry Machinery Mfg	333913	Measuring & Dispensing Pump Mfg
3334	HVAC & Commercial Refrigeration Equipment Mfg	33392	Material Handling Equipment Mfg
33341	HVAC & Commercial Refrigeration Equipment Mfg	333921	Elevator & Moving Stairway Mfg
333411	Air Purification Equipment Mfg	333922	Conveyor & Conveying Equipment Mfg
333412	Industrial & Commercial Fan & Blower Mfg	333923	Overhead Crane, Hoist & Monorail System Mfg
333414	Heating Equipment (exc Warm Air Furnaces) Mfg	333924	Ind Truck, Tractor, Trailer, Stacker Mach Mfg
333415	AC/Warm Air Htg & Commercial Refrig Equip Mfg	33399	All Other General Purpose Machinery Mfg
3335	Metalworking Machinery Mfg	333991	Power-Driven Hand Tool Mfg
33351	Metalworking Machinery Mfg	333992	Welding & Soldering Equipment Mfg
333511	Industrial Mold Mfg	333993	Packaging Machinery Mfg
333512	Machine Tool (Metal Cutting Types) Mfg	333994	Industrial Process Furnace & Oven Mfg

Note: For definitions of abbreviations and substitute words see page 765.

http://www.ntis.gov/naics

Code	Short title	Code	Short title
333995	Fluid Power Cylinder & Actuator Mfg	33451	Nav/Measuring/Medical/Control Instruments Mfg
333996	Fluid Power Pump & Motor Mfg	334510	Electromedical Apparatus Mfg
333997	Scale & Balance (except Laboratory) Mfg	334511	Search, Detection & Navigation Instrument Mfg
333999	All Oth Misc General Purpose Machinery Mfg	334512	Automatic Environmental Control Mfg
334	**Computer & Electronic Product Mfg**	334513	Industrial Process Control Mfg
		334514	Total Fluid Meter & Counting Device Mfg
3341	Computer & Peripheral Equipment Mfg	334515	Electricity Measuring/Testing Instrument Mfg
33411	Computer & Peripheral Equipment Mfg	334516	Analytical Laboratory Instrument Mfg
334111	Electronic Computer Mfg	334517	Irradiation Apparatus Mfg
334112	Computer Storage Device Mfg	334518	Watch, Clock & Part Mfg
334113	Computer Terminal Mfg	334519	Other Measuring & Controlling Device Mfg
334119	Other Computer Peripheral Equipment Mfg	3346	Mfg & Reproducing Magnetic & Optical Media
3342	Communications Equipment Mfg	33461	Mfg & Reproducing Magnetic & Optical Media
33421	Telephone Apparatus Mfg	334611	Software Reproducing
33422	Radio/TV Broadcast & Wireless Comm Equip Mfg	334612	Prerecorded CD/Tape/Record Reproducing
33429	Other Communications Equipment Mfg	334613	Magnetic and Optical Recording Media Mfg
3343	Audio & Video Equipment Mfg	**335**	**Electrical Equip, Appliance & Component Mfg**
33431	Audio & Video Equipment Mfg		
3344	Semiconductor & Oth Electronic Component Mfg	3351	Electric Lighting Equipment Mfg
33441	Semiconductor & Oth Electronic Component Mfg	33511	Electric Lamp Bulb & Part Mfg
334411	Electron Tube Mfg	33512	Lighting Fixture Mfg
334412	Bare Printed Circuit Board Mfg	335121	Residential Electric Lighting Fixture Mfg
334413	Semiconductor & Related Device Mfg	335122	Commercial Electric Lighting Fixture Mfg
334414	Electronic Capacitor Mfg	335129	Other Lighting Equipment Mfg
334415	Electronic Resistor Mfg	3352	Household Appliance Mfg
334416	Electronic Coil/Transformer/ Oth Inductor Mfg	33521	Small Electrical Appliance Mfg
334417	Electronic Connector Mfg	335211	Electric Housewares & Fan Mfg
334418	Printed Circuit Assembly (Electronic Assembly) Mfg	335212	Household Vacuum Cleaner Mfg
334419	Other Electronic Component Mfg	33522	Major Appliance Mfg
3345	Nav/Measuring/Medical/Control Instruments Mfg	335221	Household Cooking Appliance Mfg

Note: For definitions of abbreviations and substitute words see page 765.

Code	Short title	Code	Short title
335222	Household Refrigerator & Freezer Mfg	33621	Motor Vehicle Body & Trailer Mfg
335224	Household Laundry Equipment Mfg	336211	Motor Vehicle Body Mfg
335228	Other Major Household Appliance Mfg	336212	Truck Trailer Mfg
		336213	Motor Home Mfg
		336214	Travel Trailer & Camper Mfg
3353	Electrical Equipment Mfg	3363	Motor Vehicle Parts Mfg
33531	Electrical Equipment Mfg	33631	Motor Vehicle Gas Engine & Engine Parts Mfg
335311	Power/Distribution/Specialty Transformer Mfg	336311	Carburetor, Piston, Piston Ring & Valve Mfg
335312	Motor & Generator Mfg		
335313	Switchgear & Switchboard Apparatus Mfg	336312	Gasoline Engine & Engine Parts Mfg
335314	Relay & Industrial Control Mfg	33632	MV Electrical & Electronic Equipment Mfg
3359	Other Electrical Equipment & Component Mfg	336321	Vehicular Lighting Equipment Mfg
33591	Battery Mfg	336322	Oth MV Electrical & Electronic Equip Mfg
335911	Storage Battery Mfg		
335912	Primary Battery Mfg	33633	Motor Vehicle Steering & Suspension Parts Mfg
33592	Communication & Energy Wire & Cable Mfg	33634	Motor Vehicle Brake System Mfg
335921	Fiber Optic Cable Mfg	33635	MV Transmission & Power Train Parts Mfg
335929	Other Communication & Energy Wire Mfg	33636	Motor Vehicle Seating & Interior Trim Mfg
33593	Wiring Device Mfg		
335931	Current Carrying Wiring Device Mfg	33637	Motor Vehicle Metal Stamping
		33639	Other Motor Vehicle Parts Mfg
335932	Noncurrent-Carrying Wiring Device Mfg	336391	Motor Vehicle Air-Conditioning Mfg
33599	All Oth Electrical Equipment & Component Mfg	336399	All Other Motor Vehicle Parts Mfg
335991	Carbon & Graphite Product Mfg	3364	Aerospace Product & Parts Mfg
335999	All Oth Misc Electrical Equip & Component Mfg	33641	Aerospace Product & Parts Mfg
		336411	Aircraft Mfg
336	**Transportation Equipment Mfg**	336412	Aircraft Engine & Engine Parts Mfg
3361	Motor Vehicle Mfg	336413	Other Aircraft Part & Auxiliary Equipment Mfg
33611	Automobile & Light Duty Motor Vehicle Mfg		
336111	Automobile Mfg	336414	Guided Missile & Space Vehicle Mfg
336112	Light Truck & Utility Vehicle Mfg	336415	Missile/Space Veh Propulsion Unit & Parts Mfg
33612	Heavy Duty Truck Mfg		
3362	Motor Vehicle Body & Trailer Mfg	336419	Other Missile/Space Veh Parts & Aux Equip Mfg

Note: For definitions of abbreviations and substitute words see page 765.

http://www.ntis.gov/naics

Code	Short title	Code	Short title
3365	Railroad Rolling Stock Mfg	337215	Shwcase, Partition, Shelv & Locker Mfg
33651	Railroad Rolling Stock Mfg	3379	Other Furniture Related Product Mfg
3366	Ship & Boat Building		
33661	Ship & Boat Building	33791	Mattress Mfg
336611	Ship Building & Repairing	33792	Blind & Shade Mfg
336612	Boat Building		
3369	Other Transportation Equipment Mfg	**339**	**Miscellaneous Mfg**
33699	Other Transportation Equipment Mfg	3391	Medical Equipment & Supplies Mfg
336991	Motorcycle, Bicycle & Parts Mfg	33911	Medical Equipment & Supplies Mfg
336992	Mil Armored Vehicle, Tank & Tank Compn Mfg	339111	Laboratory Apparatus & Furniture Mfg
336999	All Other Transportation Equipment Mfg	339112	Surgical & Medical Instrument Mfg
		339113	Surgical Appliance & Supplies Mfg
337	**Furniture & Related Product Mfg**		
3371	HH & Institutional Furniture & Ki Cabnt Mfg	339114	Dental Equipment & Supplies Mfg
33711	Wood Kitchen Cabinet & Countertop Mfg	339115	Ophthalmic Goods Mfg
		339116	Dental Laboratories
33712	Household & Institutional Furniture Mfg	3399	Other Miscellaneous Mfg
		33991	Jewelry & Silverware Mfg
337121	Upholstered Household Furniture Mfg	339911	Jewelry (exc Costume) Mfg
337122	Nonupholstered Wood Household Furniture Mfg	339912	Silverware & Hollowware Mfg
		339913	Jewelers' Material & Lapidary Work Mfg
337124	Metal Household Furniture Manufacturing		
		339914	Costume Jewelry & Novelty Mfg
337125	Household Furniture (exc Wood & Metal) Mfg	33992	Sporting & Athletic Goods Mfg
		33993	Doll, Toy & Game Mfg
337127	Institutional Furniture Mfg	339931	Doll & Stuffed Toy Mfg
337129	Wood TV/Radio/Sewing Machine Cabinet Mfg	339932	Game, Toy & Children's Vehicle Mfg
3372	Office Furniture (including Fixtures) Mfg	33994	Office Supplies (exc Paper) Mfg
		339941	Pen & Mechanical Pencil Mfg
33721	Office Furniture (including Fixtures) Mfg	339942	Lead Pencil & Art Good Mfg
		339943	Marking Device Mfg
337211	Wood Office Furniture Mfg	339944	Carbon Paper & Inked Ribbon Mfg
337212	Custom Architectural Woodwork & Millwork Mfg		
		33995	Sign Mfg
		33999	All Other Misc Mfg
337214	Office Furniture (except Wood) Mfg	339991	Gasket, Packing & Sealing Device Mfg
		339992	Musical Instrument Mfg

Note: For definitions of abbreviations and substitute words see page 765.

http://www.ntis.gov/naics

Code	Short title	Code	Short title
339993	Fastener, Button, Needle & Pin Mfg	4215	Metal & Mineral (except Petroleum) Whsle
339994	Broom, Brush & Mop Mfg	42151	Metal Service Centers & Offices
339995	Burial Casket Mfg	42152	Coal & Other Mineral & Ore Whsle
339999	All Other Miscellaneous Mfg	4216	Electrical Goods Whsle
		42161	Elec Equip/Wiring Supp/Const Material Whsle
42	**WHOLESALE TRADE**		
		42162	Electric Appliance/TV/Radio Set Whsle
421	**Wholesale Trade, Durable Goods**		
4211	Motor Vehicle/Motor Vehicle Pt & Supply Whsle	42169	Other Electronic Parts & Equipment Whsle
42111	Automobile & Other Motor Vehicle Whsle	4217	Hardware, & Plumb & Heating Equip & Sup Whsle
42112	Motor Vehicle Supplies & New Parts Whsle	42171	Hardware Whsle
		42172	Plumbing & Heating Equipment & Supplies Whsle
42113	Tire & Tube Whsle		
42114	Motor Vehicle Parts (Used) Whsle	42173	Warm Air Heating & AC Equip & Supplies Whsle
4212	Furniture & Home Furnishing Whsle	42174	Refrigeration Equipment & Supplies Whsle
42121	Furniture Whsle		
42122	Home Furnishing Whsle	4218	Machinery, Equipment & Supplies Whsle
4213	Lumber & Other Construction Materials Whsle	42181	Const & Mining (exc Petroleum) Equip Whsle
42131	Lumber, Plywood, Millwork & Wood Panel Whsle	42182	Farm & Garden Machinery & Equipment Whsle
42132	Brick & Related Construction Material Whsle	42183	Industrial Machinery & Equipment Whsle
42133	Roofing, Siding & Insulation Material Whsle	42184	Industrial Supplies Whsle
		42185	Service Establishment Equip & Supplies Whsle
42139	Other Construction Material Whsle		
4214	Professional & Commercial Equip & Supp Whsle	42186	Transportation Equip/Supplies(exc MV) Whsle
42141	Photographic Equipment & Supplies Whsle	4219	Miscellaneous Durable Goods Whsle
42142	Office Equipment Whsle	42191	Sporting & Recreational Goods & Supply Whsle
42143	Computer & Peripheral Equip & Software Whsle	42192	Toy & Hobby Goods & Supplies Whsle
42144	Other Commercial Equipment Whsle		
42145	Medical/Dental/Hospital Equip & Supp Whsle	42193	Recyclable Material Whsle
		42194	Jewelry/Watch/Precious Stone & Metal Whsle
42146	Ophthalmic Goods Whsle		
42149	Oth Professional Equipment & Supplies Whsle	42199	Other Miscellaneous Durable Goods Whsle

Note: For definitions of abbreviations and substitute words see page 765.

http://www.ntis.gov/naics

Code	Short title
422	**Wholesale Trade, Nondurable Goods**
4221	Paper & Paper Product Whsle
42211	Printing & Writing Paper Whsle
42212	Stationery & Office Supplies Whsle
42213	Industrial & Personal Service Paper Whsle
4222	Drugs & Druggists' Sundries Whsle
42221	Drugs & Druggists' Sundries Whsle
4223	Apparel, Piece Goods & Notions Whsle
42231	Piece Goods, Notions & Other Dry Goods Whsle
42232	Men's & Boys' Clothing & Furnishings Whsle
42233	Women's/Children's/Infants' Clothing Whsle
42234	Footwear Whsle
4224	Grocery & Related Product Whsle
42241	General Line Grocery Whsle
42242	Packaged Frozen Food Whsle
42243	Dairy Product (exc Dried or Canned) Whsle
42244	Poultry & Poultry Product Whsle
42245	Confectionery Whsle
42246	Fish & Seafood Whsle
42247	Meat & Meat Product Whsle
42248	Fresh Fruit & Vegetable Whsle
42249	Other Grocery & Related Products Whsle
4225	Farm Product Raw Material Whsle
42251	Grain & Field Bean Whsle
42252	Livestock Whsle
42259	Other Farm Product Raw Material Whsle
4226	Chemical & Allied Products Whsle
42261	Plastics Materials & Basic Forms/Shapes Whsle
42269	Other Chemical & Allied Products Whsle

Code	Short title
4227	Petroleum & Petroleum Products Whsle
42271	Petroleum Bulk Stations & Terminals
42272	Petroleum Prod Whsle (exc Bulk Sta/Terminals)
4228	Beer/Wine/Distilled Alcoholic Beverage Whsle
42281	Beer & Ale Whsle
42282	Wine & Distilled Alcoholic Beverage Whsle
4229	Miscellaneous Nondurable Goods Whsle
42291	Farm Supplies Whsle
42292	Book, Periodical & Newspaper Whsle
42293	Flower/Nursery Stock/Florists' Supplies Whsle
42294	Tobacco & Tobacco Product Whsle
42295	Paint, Varnish & Supplies Whsle
42299	Other Miscellaneous Nondurable Goods Whsle
44-45	**RETAIL TRADE**
441	**Motor Vehicle & Parts Dealers**
4411	Automobile Dealers
44111	New Car Dealers
44112	Used Car Dealers
4412	Other Motor Vehicle Dealers
44121	Recreational Vehicle Dealers
44122	Motorcycle & Boat & Other MV Dealers
441221	Motorcycle Dealers
441222	Boat Dealers
441229	All Other Motor Vehicle Dealers
4413	Automotive Parts, Accessories & Tire Stores
44131	Automotive Parts, Accessories & Tire Stores
44132	Tire Dealers
442	**Furniture & Home Furnishings Stores**
4421	Furniture Stores

Note: For definitions of abbreviations and substitute words see page 765.

Code	Short title
44211	Furniture Stores
4422	Home Furnishings Stores
44221	Floor Covering Stores
44229	Other Home Furnishings Stores
442291	Window Treatment Stores
442299	All Other Home Furnishings Stores

443   Electronics & Appliance Stores

Code	Short title
4431	Electronics & Appliance Stores
44311	Appliance, TV & Other Electronics Stores
443111	Household Appliance Stores
443112	Radio, Television & Other Electronics Stores
44312	Computer & Software Stores
44313	Camera & Photographic Supplies Stores

444   Bldg Material & Garden Equip & Supp Dealers

Code	Short title
4441	Building Material & Supplies Dealers
44411	Home Centers
44412	Paint & Wallpaper Stores
44413	Hardware Stores
44419	Other Building Material Dealers
4442	Lawn & Garden Equip & Supplies Stores
44421	Outdoor Power Equipment Stores
44422	Nursery & Garden Centers

445   Food & Beverage Stores

Code	Short title
4451	Grocery Stores
44511	Grocery (except Convenience) Stores
44512	Convenience Stores
4452	Specialty Food Stores
44521	Meat Markets
44522	Fish & Seafood Markets
44523	Fruit & Vegetable Markets
44529	Other Specialty Food Stores
445291	Baked Goods Stores

Code	Short title
445292	Confectionery & Nut Stores
445299	All Other Specialty Food Stores
4453	Beer, Wine & Liquor Stores
44531	Beer, Wine & Liquor Stores

446   Health & Personal Care Stores

Code	Short title
4461	Health & Personal Care Stores
44611	Pharmacies & Drug Stores
44612	Cosmetics, Beauty Supplies & Perfume Stores
44613	Optical Goods Stores
44619	Other Health & Personal Care Stores
446191	Food (Health) Supplement Stores
446199	All Other Health & Personal Care Stores

447   Gasoline Stations

Code	Short title
4471	Gasoline Stations
44711	Gasoline Stations with Convenience Stores
44719	Other Gasoline Stations

448   Clothing & Clothing Accessories Stores

Code	Short title
4481	Clothing Stores
44811	Men's Clothing Stores
44812	Women's Clothing Stores
44813	Children's & Infants' Clothing Stores
44814	Family Clothing Stores
44815	Clothing Accessories Stores
44819	Other Clothing Stores
4482	Shoe Stores
44821	Shoe Stores
4483	Jewelry, Luggage & Leather Goods Stores
44831	Jewelry Stores
44832	Luggage & Leather Goods Stores

451   Sporting Goods, Hobby, Book & Music Stores

Code	Short title
4511	Sporting Goods/Hobby/Musical Instrumnt Stores

Note: For definitions of abbreviations and substitute words see page 765.

http://www.ntis.gov/naics

Code	Short title
45111	Sporting Goods Stores
45112	Hobby, Toy & Game Stores
45113	Sewing, Needlework & Piece Goods Stores
45114	Musical Instrument & Supplies Stores
4512	Book, Periodical & Music Stores
45121	Book Stores & News Dealers
451211	Book Stores
451212	News Dealers & Newsstands
45122	Prerecorded Tape, CD & Record Stores

452 General Merchandise Stores

Code	Short title
4521	Department Stores
45211	Department Stores
4529	Other General Merchandise Stores
45291	Warehouse Clubs & Superstores
45299	All Other General Merchandise Stores

453 Miscellaneous Store Retailers

Code	Short title
4531	Florists
45311	Florists
4532	Office Supplies, Stationery & Gift Stores
45321	Office Supplies & Stationery Stores
45322	Gift, Novelty & Souvenir Stores
4533	Used Merchandise Stores
45331	Used Merchandise Stores
4539	Other Miscellaneous Store Retailers
45391	Pet & Pet Supplies Stores
45392	Art Dealers
45393	Manufactured (Mobile) Home Dealers
45399	All Other Miscellaneous Store Retailers
453991	Tobacco Stores
453998	All Other Misc Store Retailers (exc Tobacco)

Code	Short title
454	**Nonstore Retailers**
4541	Electronic Shopping & Mail-Order Houses
45411	Electronic Shopping & Mail-Order Houses
4542	Vending Machine Operators
45421	Vending Machine Operators
4543	Direct Selling Establishments
45431	Fuel Dealers
454311	Heating Oil Dealers
454312	Liquefied Petroleum Gas (Bottled Gas) Dealers
454319	Other Fuel Dealers
45439	Other Direct Selling Establishments

48-49 TRANSPORTATION & WAREHOUSING

481 Air Transportation

Code	Short title
4811	Scheduled Air Transportation
48111	Scheduled Air Transportation
481111	Scheduled Passenger Air Transportation
481112	Scheduled Freight Air Transportation
4812	Nonscheduled Air Transportation
48121	Nonscheduled Air Transportation
481211	Nonscheduled Chartered Passenger Air Trans
481212	Nonscheduled Chartered Freight Air Trans
481219	Other Nonscheduled Air Transportation

482 Rail Transportation

Code	Short title
4821	Rail Transportation
48211	Rail Transportation
482111	Line-Haul Railroads
482112	Short Line Railroads

483 Water Transportation

Code	Short title
4831	Deep Sea, Coastal & Great Lakes Water Trans

Note: For definitions of abbreviations and substitute words see page 765.

http://www.ntis.gov/naics

Code	Short title	Code	Short title
48311	Deep Sea, Coastal & Great Lakes Water Trans	48521	Interurban & Rural Bus Transportation
483111	Deep Sea Freight Transportation	4853	Taxi & Limousine Service
483112	Deep Sea Passenger Transportation	48531	Taxi Service
		48532	Limousine Service
483113	Coastal & Great Lakes Freight Transportation	4854	School & Employee Bus Transportation
483114	Coastal & Great Lakes Passenger Trans	48541	School & Employee Bus Transportation
4832	Inland Water Transportation	4855	Charter Bus Industry
48321	Inland Water Transportation	48551	Charter Bus Industry
483211	Inland Water Freight Transportation	4859	Oth Transit & Ground Passenger Transportation
483212	Inland Water Passenger Transportation	48599	Oth Transit & Ground Passenger Transportation
		485991	Special Needs Transportation
		485999	All Other Transit & Ground Passenger Trans

484 Truck Transportation

Code	Short title	Code	Short title
4841	General Freight Trucking	**486**	**Pipeline Transportation**
48411	General Freight Trucking, Local	4861	Pipeline Transportation of Crude Oil
48412	General Freight Trucking, Long-Distance	48611	Pipeline Transportation of Crude Oil
484121	General Freight Trucking, Long-Distance, TL	4862	Pipeline Transportation of Natural Gas
484122	General Freight Trucking, Long-Distance, LTL	48621	Pipeline Transportation of Natural Gas
4842	Specialized Freight Trucking	4869	Other Pipeline Transportation
48421	Used Household & Office Goods Moving	48691	Pipeline Trans of Refined Petroleum Products
48422	Specialized Frgt (exc Used) Trucking, Local	48699	All Other Pipeline Transportation
48423	Specialized Frgt (exc Used) Trucking, LDist		

485 Transit & Ground Passenger Transportation

487 Scenic & Sightseeing Transportation

Code	Short title	Code	Short title
4851	Urban Transit Systems	4871	Scenic & Sightseeing Transportation, Land
48511	Urban Transit Systems		
485111	Mixed Mode Transit Systems	48711	Scenic & Sightseeing Transportation, Land
485112	Commuter Rail Systems	4872	Scenic & Sightseeing Transportation, Water
485113	Bus & Other Motor Vehicle Transit Systems		
485119	Other Urban Transit Systems	48721	Scenic & Sightseeing Transportation, Water
4852	Interurban & Rural Bus Transportation		

Note: For definitions of abbreviations and substitute words see page 765.

http://www.ntis.gov/naics

Code	Short title
4879	Scenic & Sightseeing Transportation, Other
48799	Scenic & Sightseeing Transportation, Other

488 Transportation Support Activities

Code	Short title
4881	Air Transportation Support Activities
48811	Airport Operations
488111	Air Traffic Control
488119	Other Airport Operations
48819	Other Air Transportation Support Activities
4882	Rail Transportation Support Activities
48821	Rail Transportation Support Activities
4883	Water Transportation Support Activities
48831	Port & Harbor Operations
48832	Marine Cargo Handling
48833	Navigational Services to Shipping
48839	Other Water Transportation Support Activities
4884	Road Transportation Support Activities
48841	Motor Vehicle Towing
48849	Other Road Transportation Support Activities
4885	Freight Transportation Arrangement
48851	Freight Transportation Arrangement
4889	Other Transportation Support Activities
48899	Other Transportation Support Activities
488991	Packing & Crating
488999	All Other Transportation Support Activities

491 Postal Service

Code	Short title
4911	Postal Service
49111	Postal Service

492 Couriers & Messengers

Code	Short title
4921	Couriers
49211	Couriers
4922	Local Messengers & Local Delivery
49221	Local Messengers & Local Delivery

493 Warehousing & Storage

Code	Short title
4931	Warehousing & Storage
49311	General Warehousing & Storage
49312	Refrigerated Warehousing & Storage
49313	Farm Product Warehousing & Storage
49319	Other Warehousing & Storage

51 INFORMATION

511 Publishing Industries

Code	Short title
5111	Newspaper/Periodical/Book/ Database Publishers
51111	Newspaper Publishers
51112	Periodical Publishers
51113	Book Publishers
51114	Database and Directory Publishers
51119	Other Publishers
511191	Greeting Card Publishers
511199	All Other Publishers
5112	Software Publishers
51121	Software Publishers

512 Motion Picture & Sound Recording Industries

Code	Short title
5121	Motion Picture & Video Industries
51211	Motion Picture & Video Production
51212	Motion Picture & Video Distribution
51213	Motion Picture & Video Exhibition
512131	Motion Picture Theaters (except Drive-Ins)
512132	Drive-In Motion Picture Theaters

Note: For definitions of abbreviations and substitute words see page 765.

Code	Short title
51219	Postprod & Other Movie & Video Industries
512191	Teleproduction & Oth Postproduction Services
512199	Other Motion Picture & Video Industries
5122	Sound Recording Industries
51221	Record Production
51222	Integrated Record Production/ Distribution
51223	Music Publishers
51224	Sound Recording Studios
51229	Other Sound Recording Industries

513 Broadcasting & Telecommunications

Code	Short title
5131	Radio & Television Broadcasting
51311	Radio Broadcasting
513111	Radio Networks
513112	Radio Stations
51312	Television Broadcasting
5132	Cable Networks & Program Distribution
51321	Cable Networks
51322	Cable & Other Program Distribution
5133	Telecommunications
51331	Wired Telecommunications Carriers
51332	Wireless Telecom Carriers (exc Satellite)
513321	Paging
513322	Cellular & Other Wireless Telecommunications
51333	Telecommunications Resellers
51334	Satellite Telecommunications
51339	Other Telecommunications

514 Information & Data Processing Services

Code	Short title
5141	Information Services
51411	News Syndicates
51412	Libraries & Archives
51419	Other Information Services
514191	On-Line Information Services
514199	All Other Information Services
5142	Data Processing Services
51421	Data Processing Services

52 FINANCE & INSURANCE

521 Monetary Authorities - Central Bank

Code	Short title
5211	Monetary Authorities - Central Bank
52111	Monetary Authorities - Central Bank

522 Credit Intermediation & Related Activities

Code	Short title
5221	Depository Credit Intermediation
52211	Commercial Banking
52212	Savings Institutions
52213	Credit Unions
52219	Other Depository Credit Intermediation
5222	Nondepository Credit Intermediation
52221	Credit Card Issuing
52222	Sales Financing
52229	Other Nondepository Credit Intermediation
522291	Consumer Lending
522292	Real Estate Credit
522293	International Trade Financing
522294	Secondary Market Financing
522298	All Oth Nondepository Credit Intermediation
5223	Activities Related to Credit Intermediation
52231	Mortgage & Nonmortgage Brokers
52232	Financial Clearinghouse & Reserve Activities
52239	Other Credit Intermediation Activities

523 Security, Commodity Contracts & Like Activity

Code	Short title
5231	Scrty & Comdty Contracts Intermed & Brokerage

Note: For definitions of abbreviations and substitute words see page 765.

Code	Short title
52311	Investment Banking & Securities Dealing
52312	Securities Brokerage
52313	Commodity Contracts Dealing
52314	Commodity Contracts Brokerage
5232	Securities & Commodity Exchanges
52321	Securities & Commodity Exchanges
5239	Other Financial Investment Activities
52391	Miscellaneous Intermediation
52392	Portfolio Management
52393	Investment Advice
52399	All Other Financial Investment Activities
523991	Trust, Fiduciary & Custody Activities
523999	Miscellaneous Financial Investment Activities
524	**Insurance Carriers & Related Activities**
5241	Insurance Carriers
52411	Direct Life/Health/Medical Insurance Carriers
524113	Direct Life Insurance Carriers
524114	Direct Health & Medical Insurance Carriers
52412	Other Direct Insurance Carriers
524126	Direct Property & Casualty Insurance Carriers
524127	Direct Title Insurance Carriers
524128	All Other Direct Insurance Carriers
52413	Reinsurance Carriers
5242	Agencies & Other Insurance Related Activities
52421	Insurance Agencies & Brokerages
52429	Other Insurance Related Activities
524291	Claims Adjusting
524292	Insurance & Pension Funds, Third Party Admin

Code	Short title
524298	All Other Insurance Related Activities
525	**Funds, Trusts & Other Financial Vehicles**
5251	Insurance & Employee Benefit Funds
52511	Pension Funds
52512	Health & Welfare Funds
52519	Other Insurance Funds
5259	Other Investment Pools & Funds
52591	Open-End Investment Funds
52592	Trusts, Estates & Agency Accounts
52593	Real Estate Investment Trusts
52599	Other Financial Vehicles
53	**REAL ESTATE & RENTAL & LEASING**
531	**Real Estate**
5311	Lessors of Real Estate
53111	Lessors of Residential Buildings & Dwellings
53112	Lessors of Nonres Bldg (exc Miniwarehouse)
53113	Lessors of Miniwarehouse & Self Storage Units
53119	Lessors of Other Real Estate Property
5312	Offices of Real Estate Agents & Brokers
53121	Offices of Real Estate Agents & Brokers
5313	Activities Related to Real Estate
53131	Real Estate Property Managers
531311	Residential Property Managers
531312	Nonresidential Property Managers
53132	Offices of Real Estate Appraisers
53139	Other Activities Related to Real Estate
532	**Rental & Leasing Services**
5321	Automotive Equipment Rental & Leasing
53211	Passenger Car Rental & Leasing

Note: For definitions of abbreviations and substitute words see page 765.

Code	Short title	Code	Short title
532111	Passenger Car Rental	541191	Title Abstract & Settlement Offices
532112	Passenger Car Leasing	541199	All Other Legal Services
53212	Truck, Utility Trailer & RV Rental & Leasing	5412	Accounting/Tax Prep/Bookkeep/ Payroll Services
5322	Consumer Goods Rental	54121	Accounting/Tax Prep/Bookkeep/ Payroll Services
53221	Consumer Electronics & Appliances Rental	541211	Offices of Certified Public Accountants
53222	Formal Wear & Costume Rental	541213	Tax Preparation Services
53223	Video Tape & Disk Rental	541214	Payroll Services
53229	Other Consumer Goods Rental	541219	Other Accounting Services
532291	Home Health Equipment Rental	5413	Architectural, Engineering & Related Services
532292	Recreational Goods Rental		
532299	All Other Consumer Goods Rental	54131	Architectural Services
5323	General Rental Centers	54132	Landscape Architectural Services
53231	General Rental Centers	54133	Engineering Services
5324	Commercial/Industrial Equip Rental & Leasing	54134	Drafting Services
		54135	Building Inspection Services
53241	Const/Trans/Mining Equip Rental & Leasing	54136	Geophysical Surveying & Mapping Services
532411	Commercial Trans Equip (exc MV) Rental/Lease	54137	Surveying/Mapping (exc Geophysical) Services
532412	Const/Mining/Forestry Equip Rental & Leasing	54138	Testing Laboratories
		5414	Specialized Design Services
53242	Office Machinery & Equipment Rental & Leasing	54141	Interior Design Services
		54142	Industrial Design Services
53249	Oth Commercial/Industrial Equip Rental/Lease	54143	Graphic Design Services
		54149	Other Specialized Design Services
533	**Lessors of Other Nonfinancial Intangible Asset**	5415	Computer Systems Design & Related Services
5331	Lessors of Other Nonfinancial Intangible Asset	54151	Computer Systems Design & Related Services
53311	Lessors of Other Nonfinancial Intangible Asset	541511	Custom Computer Programming Services
		541512	Computer Systems Design Services
54	**PROFESSIONAL, SCIENTIFIC & TECHNICAL SERVICES**	541513	Computer Facilities Management Services
541	**Professional, Scientific & Technical Services**	541519	Other Computer Related Services
		5416	Management, Sci & Tech Consulting Services
5411	Legal Services	54161	Management Consulting Services
54111	Offices of Lawyers	541611	Admin & Gen Management Consulting Services
54112	Offices of Notaries		
54119	Other Legal Services		

Note: For definitions of abbreviations and substitute words see page 765.

http://www.ntis.gov/naics

Code	Short title
541612	Human Res & Exec Search Consulting Services
541613	Marketing Consulting Services
541614	Process, Phys Dist & Log Consulting Services
541618	Other Management Consulting Services
54162	Environmental Consulting Services
54169	Oth Scientific & Technical Consulting Services
5417	Scientific R&D Services
54171	R&D in Physical, Engineering & Life Sciences
54172	R&D in Social Sciences & Humanities
5418	Advertising & Related Services
54181	Advertising Agencies
54182	Public Relations Agencies
54183	Media Buying Agencies
54184	Media Representatives
54185	Display Advertising
54186	Direct Mail Advertising
54187	Advertising Material Distribution Services
54189	Other Services Related to Advertising
5419	Oth Professional/Scientific/ Technical Service
54191	Marketing Research & Public Opinion Polling
54192	Photographic Services
541921	Photography Studios, Portrait
541922	Commercial Photography
54193	Translation & Interpretation Services
54194	Veterinary Services
54199	All Oth Prof, Scientific & Technical Services

55 MANAGEMENT OF COMPANIES & ENTERPRISES

551 Management of Companies & Enterprises

Code	Short title
5511	Management of Companies & Enterprises
55111	Management of Companies & Enterprises
551111	Offices of Bank Holding Companies
551112	Offices of Other Holding Companies
551114	Corp, Subsidiary & Regional Managing Offices

56 ADMIN/SUPPORT WASTE MGT/ REMEDIATION SERVICES

561 Administrative & Support Services

Code	Short title
5611	Office Administrative Services
56111	Office Administrative Services
5612	Facilities Support Services
56121	Facilities Support Services
5613	Employment Services
56131	Employment Placement Agencies
56132	Temporary Help Services
56133	Employee Leasing Services
5614	Business Support Services
56141	Document Preparation Services
56142	Telephone Call Centers
561421	Telephone Answering Services
561422	Telemarketing Bureaus
56143	Business Service Centers
561431	Private Mail Centers
561439	Oth Business Service Centers (incl Copy Shops)
56144	Collection Agencies
56145	Credit Bureaus
56149	Other Business Support Services
561491	Repossession Services
561492	Court Reporting & Stenotype Services
561499	All Other Business Support Services
5615	Travel Arrangement & Reservation Services

Note: For definitions of abbreviations and substitute words see page 765.

http://www.ntis.gov/naics

Code	Short title
56151	Travel Agencies
56152	Tour Operators
56159	Oth Travel Arrangement & Reservation Services
561591	Convention and Visitors Bureaus
561599	All Oth Travel Arrange & Reservation Services
5616	Investigation & Security Services
56161	Investigation, Guard & Armored Car Services
561611	Investigation Services
561612	Security Guards & Patrol Services
561613	Armored Car Services
56162	Security Systems Services
561621	Security Systems Services, (except Locksmiths)
561622	Locksmiths
5617	Services to Buildings & Dwellings
56171	Exterminating & Pest Control Services
56172	Janitorial Services
56173	Landscaping Services
56174	Carpet & Upholstery Cleaning Services
56179	Other Services to Buildings & Dwellings
5619	Other Support Services
56191	Packaging & Labeling Services
56192	Convention & Trade Show Organizers
56199	All Other Support Services

562   **Waste Management & Remediation Services**

Code	Short title
5621	Waste Collection
56211	Waste Collection
562111	Solid Waste Collection
562112	Hazardous Waste Collection
562119	Other Waste Collection
5622	Waste Treatment & Disposal
56221	Waste Treatment & Disposal
562211	Hazardous Waste Treatment & Disposal
562212	Solid Waste Landfill
562213	Solid Waste Combustors & Incinerators
562219	Other Nonhazardous Waste Treatment & Disposal
5629	Remediation & Oth Waste Management Services
56291	Remediation Services
56292	Materials Recovery Facilities
56299	All Other Waste Management Services
562991	Septic Tank & Related Services
562998	All Other Miscellaneous Waste Management

61   **EDUCATIONAL SERVICES**

611   **Educational Services**

Code	Short title
6111	Elementary & Secondary Schools
61111	Elementary & Secondary Schools
6112	Junior Colleges
61121	Junior Colleges
6113	Colleges, Universities & Professional Schools
61131	Colleges, Universities & Professional Schools
6114	Business Schools & Computer & Mgt Training
61141	Business & Secretarial Schools
61142	Computer Training
61143	Professional/Management Development Training
6115	Technical & Trade Schools
61151	Technical & Trade Schools
611511	Cosmetology & Barber Schools
611512	Flight Training
611513	Apprenticeship Training
611519	Other Technical & Trade Schools
6116	Other Schools & Instruction
61161	Fine Arts Schools
61162	Sports & Recreation Instruction
61163	Language Schools
61169	All Other Schools & Instruction
611691	Exam Preparation & Tutoring

Note: For definitions of abbreviations and substitute words see page 765.

http://www.ntis.gov/naics

Code	Short title
611692	Automobile Driving Schools
611699	All Other Miscellaneous Schools & Instruction
6117	Educational Support Services
61171	Educational Support Services

62 HEALTH CARE AND SOCIAL ASSISTANCE

621 Ambulatory Health Care Services

Code	Short title
6211	Offices of Physicians
62111	Offices of Physicians
621111	Offices of Physicians (exc Mental Health)
621112	Offices of Physicians, Mental Health
6212	Offices of Dentists
62121	Offices of Dentists
6213	Offices of Other Health Practitioners
62131	Offices of Chiropractors
62132	Offices of Optometrists
62133	Offices of Other Mental Health Practitioners
62134	Offices of PT/OT/Speech Therapy & Audiology
62139	All Oth Health Practitioners' Offices
621391	Offices of Podiatrists
621399	Offices of All Oth Misc Health Practitioners
6214	Outpatient Care Centers
62141	Family Planning Centers
62142	Outpatient Mental Health/ Substance Abuse Ctrs
62149	Other Outpatient Care Centers
621491	HMO Medical Centers
621492	Kidney Dialysis Centers
621493	Freestanding Ambulatory Surgery/ Emergency Ctr
621498	All Other Outpatient Care Centers
6215	Medical & Diagnostic Laboratories

Code	Short title
62151	Medical & Diagnostic Laboratories
621511	Medical Laboratories
621512	Diagnostic Imaging Centers
6216	Home Health Care Services
62161	Home Health Care Services
6219	Other Ambulatory Health Care Services
62191	Ambulance Services
62199	All Other Ambulatory Health Care Services
621991	Blood & Organ Banks
621999	All Oth Misc Ambulatory Health Care Services

622 Hospitals

Code	Short title
6221	General Medical & Surgical Hospitals
62211	General Medical & Surgical Hospitals
6222	Psychiatric & Substance Abuse Hospitals
62221	Psychiatric & Substance Abuse Hospitals
6223	Other Specialty Hospitals
62231	Other Specialty Hospitals

623 Nursing & Residential Care Facilities

Code	Short title
6231	Nursing Care Facilities
62311	Nursing Care Facilities
6232	Residential Mental Retardation/ Health Facil
62321	Residential Mental Retardation Facilities
62322	Residential Mental Health/Subst Abuse Facil
6233	Community Care Facilities for the Elderly
62331	Community Care Facilities for the Elderly
623311	Continuing Care Retirement Communities
623312	Homes for the Elderly

Note: For definitions of abbreviations and substitute words see page 765.

Code	Short title	Code	Short title
6239	Other Residential Care Facilities	7114	Agents/Managers for Artists & Oth Public Figu
62399	Other Residential Care Facilities	71141	Agents/Managers for Artists & Oth Public Figu
624	**Social Assistance**	7115	Independent Artists, Writers & Performers
6241	Individual & Family Services	71151	Independent Artists, Writers & Performers
62411	Child & Youth Services		
62412	Services for Elderly & Disabled Persons	**712**	**Museums, Historical Sites & Like Institutions**
62419	Other Individual & Family Services	7121	Museums, Historical Sites & Like Institutions
6242	Community/Emergency & Other Relief Services	71211	Museums
62421	Community Food Services	71212	Historical Sites
62422	Community Housing Services	71213	Zoos & Botanical Gardens
624221	Temporary Shelters	71219	Nature Parks & Other Similar Institutions
624229	Other Community Housing Services		
62423	Emergency & Other Relief Services	**713**	**Amusement, Gambling & Recreation Industries**
6243	Vocational Rehabilitation Services		
62431	Vocational Rehabilitation Services	7131	Amusement Parks & Arcades
6244	Child Day Care Services	71311	Amusement & Theme Parks
62441	Child Day Care Services	71312	Amusement Arcades
		7132	Gambling Industries
71	**ARTS, ENTERTAINMENT & RECREATION**	71321	Casinos (except Hotel Casinos)
		71329	Other Gambling Industries
711	**Perform Arts, Spectator Sports & Related Ind**	7139	Other Amusement & Recreation Industries
7111	Performing Arts Companies	71391	Golf Courses & Country Clubs
71111	Theater Companies & Dinner Theaters	71392	Skiing Facilities
71112	Dance Companies	71393	Marinas
71113	Musical Groups & Artists	71394	Fitness & Recreational Sports Centers
71119	Other Performing Arts Companies	71395	Bowling Centers
7112	Spectator Sports	71399	All Other Amusement & Recreation Industries
71121	Spectator Sports		
711211	Sports Teams and Clubs	**72**	**ACCOMMODATION & FOOD SERVICES**
711212	Racetracks		
711219	Other Spectator Sports	**721**	**Accommodation**
7113	Promoters of Entertainment Events	7211	Traveler Accommodation
71131	Promoters of Entertainment Events w/ Facility	72111	Hotels (exc Casino Hotels) & Motels
71132	Promoters of Entertainment Events w/o Facility		

Note: For definitions of abbreviations and substitute words see page 765.

http://www.ntis.gov/naics

Code	Short title	Code	Short title
72112	Casino Hotels	81112	Automotive Body/Paint/Interior & Glass Repair
72119	Other Traveler Accommodation		
721191	Bed & Breakfast Inns	811121	Automotive Body, Paint & Interior R&M
721199	All Other Traveler Accommodation		
		811122	Automotive Glass Replacement Shops
7212	RV Parks & Recreational Camps		
72121	RV Parks & Recreational Camps	81119	Other Automotive R&M
721211	RV Parks & Campgrounds	811191	Automotive Oil Change & Lubrication Shops
721214	Recreational/Vacation Camps (exc campgrounds)		
		811192	Carwashes
7213	Rooming & Boarding Houses	811198	All Other Automotive R&M
72131	Rooming & Boarding Houses	8112	Electronic & Precision Equipment R&M
722	**Food Services & Drinking Places**	81121	Electronic & Precision Equipment R&M
7221	Full-Service Restaurants	811211	Consumer Electronics R&M
72211	Full-Service Restaurants	811212	Computer & Office Machine R&M
7222	Limited-Service Eating Places		
72221	Limited-Service Eating Places	811213	Communication Equipment R&M
722211	Limited-Service Restaurants	811219	Other Electronic & Precision Equipment R&M
722212	Cafeterias		
722213	Snack & Nonalcoholic Beverage Bars	8113	Commercial Equipment (exc Auto & Elec) R&M
7223	Special Food Services	81131	Commercial Equipment (exc Auto & Elec) R&M
72231	Food Service Contractors		
72232	Caterers	8114	Personal & Household Goods R&M
72233	Mobile Food Services		
7224	Drinking Places (Alcoholic Beverages)	81141	Home/Garden Equipment & Appliance R&M
72241	Drinking Places (Alcoholic Beverages)	811411	Home & Garden Equipment R&M
		811412	Appliance R&M
81	**OTHER SERVICES (EXCEPT PUBLIC ADMINISTRATION)**	81142	Reupholstery & Furniture Repair
		81143	Footwear & Leather Goods Repair
811	**Repair & Maintenance**	81149	Other Personal & Household Goods R&M
8111	Automotive R&M	**812**	**Personal & Laundry Services**
81111	Automotive Mechanical & Electrical R&M		
		8121	Personal Care Services
811111	General Automotive Repair	81211	Hair, Nail & Skin Care Services
811112	Automotive Exhaust System Repair	812111	Barber Shops
		812112	Beauty Salons
811113	Automotive Transmission Repair	812113	Nail Salons
811118	Other Automotive Mechanical & Electrical R&M	81219	Other Personal Care Services
		812191	Diet & Weight Reducing Centers

Note: For definitions of abbreviations and substitute words see page 765.

Code	Short title
812199	Other Personal Care Services
8122	Death Care Services
81221	Funeral Homes
81222	Cemeteries & Crematories
8123	Drycleaning & Laundry Services
81231	Coin-Operated Laundries & Drycleaners
81232	Drycleaning & Laundry Services (exc Coin-Op)
81233	Linen & Uniform Supply
812331	Linen Supply
812332	Industrial Launderers
8129	Other Personal Services
81291	Pet Care (except Veterinary) Services
81292	Photofinishing
812921	Photofinishing Laboratories (except One-Hour)
812922	One-Hour Photofinishing
81293	Parking Lots & Garages
81299	All Other Personal Services

813 Religious/Grantmaking/Prof/ Like Organizations

Code	Short title
8131	Religious Organizations
81311	Religious Organizations
8132	Grantmaking & Giving Services
81321	Grantmaking & Giving Services
813211	Grantmaking Foundations
813212	Voluntary Health Organizations
813219	Other Grantmaking & Giving Services
8133	Social Advocacy Organizations
81331	Social Advocacy Organizations
813311	Human Rights Organizations
813312	Environment & Wildlife Organizations
813319	Other Social Advocacy Organizations
8134	Civic & Social Organizations
81341	Civic & Social Organizations
8139	Business/Labor/Political/Like Organizations
81391	Business Associations

Code	Short title
81392	Professional Organizations
81393	Labor Unions & Similar Labor Organizations
81394	Political Organizations
81399	Oth Similar Org (exc Business/Prof/Labor/Pol)

814 Private Households

Code	Short title
8141	Private Households
81411	Private Households

92 PUBLIC ADMINISTRATION

921 General Government Administration

Code	Short title
9211	General Government Administration
92111	Executive Offices
92112	Legislative Bodies
92113	Public Finance Activities
92114	Executive & Legislative Offices, Combined
92115	American Indian & Alaska Native Tribal Gov
92119	Other General Government Support

922 Justice, Public Order & Safety Activities

Code	Short title
9221	Justice, Public Order & Safety Activities
92211	Courts
92212	Police Protection
92213	Legal Counsel & Prosecution
92214	Correctional Institutions
92215	Parole Offices & Probation Offices
92216	Fire Protection
92219	Oth Justice/Public Order/Safety Activity

923 Administration of Human Resource Programs

Code	Short title
9231	Administration of Human Resource Programs

Note: For definitions of abbreviations and substitute words see page 765.

http://www.ntis.gov/naics

Code	Short title
92311	Administration of Education Programs
92312	Administration of Public Health Programs
92313	Administration of Other Human Resource Programs
92314	Administration of Veterans' Affairs
924	**Administration of Environmental Quality Programs**
9241	Administration of Environmental Quality Programs
92411	Admin Air/Water Resource/Solid Waste Mgt Prog
92412	Administration of Conservation Programs
925	**Admin Housing/Urban Planning/ Community Devop**
9251	Admin Housing/Urban Planning/ Community Devop
92511	Administration of Housing Programs
92512	Admin Urban Planning & Community/ Rural Devop

Code	Short title
926	**Administration of Economic Programs**
9261	Administration of Economic Programs
92611	Administration of General Economic Programs
92612	Regulation & Admin of Transportation Programs
92613	Regulation & Administration of Utilities
92614	Regulation Agricultural Marketing & Commodities
92615	Reg/License/Inspect - Misc Commercial Sectors
927	**Space Research & Technology**
9271	Space Research & Technology
92711	Space Research & Technology
928	**National Security & International Affairs**
9281	National Security & International Affairs
92811	National Security
92812	International Affairs

Note: For definitions of abbreviations and substitute words see page 765.

http://www.ntis.gov/naics

Abbreviations and Substitute Words

Abbreviation/Substitute word	Word	Abbreviation/Substitute word	Word
Access	Accessories	Finishng	Finishing
Activity	Activities	Frgt	Freight
Admin	Administration	Gas	Gasoline
Ag	Agricultural	Gen	General
AC	Air-Conditioning	Gov	Government
Alloy	Alloying	Missile	Guided Missile
Alum	Aluminu		
&	and	HH	Household
Anodize	Anodizing	Htg	Heating
Arrange	Arrangement	HVAC	Heating, Ventilation,
Artf	Artificial		Air-Conditioning
Audiology	Audiologists	Incl	Including
Auto	Automotive	Ind	Industrial; Industries
Aux	Auxiliary	Inspect	Inspection
		Instrumnt	Instrument
Bookkeep	Bookkeeping	Intermed	Intermediation
Broadcast	Broadcasting	Ki	Kitchen
Bldg	Building		
		Lamnd	Laminated
Cabnt	Cabinet	Lease	Leasing
Ctrs	Centers	LTL	Less Than Truckload
Choc	Chocolate	License	Licensing
Coin-Op	Coin-operated	Log	Logistics
Comdty	Commodities	LDist	Long-distance
Comm	Communications		
CD	Compact Disc	Mach	Machinery
Compn	Component	Mgt	Management
Const	Construction	Mfg	Manufacturing
Contr	Contractor	Mil	Military
Corp	Corporate	Misc	Miscellaneous
		Movie	Motion Picture
Devop	Development	MV	Motor Vehicle
Dist	Distribution		
Draw	Drawing	Nav	Navigational
Dryclean	Drycleaning	Nonres	Nonresidential
		NEC	Not Elsewhere Classified
Elec	Electric;Electronic		
Electropl	Electroplating	OT	Occupational Therapist
Embroid	Embroidery	Oth	Other
Engrave	Engraving		
Equip	Equipment	Pkg	Packaging
exc	except	Pt	Part
Exec	Executive	Perform	Performing
Extrude	Extruding	Photo	Photographic
		Phys	Physical
Facil	Facilities	PT	Physical Therapist
Farm	Farming	Plumb	Plumbing
Figu	Figures	Polish	Polishing
Fil	Filaments	Postprod	Postproduction

http://www.ntis.gov/naics

Abbreviation/Substitute word	Word	Abbreviation/Substitute word	Word
Pol	Political	Spd	Speed
Pwr	Power	Sta	Stations
Prep	Preparation	Subst	Substance
Press	Pressing	Supply /Supp	Supplies
Prim	Primary	Syn	Synthetic
Prod/Pro	Production	Tech	Technical
Prof	Professional	Telecom	Telecommunications
Prog	Program/Programs	TV	Television
Purch	Purchase; Purchased	Total	Totalizing
RV	Recreational Vehicle	Transmsn	Transmission
Refine	Refining	Trans	Transportation
Refrig	Refrigeration	TL	Truckload
Reg	Regulation	Turn	Turned
R&M	Repair and Maintenance	Util	Utility
R&D	Research and Development	Veg	Vegetable
Res	Resources	Veh	Vehicle
Roll	Rolling	HVAC	Ventilation, Heating, Air-Conditioning
Sci	Scientific		
Security /Scrty	Securities	Whsle	Wholesalers
Shelv	Shelving	Wirless	Wireless
Shwcase	Showcase	w/	with
/	Slash replaces comma	w/o	without
Smelt	Smelting		

Part III

Appendixes

Appendixes A and B map the 1997 NAICS to the 1987 SIC in 1997 NAICS sequence (Appendix A) and 1987 SIC sequence (Appendix B). The tables do not provide a comprehensive guide to all economic activities, but rather provide a map for the largest and most important activities defined in the 1987 SIC.

Appendix A
1997 NAICS U.S. Matched to 1987 U.S. SIC

1997 NAICS code	1997 NAICS U.S. description	1987 SIC code	1987 U.S. SIC description
11	Agriculture, Forestry, Fishing and Hunting		
111	Crop Production		
1111	Oilseed and Grain Farming		
11111	Soybean Farming	0116	Soybeans
11112	Oilseed (except Soybean) Farming	*0119	Cash Grains, NEC (oilseed, except soybean farming)
11113	Dry Pea and Bean Farming	*0119	Cash Grains, NEC (dry pea and bean farms)
11114	Wheat Farming	0111	Wheat
11115	Corn Farming	0115	Corn
		*0119	Cash Grains, NEC (popcorn farming)
11116	Rice Farming	0112	Rice
11119	Other Grain Farming		
US 111191	Oilseed and Grain Combination Farming	*0119	Cash Grains, NEC (oilseed and grain combination farms)
US 111199	All Other Grain Farming	*0119	Cash Grains, NEC (except popcorn, soybean, and dry pea and bean, and oilseed and grain combination farms)
1112	Vegetable and Melon Farming		
11121	Vegetable and Melon Farming		
CAN 111211	Potato Farming	0134	Irish Potatoes
CAN 111219	Other Vegetable (except Potato) and Melon Farming	0161	Vegetables and Melons
		*0139	Field Crops Except Cash Grains (sweet potatoes and yams)
1113	Fruit and Tree Nut Farming		
11131	Orange Groves	*0174	Citrus Fruits (orange groves and farms)
11132	Citrus (except Orange) Groves	*0174	Citrus Fruits (except, orange groves and farms)
11133	Noncitrus Fruit and Tree Nut Farming		

US—United States industry only. CAN—United States and Canadian industries are comparable. When neither US nor CAN appears, Canadian, Mexican, and United States are comparable. *—Part of; NEC—Not Elsewhere Classified.

http://www.ntis.gov/naics

1997 NAICS code	1997 NAICS U.S. description	1987 SIC code	1987 U.S. SIC description
US 111331	Apple Orchards	*0175	Deciduous Tree Fruits (apple orchards and farms)
US 111332	Grape Vineyards	0172	Grapes
US 111333	Strawberry Farming	*0171	Berry Crops (strawberry farms)
US 111334	Berry (except Strawberry) Farming	*0171	Berry Crops (except strawberry farms)
US 111335	Tree Nut Farming	0173	Tree Nuts
US 111336	Fruit and Tree Nut Combination Farming	*0179	Fruits and Tree Nuts, NEC (combination farms)
US 111339	Other Noncitrus Fruit Farming	*0175	Deciduous Tree Fruits (except apple orchards and farms)
		*0179	Fruit and Tree Nuts, NEC (except combination farms)
1114	Greenhouse, Nursery, and Floriculture Production		
11141	Food Crops Grown Under Cover		
CAN 111411	Mushroom Production	*0182	Food Crops Grown Under Cover (mushrooms, growing of)
CAN 111419	Other Food Crops Grown Under Cover	*0182	Food Crops Grown Under Cover (except mushroom, growing of)
11142	Nursery and Floriculture Production		
CAN 111421	Nursery and Tree Production	*0181	Ornamental Floriculture and Nursery Products (nursery farming)
		*0811	Timber Tracts (short rotation woody crops)
CAN 111422	Floriculture Production	*0181	Ornamental Floriculture and Nursery Products (floriculture farming)
1119	Other Crop Farming		
11191	Tobacco Farming	0132	Tobacco
11192	Cotton Farming	0131	Cotton
11193	Sugarcane Farming	*0133	Sugarcane and Sugar Beets (sugarcane farms)
11194	Hay Farming	*0139	Field Crops, Except Cash Grains, NEC (hay farms)
11199	All Other Crop Farming		
US 111991	Sugar Beet Farming	*0133	Sugarcane and Sugar Beets (sugar beet farms)

US—United States industry only. CAN—United States and Canadian industries are comparable. When neither US nor CAN appears, Canadian, Mexican, and United States are comparable. *—Part of; NEC—Not Elsewhere Classified.

http://www.ntis.gov/naics

	1997 NAICS code	1997 NAICS U.S. description	1987 SIC code	1987 U.S. SIC description
US	111992	Peanut Farming	*0139	Field Crops, Except Cash Grains, NEC (peanut farms)
US	111998	All Other Miscellaneous Crop Farming	*0139	Field Crops, Except Cash Grains, NEC (except peanut, sweet potato, yam and hay farms)
			0191	General Farms, Primarily Crop
			*0831	Forest Products (maple sap, gathering of)
			*0919	Miscellaneous Marine Products (plant aquaculture)
			*2099	Food Preparations, NEC (reducing maple sap to maple syrup)
	112	Animal Production		
	1121	Cattle Ranching and Farming		
	11211	Beef Cattle Ranching and Farming, including Feedlots		
US	112111	Beef Cattle Ranching and Farming	0212	Beef Cattle, Except Feedlots
			*0241	Dairy Farms (dairy heifer replacement farms)
US	112112	Cattle Feedlots	0211	Beef Cattle Feedlots
	11212	Dairy Cattle and Milk Production	*0241	Dairy Farms
	11213	Dual Purpose Cattle Ranching and Farming		Null Set for U.S.
	1122	Hog and Pig Farming		
	11221	Hog and Pig Farming	0213	Hogs
	1123	Poultry and Egg Production		
	11231	Chicken Egg Production	0252	Chicken Eggs
	11232	Broilers and Other Meat Type Chicken Production	0251	Broiler, Fryers, and Roaster Chickens
	11233	Turkey Production	0253	Turkey and Turkey Eggs
	11234	Poultry Hatcheries	0254	Poultry Hatcheries
	11239	Other Poultry Production	0259	Poultry and Eggs, NEC
	1124	Sheep and Goat Farming		
	11241	Sheep Farming	*0214	Sheep and Goats (sheep farms)
	11242	Goat Farming	*0214	Sheep and Goats (goat farms)
	1125	Animal Aquaculture		
	11251	Animal Aquaculture		
US	112511	Finfish Farming and Fish Hatcheries	*0273	Animal Aquaculture (finfish farms)

US—United States industry only. CAN—United States and Canadian industries are comparable. When neither US nor CAN appears, Canadian, Mexican, and United States are comparable. *—Part of; NEC—Not Elsewhere Classified.

http://www.ntis.gov/naics

	1997 NAICS code	1997 NAICS U.S. description	1987 SIC code	1987 U.S. SIC description
			*0921	Fish Hatcheries and Preserves (finfish hatcheries)
US	112512	Shellfish Farming	*0273	Animal Aquaculture (shellfish farms)
			*0921	Fish Hatcheries and Preserves (shellfish hatcheries)
US	112519	Other Animal Aquaculture	*0273	Animal Aquaculture (except finfish and shellfish)
			*0279	Animal Specialties, NEC (alligator and frog production)
	1129	Other Animal Production		
	11291	Apiculture	*0279	Animal Specialties, NEC (apiculture)
	11292	Horse and Other Equine Production	0272	Horse and Other Equine
	11293	Fur-Bearing Animal and Rabbit Production	0271	Fur-Bearing Animals and Rabbits
	11299	All Other Animal Production	0219	General Livestock, Except Dairy and Poultry
			*0279	Animal Specialties, NEC (except apiculture)
			0291	General Farms, Primarily Livestock and Animal Specialties
	113	Forestry and Logging		
	1131	Timber Tract Operations		
	11311	Timber Tract Operations	*0811	Timber Tracts (long term timber farms)
	1132	Forest Nurseries and Gathering of Forest Products		
	11321	Forest Nurseries and Gathering of Forest Products	*0831	Forest Nurseries and Gathering of Forest Products (forest products, except gathering of maple sap)
	1133	Logging		
	11331	Logging	2411	Logging
	114	Fishing, Hunting and Trapping		
	1141	Fishing		
	11411	Fishing		
US	114111	Finfish Fishing	0912	Finfish
US	114112	Shellfish Fishing	0913	Shellfish
US	114119	Other Marine Fishing	*0919	Miscellaneous Marine Products (except plant aquaculture)

US—United States industry only. CAN—United States and Canadian industries are comparable. When neither US nor CAN appears, Canadian, Mexican, and United States are comparable. *—Part of; NEC—Not Elsewhere Classified.

http://www.ntis.gov/naics

	1997 NAICS code	1997 NAICS U.S. description	1987 SIC code	1987 U.S. SIC description
	1142	Hunting and Trapping		
	11421	Hunting and Trapping	0971	Hunting and Trapping, and Game Propagation
	115	Support Activities for Agriculture and Forestry		
	1151	Support Activities for Crop Production		
	11511	Support Activities for Crop Production		
US	115111	Cotton Ginning	0724	Cotton Ginning
US	115112	Soil Preparation, Planting, and Cultivating	0711	Soil Preparation Services
			0721	Crop Planting, Cultivating, and Protecting
US	115113	Crop Harvesting, Primarily by Machine	0722	Crop Harvesting, Primarily by Machine
US	115114	Postharvest Crop Activities (except Cotton Ginning)	*0723	Crop Preparation Services For Market, Except Cotton Ginning (except custom grain grinding)
US	115115	Farm Labor Contractors and Crew Leaders	0761	Farm Labor Contractors and Crew Leaders
US	115116	Farm Management Services	0762	Farm Management Services
	1152	Support Activities for Animal Production		
	11521	Support Activities for Animal Production	*0751	Livestock Services, Except Veterinary (except custom slaughtering)
			*0752	Animal Specialty Services, Except Veterinary (horses and equines services and animal production breeding)
			*7699	Repair Services, NEC (farriers)
	1153	Support Activities for Forestry		
	11531	Support Activities for Forestry	0851	Forestry Services
	21	Mining		
	211	Oil and Gas Extraction		
	2111	Oil and Gas Extraction		
	21111	Oil and Gas Extraction		
US	211111	Crude Petroleum and Natural Gas Extraction	1311	Crude Petroleum and Natural Gas
US	211112	Natural Gas Liquid Extraction	1321	Natural Gas Liquids

US—United States industry only. CAN—United States and Canadian industries are comparable. When neither US nor CAN appears, Canadian, Mexican, and United States are comparable. *—Part of; NEC—Not Elsewhere Classified.

http://www.ntis.gov/naics

1997 NAICS code	1997 NAICS U.S. description	1987 SIC code	1987 U.S. SIC description
		*2819	Industrial Inorganic Chemicals, NEC (recovering sulfur from natural gas)
212	Mining (except Oil and Gas)		
2121	Coal Mining		
21211	Coal Mining		
US 212111	Bituminous Coal and Lignite Surface Mining	1221	Bituminous Coal and Lignite Surface Mining
US 212112	Bituminous Coal Underground Mining	1222	Bituminous Coal Underground Mining
US 212113	Anthracite Mining	1231	Anthracite Mining
2122	Metal Ore Mining		
21221	Iron Ore Mining	1011	Iron Ores
21222	Gold Ore and Silver Ore Mining		
US 212221	Gold Ore Mining	1041	Gold Ores
US 212222	Silver Ore Mining	1044	Silver Ores
21223	Copper, Nickel, Lead, and Zinc Mining		
CAN 212231	Lead Ore and Zinc Ore Mining	1031	Lead and Zinc Ores
US 212234	Copper Ore and Nickel Ore Mining	1021	Copper Ores
		*1061	Ferroalloy Ores, Except Vanadium (nickel)
21229	Other Metal Ore Mining		
US 212291	Uranium-Radium-Vanadium Ore Mining	1094	Uranium-Radium-Vanadium Ores
US 212299	All Other Metal Ore Mining	*1061	Ferroalloy Ores, Except Vanadium (other ferroalloys except nickel)
		1099	Miscellaneous Metal Ores, NEC
2123	Nonmetallic Mineral Mining and Quarrying		
21231	Stone Mining and Quarrying		
US 212311	Dimension Stone Mining and Quarrying	1411	Dimension Stone
US 212312	Crushed and Broken Limestone Mining and Quarrying	1422	Crushed and Broken Limestone
US 212313	Crushed and Broken Granite Mining and Quarrying	1423	Crushed and Broken Granite

US—United States industry only. CAN—United States and Canadian industries are comparable. When neither US nor CAN appears, Canadian, Mexican, and United States are comparable. *—Part of; NEC—Not Elsewhere Classified.

http://www.ntis.gov/naics

	1997 NAICS code	1997 NAICS U.S. description	1987 SIC code	1987 U.S. SIC description
US	212319	Other Crushed and Broken Stone Mining and Quarrying	1429	Crushed and Broken Stone, NEC
			*1499	Miscellaneous Nonmetallic Minerals, Except Fuels (bituminous limestone and bituminous sandstone)
	21232	Sand, Gravel, Clay, and Ceramic and Refractory Minerals Mining and Quarrying		
US	212321	Construction Sand and Gravel Mining	1442	Construction Sand and Gravel
US	212322	Industrial Sand Mining	1446	Industrial Sand
US	212324	Kaolin and Ball Clay Mining	1455	Kaolin and Ball Clay
			*3295	Minerals and Earths, Ground or Otherwise Treated (grinding, washing, separating, etc. of minerals in SIC 1455)
US	212325	Clay and Ceramic and Refractory Minerals Mining	1459	Clay, Ceramic, and Refractory Minerals, NEC
			*3295	Minerals and Earths, Ground or Otherwise Treated (grinding, washing, separating, etc. of minerals in SIC 1459)
	21239	Other Nonmetallic Mineral Mining and Quarrying		
US	212391	Potash, Soda, and Borate Mineral Mining	1474	Potash, Soda, and Borate Minerals
US	212392	Phosphate Rock Mining	1475	Phosphate Rock
US	212393	Other Chemical and Fertilizer Mineral Mining	1479	Chemical and Fertilizer Mineral Mining, NEC
			*3295	Minerals and Earths, Ground or Otherwise Treated (grinding, washing, separating, etc. of minerals in SIC 1479)
US	212399	All Other Nonmetallic Mineral Mining	*1499	Miscellaneous Nonmetallic Minerals, Except Fuels (except bituminous limestone and bituminous sandstone)

US—United States industry only. CAN—United States and Canadian industries are comparable. When neither US nor CAN appears, Canadian, Mexican, and United States are comparable. *—Part of; NEC—Not Elsewhere Classified.

http://www.ntis.gov/naics

1997 NAICS code	1997 NAICS U.S. description	1987 SIC code	1987 U.S. SIC description
		*3295	Minerals and Earths, Ground or Otherwise Treated (grinding, washing, separating, etc. of minerals in SIC 1499)
213	Support Activities for Mining		
2131	Support Activities for Mining		
21311	Support Activities for Mining		
CAN 213111	Drilling Oil and Gas Wells	1381	Drilling Oil and Gas Wells
US 213112	Support Activities for Oil and Gas Operations	*1382	Oil and Gas Field Exploration Services (except geophysical mapping and surveying)
		1389	Oil and Gas Field Services, NEC
US 213113	Support Activities for Coal Mining	1241	Coal Mining Services
US 213114	Support Activities for Metal Mining	*1081	Metal Mining Services (except geophysical surveying and mapping)
US 213115	Support Activities for Nonmetallic Minerals (except Fuels)	*1481	Nonmetallic Minerals Services, Except Fuels (except geophysical surveying and mapping)
22	Utilities		
221	Utilities		
CAN 2211	Electric Power Generation, Transmission and Distribution		
CAN 22111	Electric Power Generation		
CAN 221111	Hydroelectric Power Generation	*4911	Electric Services (hydroelectric power generation)
		*4931	Electric and Other Services Combined (hydroelectric power generation)
		*4939	Combination Utilities, NEC (hydroelectric power generation)
CAN 221112	Fossil Fuel Electric Power Generation	*4911	Electric Services (fossil fuel power generation)
		*4931	Electric and Other Services Combined (fossil fuel power generation)
		*4939	Combination Utilities, NEC (fossil fuel power generation)
CAN 221113	Nuclear Electric Power Generation	*4911	Electric Services (nuclear electric power generation)

US—United States industry only. CAN—United States and Canadian industries are comparable. When neither US nor CAN appears, Canadian, Mexican, and United States are comparable. *—Part of; NEC—Not Elsewhere Classified.

http://www.ntis.gov/naics

1997 NAICS code	1997 NAICS U.S. description	1987 SIC code	1987 U.S. SIC description
		*4931	Electric and Other Services Combined (nuclear power generation)
		*4939	Combination Utilities, NEC (nuclear power generation)
CAN 221119	Other Electric Power Generation	*4911	Electric Services (other electric power generation)
		*4931	Electric and Other Services Combined (other electric power generation)
		*4939	Combination Utilities, NEC (other electric power generation)
CAN 22112	Electric Power Transmission, Control, andDistribution		
CAN 221121	Electric Bulk Power Transmission and Control	*4911	Electric Services (electric power transmission and control)
		*4931	Electric and Other Services Combined (electric power transmission and control)
		*4939	Combination Utilities, NEC (electric power transmission and control)
CAN 221122	Electric Power Distribution	*4911	Electric Services (electric power distribution)
		*4931	Electric and Other Services Combined (electric power distribution)
		*4939	Combination Utilities, NEC (electric power distribution)
CAN 2212	Natural Gas Distribution		
CAN 22121	Natural Gas Distribution	*4923	Natural Gas Transmission and Distribution (distribution)
		4924	Natural Gas Distribution
		4925	Mixed, Manufactured, or Liquefied Petroleum Gas Production and/or Distribution
		*4931	Electric and Other Services Combined (natural gas distribution)
		4932	Gas and Other Services Combined (natural gas distribution)

US—United States industry only. CAN—United States and Canadian industries are comparable. When neither US nor CAN appears, Canadian, Mexican, and United States are comparable. *—Part of; NEC—Not Elsewhere Classified.

http://www.ntis.gov/naics

1997 NAICS code	1997 NAICS U.S. description	1987 SIC code	1987 U.S. SIC description
		*4939	Combination Utilities, NEC (natural gas distribution)
CAN 2213	Water, Sewage and Other Systems		
CAN 22131	Water Supply and Irrigation Systems	4941	Water Supply
		4971	Irrigation Systems
CAN 22132	Sewage Treatment Facilities	4952	Sewerage Systems
CAN 22133	Steam and Air-Conditioning Supply	4961	Steam and Air-Conditioning Supply
23	Construction		
US 233	Building, Developing, and Genera Contracting		
US 2331	Land Subdivision and Land Development		
US 23311	Land Subdivision and Land Development	6552	Land Subdividers and Developers, Except Cemeteries
US 2332	Residential Building Construction		
US 23321	Single Family Housing Construction	1521	General Contractors-Single-Family Houses
		*1531	Operative Builders (single family housing construction)
		*8741	Management Services (single family housing construction management)
US 23322	Multifamily Housing Construction	*1522	General Contractors-Residential Building, Other Than Single-Family (except hotel and motel construction)
		*1531	Operative Builders (multi-family housing construction)
		*8741	Management Services (multi-family housing construction management)
US 2333	Nonresidential Building Construction		
US 23331	Manufacturing and Industrial Building Construction	*1531	Operative Builders (manufacturing and light industrial building construction)

US—United States industry only. CAN—United States and Canadian industries are comparable. When neither US nor CAN appears, Canadian, Mexican, and United States are comparable. *—Part of; NEC—Not Elsewhere Classified.

http://www.ntis.gov/naics

1997 NAICS code	1997 NAICS U.S. description	1987 SIC code	1987 U.S. SIC description
		*1541	General Contractors-Industrial Buildings and Warehouses (except public warehouse construction)
		*8741	Management Services (manufacturing and industrial building construction management)
US 23332	Commercial and Institutional Building Construction	*1522	General Contractors-Residential Building Other than Single-Family (hotel and motel construction)
		*1531	Operative Builders (commercial and institutional building construction)
		*1541	General Contractors-Industrial Buildings and Warehouses (public warehouse construction)
		1542	General Contractors-Nonresidential Buildings, Other than Industrial Buildings and Warehouses
		*8741	Management Services (commercial and institutional building construction management)
US 234	Heavy Construction		
US 2341	Highway, Street, Bridge, and Tunnel Construction		
US 23411	Highway and Street Construction	1611	Highway and Street Construction, Except Elevated Highways
		*8741	Management Services (highway and street construction management)
US 23412	Bridge and Tunnel Construction	1622	Bridge, Tunnel, and Elevated Highway Construction
		*8741	Management Services (bridge and tunnel construction management)
US 2349	Other Heavy Construction		

US—United States industry only. CAN—United States and Canadian industries are comparable. When neither US nor CAN appears, Canadian, Mexican, and United States are comparable. *—Part of; NEC—Not Elsewhere Classified.

http://www.ntis.gov/naics

	1997 NAICS code	1997 NAICS U.S. description	1987 SIC code	1987 U.S. SIC description
US	23491	Water, Sewer, and Pipeline Construction	*1623	Water, Sewer, Pipeline, and Communications and Power Line Construction (water, sewer, and pipeline construction)
			*8741	Management Services (water, sewer, and pipeline construction management)
US	23492	Power and Communication Transmission Line Construction	*1623	Water, Sewer, Pipeline, and Communications and Power Line Construction (communications and power line construction)
			*8741	Management Services (power and communication transmission line construction management)
US	23493	Industrial Nonbuilding Structure Construction	*1629	Heavy Construction, NEC (industrial nonbuilding structures construction)
			*8741	Management Services (industrial nonbuilding structure construction management)
US	23499	All Other Heavy Construction	*1629	Heavy Construction, NEC (nonbuilding structures except industrial construction)
			*7353	Construction Equipment Rental and Leasing (construction equipment with operator)
			*8741	Management Services (other heavy construction management)
US	235	Special Trade Contractors		
US	2351	Plumbing, Heating, and Air-Conditioning Contractors		
US	23511	Plumbing, Heating, and Air-Conditioning Contractors	1711	Plumbing, Heating and Air-Conditioning
			*7699	Repair Shops and Related Services (boiler cleaning)
US	2352	Painting and Wall Covering Contractors		
US	23521	Painting and Wall Covering Contractors	1721	Painting and Paper Hanging
			*1799	Special Trade Contractors, NEC (paint and wallpaper stripping and wallpaper removal contractors)

    US—United States industry only. CAN—United States and Canadian industries are comparable. When neither US nor CAN appears, Canadian, Mexican, and United States are comparable. *—Part of; NEC—Not Elsewhere Classified.

http://www.ntis.gov/naics

1997 NAICS code	1997 NAICS U.S. description	1987 SIC code	1987 U.S. SIC description
US 2353	Electrical Contractors		
US 23531	Electrical Contractors	1731	Electrical Work
US 2354	Masonry, Drywall, Insulation, and Tile Contractors		
US 23541	Masonry and Stone Contractors	1741	Masonry, Stone Setting and Other Stone Work
US 23542	Drywall, Plastering, Acoustical, and Insulation Contractors	1742	Plastering, Drywall, Acoustical, and Insulation Work
		*1743	Terrazzo, Tile, Marble and Mosaic work (fresco work)
		*1771	Concrete Work (stucco construction)
US 23543	Tile, Marble, Terrazzo, and Mosaic Contractors	*1743	Terrazzo, Tile, Marble, and Mosaic Work (except fresco work)
US 2355	Carpentry and Floor Contractors		
US 23551	Carpentry Contractors	1751	Carpentry Work
US 23552	Floor Laying and Other Floor Contractors	1752	Floor Laying and Other Floor Work, NEC
US 2356	Roofing, Siding, and Sheet Metal Contractors		
US 23561	Roofing, Siding, and Sheet Metal Contractors	1761	Roofing, Siding, and Sheet Metal Work
US 2357	Concrete Contractors		
US 23571	Concrete Contractors	*1771	Concrete Work (except stucco construction)
US 2358	Water Well Drilling Contractors		
US 23581	Water Well Drilling Contractors	1781	Water Well Drilling
US 2359	Other Special Trade Contractors		
US 23591	Structural Steel Erection Contractors	1791	Structural Steel Erection
US 23592	Glass and Glazing Contractors	1793	Glass and Glazing Work
		*1799	Specialty Trade Contractors, NEC (tinting glass work)
US 23593	Excavation Contractors	1794	Excavation Work
US 23594	Wrecking and Demolition Contractors	1795	Wrecking and Demolition Work

US—United States industry only. CAN—United States and Canadian industries are comparable. When neither US nor CAN appears, Canadian, Mexican, and United States are comparable. *—Part of; NEC—Not Elsewhere Classified.

http://www.ntis.gov/naics

	1997 NAICS code	1997 NAICS U.S. description	1987 SIC code	1987 U.S. SIC description
US	23595	Building Equipment and Other Machinery Installation Contractors	1796	Installation or Erection of Building Equipment, NEC
US	23599	All Other Special Trade Contractors	*1799	Special Trade Contractors, NEC (except paint and wallpaper stripping, wall paper removal contractors, and tinting glass work)
	31-33	Manufacturing		
	311	Food Manufacturing		
	3111	Animal Food Manufacturing		
	31111	Animal Food Manufacturing		
CAN	311111	Dog and Cat Food Manufacturing	2047	Dog and Cat Food
CAN	311119	Other Animal Food Manufacturing	*2048	Prepared Feeds and Feed Ingredients for Animals and Fowls, Except Dogs and Cats (except slaughtering animals for pet food)
			*0723	Crop Production Services for Market, Except Cotton Ginning (custom grain grinding)
	3112	Grain and Oilseed Milling		
	31121	Flour Milling and Malt Manufacturing		
CAN	311211	Flour Milling	*2034	Dehydrated Fruits, Vegetables and Soup Mixes (vegetable flour)
			2041	Flour and Other Grain Mill Products
US	311212	Rice Milling	2044	Rice Milling
			*2099	Food Preparations, NEC (rice, uncooked and packaged with other ingredients made in rice mills)
US	311213	Malt Manufacturing	2083	Malt
	31122	Starch and Vegetable Fats and Oils Manufacturing		
CAN	311221	Wet Corn Milling	*2046	Wet Corn Milling (except refining purchased oil)
US	311222	Soybean Processing	*2075	Soybean Oil Mills (soybean processing)

US—United States industry only. CAN—United States and Canadian industries are comparable. When neither US nor CAN appears, Canadian, Mexican, and United States are comparable. *—Part of; NEC—Not Elsewhere Classified.

http://www.ntis.gov/naics

1997 NAICS code	1997 NAICS U.S. description	1987 SIC code	1987 U.S. SIC description
		*2079	Shortening, Table Oils, Margarine, and Other Edible Fats and Oils, NEC (processing soybean oil from soybeans crushed in the same establishment)
US 311223	Other Oilseed Processing	*2074	Cottonseed Oil Mills (cottonseed processing)
		*2079	Shortening, Table Oils, Margarine and Other Edible Fats and Oils, NEC (processing vegetable oils, except soybeans, from oilseeds crushed in the same establishment)
		*2076	Vegetable Oil Mills, Except Corn, Cottonseed, and Soybean (oilseed processing)
CAN 311225	Fats and Oils Refining and Blending	*2046	Wet Corn Milling (refining purchased oil)
		*2074	Cottonseed Oil Mills (processing purchased cottonseed oil)
		*2075	Soybean Oil Mills (processing purchased soybean oil)
		*2076	Vegetable Oil Mills, Except Corn, Cottonseed, and Soybean (processing purchased vegetable oils)
		*2079	Shortening, Table Oils, Margarine, and Other Edible Fats and Oils, NEC (processing fats and oils from purchased fats and oils)
31123	Breakfast Cereal Manufacturing	*2043	Cereal Breakfast Foods (breakfast cereal)
3113	Sugar and Confectionery Product Manufacturing		
31131	Sugar Manufacturing		
US 311311	Sugarcane Mills	2061	Cane Sugar, Except Refining
US 311312	Cane Sugar Refining	2062	Cane Sugar Refining
US 311313	Beet Sugar Manufacturing	2063	Beet Sugar
31132	Chocolate and Confectionery Manufacturing from Cacao Beans	*2066	Chocolate and Cocoa Products (except chocolate products, made from purchased chocolate)

US—United States industry only. CAN—United States and Canadian industries are comparable. When neither US nor CAN appears, Canadian, Mexican, and United States are comparable. *—Part of; NEC—Not Elsewhere Classified.

http://www.ntis.gov/naics

1997 NAICS code	1997 NAICS U.S. description	1987 SIC code	1987 U.S. SIC description
31133	Confectionery Manufacturing from Purchased Chocolate	*2064	Candy and Other Confectionery Products (chocolate confectionery)
		*2066	Chocolate and Cocoa Products (chocolate products made from purchased chocolate)
		*5441	Candy, Nut, and Confectionery Stores (chocolate candy stores, preparing on premises)
31134	Nonchocolate Confectionery Manufacturing	*2064	Candy and Other Confectionery Products (nonchocolate confectionery)
		*5441	Candy, Nut, and Confectionery Stores (nonchocolate candy stores, preparing on premises)
		2067	Chewing Gum
		*2099	Food Preparations, NEC (marshmallow creme)
3114	Fruit and Vegetable Preserving and Specialty Food Manufacturing		
31141	Frozen Food Manufacturing		
US 311411	Frozen Fruit, Juice, and Vegetable Manufacturing	2037	Frozen Fruits, Fruit Juices, and Vegetables
US 311412	Frozen Specialty Food Manufacturing	2038	Frozen Specialties, NEC
31142	Fruit and Vegetable Canning, Pickling, and Drying		
US 311421	Fruit and Vegetable Canning	2033	Canned Fruits, Vegetables, Preserves, Jams, and Jellies
		*2035	Pickled Fruits and Vegetables, Vegetable Sauces, and Seasonings and Salad Dressings (pickled fruits and vegetables)
US 311422	Specialty Canning	*2032	Canned Specialties (except canned puddings)
US 311423	Dried and Dehydrated Food Manufacturing	*2034	Dried and Dehydrated Fruits, Vegetables and Soup Mixes (except vegetable flour and soup mixes made from purchased dried and dehydrated ingredients made in dehydration plants)

US—United States industry only. CAN—United States and Canadian industries are comparable. When neither US nor CAN appears, Canadian, Mexican, and United States are comparable. *—Part of; NEC—Not Elsewhere Classified.

http://www.ntis.gov/naics

1997 NAICS code	1997 NAICS U.S. description	1987 SIC code	1987 U.S. SIC description
		*2099	Food Preparation, NEC (bouillon, and potatoes dried and packaged with other ingredients)
3115	Dairy Product Manufacturing		
31151	Dairy Product (except Frozen) Manufacturing		
CAN 311511	Fluid Milk Manufacturing	*2026	Fluid Milk (except ultra-high temperature)
US 311512	Creamery Butter Manufacturing	2021	Creamery Butter
US 311513	Cheese Manufacturing	2022	Natural, Processed, and Imitation Cheese
US 311514	Dry, Condensed, and Evaporated Dairy Product Manufacturing	2023	Dry, Condensed and Evaporated Dairy Products
		*2026	Fluid Milk (ultra-high temperature)
31152	Ice Cream and Frozen Dessert Manufacturing	2024	Ice Cream and Frozen Desserts
3116	Animal Slaughtering and Processing		
31161	Animal Slaughtering and Processing		
CAN 311611	Animal (except Poultry) Slaughtering	*0751	Livestock Services, Except Veterinary (custom slaughtering)
		2011	Meat Packing Plants
		*2048	Prepared Feeds and Feed Ingredients for Animals and Fowls, Except Dogs and Cats (animal slaughtering for pet food)
US 311612	Meat Processed from Carcasses	*2013	Sausages and Other Prepared Meats (except lard made from purchased materials)
		*5147	Meat and Meat Products (boxed beef)
US 311613	Rendering and Meat Byproduct Processing	*2077	Animal and Marine Fats and Oils (animal fats and oils)
		*2013	Sausages and Other Prepared Meats (lard made from purchased materials)

US—United States industry only. CAN—United States and Canadian industries are comparable. When neither US nor CAN appears, Canadian, Mexican, and United States are comparable. *—Part of; NEC—Not Elsewhere Classified.

http://www.ntis.gov/naics

	1997 NAICS code	1997 NAICS U.S. description	1987 SIC code	1987 U.S. SIC description
CAN	311615	Poultry Processing	*2015	Poultry Slaughtering and Processing (poultry processing)
	3117	Seafood Product Preparation and Packaging		
	31171	Seafood Product Preparation and Packaging		
US	311711	Seafood Canning	*2077	Animal and Marine Fats and Oils (canned marine fats and oils)
			2091	Canned and Cured Fish and Seafood
US	311712	Fresh and Frozen Seafood Processing	*2077	Animal and Marine Fats and Oils (fresh and frozen marine fats and oils)
			2092	Prepared Fresh or Frozen Fish and Seafood
	3118	Bakeries and Tortilla Manufacturing		
	31181	Bread and Bakery Product Manufacturing		
CAN	311811	Retail Bakeries	*5461	Retail Bakeries (bread, cake and related products baked and sold on premise)
US	311812	Commercial Bakeries	2051	Bread and Other Bakery Products, Except Cookies and Crackers
			*2052	Cookies and Crackers (unleavened bread and soft pretzels)
US	311813	Frozen Cakes, Pies, and Other Pastries Manufacturing	2053	Frozen Bakery Products, Except Bread
	31182	Cookie, Cracker, and Pasta Manufacturing		
CAN	311821	Cookie and Cracker Manufacturing	*2052	Cookies and Crackers (except unleavened bread and pretzels)
CAN	311822	Flour Mixes and Dough Manufacturing from Purchased Flour	2045	Prepared Flour Mixes and Doughs
CAN	311823	Dry Pasta Manufacturing	2098	Macaroni, Spaghetti, Vermicelli and Noodles

US—United States industry only. CAN—United States and Canadian industries are comparable. When neither US nor CAN appears, Canadian, Mexican, and United States are comparable. *—Part of; NEC—Not Elsewhere Classified.

http://www.ntis.gov/naics

1997 NAICS code	1997 NAICS U.S. description	1987 SIC code	1987 U.S. SIC description
		*2099	Food Preparations, NEC (dry pasta packaged with other ingredients made in dry pasta plants)
31183	Tortilla Manufacturing	*2099	Food Preparations, NEC (tortillas)
3119	Other Food Manufacturing		
31191	Snack Food Manufacturing		
CAN 311911	Roasted Nuts and Peanut Butter Manufacturing	2068	Salted and Roasted Nuts and Seeds
		*2099	Food Preparations, NEC (peanut butter)
CAN 311919	Other Snack Food Manufacturing	*2052	Cookies and Crackers (pretzel, except soft)
		2096	Potato Chips, Corn Chips, and Similar Snacks
31192	Coffee and Tea Manufacturing	*2043	Cereal Breakfast Foods (coffee substitute)
		*2087	Flavoring Extracts and Flavoring Syrups, NEC (coffee flavoring and syrups)
		2095	Roasted Coffee
		*2099	Food Preparations, NEC (tea)
31193	Flavoring Syrup and Concentrate Manufacturing	*2087	Flavoring Extracts and Flavoring Syrups (flavoring syrup and concentrate, except coffee)
31194	Seasoning and Dressing Manufacturing		
US 311941	Mayonnaise, Dressing, and Other Prepared Sauce Manufacturing	*2035	Pickled Fruits and Vegetables, Vegetable Seasonings, and Sauces and Salad Dressings (sauces and salad dressing)
		*2099	Food Preparations, NEC (vinegar, prepared dips (except dairy), and cider)
US 311942	Spice and Extract Manufacturing	*2082	Malt Beverages (malt extract)
		*2087	Flavoring Extracts and Flavoring Syrups (flavoring extracts and natural food colorings)

US—United States industry only. CAN—United States and Canadian industries are comparable. When neither US nor CAN appears, Canadian, Mexican, and United States are comparable. *—Part of; NEC—Not Elsewhere Classified.

http://www.ntis.gov/naics

1997 NAICS code	1997 NAICS U.S. description	1987 SIC code	1987 U.S. SIC description
		*2099	Food Preparations, NEC (spices, dip mix, salad dressing mix, and seasoning mix)
		*2899	Chemical Preparations, NEC (table salt)
31199	All Other Food Manufacturing		
US 311991	Perishable Prepared Food Manufacturing	*2099	Food Preparations, NEC (perishable prepared food)
US 311999	All Other Miscellaneous Food Manufacturing	*2015	Poultry Slaughtering and Processing (egg processing)
		*2032	Canned Specialties (canned puddings)
		*2034	Dried and Dehydrated Fruits, Vegetables, and Soup Mixes (soup mixes made from purchased dehydrated ingredients)
		*2087	Flavoring Extracts and Flavoring Syrups (powered drink mix)
		*2099	Food Preparations, NEC (except bouillon, marshmallow creme, spices, extracts, peanut butter, perishable prepared foods, tortillas, tea, spices, dip mix, salad dressing mix, seasoning mix, and vinegar)
312	Beverage and Tobacco Product Manufacturing		
3121	Beverage Manufacturing		
31211	Soft Drink and Ice Manufacturing		
US 312111	Soft Drink Manufacturing	*2086	Bottled and Canned Soft Drinks and Carbonated Water (except bottled water)
US 312112	Bottled Water Manufacturing	*2086	Bottled and Canned Soft Drinks and Carbonated Water (bottled water)
		*5149	Groceries and Related Products, NEC (bottling mineral or spring water)
US 312113	Ice Manufacturing	2097	Manufactured Ice
31212	Breweries	*2082	Malt Beverages (except malt extract)

US—United States industry only. CAN—United States and Canadian industries are comparable. When neither US nor CAN appears, Canadian, Mexican, and United States are comparable. *—Part of; NEC—Not Elsewhere Classified.

http://www.ntis.gov/naics

1997 NAICS code	1997 NAICS U.S. description	1987 SIC code	1987 U.S. SIC description
31213	Wineries	2084	Wines, Brandy, and Brandy Spirits
		*2085	Distilled and Blended Liquors (applejack)
31214	Distilleries	*2085	Distilled and Blended Liquors (except applejack)
3122	Tobacco Manufacturing		
31221	Tobacco Stemming and Redrying	*2141	Tobacco Stemming and Redrying (redrying and stemming)
31222	Tobacco Product Manufacturing		
US 312221	Cigarette Manufacturing	2111	Cigarettes
US 312229	Other Tobacco Product Manufacturing	2121	Cigars
		2131	Chewing and Smoking Tobacco and Snuff
		*2141	Tobacco Stemming and Redrying (reconstituted tobacco)
313	Textile Mills		
3131	Fiber, Yarn, and Thread Mills		
31311	Fiber, Yarn, and Thread Mills		
US 313111	Yarn Spinning Mills	2281	Yarn Spinning Mills
		*2299	Textile Goods, NEC (yarn of flax, hemp, jute, and ramie)
US 313112	Yarn Texturing, Throwing, and Twisting Mills	2282	Yarn Texturing, Throwing, Winding Mills
US 313113	Thread Mills	*2284	Thread Mills (except finishing)
		*2299	Textile Goods, NEC (thread of hemp, linen, and ramie)
3132	Fabric Mills		
31321	Broadwoven Fabric Mills	2211	Broadwoven Fabric Mills, Cotton
		2221	Broadwoven Fabric Mills, Manmade Fiber and Silk
		*2231	Broadwoven Fabric Mills, Wool (Including Dyeing and Finishing) (except wool finishing only)
		*2299	Textile Goods, NEC (broadwoven fabrics of jute, linen, hemp, and ramie and handwoven)
31322	Narrow Fabric Mills and Schiffli Machine Embroidery		

US—United States industry only. CAN—United States and Canadian industries are comparable. When neither US nor CAN appears, Canadian, Mexican, and United States are comparable. *—Part of; NEC—Not Elsewhere Classified.

http://www.ntis.gov/naics

1997 NAICS code	1997 NAICS U.S. description	1987 SIC code	1987 U.S. SIC description
US 313221	Narrow Fabric Mills	2241	Narrow Fabric and Other Smallware Mills: Cotton, Wool, Silk and Manmade Fiber
		*2299	Textile Goods, NEC (narrow woven fabric of jute, linen, hemp, and ramie)
US 313222	Schiffli Machine Embroidery	2397	Schiffli Machine Embroideries
31323	Nonwoven Fabric Mills	2297	Nonwoven Fabrics
		*2299	Textile Goods, NEC (nonwoven felt)
31324	Knit Fabric Mills		
US 313241	Weft Knit Fabric Mills	*2257	Weft Knit Fabric Mills (except finishing)
		*2259	Knitting Mills NEC (finished articles of weft knit fabric)
US 313249	Other Knit Fabric and Lace Mills	*2258	Lace and Warp Knit Fabric Mills (except finishing)
		*2259	Knitting Mills NEC (finished articles of warp knit fabric)
3133	Textile and Fabric Finishing and Fabric Coating Mills		
31331	Textile and Fabric Finishing Mills		
US 313311	Broadwoven Fabric Finishing Mills	*2231	Broadwoven Fabric Mills, Wool (wool broadwoven fabric finishing only)
		2261	Finishers of Broadwoven Fabrics of Cotton
		2262	Finishers of Broadwoven Fabrics of Manmade Fiber and Silk
		*5131	Piece Goods and Notions (broadwoven piece good converters)
		*7389	Business Services, NEC (sponging fabric for tailors and dressmakers)
US 313312	Textile and Fabric Finishing (except Broadwoven Fabric) Mills	*2231	Broadwoven Fabric Mills, Wool (wool finishing only, except broadwoven fabric)

US—United States industry only. CAN—United States and Canadian industries are comparable. When neither US nor CAN appears, Canadian, Mexican, and United States are comparable. *—Part of; NEC—Not Elsewhere Classified.

http://www.ntis.gov/naics

1997 NAICS code	1997 NAICS U.S. description	1987 SIC code	1987 U.S. SIC description
		*2251	Women's Full-Length and Knee-Length Hosiery, Except Socks (dyeing and finishing only)
		*2252	Hosiery, NEC (dyeing and finishing only)
		*2253	Knit Outerwear Mills (dyeing and finishing only)
		*2254	Knit Underwear and Nightwear Mills (dyeing and finishing only)
		*2257	Weft Knit Fabric Mills (finishing)
		*2258	Lace and Warp Knit Fabric Mills (finishing)
		*2259	Knitting Mills, NEC (dyeing and finishing knit gloves and mittens)
		2269	Finishers of Textiles, NEC
		*2284	Thread Mills (thread finishing)
		*2299	Textile Goods, NEC (finishing hard fiber thread and yarn)
		*5131	Piece Goods and Notions (converters, except broadwoven)
31332	Fabric Coating Mills	2295	Coated Fabrics, Not Rubberized
		*3069	Fabricated Rubber Products, NEC (rubberizing fabric or purchased textile products)
314	Textile Product Mills		
3141	Textile Furnishings Mills		
31411	Carpet and Rug Mills	2273	Carpets and Rugs
31412	Curtain and Linen Mills		
US 314121	Curtain and Drapery Mills	2391	Curtains and Draperies
		*5714	Drapery, Curtain, and Upholstery Stores (custom drapes)
US 314129	Other Household Textile Product Mills	*2392	Housefurnishings, Except Curtains and Draperies (except mops and bags)
		*5714	Drapery, Curtain, and Upholstery Stores (custom slipcovers)
3149	Other Textile Product Mills		
31491	Textile Bag and Canvas Mills		
US 314911	Textile Bag Mills	*2392	Housefurnishings, Except Curtains and Draperies (blanket, laundry, and garment storage bags)

US—United States industry only. CAN—United States and Canadian industries are comparable. When neither US nor CAN appears, Canadian, Mexican, and United States are comparable. *—Part of; NEC—Not Elsewhere Classified.

1997 NAICS code	1997 NAICS U.S. description	1987 SIC code	1987 U.S. SIC description
		2393	Textile Bags
US 314912	Canvas and Related Product Mills	2394	Canvas and Related Products
31499	All Other Textile Product Mills		
US 314991	Rope, Cordage, and Twine Mills	2298	Cordage and Twine
US 314992	Tire Cord and Tire Fabric Mills	2296	Tire Cord and Fabrics
US 314999	All Other Miscellaneous Textile Product Mills	*2299	Textile Goods, NEC (recovery and processing of fibers and waste)
		*2392	Housefurnishings, Except Curtains and Draperies (dust rags)
		*2395	Pleating, Decorative and Novelty Stitching, and Tucking for the Trade (except apparel contractors)
		*3569	General Industrial Machinery and Equipment, NEC (textile fire hose)
		*7389	Business Services, NEC (embroidery of advertising on shirts and rug binding for the trade)
		*2396	Automotive Trimmings, Apparel Findings, and Related Products (textile products except automotive trimmings; apparel bindings and trimmings; and printing and embossing on fabric articles)
		*2399	Fabricated Textile Products, NEC (except apparel, automotive seat belts, and seat and tire covers)
315	Apparel Manufacturing		
3151	Apparel Knitting Mills		
31511	Hosiery and Sock Mills		
US 315111	Sheer Hosiery Mills	*2251	Women's Full-Length and Knee-Length Hosiery, (except dyeing and finishing only)

US—United States industry only. CAN—United States and Canadian industries are comparable. When neither US nor CAN appears, Canadian, Mexican, and United States are comparable. *—Part of; NEC—Not Elsewhere Classified.

http://www.ntis.gov/naics

1997 NAICS code	1997 NAICS U.S. description	1987 SIC code	1987 U.S. SIC description
		*2252	Hosiery, NEC (girls' hosiery except dyeing and finishing only)
US 315119	Other Hosiery and Sock Mills	*2252	Hosiery, NEC (socks except dyeing and finishing only)
31519	Other Apparel Knitting Mills		
US 315191	Outerwear Knitting Mills	*2253	Knit Outerwear Mills (except dyeing and finishing only, and bath robes and lounge robes)
		*2259	Knitting Mills, NEC (gloves and mittens)
US 315192	Underwear and Nightwear Knitting Mills	*2254	Knit Underwear and Nightwear Mills (except dyeing and finishing only)
		*2259	Knitting Mills, NEC (girdles)
		*2253	Knit Outerwear Mills (bath robes and lounge robes made in knitting mills except dyeing and finishing only)
3152	Cut and Sew Apparel Manufacturing		
CAN 31521	Cut and Sew Apparel Contractors		
US 315211	Men's and Boys' Cut and Sew Apparel Contractors	*2311	Men's and Boys' Suits, Coats, and Overcoats (contractors)
		*2321	Men's and Boys' Shirts, Except Work Shirts (contractors)
		*2322	Men's and Boys' Underwear and Nightwear (contractors)
		*2323	Men's and Boys' Neckwear (contractors)
		*2325	Men's and Boys' Trousers and Slacks (contractors)
		*2326	Men's and Boys' Work Clothing (contractors)
		*2329	Men's and Boys' Clothing, NEC (contractors)
		*2341	Women's, Misses', Children's, and Infants' Underwear and Nightwear (boys' contractors)
		*2353	Hats, Caps, and Millinery (men's and boys' contractors)

US—United States industry only. CAN—United States and Canadian industries are comparable. When neither US nor CAN appears, Canadian, Mexican, and United States are comparable. *—Part of; NEC—Not Elsewhere Classified.

http://www.ntis.gov/naics

1997 NAICS code	1997 NAICS U.S. description	1987 SIC code	1987 U.S. SIC description
		*2361	Girls', Children's, and Infants' Dresses, Blouses, and Shirts (boys' contractors)
		*2369	Girls', Children's, and Infants' Outerwear, NEC (boys' contractors)
		*2371	Fur Goods (men's and boys' contractors)
		*2381	Dress and Work Gloves, Except Knit and All-Leather (men's and boys' contractors)
		*2384	Robes and Dressing Gowns (men's and boys' contractors)
		*2385	Waterproof Outerwear (men's and boys' contractors)
		*2386	Leather and Sheep-Lined Clothing (men's and boy's contractors)
		*2387	Apparel Belts (men's and boys' contractors)
		*2389	Apparel and Accessories, NEC (contractors)
		*2395	Pleating, Decorative and Novelty Stitching, and Tucking for the Trade (men's and boy's apparel contractors)
		*3151	Leather Gloves and Mittens (men's and boy's contractors)
US 315212	Women's, Girls', and Infants' Cut and Sew Apparel Contractors	*2331	Women's, Misses', and Juniors' Blouses and Shirts (contractors)
		*2335	Women's, Misses', and Juniors' Dresses (contractors)
		*2337	Women's, Misses', and Juniors' Suits, Skirts, and Coats (contractors)
		*2339	Women's, Misses', and Juniors' Outerwear, NEC (contractors)
		*2341	Women's, Misses', Children's, and Infants' Underwear and Nightwear (contractors)

http://www.ntis.gov/naics

1997 NAICS code	1997 NAICS U.S. description	1987 SIC code	1987 U.S. SIC description
		*2342	Brassieres, Girdles, and Allied Garments (contractors)
		*2353	Hats, Caps, and Millinery (women's, girls', and infants' contractors)
		*2361	Girls', Children's, and Infants' Dresses, Blouses, and Shirts (girls' and infants' contractors)
		*2369	Girls', Children's, and Infants' Outerwear, NEC (girls' and infants' contractors)
		*2371	Fur Goods (woman's, girls', and infants' contractors)
		*2381	Dress and Work Gloves, Except Knit and All-Leather (women's, girls', and infants' contractors)
		*2384	Robes and Dressing Gowns (women's, girls', and infants' contractors)
		*2385	Waterproof Outerwear (women's, girls', and infants' contractors)
		*2386	Leather and Sheep-Lined Clothing (woman's, girls', and infants' contractors)
		*2387	Apparel Belts (woman's, girls' and infants' contractors)
		*2389	Apparel and Accessories, NEC (contractors)
		*2395	Pleating, Decorative and Novelty Stitching, and Tucking for the Trade (women's, girls', and infants' apparel contractors)
		*3151	Leather Gloves and Mittens (women's, girls', and infants' contractors)
CAN 31522	Men's and Boys' Cut and Sew Apparel Manufacturing		
CAN 315221	Men's and Boys' Cut and Sew Underwear and Nightwear Manufacturing	*2322	Men's and Boys' Underwear and Nightwear (except contractors)
		*2341	Women's, Misses', Children's, and Infants' Underwear and Nightwear (boys' except contractors)

http://www.ntis.gov/naics

1997 NAICS code	1997 NAICS U.S. description	1987 SIC code	1987 U.S. SIC description
		*2369	Girls', Children's, and Infants' Outerwear, NEC (boys' robes except contractors)
		*2384	Robes and Dressing Gowns (men's except contractors)
CAN 315222	Men's and Boys' Cut and Sew Suit, Coat, and Overcoat Manufacturing	*2311	Men's and Boys' Suits, Coats, and Overcoats (except contractors)
		*2369	Girls', Children's, and Infants' Outerwear, NEC (boys' suits and coats except contractors)
		*2385	Waterproof Outerwear (men's and boys' water resistant or water repellent tailored overcoats, except contractors)
		*5699	Miscellaneous Apparel and Accessory Stores (custom tailors)
US 315223	Men's and Boys' Cut and Sew Shirt (except Work Shirt) Manufacturing	*2321	Men's and Boys' Shirts, Except Work Shirts (except contractors)
		*2361	Girls', Children's, and Infants' Dresses, Blouses, and Shirts (boys' shirts except contractors)
		*5699	Miscellaneous Apparel and Accessory Stores (custom tailors)
US 315224	Men's and Boys' Cut and Sew Trouser, Slack, and Jean Manufacturing	*2325	Men's and Boys' Trousers and Slacks (except contractors)
		*2369	Girls', Children's, and Infants' Outerwear, NEC (boys' trousers, slacks, and jeans except contractors)
US 315225	Men's and Boys' Cut and Sew Work Clothing Manufacturing	*2326	Men's and Boys' Work Clothing (except contractors)
US 315228	Men's and Boys' Cut and Sew Other Outerwear Manufacturing	*2329	Men's and Boys' Clothing, NEC (men's and boys' other outerwear except contractors)
		*2369	Girls', Children's, and Infants' Outerwear, NEC (boys' other outerwear except contractors)

US—United States industry only. CAN—United States and Canadian industries are comparable. When neither US nor CAN appears, Canadian, Mexican, and United States are comparable. *—Part of; NEC—Not Elsewhere Classified.

http://www.ntis.gov/naics

1997 NAICS code	1997 NAICS U.S. description	1987 SIC code	1987 U.S. SIC description
		*2385	Waterproof Outerwear (men's and boys' water resistant or water repellent nontailored outerwear, except rubber and plastics and contractors)
CAN 31523	Women's and Girls' Cut and Sew Apparel Manufacturing		
CAN 315231	Women's and Girls' Cut and Sew Lingerie, Loungewear, and Nightwear Manufacturing	*2341	Women's, Misses', Children's, and Infants' Underwear and Nightwear (women and girls' except contractors)
		*2342	Brassieres, Girdles, and Allied Garments (except contractors)
		*2369	Girls', Children's, and Infants' Outerwear, NEC (girls' robes except contractors)
		*2384	Robes and Dressing Gowns (women's except contractors)
		*2389	Apparel and Accessories, NEC (garters and garter belts)
CAN 315232	Women's and Girls' Cut and Sew Blouse and Shirt Manufacturing	*2331	Women's, Misses', and Juniors' Blouses and Shirts (except contractors)
		*2361	Girls', Children's, and Infants' Dresses, Blouses and Shirts (girls' blouses and shirts except contractors)
CAN 315233	Women's and Girls' Cut and Sew Dress Manufacturing	*2335	Women's, Misses', and Juniors' Dresses (except contractors)
		*2361	Girls', Children's, and Infants' Dresses, Blouses and Shirts (girls' dresses except contractors)
		*5699	Miscellaneous Apparel and Accessory Stores (custom dressmakers)
CAN 315234	Women's and Girls' Cut and Sew Suit, Coat, Tailored Jacket, and Skirt Manufacturing	*2337	Women's, Misses', and Juniors' Suits, Skirts, and Coats (except contractors)
		*2369	Girls', Children's, and Infants' Outerwear, NEC (girls' suits, coats, jackets, and skirts except contractors)

US—United States industry only. CAN—United States and Canadian industries are comparable. When neither US nor CAN appears, Canadian, Mexican, and United States are comparable. *—Part of; NEC—Not Elsewhere Classified.

http://www.ntis.gov/naics

1997 NAICS code	1997 NAICS U.S. description	1987 SIC code	1987 U.S. SIC description
		*2385	Waterproof Outerwear (women's and girls' water resistant or water repellent tailored coats, except contractors)
CAN 315239	Women's and Girls' Cut and Sew Other Outerwear Manufacturing	*2339	Women's, Misses', and Juniors' Outerwear, NEC (except contractors)
		*2369	Girls', Children's, and Infants' Outerwear, NEC (girls' except contractors)
		*2385	Waterproof Outerwear (other women's and girls' water resistant or water repellent nontailored outerwear, except rubber and plastics and contractors)
CAN 31529	Other Cut and Sew Apparel Manufacturing		
CAN 315291	Infants' Cut and Sew Apparel Manufacturing	*2341	Women's, Misses', Children's, and Infants' Underwear and Nightwear (infants' except contractors)
		*2361	Girls', Children's, and Infants' Dresses, Blouses, and Shirts (infants' except contractors)
		*2369	Girls', Children's, and Infants' Outerwear, NEC (infants' except contractors)
		*2385	Waterproof Outerwear (infants' outerwear except contractors)
CAN 315292	Fur and Leather Apparel Manufacturing	*2371	Fur Goods (except contractors)
		*2386	Leather and Sheep-Lined Clothing (except contractors)
CAN 315299	All Other Cut and Sew Apparel Manufacturing	*2329	Men's and Boys' Outerwear, NEC (athletic uniforms except contractors)
		*2339	Women's, Misses', and Juniors' Outerwear, NEC (athletic uniforms except contractors)
		*2385	Waterproof Outerwear (waterproof rubber and plastics outerwear)

US—United States industry only. CAN—United States and Canadian industries are comparable. When neither US nor CAN appears, Canadian, Mexican, and United States are comparable. *—Part of; NEC—Not Elsewhere Classified.

http://www.ntis.gov/naics

1997 NAICS code	1997 NAICS U.S. description	1987 SIC code	1987 U.S. SIC description
		*2389	Apparel and Accessories, NEC (academic and clerical outerwear, except contractors)
		*3069	Fabricated Rubber Products, NEC (rubber pants and raincoats)
3159	Apparel Accessories and Other Apparel Manufacturing		
31599	Apparel Accessories and Other Apparel Manufacturing		
US 315991	Hat, Cap, and Millinery Manufacturing	*2353	Hats, Caps, and Millinery (except contractors)
US 315992	Glove and Mitten Manufacturing	*2381	Dress and Work Gloves, Except Knit and All-Leather (except contractors)
		*3151	Leather Gloves and Mittens (except contractors)
US 315993	Men's and Boys' Neckwear Manufacturing	*2323	Men's and Boys' Neckwear (except contractors)
US 315999	Other Apparel Accessories and Other Apparel Manufacturing	*2339	Women's, Misses', and Juniors' Outerwear, NEC (scarves)
		*2385	Waterproof Outerwear (accessories such as aprons, bibs, and other miscellaneous waterproof items except contractors)
		*2387	Apparel Belts (except contractors)
		*2389	Apparel and Accessories, NEC (handkerchiefs, arm bands, etc.)
		*2396	Automotive Trimmings, Apparel Findings, and Related Products (apparel findings and trimming)
		*2399	Fabricated Textile Products, NEC (apparel and apparel accessories)
		*3069	Fabricated Rubber Products, NEC (rubber bibs, aprons and bathing caps)
316	Leather and Allied Product Manufacturing		
3161	Leather and Hide Tanning and Finishing		

US—United States industry only. CAN—United States and Canadian industries are comparable. When neither US nor CAN appears, Canadian, Mexican, and United States are comparable. *—Part of; NEC—Not Elsewhere Classified.

http://www.ntis.gov/naics

1997 NAICS code	1997 NAICS U.S. description	1987 SIC code	1987 U.S. SIC description
31611	Leather and Hide Tanning and Finishing	3111	Leather Tanning and Finishing
		*3999	Manufacturing Industries, NEC (fur dressing and finishing)
3162	Footwear Manufacturing		
31621	Footwear Manufacturing		
US 316211	Rubber and Plastics Footwear Manufacturing	3021	Rubber and Plastics Footwear
US 316212	House Slipper Manufacturing	3142	House Slippers
US 316213	Men's Footwear (except Athletic) Manufacturing	3143	Men's Footwear, Except Athletic
US 316214	Women's Footwear (except Athletic) Manufacturing	3144	Women's Footwear, Except Athletic
US 316219	Other Footwear Manufacturing	3149	Footwear Except Rubber, NEC
3169	Other Leather and Allied Product Manufacturing		
31699	Other Leather and Allied Product Manufacturing		
US 316991	Luggage Manufacturing	3161	Luggage
US 316992	Women's Handbag and Purse Manufacturing	3171	Women's Handbags and Purses
US 316993	Personal Leather Good (except Women's Handbag and Purse) Manufacturing	3172	Personal Leather Goods, Except Women's Handbags and Purses
US 316999	All Other Leather Good Manufacturing	*3131	Boot and Shoe Cut Stock and Findings (except wood heels and metal buckles)
		3199	Leather Goods, NEC
321	Wood Product Manufacturing		
3211	Sawmills and Wood Preservation		
32111	Sawmills and Wood Preservation		
US 321113	Sawmills	*2421	Sawmills and Planing Mills, General (sawmills)
		*2426	Hardwood Dimension and Flooring Mills (hardwood dimension from logs and bolts)
		*2429	Special Product Sawmills, NEC (shingle mills, shakes)

US—United States industry only. CAN—United States and Canadian industries are comparable. When neither US nor CAN appears, Canadian, Mexican, and United States are comparable. *—Part of; NEC—Not Elsewhere Classified.

http://www.ntis.gov/naics

	1997 NAICS code	1997 NAICS U.S. description	1987 SIC code	1987 U.S. SIC description
CAN	321114	Wood Preservation	2491	Wood Preserving
	3212	Veneer, Plywood, and Engineered Wood Product Manufacturing		
	32121	Veneer, Plywood, and Engineered Wood Product Manufacturing		
CAN	321211	Hardwood Veneer and Plywood Manufacturing	2435	Hardwood Veneer and Plywood
CAN	321212	Softwood Veneer and Plywood Manufacturing	2436	Softwood Veneer and Plywood
US	321213	Engineered Wood Member (except Truss) Manufacturing	*2439	Structural Wood Members, NEC (except trusses)
US	321214	Truss Manufacturing	*2439	Structural Wood Members, NEC (trusses)
US	321219	Reconstituted Wood Product Manufacturing	2493	Reconstituted Wood Products
	3219	Other Wood Product Manufacturing		
	32191	Millwork		
CAN	321911	Wood Window and Door Manufacturing	*2431	Millwork (wood windows and doors)
US	321912	Cut Stock, Resawing Lumber, and Planing	*2421	Sawmills and Planing Mills, General (lumber manufacturing from purchased lumber, softwood cut stock, wood lath, fence pickets, and planing mill products)
			*2426	Hardwood Dimension and Flooring Mills (except flooring)
			*2429	Special Product Sawmills, NEC (stave manufacturing from purchased lumber)
US	321918	Other Millwork (including Flooring)	*2426	Hardwood Dimension and Flooring Mills (hardwood flooring)
			*2421	Sawmills and Planing Mills, General (softwood flooring)
			*2431	Millwork (except wood doors and windows)

US—United States industry only. CAN—United States and Canadian industries are comparable. When neither US nor CAN appears, Canadian, Mexican, and United States are comparable. *—Part of; NEC—Not Elsewhere Classified.

http://www.ntis.gov/naics

1997 NAICS code	1997 NAICS U.S. description	1987 SIC code	1987 U.S. SIC description
32192	Wood Container and Pallet Manufacturing	*2429	Special Product Sawmills, NEC (cooperage stock)
		2441	Nailed and Lock Corner Wood Boxes and Shook
		2448	Wood Pallets and Skids
		2449	Wood Containers, NEC
		*2499	Wood Products, NEC (wood tubs and vats, jewelry, cigar boxes, and baskets, except fruit, vegetable, fish and bait)
32199	All Other Wood Product Manufacturing		
CAN 321991	Manufactured Home (Mobile Home) Manufacturing	2451	Mobile Homes
CAN 321992	Prefabricated Wood Building Manufacturing	2452	Prefabricated Wood Buildings and Components
CAN 321999	All Other Miscellaneous Wood Product Manufacturing	*2421	Sawmills and Planing Mills, General (kiln drying)
		*2429	Special Product Sawmills, NEC (excelsior and cooperage headings)
		*2499	Wood Products, NEC (other wood products)
		*3131	Boot and Shoe Cut Stock and Findings (wood heels)
322	Paper Manufacturing		
3221	Pulp, Paper, and Paperboard Mills		
32211	Pulp Mills	*2611	Pulp Mills (pulp producing mills only)
32212	Paper Mills		
CAN 322121	Paper (except Newsprint) Mills	*2611	Pulp Mills (pulp mills producing paper)
		*2621	Paper Mills (except newsprint mills)
CAN 322122	Newsprint Mills	*2621	Paper Mills (newsprint mills)
		*2611	Pulp Mills (pulp mills producing newsprint)
32213	Paperboard Mills	*2611	Pulp Mills (pulp mills producing paperboard)

US—United States industry only. CAN—United States and Canadian industries are comparable. When neither US nor CAN appears, Canadian, Mexican, and United States are comparable. *—Part of; NEC—Not Elsewhere Classified.

http://www.ntis.gov/naics

1997 NAICS code	1997 NAICS U.S. description	1987 SIC code	1987 U.S. SIC description
		2631	Paperboard Mills
3222	Converted Paper Product Manufacturing		
32221	Paperboard Container Manufacturing		
CAN 322211	Corrugated and Solid Fiber Box Manufacturing	2653	Corrugated and Solid Fiber Boxes
		*2679	Converted Paper and Paperboard Products, NEC (corrugated paper)
CAN 322212	Folding Paperboard Box Manufacturing	2657	Folding Paperboard Boxes, Including Sanitary
US 322213	Setup Paperboard Box Manufacturing	2652	Setup Paperboard Boxes
US 322214	Fiber Can, Tube, Drum, and Similar Products Manufacturing	2655	Fiber Cans, Tubes, Drums, and Similar Products
US 322215	Nonfolding Sanitary Food Container Manufacturing	2656	Sanitary Food Containers, Except Folding
32222	Paper Bag and Coated and Treated Paper Manufacturing		
US 322221	Coated and Laminated Packaging Paper and Plastics Film Manufacturing	*2671	Packaging Paper and Plastics Film, Coated and Laminated (single-web paper, paper multiweb laminated rolls and sheets for packaging uses)
US 322222	Coated and Laminated Paper Manufacturing	2672	Coated and Laminated Paper, NEC
		*2679	Converted Paper and Paperboard Products, NEC (wallpaper and gift wrap paper)
US 322223	Plastics, Foil, and Coated Paper Bag Manufacturing	*2673	Plastics, Foil, and Coated Paper Bags (except all plastics)
US 322224	Uncoated Paper and Multiwall Bag Manufacturing	2674	Uncoated Paper and Multiwall Bags
US 322225	Laminated Aluminum Foil Manufacturing for Flexible Packaging Uses	*3497	Metal Foil and Leaf (laminated aluminum foil rolls and sheets for flexible packaging uses)
US 322226	Surface-Coated Paperboard Manufacturing	*2675	Die-Cut Paper and Paperboard and Cardboard (pasted, lined, laminated, or surface-coated paperboard)

US—United States industry only. CAN—United States and Canadian industries are comparable. When neither US nor CAN appears, Canadian, Mexican, and United States are comparable. *—Part of; NEC—Not Elsewhere Classified.

http://www.ntis.gov/naics

1997 NAICS code	1997 NAICS U.S. description	1987 SIC code	1987 U.S. SIC description
32223	Stationery Product Manufacturing		
US 322231	Die-Cut Paper and Paperboard Office Supplies Manufacturing	*2675	Die-Cut Paper and Paperboard and Cardboard (file folders, tabulating cards, and other paper and paperboard office supplies)
		*2679	Converted Paper and Paperboard Products, NEC (paper supplies for business machines and other paper office supplies)
US 322232	Envelope Manufacturing	2677	Envelopes
US 322233	Stationery, Tablet, and Related Product Manufacturing	2678	Stationery, Tablets, and Related Products
32229	Other Converted Paper Product Manufacturing		
CAN 322291	Sanitary Paper Product Manufacturing	2676	Sanitary Paper Products
		*3842	Orthopedic, Prosthetic, and Surgical Appliances and Supplies (incontinent and bed pads)
CAN 322299	All Other Converted Paper Product Manufacturing	*2675	Die-Cut Paper and Paperboard and Cardboard (die-cut paper and paperboard products, except office supplies and pasted, lined, laminated, or surface-coated paperboard)
		*2679	Converted Paper and Paperboard Products, NEC (other converted paper and paperboard products, such as paper filters, crepe paper, and laminated and tiled wallboard)
323	Printing and Related Support Activities		
3231	Printing and Related Support Activities		
32311	Printing		
US 323110	Commercial Lithographic Printing	*2752	Commercial Printing, Lithographic (except quick printing)

US—United States industry only. CAN—United States and Canadian industries are comparable. When neither US nor CAN appears, Canadian, Mexican, and United States are comparable. *—Part of; NEC—Not Elsewhere Classified.

http://www.ntis.gov/naics

1997 NAICS code	1997 NAICS U.S. description	1987 SIC code	1987 U.S. SIC description
		*2771	Greeting Cards (lithographic printing of greeting cards)
US 323111	Commercial Gravure Printing	2754	Commercial Printing, Gravure
		*2771	Greeting Cards (gravure printing of greeting cards)
US 323112	Commercial Flexographic Printing	*2759	Commercial Printing, NEC (flexographic printing)
		*2771	Greeting Cards (flexographic printing of greeting cards)
CAN 323113	Commercial Screen Printing	*2396	Automotive Trimmings, Apparel Findings, and Related Products (printing and embossing on fabric articles)
		*2759	Commercial Printing, NEC (screen printing)
		*2771	Greeting Cards (screen printing of greeting cards)
CAN 323114	Quick Printing	*2752	Commercial Printing, Lithographic (quick printing)
		*2759	Commercial Printing, NEC (quick printing)
		*7334	Photocopying and Duplicating Services (instant printing)
CAN 323115	Digital Printing	*2759	Commercial Printing, NEC (digital printing, except quick printing)
CAN 323116	Manifold Business Forms Printing	2761	Manifold Business Forms
		*2782	Blankbooks, Looseleaf Binders and Devices (checkbooks)
US 323117	Books Printing	2732	Book Printing
US 323118	Blankbook, Looseleaf Binders, and Devices Manufacturing	*2782	Blankbooks, Looseleaf Binders and Devices (except checkbooks)
US 323119	Other Commercial Printing	*2759	Commercial Printing, NEC (other commercial printing except quick printing)
		*2771	Greeting Cards (other printing of greeting cards)

US—United States industry only. CAN—United States and Canadian industries are comparable. When neither US nor CAN appears, Canadian, Mexican, and United States are comparable. *—Part of; NEC—Not Elsewhere Classified.

http://www.ntis.gov/naics

1997 NAICS code	1997 NAICS U.S. description	1987 SIC code	1987 U.S. SIC description
32312	Support Activities for Printing		
US 323121	Tradebinding and Related Work	2789	Bookbinding and Related Work
US 323122	Prepress Services	2791	Typesetting
		2796	Platemaking and Related Services
324	Petroleum and Coal Products Manufacturing		
3241	Petroleum and Coal Products Manufacturing		
32411	Petroleum Refineries	2911	Petroleum Refining
32412	Asphalt Paving, Roofing, and Saturated Materials Manufacturing		
CAN 324121	Asphalt Paving Mixture and Block Manufacturing	2951	Asphalt Paving Mixtures and Blocks
CAN 324122	Asphalt Shingle and Coating Materials Manufacturing	2952	Asphalt Felts and Coatings
32419	Other Petroleum and Coal Products Manufacturing		
US 324191	Petroleum Lubricating Oil and Grease Manufacturing	2992	Lubricating Oils and Greases
US 324199	All Other Petroleum and Coal Products Manufacturing	2999	Products of Petroleum and Coal, NEC
		*3312	Blast Furnaces and Steel Mills (coke ovens)
325	Chemical Manufacturing		
3251	Basic Chemical Manufacturing		
32511	Petrochemical Manufacturing	*2865	Cyclic Organic Crudes and Intermediates, and Organic Dyes and Pigments (aromatics)
		*2869	Industrial Organic Chemicals, NEC (aliphatics)
32512	Industrial Gas Manufacturing	2813	Industrial Gases
		*2869	Industrial Organic Chemicals, NEC (fluorocarbon gases)
32513	Synthetic Dye and Pigment Manufacturing		
US 325131	Inorganic Dye and Pigment Manufacturing	*2816	Inorganic Pigments (except bone and lamp black)
		*2819	Industrial Inorganic Chemicals, NEC (inorganic dyes)

US—United States industry only. CAN—United States and Canadian industries are comparable. When neither US nor CAN appears, Canadian, Mexican, and United States are comparable. *—Part of; NEC—Not Elsewhere Classified.

http://www.ntis.gov/naics

1997 NAICS code	1997 NAICS U.S. description	1987 SIC code	1987 U.S. SIC description
US 325132	Synthetic Organic Dye and Pigment Manufacturing	*2865	Cyclic Organic Crudes and Intermediates, and Organic Dyes and Pigments (organic dyes and pigments)
32518	Other Basic Inorganic Chemical Manufacturing		
CAN 325181	Alkalies and Chlorine Manufacturing	2812	Alkalies and Chlorine
US 325182	Carbon Black Manufacturing	*2816	Inorganic pigments (bone and lamp black)
		2895	Carbon Black
US 325188	All Other Basic Inorganic Chemical Manufacturing	*2819	Industrial Inorganic Chemicals, NEC (except activated carbon and charcoal, alumina, and inorganic industrial dyes)
		*2869	Industrial Organic Chemicals, NEC (carbon bisulfide)
32519	Other Basic Organic Chemical Manufacturing		
US 325191	Gum and Wood Chemical Manufacturing	2861	Gum and Wood Chemicals
US 325192	Cyclic Crude and Intermediate Manufacturing	*2865	Cyclic Organic Crudes and Intermediates and Organic Dyes and Pigments (except aromatics and organic dyes and pigments)
US 325193	Ethyl Alcohol Manufacturing	*2869	Industrial Organic Chemicals (ethyl alcohol)
US 325199	All Other Basic Organic Chemical Manufacturing	*2869	Industrial Organic Chemicals, NEC (except aliphatics, carbon bisulfide, ethyl alcohol, and fluorocarbon gases)
		*2899	Chemical and Chemical Preparations, NEC (fatty acids)
3252	Resin, Synthetic Rubber, and Artificial and Synthetic Fibers and Filaments Manufacturing		
32521	Resin and Synthetic Rubber Manufacturing		
US 325211	Plastics Material and Resin Manufacturing	2821	Plastics Materials, Synthetic and Resins, and Nonvulcanizable Elastomers

US—United States industry only. CAN—United States and Canadian industries are comparable. When neither US nor CAN appears, Canadian, Mexican, and United States are comparable. *—Part of; NEC—Not Elsewhere Classified.

http://www.ntis.gov/naics

	1997 NAICS code	1997 NAICS U.S. description	1987 SIC code	1987 U.S. SIC description
US	325212	Synthetic Rubber Manufacturing	2822	Synthetic Rubber
	32522	Artificial and Synthetic Fibers and Filaments Manufacturing		
US	325221	Cellulosic Organic Fiber Manufacturing	2823	Cellulosic Manmade Fibers
US	325222	Noncellulosic Organic Fiber Manufacturing	2824	Manmade Organic Fibers, Except Cellulosic
	3253	Pesticide, Fertilizer, and Other Agricultural Chemical Manufacturing		
	32531	Fertilizer Manufacturing		
US	325311	Nitrogenous Fertilizer Manufacturing	2873	Nitrogenous Fertilizers
US	325312	Phosphatic Fertilizer Manufacturing	2874	Phosphatic Fertilizers
CAN	325314	Fertilizer (Mixing Only) Manufacturing	2875	Fertilizers, Mixing Only
	32532	Pesticide and Other Agricultural Chemical Manufacturing	2879	Pesticides and Agricultural Chemicals, NEC
	3254	Pharmaceutical and Medicine Manufacturing		
	32541	Pharmaceutical and Medicine Manufacturing		
US	325411	Medicinal and Botanical Manufacturing	2833	Medicinal Chemicals and Botanical Products
US	325412	Pharmaceutical Preparation Manufacturing	2834	Pharmaceutical Preparations
			*2835	In-Vitro and In-Vivo Diagnostic Substances (except in-vitro diagnostic)
US	325413	In-Vitro Diagnostic Substance Manufacturing	*2835	In-Vitro and In-Vivo Diagnostic Substances (in-vitro diagnostic substances)
US	325414	Biological Product (except Diagnostic) Manufacturing	2836	Biological Products, Except Diagnostic Substance
	3255	Paint, Coating, and Adhesive Manufacturing		
	32551	Paint and Coating Manufacturing	2851	Paints, Varnishes, Lacquers, Enamels and Allied Products

US—United States industry only. CAN—United States and Canadian industries are comparable. When neither US nor CAN appears, Canadian, Mexican, and United States are comparable. *—Part of; NEC—Not Elsewhere Classified.

http://www.ntis.gov/naics

1997 NAICS code	1997 NAICS U.S. description	1987 SIC code	1987 U.S. SIC description
		*2899	Chemicals and Chemical Preparations, NEC (frit)
32552	Adhesive Manufacturing	2891	Adhesives and Sealants
3256	Soap, Cleaning Compound, and Toilet Preparation Manufacturing		
32561	Soap and Cleaning Compound Manufacturing		
US 325611	Soap and Other Detergent Manufacturing	2841	Soaps and Other Detergents, Except Specialty Cleaners
		*2844	Toilet Preparations (toothpaste)
US 325612	Polish and Other Sanitation Good Manufacturing	2842	Specialty Cleaning, Polishing, and Sanitary Preparations
US 325613	Surface Active Agent Manufacturing	2843	Surface Active Agents, Finishing Agents, Sulfonated Oils, and Assistants
32562	Toilet Preparation Manufacturing	*2844	Perfumes, Cosmetics, and Other Toilet Preparations (except toothpaste)
3259	Other Chemical Product and Preparation Manufacturing		
32591	Printing Ink Manufacturing	2893	Printing Ink
32592	Explosives Manufacturing	2892	Explosives
32599	All Other Chemical Product and Preparation Manufacturing		
CAN 325991	Custom Compounding of Purchased Resins	3087	Custom Compounding of Purchased Plastics Resin
US 325992	Photographic Film, Paper, Plate, and Chemical Manufacturing	*3861	Photographic Equipment and Supplies (photographic films, paper, plates and chemicals)
US 325998	All Other Miscellaneous Chemical Product and Preparation Manufacturing	*2819	Industrial Inorganic Chemicals, NEC (activated carbon and charcoal)
		*2899	Chemicals and Chemical Preparations, NEC (except frit and table salt)
		*3952	Lead Pencils and Art Goods (drawing inks and india ink)
		*3999	Manufacturing Industries, NEC (matches)

US—United States industry only. CAN—United States and Canadian industries are comparable. When neither US nor CAN appears, Canadian, Mexican, and United States are comparable. *—Part of; NEC—Not Elsewhere Classified.

http://www.ntis.gov/naics

	1997 NAICS code	1997 NAICS U.S. description	1987 SIC code	1987 U.S. SIC description
			*7389	Business Services, NEC (aerosol packaging)
	326	Plastics and Rubber Products Manufacturing		
	3261	Plastics Product Manufacturing		
	32611	Unsupported Plastics Film, Sheet, and Bag Manufacturing		
CAN	326111	Unsupported Plastics Bag Manufacturing	*2673	Plastics, Foil, and Coated Paper Bags (plastics bags)
US	326112	Unsupported Plastics Packaging Film and Sheet Manufacturing	*2671	Packaging Paper and Plastics Film, Coated, and Laminated (plastics packaging film and sheet)
US	326113	Unsupported Plastics Film and Sheet (except Packaging) Manufacturing	3081	Unsupported Plastics Film and Sheets
	32612	Plastics Pipe, Pipe Fitting, and Unsupported Profile Shapes Manufacturing		
CAN	326121	Unsupported Plastics Profile Shape Manufacturing	3082	Unsupported Plastics Profile Shapes
			*3089	Plastics Product, NEC (plastics sausage casings)
CAN	326122	Plastics Pipe and Pipe Fitting Manufacturing	3084	Plastics Pipe
			*3089	Plastics Products, NEC (pipe fittings)
	32613	Laminated Plastics Plate, Sheet, and Shape Manufacturing	3083	Laminated Plastics Plate, Sheet, and Profile Shapes
	32614	Polystyrene Foam Product Manufacturing	*3086	Plastics Foam Products (polystyrene foam products)
	32615	Urethane and Other Foam Product (except Polystyrene) Manufacturing	*3086	Plastics Foam Products (urethane and other foam products)
	32616	Plastics Bottle Manufacturing	3085	Plastics Bottles
	32619	Other Plastics Product Manufacturing		
CAN	326191	Plastics Plumbing Fixture Manufacturing	3088	Plastics Plumbing Fixtures

---

US—United States industry only. CAN—United States and Canadian industries are comparable. When neither US nor CAN appears, Canadian, Mexican, and United States are comparable. *—Part of; NEC—Not Elsewhere Classified.

http://www.ntis.gov/naics

1997 NAICS code	1997 NAICS U.S. description	1987 SIC code	1987 U.S. SIC description
US 326192	Resilient Floor Covering Manufacturing	*3069	Fabricated Rubber Products, NEC (rubber resilient floor coverings)
		3996	Linoleum, Asphalted-Felt-Base, and Other Hard Surface Floor Coverings, NEC
US 326199	All Other Plastics Product Manufacturing	*3089	Plastics Products, NEC (except plastics pipe fittings and plastics sausage casings)
		*3999	Manufacturing Industries, NEC (plastics products such as combs, hair curlers, etc.)
3262	Rubber Product Manufacturing		
32621	Tire Manufacturing		
US 326211	Tire Manufacturing (except Retreading)	3011	Tires and Inner Tubes
US 326212	Tire Retreading	*7534	Tire Retreading and Repair Shops (rebuilding)
32622	Rubber and Plastics Hoses and Belting Manufacturing	3052	Rubber and Plastics Hose and Belting
32629	Other Rubber Product Manufacturing		
US 326291	Rubber Product Manufacturing for Mechanical Use	3061	Molded, Extruded, and Lathe-Cut Mechanical Rubber Goods
US 326299	All Other Rubber Product Manufacturing	*3069	Fabricated Rubber Products, NEC (except rubberized fabric and rubber resilient floor covering)
327	Nonmetallic Mineral Product Manufacturing		
3271	Clay Product and Refractory zlManufacturing		
32711	Pottery, Ceramics, and Plumbing Fixture Manufacturing		
US 327111	Vitreous China Plumbing Fixture and China and Earthenware Bathroom Accessories Manufacturing	3261	Vitreous China Plumbing Fixtures and China and Earthenware Fittings and Bathroom Accessories
US 327112	Vitreous China, Fine Earthenware, and Other Pottery Product Manufacturing	3262	Vitreous China Table and Kitchen Articles

US—United States industry only. CAN—United States and Canadian industries are comparable. When neither US nor CAN appears, Canadian, Mexican, and United States are comparable. *—Part of; NEC—Not Elsewhere Classified.

http://www.ntis.gov/naics

1997 NAICS code	1997 NAICS U.S. description	1987 SIC code	1987 U.S. SIC description
		3263	Fine Earthenware (Whiteware) Table and Kitchen Articles
		3269	Pottery Products, NEC
		*3299	Nonmetallic Mineral Products, NEC (clay statuary)
US 327113	Porcelain Electrical Supply Manufacturing	3264	Porcelain Electrical Supplies
32712	Clay Building Material and Refractories Manufacturing		
US 327121	Brick and Structural Clay Tile Manufacturing	*3251	Brick and Structural Clay Tile (except slumped brick)
US 327122	Ceramic Wall and Floor Tile Manufacturing	3253	Ceramic Wall and Floor Tile
US 327123	Other Structural Clay Product Manufacturing	3259	Structural Clay Products, NEC
US 327124	Clay Refractory Manufacturing	3255	Clay Refractories
US 327125	Nonclay Refractory Manufacturing	3297	Nonclay Refractories
3272	Glass and Glass Product Manufacturing		
32721	Glass and Glass Product Manufacturing		
US 327211	Flat Glass Manufacturing	3211	Flat Glass
US 327212	Other Pressed and Blown Glass and Glassware Manufacturing	3229	Pressed and Blown Glass and Glassware, NEC
US 327213	Glass Container Manufacturing	3221	Glass Containers
CAN 327215	Glass Product Manufacturing Made of Purchased Glass	3231	Glass Products Made of Purchased Glass
3273	Cement and Concrete Product Manufacturing		
32731	Cement Manufacturing	3241	Cement, Hydraulic
32732	Ready-Mix Concrete Manufacturing	3273	Ready-Mixed Concrete
32733	Concrete Pipe, Brick, and Block Manufacturing		
US 327331	Concrete Block and Brick Manufacturing	*3251	Brick and Structural Clay Tile (slumped brick)

US—United States industry only. CAN—United States and Canadian industries are comparable. When neither US nor CAN appears, Canadian, Mexican, and United States are comparable. *—Part of; NEC—Not Elsewhere Classified.

http://www.ntis.gov/naics

1997 NAICS code	1997 NAICS U.S. description	1987 SIC code	1987 U.S. SIC description
		3271	Concrete Block and Brick
US 327332	Concrete Pipe Manufacturing	*3272	Concrete Products, Except Block and Brick (concrete pipe)
32739	Other Concrete Product Manufacturing	*3272	Concrete Products, Except Block and Brick (concrete products, except dry mix concrete and pipe)
3274	Lime and Gypsum Product Manufacturing		
32741	Lime Manufacturing	3274	Lime
32742	Gypsum Product Manufacturing	3275	Gypsum Products
		*3299	Nonmetallic Mineral Products, NEC (moldings, ornamental and architectural plaster work and gypsum statuary)
3279	Other Nonmetallic Mineral Product Manufacturing		
32791	Abrasive Product Manufacturing	*3291	Abrasive Products (except steel wool with or without soap)
32799	All Other Nonmetallic Mineral Product Manufacturing		
US 327991	Cut Stone and Stone Product Manufacturing	3281	Cut Stone and Stone Products
US 327992	Ground or Treated Mineral and Earth Manufacturing	*3295	Minerals and Earths, Ground or Otherwise Treated (except grinding, washing, separating, etc. of nonmetallic minerals)
US 327993	Mineral Wool Manufacturing	3296	Mineral Wool
US 327999	All Other Miscellaneous Nonmetallic Mineral Product Manufacturing	*3272	Concrete Products, Except Block and Brick (dry mixture concrete)
		*3292	Asbestos Products (except brake pads and linings)
		*3299	Nonmetallic Mineral Products, NEC (except moldings, ornamental and architectural plaster work, clay and gypsum statuary)

US—United States industry only. CAN—United States and Canadian industries are comparable. When neither US nor CAN appears, Canadian, Mexican, and United States are comparable. *—Part of; NEC—Not Elsewhere Classified.

http://www.ntis.gov/naics

	1997 NAICS code	1997 NAICS U.S. description	1987 SIC code	1987 U.S. SIC description
	331	Primary Metal Manufacturing		
	3311	Iron and Steel Mills and Ferroalloy Manufacturing		
	33111	Iron and Steel Mills and Ferroalloy Manufacturing		
US	331111	Iron and Steel Mills	*3312	Steel Works, Blast Furnaces (Including Coke Ovens), and Rolling Mills (except coke ovens not integrated with steel mills and hot rolling purchased steel)
US	331112	Electrometallurgical Ferroalloy Product Manufacturing	3313	Electrometallurgical Products, Except Steel
	3312	Steel Product Manufacturing from Purchased Steel		
	33121	Iron and Steel Pipe and Tube Manufacturing from Purchased Steel	3317	Steel Pipe and Tubes
	33122	Rolling and Drawing of Purchased Steel		
CAN	331221	Rolled Steel Shape Manufacturing	*3312	Steel Works, Blast Furnaces (including coke ovens), and Rolling Mills (hot rolling purchased steel)
			3316	Cold-Rolled Steel Sheet, Strip and Bars
			*3399	Primary Metal Products, NEC (making ferrous metal powder, paste, and flake from purchased iron or steel)
CAN	331222	Steel Wire Drawing	*3315	Steel Wiredrawing and Steel Nails and Spikes (steel, wire drawing)
	3313	Alumina and Aluminum Production and Processing		
	33131	Alumina and Aluminum Production and Processing		
US	331311	Alumina Refining	*2819	Industrial Inorganic Chemicals, NEC (alumina)
US	331312	Primary Aluminum Production	3334	Primary Production of Aluminum

US—United States industry only. CAN—United States and Canadian industries are comparable. When neither US nor CAN appears, Canadian, Mexican, and United States are comparable. *—Part of; NEC—Not Elsewhere Classified.

http://www.ntis.gov/naics

	1997 NAICS code	1997 NAICS U.S. description	1987 SIC code	1987 U.S. SIC description
US	331314	Secondary Smelting and Alloying of Aluminum	*3341	Secondary Smelting and Refining of Nonferrous Metals (aluminum)
			*3399	Primary Metal Products, NEC (aluminum powder, paste, flakes, etc.)
US	331315	Aluminum Sheet, Plate, and Foil Manufacturing	3353	Aluminum Sheet, Plate, and Foil
US	331316	Aluminum Extruded Product Manufacturing	3354	Aluminum Extruded Products
US	331319	Other Aluminum Rolling and Drawing	3355	Aluminum Rolling and Drawing, NEC
			*3357	Drawing and Insulating of Nonferrous Wire (aluminum wire drawing)
	3314	Nonferrous Metal (except Aluminum) Production and Processing		
	33141	Nonferrous Metal (except Aluminum) Smelting and Refining		
US	331411	Primary Smelting and Refining of Copper	3331	Primary Smelting and Refining of Copper
US	331419	Primary Smelting and Refining of Nonferrous Metal (except Copper and Aluminum)	3339	Primary Smelting and Refining of Nonferrous Metals, Except Copper and Aluminum
	33142	Copper Rolling, Drawing, Extruding, and Alloying		
US	331421	Copper Rolling, Drawing, and Extruding	3351	Rolling, Drawing, and Extruding of Copper
US	331422	Copper Wire (except Mechanical) Drawing	*3357	Drawing and Insulating of Nonferrous Wire (copper wire drawing)
US	331423	Secondary Smelting, Refining, and Alloying of Copper	*3341	Secondary Smelting and Refining of Nonferrous Metals (copper)
			*3399	Primary Metal Products, NEC (copper powders, flakes, paste, etc.)
	33149	Nonferrous Metal (except Copper and Aluminum) Rolling, Drawing, Extruding, and Alloying		

US—United States industry only. CAN—United States and Canadian industries are comparable. When neither US nor CAN appears, Canadian, Mexican, and United States are comparable. *—Part of; NEC—Not Elsewhere Classified.

http://www.ntis.gov/naics

	1997 NAICS code	1997 NAICS U.S. description	1987 SIC code	1987 U.S. SIC description
US	331491	Nonferrous Metal (except Copper and Aluminum) Rolling, Drawing, and Extruding	3356	Rolling, Drawing, and Extruding of Nonferrous Metals, Except Copper and Aluminum
			*3357	Drawing and Insulating of Nonferrous Wire (wire drawing except copper or aluminum)
US	331492	Secondary Smelting, Refining, and Alloying of Nonferrous Metal (except Copper and Aluminum)	*3341	Secondary Smelting and Refining of Nonferrous Metals (except copper and aluminum)
			*3399	Primary Metal Products, NEC (except copper and aluminum)
	3315	Foundries		
	33151	Ferrous Metal Foundries		
CAN	331511	Iron Foundries	3321	Gray and Ductile Iron Foundries
			3322	Malleable Iron Foundries
US	331512	Steel Investment Foundries	3324	Steel Investment Foundries
US	331513	Steel Foundries (except Investment)	3325	Steel Foundries, NEC
	33152	Nonferrous Metal Foundries		
US	331521	Aluminum Die-Casting Foundries	3363	Aluminum Die-Castings
US	331522	Nonferrous (except Aluminum) Die-Casting Foundries	3364	Nonferrous Die-Castings, Except Aluminum
US	331524	Aluminum Foundries (except Die-Casting)	3365	Aluminum Foundries
US	331525	Copper Foundries (except Die-Casting)	3366	Copper Foundries
US	331528	Other Nonferrous Foundries (except Die-Casting)	3369	Nonferrous Foundries, Except Aluminum and Copper
	332	Fabricated Metal Product Manufacturing		
	3321	Forging and Stamping		
	33211	Forging and Stamping		
US	332111	Iron and Steel Forging	3462	Iron and Steel Forgings
US	332112	Nonferrous Forging	3463	Nonferrous Forgings
US	332114	Custom Roll Forming	*3449	Miscellaneous Structural Metal Work (custom roll forming)

US—United States industry only. CAN—United States and Canadian industries are comparable. When neither US nor CAN appears, Canadian, Mexican, and United States are comparable. *—Part of; NEC—Not Elsewhere Classified.

http://www.ntis.gov/naics

	1997 NAICS code	1997 NAICS U.S. description	1987 SIC code	1987 U.S. SIC description
US	332115	Crown and Closure Manufacturing	3466	Crowns and Closures
US	332116	Metal Stamping	*3469	Metal Stampings, NEC (except kitchen utensils, pots and pans for cooking, and coins)
US	332117	Powder Metallurgy Part Manufacturing	*3499	Fabricated Metal Products, NEC (powder metallurgy)
	3322	Cutlery and Handtool Manufacturing		
	33221	Cutlery and Handtool Manufacturing		
US	332211	Cutlery and Flatware (except Precious) Manufacturing	*3421	Cutlery (except tool-type shears)
			*3914	Silverware, Plated Ware, and Stainless Steel Ware (cutlery and flatware, nonprecious and precious plated)
			*3999	Manufacturing Industries, NEC (human hair clipprs, hand operated)
US	332212	Hand and Edge Tool Manufacturing	*3421	Cutlery (tool-type shears)
			3423	Hand and Edge Tools, Except Machine Tools and Handsaws
			*3523	Farm Machinery and Equipment (hand hair clippers for animals)
			*3524	Lawn and Garden Tractors and Home Lawn and Garden Equipment (nonpowered lawnmowers)
			*3545	Cutting Tools, Machine Tools Accessories, and Machinist Precision Measuring Devices (precision measuring devices)
			*3644	Noncurrent-Carrying Wiring Devices (fish wire, electrical wiring tool)
			*3999	Manufacturing Industries, NEC (tape measures)
US	332213	Saw Blade and Handsaw Manufacturing	3425	Saw Blades and Handsaws

US—United States industry only. CAN—United States and Canadian industries are comparable. When neither US nor CAN appears, Canadian, Mexican, and United States are comparable. *—Part of; NEC—Not Elsewhere Classified.

http://www.ntis.gov/naics

	1997 NAICS code	1997 NAICS U.S. description	1987 SIC code	1987 U.S. SIC description
US	332214	Kitchen Utensil, Pot, and Pan Manufacturing	*3469	Metal Stampings, NEC (kitchen utensils, pots, and pans for cooking)
	3323	Architectural and Structural Metals Manufacturing		
	33231	Plate Work and Fabricated Structural Product Manufacturing		
CAN	332311	Prefabricated Metal Building and Component Manufacturing	3448	Prefabricated Metal Buildings and Components
US	332312	Fabricated Structural Metal Manufacturing	3441	Fabricated Structural Metal
			*3449	Miscellaneous Structural Metal Work (fabricated bar joists and concrete reinforcing bars)
US	332313	Plate Work Manufacturing	*3443	Fabricated Plate Work (Boiler Shops) (fabricated plate work and metal weldments)
	33232	Ornamental and Architectural Metal Products Manufacturing		
CAN	332321	Metal Window and Door Manufacturing	3442	Metal Doors, Sash, Frames, Molding and Trim
			*3449	Miscellaneous Structural Metal Work (curtain wall)
US	332322	Sheet Metal Work Manufacturing	*3444	Sheet Metal Work (ducts, flumes, flooring, siding, dampers, etc.)
US	332323	Ornamental and Architectural Metal Work Manufacturing	3446	Architectural and Ornamental Metal Work
			*3449	Miscellaneous Structural Metal Work (metal plaster bases)
			*3523	Farm Machinery and Equipment (corrals, stalls, and holding gates)
	3324	Boiler, Tank, and Shipping Container Manufacturing		
	33241	Power Boiler and Heat Exchanger Manufacturing	*3443	Fabricated Plate Work (Boiler Shops) (power boilers and heat exchangers)
			*3559	Special Industry Machinery, NEC (nuclear control drive mechanisms)

US—United States industry only. CAN—United States and Canadian industries are comparable. When neither US nor CAN appears, Canadian, Mexican, and United States are comparable. *—Part of; NEC—Not Elsewhere Classified.

http://www.ntis.gov/naics

1997 NAICS code	1997 NAICS U.S. description	1987 SIC code	1987 U.S. SIC description
33242	Metal Tank (Heavy Gauge) Manufacturing	*3443	Fabricated Plate Work (Boiler Shops) (heavy gauge tanks)
33243	Metal Can, Box, and Other Metal Container (Light Gauge) Manufacturing		
CAN 332431	Metal Can Manufacturing	3411	Metal Cans
CAN 332439	Other Metal Container Manufacturing	3412	Metal Shipping Barrels, Drums, Kegs, and Pails
		*3429	Hardware, NEC (vacuum and insulated bottles, jugs, and chests)
		*3444	Sheet Metal Work (metal bins and vats)
		*3499	Fabricated Metal Products, NEC (metal boxes)
		*3537	Industrial Trucks, Tractors, Trailers, and Stackers (metal air cargo containers)
3325	Hardware Manufacturing		
33251	Hardware Manufacturing	*3429	Hardware, NEC (other hardware)
		*3499	Fabricated Metal Products, NEC (safe and vault locks)
3326	Spring and Wire Product Manufacturing		
33261	Spring and Wire Product Manufacturing		
CAN 332611	Spring (Heavy Gauge) Manufacturing	3493	Steel Springs, Except Wire
US 332612	Spring (Light Gauge) Manufacturing	*3495	Wire Springs (except watch and clock springs)
US 332618	Other Fabricated Wire Product Manufacturing	*3315	Steel Wiredrawing and Steel Nails and Spikes (nails, spikes, paper clips, and wire not made in wiredrawing plants)
		*3399	Primary Metal Products, NEC (nonferrous nails, brads, staples, etc.)
		*3496	Miscellaneous Fabricated Wire Products (except grocery carts)

US—United States industry only. CAN—United States and Canadian industries are comparable. When neither US nor CAN appears, Canadian, Mexican, and United States are comparable. *—Part of; NEC—Not Elsewhere Classified.

http://www.ntis.gov/naics

1997 NAICS code	1997 NAICS U.S. description	1987 SIC code	1987 U.S. SIC description
3327	Machine Shops; Turned Product; and Screw, Nut, and Bolt Manufacturing		
33271	Machine Shops	*3599	Industrial and Commercial Machinery and Equipment, NEC (machine shops)
33272	Turned Product and Screw, Nut, and Bolt Manufacturing		
US 332721	Precision Turned Product Manufacturing	3451	Screw Machine Products
US 332722	Bolt, Nut, Screw, Rivet, and Washer Manufacturing	3452	Bolts, Nuts, Screws, Rivets, and Washers
		*3429	Hardware, NEC (turnbuckles and hose clamps)
3328	Coating, Engraving, Heat Treating, and Allied Activities		
33281	Coating, Engraving, Heat Treating, and Allied Activities		
US 332811	Metal Heat Treating	3398	Metal Heat Treating
US 332812	Metal Coating, Engraving (except Jewelry and Silverware), and Allied Services to Manufacturers	*3479	Coating, Engraving, and Allied Services, NEC (except jewelry, silverware, and flatware engraving and etching)
US 332813	Electroplating, Plating, Polishing, Anodizing, and Coloring	*3399	Primary Metal Products, NEC (laminating steel)
		3471	Electroplating, Plating, Polishing, Anodizing, and Coloring
3329	Other Fabricated Metal Product Manufacturing		
33291	Metal Valve Manufacturing		
US 332911	Industrial Valve Manufacturing	3491	Industrial Valves
US 332912	Fluid Power Valve and Hose Fitting Manufacturing	3492	Fluid Power Valves and Hose Fittings
		*3728	Aircraft Parts and Auxiliary Equipment, NEC (fluid power aircraft subassemblies)

US—United States industry only. CAN—United States and Canadian industries are comparable. When neither US nor CAN appears, Canadian, Mexican, and United States are comparable. *—Part of; NEC—Not Elsewhere Classified.

http://www.ntis.gov/naics

1997 NAICS code	1997 NAICS U.S. description	1987 SIC code	1987 U.S. SIC description
US 332913	Plumbing Fixture Fitting and Trim Manufacturing	*3432	Plumbing Fixture Fittings and Trim (except shower rods and lawn hose nozzles)
US 332919	Other Metal Valve and Pipe Fitting Manufacturing	*3429	Hardware, NEC (fire hose nozzles and couplings)
		*3494	Valves and Pipe Fittings, NEC (except metal pipe hangers and supports)
		*3499	Fabricated Metal Products, NEC (metal aerosol valves)
		*3432	Plumbing Fixture Fittings and Trim (lawn hose nozzles)
33299	All Other Fabricated Metal Product Manufacturing		
CAN 332991	Ball and Roller Bearing Manufacturing	3562	Ball and Roller Bearings
US 332992	Small Arms Ammunition Manufacturing	3482	Small Arms Ammunition
US 332993	Ammunition (except Small Arms) Manufacturing	3483	Ammunition, Except for Small Arms
US 332994	Small Arms Manufacturing	3484	Small Arms
		*3841	Surgical and Medical Instruments and Apparatus (tranquilizer guns)
US 332995	Other Ordnance and Accessories Manufacturing	3489	Ordnance and Accessories, NEC
US 332996	Fabricated Pipe and Pipe Fitting Manufacturing	3498	Fabricated Pipe and Pipe Fittings
US 332997	Industrial Pattern Manufacturing	3543	Industrial Patterns
US 332998	Enameled Iron and Metal Sanitary Ware Manufacturing	3431	Enameled Iron and Metal Sanitary Ware
US 332999	All Other Miscellaneous Fabricated Metal Product Manufacturing	*3291	Abrasive Products (steel wool with or without soap)
		*3429	Hardware, NEC (fireplace fixtures, traps, handcuffs and leg irons, ladder jacks, and other like metal products)
		*3432	Plumbing Fixture Fittings and Trim (metal shower rods)

http://www.ntis.gov/naics

1997 NAICS code	1997 NAICS U.S. description	1987 SIC code	1987 U.S. SIC description
		*3494	Valves and Pipe Fittings, NEC (metal pipe hangers and supports)
		*3497	Metal Foil and Leaf (foil and foil containers)
		*3499	Fabricated Metal Products, NEC (other metal products)
		*3537	Industrial Trucks, Tractors, Trailers, and Stackers (metal pallets)
		*3599	Industrial and Commercial Machinery and Equipment, NEC (flexible metal hose)
		*3914	Silverware, Plated Ware, and Stainless Steel Ware (precious plated hollowware)
		*3999	Manufacturing Industries, NEC (other miscellaneous metal products, such as combs, hair curlers, etc.)
333	Machinery Manufacturing		
3331	Agriculture, Construction, and Mining Machinery Manufacturing		
33311	Agricultural Implement Manufacturing		
US 333111	Farm Machinery and Equipment Manufacturing	*3523	Farm Machinery and Equipment (except corrals, stalls, holding gates, hand clippers for animals, and farm conveyors/elevators)
		*3559	Industrial and Commercial Machinery and Equipment, NEC (cotton ginning machinery)
US 333112	Lawn and Garden Tractor and Home Lawn and Garden Equipment Manufacturing	*3524	Lawn and Garden Tractors and Home Lawn and Garden Equipment (except nonpowered lawnmowers)
33312	Construction Machinery Manufacturing	*3531	Construction Machinery and Equipment (except railway track maintenance equipment; winches, aerial work platforms; and automotive wrecker hoists)

US—United States industry only. CAN—United States and Canadian industries are comparable. When neither US nor CAN appears, Canadian, Mexican, and United States are comparable. *—Part of; NEC—Not Elsewhere Classified.

http://www.ntis.gov/naics

	1997 NAICS code	1997 NAICS U.S. description	1987 SIC code	1987 U.S. SIC description
	33313	Mining and Oil and Gas Field Machinery Manufacturing		
US	333131	Mining Machinery and Equipment Manufacturing	3532	Mining Machinery and Equipment, Except Oil and Gas Field Machinery and Equipment
US	333132	Oil and Gas Field Machinery and Equipment Manufacturing	3533	Oil and Gas Field Machinery and Equipment
	3332	Industrial Machinery Manufacturing		
	33321	Sawmill and Woodworking Machinery Manufacturing	3553	Woodworking Machinery
	33322	Plastics and Rubber Industry Machinery Manufacturing	*3559	Special Industry Machinery, NEC (rubber and plastics manufacturing machinery)
	33329	Other Industrial Machinery Manufacturing		
CAN	333291	Paper Industry Machinery Manufacturing	3554	Paper Industries Machinery
US	333292	Textile Machinery Manufacturing	3552	Textile Machinery
US	333293	Printing Machinery and Equipment Manufacturing	3555	Printing Trades Machinery and Equipment
US	333294	Food Product Machinery Manufacturing	3556	Food Products Machinery
US	333295	Semiconductor Machinery Manufacturing	*3559	Special Industry Machinery, NEC (semiconductor machinery manufacturing)
US	333298	All Other Industrial Machinery Manufacturing	*3559	Special Industry Machinery, NEC (except rubber and plastics manufacturing machinery, semiconductor manufacturing machinery, and automotive maintenance equipment)
			*3639	Household Appliances, NEC (household sewing machines)
	3333	Commercial and Service Industry Machinery Manufacturing		

US—United States industry only. CAN—United States and Canadian industries are comparable. When neither US nor CAN appears, Canadian, Mexican, and United States are comparable. *—Part of; NEC—Not Elsewhere Classified.

http://www.ntis.gov/naics

1997 NAICS code	1997 NAICS U.S. description	1987 SIC code	1987 U.S. SIC description
33331	Commercial and Service Industry Machinery Manufacturing		
US 333311	Automatic Vending Machine Manufacturing	3581	Automatic Vending Machines
		*3578	Calculating and Accounting Machines, Except Electronic Computers (change making machines)
US 333312	Commercial Laundry, Drycleaning, and Pressing Machine Manufacturing	3582	Commercial Laundry, Drycleaning and Pressing Machines
US 333313	Office Machinery Manufacturing	*3578	Calculating and Accounting Machinery, Except Electronic Computers (except point of sales terminals, change making machines and funds transfer devices)
		*3579	Office Machines, NEC (except timeclocks, time stamps, pencil sharpeners, stapling machines, etc.)
US 333314	Optical Instrument and Lens Manufacturing	3827	Optical Instruments and Lenses
US 333315	Photographic and Photocopying Equipment Manufacturing	*3861	Photographic Equipment and Supplies (except photographic film, paper, plates, and chemicals)
US 333319	Other Commercial and Service Industry Machinery Manufacturing	*3559	Special Industry Machinery, NEC (automotive maintenance equipment)
		3589	Service Industry Machinery, NEC
		*3599	Industrial and Commercial Machinery and Equipment, NEC (carnival amusement park equipment)
		*3699	Electrical Machinery, Equipment and Supplies, NEC (electronic teaching machines and flight simulators)
		*3999	Manufacturing Industries, NEC (beauty and barber shop equipment, except chairs)

US—United States industry only. CAN—United States and Canadian industries are comparable. When neither US nor CAN appears, Canadian, Mexican, and United States are comparable. *—Part of; NEC—Not Elsewhere Classified.

http://www.ntis.gov/naics

1997 NAICS code	1997 NAICS U.S. description	1987 SIC code	1987 U.S. SIC description
3334	Ventilation, Heating, Air-Conditioning, and Commercial Refrigeration Equipment Manufacturing		
33341	Ventilation, Heating, Air-Conditioning, and Commercial Refrigeration Equipment Manufacturing		
US 333411	Air Purification Equipment Manufacturing	*3564	Industrial and Commercial Fans and Blowers and Air Purification Equipment (air purification equipment)
US 333412	Industrial and Commercial Fan and Blower Manufacturing	*3564	Industrial and Commercial Fans and Blowers and Air Purification Equipment (fans and blowers)
US 333414	Heating Equipment (except Warm Air Furnaces) Manufacturing	3433	Heating Equipment, Except Electric and Warm Air Furnaces
		*3569	General Industrial Machinery and Equipment, NEC (electric swimming pool heaters)
		*3634	Electric Housewares and Fans (wall and baseboard heating units for permanent installation)
		*2499	Wood Products, NEC (wood cooling towers)
		*3443	Fabricated Plate Work (Boiler Shops) (metal cooling towers)
		*3444	Sheet Metal Work (sheet metal cooling towers)
US 333415	Air-Conditioning and Warm Air Heating Equipment and Commercial and Industrial Refrigeration Equipment Manufacturing	*3585	Air-Conditioning and Warm Air Heating Equipment and Commercial and Industrial Refrigeration Equipment (except motor vehicle air-conditioning)
3335	Metalworking Machinery Manufacturing		
33351	Metalworking Machinery Manufacturing		
CAN 333511	Industrial Mold Manufacturing	*3544	Special Dies and Tools, Die Sets, Jigs and Fixtures, and Industrial Molds (industrial molds)

US—United States industry only. CAN—United States and Canadian industries are comparable. When neither US nor CAN appears, Canadian, Mexican, and United States are comparable. *—Part of; NEC—Not Elsewhere Classified.

http://www.ntis.gov/naics

	1997 NAICS code	1997 NAICS U.S. description	1987 SIC code	1987 U.S. SIC description
US	333512	Machine Tool (Metal Cutting Types) Manufacturing	3541	Machine Tools, Metal Cutting Type
US	333513	Machine Tool (Metal Forming Types) Manufacturing	3542	Machine Tools, Metal Forming Type
US	333514	Special Die and Tool, Die Set, Jig, and Fixture Manufacturing	*3544	Special Dies and Tools, Die Sets, Jigs and Fixtures, and Industrial Molds (except molds)
US	333515	Cutting Tool and Machine Tool Accessory Manufacturing	*3545	Cutting Tools, Machine Tool Accessories, and Machinists' Precision Measuring Devices (except precision measuring devices)
US	333516	Rolling Mill Machinery and Equipment Manufacturing	3547	Rolling Mill Machinery and Equipment
US	333518	Other Metalworking Machinery Manufacturing	3549	Metalworking Machinery, NEC
	3336	Engine, Turbine, and Power Transmission Equipment Manufacturing		
	33361	Engine, Turbine, and Power Transmission Equipment Manufacturing		
CAN	333611	Turbine and Turbine Generator Set Units Manufacturing	3511	Steam, Gas, and Hydraulic Turbines, and Turbine Generator Set Units
US	333612	Speed Changer, Industrial High-Speed Drive, and Gear Manufacturing	3566	Speed Changers, Industrial High-Speed Drives, and Gears
US	333613	Mechanical Power Transmission Equipment Manufacturing	3568	Mechanical Power Transmission Equipment, NEC
US	333618	Other Engine Equipment Manufacturing	*3519	Internal Combustion Engines, NEC (except stationary engine radiators)
			*3699	Electrical Machinery, Equipment and Supplies, NEC (outboard electric motors)
	3339	Other General Purpose Machinery Manufacturing		
	33391	Pump and Compressor Manufacturing		

US—United States industry only. CAN—United States and Canadian industries are comparable. When neither US nor CAN appears, Canadian, Mexican, and United States are comparable. *—Part of; NEC—Not Elsewhere Classified.

http://www.ntis.gov/naics

	1997 NAICS code	1997 NAICS U.S. description	1987 SIC code	1987 U.S. SIC description
US	333911	Pump and Pumping Equipment Manufacturing	3561	Pumps and Pumping Equipment
			*3743	Railroad Equipment (locomotive fuel lubricating or cooling medium pumps)
US	333912	Air and Gas Compressor Manufacturing	3563	Air and Gas Compressors
US	333913	Measuring and Dispensing Pump Manufacturing	3586	Measuring and Dispensing Pumps
	33392	Material Handling Equipment Manufacturing		
US	333921	Elevator and Moving Stairway Manufacturing	3534	Elevators and Moving Stairways
US	333922	Conveyor and Conveying Equipment Manufacturing	*3523	Farm Machinery and Equipment (farm conveyors and elevators)
			3535	Conveyors and Conveying Equipment
US	333923	Overhead Traveling Crane, Hoist, and Monorail System Manufacturing	3536	Overhead Traveling Cranes, Hoists, and Monorail Systems
			*3531	Construction Machinery and Equipment (winches, aerial work platforms, and automobile wrecker hoists)
US	333924	Industrial Truck, Tractor, Trailer, and Stacker Machinery Manufacturing	*3496	Miscellaneous Fabricated Wire Products (grocery carts)
			*3537	Industrial Trucks, Tractors, Trailers, and Stackers (except metal pallets and metal air cargo containers)
			*3799	Transportation Equipment, NEC (wheelbarrows)
	33399	All Other General Purpose Machinery Manufacturing		
US	333991	Power-Driven Handtool Manufacturing	3546	Power-Driven Handtools
US	333992	Welding and Soldering Equipment Manufacturing	*3548	Electric and Gas Welding and Soldering Equipment (except transformers for arc-welding)

US—United States industry only. CAN—United States and Canadian industries are comparable. When neither US nor CAN appears, Canadian, Mexican, and United States are comparable. *—Part of; NEC—Not Elsewhere Classified.

http://www.ntis.gov/naics

1997 NAICS code	1997 NAICS U.S. description	1987 SIC code	1987 U.S. SIC description
		*3699	Electrical Machinery Equipment and Supplies, NEC (laser welding and soldering equipment)
US 333993	Packaging Machinery Manufacturing	3565	Packaging Machinery
US 333994	Industrial Process Furnace and Oven Manufacturing	3567	Industrial Process Furnaces and Ovens
US 333995	Fluid Power Cylinder and Actuator Manufacturing	3593	Fluid Power Cylinders and Actuators
US 333996	Fluid Power Pump and Motor Manufacturing	3594	Fluid Power Pumps and Motors
US 333997	Scale and Balance (except Laboratory) Manufacturing	3596	Scales and Balances, Except Laboratory
US 333999	All Other Miscellaneous General Purpose Machinery Manufacturing	*3599	Industrial and Commercial Machinery and Equipment, NEC (other industrial and commercial machinery and equipment)
		*3569	General Industrial Machinery and Equipment, NEC (except fire hoses and electric swimming pool heaters)
334	Computer and Electronic Product Manufacturing		
3341	Computer and Peripheral Equipment Manufacturing		
33411	Computer and Peripheral Equipment Manufacturing		
US 334111	Electronic Computer Manufacturing	3571	Electronic Computers
US 334112	Computer Storage Device Manufacturing	3572	Computer Storage Devices
US 334113	Computer Terminal Manufacturing	3575	Computer Terminals
US 334119	Other Computer Peripheral Equipment Manufacturing	*3577	Computer Peripheral Equipment, NEC (except plotter controllers and magnetic tape cleaners)
		*3578	Calculating and Accounting Machines, Except Electronic Computers (point of sale terminals and fund transfer devices)

US—United States industry only. CAN—United States and Canadian industries are comparable. When neither US nor CAN appears, Canadian, Mexican, and United States are comparable. *—Part of; NEC—Not Elsewhere Classified.

http://www.ntis.gov/naics

1997 NAICS code	1997 NAICS U.S. description	1987 SIC code	1987 U.S. SIC description
3342	Communications Equipment Manufacturing		
33421	Telephone Apparatus Manufacturing	*3661	Telephone and Telegraph Apparatus (except consumer external modems)
33422	Radio and Television Broadcasting and Wireless Communications Equipment Manufacturing	3663	Radio and Television Broadcasting and Communications Equipment
		*3679	Electronic Components, NEC (antennas)
33429	Other Communications Equipment Manufacturing	3669	Communications Equipment, NEC
3343	Audio and Video Equipment Manufacturing		
33431	Audio and Video Equipment Manufacturing	3651	Household Audio and Video Equipment
		*3679	Electronic Components, NEC (radio headphones)
3344	Semiconductor and Other Electronic Component Manufacturing		
33441	Semiconductor and Other Electronic Component Manufacturing		
US 334411	Electron Tube Manufacturing	3671	Electron Tubes
US 334412	Bare Printed Circuit Board Manufacturing	3672	Printed Circuit Boards
US 334413	Semiconductor and Related Device Manufacturing	3674	Semiconductors and Related Devices
US 334414	Electronic Capacitor Manufacturing	3675	Electronic Capacitors
US 334415	Electronic Resistor Manufacturing	3676	Electronic Resistors
US 334416	Electronic Coil, Transformer, and Other Inductor Manufacturing	3677	Electronic Coils, Transformers, and Other Inductors
US 334417	Electronic Connector Manufacturing	3678	Electronic Connectors
US 334418	Printed Circuit Assembly (Electronic Assembly) Manufacturing	*3577	Computer Peripheral Equipment, NEC (plotter controllers)

US—United States industry only. CAN—United States and Canadian industries are comparable. When neither US nor CAN appears, Canadian, Mexican, and United States are comparable. *—Part of; NEC—Not Elsewhere Classified.

http://www.ntis.gov/naics

1997 NAICS code	1997 NAICS U.S. description	1987 SIC code	1987 U.S. SIC description
		*3679	Electronic Components, NEC (printed circuit/electronic assembly manufacturing)
		*3661	Telephone and Telegraph Apparatus (consumer external modems)
us 334419	Other Electronic Component Manufacturing	*3679	Electronic Components, NEC (other electronic components)
3345	Navigational, Measuring, Electromedical, and Control Instruments Manufacturing		
33451	Navigational, Measuring, Electromedical, and Control Instruments Manufacturing		
us 334510	Electromedical and Electrotherapeutic Apparatus Manufacturing	*3842	Orthopedic, Prosthetic and Surgical Appliances and Supplies (electronic hearing aids)
		*3845	Electromedical and Electrotherapeutic Apparatus (other electromedical and electrotherapeutic apparatus)
us 334511	Search, Detection, Navigation, Guidance, Aeronautical, and Nautical System and Instrument Manufacturing	3812	Search, Detection, Navigation, Guidance, Aeronautical, and Nautical Systems and Instruments
us 334512	Automatic Environmental Control Manufacturing for Residential, Commercial, and Appliance Use	3822	Automatic Controls for Regulating Residential and Commercial Environments and Appliances
us 334513	Instruments and Related Products Manufacturing for Measuring, Displaying, and Controlling Industrial Process Variables	3823	Industrial Instruments for Measurement, Display, and Control of Process Variables; and Related Products
us 334514	Totalizing Fluid Meter and Counting Device Manufacturing	3824	Totalizing Fluid Meters and Counting Devices
		*3825	Instruments for Measuring and Testing of Electricity and Electrical Signals (automotive ammeters and voltmeters)

US—United States industry only. CAN—United States and Canadian industries are comparable. When neither US nor CAN appears, Canadian, Mexican, and United States are comparable. *—Part of; NEC—Not Elsewhere Classified.

http://www.ntis.gov/naics

1997 NAICS code	1997 NAICS U.S. description	1987 SIC code	1987 U.S. SIC description
		*3829	Measuring and Controlling Devices, NEC (motor vehicle gauges)
US 334515	Instrument Manufacturing for Measuring and Testing Electricity and Electrical Signals	*3825	Instruments for Measuring and Testing of Electricity and Electrical Signals (except automotive ammeters and voltmeters)
US 334516	Analytical Laboratory Instrument Manufacturing	3826	Laboratory Analytical Instruments
US 334517	Irradiation Apparatus Manufacturing	3844	X-Ray Apparatus and Tubes and Related Irradiation Apparatus
		*3845	Electromedical and Electrotherapeutic Apparatus (CT and CAT Scanners)
US 334518	Watch, Clock, and Part Manufacturing	*3495	Wire Springs (clock and watch springs)
		*3579	Office Machines, NEC (time clocks and other time recording devices)
		*3829	Measuring and Controlling Devices, NEC (electronic chronometers)
		*3915	Jewelers Findings and Materials and Lapidary Work (watch jewels)
		3873	Watches, Clocks, Clockwork Operated Devices, and Parts
US 334519	Other Measuring and Controlling Device Manufacturing	*3829	Measuring and Controlling Devices, NEC (except medical thermometers, electronic chronometers and motor vehicle gauges)
3346	Manufacturing and Reproducing Magnetic and Optical Media		
33461	Manufacturing and Reproducing Magnetic and Optical Media		
US 334611	Software Reproducing	*7372	Prepackaged Software (reproduction of software)

US—United States industry only. CAN—United States and Canadian industries are comparable. When neither US nor CAN appears, Canadian, Mexican, and United States are comparable. *—Part of; NEC—Not Elsewhere Classified.

http://www.ntis.gov/naics

1997 NAICS code	1997 NAICS U.S. description	1987 SIC code	1987 U.S. SIC description
US 334612	Prerecorded Compact Disc (except Software), Tape, and Record Reproducing	*3652	Phonograph Records and Prerecorded Audio Tapes and Disks (reproduction of all other media except video)
		*7819	Services Allied to Motion Picture Production (reproduction of video)
US 334613	Magnetic and Optical Recording Media Manufacturing	3695	Magnetic and Optical Recording Media
		*3577	Computer Peripheral Equipment, NEC (magnetic tape cleaners)
335	Electrical Equipment, Appliance, and Component Manufacturing		
3351	Electric Lighting Equipment Manufacturing		
33511	Electric Lamp Bulb and Part Manufacturing	3641	Electric Lamp Bulbs and Tubes
33512	Lighting Fixture Manufacturing		
US 335121	Residential Electric Lighting Fixture Manufacturing	3645	Residential Electric Lighting Fixtures
		*3999	Manufacturing Industries, NEC (lamp shades of paper or textile)
US 335122	Commercial, Industrial, and Institutional Electric Lighting Fixture Manufacturing	3646	Commercial, Industrial, and Institutional Electric Lighting Fixtures
US 335129	Other Lighting Equipment Manufacturing	3648	Lighting Equipment, NEC
		*3699	Electrical Machinery, Equipment, and Supplies, NEC (Christmas tree lighting sets, electric insect lamps, electric fireplace logs, and trouble lights)
3352	Household Appliance Manufacturing		
33521	Small Electrical Appliance Manufacturing		
US 335211	Electric Housewares and Household Fan Manufacturing	*3634	Electric Housewares and Fans (except wall and baseboard heating units for permanent installation and electronic cigarette lighters)

US—United States industry only. CAN—United States and Canadian industries are comparable. When neither US nor CAN appears, Canadian, Mexican, and United States are comparable. *—Part of; NEC—Not Elsewhere Classified.

http://www.ntis.gov/naics

	1997 NAICS code	1997 NAICS U.S. description	1987 SIC code	1987 U.S. SIC description
			*3999	Manufacturing Industries, NEC (electric hair clippers for humans)
US	335212	Household Vacuum Cleaner Manufacturing	3635	Household Vacuum Cleaners
			*3639	Household Appliances, NEC (floor waxing and floor polishing machines)
	33522	Major Appliance Manufacturing		
US	335221	Household Cooking Appliance Manufacturing	3631	Household Cooking Equipment
US	335222	Household Refrigerator and Home Freezer Manufacturing	3632	Household Refrigerators and Home and Farm Freezers
US	335224	Household Laundry Equipment Manufacturing	3633	Household Laundry Equipment
US	335228	Other Major Household Appliance Manufacturing	*3639	Household Appliances, NEC (except floor waxing and floor polishing machines, and household sewing machines)
	3353	Electrical Equipment Manufacturing		
	33531	Electrical Equipment Manufacturing		
CAN	335311	Power, Distribution, and Specialty Transformer Manufacturing	*3548	Electric and Gas Welding and Soldering Equipment (transformers for arc-welders)
			3612	Power, Distribution, and Speciality Transformers
CAN	335312	Motor and Generator Manufacturing	3621	Motors and Generators
			*7694	Armature Rewinding Shops (remanufacturing)
US	335313	Switchgear and Switchboard Apparatus Manufacturing	3613	Switchgear and Switchboard Apparatus
US	335314	Relay and Industrial Control Manufacturing	3625	Relays and Industrial Controls
	3359	Other Electrical Equipment and Component Manufacturing		

US—United States industry only. CAN—United States and Canadian industries are comparable. When neither US nor CAN appears, Canadian, Mexican, and United States are comparable. *—Part of; NEC—Not Elsewhere Classified.

1997 NAICS code	1997 NAICS U.S. description	1987 SIC code	1987 U.S. SIC description
33591	Battery Manufacturing		
US 335911	Storage Battery Manufacturing	3691	Storage Batteries
US 335912	Primary Battery Manufacturing	3692	Primary Batteries, Dry and Wet
33592	Communication and Energy Wire and Cable Manufacturing		
US 335921	Fiber Optic Cable Manufacturing	*3357	Drawing and Insulating of Nonferrous Wire (fiber optic cable-insulating only)
US 335929	Other Communication and Energy Wire Manufacturing	*3357	Drawing and Insulating of Nonferrous Wire (communication and energy wire, except fiber optic-insulating only)
33593	Wiring Device Manufacturing		
US 335931	Current-Carrying Wiring Device Manufacturing	3643	Current-Carrying Wiring Devices
US 335932	Noncurrent-Carrying Wiring Device Manufacturing	*3644	Noncurrent-Carrying Wiring Devices (except fishwire, electrical wiring tool)
33599	All Other Electrical Equipment and Component Manufacturing		
US 335991	Carbon and Graphite Product Manufacturing	3624	Carbon and Graphite Products
US 335999	All Other Miscellaneous Electrical Equipment and Component Manufacturing	3629	Electrical Industrial Apparatus, NEC
		*3699	Electrical Machinery, Equipment, and Supplies, NEC (other electrical industrial apparatus)
336	Transportation Equipment Manufacturing		
3361	Motor Vehicle Manufacturing		
33611	Automobile and Light Duty Motor Vehicle Manufacturing		
US 336111	Automobile Manufacturing	*3711	Motor Vehicles and Passenger Car Bodies (automobiles)
US 336112	Light Truck and Utility Vehicle Manufacturing	*3711	Motor Vehicles and Passenger Car Bodies (light trucks and utility vehicles)

US—United States industry only. CAN—United States and Canadian industries are comparable. When neither US nor CAN appears, Canadian, Mexican, and United States are comparable. *—Part of; NEC—Not Elsewhere Classified.

http://www.ntis.gov/naics

1997 NAICS code	1997 NAICS U.S. description	1987 SIC code	1987 U.S. SIC description
33612	Heavy Duty Truck Manufacturing	*3711	Motor Vehicles and Passenger Car Bodies (heavy duty trucks)
3362	Motor Vehicle Body and Trailer Manufacturing		
33621	Motor Vehicle Body and Trailer Manufacturing		
CAN 336211	Motor Vehicle Body Manufacturing	*3711	Motor Vehicles and Passenger Car Bodies (kit car and other passenger car bodies)
		3713	Truck and Bus Bodies
		*3714	Motor Vehicle Parts and Accessories (dump truck lifting mechanisms and fifth wheels)
CAN 336212	Truck Trailer Manufacturing	3715	Truck Trailers
US 336213	Motor Home Manufacturing	3716	Motor Homes
US 336214	Travel Trailer and Camper Manufacturing	3792	Travel Trailers and Campers
		*3799	Transportation Equipment, NEC (automobile, boat, utility and light truck trailers)
3363	Motor Vehicle Parts Manufacturing		
33631	Motor Vehicle Gasoline Engine and Engine Parts Manufacturing		
US 336311	Carburetor, Piston, Piston Ring, and Valve Manufacturing	3592	Carburetors, Pistons, Piston Rings, and Valves
US 336312	Gasoline Engine and Engine Parts Manufacturing	*3714	Motor Vehicle Parts and Accessories (gasoline engines and engine parts including rebuilt)
33632	Motor Vehicle Electrical and Electronic Equipment Manufacturing		
US 336321	Vehicular Lighting Equipment Manufacturing	3647	Vehicular Lighting Equipment
US 336322	Other Motor Vehicle Electrical and Electronic Equipment Manufacturing	3694	Electrical Equipment for Internal Combustion Engines

US—United States industry only. CAN—United States and Canadian industries are comparable. When neither US nor CAN appears, Canadian, Mexican, and United States are comparable. *—Part of; NEC—Not Elsewhere Classified.

http://www.ntis.gov/naics

1997 NAICS code	1997 NAICS U.S. description	1987 SIC code	1987 U.S. SIC description
		*3714	Motor Vehicle Parts and Accessories (wiring harness sets, other than ignition; block heaters and battery heaters; instrument board assemblies; permanent defrosters; windshield washer-wiper mechanisms; cruise control mechanisms; and other electrical equipment for internal combustion engines)
33633	Motor Vehicle Steering and Suspension Components (except Spring) Manufacturing	*3714	Motor Vehicle Parts and Accessories (steering and suspension parts)
33634	Motor Vehicle Brake System Manufacturing	*3292	Asbestos Products (asbestos brake linings and pads)
		*3714	Motor Vehicle Parts and Accessories (brake and brake systems, including assemblies)
33635	Motor Vehicle Transmission and Power Train Parts Manufacturing	*3714	Motor Vehicle Parts and Accessories (transmissions and power train parts, including rebuilding)
33636	Motor Vehicle Seating and Interior Trim Manufacturing	*2396	Automotive Trimmings, Apparel Findings, and Related Products (textile motor vehicle trimming)
		*2399	Fabricated Textile Products, NEC (seat belts, and seat and tire covers)
		*2531	Public Building and Related Furniture (seats for motor vehicles)
		*3499	Fabricated Metal Products, NEC (metal motor vehicle seat frames)
33637	Motor Vehicle Metal Stamping	3465	Automotive Stampings
33639	Other Motor Vehicle Parts Manufacturing		
US 336391	Motor Vehicle Air-Conditioning Manufacturing	*3585	Air-Conditioning and Warm Air Heating Equipment and Commercial and Industrial Refrigeration Equipment (motor vehicle air-conditioning)

US—United States industry only. CAN—United States and Canadian industries are comparable. When neither US nor CAN appears, Canadian, Mexican, and United States are comparable. *—Part of; NEC—Not Elsewhere Classified.

http://www.ntis.gov/naics

1997 NAICS code	1997 NAICS U.S. description	1987 SIC code	1987 U.S. SIC description
US 336399	All Other Motor Vehicle Parts Manufacturing	*3429	Hardware, NEC (luggage and utility racks)
		*3519	Internal Combustion Engines, NEC (stationary engine radiators)
		*3599	Industrial and Commercial Machinery and Equipment, NEC (gasoline, oil, and intake filters for internal combustion engines, except for motor vehicles)
		*3714	Motor Vehicle Parts and Accessories (except truck and bus bodies, trailers, engine and engine parts, motor vehicle electrical and electronic equipment, motor vehicle steering and suspension components, motor vehicle brake systems, and motor vehicle transmission and power train parts)
		*3799	Transportation Equipment, NEC (trailer hitches)
3364	Aerospace Product and Parts Manufacturing		
33641	Aerospace Product and Parts Manufacturing		
US 336411	Aircraft Manufacturing	*3721	Aircraft (except research and development)
		*3728	Aircraft Parts and Auxiliary Equipment, NEC (target drones)
US 336412	Aircraft Engine and Engine Parts Manufacturing	*3724	Aircraft Engines and Engine Parts (except research and development
US 336413	Other Aircraft Parts and Auxiliary Equipment Manufacturing	*3728	Aircraft Parts and Auxiliary Equipment, NEC (except fluid power aircraft subassemblies, target drones, and research and development)
US 336414	Guided Missile and Space Vehicle Manufacturing	*3761	Guided Missiles and Space Vehicles (except research and development
US 336415	Guided Missile and Space Vehicle Propulsion Unit and Propulsion Unit Parts Manufacturing	*3764	Guided Missile and Space Vehicle Propulsion Units and Propulsion Unit Parts (except research and development)

US—United States industry only. CAN—United States and Canadian industries are comparable. When neither US nor CAN appears, Canadian, Mexican, and United States are comparable. *—Part of; NEC—Not Elsewhere Classified.

http://www.ntis.gov/naics

	1997 NAICS code	1997 NAICS U.S. description	1987 SIC code	1987 U.S. SIC description
US	336419	Other Guided Missile and Space Vehicle Parts and Auxiliary Equipment Manufacturing	*3769	Guided Missile and Space Vehicle Parts and Auxiliary Equipment (except research and development)
	3365	Railroad Rolling Stock Manufacturing		
	33651	Railroad Rolling Stock Manufacturing	*3531	Construction Machinery and Equipment (railway track maintenance equipment)
			*3743	Railroad Equipment (except locomotive fuel lubricating or cooling medium pumps)
	3366	Ship and Boat Building		
	33661	Ship and Boat Building		
CAN	336611	Ship Building and Repairing	*3731	Ship Building and Repairing (except floating dry docks not associated with shipyards)
CAN	336612	Boat Building	*3732	Boat Building and Repairing (boat building)
	3369	Other Transportation Equipment Manufacturing		
	33699	Other Transportation Equipment Manufacturing		
US	336991	Motorcycle, Bicycle, and Parts Manufacturing	*3944	Games, Toys, and Children's Vehicles, Except Dolls and Bicycles (metal tricycles)
			3751	Motorcycles, Bicycles and Parts
US	336992	Military Armored Vehicle, Tank, and Tank Component Manufacturing	*3711	Motor Vehicles and Passenger Car Bodies (military armored vehicles)
			3795	Tanks and Tank Components
US	336999	All Other Transportation Equipment Manufacturing	*3799	Transportation Equipment, NEC (except automobile, boat, utility light truck trailers, trailer hitches, and wheelbarrows)
	337	Furniture and Related Product Manufacturing		
	3371	Household and Institutional Furniture and Kitchen Cabinet Manufacturing		
	33711	Wood Kitchen Cabinet and Countertop Manufacturing	2434	Wood Kitchen Cabinets

US—United States industry only. CAN—United States and Canadian industries are comparable. When neither US nor CAN appears, Canadian, Mexican, and United States are comparable. *—Part of; NEC—Not Elsewhere Classified.

1997 NAICS code	1997 NAICS U.S. description	1987 SIC code	1987 U.S. SIC description
		*5712	Furniture Stores (custom wood cabinets)
33712	Household and Institutional Furniture Manufacturing		
CAN 337121	Upholstered Household Furniture Manufacturing	2512	Wood Household Furniture, Upholstered
		*2514	Metal Household Furniture (upholstered)
		*2515	Mattress, Foundations, and Convertible Beds (convertible sofas)
		*5712	Furniture (custom made upholstered household furniture except cabinets)
US 337122	Nonupholstered Wood Household Furniture Manufacturing	*2511	Wood Household Furniture, Except Upholstered (except wood box spring frames)
		*5712	Furniture Stores (custom made wood nonupholstered household furniture except cabinets)
US 337124	Metal Household Furniture Manufacturing	*2514	Metal Household Furniture (except upholstered and metal box spring frames)
US 337125	Household Furniture (except Wood and Metal) Manufacturing	2519	Household Furniture, NEC
CAN 337127	Institutional Furniture Manufacturing	*2531	Public Building and Related Furniture (furniture made for public buildings)
		*2541	Wood Office and Store Fixtures, Partitions, Shelving, and Lockers (wood lunchroom tables and chairs)
		*2542	Office and Store Fixtures, Partitions, Shelving, and Lockers, Except Wood (lunchroom tables and chairs (except wood))
		*2599	Furniture and Fixtures, NEC (except hospital beds)
		*3952	Lead Pencils, Crayons, and Artist's Materials (drafting tables and boards)

US—United States industry only. CAN—United States and Canadian industries are comparable. When neither US nor CAN appears, Canadian, Mexican, and United States are comparable. *—Part of; NEC—Not Elsewhere Classified.

http://www.ntis.gov/naics

1997 NAICS code	1997 NAICS U.S. description	1987 SIC code	1987 U.S. SIC description
		*3999	Manufacturing Industries, NEC (beauty and barber chairs)
US 337129	Wood Television, Radio, and Sewing Machine Cabinet Manufacturing	2517	Wood Television, Radio, Phonograph, and Sewing Machine Cabinets
3372	Office Furniture (including Fixtures) Manufacturing		
33721	Office Furniture (including Fixtures) Manufacturing		
US 337211	Wood Office Furniture Manufacturing	2521	Wood Office Furniture
US 337212	Custom Architectural Woodwork and Millwork Manufacturing	*2541	Wood Office and Store Fixtures, Partitions, Shelving, and Lockers (architectural woodwork, millwork, and fixtures)
CAN 337214	Office Furniture (except Wood) Manufacturing	2522	Office Furniture, Except Wood
CAN 337215	Showcase, Partition, Shelving, and Locker Manufacturing	*2511	Wood Household Furniture, Except Upholstered (wood box spring frames)
		*2514	Metal Household Furniture (metal box spring frames)
		*2542	Office and Store Fixtures, Partitions, Shelving and Lockers, Except Wood (except lunchroom tables and chairs)
		*2541	Wood Office and Store Fixtures, Partitions, Shelving, and Lockers (except counter tops, custom architectural woodwork, millwork, lunchroom and other fixtures)
		*2426	Hardwood Dimension and Flooring Mills (wood furniture frames and finished furniture parts)
		*3089	Plastics Products, NEC (finished plastics furniture parts)
		*3429	Hardware, NEC (convertible bed sleeper mechanisms, chair glides)
		*3499	Fabricated Metal Products, NEC (metal furniture frames)

US—United States industry only. CAN—United States and Canadian industries are comparable. When neither US nor CAN appears, Canadian, Mexican, and United States are comparable. *—Part of; NEC—Not Elsewhere Classified.

http://www.ntis.gov/naics

1997 NAICS code	1997 NAICS U.S. description	1987 SIC code	1987 U.S. SIC description
3379	Other Furniture Related Product Manufacturing		
33791	Mattress Manufacturing	*2515	Mattresses, Foundations and Convertible Beds (mattresses and foundations)
33792	Blind and Shade Manufacturing	2591	Drapery Hardware and Window Blinds and Shades
339	Miscellaneous Manufacturing		
3391	Medical Equipment and Supplies Manufacturing		
33911	Medical Equipment and Supplies Manufacturing		
US 339111	Laboratory Apparatus and Furniture Manufacturing	*2599	Furniture and Fixtures, NEC (hospital beds)
		3821	Laboratory Apparatus and Furniture
		*3841	Surgical and Medical Instruments and Apparatus (operating tables)
US 339112	Surgical and Medical Instrument Manufacturing	*3841	Surgical and Medical Instruments and Apparatus (except tranquilizer guns and operating tables)
		*3829	Measuring and Controlling Devices, NEC (medical thermometers)
US 339113	Surgical Appliance and Supplies Manufacturing	*3069	Fabricated Rubber Products, NEC (rubber gloves and life jackets)
		*3842	Orthopedic, Prosthetic, and Surgical Appliances and Supplies (except electronic hearing aids)
		*3851	Ophthalmic Goods (intra ocular lenses)
US 339114	Dental Equipment and Supplies Manufacturing	3843	Dental Equipment and Supplies
US 339115	Ophthalmic Goods Manufacturing	*3851	Ophthalmic Goods (except intra ocular lenses)
		*5995	Optical Goods Stores (optical laboratories grinding of lenses to prescription)
US 339116	Dental Laboratories	8072	Dental Laboratories
3399	Other Miscellaneous Manufacturing		

US—United States industry only. CAN—United States and Canadian industries are comparable. When neither US nor CAN appears, Canadian, Mexican, and United States are comparable. *—Part of; NEC—Not Elsewhere Classified.

http://www.ntis.gov/naics

	1997 NAICS code	1997 NAICS U.S. description	1987 SIC code	1987 U.S. SIC description
	33991	Jewelry and Silverware Manufacturing		
US	339911	Jewelry (except Costume) Manufacturing	*3479	Coating, Engraving, and Allied Services, NEC (jewelry engraving and etching, including precious metal)
			3911	Jewelry, Precious Metal
US	339912	Silverware and Hollowware Manufacturing	*3479	Coating, Engraving, and Allied Services, NEC (silver and plated ware engraving and etching)
			*3914	Silverware, Plated Ware, and Stainless Steel Ware (except nonprecious and precious plated metal cutlery and flatware)
US	339913	Jewelers' Material and Lapidary Work Manufacturing	*3915	Jewelers' Findings and Materials, and Lapidary Work (except Watch Jewels)
US	339914	Costume Jewelry and Novelty Manufacturing	*3479	Coating, Engraving, and Allied Services, NEC (costume jewelry engraving and etching)
			3961	Costume Jewelry and Costume Novelties, Except Precious Metal
	33992	Sporting and Athletic Goods Manufacturing	3949	Sporting and Athletic Goods, NEC
			*3069	Fabricated Rubber Products, NEC (wet suits)
	33993	Doll, Toy, and Game Manufacturing		
US	339931	Doll and Stuffed Toy Manufacturing	3942	Dolls and Stuffed Toys
US	339932	Game, Toy, and Children's Vehicle Manufacturing	*3069	Fabricated Rubber Products, NEC (rubber toys, except dolls)
			*3944	Games, Toys, and Children's Vehicles, Except Dolls and Bicycles (except metal tricycles)
			*3999	Manufacturing Industries, NEC (embroidery kits)
	33994	Office Supplies (except Paper) Manufacturing		
US	339941	Pen and Mechanical Pencil Manufacturing	3951	Pens, Mechanical Pencils, and Parts

US—United States industry only. CAN—United States and Canadian industries are comparable. When neither US nor CAN appears, Canadian, Mexican, and United States are comparable. *—Part of; NEC—Not Elsewhere Classified.

http://www.ntis.gov/naics

	1997 NAICS code	1997 NAICS U.S. description	1987 SIC code	1987 U.S. SIC description
US	339942	Lead Pencil and Art Good Manufacturing	*2531	Public Buildings and Related Furniture (blackboards)
			*3579	Office Machines, NEC (pencil sharpeners, staplers and other office equipment)
			*3952	Lead Pencils, Crayons, and Artists' Materials (except drawing and india ink, and drafting tables and boards)
US	339943	Marking Device Manufacturing	3953	Marking Devices
US	339944	Carbon Paper and Inked Ribbon Manufacturing	3955	Carbon Paper and Inked Ribbons
	33995	Sign Manufacturing	*3993	Signs and Advertising Specialties (signs)
	33999	All Other Miscellaneous Manufacturing		
US	339991	Gasket, Packing, and Sealing Device Manufacturing	3053	Gaskets, Packing, and Sealing Devices
US	339992	Musical Instrument Manufacturing	3931	Musical Instruments
US	339993	Fastener, Button, Needle, and Pin Manufacturing	3965	Fasteners, Buttons, Needles, and Pins
			*3131	Boat and Shoe Cut Stock and Findings (metal buckles)
US	339994	Broom, Brush, and Mop Manufacturing	3991	Brooms and Brushes
			*2392	Housefurnishings, Except Curtains and Draperies (mops, floor and dust)
US	339995	Burial Casket Manufacturing	3995	Burial Caskets
US	339999	All Other Miscellaneous Manufacturing	*2499	Wood Products, NEC (mirror and picture frames)
			*3634	Electric Housewares and Fans (electronic cigarette lighters)
			*3999	Manufacturing Industries, NEC (other miscellaneous products not specially provided for previously)
	42	Wholesale Trade		
US	421	Wholesale Trade, Durable Goods		
US	4211	Motor Vehicle and Motor Vehicle Parts and Supplies Wholesalers		

US—United States industry only. CAN—United States and Canadian industries are comparable. When neither US nor CAN appears, Canadian, Mexican, and United States are comparable. *—Part of; NEC—Not Elsewhere Classified.

http://www.ntis.gov/naics

1997 NAICS code	1997 NAICS U.S. description	1987 SIC code	1987 U.S. SIC description
US 42111	Automobile and Other Motor Vehicle Wholesalers	5012	Automobiles and Other Motor Vehicles
US 42112	Motor Vehicle Supplies and New Parts Wholesalers	*5013	Motor Vehicle Supplies and New Parts (except parts sold via retail methods)
US 42113	Tire and Tube Wholesalers	*5014	Tires and Tubes (except tires sold via retail method)
US 42114	Motor Vehicle Parts (Used) Wholesalers	*5015	Motor Vehicle Parts, Used (except sold via retail method)
US 4212	Furniture and Home Furnishing Wholesalers		
US 42121	Furniture Wholesalers	*5021	Furniture (except furniture sold via retail method)
US 42122	Home Furnishing Wholesalers	*5023	Homefurnishings (except homefurnishings sold via retail method)
US 4213	Lumber and Other Construction Materials Wholesalers		
US 42131	Lumber, Plywood, Millwork, and Wood Panel Wholesalers	5031	Lumber, Plywood, Millwork, and Wood Panels
US 42132	Brick, Stone, and Related Construction Material Wholesalers	5032	Brick, Stone, and Related Construction Materials (except construction materials sold via retail method)
US 42133	Roofing, Siding, and Insulation Material Wholesalers	5033	Roofing, Siding, and Insulation Materials
US 42139	Other Construction Material Wholesalers	*5039	Construction Materials, NEC (sold via wholesale method)
US 4214	Professional and Commercial Equipment and Supplies Wholesalers		
US 42141	Photographic Equipment and Supplies Wholesalers	5043	Photographic Equipment and Supplies
US 42142	Office Equipment Wholesalers	*5044	Office Equipment (except sold via retail method)
US 42143	Computer and Computer Peripheral Equipment and Software Wholesalers	*5045	Computers and Computer Peripherals Equipment and Software (except computers, equipment, and software sold via retail method)

US—United States industry only. CAN—United States and Canadian industries are comparable. When neither US nor CAN appears, Canadian, Mexican, and United States are comparable. *—Part of; NEC—Not Elsewhere Classified.

http://www.ntis.gov/naics

1997 NAICS code	1997 NAICS U.S. description	1987 SIC code	1987 U.S. SIC description
US 42144	Other Commercial Equipment Wholesalers	5046	Commercial Equipment, NEC
US 42145	Medical, Dental, and Hospital Equipment and Supplies Wholesalers	*5047	Medical, Dental and Hospital Equipment and Supplies (except medical, dental, and hospital equipment and supplies sold via retail method)
US 42146	Ophthalmic Goods Wholesalers	5048	Ophthalmic Goods
US 42149	Other Professional Equipment and Supplies Wholesalers	*5049	Professional Equipment and Supplies, NEC (except religious and school supplies sold via retail method)
US 4215	Metal and Mineral (except Petroleum) Wholesalers		
US 42151	Metal Service Centers and Offices	5051	Metals Service Centers and Offices
US 42152	Coal and Other Mineral and Ore Wholesalers	5052	Coal and Other Mineral and Ores
US 4216	Electrical Goods Wholesalers		
US 42161	Electrical Apparatus and Equipment, Wiring Supplies, and Construction Material Wholesalers	*5063	Electrical Apparatus and Equipment, Wiring Supplies and Construction Materials (except electrical supplies sold via retail method)
US 42162	Electrical Appliance, Television, and Radio Set Wholesalers	5064	Electrical Appliances, Television and Radio Sets
US 42169	Other Electronic Parts and Equipment Wholesalers	5065	Electronic Parts and Equipment, NEC
US 4217	Hardware, and Plumbing and Heating Equipment and Supplies Wholesalers		
US 42171	Hardware Wholesalers	*5072	Hardware (except sold via retail method)
US 42172	Plumbing and Heating Equipment and Supplies (Hydronics) Wholesalers	*5074	Plumbing and Heating Equipment and Supplies (Hydronics) (except plumbing equipment sold via retail method)
US 42173	Warm Air Heating and Air-Conditioning Equipment and Supplies Wholesalers	5075	Warm Air Heating and Air-Conditioning Equipment and Supplies

US—United States industry only. CAN—United States and Canadian industries are comparable. When neither US nor CAN appears, Canadian, Mexican, and United States are comparable. *—Part of; NEC—Not Elsewhere Classified.

http://www.ntis.gov/naics

1997 NAICS code	1997 NAICS U.S. description	1987 SIC code	1987 U.S. SIC description
US 42174	Refrigeration Equipment and Supplies Wholesalers	5078	Refrigeration Equipment and Supplies
US 4218	Machinery, Equipment, and Supplies Wholesalers		
US 42181	Construction and Mining (except Oil Well) Machinery and Equipment Wholesalers	5082	Construction and Mining (Except Petroleum) Machinery and Equipment
US 42182	Farm and Garden Machinery and Equipment Wholesalers	*5083	Farm and Garden Machinery and Equipment (except lawn and garden equipment sold via retail method)
US 42183	Industrial Machinery and Equipment Wholesalers	5084	Industrial Machinery and Equipment
		*5085	Industrial Supplies (fluid power accessories)
US 42184	Industrial Supplies Wholesalers	*5085	Industrial Supplies (except fluid power accessories)
US 42185	Service Establishment Equipment and Supplies Wholesalers	*5087	Service Establishment Equipment and Supplies (except sales of the service establishment equipment and supplies sold via retail method)
US 42186	Transportation Equipment and Supplies (except Motor Vehicle) Wholesalers	5088	Transportation Equipment and Supplies, Except Motor Vehicles
		*7389	Business Services, NEC (yacht brokers)
US 4219	Miscellaneous Durable Goods Wholesalers		
US 42191	Sporting and Recreational Goods and Supplies Wholesalers	5091	Sporting and Recreational Goods and Supplies
US 42192	Toy and Hobby Goods and Supplies Wholesalers	5092	Toys and Hobby Goods and Supplies
US 42193	Recyclable Material Wholesalers	5093	Scrap and Waste Materials
US 42194	Jewelry, Watch, Precious Stone, and Precious Metal Wholesalers	5094	Jewelry, Watches, Precious Stones, and Precious Metals
US 42199	Other Miscellaneous Durable Goods Wholesalers	5099	Durable Goods, NEC

US—United States industry only. CAN—United States and Canadian industries are comparable. When neither US nor CAN appears, Canadian, Mexican, and United States are comparable. *—Part of; NEC—Not Elsewhere Classified.

http://www.ntis.gov/naics

1997 NAICS code	1997 NAICS U.S. description	1987 SIC code	1987 U.S. SIC description
		*7822	Motion Picture and Video Tape Distribution (prerecorded video tapes— distribution)
US 422	Wholesale Trade, Nondurable Goods		
US 4221	Paper and Paper Product Wholesalers		
US 42211	Printing and Writing Paper Wholesalers	5111	Printing and Writing Paper
US 42212	Stationery and Office Supplies Wholesalers	*5112	Stationery and Office Supplies (except stationery and office supplies sold via retail method)
US 42213	Industrial and Personal Service Paper Wholesalers	5113	Industrial and Personal Service Paper
US 4222	Drugs and Druggists' Sundries Wholesalers		
US 42221	Drugs and Druggists' Sundries Wholesalers	5122	Drugs, Drug Proprietaries, and Druggists' Sundries
US 4223	arel, Piece Goods, and Notions Wholesalers		
US 42231	Piece Goods, Notions, and Other Dry Goods Wholesalers	*5131	Piece Goods, Notions, and Other Dry Goods (except piece goods converters)
US 42232	Men's and Boys' Clothing and Furnishings Wholesalers	5136	Men's and Boys' Clothing and Furnishings
US 42233	Women's, Children's, and Infants' Clothing and Accessories Wholesalers	5137	Women's, Children's, and Infants' Clothing and Accessories
US 42234	Footwear Wholesalers	5139	Footwear
US 4224	Grocery and Related Product Wholesalers		
US 42241	General Line Grocery Wholesalers	5141	Groceries, General Line
US 42242	Packaged Frozen Food Wholesalers	5142	Packaged Frozen Foods
US 42243	Dairy Product (except Dried or Canned) Wholesalers	5143	Dairy Products, Except Dried or Canned
US 42244	Poultry and Poultry Product Wholesalers	5144	Poultry and Poultry Products
US 42245	Confectionery Wholesalers	5145	Confectionery
US 42246	Fish and Seafood Wholesalers	5146	Fish and Seafoods
US 42247	Meat and Meat Product Wholesalers	*5147	Meats and Meat Products (except boxed beef)

US—United States industry only. CAN—United States and Canadian industries are comparable. When neither US nor CAN appears, Canadian, Mexican, and United States are comparable. *—Part of; NEC—Not Elsewhere Classified.

http://www.ntis.gov/naics

1997 NAICS code	1997 NAICS U.S. description	1987 SIC code	1987 U.S. SIC description
US 42248	Fresh Fruit and Vegetable Wholesalers	5148	Fresh Fruits and Vegetables
US 42249	Other Grocery and Related Products Wholesalers	*5149	Groceries and Related Products, NEC (except bottling mineral or spring water)
US 4225	Farm Product Raw Material Wholesalers		
US 42251	Grain and Field Bean Wholesalers	5153	Grain and Field Beans
US 42252	Livestock Wholesalers	5154	Livestock
US 42259	Other Farm Product Raw Material Wholesalers	5159	Farm-Product Raw Materials, NEC
US 4226	Chemical and Allied Products Wholesalers		
US 42261	Plastics Materials and Basic Forms and Shapes Wholesalers	5162	Plastics Materials and Basic Forms and Shapes
US 42269	Other Chemical and Allied Products Wholesalers	5169	Chemicals and Allied Products, NEC
US 4227	Petroleum and Petroleum Products Wholesalers		
US 42271	Petroleum Bulk Stations and Terminals	*5171	Petroleum Bulk Stations and Terminals (except petroleum sold via retail method)
US 42272	Petroleum and Petroleum Products Wholesalers (except Bulk Stations and Terminals)	5172	Petroleum and Petroleum Products Wholesalers, Except Bulk Stations and Terminals
US 4228	Beer, Wine, and Distilled Alcoholic Beverage Wholesalers		
US 42281	Beer and Ale Wholesalers	5181	Beer and Ale
US 42282	Wine and Distilled Alcoholic Beverage Wholesalers	5182	Wine and Distilled Alcoholic Beverages
US 4229	Miscellaneous Nondurable Goods Wholesalers		
US 42291	Farm Supplies Wholesalers	*5191	Farm Supplies (except lawn and garden supplies sold via retail method)
US 42292	Book, Periodical, and Newspaper Wholesalers	5192	Books, Periodicals, and Newspapers

US—United States industry only. CAN—United States and Canadian industries are comparable. When neither US nor CAN appears, Canadian, Mexican, and United States are comparable. *—Part of; NEC—Not Elsewhere Classified.

http://www.ntis.gov/naics

	1997 NAICS code	1997 NAICS U.S. description	1987 SIC code	1987 U.S. SIC description
US	42293	Flower, Nursery Stock, and Florists' Supplies Wholesalers	*5193	Flowers, Nursery Stock, and Florists' Supplies (except nursery stock sold via retail method)
US	42294	Tobacco and Tobacco Product Wholesalers	5194	Tobacco and Tobacco Products
US	42295	Paint, Varnish, and Supplies Wholesalers	5198	Paints, Varnishes, and Supplies
US	42299	Other Miscellaneous Nondurable Goods Wholesalers	*5199	Nondurable Goods, NEC (except specialty advertising)
	44-45	Retail Trade		
CAN	441	Motor Vehicle and Parts Dealers		
CAN	4411	Automobile Dealers		
CAN	44111	New Car Dealers	5511	Motor Vehicle Dealers (New and Used)
CAN	44112	Used Car Dealers	5521	Motor Vehicle Dealers (Used Only)
CAN	4412	Other Motor Vehicle Dealers		
CAN	44121	Recreational Vehicle Dealers	5561	Recreational Vehicle Dealers
CAN	44122	Motorcycle, Boat, and Other Motor Vehicle Dealers		
US	441221	Motorcycle Dealers	5571	Motorcycle Dealers
US	441222	Boat Dealers	5551	Boat Dealers
US	441229	All Other Motor Vehicle Dealers	5599	Automotive Dealers, NEC
CAN	4413	Automotive Parts, Accessories, and Tire Stores		
CAN	44131	Automotive Parts and Accessories Stores	*5013	Motor Vehicle Supplies and New Parts (Wholesale) (auto parts sold via retail method)
			*5731	Radio, Television, and Consumer Electronics Stores (automobile radios)
			*5015	Motor Vehicle Parts, Used (sold via retail method)
			*5531	Auto and Home Supply Stores (auto supply stores)
CAN	44132	Tire Dealers	*5014	Tires and Tubes (Wholesale) (tires and tubes sold via retail method)
			*5531	Auto and Home Supply Stores (tires and tubes)

US—United States industry only. CAN—United States and Canadian industries are comparable. When neither US nor CAN appears, Canadian, Mexican, and United States are comparable. *—Part of; NEC—Not Elsewhere Classified.

http://www.ntis.gov/naics

1997 NAICS code	1997 NAICS U.S. description	1987 SIC code	1987 U.S. SIC description
CAN 442	Furniture and Home Furnishings Stores		
CAN 4421	Furniture Stores		
CAN 44211	Furniture Stores	*5021	Furniture (Wholesale) (sold via the retail method)
		*5712	Furniture Stores (except custom furniture and cabinets)
CAN 4422	Home Furnishings Stores		
CAN 44221	Floor Covering Stores	*5023	Homefurnishings (Wholesale) (floor covering sold via retail method)
		5713	Floor Coverings Stores
CAN 44229	Other Home Furnishings Stores		
CAN 442291	Window Treatment Stores	*5714	Drapery, Curtain, and Upholstery Stores (drapery and curtain stores)
		*5719	Miscellaneous Homefurnishings Stores (blinds and shades)
US 442299	All Other Home Furnishings Stores	*5719	Miscellaneous Homefurnishings Stores (except pottery and crafts made and sold on site and window furnishings)
		*7699	Repair Shops and Related Services, NEC (custom picture framing)
CAN 443	Electronics and Appliance Stores		
CAN 4431	Electronics and Appliance Stores		
CAN 44311	Appliance, Television, and Other Electronics Stores		
US 443111	Household Appliance Stores	5722	Household Appliance Stores
		*7623	Refrigeration and Air-Conditioning Service and Repair Shops (retailing new refrigerators from a storefront and repairing refrigerators)
		*7629	Electrical and Electronic Repair Shops, NEC (retailing new electrical and electronic appliances from a storefront and repairing appliances)

US—United States industry only. CAN—United States and Canadian industries are comparable. When neither US nor CAN appears, Canadian, Mexican, and United States are comparable. *—Part of; NEC—Not Elsewhere Classified.

http://www.ntis.gov/naics

1997 NAICS code		1997 NAICS U.S. description	1987 SIC code	1987 U.S. SIC description
US	443112	Radio, Television, and Other Electronics Stores	*5731	Radio, Television, and Consumer Electronics Stores (except auto radios)
			*5999	Miscellaneous Retail Stores, NEC (typewriters and telephones)
			*7622	Radio and Television Repair Shops (retailing new radios and TVs from a storefront and repairing radios and TVs)
CAN	44312	Computer and Software Stores	*5045	Computers and Computer Peripheral Equipment and Software (sold via retail method)
			5734	Computer and Computer Software Stores
			*7378	Computer Maintenance and Repair (retailing new computers from a storefront and repairing computers)
CAN	44313	Camera and Photographic Supplies Stores	5946	Camera and Photographic Supply Stores
CAN	444	Building Material and Garden Equipment and Supplies Dealers		
CAN	4441	Building Material and Supplies Dealers		
CAN	44411	Home Centers	*5211	Lumber and Other Building Materials Dealers (home center stores)
CAN	44412	Paint and Wallpaper Stores	*5231	Paint, Glass, and Wallpaper Stores (paint and wallpaper)
CAN	44413	Hardware Stores	*5072	Hardware (sold via retail method)
			5251	Hardware Stores
CAN	44419	Other Building Material Dealers	*5032	Brick, Stone, and Related Construction Materials (Wholesale) (sold via retail method)
			*5039	Construction Materials, NEC (Wholesale) (glass, sold via retail method)
			*5063	Electrical Apparatus and Equipment, Wiring Supplies, and Construction Materials (Wholesale) (sold via retail method)

US—United States industry only. CAN—United States and Canadian industries are comparable. When neither US nor CAN appears, Canadian, Mexican, and United States are comparable. *—Part of; NEC—Not Elsewhere Classified.

http://www.ntis.gov/naics

1997 NAICS code	1997 NAICS U.S. description	1987 SIC code	1987 U.S. SIC description
		*5074	Plumbing and Heating Equipment and Supplies (Hydronics, sold via retail method)
		*5211	Lumber and Other Building Materials Dealers (except home centers)
		*5231	Paint, Glass, and Wallpaper Stores (glass)
CAN 4442	Lawn and Garden Equipment and Supplies Stores		
CAN 44421	Outdoor Power Equipment Stores	*5083	Farm and Garden Machinery and Equipment (Wholesale) (sold via retail method)
		*5261	Retail Nurseries, Lawn and Garden Supply Stores (outdoor power equipment)
CAN 44422	Nursery and Garden Centers	*5191	Farm Supplies (sold via retail method)
		*5193	Flowers, Nursery Stock, and Florists' Supplies (sold via retail method)
		*5261	Retail Nurseries, Lawn and Garden Supply Stores (except outdoor power equipment)
CAN 445	Food and Beverage Stores		
CAN 4451	Grocery Stores		
CAN 44511	Supermarkets and Other Grocery (except Convenience) Stores	*5411	Grocery Stores (except convenience stores and grocery stores with substantial general merchandise)
CAN 44512	Convenience Stores	*5411	Grocery Stores (convenience stores without gas)
CAN 4452	Specialty Food Stores		
CAN 44521	Meat Markets	*5421	Meat and Fish (Seafood) Markets, Including Freezer Provisioners (meat except freezer provisioners)
		*5499	Miscellaneous Food Stores (poultry and poultry products)
CAN 44522	Fish and Seafood Markets	*5421	Meat and Fish (Seafood) Markets, Including Freezer Provisioners (seafood)

US—United States industry only. CAN—United States and Canadian industries are comparable. When neither US nor CAN appears, Canadian, Mexican, and United States are comparable. *—Part of; NEC—Not Elsewhere Classified.

http://www.ntis.gov/naics

	1997 NAICS code	1997 NAICS U.S. description	1987 SIC code	1987 U.S. SIC description
CAN	44523	Fruit and Vegetable Markets	5431	Fruit and Vegetable Markets
CAN	44529	Other Specialty Food Stores		
CAN	445291	Baked Goods Stores	*5461	Retail Bakeries (selling only)
CAN	445292	Confectionery and Nut Stores	5441	Candy, Nut and Confectionery Stores
CAN	445299	All Other Specialty Food Stores	*5499	Miscellaneous Food Stores (except food supplements, poultry stores, and stores with food for immediate consumption)
			5451	Dairy Products Stores
CAN	4453	Beer, Wine, and Liquor Stores		
CAN	44531	Beer, Wine, and Liquor Stores	5921	Liquor Stores
CAN	446	Health and Personal Care Stores		
CAN	4461	Health and Personal Care Stores		
CAN	44611	Pharmacies and Drug Stores	5912	Drug Stores and Proprietary Stores
CAN	44612	Cosmetics, Beauty Supplies, and Perfume Stores	*5087	Service Establishment Equipment and Supplies (beauty and barber shop equipment and supplies sold via retail method)
			*5999	Miscellaneous Retail Stores, NEC (cosmetics and perfumes)
CAN	44613	Optical Goods Stores	*5995	Optical Goods Stores (except labs grinding prescription lenses)
CAN	44619	Other Health and Personal Care Stores		
CAN	446191	Food (Health) Supplement Stores	*5499	Miscellaneous Food Stores (food supplements)
CAN	446199	All Other Health and Personal Care Stores	*5047	Medical, Dental, and Hospital Equipment and Supplies (sold via retail method)
			*5999	Miscellaneous Retail Stores, NEC (hearing aids and artificial limbs)
CAN	447	Gasoline Stations		
CAN	4471	Gasoline Stations		
CAN	44711	Gasoline Stations with Convenience Stores	*5541	Gasoline Service Station (gasoline station with convenience store)
			*5411	Grocery Stores (convenience store with gas)

US—United States industry only. CAN—United States and Canadian industries are comparable. When neither US nor CAN appears, Canadian, Mexican, and United States are comparable. *—Part of; NEC—Not Elsewhere Classified.

http://www.ntis.gov/naics

1997 NAICS code	1997 NAICS U.S. description	1987 SIC code	1987 U.S. SIC description
CAN 44719	Other Gasoline Stations	*5541	Gasoline Service Station (gasoline station without convenience store)
CAN 448	Clothing and Clothing Accessories Stores		
CAN 4481	Clothing Stores		
CAN 44811	Men's Clothing Stores	*5611	Men's and Boys' Clothing and Accessory Stores (clothing stores)
CAN 44812	Women's Clothing Stores	5621	Women's Clothing Stores
CAN 44813	Children's and Infants' Clothing Stores	5641	Children's and Infants' Wear Stores
CAN 44814	Family Clothing Stores	5651	Family Clothing Stores
CAN 44815	Clothing Accessories Stores	*5611	Men's and Boys' Clothing and Accessory Stores (accessories)
		*5632	Women's Accessory and Specialty Stores (accessories)
		*5699	Miscellaneous Apparel and Accessory Stores (accessories)
CAN 44819	Other Clothing Stores	*5699	Miscellaneous Apparel and Accessory Stores (miscellaneous apparel)
		*5632	Women's Accessory and Specialty Stores (specialty stores)
CAN 4482	Shoe Stores		
CAN 44821	Shoe Stores	5661	Shoe Stores
CAN 4483	Jewelry, Luggage, and Leather Goods Stores		
CAN 44831	Jewelry Stores	5944	Jewelry Stores
CAN 44832	Luggage and Leather Goods Stores	5948	Luggage and Leather Goods Stores
CAN 451	Sporting Goods, Hobby, Book, and Music Stores		
CAN 4511	Sporting Goods, Hobby, and Musical Instrument Stores		
CAN 45111	Sporting Goods Stores	5941	Sporting Goods Stores and Bicycle Shops
		*7699	Repair Shops and Related Services, NEC (retailing new bicycles from a storefront and repairing bicycles)

US—United States industry only. CAN—United States and Canadian industries are comparable. When neither US nor CAN appears, Canadian, Mexican, and United States are comparable. *—Part of; NEC—Not Elsewhere Classified.

http://www.ntis.gov/naics

1997 NAICS code	1997 NAICS U.S. description	1987 SIC code	1987 U.S. SIC description
CAN 45112	Hobby, Toy, and Game Stores	5945	Hobby, Toy, and Game Stores
CAN 45113	Sewing, Needlework, and Piece Goods Stores	*5714	Drapery, Curtain, and Upholstery Stores (upholstery materials)
		5949	Sewing, Needlework, and Piece Goods Stores
CAN 45114	Musical Instrument and Supplies Stores	5736	Musical Instruments Stores
CAN 4512	Book, Periodical, and Music Stores		
CAN 45121	Book Stores and News Dealers		
US 451211	Book Stores	5942	Book Stores
US 451212	News Dealers and Newsstands	5994	News Dealers and Newsstands
CAN 45122	Prerecorded Tape, Compact Disc, and Record Stores	5735	Record and Prerecorded Tape Stores
CAN 452	General Merchandise Stores		
CAN 4521	Department Stores		
CAN 45211	Department Stores	5311	Department Stores
CAN 4529	Other General Merchandise Stores		
CAN 45291	Warehouse Clubs and Superstores	*5399	Miscellaneous General Merchandise Stores (warehouse clubs and supermarket/general merchandise combination)
		*5411	Grocery Stores (grocery stores and supermarkets selling substantial amounts of nonfood items)
CAN 45299	All Other General Merchandise Stores	*5399	Miscellaneous General Merchandise Stores (except warehouse club and supermarket/general merchandise combination)
		5331	Variety Stores
		*5531	Auto and Home Supply Stores (other auto and home supply stores)
CAN 453	Miscellaneous Store Retailers		
CAN 4531	Florists		
CAN 45311	Florists	5992	Florists
CAN 4532	Office Supplies, Stationery, and Gift Stores		

US—United States industry only. CAN—United States and Canadian industries are comparable. When neither US nor CAN appears, Canadian, Mexican, and United States are comparable. *—Part of; NEC—Not Elsewhere Classified.

http://www.ntis.gov/naics

1997 NAICS code	1997 NAICS U.S. description	1987 SIC code	1987 U.S. SIC description
CAN 45321	Office Supplies and Stationery Stores	*5044	Office Equipment (sold via retail method)
		*5049	Professional Equipment and Supplies, NEC (school supplies sold via retail method)
		*5112	Stationery and Office Supplies (sold via retail method)
		5943	Stationery Stores
CAN 45322	Gift, Novelty, and Souvenir Stores	5947	Gift, Novelty, and Souvenir Shops
CAN 4533	Used Merchandise Stores		
CAN 45331	Used Merchandise Stores	*5932	Used Merchandise Stores (except pawn shops)
CAN 4539	Other Miscellaneous Store Retailers		
CAN 45391	Pet and Pet Supplies Stores	*5999	Miscellaneous Retail Stores, NEC (pet and pet supplies)
CAN 45392	Art Dealers	*5999	Miscellaneous Retail Stores, NEC (art dealer)
CAN 45393	Manufactured (Mobile) Home Dealers	5271	Mobile Home Dealers
CAN 45399	All Other Miscellaneous Store Retailers		
US 453991	Tobacco Stores	5993	Tobacco Stores and Stands
US 453998	All Other Miscellaneous Store Retailers (except Tobacco Stores)	*5999	Miscellaneous Retail Stores, NEC (except art, pet and pet supplies, hearing aids, artificial limbs, cosmetics, telephones, typewriters, personal appliances, and rough gems)
CAN 454	Nonstore Retailers		
CAN 4541	Electronic Shopping and Mail-Order Houses		
CAN 45411	Electronic Shopping and Mail-Order Houses	5961	Catalog and Mail-Order Houses
CAN 4542	Vending Machine Operators		
CAN 45421	Vending Machine Operators	5962	Automatic Merchandise Machine Operators
CAN 4543	Direct Selling Establishments		
CAN 45431	Fuel Dealers		
US 454311	Heating Oil Dealers	*5171	Petroleum Bulk Stations and Terminals (heating oil sold to final consumer)

US—United States industry only. CAN—United States and Canadian industries are comparable. When neither US nor CAN appears, Canadian, Mexican, and United States are comparable. *—Part of; NEC—Not Elsewhere Classified.

http://www.ntis.gov/naics

1997 NAICS code	1997 NAICS U.S. description	1987 SIC code	1987 U.S. SIC description
		5983	Fuel Oil Dealers
US 454312	Liquefied Petroleum Gas (Bottled Gas) Dealers	*5171	Petroleum Bulk Stations and Terminals (LP gas sold to final consumer)
		5984	Liquefied Petroleum Gas (Bottled Gas) Dealers
US 454319	Other Fuel Dealers	5989	Fuel Dealers, NEC
CAN 45439	Other Direct Selling Establishments	*5421	Meat and Fish (Seafood) Markets, Including Freezer Provisioners (freezer provisioners)
		*5963	Direct Selling Establishments (except mobile food services)
48-49	Transportation and Warehousing		
481	Air Transportation		
4811	Scheduled Air Transportation		
48111	Scheduled Air Transportation		
US 481111	Scheduled Passenger Air Transportation	*4512	Air Transportation, Scheduled (passenger)
US 481112	Scheduled Freight Air Transportation	*4512	Air Transportation, Scheduled (freight)
4812	Nonscheduled Air Transportation		
48121	Nonscheduled Air Transportation		
US 481211	Nonscheduled Chartered Passenger Air Transportation	*4522	Air Transportation, Nonscheduled (passenger)
US 481212	Nonscheduled Chartered Freight Air Transportation	*4522	Air Transportation, Nonscheduled (freight)
US 481219	Other Nonscheduled Air Transportation		Establishments that use general purpose aircraft to provide a variety of specialized flying services
482	Rail Transportation		
4821	Rail Transportation		
48211	Rail Transportation		
US 482111	Line-Haul Railroads	4011	Railroads, Line-Haul Operating
CAN 482112	Short Line Railroads	*4013	Railroad Switching and Terminal Establishments (belt line and logging railroads)

US—United States industry only. CAN—United States and Canadian industries are comparable. When neither US nor CAN appears, Canadian, Mexican, and United States are comparable. *—Part of; NEC—Not Elsewhere Classified.

http://www.ntis.gov/naics

1997 NAICS code	1997 NAICS U.S. description	1987 SIC code	1987 U.S. SIC description
483	Water Transportation		
4831	Deep Sea, Coastal, and Great Lakes Water Transportation		
48311	Deep Sea, Coastal, and Great Lakes Water Transportation		
US 483111	Deep Sea Freight Transportation	4412	Deep Sea Foreign Transportation of Freight
US 483112	Deep Sea Passenger Transportation	*4481	Deep Sea Transportation of Passengers, Except by Ferry (deep sea activities)
US 483113	Coastal and Great Lakes Freight Transportation	4424	Deep Sea Domestic Transportation of Freight
		4432	Freight Transportation on the Great Lakes - St. Lawrence Seaway
US 483114	Coastal and Great Lakes Passenger Transportation	*4481	Deep Sea Transportation of Passengers, Except by Ferry (coastal activities)
		*4482	Ferries (coastal and Great Lakes)
4832	Inland Water Transportation		
48321	Inland Water Transportation		
US 483211	Inland Water Freight Transportation	4449	Water Transportation of Freight, NEC
US 483212	Inland Water Passenger Transportation	*4482	Ferries (inland)
		*4489	Water Transportation of Passengers, NEC (water taxi)
484	Truck Transportation		
4841	General Freight Trucking		
48411	General Freight Trucking, Local	*4212	Local Trucking without Storage (general freight)
		*4214	Local Trucking with Storage (general freight)
48412	General Freight Trucking, Long-Distance		
CAN 484121	General Freight Trucking, Long-Distance, Truckload	*4213	Trucking, Except Local (general freight, truckload)
CAN 484122	General Freight Trucking, Long-Distance, Less Than Truckload	*4213	Trucking, Except Local (general freight, less than truckload)

US—United States industry only. CAN—United States and Canadian industries are comparable. When neither US nor CAN appears, Canadian, Mexican, and United States are comparable. *—Part of; NEC—Not Elsewhere Classified.

http://www.ntis.gov/naics

1997 NAICS code	1997 NAICS U.S. description	1987 SIC code	1987 U.S. SIC description
4842	Specialized Freight Trucking		
48421	Used Household and Office Goods Moving	*4212	Local Trucking Without Storage (household goods moving)
		*4213	Trucking, Except Local (household goods moving)
		*4214	Local Trucking With Storage (household goods moving)
48422	Specialized Freight (except Used Goods) Trucking, Local	*4212	Local Trucking without Storage (specialized freight)
		*4214	Local Trucking with Storage (specialized freight)
48423	Specialized Freight (except Used Goods) Trucking, Long-Distance	*4213	Trucking, Except Local (specialized freight)
485	Transit and Ground Passenger Transportation		
4851	Urban Transit Systems		
48511	Urban Transit Systems		
US 485111	Mixed Mode Transit Systems	*4111	Local and Suburban Transit (mixed mode)
US 485112	Commuter Rail Systems	*4111	Local and Suburban Transit (commuter rail)
US 485113	Bus and Other Motor Vehicle Transit Systems	*4111	Local and Suburban Transit (bus and motor vehicle)
US 485119	Other Urban Transit Systems	*4111	Local and Suburban Transit (other than mixed mode, commuter rail, and bus and motor vehicle)
4852	Interurban and Rural Bus Transportation		
48521	Interurban and Rural Bus Transportation	4131	Intercity and Rural Bus Transportation
4853	Taxi and Limousine Service		
48531	Taxi Service	4121	Taxicabs
		*4899	Communications Services, NEC (taxi cab dispatch services)
48532	Limousine Service	*4119	Local Passenger Transportation, NEC (limousine rental with driver and automobile rental with driver)
4854	School and Employee Bus Transportation		

US—United States industry only. CAN—United States and Canadian industries are comparable. When neither US nor CAN appears, Canadian, Mexican, and United States are comparable. *—Part of; NEC—Not Elsewhere Classified.

http://www.ntis.gov/naics

1997 NAICS code	1997 NAICS U.S. description	1987 SIC code	1987 U.S. SIC description
48541	School and Employee Bus Transportation	4151	School Buses
		*4119	Local Passenger Transportation, NEC (employee transportation)
4855	Charter Bus Industry		
48551	Charter Bus Industry	4141	Local Charter Bus Service
		4142	Bus Charter Services, Except Local
4859	Other Transit and Ground Passenger Transportation		
48599	Other Transit and Ground Passenger Transportation		
US 485991	Special Needs Transportation	*4119	Local Passenger Transportation, NEC (special needs transportation)
US 485999	All Other Transit and Ground Passenger Transportation	*4111	Local and Suburban Transit (airport transportation service)
		*4119	Local Passenger Transportation, NEC (hearse rental with driver and carpool and vanpool operation)
486	Pipeline Transportation		
4861	Pipeline Transportation of Crude Oil		
48611	Pipeline Transportation of Crude Oil	4612	Crude Petroleum Pipelines
4862	Pipeline Transportation of Natural Gas		
48621	Pipeline Transportation of Natural Gas	4922	Natural Gas Transmission
		*4923	Natural Gas Transmission and Distribution (transmission)
4869	Other Pipeline Transportation		
48691	Pipeline Transportation of Refined Petroleum Products	4613	Refined Petroleum Pipelines
48699	All Other Pipeline Transportation	4619	Pipelines, NEC
487	Scenic and Sightseeing Transportation		
4871	Scenic and Sightseeing Transportation, Land		

US—United States industry only. CAN—United States and Canadian industries are comparable. When neither US nor CAN appears, Canadian, Mexican, and United States are comparable. *—Part of; NEC—Not Elsewhere Classified.

http://www.ntis.gov/naics

1997 NAICS code	1997 NAICS U.S. description	1987 SIC code	1987 U.S. SIC description
48711	Scenic and Sightseeing Transportation, Land	*4119	Local Passenger Transportation, NEC (sightseeing buses and cable and cog railways, except scenic)
		*4789	Transportation Services, NEC (horse-drawn cabs and carriages)
		*7999	Amusement and Recreation Services, NEC (scenic transport operations, land)
4872	Scenic and Sightseeing Transportation, Water		
48721	Scenic and Sightseeing Transportation, Water	*4489	Water Transportation of Passengers, NEC (airboats, excursion boats, and sightseeing boats)
		*7999	Amusement and Recreation Services, NEC (charter fishing)
4879	Scenic and Sightseeing Transportation, Other		
48799	Scenic and Sightseeing Transportation, Other	*4522	Air Transportation, Nonscheduled (sightseeing planes)
		*7999	Amusement and Recreation Services, NEC (aerial tramways, scenic and amusement)
488	Support Activities for Transportation		
4881	Support Activities for Air Transportation		
48811	Airport Operations		
CAN 488111	Air Traffic Control	*4581	Airports, Flying Fields, and Airport Terminal Services (private air traffic control)
		*9621	Regulation and Administration of Transportation Programs (government air traffic control)
CAN 488119	Other Airport Operations	*4581	Airports, Flying Fields, and Airport Terminal Services (airfreight handling at airports, hangar operations, airport terminal services, aircraft storage, airports, and flying fields)

US—United States industry only. CAN—United States and Canadian industries are comparable. When neither US nor CAN appears, Canadian, Mexican, and United States are comparable. *—Part of; NEC—Not Elsewhere Classified.

http://www.ntis.gov/naics

1997 NAICS code	1997 NAICS U.S. description	1987 SIC code	1987 U.S. SIC description
		*4959	Sanitary Services, NEC (vacuuming of runways)
48819	Other Support Activities for Air Transportation	*4581	Airports, Flying Fields, and Airport Terminal Services (aircraft servicing and repairing)
4882	Support Activities for Rail Transportation		
48821	Support Activities for Rail Transportation	*4013	Railroad Switching and Terminal Establishments (all but short line railroads)
		*4741	Rental of Railroad Cars (grain leveling in railroad cars, grain trimming for railroad equipment, precooling of fruits and vegetables in connection with transportation, and railroad car cleaning, icing, ventilating, and heating)
		*4789	Transportation Services, NEC (car loading and unloading; cleaning of railroad ballasts; dining, parlor, sleeping, and other car operations; and railroad maintenance)
4883	Support Activities for Water Transportation		
48831	Port and Harbor Operations	*4491	Marine Cargo Handling (dock and pier operations)
		*4499	Water Transportation Services, NEC (lighthouse and canal operations)
48832	Marine Cargo Handling	*4491	Marine Cargo Handling (all but dock and pier operations)
48833	Navigational Services to Shipping	*4492	Towing and Tugboat Services
		*4499	Water Transportation Services, NEC (piloting vessels in and out of harbors and marine salvage)
48839	Other Support Activities for Water Transportation	*3731	Ship Building and Repairing (floating dry docks not associated with a shipyard)

US—United States industry only. CAN—United States and Canadian industries are comparable. When neither US nor CAN appears, Canadian, Mexican, and United States are comparable. *—Part of; NEC—Not Elsewhere Classified.

http://www.ntis.gov/naics

1997 NAICS code	1997 NAICS U.S. description	1987 SIC code	1987 U.S. SIC description
		*4499	Water Transportation Services, NEC (all but lighthouse operations, piloting vessels in and out of harbors, boat and ship rental, marine salvage, and canal operations)
		*4785	Fixed Facilities and Inspection and Weighing Services for Motor Vehicle Transportation (marine cargo checkers)
		*7699	Repair Shops and Related Services, NEC (ship scaling)
4884	Support Activities for Road Transportation		
48841	Motor Vehicle Towing	*7549	Automotive Services, Except Repair and Carwashes (towing)
48849	Other Support Activities for Road Transportation	4173	Terminal and Service Facilities for Motor Vehicle Passenger Transportation
		4231	Terminal and Joint Terminal Maintenance Facilities for Motor Freight Transportation
		*4785	Fixed Facilities and Inspection and Weighing Services for Motor Vehicle Transportation (all but marine cargo checkers)
4885	Freight Transportation Arrangement		
48851	Freight Transportation Arrangement	*4731	Arrangement of Transportation of Freight and Cargo (except freight rate auditors and tariff consultants)
4889	Other Support Activities for Transportation		
48899	Other Support Activities for Transportation		
US 488991	Packing and Crating	4783	Packing and Crating
US 488999	All Other Support Activities for Transportation	*4729	Arrangement of Passenger Transportation, NEC (arrangement of carpools and vanpools)
		*4789	Transportation Services, NEC (pipeline terminals and stockyards for transportation)

US—United States industry only. CAN—United States and Canadian industries are comparable. When neither US nor CAN appears, Canadian, Mexican, and United States are comparable. *—Part of; NEC—Not Elsewhere Classified.

http://www.ntis.gov/naics

1997 NAICS code	1997 NAICS U.S. description	1987 SIC code	1987 U.S. SIC description
491	Postal Service		
4911	Postal Service		
49111	Postal Service	4311	United States Postal Service
		*7389	Business Services, NEC (post office contract stations)
492	Couriers and Messengers		
4921	Couriers		
49211	Couriers	*4215	Courier Services, Except by Air (hub and spoke intercity delivery)
		4513	Air Courier Services
4922	Local Messengers and Local Delivery		
49221	Local Messengers and Local Delivery	*4215	Courier Services, Except by Air (local delivery)
493	Warehousing and Storage		
4931	Warehousing and Storage		
49311	General Warehousing and Storage	*4225	General Warehousing and Storage (all but self-storage mini-warehouse warehousing)
		*4226	Special Warehousing and Storage, NEC (warehousing in foreign trade zones)
49312	Refrigerated Warehousing and Storage	4222	Refrigerated Warehousing and Storage
		*4226	Special Warehousing and Storage, NEC (fur storage)
49313	Farm Product Warehousing and Storage	4221	Farm Product Warehousing and Storage
49319	Other Warehousing and Storage	*4226	Special Warehousing and Storage, NEC (all but fur storage and warehousing in foreign trade zones)
51	Information		
511	Publishing Industries		
5111	Newspaper, Periodical, Book, and Database Publishers		
51111	Newspaper Publishers	2711	Newspapers: Publishing, or Publishing and Printing
51112	Periodical Publishers	2721	Periodicals: Publishing, or Publishing and Printing
		*2741	Miscellaneous Publishing (shopping news)

US—United States industry only. CAN—United States and Canadian industries are comparable. When neither US nor CAN appears, Canadian, Mexican, and United States are comparable. *—Part of; NEC—Not Elsewhere Classified.

http://www.ntis.gov/naics

1997 NAICS code	1997 NAICS U.S. description	1987 SIC code	1987 U.S. SIC description
51113	Book Publishers	*2731	Books: Publishing, or Publishing and Printing (except music books)
		*2741	Miscellaneous Publishing (technical manuals and books)
51114	Database and Directory Publishers	*2741	Miscellaneous Publishing (database publishers)
		*7331	Direct Mail Advertising Services (mailing list compilers)
51119	Other Publishers		
US 511191	Greeting Card Publishers	*2771	Greeting Cards (publishing greeting cards)
US 511199	All Other Publishers	*2741	Miscellaneous Publishing (except database, sheet music, shopping news, and technical manuals and book publishing)
5112	Software Publishers		
51121	Software Publishers	*7372	Prepackaged Software (software publishing)
512	Motion Picture and Sound Recording Industries		
5121	Motion Picture and Video Industries		
51211	Motion Picture and Video Production	7812	Motion Picture and Video Tape Production
51212	Motion Picture and Video Distribution	*7822	Motion Picture and Video Tape Distribution (except video tape and cassette wholesalers)
		*7829	Services Allied to Motion Picture Distribution (commercial distribution film libraries)
51213	Motion Picture and Video Exhibition		
US 512131	Motion Picture Theaters (except Drive-Ins)	7832	Motion Picture Theaters, Except Drive-In
US 512132	Drive-In Motion Picture Theaters	7833	Drive-In Motion Picture Theaters
51219	Postproduction and Other Motion Picture and Video Industries		

US—United States industry only. CAN—United States and Canadian industries are comparable. When neither US nor CAN appears, Canadian, Mexican, and United States are comparable. *—Part of; NEC—Not Elsewhere Classified.

http://www.ntis.gov/naics

1997 NAICS code	1997 NAICS U.S. description	1987 SIC code	1987 U.S. SIC description
US 512191	Teleproduction and Other Postproduction Services	*7819	Services Allied to Motion Picture Production (teleproduction and postproduction services)
US 512199	Other Motion Picture and Video Industries	*7819	Services Allied to Motion Picture Production (except casting bureaus, wardrobe and equipment rental, talent payment services, teleproduction and other postproduction services, reproduction of videos, and film distributors and other related motion picture production services)
		*7829	Services Allied to Motion Picture Distribution (booking agencies)
5122	Sound Recording Industries		
51221	Record Production	*8999	Services, NEC (record production)
51222	Integrated Record Production/Distribution	*3652	Phonograph Records and Prerecorded Audio Tapes and Disks (integrated record companies, except duplication only)
51223	Music Publishers	*2731	Books: Publishing, or Publishing and Printing (music books)
		*2741	Miscellaneous Publishing (sheet music publishing)
		*8999	Services, NEC (music publishing)
51224	Sound Recording Studios	*7389	Business Services, NEC (recording studios)
51229	Other Sound Recording Industries	*7389	Business Services, NEC (audio taping services)
		*7922	Theatrical Producers (Except Motion Picture) and Miscellaneous Theatrical Services (producers of radio programs)
513	Broadcasting and Telecommunications		
5131	Radio and Television Broadcasting		

US—United States industry only. CAN—United States and Canadian industries are comparable. When neither US nor CAN appears, Canadian, Mexican, and United States are comparable. *—Part of; NEC—Not Elsewhere Classified.

http://www.ntis.gov/naics

1997 NAICS code	1997 NAICS U.S. description	1987 SIC code	1987 U.S. SIC description
51311	Radio Broadcasting		
US 513111	Radio Networks	*4832	Radio Broadcasting Stations (networks)
US 513112	Radio Stations	*4832	Radio Broadcasting Stations (except networks)
51312	Television Broadcasting	4833	Television Broadcasting Stations
5132	Cable Networks and Program Distribution		
51321	Cable Networks	*4841	Cable and Other Pay Television Services (cable networks)
51322	Cable and Other Program Distribution	*4841	Cable and Other Pay Television Services (except cable networks)
5133	Telecommunications		
51331	Wired Telecommunications Carriers	*4813	Telephone Communications, Except Radiotelephone (except resellers)
		4822	Telegraph and Other Message Communications
51332	Wireless Telecommunications Carriers (except Satellite)		
US 513321	Paging	*4812	Radiotelephone Communications (paging carriers)
US 513322	Cellular and Other Wireless Telecommunications	*4812	Radiotelephone Communications (cellular carriers)
		*4899	Communications Services, NEC (ship-to-shore broadcasting)
51333	Telecommunications Resellers	*4812	Radio Communications (paging and cellular resellers)
		*4813	Telephone Communications, Except Radiotelephone (wired resellers)
51334	Satellite Telecommunications	*4899	Communications Services, NEC (satellite communications)
		*4813	Telephone Communications, Except Radiotelephone (satellite with resellers)
51339	Other Telecommunications	*4899	Communications Services, NEC (except radio dispatch, ship-to-shore, and satellite communications)
514	Information Services and Data Processing Services		

US—United States industry only. CAN—United States and Canadian industries are comparable. When neither US nor CAN appears, Canadian, Mexican, and United States are comparable. *—Part of; NEC—Not Elsewhere Classified.

http://www.ntis.gov/naics

1997 NAICS code	1997 NAICS U.S. description	1987 SIC code	1987 U.S. SIC description
5141	Information Services		
51411	News Syndicates	*7383	News Syndicates (except independent news correspondents)
51412	Libraries and Archives	8231	Libraries
		*7829	Services Allied to Motion Picture Distribution (film archives)
51419	Other Information Services		
CAN 514191	On-Line Information Services	7375	Information Retrieval Services
CAN 514199	All Other Information Services	*8999	Services, NEC (miscellaneous information providers)
		*7389	Business Services, NEC (stock photo agencies, press clipping services)
5142	Data Processing Services		
51421	Data Processing Services	7374	Computer Processing and Data Preparation and Processing Services
		*7379	Computer Related Services, NEC (disk and diskette conversion and recertification)
		*7389	Business Services, NEC (microfilm services)
52	Finance and Insurance		
521	Monetary Authorities—Central Bank		
5211	Monetary Authorities—Central Bank		
CAN 52111	Monetary Authorities— Central Bank	6011	Federal Reserve Banks
522	Credit Intermediation and Related Activities		
CAN 5221	Depository Credit Intermediation		
CAN 52211	Commercial Banking	*6021	National Commercial Banks (banking)
		*6022	State Commercial Banks (commercial banking)
		6029	Commercial Banks, NEC
		*6081	Branches and Agencies of Foreign Banks (branches)

US—United States industry only. CAN—United States and Canadian industries are comparable. When neither US nor CAN appears, Canadian, Mexican, and United States are comparable. *—Part of; NEC—Not Elsewhere Classified.

http://www.ntis.gov/naics

1997 NAICS code	1997 NAICS U.S. description	1987 SIC code	1987 U.S. SIC description
US 52212	Savings Institutions	6035	Savings Institutions, Federally Chartered
		6036	Savings Institutions, Not Federally Chartered
CAN 52213	Credit Unions	6061	Credit Unions, Federally Chartered
		6062	Credit Unions, Not Federally Chartered
CAN 52219	Other Depository Credit Intermediation	*6022	State Commercial Banks (private and industrial banking)
CAN 5222	Nondepository Credit Intermediation		
CAN 52221	Credit Card Issuing	*6021	National Commercial Banks (credit card issuing)
		*6022	State Commercial Banks (credit card issuing)
		*6141	Personal Credit Institutions (credit card issuing)
		*6153	Short-Term Business Credit Institutions, Except Agricultural (credit card issuing)
CAN 52222	Sales Financing	*6141	Personal Credit Institutions (installment sales finance)
		*6153	Short Term Business Credit Institutions, Except Agricultural (business sales finance).
		*6159	Miscellaneous Business Credit Institutions (finance leasing combined with sales financing)
CAN 52229	Other Nondepository Credit Intermediation		
CAN 522291	Consumer Lending	*6141	Personal Credit Institutions (except installment sales finance and credit card issuing)
US 522292	Real Estate Credit	*6111	Foreign Trade and International Banking Institutions (Federal Land Banks)
		*6162	Mortgage Bankers and Loan Correspondents (mortgage bankers and originators)
		*6159	Miscellaneous Business Credit Institutions (farm mortgage companies)

US—United States industry only. CAN—United States and Canadian industries are comparable. When neither US nor CAN appears, Canadian, Mexican, and United States are comparable. *—Part of; NEC—Not Elsewhere Classified.

http://www.ntis.gov/naics

1997 NAICS code	1997 NAICS U.S. description	1987 SIC code	1987 U.S. SIC description
US 522293	International Trade Financing	*6081	Branches and Agencies of Foreign Banks (international trade financing)
		*6082	Foreign Trade and International Banking Institutions (international trade financing)
		*6111	Federal and Federally-Sponsored Credit Agencies (trade banks)
		*6159	Miscellaneous Business Credit Institutions (trade banks)
US 522294	Secondary Market Financing	*6111	Federal and Federally Sponsored Credit Agencies (secondary market financing)
		*6159	Miscellaneous Business Credit Institutions (secondary market financing)
US 522298	All Other Nondepository Credit Intermediation	*5932	Used Merchandise Stores (pawnshops)
		6019	Central Reserve Depository Institutions, NEC
		*6081	Branches and Agencies of Foreign Banks (agencies, except international trade financing)
		*6082	Foreign Trade and International Banking Institutions (except international trade financing)
		*6111	Federal and Federally-Sponsored Credit Agencies (except trade banks, secondary market financing and Federal Land Banks)
		*6141	Personal Credit Institutions (industrial nondeposit banks)
		*6159	Miscellaneous Business Credit Institutions (except trade banks, farm mortgage companies, secondary market, financing, and finance leasing)
CAN 5223	Activities Related to Credit Intermediation		
CAN 52231	Mortgage and Nonmortgage Loan Brokers	6163	Loan Brokers

---

US—United States industry only. CAN—United States and Canadian industries are comparable. When neither US nor CAN appears, Canadian, Mexican, and United States are comparable. *—Part of; NEC—Not Elsewhere Classified.

http://www.ntis.gov/naics

1997 NAICS code	1997 NAICS U.S. description	1987 SIC code	1987 U.S. SIC description
CAN 52232	Financial Transactions Processing, Reserve, and Clearinghouse Activities	*6099	Functions Related to Depository Banking, NEC (electronic funds transfer networks and clearinghouse associations)
		*6153	Short-Term Business Credit Institutions, Except Agricultural (credit card service)
		*7389	Business Services, NEC (credit card and validation service)
CAN 52239	Other Activities Related to Credit Intermediation	*6099	Functions Related to Depository Banking, NEC (except electronic funds transfer networks and clearinghouses, foreign currency exchanges, escrow and fiduciary agencies and deposit brokers)
		*6162	Mortgage Bankers and Loan Correspondents (mortgage servicing)
523	Securities, Commodity Contracts, and Other Financial Investments and Related Activities		
5231	Securities and Commodity Contracts Intermediation and Brokerage		
CAN 52311	Investment Banking and Securities Dealing	*6211	Security Brokers, Dealers, and Flotation Companies (security dealers and underwriters)
CAN 52312	Securities Brokerage	*6211	Security Brokers, Dealers, and Flotation Companies (security brokers)
CAN 52313	Commodity Contracts Dealing	*6099	Functions Related to Depository Banking, NEC (foreign currency exchange)
		*6799	Investors, NEC (commodity contract trading companies)
		*6221	Commodity Contracts Brokers and Dealers (commodity dealers)
CAN 52314	Commodity Contracts Brokerage	*6221	Commodity Contracts Brokers and Dealers (commodity brokers)
5232	Securities and Commodity Exchanges		
52321	Securities and Commodity Exchanges	6231	Security and Commodity Exchanges

US—United States industry only. CAN—United States and Canadian industries are comparable. When neither US nor CAN appears, Canadian, Mexican, and United States are comparable. *—Part of; NEC—Not Elsewhere Classified.

http://www.ntis.gov/naics

1997 NAICS code	1997 NAICS U.S. description	1987 SIC code	1987 U.S. SIC description
5239	Other Financial Investment Activities		
CAN 52391	Miscellaneous Intermediation	*6211	Security Brokers, Dealers, and Flotation Companies (except security and commodity dealers and security brokers and oil and gas lease brokers)
		*6153	Short-Term Business Credit Institutions, Except Agricultural (except credit card service and issuing and business sales finance)
		*6792	Oil Royalty Traders (investing on own account)
		*6799	Investors, NEC (venture capital companies, investment clubs, and speculators for own account)
CAN 52392	Portfolio Management	*6282	Investment Advice (portfolio managers)
		*6371	Pension, Health, and Welfare Funds (managers)
		*6733	Trust, Except Educational, Religious, and Charitable (managers)
		*6799	Investors, NEC (commodity contract pool operators)
CAN 52393	Investment Advice	*6282	Investment Advice (except portfolio managers)
CAN 52399	All Other Financial Investment Activities		
US 523991	Trust, Fiduciary, and Custody Activities	6091	Nondeposit Trust Facilities
		*6099	Functions Related to Depository Banking, NEC (escrow and fiduciary agencies)
		*6289	Services Allied With the Exchange of Securities or Commodities, NEC (security custodians)
		*6733	Trusts, Except Educational, Religious, and Charitable (administrators of private estates)

US—United States industry only. CAN—United States and Canadian industries are comparable. When neither US nor CAN appears, Canadian, Mexican, and United States are comparable. *—Part of; NEC—Not Elsewhere Classified.

http://www.ntis.gov/naics

	1997 NAICS code	1997 NAICS U.S. description	1987 SIC code	1987 U.S. SIC description
US	523999	Miscellaneous Financial Investment Activities	*6211	Security Brokers, Dealers, and Flotation Companies (oil and gas lease brokers' offices)
			*6289	Services Allied With the Exchange of Securities or Commodities, NEC (except security custodians)
	524	Insurance Carriers and Related Activities		
	5241	Insurance Carriers		
CAN	52411	Direct Life, Health, and Medical Insurance Carriers		
US	524113	Direct Life Insurance Carriers	*6311	Life Insurance (life insurers-direct)
			*6321	Accident and Health Insurance (disability insurers-direct)
US	524114	Direct Health and Medical Insurance Carriers	*6324	Hospital and Medical Service Plans (health and medical insurers-direct)
			*6321	Accident and Health Insurance (health and medical insurers-direct)
CAN	52412	Direct Insurance (except Life, Health, and Medical) Carriers		
US	524126	Direct Property and Casualty Insurance Carriers	*6331	Fire, Marine, and Casualty Insurance (fire, marine, and casualty insurers-direct, except contact lens insurance)
			*6351	Surety Insurance (financial responsibility insurers-direct)
US	524127	Direct Title Insurance Carriers	*6361	Title Insurance (title insurers-direct)
US	524128	Other Direct Insurance (except Life, Health, and Medical) Carriers	*6331	Fire, Marine, and Casualty Insurance (contact lens insurance)
			6399	Insurance Carriers, NEC
CAN	52413	Reinsurance Carriers	*6311	Life Insurance (reinsurers)
			*6321	Accident and Health Insurance (reinsurers)
			*6324	Hospital and Medical Service Plans (reinsurers)

US—United States industry only. CAN—United States and Canadian industries are comparable. When neither US nor CAN appears, Canadian, Mexican, and United States are comparable. *—Part of; NEC—Not Elsewhere Classified.

http://www.ntis.gov/naics

1997 NAICS code	1997 NAICS U.S. description	1987 SIC code	1987 U.S. SIC description
		*6331	Fire, Marine, and Casualty Insurance (reinsurers)
		*6351	Surety Insurance (reinsurers)
		*6361	Title Insurance (reinsurers)
5242	Agencies, Brokerages, and Other Insurance Related Activities		
CAN 52421	Insurance Agencies and Brokerages	*6411	Insurance Agents, Brokers, and Service (insurance agents and brokers)
CAN 52429	Other Insurance Related Activities		
CAN 524291	Claims Adjusting	*6411	Insurance Agents, Brokers, and Service (insurance claims adjusters)
US 524292	Third Party Administration of Insurance and Pension Funds	*6371	Pension, Health, and Welfare Funds (administrators)
		*6411	Insurance Agents, Brokers, and Service (processors)
US 524298	All Other Insurance Related Activities	*6411	Insurance Agents, Brokers, and Service (except processors, agents and brokers, and claims adjusters)
US 525	Funds, Trusts, and Other Financial Vehicles		
US 5251	Insurance and Employee Benefit Funds		
US 52511	Pension Funds	*6371	Pension, Health, and Welfare Funds (pension funds)
US 52512	Health and Welfare Funds	*6371	Pension, Health, and Welfare Funds (health and welfare funds)
US 52519	Other Insurance Funds	*6321	Accident and Health Insurance (self insurers)
		*6324	Hospital and Medical Service Plans (self insurers)
		*6331	Fire, Marine, and Casualty Insurance (self insurers)
		*6733	Trusts, Except Educational, Religious, and Charitable (vacation funds for employees)

US—United States industry only. CAN—United States and Canadian industries are comparable. When neither US nor CAN appears, Canadian, Mexican, and United States are comparable. *—Part of; NEC—Not Elsewhere Classified.

http://www.ntis.gov/naics

1997 NAICS code	1997 NAICS U.S. description	1987 SIC code	1987 U.S. SIC description
US 5259	Other Investment Pools and Funds		
US 52591	Open-End Investment Funds	6722	Management Investment Offices, Open-End
US 52592	Trusts, Estates, and Agency Accounts	*6733	Trusts, Except Educational, Religious, and Charitable (personal trusts, estates, and agency accounts)
US 52593	Real Estate Investment Trusts	6798	Real Estate Investment Trusts
US 52599	Other Financial Vehicles	*6371	Pension, Health, and Welfare Funds (profit sharing funds)
		6726	Unit Investment Trusts, Face-Amount Certificate Offices, and Closed-End Management Investment Offices
53	Real Estate and Rental and Leasing		
531	Real Estate		
5311	Lessors of Real Estate		
CAN 53111	Lessors of Residential Buildings and Dwellings	6513	Operators of Apartment Buildings
		6514	Operators of Dwellings Other Than Apartment Buildings
CAN 53112	Lessors of Nonresidential Buildings (except Miniwarehouses)	*6512	Operators of Nonresidential Buildings (other except stadium and arena owners)
CAN 53113	Lessors of Miniwarehouses and Self-Storage Units	*4225	General Warehousing and Storage (miniwarehouses and self-storage units)
CAN 53119	Lessors of Other Real Estate Property	6515	Operators of Residential Mobile Home Sites
		6517	Lessors of Railroad Property
		6519	Lessors of Real Property, NEC
5312	Offices of Real Estate Agents and Brokers		
53121	Offices of Real Estate Agents and Brokers	*6531	Real Estate Agents Managers (agents and brokers)
5313	Activities Related to Real Estate		
CAN 53131	Real Estate Property Managers		

US—United States industry only. CAN—United States and Canadian industries are comparable. When neither US nor CAN appears, Canadian, Mexican, and United States are comparable. *—Part of; NEC—Not Elsewhere Classified.

http://www.ntis.gov/naics

	1997 NAICS code	1997 NAICS U.S. description	1987 SIC code	1987 U.S. SIC description
US	531311	Residential Property Managers	*6531	Real Estate Agents and Managers (managers-residential, real estate)
US	531312	Nonresidential Property Managers	*6531	Real Estate Agents and Managers (managers-nonresidential, real estate)
CAN	53132	Offices of Real Estate Appraisers	*6531	Real Estate Agents and Managers (appraisers)
CAN	53139	Other Activities Related to Real Estate	*6531	Real Estate Agents and Managers (except real estate managers, condominium management, cemetery management, agents and brokers, and appraisers)
	532	Rental and Leasing Services		
	5321	Automotive Equipment Rental and Leasing		
	53211	Passenger Car Rental and Leasing		
CAN	532111	Passenger Car Rental	7514	Passenger Car Rental
CAN	532112	Passenger Car Leasing	7515	Passenger Car Leasing
	53212	Truck, Utility Trailer, and RV (Recreational Vehicle) Rental and Leasing	7513	Truck Rental and Leasing Without Drivers
			7519	Utility Trailers and Recreational Vehicle Rental
	5322	Consumer Goods Rental		
	53221	Consumer Electronics and Appliances Rental	*7359	Equipment Rental and Leasing, NEC (appliances, TV, VCR, and electronic equipment rental)
	53222	Formal Wear and Costume Rental	*7299	Miscellaneous Personal Services, NEC (formal wear and costume rental)
			*7819	Services Allied to Motion Picture Production (wardrobe rental for motion picture film production)
	53223	Video Tape and Disc Rental	7841	Video Tape Rental
	53229	Other Consumer Goods Rental		
US	532291	Home Health Equipment Rental	*7352	Medical Equipment Rental and Leasing (home health furniture and equipment rental and leasing)
US	532292	Recreational Goods Rental	*7999	Amusement and Recreation Services, NEC (canoe, pleasure boats, bicycles, motorcycles, moped, go carts, etc. rental)

US—United States industry only. CAN—United States and Canadian industries are comparable. When neither US nor CAN appears, Canadian, Mexican, and United States are comparable. *—Part of; NEC—Not Elsewhere Classified.

http://www.ntis.gov/naics

1997 NAICS code	1997 NAICS U.S. description	1987 SIC code	1987 U.S. SIC description
US 532299	All Other Consumer Goods Rental	*7359	Equipment Rental and Leasing, NEC (except transportation equipment, industrial equipment, and consumer electronics, appliances, and home and garden equipment)
5323	General Rental Centers		
53231	General Rental Centers	*7359	Equipment Rental and Leasing, NEC (general rental centers)
5324	Commercial and Industrial Machinery and Equipment Rental and Leasing		
53241	Construction, Transportation, Mining, and Forestry Machinery and Equipment Rental and Leasing		
US 532411	Commercial Air, Rail, and Water Transportation Equipment Rental and Leasing	*4499	Water Transportation Services, NEC (boat and ship rental, commercial)
		*4741	Rental of Railroad Cars (rental of railroad cars)
		*7359	Equipment Rental and Leasing, NEC (aircraft rental and leasing)
US 532412	Construction, Mining, and Forestry Machinery and Equipment Rental and Leasing	*7353	Heavy Construction Equipment Rental and Leasing (without operators)
		*7359	Equipment Rental and Leasing, NEC (oil field and well drilling equipment)
53242	Office Machinery and Equipment Rental and Leasing	*7359	Equipment Rental and Leasing (office machine rental and leasing)
		7377	Computer Rental and Leasing
53249	Other Commercial and Industrial Machinery and Equipment Rental and Leasing	*7352	Medical Equipment Rental and Leasing (medical machinery and equipment)
		*7359	Equipment Rental and Leasing, NEC (industrial truck and equipment rental and leasing)

US—United States industry only. CAN—United States and Canadian industries are comparable. When neither US nor CAN appears, Canadian, Mexican, and United States are comparable. *—Part of; NEC—Not Elsewhere Classified.

http://www.ntis.gov/naics

1997 NAICS code	1997 NAICS U.S. description	1987 SIC code	1987 U.S. SIC description
		*7819	Services Allied to Motion Picture Production (motion picture equipment rental)
		*7922	Theatrical Producers (Except Motion Picture) and Miscellaneous Theatrical Services (theatrical equipment rental)
533	Lessors of Nonfinancial Intangible Assets (except Copyrighted Works)		
5331	Lessors of Nonfinancial Intangible Assets (except Copyrighted Works)		
53311	Lessors of Nonfinancial Intangible Assets (except Copyrighted Works)	*6792	Oil Royalty Traders (except investors on own account)
		6794	Patent Owners and Lessors
54	Professional, Scientific, and Technical Services		
541	Professional, Scientific, and Technical Services		
5411	Legal Services		
54111	Offices of Lawyers	8111	Legal Services
54112	Offices of Notaries		Null Set for U.S.
54119	Other Legal Services		
US 541191	Title Abstract and Settlement Offices	6541	Title Abstract Offices
US 541199	All Other Legal Services	*7389	Business Services, NEC (process services, patent agents, notaries public, paralegal services)
5412	Accounting, Tax Preparation, Bookkeeping, and Payroll Services		
54121	Accounting, Tax Preparation, Bookkeeping, and Payroll Services		
US 541211	Offices of Certified Public Accountants	*8721	Accounting, Auditing, and Bookkeeping Services (auditing accountants)
CAN 541213	Tax Preparation Services	7291	Tax Return Preparation Services
US 541214	Payroll Services	*7819	Services Allied to Motion Picture Production (talent payment services)

US—United States industry only. CAN—United States and Canadian industries are comparable. When neither US nor CAN appears, Canadian, Mexican, and United States are comparable. *—Part of; NEC—Not Elsewhere Classified.

http://www.ntis.gov/naics

1997 NAICS code	1997 NAICS U.S. description	1987 SIC code	1987 U.S. SIC description
		*8721	Accounting, Auditing, and Bookkeeping Services (payroll services)
US 541219	Other Accounting Services	*8721	Accounting, Auditing, and Bookkeeping Services (other accounting services)
5413	Architectural, Engineering, and Related Services		
54131	Architectural Services	8712	Architectural Services
54132	Landscape Architectural Services	*0781	Landscape Counseling and Planning (except horticultural consulting)
		*8748	Business Consulting Services, NEC (urban planners and industrial development organizations)
54133	Engineering Services	8711	Engineering Services
		*8748	Business Consulting Services, NEC (traffic engineering consulting)
54134	Drafting Services	*7389	Business Services, NEC (drafting service)
54135	Building Inspection Services	*7389	Business Services, NEC (home and building inspection services)
54136	Geophysical Surveying and Mapping Services	*8713	Surveying Services (geophysical surveying)
		*1081	Metal Mining Services (geophysical surveying and mapping)
		*1382	Oil and Gas Field Exploration Services (geophysical surveying and mapping)
		*1481	Nonmetallic Minerals Services, Except Fuels (geophysical surveying and mapping)
54137	Surveying and Mapping (except Geophysical) Services	*7389	Business Services, NEC (map making services)
		*8713	Surveying Services (except geophysical surveying)
54138	Testing Laboratories	*8734	Testing Laboratories (except veterinary testing laboratories)

US—United States industry only. CAN—United States and Canadian industries are comparable. When neither US nor CAN appears, Canadian, Mexican, and United States are comparable. *—Part of; NEC—Not Elsewhere Classified.

http://www.ntis.gov/naics

	1997 NAICS code	1997 NAICS U.S. description	1987 SIC code	1987 U.S. SIC description
	5414	Specialized Design Services		
	54141	Interior Design Services	*7389	Business Services, NEC (interior design)
	54142	Industrial Design Services	*7389	Business Services, NEC (industrial design)
	54143	Graphic Design Services	7336	Commercial Art and Graphic Design
			*8099	Health and Allied Services, NEC (medical artists)
	54149	Other Specialized Design Services	*7389	Business Services, NEC (fashion and other design services)
	5415	Computer Systems Design and Related Services		
	54151	Computer Systems Design and Related Services		
US	541511	Custom Computer Programming Services	7371	Computer Programming Services
US	541512	Computer Systems Design Services	7373	Computer Integrated Systems Design
			*7379	Computer Related Services, NEC (computer systems consultants)
US	541513	Computer Facilities Management Services	7376	Computer Facilities Management Services
US	541519	Other Computer Related Services	*7379	Computer Related Services, NEC (except computer systems consultants and disk and diskette conversion and recertification)
	5416	Management, Scientific, and Technical Consulting Services		
	54161	Management Consulting Services		
CAN	541611	Administrative Management and General Management Consulting Services	*8742	Management Consulting Services (administrative management and general management consulting)
CAN	541612	Human Resources and Executive Search Consulting Services	*8742	Management Consulting Services (human resources and personnel management consulting)
			*7361	Employment Agencies (executive placement services)
			*8999	Services, NEC (actuarial consulting)

US—United States industry only. CAN—United States and Canadian industries are comparable. When neither US nor CAN appears, Canadian, Mexican, and United States are comparable. *—Part of; NEC—Not Elsewhere Classified.

http://www.ntis.gov/naics

1997 NAICS code	1997 NAICS U.S. description	1987 SIC code	1987 U.S. SIC description
us 541613	Marketing Consulting Services	*8742	Management Consulting Services (marketing consulting)
us 541614	Process, Physical Distribution, and Logistics Consulting Services	*8742	Management Consulting Services (manufacturing management, physical distribution, and site location consulting)
		*4731	Arrangement of Transportation of Freight and Cargo (freight rate-auditors and tariff consulting)
us 541618	Other Management Consulting Services	*8748	Business Consulting Services, NEC (except educational testing and consulting, economic consulting, safety and security, agriculture consulting, urban planning and industrial development organizations)
54162	Environmental Consulting Services	*8999	Services, NEC (environmental consultants)
54169	Other Scientific and Technical Consulting Services	*0781	Landscape Counseling and Planning (horticulture consulting)
		*8748	Business Consulting Services, NEC (safety, security, agriculture, and economic, consultants)
		*8999	Services, NEC (scientific and related consulting services)
5417	Scientific Research and Development Services		
54171	Research and Development in the Physical, Engineering, and Life Sciences	*3721	Aircraft (research and development)
		*3724	Aircraft Engines and Engine Parts (research and development)
		*3728	Aircraft Parts and Auxiliary Equipment, NEC (research and development)
		*3761	Guided missiles and Space Vehicles (research and development)
		*3764	Guided missile and Space Vehicle Propulsion Units and Propulsion Unit Parts (research and development)

US—United States industry only. CAN—United States and Canadian industries are comparable. When neither US nor CAN appears, Canadian, Mexican, and United States are comparable. *—Part of; NEC—Not Elsewhere Classified.

http://www.ntis.gov/naics

1997 NAICS code	1997 NAICS U.S. description	1987 SIC code	1987 U.S. SIC description
		*3769	Guided Missile Space Vehicle Parts and Auxiliary Equipment, NEC (research and development)
		8731	Commercial Physical and Biological Research
		*8733	Noncommercial Research Organizations (physical, engineering and life sciences)
54172	Research and Development in the Social Sciences and Humanities	*8732	Commercial Economic, Sociological, and Educational Research (social sciences and humanities)
		*8733	Noncommercial Research Organizations (social sciences and humanities)
5418	Advertising and Related Services		
54181	Advertising Agencies	7311	Advertising Agencies
54182	Public Relations Agencies	8743	Public Relations Services
54183	Media Buying Agencies	*7319	Advertising, NEC (media buying services)
54184	Media Representatives	7313	Radio, Television, and Publishers' Advertising Representatives
54185	Display Advertising	7312	Outdoor Advertising Services
		*7319	Advertising, NEC (display advertising, except outdoor)
54186	Direct Mail Advertising	*7331	Direct Mail Advertising Services (except mailing list compilers)
54187	Advertising Material Distribution Services	*7319	Advertising, NEC (advertising materials distributor)
		*7389	Business Services, NEC (distribution of telephone directories on a fee or contract basis)
54189	Other Services Related to Advertising	*7319	Advertising, NEC (except media buying, display advertising, except outdoor; and advertising material distributors)
		*5199	Nondurable Goods, NEC (advertising specialities goods distributors)

US—United States industry only. CAN—United States and Canadian industries are comparable. When neither US nor CAN appears, Canadian, Mexican, and United States are comparable. *—Part of; NEC—Not Elsewhere Classified.

http://www.ntis.gov/naics

1997 NAICS code	1997 NAICS U.S. description	1987 SIC code	1987 U.S. SIC description
		*7389	Business Services, NEC (sign painting and lettering, showcard painting, mannequin decorating service and other advertising related business services)
5419	Other Professional, Scientific, and Technical Services		
54191	Marketing Research and Public Opinion Polling	*8732	Commercial Economic, Sociological, and Educational Research (market research and opinion research)
54192	Photographic Services		
US 541921	Photography Studios, Portrait	7221	Photographic Studios, Portrait
US 541922	Commercial Photography	*7335	Commercial Photography (except when combined with a variety of aircraft based services)
		*8099	Health and Allied Services, NEC (medical photography)
54193	Translation and Interpretation Services	*7389	Business Services, NEC (translation and interpretation services)
54194	Veterinary Services	0741	Veterinary Services for Livestock
		0742	Veterinary Services for Animal Specialties
		*8734	Testing Laboratories (veterinary testing laboratories)
54199	All Other Professional, Scientific, and Technical Services	*7389	Business Services (appraisers, except insurance and real estate, and miscellaneous professional, scientific, and technical services)
55	Management of Companies and Enterprises		
551	Management of Companies and Enterprises		
5511	Management of Companies and Enterprises		
55111	Management of Companies and Enterprises		
US 551111	Offices of Bank Holding Companies	6712	Offices of Bank Holding Companies

http://www.ntis.gov/naics

1997 NAICS code	1997 NAICS U.S. description	1987 SIC code	1987 U.S. SIC description
US 551112	Offices of Other Holding Companies	6719	Offices of Holding Companies, NEC
CAN 551114	Corporate, Subsidiary, and Regional Managing Offices		These establishments were included as auxiliaries in the 1987 Standard Industrial Classification
56	Administrative and Support and Waste Management and Remediation Services		
561	Administrative and Support Services		
5611	Office Administrative Services		
56111	Office Administrative Services	*8741	Management Services (except construction management)
5612	Facilities Support Services		
56121	Facilities Support Services	8744	Facilities Support Management Services
5613	Employment Services		
56131	Employment Placement Agencies	*7299	Miscellaneous Personal Services, NEC (babysitting bureaus)
		*7361	Employment Agencies (except executive placing services)
		*7819	Services Allied to Motion Picture Production (casting bureaus)
		*7922	Theatrical Producers and Miscellaneous Theatrical Services (casting agencies)
56132	Temporary Help Services	*7363	Help Supply Services (except employee leasing service)
56133	Employee Leasing Services	*7363	Help Supply Services (except temporary help service)
5614	Business Support Services		
56141	Document Preparation Services	*7338	Secretarial and Court Reporting (except court reporting)
56142	Telephone Call Centers		
US 561421	Telephone Answering Services	*7389	Business Services, NEC (telephone answering)
US 561422	Telemarketing Bureaus	*7389	Business Services, NEC (telemarketing bureaus and telephone soliciting)

US—United States industry only. CAN—United States and Canadian industries are comparable. When neither US nor CAN appears, Canadian, Mexican, and United States are comparable. *—Part of; NEC—Not Elsewhere Classified.

http://www.ntis.gov/naics

1997 NAICS code	1997 NAICS U.S. description	1987 SIC code	1987 U.S. SIC description
56143	Business Service Centers		
US 561431	Private Mail Centers	*7389	Business Services, NEC (private mail centers and mailbox rental)
US 561439	Other Business Service Centers (including Copy Shops)	*7334	Photocopying and Duplicating Services (except instant printing)
		*7389	Business Services, NEC (other business service centers, except private mail centers and mailbox rental)
56144	Collection Agencies	7322	Adjustment and Collection Services
56145	Credit Bureaus	7323	Credit Reporting Services
56149	Other Business Support Services		
US 561491	Repossession Services	*7389	Business Services, NEC (recovery and repossession services)
US 561492	Court Reporting and Stenotype Services	*7338	Secretarial and Court Reporting (except secretarial)
US 561499	All Other Business Support Services	*7389	Business Services, NEC (business support services except telephone answering, telemarketing bureaus, private mail centers and repossession services)
5615	Travel Arrangement and Reservation Services		
56151	Travel Agencies	4724	Travel Agencies
56152	Tour Operators	4725	Tour Operators
56159	Other Travel Arrangement and Reservation Services		
US 561591	Convention and Visitors Bureaus	*7389	Business Services, NEC (convention and visitors bureaus, tourist information bureaus)
US 561599	All Other Travel Arrangement and Reservation Services	*4729	Arrangement of Passenger Transportation, NEC (except arrangement of vanpools and carpools)
		*7389	Business Services, NEC (reservation systems: hotel & restaurants and time-share condominium exchange)

US—United States industry only. CAN—United States and Canadian industries are comparable. When neither US nor CAN appears, Canadian, Mexican, and United States are comparable. *—Part of; NEC—Not Elsewhere Classified.

http://www.ntis.gov/naics

1997 NAICS code	1997 NAICS U.S. description	1987 SIC code	1987 U.S. SIC description
		*7999	Amusement and Recreation Services, NEC (ticket agencies)
		*8699	Membership Organizations, NEC (travel motor clubs)
		*7922	Theatrical Producers (except motion pictures) and Miscellaneous Theatrical Services (theatrical ticket agencies)
5616	Investigation and Security Services		
56161	Investigation, Guard, and Armored Car Services		
CAN 561611	Investigation Services	*7381	Detective, Guard, and Armored Car Services (detective services)
CAN 561612	Security Guards and Patrol Services	*7381	Detective, Guard, and Armored Car Services (guard services)
CAN 561613	Armored Car Services	*7381	Detective, Guard, and Armored Car Services (armored car services)
56162	Security Systems Services		
CAN 561621	Security Systems Services (except Locksmiths)	7382	Security Systems Services
CAN 561622	Locksmiths	*7699	Repair Shops and Related Services, NEC (locksmith shops)
5617	Services to Buildings and Dwellings		
56171	Exterminating and Pest Control Services	*4959	Sanitary Services, NEC (mosquito eradication)
		*7342	Disinfecting and Pest Control Services (exterminating and pest control)
56172	Janitorial Services	*7342	Disinfecting and Pest Control Services (except exterminating)
		*7349	Building Cleaning and Maintenance Services, NEC (except lighting maintenance services)
		*4581	Airports, Flying Fields, and Airport Terminal Services (airplane cleaning and janitorial services)

US—United States industry only. CAN—United States and Canadian industries are comparable. When neither US nor CAN appears, Canadian, Mexican, and United States are comparable. *—Part of; NEC—Not Elsewhere Classified.

http://www.ntis.gov/naics

1997 NAICS code	1997 NAICS U.S. description	1987 SIC code	1987 U.S. SIC description
56173	Landscaping Services	0782	Lawn and Garden Services
		0783	Ornamental Shrub and Tree Services
56174	Carpet and Upholstery Cleaning Services	7217	Carpet and Upholstery Cleaning
56179	Other Services to Buildings and Dwellings	*7389	Business Services, NEC (swimming pool cleaning and maintenance)
		*7349	Building Cleaning and Maintenance Services, NEC (lighting maintenance service)
		*7699	Repair Shops and Related Services, NEC (furnace, duct, chimney, gutter, and drain cleaning services)
5619	Other Support Services		
56191	Packaging and Labeling Services	*7389	Business Services, NEC (packaging and labeling services)
56192	Convention and Trade Show Organizers	*7389	Business Services, NEC (convention and trade show services)
56199	All Other Support Services	*7389	Business Services, NEC (other support services except packaging and labeling, convention and trade shows services, convention and visitor bureaus, tourist information bureaus)
562	Waste Management and Remediation Services		
CAN 5621	Waste Collection		
CAN 56211	Waste Collection		
US 562111	Solid Waste Collection	*4212	Local Trucking Without Storage (solid waste collection without disposal)
US 562112	Hazardous Waste Collection	*4212	Local Trucking Without Storage (hazardous waste collection without disposal)
US 562119	Other Waste Collection	*4212	Local Trucking Without Storage (other waste collection without disposal)

US—United States industry only. CAN—United States and Canadian industries are comparable. When neither US nor CAN appears, Canadian, Mexican, and United States are comparable. *—Part of; NEC—Not Elsewhere Classified.

http://www.ntis.gov/naics

1997 NAICS code	1997 NAICS U.S. description	1987 SIC code	1987 U.S. SIC description
CAN 5622	Waste Treatment and Disposal		
CAN 56221	Waste Treatment and Disposal		
US 562211	Hazardous Waste Treatment and Disposal	*4953	Refuse Systems (hazardous waste treatment and disposal)
US 562212	Solid Waste Landfill	*4953	Refuse Systems (solid waste landfills)
US 562213	Solid Waste Combustors and Incinerators	*4953	Refuse Systems (solid waste combustors and incinerators)
US 562219	Other Nonhazardous Waste Treatment and Disposal	*4953	Refuse Systems (other nonhazardous waste treatment and disposal)
CAN 5629	Remediation and Other Waste Management Services		
CAN 56291	Remediation Services	*1799	Special Trade Contractors, NEC (asbestos abatement and lead paint removal contractors)
		*4959	Sanitary Services, NEC (remediation services)
CAN 56292	Materials Recovery Facilities	*4953	Refuse Systems (materials recovery facilities)
CAN 56299	All Other Waste Management Services		
US 562991	Septic Tank and Related Services	*7359	Equipment Rental and Leasing, NEC (portable toilet rental)
		*7699	Repair Shops and Related Services, NEC (cesspool and septic tank cleaning)
US 562998	All Other Miscellaneous Waste Management Services	*4959	Sanitary Services, NEC (all but remediation services, malaria control, mosquito eradication, snowplowing, street sweeping, and airport runway vacuuming)
		*7699	Repair Shops and Related Services, NEC (sewer cleaning and rodding)
61	Educational Services		
611	Educational Services		
6111	Elementary and Secondary Schools		
CAN 61111	Elementary and Secondary Schools	8211	Elementary and Secondary Schools

US—United States industry only. CAN—United States and Canadian industries are comparable. When neither US nor CAN appears, Canadian, Mexican, and United States are comparable. *—Part of; NEC—Not Elsewhere Classified.

http://www.ntis.gov/naics

1997 NAICS code	1997 NAICS U.S. description	1987 SIC code	1987 U.S. SIC description
6112	Junior Colleges		
61121	Junior Colleges	8222	Junior Colleges and Technical Institutes
6113	Colleges, Universities, and Professional Schools		
61131	Colleges, Universities, and Professional Schools	8221	Colleges, Universities, and Professional Schools
6114	Business Schools and Computer and Management Training		
61141	Business and Secretarial Schools	8244	Business and Secretarial Schools
61142	Computer Training	*8243	Data Processing Schools (except computer repair training)
61143	Professional and Management Development Training	*8299	Schools and Educational Services, NEC (professional and management development training)
6115	Technical and Trade Schools		
61151	Technical and Trade Schools		
US 611511	Cosmetology and Barber Schools	*7231	Beauty Shops (beauty and cosmetology schools)
		*7241	Barber Shops (barber colleges)
US 611512	Flight Training	*8249	Vocational Schools, NEC (aviation schools, excluding flying instruction)
		*8299	Schools and Educational Services, NEC (flying instruction)
US 611513	Apprenticeship Training	*8249	Vocational Schools, NEC (vocational apprenticeship training)
US 611519	Other Technical and Trade Schools	*8249	Vocational Schools, NEC (except aviation and flight training and apprenticeship training)
		*8243	Data Processing Schools (computer repair training)
		*8299	Schools and Educational Services, NEC (modeling and cooking schools)
6116	Other Schools and Instruction		
61161	Fine Arts Schools	*8299	Schools and Educational Services, NEC (art, drama, and music schools)

US—United States industry only. CAN—United States and Canadian industries are comparable. When neither US nor CAN appears, Canadian, Mexican, and United States are comparable. *—Part of; NEC—Not Elsewhere Classified.

http://www.ntis.gov/naics

1997 NAICS code	1997 NAICS U.S. description	1987 SIC code	1987 U.S. SIC description
		*7911	Dance Studios, Schools, and Halls (dance instructors, and professional and other dance schools)
61162	Sports and Recreation Instruction	*7999	Amusement and Recreation Services, NEC (baseball, basketball, bowling, gymnastic, judo, karate, parachute, scuba and skin diving, skating, ski, swimming, tennis, and other sports instruction; and sports instructional schools and camps)
61163	Language Schools	*8299	Schools and Educational Services, NEC (language schools)
61169	All Other Schools and Instruction		
US 611691	Exam Preparation and Tutoring	*8299	Schools and Educational Services, NEC (exam preparation and tutoring)
US 611692	Automobile Driving Schools	*8299	Schools and Educational Services, NEC (automobile driving instruction)
US 611699	All Other Miscellaneous Schools and Instruction	*7999	Amusement and Recreation Services, NEC (nonathletic recreational instruction)
		*8299	Schools and Educational Services, NEC (except professional and management training, aviation and flight training, fine arts schools, language schools, exam preparation and tutoring, automobile driving schools, and educational support services)
6117	Educational Support Services		
61171	Educational Support Services	*8299	Schools and Educational Services NEC (except instruction)
		*8748	Business Consulting Services, NEC (educational test development and evaluation services, educational testing services, and educational consultants)

	1997 NAICS code	1997 NAICS U.S. description	1987 SIC code	1987 U.S. SIC description
	62	Health Care and Social Assistance		
	621	Ambulatory Health Care Services		
	6211	Offices of Physicians		
	62111	Offices of Physicians		
US	621111	Offices of Physicians (except Mental Health Specialists)	*8011	Offices and Clinics of Doctors of Medicine (except mental health specialists)
			*8031	Offices and Clinics of Doctors of Osteopathy (except mental health specialists)
US	621112	Offices of Physicians, Mental Health Specialists	*8011	Offices and Clinics of Doctors of Medicine (mental health specialists)
			*8031	Offices and Clinics of Doctors of Osteopathy (mental health specialists)
	6212	Offices of Dentists		
	62121	Offices of Dentists	8021	Offices and Clinics of Dentists
	6213	Offices of Other Health Practitioners		
	62131	Offices of Chiropractors	8041	Offices and Clinics of Chiropractors
	62132	Offices of Optometrists	8042	Offices and Clinics of Optometrists
	62133	Offices of Mental Health Practitioners (except Physicians)	*8049	Offices and Clinics of Health Practitioners, NEC (mental health practitioners except physicians)
	62134	Offices of Physical, Occupational and Speech Therapists, and Audiologists	*8049	Offices and Clinics of Health Practitioners, NEC (physical, occupational, recreational and speech therapists, and audiologists)
	62139	Offices of All Other Health Practitioners		
US	621391	Offices of Podiatrists	8043	Offices and Clinics of Podiatrists
US	621399	Offices of All Other Miscellaneous Health Practitioners	*8049	Offices and Clinics of Health Practitioners, NEC (except mental health practitioners, physical, occupational, speech therapists, and audiologists)

http://www.ntis.gov/naics

1997 NAICS code	1997 NAICS U.S. description	1987 SIC code	1987 U.S. SIC description
6214	Outpatient Care Centers		
62141	Family Planning Centers	*8093	Speciality Outpatient Facilities, NEC (family planning centers)
		*8099	Health and Allied Services, NEC (childbirth preparation)
62142	Outpatient Mental Health and Substance Abuse Centers	*8093	Specialty Outpatient Facilities, NEC (mental health facilities)
62149	Other Outpatient Care Centers		
US 621491	HMO Medical Centers	*8011	Offices and Clinics of Doctors of Medicine (HMO Medical Centers)
US 621492	Kidney Dialysis Centers	8092	Kidney Dialysis Centers
US 621493	Freestanding Ambulatory Surgical and Emergency Centers	*8011	Offices and Clinics of Doctors of Medicine (surgical and emergency centers)
US 621498	All Other Outpatient Care Centers	*8093	Specialty Outpatient Facilities, NEC (except family planning and mental health centers)
6215	Medical and Diagnostic Laboratories		
62151	Medical and Diagnostic Laboratories		
US 621511	Medical Laboratories	*8071	Medical Laboratories (except diagnostic imaging centers)
US 621512	Diagnostic Imaging Centers	*8071	Medical Laboratories (diagnostic imaging centers)
6216	Home Health Care Services		
62161	Home Health Care Services	8082	Home Health Care Services
6219	Other Ambulatory Health Care Services		
62191	Ambulance Services	*4119	Local Passenger Transportation, NEC (land ambulance)
		*4522	Air Transportation, Nonscheduled (air ambulance)
62199	All Other Ambulatory Health Care Services		
US 621991	Blood and Organ Banks	*8099	Health and Allied Services, NEC (blood and organ banks)
US 621999	All Other Miscellaneous Ambulatory Health Care Services	*8099	Health and Allied Services, NEC (except blood and organ banks, medical artists, medical photography, and childbirth preparation classes)

US—United States industry only. CAN—United States and Canadian industries are comparable. When neither US nor CAN appears, Canadian, Mexican, and United States are comparable. *—Part of; NEC—Not Elsewhere Classified.

http://www.ntis.gov/naics

1997 NAICS code	1997 NAICS U.S. description	1987 SIC code	1987 U.S. SIC description
622	Hospitals		
6221	General Medical and Surgical Hospitals		
62211	General Medical and Surgical Hospitals	8062	General Medical and Surgical Hospitals
		*8069	Specialty Hospitals, Except Psychiatric (children's hospitals)
6222	Psychiatric and Substance Abuse Hospitals		
62221	Psychiatric and Substance Abuse Hospitals	8063	Psychiatric Hospitals
		*8069	Specialty Hospitals, Except Psychiatric (substance abuse hospitals)
6223	Specialty (except Psychiatric and Substance Abuse) Hospitals		
62231	Specialty (except Psychiatric and Substance Abuse) Hospitals	*8069	Specialty Hospitals, Except Psychiatric (except children's and substance abuse hospitals)
623	Nursing and Residential Care Facilities		
6231	Nursing Care Facilities		
62311	Nursing Care Facilities	*8051	Skilled Nursing Care Facilities (except continuing care retirement communities)
		*8052	Intermediate Care Facilities (except continuing care retirement communities and mental retardation facilities)
		*8059	Nursing and Personal Care Facilities, NEC (except continuing care retirement communities)
6232	Residential Mental Retardation, Mental Health and Substance Abuse Facilities		
62321	Residential Mental Retardation Facilities	*8052	Intermediate Care Facilities (mental retardation facilities)
62322	Residential Mental Health and Substance Abuse Facilities	*8361	Residential Care (mental health and substance abuse facilities)

US—United States industry only. CAN—United States and Canadian industries are comparable. When neither US nor CAN appears, Canadian, Mexican, and United States are comparable. *—Part of; NEC—Not Elsewhere Classified.

http://www.ntis.gov/naics

	1997 NAICS code	1997 NAICS U.S. description	1987 SIC code	1987 U.S. SIC description
	6233	Community Care Facilities for the Elderly		
	62331	Community Care Facilities for the Elderly		
US	623311	Continuing Care Retirement Communities	*8051	Skilled Nursing Care Facilities (continuing care retirement communities)
			*8052	Intermediate Care Facilities (continuing care retirement communities)
			*8059	Nursing and Personal Care Facilities, NEC (continuing care retirement communities)
US	623312	Homes for the Elderly	*8361	Residential Care (homes for the elderly)
	6239	Other Residential Care Facilities		
	62399	Other Residential Care Facilities	*8361	Residential Care (except mental health and substance abuse facilities, homes for the elderly)
	624	Social Assistance		
	6241	Individual and Family Services		
	62411	Child and Youth Services	*8322	Individual and Family Social Services (child and youth services)
	62412	Services for the Elderly and Persons with Disabilities	*8322	Individual and Family Social Services (services for the elderly and disabled)
	62419	Other Individual and Family Services	*8322	Individual and Family Social Services (except services for children, youth, elderly, disabled; food, housing, emergency and relief)
	6242	Community Food and Housing, and Emergency and Other Relief Services		
	62421	Community Food Services	*8322	Individual and Family Social Services (food services)
	62422	Community Housing Services		
US	624221	Temporary Shelters	*8322	Individual and Family Social Services (temporary shelter)

US—United States industry only. CAN—United States and Canadian industries are comparable. When neither US nor CAN appears, Canadian, Mexican, and United States are comparable. *—Part of; NEC—Not Elsewhere Classified.

http://www.ntis.gov/naics

1997 NAICS code	1997 NAICS U.S. description	1987 SIC code	1987 U.S. SIC description
US 624229	Other Community Housing Services	*8322	Individual and Family Social Services (housing services except temporary shelter)
62423	Emergency and Other Relief Services	*8322	Individual and Family Social Services (emergency and relief services)
6243	Vocational Rehabilitation Services		
62431	Vocational Rehabilitation Services	8331	Job Training and Vocational Rehabilitation Services
6244	Child Day Care Services		
62441	Child Day Care Services	8351	Child Day Care Services
71	Arts, Entertainment, and Recreation		
711	Performing Arts, Spectator Sports, and Related Industries		
7111	Performing Arts Companies		
71111	Theater Companies and Dinner Theaters	*5812	Eating Places (dinner theaters)
		*7922	Theatrical Producers (Except Motion Pictures) and Miscellaneous Theatrical Services (theater companies, opera companies)
71112	Dance Companies	*7922	Theatrical Producers (Except Motion Pictures) and Miscellaneous Theatrical Services (ballet and dance companies)
71113	Musical Groups and Artists	*7929	Bands, Orchestras, Actors, and Entertainment Groups (musical groups and artists and orchestras)
71119	Other Performing Arts Companies	*7929	Bands, Orchestras, Actors, and Entertainment Groups, (except musical groups, artists, actors, and actresses)
		*7999	Amusement and Recreation Services, NEC (circus companies and traveling carnival shows)
7112	Spectator Sports		
71121	Spectator Sports		
CAN 711211	Sports Teams and Clubs	*7941	Professional Sports Clubs and Promoters (professional sports clubs)

US—United States industry only. CAN—United States and Canadian industries are comparable. When neither US nor CAN appears, Canadian, Mexican, and United States are comparable. *—Part of; NEC—Not Elsewhere Classified.

http://www.ntis.gov/naics

1997 NAICS code	1997 NAICS U.S. description	1987 SIC code	1987 U.S. SIC description
US 711212	Racetracks	*7948	Racing, Including Track Operations (track operations)
US 711219	Other Spectator Sports	*7948	Racing, Including Track Operations (except track operators)
		*7999	Amusement and Recreation Services, NEC (professional athletes)
7113	Promoters of Performing Arts, Sports, and Similar Events		
71131	Promoters of Performing Arts, Sports, and Similar Events with Facilities	*6512	Operators of Nonresidential Buildings (stadium and arena owners)
		*7922	Theatrical Producers (Except Motion Picture) and Miscellaneous Theatrical Services (theater operators)
		*7941	Professional Sports Clubs and Promoters (stadium operators)
		*7999	Amusement and Recreation Services, NEC (state fairs, agriculture fairs and county fairs with facilities)
71132	Promoters of Performing Arts, Sports, and Similar Events without Facilities	*7922	Theatrical Producers (Except Motion Picture) and Miscellaneous Theatrical Services (theatrical promoters)
		*7941	Professional Sports Clubs and Promoters (sports promoters)
		*7999	Amusement and Recreation Services, NEC (state fairs, agriculture fairs and county fairs without facilities)
7114	Agents and Managers for Artists, Athletes, Entertainers, and Other Public Figures		
71141	Agents and Managers for Artists, Athletes, Entertainers, and Other Public Figures	*7389	Business Services, NEC (agents and brokers for authors and artists and speaker bureaus)
		*7922	Theatrical Producers (Except Motion Picture) and Miscellaneous Theatrical Services (theatrical agents)

US—United States industry only. CAN—United States and Canadian industries are comparable. When neither US nor CAN appears, Canadian, Mexican, and United States are comparable. *—Part of; NEC—Not Elsewhere Classified.

http://www.ntis.gov/naics

1997 NAICS code	1997 NAICS U.S. description	1987 SIC code	1987 U.S. SIC description
		*7941	Professional Sports Clubs and Promoters (sports agents)
7115	Independent Artists, Writers, and Performers		
71151	Independent Artists, Writers, and Performers	*7819	Services Allied to Motion Picture Production (film directors and related motion picture production services, independent)
		*7699	Repair Shops and Related Services, NEC (taxidermists and antique repair and restoration, except antique car restoration)
		*7929	Bands, Orchestras, Actors, and Other Entertainers and Entertainment Groups (actors and actresses)
		*7383	News Syndicates (independent news correspondents)
		*7641	Reupholstery and Furniture Repair (antique furniture restoration)
		*7922	Theatrical Producers (Except Motion Picture) and Miscellaneous Theatrical Services (costume design, theatrical)
		*8999	Services, NEC (authors, artists, and related technical services, independent)
712	Museums, Historical Sites, and Similar Institutions		
7121	Museums, Historical Sites, and Similar Institutions		
71211	Museums	*8412	Museums and Art Galleries (except historic and heritage sites)
71212	Historical Sites	*8412	Museums and Art Galleries (historic and heritage sites)
71213	Zoos and Botanical Gardens	*8422	Arboreta and Botanical or Zoological Gardens (except nature parks and reserves)
71219	Nature Parks and Other Similar Institutions	*7999	Amusement and Recreation Services, NEC (caverns and miscellaneous commercial parks)

US—United States industry only. CAN—United States and Canadian industries are comparable. When neither US nor CAN appears, Canadian, Mexican, and United States are comparable. *—Part of; NEC—Not Elsewhere Classified.

http://www.ntis.gov/naics

1997 NAICS code	1997 NAICS U.S. description	1987 SIC code	1987 U.S. SIC description
		*8422	Arboreta and Botanical or Zoological Gardens (nature parks and reserves)
713	Amusement, Gambling, and Recreation Industries		
7131	Amusement Parks and Arcades		
71311	Amusement and Theme Parks	7996	Amusement Parks
71312	Amusement Arcades	*7993	Coin-Operated Amusement Devices (amusement arcades)
7132	Gambling Industries		
71321	Casinos (except Casino Hotels)	*7999	Amusement and Recreation Services, NEC (casinos, except hotel casinos)
71329	Other Gambling Industries	*7993	Coin-Operated Amusement Devices (slot machine operators)
		*7999	Amusement and Recreation Services, NEC (lottery, bingo, bookie, and other gambling operations)
7139	Other Amusement and Recreation Industries		
71391	Golf Courses and Country Clubs	7992	Public Golf Courses
		*7997	Membership Sports and Recreation Clubs (golf clubs)
71392	Skiing Facilities	*7999	Amusement and Recreation Services, NEC (skiing facilities)
71393	Marinas	4493	Marinas
71394	Fitness and Recreational Sports Centers	7991	Physical Fitness Facilities
		*7997	Membership Sports and Recreation Clubs (recreation clubs with facilities)
		*7999	Amusement and Recreation Services, NEC (nonmembership recreation facilities)
71395	Bowling Centers	7933	Bowling Centers
71399	All Other Amusement and Recreation Industries	*7911	Dance Studios, Schools, and Halls (except instruction)
		*7993	Amusement and Recreation Services, NEC (except amusement arcades and slot machine operators)

www.ntis.gov/naics

1997 NAICS code	1997 NAICS U.S. description	1987 SIC code	1987 U.S. SIC description
		*7997	Membership Sports and Recreation Clubs (recreation clubs without facilities)
		*7999	Amusement and Recreation Services, NEC (except circuses, professional athletes, caverns and other commercial parks, skiing facilities, casinos and other gambling operations, amusement and recreation facilities, sports instruction, sports equipment rental, ticket agencies, and amusement or scenic transport operations)
72	Accommodation and Food Services		
721	Accommodation		
7211	Traveler Accommodation		
72111	Hotels (except Casino Hotels) and Motels	*7011	Hotels and Motels (hotels and motels, except casino hotels)
		*7041	Organization Hotels and Lodging Houses, on Membership Basis (hotels)
72112	Casino Hotels	*7011	Hotels and Motels (casino hotels)
72119	Other Traveler Accommodation		
CAN 721191	Bed-and-Breakfast Inns	*7011	Hotels and Motels (bed and breakfast inns)
US 721199	All Other Traveler Accommodation	*7011	Hotels and Motels (except hotels, motels, and bed and breakfast inns)
7212	RV (Recreational Vehicle) Parks and Recreational Camps		
72121	RV (Recreational Vehicle) Parks and Recreational Camps		
CAN 721211	RV (Recreational Vehicle) Parks and Campgrounds	7033	Recreational Vehicle Parks and Campgrounds
US 721214	Recreational and Vacation Camps (except Campgrounds)	7032	Sporting and Recreational Camps

US—United States industry only. CAN—United States and Canadian industries are comparable. When neither US nor CAN appears, Canadian, Mexican, and United States are comparable. *—Part of; NEC—Not Elsewhere Classified.

http://www.ntis.gov/naics

1997 NAICS code	1997 NAICS U.S. description	1987 SIC code	1987 U.S. SIC description
7213	Rooming and Boarding Houses		
72131	Rooming and Boarding Houses	7021	Rooming and Boarding Houses
		*7041	Organization Hotels and Lodging Houses, on Membership Basis (except hotels)
722	Food Services and Drinking Places		
7221	Full-Service Restaurants		
72211	Full-Service Restaurants	*5812	Eating Places (full-service restaurants)
7222	Limited-Service Eating Places		
72221	Limited-Service Eating Places		
US 722211	Limited-Service Restaurants	*5812	Eating Places (limited-service restaurants)
US 722212	Cafeterias	*5812	Eating Places (cafeterias)
US 722213	Snack and Nonalcoholic Beverage Bars	*5812	Eating Places (snack and nonalcoholic beverage bars)
		*5461	Retail Bakeries (snacks)
7223	Special Food Services		
72231	Food Service Contractors	*4789	Transportation Services, NEC (dining car operations on a fee or contract basis)
		*5812	Eating Places (food service contractors)
72232	Caterers	*5812	Eating Places (caterers)
72233	Mobile Food Services	*5963	Direct Selling Establishments (mobile food wagons)
7224	Drinking Places (Alcoholic Beverages)		
72241	Drinking Places (Alcoholic Beverages)	5813	Drinking Places (alcoholic beverages)
81	Other Services (except Public Administration)		
811	Repair and Maintenance		
8111	Automotive Repair and Maintenance		
81111	Automotive Mechanical and Electrical Repair and Maintenance		
CAN 811111	General Automotive Repair	7538	General Automotive Repair Shops

US—United States industry only. CAN—United States and Canadian industries are comparable. When neither US nor CAN appears, Canadian, Mexican, and United States are comparable. *—Part of; NEC—Not Elsewhere Classified.

http://www.ntis.gov/naics

	1997 NAICS code	1997 NAICS U.S. description	1987 SIC code	1987 U.S. SIC description
CAN	811112	Automotive Exhaust System Repair	7533	Automotive Exhaust System Repair Shops
US	811113	Automotive Transmission Repair	7537	Automotive Transmission Repair Shops
US	811118	Other Automotive Mechanical and Electrical Repair and Maintenance	7539	Automotive Repair Shops, NEC
	81112	Automotive Body, Paint, Interior, and Glass Repair		
CAN	811121	Automotive Body, Paint, and Interior Repair and Maintenance	7532	Top, Body, and Upholstery Repair Shops and Paint Shops
CAN	811122	Automotive Glass Replacement Shops	7536	Automotive Glass Replacement Shops
			*7549	Automotive Services, Except Repair and Carwashes (automotive window tinting)
	81119	Other Automotive Repair and Maintenance		
US	811191	Automotive Oil Change and Lubrication Shops	*7549	Automotive Services, Except Repair and Carwashes (lubricating service, automotive)
CAN	811192	Car Washes	7542	Carwashes
US	811198	All Other Automotive Repair and Maintenance	*7534	Tire Retreading and Repair Shops (repair)
			*7549	Automotive Services, Except Repair and Carwashes (except automotive window tinting, lubricating, and towing)
	8112	Electronic and Precision Equipment Repair and Maintenance		
	81121	Electronic and Precision Equipment Repair and Maintenance		
US	811211	Consumer Electronics Repair and Maintenance	*7622	Radio and Television Repair Shops (other stereo, TV, VCR, and radio)
			*7629	Electrical and Electronic Repair Shops, NEC (other consumer equipment except computer, TV, stereo, VCR, and radio)

http://www.ntis.gov/naics

1997 NAICS code	1997 NAICS U.S. description	1987 SIC code	1987 U.S. SIC description
		*7699	Repair Shops and Related Services, NEC (camera repair)
US 811212	Computer and Office Machine Repair and Maintenance	*7378	Computer Maintenance and Repair (except retailing new computers from a storefront and repairing)
		*7629	Electrical and Electronic Repair Shops, NEC (business and office machine repair, electrical)
		*7699	Repair Shops and Related Services, NEC (typewriter repair)
US 811213	Communication Equipment Repair and Maintenance	*7622	Radio and Television Repair Shops (other telecommunication equipment repair)
		*7629	Electrical and Electronic Repair Shops, NEC (telephone set repair)
US 811219	Other Electronic and Precision Equipment Repair and Maintenance	*7629	Electrical and Electronic Repair Shops, NEC (electrical measuring instrument repair and calibration, medical electrical equipment repair)
		*7699	Repair Shops and Related Services, NEC (dental instrument repair, laboratory instrument repair, medical equipment and other electronic and precision equipment repair, except typewriters)
8113	Commercial and Industrial Machinery and Equipment (except Automotive and Electronic) Repair and Maintenance		
81131	Commercial and Industrial Machinery and Equipment (except Automotive and Electronic) Repair and Maintenance	*7699	Repair Shops and Related Services, NEC (other non-automotive transportation equipment and industrial machines and equipment)

US—United States industry only. CAN—United States and Canadian industries are comparable. When neither US nor CAN appears, Canadian, Mexican, and United States are comparable. *—Part of; NEC—Not Elsewhere Classified.

http://www.ntis.gov/naics

1997 NAICS code	1997 NAICS U.S. description	1987 SIC code	1987 U.S. SIC description
		*7623	Refrigeration and Air-Conditioning Services and Repair Shops (commercial refrigerator equipment repair)
		7692	Welding Repair
		*7694	Armature Rewinding Shops (repair)
8114	Personal and Household Goods Repair and Maintenance		
81141	Home and Garden Equipment and Appliance Repair and Maintenance		
CAN 811411	Home and Garden Equipment Repair and Maintenance	*7699	Repair Shops and Related Services, NEC (lawnmower repair shops, sharpening and repairing knives, saws and tools)
CAN 811412	Appliance Repair and Maintenance	*7623	Refrigeration and Air-Conditioning Service and Repair Shops (except commercial and retailing new refrigerators from a storefront and repairing)
		*7629	Electrical and Electronic Repair Shops, NEC (appliance repair, electrical; washing machine repair; electric razor repair (except retailing new appliances from a storefront))
		*7699	Repair Shops and Related Services, NEC (gas appliance repair service, sewing machine repair, stove repair shops, and other non-electrical appliance)
81142	Reupholstery and Furniture Repair	*7641	Reupholstery and Furniture Repair (except antique furniture restoration)
81143	Footwear and Leather Goods Repair	*7251	Shoe Repair and Shoeshine Parlors (shoe repair shops)
		*7699	Repair Shops and Related Services (leather goods repair shops, luggage repair shops, pocketbook repair shops)

US—United States industry only. CAN—United States and Canadian industries are comparable. When neither US nor CAN appears, Canadian, Mexican, and United States are comparable. *—Part of; NEC—Not Elsewhere Classified.

http://www.ntis.gov/naics

1997 NAICS code	1997 NAICS U.S. description	1987 SIC code	1987 U.S. SIC description
81149	Other Personal and Household Goods Repair and Maintenance	*3732	Boat Building and Repairing (pleasure boat repair)
		*7219	Laundry and Garment Services, NEC (alteration and repair)
		7631	Watch, Clock, and Jewelry Repair
		*7699	Repair Shops and Related Services, NEC (except industrial, electronic, home and garden, appliance, and leather goods)
812	Personal and Laundry Services		
CAN 8121	Personal Care Services		
CAN 81211	Hair, Nail, and Skin Care Services		
US 812111	Barber Shops	*7241	Barber Shops (except barber colleges)
US 812112	Beauty Salons	*7231	Beauty Shops (except beauty and cosmetology schools and manicure and pedicure salons)
US 812113	Nail Salons	*7231	Beauty Shops (manicure and pedicure salons)
CAN 81219	Other Personal Care Services		
US 812191	Diet and Weight Reducing Centers	*7299	Miscellaneous Personal Services, NEC (diet and weight reducing services)
US 812199	Other Personal Care Services	*7299	Miscellaneous Personal Services, NEC (personal care services)
CAN 8122	Death Care Services		
CAN 81221	Funeral Homes and Funeral Services	*7261	Funeral Services and Crematories (funeral homes and services)
CAN 81222	Cemeteries and Crematories	*6531	Real Estate Agents and Managers (cemetery management)
		6553	Cemetery Subdividers and Developers
		*7261	Funeral Services and Crematories (crematories)
CAN 8123	Drycleaning and Laundry Services		
CAN 81231	Coin-Operated Laundries and Drycleaners	7215	Coin-Operated Laundry and Drycleaning

US—United States industry only. CAN—United States and Canadian industries are comparable. When neither US nor CAN appears, Canadian, Mexican, and United States are comparable. *—Part of; NEC—Not Elsewhere Classified.

http://www.ntis.gov/naics

1997 NAICS code	1997 NAICS U.S. description	1987 SIC code	1987 U.S. SIC description
CAN 81232	Drycleaning and Laundry Services (except Coin-Operated)	7211	Power Laundries, Family and Commercial
		*7389	Business Services, NEC (apparel pressing service for the trade)
		7216	Drycleaning Plants, Except Rug Cleaning
		7212	Garment Pressing, and Agents for Laundries and Drycleaners
		*7219	Laundry and Garment Services, NEC (except diaper service and clothing alteration and repair)
CAN 81233	Linen and Uniform Supply		
US 812331	Linen Supply	7213	Linen Supply
		*7219	Laundry and Garment Services, NEC (diaper service)
US 812332	Industrial Launderers	7218	Industrial Launderers
CAN 8129	Other Personal Services		
CAN 81291	Pet Care (except Veterinary) Services	*0752	Animal Speciality Services, Except Veterinary (pet care services, except veterinary)
CAN 81292	Photofinishing		
CAN 812921	Photofinishing Laboratories (except One-Hour)	*7384	Photofinishing Laboratories (except one-hour)
CAN 812922	One-Hour Photofinishing	*7384	Photofinishing Laboratories (one-hour)
CAN 81293	Parking Lots and Garages	7521	Automobile Parking
		*7299	Miscellaneous Personal Services, NEC (valet parking services)
CAN 81299	All Other Personal Services	*7299	Miscellaneous Personal Services, NEC (except diet and weight reducing services, personal care services, valet parking services, and formal wear and costume rental service)
		*7251	Shoe Repair Shops and Shoeshine Parlors (shoeshine parlors)
		*7389	Miscellaneous Business Services (bail bonding)

US—United States industry only. CAN—United States and Canadian industries are comparable. When neither US nor CAN appears, Canadian, Mexican, and United States are comparable. *—Part of; NEC—Not Elsewhere Classified.

http://www.ntis.gov/naics

1997 NAICS code	1997 NAICS U.S. description	1987 SIC code	1987 U.S. SIC description
813	Religious, Grantmaking, Civic, Professional, and Similar Organizations		
CAN 8131	Religious Organizations		
CAN 81311	Religious Organizations	8661	Religious Organizations
CAN 8132	Grantmaking and Giving Services		
CAN 81321	Grantmaking and Giving Services		
US 813211	Grantmaking Foundations	6732	Educational, Religious, and Charitable Trusts
US 813212	Voluntary Health Organizations	*8399	Social Services, NEC (voluntary health organizations)
US 813219	Other Grantmaking and Giving Services	*8399	Social Services, NEC (grantmaking and giving)
CAN 8133	Social Advocacy Organizations		
CAN 81331	Social Advocacy Organizations		
US 813311	Human Rights Organizations	*8399	Social Services, NEC (human rights organizations)
US 813312	Environment, Conservation and Wildlife Organizations	*8399	Social Services, NEC (environment, conservation, and wildlife advocacy)
		*8699	Membership Organizations, NEC (humane societies)
US 813319	Other Social Advocacy Organizations	*8399	Social Services, NEC (except human rights, environment, conservation and wildlife organizations, grantmaking and giving, and voluntary health organizations)
CAN 8134	Civic and Social Organizations		
CAN 81341	Civic and Social Organizations	*8641	Civic, Social, and Fraternal Organizations (except condominium and homeowner associations)
		*8699	Membership Organizations, NEC (except humane societies, farm business organizations, athletic associations, and travel motor clubs)

US—United States industry only. CAN—United States and Canadian industries are comparable. When neither US nor CAN appears, Canadian, Mexican, and United States are comparable. *—Part of; NEC—Not Elsewhere Classified.

http://www.ntis.gov/naics

	1997 NAICS code	1997 NAICS U.S. description	1987 SIC code	1987 U.S. SIC description
CAN	8139	Business, Professional, Labor, Political, and Similar Organizations		
CAN	81391	Business Associations	8611	Business Associations
			*8699	Membership Organizations, NEC (farm business organizations)
CAN	81392	Professional Organizations	8621	Professional Membership Organizations
CAN	81393	Labor Unions and Similar Labor Organizations	8631	Labor Unions and Similar Labor Organizations
CAN	81394	Political Organizations	8651	Political Organizations
CAN	81399	Other Similar Organizations (except Business, Professional, Labor, and Political Organizations)	*6531	Real Estate Agents and Managers (condominium associations)
			*8641	Civic, Social, and Fraternal Organizations (condominium and homeowner associations)
			*8699	Membership Organizations, NEC (athletic associations)
	814	Private Households		
	8141	Private Households		
	81411	Private Households	8811	Private Households
	92	Public Administration		Public Administration
US	921	Executive, Legislative, and Other General Government Support		
US	9211	Executive, Legislative, and Other General Government Support		
US	92111	Executive Offices	9111	Executive Offices
US	92112	Legislative Bodies	9121	Legislative Bodies
US	92113	Public Finance Activities	9311	Public Finance, Taxation, and Monetary Policy
US	92114	Executive and Legislative Offices, Combined	9131	Executive and Legislative Office, Combined
US	92115	American Indian and Alaska Native Tribal Governments	*8641	Civic, Social, and Fraternal Organizations (Indian Tribal Councils)
US	92119	Other General Government Support	9199	General Government, NEC
US	922	Justice, Public Order, and Safety Activities		

US—United States industry only. CAN—United States and Canadian industries are comparable. When neither US nor CAN appears, Canadian, Mexican, and United States are comparable. *—Part of; NEC—Not Elsewhere Classified.

http://www.ntis.gov/naics

1997 NAICS code	1997 NAICS U.S. description	1987 SIC code	1987 U.S. SIC description
US 9221	Justice, Public Order, and Safety Activities		
US 92211	Courts	9211	Courts
US 92212	Police Protection	9221	Police Protection
US 92213	Legal Counsel and Prosecution	9222	Legal Counsel and Prosecution
US 92214	Correctional Institutions	9223	Correctional Institutions
US 92215	Parole Offices and Probation Offices	*8322	Individual and Family Social Services (parole and probation offices)
US 92216	Fire Protection	9224	Fire Protection
US 92219	Other Justice, Public Order, and Safety Activities	9229	Public Order and Safety, NEC
US 923	Administration of Human Resource Programs		
US 9231	Administration of Human Resource Programs		
US 92311	Administration of Education Programs	9411	Administration of Educational Programs
US 92312	Administration of Public Health Programs	9431	Administration of Public Health Programs
US 92313	Administration of Human Resource Programs (except Education, Public Health, and Veterans' Affairs Programs)	9441	Administration of Social, Human Resource and Income Maintenance Programs
US 92314	Administration of Veterans' Affairs	9451	Administration of Veterans' Affairs, Except Health and Insurance
US 924	Administration of Environmental Quality Programs		
US 9241	Administration of Environmental Quality Programs		
US 92411	Administration of Air and Water Resource and Solid Waste Management Programs	9511	Air and Water Resource and Solid Waste Management
US 92412	Administration of Conservation Programs	9512	Land, Mineral, Wildlife, and Forest Conservation

US—United States industry only. CAN—United States and Canadian industries are comparable. When neither US nor CAN appears, Canadian, Mexican, and United States are comparable. *—Part of; NEC—Not Elsewhere Classified.

http://www.ntis.gov/naics

1997 NAICS code	1997 NAICS U.S. description	1987 SIC code	1987 U.S. SIC description
US 925	Administration of Housing Programs, Urban Planning, and Community Development		
US 9251	Administration of Housing Programs, Urban Planning, and Community Development		
US 92511	Administration of Housing Programs	9531	Administration of Housing Programs
US 92512	Administration of Urban Planning and Community and Rural Development	9532	Administration of Urban Planning and Community and Rural Development
US 926	Administration of Economic Programs		
US 9261	Administration of Economic Programs		
US 92611	Administration of General Economic Programs	9611	Administration of General Economic Programs
US 92612	Regulation and Administration of Transportation Programs	*9621	Regulation and Administration of Transportation Programs (except air traffic control)
US 92613	Regulation and Administration of Communications, Electric, Gas, and Other Utilities	9631	Regulation and Administration of Communications, Electric, Gas, and Other Utilities
US 92614	Regulation of Agricultural Marketing and Commodities	9641	Regulation of Agricultural Marketing and Commodities
US 92615	Regulation, Licensing, and Inspection of Miscellaneous Commercial Sectors	9651	Regulation, Licensing, and Inspection of Miscellaneous Commercial Sectors
US 927	Space Research and Technology		
US 9271	Space Research and Technology		
US 92711	Space Research and Technology	9661	Space Research and Technology
US 928	National Security and International Affairs		
US 9281	National Security and International Affairs		
US 92811	National Security	9711	National Security
US 92812	International Affairs	9721	International Affairs

http://www.ntis.gov/naics

Appendix B
1987 U.S. SIC Matched to 1997 NAICS U.S.

1987 SIC code	1987 U.S. SIC description	1997 NAICS code	1997 NAICS U.S. description
0111	Wheat	11114	Wheat Farming
0112	Rice	11116	Rice Farming
0115	Corn	11115	Corn Farming (pt)
0116	Soybeans	11111	Soybean Farming
0119	Cash Grains, NEC		
	Dry Pea and Bean Farms	11113	Dry Pea and Bean Farming
	Oilseed, Except Soybean, Farms	11112	Oilseed (except Soybean) Farming
	Popcorn Farms	11115	Corn Farming (pt)
	Combination Oilseed and Grain Farms	111191	Oilseed and Grain Combination Farming
	Other Farms	111199	All Other Grain Farming
0131	Cotton	11192	Cotton Farming
0132	Tobacco	11191	Tobacco Farming
0133	Sugarcane and Sugar Beets		
	Sugar Beets	111991	Sugar Beet Farming
	Sugarcane	11193	Sugarcane Farming
0134	Irish Potatoes	111211	Potato Farming
0139	Field Crops, Except Cash Grains, NEC		
	Hay Farms	11194	Hay Farming
	Peanut Farming	111992	Peanut Farming
	Sweet Potatoes and Yam Farms	111219	Other Vegetable (except Potato) and Melon Farming (pt)
	Other Field Crop Farms	111998	All Other Miscellaneous Crop Farming (pt)
0161	Vegetables and Melons	111219	Other Vegetable (except Potato) and Melon Farming (pt)
0171	Berry Crops		
	Strawberry Farms	111333	Strawberry Farming
	Other Berry Farms	111334	Berry (except Strawberry) Farming
0172	Grapes	111332	Grape Vineyards
0173	Tree Nuts	111335	Tree Nut Farming
0174	Citrus Fruits		
	Orange Groves and Farms	11131	Orange Groves
	Other Citrus Groves and Farms	11132	Citrus (except Orange) Groves
0175	Deciduous Tree Fruits		
	Apple Orchards and Farms	111331	Apple Orchards
	Other Farms	111339	Other Noncitrus Fruit Farming (pt)

pt—Part of; NEC—Not Elsewhere Classified.

http://www.ntis.gov/naics

1987 SIC code	1987 U.S. SIC description	1997 NAICS code	1997 NAICS U.S. description
0179	Fruits and Tree Nuts, NEC		
	Combination Fruit and Tree Nut Farms	111336	Fruit and Tree Nut Combination Farming
	Other Farms	111339	Other Noncitrus Fruit Farming (pt)
0181	Ornamental Floriculture and Nursery Products		
	Floriculture Farming	111422	Floriculture Production
	Nursery Farming	111421	Nursery and Tree Production (pt)
0182	Food Crops Grown Under Cover		
	Mushrooms, Growing Of	111411	Mushroom Production
	Other Food Crops Grown Under Cover	111419	Other Food Crops Grown Under Cover
0191	General Farms, Primarily Crop	111998	All Other Miscellaneous Crop Farming (pt)
0211	Beef Cattle Feedlots	112112	Cattle Feedlots
0212	Beef Cattle, Except Feedlots	112111	Beef Cattle Ranching and Farming (pt)
0213	Hogs	11221	Hog and Pig Farming
0214	Sheep and Goats		
	Sheep Farms	11241	Sheep Farming
	Goat Farms	11242	Goat Farming
0219	General Livestock, Except Dairy and Poultry	11299	All Other Animal Production (pt)
0241	Dairy Farms		
	Dairy Heifer Replacement Farms	112111	Beef Cattle Ranching and Farming (pt)
	Dairy Farms	11212	Dairy Cattle and Milk Production
0251	Broiler, Fryers, and Roaster Chickens	11232	Broilers and Other Meat-Type Chicken Production
0252	Chicken Eggs	11231	Chicken Egg Production
0253	Turkey and Turkey Eggs	11233	Turkey Production
0254	Poultry Hatcheries	11234	Poultry Hatcheries
0259	Poultry and Eggs, NEC	11239	Other Poultry Production
0271	Fur-Bearing Animals and Rabbits	11293	Fur-Bearing Animal and Rabbit Production
0272	Horses and Other Equines	11292	Horse and Other Equine Production
0273	Animal Aquaculture		
	Finfish Farms	112511	Finfish Farming and Fish Hatcheries (pt)

pt—Part of; NEC—Not Elsewhere Classified.

1987 SIC code	1987 U.S. SIC description	1997 NAICS code	1997 NAICS U.S. description
	Shellfish Farms	112512	Shellfish Farming (pt)
	Other Animal Aquaculture	112519	Other Animal Aquaculture (pt)
0279	Animal Specialties, NEC		
	Alligator and Frog Production	112519	Other Animal Aquaculture (pt)
	Bee Farms	11291	Apiculture
	Other	11299	All Other Animal Production (pt)
0291	General Farms, Primarily Livestock and Animal Specialties	11299	All Other Animal Production (pt)
0711	Soil Preparation Services	115112	Soil Preparation, Planting, and Cultivating (pt)
0721	Crop Planting, Cultivating, and Protecting	115112	Soil Preparation, Planting, and Cultivating (pt)
0722	Crop Harvesting, Primarily by Machine	115113	Crop Harvesting, Primarily By Machine
0723	Crop Preparation Services For Market, except Cotton Ginning		
	Other	115114	Postharvest Crop Activities (except Cotton Ginning)
	Custom Grain Grinding	311119	Other Animal Food Manufacturing (pt)
0724	Cotton Ginning	115111	Cotton Ginning
0741	Veterinary Services For Livestock	54194	Veterinary Services (pt)
0742	Veterinary Services for Animal Specialties	54194	Veterinary Services (pt)
0751	Livestock Services, Except Veterinary		
	Custom Slaughtering	311611	Animal (except Poultry) Slaughtering (pt)
	Other Livestock Service, Except Veterinary	11521	Support Activities for Animal Production (pt)
0752	Animal Specialty Services, Except Veterinary		
	Horses and Equines Services and Animal Production Breeding	11521	Support Activities for Animal Production (pt)
	Pet Care Services	81291	Pet Care (except Veterinary) Services
0761	Farm Labor Contractors and Crew Leaders	115115	Farm Labor Contractors and Crew Leaders
0762	Farm Management Services	115116	Farm Management Services
0781	Landscape Counseling and Planning		
	Horticulture Consulting	54169	Other Scientific and Technical Consulting Services (pt)

pt—Part of; NEC—Not Elsewhere Classified.

http://www.ntis.gov/naics

1987 SIC code	1987 U.S. SIC description	1997 NAICS code	1997 NAICS U.S. description
	Landscape Architectural Services	54132	Landscape Architectural Services (pt)
0782	Lawn and Garden Services	56173	Landscaping Services (pt)
0783	Ornamental Shrub and Tree Services	56173	Landscaping Services (pt)
0811	Timber Tracts		
	Short Rotation Woody Crops	111421	Nursery and Tree Production (pt)
	Long Term Timber Farming	11311	Timber Tract Operations
0831	Forest Nurseries and Gathering of Forest Products		
	Maple Sap	111998	All Other Miscellaneous Crop Farming (pt)
	Other Forest Products	11321	Forest Nurseries and Gathering of Forest Products
0851	Forestry Services	11531	Support Activities for Forestry
0912	Finfish	114111	Finfish Fishing
0913	Shellfish	114112	Shellfish Fishing
0919	Miscellaneous Marine Products		
	Except Plant Aquaculture	114119	Other Marine Fishing
	Plant Aquaculture	111998	All Other Miscellaneous Crop Farming (pt)
0921	Fish Hatcheries and Preserves		
	Finfish Hatcheries	112511	Finfish Farming and Fish Hatcheries (pt)
	Shellfish Hatcheries	112512	Shellfish Farming (pt)
0971	Hunting and Trapping, and Game Propagation	11421	Hunting and Trapping
1011	Iron Ores	21221	Iron Ore Mining
1021	Copper Ores	212234	Copper Ore and Nickel Ore Mining (pt)
1031	Lead and Zinc Ores	212231	Lead Ore and Zinc Ore Mining
1041	Gold Ores	212221	Gold Ore Mining
1044	Silver Ores	212222	Silver Ore Mining
1061	Ferroalloy Ores, Except Vanadium		
	Nickel Ore Mining	212234	Copper Ore and Nickel Ore Mining (pt)
	Other Ferroalloys (except nickel)	212299	Other Metal Ore Mining (pt)
1081	Metal Mining Services		
	Metal Mining (except geophysical surveying)	213114	Support Activities for Metal Mining
	Geophysical Surveying and Mapping	54136	Geophysical Surveying and Mapping Services (pt)

pt—Part of; NEC—Not Elsewhere Classified.

http://www.ntis.gov/naics

1987 SIC code	1987 U.S. SIC description	1997 NAICS code	1997 NAICS U.S. description
1094	Uranium-Radium-Vanadium Ores	212291	Uranium-Radium-Vanadium Ore Mining
1099	Miscellaneous Metal Ores, NEC	212299	Other Metal Ore Mining (pt)
1221	Bituminous Coal and Lignite Surface Mining	212111	Bituminous Coal and Lignite Surface Mining
1222	Bituminous Coal Underground Mining	212112	Bituminous Coal Underground Mining
1231	Anthracite Mining	212113	Anthracite Mining
1241	Coal Mining Services	213113	Support Activities for Coal Mining
1311	Crude Petroleum and Natural Gas	211111	Crude Petroleum and Natural Gas Extraction
1321	Natural Gas Liquids	211112	Natural Gas Liquid Extraction (pt)
1381	Drilling Oil and Gas Wells	213111	Drilling Oil and Gas Wells
1382	Oil and Gas Field Exploration Services		
	Geophysical Mapping and Surveying	54136	Geophysical Surveying and Mapping Services (pt)
	Other Oil and Gas Field Exploration Services	213112	Support Activities for Oil and Gas Field Operations (pt)
1389	Oil and Gas Field Services, NEC	213112	Support Activities for Oil and Gas Field Operations (pt)
1411	Dimension Stone	212311	Dimension Stone Mining and Quarrying
1422	Crushed and Broken Limestone	212312	Crushed and Broken Limestone Mining and Quarrying
1423	Crushed and Broken Granite	212313	Crushed and Broken Granite Mining and Quarrying
1429	Crushed and Broken Stone, NEC	212319	Other Crushed and Broken Stone Mining and Quarrying (pt)
1442	Construction Sand and Gravel	212321	Construction Sand and Gravel Mining
1446	Industrial Sand	212322	Industrial Sand Mining
1455	Kaolin and Ball Clay	212324	Kaolin and Ball Clay Mining
1459	Clay, Ceramic, and Refractory Minerals, NEC	212325	Clay and Ceramic and Refractory Minerals Mining
1474	Potash, Soda, and Borate Minerals	212391	Potash, Soda, and Borate Mineral Mining
1475	Phosphate Rock	212392	Phosphate Rock Mining
1479	Chemical and Fertilizer Mineral Mining, NEC	212393	Other Chemical and Fertilizer Mineral Mining
1481	Nonmetallic Minerals Services Except Fuels		

pt—Part of; NEC—Not Elsewhere Classified.

http://www.ntis.gov/naics

1987 SIC code	1987 U.S. SIC description	1997 NAICS code	1997 NAICS U.S. description
	Except Geophysical Mapping and Surveying	213115	Support Activities for Nonmetallic Minerals (except Fuels)
	Geophysical Surveying and Mapping Services	54136	Geophysical Surveying and Mapping Services (pt)
1499	Miscellaneous Nonmetallic Minerals, Except Fuels		
	Bituminous Limestone and Bituminous Sandstone	212319	Other Crushed and Broken Stone Mining or Quarrying (pt)
	Except Bituminous Limestone and Bituminous Sandstone	212399	All Other Nonmetallic Mineral Mining (pt)
1521	General Contractors-Single-Family Houses	23321	Single Family Housing Construction (pt)
1522	General Contractors-Residential Buildings, Other Than Single-Family		
	Hotel and Motel Construction	23332	Commercial and Institutional Building Construction (pt)
	Except Hotel and Motel Construction	23322	Multifamily Housing Construction (pt)
1531	Operative Builders		
	Single Family Housing	23321	Single Family Housing Construction (pt)
	Multifamily Housing	23322	Multifamily Housing Construction (pt)
	Manufacturing and Light Industrial Buildings	23331	Manufacturing and Industrial Building Construction (pt)
	Commercial and Institutional Buildings	23332	Commercial and Institutional Building Construction (pt)
1541	General Contractors-Industrial Buildings and Warehouses		
	Public Warehouse Construction	23332	Commercial and Institutional Building Construction (pt)
	Except Public Warehouse Construction	23331	Manufacturing and Industrial Building Construction (pt)
1542	General Contractors-Nonresidential Buildings, Other than Industrial Buildings and Warehouses	23332	Commercial and Institutional Building Construction (pt)
1611	Highway and Street Construction, Except Elevated Highways	23411	Highway and Street Construction (pt)
1622	Bridge, Tunnel, and Elevated Highway Construction	23412	Bridge and Tunnel Construction (pt)

pt—Part of; NEC—Not Elsewhere Classified.

1987 SIC code	1987 U.S. SIC description	1997 NAICS code	1997 NAICS U.S. description
1623	Water, Sewer, Pipeline, and Communications and Power Line Construction		
	Water, Sewer and Pipelines	23491	Water, Sewer, and Pipeline Construction (pt)
	Power and Communication Transmission Lines	23492	Power and Communication Transmission Line Construction (pt)
1629	Heavy Construction, NEC		
	Industrial Nonbuilding Structures Construction	23493	Industrial Nonbuilding Structure Construction (pt)
	Nonbuilding Structures Except Industrial Construction	23499	All Other Heavy Construction (pt)
1711	Plumbing, Heating, and Air-Conditioning	23511	Plumbing, Heating, and Air-Conditioning Contractors (pt)
1721	Painting and Paper Hanging	23521	Painting and Wall Covering Contractors (pt)
1731	Electrical Work	23531	Electrical Contractors
1741	Masonry, Stone Setting, and Other Stone Work	23541	Masonry and Stone Contractors
1742	Plastering, Drywall, Acoustical, and Insulation Work	23542	Drywall, Plastering, Acoustical, and Insulation Contractors (pt)
1743	Terrazzo, Tile, Marble, and Mosaic Work		
	Fresco Work	23542	Drywall, Plastering, Acoustical, and Insulation Contractors (pt)
	Except Fresco Work	23543	Tile, Marble, Terrazzo, and Mosaic Contractors
1751	Carpentry Work	23551	Carpentry Contractors
1752	Floor Laying and Other Floor Work, NEC	23552	Floor Laying and Other Floor Contractors
1761	Roofing, Siding, and Sheet Metal Work	23561	Roofing, Siding, and Sheet Metal Contractors
1771	Concrete Work		
	Stucco Construction	23542	Drywall, Plastering, Acoustical, and Insulation Contractors (pt)
	Except Stucco Construction	23571	Concrete Contractors
1781	Water Well Drilling	23581	Water Well Drilling Contractors
1791	Structural Steel Erection	23591	Structural Steel Erection Contractors
1793	Glass and Glazing Work	23592	Glass and Glazing Contractors (pt)
1794	Excavation Work	23593	Excavation Contractors
1795	Wrecking and Demolition Work	23594	Wrecking and Demolition Contractors

pt—Part of; NEC—Not Elsewhere Classified.

http://www.ntis.gov/naics

1987 SIC code	1987 U.S. SIC description	1997 NAICS code	1997 NAICS U.S. description
1796	Installation or Erection of Building Equipment, NEC	23595	Building Equipment and Other Machinery Installation Contractors
1799	Special Trade Contractors, NEC		
	Paint and Wallpaper Stripping and Wallpaper Removal Contractors	23521	Painting and Wall Covering Contractors (pt)
	Tinted Glass Work	23592	Glass and Glazing Contractors (pt)
	Asbestos Abatement and Lead Paint Removal Contractors	56291	Remediation Services (pt)
	All Other Special Trade Contractors	23599	All Other Special Trade Contractors
2011	Meat Packing Plants	311611	Animal (except Poultry) Slaughtering (pt)
2013	Sausages and Other Prepared Meats		
	Lard Made From Purchased Material	311613	Rendering and Meat Byproduct Processing (pt)
	Except Lard Made From Purchased Material	311612	Meat Processed from Carcasses (pt)
2015	Poultry Slaughtering and Processing		
	Poultry Processing	311615	Poultry Processing
	Egg Processing	311999	All Other Miscellaneous Food Manufacturing (pt)
2021	Creamery Butter	311512	Creamery Butter Manufacturing
2022	Natural, Processed, and Imitation Cheese	311513	Cheese Manufacturing
2023	Dry, Condensed, and Evaporated Dairy Products	311514	Dry, Condensed, and Evaporated Dairy Product Manufacturing
2024	Ice Cream and Frozen Desserts	31152	Ice Cream and Frozen Dessert Manufacturing
2026	Fluid Milk		
	Ultra-High Temperature	311514	Dry, Condensed, and Evaporated Dairy Product Manufacturing (pt)
	Except Ultra-High Temperature	311511	Fluid Milk Manufacturing
2032	Canned Specialties		
	Canned Specialties	311422	Specialty Canning
	Canned Pudding	311999	All Other Miscellaneous Food Manufacturing (pt)
2033	Canned Fruits, Vegetables, Preserves, Jams, and Jellies	311421	Fruit and Vegetable Canning (pt)
2034	Dried and Dehydrated Fruits, Vegetables, and Soup Mixes		

pt—Part of; NEC—Not Elsewhere Classified.

http://www.ntis.gov/naics

1987 SIC code	1987 U.S. SIC description	1997 NAICS code	1997 NAICS U.S. description
	Dried and Dehydrated Fruits and Vegetables	311423	Dried and Dehydrated Food Manufacturing (pt)
	Soup Mixes Made from Purchased Dried and Dehydrated Vegetables	311999	All Other Miscellaneous Food Manufacturing (pt)
	Vegetable Flours	311211	Flour Milling (pt)
2035	Pickled Fruits and Vegetables, Vegetable Sauces and Seasonings, and Salad Dressings		
	Pickled Fruits and Vegetables	311421	Fruit and Vegetable Canning (pt)
	Sauces and Salad Dressings	311941	Mayonnaise, Dressing, and Other Prepared Sauce Manufacturing (pt)
2037	Frozen Fruits, Fruit Juices, and Vegetables	311411	Frozen Fruit, Juice, and Vegetable Processing
2038	Frozen Specialties, NEC	311412	Frozen Specialty Food Manufacturing
2041	Flour and Other Grain Mill Products	311211	Flour Milling (pt)
2043	Cereal Breakfast Foods		
	Coffee Substitute	31192	Coffee and Tea Manufacturing (pt)
	Breakfast Cereal	31123	Breakfast Cereal Manufacturing
2044	Rice Milling	311212	Rice Milling
2045	Prepared Flour Mixes and Doughs	311822	Flour Mixes and Dough Manufacturing from Purchased Flour
2046	Wet Corn Milling	311221	Wet Corn Milling
	Refining Purchased Oil	311225	Fats and Oils Refining and Blending (pt)
	Except Refining Purchased Oil	311221	Wet Corn Milling
2047	Dog and Cat Food	311111	Dog and Cat Food Manufacturing
2048	Prepared Feed and Feed Ingredients for Animals and Fowls, Except Dogs and Cats		
	Animal Slaughtering for Pet Food	311611	Animal (except Poultry) Slaughtering (pt)
	Except Slaughtering Animals for Pet Food	311119	Other Animal Food Manufacturing (pt)
2051	Bread and Other Bakery Products, Except Cookies and Crackers	311812	Commercial Bakeries (pt)
2052	Cookies and Crackers		
	Cookie and Cracker	311821	Cookie and Cracker Manufacturing
	Pretzels, Except Soft	311919	Other Snack Food Manufacturing (pt)

---

pt—Part of; NEC—Not Elsewhere Classified.

http://www.ntis.gov/naics

1987 SIC code	1987 U.S. SIC description	1997 NAICS code	1997 NAICS U.S. description
	Unleavened Bread and Soft Pretzels	311812	Commercial Bakeries (pt)
2053	Frozen Bakery Products, Except Bread	311813	Frozen Cakes, Pies, and Other Pastries Manufacturing
2061	Cane Sugar, Except Refining	311311	Sugarcane Mills
2062	Cane Sugar Refining	311312	Cane Sugar Refining
2063	Beet Sugar	311313	Beet Sugar Manufacturing
2064	Candy and Other Confectionery Products		
	Chocolate Confectionery	31133	Confectionery Manufacturing from Purchased Chocolate (pt)
	Nonchocolate Confectionery Manufacturing	31134	Nonchocolate Confectionery Manufacturing (pt)
2066	Chocolate and Cocoa Products		
	Chocolate Products Made From Purchased Chocolate	31133	Confectionery Manufacturing From Purchased Chocolate (pt)
	Chocolate and Confectionery Products Made From Cacao Beans	31132	Chocolate and Confectionery Manufacturing from Cacao Beans
2067	Chewing Gum	31134	Nonchocolate Confectionery Manufacturing (pt)
2068	Salted and Roasted Nuts and Seeds	311911	Roasted Nuts and Peanut Butter Manufacturing (pt)
2074	Cottonseed Oil Mills		
	Cottonseed Processing	311223	Other Oilseed Processing (pt)
	Processing Purchased Cottonseed Oil	311225	Fats and Oils Refining and Blending (pt)
2075	Soybean Oil Mills		
	Soybean Processing	311222	Soybean Processing (pt)
	Processing Purchased Soybean Oil	311225	Fats and Oils Refining and Blending (pt)
2076	Vegetable Oil Mills, Except Corn, Cottonseed, and Soybeans		
	Vegetable Oilseed Processing, except Corn, Cottonseed, and Soybeans	311223	Other Oilseed Processing (pt)
	Processing Purchased Vegetable Oils, except Corn, Cottonseed, and Soybeans	311225	Fats and Oils Refining and Blending (pt)
2077	Animal and Marine Fats and Oils		
	Animal Fats and Oils	311613	Rendering and Meat Byproduct Processing

pt—Part of; NEC—Not Elsewhere Classified.

http://www.ntis.gov/naics

1987 SIC code	1987 U.S. SIC description	1997 NAICS code	1997 NAICS U.S. description
	Canned Marine Fats and Oils	311711	Seafood Canning (pt)
	Fresh and Frozen Marine Fats and Oils	311712	Fresh and Frozen Seafood Processing (pt)
2079	Shortening, Table Oils, Margarine, and Other Edible Fats and Oils, NEC		
	Processing Fats and Oils from Purchased Fats and Oils	311225	Fats and Oils Refining and Blending (pt)
	Processing Soybean Oil from Soybeans Crushed in the Same Establishment	311222	Soybean Processing (pt)
	Processing Vegetable Oils, except Soybeans, from Oilseeds Crushed in the Same Establishment	311223	Other Oilseed Processing (pt)
2082	Malt Beverages		
	Malt Extract	311942	Spice and Extract Manufacturing (pt)
	Except Malt Extract	31212	Breweries
2083	Malt	311213	Malt Manufacturing
2084	Wines, Brandy, and Brandy Spirits	31213	Wineries (pt)
2085	Distilled and Blended Liquors		
	Applejack	31213	Wineries (pt)
	Except Applejack	31214	Distilleries
2086	Bottled and Canned Soft Drinks and Carbonated Waters		
	Soft Drinks	312111	Soft Drink Manufacturing
	Bottled Water	312112	Bottled Water Manufacturing (pt)
2087	Flavoring Extracts and Flavoring Syrups NEC		
	Coffee Flavoring and Syrups	31192	Coffee and Tea Manufacturing (pt)
	Flavoring Syrup and Concentrate, Except Coffee	31193	Flavoring Syrup and Concentrate Manufacturing
	Flavoring Extracts, Except Coffee, and Natural Food Colorings	311942	Spice and Extract Manufacturing (pt)
	Powdered Drink Mix	311999	All Other Miscellaneous Food Manufacturing (pt)
2091	Canned and Cured Fish and Seafood	311711	Seafood Canning (pt)
2092	Prepared Fresh or Frozen Fish and Seafoods	311712	Fresh and Frozen Seafood Processing (pt)

pt—Part of; NEC—Not Elsewhere Classified.

http://www.ntis.gov/naics

1987 SIC code	1987 U.S. SIC description	1997 NAICS code	1997 NAICS U.S. description
2095	Roasted Coffee	31192	Coffee and Tea Manufacturing (pt)
2096	Potato Chips, Corn Chips, and Similar Snacks	311919	Other Snack Food Manufacturing (pt)
2097	Manufactured Ice	312113	Ice Manufacturing
2098	Macaroni, Spaghetti, Vermicelli, and Noodles	311823	Dry Pasta Manufacturing (pt)
2099	Food Preparations, NEC		
	Reducing Maple Sap to Maple Syrup	111998	All Other Miscellaneous Crop Farming (pt)
	Marshmallow Creme	31134	Nonchocolate Confectionery Manufacturing (pt)
	Peanut Butter	311911	Roasted Nuts and Peanut Butter Manufacturing (pt)
	Potatoes, Dried and Packaged with Other Ingredients Made in Dehydration Plants, and Bouillon	311423	Dried and Dehydrated Food Manufacturing (pt)
	Perishable Prepared Food	311991	Perishable Prepared Food Manufacturing
	Rice, Uncooked and Packaged with Other Ingredients Made in Rice Mills	311212	Rice Milling (pt)
	Tortillas	31183	Tortilla Manufacturing
	Dry Pasta Packaged with Other Ingredients Made in Dry Pasta Plants	311823	Dry Pasta Manufacturing (pt)
	Tea	31192	Coffee and Tea Manufacturing (pt)
	Vinegar, Prepared Dips Except Dairy and Cider	311941	Mayonnaise, Dressing, and Other Prepared Sauce Manufacturing (pt)
	Spices and Extracts	311942	Spice and Extract Manufacturing (pt)
	Other	311999	All Other Miscellaneous Food Manufacturing (pt)
2111	Cigarettes	312221	Cigarette Manufacturing
2121	Cigars	312229	Other Tobacco Product Manufacturing (pt)
2131	Chewing and Smoking Tobacco and Snuff	312229	Other Tobacco Product Manufacturing (pt)
2141	Tobacco Stemming and Redrying		
	Reconstituted Tobacco	312229	Other Tobacco Product Manufacturing (pt)

pt—Part of; NEC—Not Elsewhere Classified.

http://www.ntis.gov/naics

1987 SIC code	1987 U.S. SIC description	1997 NAICS code	1997 NAICS U.S. description
	Redrying and Stemming	31221	Tobacco Stemming and Redrying
2211	Broadwoven Fabric Mills, Cotton	31321	Broadwoven Fabric Mills (pt)
2221	Broadwoven Fabric Mills, Manmade Fiber and Silk	31321	Broadwoven Fabric Mills (pt)
2231	Broadwoven Fabric Mills, Wool (Including Dyeing and Finishing)		
	Except Wool Finishing only	31321	Broadwoven Fabric Mills (pt)
	Wool Broadwoven Fabric Finishing only	313311	Broadwoven Fabric Finishing Mills (pt)
	Wool Finishing only, Except Broadwoven Fabric	313312	Textile and Fabric Finishing (except Broadwoven Fabric) Mills (pt)
2241	Narrow Fabric and Other Smallware Mills: Cotton, Wool, Silk, and Manmade Fiber	313221	Narrow Fabric Mills (pt)
2251	Women's Full-Length and Knee-Length Hosiery, Except Socks		
	Dyeing and Finishing Only	313312	Textile and Fabric Finishing (except Broadwoven Fabric) Mills (pt)
	Except Dyeing and Finishing Only	315111	Sheer Hosiery Mills (pt)
2252	Hosiery, NEC		
	Dyeing and Finishing Only	313312	Textile and Fabric Finishing (except Broadwoven Fabric) Mills (pt)
	Girls' Hosiery, Except Dyeing and Finishing Only	315111	Sheer Hosiery Mills (pt)
	Socks, Except Dyeing and Finishing Only	315119	Other Hosiery and Sock Mills
2253	Knit Outerwear Mills		
	Dyeing and Finishing Only	313312	Textile and Fabric Finishing (except Broadwoven Fabric) Mills (pt)
	Bathrobes and Lounging Robes Made in Knitting Mills Except Dyeing and Finishing Only	315192	Underwear and Nightwear Knitting Mills (pt)
	Except Dyeing and Finishing Only and Bathrobes and Lounging Robes	315191	Outerwear Knitting Mills (pt)
2254	Knit Underwear and Nightwear Mills		
	Dyeing and Finishing Only	313312	Textile and Fabric Finishing (except Broadwoven Fabric) Mills (pt)
	Except Dyeing and Finishing Only	315192	Underwear and Nightwear Knitting Mills (pt)

---

pt—Part of; NEC—Not Elsewhere Classified.

1987 SIC code	1987 U.S. SIC description	1997 NAICS code	1997 NAICS U.S. description
2257	Weft Knit Fabric Mills		
	Except Finishing	313241	Weft Knit Fabric Mills (pt)
	Finishing Only	313312	Textile and Fabric Finishing (except Broadwoven Fabric) Mills (pt)
2258	Lace and Warp Knit Fabric Mills		
	Except Finishing	313249	Other Knit Fabric and Lace Mills (pt)
	Finishing Only	313312	Textile and Fabric Finishing (except Broadwoven Fabric) Mills (pt)
2259	Knitting Mills, NEC		
	Knit Gloves and Mittens	315191	Outerwear Knitting Mills (pt)
	Girdles	315192	Underwear and Nightwear Knitting Mills (pt)
	Finished Articles of Weft Knit Fabric	313241	Weft Knit Fabric Mills (pt)
	Knit Gloves and Mittens, Dyeing and Finishing Only	313312	Textile and Fabric Finishing (except Broadwoven Fabric) Mills (pt)
	Finished Articles of Warp Knit Fabric	313249	Other Knit Fabric and Lace Mills (pt)
2261	Finishers of Broadwoven Fabrics of Cotton	313311	Broadwoven Fabric Finishing Mills (pt)
2262	Finishers of Broadwoven Fabrics of Manmade Fiber and Silk	313311	Broadwoven Fabric Finishing Mills (pt)
2269	Finishers of Textiles, NEC	313312	Textile and Fabric Finishing (except Broadwoven Fabric) Mills (pt)
2273	Carpets and Rugs	31411	Carpet and Rug Mills
2281	Yarn Spinning Mills	313111	Yarn Spinning Mills (pt)
2282	Yarn Texturizing, Throwing, Twisting, and Winding Mills	313112	Yarn Texturing, Throwing, and Twisting Mills
2284	Thread Mills		
	Except Finishing	313113	Thread Mills (pt)
	Finishing	313312	Textile and Fabric Finishing (except Broadwoven Fabric) Mills (pt)
2295	Coated Fabrics, Not Rubberized	31332	Fabric Coating Mills (pt)
2296	Tire Cord and Fabrics	314992	Tire Cord and Tire Fabric Mills
2297	Nonwoven Fabrics	31323	Nonwoven Fabric Mills (pt)
2298	Cordage and Twine	314991	Rope, Cordage and Twine Mills
2299	Textile Goods, NEC		
	Broadwoven Fabric of Jute, Linen, Hemp, and Ramie and Handwoven	31321	Broadwoven Fabric Mills (pt)

pt—Part of; NEC—Not Elsewhere Classified.

1987 SIC code	1987 U.S. SIC description	1997 NAICS code	1997 NAICS U.S. description
	Nonwoven Felt	31323	Nonwoven Fabric Mills (pt)
	Finishing Thread and Yarn of Flax, Hemp, Jute, Linen, and Ramie	313312	Textile and Fabric Finishing (except Broadwoven Fabrics) Mills (pt)
	Narrow Woven Fabric of Jute, Linen, Hemp, and Ramie	313221	Narrow Fabric Mills (pt)
	Thread of Hemp, Linen, and Ramie	313113	Thread Mills (pt)
	Yarn of Flax, Hemp, Jute, and Ramie	313111	Yarn Spinning Mills (pt)
	Recovery and Processing of Fibers and Waste	314999	All Other Miscellaneous Textile Product Mills (pt)
2311	Men's and Boys' Suits, Coats, and Overcoats		
	Contractors	315211	Men's and Boys' Cut and Sew Apparel Contractors (pt)
	Except Contractors	315222	Men's and Boys' Cut and Sew Suit, Coat, and Overcoat Manufacturing (pt)
2321	Men's and Boys' Shirts, Except Work Shirts		
	Contractors	315211	Men's and Boys' Cut and Sew Apparel Contractors (pt)
	Except Contractors	315223	Men's and Boys' Cut and Sew Shirt, (except Work Shirt) Manufacturing (pt)
2322	Men's and Boys' Underwear and Nightwear		
	Contractors	315211	Men's and Boys' Cut and Sew Apparel Contractors (pt)
	Except Contractors	315221	Men's and Boys' Cut and Sew Underwear and Nightwear Manufacturing (pt)
2323	Men's and Boys' Neckwear		
	Contractors	315211	Men's and Boys' Cut and Sew Apparel Contractors (pt)
	Except Contractors	315993	Men's and Boys' Neckwear Manufacturing
2325	Men's and Boys' Trousers and Slacks		
	Contractors	315211	Men's and Boys' Cut and Sew Apparel Contractors (pt)

pt—Part of; NEC—Not Elsewhere Classified.

http://www.ntis.gov/naics

1987 SIC code	1987 U.S. SIC description	1997 NAICS code	1997 NAICS U.S. description
	Except Contractors	315224	Men's and Boys' Cut And Sew Trouser, Slack, and Jean Manufacturing (pt)
2326	Men's and Boys' Work Clothing		
	Contractors	315211	Men's and Boys' Cut and Sew Apparel Contractors (pt)
	Except Contractors	315225	Men's and Boys' Cut and Sew Work Clothing Manufacturing
2329	Men's and Boys' Clothing, NEC		
	Contractors	315211	Men's and Boys' Cut and Sew Apparel Contractors (pt)
	Except Contractors	315228	Men's and Boys' Cut and Sew Other Outerwear Manufacturing (pt)
	Athletic Uniforms, Except Contractors	315299	All Other Cut and Sew Apparel Manufacturing (pt)
2331	Women's, Misses', and Juniors' Blouses and Shirts		
	Contractors	315212	Women's, Girls', and Infants' Cut and Sew Apparel Contractors (pt)
	Except Contractors	315232	Women's and Girls' Cut and Sew Blouse and Shirt Manufacturing (pt)
2335	Women's, Misses', and Juniors' Dresses		
	Contractors	315212	Women's, Girls', and Infants' Cut and Sew Apparel Contractors (pt)
	Except Contractors	315233	Women's and Girls' Cut and Sew Dress Manufacturing (pt)
2337	Women's, Misses' and Juniors' Suits, Skirts, and Coats		
	Contractors	315212	Women's, Girls', and Infants' Cut and Sew Apparel Contractors (pt)
	Except Contractors	315234	Women's and Girls' Cut and Sew Suit, Coat, Tailored Jacket, and Skirt Manufacturing (pt)
2339	Women's, Misses', and Juniors' Outerwear, NEC		
	Scarves, Except Contractors	315999	Other Apparel Accessories and Other Apparel Manufacturing (pt)

pt—Part of; NEC—Not Elsewhere Classified.

http://www.ntis.gov/naics

1987 SIC code	1987 U.S. SIC description	1997 NAICS code	1997 NAICS U.S. description
	Contractors	315212	Women's, Girls', and Infants' Cut and Sew Apparel Contractors (pt)
	Athletic Uniforms, Except Contractors	315299	All Other Cut and Sew Apparel Manufacturing (pt)
	All Other, Except Contractors	315239	Women's and Girls' Cut and Sew Other Outerwear Manufacturing (pt)
2341	Women's, Misses', Children's, and Infants' Underwear and Nightwear		
	Women's, Girls' and Infants' Contractors	315212	Women's, Girls', and Infants' Cut and Sew Apparel Contractors (pt)
	Boys' Contractors	315211	Men's and Boys' Cut and Sew Apparel Contractors (pt)
	Women's and Girls', Except Contractors	315231	Women's and Girls' Cut and Sew Lingerie, Loungewear, and Nightwear Manufacturing (pt)
	Boys', Except Contractors	315221	Men's and Boys' Cut and Sew Underwear and Nightwear Manufacturing (pt)
	Infants', Except Contractors	315291	Infants' Cut and Sew Apparel Manufacturing (pt)
2342	Brassieres, Girdles, and Allied Garments		
	Contractors	315212	Women's, Girls', and Infants' Cut and Sew Apparel Contractors (pt)
	Except Contractors	315231	Women's and Girls' Cut and Sew Lingerie, Loungewear, and Nightwear Manufacturing (pt)
2353	Hats, Caps, and Millinery		
	Men's and Boys' Contractors	315211	Men's and Boys' Cut and Sew Apparel Contractors (pt)
	Women's, Girls', and Infants' Contractors	315212	Women's, Girls', and Infants' Cut and Sew Apparel Contractors (pt)
	Except Contractors	315991	Hat, Cap, and Millinery Manufacturing
2361	Girls', Children's, and Infants' Dresses, Blouses, and Shirts		
	Infants' Dresses, Blouses, and Shirts, Except Contractors	315291	Infants' Cut and Sew Apparel Manufacturing (pt)
	Boys' Shirts, Except Contractors	315223	Men's and Boys' Cut and Sew Shirt, (except Work Shirt) Manufacturing (pt)

---

pt—Part of; NEC—Not Elsewhere Classified.

1987 SIC code	1987 U.S. SIC description	1997 NAICS code	1997 NAICS U.S. description
	Boys' Shirt Contractors	315211	Men's and Boys' Cut and Sew Apparel Contractors (pt)
	Girls' Blouses and Shirts, Except Contractors	315232	Women's and Girls' Cut and Sew Blouse and Shirt Manufacturing (pt)
	Girls' Dresses, Except Contractors	315233	Women's and Girls' Cut and Sew Dress Manufacturing (pt)
	Girls' and Infants' Contractors	315212	Women's, Girls', and Infants' Cut and Sew Apparel Contractors (pt)
2369	Girls', Children's, and Infants' Outerwear, NEC		
	Infants' Outerwear, NEC, Except Contractors	315291	Infants' Cut and Sew Apparel Manufacturing (pt)
	Boys' Suits and Coats, Except Contractors	315222	Men's and Boys' Cut and Sew Suit, Coat, and Overcoat Manufacturing (pt)
	Boys' Trousers and Slacks, Except Contractors	315224	Men's and Boys' Cut and Sew Trouser, Slack, and Jean Manufacturing (pt)
	Boys' Outerwear, NEC, Except Contractors	315228	Men's and Boys' Cut and Sew Other Outerwear Manufacturing (pt)
	Boys' Robes, Except Contractors	315221	Men's and Boys' Cut and Sew Underwear and Nightwear Manufacturing (pt)
	Boys' Contractors	315211	Men's and Boys' Cut and Sew Apparel Contractors (pt)
	Girls' Suits, Coats, Skirts, Etc., Except Contractors	315234	Women's and Girls' Cut and Sew Suit, Coat, Tailored Jacket, and Skirt Manufacturing (pt)
	Girls' Outerwear, NEC, Except Contractors	315239	Women's and Girls' Cut and Sew Other Outerwear Manufacturing (pt)
	Girls' Robes, Except Contractors	315231	Women's and Girls' Cut and Sew Lingerie, Loungewear, and Nightwear Manufacturing (pt)
	Girls' Contractors	315212	Women's, Girls', and Infants' Cut and Sew Apparel Contractors (pt)
2371	Fur Goods		
	Men's and Boys' Contractors	315211	Men's and Boys' Cut and Sew Apparel Contractors (pt)

—————
pt—Part of; NEC—Not Elsewhere Classified.

http://www.ntis.gov/naics

1987 SIC code	1987 U.S. SIC description	1997 NAICS code	1997 NAICS U.S. description
	Women's, Girls', and Infants' Contractors	315212	Women's, Girls', and Infants' Cut and Sew Apparel Contractors (pt)
	Except Contractors	315292	Fur and Leather Apparel Manufacturing (pt)
2381	Dress and Work Gloves, Except Knit and All-Leather		
	Men's and Boys' Contractors	315211	Men's and Boys' Cut and Sew Apparel Contractors (pt)
	Women's, Girls', and Infants' Contractors	315212	Women's, Girls', and Infants' Cut and Sew Apparel Contractors (pt)
	Except Contractors	315992	Glove and Mitten Manufacturing (pt)
2384	Robes and Dressing Gowns		
	Women's Except Contractors	315231	Women's and Girls' Cut and Sew Lingerie, Loungewear, and Nightwear Manufacturing (pt)
	Men's Except Contractors	315221	Men's and Boys' Cut and Sew Underwear and Nightwear Manufacturing (pt)
	Men's and Boys' Contractors	315211	Men's and Boys' Cut and Sew Apparel Contractors (pt)
	Women's and Girls' Contractors	315212	Women's, Girls', and Infants' Cut and Sew Apparel Contractors (pt)
2385	Waterproof Outerwear		
	Men's and Boys' Water Resistant or Water Repellent Tailored Overcoats	315222	Men's and Boys' Cut and Sew Suit, Coat, and Overcoat Manufacturing (pt)
	Women's and Girls' Water Resistant or Water Repellent Tailored Coats	315234	Women's and Girls' Cut and Sew Suit, Coat, Tailored Jacket, and Skirt Manufacturing (pt)
	Men's and Boys' Water Resistant or Water Repellent Nontailored Outerwear, except Rubber and Plastics and Contractors	315228	Men's and Boys' Cut and Sew Other Outerwear Manufacturing (pt)
	Women's and Girls' Water Resistant or Water Repellent Nontailored Outerwear, except Rubber and Plastics and Contractors	315239	Women's and Girls' Cut and Sew Other Outerwear Manufacturing (pt)

pt—Part of; NEC—Not Elsewhere Classified.

http://www.ntis.gov/naics

1987 SIC code	1987 U.S. SIC description	1997 NAICS code	1997 NAICS U.S. description
	Infants' Waterproof Outerwear Except Contractors	315291	Infants' Cut and Sew Apparel Manufacturing (pt)
	Waterproof Rubber and Plastic Outerwear, Except Contractors	315299	All Other Cut and Sew Apparel Manufacturing (pt)
	Accessories such as Aprons, Bibs, and Miscellaneous Waterproof Items, Except Contractors	315999	Other Apparel Accessories and Other Apparel Manufacturing (pt)
	Men's and Boys' Contractors	315211	Men's and Boys' Cut and Sew Apparel Contractors (pt)
	Women's and Girls' Contractors	315212	Women's, Girls', and Infants' Cut and Sew Apparel Contractors (pt)
2386	Leather and Sheep-Lined Clothing		
	Men's and Boys' Contractors	315211	Men's and Boys' Cut and Sew Apparel Contractors (pt)
	Women's, Girls', and Infants' Contractors	315212	Women's, Girls', and Infants' Cut and Sew Apparel Contractors (pt)
	Except Contractors	315292	Fur and Leather Apparel Manufacturing (pt)
2387	Apparel Belts		
	Men's and Boys' Contractors	315211	Men's and Boys' Cut and Sew Apparel Contractors (pt)
	Women's, Girls', and Infants' Contractors	315212	Women's, Girls', and Infants' Cut and Sew Apparel Contractors (pt)
	Except Contractors	315999	Other Apparel Accessories and Other Apparel Manufacturing (pt)
2389	Apparel and Accessories, NEC		
	Handkerchiefs, Arm bands, etc.	315999	Other Apparel Accessories and Other Apparel Manufacturing (pt)
	Academic and Clerical Outerwear	315299	All Other Cut and Sew Apparel Manufacturing (pt)
	Garters and Garter Belts	315231	Women's and Girls' Cut and Sew Lingerie, Loungewear, and Nightwear Manufacturing (pt)
	Women's Contractors	315212	Women's, Girls', and Infants' Cut and Sew Apparel Contractors (pt)
	Men's Contractors	315211	Men's and Boys' Cut and Sew Apparel Contractors (pt)
2391	Curtains and Draperies	314121	Curtain and Drapery Mills (pt)
2392	Housefurnishings, Except Curtains and Draperies		
	Blanket, Laundry, and Garment Storage Bags	314911	Textile Bag Mills (pt)

pt—Part of; NEC—Not Elsewhere Classified.

1987 SIC code	1987 U.S. SIC description	1997 NAICS code	1997 NAICS U.S. description
	Dust Rags	314999	All Other Miscellaneous Textile Product Mills (pt)
	Mops, Floor and Dust	339994	Broom, Brush, and Mop Manufacturing (pt)
	Other Housefurnishings	314129	Other Household Textile Product Mills (pt)
2393	Textile Bags	314911	Textile Bag Mills (pt)
2394	Canvas and Related Products	314912	Canvas and Related Product Mills (pt)
2395	Pleating, Decorative and Novelty Stitching, and Tucking for the Trade		
	Pleating and Stitching, Except Apparel Contractors	314999	All Other Miscellaneous Textile Product Mills (pt)
	Men's and Boys' Apparel Contractors	315211	Men's and Boys' Cut and Sew Apparel Contractors (pt)
	Women's, Girls', and Infants' Apparel Contractors	315212	Women's, Girls', and Infants' Cut and Sew Apparel Contractors (pt)
2396	Automotive Trimmings, Apparel Findings, and Related Products		
	Textile Automotive Trimmings	33636	Motor Vehicle Seating and Interior Trim Manufacturing (pt)
	Apparel Findings and Trimmings	315999	Other Apparel Accessories and Other Apparel Manufacturing (pt)
	Printing and Embossing on Fabric Articles	323113	Commercial Screen Printing (pt)
	Other Apparel Products	314999	All Other Miscellaneous Textile Product Mills (pt)
2397	Schiffli Machine Embroideries	313222	Schiffli Machine Embroidery
2399	Fabricated Textile Products, NEC		
	Seat Belts and Seat and Tire Covers	33636	Motor Vehicle Seating and Interior Trim Manufacturing (pt)
	Apparel and Apparel Accessories	315999	Other Apparel Accessories and Other Apparel Manufacturing (pt)
	Other Fabricated Textile Products	314999	All Other Miscellaneous Textile Product Mills (pt)
2411	Logging	11331	Logging
2421	Sawmills and Planing Mills, General		
	Lumber Manufacturing from Purchased Lumber, Softwood Cut Stock, Wood Lath and Planing Mill Products	321912	Cut Stock, Resawing Lumber, and Planing (pt)

pt—Part of; NEC—Not Elsewhere Classified.

http://www.ntis.gov/naics

1987 SIC code	1987 U.S. SIC description	1997 NAICS code	1997 NAICS U.S. description
	Sawmills	321113	Sawmills (pt)
	Softwood Flooring	321918	Other Millwork (including Flooring) (pt)
	Kiln Drying	321999	All Other Miscellaneous Wood Product Manufacturing (pt)
2426	Hardwood Dimension and Flooring Mills		
	Hardwood Flooring	321918	Other Millwork (including Flooring) (pt)
	Wood Furniture Frames	337215	Showcase, Partition, Shelving, and Locker Manufacturing (pt)
	Hardwood Dimension Lumber Made From Logs and Bolts	321113	Sawmills (pt)
	Other Hardwood Dimension Except Flooring	321912	Cut Stock, Resawing Lumber, and Planing (pt)
2429	Special Product Sawmills, NEC		
	Shingle Mills, Shakes	321113	Sawmills (pt)
	Stave Manufacturing from Purchased Lumber	321912	Cut Stock, Resawing Lumber, and Planing (pt)
	Cooperage Stock	32192	Wood Container and Pallet Manufacturing (pt)
	Excelsior and Cooperage Headings	321999	All Other Miscellaneous Wood Product Manufacturing (pt)
2431	Millwork		
	Wood Windows and Doors	321911	Wood Window and Door Manufacturing
	Except Wood Windows and Doors	321918	Other Millwork (including Flooring) (pt)
2434	Wood Kitchen Cabinets	33711	Wood Kitchen Cabinet and Countertop Manufacturing (pt)
2435	Hardwood Veneer and Plywood	321211	Hardwood Veneer and Plywood Manufacturing
2436	Softwood Veneer and Plywood	321212	Softwood Veneer and Plywood Manufacturing
2439	Structural Wood Members, NEC		
	Trusses	321214	Truss Manufacturing
	Except Trusses	321213	Engineered Wood Member (except Truss) Manufacturing
2441	Nailed and Lock Corner Wood Boxes and Shook	32192	Wood Container and Pallet Manufacturing (pt)
2448	Wood Pallets and Skids	32192	Wood Container and Pallet Manufacturing (pt)

pt—Part of; NEC—Not Elsewhere Classified.

http://www.ntis.gov/naics

1987 SIC code	1987 U.S. SIC description	1997 NAICS code	1997 NAICS U.S. description
2449	Wood Containers, NEC	32192	Wood Container and Pallet Manufacturing (pt)
2451	Mobile Homes	321991	Manufactured Home (Mobile Home) Manufacturing
2452	Prefabricated Wood Buildings and Components	321992	Prefabricated Wood Building Manufacturing
2491	Wood Preserving	321114	Wood Preservation
2493	Reconstituted Wood Products	321219	Reconstituted Wood Product Manufacturing
2499	Wood Products, NEC		
	Mirror and Picture Frames	339999	All Other Miscellaneous Manufacturing (pt)
	Wood Cooling Towers	333414	Heating Equipment (except Warm Air Furnace) Manufacturing (pt)
	Wood Tubs and Vats, Jewelry, Cigar Boxes, and Baskets, Except Fruit, Fish, and Bait	32192	Wood Container and Pallet Manufacturing (pt)
	Other Wood Products	321999	All Other Miscellaneous Wood Product Manufacturing (pt)
2511	Wood Household Furniture, Except Upholstered		
	Wood Box Spring Frames	337215	Showcase, Partition, Shelving, and Locker Manufacturing (pt)
	Except Wood Box Spring Frames	337122	Wood Household Furniture (except Upholstered) Manufacturing (pt)
2512	Wood Household Furniture, Upholstered	337121	Upholstered Household Furniture Manufacturing (pt)
2514	Metal Household Furniture		
	Except Upholstered and Metal Box Spring Frames	337124	Metal Household Furniture Manufacturing
	Upholstered	337121	Upholstered Household Furniture Manufacturing (pt)
	Metal Box Spring Frames	337215	Showcase, Partition, Shelving, and Locker Manufacturing (pt)
2515	Mattresses, Foundations, and Convertible Beds		
	Mattresses and Foundations	33791	Mattress Manufacturing
	Convertible Sofas	337121	Upholstered Household Furniture Manufacturing (pt)
2517	Wood Television, Radio, Phonograph and Sewing Machine Cabinets	337129	Wood Television, Radio, and Sewing Machine Cabinet Manufacturing

pt—Part of; NEC—Not Elsewhere Classified.

1987 SIC code	1987 U.S. SIC description	1997 NAICS code	1997 NAICS U.S. description
2519	Household Furniture, NEC	337125	Household Furniture (except Wood and Metal) Manufacturing
2521	Wood Office Furniture	337211	Wood Office Furniture Manufacturing
2522	Office Furniture, Except Wood	337214	Office Furniture (except Wood) Manufacturing
2531	Public Building and Related Furniture		
	Seats for Motor Vehicles	33636	Motor Vehicle Seating and Interior Trim Manufacturing (pt)
	Furniture Made for Public Buildings	337127	Institutional Furniture Manufacturing (pt)
	Blackboards	339942	Lead Pencil and Art Good Manufacturing (pt)
2541	Wood Office and Store Fixtures, Partitions, Shelving, and Lockers		
	Wood Lunchroom Tables and Chairs	337127	Institutional Furniture Manufacturing (pt)
	Custom Architectural Woodwork, Millwork and Fixtures	337212	Custom Architectural Woodwork and Millwork Manufacturing
	Except Countertops, Custom Architectural Woodwork, Millwork, and Fixtures	337215	Showcase, Partition, Shelving, and Locker Manufacturing (pt)
2542	Office and Store Fixtures, Partitions, Shelving, and Lockers, Except Wood		
	Lunchroom Tables and Chairs (except wood)	337127	Institutional Furniture Manufacturing (pt)
	Except Lunchroom Tables and Chairs (except wood)	337215	Showcase, Partition, Shelving, and Locker Manufacturing (pt)
2591	Drapery Hardware and Window Blinds and Shades	33792	Blind and Shade Manufacturing
2599	Furniture and Fixtures, NEC		
	Hospital Beds	339111	Laboratory Apparatus and Furniture Manufacturing (pt)
	Except Hospital Beds	337127	Institutional Furniture Manufacturing (pt)
2611	Pulp Mills		
	Pulp Producing Mills Only	32211	Pulp Mills
	Pulp Mills Producing Paper	322121	Paper (except Newsprint) Mills (pt)
	Pulp Mills Producing Newsprint	322122	Newsprint Mills (pt)
	Pulp Mills Producing Paperboard	32213	Paperboard Mills (pt)
2621	Paper Mills		
	Except Newsprint Mills	322121	Paper (except Newsprint) Mills (pt)
	Newsprint Mills	322122	Newsprint Mills (pt)
2631	Paperboard Mills	32213	Paperboard Mills (pt)

pt—Part of; NEC—Not Elsewhere Classified.

1987 SIC code	1987 U.S. SIC description	1997 NAICS code	1997 NAICS U.S. description
2652	Setup Paperboard Boxes	322213	Setup Paperboard Box Manufacturing
2653	Corrugated and Solid Fiber Boxes	322211	Corrugated and Solid Fiber Box Manufacturing (pt)
2655	Fiber Cans, Tubes, Drums, and Similar Products	322214	Fiber Can, Tube, Drum, and Similar Products Manufacturing
2656	Sanitary Food Containers, Except Folding	322215	Nonfolding Sanitary Food Container Manufacturing
2657	Folding Paperboard Boxes, Including Sanitary	322212	Folding Paperboard Box Manufacturing
2671	Packaging Paper and Plastics Film, Coated and Laminated		
	Single-Web Paper, Paper Multiweb Laminated Rolls and Sheets for Packaging Uses	322221	Coated and Laminated Packaging Paper and Plastics Film Manufacturing
	Plastics Packaging Film and Sheet	326112	Unsupported Plastics Packaging Film and Sheet Manufacturing
2672	Coated and Laminated Paper, NEC	322222	Coated and Laminated Paper Manufacturing (pt)
2673	Plastics, Foil, and Coated Paper Bags		
	Except All Plastics	322223	Plastics, Foil, and Coated Paper Bag Manufacturing
	Plastics Bags	326111	Unsupported Plastics Bag Manufacturing
2674	Uncoated Paper and Multiwall Bags	322224	Uncoated Paper and Multiwall Bag Manufacturing
2675	Die-Cut Paper and Paperboard and Cardboard		
	File Folders, Tabulating Cards, and Other Paper and Paperboard Office Supplies	322231	Die-Cut Paper and Paperboard Office Supplies Manufacturing (pt)
	Pasted, Lined, Laminated, or Surface-Coated Paperboard	322226	Surface-Coated Paperboard Manufacturing
	Die-Cut Paper and Paperboard Products, Except Office Supplies and Pasted, Lined, Laminated, or Surface-Coated Paperboard	322299	All Other Converted Paper Product Manufacturing (pt)
2676	Sanitary Paper Products	322291	Sanitary Paper Product Manufacturing (pt)

---

pt—Part of; NEC—Not Elsewhere Classified.

http://www.ntis.gov/naics

1987 SIC code	1987 U.S. SIC description	1997 NAICS code	1997 NAICS U.S. description
2677	Envelopes	322232	Envelope Manufacturing
2678	Stationery, Tablets, and Related Products	322233	Stationery, Tablet, and Related Product Manufacturing
2679	Converted Paper and Paperboard Products, NEC		
	Corrugated Paper	322211	Corrugated and Solid Fiber Box Manufacturing (pt)
	Wallpaper and Gift Wrap Paper	322222	Coated and Laminated Paper Manufacturing (pt)
	Paper Supplies for Business Machines and Other Paper Office Supplies	322231	Die-Cut Paper and Paperboard Office Supplies Manufacturing (pt)
	Other Converted Paper and Paperboard Products such as Paper Filters, Crepe Paper, and Laminated and Tiled Wallboard	322299	All Other Converted Paper Product Manufacturing (pt)
2711	Newspapers: Publishing, or Publishing and Printing	51111	Newspaper Publishers
2721	Periodicals: Publishing, or Publishing and Printing	51112	Periodical Publishers (pt)
2731	Books: Publishing, or Publishing and Printing		
	Music Book Publishing	51223	Music Publishers (pt)
	All Other Book Publishers	51113	Book Publishers
2732	Book Printing	323117	Book Printing
2741	Miscellaneous Publishing		
	Database Publishing	51114	Database and Directory Publishers (pt)
	Shopping News	51112	Periodical Publishers (pt)
	Technical Manuals and Books	51113	Book Publishers (pt)
	Sheet Music Publishers	51223	Music Publishers (pt)
	Miscellaneous Publishing, Except Database, Shopping News, Technical Manuals and Books, and Sheet Music	511199	All Other Publishers
2752	Commercial Printing, Lithographic		
	Quick Printing	323114	Quick Printing (pt)
	Except Quick Printing	323110	Commercial Lithographic Printing (pt)

pt—Part of; NEC—Not Elsewhere Classified.

1987 SIC code	1987 U.S. SIC description	1997 NAICS code	1997 NAICS U.S. description
2754	Commercial Printing, Gravure	323111	Commercial Gravure Printing (pt)
2759	Commercial Printing, NEC		
	Screen Printing	323113	Commercial Screen Printing (pt)
	Flexographic Printing	323112	Commercial Flexographic Printing (pt)
	Quick Printing	323114	Quick Printing (pt)
	Digital Printing, except Quick Printing	323115	Digital Printing
	Other Commercial Printing	323119	Other Commercial Printing (pt)
2761	Manifold Business Forms	323116	Manifold Business Form Printing (pt)
2771	Greeting Cards		
	Lithographic Printing of Greeting Cards	323110	Commercial Lithographic Printing (pt)
	Gravure Printing of Greeting Cards	323111	Commercial Gravure Printing (pt)
	Flexographic Printing of Greeting Cards	323112	Commercial Flexographic Printing (pt)
	Screen Printing of Greeting Cards	323113	Commercial Screen Printing (pt)
	Other Printing of Greeting Cards	323119	Other Commercial Printing (pt)
	Publishing Greeting Cards	511191	Greeting Card Publishers
2782	Blankbooks, Looseleaf Binders and Devices		
	Printing of Checkbooks	323116	Manifold Business Form Printing (pt)
	Blankbooks, Looseleaf Binders and Devices	323118	Blankbook, Looseleaf Binder, and Device Manufacturing
2789	Bookbinding and Related Work	323121	Tradebinding and Related Work
2791	Typesetting	323122	Prepress Services (pt)
2796	Platemaking and Related Services	323122	Prepress Services (pt)
2812	Alkalies and Chlorine	325181	Alkalies and Chlorine Manufacturing
2813	Industrial Gases	32512	Industrial Gas Manufacturing (pt)
2816	Inorganic Pigments		
	Except Bone and Lamp Black	325131	Inorganic Dye and Pigment Manufacturing (pt)
	Bone and Lamp Black	325182	Carbon Black Manufacturing (pt)
2819	Industrial Inorganic Chemicals, NEC		
	Recovering Sulfur from Natural Gas	211112	Natural Gas Liquid Extraction (pt)

pt—Part of; NEC—Not Elsewhere Classified.

http://www.ntis.gov/naics

1987 SIC code	1987 U.S. SIC description	1997 NAICS code	1997 NAICS U.S. description
	Activated Carbon and Charcoal	325998	All Other Miscellaneous Chemical Product and Preparation Manufacturing (pt)
	Alumina	331311	Alumina Refining
	Inorganic Dyes	325131	Inorganic Dye and Pigment Manufacturing (pt)
	Other	325188	All Other Basic Inorganic Chemical Manufacturing (pt)
2821	Plastics Material and Synthetic Resins, and Nonvulcanizable Elastomers	325211	Plastics Material and Resin Manufacturing
2822	Synthetic Rubber	325212	Synthetic Rubber Manufacturing
2823	Cellulosic Manmade Fibers	325221	Cellulosic Organic Fiber Manufacturing
2824	Manmade Organic Fibers, Except Cellulosic	325222	Noncellulosic Organic Fiber Manufacturing
2833	Medicinal Chemicals and Botanical Products	325411	Medicinal and Botanical Manufacturing
2834	Pharmaceutical Preparations	325412	Pharmaceutical Preparation Manufacturing (pt)
2835	In Vitro and In Vivo Diagnostic Substances		
	Except In Vitro Diagnostic	325412	Pharmaceutical Preparation Manufacturing (pt)
	In Vitro Diagnostic Substances	325413	In-Vitro Diagnostic Substance Manufacturing
2836	Biological Products, Except Diagnostic Substances	325414	Biological Product (except Diagnostic) Manufacturing
2841	Soaps and Other Detergents, Except Speciality Cleaners	325611	Soap and Other Detergent Manufacturing (pt)
2842	Speciality Cleaning, Polishing, and Sanitary Preparations	325612	Polish and Other Sanitation Good Manufacturing
2843	Surface Active Agents, Finishing Agents, Sulfonated Oils, and Assistants	325613	Surface Active Agent Manufacturing
2844	Perfumes, Cosmetics, and Other Toilet Preparations		
	Toilet Preparations, Except Toothpaste	32562	Toilet Preparation Manufacturing
	Toothpaste	325611	Soap and Other Detergent Manufacturing (pt)

---

pt—Part of; NEC—Not Elsewhere Classified.

http://www.ntis.gov/naics

1987 SIC code	1987 U.S. SIC description	1997 NAICS code	1997 NAICS U.S. description
2851	Paints, Varnishes, Lacquers, Enamels, and Allied Products	32551	Paint and Coating Manufacturing (pt)
2861	Gum and Wood Chemicals	325191	Gum and Wood Chemical Manufacturing
2865	Cyclic Organic Crudes and Intermediates, and Organic Dyes and Pigments		
	Aromatics	32511	Petrochemical Manufacturing (pt)
	Organic Dyes and Pigments	325132	Synthetic Organic Dye and Pigment Manufacturing
	Other	325192	Cyclic Crude and Intermediate Manufacturing
2869	Industrial Organic Chemicals, NEC		
	Aliphatics	32511	Petrochemical Manufacturing (pt)
	Carbon Bisulfide	325188	All Other Inorganic Chemical Manufacturing (pt)
	Ethyl Alcohol	325193	Ethyl Alcohol Manufacturing
	Fluorocarbon Gases	32512	Industrial Gas Manufacturing (pt)
	Other	325199	All Other Basic Organic Chemical Manufacturing (pt)
2873	Nitrogenous Fertilizers	325311	Nitrogenous Fertilizer Manufacturing
2874	Phosphatic Fertilizers	325312	Phosphatic Fertilizer Manufacturing
2875	Fertilizers, Mixing Only	325314	Fertilizer (Mixing Only) Manufacturing
2879	Pesticides and Agricultural Chemicals, NEC	32532	Pesticide and Other Agricultural Chemical Manufacturing
2891	Adhesives and Sealants	32552	Adhesive Manufacturing
2892	Explosives	32592	Explosives Manufacturing
2893	Printing Ink	32591	Printing Ink Manufacturing
2895	Carbon Black	325182	Carbon Black Manufacturing (pt)
2899	Chemicals and Chemical Preparations, NEC		
	Frit	32551	Paint and Coating Manufacturing (pt)
	Table Salt	311942	Spice and Extract Manufacturing (pt)
	Fatty Acids	325199	All Other Basic Organic Chemical Manufacturing (pt)
	Other	325998	All Other Miscellaneous Chemical Product and Preparation Manufacturing (pt)

---

pt—Part of; NEC—Not Elsewhere Classified.

http://www.ntis.gov/naics

1987 SIC code	1987 U.S. SIC description	1997 NAICS code	1997 NAICS U.S. description
2911	Petroleum Refining	32411	Petroleum Refineries
2951	Asphalt Paving Mixtures and Blocks	324121	Asphalt Paving Mixture and Block Manufacturing
2952	Asphalt Felts and Coatings	324122	Asphalt Shingle and Coating Materials Manufacturing
2992	Lubricating Oils and Greases	324191	Petroleum Lubricating Oil and Grease Manufacturing
2999	Products of Petroleum and Coal, NEC	324199	All Other Petroleum and Coal Products Manufacturing (pt)
3011	Tires and Inner Tubes	326211	Tire Manufacturing (except Retreading)
3021	Rubber and Plastics Footwear	316211	Rubber and Plastics Footwear Manufacturing
3052	Rubber and Plastics Hose and Belting	32622	Rubber and Plastics Hoses and Belting Manufacturing
3053	Gaskets, Packing, and Sealing Devices	339991	Gasket, Packing, and Sealing Device Manufacturing
3061	Molded, Extruded, and Lathe-Cut Mechanical Rubber Goods	326291	Rubber Product Manufacturing for Mechanical Use
3069	Fabricated Rubber Products, NEC		
	Rubberizing Fabric or Purchased Textile Products	31332	Fabric Coating Mills (pt)
	Rubber Pants and Raincoats	315299	All Other Cut and Sew Apparel Manufacturing (pt)
	Rubber Bibs, Aprons, and Bathing Caps	315999	Other Apparel Accessories and Other Apparel (pt)
	Rubber Gloves and Life Jackets	339113	Surgical Appliance and Supplies Manufacturing (pt)
	Rubber Wet Suits	33992	Sporting and Athletic Goods Manufacturing (pt)
	Rubber Toys, Except Dolls	339932	Game, Toy, and Children's Vehicle Manufacturing (pt)
	Rubber Resilient Floor Covering	326192	Resilient Floor Covering Manufacturing (pt)
	Other	326299	All Other Rubber Product Manufacturing
3081	Unsupported Plastics Film and Sheet	326113	Unsupported Plastics Film and Sheet (except Packaging) Manufacturing
3082	Unsupported Plastics Profile Shapes	326121	Unsupported Plastics Profile Shape Manufacturing (pt)

pt—Part of; NEC—Not Elsewhere Classified.

1987 SIC code	1987 U.S. SIC description	1997 NAICS code	1997 NAICS U.S. description
3083	Laminated Plastics Plate, Sheet, and Profile Shapes	32613	Laminated Plastics Plate, Sheet, and Shape Manufacturing
3084	Plastics Pipe	326122	Plastics Pipe and Pipe Fitting Manufacturing (pt)
3085	Plastics Bottles	32616	Plastics Bottle Manufacturing
3086	Plastics Foam Products		
	Urethane and Other Foam Products	32615	Urethane and Other Foam Product (except Polystyrene) Manufacturing
	Polystyrene Foam Products	32614	Polystyrene Foam Product Manufacturing
3087	Custom Compounding of Purchased Plastics Resins	325991	Custom Compounding of Purchased Resins
3088	Plastics Plumbing Fixtures	326191	Plastics Plumbing Fixtures Manufacturing
3089	Plastics Products, NEC		
	Pipe Fittings	326122	Plastics Pipe and Pipe Fitting Manufacturing (pt)
	Plastics Sausage Casings	326121	Unsupported Plastics Profile Shape Manufacturing (pt)
	Finished Plastics Furniture Parts	337215	Showcase, Partition, Shelving, and Locker Manufacturing (pt)
	Other	326199	All Other Plastics Product Manufacturing (pt)
3111	Leather Tanning and Finishing	31611	Leather and Hide Tanning and Finishing (pt)
3131	Boot and Shoe Cut Stock and Findings		
	Wood Heels	321999	All Other Miscellaneous Wood Product Manufacturing (pt)
	Metal Buckles	339993	Fastener, Button, Needle, and Pin Manufacturing (pt)
	Except Wood Heels and Metal Buckles	316999	All Other Leather Good Manufacturing (pt)
3142	House Slippers	316212	House Slipper Manufacturing
3143	Men's Footwear, Except Athletic	316213	Men's Footwear (except Athletic) Manufacturing
3144	Women's Footwear, Except Athletic	316214	Women's Footwear (except Athletic) Manufacturing
3149	Footwear, Except Rubber, NEC	316219	Other Footwear Manufacturing
3151	Leather Gloves and Mittens		
	Men's and Boys' Contractors	315211	Men's and Boys' Cut and Sew Apparel Contractors (pt)

pt—Part of; NEC—Not Elsewhere Classified.

http://www.ntis.gov/naics

1987 SIC code	1987 U.S. SIC description	1997 NAICS code	1997 NAICS U.S. description
	Women's, Girls', and Infants' Contractors	315212	Women's, Girls', and Infants' Cut and Sew Apparel Contractors (pt)
	Except Contractors	315992	Glove and Mitten Manufacturing (pt)
3161	Luggage	316991	Luggage Manufacturing
3171	Women's Handbags and Purses	316992	Women's Handbag and Purse Manufacturing
3172	Personal Leather Goods, Except Women's Handbags and Purses	316993	Personal Leather Good (except Women's Handbag and Purse) Manufacturing
3199	Leather Goods, NEC	316999	All Other Leather Good Manufacturing (pt)
3211	Flat Glass	327211	Flat Glass Manufacturing
3221	Glass Containers	327213	Glass Container Manufacturing
3229	Pressed and Blown Glass and Glassware, NEC	327212	Other Pressed and Blown Glass and Glassware Manufacturing
3231	Glass Products, Made of Purchased Glass	327215	Glass Product Manufacturing Made of Purchased Glass
3241	Cement, Hydraulic	32731	Cement Manufacturing
3251	Brick and Structural Clay Tile		
	Slumped Brick	327331	Concrete Block and Brick Manufacturing (pt)
	Except Slump Brick	327121	Brick and Structural Clay Tile Manufacturing
3253	Ceramic Wall and Floor Tile	327122	Ceramic Wall and Floor Tile Manufacturing
3255	Clay Refractories	327124	Clay Refractory Manufacturing
3259	Structural Clay Products, NEC	327123	Other Structural Clay Product Manufacturing
3261	Vitreous China Plumbing Fixtures and China and Earthenware Fittings and Bathroom Accessories	327111	Vitreous China Plumbing Fixture and China and Earthenware Bathroom Accessories Manufacturing
3262	Vitreous China Table and Kitchen Articles	327112	Vitreous China, Fine Earthenware, and Other Pottery Product Manufacturing (pt)
3263	Fine Earthenware (Whiteware) Table and Kitchen Articles	327112	Vitreous China, Fine Earthenware, and Other Pottery Product Manufacturing (pt)
3264	Porcelain Electrical Supplies	327113	Porcelain Electrical Supply Manufacturing

pt—Part of; NEC—Not Elsewhere Classified.

1987 SIC code	1987 U.S. SIC description	1997 NAICS code	1997 NAICS U.S. description
3269	Pottery Products, NEC	327112	Vitreous China, Fine Earthenware, and Other Pottery Product Manufacturing (pt)
3271	Concrete Block and Brick	327331	Concrete Block and Brick Manufacturing
3272	Concrete Products, Except Block and Brick		
	Dry Mixture Concrete	327999	All Other Miscellaneous Nonmetallic Mineral Product Manufacturing (pt)
	Concrete Pipes	327332	Concrete Pipe Manufacturing
	Other Concrete Products	32739	Other Concrete Product Manufacturing
3273	Ready-Mixed Concrete	32732	Ready-Mix Concrete Manufacturing
3274	Lime	32741	Lime Manufacturing
3275	Gypsum Products	32742	Gypsum Product Manufacturing (pt)
3281	Cut Stone and Stone Products	327991	Cut Stone and Stone Product Manufacturing
3291	Abrasive Products		
	Steel Wool With or Without Soap	332999	All Other Miscellaneous Fabricated Metal Product Manufacturing (pt)
	Abrasive Products (Except Steel Wool With or Without Soap)	32791	Abrasive Product Manufacturing
3292	Asbestos Products		
	Asbestos Brake Linings and Pads	33634	Motor Vehicle Brake System Manufacturing (pt)
	Other Asbestos Products	327999	All Other Miscellaneous Nonmetallic Mineral Product Manufacturing (pt)
3295	Minerals and Earths, Ground or Otherwise Treated		
	Grinding, Washing, Separating, etc. of Minerals in SIC 1455	212324	Kaolin and Ball Clay Mining (pt)
	Grinding, Washing, Separating, etc. of Minerals in SIC 1459	212325	Clay and Ceramic and Refractory Minerals Mining (pt)
	Grinding, Washing, Separating, etc. of Minerals in SIC 1479	212393	Other Chemical and Fertilizer Mineral Mining (pt)
	Grinding, Washing, Separating, etc. of Minerals in SIC 1499	212399	All Other Nonmetallic Mineral Mining (pt)
	Except Grinding, Washing, Separating, etc.	327992	Ground or Treated Mineral and Earth Manufacturing

pt—Part of; NEC—Not Elsewhere Classified.

http://www.ntis.gov/naics

1987 SIC code	1987 U.S. SIC description	1997 NAICS code	1997 NAICS U.S. description
3296	Mineral Wool	327993	Mineral Wool Manufacturing
3297	Nonclay Refractories	327125	Nonclay Refractory Manufacturing
3299	Nonmetallic Mineral Products, NEC		
	Clay Statuary	327112	Vitreous China, Fine Earthenware, and Other Pottery Product Manufacturing (pt)
	Moldings, Ornamental and Architectural Plaster Work, and Gypsum Statuary	32742	Gypsum Product Manufacturing (pt)
	Other Nonmetallic Mineral Products	327999	All Other Miscellaneous Nonmetallic Mineral Product Manufacturing (pt)
3312	Steel Works, Blast Furnaces (Including Coke Ovens), and Rolling Mills		
	Coke Ovens, Not Integrated With Steel Mills	324199	All Other Petroleum and Coal Products Manufacturing (pt)
	Hot Rolling Purchased Steel	331221	Rolled Steel Shape Manufacturing (pt)
	Except Coke Ovens Not Integrated with Steel Mills and Hot Rolling Purchased Steel	331111	Iron and Steel Mills (pt)
3313	Electrometallurgical Products, Except Steel	331112	Electrometallurgical Ferroalloy Product Manufacturing
3315	Steel Wiredrawing and Steel Nails and Spikes		
	Steel Wire Drawing	331222	Steel Wire Drawing
	Nails, Spikes, Paper Clips, and Wire, Not Made in Wire Drawing Plants	332618	Other Fabricated Wire Product Manufacturing (pt)
3316	Cold-Rolled Steel Sheet, Strip, and Bars	331221	Rolled Steel Shape Manufacturing (pt)
3317	Steel Pipe and Tubes	33121	Iron and Steel Pipe and Tube Manufacturing from Purchased Steel
3321	Gray and Ductile Iron Foundries	331511	Iron Foundries (pt)
3322	Malleable Iron Foundries	331511	Iron Foundries (pt)
3324	Steel Investment Foundries	331512	Steel Investment Foundries
3325	Steel Foundries, NEC	331513	Steel Foundries (except Investment)
3331	Primary Smelting and Refining of Copper	331411	Primary Smelting and Refining of Copper

pt—Part of; NEC—Not Elsewhere Classified.

http://www.ntis.gov/naics

1987 SIC code	1987 U.S. SIC description	1997 NAICS code	1997 NAICS U.S. description
3334	Primary Production of Aluminum	331312	Primary Aluminum Production
3339	Primary Smelting and Refining of Nonferrous Metals, Except Copper and Aluminum	331419	Primary Smelting and Refining of Nonferrous Metals (except Copper and Aluminum)
3341	Secondary Smelting and Refining of Nonferrous Metals		
	Aluminum	331314	Secondary Smelting and Alloying of Aluminum (pt)
	Copper	331423	Secondary Smelting, Refining, and Alloying of Copper (pt)
	Except Aluminum and Copper	331492	Secondary Smelting, Refining, and Alloying of Nonferrous Metals (except Copper and Aluminum) (pt)
3351	Rolling, Drawing, and Extruding of Copper	331421	Copper Rolling, Drawing, and Extruding
3353	Aluminum Sheet, Plate, and Foil	331315	Aluminum Sheet, Plate, and Foil Manufacturing
3354	Aluminum Extruded Products	331316	Aluminum Extruded Product Manufacturing
3355	Aluminum Rolling and Drawing, NEC	331319	Other Aluminum Rolling and Drawing, (pt)
3356	Rolling, Drawing, and Extruding of Nonferrous Metals, Except Copper and Aluminum	331491	Nonferrous Metal (except Copper and Aluminum) Rolling, Drawing, and Extruding (pt)
3357	Drawing and Insulating of Nonferrous Wire		
	Aluminum Wire Drawing	331319	Other Aluminum Rolling and Drawing (pt)
	Copper Wire Drawing	331422	Copper Wire (except Mechanical) Drawing
	Wire Drawing Except Copper or Aluminum	331491	Nonferrous Metal (except Copper and Aluminum) Rolling, Drawing, and Extruding (pt)
	Fiber Optic Cable - Insulating Only	335921	Fiber Optic Cable Manufacturing
	All Other	335929	Other Communication and Energy Wire Manufacturing
3363	Aluminum Die-Castings	331521	Aluminum Die-Casting Foundries
3364	Nonferrous Die-Castings, Except Aluminum	331522	Nonferrous (except Aluminum) Die-Casting Foundries
3365	Aluminum Foundries	331524	Aluminum Foundries (except Die-Casting)

pt—Part of; NEC—Not Elsewhere Classified.

http://www.ntis.gov/naics

1987 SIC code	1987 U.S. SIC description	1997 NAICS code	1997 NAICS U.S. description
3366	Copper Foundries	331525	Copper Foundries (except Die-Casting)
3369	Nonferrous Foundries, Except Aluminum and Copper	331528	Other Nonferrous Foundries (except Die-Casting)
3398	Metal Heat Treating	332811	Metal Heat Treating
3399	Primary Metal Products, NEC		
	Aluminum Powder, Paste, Flakes, etc.	331314	Secondary Smelting and Alloying of Aluminum (pt)
	Copper Powder, Flakes, Paste, etc.	331423	Secondary Smelting, Refining, and Alloying of Copper (pt)
	Other Nonferrous Powder, Paste, Flakes, etc.	331492	Secondary Smelting, Refining, and Alloying of Nonferrous Metals (except Copper and Aluminum) (pt)
	Making Ferrous Metal Powder, Paste, and Flake From Purchased Iron or Steel	331221	Rolled Steel Shape Manufacturing (pt)
	Nonferrous Nails, Brads, Staples, etc.	332618	Other Fabricated Wire Product Manufacturing (pt)
	Laminated Steel	332813	Electroplating, Plating, Polishing, Anodizing, and Coloring (pt)
3411	Metal Cans	332431	Metal Can Manufacturing
3412	Metal Shipping Barrels, Drums, Kegs, and Pails	332439	Other Metal Container Manufacturing (pt)
3421	Cutlery		
	Except Tool-Type Shears	332211	Cutlery and Flatware (except Precious) Manufacturing (pt)
	Tool-Type Shears	332212	Hand and Edge Tool Manufacturing (pt)
3423	Hand and Edge Tools, Except Machine Tools and Handsaws	332212	Hand and Edge Tool Manufacturing (pt)
3425	Saw Blades and Handsaws	332213	Saw Blade and Handsaw Manufacturing
3429	Hardware, NEC		
	Fireplace Fixtures, Traps, Handcuffs and Leg Irons, Ladder Jacks, and Other Like Metal Products	332999	All Other Miscellaneous Fabricated Metal Products Manufacturing (pt)
	Vacuum and Insulated Bottles, Jugs, and Chests	332439	Other Metal Container Manufacturing (pt)
	Turnbuckles and Hose Clamps	332722	Bolt, Nut, Screw, Rivet, and Washer Manufacturing (pt)

---

pt—Part of; NEC—Not Elsewhere Classified.

1987 SIC code	1987 U.S. SIC description	1997 NAICS code	1997 NAICS U.S. description
	Luggage and Utility Racks	336399	All Other Motor Vehicle Parts Manufacturing (pt)
	Fire Hose Nozzles and Couplings	332919	Other Metal Valve and Pipe Fitting Manufacturing (pt)
	Convertible Bed Sleeper Mechanisms and Chair Glides	337215	Showcase, Partition, Shelving, and Locker Manufacturing (pt)
	Other Hardware	33251	Hardware Manufacturing (pt)
3431	Enameled Iron and Metal Sanitary Ware	332998	Enameled Iron and Metal Sanitary Ware Manufacturing
3432	Plumbing Fixture Fittings and Trim		
	Plumbing Fixture Fittings and Trim, Except Metal Shower Rods and Lawn Hose Nozzels	332913	Plumbing Fixture Fitting and Trim Manufacturing
	Lawn Hose Nozzels	332919	Other Metal Valve and Pipe Fitting Manufacturing (pt)
	Metal Shower Rods	332999	All Other Miscellaneous Fabricated Metal Product Manufacturing (pt)
3433	Heating Equipment, Except Electric and Warm Air Furnaces	333414	Heating Equipment Manufacturing, (except Warm Air Furnaces) (pt)
3441	Fabricated Structural Metal	332312	Fabricated Structural Metal Manufacturing (pt)
3442	Metal Doors, Sash, Frames, Molding, and Trim Manufacturing	332321	Metal Window and Door Manufacturing (pt)
3443	Fabricated Plate Work (Boiler Shops)		
	Fabricated Plate Work and Metal Weldments	332313	Plate Work Manufacturing
	Power Boilers and Heat Exchanges	33241	Power Boiler and Heat Exchanger Manufacturing (pt)
	Heavy Gauge Tanks	33242	Metal Tank (Heavy Gauge) Manufacturing
	Metal Cooling Towers	333414	Heating Equipment (except Warm Air Furnaces) Manufacturing (pt)
3444	Sheet Metal Work		
	Ducts, Flumes, Flooring, Siding, Dampers, etc.	332322	Sheet Metal Work Manufacturing
	Metal Bins and Vats	332439	Other Metal Container Manufacturing (pt)
	Cooling Towers	333414	Heating Equipment (except Warm Air Furnaces) Manufacturing (pt)
3446	Architectural and Ornamental Metal Work	332323	Ornamental and Architectural Metal Work Manufacturing (pt)

pt—Part of; NEC—Not Elsewhere Classified.

http://www.ntis.gov/naics

1987 SIC code	1987 U.S. SIC description	1997 NAICS code	1997 NAICS U.S. description
3448	Prefabricated Metal Buildings and Components	332311	Prefabricated Metal Building and Component Manufacturing
3449	Miscellaneous Structural Metal Work		
	Custom Roll Forming	332114	Custom Roll Forming
	Fabricated Bar Joists and Concrete Reinforcing Bars	332312	Fabricated Structural Metal Manufacturing (pt)
	Curtain Wall	332321	Metal Window and Door Manufacturing (pt)
	Metal Plaster Bases	332323	Ornamental and Architectural Metal Work Manufacturing (pt)
3451	Screw Machine Products	332721	Precision Turned Product Manufacturing
3452	Bolts, Nuts, Screws, Rivets, and Washers	332722	Bolt, Nut, Screw, Rivet, and Washer Manufacturing (pt)
3462	Iron and Steel Forgings	332111	Iron and Steel Forging
3463	Nonferrous Forgings	332112	Nonferrous Forging
3465	Automotive Stamping	33637	Motor Vehicle Metal Stamping
3466	Crowns and Closures	332115	Crown and Closure Manufacturing
3469	Metal Stamping, NEC		
	Metal Stamping, NEC (Except Kitchen Utensils, Pots and Pans for Cooking, and Coins)	332116	Metal Stamping
	Kitchen Utensils and Pots and Pans for Cooking	332214	Kitchen Utensil, Pot, and Pan Manufacturing
3471	Electroplating, Plating, Polishing, Anodizing, and Coloring	332813	Electroplating, Plating, Polishing, Anodizing, and Coloring (pt)
3479	Coating, Engraving, and Allied Services, NEC		
	Jewelry Engraving and Etching, Costume Jewelry	339914	Costume Jewelry and Novelty Manufacturing (pt)
	Jewelry Engraving and Etching, Precious Metal	339911	Jewelry (except Costume) Manufacturing (pt)
	Silverware and Flatware Engraving and Etching	339912	Silverware and Hollowware Manufacturing (pt)
	Other Coating, Engraving and Allied Services	332812	Metal Coating, Engraving (except Jewelry and Silverware), and Allied Services to Manufacturers
3482	Small Arms Ammunition	332992	Small Arms Ammunition Manufacturing
3483	Ammunition, Except for Small Arms	332993	Ammunition (except Small Arms) Manufacturing

pt—Part of; NEC—Not Elsewhere Classified.

http://www.ntis.gov/naics

1987 SIC code	1987 U.S. SIC description	1997 NAICS code	1997 NAICS U.S. description
3484	Small Arms	332994	Small Arms Manufacturing (pt)
3489	Ordnance and Accessories, NEC	332995	Other Ordnance and Accessories Manufacturing
3491	Industrial Valves	332911	Industrial Valve Manufacturing
3492	Fluid Power Valves and Hose Fittings	332912	Fluid Power Valve and Hose Fitting Manufacturing (pt)
3493	Steel Springs, Except Wire	332611	Spring (Heavy Gauge) Manufacturing
3494	Valves and Pipe Fittings, NEC		
	Except Metal Pipe Hangers and Supports	332919	Other Metal Valve and Pipe Fitting Manufacturing (pt)
	Metal Pipe Hangers and Supports	332999	All Other Miscellaneous Fabricated Metal Product Manufacturing (pt)
3495	Wire Springs		
	Wire Springs (Except Watch and Clock Springs)	332612	Spring (Light Gauge) Manufacturing
	Watch and Clock Springs	334518	Watch, Clock, and Part Manufacturing (pt)
3496	Miscellaneous Fabricated Wire Products		
	Grocery Carts	333924	Industrial Truck, Tractor, Trailer, and Stacker Machinery Manufacturing (pt)
	Except Grocery Carts	332618	Other Fabricated Wire Product Manufacturing (pt)
3497	Metal Foil and Leaf		
	Laminated Aluminum Foil Rolls/Sheets for Flexible Packaging Uses	322225	Laminated Aluminum Foil Manufacturing for Flexible Packaging Uses
	Foil and Foil Containers	332999	All Other Miscellaneous Fabricated Metal Product Manufacturing (pt)
3498	Fabricated Pipe and Pipe Fittings	332996	Fabricated Pipe and Pipe Fitting Manufacturing
3499	Fabricated Metal Products, NEC		
	Metal Furniture Frames	337215	Showcase, Partition, Shelving, and Locker Manufacturing (pt)
	Metal Motor Vehicle Seat Frames	33636	Motor Vehicle Seating and Interior Trim Manufacturing (pt)
	Powder Metallurgy	332117	Powder Metallurgy Part Manufacturing
	Metal Boxes	332439	Other Metal Container Manufacturing (pt)

pt—Part of; NEC—Not Elsewhere Classified.

1987 SIC code	1987 U.S. SIC description	1997 NAICS code	1997 NAICS U.S. description
	Safe and Vault Locks	33251	Hardware Manufacturing (pt)
	Metal Aerosol Valves	332919	Other Metal Valve and Pipe Fitting Manufacturing (pt)
	Other Metal Products	332999	All Other Miscellaneous Fabricated Metal Product Manufacturing (pt)
3511	Steam, Gas, and Hydraulic Turbines, and Turbine Generator Set Units	333611	Turbine and Turbine Generator Set Unit Manufacturing
3519	Internal Combustion Engines, NEC		
	Stationary Engine Radiators	336399	All Other Motor Vehicle Parts Manufacturing (pt)
	Except Stationary Engine Radiators	333618	Other Engine Equipment Manufacturing (pt)
3523	Farm Machinery and Equipment		
	Farm Machinery and Equipment (Except Corrals, Stalls, Holding Gates, Hand Hair Clippers for Animals, Farm Conveyors, and Elevators)	333111	Farm Machinery and Equipment Manufacturing
	Corrals, Stalls, Holding Gates	332323	Ornamental and Architectural Metal Work Manufacturing (pt)
	Hand Hair Clippers for Animals	332212	Hand and Edge Tool Manufacturing (pt)
	Farm Conveyors and Farm Elevators, Stackers, and Bale Throwers	333922	Conveyor and Conveying Equipment Manufacturing (pt)
3524	Lawn and Garden Tractors and Home Lawn and Garden Equipment		
	Lawn and Garden Tractors and Home Lawn and Garden Equipment (Except Nonpowered Lawnmowers)	333112	Lawn and Garden Tractor and Home Lawn and Garden Equipment Manufacturing
	Nonpowered Lawnmowers	332212	Hand and Edge Tool Manufacturing (pt)
3531	Construction Machinery and Equipment		
	Railway Track Maintenance Equipment	33651	Railroad Rolling Stock Manufacturing (pt)
	Winches, Aerial Work Platforms, and Automotive Wrecker Hoists	333923	Overhead Traveling Crane, Hoist, and Monorail System Manufacturing (pt)
	Other Construction Machinery and Equipment		

---

pt—Part of; NEC—Not Elsewhere Classified.

1987 SIC code	1987 U.S. SIC description	1997 NAICS code	1997 NAICS U.S. description
		33312	Construction Machinery Manufacturing
3532	Mining Machinery and Equipment, Except Oil and Gas Field Machinery and Equipment	333131	Mining Machinery and Equipment Manufacturing
3533	Oil and Gas Field Machinery and Equipment	333132	Oil and Gas Field Machinery and Equipment Manufacturing
3534	Elevators and Moving Stairways	333921	Elevator and Moving Stairway Manufacturing
3535	Conveyors and Conveying Equipment	333922	Conveyor and Conveying Equipment Manufacturing (pt)
3536	Overhead Traveling Cranes, Hoists, and Monorail Systems	333923	Overhead Traveling Crane, Hoist, and Monorail System Manufacturing (pt)
3537	Industrial Trucks, Tractors, Trailers, and Stackers		
	Industrial Trucks, Tractors, Trailers, and Stackers (Except Metal Pallets and Air Cargo Containers)	333924	Industrial Truck, Tractor, Trailer, and Stacker Machinery Manufacturing
	Metal Pallets	332999	All Other Miscellaneous Fabricated Metal Product Manufacturing (pt)
	Metal Air Cargo Containers	332439	Other Metal Container Manufacturing (pt)
3541	Machine Tools, Metal Cutting Type	333512	Machine Tool (Metal Cutting Types) Manufacturing
3542	Machine Tools, Metal Forming Type	333513	Machine Tool (Metal Forming Types) Manufacturing
3543	Industrial Patterns	332997	Industrial Pattern Manufacturing
3544	Special Dies and Tools, Die Sets, Jigs and Fixtures, and Industrial Molds		
	Except Industrial Molds	333514	Special Die and Tool, Die Set, Jig, and Fixture Manufacturing
	Industrial Molds	333511	Industrial Mold Manufacturing
3545	Cutting Tools, Machine Tool Accessories, and Machinists' Precision Measuring Devices		
	Cutting Tools, Machine Tool Accessories, and Machinists' Precision Measuring Devices (Except Precision Measuring Devices)	333515	Cutting Tool and Machine Tool Accessory Manufacturing

pt—Part of; NEC—Not Elsewhere Classified.

http://www.ntis.gov/naics

1987 SIC code	1987 U.S. SIC description	1997 NAICS code	1997 NAICS U.S. description
	Precision Measuring Devices	332212	Hand and Edge Tool Manufacturing (pt)
3546	Power-Driven Handtools	333991	Power-Driven Handtool Manufacturing
3547	Rolling Mill Machinery and Equipment	333516	Rolling Mill Machinery and Equipment Manufacturing
3548	Electric and Gas Welding and Soldering Equipment		
	Except Transformers for Arc-Welding	333992	Welding and Soldering Equipment Manufacturing
	Transformers for Arc-Welding	335311	Power, Distribution, and Specialty Transformer Manufacturing (pt)
3549	Metalworking Machinery, NEC	333518	Other Metalworking Machinery Manufacturing
3552	Textile Machinery	333292	Textile Machinery Manufacturing
3553	Woodworking Machinery	33321	Sawmill and Woodworking Machinery Manufacturing
3554	Paper Industries Machinery	333291	Paper Industry Machinery Manufacturing
3555	Printing Trades Machinery and Equipment	333293	Printing Machinery and Equipment Manufacturing
3556	Food Products Machinery	333294	Food Product Machinery Manufacturing
3559	Special Industry Machinery, NEC		
	Rubber and Plastics Manufacturing Machinery	33322	Plastics and Rubber Industry Machinery Manufacturing
	Nuclear Control Drive Mechanisms	33241	Power Boiler and Heat Exchanger Manufacturing (pt)
	Automotive Maintenance Equipment	333319	Other Commercial and Service Industry Machinery Manufacturing (pt)
	Semiconductor Machinery Manufacturing	333295	Semiconductor Manufacturing Machinery
	Cotton Ginning Machinery	333111	Farm Machinery and Equipment Manufacturing (pt)
	Except Rubber and Plastics Manufacturing Machinery, Semiconductor Manufacturing Machinery, Automotive Maintenance Equipment,		

pt—Part of; NEC—Not Elsewhere Classified.

1987 SIC code	1987 U.S. SIC description	1997 NAICS code	1997 NAICS U.S. description
	Cotton Ginning Machinery, and Nuclear Control Device Mechanisms	333298	All Other Industrial Machinery Manufacturing (pt)
3561	Pumps and Pumping Equipment	333911	Pump and Pumping Equipment Manufacturing (pt)
3562	Ball and Roller Bearings	332991	Ball and Roller Bearing Manufacturing
3563	Air and Gas Compressors	333912	Air and Gas Compressor Manufacturing
3564	Industrial and Commercial Fans and Blowers and Air Purification Equipment		
	Air Purification Equipment	333411	Air Purification Equipment Manufacturing
	Fans and Blowers	333412	Industrial and Commercial Fan and Blower Manufacturing
3565	Packaging Machinery	333993	Packaging Machinery Manufacturing
3566	Speed Changers, Industrial High-Speed Drives, and Gears	333612	Speed Changer, Industrial High-Speed Drive, and Gear Manufacturing
3567	Industrial Process Furnaces and Ovens	333994	Industrial Process Furnace and Oven Manufacturing
3568	Mechanical Power Transmission Equipment, NEC	333613	Mechanical Power Transmission Equipment Manufacturing
3569	General Industrial Machinery and Equipment, NEC		
	Electric Swimming Pool Heaters	333414	Heating Equipment (except Warm Air Furnace) Manufacturing (pt)
	Textile Fire Hose	314999	All Other Miscellaneous Textile Product Mills (pt)
	Except Electric Swimming Pool Heaters and Textile Fire Hoses	333999	All Other Miscellaneous General Purpose Machinery Manufacturing (pt)
3571	Electronic Computers	334111	Electronic Computer Manufacturing
3572	Computer Storage Devices	334112	Computer Storage Device Manufacturing
3575	Computer Terminals	334113	Computer Terminal Manufacturing
3577	Computer Peripheral Equipment, NEC		

pt—Part of; NEC—Not Elsewhere Classified.

http://www.ntis.gov/naics

1987 SIC code	1987 U.S. SIC description	1997 NAICS code	1997 NAICS U.S. description
	Plotter Controllers	334418	Printed Circuit Assembly (Electronic Assembly) Manufacturing (pt)
	Magnetic Tape Cleaner	334613	Magnetic Optical Recording Media Manufacturing (pt)
	Except Plotter Controllers and Magnetic Tape Cleaners	334119	Other Computer Peripheral Equipment Manufacturing (pt)
3578	Calculating and Accounting Machines, Except Electronic Computers		
	Point of Sales Terminals and Fund Transfer Devices	334119	Other Computer Peripheral Equipment Manufacturing (pt)
	Change Making Machines	333311	Automatic Vending Machine Manufacturing (pt)
	Calculating and Accounting Machines, Except Point of Sales Terminals and Fund Transfer Devices, and Change Making Machines	333313	Office Machinery Manufacturing (pt)
3579	Office Machines, NEC		
	Pencil Sharpeners, Staplers, and Other Office Equipment	339942	Lead Pencil and Art Good Manufacturing (pt)
	Time Clocks and Other Time Recording Devices	334518	Watch, Clock, and Part Manufacturing (pt)
	Other Office Machines	333313	Office Machinery Manufacturing (pt)
3581	Automatic Vending Machines	333311	Automatic Vending Machine Manufacturing
3582	Commercial Laundry, Drycleaning, and Pressing Machines	333312	Commercial Laundry, Drycleaning, and Pressing Machine Manufacturing
3585	Air-Conditioning and Warm Air Heating Equipment and Commercial and Industrial Refrigeration Equipment		
	Motor Vehicle Air-Conditioning	336391	Motor Vehicle Air-Conditioning Manufacturing
	Except Motor Vehicle Air-Conditioning	333415	Air-Conditioning and Warm Air Heating Equipment and Commercial and Industrial Refrigeration Equipment Manufacturing

pt—Part of; NEC—Not Elsewhere Classified.

http://www.ntis.gov/naics

1987 SIC code	1987 U.S. SIC description	1997 NAICS code	1997 NAICS U.S. description
3586	Measuring and Dispensing Pumps	333913	Measuring and Dispensing Pump Manufacturing
3589	Service Industry Machinery, NEC	333319	Other Commercial and Service Industry Machinery Manufacturing (pt)
3592	Carburetors, Pistons, Piston Rings, and Valves	336311	Carburetor, Piston, Piston Ring, and Valve Manufacturing
3593	Fluid Power Cylinders and Actuators	333995	Fluid Power Cylinder and Actuator Manufacturing
3594	Fluid Power Pumps and Motors	333996	Fluid Power Pump and Motor Manufacturing
3596	Scales and Balances, Except Laboratory	333997	Scale and Balance (except Laboratory) Manufacturing
3599	Industrial and Commercial Machinery and Equipment, NEC		
	Gasoline, Oil and Intake Filters for Internal Combustion Engines, Except Motor Vehicle	336399	All Other Motor Vehicle Part Manufacturing (pt)
	Flexible Metal Hose	332999	All Other Miscellaneous Fabricated Metal Product Manufacturing (pt)
	Carnival Amusement Park Equipment	333319	Other Commercial and Service Industry Machinery Manufacturing (pt)
	Machine Shops	33271	Machine Shops
	Other Industrial and Commercial Machinery and Equipment	333999	All Other Miscellaneous General Purpose Machinery Manufacturing (pt)
3612	Power, Distribution, and Specialty Transformers	335311	Power, Distribution, and Specialty Transformer Manufacturing (pt)
3613	Switchgear and Switchboard Apparatus	335313	Switchgear and Switchboard Apparatus Manufacturing
3621	Motors and Generators	335312	Motor and Generator Manufacturing (pt)
3624	Carbon and Graphite Products	335991	Carbon and Graphite Product Manufacturing
3625	Relays and Industrial Controls	335314	Relay and Industrial Control Manufacturing
3629	Electrical Industrial Apparatus, NEC	335999	All Other Miscellaneous Electrical Equipment and Component Manufacturing (pt)
3631	Household Cooking Equipment	335221	Household Cooking Appliance Manufacturing

---

pt—Part of; NEC—Not Elsewhere Classified.

http://www.ntis.gov/naics

1987 SIC code	1987 U.S. SIC description	1997 NAICS code	1997 NAICS U.S. description
3632	Household Refrigerators and Home and Farm Freezers	335222	Household Refrigerator and Home Freezer Manufacturing
3633	Household Laundry Equipment	335224	Household Laundry Equipment Manufacturing
3634	Electric Housewares and Fans Except Wall and Baseboard Heating Units for Permanent Installation, and Electronic Cigarette Lighters	335211	Electric Housewares and Household Fan Manufacturing
	Electronic Cigarette Lighters	339999	All Other Miscellaneous Manufacturing (pt)
	Wall and Baseboard Heating Units For Permanent Installation	333414	Heating Equipment (except Warm Air Furnaces) Manufacturing (pt)
3635	Household Vacuum Cleaners	335212	Household Vacuum Cleaner Manufacturing (pt)
3639	Household Appliances, NEC		
	Floor Waxing and Floor Polishing Machines	335212	Household Vacuum Cleaner Manufacturing (pt)
	Household Sewing Machines	333298	All Other Industrial Machinery Manufacturing (pt)
	Other Household Appliances	335228	Other Major Household Appliance Manufacturing
3641	Electric Lamp Bulbs and Tubes	33511	Electric Lamp Bulb and Part Manufacturing
3643	Current-Carrying Wiring Devices	335931	Current-Carrying Wiring Device Manufacturing
3644	Noncurrent-Carrying Wiring Devices		
	Fish Wire, Electrical Wiring Tool	332212	Hand and Edge Tool Manufacturing (pt)
	All Other Noncurrent-Carrying Wiring Devices	335932	Noncurrent-Carrying Wiring Device Manufacturing
3645	Residential Electric Lighting Fixtures	335121	Residential Electric Lighting Fixture Manufacturing (pt)
3646	Commercial, Industrial, and Institutional Electric Lighting Fixtures	335122	Commercial, Industrial, and Institutional Electric Lighting Fixture Manufacturing
3647	Vehicular Lighting Equipment	336321	Vehicular Lighting Equipment Manufacturing
3648	Lighting Equipment, NEC	335129	Other Lighting Equipment Manufacturing (pt)

pt—Part of; NEC—Not Elsewhere Classified.

1987 SIC code	1987 U.S. SIC description	1997 NAICS code	1997 NAICS U.S. description
3651	Household Audio and Video Equipment	33431	Audio and Video Equipment Manufacturing
3652	Phonograph Records and Prerecorded Audio Tapes and Disks		
	Reproduction of Recording Media	334612	Prerecorded Compact Disc (Except Software), Tape, and Record Reproducing (pt)
	Integrated Record Companies, Except Duplication Only	51222	Integrated Record Production/ Distribution
3661	Telephone and Telegraph Apparatus		
	Telephone and Telegraph Apparatus, Except Consumer External Modems	33421	Telephone Apparatus Manufacturing
	Consumer External Modems	334418	Printed Circuit Assembly (Electronic Assembly) Manufacturing (pt)
3663	Radio and Television Broadcasting and Communications Equipment	33422	Radio and Television Broadcasting and Wireless Communications Equipment Manufacturing (pt)
3669	Communications Equipment, NEC	33429	Other Communications Equipment Manufacturing
3671	Electron Tubes	334411	Electron Tube Manufacturing
3672	Printed Circuit Boards	334412	Bare Printed Circuit Board Manufacturing
3674	Semiconductors and Related Devices	334413	Semiconductor and Related Device Manufacturing
3675	Electronic Capacitors	334414	Electronic Capacitor Manufacturing
3676	Electronic Resistors	334415	Electronic Resistor Manufacturing
3677	Electronic Coils, Transformers, and Other Inductors	334416	Electronic Coil, Transformer, and Other Inductor Manufacturing (pt)
3678	Electronic Connectors	334417	Electronic Connector Manufacturing
3679	Electronic Components, NEC		
	Antennas	33422	Radio and Television Broadcasting and Wireless Communications Equipment Manufacturing (pt)
	Radio Headphones	33431	Audio and Video Equipment Manufacturing (pt)
	Printed Circuit/Electronics Assembly	334418	Printed Circuit Assembly (Electronic Assembly) Manufacturing (pt)
	Other Electronic Components	334419	Other Electronic Component Manufacturing

pt—Part of; NEC—Not Elsewhere Classified.

http://www.ntis.gov/naics

1987 SIC code	1987 U.S. SIC description	1997 NAICS code	1997 NAICS U.S. description
3691	Storage Batteries	335911	Storage Battery Manufacturing
3692	Primary Batteries, Dry and Wet	335912	Primary Battery Manufacturing
3694	Electrical Equipment for Internal Combustion Engines	336322	Other Motor Vehicle Electrical and Electronic Equipment Manufacturing (pt)
3695	Magnetic and Optical Recording Media	334613	Magnetic and Optical Recording Media Manufacturing
3699	Electrical Machinery, Equipment, and Supplies, NEC		
	Electronic Teaching Machines and Flight Simulators	333319	Other Commercial and Service Industry Machinery Manufacturing (pt)
	Outboard Electric Motors	333618	Other Engine Equipment Manufacturing (pt)
	Laser Welding and Soldering Equipment	333992	Welding and Soldering Equipment Manufacturing (pt)
	Other Lasers		Classify According to Function
	Christmas Tree Lighting Sets, Electric Insect Lamps, Electric Fireplace Logs, and Trouble Lights	335129	Other Lighting Equipment Manufacturing (pt)
	Other Electrical Machinery, Equipment, and Supplies	335999	All Other Miscellaneous Electrical Equipment and Component Manufacturing (pt)
3711	Motor Vehicles and Passenger Car Bodies		
	Automobiles	336111	Automobile Manufacturing
	Light Truck and Utility Vehicles	336112	Light Truck and Utility Vehicle Manufacturing
	Heavy Duty Trucks	33612	Heavy Duty Truck Manufacturing
	Kit Car and Other Passenger Car Bodies	336211	Motor Vehicle Body Manufacturing (pt)
	Military Armored Vehicles	336992	Military Armored Vehicle, Tank, and Tank Component Manufacturing (pt)
3713	Truck and Bus Bodies	336211	Motor Vehicle Body Manufacturing (pt)
3714	Motor Vehicle Parts and Accessories		
	Dump-Truck Lifting Mechanisms and Fifth Wheels	336211	Motor Vehicle Body Manufacturing (pt)

———

pt—Part of; NEC—Not Elsewhere Classified.

1987 SIC code	1987 U.S. SIC description	1997 NAICS code	1997 NAICS U.S. description
	Gasoline Engines Including Rebuilt and Engine Parts Including Rebuilt for Motor Vehicles	336312	Gasoline Engine and Engine Parts Manufacturing
	Wiring Harness Sets, Other than Ignition; Block Heaters and Battery Heaters; Instrument Board Assemblies; Permanent Defroster; Windshield Washer-Wiper Mechanisms; Cruise Control Mechanisms; and Other Electrical Equipment for Internal Combustion Engines	336322	Other Motor Vehicle Electrical and Electronic Equipment Manufacturing (pt)
	Steering and Suspension Parts	33633	Motor Vehicle Steering and Suspension Components (except Spring) Manufacturing
	Brake and Brake Systems, Including Assemblies	33634	Motor Vehicle Brake System Manufacturing (pt)
	Transmissions and Power Train Parts, Including Rebuilding	33635	Motor Vehicle Transmission and Power Train Parts Manufacturing
	Other Motor Vehicle Parts	336399	All Other Motor Vehicle Parts Manufacturing (pt)
3715	Truck Trailers	336212	Truck Trailer Manufacturing
3716	Motor Homes	336213	Motor Home Manufacturing
3721	Aircraft		
	Research and Development	54171	Research and Development in the Physical, Engineering, and Life Sciences (pt)
	Except Research and Development	336411	Aircraft Manufacturing (pt)
3724	Aircraft Engines and Engine Parts		
	Except Research and Development	336412	Aircraft Engine and Engine Parts Manufacturing (pt)
	Research and Development	54171	Research and Development in the Physical, Engineering, and Life Sciences (pt)
3728	Aircraft Parts and Auxiliary Equipment, NEC		
	Fluid Power Aircraft Subassemblies	332912	Fluid Power Valve and Hose Fitting Manufacturing (pt)

pt—Part of; NEC—Not Elsewhere Classified.

http://www.ntis.gov/naics

1987 SIC code	1987 U.S. SIC description	1997 NAICS code	1997 NAICS U.S. description
	Research and Development	54171	Research and Development in the Physical, Engineering, and Life Sciences (pt)
	Target Drones	336411	Aircraft Manufacturing (pt)
	Except Fluid Power Aircraft Subassemblies, Target Drones, and Research and Development	336413	Other Aircraft Parts and Auxiliary Equipment Manufacturing
3731	Ship Building and Repairing		
	Floating Dry Docks Not Associated With Shipyards	48839	Other Support Activities for Water Transportation (pt)
	Ship Building and Repairing Except Floating Dry Docks Not Associated With Shipyards	336611	Ship Building and Repairing
3732	Boat Building and Repairing		
	Boat Repair	81149	Other Personal and Household Goods Repair and Maintenance (pt)
	Boat Building	336612	Boat Building
3743	Railroad Equipment		
	Locomotive Fuel Lubricating or Cooling Medium Pumps	333911	Pump and Pumping Equipment Manufacturing (pt)
	Other Railroad Equipment	33651	Railroad Rolling Stock Manufacturing (pt)
3751	Motorcycles, Bicycles, and Parts	336991	Motorcycle, Bicycle, and Parts Manufacturing (pt)
3761	Guided Missiles and Space Vehicles		
	Except Research and Development	336414	Guided Missile and Space Vehicle Manufacturing
	Research and Development	54171	Research and Development in the Physical, Engineering, and Life Sciences (pt)
3764	Guided Missile and Space Vehicle Propulsion Units and Propulsion Unit Parts		Research and Development in the Physical, Engineering, and Life Sciences (pt)
	Except Research and Development	336415	Guided Missile and Space Vehicle Propulsion Unit and Propulsion Unit Parts Manufacturing
	Research and Development	54171	Research and Development in the Physical, Engineering, and Life Sciences (pt)
3769	Guided Missile Space Vehicle Parts and Auxiliary Equipment, NEC		

pt—Part of; NEC—Not Elsewhere Classified.

http://www.ntis.gov/naics

1987 SIC code	1987 U.S. SIC description	1997 NAICS code	1997 NAICS U.S. description
	Except Research and Development	336419	Other Guided Missile and Space Vehicle Parts and Auxiliary Equipment Manufacturing
	Research and Development	54171	Research and Development in the Physical, Engineering, and Life Sciences (pt)
3792	Travel Trailers and Campers	336214	Travel Trailer and Camper Manufacturing (pt)
3795	Tanks and Tank Components	336992	Military Armored Vehicle, Tank, and Tank Component Manufacturing (pt)
3799	Transportation Equipment, NEC Automobile, Boat, Utility and Light Truck Trailers	336214	Travel Trailer and Camper Manufacturing (pt)
	Trailer Hitches	336399	All Other Motor Vehicle Parts Manufacturing (pt)
	Wheelbarrows	333924	Industrial Truck, Tractor, Trailer, and Stacker Machinery Manufacturing (pt)
	Other Transportation Equipment	336999	All Other Transportation Equipment Manufacturing
3812	Search, Detection, Navigation, Guidance, Aeronautical, and Nautical Systems and Instruments	334511	Search, Detection, Navigation, Guidance, Aeronautical, and Nautical System and Instrument Manufacturing
3821	Laboratory Apparatus and Furniture	339111	Laboratory Apparatus and Furniture Manufacturing (pt)
3822	Automatic Controls for Regulating Residential and Commercial Environments and Appliances	334512	Automatic Environmental Control Manufacturing for Regulating Residential, Commercial, and Appliance Use
3823	Industrial Instruments for Measurement, Display, and Control of Process Variables; and Related Products	334513	Instruments and Related Product Manufacturing for Measuring Displaying, and Controlling Industrial Process Variables
3824	Totalizing Fluid Meters and Counting Devices	334514	Totalizing Fluid Meter and Counting Device Manufacturing (pt)
3825	Instruments for Measuring and Testing of Electricity and Electrical Signals		

pt—Part of; NEC—Not Elsewhere Classified.

1987 SIC code	1987 U.S. SIC description	1997 NAICS code	1997 NAICS U.S. description
	Automotive Ammeters and Voltmeters	334514	Totalizing Fluid Meters and Counting Device Manufacturing (pt)
	Except Automotive Ammeters and Voltmeters	334515	Instrument Manufacturing for Measuring and Testing Electricity and Electrical Signals
3826	Laboratory Analytical Instruments	334516	Analytical Laboratory Instrument Manufacturing
3827	Optical Instruments and Lenses	333314	Optical Instrument and Lens Manufacturing
3829	Measuring and Controlling Devices, NEC		
	Motor Vehicle Gauges	334514	Totalizing Fluid Meter and Counting Device Manufacturing (pt)
	Medical Thermometers	339112	Surgical and Medical Instrument Manufacturing (pt)
	Electronic Chronometers	334518	Watch, Clock, and Part Manufacturing
	Except Medical Thermometers, Electronic Chronometers, and Motor Vehicle Gauges	334519	Other Measuring and Controlling Device Manufacturing
3841	Surgical and Medical Instruments and Apparatus		
	Tranquilizer Guns	332994	Small Arms Manufacturing (pt)
	Operating Tables	339111	Laboratory Apparatus and Furniture Manufacturing (pt)
	Except Tranquilizer Guns and Operating Tables	339112	Surgical and Medical Instrument Manufacturing (pt)
3842	Orthopedic, Prosthetic, and Surgical Appliances and Supplies		
	Incontinent and Bed Pads	322291	Sanitary Paper Product Manufacturing (pt)
	Orthopedic, Prosthetic, and Surgical Appliances and Supplies, except Electronic Hearing Aids	339113	Surgical Appliance and Supplies Manufacturing
	Electronic Hearing Aids	334510	Electromedical and Electrotherapeutic Apparatus Manufacturing (pt)
3843	Dental Equipment and Supplies	339114	Dental Equipment and Supplies Manufacturing

_____

pt—Part of; NEC—Not Elsewhere Classified.

1987 SIC code	1987 U.S. SIC description	1997 NAICS code	1997 NAICS U.S. description
3844	X-ray Apparatus and Tubes and Related Irradiation Apparatus	334517	Irradiation Apparatus Manufacturing (pt)
3845	Electromedical and Electrotherapeutic Apparatus		
	CT and CAT Scanners	334517	Irradiation Apparatus Manufacturing (pt)
	Other Electromedical and Electrotherapeutic Apparatus	334510	Electromedical and Electrotherapeutic Apparatus Manufacturing (pt)
3851	Ophthalmic Goods		
	Intra Ocular Lenses	339113	Surgical and Medical Instrument Manufacturing (pt)
	Except Intra Ocular Lenses	339115	Ophthalmic Goods Manufacturing (pt)
3861	Photographic Equipment and Supplies		
	Photographic Equipment and Supplies (Except Photographic Film, Paper, Plates and Chemicals)	333315	Photographic and Photocopying Equipment Manufacturing
	Photographic Film, Paper, Plates and Chemicals	325992	Photographic Film, Paper, Plate, and Chemical Manufacturing
3873	Watches, Clocks, Clockwork Operated Devices and Parts	334518	Watch, Clock, and Part Manufacturing (pt)
3911	Jewelry, Precious Metal	339911	Jewelry (except Costume) Manufacturing (pt)
3914	Silverware, Plated Ware, and Stainless Steel Ware		
	Cutlery and Flatware Nonprecious and Precious Plated	332211	Cutlery and Flatware (except Precious) Manufacturing (pt)
	Precious Plated Hollowware	332999	All Other Miscellaneous Fabricated Metal Product Manufacturing (pt)
	Silverware, Plated Ware, and Stainless Steel Ware (Except Nonprecious and Precious Plated Metal Cutlery and Flatware)	339912	Silverware and Hollowware Manufacturing (pt)
3915	Jewelers' Findings and Materials, and Lapidary Work		
	Watch Jewels	334518	Watch, Clock, and Part Manufacturing (pt)
	Except Watch Jewels	339913	Jewelers' Material and Lapidary Work Manufacturing

---

pt—Part of; NEC—Not Elsewhere Classified.

1987 SIC code	1987 U.S. SIC description	1997 NAICS code	1997 NAICS U.S. description
3931	Musical Instruments	339992	Musical Instrument Manufacturing
3942	Dolls and Stuffed Toys	339931	Doll and Stuffed Toy Manufacturing
3944	Games, Toys, and Children's Vehicles, Except Dolls and Bicycles		
	Metal Tricycles	336991	Motorcycle, Bicycle, and Parts Manufacturing (pt)
	Other Games, Toys, and Children's Vehicles	339932	Game, Toy, and Children's Vehicle Manufacturing
3949	Sporting and Athletic Goods, NEC	33992	Sporting and Athletic Good Manufacturing
3951	Pens, Mechanical Pencils, and Parts	339941	Pen and Mechanical Pencil Manufacturing
3952	Lead Pencils, Crayons, and Artist's Materials		
	Drafting Tables and Boards	337127	Institutional Furniture Manufacturing (pt)
	Drawing and India Ink	325998	All Other Miscellaneous Chemical and Preparation Manufacturing (pt)
	Other	339942	Lead Pencil and Art Good Manufacturing (pt)
3953	Marking Devices	339943	Marking Device Manufacturing
3955	Carbon Paper and Inked Ribbons	339944	Carbon Paper and Inked Ribbon Manufacturing
3961	Costume Jewelry and Costume Novelties, Except Precious Metals	339914	Costume Jewelry and Novelty Manufacturing (pt)
3965	Fasteners, Buttons, Needles, and Pins	339993	Fastener, Button, Needle, and Pin Manufacturing (pt)
3991	Brooms and Brushes	339994	Broom, Brush, and Mop Manufacturing (pt)
3993	Signs and Advertising Specialties		
	Signs	33995	Sign Manufacturing
	Advertising Specialties		Classified According to the Product Produced
3995	Burial Caskets	339995	Burial Casket Manufacturing
3996	Linoleum, Asphalted-Felt-Base, and Other Hard Surface Floor Coverings, NEC	326192	Resilient Floor Covering Manufacturing (pt)
3999	Manufacturing Industries, NEC		
	Beauty and Barber Chairs	337127	Institutional Furniture Manufacturing (pt)

pt—Part of; NEC—Not Elsewhere Classified.

1987 SIC code	1987 U.S. SIC description	1997 NAICS code	1997 NAICS U.S. description
	Other Beauty and Barber Shop Equipment	333319	Other Commercial and Service Industry Machinery Manufacturing (pt)
	Fur Dressing and Bleaching	31611	Leather and Hide Tanning and Finishing (pt)
	Lamp Shades of Paper or Textile	335121	Residential Electric Lighting Fixture Manufacturing (pt)
	Matches	325998	All Other Miscellaneous Chemical Product and Preparation Manufacturing (pt)
	Metal Products, Such As Combs, Hair Curlers, Etc.	332999	All Other Miscellaneous Fabricated Metal Product Manufacturing (pt)
	Plastics Products, Such As Combs, Hair Curlers, Etc.	326199	All Other Plastics Product Manufacturing (pt)
	Electric Hair Clippers for Humans	335211	Electric Housewares and Household Fan Manufacturing (pt)
	Tape Measures	332212	Hand and Edge Tool Manufacturing (pt)
	Human Hair Clippers, Hand Operated	332211	Cutlery and Flatware (except Precious) Manufacturing (pt)
	Embroidery Kits	339932	Game, Toy, and Children's Vehicle Manufacturing (pt)
	Other	339999	All Other Miscellaneous Manufacturing (pt)
4011	Railroads, Line-haul Operating	482111	Line-Haul Railroads
4013	Railroad Switching and Terminal Establishments		
	Beltline and Logging Railroads	482112	Short Line Railroads
	Other	48821	Support Activities for Rail Transportation (pt)
4111	Local and Suburban Transit		
	Mixed Mode Transit Systems	485111	Mixed Mode Transit Systems
	Commuter Rail Systems	485112	Commuter Rail Systems
	Bus and Motor Vehicle Transit Systems	485113	Bus and Other Motor Vehicle Transit Systems
	Other Urban Transit Systems	485119	Other Urban Transit Systems
	Airport Limousine Transportation	485999	All Other Transit and Ground Passenger Transportation (pt)
4119	Local Passenger Transportation, NEC		

pt—Part of; NEC—Not Elsewhere Classified.

http://www.ntis.gov/naics

1987 SIC code	1987 U.S. SIC description	1997 NAICS code	1997 NAICS U.S. description
	Ambulances	62191	Ambulance Service (pt)
	Employee Transportation	48541	School and Employee Bus Transportation (pt)
	Sightseeing Buses and Cable and Cog Railways, Except Scenic	48711	Scenic and Sightseeing Transportation, Land (pt)
	Special Needs Transportation	485991	Special Needs Transportation
	Hearse Rental with Driver and Carpool and Vanpool Operations	485999	All Other Transit and Ground Passenger Transportation (pt)
	Automobile Rental with Driver and Limousine Rental with Driver	48532	Limousine Service
4121	Taxicabs	48531	Taxi Service (pt)
4131	Intercity and Rural Bus Transportation	48521	Interurban and Rural Bus Transportation
4141	Local Bus Charter Service	48551	Charter Bus Industry (pt)
4142	Bus Charter Service, Except Local	48551	Charter Bus Industry (pt)
4151	School Buses	48541	School and Employee Bus Transportation (pt)
4173	Terminal and Service Facilities for Motor Vehicle Passenger Transportation	48849	Other Support Activities for Road Transportation (pt)
4212	Local Trucking Without Storage		
	Solid Waste Collection Without Disposal	562111	Solid Waste Collection
	Hazardous Waste Collection Without Disposal	562112	Hazardous Waste Collection
	Other Waste Collection Without Disposal	562119	Other Waste Collection
	Local General Freight Trucking Without Storage	48411	General Freight Trucking, Local (pt)
	Household Goods Moving Without Storage	48421	Used Household and Office Goods Moving (pt)
	Local Specialized Freight Trucking Without Storage	48422	Specialized Freight (except Used Goods) Trucking, Local (pt)
4213	Trucking, Except Local		
	Long-distance Truckload General Freight Trucking	484121	General Freight Trucking, Long-Distance, Truckload
	Long-distance Less Than Truckload General Freight Trucking	484122	General Freight Trucking, Long-Distance, Less Than Truckload
	Long-distance Household Goods Moving	48421	Used Household and Office Goods Moving (pt)

pt—Part of; NEC—Not Elsewhere Classified.

http://www.ntis.gov/naics

1987 SIC code	1987 U.S. SIC description	1997 NAICS code	1997 NAICS U.S. description
	Long-distance Specialized Freight Trucking	48423	Specialized Freight (except Used Goods) Trucking, Long-Distance
4214	Local Trucking with Storage		
	Local General Freight Trucking with Storage	48411	General Freight Trucking, Local (pt)
	Local Household Goods Moving	48421	Used Household and Office Goods Moving (pt)
	Local Specialized Freight Trucking with Storage	48422	Specialized Freight (except Used Goods) Trucking, Local (pt)
4215	Courier Services Except by Air		
	Hub and Spoke Intercity Delivery	49211	Couriers (pt)
	Local Delivery	49221	Local Messengers and Local Delivery
4221	Farm Product Warehousing and Storage	49313	Farm Product Warehousing and Storage
4222	Refrigerated Warehousing and Storage	49312	Refrigerated Warehousing and Storage (pt)
4225	General Warehousing and Storage		
	General Warehousing and Storage	49311	General Warehousing and Storage (pt)
	Miniwarehouses and Self-Storage Units	53113	Lessors of Miniwarehouses and Self Storage Units
4226	Special Warehousing and Storage, NEC		
	Fur Storage	49312	Refrigerated Warehousing and Storage (pt)
	General Warehousing in Foreign Trade Zones	49311	General Warehousing and Storage (pt)
	Other	49319	Other Warehousing and Storage
4231	Terminal and Joint Terminal Maintenance Facilities for Motor Freight Transportation	48849	Other Support Activities for Road Transportation (pt)
4311	United States Postal Service	49111	Postal Service (pt)
4412	Deep Sea Foreign Transportation of Freight	483111	Deep Sea Freight Transportation
4424	Deep Sea Domestic Transportation of Freight	483113	Coastal and Great Lakes Freight Transportation (pt)
4432	Freight Transportation on the Great Lakes - St. Lawrence Seaway	483113	Coastal and Great Lakes Freight Transportation (pt)
4449	Water Transportation of Freight, NEC	483211	Inland Water Freight Transportation

pt—Part of; NEC—Not Elsewhere Classified.

http://www.ntis.gov/naics

1987 SIC code	1987 U.S. SIC description	1997 NAICS code	1997 NAICS U.S. description
4481	Deep Sea Transportation of Passengers, Except by Ferry		
	Deep Sea Passenger Transportation	483112	Deep Sea Passenger Transportation
	Coastal and Great Lakes Passenger Transportation	483114	Coastal and Great Lakes Passenger Transportation (pt)
4482	Ferries		
	Coastal and Great Lakes Ferries	483114	Coastal and Great Lakes Passenger Transportation (pt)
	Inland Water Ferries	483212	Inland Water Passenger Transportation (pt)
4489	Water Transportation of Passengers, NEC		
	Water Taxis	483212	Inland Water Passenger Transportation (pt)
	Airboats, Excursion Boats, and Sightseeing Boats	48721	Scenic and Sightseeing Transportation, Water (pt)
4491	Marine Cargo Handling		
	Dock and Pier Operations	48831	Port and Harbor Operations (pt)
	Except Dock and Pier Operations	48832	Marine Cargo Handling
4492	Towing and Tugboat Services	48833	Navigational Services to Shipping (pt)
4493	Marinas	71393	Marinas
4499	Water Transportation Services, NEC		
	Boat and Ship Rental	532411	Commercial Air, Rail, and Water Transportation Equipment Rental and Leasing (pt)
	Lighthouse and Canal Operations	48831	Port and Harbor Operations (pt)
	Marine Salvage and Piloting Vessels In and Out of Harbors	48833	Navigational Services to Shipping (pt)
	Other	48839	Other Support Activities for Water Transportation (pt)
4512	Air Transportation, Scheduled		
	Scheduled Passenger Air Transportation	481111	Scheduled Passenger Air Transportation
	Scheduled Freight Air Transportation	481112	Scheduled Freight Air Transportation
4513	Air Courier Services	49211	Couriers (pt)
4522	Air Transportation, Nonscheduled		
	Air Ambulance	62191	Ambulance Services (pt)
	Nonscheduled Charter Freight Air Transportation	481212	Nonscheduled Chartered Freight Air Transportation

pt—Part of; NEC—Not Elsewhere Classified.

1987 SIC code	1987 U.S. SIC description	1997 NAICS code	1997 NAICS U.S. description
	Nonscheduled Charter Passenger Air Transportation	481211	Nonscheduled Chartered Passenger Air Transportation
	Sightseeing Aircraft	48799	Scenic and Sightseeing Transportation, Other (pt)
4581	Airports, Flying Fields, and Airport Terminal Services		
	Air Traffic Control	488111	Air Traffic Control (pt)
	Airfreight Handling at Airports, Hangar Operations, Airport Terminal Services, Aircraft Storage, Airports, and Flying Fields	488119	Other Airport Operations (pt)
	Aircraft Cleaning and Janitorial Services	56172	Janitorial Services (pt)
	Aircraft Servicing and Repairing	48819	Other Support Activities for Air Transportation
4612	Crude Petroleum Pipelines	48611	Pipeline Transportation of Crude Oil
4613	Refined Petroleum Pipelines	48691	Pipeline Transportation of Refined Petroleum Products
4619	Pipelines, NEC	48699	All Other Pipeline Transportation
4724	Travel Agencies	56151	Travel Agencies
4725	Tour Operators	56152	Tour Operators
4729	Arrangement of Passenger Transportation, NEC		
	Arrangement of Carpools and Vanpools	488999	All Other Support Activities for Transportation (pt)
	Except Arrangement of Carpools and Vanpools	561599	All Other Travel Arrangement and Reservation Services (pt)
4731	Arrangement of Transportation of Freight and Cargo		
	Freight Rate Auditors and Tariff Consultants	541614	Process, Physical Distribution, and Logistics Consulting Services (pt)
	Except Freight Rate Auditors and Tariff Consultants	48851	Freight Transportation Arrangement
4741	Rental of Railroad Cars		
	Rental of Railroad Cars	532411	Commercial Air, Rail, and Water Transportation Equipment Rental and Leasing (pt)
	Grain Leveling in Railroad Cars, Grain Trimming for Railroad Equipment, Precooling of Fruits and Vegetables in Connection with Transportation, and Railroad Car Cleaning, Icing, Ventilating and Heating	48821	Support Activities for Rail Transportation (pt)

pt—Part of; NEC—Not Elsewhere Classified.

http://www.ntis.gov/naics

1987 SIC code	1987 U.S. SIC description	1997 NAICS code	1997 NAICS U.S. description
4783	Packing and Crating	488991	Packing and Crating
4785	Fixed Facilities and Inspection and Weighing Services for Motor Vehicle Transportation		
	Marine Cargo Checkers	48839	Other Support Activities for Water Transportation (pt)
	Except Marine Cargo Checkers	48849	Other Support Activities for Road Transportation (pt)
4789	Transportation Services, NEC		
	Pipeline Terminals and Stockyards for Transportation	488999	All Other Support Activities for Transportation (pt)
	Horse-drawn Cabs and Carriages	48711	Scenic and Sightseeing Transportation, Land (pt)
	Dining Car Operations on a Fee or Contract Basis	72231	Food Service Contractors
	Other	48821	Support Activities for Rail Transportation (pt)
4812	Radiotelephone Communications		
	Paging Carriers	513321	Paging
	Cellular Carriers	513322	Cellular and Other Wireless Telecommunications (pt)
	Paging and Cellular Resellers	51333	Telecommunications Resellers (pt)
4813	Telephone Communications, Except Radiotelephone		
	Except Resellers	51331	Wired Telecommunications Carriers (pt)
	Wired Resellers	51333	Telecommunications Resellers (pt)
	Satellite Resellers	51334	Satellite Telecommunications (pt)
4822	Telegraph and Other Message Communications	51331	Wired Telecommunications Carriers (pt)
4832	Radio Broadcasting Stations		
	Networks	513111	Radio Networks
	Stations	513112	Radio Stations
4833	Television Broadcasting Stations	51312	Television Broadcasting
4841	Cable and Other Pay Television Services		
	Cable Networks	51321	Cable Networks
	Except Cable Networks	51322	Cable and Other Program Distribution

---

pt—Part of; NEC—Not Elsewhere Classified.

1987 SIC code	1987 U.S. SIC description	1997 NAICS code	1997 NAICS U.S. description
4899	Communications Services, NEC		
	Taxi Cab Dispatch	48531	Taxi Service (pt)
	Ship-to-Shore Broadcasting Communications	513322	Cellular and Other Wireless Telecommunications (pt)
	Satellite Communications	51334	Satellite Telecommunications (pt)
	Except Taxi Cab Dispatch Ship-to-Shore Communications and Satellite Communications	51339	Other Telecommunications
4911	Electric Services		
	Hydroelectric Power Generation	221111	Hydroelectric Power Generation (pt)
	Electric Power Generation by Fossil Fuels	221112	Fossil Fuel Electric Power Generation (pt)
	Electric Power Generation by Nuclear Fuels	221113	Nuclear Electric Power Generation (pt)
	Other Electric Power Generation	221119	Other Electric Power Generation (pt)
	Electric Power Transmission and Control	221121	Electric Bulk Power Transmission and Control (pt)
	Electric Power Distribution	221122	Electric Power Distribution (pt)
4922	Natural Gas Transmission	48621	Pipeline Transportation of Natural Gas (pt)
4923	Natural Gas Transmission and Distribution		
	Distribution	22121	Natural Gas Distribution (pt)
	Transmission	48621	Pipeline Transportation of Natural Gas (pt)
4924	Natural Gas Distribution	22121	Natural Gas Distribution (pt)
4925	Mixed, Manufactured, or Liquefied Petroleum Gas Production and/or Distribution	22121	Natural Gas Distribution (pt)
4931	Electric and Other Services Combined		
	Hydroelectric Power Generation When Combined with Other Services	221111	Hydroelectric Power Generation (pt)
	Electric Power Generation by Fossil Fuels When Combined with Other Services	221112	Fossil Fuel Electric Power Generation (pt)
	Electric Power Generation by Nuclear Fuels When Combined with Other Services	221113	Nuclear Electric Power Generation (pt)

pt   Part of; NEC—Not Elsewhere Classified.

http://www.ntis.gov/naics

1987 SIC code	1987 U.S. SIC description	1997 NAICS code	1997 NAICS U.S. description
	Other Electric Power Generation When Combined with Other Services	221119	Other Electric Power Generation (pt)
	Electric Power Transmission When Combined with Other Services	221121	Electric Bulk Power Transmission and Control (pt)
	Electric Power Distribution When Combined with Other Services	221122	Electric Power Distribution (pt)
	Natural Gas When Combined with Electric Services	22121	Natural Gas Distribution (pt)
4932	Gas and Other Services Combined	22121	Natural Gas Distribution (pt)
4939	Combination Utilities, NEC		
	Hydroelectric Power Generation When Combined with Other Services	221111	Hydroelectric Power Generation (pt)
	Electric Power Generation by Fossil Fuels When Combined with Other Services	221112	Fossil Fuel Electric Power Generation (pt)
	Electric Power Generation by Nuclear Fuels When Combined with Other Services	221113	Nuclear Electric Power Generation (pt)
	Other Power Generation When Combined with Other Services	221119	Other Electric Power Generation (pt)
	Electric Power Transmission When Combined with Other Services	221121	Electric Bulk Power Transmission and Control (pt)
	Electric Power Distribution When Combined with Other Services	221122	Electric Power Distribution (pt)
	Natural Gas Distribution when Combined with Other Services	22121	Natural Gas Distribution (pt)
4941	Water Supply	22131	Water Supply and Irrigation Systems (pt)
4952	Sewerage Systems	22132	Sewage Treatment Facilities
4953	Refuse Systems		
	Materials Recovery Facilities	56292	Materials Recovery Facilities
	Hazardous Waste Treatment and Disposal	562211	Hazardous Waste Treatment and Disposal
	Solid Waste Landfills	562212	Solid Waste Landfills
	Solid Waste Combustors and Incinerators	562213	Solid Waste Combustors and Incinerators
	Other Nonhazardous Waste Treatment and Disposal	562219	Other Nonhazardous Waste Treatment and Disposal

pt—Part of; NEC—Not Elsewhere Classified.

http://www.ntis.gov/naics

1987 SIC code	1987 U.S. SIC description	1997 NAICS code	1997 NAICS U.S. description
4959	Sanitary Services, NEC		
	Vacuuming of Airport Runways	488119	Other Airport Operations (pt)
	Remediation Services	56291	Remediation Services (pt)
	Malaria Control and Mosquito Eradication	56171	Exterminating and Pest Control Services (pt)
	Other	562998	All Other Miscellaneous Waste Management Services
4961	Steam and Air-Conditioning Supply	22133	Steam and Air-Conditioning Supply
4971	Irrigation Systems	22131	Water Supply and Irrigation Systems (pt)
5012	Automobiles and Other Motor Vehicles	42111	Automobile and Other Motor Vehicle Wholesalers
5013	Motor Vehicle Supplies and New Parts		
	Sold Via Retail Method	44131	Automotive Parts and Accessories Stores (pt)
	Sold Via Wholesale Method	42112	Motor Vehicle Supplies and New Part Wholesalers
5014	Tires and Tubes		
	Sold Via Retail Method	44132	Tire Dealers (pt) - Retail
	Sold Via Wholesale Method	42113	Tire and Tube Wholesalers
5015	Motor Vehicle Parts, Used		
	Sold Via Retail Method	44131	Automotive Parts and Accessories (pt)
	Sold Via Wholesale Method	42114	Motor Vehicle Part (Used) Wholesalers
5021	Furniture		
	Sold Via Retail Method	44211	Furniture Stores (pt)
	Sold Via Wholesale Method	42121	Furniture Wholesalers
5023	Home Furnishings		
	Sold Via Retail Method	44221	Floor Covering Stores (pt)
	Sold Via Wholesale Method	42122	Home Furnishing Wholesalers
5031	Lumber, Plywood, Millwork, and Wood Panels	42131	Lumber, Plywood, Millwork, and Wood Panel Wholesalers
5032	Brick, Stone and Related Construction Materials		
	Sold Via Retail Method	44419	Other Building Material Dealers (pt)
	Sold Via Wholesale Method	42132	Brick, Stone and Related Construction Material Wholesalers
5033	Roofing, Siding, and Insulation Materials	42133	Roofing, Siding, and Insulation Material Wholesalers

pt—Part of; NEC—Not Elsewhere Classified.

http://www.ntis.gov/naics

1987 SIC code	1987 U.S. SIC description	1997 NAICS code	1997 NAICS U.S. description
5039	Construction Materials, NEC		
	Sold Via Retail Method	44419	Other Building Material Dealers (pt)
	Sold Via Wholesale Method	42139	Other Construction Material Wholesalers
5043	Photographic Equipment and Supplies	42141	Photographic Equipment and Supplies Wholesalers
5044	Office Equipment		
	Sold Via Retail Method	45321	Office Supplies and Stationery Stores (pt)
	Sold Via Wholesale Method	42142	Office Equipment Wholesalers
5045	Computers and Computer Peripheral Equipment and Software		
	Sold Via Wholesale Method	42143	Computer and Computer Peripheral Equipment and Software Wholesalers
	Sold Via Retail Method	44312	Computer and Software Stores (pt) - Retail
5046	Commercial Equipment, NEC	42144	Other Commercial Equipment Wholesalers
5047	Medical, Dental, and Hospital Equipment and Supplies		
	Sold Via Wholesale Method	42145	Medical, Dental, and Hospital Equipment and Supplies Wholesalers
	Sold Via Retail Method	446199	All Other Health and Personal Care Stores (pt) - Retail
5048	Ophthalmic Goods	42146	Ophthalmic Goods Wholesalers
5049	Professional Equipment and Supplies, NEC		
	Sold Via Wholesale Method	42149	Other Professional Equipment and Supplies Wholesalers
	Sold Via Retail Method	45321	Office Supplies and Stationery Stores (pt) - Retail
5051	Metals Service Centers and Offices	42151	Metals Service Centers and Offices
5052	Coal and Other Minerals and Ores	42152	Coal and Other Mineral and Ore Wholesalers
5063	Electrical Apparatus and Equipment Wiring Supplies, and Construction Materials		
	Sold Via Retail Method	44419	Other Building Material Dealers (pt)

---

pt—Part of; NEC—Not Elsewhere Classified.

http://www.ntis.gov/naics

1987 SIC code	1987 U.S. SIC description	1997 NAICS code	1997 NAICS U.S. description
	Sold Via Wholesale Method	42161	Electrical Apparatus and Equipment, Wiring Supplies, and Construction Material Wholesalers
5064	Electrical Appliances, Television and Radio Sets	42162	Electrical Appliance, Television, and Radio Set Wholesalers
5065	Electronic Parts and Equipment, NEC	42169	Other Electronic Parts and Equipment Wholesalers
5072	Hardware		
	Sold Via Retail Method	44413	Hardware Stores (pt) - Retail
	Sold Via Wholesale Method	42171	Hardware Wholesalers
5074	Plumbing and Heating Equipment and Supplies (Hydronics)		
	Sold Via Retail Method	44419	Other Building Material Dealers (pt)- Retail
	Sold Via Wholesale Method	42172	Plumbing and Heating Equipment and Supplies (Hydronics) Wholesalers
5075	Warm Air Heating and Air-Conditioning Equipment and Supplies	42173	Warm Air Heating and Air-Conditioning Equipment and Supplies Wholesalers
5078	Refrigeration Equipment and Supplies	42174	Refrigeration Equipment and Supplies Wholesalers
5082	Construction and Mining (Except Petroleum) Machinery and Equipment	42181	Construction and Mining (except Petroleum) Machinery and Equipment Wholesalers
5083	Farm and Garden Machinery and Equipment		
	Sold Via Wholesale Method	42182	Farm and Garden Machinery and Equipment Wholesalers
	Sold Via Retail Method	44421	Outdoor Power Equipment Stores (pt) - Retail
5084	Industrial Machinery and Equipment	42183	Industrial Machinery and Equipment Wholesalers (pt)
5085	Industrial Supplies		
	Fluid Power Accessories	42183	Industrial Machinery and Equipment Wholesalers (pt)
	Except Fluid Power Accessories	42184	Industrial Supplies Wholesalers
5087	Service Establishment Equipment and Supplies		
	Sold Via Wholesale Method	42185	Service Establishment Equipment and Supplies Wholesalers

---

pt—Part of; NEC—Not Elsewhere Classified.

1987 SIC code	1987 U.S. SIC description	1997 NAICS code	1997 NAICS U.S. description
	Sold Via Retail Method Beauty and Barber Shop Equipment and Supplies	44612	Cosmetics, Beauty Supplies, and Perfume Stores (pt)
5088	Transportation Equipment and Supplies, Except Motor Vehicles	42186	Transportation Equipment and Supplies (except Motor Vehicles) Wholesalers
5091	Sporting and Recreational Goods and Supplies	42191	Sporting and Recreational Goods and Supplies Wholesalers
5092	Toys and Hobby Goods and Supplies	42192	Toy and Hobby Goods and Supplies Wholesalers
5093	Scrap and Waste Materials	42193	Recyclable Material Wholesalers
5094	Jewelry, Watches, Precious Stones, and Precious Metals	42194	Jewelry, Watch, Precious Stone, and Precious Metal Wholesalers
5099	Durable Goods, NEC	42199	Other Miscellaneous Durable Goods Wholesalers (pt)
5111	Printing and Writing Paper	42211	Printing and Writing Paper Wholesalers
5112	Stationery and Office Supplies Sold Via Retail Method	45321	Office Supplies and Stationery Stores (pt)
	Sold Via Wholesale Method	42212	Stationery and Office Supplies Wholesalers
5113	Industrial and Personal Service Paper	42213	Industrial and Personal Service Paper Wholesalers
5122	Drugs, Drug Proprietaries, and Druggists' Sundries	42221	Drugs and Druggists' Sundries Wholesalers
5131	Piece Goods, Notions, and Other Dry Goods		
	Converters, Broadwoven Piece Good Fabric	313311	Broadwoven Fabric Finishing Mills (pt)
	Converters, Except Broadwoven Fabric	313312	Textile and Fabric Finishing (except Broadwoven Fabric) Mills (pt)
	Except Converters	42231	Piece Goods, Notions, and Other Dry Goods Wholesalers
5136	Men's and Boys' Clothing and Furnishings	42232	Men's and Boys' Clothing and Furnishings Wholesalers
5137	Women's, Children's, and Infants' Clothing and Accessories	42233	Women's, Children's, and Infants' Clothing and Accessories Wholesalers
5139	Footwear	42234	Footwear Wholesalers
5141	Groceries, General Line	42241	General Line Grocery Wholesalers
5142	Packaged Frozen Foods	42242	Packaged Frozen Food Wholesalers
5143	Dairy Products, Except Dried or Canned	42243	Dairy Products (except Dried or Canned) Wholesalers

pt—Part of; NEC—Not Elsewhere Classified.

1987 SIC code	1987 U.S. SIC description	1997 NAICS code	1997 NAICS U.S. description
5144	Poultry and Poultry Products	42244	Poultry and Poultry Product Wholesalers
5145	Confectionery	42245	Confectionery Wholesalers
5146	Fish and Seafoods	42246	Fish and Seafood Wholesalers
5147	Meats and Meat Products		
	Boxed Beef	311612	Meat Processed from Carcasses (pt)
	Except Boxed Beef	42247	Meat and Meat Product Wholesalers
5148	Fresh Fruits and Vegetables	42248	Fresh Fruit and Vegetable Wholesalers
5149	Groceries and Related Products, NEC		
	Bottling Mineral or Spring Water	312112	Bottled Water Manufacturing (pt)
	Except Bottling Mineral or Spring Water	42249	Other Grocery and Related Product Wholesalers
5153	Grain and Field Beans	42251	Grain and Field Bean Wholesalers
5154	Livestock	42252	Livestock Wholesalers
5159	Farm-Product Raw Materials, NEC	42259	Other Farm Product Raw Material Wholesalers
5162	Plastics Materials and Basic Forms and Shapes	42261	Plastics Materials and Basic Forms and Shapes Wholesalers
5169	Chemicals and Allied Products, NEC	42269	Other Chemical and Allied Products Wholesalers
5171	Petroleum Bulk Stations and Terminals		
	Heating Oil Sold Via Retail Method	454311	Heating Oil Dealers (pt)
	LP Gas Sold Via Retail Method	454312	Liquefied Petroleum Gas (Bottled Gas) Dealers (pt)
	Sold Via Wholesale Method	42271	Petroleum Bulk Stations and Terminals
5172	Petroleum and Petroleum Products Wholesalers, Except Bulk Stations and Terminals	42272	Petroleum and Petroleum Products Wholesalers (except Bulk Stations and Terminals)
5181	Beer and Ale	42281	Beer and Ale Wholesalers
5182	Wine and Distilled Alcoholic Beverages	42282	Wine and Distilled Alcoholic Beverage Wholesalers
5191	Farm Supplies		
	Lawn and Garden Supplies Sold Via Retail Method	44422	Nursery and Garden Centers (pt) - Retail
	Except Lawn and Garden Supplies Sold Via Retail Method	42291	Farm Supplies Wholesalers

pt—Part of; NEC—Not Elsewhere Classified.

http://www.ntis.gov/naics

1987 SIC code	1987 U.S. SIC description	1997 NAICS code	1997 NAICS U.S. description
5192	Books, Periodicals, and Newspapers	42292	Book, Periodical, and Newspaper Wholesalers
5193	Flowers, Nursery Stock, and Florists' Supplies		
	Sold Via Wholesale Method	42293	Flower, Nursery Stock, and Florists' Supplies Wholesalers
	Sold Via Retail Method	44422	Nursery and Garden Centers (pt) - Retail
5194	Tobacco and Tobacco Products	42294	Tobacco and Tobacco Product Wholesalers
5198	Paint, Varnishes, and Supplies	42295	Paint, Varnish, and Supplies Wholesalers
5199	Nondurable Goods, NEC		
	Advertising Specialties Goods Distributors	54189	Other Services Related to Advertising (pt)
	Except Advertising Specialty	42299	Other Miscellaneous Nondurable Goods Wholesalers
5211	Lumber and Other Building Materials Dealers		
	Home Centers	44411	Home Centers
	Except Home Centers	44419	Other Building Material Dealers (pt)
5231	Paint, Glass, and Wallpaper Stores		
	Paint and Wallpaper	44412	Paint and Wallpaper Stores (pt)
	Glass Stores	44419	Other Building Material Dealers (pt)
5251	Hardware Stores	44413	Hardware Stores (pt)
5261	Retail Nurseries, Lawn and Garden Supply Stores		
	Except Outdoor Power Equipment	44422	Nursery and Garden Centers (pt)
	Outdoor Power Equipment Stores	44421	Outdoor Power Equipment Stores (pt)
5271	Mobile Home Dealers	45393	Manufactured (Mobile) Home Dealers
5311	Department Stores	45211	Department Stores
5331	Variety Stores	45299	All Other General Merchandise Stores (pt)
5399	Miscellaneous General Merchandise Stores		
	Warehouse Clubs and General Merchandise Combination Stores	45291	Warehouse Clubs and Superstores (pt)

pt—Part of; NEC—Not Elsewhere Classified.

http://www.ntis.gov/naics

1987 SIC code	1987 U.S. SIC description	1997 NAICS code	1997 NAICS U.S. description
	All Other General Merchandise Stores	45299	All Other General Merchandise Stores (pt)
5411	Grocery Stores		
	Convenience Stores with Gas	44711	Gasoline Stations with Convenience Stores (pt)
	Supermarkets and Grocery Stores with Little General Merchandise	44511	Supermarkets and Other Grocery (except Convenience) Stores
	Supermarkets and Grocery Stores with Substantial General Merchandise	45291	Warehouse Clubs and Superstores (pt)
	Convenience Stores without Gas	44512	Convenience Stores
5421	Meat and Fish (Seafood) Markets, Including Freezer Provisioners		
	Freezer Provisioners	45439	Other Direct Selling Establishments (pt)
	Meat Markets	44521	Meat Markets (pt)
	Fish and Seafood Markets	44522	Fish and Seafood Markets
5431	Fruit and Vegetable Markets	44523	Fruit and Vegetable Markets
5441	Candy, Nut, and Confectionery Stores		
	Confectionery and Nut Stores	445292	Confectionery and Nut Stores
	Chocolate Candy Stores, Preparing Candy on Premises	31133	Confectionery Manufacturing from Purchased Chocolate (pt)
	Nonchocolate Candy Stores, Preparing Candy on Premises	31134	Nonchocolate Confectionery Manufacturing (pt)
5451	Dairy Products Stores	445299	All Other Specialty Food Stores (pt)
5461	Retail Bakeries		
	Doughnut Shops, Pretzel Shops, Cookie Shops, Bagel Shops, and Other Such Shops that Make and Sell for Immediate Consumption	722213	Snack and Nonalcoholic Beverage Bars (pt)
	Bakeries That Make and Sell at the Same Location	311811	Retail Bakeries
	Sales Only of All Other Baked Goods	445291	Baked Goods Stores
5499	Miscellaneous Food Stores		
	Poultry and Poultry Products	44521	Meat Markets (pt)
	Food Supplement Stores	446191	Food (Health) Supplement Stores
	All Other Miscellaneous Food Stores	445299	All Other Specialty Food Stores (pt)

pt—Part of; NEC—Not Elsewhere Classified.

1987 SIC code	1987 U.S. SIC description	1997 NAICS code	1997 NAICS U.S. description
5511	Motor Vehicle Dealers (New and Used)	44111	New Car Dealers
5521	Motor Vehicle Dealers (Used Only)	44112	Used Car Dealers
5531	Auto and Home Supply Stores		
	Tire Dealers	44132	Tire Dealers (pt)
	Auto Supply Stores	44131	Automotive Parts and Accessories Stores (pt)
	Other Auto and Home Supply Stores	45299	All Other General Merchandise (pt)
5541	Gasoline Service Stations		
	With Convenience Store	44711	Gasoline Stations with Convenience Store (pt)
	Except with Convenience Stores	44719	Other Gasoline Stations
5551	Boat Dealers	441222	Boat Dealers
5561	Recreational Vehicle Dealers	44121	Recreational Vehicle Dealers
5571	Motorcycle Dealers	441221	Motorcycle Dealers
5599	Automotive Dealers, NEC	441229	All Other Motor Vehicle Dealers
5611	Men's and Boys' Clothing and Accessory Stores		
	Men's Clothing Stores	44811	Men's Clothing Stores
	Men's Accessory Stores	44815	Clothing Accessories Stores (pt)
5621	Women's Clothing Stores	44812	Women's Clothing Stores
5632	Women's Accessory and Specialty Stores		
	Specialty Stores	44819	Other Clothing Stores (pt)
	Accessory Stores	44815	Clothing Accessories Stores (pt)
5641	Children's and Infants' Wear Stores	44813	Children's and Infants' Clothing Stores
5651	Family Clothing Stores	44814	Family Clothing Stores
5661	Shoe Stores	44821	Shoe Stores
5699	Miscellaneous Apparel and Accessory Stores		
	Custom Tailors and Seamstresses	315	Included in Apparel Manufacturing Subsector Based on Type of Garment Produced
	Miscellaneous Apparel	44819	Other Clothing Stores (pt)
	Miscellaneous Accessories	44815	Clothing Accessories Stores (pt)
5712	Furniture Stores		
	Custom Made Wood Nonupholstered Furniture, Except Cabinets and Upholstered	337122	Nonupholstered Wood Household Furniture Manufacturing (pt)

pt—Part of; NEC—Not Elsewhere Classified.

1987 SIC code	1987 U.S. SIC description	1997 NAICS code	1997 NAICS U.S. description
	Custom Wood Cabinets	33711	Wood Kitchen Cabinet and Countertop Manufacturing (pt)
	Upholstered Custom Made Furniture	337121	Upholstered Household Furniture Manufacturing (pt)
	Except Custom Cabinet and Furniture Builders	44211	Furniture Stores (pt)
5713	Floor Covering Stores	44221	Floor Covering Stores (pt)
5714	Drapery, Curtain, and Upholstery Stores		
	Drapery and Curtain Stores	442291	Window Treatment Stores (pt)
	Upholstery Stores	45113	Sewing, Needlework and Piece Goods Stores (pt)
	Custom Drapes	314121	Curtain and Drapery Mills (pt)
	Custom Slipcovers	314129	Other Household Textile Product Mills (pt)
5719	Miscellaneous Homefurnishings Stores		
	Blinds and Shades	442291	Window Treatment Stores (pt)
	Pottery and Crafts Made and Sold on Site		Included in Manufacturing sector based on article produced
	Except Blinds, Shades, and Pottery and Crafts Made and Sold on Site	442299	All Other Home Furnishings Stores (pt)
5722	Household Appliance Stores	443111	Household Appliance Stores
5731	Radio, Television, and Consumer Electronics Stores		
	Except Auto Radio Stores	443112	Radio, Television, and Other Electronics Stores (pt)
	Auto Radio Stores	44131	Automotive Parts and Accessories Stores (pt)
5734	Computer and Computer Software Stores	44312	Computer and Software Stores (pt)
5735	Record and Prerecorded Tape Stores	45122	Prerecorded Tape, Compact Disc, and Record Stores
5736	Musical Instrument Stores	45114	Musical Instrument and Supplies Stores
5812	Eating and Drinking Places		
	Full Service Restaurants	72211	Full-Service Restaurants
	Limited Service Restaurants	722211	Limited-Service Restaurants
	Cafeterias	722212	Cafeterias
	Snack and Nonalcoholic Beverage Bars	722213	Snack and Nonalcoholic Beverage Bars (pt)

pt—Part of; NEC—Not Elsewhere Classified.

http://www.ntis.gov/naics

1987 SIC code	1987 U.S. SIC description	1997 NAICS code	1997 NAICS U.S. description
	Food Service Contractors	72231	Food Service Contractors
	Caterers	72232	Caterers
	Dinner Theaters	71111	Theater Companies and Dinner Theaters (pt)
5813	Drinking Places (Alcoholic Beverages)	72241	Drinking Places (Alcoholic Beverages)
5912	Drug Stores and Proprietary Stores	44611	Pharmacies and Drug Stores
5921	Liquor Stores	44531	Beer, Wine, and Liquor Stores
5932	Used Merchandise Stores		
	Pawnshops	522298	All Other Nondepository Credit Intermediation
	Except pawn shops	45331	Used Merchandise Stores
5941	Sporting Goods Stores and Bicycle Shops	45111	Sporting Goods Stores
5942	Book Stores	451211	Book Stores
5943	Stationery Stores	45321	Office Supplies and Stationery Stores (pt)
5944	Jewelry Stores	44831	Jewelry Stores
5945	Hobby, Toy, and Game Shops	45112	Hobby, Toy, and Game Stores
5946	Camera and Photographic Supply Stores	44313	Camera and Photographic Supplies Stores
5947	Gift, Novelty, and Souvenir Shops	45322	Gift, Novelty, and Souvenir Stores
5948	Luggage and Leather Goods Stores	44832	Luggage and Leather Goods Stores
5949	Sewing, Needlework, and Piece Goods Stores	45113	Sewing, Needlework, and Piece Goods Stores (pt)
5961	Catalog and Mail-Order Houses	45411	Electronic Shopping and Mail-Order Houses
5962	Automatic Merchandising Machine Operator	45421	Vending Machine Operators
5963	Direct Selling Establishments		
	Mobile Food Wagons	72233	Mobile Food Services
	All Other Direct Selling Establishments	45439	Other Direct Selling Establishments (pt)
5983	Fuel Oil Dealers	454311	Heating Oil Dealers (pt)
5984	Liquefied Petroleum Gas (Bottled Gas) Dealers	454312	Liquefied Petroleum Gas (Bottled Gas) Dealers (pt)
5989	Fuel Dealers, NEC	454319	Other Fuel Dealers
5992	Florists	45311	Florists
5993	Tobacco Stores and Stands	453991	Tobacco Stores
5994	News Dealers and Newsstands	451212	News Dealers and Newsstands
5995	Optical Goods Stores		
	Optical Stores Grinding Prescription Lenses, except 1-Hour Labs	339115	Ophthalmic Goods Manufacturing (pt)

---

pt—Part of; NEC—Not Elsewhere Classified.

1987 SIC code	1987 U.S. SIC description	1997 NAICS code	1997 NAICS U.S. description
	Except Optical Laboratories Grinding Prescription Lenses	44613	Optical Goods Stores
5999	Miscellaneous Retail Stores, NEC		
	Cosmetic Stores	44612	Cosmetics, Beauty Supplies, and Perfume Stores (pt)
	Hearing Aid and Artificial Limb Stores	446199	All Other Health and Personal Care Stores (pt)
	Pets and Pet Supply Stores	45391	Pet and Pet Supplies Stores
	Art Dealers	45392	Art Dealers
	Telephone and Typewriter Stores	443112	Radio, Television, and Other Electronics Stores (pt)
	Other Miscellaneous Retail Stores	453998	All Other Miscellaneous Store Retailers (except Tobacco Stores) (pt)
6011	Federal Reserve Banks	52111	Monetary Authorities-Central Banks
6019	Central Reserve Depository Institutions, NEC	522298	All Other Nondepository Credit Intermediation (pt)
6021	National Commercial Banks		
	Commercial Banks	52211	Commercial Banking (pt)
	Credit Card Issuing	52221	Credit Card Issuing (pt)
6022	State Commercial Banks		
	Commercial Banks	52211	Commercial Banking (pt)
	Credit Card Issuing	52221	Credit Card Issuing (pt)
	Private and Industrial Banking	52219	Other Depository Intermediation
6029	Commercial Banks, NEC	52211	Commercial Banking (pt)
6035	Savings Institutions, Federally Chartered	52212	Savings Institutions (pt)
6036	Savings institutions, Not Federally Chartered	52212	Savings Institutions (pt)
6061	Credit Unions, Federally Chartered	52213	Credit Unions (pt)
6062	Credit Unions, Not Federally Chartered	52213	Credit Unions (pt)
6081	Branches and Agencies of Foreign Banks		
	International Trade Financing	522293	International Trade Financing (pt)
	Branches of Foreign Banks	52211	Commercial Banking (pt)
	Agencies of Foreign Banks, Except International Trade Financing	522298	All Other Nondepository Credit Intermediation (pt)
6082	Foreign Trade and International Banking Institutions		

pt—Part of; NEC—Not Elsewhere Classified.

1987 SIC code	1987 U.S. SIC description	1997 NAICS code	1997 NAICS U.S. description
	International Trade Financing	522293	International Trade Financing (pt)
	Except International Trade Financing	522298	All Other Nondepository Credit Intermediation (pt)
6091	Nondeposit Trust Facilities	523991	Trust, Fiduciary, and Custody Activities (pt)
6099	Functions Related to Deposit Banking, NEC		
	Clearinghouses and Electronic Funds Transfer	52232	Financial Transactions Processing, Reserve, and Clearinghouse Activities (pt)
	Foreign Currency Exchange	52313	Commodity Contracts Dealing (pt)
	Escrow and Fiduciary Agencies	523991	Trust, Fiduciary, and Custody Activities (pt)
	Other	52239	Other Activities Related to Credit Intermediation (pt)
6111	Federal and Federally-Sponsored Credit Agencies		
	Federal Land Banks	522292	Real Estate Credit (pt)
	Trade Banks	522293	International Trade Financing (pt)
	Secondary Market Financing	522294	Secondary Market Financing
	Other	522298	All Other Nondepository Credit Intermediation (pt)
6141	Personal Credit Institutions		
	Credit Card Issuing	52221	Credit Card Issuing (pt)
	Installment Sales Financing	52222	Sales Financing (pt)
	Industrial Nondeposit Banks	522298	All Other Nondepository Credit Intermediation (pt)
	Other	522291	Consumer Lending
6153	Short-Term Business Credit Institutions, Except Agricultural		
	Credit Card Issuing	52221	Credit Card Issuing (pt)
	Business Sales Finance	52222	Sales Financing (pt)
	Credit Card Service	52232	Financial Transactions Processing, Reserve, and Clearinghouse Activities (pt)
	Other	52391	Miscellaneous Intermediation (pt)
6159	Miscellaneous Business Credit Institutions		
	Finance Leasing Combined With Loan Making	522	Included in Credit Intermediation and Related Activities Subsector by Type of Credit

pt—Part of; NEC—Not Elsewhere Classified.

http://www.ntis.gov/naics

1987 SIC code	1987 U.S. SIC description	1997 NAICS code	1997 NAICS U.S. description
	Finance Leasing Combined With Sales Financing	52222	Sales Financing (pt)
	Farm Mortgage Companies	522292	Real Estate Credit (pt)
	Finance Leasing Without Loan Making	532	Included in Rental and Leasing Services Subsector by Type of Equipment and Method of Operation
	Trade Banks	522293	International Trade Financing (pt)
	Secondary Market Financing	522294	Secondary Market Financing (pt)
	All Other	522298	All Other Nondepository Credit Intermediation (pt)
6162	Mortgage Bankers and Loan Correspondents		
	Mortgage Bankers and Originators	522292	Real Estate Credit
	Mortgage Servicing	52239	Other Activities Related to Credit Intermediation (pt)
6163	Loan Brokers	52231	Mortgage and Nonmortgage Loan Brokers
6211	Security Brokers, Dealers, and Flotation Companies		
	Security Dealers and Underwriters	52311	Investment Banking and Securities Dealing
	Security Brokers	52312	Securities Brokerage
	Dealers and Brokers, Except Securities, Commodities, and Oil and Gas Lease	52391	Miscellaneous Intermediation (pt)
	Oil and Gas Lease Brokers' Offices	523999	Miscellaneous Financial Investment Activities (pt)
6221	Commodity Contracts Brokers and Dealers		
	Commodity Dealers	52313	Commodity Contracts Dealing (pt)
	Commodity Brokers	52314	Commodity Contracts Brokerage
6231	Security and Commodity Exchanges	52321	Securities and Commodity Exchanges
6282	Investment Advice		
	Portfolio Managers	52392	Portfolio Management (pt)
	Other	52393	Investment Advice
6289	Services Allied With the Exchange of Securities or Commodities, NEC		
	Securities Custodians	523991	Trust, Fiduciary, and Custody Activities (pt)

pt—Part of; NEC—Not Elsewhere Classified.

http://www.ntis.gov/naics

1987 SIC code	1987 U.S. SIC description	1997 NAICS code	1997 NAICS U.S. description
	Other	523999	Miscellaneous Financial Investment Activities (pt)
6311	Life Insurance		
	Life Insurers, Direct	524113	Direct Life Insurance Carriers
	Reinsurance Carriers, Life	52413	Reinsurance Carriers (pt)
6321	Accident and Health Insurance		
	Disability Insurers, Direct	524113	Direct Life Insurance Carriers (pt)
	Accident and Health Insurers, Direct	524114	Direct Health and Medical Insurance Carriers (pt)
	Self Insurers	52519	Other Insurance Funds (pt)
	Reinsurance Carriers, Accident and Health	52413	Reinsurance Carriers (pt)
6324	Hospital and Medical Service Plans		
	Health and Medical Insurers, Direct	524114	Direct Health and Medical Insurance Carriers (pt)
	Self Insurers	52519	Other Insurance Funds (pt)
	Reinsurance Carriers, Health and Medical	52413	Reinsurance Carriers (pt)
6331	Fire, Marine, and Casualty Insurance		
	Fire, Marine, and Casualty Insurers, Direct	524126	Direct Property and Casualty Insurance Carriers (pt)
	Contact Lens Insurance	524128	Other Direct Insurance (except Life, Health, and Medical) Carriers (pt)
	Self Insurers	52519	Other Insurance Funds (pt)
	Reinsurance Carriers, Fire, Marine, and Casualty	52413	Reinsurance Carriers (pt)
6351	Surety Insurance		
	Financial Responsibility Insurers, Direct	524126	Direct Property and Casualty Insurance Carriers (pt)
	Reinsurance Carriers, Financial Responsibility	52413	Reinsurance Carriers (pt)
6361	Title Insurance		
	Title Insurers, Direct	524127	Direct Title Insurance Carriers
	Reinsurance Carriers, Title	52413	Reinsurance Carriers (pt)
6371	Pension, Health, and Welfare Funds		
	Managers	52392	Portfolio Management (pt)
	Administrators	524292	Third Party Administration of Insurance and Pension Funds (pt)

---

pt—Part of; NEC—Not Elsewhere Classified.

1987 SIC code	1987 U.S. SIC description	1997 NAICS code	1997 NAICS U.S. description
	Pension Funds	52511	Pension Funds
	Health and Welfare Funds	52512	Health and Welfare Funds
	Profit Sharing Funds	52599	Other Financial Vehicles (pt)
6399	Insurance Carriers, NEC	524128	Other Direct Insurance (except Life, Health, and Medical) Carriers
6411	Insurance Agents, Brokers, and Service		
	Insurance Agents and Brokers	52421	Insurance Agencies and Brokerages
	Claim Adjusters	524291	Claims Adjusting
	Claim Processors	524292	Third Party Administrators of Insurance and Pension Funds (pt)
	Other	524298	All Other Insurance Related Activities
6512	Operators of Nonresidential Buildings		
	Stadium and Arena Owners	71131	Promoters of Performing Arts, Sports, and Similar Events with Facilities (pt)
	Except Stadium and Arena Owners	53112	Lessors of Nonresidential Buildings (except Miniwarehouses)
6513	Operators of Apartment Buildings	53111	Lessors of Residential Buildings and Dwellings (pt)
6514	Operators of Dwellings Other Than Apartment Buildings	53111	Lessors of Residential Buildings and Dwellings (pt)
6515	Operators of Residential Mobile Home Sites	53119	Lessors of Other Real Estate Property (pt)
6517	Lessors of Railroad Property	53119	Lessors of Other Real Estate Property (pt)
6519	Lessors of Real Property, NEC	53119	Lessors of Other Real Estate Property (pt)
6531	Real Estate Agents and Managers		
	Real Estate Agents and Brokers	53121	Offices of Real Estate Agents and Brokers
	Condominium Associations	81399	Other Similar Organizations (except Business, Professional, Labor, and Political Organizations) (pt)
	Residential Property Managers	531311	Residential Property Managers
	Nonresidential Property Managers	531312	Nonresidential Property Managers
	Real Estate Appraisers	53132	Offices of Real Estate Appraisers
	Cemetery Management	81222	Cemeteries and Crematories (pt)
	Other	53139	Other Activities Related to Real Estate

pt—Part of; NEC—Not Elsewhere Classified.

http://www.ntis.gov/naics

1987 SIC code	1987 U.S. SIC description	1997 NAICS code	1997 NAICS U.S. description
6541	Title Abstract Offices	541191	Title Abstract and Settlement Offices
6552	Land Subdividers and Developers, Except Cemeteries	23311	Land Subdivision and Land Development
6553	Cemetery Subdividers and Developers	81222	Cemeteries and Crematories (pt)
6712	Offices of Bank Holding Companies	551111	Offices of Bank Holding Companies
6719	Offices of Holding Companies, NEC	551112	Offices of Other Holding Companies
6722	Management Investment Offices, Open-End	52591	Open-End Investment Funds
6726	Unit Investment Trusts, Face-Amount Certificate Offices, and Closed-End Management Investment Offices	52599	Other Financial Vehicles
6732	Education, Religious, and Charitable Trusts	813211	Grantmaking Foundations
6733	Trusts, Except Educational, Religious, and Charitable		
	Managers	52392	Portfolio Management (pt)
	Administrators of Private Estates	523991	Trust, Fiduciary, and Custody Services (pt)
	Vacation Funds for Employees	52519	Other Insurance Funds (pt)
	Personal Trusts, Estates, and Agency Accounts	52592	Trusts, Estates, and Agency Accounts
6792	Oil Royalty Traders		
	Investing on Own Account	52391	Miscellaneous Intermediation (pt)
	Oil Royalty Companies	53311	Lessors of Nonfinancial Intangible Assets (except Copyrighted Works) (pt)
6794	Patent Owners and Lessors	53311	Lessors of Nonfinancial Intangible Assets (except Copyrighted Works) (pt)
6798	Real Estate Investment Trusts	52593	Real Estate Investment Trusts
6799	Investors, NEC		
	Venture Capital Companies, Investment Clubs, and Operators on Own Account	52391	Miscellaneous Intermediation (pt)
	Commodity Contract Pool Operators	52392	Portfolio Management (pt)
	Commodity Contract Trading Companies	52313	Commodity Contracts Dealing (pt)

pt—Part of; NEC—Not Elsewhere Classified.

http://www.ntis.gov/naics

1987 SIC code	1987 U.S. SIC description	1997 NAICS code	1997 NAICS U.S. description
7011	Hotels and Motels		
	Hotels and Motels, except Casino Hotels	72111	Hotels (except Casino Hotels) and Motels (pt)
	Casino Hotels	72112	Casino Hotels
	Bed and Breakfast Inns	721191	Bed and Breakfast Inns
	Other	721199	All Other Traveler Accommodation
7021	Rooming and Boarding Houses	72131	Rooming and Boarding Houses (pt)
7032	Sporting and Recreational Camps	721214	Recreational and Vacation Camps (except Campgrounds)
7033	Recreational Vehicle Parks and Campsites	721211	RV (Recreational Vehicle Parks) and Campgrounds
7041	Organization Hotels and Lodging Houses, on Membership Basis		
	Organization Hotels	72111	Hotels (except Casino Hotels) and Motels (pt)
	Other	72131	Rooming and Boarding Houses (pt)
7211	Power Laundries, Family and Commercial	81232	Drycleaning and Laundry Services (except Coin-Operated) (pt)
7212	Garment Pressing, and Agents for Laundries and Drycleaners	81232	Drycleaning and Laundry Services (except Coin-Operated) (pt)
7213	Linen Supply	812331	Linen Supply (pt)
7215	Coin-Operated Laundries and Drycleaning	81231	Coin-Operated Laundries and Drycleaners
7216	Drycleaning Plants, Except Rug Cleaning	81232	Drycleaning and Laundry Services (except Coin-Operated) (pt)
7217	Carpet and Upholstery Cleaning	56174	Carpet and Upholstery Cleaning Services
7218	Industrial Launderers	812332	Industrial Launderers
7219	Laundry and Garment Services, NEC		
	Diaper Service	812331	Linen Supply (pt)
	Clothing Alteration and Repair	81149	Other Personal and Household Goods Repair and Maintenance (pt)
	Except Diaper Service and Clothing Alteration and Repair	81232	Drycleaning and Laundry Services (except Coin-Operated)
7221	Photographic Studios, Portrait	541921	Photographic Studios, Portrait
7231	Beauty Shops		
	Beauty Shops and Salons	812112	Beauty Salons
	Manicure and Pedicure Salons	812113	Nail Salons
	Beauty and Cosmetology Schools	611511	Cosmetology and Barber Schools (pt)

_____
pt—Part of; NEC—Not Elsewhere Classified.

1987 SIC code	1987 U.S. SIC description	1997 NAICS code	1997 NAICS U.S. description
7241	Barber Shops		
	Barber Shops	812111	Barber Shops
	Barber Colleges	611511	Cosmetology and Barber Schools (pt)
7251	Shoe Repair Shops and Shoeshine Parlors		
	Shoe Repair Shops	81143	Footwear and Leather Goods Repair (pt)
	Shoeshine Parlors	81299	All Other Personal Services (pt)
7261	Funeral Services and Crematories		
	Crematories	81222	Cemeteries and Crematories (pt)
	Funeral Homes and Funeral Services	81221	Funeral Homes
7291	Tax Return Preparation Services	541213	Tax Preparation Services
7299	Miscellaneous Personal Services, NEC		
	Babysitting Bureaus	56131	Employment Placement Agencies (pt)
	Diet and Weight Reducing Services	812191	Diet and Weight Reducing Centers
	Valet Parking Services	81293	Parking Lots and Garages (pt)
	Formal Wear and Costume Rental	53222	Formal Wear and Costume Rental (pt)
	Personal Care Services	812199	Other Personal Care Services
	All Other Miscellaneous Personal Services, NEC	81299	All Other Personal Services (pt)
7311	Advertising Agencies	54181	Advertising Agencies
7312	Outdoor Advertising Services	54185	Display Advertising (pt)
7313	Radio, Television, and Publishers' Advertising Representatives	54184	Media Representatives
7319	Advertising, NEC		
	Media Buying Services	54183	Media Buying Agencies
	Display Advertising, Except Outdoor	54185	Display Advertising (pt)
	Advertising Materials Distributor Services	54187	Advertising Material Distribution Services
	Other	54189	Other Services Related to Advertising (pt)
7322	Adjustment and Collection Services	56144	Collection Agencies
7323	Credit Reporting Services	56145	Credit Bureaus
7331	Direct Mail Advertising Services		
	Mailing List Compilers	51114	Database and Directory Publishers (pt)

---

pt—Part of; NEC—Not Elsewhere Classified.

http://www.ntis.gov/naics

1987 SIC code	1987 U.S. SIC description	1997 NAICS code	1997 NAICS U.S. description
	Other	54186	Direct Mail Advertising
7334	Photocopying and Duplicating Services		
	Instant Printing	323114	Quick Printing (pt)
	Photocopying and Duplicating Services, Except Instant Printing	561439	Other Business Service Centers (including Copy Shops) (pt)
7335	Commercial Photography	541922	Commercial Photography (pt)
7336	Commercial Art and Graphic Design	54143	Graphic Design Services (pt)
7338	Secretarial and Court Reporting Services		
	Secretarial Services	56141	Document Preparation Services
	Court Reporting Services	561492	Court Reporting and Stenotype Services
7342	Disinfecting and Pest Control Services		
	Disinfecting Services	56172	Janitorial Services (pt)
	Exterminating and Pest Control Services	56171	Exterminating and Pest Control Services (pt)
7349	Building Cleaning and Maintenance Services, NEC		
	Lighting Maintenance Services	56179	Other Services to Buildings and Dwellings (pt)
	Except Lighting Maintenance Services	56172	Janitorial Services (pt)
7352	Medical Equipment Rental and Leasing		
	Home Health Furniture and Equipment Rental and Leasing	532291	Home Health Equipment Rental
	Medical Machinery Rental and Leasing	53249	Other Commercial and Industrial Machinery and Equipment Rental and Leasing (pt)
7353	Heavy Construction Equipment Rental and Leasing		
	With Operator	23499	All Other Heavy Construction (pt)
	Without Operator	532412	Construction, Mining, and Forestry Machinery and Equipment Rental and Leasing (pt)
7359	Equipment Rental and Leasing, NEC		
	Consumer Electronics and Appliances Rental	53221	Consumer Electronics and Appliances Rental

pt—Part of; NEC—Not Elsewhere Classified.

http://www.ntis.gov/naics

1987 SIC code	1987 U.S. SIC description	1997 NAICS code	1997 NAICS U.S. description
	General Rental Centers	53231	General Rental Centers
	Residential Furniture, Party Supplies, and All Other Miscellaneous Consumer Goods Rental and Leasing	532299	All Other Consumer Goods Rental
	Oilfield and Well Drilling Machinery and Equipment Rental and Leasing	532412	Construction, Mining, and Forestry Machinery and Equipment Rental and Leasing (pt)
	Aircraft Rental and Leasing	532411	Commercial Air, Rail, and Water Transportation Equipment Rental and Leasing (pt)
	Portable Toilet Rental	562991	Septic Tank and Related Services (pt)
	Office Machinery and Equipment Rental and Leasing	53242	Office Machinery and Equipment Rental and Leasing (pt)
	Industrial Trucks Rental and Leasing	53249	Other Commercial and Industrial Machinery and Equipment Rental and Leasing (pt)
7361	Employment Agencies		
	Executive Placing Services	541612	Human Resources and Executive Search Consulting Services (pt)
	Except Executive Placing Services	56131	Employment Placement Agencies (pt)
7363	Help Supply Services		
	Temporary Help Supply	56132	Temporary Help Services
	Employee Leasing Services	56133	Employee Leasing Services
7371	Computer Programming Services	541511	Custom Computer Programming Services
7372	Prepackaged Software		
	Software Publishing	51121	Software Publishers
	Reproduction of Software	334611	Software Reproducing
7373	Computer Integrated Systems Design	541512	Computer Systems Design Services (pt)
7374	Computer Processing and Data Preparation and Processing Services	51421	Data Processing Services
7375	Information Retrieval Services	514191	On-Line Information Services
7376	Computer Facilities Management Services	541513	Computer Facilities Management Services
7377	Computer Rental and Leasing	53242	Office Machinery and Equipment Rental and Leasing (pt)

———————
pt—Part of; NEC—Not Elsewhere Classified.

http://www.ntis.gov/naics

1987 SIC code	1987 U.S. SIC description	1997 NAICS code	1997 NAICS U.S. description
7378	Computer Maintenance and Repair		
	Retailing Computers From a Storefront and Repairing	44312	Computer and Software Stores (pt)
	All Other Repair	811212	Computer and Office Machine Repair and Maintenance (pt)
7379	Computer Related Services, NEC		
	Disk and Diskette Conversion and Recertification	51421	Data Processing Services (pt)
	Computer Systems Consultants	541512	Computer Systems Design Services (pt)
	Except Computer Systems Consultants and Disk and Diskette Conversion and Recertification	541519	Other Computer Related Services
7381	Detective, Guard, and Armored Car Services		
	Detective Services	561611	Investigation Services
	Guard Services	561612	Security Guards and Patrol Services
	Armored Car Services	561613	Armored Car Services
7382	Security Systems Services	561621	Security Systems Services (except Locksmiths) (pt)
7383	News Syndicates		
	Independent Correspondents	71151	Independent Artists, Writers, and Performers (pt)
	Except Independent Correspondents	51411	News Syndicates
7384	Photofinishing Laboratories		
	Photofinishing Laboratories (Except 1-Hour)	812921	Photofinishing Laboratories (except One-Hour)
	One-Hour Photofinishing	812922	One-Hour Photo Finishing
7389	Business Services, NEC		
	Sound Recording Studios	51224	Sound Recording Studios
	Audio Taping Services	51229	Other Sound Recording Industries (pt)
	Stock Photo Agencies and Press Clipping Services	514199	All Other Information Services (pt)
	Process Services, Patent Agents, Notaries Public and Paralegal Services	541199	All Other Legal Services
	Bail Bonding	81299	All Other Personal Services (pt)
	Mapmaking Services	54137	Surveying and Mapping (except Geophysical) Services (pt)

---

pt—Part of; NEC—Not Elsewhere Classified.

1987 SIC code	1987 U.S. SIC description	1997 NAICS code	1997 NAICS U.S. description
	Interior Design	54141	Interior Design Services
	Industrial Design	54142	Industrial Design Services
	Drafting Service	54134	Drafting Services
	Fashion and Other Design Services	54149	Other Specialized Design Services
	Sign Painting and Lettering Shops, Showcard Painting, Mannequin Decorating Services, and Other Advertising Related Business Services	54189	Other Services Related to Advertising (pt)
	Translation and Interpretation Services	54193	Translation and Interpretation Services
	Home and Building Inspection Services	54135	Building Inspection Services
	Appraisers, Except Insurance and Real Estate, and Miscellaneous Professional, Scientific, and Technical Services	54199	All Other Professional, Scientific, and Technical Services
	Microfilm Services	51421	Data Processing Services (pt)
	Agents and Brokers for Authors and Artists and Speaker Bureaus	71141	Agents and Managers for Artists, Athletes, Entertainers, and Other Public Figures (pt)
	Yacht Brokers	42186	Transportation Equipment and Supplies (except Motor Vehicle) Wholesalers
	Telephone Answering Services	561421	Telephone Answering Services
	Aerosol Packaging	325998	All Other Miscellaneous Chemical Product and Preparation Manufacturing (pt)
	Telemarketing Bureaus and Telephone Soliciting Services	561422	Telemarketing Bureaus
	Private Mail Centers and Mail Box Rental	561431	Private Mail Centers
	Business Service Centers, Except Private Mail Centers and Mail Box Rental	561439	Other Business Service Centers (including Copy Shops)
	Embroidery of Advertising on Shirts and Rug Binding for the Trade	314999	All Other Miscellaneous Textile Product Mills (pt)
	Sponging Fabric for Tailors and Dressmakers	313311	Broadwoven Fabric Finishing Mills (pt)

pt—Part of; NEC—Not Elsewhere Classified.

http://www.ntis.gov/naics

1987 SIC code	1987 U.S. SIC description	1997 NAICS code	1997 NAICS U.S. description
	Distribution of Telephone Directories on a Fee or Contract Basis	54187	Advertising Material Distribution Services
	Post Office Contract Stations	49111	Postal Services (pt)
	Apparel Pressing for the Trade	81232	Drycleaning and Laundry Services (except Coin-Operated)
	Recovery and Repossession	561491	Repossession Services (pt)
	Packaging and Labeling Services	56191	Packaging and Labeling Services
	Swimming Pool Cleaning and Maintenance	56179	Other Services to Buildings and Dwellings (pt)
	Hotel and Restaurant Reservation Services and Time Share Condominium Exchange	561599	All Other Travel Arrangement and Reservation Services (pt)
	Convention and Trade Show Services	56192	Convention and Trade Show Organizers
	Convention and Visitors Bureaus and Tourist Information Service	561591	Convention and Visitors Bureaus
	Credit Card and Check Validation Services	52232	Financial Transactions, Processing, Reserve, and Clearinghouse Activities (pt)
	Business Support Services, Except Telephone Answering, Telemarketing Bureaus, Private Mail Centers, and Repossession Services	561499	All Other Business Support Services
	All Other Support Services	56199	All Other Support Services
7513	Truck Rental and Leasing, Without Drivers	53212	Truck, Utility Trailer, and RV (Recreational Vehicle) Rental and Leasing (pt)
7514	Passenger Car Rental	532111	Passenger Cars Rental
7515	Passenger Car Leasing	532112	Passenger Cars Leasing
7519	Utility Trailer and Recreational Vehicle Rental	53212	Truck, Utility Trailer and RV (Recreational Vehicles) Rental and Leasing (pt)
7521	Automobile Parking	81293	Parking Lots and Garages (pt)
7532	Top, Body, and Upholstery Repair Shops and Paint Shops	811121	Automotive Body, Paint, and Interior Repair and Maintenance
7533	Automotive Exhaust System Repair Shops	811112	Automotive Exhaust System Repair
7534	Tire Retreading and Repair Shops		
	Retreading	326212	Tire Retreading
	Repair	811198	All Other Automotive Repair and Maintenance (pt)

_____
pt—Part of; NEC—Not Elsewhere Classified.

http://www.ntis.gov/naics

1987 SIC code	1987 U.S. SIC description	1997 NAICS code	1997 NAICS U.S. description
7536	Automotive Glass Replacement Shops	811122	Automotive Glass Replacement Shops (pt)
7537	Automotive Transmission Repair Shops	811113	Automotive Transmission Repair
7538	General Automotive Repair Shops	811111	General Automotive Repair
7539	Automotive Repair Shops, NEC	811118	Other Automotive Mechanical and Electrical Repair and Maintenance
7542	Carwashes	811192	Carwashes
7549	Automotive Services, Except Repair and Carwashes		
	Automotive Window Tinting	811122	Automotive Glass Replacement Shops (pt)
	Lubricating Services, Automotive	811191	Automotive Oil Change and Lubrication Shops
	Towing	48841	Motor Vehicle Towing
	Except Automotive Window Tinting, Lubricating Services, and Towing	811198	All Other Automotive Repair and Maintenance (pt)
7622	Radio and Television Repair Shops		
	Retailing New Electronic Equipment from a Storefront and Repairing	443112	Radio, Television, and Other Electronics Stores (pt)
	Other Stereo, TV, VCR, and Radio Repair	811211	Consumer Electronics Repair and Maintenance (pt)
	Other Telecommunications Equipment Repair	811213	Communication Equipment Repair and Maintenance (pt)
7623	Refrigeration and Air-Conditioning Services and Repair Shops		
	Retailing New Refrigerators from a Storefront and Repairing Refrigerators	443111	Household Appliance Stores (pt)
	Commercial Refrigerator Equipment Repair	81131	Commercial and Industrial Machinery and Equipment (except Automotive and Electronic) Repair and Maintenance (pt)
	Except Commercial and Retailing New Refrigerators from a Storefront and Repairing Refrigerators	811412	Appliance Repair and Maintenance (pt)
7629	Electrical and Electronic Repair Shops, NEC		

pt—Part of; NEC—Not Elsewhere Classified.

1987 SIC code	1987 U.S. SIC description	1997 NAICS code	1997 NAICS U.S. description
	Retailing New Electrical and Electronic Appliances from a Storefront and Repairing	443111	Household Appliance Stores (pt)
	Business and Office Machine Repair, Electrical	811212	Computer and Office Machine Repair and Maintenance (pt)
	Telephone Set Repair	811213	Communication Equipment Repair and Maintenance (pt)
	Electrical Measuring Instrument Repair and Calibration, Medical Equipment Repair, Electrical	811219	Other Electronic and Precision Equipment Repair and Maintenance (pt)
	Appliance Repair, Electrical; Washing Machine Repair; Electric Razor Repair (Except Retailing New Appliances From a Storefront)	811412	Appliance Repair and Maintenance (pt)
	Other Consumer Electronic Equipment Repair Except Computer, Radio, Television, Stereo, and VCR	811211	Consumer Electronics Repair and Maintenance (pt)
7631	Watch, Clock, and Jewelry Repair	81149	Other Personal and Household Goods Repair and Maintenance (pt)
7641	Reupholstery and Furniture Repair		
	Antique Furniture Restoration	71151	Independent Artists, Writers, and Performers (pt)
	Except Antique Furniture Restoration	81142	Reupholstery and Furniture Repair
7692	Welding Repair	81131	Commercial and Industrial Machinery and Equipment (except Automotive and Electronic) Repair and Maintenance (pt)
7694	Armature Rewinding Shops		
	Repair	81131	Commercial and Industrial Machinery and Equipment (except Automotive and Electronic) Repair and Maintenance (pt)
	Remanufacturing	335312	Motor and Generator Manufacturing (pt)
7699	Repair Shops and Related Services, NEC		
	Boiler Cleaning	23511	Plumbing, Heating, and Air-Conditioning Contractors (pt)

pt—Part of; NEC—Not Elsewhere Classified.

http://www.ntis.gov/naics

1987 SIC code	1987 U.S. SIC description	1997 NAICS code	1997 NAICS U.S. description
	Custom Picture Framing	442299	All Other Home Furnishings Stores (pt)
	Locksmith Shops	561622	Locksmiths
	Cesspool and Septic Tank Cleaning	562991	Septic Tank and Related Services (pt)
	Furnace Ducts, Chimney, and Gutter Cleaning Services	56179	Other Services to Buildings and Dwellings (pt)
	Sewer Cleaning and Rodding	562998	All Other Miscellaneous Waste Management Services (pt)
	Ship Scaling	48839	Other Supporting Activities for Water Transportation (pt)
	Other Non-Automotive Transportation Equipment and Industrial Machinery and Equipment	81131	Commercial and Industrial Machinery and Equipment (except Automotive and Electronic) Repair and Maintenance (pt)
	Retailing New Bicycles from a Storefront and Repairing Bicycles	45111	Sporting Goods Stores (pt)
	Farriers	11521	Support Activities for Animal Production (pt)
	Camera Repair	811211	Consumer Electronics Repair and Maintenance (pt)
	Typewriter Repair	811212	Computer and Office Machine Repair and Maintenance (pt)
	Dental Instrument Repair, Laboratory Instrument Repair, Medical Equipment and Other Electronic and Precision Equipment Repair, Except Typewriters	811219	Other Electronic and Precision Equipment Repair and Maintenance (pt)
	Lawnmower Repair Shops, Sharpening and Repairing Knives, Saws and Tools	811411	Home and Garden Equipment Repair and Maintenance
	Taxidermists, and Antique Repair and Maintenance, Except Antique Car Restoration	71151	Independent Artists, Writers, and Performers
	Gas Appliance Repair Service, Sewing Machine Repair, Stove Repair Shops, and Other Nonelectrical Appliances	811412	Appliance Repair and Maintenance (pt)
	Leather Goods Repair Shops, Luggage Repair Shops, Pocketbook Repair Shops	81143	Footwear and Leather Goods Repair (pt)

pt—Part of; NEC—Not Elsewhere Classified.

http://www.ntis.gov/naics

1987 SIC code	1987 U.S. SIC description	1997 NAICS code	1997 NAICS U.S. description
	Except Industrial, Electronic, Home and Garden, Appliance, Locksmith, and Leather Goods	81149	Other Personal and Household Goods Repair and Maintenance (pt)
7812	Motion Picture and Video Tape Production	51211	Motion Picture and Video Production
7819	Services Allied to Motion Picture Production		
	Teleproduction and Post-Production Services	512191	Teleproduction and Other Post-Production Services
	Casting Bureaus	56131	Employment Placement Agencies (pt)
	Wardrobe Rental (Motion Pictures)	53222	Formal Wear and Costumes Rental (pt)
	Rental of Motion Picture Equipment	53249	Other Commercial and Industrial Machinery and Equipment Rental and Leasing (pt)
	Talent Payment Services	541214	Payroll Services (pt)
	Film Directors and Related Motion Picture Production Services, Independent	71151	Independent Artists, Writers, and Performers (pt)
	Reproduction of Video	334612	Prerecorded Compact Disc (Except Software), Tape, and Record Manufacturing (pt)
	All Other Services	512199	Other Motion Picture and Video Industries (pt)
7822	Motion Picture and Video Tape Distribution		
	Prerecorded Video Tapes (Wholesaling of)	42199	Other Miscellaneous Durable Goods Wholesalers (pt)
	All Other	51212	Motion Picture and Video Distribution (pt)
7829	Services Allied to Motion Picture Distribution		
	Booking Agencies	512199	Other Motion Picture and Video Industries (pt)
	Film Archives	51412	Libraries and Archives (pt)
	Commercial Distribution Film Libraries	51212	Motion Picture and Video Distribution (pt)
7832	Motion Picture Theaters, Except Drive-In	512131	Motion Picture Theaters, Except Drive-In

pt—Part of; NEC—Not Elsewhere Classified.

http://www.ntis.gov/naics

1987 SIC code	1987 U.S. SIC description	1997 NAICS code	1997 NAICS U.S. description
7833	Drive-In Motion Picture Theaters	512132	Drive-In Motion Picture Theaters
7841	Video Tape Rental	53223	Video Tapes and Disc Rental
7911	Dance Studios, Schools, and Halls		
	Dance Studios and Halls	71399	All Other Amusement and Recreation Industries (pt)
	Dance Schools	61161	Fine Arts Schools (pt)
7922	Theatrical Producers (Except Motion Picture) and Miscellaneous Theatrical Services		
	Casting Agencies	56131	Employment Placement Agencies (pt)
	Theater and Opera Companies	71111	Theater Companies and Dinner Theaters (pt)
	Theatrical Agents	71141	Agents and Managers for Artists, Athletes, Entertainers, and Other Public Figures (pt)
	Theatrical Ticket Agencies	561599	All Other Travel Arrangement and Reservation Services (pt)
	Costume Design, Theatrical	71151	Independent Artists, Writers, and Performers (pt)
	Ballet and Dance Companies	71112	Dance Companies
	Theater Operators	71131	Promoters of Performing Arts, Sports, and Similar Events with Facilities (pt)
	Theatrical Promoters	71132	Promoters of Performing Arts, Sports, and Similar Events without Facilities (pt)
	Producers of Radio Programs	51229	Other Sound Recording Industries (pt)
	Theatrical Equipment Rental	53249	Other Commercial and Industrial Machinery and Equipment Rental and Leasing (pt)
7929	Bands, Orchestras, Actors, and Other Entertainers and Entertainment Groups		
	Musical Groups and Artists, Orchestras	71113	Musical Groups and Artists
	Actors and Actresses	71151	Independent Artists, Writers, and Performers (pt)
	Except Musical Groups and Artists, Actors and Actresses	71119	Other Performing Arts Companies (pt)

pt—Part of; NEC—Not Elsewhere Classified.

1987 SIC code	1987 U.S. SIC description	1997 NAICS code	1997 NAICS U.S. description
7933	Bowling Centers	71395	Bowling Centers
7941	Professional Sports Clubs and Promoters		
	Professional Sports Clubs	711211	Sports Teams and Clubs
	Sports Agents	71141	Agents and Managers for Artists, Athletes, Entertainers, and Other Public Figures (pt)
	Sports Promoters	71132	Promoters of Arts, Sports, and Similar Events without Facilities (pt)
	Stadium Operators	71131	Promoters of Arts, Sports, and Similar Events with Facilities (pt)
7948	Racing, Including Track Operations		
	Racetrack Operators	711212	Racetracks
	Racing, except Track Operators	711219	Other Spectator Sports (pt)
7991	Physical Fitness Facilities	71394	Fitness and Recreational Sports Centers (pt)
7992	Public Golf Courses	71391	Golf Courses and Country Clubs (pt)
7993	Coin-Operated Amusement Devices		
	Amusement Arcades	71312	Amusement Arcades
	Gambling (Slot Machine) Operators	71329	Other Gambling Industries (pt)
	Except Amusement Arcades and Slot Machine Operators	71399	All Other Amusement and Recreation Industries (pt)
7996	Amusement Parks	71311	Amusement and Theme Parks
7997	Membership Sports and Recreation Clubs		
	Golf Clubs	71391	Golf Courses and Country Clubs (pt)
	Recreation Clubs with Facilities	71394	Fitness and Recreational Sports Centers (pt)
	Recreation Clubs Without Facilities	71399	All Other Amusement and Recreation Industries (pt)
7999	Amusement and Recreation Services, NEC		
	Ticket Agencies	561599	All Other Travel Arrangement and Reservation Services (pt)
	Aerial Tramways, Scenic and Amusement	48799	Scenic and Sightseeing Transportation, Other (pt)
	Circus Companies and Traveling Carnival Shows	71119	Other Performing Arts Companies (pt)

pt—Part of; NEC—Not Elsewhere Classified.

http://www.ntis.gov/naics

1987 SIC code	1987 U.S. SIC description	1997 NAICS code	1997 NAICS U.S. description
	Professional Athletes	711219	Other Spectator Sports (pt)
	Skiing Facilities	71392	Skiing Facilities
	Nonmembership Recreation Facilities	71394	Fitness and Recreational Sports Centers (pt)
	Casinos, except Casino Hotels	71321	Casinos (except Casino Hotels)
	Lottery, Bingo, Bookie and Other Gaming Operations	71329	Other Gambling Industries (pt)
	Caverns and Miscellaneous Commercial Parks	71219	Nature Parks and Other Similar Institutions (pt)
	Sports Instruction	61162	Sports and Recreation Instruction
	Nonathletic Recreational Instruction	611699	All Other Miscellaneous Schools and Instruction (pt)
	State Fairs, Agriculture Fairs, and County Fairs with Facilities	71131	Promoters of Performing Arts, Sports, and Similar Events with Facilities (pt)
	State Fairs, Agriculture Fairs, and County Fairs without Facilities	71132	Promoters of Performing Arts, Sports, and Similar Events without Facilities (pt)
	Sports Equipment Rental	532292	Recreational Goods Rental
	Scenic Transport Operations, Land	48711	Scenic and Sightseeing Transportation, Land (pt)
	Charter Fishing	48721	Scenic and Sightseeing Transportation, Water (pt)
	Amusement and Recreation Services, NEC (except circuses, professional athletes, caverns and other commercial parks, skiing facilities, casinos and other gambling operations, amusement and recreation facilities, sports instruction, sports equipment rental, and amusement or scenic transport operations)	71399	All Other Amusement and Recreation Industries (pt)
8011	Offices and Clinics of Doctors of Medicine		
	Surgical and Emergency Centers	621493	Freestanding Ambulatory Surgical and Emergency Centers
	HMO Medical Centers	621491	HMO Medical Centers
	Offices of Physicians, Mental Health Specialists	621112	Offices of Physicians, Mental Health Specialists (pt)
	Offices of Physicians Except Mental Health	621111	Offices of Physicians, (except Mental Health Specialists) (pt)

pt—Part of; NEC—Not Elsewhere Classified.

1987 SIC code	1987 U.S. SIC description	1997 NAICS code	1997 NAICS U.S. description
8021	Offices and Clinics of Dentists	62121	Offices of Dentists
8031	Offices and Clinics of Doctors of Osteopathy		
	Offices of Doctors of Osteopathy, Except Mental Health	621111	Offices of Physicians (except Mental Health Specialists) (pt)
	Offices of Doctors of Osteopathy, Mental Health Specialists	621112	Offices of Physicians, Mental Health Specialists (pt)
8041	Offices and Clinics of Chiropractors	62131	Offices of Chiropractors
8042	Offices and Clinics of Optometrists	62132	Offices of Optometrists
8043	Offices and Clinics of Podiatrists	621391	Offices of Podiatrists
8049	Offices and Clinics of Health Practitioners, NEC		
	Mental Health Practitioners, Except Physicians	62133	Offices of Mental Health Practitioners (except Physicians)
	Offices of Physical, Occupational, Recreational, and Speech Therapists and Audiologists	62134	Offices of Physical, Occupational, and Speech Therapists and Audiologists
	Other Offices of Health Practitioners	621399	Offices of All Other Miscellaneous Health Practitioners
8051	Skilled Nursing Care Facilities		
	Continuing Care Retirement Communities	623311	Continuing Care Retirement Communities (pt)
	All Other Skilled Nursing Care Facilities	62311	Nursing Care Facilities (pt)
8052	Intermediate Care Facilities		
	Continuing Care Retirement Communities	623311	Continuing Care Retirement Communities (pt)
	Mental Retardation Facilities	62321	Residential Mental Retardation Facilities
	Other Intermediate Care Facilities	62311	Nursing Care Facilities (pt)
8059	Nursing and Personal Care Facilities, NEC		
	Continuing Care Retirement Communities	623311	Continuing Care Retirement Communities (pt)
	Other Nursing and Personal Care Facilities	62311	Nursing Care Facilities (pt)
8062	General Medical and Surgical Hospitals	62211	General Medical and Surgical Hospitals (pt)
8063	Psychiatric Hospitals	62221	Psychiatric and Substance Abuse Hospitals (pt)
8069	Specialty Hospitals, Except Psychiatric		

---

pt—Part of; NEC—Not Elsewhere Classified.

1987 SIC code	1987 U.S. SIC description	1997 NAICS code	1997 NAICS U.S. description
	Children's Hospitals	62211	General Medical and Surgical Hospitals (pt)
	Substance Abuse Hospitals	62221	Psychiatric and Substance Abuse Hospitals (pt)
	Other Specialty Hospitals	62231	Specialty (except Psychiatric and Substance Abuse) Hospitals
8071	Medical Laboratories		
	Diagnostic Imaging Centers	621512	Diagnostic Imaging Centers
	Medical Laboratories, Except Diagnostic Imaging Centers	621511	Medical Laboratories
8072	Dental Laboratories	339116	Dental Laboratories
8082	Home Health Care Services	62161	Home Health Care Services
8092	Kidney Dialysis Centers	621492	Kidney Dialysis Centers
8093	Specialty Outpatient Facilities, NEC		
	Family Planning Centers	62141	Family Planning Centers (pt)
	Outpatient Mental Health Facilities	62142	Outpatient Mental Health and Substance Abuse Centers
	Other Specialty Outpatient Facilities	621498	All Other Outpatient Care Facilities
8099	Health and Allied Services, NEC		
	Blood and Organ Banks	621991	Blood and Organ Banks
	Medical artists	54143	Graphic Design Services (pt)
	Medical Photography	541922	Commercial Photography (pt)
	Childbirth Preparation Classes	62141	Family Planning Centers (pt)
	Other Health and Allied Services	621999	All Other Miscellaneous Ambulatory Health Care Services
8111	Legal Services	54111	Offices of Lawyers
8211	Elementary and Secondary Schools	61111	Elementary and Secondary Schools
8221	Colleges, Universities, and Professional Schools	61131	Colleges, Universities, and Professional Schools
8222	Junior Colleges and Technical Institutes	61121	Junior Colleges
8231	Libraries	51412	Libraries and Archives
8243	Data Processing Schools		
	Computer Repair Training	611519	Other Technical and Trade Schools (pt)
	Except Computer Repair Training	61142	Computer Training
8244	Business and Secretarial Schools	61141	Business and Secretarial Schools
8249	Vocational Schools, NEC		
	Vocational Apprenticeship Training	611513	Apprenticeship Training

pt—Part of; NEC—Not Elsewhere Classified.

http://www.ntis.gov/naics

1987 SIC code	1987 U.S. SIC description	1997 NAICS code	1997 NAICS U.S. description
	Aviation Schools	611512	Flight Training (pt)
	Other Technical and Trade Schools	611519	Other Technical and Trade Schools (pt)
8299	Schools and Educational Services, NEC		
	Flying Instruction	611512	Flight Training (pt)
	Automobile Driving Instruction	611692	Automobile Driving Schools
	Curriculum Development, Educational	61171	Educational Support Services (pt)
	Exam Preparation and Tutoring	611691	Exam Preparation and Tutoring
	Art Drama and Music Schools	61161	Fine Arts Schools (pt)
	Language Schools	61163	Language Schools
	Professional and Management Development Training	61143	Professional and Management Development Training Schools
	Cooking and Modeling Schools	611519	Other Technical and Trade Schools (pt)
	All Other Schools and Educational Services, NEC	611699	All Other Miscellaneous Schools and Instruction
8322	Individual and Family Social Services		
	Child and Youth Services	62411	Child and Youth Services
	Community Food Services	62421	Community Food Services
	Community Housing Services, Except Temporary Shelters	624229	Other Community Housing Services
	Emergency and Other Relief Services	62423	Emergency and Other Relief Services
	Services for the Elderly and Persons with Disabilities	62412	Services for the Elderly and Persons with Disabilities
	Temporary Shelter	624221	Temporary Shelters
	Parole Offices and Probation Offices	92215	Parole Offices and Probation Offices
	Other Individual and Family Services	62419	Other Individual and Family Services
8331	Job Training and Vocational Rehabilitation Services	62431	Vocational Rehabilitation Services
8351	Child Day Care Services	62441	Child Day Care Services (pt)
8361	Residential Care		
	Homes for the Elderly	623312	Homes for the Elderly
	Mental Health and Substance Abuse Facilities	62322	Residential Mental Health and Substance Abuse Facilities

pt—Part of; NEC—Not Elsewhere Classified.

http://www.ntis.gov/naics

1987 SIC code	1987 U.S. SIC description	1997 NAICS code	1997 NAICS U.S. description
	Other Residential Care	62399	Other Residential Care Facilities
8399	Social Services, NEC		
	Voluntary Health Organizations	813212	Voluntary Health Organizations
	Grantmaking and Giving	813219	Other Grantmaking and Giving Services
	Human Rights Organizations	813311	Human Rights Organizations
	Environment, Conservation, and Wildlife Organizations	813312	Environment, Conservation, and Wildlife Organizations (pt)
	All Other Social Advocacy Organizations	813319	Other Social Advocacy Organizations
8412	Museums and Art Galleries		
	Museums	71211	Museums
	Historical and Heritage Sites	71212	Historical Sites
8422	Arboreta and Botanical or Zoological Gardens		
	Botanical and Zoological Gardens	71213	Zoos and Botanical Gardens
	Nature Parks and Reserves	71219	Nature Parks and Other Similar Institutions (pt)
8611	Business Associations	81391	Business Associations (pt)
8621	Professional Membership Organizations	81392	Professional Organizations
8631	Labor Unions and Similar Labor Organizations	81393	Labor Unions and Similar Labor Organizations
8641	Civic, Social, and Fraternal Associations		
	Civic and Social Associations	81341	Civic and Social Organizations (except Business, Professional, Labor, and Political Organizations) (pt)
	Homeowner and Condominium Associations	81399	Other Similar Organizations (pt)
	American Indian and Alaska Native Tribal Governments	92115	American Indian and Alaska Native Tribal Governments
8651	Political Organizations	81394	Political Organizations
8661	Religious Organizations	81311	Religious Organizations
8699	Membership Organizations, NEC		
	Except Humane Societies, Farm Business Organizations, Athletic Associations, and Travel Motor Clubs	81341	Civic and Social Organizations (pt)

---

pt—Part of; NEC—Not Elsewhere Classified.

1987 SIC code	1987 U.S. SIC description	1997 NAICS code	1997 NAICS U.S. description
	Farm Business Organizations	81391	Business Associations (pt)
	Humane Societies	813312	Environment, Conservation, and Wildlife Organizations (pt)
	Travel Motor Clubs	561599	All Other Travel Arrangement and Reservation Services (pt)
	Athletic Associations	81399	Other Similar Organizations (except Business, Professional, Labor, and Political Organizations) (pt)
8711	Engineering Services	54133	Engineering Services (pt)
8712	Architectural Services	54131	Architectural Services
8713	Surveying Services		
	Geophysical Surveying Services	54136	Geophysical Surveying and Mapping Services (pt)
	Except Geophysical Surveying	54137	Surveying and Mapping (except Geophysical) Services (pt)
8721	Accounting, Auditing, and Bookkeeping Services		
	Auditing Accountants	541211	Offices of Certified Public Accountants
	Payroll Services	541214	Payroll Services (pt)
	Other Accounting Services	541219	Other Accounting Services
8731	Commercial Physical and Biological Research	54171	Research and Development in the Physical, Engineering, and Life Sciences (pt)
8732	Commercial Economic, Sociological, and Educational Research		
	Social Sciences and Humanities	54172	Research and Development in the Social Sciences and Humanities (pt)
	Market Research and Opinion Research	54191	Marketing Research and Public Opinion Polling
8733	Noncommercial Research Organizations		
	Physical, Engineering, and Life Services	54171	Research and Development in the Physical, Engineering, and Life Sciences (pt)
	Social Sciences and Humanities	54172	Research and Development in the Social Sciences and Humanities (pt)
8734	Testing Laboratories		
	Veterinary Testing Labs	54194	Veterinary Services (pt)
	Except Veterinary Testing Labs	54138	Testing Laboratories
8741	Management Services		
	Except Construction Management Services	56111	Office Administrative Services

pt—Part of; NEC—Not Elsewhere Classified.

http://www.ntis.gov/naics

1987 SIC code	1987 U.S. SIC description	1997 NAICS code	1997 NAICS U.S. description
	Construction Management Services	23	Included in Construction Sector By Type of Construction
8742	Management Consulting Services		
	Administrative and General Management Consulting	541611	Administrative Management and General Management Consulting Services
	Human Resources and Personnel Management Consulting	541612	Human Resources and Executive Search Services (pt)
	Marketing Consulting	541613	Marketing Consulting Services
	Manufacturing Management, Physical Distribution, and Site Location Consulting	541614	Process, Physical Distribution, and Logistics Consulting Services (pt)
8743	Public Relations Services	54182	Public Relations Agencies
8744	Facilities Support Management Services	56121	Facilities Support Services
8748	Business Consulting Services, NEC		
	Educational Test Development and Evaluation Services, Educational Testing, and Educational Consulting	61171	Educational Support Services (pt)
	Safety Consulting and Security Consulting	54169	Other Scientific and Technical Consulting Services (pt)
	Agriculture Consulting and Economic Consulting	54169	Other Scientific and Technical Consulting Services (pt)
	Urban Planners and Industrial Development Organizations	54132	Landscape Architectural Services (pt)
	Traffic Engineering Consulting	54133	Engineering Services (pt)
	All Other Business Consulting Services	541618	Other Management Consulting Services
8811	Private Households	81411	Private Households
8999	Services, NEC		
	Authors, Artists, and Related Technical Services, Independent	71151	Independent Artists, Writers, and Performers (pt)
	Record Production	51221	Record Production
	Scientific and Related Consulting Services	54169	Other Scientific and Technical Consulting Services (pt)
	Music Publishing	51223	Music Publishers (pt)
	Actuarial Consulting	541612	Human Resources and Executive Search Consulting Services (pt)

pt—Part of; NEC—Not Elsewhere Classified.

http://www.ntis.gov/naics

1987 SIC code	1987 U.S. SIC description	1997 NAICS code	1997 NAICS U.S. description
	All Other Information Providers	514199	All Other Information Services (pt)
	Environmental Consultants	54162	Environmental Consulting Services
9111	Executive Offices	92111	Executive Offices
9121	Legislative Bodies	92112	Legislative Bodies
9131	Executive and Legislative Offices, Combined	92114	Executive and Legislative Offices, Combined
9199	General Government, NEC	92119	Other General Government Support
9211	Courts	92211	Courts
9221	Police Protection	92212	Police Protection
9222	Legal Counsel and Prosecution	92213	Legal Counsel and Prosecution
9223	Correctional Institutions	92214	Correctional Institutions
9224	Fire Protection	92216	Fire Protection
9229	Public Order and Safety, NEC	92219	Other Justice, Public Order, and Safety
9311	Public Finance, Taxation, and Monetary Policy	92113	Public Finance Activities
9411	Administration of Educational Programs	92311	Administration of Education Programs
9431	Administration of Public Health Programs	92312	Administration of Public Health Programs
9441	Administration of Social, Human Resource and Income Maintenance Programs	92313	Administration of Human Resource Programs (except Education, Public Health, and Veterans' Affairs Programs)
9451	Administration of Veterans' Affairs, Except Health Insurance	92314	Administration of Veterans' Affairs
9511	Air and Water Resource and Solid Waste Management	92411	Administration of Air and Water Resource and Solid Waste Management Programs
9512	Land, Mineral, Wildlife, and Forest Conservation	92412	Administration of Conservation Programs
9531	Administration of Housing Programs	92511	Administration of Housing Programs
9532	Administration of Urban Planning and Community and Rural Development	92512	Administration of Urban Planning and Community and Rural Development
9611	Administration of General Economic Programs	92611	Administration of General Economic Programs
9621	Regulation and Administration of Transportation Programs		

pt—Part of; NEC—Not Elsewhere Classified.

http://www.ntis.gov/naics

1987 SIC code	1987 U.S. SIC description	1997 NAICS code	1997 NAICS U.S. description
	Air Traffic Control	488111	Air Traffic Control (pt)
	Except Air Traffic Control	92612	Regulation and Administration of Transportation Programs
9631	Regulation and Administration of Communications, Electric, Gas, and Other Utilities	92613	Regulation and Administration of Communications, Electric, Gas, and Other Utilities
9641	Regulation of Agricultural Marketing and Commodities	92614	Regulation of Agricultural Marketing and Commodities
9651	Regulation, Licensing, and Inspection of Miscellaneous Commercial Sectors	92615	Regulation, Licensing, and Inspection of Miscellaneous Commercial Sectors
9661	Space Research and Technology	92711	Space Research and Technology
9711	National Security	92811	National Security
9721	International Affairs	92812	International Affairs

pt—Part of; NEC—Not Elsewhere Classified.

Part IV

Alphabetic Index

Alphabetic Index

http://www.ntis.gov/naics

325998	Additive preparations for gasoline (e.g., anti-knock preparations, detergents, gum inhibitors) manufacturing
561499	Address bar coding services
511140	Address list compilers
511140	Address list publishers
511140	Address list publishers and printing combined
323112	Address lists flexographic printing without publishing
323111	Address lists gravure printing without publishing
323110	Address lists lithographic (offset) printing without publishing
323119	Address lists printing (except flexographic, gravure, lithographic, screen) without publishing
323113	Address lists screen printing without publishing
421420	Addressing machines wholesaling
322222	Adhesive tape (except medical) made from purchased materials
339113	Adhesive tape, medical, manufacturing
325520	Adhesives (except asphalt, dental, gypsum base) manufacturing
422690	Adhesives and sealants wholesaling
325199	Adipic acid manufacturing
233320	Administration building construction
541611	Administrative management consulting services
561110	Administrative management services
327123	Adobe brick manufacturing
624110	Adoption agencies
624110	Adoption services, child
611691	Adult literacy instruction
541810	Advertising agencies
541810	Advertising agency consulting services
541870	Advertising material (e.g., coupons, flyers, samples) direct distribution services
541860	Advertising material preparation services for mailing or other direct distribution
323110	Advertising materials (e.g., coupons, flyers) lithographic (offset) printing without publishing
541840	Advertising media representatives (i.e., independent of media owners)
541850	Advertising services, indoor or outdoor display
541890	Advertising specialty (e.g., keychain, magnet, pen) distribution services
541850	Advertising, aerial
921110	Advisory commissions, executive government
921120	Advisory commissions, legislative
487990	Aerial cable car, scenic and sightseeing, operation
115112	Aerial dusting or spraying (i.e., using specialized or dedicated aircraft)
541360	Aerial geophysical surveying services
541370	Aerial surveying (except geophysical) services
487990	Aerial tramway, scenic and sightseeing, operation
333923	Aerial work platforms manufacturing
713940	Aerobic dance and exercise centers
421860	Aeronautical equipment and supplies wholesaling
334511	Aeronautical systems and instruments manufacturing
325998	Aerosol can filling on a job order or contract basis
332431	Aerosol cans manufacturing
325998	Aerosol packaging services
332919	Aerosol valves manufacturing
325620	After-shave preparations manufacturing
325411	Agar-agar grinding manufacturing
111998	Agave farming
524210	Agencies, insurance
522310	Agencies, loan
531210	Agencies, real estate
711410	Agents, artists'
711410	Agents, authors'
711410	Agents, celebrities'
711410	Agents, entertainers'
711410	Agents, modeling
711410	Agents, public figures'
531210	Agents, real estate

488510	Agents, shipping
711410	Agents, sports figures'
711410	Agents, talent
711410	Agents, theatrical talent
212210	Agglomerates, iron ore, beneficiating
551112	Agreement corporation (except international trade financing)
522293	Agreement corporations (i.e., international trade financing)
524126	Agricultural (i.e., crop, livestock) insurance carriers, direct
422910	Agricultural chemicals wholesaling
541690	Agricultural consulting services
926140	Agricultural cooperative extension program administration
522298	Agricultural credit institutions, making loans or extending credit (except real estate, sales financing)
711320	Agricultural fair managers without facilities
711320	Agricultural fair organizers without facilities
711320	Agricultural fair promoters without facilities
332212	Agricultural handtools (e.g., hay forks, hoes, rakes, spades), nonpowered, manufacturing
327410	Agricultural lime manufacturing
422910	Agricultural limestone wholesaling
532490	Agricultural machinery and equipment rental or leasing
811310	Agricultural machinery and equipment repair and maintenance services
421820	Agricultural machinery and equipment wholesaling
511120	Agricultural magazine and periodical publishers
511120	Agricultural magazine and periodical publishers and printing combined
323112	Agricultural magazines and periodicals flexographic printing without publishing
323111	Agricultural magazines and periodicals gravure printing without publishing
323110	Agricultural magazines and periodicals lithographic (offset) printing without publishing
323119	Agricultural magazines and periodicals printing (except flexographic, gravure, lithographic, screen) without publishing
323113	Agricultural magazines and periodicals screen printing without publishing
484220	Agricultural products trucking, local
115115	Agriculture production or harvesting crews
541710	Agriculture research and development laboratories or services
541690	Agrology consulting services
541690	Agronomy consulting services
928110	Air Force
336399	Air bag assemblies manufacturing
336612	Air boat building
336340	Air brake systems and parts, automotive, truck, and bus, manufacturing
481212	Air cargo carriers (except air couriers), nonscheduled
481112	Air cargo carriers (except air couriers), scheduled
332439	Air cargo containers, metal, manufacturing
335313	Air circuit breakers manufacturing
481111	Air commuter carriers, scheduled
333912	Air compressors manufacturing
492110	Air courier services
336399	Air filters, automotive, truck, and bus, manufacturing
481211	Air passenger carriers, nonscheduled
481111	Air passenger carriers, scheduled
421730	Air pollution control equipment and supplies wholesaling
333411	Air purification equipment, stationary, manufacturing
333411	Air scrubbing systems manufacturing
711310	Air show managers with facilities
711320	Air show managers without facilities

711310	Air show organizers with facilities
711320	Air show organizers without facilities
711310	Air show promoters with facilities
711320	Air show promoters without facilities
481211	Air taxi services
334511	Air traffic control radar systems and equipment manufacturing
488111	Air traffic control services (except military)
928110	Air traffic control, military
333411	Air washers (i.e., air scrubbers) manufacturing
336391	Air-conditioners, motor vehicle, manufacturing
421620	Air-conditioners, room, wholesaling
333415	Air-conditioners, unit (e.g., motor home, travel trailer, window), manufacturing
333415	Air-conditioning and warm air heating combination units manufacturing
333415	Air-conditioning compressors (except motor vehicle) manufacturing
333415	Air-conditioning condensers and condensing units manufacturing
333415	Air-conditioning equipment (except motor vehicle) manufacturing
421730	Air-conditioning equipment (except room units) wholesaling
235110	Air-conditioning installation contractors
487210	Airboat (i.e., swamp buggy) operation
334220	Airborne radio communications equipment manufacturing
332995	Aircraft artillery manufacturing
336413	Aircraft assemblies, subassemblies, and parts (except engines) manufacturing
336413	Aircraft auxiliary parts (e.g., crop dusting, external fuel tanks, inflight refueling equipment) manufacturing
481219	Aircraft charter services (i.e., general purpose aircraft used for a variety of specialty air and flying services)
481211	Aircraft charter services, passenger
336413	Aircraft control surface assemblies manufacturing
336411	Aircraft conversions (i.e., major modifications to system)
441229	Aircraft dealers
336412	Aircraft engine and engine parts (except carburetors, pistons, piston rings, valves) manufacturing
334519	Aircraft engine instruments manufacturing
336412	Aircraft engine overhauling
336412	Aircraft engine rebuilding
421860	Aircraft engines and parts wholesaling
421860	Aircraft equipment and supplies wholesaling
488190	Aircraft ferrying services
334511	Aircraft flight instruments (except engine instruments) manufacturing
336413	Aircraft fuselage wing tail and similar assemblies manufacturing
488119	Aircraft hangar rental
332510	Aircraft hardware, metal, manufacturing
488190	Aircraft inspection services
561720	Aircraft janitorial services
336321	Aircraft lighting fixtures manufacturing
333924	Aircraft loading hoists manufacturing
488190	Aircraft maintenance and repair services (except factory conversion, factory overhaul, factory rebuilding)
336411	Aircraft manufacturing
336411	Aircraft overhauling
488119	Aircraft parking service
336413	Aircraft propellers and parts manufacturing
336411	Aircraft rebuilding (i.e., restoration to original design specifications)
532411	Aircraft rental and leasing
336360	Aircraft seats manufacturing
488190	Aircraft testing services

326211	Aircraft tire manufacturing
336412	Aircraft turbines manufacturing
421860	Aircraft wholesaling
336413	Airframe assemblies (except for guided missiles) manufacturing
336419	Airframe assemblies for guided missiles manufacturing
325612	Airfreshners manufacturing
722310	Airline food service contractors
561599	Airline reservation services
561599	Airline ticket offices
488119	Airport baggage handling services
488119	Airport cargo handling services
335311	Airport lighting transformers manufacturing
485999	Airport limousine services (i.e., shuttle)
488119	Airport operators (e.g., civil, international, national)
234110	Airport runway construction
488119	Airport runway maintenance services
485999	Airport shuttle services
421610	Alarm apparatus, electric, wholesaling
561621	Alarm system monitoring services
334290	Alarm systems and equipment manufacturing
561621	Alarm systems sales combined with installation, maintenance, or monitoring services
323118	Albums (e.g., photo, scrap) manufacturing
422120	Albums, photo, wholesaling
422690	Alcohol, industrial, wholesaling
922120	Alcohol, tobacco, and firearms control
926150	Alcoholic beverage control boards
722410	Alcoholic beverage drinking places
312140	Alcoholic beverages (except brandy) distilling
422810	Alcoholic beverages (except distilled spirits, wine) wholesaling
312130	Alcoholic beverages, brandy, distilling
422820	Alcoholic beverages, wine and distilled spirits wholesaling
624190	Alcoholism counseling (except medical treatment), nonresidential
623220	Alcoholism rehabilitation facilities (except licensed hospitals), residential
622210	Alcoholism rehabilitation hospitals
624190	Alcoholism self-help organizations
621420	Alcoholism treatment centers and clinics (except hospitals), outpatient
325199	Aldehydes manufacturing
312120	Ale brewing
422810	Ale wholesaling
111940	Alfalfa hay farming
311119	Alfalfa meal, dehydrated, manufacturing
311119	Alfalfa prepared as feed for animals
111998	Alfalfa seed farming
422910	Alfalfa wholesaling
311119	Alfalfa, cubed, manufacturing
111998	Algae farming
325199	Alginates (e.g., calcium, potassium, sodium) manufacturing
333319	Alignment equipment, motor vehicle, manufacturing
325110	Aliphatic (e.g., hydrocarbons) (except acetylene) made from refined petroleum or liquid hydrocarbons
324110	Aliphatic chemicals (i.e., acyclic) made in petroleum refineries
325181	Alkalies manufacturing
422690	Alkalies wholesaling
335912	Alkaline cell primary batteries manufacturing
335911	Alkaline cell storage batteries (i.e., nickel-cadmium, nickel-iron, silver oxide-zinc) manufacturing
325211	Alkyd resins manufacturing
421110	All terrain vehicles (ATV's) wholesaling
336999	All terrain vehicles (ATV's), wheeled or tracked, manufacturing
441221	All-terrain vehicle (ATV) dealers
325414	Allergenic extracts (except diagnostic substances) manufacturing

http://www.ntis.gov/naics

112519	Alligator production, farm raising
331314	Alloying purchased aluminum metals
331423	Alloying purchased copper
331423	Alloying purchased copper metals
331492	Alloying purchased nonferrous metals (except aluminum, copper)
323121	Almanac binding without printing
511130	Almanac publishers
511130	Almanac publishers and printing combined
323117	Almanacs printing and binding without publishing
323117	Almanacs printing without publishing
111335	Almond farming
111998	Aloe farming
713920	Alpine skiing facilities without accommodations
721110	Alpine skiing facilities with accommodations (i.e., ski resort)
334515	Alternator and generator testers manufacturing
336322	Alternators and generators for internal combustion engines manufacturing
331311	Alumina refining
327125	Aluminous refractory cement manufacturing
331312	Aluminum alloys made from bauxite or alumina producing primary aluminum and manufacturing
331314	Aluminum alloys made from scrap or dross
331316	Aluminum bar made by extruding purchased aluminum
331316	Aluminum bar made in integrated secondary smelting and extruding mills
331314	Aluminum billet made from purchased aluminum
331314	Aluminum billet made in integrated secondary smelting and rolling mills
332431	Aluminum cans manufacturing
331524	Aluminum castings (except die-castings), unfinished, manufacturing
325188	Aluminum compounds, not specified elsewhere by process, manufacturing
331521	Aluminum die-casting foundries
331521	Aluminum die-castings, unfinished, manufacturing
331314	Aluminum flakes made from purchased aluminum
331315	Aluminum foil made by flat rolling purchased aluminum
331315	Aluminum foil made in integrated secondary smelting and flat rolling mills
332112	Aluminum forgings made from purchased metals, unfinished
331524	Aluminum foundries (except die-casting)
332999	Aluminum freezer foil not made in rolling mills
331314	Aluminum ingot made from purchased aluminum
331314	Aluminum ingot, secondary smelting of aluminum and manufacturing
332999	Aluminum ladders manufacturing
327910	Aluminum oxide (fused) abrasives manufacturing
331311	Aluminum oxide refining
331316	Aluminum pipe made by extruding purchased aluminum
331316	Aluminum pipe made in integrated secondary smelting and extruding mills
331315	Aluminum plate made by continuous casting purchased aluminum
331315	Aluminum plate made by flat rolling purchased aluminum
331315	Aluminum plate made in integrated secondary smelting and continuous casting mills
331315	Aluminum plate made in integrated secondary smelting and flat rolling mills
331312	Aluminum producing from alumina
331314	Aluminum recovering from scrap and making ingot and billet (except by rolling)

331316	Aluminum rod made by extruding purchased aluminum
331316	Aluminum rod made in integrated secondary smelting and extruding mills
331312	Aluminum shapes (e.g., bar, ingot, rod, sheet) made by producing primary aluminum and manufacturing
331315	Aluminum sheet made by flat rolling purchased aluminum
331315	Aluminum sheet made in integrated secondary smelting and flat rolling mills
331316	Aluminum tube blooms made by extruding purchased aluminum
331316	Aluminum tube blooms made in integrated secondary smelting and extruding mills
331316	Aluminum tube made by drawing or extruding purchased aluminum
331316	Aluminum tube made in integrated secondary smelting and drawing plants
331316	Aluminum tube made in integrated secondary smelting and extruding mills
331315	Aluminum welded tube made by flat rolling purchased aluminum
331315	Aluminum welded tube made in integrated secondary smelting and flat rolling mills
813410	Alumni associations
813410	Alumni clubs
325188	Alums (e.g., aluminum ammonium sulfate, aluminum potassium sulfate) manufacturing
713990	Amateur sports teams, recreational
922160	Ambulance and fire service combined
336213	Ambulance bodies manufacturing
621910	Ambulance services, air or ground
336211	Ambulances assembling on purchased chassis
421110	Ambulances wholesaling
621493	Ambulatory surgical centers and clinics, freestanding
921150	American Indian or Alaska Native tribal councils
921150	American Indian or Alaska Native tribal courts
921150	American Indian or Alaska Native, tribal chief's or chairman's office
325211	Amino resins manufacturing
422690	Ammonia (except fertilizer material) wholesaling
325311	Ammonia, anhydrous and aqueous, manufacturing
422910	Ammonia, fertilizer material, wholesaling
325612	Ammonia, household-type, manufacturing
325188	Ammonium compounds, not specified elsewhere by process, manufacturing
325311	Ammonium nitrate manufacturing
325312	Ammonium phosphates manufacturing
325311	Ammonium sulfate manufacturing
421990	Ammunition (except sporting) wholesaling
332993	Ammunition (i.e., more than 30 mm., more than 1.18 inch) manufacturing
332992	Ammunition, small arms (i.e., 30 mm. or less, 1.18 inch or less), manufacturing
325411	Amphetamines, uncompounded, manufacturing
334310	Amplifiers (e.g., auto, home, musical instrument, public address) manufacturing
334220	Amplifiers, (e.g., RF power and IF), broadcast and studio equipment, manufacturing
713120	Amusement arcades
233320	Amusement building construction
713990	Amusement device (except gambling) concession operators (i.e., supplying and servicing in others' facilities)
713120	Amusement device (except gambling) parlors, coin-operated
339999	Amusement machines, coin-operated, manufacturing

421850	Amusement park equipment wholesaling
713110	Amusement parks (e.g., theme, water)
713990	Amusement ride concession operators (i.e., supplying and servicing in others' facilities)
325412	Analgesic preparations manufacturing
334111	Analog computers manufacturing
421490	Analytical instruments (e.g., chromatographic, photometers, spectrographs) wholesaling
334515	Analyzers for testing electrical characteristics manufacturing
334513	Analyzers, industrial process control type, manufacturing
235990	Anchored earth retention construction contractors
339112	Anesthesia apparatus manufacturing
325412	Anesthetic preparations manufacturing
332911	Angle valves, industrial-type, manufacturing
325311	Anhydrous ammonia manufacturing
311512	Anhydrous butterfat manufacturing
112519	Animal aquaculture (except finfish, shellfish)
813910	Animal breeders' associations
712130	Animal exhibits, live
311611	Animal fats (except poultry and small game) produced in slaughtering plants
311613	Animal fats rendering
422910	Animal feeds (except pet food) wholesaling
311119	Animal feeds, prepared (except dog and cat), manufacturing
311111	Animal feeds, prepared, dog and cat, manufacturing
812910	Animal grooming services
422590	Animal hair wholesaling
541940	Animal hospitals
311613	Animal oil rendering
926140	Animal quarantine service, government
813312	Animal rights organizations
712130	Animal safari parks
115210	Animal semen banks
812910	Animal shelters
114210	Animal trapping, commercial
332999	Animal traps, metal (except wire), manufacturing
813312	Animal welfare associations or leagues
336999	Animal-drawn vehicles and parts manufacturing
711510	Animated cartoon artists, independent
512120	Animated cartoon distribution
512110	Animated cartoon production
512110	Animated cartoon production and distribution
315119	Anklets, sheer hosiery or socks, knitting or knitting and finishing
332811	Annealing metals for the trade
711510	Announcers, independent radio and television
524113	Annuities underwriting
332991	Annular ball bearings manufacturing
332813	Anodizing metals and metal products for the trade
421620	Answering machines, telephone, wholesaling
561421	Answering services, telephone
421690	Antennas wholesaling
334220	Antennas, satellite, manufacturing
334220	Antennas, transmitting and receiving, manufacturing
212113	Anthracite beneficiating (e.g., crushing, screening, washing, cleaning, sizing)
212113	Anthracite mining and/or beneficiating
325620	Antiperspirants, personal, manufacturing
813319	Antipoverty advocacy organizations
332913	Antiscald bath and shower valves manufacturing
332995	Antiaircraft artillery manufacturing
325412	Antibacterial preparations manufacturing
325412	Antibiotic preparations manufacturing
422210	Antibiotics wholesaling
325411	Antibiotics, uncompounded, manufacturing
325998	Antifreeze preparations manufacturing

422690	Antifreeze wholesaling
325412	Antihistamine preparations manufacturing
325131	Antimony based pigments manufacturing
212299	Antimony ores mining and/or beneficiating
325412	Antineoplastic preparations manufacturing
325412	Antipyretic preparations manufacturing
811121	Antique and classic automotive restoration
441120	Antique auto dealers
811420	Antique furniture repair and restoration shops
453310	Antique shops
325998	Antiscaling compounds manufacturing
325412	Antiseptic preparations manufacturing
422210	Antiseptics wholesaling
325412	Antispasmodic preparations manufacturing
332995	Antitank rocket launchers manufacturing
531110	Apartment building rental or leasing
531311	Apartment managers' offices
531110	Apartment rental or leasing
233220	Apartments (e.g., garden, high-rise) construction
446110	Apothecaries
448150	Apparel accessory stores
314999	Apparel fillings (e.g., cotton mill waste, kapok) manufacturing
315999	Apparel findings and trimmings cut and sewn from purchased fabric (except apparel contractors)
561910	Apparel folding and packaging services
448130	Apparel stores, children's and infants' clothing
448110	Apparel stores, men's and boys' clothing
453310	Apparel stores, used clothing
448120	Apparel stores, women's and girls' clothing
315211	Apparel trimmings and findings, men's and boys', cut and sew apparel contractors
315212	Apparel trimmings and findings, women's, girls', and infants', cut and sew apparel contractors
313221	Apparel webbings manufacturing
315292	Apparel, fur (except apparel contractors), manufacturing
315211	Apparel, fur, men's and boys', cut and sew apparel contractors
315212	Apparel, fur, women's, girls', and infants', cut and sew apparel contractors
315211	Apparel, men's and boys', cut and sew apparel contractors
315212	Apparel, women's, girls', and infants', cut and sew contractors
111331	Apple orchards
334512	Appliance controls manufacturing
335999	Appliance cords made from purchased insulated wire
332510	Appliance hardware, metal, manufacturing
334512	Appliance regulators (except switches) manufacturing
532210	Appliance rental
443111	Appliance stores, household-type
453310	Appliance stores, household-type, used
334518	Appliance timers manufacturing
811412	Appliance, household-type, repair and maintenance services without retailing new appliances
421720	Appliances, gas (except dryers, freezers, refrigerators), wholesaling
421620	Appliances, household-type (except gas ranges, gas water heaters), wholesaling
421450	Appliances, surgical, wholesaling
541511	Applications software programming services, custom computer
315211	Appliqueing on men's and boys' apparel
314999	Appliqueing on textile products (except apparel)
323118	Appointment books and refills manufacturing

541990	Appraisal (except real estate) services
531320	Appraisers' offices, real estate
611513	Apprenticeship training programs
111339	Apricot farming
316999	Aprons, leather (e.g., blacksmith's, welder's), manufacturing
315999	Aprons, waterproof (e.g., plastics, rubberized fabric), rubberizing fabric and manufacturing aprons
315212	Aprons, waterproof (including plastics, rubberized fabric), woman's, girls', and infants', cut and sew apparel contractors
315999	Aprons, waterproof (including rubberized fabric, plastics), cut and sewn from purchased fabric (except apparel contractors)
315211	Aprons, waterproof (including rubberized fabric, plastics), men's and boys', cut and sew apparel contractors
712130	Aquariums
327215	Aquariums made from purchased glass
234910	Aqueduct construction
541990	Arbitration and conciliation services (except by attorney, paralegal)
712130	Arboreta
561730	Arborist services
333992	Arc welding equipment manufacturing
335311	Arc-welding transformers, separate solid-state, manufacturing
713120	Arcades, amusement
541720	Archeological research and development services
712120	Archeological sites (i.e., public display)
713990	Archery ranges
421490	Architect's equipment and supplies wholesaling
541310	Architects' (except landscape) offices
813920	Architects' associations
541320	Architects' offices, landscape
541310	Architectural (except landscape) consultants' offices
541310	Architectural (except landscape) design services
541310	Architectural (except landscape) services
327331	Architectural block, concrete (e.g., fluted, ground face, screen, slump, split), manufacturing
325510	Architectural coatings (i.e., paint) manufacturing
332323	Architectural metalwork manufacturing
421390	Architectural metalwork wholesaling
327112	Architectural sculptures, clay, manufacturing
327991	Architectural sculptures, stone, manufacturing
541320	Architectural services, landscape
327123	Architectural terra cotta manufacturing
327390	Architectural wall panels, precast concrete, manufacturing
337212	Architectural woodwork and fixtures (i.e., custom designed interiors) manufacturing
514120	Archives
335129	Area and sports luminaries (e.g., stadium lighting fixtures), electric, manufacturing
711310	Arena operators
531120	Arena, no promotion of events, rental or leasing
325120	Argon manufacturing
335312	Armature rewinding on a factory basis
811310	Armature rewinding services (except on an assembly line or factory basis)
335312	Armatures, industrial, manufacturing
928110	Armed forces
331422	Armored cable made from purchased copper in wire drawing plants
331422	Armored cable, copper, made in integrated secondary smelting and drawing plants
561613	Armored car services

336992	Armored military vehicles and parts manufacturing
928110	Army
422690	Aromatic chemicals wholesaling
113210	Aromatic wood gathering
488999	Arrangement of car pools and vanpools
335931	Arrestors and coils, lighting, manufacturing
325320	Arsenate insecticides manufacturing
611610	Art (except commercial or graphic) instruction
453920	Art auctions
453920	Art dealers
712110	Art galleries (except retail)
453920	Art galleries retailing art
327420	Art goods (e.g., gypsum, plaster of paris) manufacturing
422990	Art goods wholesaling
712110	Art museums
314999	Art needlework on clothing for the trade
323111	Art print gravure printing without publishing
511199	Art print publishers
511199	Art print publishers and printing combined
323112	Art prints flexographic printing without publishing
323110	Art prints lithographic (offset) printing without publishing
323119	Art prints printing (except flexographic, gravure, lithographic, screen) without publishing
323113	Art prints screen printing without publishing
511199	Art publishers
711510	Art restorers, independent
611610	Art schools (except academic), fine
611519	Art schools, commercial or graphic
541430	Art services, commercial
541430	Art services, graphic
541430	Art studios, commercial
453998	Art supply stores
621340	Art therapists' offices (e.g., centers, clinics)
111219	Artichoke farming, field, bedding plant and seed production
422990	Artificial Christmas trees wholesaling
115210	Artificial insemination services for livestock
115210	Artificial insemination services for pets
339113	Artificial limbs manufacturing
312111	Artificially carbonated waters manufacturing
332993	Artillery (i.e., more than 30 mm., more than 1.18 inch) manufacturing
339942	Artist's paint manufacturing
339942	Artist's supplies (except paper) manufacturing
711510	Artists (except commercial, musical), independent
711410	Artists' agents or managers
422990	Artists' supplies wholesaling
541430	Artists, independent commercial
541430	Artists, independent graphic
541430	Artists, independent medical
926110	Arts and cultural program administration, government
711310	Arts event managers with facilities
711320	Arts event managers without facilities
711310	Arts event organizers with facilities
711320	Arts event organizers without facilities
711310	Arts event promoters with facilities
711320	Arts event promoters without facilities
711320	Arts festival promoters without facilities
562910	Asbestos abatement services
562910	Asbestos removal contractors
562111	Ash collection services
562111	Ash hauling, local
327215	Ashtrays made from purchased glass
327212	Ashtrays, glass, made in glass making plants
327112	Ashtrays, pottery, manufacturing
111219	Asparagus farming, field, bedding plant and seed production
324110	Asphalt and asphaltic materials made in petroleum refineries

http://www.ntis.gov/naics

322121   Asphalt paper made in paper mills

234110   Asphalt paving (e.g., public sidewalks, roads, streets) contractors

324121   Asphalt paving blocks made from purchased asphaltic materials

324121   Asphalt paving mixtures made from purchased asphaltic materials

324110   Asphalt paving mixtures made in petroleum refineries

324122   Asphalt roofing cements made from purchased asphaltic materials

324122   Asphalt roofing coatings made from purchased asphaltic materials

324122   Asphalt saturated boards made from purchased asphaltic materials

324122   Asphalt saturated mats and felts made from purchased asphaltic materials and paper

324122   Asphalt shingles made from purchased asphaltic materials

235520   Asphalt tile construction contractors

212399   Asphalt, native, mining and/or beneficiating

235710   Asphalting of private driveways and parking areas construction contractors

541380   Assaying services

336213   Assembly line conversions of purchased vans and mini-vans

336312   Assembly line rebuilding of automotive and truck gasoline engines

336350   Assembly line rebuilding of automotive, truck, and bus transmissions

333518   Assembly machines manufacturing

233310   Assembly plant construction

336120   Assembly plants, heavy trucks, and buses on chassis of own manufacture

336112   Assembly plants, light trucks on chassis of own manufacture

336112   Assembly plants, mini-vans on chassis of own manufacture

336111   Assembly plants, passenger car, on chassis of own manufacture

336112   Assembly plants, sport utility vehicles on chassis of own manufacture

921130   Assessor's offices, tax

325613   Assistants, textile and leather finishing, manufacturing

623311   Assisted-living facilities with on-site nursing facilities

623312   Assisted-living facilities without on-site nursing care facilities

813311   Associations for retired persons, advocacy

812990   Astrology services

711219   Athletes, independent (i.e., participating in live sports events)

813990   Athletic associations, regulatory

315228   Athletic clothing (except team athletic uniforms), men's, boys' and unisex (i.e., sized without regard to gender), cut and sewn from purchased fabric (except apparel contractors)

315239   Athletic clothing (except team athletic uniforms), women's, misses', and girls', cut and sewn from purchased fabric (except apparel contractors)

315191   Athletic clothing made in apparel knitting mills

315211   Athletic clothing, men's and boys', cut and sew apparel contractors

315212   Athletic clothing, women's, girls', and infants', cut and sew apparel contractors

713940   Athletic club facilities, physical fitness

713990   Athletic clubs (i.e., sports teams) not operating sports facilities, recreational

234990   Athletic field construction

422340   Athletic footwear wholesaling

339920   Athletic goods (except ammunition, clothing, footwear, small arms) manufacturing

421910   Athletic goods (except apparel, footwear, nonspecialty) wholesaling

813990	Athletic leagues (i.e., regulating bodies)
448210	Athletic shoe (except bowling, golf, spiked) stores
316219	Athletic shoes (except rubber or plastics soled with fabric upper) manufacturing
316211	Athletic shoes, plastics or plastics soled fabric upper (except cleated), manufacturing
316211	Athletic shoes, rubber or rubber soled fabric uppers (except cleated), manufacturing
315119	Athletic socks, knitting or knitting and finishing
421910	Athletic uniforms wholesaling
315299	Athletic uniforms, team, cut and sewn from purchased fabric (except apparel contractors)
315211	Athletic uniforms, team, men's and boys', cut and sew apparel contractors
315212	Athletic uniforms, team, women's, girls', and infants, cut and sew apparel contractors
511199	Atlas publishers
511199	Atlas publishers and printing combined
323112	Atlases flexographic printing without publishing
323111	Atlases gravure printing without publishing
323110	Atlases lithographic (offset) printing without publishing
323119	Atlases printing (except flexographic, gravure, lithographic, screen) without publishing
323113	Atlases screen printing without publishing
316991	Attache cases, all materials, manufacturing
333412	Attic fans manufacturing
922130	Attorney generals' offices
541110	Attorneys' offices
453998	Auction houses (general merchandise)
422590	Auction markets, horses and mules

422520	Auction markets, livestock (except horses, mules)
422590	Auction markets, tobacco
561990	Auctioneers, independent
421990	Audio and video tapes and disks, prerecorded, wholesaling
337129	Audio cabinets (i.e., housings), wood, manufacturing
421620	Audio equipment, household-type, wholesaling
512290	Audio recording of meetings or conferences
512240	Audio recording post-production services
421690	Audiotapes, blank, wholesaling
532490	Audio visual equipment rental or leasing
621340	Audiologists' offices (e.g., centers, clinics)
334613	Audiotape, blank, manufacturing
541211	Auditing accountants' (i.e., CPAs) offices
541211	Auditing services (i.e., CPA services), accounts
531120	Auditorium rental or leasing
541211	Auditors' (i.e., CPAs) offices, accounts
711410	Authors' agents or managers
711510	Authors, independent
421120	Auto body shop supplies wholesaling
336411	Autogiros manufacturing
522320	Automated clearinghouses, bank or check (except central bank)
514210	Automated data processing services
332911	Automatic (i.e., controlling-type, regulating) valves, industrial-type, manufacturing
454210	Automatic merchandising machine operators
334119	Automatic teller machines (ATM) manufacturing
421420	Automatic teller machines (ATM) wholesaling
336350	Automatic transmissions, automotive, truck, and bus, manufacturing
421120	Automobile accessories (except tires, tubes) wholesaling

http://www.ntis.gov/naics

334220	Automobile antennas manufacturing
421110	Automobile auctions
336211	Automobile bodies, passenger car, manufacturing
484220	Automobile carrier trucking, local
484230	Automobile carrier trucking, long-distance
813410	Automobile clubs (except road and travel services)
561599	Automobile clubs, road and travel services
441110	Automobile dealers, new only or new and used
441120	Automobile dealers, used only
611692	Automobile driving schools
522220	Automobile financing
421120	Automobile glass wholesaling
332510	Automobile hardware, metal, manufacturing
541420	Automobile industrial design services
524126	Automobile insurance carriers, direct
532112	Automobile leasing
333921	Automobile lifts (i.e., garage-type, service station) manufacturing
812930	Automobile parking garages or lots
441310	Automobile parts dealers
325612	Automobile polishes and cleaners manufacturing
541380	Automobile proving and testing grounds
711212	Automobile racetracks
711219	Automobile racing teams
334310	Automobile radio receivers manufacturing
532111	Automobile rental
485320	Automobile rental with driver (except shuttle service, taxis)
561491	Automobile repossession services
336360	Automobile seat covers manufacturing
421120	Automobile service station equipment wholesaling
335911	Automobile storage batteries manufacturing
332611	Automobile suspension springs manufacturing
336212	Automobile transporter trailers, multi-car, manufacturing
336214	Automobile transporter trailers, single car, manufacturing
333923	Automobile wrecker (i.e., tow truck) hoists manufacturing
336211	Automobile wrecker truck bodies manufacturing
336211	Automobile wreckers assembling on purchased chassis
336111	Automobiles assembling on chassis of own manufacture
421110	Automobiles wholesaling
811198	Automotive air-conditioning repair shops
441310	Automotive audio equipment stores
811121	Automotive body shops
811118	Automotive brake repair shops
422690	Automotive chemicals (except lubrication greases, lubrication oils) wholesaling
811192	Automotive detailing services (i.e., cleaning, polishing)
334515	Automotive electrical engine diagnostic equipment manufacturing
811118	Automotive electrical repair shops
335931	Automotive electrical switches manufacturing
334519	Automotive emissions testing equipment manufacturing
811198	Automotive emissions testing services
811111	Automotive engine repair and replacement shops
811112	Automotive exhaust system repair and replacement shops
811118	Automotive front end alignment shops
811122	Automotive glass shops
336322	Automotive harness and ignition sets manufacturing
335110	Automotive light bulbs manufacturing
336321	Automotive lighting fixtures manufacturing
811191	Automotive oil change and lubrication shops

811121	Automotive paint shops
441310	Automotive parts and supply stores
441310	Automotive parts dealers, used
421120	Automotive parts, new, wholesaling
811118	Automotive radiator repair shops
421620	Automotive radios wholesaling
811111	Automotive repair and replacement shops, general
811198	Automotive rustproofing and undercoating shops
334290	Automotive theft alarm systems manufacturing
441320	Automotive tire dealers
811198	Automotive tire repair (except retreading) shops
811113	Automotive transmission repair shops
811118	Automotive tune-up shops
811121	Automotive upholstery shops
811192	Automotive washing and polishing
336330	Automotive, truck and bus steering assemblies and parts manufacturing
336330	Automotive, truck and bus suspension assemblies and parts (except springs) manufacturing
335311	Autotransformers manufacturing
712130	Aviaries
813319	Aviation advocacy organizations
481219	Aviation clubs providing a variety of air transportation activities to the general public
488119	Aviation clubs, primarily providing flying field services to the general public
713990	Aviation clubs, recreational
611512	Aviation schools
111339	Avocado farming
421390	Awnings (except canvas) wholesaling
314912	Awnings and canopies, outdoor, made from purchased fabrics
422990	Awnings, canvas, wholesaling
326199	Awnings, rigid plastics or fiberglass, manufacturing
332322	Awnings, sheet metal, manufacturing
332212	Axes manufacturing
336350	Axle bearings, automotive, truck, and bus, manufacturing
111421	Azalea farming
325920	Azides explosive materials manufacturing
325132	Azine dyes manufacturing
325132	Azo dyes manufacturing
325192	Azobenzene manufacturing
332994	BB guns manufacturing
332992	BB shot manufacturing
448130	Baby clothing shops
422330	Baby clothing wholesaling
311422	Baby foods (including meats) canning
422490	Baby foods, canned, wholesaling
311514	Baby formula, fresh, processed, and bottled, manufacturing
624410	Babysitting services, child day care
561310	Babysitting bureaus (i.e., registries)
333120	Backhoes manufacturing
311612	Bacon, slab and sliced, made from purchased carcasses
311611	Bacon, slab and sliced, produced in slaughtering plants
325414	Bacterial vaccines manufacturing
621511	Bacteriological laboratories, medical
541710	Bacteriological research and development laboratories or services
314999	Badges, fabric, manufacturing
332999	Badges, metal, manufacturing
326199	Badges, plastics, manufacturing
333993	Bag opening, filling, and closing machines manufacturing
722110	Bagel shops, full service
722213	Bagel shops, on premise baking and carryout service
311812	Bagels made in commercial bakeries
322223	Bags (except plastics only) made by laminating or coating combinations of purchased plastics, foil and paper
316991	Bags (i.e., luggage), all materials, manufacturing
313249	Bags and bagging fabric made in warp knitting mills
313241	Bags and bagging fabrics made in weft knitting mills

316991	Bags, athletic, manufacturing
322223	Bags, coated paper, made from purchased paper
322223	Bags, foil, made from purchased foil
313111	Bags, hemp, made from purchased fiber
322224	Bags, multiwall, made from purchased uncoated paper
422130	Bags, paper and disposable plastics, wholesaling
322224	Bags, paper, uncoated, made from purchased paper
314911	Bags, plastic, made from purchased woven plastics
326111	Bags, plastics film, single wall or multiwall, manufacturing
314911	Bags, rubberized fabric, manufacturing
314999	Bags, sleeping, manufacturing
314911	Bags, textile, made from purchased woven or knitted materials
422990	Bags, textile, wholesaling
322224	Bags, uncoated paper, made from purchased paper
812990	Bail bonding services
421910	Bait, artificial, wholesaling
422990	Bait, live, wholesaling
311422	Baked beans canning
311813	Baked goods (except bread, bread-type rolls), frozen, manufacturing
445210	Baked ham stores
311811	Bakeries with baking from flour on the premises, retailing not for immediate consumption
333294	Bakery machinery and equipment manufacturing
333294	Bakery ovens manufacturing
422490	Bakery products (except frozen) wholesaling
311812	Bakery products, fresh (i.e., bread, cakes, doughnuts, pastries), made in commercial bakeries
422420	Bakery products, frozen, wholesaling
445291	Bakery stores, retailing only (except immediate consumption)
311320	Baking chocolate made from cacao beans
311330	Baking chocolate made from purchased chocolate
311999	Baking powder manufacturing
333997	Balances (except laboratory-type) manufacturing
421440	Balances and scales (except laboratory) wholesaling
421490	Balances and scales, laboratory, wholesaling
339111	Balances and scales, laboratory-type, manufacturing
333319	Balancing equipment, motor vehicle, manufacturing
333111	Balers, farm-type (e.g., cotton, hay, straw), manufacturing
333999	Baling machinery (e.g., paper, scrap metal) manufacturing
332991	Ball bearings manufacturing
212324	Ball clay mining and/or beneficiating
333613	Ball joints (except aircraft, motor vehicle) manufacturing
339941	Ball point pens manufacturing
332911	Ball valves, industrial-type, manufacturing
335311	Ballasts (i.e., transformers) manufacturing
711120	Ballet companies
711510	Ballet dancers, independent
711120	Ballet productions, live theatrical
316219	Ballet slippers manufacturing
453220	Balloon shops
812990	Balloon-o-gram services
326199	Balloons, plastics, manufacturing
326299	Balloons, rubber, manufacturing
713990	Ballrooms
339932	Balls, rubber (except athletic equipment), manufacturing
113210	Balsam needles gathering
111339	Banana farming
315299	Band uniforms cut and sewn from purchased fabric (except apparel contractors)
315211	Band uniforms, men's and boys', cut and sew apparel contractors

315212 Band uniforms, women's, girls', and infants', cut and sew apparel contractors

339113 Bandages and dressings, surgical and orthopedic, manufacturing

422210 Bandages wholesaling

711130 Bands

333210 Bandsaws, woodworking-type, manufacturing

233320 Bank building construction

522320 Bank clearinghouse associations

524128 Bank deposit insurance carriers, direct

551111 Bank holding companies (except managing)

523991 Bank trust offices

813910 Bankers' associations

926150 Banking regulatory agencies

523110 Banking, investment

525920 Bankruptcy estates

521110 Banks, Federal Reserve

522110 Banks, commercial

522210 Banks, credit card

522190 Banks, private (i.e., unincorporated)

522120 Banks, savings

522293 Banks, trade (i.e., international trade financing)

314999 Banners made from purchased fabrics

332323 Bannisters, metal, manufacturing

722320 Banquet halls with catering staff

327991 Baptismal fonts, cut stone, manufacturing

813920 Bar associations

561499 Bar code imprinting services

331316 Bar made by extruding purchased aluminum

331319 Bar made by rolling purchased aluminum

325611 Bar soaps manufacturing

331316 Bar, aluminum, made in integrated secondary smelting and extruding mills

331319 Bar, aluminum, made in integrated secondary smelting and rolling mills

311421 Barbecue sauce manufacturing

335221 Barbecues, grills, and braziers manufacturing

332618 Barbed wire made from purchased wire

611511 Barber colleges

421850 Barber shop equipment and supplies wholesaling

812111 Barber shops

325411 Barbiturates, uncompounded, manufacturing

336611 Barge building

332312 Barge sections, prefabricated metal, manufacturing

483211 Barge transportation, canal

483113 Barge transportation, coastal or Great Lakes

212393 Barite mining and/or beneficiating

327992 Barite processing beyond beneficiation

325188 Barium compounds, not specified elsewhere by process, manufacturing

327992 Barium processing beyond beneficiation

113210 Bark gathering

111199 Barley farming, field and seed production

311119 Barley feed, chopped, crushed or ground, manufacturing

311211 Barley flour manufacturing

311213 Barley, malt, manufacturing

332994 Barrels, gun (i.e., 30 mm. or less, 1.18 inch or less), manufacturing

332995 Barrels, gun (i.e., more than 30 mm., more than 1.18 inch), manufacturing

332439 Barrels, metal, manufacturing

421840 Barrels, new and reconditioned, wholesaling

321920 Barrels, wood, coopered, manufacturing

541110 Barristers' offices

722410 Bars (i.e., drinking places), alcoholic beverage

332312 Bars, concrete reinforcing, manufacturing

331111 Bars, iron, made in steel mills

421510 Bars, metal (except precious), wholesaling

331221 Bars, steel, made in cold rolling mills

331111	Bars, steel, made in steel mills
611519	Bartending schools
561990	Bartering services
325131	Barytes based pigments manufacturing
212319	Basalt crushed and broken stone mining and/or beneficiating
561210	Base facilities operation support services
315211	Baseball caps (except plastics), men's and boys', cut and sew apparel contractors
315212	Baseball caps (except plastics), women's, girls', and infants', cut and sew apparel contractors
315991	Baseball caps cut and sewn from purchased fabric (except apparel contractors)
711211	Baseball clubs, professional or semiprofessional
713990	Baseball clubs, recreational
421730	Baseboard heaters, electric, non-portable, wholesaling
333414	Baseboard heating equipment manufacturing
711211	Basketball clubs, professional or semiprofessional
713990	Basketball clubs, recreational
422990	Baskets wholesaling
331222	Baskets, iron or steel, made in wire drawing plants
332618	Baskets, metal, made from purchased wire
321920	Baskets, wood (e.g., round stave, veneer), manufacturing
335211	Bath fans, residential, manufacturing
314110	Bath mats and bath sets made in carpet mills
442299	Bath shops
713990	Bathing beaches
315999	Bathing caps, rubber, manufacturing
315191	Bathing suits made in apparel knitting mills
315291	Bathing suits, infants', cut and sewn from purchased fabric (except apparel contractors)
315211	Bathing suits, men's and boys', cut and sew apparel contractors
315228	Bathing suits, men's and boys', cut and sewn from purchased fabric (except apparel contractors)
315212	Bathing suits, women's, girls', and infants', cut and sew apparel contractors
315239	Bathing suits, women's, misses', and girls', cut and sewn from purchased fabric (except apparel contractors)
315192	Bathrobes made in apparel knitting mills
315291	Bathrobes, infants', cut and sewn from purchased fabric (except apparel contractors)
315211	Bathrobes, men's and boys', cut and sew apparel contractors
315221	Bathrobes, men's and boys', cut and sewn from purchased fabric (except apparel contractors)
315212	Bathrobes, women's, girls', and infants', cut and sew apparel contractors
315231	Bathrobes, women's, misses', and girls', cut and sewn from purchased fabric (except apparel contractors)
421220	Bathroom accessories wholesaling
327111	Bathroom accessories, vitreous china and earthenware, manufacturing
326199	Bathroom and toilet accessories, plastics, manufacturing
333997	Bathroom scales manufacturing
337110	Bathroom vanities (except freestanding), stock or custom wood, manufacturing
812199	Baths, steam or turkish
332998	Bathtubs, metal, manufacturing
326191	Bathtubs, plastics, manufacturing
421610	Batteries (except automotive) wholesaling
421120	Batteries, automotive, wholesaling
335912	Batteries, primary, dry or wet, manufacturing
335911	Batteries, rechargeable, manufacturing

335911	Batteries, storage, manufacturing
311822	Batters, prepared, made from purchased flour
311211	Batters, prepared, made in flour mills
335999	Battery chargers, solid-state, manufacturing
334515	Battery testers, electrical, manufacturing
712120	Battlefields
314999	Batts and batting (except nonwoven fabrics) manufacturing
212299	Bauxite mining and/or beneficiating
454390	Bazaars (i.e., temporary stands)
532292	Beach chair rental
713990	Beach clubs, recreational
562998	Beach maintenance and cleaning services
532292	Beach umbrella rental
713990	Beaches, bathing
314999	Beading on textile products (except apparel) for the trade
333292	Beaming machinery for yarn manufacturing
313112	Beaming yarn
321113	Beams, wood, made from logs or bolts
111219	Bean (except dry) farming, field and seed production
111130	Bean farming, dry, field and seed production
311422	Beans, baked, canning
422510	Beans, dry, wholesaling
336312	Bearings (e.g., camshaft, crankshaft, connecting rod), automotive and truck gasoline engine, manufacturing
421840	Bearings wholesaling
332991	Bearings, ball and roller, manufacturing
333613	Bearings, plain (except internal combustion engine), manufacturing
812112	Beautician services
611511	Beauty schools
812112	Beauty and barber shops, combined
711310	Beauty pageant managers with facilities
711320	Beauty pageant managers without facilities
711310	Beauty pageant organizers with facilities
711320	Beauty pageant organizers without facilities
711310	Beauty pageant promoters with facilities
711320	Beauty pageant promoters without facilities
421850	Beauty parlor equipment and supplies wholesaling
812112	Beauty parlors
422210	Beauty preparations wholesaling
812112	Beauty salons
812112	Beauty shops
422210	Beauty supplies wholesaling
446120	Beauty supply stores
721191	Bed-and-breakfast inns
337122	Bed frames, wood household-type, manufacturing
111422	Bedding plant growing (except vegetable and melon bedding plants)
337122	Beds (except hospital), wood household-type, manufacturing
337124	Beds (including cabinet and folding), metal household-type (except hospital), manufacturing
339111	Beds, hospital, manufacturing
421450	Beds, hospital, wholesaling
314129	Bedspreads and bed sets made from purchased fabrics
313249	Bedspreads and bed sets made in lace mills
313249	Bedspreads and bed sets made in warp knitting mills
313241	Bedspreads and bed sets made in weft knitting mills
112910	Bee production (i.e., apiculture)
311611	Beef carcasses, half carcasses, primal and sub-primal cuts, produced in slaughtering plants
112112	Beef cattle feedlots (except stockyards for transportation)
112111	Beef cattle ranching or farming
311611	Beef produced in slaughtering plants
311612	Beef stew made from purchased carcasses

311612	Beef, primal and sub-primal cuts, made from purchased carcasses
422910	Beekeeping supplies wholesaling
513321	Beeper (i.e., radio pager) communication carriers
312120	Beer brewing
333415	Beer cooling and dispensing equipment manufacturing
445310	Beer stores, packaged
422810	Beer wholesaling
112910	Beeswax production
111219	Beet farming (except sugar beets), field, bedding plant and seed production
311313	Beet pulp, dried, manufacturing
311313	Beet sugar refining
541720	Behavioral research and development services
335999	Bells, electric, manufacturing
422310	Belt and buckle assembly kits wholesaling
333922	Belt conveyor systems manufacturing
313221	Belting fabrics, narrow woven
316999	Belting for machinery, leather, manufacturing
316110	Belting leather, manufacturing
314999	Belting made from purchased fabrics
421840	Belting, industrial, wholesaling
326220	Belting, rubber (e.g., conveyor, elevator, transmission), manufacturing
482112	Beltline railroads
315999	Belts, apparel (e.g., fabric, leather, vinyl), cut and sewn from purchased fabric (except apparel contractors)
315211	Belts, apparel (e.g., fabric, leather, vinyl), men's and boys', cut and sew apparel contractors
315212	Belts, apparel (e.g., fabric, leather, vinyl), women's, girls', and infants', cut and sew apparel contractors
316999	Belts, leather safety, manufacturing
337127	Benches, park-type (except concrete, stone), manufacturing
337127	Benches, public building-type, manufacturing
337127	Benches, work, manufacturing
333513	Bending and forming machines, metalworking, manufacturing
541612	Benefit consulting services
212325	Bentonite mining and/or beneficiating
325192	Benzaldehyde manufacturing
325110	Benzene made from refined petroleum or liquid hydrocarbons
324110	Benzene made in petroleum refineries
311421	Berries, canned, manufacturing
422480	Berries, fresh, wholesaling
115113	Berries, machine harvesting
111334	Berry (except strawberry) farming
334517	Beta-ray irradiation equipment manufacturing
813910	Better business bureaus
722213	Beverage (e.g., coffee, juice, soft drink) bars, nonalcoholic, fixed location
311930	Beverage bases manufacturing
422490	Beverage bases wholesaling
422490	Beverage concentrates wholesaling
421740	Beverage coolers, mechanical, wholesaling
311930	Beverage flavorings (except coffee based) manufacturing
722330	Beverage stands, nonalcoholic, mobile
311930	Beverage syrups (except coffee based) manufacturing
422810	Beverages, alcoholic (except distilled spirits, wine), wholesaling
312120	Beverages, beer, ale, and malt liquors, manufacturing
311514	Beverages, dietary, dairy and nondairy based
312111	Beverages, fruit and vegetable drinks, cocktails, and ades, manufacturing
311421	Beverages, fruit and vegetable juice, manufacturing
312140	Beverages, liquors (except brandies), manufacturing
311511	Beverages, milk based (except dietary), manufacturing

312112	Beverages, naturally carbonated bottled water, manufacturing
312111	Beverages, soft drink (including artificially carbonated waters), manufacturing
422820	Beverages, wine and distilled spirits, wholesaling
312130	Beverages, wines and brandies, manufacturing
314999	Bias bindings made from purchased fabrics
813110	Bible societies
315999	Bibs and aprons, waterproof (e.g., plastics, rubber, similar materials), cut and sewn from purchased fabric (except apparel contractors)
315211	Bibs and aprons, waterproof (e.g., plastics, rubber, similar materials), men's and boys', cut and sew apparel contractors
315999	Bibs and aprons, waterproof (e.g., plastics, rubber, similar materials), rubberizing fabric and manufacturing bibs and aprons
315212	Bibs and aprons, waterproof (e.g., plastics, rubber, similar materials), women's, girls', and infants', cut and sew apparel contractors
315212	Bibs, waterproof, cut and sew apparel contractors
451110	Bicycle (except motorized) shops
453310	Bicycle (except motorized) shops, used
492210	Bicycle courier
532292	Bicycle rental
811490	Bicycle repair and maintenance shops without retailing new bicycles
441221	Bicycle shops, motorized
421910	Bicycles (except motorized) wholesaling
336991	Bicycles and parts manufacturing
421110	Bicycles, motorized, wholesaling
561440	Bill collection services
541850	Billboard display advertising services
339950	Billboards manufacturing
316993	Billfolds, all materials, manufacturing
339920	Billiard equipment and supplies manufacturing
421910	Billiard equipment and supplies wholesaling
713990	Billiard parlors
713990	Billiard rooms
541219	Billing services
422120	Binders, looseleaf, wholesaling
333293	Bindery machinery manufacturing
314999	Binding carpets and rugs for the trade
422310	Binding, textile, wholesaling
314999	Bindings, bias, made from purchased fabrics
313221	Bindings, narrow woven, manufacturing
713290	Bingo halls
713290	Bingo parlors
333314	Binoculars manufacturing
421460	Binoculars wholesaling
332439	Bins, metal, manufacturing
421390	Bins, storage, wholesaling
621498	Biofeedback centers and clinics, outpatient
339113	Biohazard protective clothing and accessories manufacturing
541380	Biological (except medical, veterinary) testing laboratories or services
541690	Biological consulting services
422210	Biologicals and allied products wholesaling
541710	Biology research and development laboratories or services
541710	Biotechnology research and development laboratories or services
311119	Bird feed, prepared, manufacturing
112990	Bird production (e.g., canaries, love birds, parakeets, parrots)
561710	Bird proofing services
712190	Bird sanctuaries
621410	Birth control clinics
326299	Birth control devices (i.e., diaphragms, prophylactics) manufacturing
325412	Birth control pills manufacturing
311812	Biscuits, bread-type, made in commercial bakeries

112990	Bison production
333515	Bits and knives for metalworking lathes, planers, and shapers manufacturing
333515	Bits, drill, metalworking, manufacturing
332212	Bits, edge tool, woodworking, manufacturing
333120	Bits, rock drill, construction and surface mining-type, manufacturing
333132	Bits, rock drill, oil and gas field-type, manufacturing
333131	Bits, rock drill, underground mining-type, manufacturing
212111	Bituminous coal and lignite surface mine site development for own account
212111	Bituminous coal or lignite beneficiating (e.g., cleaning, crushing, screening, washing)
213113	Bituminous coal or lignite surface mine site development on a contract basis
212111	Bituminous coal surface mining and/or beneficiating
212112	Bituminous coal underground mine site development for own account
212112	Bituminous coal underground mining or mining and beneficiating
212319	Bituminous limestone mining and/or beneficiating
212319	Bituminous sandstone mining and/or beneficiating
421510	Black plate wholesaling
111334	Blackberry farming
421490	Blackboards wholesaling
339942	Blackboards, framed, manufacturing
327991	Blackboards, unframed, slate, manufacturing
311312	Blackstrap invert made from purchased raw cane sugar
311311	Blackstrap molasses made in sugarcane mill
421710	Blades (e.g., knife, saw) wholesaling
332211	Blades, knife and razor, manufacturing
422210	Blades, razor, wholesaling
332213	Blades, saw, all types, manufacturing
334613	Blank tapes, audio and video, manufacturing
421690	Blank tapes, audio and video, wholesaling
323118	Blankbooks and refills manufacturing
422120	Blankbooks wholesaling
314129	Blankets (except electric) made from purchased fabrics or felts
421220	Blankets (except electric) wholesaling
313210	Blankets and bedspreads made in broadwoven fabric mills
335211	Blankets, electric, manufacturing
421620	Blankets, electric, wholesaling
327212	Blanks for electric light bulbs, glass, made in glass making plants
327215	Blanks, ophthalmic lens and optical glass, made from purchased glass
327212	Blanks, ophthalmic lens and optical glass, made in glass making plants
311411	Blast freezing on a contract basis
327992	Blast furnace slag processing
331111	Blast furnaces
325920	Blasting accessories (e.g., caps, fuses, ignitors, squibbs) manufacturing
325920	Blasting powders manufacturing
337127	Bleacher seating manufacturing
422690	Bleaches wholesaling
325612	Bleaches, formulated for household use, manufacturing
325188	Bleaching agents, inorganic, manufacturing
325199	Bleaching agents, organic, manufacturing
313311	Bleaching broadwoven fabrics
333292	Bleaching machinery for textiles manufacturing
313312	Bleaching textile products, apparel, and fabrics (except broadwoven)
311211	Blended flour made in flour mills
325620	Blending and compounding perfume bases

311119	Blending animal feed
312130	Blending brandy
312140	Blending distilled beverages (except brandy)
312130	Blending wines
336411	Blimps (i.e., aircraft) manufacturing
337920	Blinds (e.g., mini, venetian, vertical), all materials, manufacturing
421220	Blinds and shades, window, wholesaling
561910	Blister packaging services
333923	Block and tackle manufacturing
312113	Block ice manufacturing
324121	Blocks, asphalt paving, made from purchased asphaltic materials
327331	Blocks, concrete and cinder, manufacturing
327212	Blocks, glass, made in glass making plants
621511	Blood analysis laboratories
334516	Blood bank process equipment manufacturing
621991	Blood banks
325414	Blood derivatives manufacturing
422210	Blood derivatives wholesaling
621991	Blood donor stations
325413	Blood glucose test kits manufacturing
422210	Blood plasma wholesaling
339112	Blood pressure apparatus manufacturing
621999	Blood pressure screening facilities
621999	Blood pressure screening services
812990	Blood pressure testing machine concession operators, coin-operated
339111	Blood testing apparatus, laboratory-type, manufacturing
339112	Blood transfusion equipment manufacturing
315191	Blouses made in apparel knitting mills
315291	Blouses, infants', manufacturing
315212	Blouses, women's, girls', and infants', cut and sew apparel contractors
315232	Blouses, women's, misses', and girls', cut and sewn from purchased fabric (except apparel contractors)
335211	Blow dryers, household-type electric, manufacturing
333220	Blow molding machinery for plastics manufacturing
421830	Blowers, industrial, wholesaling
333112	Blowers, leaf, manufacturing
111334	Blueberry farming
114111	Bluefish fishing
541340	Blueprint drafting services
421420	Blueprinting equipment wholesaling
561439	Blueprinting services
921130	Board of Governors, Federal Reserve
327420	Board, gypsum, manufacturing
321219	Board, particle, manufacturing
115210	Boarding horses
721310	Boarding houses
611110	Boarding schools, elementary or secondary
812910	Boarding services, pet
813910	Boards of trade
324122	Boards, asphalt saturated, made from purchased asphaltic materials
321999	Boards, bulletin, wood and cork, manufacturing
321113	Boards, wood, made from logs or bolts
321912	Boards, wood, resawing purchased lumber
336321	Boat and ship lighting fixtures manufacturing
441222	Boat dealers, new and used
541330	Boat engineering design services
484220	Boat hauling, truck, local
484230	Boat hauling, truck, long-distance
333923	Boat lifts manufacturing
532411	Boat rental or leasing, commercial
532292	Boat rental, pleasure
336212	Boat transporter trailers, multi-unit, manufacturing
336214	Boat transporter trailers, single-unit, manufacturing
336612	Boat yards (i.e., boat manufacturing facilities)

http://www.ntis.gov/naics

487210	Boat, fishing charter, operation
811490	Boat, pleasure, repair and maintenance services without retailing new boats
713930	Boating clubs with marinas
713990	Boating clubs without marinas
421860	Boats (except pleasure) wholesaling
336612	Boats (i.e., suitable or intended for personal use) manufacturing
326199	Boats, inflatable plastics, manufacturing
421910	Boats, pleasure (e.g., canoes, motorboats, sailboats), wholesaling
333292	Bobbins, textile machinery, manufacturing
713990	Boccie ball courts
421110	Bodies, motor vehicle, wholesaling
713940	Body building studios, physical fitness
561612	Body guard services
811121	Body shops, automotive
235110	Boiler chipping, scaling, cleaning
235110	Boiler cleaning
811310	Boiler repair and maintenance shops (except manufacturing)
421720	Boilers (e.g., heating, hot water, power, steam) wholesaling
333414	Boilers, heating, manufacturing
332410	Boilers, power, manufacturing
332722	Bolts, metal, manufacturing
326199	Bolts, nuts, and rivets, plastics, manufacturing
332993	Bomb loading and assembling plants
332993	Bombs manufacturing
523110	Bond dealing (i.e., acting as a principal in dealing securities to investors)
493190	Bonded warehousing (except farm products, general merchandise, refrigerated)
493130	Bonded warehousing, farm products (except refrigerated)
493110	Bonded warehousing, general merchandise
493120	Bonded warehousing, refrigerated
524126	Bonding, fidelity or surety insurance, direct
812990	Bondsperson services
325182	Bone black manufacturing
327112	Bone china manufacturing
311119	Bone meal prepared as feed for animals and fowls
339999	Bone novelties manufacturing
339112	Bone plates and screws manufacturing
323121	Book binding shops
323121	Book binding without printing
454110	Book clubs, not publishing, mail-order
813410	Book discussion clubs
322222	Book paper made by coating purchased paper
322222	Book paper, coated, made from purchased paper
322121	Book paper, coated, made in paper mills
511130	Book publishers (e.g., hardback, paperback, tape)
511130	Book publishers and printing combined
511130	Book publishers publishing all formats
451211	Book stores
453310	Book stores, used
333293	Bookbinding machines manufacturing
323121	Bookbinding without printing
337125	Bookcases (except wood and metal), household-type, manufacturing
337214	Bookcases (except wood), office-type, manufacturing
337124	Bookcases, metal household-type, manufacturing
337122	Bookcases, wood household-type, manufacturing
337211	Bookcases, wood office-type, manufacturing
713290	Bookies
512199	Booking agencies, motion picture
512199	Booking agencies, motion picture or video productions
711320	Booking agencies, theatrical (except motion picture)

http://www.ntis.gov/naics

541219   Bookkeepers' offices
421420   Bookkeeping machines wholesaling
541219   Bookkeeping services
713290   Bookmakers
323117   Books printing and binding without publishing
323117   Books printing without publishing
422920   Books wholesaling
422120   Books, sales or receipt, wholesaling
323116   Books, sales, manifold, printing
813410   Booster clubs
421850   Boot and shoe cut stock and findings wholesaling
316999   Boot and shoe cut stock and findings, leather, manufacturing
316219   Boots, dress and casual (except plastics, rubber), children's and infants', manufacturing
316213   Boots, dress and casual (except plastics, rubber), men's, manufacturing
316214   Boots, dress and casual (except plastics, rubber), women's, manufacturing
316219   Boots, hiking (except rubber, plastics), children's and infants', manufacturing
316213   Boots, hiking (except rubber, plastics), men's, manufacturing
316214   Boots, hiking (except rubber, plastics), women's, manufacturing
316211   Boots, plastics or plastics soled fabric upper, manufacturing
316211   Boots, rubber or rubber soled fabric upper, manufacturing
212391   Borate, natural, mining and/or beneficiating
325320   Bordeaux mixture insecticides manufacturing
333512   Boring machines, metalworking, manufacturing
333512   Boring, drilling, and milling machine combinations, metalworking, manufacturing
212391   Boron compounds prepared at beneficiating plants
325188   Boron compounds, not specified elsewhere by process, manufacturing

212391   Boron mineral mining and/or beneficiating
712130   Botanical gardens
325320   Botanical insecticides manufacturing
422210   Botanicals wholesaling
541710   Botany research and development laboratories or services
326199   Bottle caps and lids, plastics, manufacturing
332115   Bottle caps and tops, metal, stamping
561990   Bottle exchanges
454312   Bottled gas dealers, direct selling
422490   Bottled water (except water treating) wholesaling
454390   Bottled water providers, direct selling
421840   Bottles (except waste) wholesaling
327213   Bottles (i.e., bottling, canning, packaging), glass, manufacturing
326160   Bottles, plastics, manufacturing
332439   Bottles, vacuum, manufacturing
421930   Bottles, waste, wholesaling
312111   Bottling flavored water
333993   Bottling machinery (e.g., capping, filling, labeling, sterilizing, washing) manufacturing
421830   Bottling machinery and equipment wholesaling
311422   Bouillon canning
311423   Bouillon made in dehydration plants
422590   Bovine semen wholesaling
713950   Bowling alleys
713950   Bowling centers
421910   Bowling equipment and supplies wholesaling
451110   Bowling equipment and supply stores
713990   Bowling leagues or teams, recreational
339920   Bowling pin machines, automatic, manufacturing
326199   Bowls and bowl covers, plastics, manufacturing
321920   Box shook manufacturing
337910   Box springs, assembled, made from purchased spring
311612   Boxed beef made from purchased carcasses

http://www.ntis.gov/naics

311611	Boxed beef produced in slaughtering plants
311612	Boxed meat produced from purchased carcasses
311611	Boxed meats produced in slaughtering plants
711219	Boxers, independent professional
421840	Boxes and crates, industrial (except disposable plastics, paperboard, waste), wholesaling
322211	Boxes, corrugated and solid fiber, made from purchased paper or paperboard
335932	Boxes, electrical wiring (e.g., junction, outlet, switch), manufacturing
322212	Boxes, folding (except corrugated), made from purchased paperboard
332439	Boxes, light gauge metal, manufacturing
422130	Boxes, paperboard and disposable plastics, wholesaling
322215	Boxes, sanitary food (except folding), made from purchased paper or paperboard
322213	Boxes, setup (i.e., not shipped flat), made from purchased paperboard
322211	Boxes, shipping, laminated paper and paperboard, made from purchased paperboard
336211	Boxes, truck (e.g., cargo, dump, utility, van), assembled on purchased chassis
421930	Boxes, waste, wholesaling
321920	Boxes, wood, manufacturing
711211	Boxing clubs, professional or semiprofessional
713990	Boxing clubs, recreational
337215	Boxspring frames manufacturing
813410	Boy guiding organizations
611620	Boys' camps, sports instruction
611620	Boys' camps, sports instructor
315119	Boys' socks manufacturing
115112	Bracing of orchard trees and vines
332510	Brackets (i.e., builder's hardware-type), metal, manufacturing
339911	Bracelets, precious metal, manufacturing
421710	Brads wholesaling
332618	Brads, metal, made from purchased wire
313221	Braiding narrow fabrics
336340	Brake and brake parts, automotive, truck, and bus, manufacturing
336340	Brake caliper assemblies, automotive, truck, and bus, manufacturing
336340	Brake cylinders, master and wheel, automotive, truck, and bus, manufacturing
336340	Brake discs (rotor), automotive, truck, and bus, manufacturing
336340	Brake drums, automotive, truck, and bus, manufacturing
325998	Brake fluid, synthetic, manufacturing
324191	Brake fluids, petroleum, made from refined petroleum
336340	Brake hose assemblies manufacturing
336340	Brake lining, automotive, truck, and bus, manufacturing
336340	Brake pads and shoes, automotive, truck, and bus, manufacturing
811118	Brake repair shops, automotive
333613	Brakes and clutches (except electromagnetic industrial controls, motor vehicle) manufacturing
335314	Brakes and clutches, electromagnetic, manufacturing
336510	Brakes and parts for railroad rolling stock manufacturing
335314	Brakes, electromagnetic, manufacturing
311212	Bran and other residues of milling rice
522110	Branches of foreign banks
521110	Branches, Federal Reserve Bank
533110	Brand name licensing
115210	Branding
312130	Brandy distilling
331522	Brass die-castings, unfinished, manufacturing
331525	Brass foundries (except die-casting)
421720	Brass goods, plumbers', wholesaling
315212	Brassieres cut and sew apparel contractors

315231	Brassieres cut and sewn from purchased fabric (except apparel contractors)
332323	Brasswork, ornamental, manufacturing
332811	Brazing (i.e., hardening) metals and metal products for the trade
311822	Bread and bread-type roll mixes made from purchased flour
311812	Bread and bread-type rolls made in commercial bakeries
335211	Bread machines, household-type electric, manufacturing
311340	Breakfast bars, nonchocolate covered, manufacturing
311230	Breakfast cereals manufacturing
422490	Breakfast cereals wholesaling
112990	Breeding of pets (e.g., birds, cats, dogs)
312120	Breweries
311211	Brewers' and distillers' flakes and grits, corn, manufacturing
311213	Brewers' malt manufacturing
311212	Brewers' rice manufacturing
333294	Brewery machinery manufacturing
421320	Bricks (except refractory) wholesaling
327121	Bricks (i.e., common, face, glazed, hollow, vitrified), clay, manufacturing
327123	Bricks, adobe, manufacturing
327124	Bricks, clay refractory, manufacturing
327331	Bricks, concrete, manufacturing
327215	Bricks, glass, made from purchased glass
327212	Bricks, glass, made in glass making plants
327125	Bricks, nonclay refractory, manufacturing
235410	Bricklaying construction contractors
315233	Bridal dresses or gowns, custom made
315233	Bridal dresses or gowns, women's, misses', and girls', cut and sewn from purchased fabric (except apparel contractors)

448190	Bridal gown shops (except custom)
532220	Bridal wear rental
333999	Bridge and gate lifting machinery manufacturing
611699	Bridge and other card game instruction
713990	Bridge clubs, recreational
234120	Bridge construction
235210	Bridge painting construction contractors
332312	Bridge sections, prefabricated metal, manufacturing
488490	Bridge, tunnel, and highway operations
339116	Bridges, custom made in dental laboratories
316991	Briefcases, all materials, manufacturing
315291	Briefs, infants', cut and sewn from purchased fabric (except apparel contractors)
315192	Briefs, underwear, made in apparel knitting mills
315211	Briefs, underwear, men's and boys', cut and sew apparel contractors
315221	Briefs, underwear, men's and boys', cut and sewn from purchased fabric (except apparel contractors)
315231	Briefs, underwear, women's, misses', and girls', cut and sewn from purchased fabric (except apparel contractors)
315212	Briefs, women's, girls', and infants', cut and sew apparel contractors
311421	Brining of fruits and vegetables
324199	Briquettes, petroleum, made from refined petroleum
422590	Bristles wholesaling
333512	Broaching machines, metalworking, manufacturing
334220	Broadcast equipment (including studio), for radio and television, manufacturing
541910	Broadcast media rating services
421690	Broadcasting equipment wholesaling
513111	Broadcasting networks, radio
513120	Broadcasting networks, television

http://www.ntis.gov/naics

611519	Broadcasting schools
513112	Broadcasting stations, radio
513120	Broadcasting stations, television
513112	Broadcasting studio, radio station
711110	Broadway theaters
313210	Broadwoven fabrics (except rugs, tire fabrics) weaving
313311	Broadwoven fabrics finishing
111219	Broccoli farming, field, bedding plant and seed production
112320	Broiler chicken production
523140	Brokerages, commodity contracts
524210	Brokerages, insurance
522310	Brokerages, loan
522310	Brokerages, mortgage
531210	Brokerages, real estate
523120	Brokerages, securities
531210	Brokers' offices, real estate
325188	Bromine manufacturing
331525	Bronze foundries (except die-casting)
422590	Broomcorn wholesaling
421220	Brooms and brushes, household-type, wholesaling
339994	Brooms, hand and machine, manufacturing
311422	Broth (except seafood) canning
311313	Brown beet sugar refining
311313	Brown sugar made from beet sugar
311312	Brown sugar made from purchased raw cane sugar
311311	Brown sugar made in sugarcane mill
562119	Brush collection services
562119	Brush hauling, local
562119	Brush removal services
335991	Brushes and brush stock contacts, electric, carbon and graphite, manufacturing
339942	Brushes, artists', manufacturing
339994	Brushes, household-type and industrial, manufacturing
339994	Brushes, paint (except artists'), manufacturing
335991	Brushplates, carbon or graphite, manufacturing
111219	Brussel sprout farming, field, bedding plant and seed production
339993	Buckles and buckle parts (including shoe) manufacturing
333512	Buffing and polishing machines, metalworking, manufacturing
327910	Buffing and polishing wheels, abrasive and nonabrasive, manufacturing
325612	Buffing compounds manufacturing
332813	Buffing metals and metal products for the trade
332510	Builder's hardware, metal, manufacturing
233320	Building alterations, nonresidential, commercial and institutional buildings, general construction contractors
233220	Building alterations, residential (except single family), general construction contractors
233210	Building alterations, single family, general construction contractors
541310	Building architectural design services
421310	Building board (e.g., fiber, flake, particle) wholesaling
561720	Building cleaning services, interior
561720	Building cleaning services, janitorial
233220	Building construction, residential (except single family), general construction contractors
233210	Building construction, single family, general construction contractors
561790	Building exterior cleaning services (except sand blasting, window cleaning)
235910	Building front metal, construction contractors
541350	Building inspection bureaus
541350	Building inspection services
926150	Building inspections, government
326199	Building materials (e.g., fascia, panels, siding, soffit), plastics, manufacturing
444190	Building materials supply dealers
421390	Building materials, fiberglass (except insulation, roofing, siding), wholesaling
421390	Building paper wholesaling
925110	Building standards agencies, government

421320	Building stone wholesaling
531110	Building, apartment, rental or leasing
213112	Building, erecting, repairing, and dismantling oil and gas field rigs and derricks on a contract basis
531120	Building, nonresidential (except miniwarehouse), rental or leasing
531110	Building, residential, rental or leasing
321992	Buildings, prefabricated and portable, wood, manufacturing
332311	Buildings, prefabricated metal, manufacturing
421390	Buildings, prefabricated nonwood, wholesaling
421310	Buildings, prefabricated wood, wholesaling
327999	Built-up mica manufacturing
335110	Bulbs, electric light, complete, manufacturing
422710	Bulk gasoline stations
484220	Bulk liquids trucking, local
484230	Bulk liquids trucking, long-distance
484110	Bulk mail truck transportation, contract, local
484121	Bulk mail truck transportation, contract, long-distance
493190	Bulk petroleum storage
422710	Bulk stations, petroleum
332420	Bulk storage tanks, heavy gauge metal, manufacturing
115210	Bull testing stations
532412	Bulldozer rental or leasing without operator
333120	Bulldozers manufacturing
321999	Bulletin boards, wood and cork, manufacturing
339113	Bulletproof vests manufacturing
212221	Bullion, gold, produced at the mine
212222	Bullion, silver, produced at the mine
336399	Bumpers and bumperettes assembled, automotive, truck, and bus, manufacturing
561621	Burglar alarm monitoring services
561621	Burglar alarm sales combined with installation, maintenance, or monitoring services
334290	Burglar alarm systems and equipment manufacturing
339995	Burial caskets and cases manufacturing
421850	Burial caskets wholesaling
315299	Burial garments cut and sewn from purchased fabric (except apparel contractors)
339995	Burial vaults (except concrete, stone) manufacturing
327390	Burial vaults, concrete and precast terrazzo, manufacturing
327991	Burial vaults, stone, manufacturing
422990	Burlap wholesaling
711110	Burlesque companies
335311	Burner ignition transformers manufacturing
421720	Burners, fuel oil and distillate oil, wholesaling
333414	Burners, heating, manufacturing
332811	Burning metals and metal products for the trade
321999	Burnt wood articles manufacturing
314999	Burnt-out laces manufacturing
112920	Burro production
335313	Bus bar structures, switchgear-type, manufacturing
335931	Bus bars, electrical conductors (except switchgear-type), manufacturing
336211	Bus bodies assembling on purchased chassis
336211	Bus bodies manufacturing
541850	Bus card advertising services
485510	Bus charter services (except scenic, sightseeing)
541850	Bus display advertising services
485210	Bus line operation, intercity
485113	Bus line, local (except mixed mode)
485410	Bus operation, school and employee
485113	Bus services, urban and suburban (except mixed mode)
488490	Bus terminal operation, independent
561599	Bus ticket offices
336120	Buses (except trackless trolley) assembling on chassis of own manufacture
421110	Buses wholesaling
487110	Buses, scenic and sightseeing operation
336510	Buses, trackless trolley, manufacturing

333613	Bushings, plain (except internal combustion engine), manufacturing
813910	Business associations
611310	Business colleges or schools offering baccalaureate or graduate degrees
323112	Business directories flexographic printing without publishing
323111	Business directories gravure printing without publishing
323110	Business directories lithographic (offset) printing without publishing
323119	Business directories printing (except flexographic, gravure, lithographic, screen) without publishing
323113	Business directories screen printing without publishing
511140	Business directory publishers
511140	Business directory publishers and printing combined
323112	Business forms (except manifold) flexographic printing without publishing
323111	Business forms (except manifold) gravure printing without publishing
323110	Business forms (except manifold) lithographic printing
323119	Business forms (except manifold) printing (except flexographic, gravure, lithographic, screen) without publishing
323113	Business forms (except manifold) screen printing without publishing
323116	Business forms, manifold, printing
421420	Business machines and equipment (except computers) wholesaling
541611	Business management consulting services
561110	Business management services
541720	Business research and development services
611410	Business schools not offering academic degrees
561439	Business service centers (except private mail centers)
561439	Business service centers (except private mail centers) providing range of office support services (except printing)

541611	Business start-up consulting services
325110	Butadiene made from refined petroleum or liquid hydrocarbons
325212	Butadiene rubber (i.e., polybutadiene) manufacturing
325110	Butane made from refined petroleum or liquid hydrocarbons
445210	Butcher shops
311512	Butter manufacturing
422430	Butter wholesaling
311512	Butter, creamery and whey, manufacturing
332911	Butterfly valves, industrial-type, manufacturing
311511	Buttermilk manufacturing
339993	Buttons (except precious metal, precious stones, semiprecious stones) manufacturing
339911	Buttons, precious metal, precious stones, semiprecious stones, manufacturing
325212	Butyl rubber manufacturing
324110	Butylene (i.e., butene) made in petroleum refineries
325110	Butylene made from refined petroleum or liquid hydrocarbons
531210	Buying real estate for others (i.e., agents, brokers)
541512	CAD (computer-aided design) systems integration design services
541512	CAE (computer-aided engineering) systems integration design services
541512	CAM (computer-aided manufacturing) systems integration design services
334220	CB (citizens band) radios manufacturing
334112	CD-ROM drives manufacturing
334611	CD-ROM, software, mass reproducing
525990	CMOs (collateralized mortgage obligations)
541211	CPAs' (certified public accountants) offices
334411	CRT (cathode ray tube) manufacturing
621512	CT-SCAN (computer tomography) centers

334517	CT/CAT (computerized axial tomography) scanners manufacturing
485310	Cab (i.e., taxi) services
336112	Cab and chassis, light trucks and vans, manufacturing
111219	Cabbage farming, field, bedding plant and seed production
336612	Cabin cruiser
332510	Cabinet hardware, metal, manufacturing
444190	Cabinet stores, kitchen (except custom), to be installed
337129	Cabinets (i.e., housings), wood (e.g., sewing machines, stereo, television), manufacturing
337110	Cabinets, kitchen (except freestanding), stock or custom wood, manufacturing
421310	Cabinets, kitchen, built in, wholesaling
421210	Cabinets, kitchen, free standing, wholesaling
337124	Cabinets, metal (i.e., bathroom, kitchen) (except freestanding), manufacturing
337124	Cabinets, metal household-type, freestanding, manufacturing
337124	Cabinets, metal, radio and television, manufacturing
337122	Cabinets, wood household-type, freestanding, manufacturing
513220	Cable TV providers (except networks)
513210	Cable broadcasting networks
485119	Cable car systems (except mixed mode), commuter
487110	Cable car, land, scenic and sightseeing operation
334220	Cable decoders manufacturing
234920	Cable laying
513220	Cable program distribution operators
234920	Cable television line construction
513210	Cable television networks
334220	Cable television transmission and receiving equipment manufacturing
331422	Cable, copper (e.g., armored, bare, insulated), made from purchased copper in wire drawing plants
331422	Cable, copper (e.g., armored, bare, insulated), made in integrated secondary smelting and drawing plants
335929	Cable, nonferrous, insulated, or armored, made from purchased nonferrous wire
332618	Cable, noninsulated wire, made from purchased wire
421510	Cable, wire (except insulated), wholesaling
333111	Cabs for agricultural machinery manufacturing
333120	Cabs for construction machinery manufacturing
333924	Cabs for industrial trucks manufacturing
111339	Cactus fruit farming
541370	Cadastral surveying services
337215	Cafeteria fixtures manufacturing
722310	Cafeteria food service contractors (e.g., government office cafeterias, hospital cafeterias, school cafeterias)
337127	Cafeteria tables and benches manufacturing
722212	Cafeterias
332618	Cages made from purchased wire
311999	Cake frosting manufacturing
311999	Cake frosting mixes manufacturing
311822	Cake mixes made from purchased flour
311340	Cake ornaments, confectionery, manufacturing
311813	Cake, frozen, manufacturing
311812	Cakes, baking (except frozen), made in commercial bakeries
212312	Calcareous tufa crushed and broken stone mining and/or beneficiating
324199	Calcining petroleum coke from refined petroleum
327410	Calcium hydroxide (i.e., hydrated lime) manufacturing
325188	Calcium hypochlorite manufacturing
325188	Calcium inorganic compounds, not specified elsewhere by process, manufacturing

325199	Calcium organic compounds, not specified elsewhere by process, manufacturing
327410	Calcium oxide (i.e., quicklime) manufacturing
421420	Calculators and calculating machines wholesaling
333313	Calculators manufacturing
511199	Calendar publishers
511199	Calendar publishers and printing combined
453998	Calendar shops
323112	Calendars flexographic printing without publishing
323111	Calendars gravure printing without publishing
323110	Calendars lithographic (offset) printing without publishing
323119	Calendars printing (except flexographic, lithographic, gravure, screen) without publishing
323113	Calendars screen printing without publishing
313311	Calendering broadwoven fabrics
333220	Calendering machinery for plastics manufacturing
333292	Calendering machinery for textiles manufacturing
313312	Calendering textile products, apparel, and fabrics (except broadwoven)
112111	Calf (e.g., feeder, stocker, veal) production
541380	Calibration and certification testing laboratories or services
336340	Calipers, brake, automotive, truck, and bus, manufacturing
334310	Camcorders manufacturing
326211	Camelback (i.e., retreading material) manufacturing
333220	Camelback (i.e., retreading materials) machinery manufacturing
316991	Camera carrying bags, all materials, manufacturing
421410	Camera equipment and supplies, photographic, wholesaling

333314	Camera lenses manufacturing
811211	Camera repair shops without retailing new cameras
443130	Camera shops, photographic
711510	Cameramen, independent (freelance)
333315	Cameras (except digital, television, video) manufacturing
334220	Cameras, television, manufacturing
337125	Camp furniture, reed and rattan, manufacturing
813940	Campaign organizations, political
441210	Camper dealers, recreational
336214	Camper units, slide-in, for pick-up trucks, manufacturing
721211	Campgrounds
421910	Camping equipment and supplies wholesaling
336214	Camping trailers and chassis manufacturing
421110	Camping trailers wholesaling
721214	Camps (except day, instructional)
713990	Camps (except instructional), day
623990	Camps, boot or disciplinary (except correctional), for delinquent youth
611620	Camps, sports instruction
333513	Can forming machines, metalworking, manufacturing
332431	Can lids and ends, metal, manufacturing
332212	Can openers (except electric) manufacturing
335211	Can openers, household-type electric, manufacturing
483211	Canal barge transportation
234990	Canal construction
488310	Canal maintenance services (except dredging)
488310	Canal operation
483212	Canal passenger transportation
541710	Cancer research laboratories or services
311340	Candied fruits and fruit peel manufacturing
453998	Candle shops
339999	Candles manufacturing
422990	Candles wholesaling
311320	Candy bars, chocolate (including chocolate covered), made from cacao beans

311340 Candy bars, nonchocolate, manufacturing

311330 Candy stores, chocolate, candy made on premises not for immediate consumption

311340 Candy stores, nonchocolate, candy made on premises, not for immediate consumption

445292 Candy stores, packaged, retailing only

422450 Candy wholesaling

311320 Candy, chocolate, made from cacao beans

111930 Cane farming, sugar, field production

311312 Cane sugar made from purchased raw cane sugar

311311 Cane sugar made in sugarcane mill

422490 Cane sugar, refined, wholesaling

311312 Cane syrup made from purchased raw cane sugar

311311 Cane syrup made in sugarcane mill

339999 Canes (except orthopedic) manufacturing

332993 Canisters, ammunition, manufacturing

422490 Canned foods (e.g., fish, meat, seafood, soups) wholesaling

311611 Canned meats (except poultry) produced in slaughtering plants

311911 Canned nuts manufacturing

311711 Cannery, fish

311711 Cannery, shellfish

311421 Canning fruits and vegetables

311421 Canning jams and jellies

333993 Canning machinery manufacturing

311615 Canning poultry (except baby and pet food)

311422 Canning soups (except seafood)

421840 Canning supplies wholesaling

311711 Canning, fish, crustacea, and molluscs

332995 Cannons manufacturing

532292 Canoe rental

713990 Canoeing, recreational

311225 Canola (rapeseed) oil, cake and meal, made from purchased oils

311223 Canola (rapeseed) oil, cake and meal, made in crushing mills

111120 Canola farming, field and seed production

332322 Canopies, sheet metal, manufacturing

332431 Cans, aluminum, manufacturing

332431 Cans, metal, manufacturing

332431 Cans, steel, manufacturing

111219 Cantaloupe farming, field, bedding plant and seed production

722213 Canteens, fixed location

722330 Canteens, mobile

314911 Canvas bags manufacturing

314912 Canvas products (except bags) made from purchased canvas or canvas substitutes

422990 Canvas products wholesaling

316211 Canvas shoes, plastics soled fabric upper, manufacturing

316211 Canvas shoes, rubber soled fabric upper, manufacturing

454390 Canvassers (door-to-door), headquarters for retail sale of merchandise, direct selling

335999 Capacitors (except electronic), fixed and variable, manufacturing

334414 Capacitors, electronic, fixed and variable, manufacturing

421690 Capacitors, electronic, wholesaling

333993 Capping, sealing, and lidding packaging machinery manufacturing

325199 Caprolactam manufacturing

315991 Caps (except fur, leather) cut and sewn from purchased fabric (except apparel contractors)

315991 Caps (i.e., apparel accessory) cut and sewn from purchased fabric (except fur, leather, apparel contractors)

315211 Caps (i.e., apparel accessory), men's and boys', cut and sew apparel contractors

315212 Caps (i.e., apparel accessory), women's, girls', and infants', cut and sew apparel contractors

315299 Caps and gowns, academic, cut and sewn from purchased fabric (except apparel contractors)

315211	Caps and gowns, academic, men's and boys', cut and sew apparel contractors
315212	Caps and gowns, academic, women's and girls', cut and sew apparel contractors
332115	Caps and tops, bottle, metal, stamping
336214	Caps for pick-up trucks manufacturing
315191	Caps made in apparel knitting mills
325920	Caps, blasting and detonating, manufacturing
334290	Car alarm manufacturing
336211	Car bodies, kit, manufacturing
811192	Car detailers
532112	Car leasing
483212	Car lighters (i.e., ferries), inland waters (except on Great Lakes system)
488999	Car pools, arrangement of
532111	Car rental
532111	Car rental agencies
561599	Car rental reservation services
811111	Car repair shops, general
337125	Car seats, infant (except metal), manufacturing
334310	Car stereos manufacturing
421850	Car wash equipment and supplies wholesaling
811192	Car washes
325188	Carbides (e.g., boron, calcium, silicon, tungsten) manufacturing
325182	Carbon black manufacturing
325120	Carbon dioxide manufacturing
335991	Carbon electrodes and contacts, electric, manufacturing
325188	Carbon inorganic compounds manufacturing
334290	Carbon monoxide detectors manufacturing
421690	Carbon monoxide detectors, electronic, wholesaling
325199	Carbon organic compounds, not specified elsewhere by process, manufacturing
339944	Carbon paper manufacturing
335991	Carbon specialties for aerospace use (except gaskets) manufacturing

335991	Carbon specialties for electrical use manufacturing
335991	Carbon specialties for mechanical use (except gaskets) manufacturing
325998	Carbon, activated, manufacturing
312111	Carbonated soda manufacturing
312111	Carbonated soft drinks manufacturing
313312	Carbonizing textile fibers
336311	Carburetors, all types, manufacturing
713290	Card rooms (e.g., poker rooms)
453220	Card shops, greeting
313111	Carded yarn manufacturing
325412	Cardiac preparations manufacturing
333292	Carding machinery for textiles manufacturing
313312	Carding textile fibers
323112	Cards (e.g., business, greeting, playing, postcards, trading) flexographic printing without publishing
323111	Cards (e.g., business, greeting, playing, postcards, trading) gravure printing without publishing
323110	Cards (e.g., business, greeting, playing, postcards, trading) lithographic (offset) printing without publishing
323119	Cards (e.g., business, greeting, playing, postcards, trading) printing (except flexographic, gravure, lithographic, screen) without publishing
323113	Cards (e.g., business, greeting, playing, postcards, trading) screen printing without publishing
322299	Cards, die-cut (except office supply) made from purchased paper or paperboard
322231	Cards, die-cut office supply (e.g., index, library, time recording), made from purchased paper or paperboard
422120	Cards, greeting, wholesaling
******	Cards, publishing—see specific product

481112	Cargo carriers, air, scheduled
488390	Cargo checkers, marine
336611	Cargo ship building
488390	Cargo surveyors, marine
488490	Cargo surveyors, truck transportation
333319	Carnival and amusement park rides manufacturing
333319	Carnival and amusement park shooting gallery machinery manufacturing
421850	Carnival equipment wholesaling
713990	Carnival ride concession operators (i.e., supplying and servicing in others' facilities)
711190	Carnival traveling shows
333922	Carousel conveyors (e.g., luggage) manufacturing
332212	Carpenter's handtools, nonelectric (except saws), manufacturing
235510	Carpentry (rough and framing) construction contractors
235510	Carpentry (trim and finish) construction contractors
333319	Carpet and floor cleaning equipment, electric commercial-type, manufacturing
335212	Carpet and floor cleaning equipment, household-type electric, manufacturing
532490	Carpet and rug cleaning equipment rental or leasing
313111	Carpet and rug yarn spinning
561740	Carpet cleaning services
314999	Carpet cutting and binding
235520	Carpet laying or removal construction contractors
313230	Carpet paddings, nonwoven, manufacturing
442210	Carpet stores
333319	Carpet sweepers, mechanical, manufacturing
421220	Carpet wholesaling
314110	Carpets and rugs made from textile materials
487110	Carriage, horse-drawn, operation
334210	Carrier equipment (i.e., analog, digital), telephone, manufacturing
111219	Carrot farming, field, bedding plant and seed production
311991	Carrots, cut, peeled or sliced fresh, manufacturing
722211	Carryout restaurants
336111	Cars, electric, for highway use, assembling on chassis of own manufacture
333131	Cars, mining, manufacturing
541370	Cartographic surveying services
333993	Carton filling machinery manufacturing
322299	Cartons, egg, molded pulp manufacturing
322212	Cartons, folding (except milk), made from purchased paperboard
322215	Cartons, milk, made from purchased paper or paperboard
711510	Cartoonists, independent
422120	Cartridge toner wholesaling
332992	Cartridges (i.e., 30 mm. or less, 1.18 inch or less) manufacturing
333924	Carts, grocery, made from purchased wire
333319	Carwashing machinery manufacturing
311514	Casein, dry and wet, manufacturing
316991	Cases, musical instrument, manufacturing
333313	Cash registers (i.e., point of sales terminals) manufacturing
421420	Cash registers wholesaling
326121	Casings, sausage, nonrigid plastics, manufacturing
332322	Casings, sheet metal, manufacturing
233320	Casino construction
721120	Casino hotels
713210	Casinos (except casino hotels)
332510	Casket hardware, metal, manufacturing
339995	Caskets, burial, manufacturing
421850	Caskets, burial, wholesaling
334612	Cassette tapes, pre-recorded audio, mass reproducing
421990	Cassettes, prerecorded audio and video, wholesaling
331511	Cast iron pipe and pipe fittings manufacturing
421510	Cast iron pipe wholesaling
327390	Cast stone, concrete (except structural), manufacturing

332510	Casters, furniture, manufacturing
561310	Casting agencies (i.e., motion picture, theatrical, video)
561310	Casting bureaus (e.g., motion picture, theatrical, video)
331528	Castings (except die-castings), nonferrous metals (except aluminum, copper), unfinished manufacturing
331524	Castings (except die-castings), unfinished, aluminum, manufacturing
331525	Castings (except die-castings), unfinished, copper, manufacturing
331513	Castings, steel (except investment), unfinished, manufacturing
331511	Castings, unfinished iron (e.g., ductile, gray, malleable, semisteel), manufacturing
311223	Castor oil and pomace made in crushing mills
316213	Casual shoes (except athletic, plastic, rubber), men's, manufacturing
316214	Casual shoes (except athletic, rubber, plastic), women's, manufacturing
316219	Casual shoes (except rubber, plastics), children's and infants', manufacturing
524126	Casualty insurance carriers, direct
311111	Cat food manufacturing
325998	Cat litter manufacturing
112990	Cat production
511199	Catalog (i.e., mail order, store merchandise) publishers
511199	Catalog (i.e., mail order, store merchandise) publishers and printing combined
454110	Catalog (i.e., order taking) offices of mail-order houses
511140	Catalog of collections publishers
511140	Catalog of collections publishers and printing combined
452990	Catalog showrooms, general merchandise (except catalog mail-order)
323112	Catalogs flexographic printing without publishing
323111	Catalogs gravure printing without publishing
323110	Catalogs lithographic (offset) printing without publishing
323112	Catalogs of collections flexographic printing without publishing
323111	Catalogs of collections gravure printing without publishing
323110	Catalogs of collections lithographic (offset) printing without publishing
323119	Catalogs of collections printing (except flexographic, gravure, lithographic, screen) without publishing
323113	Catalogs of collections screen printing without publishing
323119	Catalogs printing (except flexographic, gravure, lithographic, screen) without publishing
323113	Catalogs screen printing without publishing
336399	Catalytic converters, engine exhaust, automotive, truck, and buses manufacturing
562998	Catch basin cleaning services
722320	Caterers
112511	Catfish production, farm raising
325412	Cathartic preparations manufacturing
339112	Catheters manufacturing
334411	Cathode ray tubes (CRT) manufacturing
311421	Catsup manufacturing
112111	Cattle farming or ranching
112112	Cattle feedlots (except stockyards for transportation)
311119	Cattle feeds, supplements, concentrates, and premixes, manufacturing
422520	Cattle wholesaling
111219	Cauliflower farming, field, bedding plant and seed production
325520	Caulking compounds (except gypsum base) manufacturing
332212	Caulking guns, nonpowered, manufacturing
422690	Caulking materials wholesaling
325181	Caustic soda (i.e., sodium hydroxide) manufacturing

422690	Caustic soda wholesaling
712190	Caverns (i.e., natural wonder tourist attractions)
235420	Ceiling construction contractors
444190	Ceiling fan stores
335211	Ceiling fans, residential, manufacturing
335122	Ceiling lighting fixtures, commercial, industrial, and institutional, manufacturing
335121	Ceiling lighting fixtures, residential, manufacturing
711410	Celebrities' agents or managers
711510	Celebrity spokespersons, independent
111219	Celery farming, field, bedding plant and seed production
212393	Celestite mining and/or beneficiating
325221	Cellophane film or sheet manufacturing
422120	Cellophane tape wholesaling
513322	Cellular telephone communication carriers
334220	Cellular telephones manufacturing
421690	Cellular telephones wholesaling
325211	Cellulose resins manufacturing
325221	Cellulosic fibers and filaments manufacturing
325221	Cellulosic filament yarn manufacturing
325221	Cellulosic staple fibers manufacturing
327310	Cement (e.g., hydraulic, masonry, portland, pozzolana) manufacturing
327310	Cement clinker manufacturing
212312	Cement rock crushed and broken stone mining and/or beneficiating
421320	Cement wholesaling
327420	Cement, Keene's (i.e., tiling plaster), manufacturing
325520	Cement, rubber, manufacturing
421830	Cement-making machinery wholesaling
213112	Cementing oil and gas well casings on a contract basis
324122	Cements, asphalt roofing, made from purchased asphaltic materials
339114	Cements, dental, manufacturing
812220	Cemetery associations (i.e., operators)
812220	Cemeteries
453998	Cemetery memorial dealers (e.g., headstones, markers, vaults)
561730	Cemetery plot care services
421730	Central heating equipment, warm-air, wholesaling
325412	Central nervous system stimulant preparations manufacturing
334210	Central office and switching equipment, telephone, manufacturing
335212	Central vacuuming systems, household-type, manufacturing
327320	Central-mixed concrete manufacturing
551114	Centralized administrative offices
333911	Centrifugal pumps manufacturing
333999	Centrifuges, industrial-type, manufacturing
325411	Cephalosporin, uncompounded, manufacturing
325131	Ceramic colors manufacturing
421320	Ceramic construction materials (except refractory) wholesaling
327999	Ceramic fiber manufacturing
333994	Ceramic kilns and furnaces manufacturing
444190	Ceramic tile stores
327122	Ceramic tiles, floor and wall, manufacturing
311211	Cereal grain flour manufacturing
422490	Cereal products wholesaling
541710	Cerebral palsy research laboratories or services
523120	Certificate of deposit (CD) brokers' offices
523930	Certified financial planners, customized, fees paid by client
541211	Certified public accountants' (CPAs) offices
325188	Cesium and cesium compounds, not specified elsewhere by process, manufacturing

562991	Cesspool cleaning services
332323	Chain ladders, metal, manufacturing
332618	Chain link fencing and fence gates made from purchased wire
332618	Chain made from purchased wire
332213	Chain saw blades manufacturing
333991	Chain saws, handheld power-driven, manufacturing
332618	Chain, welded, made from purchased wire
339911	Chains or necklace, precious metal, manufacturing
333613	Chains, power transmission, manufacturing
421830	Chainsaws wholesaling
337215	Chair seats for furniture manufacturing
337122	Chairs (except upholstered), wood household-type, manufacturing
337214	Chairs (except wood), office-type, manufacturing
337127	Chairs, barber and beauty (i.e., hydraulic), manufacturing
337127	Chairs, barber, beauty shop (i.e., hydraulic), manufacturing
339114	Chairs, dentist's, manufacturing
337124	Chairs, metal household-type (except upholstered), manufacturing
337127	Chairs, portable folding, auditorium-type, manufacturing
337127	Chairs, stacking, auditorium-type, manufacturing
337121	Chairs, upholstered household-type (except dining room, kitchen), manufacturing
337211	Chairs, wood office-type, manufacturing
339942	Chalk (e.g., artist's, blackboard, carpenter's, marking, tailor's), manufacturing
339942	Chalkboards, framed, manufacturing
813910	Chambers of commerce
422990	Chamois, leather, wholesaling
312130	Champagne method sparkling wine, manufacturing
335122	Chandeliers, commercial, industrial, and institutional electric, manufacturing
335121	Chandeliers, residential, manufacturing
333311	Change making machines manufacturing
234990	Channel construction
325191	Charcoal (except activated) manufacturing
325191	Charcoal briquettes, wood, manufacturing
422990	Charcoal wholesaling
325998	Charcoal, activated, manufacturing
813211	Charitable trusts, awarding grants
481212	Charter air freight services
481211	Charter air passenger services
485510	Charter bus services (except scenic, sightseeing)
487210	Charter fishing boat operation
332812	Chasing metals and metal products for the trade
336111	Chassis, automobile, manufacturing
336120	Chassis, heavy truck, with or without cabs, manufacturing
336112	Chassis, light truck and utility, manufacturing
421110	Chassis, motor vehicle, wholesaling
561310	Chauffeur registries
522390	Check cashing services
521110	Check clearing activities of the central bank
522320	Check clearing services (except central banks)
522320	Check clearinghouse services (except central banks)
421420	Check handling machines wholesaling
812990	Check room services
522320	Check validation services
332911	Check valves, industrial-type, manufacturing
316993	Checkbook covers, (except metal), manufacturing
339911	Checkbook covers, precious metal, manufacturing
323116	Checkbooks and refills printing
311513	Cheese (except cottage cheese) manufacturing
311513	Cheese analogs manufacturing
311941	Cheese based salad dressing manufacturing

422450	Cheese confections (e.g., curls, puffs) wholesaling
311919	Cheese curls and puffs manufacturing
311513	Cheese products, imitation or substitute, manufacturing
311513	Cheese spreads manufacturing
422430	Cheese wholesaling
311511	Cheese, cottage, manufacturing
311513	Cheese, imitation or substitute, manufacturing
311513	Cheese, natural (except cottage cheese), manufacturing
234930	Chemical complexes or facility construction
541690	Chemical consulting services
541330	Chemical engineering services
313311	Chemical finishing (e.g., fire, mildew, water resistance) broadwoven fabrics
313312	Chemical finishing (e.g., fire, mildew, water resistance) fabrics (except broadwoven and textile products)
422690	Chemical gases wholesaling
421830	Chemical industries machinery and equipment wholesaling
333298	Chemical processing machinery and equipment manufacturing
541710	Chemical research and development laboratories or services
327112	Chemical stoneware (i.e., pottery products) manufacturing
326191	Chemical toilets, plastics, manufacturing
115112	Chemical treatment of soil for crops
213112	Chemically treating oil and gas wells (e.g., acidizing, bailing, swabbing) on a contract basis
422690	Chemicals (except agriculture) (e.g., automotive, household, industrial, photographic) wholesaling
422910	Chemicals, agricultural, wholesaling
111339	Cherry farming
311340	Chewing gum manufacturing
422450	Chewing gum wholesaling
312229	Chewing tobacco manufacturing
422940	Chewing tobacco wholesaling
112310	Chicken egg production
311119	Chicken feeds, prepared, manufacturing
112340	Chicken hatcheries
112320	Chicken production (except egg laying)
422590	Chicks wholesaling
624410	Child day care centers
624410	Child day care services
623990	Child group foster homes
624110	Child guidance agencies
624110	Child welfare services
621410	Childbirth preparation classes
721214	Children's camps (except day, instructional)
422330	Children's clothing wholesaling
511199	Children's coloring book publishers
316219	Children's shoes (except orthopedic extension, plastics, rubber) manufacturing
421920	Children's vehicles (except bicycles) wholesaling
311422	Chili con carne canning
311942	Chili pepper or powder manufacturing
311421	Chili sauce manufacturing
335999	Chimes, electric, manufacturing
327390	Chimney caps, concrete, manufacturing
561790	Chimney cleaning services
327112	China cooking ware manufacturing
327112	China tableware, vitreous, manufacturing
442299	Chinaware stores
421440	Chinaware, commercial, wholesaling
421220	Chinaware, household-type, wholesaling
112930	Chinchilla production
311422	Chinese foods canning
311999	Chinese noodles, fried, manufacturing
321219	Chipboard manufacturing
321113	Chipper mills (except portable)
333112	Chippers (i.e., shredders), lawn and garden-type, manufacturing
333120	Chippers, portable, commercial (e.g., brush, limb, log), manufacturing

333291	Chippers, stationary (e.g., log), manufacturing
422450	Chips (e.g., corn, potato) wholesaling
621310	Chiropractors' offices (e.g., centers, clinics)
332212	Chisels manufacturing
325212	Chlorinated rubber, synthetic, manufacturing
325188	Chlorine compounds, not specified elsewhere by process, manufacturing
325188	Chlorine dioxide manufacturing
325181	Chlorine manufacturing
325212	Chloroprene rubber manufacturing
311330	Chocolate (coating, instant, liquor, syrups) made from purchased chocolate
311320	Chocolate (e.g., coatings, instant, liquor, syrups) made from cacao beans
422490	Chocolate (except candy) wholesaling
311320	Chocolate bars made from cocoa beans
422450	Chocolate candy wholesaling
311330	Chocolate coatings and syrups made from purchased chocolate
311330	Chocolate covered candy bars made from purchased chocolate
311330	Chocolate covered granola bars made from purchased chocolate
311511	Chocolate drink (milk based) manufacturing
311511	Chocolate milk manufacturing
311320	Chocolate, confectionery, made from cacao beans
711130	Choirs
334416	Chokes for electronic circuitry manufacturing
115113	Chopping and silo filling
711510	Choreographers, independent
311711	Chowders, fish and seafood, canning
311712	Chowders, frozen fish and seafood, manufacturing
621399	Christian Science practitioners' offices (e.g., centers, clinics)
422990	Christmas ornaments wholesaling
453220	Christmas stores
333132	Christmas tree assemblies, oil and gas field-type, manufacturing
111421	Christmas tree growing
335129	Christmas tree lighting sets, electric, manufacturing
339999	Christmas tree ornaments (except electric, glass) manufacturing
327215	Christmas tree ornaments made from purchased glass
327212	Christmas tree ornaments, glass, made in glass making plants
422990	Christmas trees (e.g., artificial, cut) wholesaling
339999	Christmas trees, artificial, manufacturing
454390	Christmas trees, cut, direct selling
334513	Chromatographs, industrial process-type, manufacturing
325131	Chrome pigments (e.g., chrome green, chrome orange, chrome yellow) manufacturing
325188	Chromium compounds, not specified elsewhere by process, manufacturing
331419	Chromium refining, primary
334518	Chronographs manufacturing
334518	Chronometers manufacturing
337127	Church furniture (except concrete, stone) manufacturing
421490	Church supplies (except plated ware, silverware) wholesaling
233320	Church, synagogue, mosque, temple, and related building construction
813110	Churches
311941	Cider vinegar manufacturing
311941	Cider, nonalcoholic, manufacturing
339911	Cigar cases, precious metal, manufacturing
312229	Cigar manufacturing
453991	Cigar stores
339911	Cigarette cases, precious metal, manufacturing
339999	Cigarette holders manufacturing
339999	Cigarette lighters (except precious metal) manufacturing

422990	Cigarette lighters wholesaling
333298	Cigarette making machinery manufacturing
453991	Cigarette stands, permanent
454390	Cigarette stands, temporary
333311	Cigarette vending machines manufacturing
312221	Cigarettes manufacturing
422940	Cigarettes wholesaling
422940	Cigars wholesaling
327331	Cinder (clinker) block, concrete, manufacturing
233320	Cinema construction
512131	Cinemas
711510	Cinematographers, independent
333298	Circuit board making machinery manufacturing
421690	Circuit boards wholesaling
334412	Circuit boards, printed, bare, manufacturing
421610	Circuit breakers wholesaling
335313	Circuit breakers, air, manufacturing
335313	Circuit breakers, power, manufacturing
334515	Circuit testers manufacturing
421690	Circuits, integrated, wholesaling
313241	Circular (i.e., weft) fabrics knitting
541870	Circular direct distribution services
333292	Circular knitting machinery manufacturing
333991	Circular saws, handheld power-driven, manufacturing
333210	Circular saws, woodworking-type, stationary, manufacturing
711190	Circus companies
711190	Circuses
334220	Citizens band (CB) radios manufacturing
325199	Citrates, not specified elsewhere by process, manufacturing
111320	Citrus groves (except orange)
311119	Citrus pulp, cattle feed, manufacturing
311411	Citrus pulp, frozen, manufacturing
485113	City bus services (except mixed mode)

541320	City planning services
813410	Civic associations
541330	Civil engineering services
813311	Civil liberties organizations
921190	Civil rights commissions
921190	Civil service commissions
524291	Claims adjusting, insurance
524292	Claims processing services, insurance, third-party
114112	Clam digging
112512	Clam production, farm raising
813410	Classic car clubs
212325	Clay (except kaolin, ball) mining and/or beneficiating
327112	Clay and ceramic statuary manufacturing
421320	Clay construction materials (except refractory) wholesaling
327124	Clay refractories (e.g., mortar, brick, tile, block) manufacturing
212324	Clay, ball, mining and/or beneficiating
212325	Clay, fire, mining and/or beneficiating
339942	Clay, modeling, manufacturing
233310	Clean room construction, general construction contractors
339113	Clean room suits and accessories manufacturing
561790	Cleaning (e.g., power sweeping, washing) driveways and parking lots
311212	Cleaning and polishing rice
561790	Cleaning building exteriors (except sand blasting, window cleaning)
561740	Cleaning carpets
422690	Cleaning compounds and preparations wholesaling
335999	Cleaning equipment, ultrasonic (except dental, medical), manufacturing
561720	Cleaning homes
561720	Cleaning new building interiors after construction
561720	Cleaning offices
561740	Cleaning plants, carpet and rug
115210	Cleaning poultry houses
561740	Cleaning rugs

561740	Cleaning services, carpet and rug
561720	Cleaning shopping centers
561790	Cleaning swimming pools
321918	Clear and finger joint wood moldings manufacturing
522320	Clearinghouses, bank or check
316219	Cleated athletic shoes manufacturing
315299	Clerical vestments cut and sewn from purchased fabric (except apparel contractors)
315191	Clerical vestments made in apparel knitting mills
315211	Clerical vestments, men's and boys, cut and sew apparel contractors
315212	Clerical vestments, women's and girls', cut and sew apparel contractors
316211	Climbing shoes, plastics or plastics soled fabric upper, manufacturing
621330	Clinical psychologists' offices (e.g., centers, clinics)
******	Clinics, medical—see type
621498	Clinics/centers of health practitioners from more than one industry practicing within the same establishment
321999	Clipboards, wood, manufacturing
332212	Clippers for animal use, nonelectric, manufacturing
332211	Clippers, fingernail and toenail, manufacturing
334518	Clock materials and parts (except crystals) manufacturing
334518	Clock or watch springs, precision, made from purchased wire
334310	Clock radios manufacturing
811490	Clock repair shops without retailing new clocks
448310	Clock shops
334518	Clocks assembling from purchased components
421940	Clocks wholesaling
561492	Closed captioning services, real-time (i.e., simultaneous)
512191	Closed captioning services, taped material
513220	Closed circuit television (CCTV)
334220	Closed circuit television equipment manufacturing
525990	Closed-end investment funds (except REITs)
332115	Closures, metal, stamping
422130	Closures, paper and disposable plastics, wholesaling
327910	Cloth (e.g., aluminum oxide, garnet, emery, silicon carbide) coated manufacturing
561990	Cloth cutting, bolting, or winding for the trade
332618	Cloth, woven wire, made from purchased wire
422990	Clothes hangers wholesaling
326199	Clothes hangers, plastics, manufacturing
448150	Clothing accessories stores
422330	Clothing accessories, women's, children's, and infants', wholesaling
541490	Clothing design services
532220	Clothing rental (except industrial launderer, linen supply)
448130	Clothing stores, children's and infants'
448140	Clothing stores, family
448110	Clothing stores, men's and boys'
453310	Clothing stores, used
448120	Clothing stores, women's and girls'
315292	Clothing, fur (except apparel contractors), manufacturing
315211	Clothing, fur, men's and boys', cut and sew apparel contractors
315212	Clothing, fur, women's, girls', and infants', cut and sew apparel contractors
315292	Clothing, leather or sheep-lined (except apparel contractors), manufacturing
315211	Clothing, leather or sheep-lined, men's and boys', cut and sew apparel contractors
315212	Clothing, leather or sheep-lined, women's, girls', and infants', cut and sew apparel contractors
422320	Clothing, men's and boys', wholesaling

315291 Clothing, water resistant, infants', cut and sewn from purchased fabric (except apparel contractors)

315211 Clothing, water resistant, men's and boy's, cut and sew apparel contractors

315228 Clothing, water resistant, not specified elsewhere, men's and boys', cut and sewn from purchased fabric (except apparel contractors)

315212 Clothing, water resistant, women's, girls' and infants', cut and sew apparel contractors

315291 Clothing, water-repellent, infants', cut and sewn from purchased fabric (except apparel contractors)

315211 Clothing, water-repellent, men's and boys', cut and sew apparel contractors

315228 Clothing, water-repellent, not specified elsewhere, men's and boys', cut and sewn from purchased fabric (except apparel contractors)

315239 Clothing, water-repellent, not specified elsewhere, women's, misses', and girls', cut and sewn from purchased fabric (except apparel contractors)

315212 Clothing, water-repellent, women's, girls', and infants', cut and sew apparel contractors

315299 Clothing, waterproof, cut and sewn from purchased fabric (except apparel contractors)

315211 Clothing, waterproof, men's and boys', cut and sew apparel contractors

315212 Clothing, waterproof, women's, girls', and infants', cut and sew apparel contractors

422330 Clothing, women's, children's, and infants', wholesaling

339994 Cloths (except chemically treated), dusting and polishing, manufacturing

325612 Cloths, dusting and polishing, chemically treated, manufacturing

111940 Clover hay farming

111998 Clover seed farming

333613 Clutches and brakes (except electromagnetic industrial controls, motor vehicle) manufacturing

234930 Co-generation plant construction

212113 Coal beneficiating plants, anthracite

212111 Coal beneficiating plants, bituminous or lignite (surface or underground)

333131 Coal breakers, cutters, and pulverizers manufacturing

454319 Coal dealers, direct selling

213113 Coal mining support services (tunneling, blasting, training, overburden removal)

486990 Coal pipeline transportation

325192 Coal tar distillates manufacturing

422690 Coal tar products, primary and intermediate, wholesaling

325211 Coal tar resins manufacturing

421520 Coal wholesaling

212113 Coal, anthracite, mining and/or beneficiating

212111 Coal, bituminous, beneficiating

212112 Coal, bituminous, underground mining or mining and beneficiating

926120 Coast Guard (except academy)

483113 Coastal freight transportation to and from domestic ports

483114 Coastal passenger transportation to and from domestic ports

483113 Coastal shipping of freight to and from domestic ports

448190 Coat stores

332812 Coating metals and metal products for the trade

322222 Coating purchased papers for nonpackaging applications (except photosensitive paper)

322221 Coating purchased papers for packaging applications

311320 Coatings, chocolate, made from cacao beans

315239 Coats (except fur, leather, tailored, waterproof), women's, misses', and girls', cut and sewn from purchased fabric (except apparel contractors)

315228 Coats (except fur, leather, tailored, waterproof, work), men's and boys', cut and sewn from purchased fabric (except apparel contractors)

315292 Coats (including tailored), leather or sheep-lined (except apparel contractors), manufacturing

315212 Coats (including tailored, leather, or sheep-lined), women's, girls', and infants', cut and sew apparel contractors

315212 Coats, artificial leather, women's, girls', and infants', cut and sew apparel contractors

315292 Coats, fur (except apparel contractors), manufacturing

315212 Coats, fur, women's, girls', and infants', cut and sew apparel contractors

315291 Coats, infants' (except waterproof), cut and sewn from purchased fabric (except apparel contractors)

315292 Coats, leather, (except apparel contractors)

315212 Coats, leather, women's, girls', and infants', cut and sew apparel contractors

315211 Coats, men's and boys', cut and sew apparel contractors

315222 Coats, tailored (except fur, leather), men's and boys', cut and sewn from purchased fabric (except apparel contractors)

315234 Coats, tailored (except fur, leather), women's, misses', and girls', cut and sewn from purchased fabric

315999 Coats, waterproof (e.g., plastics, rubberized fabric, similar materials) rubberizing fabric and manufacturing coats

315211 Coats, waterproof (i.e., plastic, rubberized fabric, similar materials), men's and boy's, cut and sew apparel contractors

315212 Coats, waterproof (i.e., plastics, rubberized fabric, similar materials), women's, girls', and infants', cut and sew apparel contractors

315999 Coats, waterproof, (e.g., plastics, rubberized fabric, similar materials) cut and sewn from purchased fabric (except apparel contractors)

315212 Coats, women's, girls', and infants', cut and sew apparel contractors

421610 Coaxial cable wholesaling

335929 Coaxial cable, nonferrous, made from purchased nonferrous wire

334417 Coaxial connectors manufacturing

325188 Cobalt compounds, not specified elsewhere by process, manufacturing

331419 Cobalt refining, primary

332913 Cocks, drain, plumbing, manufacturing

722410 Cocktail lounges

311999 Cocktail mixes, dry, manufacturing

422820 Cocktails, alcoholic, premixed, wholesaling

311320 Cocoa (e.g., instant, mix, mixed with other ingredients, powder drink, powdered) made from cacao beans

422590 Cocoa beans wholesaling

311320 Cocoa butter made from cocoa beans

311330 Cocoa, powdered drink, prepared, made from purchased chocolate

311330 Cocoa, powdered, made from purchased chocolate

311330 Cocoa, powdered, mixed with other ingredients, made from purchased chocolate

311225 Coconut oil made from purchased oils

311223 Coconut oil made in crushing mills

311999 Coconut, desiccated and shredded, manufacturing

114111 Cod catching

311711 Cod liver oil extraction, crude, produced in a cannery

311712 Cod liver oil extraction, crude, produced in a fresh and frozen seafood plant

333993 Coding, dating, and imprinting packaging machinery manufacturing

445299 Coffee and tea (i.e., packaged) stores

722330 Coffee carts, mobile

311920 Coffee concentrates (i.e., instant coffee) manufacturing

311920 Coffee extracts manufacturing

111339 Coffee farming

311920 Coffee flavoring and syrups (i.e., made from coffee) manufacturing

333319 Coffee makers and urns, commercial-type, manufacturing

335211 Coffee makers, household-type electric, manufacturing

311920 Coffee roasting

722213 Coffee shops, on premise brewing

311920 Coffee substitute manufacturing

422490 Coffee wholesaling

311920 Coffee, blended, manufacturing

312111 Coffee, iced, manufacturing

311920 Coffee, instant and freeze dried, manufacturing

454390 Coffee-break service providers, direct selling

541720 Cognitive research and development services

333518 Coil winding and cutting machinery, metalworking, manufacturing

332612 Coiled springs (except clock, watch), light gauge, manufacturing

332611 Coiled springs, heavy gauge, manufacturing

336322 Coils, ignition, internal combustion engines, manufacturing

561990 Coin pick-up services, parking meter

316993 Coin purses (except metal) manufacturing

339911 Coin purses, precious metal, manufacturing

339999 Coin-operated amusement machines (except jukebox) manufacturing

812310 Coin-operated drycleaners and laundries

713290 Coin-operated gambling device concession operators (i.e., supplying and servicing in others' facilities)

339999 Coin-operated gambling devices manufacturing

421990 Coin-operated game machines wholesaling

334310 Coin-operated jukebox manufacturing

713990 Coin-operated nongambling amusement device concession operators (i.e., supplying and servicing in others' facilities)

812990 Coin-operated personal service machine (e.g., blood pressure, locker, photographic, scale, shoeshine) concession operators

421440 Coin-operated phonographs and vending machines wholesaling

333311 Coin-operated vending machines manufacturing

339911 Coins minting

421940 Coins wholesaling

221210 Coke oven gas, production and distribution

324199 Coke oven products (e.g., coke, gases, tars) made in coke oven establishments

331111 Coke oven products made in steel mills

421520 Coke wholesaling

324110 Coke, petroleum, made in petroleum refineries

332111 Cold forgings made from purchased iron or steel, unfinished

332112 Cold forgings made from purchased nonferrous metals, unfinished

325412 Cold remedies manufacturing

333516 Cold rolling mill machinery, metalworking, manufacturing

331221 Cold rolling steel shapes (e.g., bar, plate, rod, sheet, strip) made from purchased steel

421740 Cold storage machinery wholesaling

493120 Cold storage warehousing

311991 Cole slaw, fresh, manufacturing

311612 Collagen sausage casings made from purchased hides

316999	Collars, dog, manufacturing
525990	Collateralized mortgage obligations (CMOs)
453220	Collectible gift shops (e.g., crystal, pewter, porcelain)
561440	Collection agencies
221320	Collection, treatment, and disposal of waste through a sewer system
453998	Collector's items shops (e.g., autograph, card, coin, stamp)
454110	Collector's items, mail-order houses
611691	College board preparation centers
611310	Colleges (except junior colleges)
611511	Colleges, barber and beauty
611210	Colleges, community
611210	Colleges, junior
325620	Colognes manufacturing
422210	Colognes wholesaling
812199	Color consulting services (i.e., personal care services)
325131	Color pigments, inorganic (except bone black, carbon black, lamp black), manufacturing
325132	Color pigments, organic (except animal black, bone black), manufacturing
323122	Color separation services, for the printing trade
316110	Coloring leather
332813	Coloring metals and metal products (except coating) for the trade
212299	Columbite mining and/or beneficiating
327420	Columns, architectural or ornamental plaster work, manufacturing
112990	Combination livestock farming (except dairy, poultry)
333111	Combines (i.e., harvester-threshers) manufacturing
313312	Combing and converting top
333292	Combing machinery for textiles manufacturing
313312	Combing textile fibers
115113	Combining, agricultural
326199	Combs, plastics, manufacturing
541330	Combustion engineering consulting services

562211	Combustors, hazardous waste
562213	Combustors, nonhazardous solid waste
711510	Comedians, independent
711110	Comedy troupes
812990	Comfort station operation
314129	Comforters made from purchased fabrics
511120	Comic book publishers
511120	Comic book publishers and printing combined
323112	Comic books flexographic printing without publishing
323111	Comic books gravure printing without publishing
323110	Comic books lithographic (offset) printing without publishing
323119	Comic books printing (except flexographic, gravure, lithographic, screen) without publishing
323113	Comic books screen printing without publishing
811310	Commercial and industrial machinery repair and maintenance services
541430	Commercial art services
541430	Commercial artists, independent
311812	Commercial bakeries
522110	Commercial banking
522110	Commercial banks
233320	Commercial building construction
531120	Commercial building rental or leasing
561450	Commercial credit reporting bureaus
541430	Commercial illustration services
541430	Commercial illustrators, independent
335122	Commercial lighting fixtures, electric, manufacturing
523120	Commercial note brokers' offices
541922	Commercial photography services
531210	Commercial real estate agencies
531210	Commercial real estate agents' offices
531312	Commercial real estate property managers' offices
811310	Commercial refrigeration equipment repair and maintenance services

422120 Commercial stationery suppliers wholesaling

512110 Commercials, television, production

445110 Commissaries, primarily groceries

522298 Commodity Credit Corporation

523140 Commodity contracts brokerages

523130 Commodity contracts dealing (i.e., acting as a principal in dealing commodities to investors)

523210 Commodity contracts exchanges

523140 Commodity contracts floor brokers

523130 Commodity contracts floor traders (i.e., acting as a principal in dealing commodities to investors)

523140 Commodity futures brokerages

541990 Commodity inspection services

212325 Common clay mining and/or beneficiating

923120 Communicable disease program administration

541430 Communication design services, visual

235310 Communication equipment construction contractors

811213 Communication equipment repair and maintenance services

926130 Communications commissions

421690 Communications equipment wholesaling

334220 Communications equipment, mobile and microwave, manufacturing

334210 Communications headgear, telephone, manufacturing

926130 Communications licensing commissions and agencies

335929 Communications wire and cable, nonferrous, made from purchased nonferrous wire

311812 Communion wafer manufacturing

813319 Community action advocacy organizations

624190 Community action service agencies

624120 Community centers (except recreational only), adult

624110 Community centers (except recreational only), youth

813219 Community chests

611210 Community colleges

813211 Community foundations

621498 Community health centers and clinics, outpatient

923120 Community health programs administration

923130 Community social service program administration

711110 Community theaters

335312 Commutators, electric motor, manufacturing

481111 Commuter air carriers, scheduled

485113 Commuter bus operation (except mixed mode)

485112 Commuter rail systems (except mixed mode)

485111 Commuter transit systems, mixed mode (e.g., bus, commuter rail, subway combination)

334310 Compact disc players (e.g., automotive, household-type) manufacturing

421990 Compact discs (CDs), prerecorded, wholesaling

334611 Compact discs (i.e., CD-ROM), software, mass reproducing

334612 Compact discs, prerecorded audio, mass reproducing

334613 Compact discs, recordable or rewritable, blank, manufacturing

335110 Compact fluorescent light bulbs manufacturing

339911 Compacts, precious metal, manufacturing

624120 Companion services for disabled persons, the elderly, and persons diagnosed with mental retardation

334511 Compasses, gyroscopic and magnetic (except portable), manufacturing

334519 Compasses, portable magnetic-type, manufacturing

541612 Compensation consulting services

541612 Compensation planning services

511140 Compiling mailing lists

311119 Complete feed, livestock, manufacturing

711510	Composers, independent
322214	Composite cans (i.e., foil-fiber and other combinations) manufacturing
******	Composite materials—classified according to the major constituent component (i.e., carbon, carbon graphite, ceramics, glass, metal, polymers, etc.)
562219	Compost dumps
325314	Compost manufacturing
325120	Compressed and liquefied industrial gas manufacturing
422690	Compressed gases (except LP gas) wholesaling
333220	Compression molding machinery for plastics manufacturing
339991	Compression packings manufacturing
421830	Compressors (except air-conditioning, refrigeration) wholesaling
333912	Compressors, air and gas, general purpose-type, manufacturing
421730	Compressors, air-conditioning, wholesaling
336391	Compressors, motor vehicle air-conditioning, manufacturing
421740	Compressors, refrigeration, wholesaling
541710	Computer and related hardware research and development laboratories or services
421430	Computer boards, loaded, wholesaling
421690	Computer boards, unloaded, wholesaling
235310	Computer cable construction contractors
421690	Computer chips wholesaling
541519	Computer disaster recovery services
813410	Computer enthusiasts clubs
811212	Computer equipment repair and maintenance services without retailing new computers
443120	Computer equipment stores
323116	Computer forms (manifold or continuous) printing
337124	Computer furniture, metal household-type, manufacturing
337122	Computer furniture, wood household-type, manufacturing
514210	Computer input preparation services
334119	Computer input/output equipment (except terminals) manufacturing
422120	Computer paper supplies wholesaling
322231	Computer paper, single layered continuous, die-cut, made from purchased paper
421430	Computer peripheral equipment wholesaling
421430	Computer printers wholesaling
541511	Computer program or software development, custom
611420	Computer programming schools
541511	Computer programming services, custom
532420	Computer rental or leasing
611519	Computer repair training
334111	Computer servers manufacturing
541511	Computer software analysis and design services, custom
541511	Computer software programming services, custom
511210	Computer software publishers, packaged
511210	Computer software publishing and reproduction
511210	Computer software publishing including design and development, packaged (i.e., establishments known as publishers)
541511	Computer software support services, custom
334613	Computer software tapes and disks, blank, rigid and floppy, manufacturing
611420	Computer software training
454110	Computer software, mail-order houses
421430	Computer software, packaged, wholesaling
443120	Computer stores
541513	Computer systems facilities (i.e., clients' facilities) management and operation services
541512	Computer systems integration analysis and design services

541512 Computer systems integration design consulting services

541512 Computer systems integrator services

334113 Computer terminals manufacturing

514210 Computer time leasing

514210 Computer time rental

514210 Computer time sharing services

621512 Computer tomography (CT-SCAN) centers

611420 Computer training (except repair)

541512 Computer-aided design (CAD) systems integration design services

541512 Computer-aided engineering (CAE) systems integration design services

541512 Computer-aided manufacturing (CAM) systems integration design services

334517 Computerized axial tomography (CT/CAT) scanners manufacturing

334512 Computerized environmental control systems for buildings manufacturing

334111 Computers manufacturing

421430 Computers wholesaling

325411 Concentrated medicinal chemicals, uncompounded, manufacturing

311930 Concentrates, drink (except frozen fruit juice), manufacturing

311930 Concentrates, flavoring (except coffee based), manufacturing

311411 Concentrates, frozen fruit juice, manufacturing

421520 Concentrates, metallic, wholesaling

711130 Concert artists, independent

711320 Concert booking agencies

711310 Concert hall operators

711310 Concert managers with facilities

711320 Concert managers without facilities

711310 Concert organizers with facilities

711320 Concert organizers without facilities

711310 Concert promoters with facilities

711320 Concert promoters without facilities

713990 Concession operators, amusement device (except gambling) and ride

722330 Concession stands, mobile

926150 Conciliation and mediation services, government

234110 Concrete (e.g., roads, highways, public sidewalks, streets) construction contractors

325998 Concrete additive preparations (e.g., curing, hardening) manufacturing

327320 Concrete batch plants (including temporary)

235410 Concrete block laying construction contractors

235940 Concrete breaking and cutting construction contractors

421320 Concrete building products wholesaling

235710 Concrete construction contractors (i.e., parking areas, private driveways, sidewalks)

327390 Concrete furniture (e.g., benches, tables) manufacturing

333120 Concrete mixing machinery, portable, manufacturing

421810 Concrete processing equipment wholesaling

235910 Concrete products (e.g., structural precast or prestressed), placement, construction contractors

327390 Concrete products, precast (except block, brick and pipe), manufacturing

332312 Concrete reinforcing bars manufacturing

421510 Concrete reinforcing bars wholesaling

332618 Concrete reinforcing mesh made from purchased wire

327390 Concrete tanks manufacturing

327999 Concrete, dry mixture, manufacturing

311514 Condensed milk manufacturing

311514 Condensed, evaporated or powdered whey, manufacturing

334414 Condensers, electronic, manufacturing

421690 Condensers, electronic, wholesaling

332410 Condensers, steam, manufacturing

421830 Condensing units (except air-conditioning, refrigeration) wholesaling

421730 Condensing units, air-conditioning, wholesaling

421740   Condensing units, refrigeration, wholesaling
326299   Condom manufacturing
813990   Condominium corporations
531312   Condominium managers' offices, commercial
531311   Condominium managers' offices, residential
813990   Condominium owners' associations
561599   Condominium time share exchange services
233220   Condominiums, multifamily, construction
327123   Conduit, vitrified clay, manufacturing
335932   Conduits and fittings, electrical, manufacturing
327332   Conduits, concrete, manufacturing
311821   Cones, ice cream, manufacturing
327112   Cones, pyrometric, earthenware, manufacturing
311313   Confectioner's beet sugar manufacturing
311312   Confectioner's powdered sugar made from purchased raw cane sugar
311320   Confectionery chocolate made from cacao beans
722213   Confectionery snack shops, made on premises with carryout services
445292   Confectionery stores, packaged, retailing only
422450   Confectionery wholesaling
311340   Confectionery, nonchocolate, manufacturing
336312   Connecting rods, automotive and truck gasoline engine, manufacturing
334417   Connectors, electronic (e.g., coaxial, cylindrical, printed circuit, rack and panel), manufacturing
421690   Connectors, electronic, wholesaling
335313   Connectors, power, manufacturing
335931   Connectors, twist on wire (i.e., nuts), manufacturing
813312   Conservation advocacy organizations
924120   Conservation and reclamation agencies

712190   Conservation areas
712130   Conservatories, botanical
711510   Conservators, independent
453310   Consignment shops, used
336350   Constant velocity joints, automotive, truck, and bus, manufacturing
813940   Constituencies' associations, political party
325520   Construction adhesives (except asphalt, gypsum base) manufacturing
813910   Construction associations
541330   Construction engineering services
532412   Construction machinery and equipment rental or leasing without operator
811310   Construction machinery and equipment repair and maintenance services
421810   Construction machinery and equipment wholesaling
333120   Construction machinery manufacturing
234120   Construction management firms, bridge and tunnel
233320   Construction management firms, commercial and institutional building firms
234110   Construction management firms, highway and street
234930   Construction management firms, industrial nonbuilding
233310   Construction management firms, manufacturing and industrial building
233220   Construction management firms, multifamily
234990   Construction management firms, nonbuilding (except industrial)
234920   Construction management firms, power and communication transmission line
233210   Construction management firms, single family
234910   Construction management firms, water, sewer and pipeline
421610   Construction materials, electrical, wholesaling

212321 Construction sand and gravel beneficiating (e.g., grinding, screening, washing)

212321 Construction sand or gravel dredging

333120 Construction-type tractors and attachments manufacturing

****** Consultants—see specific activity

813920 Consultants' associations

541330 Consulting engineers' offices

812990 Consumer buying services

541990 Consumer credit counseling services

561450 Consumer credit reporting bureaus

532210 Consumer electronics rental

811211 Consumer electronics repair and maintenance services without retailing new consumer electronics

421620 Consumer electronics wholesaling

522291 Consumer finance companies (i.e., unsecured cash loans)

922190 Consumer product safety commissions

926110 Consumer protection offices

443112 Consumer-type electronic stores (e.g., radio, television, video camera)

334514 Consumption meters (e.g., gas, water) manufacturing

524128 Contact lens insurance, direct

339115 Contact lenses manufacturing

421460 Contact lenses wholesaling

335931 Contacts, electrical (except carbon and graphite), manufacturing

335991 Contacts, electrical, carbon and graphite, manufacturing

336611 Container ship building

327213 Containers for packaging, bottling, and canning, glass, manufacturing

332439 Containers, air cargo, metal, manufacturing

332999 Containers, foil (except bags), manufacturing

421840 Containers, industrial, wholesaling

332439 Containers, light gauge metal (except cans), manufacturing

422130 Containers, paper and disposable plastics, wholesaling

321920 Containers, wood, manufacturing

623311 Continuing care retirement communities

325412 Contraceptive preparations manufacturing

****** Contractors—see specific activity

813910 Contractors' associations

315211 Contractors, men's and boys', cut and sew apparel

315212 Contractors, women's, girls' and infants', cut and sew apparel

335313 Control panels, electric power distribution, manufacturing

332912 Control valves, fluid power, manufacturing

332911 Control valves, industrial-type, manufacturing

921130 Controller's and comptrollers' offices, government

334513 Controllers for process variables (e.g., electric, electronic, mechanical, pneumatic operation) manufacturing

334290 Controlling equipment, street light, manufacturing

335314 Controls and control accessories, industrial, manufacturing

335314 Controls for adjustable speed drives manufacturing

623220 Convalescent homes or hospitals for psychiatric patients

446199 Convalescent supply stores

335221 Convection ovens (including portable), household-type, manufacturing

445120 Convenience food stores

447110 Convenience food with gasoline stations

335931 Convenience outlets, electric, manufacturing

561591 Convention and visitors bureaus

561591 Convention bureaus

531120 Convention center, no promotion of events, rental or leasing

561920 Convention managers

561920 Convention organizers

561920 Convention promoters

561920 Convention services

813110 Convents (except schools)

313311	Converters, broadwoven piece goods
337121	Convertible sofas (except futons) manufacturing
336399	Convertible tops for automotive, truck, and bus, manufacturing
313311	Converting textiles, broadwoven
313312	Converting textiles, narrow woven
316110	Convertors, leather
313312	Convertors, narrow woven piece goods
421830	Conveying equipment (except farm) wholesaling
421820	Conveying equipment, farm, wholesaling
333922	Conveyors, farm-type, manufacturing
311822	Cookie dough made from purchased flour
722213	Cookie shops, on premise baking and carryout service
311821	Cookies manufacturing
422490	Cookies wholesaling
335211	Cooking appliances (except convection, microwave ovens), household-type electric portable, manufacturing
311320	Cooking chocolate made from cacao beans
333319	Cooking equipment (i.e., fryers, microwave ovens, ovens, ranges), commercial-type, manufacturing
421440	Cooking equipment, commercial, wholesaling
421620	Cooking equipment, electric household-type, wholesaling
421720	Cooking equipment, gas, household-type, wholesaling
422490	Cooking oils wholesaling
332214	Cooking utensils, fabricated metal, manufacturing
421220	Cooking utensils, household-type, wholesaling
327112	Cooking ware (e.g., stoneware, coarse earthenware, pottery), manufacturing
327215	Cooking ware made from purchased glass

327212	Cooking ware made in glass making plants
327112	Cooking ware, china, manufacturing
327112	Cooking ware, fine earthenware, manufacturing
221330	Cooled air distribution
326199	Coolers or ice chests, plastics (except foam), manufacturing
326140	Coolers or ice chests, polystyrene foam, manufacturing
333415	Coolers, refrigeration, manufacturing
333415	Coolers, water, manufacturing
333415	Cooling towers manufacturing
321920	Cooperage manufacturing
321920	Cooperage stock (e.g., heading, hoops, stoves) manufacturing
321920	Cooperage stock mills
421840	Cooperage stock wholesaling
531311	Cooperative apartment managers' offices
233220	Cooperative construction
813990	Cooperative owners' associations
532420	Copier rental or leasing
327123	Coping, wall, clay, manufacturing
327390	Copings, concrete, manufacturing
331525	Copper alloy castings (except die-castings), unfinished, manufacturing
331423	Copper alloys (e.g., brass, bronze) made from purchased metal or scrap
331411	Copper alloys made in primary copper smelting and refining mills
331423	Copper and copper-based shapes (e.g., cake, ingot, slag, wire bar) made from purchased metal or scrap
325131	Copper base pigments manufacturing
212234	Copper beneficiating plants
325188	Copper compounds, not specified elsewhere by process, manufacturing
331411	Copper concentrate refining
331522	Copper die-casting foundries
331522	Copper die-castings, unfinished, manufacturing

331421	Copper foil made from purchased metal or scrap
332999	Copper foil not made in rolling mills
332112	Copper forgings made from purchased metals, unfinished
331525	Copper foundries (except die-casting)
212234	Copper ore concentrates recovery
212234	Copper ore mine site development for own account
212234	Copper ores mining and/or beneficiating
331423	Copper powder, flakes, and paste made from purchased copper
331421	Copper products (except communication wire, energy wire) made by drawing purchased copper
331421	Copper products (except communication wire, energy wire) made by rolling, drawing, or extruding purchased copper
331421	Copper products (except communication wire, energy wire) made in integrated secondary smelting and extruding mills
331421	Copper products (except communication wire, energy wire) made in integrated secondary smelting mills and drawing plants
331423	Copper secondary smelting and alloying
331423	Copper secondary smelting and refining from purchased metal or scrap
331411	Copper shapes (e.g., bar, billet, ingot, plate, sheet) made in primary copper smelting and refining mills
331411	Copper smelting and refining, primary
561439	Copy centers (except combined with printing services)
561439	Copy shops (except combined with printing services)
421420	Copying machines wholesaling
314991	Cord (except tire, wire) manufacturing

314992	Cord for reinforcing rubber tires, industrial belting, and fuel cells manufacturing
314991	Cordage (except wire) manufacturing
421840	Cordage wholesaling
334210	Cordless telephones (except cellular) manufacturing
313221	Cords and braids, narrow woven, manufacturing
333131	Core drills, underground mining-type, manufacturing
332997	Cores, sand foundry, manufacturing
321999	Cork products (except gaskets) manufacturing
421840	Cork wholesaling
321999	Corks, bottle, manufacturing
311230	Corn breakfast foods manufacturing
311919	Corn chips and related corn snacks manufacturing
422450	Corn chips and related corn snacks wholesaling
311340	Corn confections manufacturing
311221	Corn dextrin manufacturing
111150	Corn farming (except sweet corn), field and seed production
311211	Corn flour manufacturing
311211	Corn meal made in flour mills
311225	Corn oil made from purchased oils
311221	Corn oil mills
311221	Corn oil, crude and refined, made by wet milling corn
333319	Corn popping machines, commercial-type, manufacturing
115114	Corn shelling
311221	Corn starch manufacturing
311221	Corn sweeteners (e.g., dextrose, fructose, glucose) made by wet milling corn
311999	Corn syrups made from purchased sweeteners
112320	Cornish hen production
923120	Coroners' offices
813211	Corporate foundations, awarding grants
541430	Corporate identification (i.e., logo) design services

541110	Corporate law offices
551114	Corporate offices
332323	Corrals, metal, manufacturing
561210	Correctional facility operation on a contract or fee basis
922140	Correctional institutions
322211	Corrugated and solid fiber boxes made from purchased paper or paperboard
322211	Corrugated and solid fiberboard pads made from purchased paper or paperboard
322211	Corrugated paper made from purchased paper or paperboard
315231	Corsets and allied garments (except surgical), women's, misses', and girls', cut and sewn from purchased fabric (except apparel contractors)
325411	Cortisone, uncompounded, manufacturing
325620	Cosmetic creams, lotions, and oils manufacturing
446120	Cosmetics stores
422210	Cosmetics wholesaling
812112	Cosmetology salons or shops
611511	Cosmetology schools
541490	Costume design services (except independent theatrical costume designers)
711510	Costume designers, independent theatrical
339914	Costume jewelry manufacturing
448150	Costume jewelry stores
421940	Costume jewelry wholesaling
532220	Costume rental
448190	Costume shops (including theatrical)
315299	Costumes (e.g., lodge, masquerade, theatrical) cut and sewn from purchased fabric (except apparel contractors)
315212	Costumes (e.g., lodge, masquerade, theatrical) women's, girls' and infants', cut and sew apparel contractors
315211	Costumes (e.g., lodge, masquerade, theatrical), men's and boys', cut and sew apparel contractors
311511	Cottage cheese manufacturing
332722	Cotter pins, metal, manufacturing
422990	Cotton (except raw) wholesaling
339113	Cotton and cotton balls, absorbent, manufacturing
314999	Cotton battings (except nonwoven batting) manufacturing
313210	Cotton fabrics, broadwoven, weaving
111920	Cotton farming, field and seed production
115111	Cotton ginning
333111	Cotton ginning machinery manufacturing
115113	Cotton, machine harvesting
422590	Cotton, raw, wholesaling
311225	Cottonseed oil made from purchased oils
311223	Cottonseed oil, cake and meal, made in crushing mills
337121	Couches, upholstered, manufacturing
311340	Cough drops (except medicated) manufacturing
325412	Cough drops, medicated, manufacturing
325412	Cough medicines manufacturing
621410	Counseling services, family planning
541110	Counselors' at law offices
337215	Counter units (except refrigerated) manufacturing
334511	Countermeasure sets (e.g., active countermeasures, jamming equipment) manufacturing
334514	Counters (e.g., electrical, electronic, mechanical), totalizing, manufacturing
333415	Counters and display cases, refrigerated, manufacturing
337215	Countertops (except kitchen and bathroom), wood or plastics laminated on wood, manufacturing
337110	Countertops (i.e., kitchen, bathroom), wood or plastics laminated on wood, manufacturing

http://www.ntis.gov/naics

561450	Credit bureaus
522210	Credit card banks
522210	Credit card issuing
812990	Credit card notification services (i.e., lost or stolen card reporting)
522320	Credit card processing services
561450	Credit investigation services
524113	Credit life insurance carriers, direct
561450	Credit rating services
561450	Credit reporting bureaus
522130	Credit unions
333999	Cremating ovens manufacturing
812220	Crematories (except combined with funeral homes)
325192	Creosote made by distillation of coal tar
325191	Creosote made by distillation of wood tar
321114	Creosoting of wood
322299	Crepe paper made from purchased paper
325192	Cresols made by distillation of coal tar
325192	Cresylic acids made from refined petroleum or natural gas
115115	Crew leaders, farm labor
337124	Cribs (i.e., baby beds), metal, manufacturing
337122	Cribs (i.e., baby beds), wood, manufacturing
112990	Cricket production
922120	Criminal investigation offices, government
922190	Criminal justice statistics centers, government
541110	Criminal law offices
624190	Crisis intervention centers
314999	Crochet ware made from purchased materials
327112	Crockery manufacturing
311812	Croissants, baking, made in commercial bakeries
115114	Crop cleaning
115112	Crop dusting
421820	Crop preparation machinery (e.g., cleaning, conditioning, drying) wholesaling

115112	Crop spraying
713920	Cross country skiing facilities without accommodations
332911	Cross valves, industrial-type, manufacturing
311812	Croutons and bread crumbs made in commercial bakeries
421840	Crowns and closures, metal, wholesaling
332115	Crowns, metal (e.g., bottle, can), stamping
311221	Crude corn oil manufacturing
486110	Crude oil pipeline transportation
324110	Crude oil refining
422710	Crude oil terminals
422720	Crude oil wholesaling (except bulk stations, terminals)
211111	Crude petroleum production
324110	Crude petroleum refineries
422990	Crude rubber wholesaling
336322	Cruise control mechanisms, electronic, automotive, truck, and bus, manufacturing
483114	Cruise lines (i.e., deep sea passenger transportation to and from domestic ports)
483112	Cruise lines (i.e., deep sea passenger transportation to or from foreign ports)
561599	Cruise ship ticket offices
713210	Cruises, gambling
421320	Crushed stone wholesaling
333120	Crushing machinery, portable, manufacturing
333131	Crushing machinery, stationary, manufacturing
333120	Crushing, pulverizing, and screening machinery, portable, manufacturing
112512	Crustacean production, farm raising
339113	Crutches and walkers manufacturing
421450	Crutches wholesaling
311340	Crystallized fruits and fruit peel manufacturing
334419	Crystals and crystal assemblies, electronic, manufacturing
111219	Cucumber farming (except under cover), field, bedding plant and seed production

339911 Cuff links, precious metal, manufacturing
611519 Culinary arts schools
111422 Cultivated florist greens growing
421820 Cultivating machinery and equipment wholesaling
115112 Cultivation services
333111 Cultivators, farm-type, manufacturing
333112 Cultivators, powered, lawn and garden-type, manufacturing
926110 Cultural and arts development support program administration
325414 Culture media manufacturing
326191 Cultured marble plumbing fixtures manufacturing
326199 Cultured marble products (except plumbing fixtures) manufacturing
112512 Cultured pearl production, farm raising
326199 Cultured stone products (except plumbing fixtures) manufacturing
327332 Culvert pipe, concrete, manufacturing
325110 Cumene made from refined petroleum or liquid hydrocarbons
324110 Cumene made in petroleum refineries
322299 Cups, molded pulp, manufacturing
422130 Cups, paper and disposable plastics, wholesaling
421220 Cups, plastics (except disposable), wholesaling
326199 Cups, plastics (except foam), manufacturing
326140 Cups, polystyrene foam, manufacturing
327991 Curbing, granite and stone, manufacturing
311513 Curds, cheese, made in a cheese plant, manufacturing
422460 Cured fish wholesaling
311612 Cured meats (e.g., brined, dried, and salted) made from purchased carcasses
311711 Curing fish and seafood
453220 Curio shops
422990 Curios wholesaling

713990 Curling facilities
335211 Curling irons, household-type electric, manufacturing
111334 Currant farming
421420 Currency handling machines wholesaling
335311 Current limiting reactors, electrical, manufacturing
334515 Current measuring equipment manufacturing
421610 Current-carrying wiring devices wholesaling
316110 Currying furs
316110 Currying leather
442291 Curtain and drapery stores, packaged
337920 Curtain or drapery fixtures (e.g., poles, rods, rollers) manufacturing
337920 Curtain rods and fittings manufacturing
235910 Curtain wall construction contractors
332321 Curtain wall, metal, manufacturing
313210 Curtains and draperies made in broadwoven fabric mills
314121 Curtains and draperies, window, made from purchased fabrics
313249 Curtains made in lace mills
313249 Curtains made in warp knitting mills
313241 Curtains made in weft knitting mills
421220 Curtains wholesaling
314129 Cushions (except carpet, springs) made from purchased fabrics
326150 Cushions, carpet and rug, urethane and other foam plastics (except polystrene), manufacturing
311520 Custard, frozen, manufacturing
561720 Custodial services
337212 Custom architectural millwork and fixtures, manufacturing on a job shop basis
233210 Custom built house construction
325991 Custom compounding (i.e., blending and mixing) of purchased plastics resins

http://www.ntis.gov/naics

337212	Custom design interiors (i.e., coordinated furniture, architectural woodwork, fixtures), manufacturing
115114	Custom feed mixing and grinding
442299	Custom picture frame shops
333513	Custom roll forming machines, metalworking, manufacturing
332114	Custom roll forming metal products
311611	Custom slaughtering
315223	Custom tailors, men's and boys' dress shirts, cut and sewn from purchased fabric
315222	Custom tailors, men's and boys' suits, cut and sewn from purchased fabric
315233	Custom tailors, women's, misses' and girls' dresses cut and sewn from purchased fabric (except apparel contractors)
541613	Customer service management consulting services
488510	Customs brokers
921130	Customs bureaus
541614	Customs consulting services
327215	Cut and engraved glassware made from purchased glass
315211	Cut and sew apparel contractors, men's and boys'
111422	Cut flower growing
111422	Cut rose growing
316999	Cut stock for boots and shoes manufacturing
321912	Cut stock manufacturing
327991	Cut stone bases (e.g., desk sets pedestals, lamps, plaques and similar small particles) manufacturing
327991	Cut stone products (e.g., blocks, statuary) manufacturing
811490	Cutlery (e.g., knives, scissors) sharpening, household-type
421710	Cutlery wholesaling
332211	Cutlery, nonprecious and precious plated metal, manufacturing
339912	Cutlery, precious (except precious plated) metal, manufacturing
332212	Cutters, glass, manufacturing
332212	Cutting dies (except metal cutting) manufacturing
333514	Cutting dies, metalworking, manufacturing
315211	Cutting fabric owned by others for men's and boys' apparel
315212	Cutting fabric owned by others for women's, girls', and infants' apparel
333512	Cutting machines, metalworking, manufacturing
422470	Cutting of purchased carcasses (except boxed meat cut on an assembly-line basis) wholesaling
324191	Cutting oils made from refined petroleum
113310	Cutting timber
327215	Cutting, engraving, etching, painting or polishing purchased glass
211112	Cycle condensate production
325110	Cyclic aromatic hydrocarbons made from refined petroleum or liquid hydrocarbons
324110	Cyclic aromatic hydrocarbons made in petroleum refineries
422690	Cyclic crudes and intermediates wholesaling
325192	Cyclic crudes made by distillation of coal tar
325192	Cyclohexane manufacturing
325191	Cycloterpenes manufacturing
336312	Cylinder heads, automotive and truck gasoline engine, manufacturing
327332	Cylinder pipe, prestressed concrete, manufacturing
333995	Cylinders, fluid power, manufacturing
336340	Cylinders, master brake (new and rebuilt), manufacturing
332420	Cylinders, pressure, manufacturing
334417	Cylindrical connectors, electronic, manufacturing
332991	Cylindrical roller bearings manufacturing
621310	DCs' (doctors of chiropractic) offices (e.g., centers, clinics)

621210	DDSs' (doctors of dental surgery) offices (e.g., centers, clinics)
621210	DMDs' (doctors of dental medicine) offices (e.g., centers, clinics)
621112	DOs' (doctors of osteopathy), mental health, offices (e.g., centers, clinics)
621111	DOs' (doctors of osteopathy, except mental health) offices (e.g., centers, clinics)
621391	DPs' (doctors of podiatry) offices (e.g., centers, clinics)
334310	DVD (digital video disc) players manufacturing
112120	Dairy cattle farming
422430	Dairy depots wholesaling
311514	Dairy food canning
112111	Dairy heifer replacement production
541690	Dairy herd consulting services
115210	Dairy herd improvement associations
445299	Dairy product stores
422430	Dairy products (except canned, dried) wholesaling
422490	Dairy products, dried or canned, wholesaling
422430	Dairy products, frozen, wholesaling
112410	Dairy sheep farming
234990	Dam, dike, and dock construction
334512	Damper operators (e.g., electric, pneumatic, thermostatic) manufacturing
332322	Dampers, sheet metal, manufacturing
711130	Dance bands
713940	Dance centers, aerobic
711120	Dance companies
713990	Dance halls
611610	Dance instruction
711120	Dance productions, live theatrical
611610	Dance schools
611610	Dance studios
711120	Dance theaters
711120	Dance troupes
711510	Dancers, independent
334210	Data communications equipment (e.g., bridges, gateways, routers) manufacturing
514210	Data entry services
514210	Data processing computer services
541513	Data processing facilities (i.e., clients' facilities) management and operation services
514210	Data processing services (except payroll services, financial transition processing services)
511140	Database and directory publishers
511140	Database and directory publishers and printing combined
511140	Database publishers
511140	Database publishers and printing combined
323112	Databases flexographic printing without publishing
323111	Databases gravure printing without publishing
323110	Databases lithographic (offset) printing without publishing
323119	Databases printing (except flexographic, gravure, lithographic, screen) without publishing
323113	Databases screen printing without publishing
111339	Date farming
311340	Dates, sugared and stuffed, manufacturing
812990	Dating services
******	Day camps, instructional—see type of instruction
624120	Day care centers for disabled persons, the elderly, and persons diagnosed with mental retardation
624120	Day care centers, adult
624410	Day care centers, child or infant
624410	Day care services, child or infant
******	Dealers—see type
561440	Debt collection services
327215	Decorated glassware made from purchased glass
327112	Decorating china (e.g., encrusting gold, silver, other metal on china) for the trade
541410	Decorating consulting services, interior
335121	Decorative area lighting fixtures, residential, manufacturing

327212	Decorative glassware made in glass making plants
315211	Decorative stitching contractors on men's and boys' apparel
314999	Decorative stitching on textile articles and apparel
321918	Decorative wood moldings (e.g., base, chair rail, crown, shoe) manufacturing
483113	Deep sea freight transportation to or from domestic ports
483111	Deep sea freight transportation to or from foreign ports
483114	Deep sea passenger transportation to and from domestic ports
483112	Deep sea passenger transportation to or from foreign ports
112990	Deer production
334510	Defibrilators manufacturing
325320	Defoliants manufacturing
325612	Degreasing preparations, household-type, manufacturing
325998	Degreasing preparations for machinery parts manufacturing
333415	Dehumidifiers (except portable electric) manufacturing
335211	Dehumidifiers, portable electric, manufacturing
311514	Dehydrated milk manufacturing
311423	Dehydrating fruits and vegetables
311423	Dehydrating potato products (e.g., flakes, granules)
322110	Deinking recovered paper
722211	Delicatessen restaurants
445210	Delicatessens (except grocery store, restaurants)
445110	Delicatessens primarily retailing a range of grocery items and meats
561440	Delinquent account collection services
623990	Delinquent youth halfway group homes
115114	Delinting cottonseed
492210	Delivery service (except as part of intercity carrier network, U.S. Postal Service)
541720	Demographic research and development services
235940	Demolition of buildings or other structures construction contractors
541890	Demonstration services, merchandise
336212	Demountable cargo containers manufacturing
334513	Density and specific gravity instruments, industrial process-type, manufacturing
621512	Dental X-ray laboratories
339114	Dental alloys for amalgams manufacturing
339114	Dental chairs manufacturing
339114	Dental equipment and instruments manufacturing
421450	Dental equipment and supplies wholesaling
325620	Dental floss manufacturing
339114	Dental glues and cements manufacturing
611519	Dental hygienist schools
621399	Dental hygienists' offices (e.g., centers, clinics)
339114	Dental impression materials manufacturing
339114	Dental instrument delivery systems manufacturing
339116	Dental laboratories
339114	Dental laboratory equipment manufacturing
541710	Dental research and development laboratories or services
621210	Dental surgeons' offices (e.g., centers, clinics)
325611	Dentifrices manufacturing
422210	Dentifrices wholesaling
813920	Dentists' associations
621210	Dentists' offices (e.g., centers, clinics)
421450	Dentists' professional supplies wholesaling
325620	Denture adhesives manufacturing
325620	Denture cleaners, effervescent, manufacturing
339116	Dentures, custom made in dental laboratories
621399	Denturists' offices (e.g., centers, clinics)

561720   Deodorant servicing of rest rooms

325612   Deodorants (except personal) manufacturing

422690   Deodorants (except personal) wholesaling

325620   Deodorants, personal, manufacturing

422210   Deodorants, personal, wholesaling

561720   Deodorizing services

452110   Department stores

812199   Depilatory (i.e., hair removal) salons

325620   Depilatory preparations manufacturing

524128   Deposit or share insurance carriers, direct

339113   Depressors, tongue, manufacturing

332995   Depth charge projectors manufacturing

332993   Depth charges manufacturing

325412   Dermatological preparations manufacturing

333132   Derricks, oil and gas field-type, manufacturing

327992   Desiccants, activated clay, manufacturing

316999   Desk sets, leather, manufacturing

337214   Desks (except wood), office-type, manufacturing

337122   Desks, wood household-type, manufacturing

337211   Desks, wood office-type, manufacturing

561410   Desktop publishing services

422430   Desserts, dairy, wholesaling

311520   Desserts, frozen (except bakery), manufacturing

311813   Desserts, frozen bakery, manufacturing

811192   Detailing services (i.e., cleaning and polishing), automotive

561611   Detective agencies

922140   Detention centers

325611   Detergents (e.g., dishwashing, industrial, laundry) manufacturing

422690   Detergents wholesaling

325920   Detonating caps, cord, fuses, and primers manufacturing

332993   Detonators, ammunition (i.e., more than 30 mm., more than 1.18 inch), manufacturing

621420   Detoxification centers and clinics (except hospitals), outpatient

622210   Detoxification hospitals

325992   Developers, prepared photographic, manufacturing

336411   Developing and producing prototypes for aircraft

336412   Developing and producing prototypes for aircraft engines and engine parts

336413   Developing and producing prototypes for aircraft parts (except engines) and auxiliary equipment

336414   Developing and producing prototypes for complete guided missiles and space vehicles

336419   Developing and producing prototypes for guided missile and space vehicle components

336415   Developing and producing prototypes for guided missile and space vehicle engines

333315   Developing equipment, film, manufacturing

926110   Development assistance program administration

813311   Developmentally disabled advocacy organizations

311221   Dextrin made by wet milling corn

325412   Diagnostic biological preparations (except in-vitro) manufacturing

334510   Diagnostic equipment, MRI (magnetic resonance imaging), manufacturing

334510   Diagnostic equipment, electromedical, manufacturing

421450   Diagnostic equipment, medical, wholesaling

621512   Diagnostic imaging centers (medical)

325413   Diagnostic substances, in-vitro, manufacturing

422210   Diagnostics, in-vitro and in-vivo, wholesaling

621492	Dialysis centers and clinics
334510	Dialysis equipment, electromedical, manufacturing
339913	Diamond cutting and polishing
327910	Diamond dressing wheels manufacturing
421940	Diamonds (except industrial) wholesaling
421840	Diamonds, industrial, wholesaling
315212	Diaper covers, water resistant and waterproof, cut and sew apparel contractors
315291	Diaper covers, waterproof, infants', cut and sewn from purchased fabric (except apparel contractors)
812331	Diaper supply services
314999	Diapers (except disposable) made from purchased fabrics
422330	Diapers (except paper) wholesaling
322291	Diapers, disposable, made from purchased paper or textile fiber
422130	Diapers, paper, wholesaling
326299	Diaphragms (i.e., birth control device), rubber, manufacturing
511199	Diary and time scheduler publishers
327992	Diatomaceous earth processing beyond beneficiation
212399	Diatomite mining and/or beneficiating
421420	Dictating machines wholesaling
561410	Dictation services
323117	Dictionaries printing and binding without publishing
323117	Dictionaries printing without publishing
323121	Dictionary binding without printing
511130	Dictionary publishers
511130	Dictionary publishers and printing combined
333511	Die-casting dies manufacturing
331521	Die-castings, aluminum, unfinished, manufacturing
331522	Die-castings, nonferrous metals (except aluminum), unfinished, manufacturing
322299	Die-cut paper products (except for office use) made from purchased paper or paperboard
322231	Die-cut paper products for office use made from purchased paper or paperboard
333994	Dielectric industrial heating equipment manufacturing
333515	Dies and taps (i.e., a machine tool accessory) manufacturing
332212	Dies, cutting (except metal cutting), manufacturing
333514	Dies, metalworking (except threading), manufacturing
333514	Dies, steel rule, metal cutting, manufacturing
333618	Diesel and semidiesel engines manufacturing
812191	Diet centers, non-medical
812191	Diet workshops
311514	Dietary drinks, dairy and nondairy based, manufacturing
621399	Dieticians' offices (e.g., centers, clinics)
813920	Dieticians' associations
336350	Differential and rear axle assemblies, automotive, truck, and bus, manufacturing
325412	Digestive system preparations manufacturing
334119	Digital cameras manufacturing
334111	Digital computers manufacturing
323115	Digital printing (e.g., graphics, high resolution)
333293	Digital printing presses manufacturing
334515	Digital test equipment (e.g., electronic and electrical circuits and equipment testing) manufacturing
334310	Digital video disc players manufacturing
325411	Digitoxin, uncompounded, manufacturing
321113	Dimension lumber, made from logs or bolts
321912	Dimension lumber, resawing purchased lumber
321912	Dimension stock, wood, manufacturing
327991	Dimension stone dressing and manufacturing

327991	Dimension stone for buildings manufacturing
212311	Dimension stone mining or quarrying
335931	Dimmer switches, outlet box mounting-type, manufacturing
337124	Dinette sets, metal household-type, manufacturing
336612	Dinghy (except inflatable rubber) manufacturing
326299	Dinghies, inflatable rubber, manufacturing
337124	Dining room chairs (including upholstered), metal, manufacturing
337125	Dining room chairs (including upholstered), plastics manufacturing
337122	Dining room chairs (including upholstered), wood, manufacturing
337124	Dining room furniture, metal household-type, manufacturing
337122	Dining room furniture, wood household-type, manufacturing
487210	Dinner cruises
711110	Dinner theaters
311412	Dinners, frozen (except seafood-based), manufacturing
311712	Dinners, frozen seafood, manufacturing
422420	Dinners, frozen, wholesaling
326199	Dinnerware, plastics (except polystyrene foam), manufacturing
326140	Dinnerware, polystyrene foam, manufacturing
334515	Diode and transistor testers manufacturing
421690	Diodes wholesaling
334413	Diodes, solid-state (e.g., germanium, silicon), manufacturing
212313	Diorite crushed and broken stone mining and/or beneficiating
325192	Diphenylamine manufacturing
928120	Diplomatic services
311941	Dips (except cheese and sour cream based) manufacturing
325320	Dips (i.e., pesticides), cattle and sheep, manufacturing
311513	Dips, cheese based, manufacturing
311511	Dips, sour cream based, manufacturing
334112	Direct access storage devices manufacturing
513220	Direct broadcast satellite (DBS)
325132	Direct dyes manufacturing
541860	Direct mail advertising services
541860	Direct mail or other direct distribution advertising campaign services
454110	Direct mailers (i.e., selling own merchandise)
331111	Direct reduction of iron ore
454390	Direct selling of merchandise (door-to-door)
513220	Direct-to-home satellite systems
812210	Director services, funeral
323112	Directories flexographic printing without publishing
323111	Directories gravure printing without publishing
323110	Directories lithographic (offset) printing without publishing
323119	Directories printing (except flexographic, gravure, lithographic, screen) without publishing
323113	Directories screen printing without publishing
711510	Directors (i.e., film, motion picture, music, theatrical), independent
511140	Directory and database publishers
511140	Directory compilers
511140	Directory publishers
511140	Directory publishers and printing combined
541870	Directory, telephone, distribution on a contract basis
524113	Disability insurance carriers, direct
623990	Disabled group homes without nursing care
922190	Disaster preparedness and management offices, government
624230	Disaster relief services
711510	Disc jockeys, independent
713990	Discotheques (except those serving alcoholic beverages)

812990	Discount buying services
511199	Discount coupon book publishers
511199	Discount coupon book publishers and printing combined
323112	Discount coupon books flexographic printing without publishing
323111	Discount coupon books gravure printing without publishing
323110	Discount coupon books lithographic (offset) printing without publishing
323119	Discount coupon books printing (except flexographic, gravure, lithographic, screen) without publishing
323113	Discount coupon books screen printing without publishing
452110	Discount department stores
813212	Disease awareness fundraising organizations
813212	Disease research (e.g., cancer, heart) fundraising organizations
421220	Dishes, household-type (except disposable plastics, paper), wholesaling
422130	Dishes, paper and disposable plastics, wholesaling
327112	Dishes, pottery, manufacturing
321999	Dishes, wood, manufacturing
335228	Dishwashers, household-type, manufacturing
421620	Dishwashers, household-type, wholesaling
421440	Dishwashing equipment, commercial-type, wholesaling
333319	Dishwashing machines, commercial-type, manufacturing
325612	Disinfectants, household-type and industrial, manufacturing
332611	Disk and ring springs, heavy gauge, manufacturing
334112	Disk drives, computer, manufacturing
421430	Disk drives, computer, wholesaling
334613	Diskettes, blank, manufacturing
421690	Diskettes, blank, wholesaling
235950	Dismantling of machinery and other industrial equipment construction contractors
333913	Dispensing and measuring pumps (e.g., gasoline, lubricants) manufacturing

325132	Disperse dyes manufacturing
541850	Display advertising services
421440	Display cases (except refrigerated) wholesaling
337215	Display cases and fixtures (except refrigerated) manufacturing
333415	Display cases, refrigerated, manufacturing
421740	Display cases, refrigerated, wholesaling
334513	Display instruments, industrial process control-type, manufacturing
541890	Display lettering services
339950	Displays (e.g., counter, floor, point-of-purchase) manufacturing
335912	Disposable flashlight batteries manufacturing
422130	Disposable plastics products (e.g., boxes, cups, cutlery, dishes, sanitary food containers) wholesaling
325191	Distillates, wood, manufacturing
422820	Distilled alcoholic beverages wholesaling
325998	Distilled water manufacturing
311213	Distiller's malt manufacturing
312140	Distilleries
312140	Distilling alcoholic beverages (except brandy)
312130	Distilling brandy
333298	Distilling equipment (except beverage) manufacturing
333294	Distilling equipment, beverage, manufacturing
312140	Distilling potable liquor (except brandy)
421610	Distribution equipment, electrical, wholesaling
234910	Distribution line construction, oil and gas fields
221330	Distribution of cooled air
221122	Distribution of electric power
221330	Distribution of heated air
221210	Distribution of natural gas
221330	Distribution of steam heat
335311	Distribution transformers, electric, manufacturing
336322	Distributor cap and rotor for internal combustion engines manufacturing

336322	Distributors for internal combustion engines manufacturing
813910	Distributors' associations
551114	District and regional offices
922130	District attorneys' offices
325412	Diuretic preparations manufacturing
451110	Diving equipment stores
561990	Diving services on a contract or fee basis
488330	Docking and undocking marine vessel services
488310	Docking facility operations
621310	Doctors of chiropractic (DCs) offices (e.g., centers, clinics)
621210	Doctors of dental medicine (DMDs) offices (e.g., centers, clinics)
621210	Doctors of dental surgery (DDSs) offices (e.g., centers, clinics)
621320	Doctors of optometry (ODs) offices (e.g., centers, clinics)
621112	Doctors of osteopathy (DOs), mental health, offices (e.g., centers, clinics)
621111	Doctors of osteopathy (DOs, except mental health) offices (e.g., centers, clinics)
621391	Doctors of podiatry (DPs) offices (e.g., centers, clinics)
621330	Doctors of psychology offices (e.g., centers, clinics)
561439	Document copying services (except combined with printing services)
561439	Document duplicating services (except combined with printing services)
561410	Document preparation services
561410	Document transcription services
311111	Dog food manufacturing
316999	Dog furnishings (e.g., collars, harnesses, leashes, muzzles), manufacturing
711219	Dog owners, race (i.e., racing dogs)
812910	Dog pounds
112990	Dog production
711212	Dog racetracks
711219	Dog racing kennels
322299	Doilies, paper, made from purchased paper
339932	Doll carriages and carts manufacturing
339931	Doll clothing manufacturing
452990	Dollar stores
421920	Dolls wholesaling
339931	Dolls, doll parts, and doll clothing (except wigs) manufacturing
212312	Dolomite crushed and broken stone mining and/or beneficiating
327410	Dolomite, dead-burned, manufacturing
327410	Dolomitic lime manufacturing
114111	Dolphin fishing
332321	Door frames and sash, metal, manufacturing
321911	Door frames and sash, wood and covered wood, manufacturing
332510	Door locks manufacturing
332510	Door opening and closing devices (except electrical) manufacturing
335999	Door opening and closing devices, electrical, manufacturing
321911	Door units, prehung, wood and covered wood, manufacturing
541870	Door-to-door distribution of advertising materials (e.g., coupons, flyers, samples)
454390	Door-to-door retailing of merchandise, direct selling
314110	Doormats, all materials (except entirely of rubber or plastics), manufacturing
326199	Doormats, plastics, manufacturing
326299	Doormats, rubber, manufacturing
421310	Doors and door frames wholesaling
326199	Doors and door frames, plastics, manufacturing
332321	Doors, metal, manufacturing
327215	Doors, unframed glass, made from purchased glass
321911	Doors, wood and covered wood, manufacturing
336612	Dories building
721310	Dormitories
233220	Dormitory construction, general construction contractors
333294	Dough mixing machinery (i.e., food manufacturing-type) manufacturing
722110	Doughnut shops, full service
722213	Doughnut shops, on premise baking and carryout service

311812	Doughnuts (except frozen) made in commercial bakeries
311813	Doughnuts, frozen, manufacturing
422420	Doughs, frozen, wholesaling
311211	Doughs, prepared, made in flour mills
311822	Doughs, refrigerated or frozen, made from purchased flour
332722	Dowel pins, metal, manufacturing
321999	Dowels, wood, manufacturing
315291	Down-filled clothing, infants', cut and sewn from purchased fabric (except apparel contractors)
315211	Down-filled clothing, men's and boys', cut and sew apparel contractors
315228	Down-filled clothing, men's and boys', cut and sewn from purchased fabric (except apparel contractors)
315212	Down-filled clothing, women's, girls' and infants' cut and sew apparel contractors
315239	Down-filled clothing, women's, misses', and girls', cut and sewn from purchased fabric (except apparel contractors)
713920	Downhill skiing facilities without accommodations
332322	Downspouts, sheet metal, manufacturing
334519	Drafting instruments manufacturing
421490	Drafting instruments wholesaling
339942	Drafting materials (except instruments and tables) manufacturing
541340	Drafting services
337127	Drafting tables and boards manufacturing
421490	Drafting tables wholesaling
541340	Draftsmen's offices
711212	Drag strips
333120	Draglines, crawler, manufacturing
561790	Drain cleaning services
332913	Drain cocks, plumbing, manufacturing
325612	Drain pipe cleaners manufacturing
327123	Drain tile, clay, manufacturing
234990	Drainage project construction
611610	Drama schools (except academic)
314121	Draperies made from purchased fabrics or sheet goods
421220	Draperies wholesaling
339113	Drapes, surgical, disposable, manufacturing
325998	Drawing inks manufacturing
331222	Drawing iron or steel wire from purchased iron or steel
331222	Drawing iron or steel wire from purchased iron or steel and fabricating wire products
333292	Drawing machinery for textiles manufacturing
336611	Dredge building
333120	Dredging machinery manufacturing
234990	Dredging, general construction contractors
315992	Dress and semidress gloves cut and sewn from purchased fabric (except apparel contractors)
315191	Dress and semidress gloves made in apparel knitting mills
315211	Dress and semidress gloves, men's and boys', cut and sew apparel contractors
315212	Dress and semidress gloves, women's, girls', and infants', cut and sew apparel contractors
316219	Dress shoes, children's and infants', manufacturing
316213	Dress shoes, men's, manufacturing
316214	Dress shoes, women's, manufacturing
448190	Dress shops
422990	Dressed furs and skins wholesaling
337124	Dressers, metal, manufacturing
337122	Dressers, wood, manufacturing
315191	Dresses made in apparel knitting mills
422330	Dresses wholesaling
315191	Dresses, hand-knit, manufacturing
315291	Dresses, infants', cut and sewn from purchased fabric (except apparel contractors)

315233	Dresses, women's, misses', and girls', cut and sewn from purchased fabric (except apparel contractors)
315212	Dresses, women's, misses', girls', and infants', cut and sew apparel contractors
316110	Dressing (i.e., bleaching, blending, currying, scraping, tanning) furs
316110	Dressing hides
311615	Dressing small game
421450	Dressings, medical, wholesaling
339113	Dressings, surgical, manufacturing
422490	Dried foods (e.g., fruits, milk, vegetables) wholesaling
325510	Driers, paint, and varnish, manufacturing
333515	Drill bits, metalworking, manufacturing
332212	Drill bits, woodworking, manufacturing
333512	Drill presses, metalworking, manufacturing
235930	Drilled shaft construction contractors
339913	Drilling pearls
336611	Drilling and production platforms, floating, oil and gas, building
333132	Drilling equipment, oil and gas field-type, manufacturing
333131	Drilling equipment, underground mining-type, manufacturing
213111	Drilling for gas on a contract basis
213111	Drilling for oil on a contract basis
333512	Drilling machines, metalworking, manufacturing
325998	Drilling mud compounds, conditioners, and additives (except bentonites) manufacturing
422690	Drilling muds wholesaling
333132	Drilling rigs, oil and gas field-type, manufacturing
213111	Drilling water intake wells, oil and gas field on a contract basis
333131	Drills, core, underground mining-type, manufacturing
339114	Drills, dental, manufacturing
332212	Drills, hand held, nonelectric, manufacturing
333991	Drills, handheld power-driven (except heavy construction and mining type), manufacturing
333131	Drills, rock, underground mining-type, manufacturing
311999	Drink powder mixes (except chocolate, coffee, milk based, tea) manufacturing
311320	Drink powdered mixes, cocoa, made from cacao
311330	Drink powdered mixes, cocoa, made from purchased cocoa
311511	Drink, chocolate milk, manufacturing
332998	Drinking fountains (except mechanically refrigerated), metal, manufacturing
333415	Drinking fountains, refrigerated, manufacturing
327111	Drinking fountains, vitreous china, non-refrigerated, manufacturing
722410	Drinking places (i.e., bars, lounges, taverns), alcoholic
312111	Drinks, fruit (except juice), manufacturing
336350	Drive shafts and half shafts, automotive, truck, and bus, manufacturing
512132	Drive-in motion picture theaters
711219	Drivers, harness or race car
333612	Drives, high-speed industrial (except hydrostatic), manufacturing
561790	Driveway cleaning (e.g., power sweeping, washing) services
713990	Driving ranges, golf
488490	Driving services (e.g., automobile, truck delivery)
332111	Drop forgings made from purchased iron or steel, unfinished
812320	Drop-off and pick-up sites for laundries and drycleaners
813319	Drug abuse prevention advocacy organizations
t623220	Drug addiction rehabilitation facilities (except licensed hospitals), residential
622210	Drug addiction rehabilitation hospitals

http://www.ntis.gov/naics

624190	Drug addiction self-help organizations
621420	Drug addiction treatment centers and clinics (except hospitals), outpatient
922120	Drug enforcement agencies and offices
422210	Drug proprietaries wholesaling
446110	Drug stores
422210	Druggists' sundries wholesaling
422210	Drugs wholesaling
711130	Drum and bugle corps (i.e., drill teams)
332439	Drums, light gauge metal, manufacturing
421840	Drums, new and reconditioned, wholesaling
326199	Drums, plastics (i.e., containers), manufacturing
813319	Drunk driving prevention advocacy organizations
422510	Dry beans wholesaling
484230	Dry bulk carrier, truck, long-distance
335912	Dry cell primary batteries, single and multiple cell, manufacturing
335912	Dry cells, primary (e.g., AAA, AA, C, D, 9V), manufacturing
325120	Dry ice (i.e., solid carbon dioxide) manufacturing
422690	Dry ice wholesaling
311514	Dry milk manufacturing
311514	Dry milk products and mixture manufacturing
311514	Dry milk products for animal feed manufacturing
327999	Dry mix concrete manufacturing
311822	Dry mixes made from purchased flour
311823	Dry pasta manufacturing
311823	Dry pasta packaged with other ingredients made in dry pasta plants
812320	Drycleaner drop-off and pick-up sites
812320	Drycleaners (except coin-operated)
333312	Drycleaning equipment and machinery manufacturing

421850	Drycleaning equipment and supplies wholesaling
812310	Drycleaning machine routes (i.e., concession operators), coin-operated or similar self-service
325612	Drycleaning preparations manufacturing
336611	Drydock, floating, building
488390	Drydocks, floating (i.e., routine repair and maintenance of ships and boats)
335224	Dryers, clothes, household-type, gas and electric, manufacturing
421620	Dryers, hair, wholesaling
333312	Dryers, laundry (except household-type), manufacturing
311711	Drying fish and seafood
333292	Drying machinery for textiles manufacturing
235420	Drywall construction contractors
421320	Drywall supplies wholesaling
112390	Duck production
561790	Duct cleaning services
331511	Ductile iron foundries
335313	Ducts for electrical switchboard apparatus manufacturing
332322	Ducts, sheet metal, manufacturing
721214	Dude ranches
336212	Dump trailer manufacturing
484220	Dump trucking (e.g., gravel, sand, top soil)
562119	Dump trucking of rubble or brush with collection or disposal
336211	Dump-truck lifting mechanisms manufacturing
562219	Dumps, compost
562212	Dumps, nonhazardous solid waste (e.g., trash)
233220	Duplexes, double (i.e., one unit above the other) multifamily, construction
233210	Duplexes, single family, construction
532420	Duplicating machine (e.g., copier) rental or leasing
333411	Dust and fume collecting equipment manufacturing

314999	Dust cloths made from purchased fabrics
421730	Dust collection equipment wholesaling
333111	Dusters, farm-type, manufacturing
115112	Dusting crops
445310	Duty free liquor shops
531110	Dwelling rental or leasing
313311	Dyeing broadwoven fabrics
316110	Dyeing furs
316110	Dyeing leather
333292	Dyeing machinery for textiles manufacturing
313312	Dyeing textile products and fabrics (except broadwoven fabrics)
422690	Dyes, industrial, wholesaling
325131	Dyes, inorganic, manufacturing
325191	Dyes, natural, manufacturing
325132	Dyes, synthetic organic, manufacturing
422690	Dyestuffs wholesaling
325920	Dynamite manufacturing
335932	EMTs (electrical metallic tube) manufacturing
812199	Ear piercing services
532412	Earth moving equipment rental or leasing without operator
334220	Earth station communications equipment manufacturing
513390	Earth stations (except satellite telecommunication carriers)
513340	Earth stations for satellite communication carriers
327112	Earthenware table and kitchen articles, coarse, manufacturing
327112	Earthenware, commercial and household, semivitreous, manufacturing
422130	Eating utensils, disposable plastics, wholesaling
332322	Eaves, sheet metal, manufacturing
327420	Ecclesiastical statuary, gypsum, manufacturing
327999	Ecclesiastical statuary, paper mache, manufacturing
327991	Ecclesiastical statuary, stone, manufacturing

541690	Economic consulting services
926110	Economic development agencies, government
928120	Economic development assistance (i.e., international), government
541720	Economic research and development services
522298	Edge Act corporations (except international trade financing)
522293	Edge Act corporations (i.e., international trade financing)
332212	Edge tools, woodworking (e.g., augers, bits, countersinks), manufacturing
561410	Editing services
923110	Education offices, nonoperating
923110	Education program administration
923110	Education statistics centers, government
611710	Educational consultants
611710	Educational guidance counseling services
611710	Educational testing evaluation services
611710	Educational testing services
813211	Educational trusts, awarding grants
813920	Educators' associations
114111	Eel fishing
541614	Efficiency management (i.e., efficiency expert) consulting services
311823	Egg noodles, dry, manufacturing
311991	Egg noodles, fresh, manufacturing
112310	Egg production, chicken
112330	Egg production, turkey
311999	Egg substitutes manufacturing
312140	Eggnog, alcoholic, manufacturing
311514	Eggnog, canned, nonalcoholic, manufacturing
311511	Eggnog, fresh, nonalcoholic, manufacturing
311511	Eggnog, nonalcoholic (except canned), manufacturing
111219	Eggplant farming (except under cover), field, bedding plant and seed production
111419	Eggplant farming, grown under cover

http://www.ntis.gov/naics

422440	Eggs wholesaling
311999	Eggs, processed, manufacturing
313221	Elastic fabrics, narrow woven, manufacturing
339113	Elastic hosiery, orthopedic, manufacturing
325222	Elastomeric fibers and filaments manufacturing
325211	Elastomers (except synthetic rubber) manufacturing
325212	Elastomers, synthetic rubber, manufacturing
332322	Elbows for conductor pipe, hot air ducts, and stovepipe, sheet metal, manufacturing
332919	Elbows, pipe, metal (except made from purchased pipe), manufacturing
921190	Election boards
336111	Electric automobiles for highway use manufacturing
335999	Electric bells manufacturing
335211	Electric blankets manufacturing
421620	Electric blankets wholesaling
335311	Electric furnace transformers manufacturing
335110	Electric light bulbs, complete, manufacturing
811310	Electric motor repair and maintenance services, commercial or industrial
421610	Electric motors, wiring supplies, and lighting fixtures wholesaling
333618	Electric outboard motors manufacturing
221122	Electric power brokers
221121	Electric power control
221122	Electric power distribution systems
221119	Electric power generation, (except fossil fuel, hydroelectric, nuclear)
221112	Electric power generation, fossil fuel (e.g., coal, oil, gas)
221111	Electric power generation, hydroelectric
221113	Electric power generation, nuclear
221119	Electric power generation, solar
221119	Electric power generation, tidal
221119	Electric power generation, wind
234920	Electric power transmission line and tower construction
221121	Electric power transmission systems
335211	Electric space heaters, portable, manufacturing
333415	Electric warm air (i.e., forced air) furnaces manufacturing
235310	Electrical construction contractors
541330	Electrical engineering services
811310	Electrical generating and transmission equipment repair and maintenance services
541360	Electrical geophysical surveying services
336322	Electrical ignition cable sets for internal combustion engines manufacturing
335932	Electrical metallic tube (EMTs) manufacturing
561990	Electrical meter reading services, contract
334515	Electrical power measuring equipment manufacturing
235310	Electrical repair construction contractors
811118	Electrical repair shops, automotive
339950	Electrical signs manufacturing
421440	Electrical signs wholesaling
444190	Electrical supply stores
541380	Electrical testing laboratories or services
334515	Electricity and electrical signal measuring instruments manufacturing
335999	Electrochemical generators (i.e., fuel cells) manufacturing
335991	Electrodes for thermal and electrolytic uses, carbon and graphite, manufacturing
333992	Electrodes, welding, manufacturing
812199	Electrolysis (i.e., hair removal) salons
334513	Electromagnetic flowmeters manufacturing
541360	Electromagnetic geophysical surveying services
334510	Electromedical diagnostic equipment manufacturing

334510	Electromedical equipment manufacturing
421450	Electromedical equipment wholesaling
334510	Electromedical therapy equipment manufacturing
331112	Electrometallurical ferroalloy manufacturing
333992	Electron beam welding equipment manufacturing
334516	Electron microscopes manufacturing
333298	Electron tube machinery manufacturing
334411	Electron tube parts (e.g., bases, getters, guns) (except glass blanks) manufacturing
327215	Electron tube parts, glass blanks, made from purchased glass
327212	Electron tube parts, glass blanks, made in glass making plants
334411	Electron tubes manufacturing
514210	Electronic data processing services
511140	Electronic database publishers
611519	Electronic equipment repair training
522320	Electronic funds transfer services
421920	Electronic games wholesaling
334511	Electronic guidance systems and equipment manufacturing
421690	Electronic parts (e.g., condensers, connectors, switches) wholesaling
323122	Electronic prepress services for the printing trade
541710	Electronic research and development laboratories or services
541380	Electronic testing laboratories or services
339932	Electronic toys and games manufacturing
421690	Electronic tubes (e.g., industrial, receiving, transmitting) wholesaling
332813	Electroplating metals and formed products for the trade
333411	Electrostatic precipitation equipment manufacturing
323122	Electrotype plate preparation services
611110	Elementary schools
235950	Elevator installation contractors
421830	Elevators wholesaling
333921	Elevators, passenger and freight, manufacturing
325998	Embalming fluids manufacturing
812210	Embalming services
928120	Embassies
316110	Embossing leather
339943	Embossing stamps manufacturing
313222	Embroideries, Schiffli machine, manufacturing
315211	Embroidering contractors on men's and boys' apparel
315212	Embroidering contractors on women's, misses', girls', and infants' apparel
314999	Embroidering on textile products (except apparel) for the trade
339932	Embroidery kits manufacturing
333292	Embroidery machinery manufacturing
422310	Embroidery products wholesaling
335122	Emergency lighting (i.e., battery backup) manufacturing
621493	Emergency medical centers and clinics, freestanding
922190	Emergency planning and management offices, government
624230	Emergency relief services
488410	Emergency road services (i.e., tow service)
624221	Emergency shelters (except for victims of domestic or international disasters or conflicts)
624230	Emergency shelters for victims of domestic or international disasters or conflicts
541612	Employee assessment consulting services
541612	Employee benefit consulting services
525110	Employee benefit pension plans
525120	Employee benefit plans (except pension)
524292	Employee benefit plans, third-party administrative processing services

485410	Employee bus services
541612	Employee compensation consulting services
561330	Employee leasing services
813930	Employees' associations for improvement of wages and working conditions
561310	Employment agencies
561310	Employment placement agencies or services
561310	Employment referral agencies or services
561310	Employment registries
112390	Emu production
325613	Emulsifiers (i.e., surface-active agents) manufacturing
332214	Enameled metal cutting utensils
332812	Enameling metals and metal products for the trade
339114	Enamels, dental, manufacturing
323121	Encyclopedia binding without printing
511130	Encyclopedia publishers
511130	Encyclopedia publishers and printing combined
323117	Encyclopedias printing and binding without publishing
323117	Encyclopedias printing without publishing
337124	End tables, metal, manufacturing
337122	End tables, wood, manufacturing
111419	Endive farming, grown under cover
422210	Endocrine substances wholesaling
334510	Endoscopic equipment, electromedical (e.g., bronchoscopes, colonoscopes, cystoscopes), manufacturing
541690	Energy consulting services
336312	Engine block assemblies, automotive and truck gasoline, manufacturing
325998	Engine degreasers manufacturing
336311	Engine intake and exhaust valves manufacturing
811111	Engine repair and replacement shops, automotive
421120	Engine testing equipment, motor vehicle, wholesaling

541330	Engineering consulting services
541330	Engineering design services
541710	Engineering research and development laboratories or services
541330	Engineering services
813920	Engineers' associations
421490	Engineers' equipment and supplies wholesaling
541330	Engineers' offices
336412	Engines and engine parts, aircraft (except carburetors, pistons, piston rings, valves), manufacturing
336312	Engines and parts (except diesel), automotive and truck, manufacturing
421860	Engines and parts, aircraft, wholesaling
421120	Engines and parts, automotive, new, wholesaling
421860	Engines and turbines, marine, wholesaling
333618	Engines, diesel locomotive, manufacturing
421830	Engines, internal combustion (except aircraft, automotive), wholesaling
333618	Engines, internal combustion (except aircraft, nondiesel automotive), manufacturing
333618	Engines, natural gas, manufacturing
111419	English pea farming, grown under cover
339911	Engraving and etching precious (except precious plated) metal jewelry and flatware
339912	Engraving and etching precious metal flatware
332812	Engraving metals and metal products (except printing plates) for the trade
323122	Engraving printing plate, for the printing trade
333315	Enlargers, photographic, manufacturing
711130	Ensembles, musical
711410	Entertainers' agents or managers
711510	Entertainers, independent

541710	Entomological research and development laboratories or services
115112	Entomological service, agricultural
541690	Entomology consulting services
422110	Envelope paper, bulk, wholesaling
333313	Envelope stuffing, sealing, and addressing machinery manufacturing
322232	Envelopes (i.e., mailing, stationery) made from any material
422120	Envelopes wholesaling
541380	Environmental testing laboratories or services
813312	Environmental advocacy organizations
541620	Environmental consulting services
541330	Environmental engineering services
924110	Environmental protection program administration
562910	Environmental remediation services
541710	Environmental research and development laboratories or services
325199	Enzyme proteins (i.e., basic synthetic chemicals) (except pharmaceutical use) manufacturing
325411	Enzyme proteins (i.e., basic synthetic chemicals), pharmaceutical use, manufacturing
325520	Epoxy adhesives manufacturing
325211	Epoxy resins manufacturing
923130	Equal employment opportunity offices
115210	Equine boarding
522220	Equipment finance leasing
326299	Erasers, rubber or rubber and abrasive combined, manufacturing
541330	Erosion control engineering services
235950	Escalator installation contractors
333921	Escalators manufacturing
421830	Escalators wholesaling
111219	Escarole farming (except under cover), field, bedding plant and seed production
111419	Escarole farming, grown under cover

812990	Escort services, social
523991	Escrow agencies (except real estate)
531390	Escrow agencies, real estate
325998	Essential oils manufacturing
422690	Essential oils wholesaling
325199	Essential oils, synthetic, manufacturing
541110	Estate law offices
325199	Esters, not specified elsewhere by process, manufacturing
115310	Estimating timber
332812	Etching metals and metal products (except printing plates) for the trade
325110	Ethane made from refined petroleum or liquid hydrocarbons
325193	Ethanol, nonpotable, manufacturing
813410	Ethnic associations
422820	Ethyl alcohol wholesaling
325193	Ethyl alcohol, nonpotable, manufacturing
312140	Ethyl alcohol, potable, manufacturing
325110	Ethylbenzene made from refined petroleum or liquid hydrocarbons
325199	Ethylene glycol manufacturing
325110	Ethylene made from refined petroleum or liquid hydrocarbons
324110	Ethylene made in petroleum refineries
325199	Ethylene oxide manufacturing
325212	Ethylene-propylene rubber manufacturing
325211	Ethylene-vinyl acetate resins manufacturing
311514	Evaporated milk manufacturing
333415	Evaporative condensers (i.e., heat transfer equipment) manufacturing
611691	Exam preparation services
421810	Excavating machinery and equipment wholesaling
213112	Excavating mud pits, slush pits, and cellars at oil and gas fields on a contract basis
235930	Excavation construction contractors
523999	Exchange clearinghouses, commodities or securities

332410	Exchangers, heat, manufacturing
523210	Exchanges, commodity contracts
523210	Exchanges, securities
335312	Exciter assemblies, motor and generator, manufacturing
487210	Excursion boat operation
921140	Executive and legislative office combinations
561110	Executive management services
921110	Executive offices, federal, state, and local (e.g., governor, mayor, president)
541612	Executive placement consulting services
541612	Executive search consulting services
713940	Exercise centers
451110	Exercise equipment stores
339920	Exercise machines manufacturing
336399	Exhaust and tail pipes, automotive, truck, and bus, manufacturing
333412	Exhaust fans, industrial and commercial-type, manufacturing
811112	Exhaust system repair and replacement shops, automotive
336399	Exhaust systems and parts, automotive, truck, and bus, manufacturing
624190	Exoffender rehabilitation agencies
332312	Expansion joints, metal, manufacturing
541710	Experimental farms
213113	Exploration services for coal (except geophysical surveying and mapping) on a contract basis
213114	Exploration services for metal (except geophysical surveying and mapping) on a contract basis
213115	Exploration services for nonmetallic minerals (except geophysical surveying and mapping) on a contract basis
213112	Exploration services for oil and gas (except geophysical surveying and mapping) on a contract basis
422690	Explosives (except ammunition, fireworks) wholesaling
325920	Explosives manufacturing
522293	Export trading companies (i.e., international trade financing)
522293	Export-Import banks
335999	Extension cords made from purchased insulated wire
321999	Extension ladders, wood, manufacturing
325320	Exterminating chemical products (e.g., fungicides, insecticides, pesticides) manufacturing
561710	Exterminating services
421990	Extinguishers, fire, wholesaling
311920	Extracts, essences and preparations, coffee, manufacturing
311920	Extracts, essences and preparations, tea, manufacturing
311942	Extracts, food (except coffee, meat), manufacturing
311942	Extracts, malt, manufacturing
325191	Extracts, natural dyeing and tanning, manufacturing
326291	Extruded, molded or lathe-cut rubber goods manufacturing
333220	Extruding machinery for plastics and rubber manufacturing
333292	Extruding machinery for yarn manufacturing
331319	Extrusion billet made by rolling purchased aluminum
331319	Extrusion billet, aluminum, made in integrated secondary smelting and rolling mills
333514	Extrusion dies for use with all materials manufacturing
331319	Extrusion ingot made by rolling purchased aluminum
331319	Extrusion ingot, aluminum, made in integrated secondary smelting and rolling mills
325412	Eye and ear preparations manufacturing
621991	Eye banks
339112	Eye examining instruments and apparatus manufacturing
325620	Eye make-up (e.g., eye shadow, eyebrow pencil, mascara) manufacturing
316993	Eyeglass cases, all materials, manufacturing

339115	Eyeglass frames (i.e., fronts and temples), ophthalmic, manufacturing
421460	Eyeglasses wholesaling
339115	Eyes, glass and plastics, manufacturing
522294	FHLMC (Federal Home Loan Mortgage Corporation)
522294	FNMA (Federal National Mortgage Association)
313312	Fabric (except broadwoven) finishing
451130	Fabric shops
325612	Fabric softeners manufacturing
332312	Fabricated bar joists manufacturing
332996	Fabricated pipe and pipe fittings made from purchased pipe
332313	Fabricated plate work manufacturing
314991	Fabricated rope products (e.g., nets, slings) made in cordage or twine mills
332312	Fabricated structural metal manufacturing
321213	Fabricated structural wood members (except trusses) manufacturing
313210	Fabrics (except rug, tire fabrics), broadwoven, weaving
314992	Fabrics for reinforcing rubber tires, industrial belting, and fuel cells manufacturing
313311	Fabrics, broadwoven, finishing
313311	Fabrics, broadwoven, mercerizing
313249	Fabrics, knit, made in warp knit fabric mills
313241	Fabrics, knit, made in weft knit fabric mills
313249	Fabrics, lace, made in lace mills
313221	Fabrics, narrow woven, weaving
313230	Fabrics, nonwoven, manufacturing
422310	Fabrics, textile (except burlap, felt), wholesaling
332618	Fabrics, woven wire, made from purchased wire
325620	Face creams (e.g., cleansing, moisturizing) manufacturing
335932	Face plates (i.e., outlet or switch covers) manufacturing

525990	Face-amount certificate funds
812112	Facial salons
422130	Facial tissue wholesaling
322291	Facial tissues made from purchased paper
322121	Facial tissues made in paper mills
561210	Facilities (except computer operation) support services
541513	Facilities (i.e., clients' facilities) management and operation services, computer systems or data processing
541513	Facilities (i.e., clients' facilities) support services, computer systems or data processing
513310	Facilities-based telecommunication carriers (except wireless)
334210	Facsimile equipment, standalone, manufacturing
532420	Facsimile machine rental or leasing
811213	Facsimile machine repair and maintenance services
421690	Facsimile machines wholesaling
522298	Factoring accounts receivable
233310	Factory construction
711310	Fair managers with facilities, agricultural
711310	Fair organizers with facilities, agricultural
711310	Fair promoters with facilities, agricultural
711320	Fair promoters without facilities, agricultural
448140	Family clothing stores
713120	Family fun centers
541110	Family law offices
621410	Family planning centers
621410	Family planning counseling services
722110	Family restaurants, full service
722211	Family restaurants, limited service
624190	Family social service agencies
624190	Family welfare services
335211	Fans (except attic), household-type electric, manufacturing
336322	Fans, electric cooling, automotive, truck, and bus, manufacturing
421620	Fans, household-type, wholesaling
333412	Fans, industrial and commercial-type, manufacturing

http://www.ntis.gov/naics

421830	Fans, industrial, wholesaling
334514	Fare collection equipment manufacturing
311211	Farina (except breakfast food) made in flour mills
311230	Farina, breakfast cereal, manufacturing
233320	Farm building construction
813910	Farm bureaus
532490	Farm equipment rental or leasing
813410	Farm granges
115115	Farm labor contractors
421820	Farm machinery and equipment wholesaling
115116	Farm management services
493130	Farm product warehousing and storage (except refrigerated)
493120	Farm product warehousing and storage, refrigerated
422910	Farm supplies wholesaling
333111	Farm tractors and attachments manufacturing
333922	Farm-type conveyers manufacturing
******	Farming—see type
813910	Farmers' associations
813910	Farmers' unions
531190	Farmland rental or leasing
115210	Farriers
112210	Farrow-to-finish operations
541490	Fashion design services
722211	Fast food restaurants
421710	Fasteners (e.g., bolts, nuts, rivets, screws) wholesaling
339993	Fasteners (e.g., glove, hook-and-eye, slide, snap) manufacturing
311611	Fats, animal (except poultry, small game), produced in slaughtering plants
311613	Fats, animal, rendering
112112	Fattening cattle
325199	Fatty acids (e.g., margaric, oleic, stearic) manufacturing
325199	Fatty alcohols manufacturing
327111	Faucet handles, vitreous china and earthenware, manufacturing
332913	Faucets, plumbing, manufacturing
811213	Fax machine repair and maintenance services
422590	Feathers wholesaling
514110	Feature syndicates (i.e., advice columns, comic, news)
522294	Federal Agricultural Mortgage Corporation
926120	Federal Aviation Administration (except air traffic control)
522298	Federal Home Loan Banks (FHLB)
522294	Federal Home Loan Mortgage Corporation (FHLMC)
522294	Federal National Mortgage Association (FNMA)
521110	Federal Reserve Banks or Branches
921130	Federal Reserve Board of Governors
522130	Federal credit unions
922120	Federal police services
522120	Federal savings and loan associations (S&L)
522120	Federal savings banks
813219	Federated charities
813930	Federation of workers, labor organizations
813930	Federations of labor
422910	Feed additives wholesaling
314911	Feed bags made from purchased woven or knitted materials
311119	Feed concentrates, animal, manufacturing
311514	Feed grade dry milk products manufacturing
311119	Feed premixes, animal, manufacturing
333111	Feed processing equipment, farm-type, manufacturing
444220	Feed stores (except pet)
453910	Feed stores, pet
311119	Feed supplements, animal (except cat, dog), manufacturing
311111	Feed supplements, dog and cat, manufacturing
112112	Feed yards (except stockyards for transportation), cattle
112210	Feeder pig farming
335311	Feeder voltage regulators and boosters (i.e., electrical transformers) manufacturing

421820	Feeders, animal, wholesaling
112112	Feedlots (except stockyards for transportation), cattle
112210	Feedlots (except stockyards for transportation), hog
112410	Feedlots (except stockyards for transportation), lamb
422910	Feeds (except pet) wholesaling
311111	Feeds, prepared for dog and cat, manufacturing
311119	Feeds, prepared, for animals (except cat, dog) manufacturing
311119	Feeds, specialty (e.g., guinea pig, mice, mink), manufacturing
212325	Feldspar mining and/or beneficiating
327992	Feldspar processing beyond beneficiation
339941	Felt tip markers manufacturing
422990	Felt wholesaling
322121	Felts, asphalt, made in paper mills
313210	Felts, broadwoven, weaving
313230	Felts, nonwoven, manufacturing
235990	Fence construction contractors
332323	Fences and gates (except wire), metal, manufacturing
421390	Fencing (except wood) wholesaling
332618	Fencing and fence gates made from purchased wire
421390	Fencing and fencing accessories, wire, wholesaling
444190	Fencing dealers
321999	Fencing, prefabricated sections, wood, manufacturing
421310	Fencing, wood, wholesaling
333298	Fermentation equipment, chemical, manufacturing
332420	Fermention tanks, heavy gauge metal tanks, manufacturing
212299	Ferralloy ores (except vanadium) (e.g., chromium, columbium, molybdenum, tungsten) mining and/or beneficiating
331112	Ferroalloys manufacturing
421510	Ferroalloys wholesaling
332111	Ferrous forgings made from purchased iron or steel, unfinished
421510	Ferrous metals wholesaling
483114	Ferry passenger transportation, Great Lakes

336611	Ferryboat building
621410	Fertility clinics
422910	Fertilizer and fertilizer materials wholesaling
115112	Fertilizer application for crops
325314	Fertilizers, mixed, made in plants not manufacturing fertilizer materials
325311	Fertilizers, mixed, made in plants producing nitrogenous fertilizer materials
325312	Fertilizers, mixed, made in plants producing phosphatic fertilizer materials
325311	Fertilizers, natural organic (except compost), manufacturing
325311	Fertilizers, of animal waste origin, manufacturing
325311	Fertilizers, of sewage origin, manufacturing
561730	Fertilizing lawns
333111	Fertilizing machinery, farm-type, manufacturing
711310	Festival managers with facilities
711320	Festival managers without facilities
711310	Festival organizers with facilities
711320	Festival organizers without facilities
711310	Festival promoters with facilities
711320	Festival promoters without facilities
325412	Fever remedy preparations manufacturing
322214	Fiber cans and drums (i.e., all-fiber, nonfiber ends of any material) made from purchased paperboard
422130	Fiber cans and drums wholesaling
322214	Fiber drums made from purchased paperboard
337125	Fiber furniture (except upholstered), household-type, manufacturing
235310	Fiber optic cable construction contractors
335921	Fiber optic cable manufacturing
334417	Fiber optic connectors manufacturing
322214	Fiber spools, reels, blocks made from purchased paperboard
322214	Fiber tubes made from purchased paperboard

http://www.ntis.gov/naics

314999	Fiber, textile recovery from textile mill waste and rags
321219	Fiberboard manufacturing
421310	Fiberboard wholesaling
421390	Fiberglass building materials (except insulation, roofing, siding) wholesaling
327993	Fiberglass insulation products manufacturing
325221	Fibers and filaments, cellulosic, manufacturing and texturizing
325222	Fibers and filaments, noncellulosic, manufacturing and texturizing
327212	Fibers, glass, textile, made in glass making plants
422690	Fibers, manmade, wholesaling
422590	Fibers, vegetable, wholesaling
323121	Fiction book binding without printing
323117	Fiction books printing and binding without publishing
323117	Fiction books printing without publishing
524126	Fidelity insurance carriers, direct
523991	Fiduciary agencies (except real estate)
334515	Field strength and intensity measuring equipment, electrical, manufacturing
336211	Fifth wheel assemblies manufacturing
111339	Fig farming
711219	Figure skaters, independent
111335	Filbert farming
422120	File cards and folders wholesaling
322231	File folders (e.g., accordion, expanding, hanging, manila) made from purchased paper and paperboard
332212	Files, handheld, manufacturing
337214	Filing cabinets (except wood), office-type, manufacturing
337211	Filing cabinets, wood, office type, manufacturing
325510	Fillers, wood (e.g., dry, liquid, paste), manufacturing
314999	Filling (except nonwoven textile), upholstery, manufacturing

333315	Film developing equipment manufacturing
421410	Film developing equipment wholesaling
512120	Film distribution agencies
512120	Film distribution, motion picture and video
512131	Film festivals exhibitors
512120	Film libraries, commercial distribution
512199	Film libraries, motion picture or video, stock footage
512191	Film or tape closed captioning
512191	Film or video transfer services
512199	Film processing laboratories, motion picture
711510	Film producers, independent
512110	Film studios producing films
421410	Film, photographic, wholesaling
326113	Film, plastics (except packaging), manufacturing
326112	Film, plastics, packaging, manufacturing
325992	Film, sensitized (e.g., camera, motion picture, X-ray), manufacturing
512110	Films, motion picture production
512110	Films, motion picture production and distribution
327112	Filtering media, pottery, manufacturing
336399	Filters (e.g., air, engine oil, fuel) automotive, truck, and bus, manufacturing
333411	Filters, air-conditioner, manufacturing
334419	Filters, electronic component-type, manufacturing
333411	Filters, furnace, manufacturing
333999	Filters, industrial and general line (except internal combustion engine, warm air furnace), manufacturing
322299	Filters, paper, made from purchased paper
522291	Finance companies (i.e., unsecured cash loans)

523140	Financial futures brokerages
523930	Financial investment advice services, customized, fees paid by client
511120	Financial magazine and periodical publishers
511120	Financial magazine and periodical publishers and printing combined
323112	Financial magazines and periodicals flexographic printing without publishing
323111	Financial magazines and periodicals gravure printing without publishing
323110	Financial magazines and periodicals lithographic (offset) printing without publishing
323119	Financial magazines and periodicals printing (except flexographic, gravure, lithographic, screen) without publishing
323113	Financial magazines and periodicals screen printing without publishing
541611	Financial management consulting (except investment advice) services
523930	Financial planning services, customized, fees paid by client
522320	Financial transactions processing (except central bank)
521110	Financial transactions processing of the central bank
339913	Findings, jeweler's, manufacturing
611610	Fine arts schools (except academic)
722110	Fine dining restaurants, full service
422110	Fine paper, bulk, wholesaling
114111	Finfish fishing (e.g., flounder, salmon, trout)
112511	Finfish production, farm raising
112511	Finfish, hatcheries
321213	Finger joint lumber manufacturing
561611	Fingerprint services
314110	Finishing (e.g., dyeing) rugs and carpets
325613	Finishing agents, textile and leather, manufacturing
316110	Finishing hides and skins on a contract basis
316110	Finishing leather
333292	Finishing machinery for textile manufacturing
313311	Finishing plants, broadwoven fabric
561621	Fire alarm monitoring services
561621	Fire alarm sales combined with installation, maintenance, or monitoring services
922160	Fire departments (e.g., government, volunteer)
334290	Fire detection and alarm systems manufacturing
332323	Fire escapes, metal, manufacturing
325998	Fire extinguisher chemical preparations manufacturing
422690	Fire extinguisher preparations wholesaling
421990	Fire extinguishers wholesaling
339999	Fire extinguishers, portable, manufacturing
611519	Fire fighter training schools
314999	Fire hose, textile, made from purchased materials
332911	Fire hydrant valves manufacturing
332911	Fire hydrants, complete, manufacturing
524126	Fire insurance carriers, direct
922160	Fire marshals' offices
115310	Fire prevention, forest
325998	Fire retardant chemical preparations manufacturing
421990	Firearms (except sporting) wholesaling
813319	Firearms advocacy organizations
332994	Firearms manufacturing
421910	Firearms, sporting, wholesaling
336611	Fireboat building
327124	Firebrick, clay refractories, manufacturing
922160	Firefighting (except forest), volunteer and government
421850	Firefighting equipment and supplies wholesaling
922160	Firefighting services (including volunteer)
339113	Firefighting suits and accessories manufacturing
115310	Firefighting, forest
332999	Fireplace fixtures and equipment manufacturing
333414	Fireplace inserts (i.e., heat directing) manufacturing

335129	Fireplace logs, electric, manufacturing
421720	Fireplaces, gas, wholesaling
321999	Firewood and fuel wood containing fuel binder manufacturing
454319	Firewood dealers, direct selling
421990	Firewood wholesaling
713990	Fireworks display services
325998	Fireworks manufacturing
453998	Fireworks shops (i.e., permanent location)
421920	Fireworks wholesaling
327112	Firing china for the trade
339113	First aid, snake bite, or burn kits manufacturing
421450	First-aid kits wholesaling
422210	First-aid supplies wholesaling
422460	Fish (except canned, packaged frozen) wholesaling
924120	Fish and game agencies
311711	Fish and marine animal oils produced in a cannery
311712	Fish and marine animal oils produced in a fresh and frozen seafood plant
311711	Fish and seafood chowder canning
924120	Fish and wildlife conservation program administration
311711	Fish egg bait canning
334511	Fish finders (i.e., sonar) manufacturing
311119	Fish food for feeding fish manufacturing
311712	Fish freezing (e.g., blocks, fillets, ready-to-serve products)
325411	Fish liver oils, medicinal, uncompounded, manufacturing
445220	Fish markets
311711	Fish meal produced in a cannery
311712	Fish meal produced in a fresh and frozen seafood plant
311711	Fish, canned and cured, manufacturing
422490	Fish, canned, wholesaling
311711	Fish, curing, drying, pickling, salting, and smoking

311712	Fish, fresh or frozen, manufacturing
311712	Fish, fresh prepared, manufacturing
422420	Fish, packaged frozen, wholesaling
422990	Fish, tropical, wholesaling
541710	Fisheries research and development laboratories or services
114111	Fisheries, finfish
114112	Fisheries, shellfish
487210	Fishing boat charter operation
336611	Fishing boat, commercial, building
721214	Fishing camps with accommodation facilities
713990	Fishing clubs, recreational
421910	Fishing equipment and supplies (except commercial) wholesaling
713990	Fishing guide services
314999	Fishing nets made from purchased materials
713990	Fishing piers
114210	Fishing preserves
451110	Fishing supply stores (e.g., bait)
339920	Fishing tackle and equipment (except lines, nets, seines) manufacturing
713940	Fitness centers
421910	Fitness equipment and supplies wholesaling
713940	Fitness salons
713940	Fitness spas without accommodations
326122	Fittings and unions, rigid plastics pipe, manufacturing
421720	Fittings and valves, plumber's, wholesaling
331511	Fittings, soil and pressure pipe, cast iron, manufacturing
337920	Fixtures (e.g., poles, rods, rollers), curtain and drapery, manufacturing
421610	Fixtures, electric lighting, wholesaling
421440	Fixtures, store (except refrigerated), wholesaling
337215	Fixtures, store display, manufacturing
453998	Flag and banner shops
561990	Flagging (i.e., traffic control) services

332323	Flagpoles, metal, manufacturing
321999	Flagpoles, wood, manufacturing
314999	Flags, textile (e.g., banners, bunting, emblems, pennants), made from purchased fabrics
212311	Flagstone mining or quarrying
327991	Flagstones cutting
331314	Flakes, aluminum, made from purchased aluminum
331221	Flakes made from purchased iron or steel
331111	Flakes, iron or steel, made in steel mills
332995	Flame throwers manufacturing
332919	Flanges and flange unions, pipe, metal, manufacturing
325998	Flares manufacturing
335110	Flash bulbs, photographic, manufacturing
335129	Flashlights manufacturing
421610	Flashlights wholesaling
313249	Flat (i.e., warp) fabrics knitting
327211	Flat glass (e.g., float, plate) manufacturing
421390	Flat glass wholesaling
334119	Flat panel displays (i.e., complete units), computer peripheral equipment, manufacturing
332612	Flat springs (except clock, watch), light gauge, manufacturing
332611	Flat springs, heavy gauge, manufacturing
336212	Flatbed trailers, commercial, manufacturing
421220	Flatware (except plated, precious) wholesaling
332211	Flatware, nonprecious and precious plated metal, manufacturing
421940	Flatware, precious and plated, wholesaling
311942	Flavor extracts (except coffee) manufacturing
311511	Flavored milk drinks manufacturing
311930	Flavoring concentrates (except coffee based) manufacturing
422490	Flavoring extracts (except for fountain use) wholesaling
325199	Flavoring materials (i.e., basic synthetic chemicals such as coumarin) manufacturing
311930	Flavoring pastes, powders, and syrups for soft drink manufacturing
111120	Flaxseed farming, field and seed production
311225	Flaxseed oil made from purchased oils
311223	Flaxseed oil made in crushing mills
531190	Flea market space (except under roof) rental or leasing
531120	Flea market space, under roof, rental or leasing
454390	Flea markets, temporary location, direct selling
453310	Flea markets, used merchandise, permanent
325320	Flea powders or sprays manufacturing
334112	Flexible (i.e., floppy) magnetic disk drives manufacturing
332999	Flexible metal hose and tubing manufacturing
322221	Flexible packaging sheet materials (except foil-paper laminates) made by coating or laminating purchased paper
322225	Flexible packaging sheet materials made by laminating purchased foil
334412	Flexible wiring boards, bare, manufacturing
323122	Flexographic plate preparation services
323112	Flexographic printing (except books, manifold business forms, printing grey goods)
333293	Flexographic printing presses manufacturing
334511	Flight and navigation sensors, transmitters, and displays manufacturing
611519	Flight attendant schools
334511	Flight recorders (i.e., black boxes) manufacturing
333319	Flight simulation machinery manufacturing

611512	Flight training schools
327992	Flint processing beyond beneficiation
321113	Flitches (i.e., veneer stock) made in sawmills
561990	Float decorating services
541490	Float design services
713210	Floating casinos (i.e., gambling cruises, riverboat casinos)
311711	Floating factory ships seafood processing
234990	Flood control project construction
335129	Floodlights (i.e., lighting fixtures) manufacturing
442210	Floor covering stores (except wood or ceramic tile only)
444190	Floor covering stores, wood or ceramic tile only
421220	Floor coverings wholesaling
326192	Floor coverings, linoleum, manufacturing
326192	Floor coverings, resilient, manufacturing
326192	Floor coverings, rubber, manufacturing
326192	Floor coverings, vinyl, manufacturing
235520	Floor laying, finishing, or refinishing construction contractors
326299	Floor mats (e.g., bath, door), rubber, manufacturing
325612	Floor polishes and waxes manufacturing
333319	Floor sanding, washing, and polishing machines, commercial-type, manufacturing
335212	Floor scrubbing and shampooing machines, household-type electric, manufacturing
327122	Floor tile, ceramic, manufacturing
321214	Floor trusses, wood, manufacturing
335212	Floor waxers and polishers, household-type electric, manufacturing
332323	Flooring, open steel (i.e., grating), manufacturing
332322	Flooring, sheet metal, manufacturing
321918	Flooring, wood, manufacturing
421310	Flooring, wood, wholesaling
334112	Floppy disk drives manufacturing
561422	Floral wire services (i.e., telemarketing services)
422930	Florist's supplies wholesaling
453110	Florists
327112	Florists' articles, red earthenware, manufacturing
114111	Flounder fishing
314911	Flour bags made from purchased woven or knitted materials
311211	Flour mixes made in flour mills
422490	Flour wholesaling
311822	Flour, blended or self-rising, made from purchased flour
311211	Flour, blended, prepared, or self-rising (except rice), made in flour mills
311213	Flour, malt, manufacturing
311212	Flour, rice, manufacturing
334513	Flow instruments, industrial process-type, manufacturing
327420	Flower boxes, plaster of paris, manufacturing
111421	Flower bulb growing
422910	Flower bulbs wholesaling
111422	Flower growing
327112	Flower pots, red earthenware, manufacturing
111422	Flower seed production
453998	Flower shops, artificial or dried
453110	Flower shops, fresh
422930	Flowers wholesaling
339999	Flowers, artificial (except glass, plastics), manufacturing
327123	Flue lining, clay, manufacturing
332322	Flues, stove and furnace, sheet metal, manufacturing
311511	Fluid milk substitutes processing
333995	Fluid power actuators manufacturing
332912	Fluid power aircraft subassemblies manufacturing
333995	Fluid power cylinders manufacturing
332912	Fluid power hose assemblies manufacturing

333996	Fluid power motors manufacturing
333996	Fluid power pumps manufacturing
332912	Fluid power valves and hose fittings manufacturing
421830	Fluid-power transmission equipment wholesaling
332322	Flumes, sheet metal, manufacturing
335311	Fluorescent ballasts (i.e., transformers) manufacturing
325132	Fluorescent dyes manufacturing
335110	Fluorescent lamp tubes, electric, manufacturing
325188	Fluorine manufacturing
325211	Fluoro-polymer resins manufacturing
325120	Fluorocarbon gases manufacturing
212393	Fluorspar mining and/or beneficiating
332998	Flush tanks, metal, manufacturing
332913	Flush valves, plumbing, manufacturing
325998	Fluxes (e.g., brazing, galvanizing, soldering, welding) manufacturing
541870	Flyer direct distribution (except direct mail) services
713990	Flying clubs, recreational
488119	Flying field operators
611512	Flying instruction
336312	Flywheels and ring gears, automotive and truck gasoline engine, manufacturing
326140	Foam polystyrene products manufacturing
422990	Foam rubber wholesaling
322223	Foil bags, made from purchased foil
332999	Foil containers (except bags) manufacturing
332999	Foil not made in rolling mills
322225	Foil sheet, laminating purchased foil sheets for packaging applications
331315	Foil, aluminum, made by flat rolling purchased aluminum
331315	Foil, aluminum, made in integrated secondary smelting and flat rolling mills
331421	Foil, copper, made from purchased metal or scrap
331491	Foil, gold, made by rolling purchased metals or scrap

331491	Foil, nickel, made by rolling purchased metals or scrap
331491	Foil, silver, made by rolling purchased metals or scrap
422120	Folders, file, wholesaling
561910	Folding and packaging services, textile and apparel
322212	Folding boxes (except corrugated) made from purchased paperboard
322212	Folding paper and paperboard containers (except corrugated) made from purchased paperboard
111422	Foliage growing
445110	Food (i.e., groceries) stores
446191	Food (i.e., health) supplement stores
336999	Food (vendor) carts on wheels manufacturing
624210	Food banks
722330	Food carts, mobile
333294	Food choppers, grinders, mixers, and slicers (i.e., food manufacturing-type) manufacturing
325132	Food coloring, synthetic, manufacturing
311942	Food colorings, natural, manufacturing
722310	Food concession contractors (e.g., convention facilities, entertainment facilities, sporting facilities)
322299	Food containers made from molded pulp
326140	Food containers, polystyrene foam, manufacturing
322215	Food containers, sanitary (except folding), made from purchased paper or paperboard
322212	Food containers, sanitary, folding, made from purchased paperboard
311942	Food extracts (except coffee, meat) manufacturing
926140	Food inspection agencies
333993	Food packaging machinery manufacturing
421830	Food processing machinery and equipment wholesaling
233310	Food products manufacturing or packaging plant construction
541710	Food research and development laboratories or services

722310   Food service contractors, airline

722310   Food service contractors, cafeteria

722310   Food service contractors, concession operator (e.g., convention facilities, entertainment facilities, sporting facilities)

421440   Food service equipment (except refrigerated), commercial, wholesaling

541380   Food testing laboratories or services

322299   Food trays, molded pulp, manufacturing

333319   Food warming equipment, commercial-type, manufacturing

311991   Food, prepared, perishable, packaged for individual resale

711211   Football clubs, professional or semiprofessional

713990   Football clubs, recreational

316211   Footholds, plastics or plastics soled fabric upper, manufacturing

315119   Footies, sheer, knitting or knitting and finishing

451110   Footwear (e.g., bowling, golf, spiked), specialty sports, stores

316211   Footwear (except house slippers), plastics or plastics soled fabric uppers, manufacturing

333298   Footwear making or repairing machinery manufacturing

326199   Footwear parts (e.g., heels, soles), plastics, manufacturing

326299   Footwear parts (e.g., heels, soles, soling strips), rubber, manufacturing

422340   Footwear wholesaling

316219   Footwear, athletic (except rubber or plastics soled with fabric upper), manufacturing

316219   Footwear, children's (except house slippers, orthopedic extension, plastics, rubber), manufacturing

316219   Footwear, children's, leather or vinyl upper with rubber or plastics soles, manufacturing

316213   Footwear, men's (except house slippers, athletic, orthopedic extension, plastics, rubber), manufacturing

316213   Footwear, men's leather or vinyl upper with rubber or plastics soles, manufacturing

316214   Footwear, women's (except house slippers, athletic, orthopedic extension, plastics, rubber) manufacturing

316214   Footwear, women's leather or vinyl upper with rubber or plastics soles, manufacturing

339112   Forceps, surgical, manufacturing

523130   Foreign currency exchange dealing (i.e., acting as a principal in dealing commodities to investors)

523130   Foreign currency exchange services (i.e., selling to the public)

928120   Foreign economic and social development services, government

541380   Forensic (except medical) laboratories or services

621511   Forensic laboratories, medical

621111   Forensic pathologists' offices (e.g., centers, clinics)

113210   Forest nurseries for reforestation, growing trees

421990   Forest products (except lumber) wholesaling

532412   Forestry machinery and equipment rental or leasing

811310   Forestry machinery and equipment repair and maintenance services

421810   Forestry machinery and equipment wholesaling

541710   Forestry research and development laboratories or services

115310   Forestry services

332111   Forgings made from purchased iron or steel, unfinished

331111   Forgings, iron or steel, made in steel mills

421830   Forklift trucks (except log) wholesaling

333924   Forklifts manufacturing

332212   Forks, handtools (e.g., garden, hay, manure), manufacturing

532220   Formal wear rental

325199   Formaldehyde manufacturing

333513   Forming machines (except drawing), metalworking, manufacturing

421420	Forms handling machines wholesaling
422120	Forms, paper (e.g., business, office, sales), wholesaling
812990	Fortune-telling services
624110	Foster home placement services
235410	Foundation (e.g., block, brick, stone) construction contractors
235930	Foundation drilling construction contractors
315212	Foundation garments, women's and girls', cut and sew apparel contractors
315231	Foundation garments, women's, misses', and girls', cut and sewn from purchased fabric (except apparel contractors)
325620	Foundations (i.e., make-up) manufacturing
235710	Foundations of buildings, poured concrete, construction contractors
331528	Foundries (except die-casting), nonferrous metals (except aluminum, copper)
331524	Foundries, aluminum (except die-casting)
331525	Foundries, copper (except die-casting)
331521	Foundries, die-casting, aluminum
331522	Foundries, die-casting, nonferrous metals (except aluminum)
331511	Foundries, iron (i.e., ductile, gray, malleable, semisteel)
331513	Foundries, steel (except investment)
331512	Foundries, steel investment
333511	Foundry casting molds manufacturing
325998	Foundry core oil, wash, and wax manufacturing
332997	Foundry cores manufacturing
421830	Foundry machinery and equipment wholesaling
421510	Foundry products wholesaling
422450	Fountain fruits and syrups wholesaling
339941	Fountain pens manufacturing
332999	Fountains (except drinking), metal, manufacturing
332998	Fountains, drinking (except mechanically refrigerated), manufacturing
421720	Fountains, drinking (except refrigerated), wholesaling
421740	Fountains, drinking, refrigerated, wholesaling
327420	Fountains, plaster of paris, manufacturing
333415	Fountains, refrigerated drinking, manufacturing
713920	Four season ski resorts without accommodations
333291	Fourdrinier machinery manufacturing
332618	Fourdrinier wire cloth made from purchased wire
112930	Fox production
335312	Fractional horsepower electric motors manufacturing
211112	Fractionating natural gas liquids
421220	Frames and pictures wholesaling
332321	Frames, door and window, metal, manufacturing
332999	Frames, metal, lamp shade, manufacturing
332999	Frames, metal, umbrella and parasol, manufacturing
339999	Frames, mirror and picture, all materials, manufacturing
421460	Frames, ophthalmic, wholesaling
533110	Franchise agreements, leasing, selling or licensing, without providing other services
813410	Fraternal associations or lodges, social or civic
813410	Fraternal lodges
813410	Fraternal organizations
813410	Fraternities (except residential)
721310	Fraternity houses
621493	Freestanding ambulatory surgical centers and clinics
621493	Freestanding emergency medical centers and clinics
311423	Freeze-dried, food processing, fruits and vegetables
335222	Freezers, chest and upright household-type, manufacturing

421620	Freezers, household-type, wholesaling
333415	Freezing equipment, industrial and commercial-type, manufacturing
311712	Freezing fish (e.g., blocks, fillets, ready-to-serve products)
488210	Freight car cleaning services
481112	Freight carriers (except air couriers), air, scheduled
481212	Freight charter services, air
488510	Freight forwarding
482111	Freight railways, line-haul
482112	Freight railways, short-line or beltline
541614	Freight rate auditor services
541614	Freight rate consulting services
483113	Freight shipping on the Great Lakes system (including the St Lawrence Seaway)
541614	Freight traffic consulting services
481212	Freight transportation, air, charter services
481212	Freight transportation, air, nonscheduled
483113	Freight transportation, deep sea, to and from domestic ports
483111	Freight transportation, deep sea, to or from foreign ports
483211	Freight transportation, inland waters (except on Great Lakes system)
311411	French fries, frozen, pre-cooked, manufacturing
311412	French toast, frozen, manufacturing
235420	Fresco construction contractors
422460	Fresh fish wholesaling
422480	Fresh fruits, vegetables and berries wholesaling
422470	Fresh meats wholesaling
422440	Fresh poultry wholesaling
422460	Fresh seafood wholesaling
313221	Fringes weaving
325510	Frit manufacturing
114119	Frog fishing
112519	Frog production, farm raising
811118	Front end alignment shops, automotive
421820	Frost protection machinery wholesaling
311999	Frosting, prepared, manufacturing
311411	Frozen ades, drinks and cocktail mixes, manufacturing
311812	Frozen bread and bread-type rolls, made in commercial bakeries
311813	Frozen cake manufacturing
311411	Frozen citrus pulp manufacturing
311520	Frozen custard manufacturing
722213	Frozen custard stands, fixed location
311520	Frozen desserts (except bakery) manufacturing
311412	Frozen dinners (except seafood-based) manufacturing
311822	Frozen doughs made from purchased flour
422460	Frozen fish (except packaged) wholesaling
454390	Frozen food and freezer plan providers, direct selling
311412	Frozen food entrees (except seafood based), packaged, manufacturing
422420	Frozen foods, packaged (except dairy products), wholesaling
311411	Frozen fruits, fruit juices, and vegetables, manufacturing
311612	Frozen meat pies (i.e., tourtires) made from purchased carcasses
445210	Frozen meat stores
422470	Frozen meats (except packaged) wholesaling
311412	Frozen pizza manufacturing
311412	Frozen pot pies manufacturing
422440	Frozen poultry (except packaged) wholesaling
311412	Frozen rice dishes manufacturing
422460	Frozen seafood (except packaged) wholesaling
311412	Frozen side dishes manufacturing
311412	Frozen soups (except seafood) manufacturing
311412	Frozen waffles manufacturing
111336	Fruit and tree nut combination farming
445230	Fruit and vegetable stands, permanent
311423	Fruit and vegetables, dehydrating, manufacturing

311421	Fruit brining
311421	Fruit butters manufacturing
312111	Fruit drinks (except juice), manufacturing
311942	Fruit extracts (except coffee) manufacturing
111419	Fruit farming, grown under cover
311211	Fruit flour, meal, and powders, manufacturing
311421	Fruit juice canning
311411	Fruit juice concentrates, frozen, manufacturing
311421	Fruit juices, fresh, manufacturing
445230	Fruit markets
311340	Fruit peel products (e.g., candied, crystallized, glace, glazed) manufacturing
311421	Fruit pickling
311421	Fruit pie fillings, canning
311520	Fruit pops, frozen, manufacturing
115114	Fruit precooling
445230	Fruit stands, permanent
454390	Fruit stands, temporary
111421	Fruit stock (e.g., plants, seedlings, trees) growing
311930	Fruit syrups, flavoring, manufacturing
115113	Fruit, machine harvesting
311340	Fruits (e.g., candied, crystallized, glazed) manufacturing
311423	Fruits dehydrating (except sun drying)
311421	Fruits pickling
311421	Fruits, canned, manufacturing
422490	Fruits, canned, wholesaling
422480	Fruits, fresh, wholesaling
311411	Fruits, frozen, manufacturing
422420	Fruits, frozen, wholesaling
112320	Fryer chicken production
311320	Fudge, chocolate, made from cacao beans
311330	Fudge, chocolate, made from purchased chocolate
311340	Fudge, nonchocolate, manufacturing
324199	Fuel briquettes or boulets made from refined petroleum
335999	Fuel cells, electrochemical generators, manufacturing
334413	Fuel cells, solid-state, manufacturing
336312	Fuel injection systems and parts, automotive and truck gasoline engine, manufacturing
422710	Fuel oil bulk stations and terminals
235110	Fuel oil burner construction contractors
422720	Fuel oil truck jobbers
422720	Fuel oil wholesaling (except bulk stations, terminals)
324110	Fuel oils manufacturing
325188	Fuel propellants, solid inorganic, not specified elsewhere by process, manufacturing
325199	Fuel propellants, solid organic, not specified elsewhere by process, manufacturing
336322	Fuel pumps, electric, automotive, truck, and bus, manufacturing
336312	Fuel pumps, mechanical, automotive and truck gasoline engine, manufacturing
421520	Fuel, coal and coke, wholesaling
422720	Fueling aircraft (except on contract basis)
488190	Fueling aircraft on a contract or fee basis
324110	Fuels, jet, manufacturing
722110	Full service restaurants
212325	Fuller's earth mining and/or beneficiating
327992	Fuller's earth processing beyond beneficiating
115114	Fumigating grain
561710	Fumigating services
561499	Fundraising campaign organization services on a contract or fee basis
334119	Funds transfer devices manufacturing
525110	Funds, employee benefit pension
525120	Funds, health and welfare
525990	Funds, mutual, closed-end
525910	Funds, mutual, open-ended
525110	Funds, pension
525190	Funds, self-insurance (except employee benefit funds)

812210	Funeral director services
812210	Funeral homes
812210	Funeral homes combined with crematories
524128	Funeral insurance carriers, direct
812210	Funeral parlors
325320	Fungicides manufacturing
448190	Fur apparel stores
315292	Fur clothing (except apparel contractors) manufacturing
422330	Fur clothing wholesaling
315211	Fur clothing, men's and boys', cut and sew apparel contractors
315212	Fur clothing, women's, girls', and infants', cut and sew apparel contractors
421930	Fur cuttings and scraps wholesaling
541490	Fur design services
315211	Fur finishers, liners, and buttonhole makers, men's and boys', cut and sew apparel contractors
315212	Fur finishers, liners, and buttonhole makers, women's, girls', and infants', cut and sew apparel contractors
811490	Fur garment repair shops without retailing new fur garments
493120	Fur storage warehousing for the trade
316110	Fur stripping
333411	Furnace filters manufacturing
332322	Furnace flues, sheet metal, manufacturing
333414	Furnaces (except forced air), heating, manufacturing
421720	Furnaces, (except forced air), heating, wholesaling
333414	Furnaces, floor and wall, manufacturing
421830	Furnaces, industrial process, wholesaling
333994	Furnaces, industrial-type, manufacturing
333415	Furnaces, warm air (i.e., forced air), manufacturing
421730	Furnaces, warm air (i.e., forced air), wholesaling
422320	Furnishings (except shoes), men's and boys', wholesaling
422330	Furnishings (except shoes), women's, girls' and infants', wholesaling
448150	Furnishings stores, men's and boys'
448150	Furnishings stores, women's and girls'
421210	Furniture (except drafting tables, hospital beds, medical furniture) wholesaling
337124	Furniture (except upholstered), metal household-type, manufacturing
337214	Furniture (except wood), office-type, padded, upholstered, or plain, manufacturing
337125	Furniture (except wood, metal, upholstered) indoor and outdoor household-type, manufacturing
532299	Furniture (i.e., residential) rental centers
442110	Furniture and appliance stores (i.e., primarily retailing furniture)
561740	Furniture cleaning services
541420	Furniture design services
321912	Furniture dimension stock, unfinished wood, manufacturing
337215	Furniture frames and parts, metal, manufacturing
337215	Furniture frames, wood, manufacturing
332510	Furniture hardware, metal, manufacturing
484210	Furniture moving, used
421210	Furniture parts wholesaling
337215	Furniture parts, finished metal, manufacturing
337215	Furniture parts, finished plastics, manufacturing
337215	Furniture parts, finished wood, manufacturing
325612	Furniture polishes and waxes manufacturing
811420	Furniture refinishing shops
811420	Furniture repair shops
811420	Furniture reupholstering shops
332612	Furniture springs, unassembled, made from purchased wire
442110	Furniture stores (e.g., household, office, outdoor)

453310	Furniture stores, used
327215	Furniture tops, glass (e.g., beveled, cut, polished), made from purchased glass
314999	Furniture trimmings made from purchased fabrics
327991	Furniture, cut stone (i.e., benches, tables, church), manufacturing
337127	Furniture, factory-type (e.g., cabinets, stools, tool stands, work benches), manufacturing
532291	Furniture, home health, rental
339111	Furniture, hospital (e.g., hospital beds, operating room furniture), manufacturing
337121	Furniture, household-type, upholstered on frames of any material, manufacturing
532490	Furniture, institutional (i.e. public building), rental or leasing
337127	Furniture, institutional, manufacturing
339111	Furniture, laboratory-type (e.g., benches, cabinets, stools, tables), manufacturing
532420	Furniture, office, rental or leasing
337211	Furniture, office-type, padded, upholstered, or plain wood, manufacturing
337124	Furniture, outdoor metal household-type (e.g., beach, garden, lawn, porch), manufacturing
337122	Furniture, outdoor wood household-type (e.g., beach, garden, lawn, porch), manufacturing
337127	Furniture, public building (e.g., church, library, school, theater), manufacturing
532299	Furniture, residential, rental or leasing
337127	Furniture, restaurant-type, manufacturing
337122	Furniture, unassembled or knock-down wood household-type, manufacturing
337122	Furniture, unfinished wood household-type, manufacturing
337122	Furniture, wood household-type, not upholstered (except TV and radio housings, and sewing machine cabinets), manufacturing
448190	Furriers
422990	Furs, dressed, wholesaling
422590	Furs, raw, wholesaling
335313	Fuse clips and blocks, electric, manufacturing
332993	Fuses ammunition (i.e., more than 30 mm., more than 1.18 inch) manufacturing
421610	Fuses, electric, wholesaling
335313	Fuses, electrical, manufacturing
337122	Futon frames manufacturing
523140	Futures commodity contracts brokerages
523130	Futures commodity contracts dealing (i.e., acting as a principal in dealing commodities to investors)
523210	Futures commodity contracts exchanges
335931	GFCI (ground fault circuit interrupters) manufacturing
522294	GNMA (Government National Mortgage Association)
334220	GPS (global positioning system) equipment manufacturing
712110	Galleries, art (except retail)
453920	Galleries, art, retail
713990	Galleries, shooting
316211	Galoshes, plastics or plastics soled fabric upper, manufacturing
316211	Galoshes, rubber, or rubber soled fabric upper, manufacturing
333516	Galvanizing machinery manufacturing
331111	Galvanizing metals and metal formed products made in steel mills
332812	Galvanizing metals and metal products for the trade
713290	Gambling control boards, operating gambling activities
713210	Gambling cruises
713290	Gambling device arcades or parlors, coin-operated

http://www.ntis.gov/naics

713290	Gambling device concession operators (i.e., supplying and servicing in others' facilities), coin-operated
334611	Game cartridge software, mass reproducing
114210	Game preserves, commercial
114210	Game retreats
421430	Game software wholesaling
451120	Game stores (including electronic)
924120	Game wardens
339932	Games (except coin operated), children's and adult, manufacturing
421920	Games (except coin-operated) wholesaling
334611	Games, computer software, mass reproducing
511210	Games, computer software, publishing
334517	Gamma ray irradiation equipment manufacturing
335999	Garage door openers manufacturing
332321	Garage doors, metal, manufacturing
321911	Garage doors, wood, manufacturing
233320	Garage, commercial or institutional, construction contractors
812930	Garages, automobile parking
811111	Garages, general automotive repair (except gasoline service stations)
332439	Garbage cans, light gauge metal, manufacturing
562111	Garbage collection services
562213	Garbage disposal combustors or incinerators
562212	Garbage disposal landfills
421440	Garbage disposal units, commercial-type, wholesaling
333319	Garbage disposal units, commercial-type, manufacturing
335228	Garbage disposal units, household-type, manufacturing
421620	Garbage disposal units, household-type, wholesaling
562212	Garbage dumps
562111	Garbage hauling, local
333994	Garbage incinerators (except precast concrete) manufacturing
327390	Garbage incinerators, precast concrete, manufacturing
562111	Garbage pick-up services
336211	Garbage truck bodies manufacturing
336120	Garbage trucks assembling on chassis of own manufacture
336211	Garbage trucks assembling on purchased chassis
444220	Garden centers
813410	Garden clubs
811411	Garden equipment repair and maintenance services without retailing new garden equipment
327390	Garden furniture, precast concrete, manufacturing
327991	Garden furniture, stone, manufacturing
337122	Garden furniture, wood, manufacturing
326220	Garden hose, rubber or plastics, manufacturing
421820	Garden machinery and equipment wholesaling
333112	Garden machinery and equipment, powered, manufacturing
561730	Garden maintenance services
541320	Garden planning services
327112	Garden pottery manufacturing
444210	Garden power equipment stores
422910	Garden supplies (e.g., fertilizers, pesticides) wholesaling
811411	Garden tool sharpening and repair services
532490	Garden tractor rental or leasing
712130	Gardens, zoological or botanical
111219	Garlic farming (except under cover), field, bedding plant and seed production
111419	Garlic farming under cover
811490	Garment alteration and/or repair shops without retailing new garments
812320	Garment cleaning (e.g., fur, leather, suede) services
314911	Garment storage bags manufacturing
315292	Garments, leather or sheep-lined (except apparel contractors), manufacturing

315211	Garments, leather or sheep-lined, men's and boys', cut and sew apparel contractors
315212	Garments, leather or sheep-lined, women's, girls', and infants', cut and sew apparel contractors
313320	Garments, oiling (i.e., waterproofing)
314999	Garnetting of textile waste and rags
315212	Garter belts cut and sew apparel contractors
315231	Garter belts cut and sewn from purchased fabric (except apparel contractors)
315212	Garters, women's, cut and sew apparel contractors
315231	Garters, women's, misses', and girls', cut and sewn from purchased fabric (except apparel contractors)
334513	Gas chromatographic instruments, industrial process-type, manufacturing
334516	Gas chromatographic instruments, laboratory-type, manufacturing
333414	Gas fireplaces manufacturing
421720	Gas fireplaces wholesaling
421720	Gas hot water heaters wholesaling
523999	Gas lease brokers' offices
335129	Gas lighting fixtures manufacturing
421990	Gas lighting fixtures wholesaling
561990	Gas meter reading services, contract
421720	Gas ranges wholesaling
333414	Gas space heaters manufacturing
332420	Gas storage tanks, heavy gauge metal, manufacturing
336399	Gas tanks assembled, automotive, truck, and bus, manufacturing
333611	Gas turbine generator set units manufacturing
333611	Gas turbines (except aircraft) manufacturing
336412	Gas turbines, aircraft, manufacturing
332911	Gas valves, industrial-type, manufacturing
333992	Gas welding equipment manufacturing
333992	Gas welding rods, coated or cored, manufacturing
213111	Gas well drilling on a contract basis
333132	Gas well machinery and equipment manufacturing
213112	Gas, compressing natural, in the field on a contract basis
221210	Gas, manufactured, production and distribution
221210	Gas, natural, distribution
211111	Gas, natural, extraction
486210	Gas, natural, pipeline operation
422690	Gases, compressed and liquefied (except liquefied petroleum gas), wholesaling
325120	Gases, industrial (i.e., compressed, liquefied, solid), manufacturing
339991	Gasket, packing, and sealing devices manufacturing
339991	Gaskets manufacturing
421840	Gaskets wholesaling
334514	Gasmeters, consumption registering, manufacturing
422710	Gasoline bulk stations and terminals
336412	Gasoline engine parts (except carburetors, pistons, piston rings, valves), aircraft, manufacturing
336312	Gasoline engine parts (except carburetors, pistons, piston rings, valves), automotive and truck, manufacturing
333618	Gasoline engines (except aircraft, automotive, truck) manufacturing
336412	Gasoline engines, aircraft, manufacturing
336312	Gasoline engines, automotive and truck, manufacturing
324110	Gasoline made in petroleum refineries
421120	Gasoline marketing equipment wholesaling
333913	Gasoline measuring and dispensing pumps manufacturing
486910	Gasoline pipeline transportation
421120	Gasoline service station equipment wholesaling
447110	Gasoline stations with convenience stores
447190	Gasoline stations without convenience stores

422720	Gasoline wholesaling (except bulk stations, terminals)
447110	Gasoline with convenience stores
211112	Gasoline, natural, production
313312	Gassing yarn (i.e., singeing)
333999	Gate and bridge lifting machinery manufacturing
332911	Gate valves, industrial-type, manufacturing
332323	Gates, holding, sheet metal, manufacturing
332323	Gates, metal (except wire), manufacturing
113210	Gathering of forest products (e.g., barks, gums, needles, seeds)
334514	Gauges (e.g., oil pressure, water temperature, speedometer, tachometer), motor vehicle, manufacturing
339113	Gauze, surgical, made from purchased fabric
313210	Gauzes, surgical, made in broadwoven fabric mills
321999	Gavels, wood, manufacturing
332212	Gear pullers, handtools, manufacturing
333612	Gearmotors (i.e., power transmission equipment) manufacturing
336350	Gears (e.g., crown, pinion, spider), automotive, truck, and bus, manufacturing
333612	Gears, power transmission (except aircraft, motor vehicle), manufacturing
112390	Geese production
334519	Geiger counters manufacturing
325998	Gelatin capsules, empty, manufacturing
311999	Gelatin dessert preparations manufacturing
311999	Gelatin for cooking manufacturing
422490	Gelatin, edible, wholesaling
422690	Gelatin, inedible, wholesaling
212399	Gem stone (e.g., amethyst, garnet, agate, ruby, sapphire, jade) mining and/or beneficiating
421940	Gem stones wholesaling
812990	Genealogical investigation services
921190	General accounting offices, government
811111	General automotive repair shops
112990	General combination animal farming
111998	General combination crop farming (except fruit and nut combinations, oilseed and grain, vegetable)
926110	General economics statistical agencies
484110	General freight trucking, local
484122	General freight trucking, long-distance, less-than-truckload (LTL)
484121	General freight trucking, long-distance, truckload
541611	General management consulting services
622110	General medical and surgical hospitals
421990	General merchandise, durable goods, wholesaling
422990	General merchandise, nondurable goods, wholesaling
921190	General public administration
532310	General rental centers
921190	General services departments, government
452990	General stores
493110	General warehousing and storage
422210	General-line drugs wholesaling
422410	General-line groceries wholesaling
421840	General-line industrial supplies wholesaling
421930	General-line scrap wholesaling
421830	General-purpose industrial machinery and equipment wholesaling
335313	Generator control and metering panels, switchgear-type, manufacturing
335312	Generator sets, prime mover (except turbine generator sets), manufacturing
333611	Generator sets, turbine (e.g., gas, hydraulic, steam), manufacturing

335311 Generator voltage regulators, electric induction and step-type (except engine electrical equipment), manufacturing

335312 Generators and sets, electric (except internal combustion engine, welding, turbine generator sets), manufacturing

336322 Generators for internal combustion engines manufacturing

334517 Generators, X-ray, manufacturing

421610 Generators, electrical (except motor vehicle), wholesaling

421120 Generators, motor vehicle electrical, new, wholesaling

421140 Generators, motor vehicle electrical, used, wholesaling

332995 Generators, smoke, manufacturing

541710 Genetics research and development laboratories or services

541690 Geochemical consulting services

541370 Geodetic surveying services

541370 Geographic information system (GIS) base mapping services

541330 Geological engineering services

541710 Geological research and development laboratories or services

924120 Geological research program administration

541360 Geological surveying services

541330 Geophysical engineering services

334519 Geophysical instruments manufacturing

541360 Geophysical mapping services

541360 Geophysical surveying services

541370 Geospatial mapping services

541380 Geotechnical testing laboratories or services

235810 Geothermal drilling construction contractors

453220 Gift shops

322222 Gift wrap, laminated foil, made from purchased foil

322222 Gift wrap, laminated, made from purchased paper

422120 Gift wrapping paper wholesaling

561910 Gift wrapping services

115111 Ginning cotton

113210 Ginseng gathering

327390 Girders and beams, prestressed concrete, manufacturing

327390 Girders, prestressed concrete, manufacturing

315192 Girdles and other foundation garments made in apparel knitting mills

315212 Girdles, women's, cut and sew apparel contractors

315231 Girdles, women's, misses', and girls', cut and sewn from purchased fabric (except apparel contractors)

813410 Girl guiding organizations

611620 Girls' camps, sports instruction

315111 Girls' hosiery, sheer, full length or knee length, knitting and finishing

315119 Girls' socks manufacturing

325411 Glandular derivatives, uncompounded, manufacturing

325412 Glandular medicinal preparations manufacturing

327215 Glass blanks for electric light bulbs made from purchased glass

327212 Glass blanks for electric light bulbs made in glass making plants

327212 Glass fiber, textile type, made in glass making plants

327212 Glass fiber, unsheathed, made in glass making plants

235920 Glass installation (except automotive) construction contractors

811122 Glass installation, automotive repair

327212 Glass making and blowing by hand

333298 Glass making machinery (e.g., blowing, forming, molding) manufacturing

327213 Glass packaging containers manufacturing

327215 Glass products (except packaging containers) made from purchased glass

327212	Glass products (except packaging containers) made in a glass making plants
212322	Glass sand quarrying and/or beneficiating
421930	Glass scrap wholesaling
811122	Glass shops, automotive
444190	Glass stores
235920	Glass tinting (except automotive) construction contractors
235920	Glass work (except automotive) construction contractors
327215	Glass, automotive, made from purchased glass
327212	Glass, automotive, made in glass making plants
421120	Glass, automotive, wholesaling
327211	Glass, plate, made in glass making plants
421390	Glass, plate, wholesaling
327215	Glassware for industrial, scientific, and technical use made from purchased glass
327212	Glassware for industrial, scientific, and technical use made in glass making plants
327215	Glassware for lighting fixtures made from purchased glass
327212	Glassware for lighting fixtures made in glass making plants
442299	Glassware stores
327215	Glassware, cutting and engraving, made from purchased glass
421220	Glassware, household-type, wholesaling
421450	Glassware, medical, wholesaling
325510	Glaziers' putty manufacturing
235920	Glazing construction contractors
315292	Glazing furs
487990	Glider excursions
336411	Gliders (i.e., aircraft) manufacturing
334220	Global positioning system (GPS) equipment manufacturing
511199	Globe cover and map publishers
511199	Globe cover and map publishers and printing combined
323112	Globe covers and maps flexographic printing without publishing
323111	Globe covers and maps gravure printing without publishing
323110	Globe covers and maps lithographic (offset) printing without publishing
323119	Globe covers and maps printing (except flexographic, gravure, lithographic, screen) without publishing
323113	Globe covers and maps screen printing without publishing
332911	Globe valves, industrial-type, manufacturing
339999	Globes, geographical, manufacturing
315992	Gloves and mittens (except athletic), leather, fabric, fur, or combinations, cut and sewn from purchased fabric (except apparel contractors)
315211	Gloves and mittens (except athletic), leather, fabric, fur, or combinations, men's and boys', cut and sew apparel contractors
315212	Gloves and mittens (except athletic), leather, fabric, fur, or combinations, women's, girls', and infants', cut and sew apparel contractors
315992	Gloves and mittens, woven or knit, cut and sewn from purchased fabric (except apparel contractors), manufacturing
315212	Gloves and mittens, woven or knit, women's, girls', and infants', cut and sew apparel contractors
315191	Gloves, knit, made in apparel knitting mills
315211	Gloves, leather (except athletic), men's and boys', cut and sew apparel contractors
315212	Gloves, leather (except athletic), women's, girls', and infants', cut and sew apparel contractors
422320	Gloves, men's and boys', wholesaling
326199	Gloves, plastics, manufacturing
339113	Gloves, rubber (e.g., electrician's, examination, household-type, surgeon's), manufacturing

339920 Gloves, sport and athletic (e.g., baseball, boxing, racketball, handball), manufacturing

422330 Gloves, women's, children's, and infants', wholesaling

339114 Glue, dental, manufacturing

325520 Glues (except dental) manufacturing

422690 Glues wholesaling

311221 Gluten feed, flour, and meal, made by wet milling corn

311221 Gluten manufacturing

325611 Glycerin (i.e., glycerol), natural, manufacturing

325199 Glycerin (i.e., glycerol), synthetic, manufacturing

325411 Glycosides, uncompounded, manufacturing

212313 Gneiss crushed and broken stone mining and/or beneficiating

112420 Goat farming (e.g., meat, milk, mohair production)

422520 Goats wholesaling

713990 Gocart raceways (i.e., amusement rides)

713990 Gocart tracks (i.e., amusement rides)

336999 Gocarts (except children's) manufacturing

421910 Gocarts wholesaling

339115 Goggles (e.g., industrial, safety, sun, underwater) manufacturing

331419 Gold bullion or dore bar produced at primary metal refineries

332999 Gold foil and leaf not made in rolling mills

331491 Gold foil made by rolling purchased metals or scrap

212221 Gold ore mine site development for own account

212221 Gold ore mining and/or beneficiating plants

212221 Gold ores, concentrates, bullion, and/or precipitates mining and/or beneficiating

331419 Gold refining, primary

813410 Golden age clubs

713910 Golf and country clubs

441229 Golf cart dealers, powered

421910 Golf carts (except motorized passenger) wholesaling

336999 Golf carts and similar motorized passenger carriers manufacturing

421860 Golf carts, motorized passenger, wholesaling

336999 Golf carts, powered, manufacturing

234990 Golf course construction

541320 Golf course design services

713910 Golf courses (except miniature, pitch-n-putt)

713990 Golf courses, miniature

713990 Golf courses, pitch-n-putt

713990 Golf driving ranges

713990 Golf practice ranges

451110 Golf pro shops

316219 Golf shoes, men's cleated, manufacturing

316219 Golf shoes, women's cleated, manufacturing

711219 Golfers, independent professional (i.e., participating in sports events)

339920 Golfing equipment (e.g., bags, balls, caddy carts, clubs, tees) manufacturing

445299 Gourmet food stores

522294 Government National Mortgage Association (GNMA)

561210 Government base facilities operation support services

315212 Gowns, wedding, women's, cut and sew apparel contractors

315233 Gowns, wedding, women's, misses', and girls', cut and sewn from purchased fabric (except apparel contractors)

333120 Graders, road, manufacturing

235930 Grading for buildings, construction contractors

315299 Graduation caps and gowns cut and sewn from purchased fabric (except apparel contractors)

315211 Graduation caps and gowns, men's and boys', cut and sew apparel contractors

315212 Graduation caps and gowns, women's and girls', cut and sew apparel contractors

311821 Graham wafers manufacturing

312140 Grain alcohol, beverage, manufacturing

115114	Grain cleaning
115114	Grain drying
422510	Grain elevators wholesaling grain
493130	Grain elevators, storage only
115114	Grain fumigation
115114	Grain grinding (except custom grinding for animal feed)
311119	Grain grinding, custom, for animal feed
488210	Grain leveling and trimming in railroad cars
333294	Grain milling machinery manufacturing
311211	Grain mills (except animal feed, breakfast cereal, rice)
311119	Grain mills, animal feed
311230	Grain mills, breakfast cereal
311212	Grain mills, rice
422510	Grain wholesaling
311230	Grain, breakfast cereal, manufacturing
312120	Grain, brewers' spent, manufacturing
115113	Grain, machine harvesting
327910	Grains, abrasive, natural and artificial, manufacturing
813410	Granges
212313	Granite beneficiating plants (e.g., grinding or pulverizing)
212313	Granite crushed and broken stone mining and/or beneficiating
212311	Granite mining or quarrying
311320	Granola bars and clusters, chocolate, made from cacao beans
311330	Granola bars and clusters, chocolate, made from purchased chocolate
311340	Granola bars and clusters, nonchocolate, manufacturing
311230	Granola, cereal (except bars and clusters), manufacturing
813211	Grantmaking foundations
311313	Granulated beet sugar manufacturing
311312	Granulated cane sugar made from purchased raw cane sugar
311311	Granulated cane sugar made from sugar cane
333220	Granulator and pelletizer machinery for plastics manufacturing
312130	Grape farming and making wine
111332	Grape farming without making wine
111320	Grapefruit groves
311423	Grapes, artificially drying
541430	Graphic art and related design services
541430	Graphic artists, independent
611519	Graphic arts schools
541430	Graphic design services
335991	Graphite electrodes and contacts, electric, manufacturing
335991	Graphite specialties for aerospace use (except gaskets) manufacturing
335991	Graphite specialties for electrical use manufacturing
335991	Graphite specialties for mechanical use (except gaskets) manufacturing
327992	Graphite, natural (e.g., ground, pulverized, refined, blended), manufacturing
111940	Grass hay farming
111998	Grass seed farming
332323	Gratings (i.e., open steel flooring) manufacturing
212321	Gravel quarrying and/or beneficiating
541360	Gravity geophysical surveying services
323122	Gravure plate and cylinder preparation services
323111	Gravure printing (except books, manifold business forms, printing grey goods)
333293	Gravure printing presses manufacturing
311422	Gravy canning
311942	Gravy mixes, dry, manufacturing
331511	Gray iron foundries
531190	Grazing land rental or leasing
311613	Grease rendering
311225	Grease, inedible, animal and vegetable, refining and blending purchased oils
422990	Greases, inedible animal and vegetable, wholesaling
324191	Greases, petroleum lubricating, made from refined petroleum

483113	Great Lakes freight transportation
483114	Great Lakes passenger transportation
111219	Green bean farming, field and seed production
111219	Green lima bean farming, field and seed production
111219	Green pea farming, field and seed production
511191	Greeting card publishers
511191	Greeting card publishers and printing combined
453220	Greeting card shops
323112	Greeting cards (e.g., birthday, holiday, sympathy) flexographic printing without publishing
323111	Greeting cards (e.g., birthday, holiday, sympathy) gravure printing without publishing
323110	Greeting cards (e.g., birthday, holiday, sympathy) lithographic (offset) printing without publishing
323119	Greeting cards (e.g., birthday, holiday, sympathy) printing (except flexographic, gravure, lithographic, screen) without publishing
323113	Greeting cards (e.g., birthday, holiday, sympathy) screen printing without publishing
422120	Greeting cards wholesaling
332994	Grenade launchers manufacturing
332993	Grenades, hand or projectile, manufacturing
711212	Greyhound dog racetracks
332618	Grilles and grillwork made from purchased wire
332323	Grills and grillwork, sheet metal, manufacturing
332323	Grillwork, ornamental metal, manufacturing
325411	Grinding and milling botanicals (i.e., for medicinal use)
327910	Grinding balls, ceramic, manufacturing
333512	Grinding machines, metalworking, manufacturing
311942	Grinding spices
327910	Grinding wheels manufacturing
311211	Grits and flakes, corn brewer's, manufacturing
422410	Groceries, general-line, wholesaling
322224	Grocers' bags and sacks made from purchased uncoated paper
333924	Grocery carts made from purchased wire
492210	Grocery delivery services (i.e., independent service from grocery store)
445110	Grocery stores
421840	Grommets wholesaling
812910	Grooming services, animal
335931	Ground fault circuit interrupters (GFCI) manufacturing
322122	Groundwood paper products (e.g., publication and printing paper, tablet stock, wallpaper base) made in newsprint mills
422110	Groundwood paper, bulk, wholesaling
322121	Groundwood paper, coated, laminated, or treated in paper mills
322121	Groundwood paper, coated, made in paper mills
322122	Groundwood paper, newsprint, made in paper mills
322110	Groundwood pulp manufacturing
623990	Group foster homes for children
623110	Group homes for the disabled with nursing care
623990	Group homes for the disabled without nursing care
623990	Group homes for the hearing impaired
623990	Group homes for the visually impaired
623210	Group homes, mental retardation
621491	Group hospitalization plans providing health care services
524114	Group hospitalization plans without providing health care services
114111	Grouper fishing
813910	Growers' associations
561612	Guard dog services
812910	Guard dog training services

561612	Guard services
332322	Guardrails, sheet metal highway, manufacturing
721199	Guest houses
812910	Guide dog training services
713990	Guide services (i.e., fishing, hunting, tourist)
511199	Guide, street map, publishers
511199	Guide, street map, publishers and printing combined
421860	Guided missiles and space vehicles wholesaling
336414	Guided missiles, complete, assembling
336415	Guided missile and space vehicle engine manufacturing
541710	Guided missile and space vehicle engine research and development
336414	Guided missile and space vehicle manufacturing
336419	Guided missile and space vehicle parts (except engines) manufacturing
541710	Guided missile and space vehicle parts (except engines) research and development
323112	Guides, street map, flexographic printing without publishing
323111	Guides, street map, gravure printing without publishing
323110	Guides, street map, lithographic (offset) printing without publishing
323119	Guides, street map, printing (except flexographic, gravure, lithographic, screen) without publishing
323113	Guides, street map, screen printing without publishing
113210	Gum (i.e., forest product) gathering
325191	Gum and wood chemicals manufacturing
422690	Gum and wood chemicals wholesaling
311340	Gum, chewing, manufacturing
422450	Gum, chewing, wholesaling
322222	Gummed paper products (e.g., labels, sheets, tapes) made from purchased paper
422130	Gummed tapes (except cellophane) wholesaling
422120	Gummed tapes, cellophane, wholesaling
332994	Gun barrels (i.e., 30 mm. or less, 1.18 inch or less) manufacturing
332995	Gun barrels (i.e., more than 30 mm., more than 1.18 inch) manufacturing
713990	Gun clubs, recreational
813319	Gun control organizations
332994	Gun magazines (i.e., 30 mm. or less, 1.18 inch or less) manufacturing
332995	Gun magazines (i.e., more than 30 mm., more than 1.18 inch) manufacturing
451110	Gun shops
333314	Gun sighting and fire control equipment and instruments, optical, manufacturing
333314	Gun sights, optical, manufacturing
332612	Gun springs manufacturing
334413	Gun effect devices manufacturing
421990	Guns (except sporting) wholesaling
332994	Guns (i.e., 30 mm. or less, 1.18 inch or less) manufacturing
332995	Guns (i.e., more than 30 mm., more than 1.18 inch) manufacturing
332212	Guns, caulking, nonpowered, manufacturing
421910	Guns, sporting equipment, wholesaling
451110	Gunsmith shops retailing new guns
811490	Gunsmith shops without retailing new guns
561790	Gutter cleaning services
332114	Gutters and down spouts sheet metal, custom roll formed, manufacturing
421330	Gutters and down spouts wholesaling
326199	Gutters and down spouts, plastics, manufacturing
234110	Gutters, concrete, street and highway construction
332322	Gutters, sheet metal (except custom roll formed), manufacturing
339920	Gymnasium and playground equipment, manufacturing

713940   Gymnasiums
327420   Gypsum building products
         manufacturing
421390   Gypsum building products
         wholesaling
212399   Gypsum mining and/or beneficiating
327420   Gypsum products (e.g., block,
         board, plaster, lath, rock, tile)
         manufacturing
334511   Gyroscopes manufacturing
311221   HFCS (high fructose corn syrup)
         manufacturing
325413   HIV test kits manufacturing
621491   HMO (health maintenance
         organization) medical centers and
         clinics
334511   HUD (heads-up display) systems,
         aeronautical, manufacturing
114111   Haddock fishing
422310   Hair accessories wholesaling
326299   Hair care products (e.g., combs,
         curlers), rubber, manufacturing
333111   Hair clippers for animal use,
         electric, manufacturing
332212   Hair clippers for animal use,
         nonelectric, manufacturing
335211   Hair clippers for human use,
         electric, manufacturing
332211   Hair clippers for human use,
         nonelectric, manufacturing
332999   Hair curlers, metal, manufacturing
335211   Hair driers, electric (except
         equipment designed for beauty
         parlor use), manufacturing
421620   Hair dryers wholesaling
339999   Hair nets, made from purchased
         netting
325620   Hair preparations (e.g., conditioners,
         dyes, rinses, shampoos)
         manufacturing
422210   Hair preparations (except
         professional) wholesaling
421850   Hair preparations, professional,
         wholesaling
812199   Hair removal (i.e., dipilatory,
         electrolysis) services
812199   Hair replacement services (except
         by offices of physicians)

812112   Hair stylist salons or shops, unisex
         or women's
812111   Hair stylist services, men's
812112   Hair stylist services, unisex or
         women's
812111   Hair stylist shops, men's
812199   Hair weaving services
422990   Hairbrushes wholesaling
339994   Hairbrushes manufacturing
812112   Hairdresser services
812112   Hairdressing salons or shops, unisex
         or women's
339999   Hairpieces (e.g., toupees, wigs,
         wiglets) manufacturing
422990   Hairpieces (e.g., toupees, wigs,
         wiglets) wholesaling
332612   Hairsprings (except clock, watch)
         manufacturing
623990   Halfway group homes for
         delinquents and exoffenders
623220   Halfway houses for patients with
         mental health illnesses
623220   Halfway houses, substance abuse
         (e.g., alcoholism, drug addiction)
334413   Hall effect devices manufacturing
712110   Halls of fame
335110   Halogen light bulbs manufacturing
325192   Halogenated aromatic hydrocarbon
         derivatives manufacturing
325199   Halogenated hydrocarbon
         derivatives (except aromatic)
         manufacturing
311340   Halvah manufacturing
332111   Hammer forgings made from
         purchased iron or steel, unfinished
332112   Hammer forgings made from
         purchased nonferrous metals,
         unfinished
332212   Hammers, handtools, manufacturing
337124   Hammocks, metal framed,
         manufacturing
337122   Hammocks, wood framed,
         manufacturing
311611   Hams (except poultry) produced in
         slaughtering plants
311612   Hams, canned, made from
         purchased carcasses

http://www.ntis.gov/naics

311615	Hams, poultry, manufacturing
311612	Hams, preserved (except poultry), made from purchased carcasses
327215	Hand blowing purchased glass
334111	Hand held computers (e.g., PDAs) manufacturing
313249	Hand knitting lace or warp fabric products
339943	Hand operated stamps (e.g., canceling, postmark, shoe, textile marking), manufacturing
325611	Hand soaps (e.g., hard, liquid, soft) manufacturing
334518	Hand stamps (e.g., date, time), timing mechanism operated, manufacturing
333991	Hand tools, power-driven, manufacturing
333924	Hand trucks manufacturing
448150	Handbag stores
422330	Handbags wholesaling
316992	Handbags, women's, all materials (except precious metal), manufacturing
713940	Handball club facilities
541870	Handbill direct distribution services
332999	Handcuffs manufacturing
332212	Handheld edge tools (except saws, scissors-type), nonelectric, manufacturing
485991	Handicapped passenger transportation services
321912	Handle stock, sawed or planed, manufacturing
321999	Handles (e.g., broom, mop, hand tool), wood, manufacturing
422990	Handles (e.g., broom, mop, paint) wholesaling
326199	Handles (e.g., brush, tool, umbrella), plastics, manufacturing
327111	Handles, faucet, vitreous china and earthenware, manufacturing
332212	Handtool metal blades (e.g., putty knives, scrapers, screw drivers) manufacturing
421710	Handtools (except motor vehicle mechanics', machinists' precision) wholesaling
332212	Handtools, machinists' precision, manufacturing
421830	Handtools, machinists' precision, wholesaling
332212	Handtools, motor vehicle mechanics', manufacturing
421120	Handtools, motor vehicle mechanics', wholesaling
444130	Handtools, power-driven, repair and maintenance services retailing new power-driven handtools
811411	Handtools, power-driven, repair and maintenance services without retailing new power-driven handtools
541990	Handwriting analysis services
336411	Hang gliders manufacturing
488119	Hangar rental, aircraft
321999	Hangers, wooden, garment, manufacturing
234990	Harbor dredging construction contractors
488310	Harbor maintenance services (except dredging)
488310	Harbor operation
487210	Harbor sightseeing tours
488330	Harbor tugboat services
311340	Hard candies manufacturing
334112	Hard disk drives manufacturing
334613	Hard drive media manufacturing
313111	Hard fiber spun yarns made from purchased fiber
339113	Hard hats manufacturing
421710	Hardware (except motor vehicle) wholesaling
444130	Hardware stores
421120	Hardware, motor vehicle, wholesaling
326199	Hardware, plastics, manufacturing
335932	Hardware, transmission pole and line, manufacturing
421610	Hardware, transmission pole and line, wholesaling
321912	Hardwood dimension lumber and stock, resawing purchased lumber
321211	Hardwood veneer or plywood manufacturing
334419	Harness assemblies for electronic use manufacturing

711219	Harness drivers
422910	Harness equipment wholesaling
332999	Harness parts, metal, manufacturing
711212	Harness racetracks
113210	Harvesting berries or nuts from native and non-cultivated plants
333111	Harvesting machinery and equipment, agriculture, manufacturing
421820	Harvesting machinery and equipment, agriculture, wholesaling
448150	Hat and cap stores
315991	Hat bodies (e.g., fur-felt, straw, wool-felt) cut and sewn from purchased fabric (except apparel contractors)
315211	Hat bodies (e.g., fur-felt, straw, wool-felt), men's and boys', cut and sew apparel contractors
315212	Hat bodies (e.g., fur-felt, straw, wool-felt), women's, girls', and infants', cut and sew apparel contractors
112511	Hatcheries, finfish
112340	Hatcheries, poultry
332212	Hatchets manufacturing
315991	Hats (except fur, knitting mill products, leather) cut and sewn from purchased fabric (except apparel contractors)
422320	Hats and caps, men's and boys', wholesaling
422330	Hats and caps, women's, girls' and infants', wholesaling
322299	Hats made from purchased paper
315191	Hats made in apparel knitting mills
315212	Hats, fur, women's, girls', and infants', cut and sew apparel contractors
315212	Hats, leather, women's, girls', and infants', cut and sew apparel contractors
315211	Hats, men's and boys', cut and sew apparel contractors
315212	Hats, women's, girls', and infants', cut and sew apparel contractors
111940	Hay farming (e.g., alfalfa hay, clover hay, grass hay)
115113	Hay mowing, raking, baling, and chopping
111998	Hay seed farming
422910	Hay wholesaling
311119	Hay, cubed, manufacturing
333111	Haying machines manufacturing
421820	Haying machines wholesaling
562112	Hazardous waste collection services
562211	Hazardous waste disposal facilities
562211	Hazardous waste disposal facilities combined with collection and/or local hauling of hazardous waste
562211	Hazardous waste treatment facilities
562211	Hazardous waste treatment facilities combined with collection and/or local hauling of hazardous waste
551114	Head offices
311212	Head rice manufacturing
315999	Headbands, women's and girls', cut and sewn from purchased fabric (except apparel contractors)
315212	Headbands, women's, girls', and infants', cut and sew apparel contractors
337122	Headboards, wood, manufacturing
334419	Heads (e.g., recording, read/write), manufacturing
334511	Heads-up display (HUD) systems, aeronautical, manufacturing
446110	Health and beauty aids stores
525120	Health and welfare funds
713940	Health club facilities, physical fitness
422490	Health foods (except fresh fruits, vegetables) wholesaling
422480	Health foods, fresh fruits and vegetables, wholesaling
524114	Health insurance carriers, direct
621491	Health maintenance organization (HMO) medical centers and clinics
813920	Health professionals' associations
926150	Health professions licensure agencies
923120	Health program administration
541710	Health research and development laboratories or services
813212	Health research fundraising organizations

621999 Health screening services (except by offices of health practitioners)

621111 Health screening services in physicians' offices

721110 Health spas (i.e., physical fitness facilities) with accommodations

713940 Health spas without accommodations, physical fitness

713940 Health studios, physical fitness

446199 Hearing aid stores

421450 Hearing aids wholesaling

334510 Hearing aids, electronic, manufacturing

621999 Hearing testing services (except by offices of audiologists)

336211 Hearse bodies manufacturing

532111 Hearse rental

485320 Hearse rental with driver

336111 Hearses assembling on chassis of own manufacture

336211 Hearses assembling on purchased chassis

332410 Heat exchangers manufacturing

333415 Heat pumps manufacturing

421730 Heat pumps wholesaling

332811 Heat treating metals and metal products for the trade

333994 Heat treating ovens, industrial process-type, manufacturing

221330 Heated air distribution

335211 Heaters, portable electric space, manufacturing

421620 Heaters, portable electric, wholesaling

333414 Heaters, space (except portable electric), manufacturing

333414 Heaters, swimming pool, manufacturing

333415 Heating and air conditioning combination units manufacturing

334512 Heating and cooling system controls, residential and commercial, manufacturing

421720 Heating boilers, steam and hot water, wholesaling

235110 Heating construction contractors

541330 Heating engineering consulting services

333414 Heating equipment, hot water (except hot water heaters), manufacturing

421720 Heating equipment, hot water, wholesaling

421730 Heating equipment, warm air (i.e. forced air), wholesaling

333415 Heating equipment, warm air (i.e., forced air), manufacturing

454311 Heating oil dealers, direct selling

333414 Heating units, baseboard, manufacturing

234990 Heavy construction equipment rental with operator

532412 Heavy construction equipment rental without operator

811310 Heavy machinery and equipment repair and maintenance services

336120 Heavy trucks assembling on chassis of own manufacture

336211 Heavy trucks assembling on purchased chassis

332212 Hedge shears and trimmers, nonelectric, manufacturing

333112 Hedge trimmers, powered, manufacturing

332611 Helical springs, hot wound heavy gauge, manufacturing

332612 Helical springs, light gauge, manufacturing

481212 Helicopter carriers, freight, nonscheduled

481112 Helicopter freight carriers, scheduled

481211 Helicopter passenger carriers (except scenic, sightseeing), nonscheduled

481111 Helicopter passenger carriers, scheduled

487990 Helicopter ride, scenic and sightseeing, operation

336411 Helicopters manufacturing

325120 Helium manufacturing

325120 Helium recovery from natural gas

339113 Helmets (except athletic), safety (e.g., motorized vehicle crash helmets, space helmets), manufacturing

339920	Helmets, athletic (except motorized vehicle crash helmets), manufacturing
561320	Help supply services
325412	Hematology in-vivo diagnostic substances manufacturing
334516	Hematology instruments manufacturing
325414	Hematology products (except diagnostic substances) manufacturing
313111	Hemp bags made from purchased fiber
313111	Hemp ropes made from purchased fiber
111419	Herb farming, grown under cover
111998	Herb farming, open field
111421	Herbaceous perennial growing
712110	Herbariums
325320	Herbicides manufacturing
711310	Heritage festival managers with facilities
711320	Heritage festival managers without facilities
711310	Heritage festival organizers with facilities
711320	Heritage festival organizers without facilities
711310	Heritage festival promoters with facilities
711320	Heritage festival promoters without facilities
712120	Heritage villages
325199	Heterocyclic chemicals, not specified elsewhere by process, manufacturing
311611	Hides and skins produced in slaughtering plants
316110	Hides and skins, finishing on a contract basis
422590	Hides wholesaling
316110	Hides, tanning, currying, dressing, and finishing
311221	High fructose corn syrup (HFCS) manufacturing
331112	High percentage nonferrous alloying elements (i.e., ferroalloys) manufacturing
611110	High schools
332312	Highway bridge sections, prefabricated metal, manufacturing
234110	Highway construction (except elevated)
234120	Highway construction, elevated
234110	Highway guardrail construction contractors
332322	Highway guardrails, sheet metal, manufacturing
922120	Highway patrols, police
336120	Highway tractors assembled on chassis of own manufacture
336211	Highway tractors assembling on purchased chassis
332510	Hinges, metal, manufacturing
813410	Historical clubs
712120	Historical forts
712110	Historical museums
712120	Historical ships
712120	Historical sites
336399	Hitches, trailer, automotive, truck, and bus, manufacturing
451120	Hobby shops
421920	Hobbyists' supplies wholesaling
711211	Hockey clubs, professional or semiprofessional
713990	Hockey clubs, recreational
339920	Hockey skates manufacturing
115112	Hoeing
332212	Hoes, garden and mason's handtools, manufacturing
112210	Hog and pig (including breeding, farrowing, nursery, and finishing activities) farming
112210	Hog feedlots (except stockyards for transportation)
422520	Hogs wholesaling
333923	Hoists (except aircraft loading) manufacturing
421830	Hoists (except automotive) wholesaling
333924	Hoists, aircraft loading, manufacturing
421120	Hoists, automotive, wholesaling
551112	Holding companies (except bank, managing)

http://www.ntis.gov/naics

551114	Holding companies that manage
551111	Holding companies, bank (except managing)
316999	Holsters, leather, manufacturing
452990	Home and auto supply stores
332115	Home canning lids and rings, metal stamping
444110	Home centers, building materials
624229	Home construction organizations, work (sweat) equity
454390	Home delivery newspaper routes, direct selling
337124	Home entertainment centers, metal, manufacturing
337122	Home entertainment centers, wood, manufacturing
522292	Home equity credit lending
621610	Home health care agencies
532291	Home health furniture and equipment rental
444110	Home improvement centers
541350	Home inspection services
453998	Home security equipment stores
334310	Home stereo systems manufacturing
334310	Home tape recorders and players (e.g., cartridge, cassette, reel) manufacturing
334310	Home theater audio and video equipment manufacturing
333512	Home workshop metal cutting machine tools (except hand tools, welding equipment) manufacturing
442299	Homefurnishings stores
421220	Homefurnishings wholesaling
624120	Homemaker's service for elderly or disabled persons, non-medical
621399	Homeopaths' offices (e.g., centers, clinics)
813990	Homeowners' associations
524126	Homeowners' insurance carriers, direct
524128	Homeowners' warranty insurance carriers, direct
623220	Homes for emotionally disturbed adults or children
623110	Homes for the elderly with nursing care
623312	Homes for the elderly without nursing care

623990	Homes for unwed mothers
623210	Homes with or without health care, mental retardation
623220	Homes, psychiatric convalescent
311211	Hominy grits (except breakfast food), manufacturing
311230	Hominy grits, prepared as cereal breakfast food, manufacturing
333294	Homogenizing machinery, food, manufacturing
311511	Homogenizing milk
112910	Honey bee production
311999	Honey processing
422490	Honey wholesaling
111219	Honeydew melon farming, field, bedding plant and seed production
333512	Honing and lapping machines manufacturing
332322	Hoods, range (except household-type), sheet metal, manufacturing
335211	Hoods, range, household-type, manufacturing
115210	Hoof trimming
339993	Hook and eye fasteners (i.e., sewing accessories) manufacturing
332722	Hook and eye latches manufacturing
332722	Hooks (i.e., general purpose fasteners), metal, manufacturing
332212	Hooks, handtools (e.g., baling, bush, grass, husking), manufacturing
332722	Hooks, metal screw, manufacturing
311942	Hop extract manufacturing
422490	Hop extract wholesaling
111998	Hop farming
422590	Hops wholesaling
325413	Hormone in-vitro diagnostic substances manufacturing
325412	Hormone preparations (except in-vitro diagnostics) manufacturing
325411	Hormones and derivatives, uncompounded, manufacturing
112920	Horse (including thoroughbreds) production
711212	Horse racetracks
711219	Horse racing stables
713990	Horse rental services, recreational saddle

711310	Horse show managers with facilities
711320	Horse show managers without facilities
711310	Horse show organizers with facilities
711320	Horse show organizers without facilities
711310	Horse show promoters with facilities
711320	Horse show promoters without facilities
336214	Horse trailers (except fifth-wheel-type) manufacturing
336212	Horse trailers, fifth-wheel-type, manufacturing
487110	Horse-drawn carriage operation
713990	Horseback riding, recreational
311611	Horsemeat produced in slaughtering plants
311111	Horsemeat, processing, for dog and cat food
311421	Horseradish (except sauce) canning
311941	Horseradish, prepared sauce, manufacturing
115210	Horses (except racehorses), boarding
422590	Horses wholesaling
115210	Horses, training (except racehorses)
541690	Horticultural consulting services
332912	Hose couplings and fittings, fluid power, manufacturing
332919	Hose couplings, metal (except fluid power), manufacturing
332999	Hose, flexible metal, manufacturing
421840	Hose, industrial, wholesaling
326220	Hoses, reinforced, made from purchased rubber or plastics manufacturing
326220	Hoses, rubberized fabric, manufacturing
315119	Hosiery (except sheer), women's girls' and infants', manufacturing
333292	Hosiery machines manufacturing
448190	Hosiery stores
422320	Hosiery, men's and boys', wholesaling

315111	Hosiery, sheer, women's, misses', and girls' full-length and knee-length, knitting or knitting and finishing
422330	Hosiery, women's and girls', wholesaling
422330	Hosiery, women's, children's, and infants', wholesaling
621610	Hospice care services, in home
623110	Hospices, inpatient care
813920	Hospital administrators' associations
524114	Hospital and medical service plans, direct, without providing health care services
813910	Hospital associations
339111	Hospital beds manufacturing
421450	Hospital beds wholesaling
233320	Hospital construction
421450	Hospital equipment and supplies wholesaling
339111	Hospital furniture (e.g., hospital beds, operating room furniture) manufacturing
532291	Hospital furniture and equipment rental (i.e. home use)
421450	Hospital furniture wholesaling
315211	Hospital service apparel, washable, men's and boys', cut and sew apparel contractors
315225	Hospital service apparel, washable, men's and boys', cut and sewn from purchased fabric (except apparel contractors)
315239	Hospital service apparel, washable, women's, misses', and girls', cut and sewn from purchased fabric (except apparel contractors)
62****	Hospitals (see type)
541940	Hospitals, animal
622110	Hospitals, general medical and surgical
622210	Hospitals, mental (except mental retardation)
623210	Hospitals, mental retardation
622210	Hospitals, psychiatric (except convalescent)
623220	Hospitals, psychiatric convalescent
622310	Hospitals, specialty (except psychiatric, substance abuse)

http://www.ntis.gov/naics

622210	Hospitals, substance abuse
721199	Hostels
487990	Hot air balloon ride, scenic and sightseeing, operation
333311	Hot beverage vending machines manufacturing
332812	Hot dip galvanizing metals and metal products for the trade
311612	Hot dogs (except poultry) made from purchased carcasses
311611	Hot dogs (except poultry) produced in slaughtering plants
311615	Hot dogs, poultry, manufacturing
332111	Hot forgings made from purchased iron or steel, unfinished
332112	Hot forgings made from purchased nonferrous metals, unfinished
331111	Hot-rolling iron or steel products in steel mills
333516	Hot-rolling mill machinery, metalworking, manufacturing
331221	Hot-rolling purchased steel
453998	Hot tub stores
421910	Hot tubs wholesaling
321920	Hot tubs, coopered, manufacturing
326191	Hot tubs, plastics or fiberglass, manufacturing
335228	Hot water heaters (including nonelectric), household-type, manufacturing
233320	Hotel construction
421440	Hotel equipment and supplies (except furniture) wholesaling
421210	Hotel furniture wholesaling
561110	Hotel management services (except complete operation of client's business)
721110	Hotel management services (i.e., providing management and operating staff to run hotel)
561599	Hotel reservation services
721110	Hotels (except casino hotels)
721110	Hotels with golf courses, tennis courts, and/or other health spa facilities (i.e., resorts)
721120	Hotels, casino
721110	Hotels, membership
624190	Hotline centers
235990	House moving construction contractors

235210	House painting construction contractors
812990	House sitting services
316212	House slippers manufacturing
316212	House slippers, plastics or plastics soled fabric upper, manufacturing
316212	House slippers, rubber or rubber soled fabric upper, manufacturing
454390	House-to-house direct selling
443111	Household-type appliance stores
421620	Household-type appliances, electrical, wholesaling
327112	Household-type earthenware, semivitreous, manufacturing
421210	Household-type furniture wholesaling
337121	Household-type furniture, upholstered, manufacturing
337122	Household-type furniture, wood, not upholstered (except TV and radio housings and sewing machine cabinets), manufacturing
421620	Household-type laundry equipment (e.g., dryers, washers) wholesaling
814110	Households, private, employing (e.g., cooks, maids, chauffeurs, gardeners)
814110	Households, private, employing domestic personnel
721199	Housekeeping cabins
721199	Housekeeping cottages
561720	Housekeeping services (i.e., cleaning services)
321991	Houses, prefabricated mobile homes, manufacturing
321992	Houses, prefabricated, wood (except mobile homes), manufacturing
421220	Housewares (except electric) wholesaling
442299	Housewares stores
421620	Housewares, electric, wholesaling
624229	Housing assistance agencies
531110	Housing authorities operating residential buildings
925110	Housing authorities, nonoperating
233220	Housing construction, multifamily
233210	Housing construction, single family
922120	Housing police, government
624229	Housing repair organizations, volunteer

336612 Hovercraft building
332995 Howitzers manufacturing
212299 Huebnerite mining and/or beneficiating
541612 Human resource consulting services
813311 Human rights advocacy organizations
921190 Human rights commissions, government
813312 Humane societies
541720 Humanities research and development services
421730 Humidifiers and dehumidifiers (except portable) wholesaling
421620 Humidifiers and dehumidifiers, portable, wholesaling
335211 Humidifiers, portable electric, manufacturing
333415 Humidifying equipment (except portable) manufacturing
334512 Humidistats (e.g., duct, skeleton, wall) manufacturing
334513 Humidity instruments, industrial process type, manufacturing
721214 Hunting camps with accommodation facilities
713990 Hunting clubs, recreational
713990 Hunting guide services
114210 Hunting preserves
334111 Hybrid computers manufacturing
334413 Hybrid integrated circuits manufacturing
327410 Hydrated lime (i.e., calcium hydroxide), manufacturing
332912 Hydraulic aircraft subassemblies manufacturing
333995 Hydraulic cylinders, fluid power, manufacturing
811310 Hydraulic equipment repair and maintenance services
324110 Hydraulic fluids made in petroleum refineries
324191 Hydraulic fluids, petroleum, made from refined petroleum
325998 Hydraulic fluids, synthetic, manufacturing
332912 Hydraulic hose fittings, fluid power, manufacturing

326220 Hydraulic hoses (without fitting), rubber or plastics, manufacturing
421830 Hydraulic power transmission equipment wholesaling
421830 Hydraulic pumps and parts wholesaling
333996 Hydraulic pumps, fluid power, manufacturing
336340 Hydraulic slave cylinders, automotive, truck, and bus clutch, manufacturing
332912 Hydraulic valves, fluid power, manufacturing
325188 Hydrochloric acid manufacturing
234990 Hydroelectric plant construction
336611 Hydrofoil vessel building and repairing in shipyard
325120 Hydrogen manufacturing
311225 Hydrogenating purchased oil
541370 Hydrographic mapping services
541370 Hydrographic surveying services
541690 Hydrology consulting services
421720 Hydronic heating equipment and supplies wholesaling
333414 Hydronic heating equipment manufacturing
334512 Hydronic limit, pressure, and temperature controls, manufacturing
111419 Hydroponic crop farming
333996 Hydrostatic drives manufacturing
541380 Hydrostatic testing laboratories or services
339113 Hydrotherapy equipment manufacturing
621399 Hypnotherapists' offices (e.g., centers, clinics)
325411 Hypnotic drugs, uncompounded, manufacturing
339112 Hypodermic needles and syringes manufacturing
321213 I-joists, wood, fabricating
514191 ISP (internet service providers)
339112 IV apparatus manufacturing
312113 Ice (except dry ice) manufacturing
422990 Ice (except dry ice) wholesaling

332439	Ice chests or coolers, metal, manufacturing
326199	Ice chests or coolers, plastics (except plastics foam) manufacturing
326140	Ice chests or coolers, polystyrene foam, manufacturing
326150	Ice chests or coolers, urethane or other plastics foam (except polystyrene) manufacturing
445299	Ice cream (i.e., packaged) stores
422430	Ice cream and ices wholesaling
311821	Ice cream cones manufacturing
311520	Ice cream manufacturing
311514	Ice cream mix manufacturing
722213	Ice cream parlors
311520	Ice cream specialties manufacturing
722330	Ice cream truck vendors
333311	Ice cream vending machines manufacturing
422430	Ice cream wholesaling
333415	Ice making machinery manufacturing
421740	Ice making machines wholesaling
311520	Ice milk manufacturing
311514	Ice milk mix manufacturing
311520	Ice milk specialties manufacturing
339920	Ice skates manufacturing
711190	Ice skating companies
713940	Ice skating rinks
711190	Ice skating shows
325120	Ice, dry, manufacturing
422690	Ice, dry, wholesaling
312111	Iced coffee manufacturing
312111	Iced tea manufacturing
311520	Ices, flavored sherbets, manufacturing
421410	Identity recorders wholesaling
334512	Ignition controls for gas appliances and furnaces, automatic, manufacturing
336322	Ignition points and condensers for internal combustion engines manufacturing
336322	Ignition wiring harness for internal combustion engines manufacturing
335122	Illuminated indoor lighting fixtures (e.g., directional, exit) manufacturing
541430	Illustrators, independent commercial
212299	Ilmenite ores mining and/or beneficiating
327420	Images, small gypsum, manufacturing
327999	Images, small papier-mache, manufacturing
323122	Imagesetting services, prepress
624230	Immigrant resettlement services
928120	Immigration services
334516	Immunology instruments, laboratory, manufacturing
333991	Impact wrenches, handheld power-driven, manufacturing
334515	Impedance measuring equipment manufacturing
339113	Implants, surgical, manufacturing
339114	Impression material, dental, manufacturing
711110	Improvisational theaters
325413	In-vitro diagnostic substances manufacturing
325412	In-vivo diagnostic substances manufacturing
325998	Incense manufacturing
334512	Incinerator control systems, residential and commercial-type, manufacturing
333994	Incinerators (except precast concrete) manufacturing
562211	Incinerators, hazardous waste, operating
562213	Incinerators, nonhazardous solid waste
327390	Incinerators, precast concrete, manufacturing
541213	Income tax compilation services
541213	Income tax return preparation services
333313	Incoming mail handling equipment (e.g., opening, scanning, sorting) manufacturing
339113	Incubators, infant, manufacturing
339111	Incubators, laboratory-type, manufacturing
333111	Incubators, poultry, manufacturing
334513	Indicators, industrial process control-type, manufacturing

523910 Individuals investing in financial contracts on own account

541850 Indoor display advertising services

713120 Indoor play areas

333994 Induction heating equipment, industrial process-type, manufacturing

334416 Inductors, electronic component-type (e.g., chokes, coils, transformers), manufacturing

233310 Industrial and manufacturing building construction contractors

813910 Industrial associations

522190 Industrial banks (i.e., known as), depository

522298 Industrial banks (i.e., known as), nondepository

314992 Industrial belting reinforcement, cord and fabric, manufacturing

722310 Industrial caters (i.e., providing food services on a contractural arrangement (except single event base))

422690 Industrial chemicals wholesaling

421840 Industrial containers wholesaling

421610 Industrial controls, electrical, wholesaling

541420 Industrial design consulting services

533110 Industrial design licensing

541420 Industrial design services

541330 Industrial engineering services

811310 Industrial equipment and machinery repair and maintenance services

315239 Industrial garments, women's, misses', and girls', cut and sewn from purchased fabric (except apparel contractors)

325120 Industrial gases manufacturing

422690 Industrial gases wholesaling

813930 Industrial labor unions

541320 Industrial land use planning services

812332 Industrial launderers

335122 Industrial lighting fixtures, electric, manufacturing

336510 Industrial locomotives and parts manufacturing

421830 Industrial machinery and equipment (except electrical) wholesaling

333511 Industrial molds (except steel ingot) manufacturing

331511 Industrial molds, steel ingot, manufacturing

332997 Industrial pattern manufacturing

234930 Industrial plant appurtenance construction

334513 Industrial process control instruments manufacturing

541710 Industrial research and development laboratories or services

421450 Industrial safety devices (e.g., eye shields, face shields, first-aid kits) wholesaling

325998 Industrial salt manufacturing

422690 Industrial salt wholesaling

212322 Industrial sand beneficiating (e.g., screening, washing)

212322 Industrial sand sandpits and dredging

333997 Industrial scales manufacturing

234930 Industrial structures, construction (except building)

421840 Industrial supplies (except disposable plastics, paper) wholesaling

422130 Industrial supplies, disposable plastics, paper, wholesaling

541380 Industrial testing laboratories or services

621340 Industrial therapists' offices (e.g., centers, clinics)

811310 Industrial truck (e.g., forklifts) repair and maintenance services

333924 Industrial trucks and tractors manufacturing

421830 Industrial trucks, tractors, or trailers wholesaling

812332 Industrial uniform supply services

421930 Industrial wastes to be reclaimed wholesaling

311611 Inedible products (e.g., hides, skins, pulled wool, wool grease) produced in slaughtering plants

334511 Inertial navigation systems, aeronautical, manufacturing

311422	Infant and junior food canning
311230	Infant cereals, dry, manufacturing
624410	Infant day care centers
624410	Infant day care services
339113	Infant incubators manufacturing
311514	Infant's formulas manufacturing
316219	Infant's shoes (except plastics, rubber), manufacturing
315291	Infants' apparel cut and sewn from purchased fabric (except apparel contractors)
422330	Infants' clothing wholesaling
315212	Infants' cut and sew apparel contractors
514191	Information access services, on-line
541512	Information management computer systems integration design services
514199	Information search services, on a contract or fee basis
333994	Infrared ovens, industrial, manufacturing
334413	Infrared sensors, solid-state, manufacturing
621498	Infusion therapy centers and clinics, outpatient
331319	Ingot made by rolling purchased aluminum
331111	Ingot made in steel mills
331319	Ingot, aluminum, made in integrated secondary smelting and rolling mills
421510	Ingots (except precious) wholesaling
421940	Ingots, precious, wholesaling
621399	Inhalation therapists' offices (e.g., centers, clinics)
325998	Inhibitors (e.g., corrosion, oxidation, polymerization) manufacturing
333220	Injection molding machinery for plastics manufacturing
422120	Ink, writing, wholesaling
339944	Inked ribbons manufacturing
422120	Inked ribbons wholesaling
325910	Inkjet cartridges manufacturing
325910	Inkjet inks manufacturing
325910	Inks, printing, manufacturing
421840	Inks, printing, wholesaling

325998	Inks, writing, manufacturing
326211	Inner tubes manufacturing
422690	Inorganic chemicals wholesaling
325131	Inorganic pigments (except bone black, carbon black, lamp black) manufacturing
334119	Input/output equipment, computer (except terminals), manufacturing
115112	Insect control for crops
335129	Insect lamps, electric, manufacturing
325320	Insecticides manufacturing
541350	Inspection bureaus, building
488490	Inspection or weighing services, truck transportation
488190	Inspection services, aircraft
541350	Inspection services, building or home
235950	Installation of machinery and other industrial equipment construction contractors
213112	Installing production equipment at the oil or gas field on a contract basis
522220	Installment sales financing
311920	Instant coffee manufacturing
311230	Instant hot cereals manufacturing
311920	Instant tea manufacturing
233320	Institutional building construction
337127	Institutional furniture manufacturing
335122	Institutional lighting fixtures, electric, manufacturing
******	Instruction—see type of training
512110	Instructional video production
336322	Instrument control panels (i.e., assembling purchased gauges), automotive, truck, and bus, manufacturing
334511	Instrument landing system instrumentation, airborne or airport, manufacturing
333314	Instrument lenses manufacturing
334514	Instrument panels, assembling gauges made in the same establishment
332612	Instrument springs, precision (except clock, watch), manufacturing

335311	Instrument transformers (except complete instruments) for metering or protective relaying use manufacturing	524298	Insurance advisory services
		524210	Insurance agencies
		524210	Insurance brokerages
421830	Instruments (except electrical) (e.g., controlling, indicating, recording) wholesaling	524113	Insurance carriers, disability, direct
		524126	Insurance carriers, fidelity, direct
		524114	Insurance carriers, health, direct
334513	Instruments for industrial process control manufacturing	524113	Insurance carriers, life, direct
		524126	Insurance carriers, property and casualty, direct
334511	Instruments, aeronautical, manufacturing	524126	Insurance carriers, surety, direct
339992	Instruments, musical, manufacturing	524127	Insurance carriers, title, direct
421990	Instruments, musical, wholesaling	524291	Insurance claims adjusting
421490	Instruments, professional and scientific, wholesaling	524291	Insurance claims investigation services
331422	Insulated wire or cable made from purchased copper in wire drawing plants	524292	Insurance claims processing services, third party
		926150	Insurance commissions, government
331319	Insulated wire or cable made in aluminum wire drawing plants	524292	Insurance fund, third party administrative services (except claims adjusting only)
421610	Insulated wire or cable wholesaling	524298	Insurance investigation services (except claims investigation)
331422	Insulated wire or cable, copper, made in integrated secondary smelting and drawing plants	524292	Insurance plan administrative services (except claims adjusting only), third-party
322299	Insulating batts, fills, or blankets made from purchased paper	524298	Insurance rate making services
		524291	Insurance settlement offices
327993	Insulating batts, fills, or blankets, fiberglass, manufacturing	524113	Insurance underwriting, disability, direct
327215	Insulating glass, sealed units, made from purchased glass	524114	Insurance underwriting, health and medical, direct
327211	Insulating glass, sealed units, made in glass making plants	524113	Insurance underwriting, life, direct
235990	Insulating pipes and boilers construction contractors	524126	Insurance underwriting, property and casualty, direct
335929	Insulating purchased wire	524127	Insurance underwriting, title, direct
		813910	Insurers' associations
326150	Insulation and cushioning, foam plastics (except polystrene), manufacturing	335312	Integral horsepower electric motors manufacturing
		421690	Integrated circuits wholesaling
326140	Insulation and cushioning, polystyrene foam plastics, manufacturing	334413	Integrated microcircuits manufacturing
		512220	Integrated record companies (i.e., releasing, promoting, distributing)
321219	Insulation board, cellular fiber or hard pressed wood, manufacturing	512220	Integrated record production and distribution
235420	Insulation construction contractors	334515	Integrated-circuit testers manufacturing
325412	Insulin preparations manufacturing		
325411	Insulin, uncompounded, manufacturing		

485210	Intercity bus line operation
483113	Intercoastal freight transportation to and from domestic ports
334290	Intercom systems and equipment manufacturing
483114	Intercostal transportation of passengers to and from domestic ports
541410	Interior decorating consulting services
541410	Interior design consulting services
541410	Interior design services
623210	Intermediate care facilities, mental retardation
921130	Internal Revenue Service
333618	Internal combustion engines (except aircraft, nondiesel automotive, nondiesel truck) manufacturing
421830	Internal combustion engines (except aircraft, nondiesel automotive, nondiesel truck) wholesaling
336412	Internal combustion engines, aircraft, manufacturing
336312	Internal combustion engines, automotive and truck gasoline, manufacturing
928120	International Monetary Fund
522293	International trade financing
514191	Internet access providers
514191	Internet service providers (ISP)
541940	Internists' offices, veterinary
541930	Interpretation services, language
485210	Interurban bus line operation
483211	Intracoastal transportation of freight
483212	Intracoastal transportation of passengers
339113	Intrauterine devices manufacturing
812990	Introduction services, social
532291	Invalid equipment rental (i.e. home use)
561990	Inventory computing services
541614	Inventory planning and control management consulting services
561990	Inventory taking services
311312	Invert sugar made from purchased raw cane sugar
335312	Inverters, rotating electrical, manufacturing

335999	Inverters, solid-state, manufacturing
561611	Investigation services (except credit), private
561450	Investigation services, credit
561611	Investigators, private
523930	Investment advisory services, customized, fees paid by client
523110	Investment banking
331512	Investment castings, steel, unfinished, manufacturing
523910	Investment clubs
525990	Investment funds, closed-end
525910	Investment funds, open-ended
325188	Iodine, crude or resublimed, manufacturing
325211	Ion exchange resins manufacturing
325211	Ionomer resins manufacturing
421390	Iron and steel architectural shapes wholesaling
325131	Iron based pigments manufacturing
331511	Iron castings, unfinished, manufacturing
325188	Iron compounds, not specified elsewhere by process, manufacturing
332111	Iron forgings made from purchased iron, unfinished
331511	Iron foundries
212210	Iron ore (e.g., hematite, magnetite, siderite, taconite) mining and/or beneficiating
212210	Iron ore agglomerates mining and/or beneficiating
212210	Iron ore beneficiating plants (e.g., agglomeration, sintering)
212210	Iron ore mine site development for own account
331111	Iron, pig, manufacturing
332999	Ironing boards, metal, manufacturing
335211	Irons, household-type electric, manufacturing
334517	Irradiation apparatus and tubes (e.g., industrial, medical diagnostic, medical therapeutic, research, scientific), manufacturing

115114	Irradiation of fruits and vegetables
926130	Irrigation districts, nonoperating
421820	Irrigation equipment wholesaling
327332	Irrigation pipe, concrete, manufacturing
332322	Irrigation pipe, sheet metal, manufacturing
221310	Irrigation system operation
325211	Isobutylene polymer resins manufacturing
325192	Isocyanates manufacturing
335311	Isolation transformers manufacturing
325199	Isopropyl alcohol manufacturing
421330	Insulation materials wholesaling
311422	Italian foods canning
333120	Jack hammers manufacturing
315191	Jackets made in apparel knitting mills
315292	Jackets, fur (except apparel contractors), manufacturing
315211	Jackets, fur, men's and boys', cut and sew apparel contractors
315212	Jackets, fur, women's, girls', and infants', cut and sew apparel contractors
315291	Jackets, infants', cut and sewn from purchased fabric (except apparel contractors)
315292	Jackets, leather (except welders') or sheep-lined (except apparel contractors), manufacturing
315211	Jackets, leather (except welders') or sheep-lined, men's and boys', cut and sew apparel contractors
315212	Jackets, leather (except welders') or sheep-lined, women's, girls', and infants', cut and sew apparel contractors
315211	Jackets, men's and boys', cut and sew apparel contractors
315225	Jackets, nontailored work, men's and boys', cut and sewn from purchased fabric (except apparel contractors)
315239	Jackets, nontailored work, women's, misses', and girls', cut and sewn from purchased fabric (except apparel contractors)
315239	Jackets, nontailored, women's, misses', and girls', cut and sewn from purchased fabric (except apparel contractors)
315228	Jackets, not tailored (except work), men's and boys', cut and sewn from purchased fabric (except apparel contractors)
315222	Jackets, tailored (except fur, leather, sheep-lined), men's and boys', cut and sewn from purchased fabric (except apparel contractors)
315234	Jackets, tailored (except fur, sheep-lined), women's, misses', and girls', cut and sewn from purchased fabric (except apparel contractors)
315211	Jackets, tailored, men's and boys', cut and sew apparel contractors
315212	Jackets, tailored, women's, girls', and infants', cut and sew apparel contractors
316999	Jackets, welder's, leather, manufacturing
315212	Jackets, women's, girls', and infants', cut and sew apparel contractors
332212	Jacks (except hydraulic, pneumatic) manufacturing
333999	Jacks, hydraulic and pneumatic, manufacturing
561210	Jail operation on a contract or fee basis
922140	Jails
422690	Janitorial chemicals wholesaling
421850	Janitorial equipment and supplies wholesaling
561720	Janitorial services
327213	Jars for packaging, bottling, and canning, glass, manufacturing
315211	Jean-cut casual slacks, men's and boys', cut and sew apparel contractors
315224	Jean-cut casual slacks, men's and boys', cut and sewn from purchased fabric (except apparel contractors)

315212	Jean-cut casual slacks, women's, girls, and infants', cut and sew apparel contractors
315239	Jean-cut casual slacks, women's, misses', and girls', cut and sewn from purchased fabric (except apparel contractors)
315291	Jeans, infants', cut and sewn from purchased fabric (except apparel contractors)
315211	Jeans, men's and boys', cut and sew apparel contractors
315239	Jeans, women's, misses', and girls', cut and sewn from purchased fabric (except apparel contractors)
315212	Jeans, women's, misses', girls', and infants', cut and sew apparel contractors
311421	Jellies and jams manufacturing
422490	Jellies and jams wholesaling
311340	Jelly candies manufacturing
315191	Jerseys made in apparel knitting mills
315211	Jerseys, men's and boys', cut and sew apparel contractors
315223	Jerseys, men's and boys', cut and sewn from purchased fabric (except apparel contractors)
315212	Jerseys, women's, girls', and infants', cut and sew apparel contractors
315232	Jerseys, women's, misses', and girls', cut and sewn from purchased fabric (except apparel contractors)
324110	Jet fuels manufacturing
336412	Jet propulsion and internal combustion engines and parts, aircraft, manufacturing
339913	Jeweler's findings and materials manufacturing
332212	Jeweler's handtools, nonelectric, manufacturing
421940	Jewelers' findings wholesaling
422990	Jewelry boxes wholesaling
541490	Jewelry design services
811490	Jewelry repair shops without retailing new jewelry
448150	Jewelry stores, costume
448310	Jewelry stores, precious
421940	Jewelry wholesaling
339914	Jewelry, costume, manufacturing
339911	Jewelry, precious metal, manufacturing
333514	Jigs (e.g., checking, gauging, inspection) manufacturing
333514	Jigs and fixtures for use with machine tools manufacturing
333991	Jigsaws, handheld power-driven, manufacturing
624310	Job counseling, vocational rehabilitation or habilitation
336370	Job stampings, automotive, metal, manufacturing
624310	Job training, vocational rehabilitation or habilitation
711219	Jockeys, horse racing
315191	Jogging suits made in apparel knitting mills
315291	Jogging suits, infants', cut and sewn from purchased fabric (except apparel contractors)
315211	Jogging suits, men's and boys', cut and sew apparel contractors
315228	Jogging suits, men's and boys', cut and sewn from purchased fabric (except apparel contractors)
315212	Jogging suits, women's, girls', and infants', cut and sew apparel contractors
315239	Jogging suits, women's, misses', and girls', cut and sewn from purchased fabric (except apparel contractors)
325520	Joint compounds (except gypsum base) manufacturing
327420	Joint compounds, gypsum based, manufacturing
333613	Joints, universal (except aircraft, motor vehicle), manufacturing
336413	Joints, universal, aircraft, manufacturing
336350	Joints, universal, automotive, truck, and bus, manufacturing

332312	Joists, fabricated bar, manufacturing
332322	Joists, sheet metal, manufacturing
711510	Journalists, independent (freelance)
334119	Joystick devices manufacturing
326150	Jugs, vacuum, foam plastics (except polystyrene), manufacturing
332439	Jugs, vacuum, light gauge metal, manufacturing
326140	Jugs, vacuum, polystyrene foam plastics, manufacturing
311520	Juice pops, frozen, manufacturing
422490	Juices, canned or fresh, wholesaling
422420	Juices, frozen, wholesaling
311411	Juices, fruit or vegetable concentrates, frozen, manufacturing
311421	Juices, fruit or vegetable, canned manufacturing
311421	Juices, fruit or vegetable, fresh, manufacturing
311411	Juices, fruit or vegetable, frozen, manufacturing
713990	Jukebox concession operators (i.e., supplying and servicing in others' facilities)
334310	Jukeboxes manufacturing
335932	Junction boxes, electrical wiring, manufacturing
813910	Junior chambers of commerce
611210	Junior colleges
611110	Junior high schools
422310	Jute piece goods (except burlap) wholesaling
337124	Juvenile furniture (except upholstered), metal manufacturing
337122	Juvenile furniture (except upholstered), wood, manufacturing
337121	Juvenile furniture, upholstered, manufacturing
623990	Juvenile halfway group homes
511120	Juvenile magazine and periodical publishers
511120	Juvenile magazine and periodical publishers and printing combined
323112	Juvenile magazines and periodicals flexographic printing without publishing
323111	Juvenile magazines and periodicals gravure printing without publishing
323110	Juvenile magazines and periodicals lithographic (offset) printing without publishing
323119	Juvenile magazines and periodicals printing (except flexographic, gravure, lithographic, screen) without publishing
323113	Juvenile magazines and periodicals screen printing without publishing
212324	Kaolin mining and/or beneficiating
327992	Kaolin, processing beyond beneficiation
713990	Kayaking, recreational
327420	Keene's cement manufacturing
321920	Kegs, wood, coopered, manufacturing
311119	Kelp meal and pellets, animal feed manufacturing
711219	Kennels, dog racing
812910	Kennels, pet boarding
324110	Kerosene manufacturing
333414	Kerosene space heaters manufacturing
311421	Ketchup manufacturing
325199	Ketone compounds, not specified elsewhere by process, manufacturing
332510	Key blanks manufacturing
316993	Key cases (except metal) manufacturing
339911	Key cases, precious metal, manufacturing
811490	Key duplicating shops
334119	Keyboards, computer peripheral equipment, manufacturing
336322	Keyless entry systems, automotive, truck, and bus, manufacturing
421710	Keys and locks wholesaling
334210	Keysets, telephone, manufacturing
621492	Kidney dialysis centers and clinics
321999	Kiln drying lumber
327124	Kiln furniture, clay, manufacturing
333994	Kilns (except cement, chemical, wood) manufacturing
333298	Kilns (i.e., cement, chemical, wood) manufacturing

421830	Kilns, industrial, wholesaling
611110	Kindergartens
334519	Kinematic test and measuring equipment manufacturing
561910	Kit assembling and packaging services
336211	Kit car bodies manufacturing
421620	Kitchen appliances, household-type, electric, wholesaling
327112	Kitchen articles, coarse earthenware, manufacturing
444190	Kitchen cabinet (except custom) stores
337110	Kitchen cabinets (except freestanding), stock or custom wood, manufacturing
421310	Kitchen cabinets, built in, wholesaling
337122	Kitchen chairs (e.g., upholstered), wood, manufacturing
337124	Kitchen chairs (including upholstered), metal, manufacturing
337125	Kitchen chairs (including upholstered), plastics manufacturing
325612	Kitchen degreasing and cleaning preparations manufacturing
337124	Kitchen furniture, household-type, metal, manufacturing
332214	Kitchen utensils, fabricated metal (e.g., colanders, garlic presses, ice scream scoops, spatulas), manufacturing
326199	Kitchen utensils, plastics, manufacturing
442299	Kitchenware stores
327112	Kitchenware, commercial and household-type, vitreous china, manufacturing
327112	Kitchenware, semivitreous earthenware, manufacturing
321999	Kitchenware, wood, manufacturing
339932	Kites manufacturing
111339	Kiwi fruit farming
334411	Klystron tubes manufacturing
314911	Knapsacks (e.g., backpacks, book bags) manufacturing
314911	Knapsacks, made from purchased woven or knitted materials

332211	Knife blades manufacturing
335313	Knife switches, electric power switchgear-type, manufacturing
313113	Knitting and crocheting thread manufacturing
313249	Knitting and finishing lace
313249	Knitting and finishing warp fabric
313241	Knitting and finishing weft fabric
313249	Knitting lace
333292	Knitting machinery manufacturing
313249	Knitting warp fabric
313241	Knitting weft fabric
332211	Knives (e.g., hunting, pocket, table nonprecious, table precious plated) manufacturing
421710	Knives (except disposable plastics) wholesaling
333515	Knives and bits for metalworking lathes, planers, and shapers manufacturing
332212	Knives and bits for woodworking lathes, planers, and shapers manufacturing
422130	Knives, disposable plastics, wholesaling
335211	Knives, household-type electric carving, manufacturing
339112	Knives, surgical, manufacturing
321999	Knobs, wood, manufacturing
334419	LCD (liquid crystal display) screen units manufacturing
334413	LED (light emitting diode) manufacturing
621399	LPNs' (licensed practical nurses) offices (e.g., centers, clinics)
484122	LTL (less-than-truckload) long-distance freight trucking
321213	LVL (laminated veneer lumber) manufacturing
339942	Label making equipment, handheld, manufacturing
333993	Labeling (i.e., packaging) machinery manufacturing
561910	Labeling services
323110	Labels lithographic (offset) printing on a job-order basis

313221 Labels weaving
422310 Labels, textile, wholesaling
561320 Labor (except farm) contractors (i.e., personnel suppliers)
561320 Labor (except farm) pools
115115 Labor contractors, farm
813930 Labor federations
561330 Labor leasing services
926150 Labor management negotiations boards, government
541612 Labor relations consulting services
813930 Labor unions (except apprenticeship programs)
54 Laboratories (see specific type)
621512 Laboratories, dental X-ray
621511 Laboratories, medical (except radiological, X-ray)
621512 Laboratories, medical radiological or X-ray
334516 Laboratory analytical instruments (except optical) manufacturing
333314 Laboratory analytical optical instruments (e.g., microscopes) manufacturing
311119 Laboratory animal feed manufacturing
112990 Laboratory animal production (e.g., guinea pigs, mice, rats)
315211 Laboratory coats, men's and boys', cut and sew apparel contractors
315225 Laboratory coats, men's and boys', cut and sewn from purchased fabric (except apparel contractors)
315212 Laboratory coats, women's, cut and sew apparel contractors
315239 Laboratory coats, women's, misses', and girls', cut and sewn from purchased fabric (except apparel contractors)
421490 Laboratory equipment (except dental, medical, ophthalmic) wholesaling
421450 Laboratory equipment, dental and medical, wholesaling
512199 Laboratory services, motion picture
541380 Laboratory testing (except medical, veterinary) services
621511 Laboratory testing services, medical (except radiological, X-ray)

621512 Laboratory testing services, medical radiological or X-ray
541940 Laboratory testing services, veterinary
233320 Laboratory, commercial and educational, construction
339111 Laboratory-type equipment (e.g., balances, centrifuges, furnaces) manufacturing
339111 Laboratory-type furniture (e.g., benches, cabinets, stools, tables) (except dental) manufacturing
333292 Lace and net making machinery manufacturing
313249 Lace manufacturing
313249 Lace products (except apparel) made in lace mills
314999 Lace, burnt-out, manufacturing
313221 Laces (e.g. shoe), textile, manufacturing
316999 Laces (e.g., shoe), leather, manufacturing
332812 Lacquering metals and metal products for the trade
325510 Lacquers manufacturing
422950 Lacquers wholesaling
311514 Lactose manufacturing
421830 Ladders wholesaling
321999 Ladders, extension, wood, manufacturing
326199 Ladders, fiberglass, manufacturing
332323 Ladders, metal chain, manufacturing
332323 Ladders, permanently installed, metal, manufacturing
332999 Ladders, portable metal, manufacturing
312120 Lager brewing
483211 Lake freight transportation (except on Great Lakes system)
483113 Lake freight transportation, Great Lakes
483212 Lake passenger transportation (except on Great Lakes system)
483114 Lake passenger transportation, Great Lakes
325132 Lakes (i.e., organic pigments) manufacturing

311611	Lamb carcasses, half carcasses, primal and sub-primal cuts, produced in slaughtering plants
112410	Lamb feedlots (except stockyards for transportation)
311612	Lamb, primal and sub-primal cuts, made from purchased carcasses
332999	Laminated aluminum foil (except bags, liners) manufacturing
327215	Laminated glass made from purchased glass
327211	Laminated glass made in glass making plants
326130	Laminated plastics plate, rod, and sheet, manufacturing
321213	Laminated structural wood members (except trusses) manufacturing
321213	Laminated veneer lumber (LVL) manufacturing
322225	Laminating foil for flexible packaging applications
332813	Laminating metals and metal formed products without fabricating
322222	Laminating purchased foil sheets for nonpackaging applications
322226	Laminating purchased paperboard
322222	Laminating purchased papers for nonpackaging applications
322221	Laminating purchased papers for packaging applications
313320	Laminating purchased textiles
327112	Lamp bases, pottery, manufacturing
325182	Lamp black manufacturing
335110	Lamp bulb parts (except glass blanks), electric, manufacturing
335110	Lamp bulbs and tubes, electric (e.g., fluorescent, incandescent filament, vapor), manufacturing
335931	Lamp holders manufacturing
332999	Lamp shade frames, metal, manufacturing
335121	Lamp shades (except glass, plastics), residential, manufacturing
327215	Lamp shades made from purchased glass
327212	Lamp shades made in glass making plants

326199	Lamp shades, plastics, manufacturing
442299	Lamp shops, electric
421220	Lamps (i.e., lighting fixtures) wholesaling
335122	Lamps (i.e., lighting fixtures), commercial, industrial, and institutional, manufacturing
335121	Lamps (i.e., lighting fixtures), residential, electric, manufacturing
335129	Lamps, insect, electric fixture, manufacturing
924120	Land management program administration
421820	Land preparation machinery, agricultural, wholesaling
333120	Land preparation machinery, construction, manufacturing
421810	Land preparation machinery, construction, wholesaling
925120	Land redevelopment agencies, government
531190	Land rental or leasing
233110	Land subdividers and developers (except cemeteries)
541370	Land surveying services
335312	Land transportation motors and generators manufacturing
541320	Land use design services
541320	Land use planning services
562212	Landfills
541320	Landscape architects' offices
541320	Landscape architectural services
561730	Landscape care and maintenance services
541320	Landscape consulting services
561730	Landscape contractors (except construction)
541320	Landscape design services
561730	Landscape installation services
541320	Landscape planning services
561730	Landscaping services (except planning)
541720	Language research and development services
611630	Language schools
541930	Language services (e.g., interpretation, sign, translation)

335129 Lanterns (e.g., carbide, electric, gas, gasoline, kerosene) manufacturing

339913 Lapidary work manufacturing

311613 Lard made from purchased fat

311611 Lard produced in slaughtering plants

422470 Lard wholesaling

334413 Laser diodes manufacturing

532230 Laser disc, video, rental

334612 Laser disks, prerecorded video, mass reproducing

334510 Laser equipment, electromedical, manufacturing

333992 Laser welding equipment manufacturing

326299 Latex foam rubber manufacturing

325510 Latex paint (i.e., water based) manufacturing

325212 Latex rubber, synthetic, manufacturing

327420 Lath, gypsum, manufacturing

321912 Lath, wood, manufacturing

333512 Lathes, metalworking, manufacturing

333210 Lathes, woodworking-type, manufacturing

321912 Lathmills, wood

812332 Launderers, industrial

812320 Laundries (except coin-operated, linen supply, uniform supply)

812310 Laundries, coin-operated or similar self-service

812331 Laundries, linen and uniform supply

812310 Laundromats

314911 Laundry bags made from purchased woven or knitted materials

812320 Laundry drop-off and pick-up sites

335224 Laundry equipment (e.g., dryers, washers), household-type, manufacturing

812310 Laundry machine routes (i.e., concession operators), coin-operated or similar self-service

333312 Laundry machinery and equipment (except household-type) manufacturing

421620 Laundry machinery and equipment, household-type (e.g., dryers, washers), wholesaling

421850 Laundry machinery, equipment, and supplies, commercial, wholesaling

314999 Laundry nets made from purchased materials

333312 Laundry pressing machines (except household-type) manufacturing

812320 Laundry services (except coin-operated, linen supply, uniform supply)

812310 Laundry services, coin-operated or similar self-service

812332 Laundry services, industrial

812331 Laundry services, linen supply

325611 Laundry soap, chips, and powder manufacturing

422690 Laundry soap, chips, and powder, wholesaling

332998 Laundry tubs, metal, manufacturing

326191 Laundry tubs, plastics, manufacturing

332998 Lavatories, metal, manufacturing

327111 Lavatories, vitreous china, manufacturing

541110 Law firms

541110 Law offices

333112 Lawn and garden equipment manufacturing

811411 Lawn and garden equipment repair and maintenance services without retailing new lawn and garden equipment

713990 Lawn bowling clubs

561730 Lawn care services (e.g., fertilizing, mowing, seeding, spraying)

422910 Lawn care supplies (e.g., chemicals, fertilizers, pesticides) wholesaling

332212 Lawn edgers, nonpowered, manufacturing

333112 Lawn edgers, powered, manufacturing

337125 Lawn furniture (except concrete, metal, stone, wood) manufacturing

337124 Lawn furniture, metal, manufacturing

337122 Lawn furniture, wood, manufacturing

332919	Lawn hose nozzles and lawn sprinklers manufacturing
421820	Lawn maintenance machinery and equipment wholesaling
561730	Lawn maintenance services
811411	Lawn mower repair and maintenance shops without retailing new lawn mowers
421820	Lawn mowers wholesaling
444210	Lawn power equipment stores
444220	Lawn supply stores
333112	Lawnmowers (except agricultural-type), powered, manufacturing
333111	Lawnmowers, agricultural-type, powered, manufacturing
332212	Lawnmowers, nonpowered, manufacturing
541110	Lawyers' offices
212291	Leaching of uranium, radium, or vanadium ores
335911	Lead acid storage batteries manufacturing
325131	Lead based pigments manufacturing
332999	Lead foil not made in rolling mills
212231	Lead ore mine site development for own account
212231	Lead ore mining and/or beneficiating
562910	Lead paint abatement services
562910	Lead paint removal contractors
331419	Lead smelting and refining, primary
327992	Lead, black (i.e., natural graphite), ground, refined, or blended, manufacturing
212231	Lead-zinc ore mining and/or beneficiating
333112	Leaf blowers manufacturing
332611	Leaf springs manufacturing
422590	Leaf tobacco wholesaling
813920	Learned societies
611691	Learning centers offering remedial courses
541720	Learning disabilities research and development services
211111	Lease condensate production
316999	Leashes, dog, manufacturing
******	Leasing—see type of property or article being leased
522220	Leasing in combination with sales financing
316999	Leather belting manufacturing
315292	Leather clothing (except apparel contractors) manufacturing
315212	Leather clothing manufacturing, women's, girls', and infants', cut and sew apparel contractors
315211	Leather clothing, men's and boys', cut and sew apparel contractors
448190	Leather coat stores
316110	Leather converters
422990	Leather cut stock (except boot, shoe) wholesaling
316999	Leather cut stock for shoe and boot manufacturing
422340	Leather cut stock for shoe and boot wholesaling
316219	Leather footwear (except house slippers, men's, women's) manufacturing
316213	Leather footwear, men's (except athletic, slippers), manufacturing
316212	Leather footwear, slippers, manufacturing
316214	Leather footwear, women's (except athletic, slippers), manufacturing
339920	Leather gloves, athletic, manufacturing
422990	Leather goods (except belting, footwear, handbags, gloves, luggage) wholesaling
811430	Leather goods repair shops without retailing new leather goods
448320	Leather goods stores
316993	Leather goods, small personal (e.g., coin purses, eyeglass cases, key cases), manufacturing
316992	Leather handbags and purses manufacturing
316212	Leather house slippers manufacturing
316991	Leather luggage manufacturing
316110	Leather tanning, currying, and finishing
316219	Leather upper athletic footwear manufacturing
333298	Leather working machinery manufacturing

541110 Legal aid services

315291 Leggings, infants', cut and sewn from purchased fabric (except apparel contractors)

316999 Leggings, welder's, leather, manufacturing

315239 Leggings, women's, misses' and girls', cut and sewn from purchased fabric (except apparel contractors)

921140 Legislative and executive office combinations

921120 Legislative bodies (e.g., federal, local, and state)

921120 Legislative commissions

111320 Lemon groves

421460 Lens blanks, ophthalmic, wholesaling

327215 Lens blanks, optical and ophthalmic, made from purchased glass

327212 Lens blanks, optical and ophthalmic, made in glass making plants

326199 Lens blanks, plastics ophthalmic or optical, manufacturing

333314 Lens coating (except ophthalmic)

339115 Lens coating, ophthalmic

333314 Lens grinding (except ophthalmic)

339115 Lens grinding, ophthalmic (except in retail stores)

446130 Lens grinding, ophthalmic, in retail stores

333314 Lens mounting (except ophthalmic)

339115 Lens mounts, ophthalmic, manufacturing

333314 Lens polishing (except ophthalmic)

339115 Lens polishing, ophthalmic

333314 Lenses (except ophthalmic) manufacturing

339115 Lenses, ophthalmic, manufacturing

111130 Lentil farming, dry, field and seed production

315191 Leotards made in apparel knitting mills

315239 Leotards, women's, misses', and girls', cut and sewn from purchased fabric (except apparel contractors)

****** Lessors—see specific type of asset or property being rented or leased

333313 Letter folding, stuffing, and sealing machinery manufacturing

561410 Letter writing services

323122 Letterpress plate preparation services

333293 Letterpress printing presses manufacturing

339950 Letters for signs manufacturing

322231 Letters, die-cut, made from purchased cardboard

111219 Lettuce farming, field, bedding plant and seed production

332212 Levels, carpenter's, manufacturing

524126 Liability insurance carriers, direct

514120 Libraries (except motion picture stock footage, motion picture commercial distribution)

512199 Libraries, motion picture stock footage film

512199 Libraries, videotape, stock footage

561990 License issuing services (except government), motor vehicle

621399 Licensed practical nurses' (LPNs) offices (e.g., centers, clinics)

926130 Licensing and inspecting of utilities

926150 Licensing and permit issuance for business operations, government

926150 Licensing and permit issuance for professional occupations, government

311340 Licorice candy manufacturing

332431 Lids and ends, can, metal, manufacturing

332115 Lids, jar, metal, stamping

561611 Lie detection services

334519 Lie detectors manufacturing

524210 Life insurance agencies

524113 Life insurance carriers, direct

339113 Life preservers manufacturing

326199 Life rafts, inflatable plastics, manufacturing

326299 Life rafts, inflatable rubberized fabric, manufacturing

541710 Life sciences research and development laboratories or services

421830	Lift trucks, industrial, wholesaling
333298	Light bulb and tube (i.e., electric lamp) machinery manufacturing
335110	Light bulbs manufacturing
421610	Light bulbs wholesaling
335110	Light bulbs, sealed beam automotive, manufacturing
334413	Light emitting diodes (LED) manufacturing
333315	Light meters, photographic, manufacturing
336510	Light rail cars and equipment manufacturing
485119	Light rail systems (except mixed mode), commuter
441110	Light utility truck dealers, new only or new and used
441120	Light utility truck dealers, used only
336112	Light utility trucks assembling on chassis of own manufacture
325998	Lighter fluids (e.g., charcoal, cigarette) manufacturing
339999	Lighters, cigar and cigarette (except motor vehicle, precious metal), manufacturing
339911	Lighters, cigar and cigarette, clad with precious metal, manufacturing
422990	Lighters, cigar and cigarette, wholesaling
488310	Lighthouse operation
421990	Lighting equipment, gas, wholesaling
444190	Lighting fixture stores
335129	Lighting fixtures, airport (e.g., approach, ramp, runway, taxi), manufacturing
335122	Lighting fixtures, commercial electric, manufacturing
421610	Lighting fixtures, electric, wholesaling
335122	Lighting fixtures, industrial electric, manufacturing
335122	Lighting fixtures, institutional electric, manufacturing
335129	Lighting fixtures, nonelectric (e.g., propane, kerosene, carbide), manufacturing
335121	Lighting fixtures, residential electric, manufacturing

561790	Lighting maintenance services (e.g., bulb and fuse replacement and cleaning)
235310	Lighting system construction contractors
711510	Lighting technicians, theatrical, independent
335311	Lighting transformers manufacturing
335931	Lightning arrestors and coils manufacturing
325211	Lignin plastics manufacturing
212111	Lignite surface mining and/or beneficiating
339113	Limbs, artificial, manufacturing
421320	Lime (except agricultural) wholesaling
327410	Lime production
422910	Lime, agricultural, wholesaling
212312	Limestone (except bituminous) crushed and broken stone mining and/or beneficiating
212312	Limestone beneficiating plants (e.g., grinding or pulverizing)
212311	Limestone mining or quarrying
212319	Limestone, bituminous, mining and/or beneficiating
334512	Limit controls (e.g., air-conditioning, appliance, heating) manufacturing
532111	Limousine rental without driver
485320	Limousine services (except shuttle services)
485320	Limousines for hire with driver (except taxis)
561730	Line slash (i.e., rights of way) maintenance services
335311	Line voltage regulators (i.e., electric transformers) manufacturing
332991	Linear ball bearings manufacturing
332991	Linear roller bearings manufacturing
442299	Linen stores
812331	Linen supply services
421220	Linens (e.g., bath, bed, table) wholesaling
314129	Linens made from purchased materials

448190	Lingerie stores
422330	Lingerie wholesaling
315212	Lingerie, women's, cut and sew apparel contractors
315231	Lingerie, women's, misses', and girls', cut and sewn from purchased fabric (except apparel contractors)
314999	Linings, casket, manufacturing
315211	Linings, hat, men's, cut and sew apparel contractors
315999	Linings, hat, men's, cut and sewn from purchased fabric (except apparel contractors)
314999	Linings, luggage, manufacturing
235520	Linoleum construction contractors
326192	Linoleum floor coverings manufacturing
311225	Linseed oil made from purchased oils
311223	Linseed oil, cake and meal, made in crushing mills
327390	Lintels, concrete, manufacturing
325412	Lip balms manufacturing
325620	Lipsticks manufacturing
422690	Liquefied gases (except LP) wholesaling
422710	Liquefied petroleum gas (LPG) bulk stations and terminals
332420	Liquefied petroleum gas (LPG) cylinders manufacturing
454312	Liquefied petroleum gas (LPG) dealers, direct selling
324110	Liquefied petroleum gas (LPG) made in refineries
422720	Liquefied petroleum gas (LPG) wholesaling (except bulk stations, terminals)
311313	Liquid beet syrup manufacturing
211112	Liquid hydrocarbons recovered from oil and gas field gases
311313	Liquid sugar made from beet sugar
311312	Liquid sugar made from purchased raw cane sugar
311311	Liquid sugar made in sugarcane mill

211112	Liquids, natural gas (e.g., ethane, isobutane, natural gasoline, propane) recovered from oil and gas field gases
445310	Liquor stores, package
311320	Liquor, chocolate, made from cacao beans
311330	Liquor, chocolate, made from purchased chocolate
422820	Liquors wholesaling
312130	Liquors, brandy, distilling and blending
422820	Liquors, distilled, wholesaling
312140	Liquors, distilling and blending (except brandy)
531390	Listing services, real estate
711410	Literary agents
335912	Lithium batteries, primary, manufacturing
325188	Lithium compounds, not specified elsewhere by process, manufacturing
323122	Lithographic plate preparation services
323110	Lithographic printing (except books, manifold business forms, printing grey goods, quick printing)
333293	Lithographic printing presses manufacturing
711310	Live arts center operators
422990	Live bait wholesaling
711310	Live theater operators
422520	Livestock (except horses, mules) wholesaling
422520	Livestock auction markets (except horses, mules)
422590	Livestock auction markets, horses and mules
541690	Livestock breeding consulting services
115210	Livestock breeding services (except consulting)
422910	Livestock feeds wholesaling
311119	Livestock feeds, supplements, concentrates and premixes, manufacturing

115210	Livestock spraying
484220	Livestock trucking, local
484230	Livestock trucking, long-distance
541940	Livestock veterinary services
422590	Livestock, horses and mules, wholesaling
337124	Living room furniture (except upholstered), metal, manufacturing
337122	Living room furniture (except upholstered), wood, manufacturing
337121	Living room furniture, upholstered, manufacturing
112990	Llama production
334418	Loaded computer boards manufacturing
421430	Loaded computer boards wholesaling
333120	Loaders, shovel, manufacturing
488320	Loading and unloading services at ports and harbors
488210	Loading and unloading services at rail terminals
334418	Loading printed circuit boards
522310	Loan brokerages
522310	Loan brokers' or agents' offices (i.e., independent)
522291	Loan companies (i.e., consumer, personal, small, student)
522390	Loan servicing
541820	Lobbying services
114112	Lobster fishing
334210	Local area network (LAN) communications equipment (e.g., bridges, gateways, routers) manufacturing
541512	Local area network (LAN) computer systems integration design services
611420	Local area network (LAN) management training
485113	Local bus services (except mixed mode)
492210	Local letter and parcel delivery services (except as part of intercity carrier network, U.S. Postal Service)
492110	Local letter and parcel delivery services as part of intercity courier network
485112	Local passenger rail systems (except mixed mode)
813940	Local political organizations
513310	Local telephone carriers (except wireless)
485111	Local transit systems, mixed mode (e.g., bus, commuter rail, subway combinations)
454390	Locker meat provisioners, direct selling
337215	Lockers (except refrigerated) manufacturing
421440	Lockers (except refrigerated) wholesaling
812990	Lockers, coin operated, rental
333415	Lockers, refrigerated, manufacturing
421740	Lockers, refrigerated, wholesaling
332510	Locks (except coin-operated, time locks) manufacturing
333311	Locks, coin-operated, manufacturing
421710	Locks, security, wholesaling
561622	Locksmith services
561622	Locksmith services with or without sales of locking devices, safes, and security vaults
561622	Locksmith shops
488210	Locomotive and rail car repair (except factory conversion, factory overhaul, factory rebuilding)
336321	Locomotive and railroad car light fixtures manufacturing
333618	Locomotive diesel engines manufacturing
336510	Locomotives manufacturing
336510	Locomotives rebuilding
212221	Lode gold mining and/or beneficiating
113310	Logging
541330	Logging engineering services
421810	Logging equipment wholesaling
336212	Logging trailers manufacturing
334515	Logic circuit testers manufacturing
541614	Logistics management consulting services
513310	Long-distance telephone carriers (except wireless)
513330	Long-distance telephone resellers (except satellite)

488320 Longshoremen services
333292 Looms for textiles manufacturing
323118 Looseleaf binders and devices manufacturing
422120 Looseleaf binders wholesaling
322233 Looseleaf fillers and paper made from purchased paper
322121 Looseleaf fillers and paper made in paper mills
325620 Lotions (e.g., body, face, hand) manufacturing
713290 Lottery control boards (i.e., operating lotteries)
921130 Lottery control boards, nonoperating
713290 Lottery ticket sales agents (except retail stores)
334310 Loudspeakers manufacturing
722410 Lounges, cocktail
315192 Lounging robes and dressing gowns made in apparel knitting mills
315291 Lounging robes and dressing gowns, infants', cut and sewn from purchased fabric (except apparel contractors)
315211 Lounging robes and dressing gowns, men's and boys', cut and sew apparel contractors
315221 Lounging robes and dressing gowns, men's and boys', cut and sewn from purchased fabric (except apparel contractors)
315212 Lounging robes and dressing gowns, women's, girls', and infants', cut and sew apparel contractors
311340 Lozenges, nonmedicated, candy, manufacturing
422710 Lubricating oils and greases bulk stations and terminals
324110 Lubricating oils and greases made in petroleum refineries
422720 Lubricating oils and greases wholesaling (except bulk stations, terminals)
324191 Lubricating oils and greases, petroleum, made from refined petroleum
325998 Lubricating oils and greases, synthetic, manufacturing

336510 Lubrication systems, locomotive (except pumps), manufacturing
332510 Luggage hardware, metal, manufacturing
314999 Luggage linings manufacturing
336399 Luggage racks, car top, automotive, truck, and bus, manufacturing
811430 Luggage repair shops without retailing new luggage
448320 Luggage stores
421990 Luggage wholesaling
316991 Luggage, all materials, manufacturing
335931 Lugs and connectors, electrical, manufacturing
421610 Lugs and connectors, electrical, wholesaling
421310 Lumber (e.g., dressed, finished, rough) wholesaling
321113 Lumber (i.e., rough, dressed) made from logs or bolts
561990 Lumber grading services
444190 Lumber retailing yards
493190 Lumber storage terminals
321113 Lumber, hardwood dimension, made from logs or bolts
321912 Lumber, hardwood dimension, resawing purchased lumber
321999 Lumber, kiln drying
321213 Lumber, parallel strand, manufacturing
321113 Lumber, softwood dimension, made from logs or bolts
321912 Lumber, softwood dimension, resawing purchased lumber
332439 Lunch boxes, light gauge metal, manufacturing
311612 Luncheon meat (except poultry) made from purchased carcasses
311611 Luncheon meat (except poultry) produced in slaughtering plants
311615 Luncheon meat, poultry, manufacturing
532111 Luxury automobile rental
485320 Luxury automobiles for hire with driver (except taxis)
321219 MDF (medium density fiberboard) manufacturing

http://www.ntis.gov/naics

621112	MDs' (medical doctors), mental health, offices (e.g., centers, clinics)
621111	MDs' (medical doctors, except mental health) offices (e.g., centers, clinics)
334413	MOS (metal oxide silicon) devices manufacturing
562920	MRF (materials recovery facilities)
621512	MRI (magnetic resonance imaging) centers
334510	MRI (magnetic resonance imaging) medical diagnostic equipment manufacturing
111335	Macadamia farming
422490	Macaroni wholesaling
311823	Macaroni, dry, manufacturing
311991	Macaroni, fresh, manufacturing
332994	Machine guns (i.e., 30 mm. or less, 1.18 inch or less) manufacturing
332995	Machine guns (i.e., more than 30 mm., more than 1.18 inch) manufacturing
332212	Machine knives (except metal cutting) manufacturing
235950	Machine rigging construction contractors
332710	Machine shops
333515	Machine tool attachments and accessories manufacturing
335311	Machine tool transformers manufacturing
421830	Machine tools and accessories wholesaling
333512	Machine tools, metal cutting, manufacturing
333513	Machine tools, metal forming, manufacturing
421420	Machines, office, wholesaling
332212	Machinist's precision measuring tools (except optical) manufacturing
421830	Machinists' precision measuring tools wholesaling
114111	Mackerel fishing
541840	Magazine advertising representatives (i.e., independent of media owners)
511120	Magazine publishers
511120	Magazine publishers and printing combined
511120	Magazine publishers, publishing only
451212	Magazine stands (i.e., permanent)
323112	Magazines and periodicals flexographic printing without publishing
323111	Magazines and periodicals gravure printing without publishing
323110	Magazines and periodicals lithographic (offset) printing without publishing
323119	Magazines and periodicals printing (except flexographic, gravure, lithographic, screen) without publishing
323113	Magazines and periodicals screen printing without publishing
422920	Magazines wholesaling
711190	Magic shows
451120	Magic supply stores
711510	Magicians, independent
327125	Magnesia refractory cement manufacturing
212325	Magnesite mining and/or beneficiating
327992	Magnesite, crude (e.g., calcined, dead-burned, ground), manufacturing
325188	Magnesium compounds, not specified elsewhere by process, manufacturing
331491	Magnesium foil made by rolling purchased metals or scrap
332999	Magnesium foil not made in rolling mills
331419	Magnesium refining, primary
331422	Magnet wire, insulated, made from purchased copper in wire drawing plants
334613	Magnetic and optical media, blank, manufacturing
541360	Magnetic geophysical surveying services
334119	Magnetic ink recognition devices, computer peripheral equipment, manufacturing

334613	Magnetic recording media for tapes, cassettes, and disks, manufacturing
621512	Magnetic resonance imaging (MRI) centers
334510	Magnetic resonance imaging (MRI) medical diagnostic equipment manufacturing
334613	Magnetic tapes, cassettes and disks, blank, manufacturing
421690	Magnetic tapes, cassettes, and disks, blank, wholesaling
334112	Magnetic/optical combination storage units for computers manufacturing
334411	Magnetron tubes manufacturing
327113	Magnets, permanent, ceramic or ferrite, manufacturing
332999	Magnets, permanent, metallic, manufacturing
333314	Magnifying instruments, optical, manufacturing
561310	Maid registries
561720	Maid services (i.e., cleaning services)
333313	Mail handling machinery, post office-type, manufacturing
561499	Mail presorting services
454110	Mail-order houses
561431	Mailbox rental centers, private
561431	Mailbox rental services combined with one or more other office support services, private
332439	Mailboxes, light gauge metal, manufacturing
511140	Mailing list compiling services
511140	Mailing list publishers
421420	Mailing machines wholesaling
334111	Mainframe computers manufacturing
488190	Maintenance and repair services, aircraft (except factory conversion, factory overhaul, factory rebuilding)
561730	Maintenance of plants and shrubs in buildings
488210	Maintenance of rights-of-way and structures, railway

488119	Maintenance services, runway
488310	Maintenance services, waterfront terminal (except dredging)
711211	Major league baseball clubs
812112	Make-up (except permanent) salons
325620	Make-up (i.e., cosmetics) manufacturing
812199	Make-up salons, permanent
337125	Malacca furniture (except upholstered), household-type, manufacturing
331511	Malleable iron foundries
332212	Mallets (e.g., rubber, wood) manufacturing
524126	Malpractice insurance carriers, direct
311942	Malt extract and syrups manufacturing
422490	Malt extract wholesaling
311213	Malt flour manufacturing
312120	Malt liquor brewing
311213	Malt manufacturing
422490	Malt wholesaling
311514	Malted milk manufacturing
311213	Malting (germinating and drying grains)
311221	Maltodextrins manufacturing
621512	Mammogram (i.e., breast imaging) centers
325221	Manmade cellulosic fibers manufacturing
325222	Manmade fibers and filaments (except cellulosic) manufacturing
422690	Manmade fibers wholesaling
711410	Management agencies for artists, entertainers, and other public figures
611430	Management development training
561110	Management services (except complete operation of client's business)
115116	Management services, farm
711310	Managers of agricultural fairs with facilities
711320	Managers of agricultural fairs without facilities
711310	Managers of arts events with facilities

711320	Managers of arts events without facilities
711310	Managers of festivals with facilities
711320	Managers of festivals without facilities
711310	Managers of live performing arts productions (e.g., concerts) with facilities
711320	Managers of live performing arts productions (e.g., concerts) without facilities
711310	Managers of sports events with facilities
711320	Managers of sports events without facilities
711410	Managers, authors'
711410	Managers, celebrities'
561920	Managers, convention
711410	Managers, entertainers'
711410	Managers, pubic figures'
711410	Managers, sports figures'
561920	Managers, trade fair or show
531312	Managing commercial real estate
523920	Managing investment funds
523920	Managing mutual funds
561110	Managing offices of professionals (e.g., dentists, physicians, surgeons)
523920	Managing personal investment trusts
531311	Managing residential real estate
523920	Managing trusts
111320	Mandarin groves
212210	Manganiferous ores valued for iron content, mining and/or beneficiating
212299	Manganiferousares ores (not valued for iron content) mining and/or beneficiating
812113	Manicure and pedicure salons
812113	Manicurist services
323116	Manifold business forms printing
336312	Manifolds (i.e., intake and exhaust), automotive and truck gasoline engine, manufacturing
313210	Manmade fabrics, broadwoven, weaving
541890	Mannequin decorating services
339999	Mannequins manufacturing
421440	Mannequins wholesaling
561320	Manpower pools
421390	Manufactured (i.e., mobile) homes wholesaling
321991	Manufactured (mobile) buildings for commercial use (e.g., banks, offices) manufacturing
321991	Manufactured (mobile) classrooms manufacturing
453930	Manufactured (mobile) home dealers
453930	Manufactured (mobile) home parts and accessory dealers
321991	Manufactured (mobile) homes manufacturing
813910	Manufacturers' associations
532490	Manufacturing machinery and equipment rental or leasing
541614	Manufacturing management consulting services
541614	Manufacturing operations improvement consulting services
511199	Map publishers
511199	Map publishers and printing combined
111998	Maple sap concentrating (i.e., producing pure maple syrup in the field)
111998	Maple sap gathering
111998	Maple syrup (i.e., maple sap reducing)
311999	Maple syrup mixing into other products
541370	Mapping (except geophysical) services
541360	Mapping services, geophysical
422920	Maps (except globe, school, wall) wholesaling
323112	Maps flexographic printing without publishing
323111	Maps gravure printing without publishing
323110	Maps lithographic (offset) printing without publishing
323119	Maps printing (except flexographic, gravure, lithographic, screen) without publishing

323113 Maps screen printing without publishing

212319 Marble crushed and broken stone mining and/or beneficiating

212311 Marble mining or quarrying

235430 Marble, granite, and slate work (interior) construction contractors

235410 Marble, granite, and slatework (i.e., exterior) construction contractors

422490 Margarine wholesaling

311225 Margarine-butter blend made from purchased fats and oils

311225 Margarines (including imitation) made from purchased fats and oils

713930 Marinas

928110 Marine Corps

488390 Marine cargo checkers and surveyors

488320 Marine cargo handling services

541330 Marine engineering services

333618 Marine engines manufacturing

332510 Marine hardware, metal, manufacturing

524126 Marine insurance carriers, direct

332410 Marine power boilers manufacturing

334220 Marine radio communications equipment manufacturing

488330 Marine salvaging services

447190 Marine service stations

488510 Marine shipping agency

335911 Marine storage batteries manufacturing

421860 Marine supplies (except pleasure) wholesaling

421910 Marine supplies, pleasure, wholesaling

441222 Marine supply dealers

541990 Marine surveyor (i.e., ship appraiser) services

488330 Marine vessel traffic reporting services

339942 Marker boards (i.e., whiteboards) manufacturing

541910 Marketing analysis services

541613 Marketing consulting services

541613 Marketing management consulting services

541910 Marketing research services

339943 Marking devices manufacturing

422120 Marking devices wholesaling

212312 Marl crushed and broken stone mining and/or beneficiating

311421 Marmalade manufacturing

624190 Marriage counseling services (except by offices of mental health practitioners)

311340 Marshmallow creme manufacturing

311340 Marshmallows manufacturing

611620 Martial arts instruction, camps, or schools

311340 Marzipan (i.e., candy) manufacturing

332212 Mason's handtools manufacturing

421320 Mason's materials wholesaling

235410 Masonry construction contractors

334516 Mass spectrometers manufacturing

234990 Mass transit construction

812199 Massage parlors

512210 Master recording leasing and licensing

422690 Mastics (except construction) wholesaling

325998 Matches and match books manufacturing

422990 Matches and match books wholesaling

811310 Materials handling equipment repair and maintenance services

532490 Materials handling machinery and equipment rental or leasing

421830 Materials handling machinery and equipment wholesaling

562920 Materials recovery facilities (MRF)

448120 Maternity shops

541710 Mathematics research and development laboratories or services

332618 Mats and matting made from purchased wire

332612 Mattress springs and spring units made from purchased wire

442110 Mattress stores (including waterbeds)

337910 Mattresses (i.e., box spring, innerspring, noninnerspring) manufacturing

337910	Mattresses made from felt, foam rubber, urethane and similar materials
421210	Mattresses wholesaling
326199	Mattresses, air, plastics, manufacturing
326299	Mattresses, air, rubber, manufacturing
311812	Matzo baking made in commercial bakeries
812220	Mausoleums
311941	Mayonnaise manufacturing
624210	Meal delivery programs
311119	Meal, alfalfa, manufacturing
311119	Meal, bone, prepared as feed for animals and fowls, manufacturing
311211	Meal, corn, for human consumption made in flour mills
421830	Measuring and testing equipment (except automotive) wholesaling
333515	Measuring attachments (e.g., sine bars) for machine tool manufacturing
334515	Measuring instruments and meters, electric, manufacturing
334513	Measuring instruments, industrial process control-type, manufacturing
332212	Measuring tools, machinist's (except optical), manufacturing
311613	Meat and bone meal and tankage, produced in rendering plant
311612	Meat canning (except baby, pet food, poultry), made from purchased carcasses
311611	Meat canning (except poultry) produced in slaughtering plants
311422	Meat canning, baby food, manufacturing
311111	Meat canning, dog and cat, pet food, made from purchased carcasses
311615	Meat canning, poultry (except baby and pet food), manufacturing
445210	Meat markets
311615	Meat products (e.g., hot dogs, luncheon meats, sausages) made from a combination of poultry and other meats

311612	Meat products canning (except baby, pet food, poultry) made from purchased carcasses
311111	Meat products, dog and cat, pet food, canning, made from purchased carcasses
311612	Meats (except poultry), cured or smoked, made from purchased carcasses
422470	Meats and meat products (except canned, packaged frozen) wholesaling
311611	Meats fresh, chilled or frozen (except poultry and small game), produced in slaughtering plants
422490	Meats, canned, wholesaling
311611	Meats, cured or smoked, produced in slaughtering plants
422470	Meats, cured or smoked, wholesaling
311612	Meats, fresh or chilled (except poultry and small game), frozen, made from purchased carcasses
422470	Meats, fresh, wholesaling
422470	Meats, frozen (except packaged), wholesaling
422420	Meats, packaged frozen, wholesaling
333924	Mechanic's creepers manufacturing
332212	Mechanic's handtools, nonpowered, manufacturing
421120	Mechanic's tools wholesaling
235110	Mechanical construction contractors
541330	Mechanical engineering services
313311	Mechanical finishing of broadwoven fabrics
339941	Mechanical pencils manufacturing
811310	Mechanical power transmission equipment repair and maintenance services
421840	Mechanical power transmission supplies (e.g., gears, pulleys, sprockets) wholesaling
326291	Mechanical rubber goods (i.e., extruded, lathe-cut, molded) manufacturing
421840	Mechanical rubber goods wholesaling

541380	Mechanical testing laboratories or services
333311	Mechanisms for coin-operated machines manufacturing
334518	Mechanisms, clockwork operated device, manufacturing
339942	Mechanical pencil refills manufacturing
541840	Media advertising representatives (i.e., independent of media owners)
541830	Media buying agencies
541830	Media buying services
541840	Media representatives (i.e., independent of media owners)
926150	Mediation and conciliation services, government
624190	Mediation, social service, family, agencies
621512	Medical X-ray laboratories
811219	Medical and surgical equipment repair and maintenance services
541430	Medical art services
541430	Medical artists, independent
531120	Medical building rental or leasing
621112	Medical doctors' (MDs), mental health, offices (e.g. centers, clinics)
621111	Medical doctors' (MDs, except mental health) offices (e.g., centers, clinics)
532490	Medical equipment (except home health furniture and equipment) rental or leasing
421450	Medical equipment wholesaling
421450	Medical furniture wholesaling
327215	Medical glassware made from purchased glass
327212	Medical glassware made in glass making plants
421450	Medical glassware wholesaling
541430	Medical illustration services
541430	Medical illustrators, independent
421450	Medical instruments wholesaling
524114	Medical insurance carriers, direct
621511	Medical laboratories (except radiological, X-ray)
621512	Medical laboratories, radiological or X-ray
541922	Medical photography services
621512	Medical radiological laboratories
541710	Medical research and development laboratories or services
422210	Medical sundries, rubber, wholesaling
421450	Medical supplies wholesaling
339112	Medical thermometers manufacturing
334510	Medical ultrasound equipment manufacturing
923130	Medicare and Medicaid administration
325411	Medicinal chemicals, uncompounded, manufacturing
337110	Medicine cabinets (except freestanding), wood household-type, manufacturing
337124	Medicine cabinets, metal household-type, manufacturing
321219	Medium density fiberboard (MDF) manufacturing
325211	Melamine resins manufacturing
111219	Melon farming (e.g., cantaloupe, casaba, honeydew, watermelon), field, bedding plant and seed production
111419	Melon farming, grown under cover
813410	Membership associations, civic or social
812220	Memorial gardens (i.e., burial places)
334418	Memory boards manufacturing
422320	Men's and boys' clothing wholesaling
422320	Men's and boys' furnishings (except shoes) wholesaling
315119	Men's socks knitting or knitting and finishing
114111	Menhaden fishing
622210	Mental (except mental retardation) hospitals
621420	Mental health centers and clinics (except hospitals), outpatient
623220	Mental health facilities, residential
623220	Mental health halfway houses
622210	Mental health hospitals
621112	Mental health physicians' offices (e.g., centers, clinics)

http://www.ntis.gov/naics

923120	Mental health program administration
623210	Mental retardation facilities (e.g., homes, hospitals, intermediate care facilities), residential
561450	Mercantile credit reporting bureaus
421440	Merchandising machines, coin-operated, wholesaling
926120	Merchant Marine (except academy)
813910	Merchants' associations
325188	Mercury compounds, not specified elsewhere by process, manufacturing
212299	Mercury ores mining and/or beneficiating
332618	Mesh made from purchased wire
331422	Mesh, wire, made from purchased copper in wire drawing plants
331319	Mesh, wire, made in aluminum wire drawing plants
331111	Mesh, wire, made in steel mills
331222	Mesh, wire, made in wire drawing mills
331491	Mesh, wire, nonferrous metals (except aluminum, copper), made from purchased nonferrous metals (except aluminum, copper) in wire drawing plants
561421	Message services, telephone answering
492210	Messenger service
332431	Metal cans manufacturing
333512	Metal cutting machine tools manufacturing
332213	Metal cutting saw blades manufacturing
422690	Metal cyanides wholesaling
334519	Metal detectors manufacturing
339113	Metal fabric and mesh safety gloves manufacturing
332999	Metal foil containers (except bags) manufacturing
333513	Metal forming machine tools manufacturing
337121	Metal framed furniture, household-type, upholstered, manufacturing
339943	Metal hand stamps manufacturing
333994	Metal melting furnaces, industrial, manufacturing
213114	Metal mining support services (shaft sinking, tunneling, blasting)
336370	Metal motor vehicle body parts stamping
334413	Metal oxide silicon (MOS) devices manufacturing
325612	Metal polishes (i.e., tarnish removers) manufacturing
331314	Metal powder and flake made from purchased aluminum
331423	Metal powder and flake made from purchased copper
331221	Metal powder and flake made from purchased iron
331492	Metal powder and flake nonferrous (except aluminum, copper) made from purchased metal
331111	Metal powder and flake, iron or steel, manufacturing
421510	Metal products (e.g., bars, ingots, plates, rods, shapes, sheets) wholesaling
421930	Metal scrap and waste wholesaling
332116	Metal stampings (except automotive, cans, cooking, closures, crowns), unfinished, manufacturing
421520	Metallic concentrates wholesaling
325131	Metallic pigments, inorganic, manufacturing
313320	Metallizing purchased textiles
541380	Metallurgical testing laboratories or services
421510	Metals sales offices
421510	Metals service centers
421510	Metals, ferrous and nonferrous, wholesaling
421940	Metals, precious, wholesaling
333512	Metalworking lathes manufacturing
532490	Metalworking machinery and equipment rental or leasing
421830	Metalworking machinery and equipment wholesaling
334519	Meteorological instruments manufacturing

541990	Meteorological services
561990	Meter reading services, contract
334514	Metering devices (except electrical and industrial process control) manufacturing
334514	Meters (except electrical and industrial process control) manufacturing
421830	Meters (except electrical, parking) wholesaling
334515	Meters, electrical (i.e., graphic recording, panelboard, pocket, portable), manufacturing
421610	Meters, electrical, wholesaling
334513	Meters, industrial process control-type, manufacturing
334514	Meters, parking, manufacturing
421850	Meters, parking, wholesaling
325199	Methyl alcohol (i.e., methanol), synthetic, manufacturing
325191	Methyl alcohol (methanol), natural, manufacturing
311422	Mexican foods canning
311412	Mexican foods, frozen, manufacturing
212399	Mica mining and/or beneficiating
327992	Mica processing beyond beneficiation
327999	Mica products manufacturing
311119	Micro and macro premixes, livestock, manufacturing
334516	Microbiology instruments manufacturing
334111	Microcomputers manufacturing
334413	Microcontroller chip manufacturing
333315	Microfiche equipment (e.g., cameras, projectors, readers) manufacturing
333315	Microfilm equipment (e.g., cameras, projectors, readers) manufacturing
421420	Microfilm equipment and supplies wholesaling
334310	Microphones manufacturing
334413	Microprocessor chip manufacturing
333314	Microscopes (except electron, proton) manufacturing
334516	Microscopes, electron and proton, manufacturing
334220	Microwave communications equipment manufacturing
334419	Microwave components manufacturing
335221	Microwave ovens (including portable), household-type, manufacturing
333319	Microwave ovens, commercial-type, manufacturing
513330	Microwave telecommunication resellers
611110	Middle schools
621399	Midwives' offices (e.g., centers, clinics)
721310	Migrant workers' camps
611310	Military academies, college level
611110	Military academies, elementary or secondary
314999	Military insignia, textile, manufacturing
928110	Military police
928110	Military training schools (except academies)
421860	Military vehicles (except trucks) wholesaling
311511	Milk based drinks (except dietary) manufacturing
311514	Milk based drinks, dietary, manufacturing
311511	Milk drink, chocolate, manufacturing
311511	Milk pasteurizing
311511	Milk processing (e.g., bottling, homogenizing, pasteurizing, vitaminizing) manufacturing
112120	Milk production, dairy cattle
311511	Milk substitutes manufacturing
311511	Milk, acidophilus, manufacturing
422490	Milk, canned or dried, wholesaling
311514	Milk, concentrated, condensed, dried, evaporated, and powdered, manufacturing
311511	Milk, fluid (except canned), manufacturing
422430	Milk, fluid (except canned), wholesaling

311514	Milk, malted, manufacturing
311514	Milk, powdered, manufacturing
311514	Milk, ultra-high temperature, manufacturing
112120	Milking dairy cattle
112420	Milking dairy goat
112410	Milking dairy sheep
421820	Milking machinery and equipment wholesaling
333111	Milking machines manufacturing
311514	Milkshake mixes manufacturing
314999	Mill menders, contract, woven fabrics
421840	Mill supplies wholesaling
315991	Millinery cut and sewn from purchased fabric (except apparel contractors)
422310	Millinery supplies wholesaling
315999	Millinery trimmings cut and sewn from purchased fabric (except apparel contractors)
315211	Millinery trimmings, men's and boys', cut and sew apparel contractors
315212	Millinery trimmings, women's, girls', and infants', cut and sew apparel contractors
422330	Millinery wholesaling
315211	Millinery, men's and boys', cut and sew apparel contractors
315212	Millinery, women's, girls', and infants', cut and sew apparel contractors
333512	Milling machines, metalworking, manufacturing
311212	Milling rice
421310	Millwork wholesaling
337212	Millwork, custom architectural, manufacturing
111199	Milo farming, field and seed production
711110	Mime theaters
333922	Mine conveyors manufacturing
562910	Mine reclamation services, integrated (e.g., demolition, hazardous material removal, soil remediation)
325131	Mineral colors and pigments manufacturing
311119	Mineral feed supplements (except cat, dog) manufacturing
311111	Mineral feed supplements, dog and cat, manufacturing
333131	Mineral processing and beneficiating machinery manufacturing
523910	Mineral royalties or leases dealing (i.e., acting as a principal in dealing royalties or leases to investors)
311119	Mineral supplements, animal (except cat, dog), manufacturing
422910	Mineral supplements, animal, wholesaling
311111	Mineral supplements, dog and cat, manufacturing
327993	Mineral wool insulation materials manufacturing
327993	Mineral wool products (e.g., board, insulation, tile) manufacturing
421520	Minerals (except construction materials, petroleum) wholesaling
332993	Mines, ammunition, manufacturing
713990	Miniature golf courses
334111	Minicomputers manufacturing
331111	Minimills, steel
******	Mining—see type
234930	Mining appurtenance construction contractors
813910	Mining associations
333131	Mining cars manufacturing
541330	Mining engineering services
336510	Mining locomotives and parts manufacturing
421810	Mining machinery and equipment (except petroleum) wholesaling
532412	Mining machinery and equipment rental or leasing
811310	Mining machinery and equipment repair and maintenance services
421830	Mining machinery and equipment, petroleum, wholesaling
336112	Minivans assembling on chassis of own manufacture
531130	Miniwarehouse rental or leasing
112930	Mink production
112511	Minnow production, farm raising
711211	Minor league baseball clubs

111998	Mint farming
421220	Mirrors (except automotive) wholesaling
421120	Mirrors, automotive, wholesaling
327215	Mirrors, framed or unframed, made from purchased glass
333314	Mirrors, optical, manufacturing
332993	Missile warheads manufacturing
561611	Missing person tracing services
813110	Missions, religious organization
332212	Miter boxes manufacturing
311514	Mix, ice cream, manufacturing
312140	Mixed drinks, alcoholic, manufacturing
111940	Mixed hay farming
485111	Mixed mode transit systems (e.g., bus, commuter rail, subway combinations)
422490	Mixes (e.g., cake, dessert, pie) wholesaling
311211	Mixes, flour (e.g., biscuit, cake, doughnut, pancake) made in flour mills
311822	Mixes, flour (e.g., biscuit, cake, doughnut, pancake), made from purchased flour
325314	Mixing purchased fertilizer materials
531190	Mobile (manufactured) home parks
531110	Mobile (manufactured) home, on site, rental or leasing
321991	Mobile (manufactured) homes, manufacturing
334220	Mobile communications equipment manufacturing
311119	Mobile feed mill
722330	Mobile food stands
453930	Mobile home dealers, manufactured
321991	Mobile home manufacturing
235990	Mobile home site setup and tie down construction contractors
484220	Mobile home towing services, local
484230	Mobile home towing services, long-distance
333924	Mobile straddle carriers manufacturing
339932	Model kits manufacturing
421920	Model kits wholesaling
339932	Model railroad manufacturing
561310	Model registries
561320	Model supply services
711410	Modeling agents
339942	Modeling clay manufacturing
611519	Modeling schools
711410	Models' agents or managers
711510	Models, independent
421690	Modems wholesaling
334210	Modems, carrier equipment, manufacturing
337214	Modular furniture systems (except wood frame), office-type, manufacturing
337211	Modular furniture systems, wood frame office-type, manufacturing
233210	Modular house assembly and installation on site, construction
422590	Mohair, raw, wholesaling
334516	Moisture analyzers, laboratory-type, manufacturing
334513	Moisture meters, industrial process-type, manufacturing
311312	Molasses made from purchased raw cane sugar
311313	Molasses made from sugar beets
311311	Molasses made in sugarcane mill
422490	Molasses wholesaling
311312	Molasses, blackstrap, made from purchased raw cane sugar
311311	Molasses, blackstrap, made in sugarcane mill
339991	Molded packings and seals manufacturing
322299	Molded pulp products (e.g., egg cartons, food containers, food trays) manufacturing
421310	Molding (e.g., sheet metal, wood) wholesaling
332321	Molding and trim (except motor vehicle), metal, manufacturing
212322	Molding sand quarrying and/or beneficiating
336370	Moldings and trim, motor vehicle, stamping
321918	Moldings, clear and finger joint wood, manufacturing

http://www.ntis.gov/naics

321918	Moldings, wood and covered wood, manufacturing
333511	Molds (except steel ingot), industrial, manufacturing
331511	Molds for casting steel ingots manufacturing
333511	Molds for forming materials (e.g., glass, plastics, rubber) manufacturing
333511	Molds for metal casting (except steel ingot) manufacturing
331511	Molds, steel ingot, industrial, manufacturing
112512	Mollusk production, farm raising
212299	Molybdenum ores mining and/or beneficiating
813110	Monasteries (except schools)
332999	Money chests, metal, manufacturing
525990	Money market mutual funds, closed-end
525910	Money market mutual funds, open-ended
522390	Money order issuance services
334119	Monitors, computer peripheral equipment, manufacturing
334413	Monolithic integrated circuits (solid-state) manufacturing
333923	Monorail systems (except passenger-type) manufacturing
485119	Monorail transit systems (except mixed mode), commuter
487110	Monorail, scenic and sightseeing, operation
453998	Monument (i.e., burial marker) dealers
421990	Monuments and grave markers wholesaling
327991	Monuments and tombstone, cut stone (except finishing or lettering to order only), manufacturing
441221	Moped dealers
532292	Moped rental
336991	Mopeds and parts manufacturing
421110	Mopeds wholesaling
339994	Mops, floor and dust, manufacturing
325132	Mordant dyes manufacturing
325613	Mordants manufacturing
522190	Morris Plans (i.e., known as), depository
522298	Morris Plans (i.e., known as), nondepository
332993	Mortar shells manufacturing
332995	Mortars manufacturing
522292	Mortgage banking (i.e., nondepository mortgage lending)
522310	Mortgage brokerages
522310	Mortgage brokers' or agents' offices (i.e., independent)
522292	Mortgage companies
524126	Mortgage guaranty insurance carriers, direct
812210	Mortician services
812210	Mortuaries
235430	Mosaic construction contractors (except fresco)
327122	Mosaic tile, ceramic, manufacturing
813110	Mosques, religious
561710	Mosquito eradication services
113210	Moss gathering
233320	Motel construction
561110	Motel management services (except complete operation of client's business)
721110	Motels
325320	Moth repellants manufacturing
421430	Mother boards wholesaling
512110	Motion picture and video production
512110	Motion picture and video production and distribution
512191	Motion picture animation, post-production
512199	Motion picture booking agencies
333315	Motion picture cameras manufacturing
421410	Motion picture cameras, equipment, and supplies wholesaling
541690	Motion picture consulting services
711510	Motion picture directors, independent
512120	Motion picture distribution exclusive of production
532490	Motion picture equipment rental or leasing

512131 Motion picture exhibition
512131 Motion picture exhibitors, itinerant
512199 Motion picture film laboratories
512120 Motion picture film libraries
512199 Motion picture film libraries, stock footage
325992 Motion picture film manufacturing
512199 Motion picture film reproduction for theatrical distribution
512199 Motion picture laboratories
512191 Motion picture or video editing services
512191 Motion picture or video post-production services
512191 Motion picture or video titling
711510 Motion picture producers, independent
512110 Motion picture production
512110 Motion picture production and distribution
512191 Motion picture production special effects, post-production
333315 Motion picture projectors manufacturing
512110 Motion picture studios, producing motion pictures
512132 Motion picture theaters, drive-in
512131 Motion picture theaters, indoor
532220 Motion picture wardrobe and costume rental
485210 Motor coach operation, interurban and rural
335314 Motor control accessories (including overload relays) manufacturing
335314 Motor controls, electric, manufacturing
421610 Motor controls, electric, wholesaling
484110 Motor freight carrier, general, local
484122 Motor freight carrier, general, long-distance, less-than-truckload (LTL)
484121 Motor freight carrier, general, long-distance, truckload
484210 Motor freight carrier, used household goods
441210 Motor home dealers
421110 Motor homes wholesaling
336213 Motor homes, self-contained, assembling on purchased chassis

336120 Motor homes, self-contained, mounted on heavy truck chassis of own manufacture
336112 Motor homes, self-contained, mounted on light duty truck chassis of own manufacture
721110 Motor hotels
721110 Motor inns
324191 Motor oils, petroleum, made from refined petroleum
325998 Motor oils, synthetic, manufacturing
811310 Motor repair and maintenance services, commercial or industrial
335314 Motor starters, contractors, and controllers, industrial, manufacturing
561599 Motor travel clubs
333997 Motor truck scales manufacturing
332510 Motor vehicle hardware, metal, manufacturing
334514 Motor vehicle instruments (e.g., fuel level gauges, oil pressure, speedometers, tachometers, water temperature) manufacturing
336360 Motor vehicle interior systems (e.g., headliners, panels, seats, trims) manufacturing
561990 Motor vehicle license issuing services, private franchise
926120 Motor vehicle licensing offices, government
336370 Motor vehicle metal bumper stampings
336370 Motor vehicle metal parts stamping
336370 Motor vehicle metal stampings (e.g., body parts, fenders, hub caps, tops, trim) manufacturing
326199 Motor vehicle moldings and extrusions, plastics, manufacturing
421120 Motor vehicle parts and accessories, new, wholesaling
421140 Motor vehicle parts, used, wholesaling
336360 Motor vehicle seat frames, metal, manufacturing
336360 Motor vehicle seats manufacturing
421130 Motor vehicle tires and tubes wholesaling

326211	Motor vehicle tires manufacturing
488410	Motor vehicle towing services
336360	Motor vehicle trimmings manufacturing
421110	Motor vehicles wholesaling
811490	Motorboat (i.e., inboard and outboard) repair and maintenance services
336612	Motorboat, inboard or outboard, building
441221	Motorcycle dealers
441221	Motorcycle parts and accessories dealers
421120	Motorcycle parts, new, wholesaling
711212	Motorcycle racetracks
711219	Motorcycle racing teams
532292	Motorcycle rental
811490	Motorcycle repair shops without retailing new motorcycles
336991	Motorcycles and parts manufacturing
421110	Motorcycles wholesaling
335312	Motors, electric (except engine starting motors, gearmotors, outboard), manufacturing
421610	Motors, electric, wholesaling
333996	Motors, fluid power, manufacturing
333618	Motors, outboard, manufacturing
421910	Motors, outboard, wholesaling
336322	Motors, starter, for internal combustion engines, manufacturing
713990	Mountain hiking, recreational
561910	Mounting merchandise on cards
334119	Mouse devices, computer peripheral equipment, manufacturing
325620	Mouthwashes (except medicinal) manufacturing
325412	Mouthwashes, medicated, manufacturing
334518	Movements, watch or clock, manufacturing
512110	Movie production and distribution
512131	Movie theaters (except drive-in)
512132	Movie theaters, drive-in
561730	Mowing services (e.g., highway, lawn, road strip)
811112	Muffler repair and replacement shops

336399	Mufflers and resonators, automotive, truck, and bus, manufacturing
315191	Mufflers made in apparel knitting mills
421120	Mufflers, exhaust, wholesaling
315211	Mufflers, men's and boys', cut and sew apparel contractors
315993	Mufflers, men's and boys', cut and sewn from purchased fabric (except apparel contractors)
315999	Mufflers, women's and girls', cut and sewn from purchased fabric (except apparel contractors)
315212	Mufflers, women's, girls', and infants', cut and sew apparel contractors
422910	Mulch wholesaling
333112	Mulchers, lawn and garden-type, manufacturing
112920	Mule production
422590	Mules wholesaling
334515	Multimeters manufacturing
334210	Multiplex equipment, telephone, manufacturing
624190	Multiservice centers, neighborhood
233320	Municipal building construction
212391	Muriate of potash, mining
325412	Muscle relaxant preparations manufacturing
712110	Museums
111411	Mushroom farming
111411	Mushroom spawn farming
311421	Mushrooms canning
711510	Music arrangers, independent
512230	Music book (i.e., bound sheet music) publishers and printing combined
512230	Music book (i.e., bound sheet music) publishers
339999	Music boxes manufacturing
512230	Music copyright buying and licensing
711310	Music festival promoters with facilities
611610	Music instruction (e.g., guitar, piano)
512230	Music publishers

339992	Music rolls, perforated, manufacturing
611610	Music schools (except academic)
451220	Music stores (e.g., cassette, compact disc, record, tape)
453310	Music stores (e.g., cassette, instrument, record, tape), used
451140	Music stores (i.e., instrument)
621340	Music therapists' offices (e.g., centers, clinics)
512110	Music video production
512110	Music video production and distribution
323112	Music, sheet, flexographic printing without publishing
323111	Music, sheet, gravure printing without publishing
323110	Music, sheet, lithographic (offset) printing without publishing
323119	Music, sheet, printing (except flexographic, gravure, lithographic, screen) without publishing
512230	Music, sheet, publishers and printing combined
512230	Music, sheet, publishing (i.e., establishment known as publishers)
323113	Music, sheet, screen printing without publishing
422990	Music, sheet, wholesaling
711130	Musical artists, independent
711130	Musical groups (except musical theater groups)
339992	Musical instrument accessories (e.g., mouthpieces, reeds, stands, traps) manufacturing
421990	Musical instrument accessories and supplies wholesaling
316991	Musical instrument cases, all materials, manufacturing
532299	Musical instrument rental
811490	Musical instrument repair shops without retailing new musical instruments
339992	Musical instruments (except toy) manufacturing
421990	Musical instruments wholesaling
339932	Musical instruments, toy, manufacturing
711130	Musical productions (except musical theater productions), live
512220	Musical recording, releasing, promoting, and distributing
421990	Musical recordings (e.g., compact discs, records, tapes) wholesaling
711110	Musical theater companies or groups
711110	Musical theater productions, live
711130	Musicians, independent
114112	Mussel fishing
112512	Mussel production, farm raising
311941	Mustard, prepared, manufacturing
523120	Mutual fund agencies (i.e., brokerages)
523920	Mutual fund managing
525990	Mutual funds, closed-end
525910	Mutual funds, open-ended
522120	Mutual savings banks
333991	Nail guns, handheld power-driven, manufacturing
325620	Nail polish remover manufacturing
325620	Nail polishes manufacturing
812113	Nail salons
333991	Nailers and staplers, handheld power-driven, manufacturing
421510	Nails wholesaling
331319	Nails, aluminum, made in wire drawing plants
332618	Nails, brads, and staples made from purchased wire
331222	Nails, iron or steel, made in wire drawing plants
331491	Nails, nonferrous metals (except aluminum, copper), made from purchased nonferrous metals (except aluminum, copper) in wire drawing plants
339950	Name plate blanks manufacturing
332999	Name plate blanks, metal, manufacturing
325192	Naphtha made by distillation of coal tar
325192	Naphthalene made from refined petroleum or natural gas
314129	Napkins made from purchased fabrics

422130	Napkins, paper, wholesaling
322291	Napkins, table, made from purchased paper
322121	Napkins, table, made in paper mills
313311	Napping broadwoven fabrics
313312	Napping textile products and fabrics (except broadwoven fabrics)
313221	Narrow fabrics weaving
927110	National Aeronautics and Space Administration
522298	National Credit Union Administration (NCUA)
928110	National Guard
712190	National parks
311422	Nationality specialty foods canning
311412	Nationality specialty foods, frozen, manufacturing
327310	Natural (i.e., calcined earth) cement manufacturing
212399	Natural abrasives (e.g., emery, grindstones, hones, pumice) (except sand) mining and/or beneficiating
313113	Natural fiber (i.e., hemp, linen, ramie) thread manufacturing
313210	Natural fiber fabrics (i.e., jute, linen, hemp, ramie), broadwoven, weaving
313221	Natural fiber fabrics (i.e., jute, linen, hemp, ramie), narrow woven, weaving
313111	Natural fiber spun yarns (i.e., hemp, jute, ramie, flax) made from purchased fiber
221210	Natural gas brokers
221210	Natural gas distribution systems
333618	Natural gas engines manufacturing
211112	Natural gas liquids (e.g., ethane, isobutane, natural gasoline, propane) recovered from oil and gas field gases
486910	Natural gas liquids pipeline transportation
221210	Natural gas marketers
486210	Natural gas pipeline transportation
211111	Natural gas production
486210	Natural gas transmission (i.e., processing plants to local distribution systems)

211112	Natural gasoline recovered from oil and gas field gases
325199	Natural nonfood coloring, manufacturing
813312	Natural resource preservation organizations
712190	Natural wonder tourist attractions (e.g., caverns, waterfalls)
312112	Naturally carbonated water, purifying and bottling
712190	Nature centers
712190	Nature parks
712190	Nature preserves
712190	Nature reserves
621399	Naturopaths' offices (e.g., centers, clinics)
334511	Nautical systems and instruments manufacturing
336611	Naval ship building
325191	Naval stores, gum or wood, manufacturing
811219	Navigational instruments (e.g., radar, sonar) repair and maintenance services
421860	Navigational instruments (except electronic) wholesaling
334511	Navigational instruments manufacturing
421690	Navigational instruments, electronic (e.g., radar, sonar), wholesaling
928110	Navy
312120	Near beer brewing
315191	Neckties made in apparel knitting mills
315211	Neckties, men's and boys', cut and sew apparel contractors
315993	Neckties, men's and boys', cut and sewn from purchased fabric (except apparel contractors)
422320	Neckties, men's and boys', wholesaling
315999	Neckties, women's and girls', cut and sewn from purchased fabric (except apparel contractors)
315212	Neckties, women's, girls', and infants', cut and sew apparel contractors

448150	Neckwear stores
111339	Nectarine farming
332991	Needle roller bearings manufacturing
451130	Needlecraft sewing supply stores
339993	Needles (except hypodermic, phonograph, styli) manufacturing
333292	Needles for knitting machinery manufacturing
339112	Needles, hypodermic and suture, manufacturing
334419	Needles, phonograph and styli, manufacturing
315192	Negligees made in apparel knitting mills
315212	Negligees, women's, cut and sew apparel contractors
315231	Negligees, women's, misses', and girls', cut and sewn from purchased fabric (except apparel contractors)
813319	Neighborhood development advocacy organizations
325120	Neon manufacturing
339950	Neon signs manufacturing
325212	Neoprene manufacturing
212325	Nepheline syenite mining and/or beneficiating
333292	Net and lace making machinery manufacturing
422310	Net goods wholesaling
313249	Netting made in warp knitting mills
313241	Netting made in weft knitting mills
313249	Netting made on a lace or net machine
326199	Netting, plastics, manufacturing
332618	Netting, woven, made from purchased wire
513111	Network broadcasting service, radio
513111	Network radio broadcasting
541512	Network systems integration design services, computer
513120	Network television broadcasting
513210	Networks, cable television
441110	New car dealers
541613	New product development consulting services
451212	News dealers
514110	News picture gathering and distributing services
514110	News reporting services
514110	News service syndicates
514110	News ticker services
511120	Newsletter publishers
511120	Newsletter publishers and printing combined
323112	Newsletters flexographic printing without publishing
323111	Newsletters gravure printing without publishing
323110	Newsletters lithographic (offset) printing without publishing
323119	Newsletters printing (except flexographic, gravure, lithographic, screen) without publishing
323113	Newsletters screen printing without publishing
541840	Newspaper advertising representatives (i.e., independent of media owners)
422920	Newspaper agencies wholesaling
511110	Newspaper branch offices
711510	Newspaper columnists, independent (freelance)
511110	Newspaper publishers
511110	Newspaper publishers and printing combined
323112	Newspapers flexographic printing without publishing
323111	Newspapers gravure printing without publishing
323110	Newspapers lithographic (offset) printing without publishing
323119	Newspapers printing (except flexographic, gravure, lithographic, screen) without publishing
323113	Newspapers screen printing without publishing
422920	Newspapers wholesaling
322122	Newsprint mills
322122	Newsprint paper, manufacturing
422110	Newsprint wholesaling
451212	Newsstands (i.e., permanent)
325188	Nickel compounds, not specified elsewhere by process, manufacturing

http://www.ntis.gov/naics

212234	Nickel concentrates recovery
332999	Nickel foil not made in rolling mills
212234	Nickel ore beneficiating plants
212234	Nickel ore mine site development for own account
212234	Nickel ores mining and/or beneficiating
331419	Nickel refining, primary
713990	Night clubs without alcoholic beverages
722410	Night clubs, alcoholic beverage
315192	Nightgowns made in apparel knitting mills
315291	Nightgowns, infants', cut and sewn from purchased fabric (except apparel contractors)
315211	Nightgowns, men's and boys', cut and sew apparel contractors
315221	Nightgowns, men's and boys', cut and sewn from purchased fabric (except apparel contractors)
315212	Nightgowns, women's, girls', and infants', cut and sew apparel contractors
315231	Nightgowns, women's, misses', and girls', cut and sewn from purchased fabric (except apparel contractors)
315192	Nightshirts made in apparel knitting mills
315291	Nightshirts, infants', cut and sewn from purchased fabric (except apparel contractors)
315211	Nightshirts, men's and boys', cut and sew apparel contractors
315221	Nightshirts, men's and boys', cut and sewn from purchased fabric (except apparel contractors)
315212	Nightshirts, women's, girls', and infants', cut and sew apparel contractors
315231	Nightshirts, women's, misses', and girls', cut and sewn from purchased fabric (except contractors)
315192	Nightwear made in apparel knitting mills
315291	Nightwear, infants', cut and sewn from purchased fabric (except apparel contractors)
315211	Nightwear, men's and boys', cut and sew apparel contractors
315221	Nightwear, men's and boys', cut and sewn from purchased fabric (except apparel contractors)
422320	Nightwear, men's and boys', wholesaling
315212	Nightwear, women's, girls', and infants', cut and sew apparel contractors
315231	Nightwear, women's, misses', and girls', cut and sewn from purchased fabric (except apparel contractors)
326299	Nipples and teething rings, rubber, manufacturing
325192	Nitrated hydrocarbon derivatives manufacturing
325311	Nitric acid manufacturing
325212	Nitrile rubber manufacturing
325211	Nitrocellulose (i.e., pyroxylin) resins manufacturing
325120	Nitrogen manufacturing
325314	Nitrogenous fertilizers made by mixing purchased materials
325311	Nitrogenous fertilizer materials manufacturing
325920	Nitroglycerin explosive materials manufacturing
325192	Nitrosated hydrocarbon derivatives manufacturing
325120	Nitrous oxide manufacturing
541380	Non-destructive testing laboratories or services
312120	Nonalcoholic beer brewing
312130	Nonalcoholic wines manufacturing
234990	Nonbuilding structures (except industrial) contractor
234930	Nonbuilding structures, industrial construction
325222	Noncellulosic fibers and filaments manufacturing
325222	Noncellulosic filament yarn manufacturing
325222	Noncellulosic staple fibers and filaments manufacturing

111339 Noncitrus fruit farming

327125 Nonclay refractories (e.g., block, brick, mortar, tile) manufacturing

311514 Nondairy creamers, dry, manufacturing

311511 Nondairy creamers, liquid, manufacturing

311514 Nonfat dry milk manufacturing

331522 Nonferrous (except aluminum) die-casting foundries

331492 Nonferrous alloys (except aluminum, copper) made from purchased nonferrous metals

331492 Nonferrous alloys (except aluminum, copper) made in integrated secondary smelting and alloying plants

331419 Nonferrous metal (except aluminum, copper) shapes made in primary nonferrous metal smelting and refining mills

331491 Nonferrous metal shapes (except aluminum, copper) made by rolling, drawing, or extruding purchased nonferrous metal

331491 Nonferrous metal shapes (except aluminum, copper) made in integrated secondary smelting and extruding mills

331491 Nonferrous metal shapes (except aluminum, copper) made in integrated secondary smelting and rolling mills

331491 Nonferrous metal shapes (except aluminum, copper) made in integrated secondary smelting mills and wire drawing plants

331528 Nonferrous metals (except aluminum, copper) foundries (except die-casting)

331419 Nonferrous metals (except aluminum, copper) made in primary nonferrous metal smelting and refining mills

331419 Nonferrous metals (except aluminum, copper) smelting and refining, primary

331528 Nonferrous metals (except aluminum, copper) unfinished castings (except die-castings) manufacturing

421510 Nonferrous metals (except precious) wholesaling

331491 Nonferrous wire (except aluminum, copper) made from purchased nonferrous metals (except aluminum, copper) in wire drawing plants

331491 Nonferrous wire (except aluminum, copper) made in integrated secondary smelting mills and wire drawing plants

323121 Nonfiction book binding without printing

323117 Nonfiction books printing and binding without publishing

323117 Nonfiction books printing without publishing

562219 Nonhazardous waste treatment and disposal facilities (except combustors, incinerators, landfills, sewer systems, sewage treatment facilities)

213115 Nonmetallic minerals mining support services (e.g., blasting, shaft sinking, tunneling) on a contract basis

325412 Nonprescription drug preparations manufacturing

422210 Nonprescription drugs wholesaling

531120 Nonresidential building (except miniwarehouse) rental or leasing

481212 Nonscheduled air freight transportation

481211 Nonscheduled air passenger transportation

332214 Nonstick metal cooking utensils

337122 Nonupholstered, household-type, custom wood furniture, manufacturing

313230 Nonwoven fabric tapes manufacturing

313230 Nonwoven fabrics manufacturing

313230 Nonwoven felts manufacturing

311999 Noodle mixes made from purchased dry ingredients

311423	Noodle mixes made in dehydration plants
311823	Noodle mixes made in dry pasta plants
311823	Noodles, dry, manufacturing
311991	Noodles, fresh, manufacturing
311999	Noodles, fried, manufacturing
541199	Notary public services
322233	Notebooks (including mechanically bound by wire, or plastics) made from purchased paper
422120	Notebooks wholesaling
453220	Novelty shops
332919	Nozzles, fire fighting, manufacturing
332919	Nozzles, lawn hose, manufacturing
332911	Nuclear application valves manufacturing
541690	Nuclear energy consulting services
926130	Nuclear energy inspection and regulation offices
325188	Nuclear fuel scrap reprocessing
325412	Nuclear medicine (e.g., radioactive isotopes) preparations manufacturing
234930	Nuclear reactor containment structure construction
332410	Nuclear reactor steam supply systems manufacturing
332410	Nuclear reactors control rod drive mechanisms manufacturing
332410	Nuclear reactors manufacturing
333512	Numerically controlled metal cutting machine tools manufacturing
621610	Nurse associations, visiting
561310	Nurse registries
113210	Nurseries for reforestation growing trees
444220	Nursery and garden centers without tree production
337124	Nursery furniture, metal, manufacturing
624410	Nursery schools
422930	Nursery stock (except plant bulbs, seeds) wholesaling
111421	Nursery stock growing
111421	Nursery with tree production (except for reforestation)

813920	Nurses' associations
621399	Nurses', licensed practical or registered, offices (e.g., centers, clinics)
623110	Nursing care facilities
623110	Nursing homes
611519	Nursing schools (except academic)
445292	Nut (i.e., packaged) stores
115114	Nut hulling and shelling
446191	Nutrition (i.e., food supplement) stores
621399	Nutritionists' offices (e.g., centers, clinics)
422450	Nuts (e.g., canned, roasted, salted) wholesaling
311320	Nuts, chocolate covered, made from cacao beans
311330	Nuts, chocolate covered, made from purchased chocolate
311340	Nuts, covered (except chocolate covered), manufacturing
311911	Nuts, kernels and seeds, roasting and processing
115113	Nuts, machine harvesting
332722	Nuts, metal, manufacturing
311911	Nuts, salted, roasted, cooked, canned, manufacturing
422590	Nuts, unprocessed or shelled only, wholesaling
325222	Nylon fibers and filaments manufacturing
315111	Nylon hosiery, sheer, women's, misses', and girls' full-length and knee-length, knitting or knitting and finishing
325211	Nylon resins manufacturing
315111	Nylons, sheer, women's, misses', and girls' full-length and knee-length, knitting or knitting and finishing
621320	ODs' (doctors of optometry) offices (e.g., centers, clinics)
321219	OSB (oriented strandboard) manufacturing
321999	Oars, wood, manufacturing
111199	Oat farming, field and seed production
311230	Oatmeal (i.e., cereal breakfast food) manufacturing

311230	Oats, breakfast cereal, manufacturing
311230	Oats, rolled (i.e., cereal breakfast food), manufacturing
812910	Obedience training services, pet
713990	Observation towers
926150	Occupational safety and health standards agencies
813920	Occupational therapists' associations
621340	Occupational therapists' offices (e.g., centers, clinics)
541710	Oceanographic research and development laboratories or services
336999	Off-highway tracked vehicles (except construction, armored military) manufacturing
333120	Off-highway trucks manufacturing
713290	Off-track betting parlors
561110	Office administration services
541512	Office automation computer systems integration design services
233320	Office building construction
531120	Office building rental or leasing
561720	Office cleaning services
421420	Office equipment wholesaling
337214	Office furniture (except wood), padded, upholstered, or plain (except wood), manufacturing
532420	Office furniture rental or leasing
442110	Office furniture stores
421210	Office furniture wholesaling
337211	Office furniture, padded, upholstered, or plain wood, manufacturing
561320	Office help supply services
811212	Office machine repair and maintenance services (except communication equipment)
532420	Office machinery and equipment rental or leasing
421420	Office machines wholesaling
561110	Office management services
322121	Office paper (e.g., computer printer, photocopy, plain paper) made in paper mills
322233	Office paper (e.g., computer printer, photocopy, plain paper), cut sheet, made from purchased paper
422120	Office supplies (except furniture, machines) wholesaling
322231	Office supplies, die-cut paper, made from purchased paper or paperboard
561320	Office supply pools
453210	Office supply stores
323122	Offset plate preparation services
323110	Offset printing (except books, manifold business forms, printing grey goods)
333293	Offset printing presses manufacturing
334515	Ohmmeters manufacturing
325998	Oil additive preparations manufacturing
422690	Oil additives wholesaling
211111	Oil and gas field development for own account
211111	Oil and gas field exploration for own account
213112	Oil and gas field services (except contract drilling) on a contract basis
333132	Oil and gas field-type drilling machinery and equipment (except offshore floating platforms) manufacturing
336611	Oil and gas offshore floating platforms manufacturing
213111	Oil and gas well drilling services (redrilling, spudding, tailing) on a contract basis
333414	Oil burners, heating, manufacturing
421720	Oil burners, heating, wholesaling
811191	Oil change and lubrication shops, automotive
422690	Oil drilling muds wholesaling
336399	Oil filters, automotive, truck, and bus, manufacturing
422590	Oil kernels wholesaling
523999	Oil lease brokers' offices
333913	Oil measuring and dispensing pumps manufacturing
422590	Oil nuts wholesaling
234930	Oil refinery construction
533110	Oil royalty companies
533110	Oil royalty leasing

211111	Oil shale mining and/or beneficiating
562910	Oil spill cleanup services
332420	Oil storage tanks, heavy gauge metal, manufacturing
213111	Oil well drilling on a contract basis
421830	Oil well machinery and equipment wholesaling
421830	Oil well supply houses wholesaling
311613	Oil, animal, rendering
311221	Oil, corn crude and refined, made by wet milling corn
311225	Oil, olive, made from purchased oils
422710	Oil, petroleum, bulk stations and terminals
422720	Oil, petroleum, wholesaling (except bulk stations, terminals)
311225	Oil, vegetable stearin, made from purchased oils
421930	Oil, waste, wholesaling
333911	Oil-well and oil-field pumps manufacturing
313320	Oiling of purchased textiles and apparel
325998	Oils (e.g., cutting, lubricating), synthetic, manufacturing
325192	Oils made by distillation of coal tar
422490	Oils, cooking and salad, wholesaling
324110	Oils, fuel, manufacturing
422990	Oils, inedible, animal or vegetable, wholesaling
324191	Oils, lubricating petroleum, made from refined petroleum
325998	Oils, lubricating, synthetic, manufacturing
324191	Oils, petroleum lubricating, re-refining used
325613	Oils, soluble (i.e., textile finishing assistants), manufacturing
325411	Oils, vegetable and animal, medicinal, uncompounded, manufacturing
325191	Oils, wood, made by distillation of wood
111191	Oilseed and grain combination farming, field and seed production
422990	Oilseed cake and meal wholesaling
111120	Oilseed farming (except soybean), field and seed production
422590	Oilseeds wholesaling
325199	Oleic acid (i.e., red oil) manufacturing
325188	Oleum (i.e., fuming sulfuric acid) manufacturing
111339	Olive farming
311225	Olive oil made from purchased oils
311223	Olive oil made in crushing mills
514191	On-line access service providers
812922	One-hour photofinishing services
111219	Onion farming, field, bedding plant and seed production
711110	Opera companies
711130	Opera singers, independent
927110	Operating and launching government satellites
541614	Operations research consulting services
233320	Operative builders of commercial and institutional buildings
233310	Operative builders of manufacturing and industrial buildings
233220	Operative builders of multifamily housing
233210	Operative builders of single family housing
421460	Ophthalmic goods (except cameras) wholesaling
339112	Ophthalmic instruments and apparatus (except laser surgical) manufacturing
541910	Opinion research services
325411	Opium and opium derivatives (i.e., basic chemicals) manufacturing
334112	Optical disk drives manufacturing
421460	Optical goods (except cameras) wholesaling
446130	Optical goods stores (except offices of optometrists)
333314	Optical gun sighting and fire control equipment and instruments manufacturing
811219	Optical instrument repair and maintenance services
334119	Optical readers and scanners manufacturing

514210 Optical scanning services

333314 Optical test and inspection equipment manufacturing

334413 Optoelectronic devices manufacturing

421460 Optometric equipment and supplies wholesaling

813920 Optometrists' associations

621320 Optometrists' offices (e.g., centers, clinics)

325412 Oral contraceptive preparations manufacturing

621210 Oral pathologists' offices (e.g., centers, clinics)

111310 Orange groves

115112 Orchard cultivation services (e.g., bracing, planting, pruning, removal, spraying, surgery)

711510 Orchestra conductors, independent

711130 Orchestras

454110 Order taking offices of mail-order houses

421520 Ore concentrates wholesaling

421520 Ores (e.g., gold, iron, lead, silver, zinc) wholesaling

621991 Organ banks, body

621991 Organ donor centers, body

422690 Organic chemicals wholesaling

325132 Organic pigments, dyes, lakes, and toners manufacturing

541612 Organization development consulting services

711310 Organizers of agricultural fairs with facilities

711320 Organizers of agricultural fairs without facilities

711310 Organizers of arts events with facilities

711320 Organizers of arts events without facilities

711310 Organizers of festivals with facilities

711320 Organizers of festivals without facilities

711310 Organizers of live performing arts productions (e.g., concerts) with facilities

711320 Organizers of live performing arts productions (e.g., concerts) without facilities

711310 Organizers of sports events with facilities

711320 Organizers of sports events without facilities

325199 Organo-inorganic compound manufacturing

321219 Oriented strandboard (OSB) manufacturing

327420 Ornamental and architectural plaster work (e.g., columns, mantels, molding) manufacturing

112511 Ornamental fish production, farm raising

421390 Ornamental ironwork wholesaling

235990 Ornamental metalwork construction contractors

332323 Ornamental metalwork manufacturing

111422 Ornamental plant growing

321918 Ornamental woodwork (e.g., cornices, mantels) manufacturing

339999 Ornaments, Christmas tree (except electric, glass), manufacturing

335129 Ornaments, Christmas tree, electric, manufacturing

327212 Ornaments, Christmas tree, glass, made in glass making plants

327215 Ornaments, Christmas tree, made from purchased glass

623990 Orphanages

339116 Orthodontic appliance, custom made in dental laboratories

339114 Orthodontic appliances manufacturing

621210 Orthodontists' offices (e.g., centers, clinics)

339113 Orthopedic canes manufacturing

339113 Orthopedic devices manufacturing

339113 Orthopedic extension shoes manufacturing

339113 Orthopedic hosiery, elastic, manufacturing

327420 Orthopedic plaster, gypsum, manufacturing

316219 Orthopedic shoes (except extension shoes), children's, manufacturing

316213	Orthopedic shoes (except extension shoes), men's, manufacturing
316214	Orthopedic shoes (except extension shoes), women's, manufacturing
448210	Orthopedic shoes stores
334515	Oscilloscopes manufacturing
621111	Osteopathic physicians' (except mental health) offices (e.g., centers, clinics)
112390	Ostrich production
441222	Outboard motor dealers
811490	Outboard motor repair shops
333618	Outboard motors manufacturing
421910	Outboard motors wholesaling
713990	Outdoor adventure operations (e.g., white water rafting) without accommodations
721214	Outdoor adventure retreats with accommodation facilities
541850	Outdoor display advertising services
421210	Outdoor furniture wholesaling
451110	Outdoor sporting equipment stores
315191	Outerwear handknitted for the trade
335932	Outlet boxes, electrical wiring, manufacturing
335931	Outlets (i.e., receptacles), electrical, manufacturing
621420	Outpatient mental health centers and clinics (except hospitals)
621420	Outpatient treatment centers and clinics (except hospitals) for substance abuse (i.e., alcoholism, drug addiction)
421720	Ovens (except electric), household-type, wholesaling
333294	Ovens, bakery, manufacturing
333319	Ovens, commercial-type, manufacturing
421440	Ovens, commercial-type, wholesaling
421620	Ovens, electric household-type, wholesaling
333994	Ovens, industrial process-type, manufacturing
421830	Ovens, industrial, wholesaling
315211	Overalls, work, men's and boys', cut and sew apparel contractors
315225	Overalls, work, men's and boys', cut and sewn from purchased fabric (except apparel contractors)
315211	Overcoats, men's and boys', cut and sew apparel contractors
315222	Overcoats, men's and boys', cut and sewn from purchased fabric (except apparel contractors)
315212	Overcoats, women's, girls', and infants', cut and sew apparel contractors
315234	Overcoats, women's, misses', and girls', cut and sewn from purchased fabric (except apparel contractors)
333922	Overhead conveyors manufacturing
333315	Overhead projectors (except computer peripheral) manufacturing
334119	Overhead projectors, computer peripheral-type, manufacturing
333923	Overhead traveling cranes manufacturing
234120	Overpass construction
316211	Overshoes, plastics or plastics soled fabric upper, manufacturing
316211	Overshoes, rubber, or rubber soled fabric, manufacturing
325199	Oxalates (e.g., ammonium oxalate, ethyl oxalate, sodium oxalate) manufacturing
339991	Oxial mechanical face seals manufacturing
532291	Oxygen equipment rental (i.e. home use)
325120	Oxygen manufacturing
339112	Oxygen tents manufacturing
114112	Oyster dredging
112512	Oyster production, farm raising
813940	PACs (Political Action Committees)
334210	PBX (private branch exchange) equipment manufacturing
561330	PEO (professional employer organizations)
334510	PET (position emission tomography) scanners manufacturing

621999	Pacemaker monitoring services
334510	Pacemakers manufacturing
713990	Pack trains (i.e., trail riding), recreational
445310	Package stores (i.e., liquor)
511210	Packaged computer software publishers
511210	Packaged computer software publishing (i.e., establishments known as publishers)
326112	Packaging film, plastics, single-web or multiweb, manufacturing
115114	Packaging fresh or farm-dried fruits and vegetables
541420	Packaging industrial design services
333993	Packaging machinery manufacturing
421840	Packaging material wholesaling
561910	Packaging services (except packing and crating for transportation)
326150	Packaging, foam plastics (except polystyrene), manufacturing
326199	Packaging, plastics (e.g., blister, bubble), manufacturing
488991	Packing and preparing goods for shipping
321920	Packing crates, wood, manufacturing
115114	Packing fruits and vegetables
421830	Packing machinery and equipment wholesaling
421840	Packing materials wholesaling
314999	Padding and wadding (except nonwoven fabric) manufacturing
422310	Paddings, apparel, wholesaling
321999	Paddles, wood, manufacturing
332510	Padlocks manufacturing
314129	Pads and protectors (e.g., ironing board, mattress, table), textile, made from purchased fabrics or felts
313230	Pads and wadding, nonwoven, manufacturing
322211	Pads, corrugated and solid fiberboard, made from purchased paper or paperboard
322233	Pads, desk, made from purchased paper
332999	Pads, soap impregnated scouring, manufacturing

334220	Pagers manufacturing
513321	Paging services
326199	Pails, plastics, manufacturing
321920	Pails, wood, manufacturing
621498	Pain therapy centers and clinics, outpatient
325510	Paint and varnish removers manufacturing
333994	Paint baking and drying ovens manufacturing
339994	Paint rollers manufacturing
422950	Paint rollers wholesaling
811121	Paint shops, automotive
333991	Paint spray guns, handheld pneumatic, manufacturing
333912	Paint sprayers (i.e., compressor and spray gun unit) manufacturing
444120	Paint stores
325510	Paint thinner and reducer preparations manufacturing
325510	Paintbrush cleaners manufacturing
339994	Paintbrushes manufacturing
422950	Paintbrushes wholesaling
422950	Painter's supplies (except artist's, turpentine) wholesaling
711510	Painting restorers, independent
235210	Painting, exterior (except roof) and interior, construction contractors
235610	Painting, roof, construction contractors
325510	Paints (except artist's) manufacturing
422950	Paints (except artist's) wholesaling
339942	Paints, artist's, manufacturing
422990	Paints, artist's, wholesaling
315192	Pajamas made in apparel knitting mills
315291	Pajamas, infants', cut and sewn from purchased fabric (except apparel contractors)
315211	Pajamas, men's and boys', cut and sew apparel contractors
315221	Pajamas, men's and boys', cut and sewn from purchased fabric (except apparel contractors)
315231	Pajamas, women's and girls', cut and sewn from purchased fabric (except apparel contractors)

315212	Pajamas, women's, girls', and infants', cut and sew apparel contractors
339942	Palettes, artist's, manufacturing
321920	Pallet parts, wood, manufacturing
421830	Pallets and skids wholesaling
322211	Pallets, corrugated and solid fiber, made from purchased paper or paperboard
332999	Pallets, metal, manufacturing
321920	Pallets, wood or wood and metal combination, manufacturing
812990	Palm reading services
311225	Palm-kernel oil made from purchased oils
311223	Palm-kernel oil, cake, and meal made in crushing mills
323121	Pamphlet binding without printing
511130	Pamphlet publishers
511130	Pamphlet publishers and printing combined
323117	Pamphlets printing and binding without publishing
323117	Pamphlets printing without publishing
422920	Pamphlets wholesaling
311822	Pancake mixes made from purchased flour
311999	Pancake syrups (except pure maple) manufacturing
311412	Pancakes, frozen, manufacturing
335313	Panelboards, electric power distribution, manufacturing
421610	Panelboards, electric power distribution, wholesaling
235510	Paneling construction contractors
421310	Paneling wholesaling
332311	Panels, prefabricated metal building, manufacturing
321992	Panels, prefabricated wood building, manufacturing
315192	Panties made in apparel knitting mills
315291	Panties, infants', cut and sewn from purchased fabric (except apparel contractors)
315212	Panties, women's and girls', cut and sew apparel contractors

315231	Panties, women's, misses', and girls', cut and sewn from purchased fabric (except apparel contractors)
315211	Pants, dress, men's and boys', cut and sew apparel contractors
315224	Pants, dress, men's and boys', cut and sewn from purchased fabric (except apparel contractors)
315212	Pants, infants', cut and sew apparel contractors
315291	Pants, infants', cut and sewn from purchased fabric (except apparel contractors)
315292	Pants, leather (except apparel contractors), manufacturing
315211	Pants, leather, men's and boys', cut and sew apparel contractors
315211	Pants, men's and boys', cut and sew apparel contractors
315191	Pants, outerwear, made in apparel knitting mills
315291	Pants, sweat, infant's, cut and sewn from purchased fabric (except apparel contractors)
315228	Pants, sweat, men's and boys', cut and sewn from purchased fabric (except apparel contractors)
315212	Pants, sweat, women's, girls', and infants', cut and sew apparel contractors
315211	Pants, unisex sweat, cut and sew apparel contractors
315228	Pants, unisex sweat, cut and sewn from purchased fabric (except apparel contractors)
315299	Pants, waterproof outerwear (except infants'), cut and sewn from purchased fabric (except apparel contractors)
315211	Pants, waterproof outerwear, men's and boys', cut and sew apparel contractors
315212	Pants, waterproof outerwear, women's, girls', and infants', cut and sew apparel contractors
315212	Pants, women's, girls', and infants', cut and sew apparel contractors

315239	Pants, women's, misses', and girls', cut and sewn from purchased fabric (except apparel contractors)
315211	Pants, work (except dungarees, jeans), men's and boys', cut and sew apparel contractors
315225	Pants, work (except dungarees, jeans), men's and boys', cut and sewn from purchased fabric (except apparel contractors)
315291	Pantsuits, infants', cut and sewn from purchased fabric (except apparel contractors)
315212	Pantsuits, women's, girls', and infants', cut and sew apparel contractors
315234	Pantsuits, women's, misses', and girls', cut and sewn from purchased fabric (except apparel contractors)
315111	Panty hose, women's and girls', knitting or knitting and finishing
111339	Papaya farming
327910	Paper (e.g., aluminum oxide, emery, garnet, silicon carbide), abrasive coated, made from purchased paper
422110	Paper (e.g., fine, printing, writing), bulk, wholesaling
322121	Paper (except newsprint, uncoated groundwood) manufacturing
322121	Paper (except newsprint, uncoated groundwood) products made in paper mills
322121	Paper (except newsprint, uncoated groundwood), coated, laminated or treated, made in paper mills
422130	Paper (except office supplies, printing paper, stationery, writing paper) wholesaling
333291	Paper and paperboard converting machinery manufacturing
421830	Paper and pulp industries manufacturing machinery wholesaling
422130	Paper bags wholesaling
322223	Paper bags, coated, made from purchased paper
322224	Paper bags, uncoated, made from purchased paper
332618	Paper clips made from purchased wire
339942	Paper cutters, office-type, manufacturing
322299	Paper dishes (e.g., cups, plates) made from purchased molded pulp
322215	Paper dishes (e.g., cups, plates) made from purchased paper or paperboard
235210	Paper hanging or removal construction contractors
332618	Paper machine wire cloth made from purchased wire
333291	Paper making machinery manufacturing
322121	Paper mills (except newsprint, uncoated groundwood paper mills)
322122	Paper mills, newsprint
322122	Paper mills, uncoated groundwood
322291	Paper napkins and tablecloths made from purchased paper
322299	Paper novelties made from purchased paper
322215	Paper plates made from purchased paper or paperboard
322299	Paper products (except office supply), die-cut, made from purchased paper or paperboard
322231	Paper products, die-cut office supply, made from purchased paper or paperboard
322121	Paper stock for conversion into paper products (e.g., bag and sack stock, envelope stock, tissue stock, wallpaper stock) manufacturing
322291	Paper towels made from purchased paper
322121	Paper towels made in paper mills
313111	Paper yarn manufacturing
322121	Paper, asphalt, made in paper mills
421390	Paper, building, wholesaling
339944	Paper, carbon, manufacturing
322211	Paper, corrugated, made from purchased paper or paperboard
322122	Paper, newsprint and uncoated groundwood, manufacturing

http://www.ntis.gov/naics

422120	Paper, office (e.g., carbon, computer, copier, typewriter), wholesaling
325992	Paper, photographic sensitized, manufacturing
421930	Paper, scrap, wholesaling
339944	Paper, stencil, manufacturing
322130	Paperboard (e.g., can/drum stock, container board, corrugating medium, folding carton stock, linerboard, tube) manufacturing
422130	Paperboard and paperboard products (except office supplies) wholesaling
322130	Paperboard coating, laminating, or treating in paperboard mills
333291	Paperboard making machinery manufacturing
322130	Paperboard mills
322130	Paperboard products (e.g., containers) made in paperboard mills
322226	Paperboard, pasted, lined, laminated, or surface coated, made from purchased paperboard
713990	Para sailing, recreational
314999	Parachutes manufacturing
541199	Paralegal services
321213	Parallel strand lumber manufacturing
621399	Paramedics' offices (e.g., centers, clinics)
485991	Paratransit transportation services
561431	Parcel mailing services combined with one or more other office support services, private
561431	Parcel mailing services, private
922150	Pardon boards and offices
813410	Parent-teachers' associations
234990	Park construction
922120	Park police
812930	Parking garages, automobile
561790	Parking lot cleaning (e.g., power sweeping, washing) services
812930	Parking lots, automobile
334514	Parking meters manufacturing
561612	Parking security services
488119	Parking services, aircraft
812930	Parking services, valet
233320	Parking structure construction
713110	Parks (e.g., theme, water), amusement
924120	Parks and recreation commission, government
712190	Parks, national
712190	Parks, nature
712130	Parks, wild animal
611310	Parochial schools, college level
611110	Parochial schools, elementary or secondary
922150	Parole offices
321918	Parquet flooring, hardwood, manufacturing
335999	Particle accelerators, high voltage, manufacturing
321219	Particleboard manufacturing
421310	Particleboard wholesaling
337215	Partitions for floor attachment, prefabricated, manufacturing
421440	Partitions wholesaling
322211	Partitions, corrugated and solid fiber, made from purchased paper or paperboard
337215	Partitions, freestanding, prefabricated, manufacturing
332323	Partitions, ornamental metal, manufacturing
441310	Parts and accessories dealers, automotive
421120	Parts, new, motor vehicle, wholesaling
421140	Parts, used, motor vehicle, wholesaling
532299	Party (i.e., banquet) equipment rental
454390	Party plan merchandisers, direct selling
812990	Party planning services
532299	Party rental supply centers
481211	Passenger air transportation, nonscheduled
481111	Passenger air transportation, scheduled
233320	Passenger and freight terminal building construction
333922	Passenger baggage belt loaders (except industrial truck) manufacturing

532112	Passenger car leasing
532111	Passenger car rental
481211	Passenger carriers, air, nonscheduled
481111	Passenger carriers, air, scheduled
485320	Passenger limousine rental with driver (except shuttle service, taxi)
482111	Passenger railways, line-haul
336611	Passenger ship building
483114	Passenger transportation, coastal or Great Lakes
483114	Passenger transportation, deep sea, to and from domestic ports
483112	Passenger transportation, deep sea, to or from foreign ports
483212	Passenger transportation, inland waters (except on Great Lakes system)
532112	Passenger van leasing
532111	Passenger van rental
485320	Passenger van rental with driver (except shuttle service, taxi)
541921	Passport photography services
311422	Pasta based products canning
311999	Pasta mixes made from purchased dry ingredients
311823	Pasta, dry, manufacturing
311991	Pasta, fresh, manufacturing
331221	Paste made from purchased iron or steel
325520	Pastes, adhesive, manufacturing
311421	Pastes, fruit and vegetable, canning
333294	Pasteurizing equipment, food, manufacturing
311511	Pasteurizing milk
311812	Pastries (e.g., Danish, French), fresh, made in commercial bakeries
311813	Pastries (e.g., Danish, French), frozen, manufacturing
311822	Pastries, uncooked, manufacturing
541199	Patent agent services (i.e., patent filing and searching services)
541110	Patent attorneys' offices
541990	Patent broker services (i.e., patent marketing services)
533110	Patent buying and licensing
533110	Patent leasing
621111	Pathologists' (except oral, speech, voice) offices (e.g., centers, clinics)
621210	Pathologists', oral, offices (e.g., centers, clinics)
621340	Pathologists', speech or voice, offices (e.g., centers, clinics)
621511	Pathology laboratories, medical
334510	Patient monitoring equipment (e.g., intensive care, coronary care unit) manufacturing
421450	Patient monitoring equipment wholesaling
327331	Patio block, concrete, manufacturing
235710	Patio construction contractors
336611	Patrol boat building
561612	Patrol services, security
541990	Patrolling (i.e., visual inspection) of electric transmission or gas lines
511199	Pattern and plan (e.g., clothing patterns) publishers
511199	Pattern and plan (e.g., clothing patterns) publishers and printing combined
332997	Patterns (except shoe), industrial, manufacturing
421830	Patterns (except shoe), industrial, wholesaling
323112	Patterns and plans (e.g., clothing patterns) flexographic printing without publishing
323111	Patterns and plans (e.g., clothing patterns) gravure printing without publishing
323110	Patterns and plans (e.g., clothing patterns) lithographic (offset) printing without publishing
323119	Patterns and plans (e.g., clothing patterns) printing (except flexographic, gravure, lithographic, screen) without publishing
323113	Patterns and plans (e.g., clothing patterns) screen printing without publishing

http://www.ntis.gov/naics

339999	Patterns, shoe, manufacturing
421850	Patterns, shoe, wholesaling
324121	Paving blocks and mixtures made from purchased asphaltic materials
327331	Paving blocks, concrete, manufacturing
327121	Paving brick, clay, manufacturing
333120	Paving machinery manufacturing
522298	Pawnshops
812990	Pay telephone equipment concession operators
513210	Pay television networks
541214	Payroll processing services
111219	Pea (except dry) farming, field and seed production
111130	Pea farming, dry, field and seed production
928120	Peace Corps
813319	Peace advocacy organizations
111339	Peach farming
311911	Peanut butter blended with jelly manufacturing
311911	Peanut butter manufacturing
311223	Peanut cake, meal, and oil made in crushing mills
111992	Peanut farming
311225	Peanut oil made from purchased oils
115113	Peanut, machine harvesting
111339	Pear farming
339913	Pearl drilling, peeling, or sawing
421940	Pearls wholesaling
339914	Pearls, costume, manufacturing
212399	Peat mining and/or beneficiating
111335	Pecan farming
311942	Pectin manufacturing
621111	Pediatricians' (except mental health) offices (e.g., centers, clinics)
621112	Pediatricians', mental health, offices (e.g., centers, clinics)
812113	Pedicure and manicure salons
812113	Pedicurist services
115210	Pedigree (i.e., livestock, pets, poultry) record services
334514	Pedometers manufacturing
813920	Peer review boards
332994	Pellet guns manufacturing
332992	Pellets, air rifle and pistol, manufacturing
316110	Pelts bleaching, currying, dyeing, scraping, and tanning
422590	Pelts, raw, wholesaling
339941	Pen refills and cartridges manufacturing
339942	Pencil leads manufacturing
339942	Pencil sharpeners manufacturing
339942	Pencils (except mechanical) manufacturing
422120	Pencils wholesaling
339941	Pencils, mechanical, manufacturing
325613	Penetrants manufacturing
325412	Penicillin preparations manufacturing
325411	Penicillin, uncompounded, manufacturing
922140	Penitentiaries
339941	Pens manufacturing
422120	Pens, writing, wholesaling
523920	Pension fund managing
524292	Pension fund, third party administrative services
525110	Pension funds
525110	Pension plans (e.g., employee benefit, retirement)
111219	Pepper (e.g., bell, chili, green, hot, red, sweet) farming
311942	Pepper (i.e., spice) manufacturing
711510	Performers (i.e., entertainers), independent
711510	Performing artists, independent
711310	Performing arts center operators
611610	Performing arts schools (except academic)
325199	Perfume materials (i.e., basic synthetic chemicals, such as terpineol) manufacturing
446120	Perfume stores
325620	Perfumes manufacturing
422210	Perfumes wholesaling
511120	Periodical publishers
511120	Periodical publishers and printing combined
422920	Periodicals wholesaling
621210	Periodontists' offices (e.g., centers, clinics)
334418	Peripheral controller boards manufacturing

421430 Peripheral equipment, computer, wholesaling

333314 Periscopes manufacturing

327992 Perlite aggregates manufacturing

212399 Perlite mining and/or beneficiating

327992 Perlite, expanded, manufacturing

325620 Permanent wave preparations manufacturing

325188 Peroxides, inorganic, manufacturing

325199 Peroxides, organic, manufacturing

513322 Personal communication services (PCS) (i.e., communication carriers)

334418 Personal computer modems manufacturing

334111 Personal computers manufacturing

522291 Personal credit institutions (i.e., unsecured cash loans)

525920 Personal estates (i.e., managing assets)

551112 Personal holding companies

525920 Personal investment trusts

523991 Personal investments trust administration

523920 Personal investments trusts, managing

316993 Personal leather goods (e.g., coin purses, eyeglass cases, key cases), small, manufacturing

339113 Personal safety devices, not specified elsewhere, manufacturing

422130 Personal sanitary paper products wholesaling

525920 Personal trusts

441221 Personal watercraft dealers

336999 Personal watercraft manufacturing

532292 Personal watercraft rental

561320 Personnel (e.g., industrial, office) suppliers

813920 Personnel management associations

541612 Personnel management consulting services

921190 Personnel offices, government

325320 Pest (e.g., ant, rat, roach, rodent) control poison manufacturing

561710 Pest control (except agricultural, forestry) services

115112 Pest control services, agricultural

115310 Pest control services, forestry

422690 Pesticides (except agricultural) wholesaling

325320 Pesticides manufacturing

422910 Pesticides, agricultural, wholesaling

812910 Pet boarding services

812220 Pet cemeteries

311119 Pet food (except cat, dog) manufacturing

422490 Pet food wholesaling

311111 Pet food, dog and cat, manufacturing

812910 Pet grooming services

541940 Pet hospitals

453910 Pet shops

812910 Pet sitting services

422990 Pet supplies (except pet food) wholesaling

453910 Pet supply stores

812910 Pet training services

324110 Petrochemicals made in petroleum refineries

422710 Petroleum and petroleum products bulk stations and terminals

422720 Petroleum and petroleum products wholesaling (except bulk stations, terminals)

422720 Petroleum brokers

324110 Petroleum coke made in petroleum refineries

541330 Petroleum engineering services

324199 Petroleum jelly made from refined petroleum

324110 Petroleum jelly made in petroleum refineries

324191 Petroleum lubricating oils made from refined petroleum

324110 Petroleum lubricating oils made in petroleum refineries

486110 Petroleum pipelines, crude

486910 Petroleum pipelines, refined

324110 Petroleum refineries

333298 Petroleum refining machinery manufacturing

332420 Petroleum storage tanks, heavy gauge metal, manufacturing

324199 Petroleum waxes made from refined petroleum

http://www.ntis.gov/naics

211111	Petroleum, crude, production (i.e., extraction)
422990	Pets wholesaling
325412	Pharmaceutical preparations (e.g., capsules, liniments, ointments, tablets) manufacturing
422210	Pharmaceuticals wholesaling
446110	Pharmacies
813920	Pharmacists' associations
112390	Pheasant production
325192	Phenol manufacturing
325211	Phenolic resins manufacturing
813211	Philanthropic trusts, awarding grants
334612	Phonograph records manufacturing
421990	Phonograph records wholesaling
421440	Phonographs, coin-operated, wholesaling
212392	Phosphate rock mining and/or beneficiating
325312	Phosphatic fertilizer materials manufacturing
325314	Phosphatic fertilizers made by mixing purchased materials
325312	Phosphoric acid manufacturing
325188	Phosphorus compounds, not specified elsewhere by process, manufacturing
323118	Photo albums and refills manufacturing
422120	Photo albums wholesaling
421410	Photo finishing equipment wholesaling
711510	Photo journalists, independent (freelance)
422120	Photocopy supplies wholesaling
333315	Photocopying machines manufacturing
561439	Photocopying services (except combined with printing services)
334413	Photoelectric cells, solid-state (e.g., electronic eye), manufacturing
323122	Photoengraving plate preparation services
812921	Photofinishing labs (except one-hour)
812922	Photofinishing labs, one-hour
812921	Photofinishing services (except one-hour)
812922	Photofinishing services, one-hour
335110	Photoflash and photoflood lamp bulbs and tubes manufacturing
541370	Photogrammetric mapping services
322299	Photograph folders, mats, and mounts manufacturing
541922	Photographers specializing in aerial photography
711510	Photographers, independent artistic
325992	Photographic chemicals manufacturing
333315	Photographic equipment (except lenses) manufacturing
421410	Photographic equipment and supplies wholesaling
532210	Photographic equipment rental
811211	Photographic equipment repair shops without retailing new photographic equipment
325992	Photographic film, cloth, paper, and plate, sensitized, manufacturing
333314	Photographic lenses manufacturing
812990	Photographic machine concession operators, coin-operated
443130	Photographic supply stores
326113	Photographic, micrographic, and X-ray plastics, sheet, and film (except sensitized), manufacturing
611610	Photography schools, art
541922	Photography services, commercial
541921	Photography services, portrait (e.g., still, video)
541922	Photography studios, commercial
541921	Photography studios, portrait
325992	Photosensitized paper manufacturing
334413	Photovoltaic devices, solid-state, manufacturing
325192	Phthalic anhydride manufacturing
541614	Physical distribution consulting services
621999	Physical fitness evaluation services (except by offices of health practitioners)
713940	Physical fitness facilities
334519	Physical properties testing and inspection equipment manufacturing

622310	Physical rehabilitation hospitals
541710	Physical science research and development laboratories or services
621340	Physical therapists' offices (e.g., centers, clinics)
621111	Physicians' (except mental health) offices (e.g., centers, clinics)
621112	Physicians', mental health, offices (e.g., centers, clinics)
541690	Physics consulting services
541710	Physics research and development laboratories or services
621340	Physiotherapists' offices (e.g., centers, clinics)
339112	Physiotherapy equipment (except electrotherapeutic) manufacturing
451140	Piano stores
336112	Pick-up trucks, light duty, assembling on chassis of own manufacture
311712	Picking crab meat
333516	Picklers and pickling machinery, metalworking, manufacturing
311421	Pickles manufacturing
311421	Pickling fruits and vegetables
332212	Picks (i.e., handtools) manufacturing
336214	Pickup canopies, caps, or covers manufacturing
713990	Picnic grounds
442299	Picture frame shops, custom
311822	Pie crust shells, uncooked, made from purchased flour
422310	Piece goods (except burlap, felt) wholesaling
422990	Piece goods, burlap and felt, wholesaling
713110	Piers, amusement
422420	Pies (e.g., fruit, meat, poultry), frozen, wholesaling
311812	Pies, fresh, made in commercial bakeries
311812	Pies, frozen, manufacturing
334419	Piezoelectric crystals manufacturing
334419	Piezoelectric devices manufacturing
112210	Pig farming
331111	Pig iron manufacturing
421510	Pig iron wholesaling

325132	Pigments (except animal black, bone black), organic, manufacturing
325131	Pigments (except bone black, carbon black, lamp black), inorganic, manufacturing
212393	Pigments, natural, mineral, mining and/or beneficiating
422950	Pigments, paint, wholesaling
313249	Pile fabrics made in warp knitting mills
313241	Pile fabrics made in weft knitting mills
333120	Pile-driving equipment manufacturing
321114	Pilings, round wood, cutting and treating
321114	Pilings, wood, treating
314129	Pillowcases, bed, made from purchased fabrics
314129	Pillows, bed, made from purchased materials
488490	Pilot car services (i.e., wide load warning services)
488330	Piloting services, water transportation
713120	Pinball arcades
713990	Pinball machine concession operators (i.e., supplying and servicing in others' facilities)
339999	Pinball machines, coin-operated, manufacturing
113210	Pine gum extracting
111339	Pineapple farming
325191	Pinene manufacturing
713990	Ping pong parlors
339993	Pins (except precious) manufacturing
339911	Pins and brooches, precious metal, manufacturing
712120	Pioneer villages
331210	Pipe (e.g., heavy riveted, lock joint, seamless, welded) made from purchased iron or steel
332996	Pipe and pipe fittings made from purchased metal pipe
331511	Pipe and pipe fittings, cast iron, manufacturing

http://www.ntis.gov/naics

333516	Pipe and tube rolling mill machinery, metalworking, manufacturing
332996	Pipe couplings made from purchased metal pipe
331511	Pipe couplings, cast iron, manufacturing
332996	Pipe fabricating (i.e., bending, cutting, threading) made from purchased metal pipe
326122	Pipe fittings, rigid plastics, manufacturing
332999	Pipe hangers and supports, metal, manufacturing
331316	Pipe made by extruding purchased aluminum
325520	Pipe sealing compounds manufacturing
422940	Pipe tobacco wholesaling
312229	Pipe tobacco, prepared, manufacturing
331316	Pipe, aluminum, made in integrated secondary smelting and extruding mills
327332	Pipe, concrete, manufacturing
332313	Pipe, fabricated metal plate, manufacturing
331111	Pipe, iron or steel, made in steel mills
421510	Pipe, metal, wholesaling
326122	Pipe, rigid plastics, manufacturing
332322	Pipe, sheet metal, manufacturing
234910	Pipeline (e.g., gas, oil, sewer, water) construction
541990	Pipeline inspection (i.e., visual) services
421830	Pipeline machinery and equipment wholesaling
488999	Pipeline terminal facilities, independently operated
486990	Pipeline transportation (except crude oil, natural gas, refined petroleum products)
486110	Pipeline transportation, crude oil
486910	Pipeline transportation, gasoline and other refined petroleum products
486210	Pipeline transportation, natural gas
339999	Pipes, smoker's, manufacturing
111335	Pistachio farming
332994	Pistols manufacturing

336311	Pistons and piston rings manufacturing
421830	Pistons, hydraulic and pneumatic, wholesaling
325192	Pitch made by distillation of coal tar
325191	Pitch, wood, manufacturing
325411	Pituitary gland derivatives, uncompounded, manufacturing
722211	Pizza delivery shops
311822	Pizza doughs made from purchased flour
722110	Pizza parlors, full service
722211	Pizza parlors, limited service
422490	Pizzas (except frozen) wholesaling
311991	Pizzas, fresh, manufacturing
311412	Pizzas, frozen, manufacturing
422420	Pizzas, frozen, wholesaling
722110	Pizzerias, full service
722211	Pizzerias, limited-service (e.g., take-out)
314129	Placemats, all materials, made from purchased materials
561310	Placement agencies or services, employment
813110	Places of worship
334417	Planar cable connectors manufacturing
333210	Planers woodworking-type, stationary, manufacturing
332212	Planes, handheld, nonpowered, manufacturing
712110	Planetariums
321912	Planing mills (except millwork)
321918	Planing mills, millwork
321912	Planing purchased lumber
525120	Plans, health and welfare related employee benefit
525110	Plans, pension
422990	Plant food wholesaling
325312	Plant foods, mixed, made in plants producing phosphatic fertilizer materials
561730	Plant maintenance services
111339	Plantain farming
115112	Planting crops
421820	Planting machinery and equipment, farm-type, wholesaling
333111	Planting machines, farm-type, manufacturing

621991	Plasmapheresis centers
325414	Plasmas manufacturing
422210	Plasmas, blood, wholesaling
327420	Plaster and plasterboard, gypsum, manufacturing
327420	Plaster of paris manufacturing
327420	Plaster of paris products (e.g., columns, statuary, urns) manufacturing
327420	Plaster, gypsum, manufacturing
235420	Plastering (i.e., ornamental, plain) construction contractors
325510	Plastic wood fillers manufacturing
325199	Plasticizers (i.e., basic synthetic chemicals) manufacturing
422610	Plasticizers wholesaling
337125	Plastics (including fiberglass) furniture (except upholstered), household-type, manufacturing
326220	Plastics and rubber belts and hoses (without fittings) manufacturing
325211	Plastics and synthetic resins regenerating, precipitating, and coagulating
422130	Plastics bags wholesaling
422610	Plastics basic shapes wholesaling
313320	Plastics coating of textiles and apparel
326113	Plastics film and unlaminated sheet (except packaging) manufacturing
422990	Plastics foam (except disposable) wholesaling
421840	Plastics foam packing and packaging materials wholesaling
422130	Plastics foam products, disposable (except packaging, packing), wholesaling
421830	Plastics industries machinery, equipment, and supplies wholesaling
337110	Plastics laminated over particleboard (e.g., fixture tops) manufacturing
422610	Plastics materials (e.g., film, rod, shape, sheet, tubing) wholesaling
315299	Plastics rainwear cut and sewn from purchased fabric (except apparel contractors)
315211	Plastics rainwear, men's and boys', cut and sewn apparel contractors
315212	Plastics rainwear, women's, girls', and infants', cut and sew apparel contractors
325991	Plastics resins compounding from recycled materials
422610	Plastics resins wholesaling
325991	Plastics resins, custom compounding of purchased
421930	Plastics scrap wholesaling
333220	Plastics working machinery manufacturing
421390	Plate glass wholesaling
332313	Plate work (e.g., bending, cutting, punching, shaping, welding), fabricated metal, manufacturing
331315	Plate, aluminum, made by continuous casting purchased aluminum
331315	Plate, aluminum, made by flat rolling purchased aluminum
331315	Plate, aluminum, made in integrated secondary smelting and continuous casting mills
331315	Plate, aluminum, made in integrated secondary smelting and flat rolling mills
331111	Plate, iron or steel, made in steel mills
332211	Plated metal cutlery manufacturing
421940	Plated metal cutlery or flatware wholesaling
332211	Plated metal flatware manufacturing
332999	Plated ware (e.g., ecclesiastical ware, hollowware, toilet ware) manufacturing
335932	Plates (i.e., outlet or switch covers), face, manufacturing
322299	Plates, molded pulp, manufacturing
326140	Plates, polystyrene foam, manufacturing
332813	Plating metals and metal products for the trade
332999	Platinum foil and leaf not made in rolling mills
212299	Platinum mining and/or beneficiating

331419	Platinum refining, primary
421910	Playground equipment and supplies wholesaling
711510	Playwrights, independent
336612	Pleasure boats manufacturing
421910	Pleasure boats wholesaling
332212	Pliers, handtools, manufacturing
327331	Plinth blocks, precast terrazzo, manufacturing
334119	Plotters, computer, manufacturing
115112	Plowing
333111	Plows, farm-type, manufacturing
332911	Plug valves, industrial-type, manufacturing
111339	Plum farming
421720	Plumber's brass goods wholesaling
332212	Plumber's handtools, nonpowered, manufacturing
332919	Plumbing and heating inline valves (e.g., check, cutoffs, stop) manufacturing
421720	Plumbing and heating valves wholesaling
235110	Plumbing construction contractors
532490	Plumbing equipment rental or leasing
421720	Plumbing equipment wholesaling
332913	Plumbing fittings and couplings (e.g., compression fittings, metal elbows, metal unions) manufacturing
332913	Plumbing fixture fittings and trim, all materials, manufacturing
326191	Plumbing fixtures (e.g., shower stalls, toilets, urinals), plastics or fiberglass, manufacturing
421720	Plumbing fixtures wholesaling
332998	Plumbing fixtures, metal, manufacturing
327111	Plumbing fixtures, vitreous china, manufacturing
421720	Plumbing supplies wholesaling
444190	Plumbing supply stores
421310	Plywood wholesaling
321211	Plywood, faced with nonwood materials, hardwood, manufacturing
321212	Plywood, faced with nonwood materials, softwood, manufacturing
321211	Plywood, hardwood, manufacturing
321212	Plywood, softwood, manufacturing
332912	Pneumatic aircraft subassemblies manufacturing
333995	Pneumatic cylinders, fluid power, manufacturing
326220	Pneumatic hose (without fittings), rubber or plastics, manufacturing
332912	Pneumatic hose fittings, fluid power, manufacturing
421830	Pneumatic pumps and parts wholesaling
333996	Pneumatic pumps, fluid power, manufacturing
333922	Pneumatic tube conveyors manufacturing
332912	Pneumatic valves, fluid power, manufacturing
339911	Pocketbooks, precious metal, manufacturing
339911	Pocketbooks, precious metal, men's, manufacturing
339911	Pocketbooks, precious metal, women's, manufacturing
621391	Podiatrists' offices (e.g., centers, clinics)
813410	Poetry clubs
711510	Poets, independent
334119	Point of sale terminals manufacturing
421420	Point of sale terminals wholesaling
334119	Pointing devices, computer peripheral equipment, manufacturing
421610	Pole line hardware wholesaling
327390	Poles, concrete, manufacturing
421510	Poles, metal, wholesaling
321114	Poles, round wood, cutting and treating
321113	Poles, wood, made from from log or bolts
321114	Poles, wood, treating
922120	Police departments (except American Indian or Alaska Native)
453998	Police supply stores
611519	Police training schools
921150	Police, American Indian or Alaska Native tribal

311212 Polished rice manufacturing

325612 Polishes (e.g., automobile, furniture, metal, shoe) manufacturing

422690 Polishes (e.g., automobile, furniture, metal, shoe, stove) wholesaling

333512 Polishing and buffing machines, metalworking, manufacturing

332813 Polishing metals and metal products for the trade

325612 Polishing preparations manufacturing

327910 Polishing wheels manufacturing

813940 Political action committees (PACs)

813940 Political campaign organizations

541820 Political consulting services

541910 Political opinion polling services

813940 Political organizations or clubs

115112 Pollinating

421830 Pollution control equipment (except air) wholesaling

421730 Pollution control equipment, air, wholesaling

924110 Pollution control program administration

541380 Pollution testing (except automotive emissions testing) services

325211 Polyamide resins manufacturing

325222 Polyester fibers and filaments manufacturing

325211 Polyester resins manufacturing

325211 Polyethylene resins manufacturing

325212 Polyethylene rubber manufacturing

325211 Polyethylene terephathalate (PET) resins manufacturing

334519 Polygraph machines manufacturing

561611 Polygraph services

325211 Polyisobutylene resins manufacturing

325212 Polyisobutylene rubber manufacturing

325222 Polyolefin fibers and filaments manufacturing

325211 Polypropylene resins manufacturing

326140 Polystyrene foam packaging manufacturing

325211 Polystyrene resins manufacturing

325212 Polysulfide rubber manufacturing

326150 Polyurethane foam products manufacturing

325211 Polyurethane resins manufacturing

325211 Polyvinyl alcohol resins manufacturing

325211 Polyvinyl resins manufacturing

315299 Ponchos and similar waterproof raincoats (except infants') cut and sewn from purchased fabric (except apparel contractors)

315291 Ponchos and similar waterproof raincoats, infants', cut and sewn from purchased fabric (except apparel contractors)

315211 Ponchos and similar waterproof raincoats, men's and boys', cut and sew apparel contractors

315212 Ponchos and similar waterproof raincoats, women's, girls', and infants', cut and sew apparel contractors

112920 Pony production

713990 Pool halls

713990 Pool parlors

713990 Pool rooms

312111 Pop, soda, manufacturing

311919 Popcorn (except candy covered), popped, manufacturing

311999 Popcorn (except popped) manufacturing

311340 Popcorn balls manufacturing

111150 Popcorn farming, field and seed production

422450 Popcorn wholesaling

311340 Popcorn, candy covered popped, manufacturing

327113 Porcelain parts, electrical and electronic device, molded, manufacturing

327112 Porcelain, chemical, manufacturing

337124 Porch swings, metal, manufacturing

311422 Pork and beans canning

311611 Pork carcasses, half carcasses, and primal and sub-primal cuts produced in slaughtering plants

311919 Pork rinds manufacturing

311612 Pork, primal and sub-primal cuts, made from purchased carcasses

926120 Port authorities and districts, nonoperating

488310	Port facility operation
332311	Portable buildings, prefabricated metal, manufacturing
321992	Portable buildings, prefabricated wood, manufacturing
332998	Portable chemical toilets, metal, manufacturing
334111	Portable computers manufacturing
335211	Portable cooking appliances (except convection, microwave ovens), household-type electric, manufacturing
335211	Portable electric space heaters manufacturing
335211	Portable hair dryers, electric, manufacturing
335211	Portable humidifiers and dehumidifiers manufacturing
334310	Portable stereo systems manufacturing
562991	Portable toilet pumping (i.e., cleaning) services
562991	Portable toilet renting and/or servicing
326191	Portable toilets, plastics, manufacturing
312120	Porter brewing
812990	Porter services
422810	Porter wholesaling
523920	Portfolio fund managing
541921	Portrait photography services
541921	Portrait photography studios
334510	Position emission tomography (PET) scanners manufacturing
336312	Positive crankcase ventilation (PCV) valves, engine, manufacturing
332212	Post hole diggers, nonpowered, manufacturing
333120	Post hole diggers, powered, manufacturing
512191	Post-production facilities, motion picture or video
512191	Post-synchronization sound dubbing
333313	Postage meters manufacturing
421420	Postage meters wholesaling
491110	Postal delivery services, local, operated by U.S. Postal Service
491110	Postal delivery services, local, operated on a contract basis
491110	Postal services operated by U.S. Postal Service
491110	Postal stations operated by U.S. Postal Service
491110	Postal stations operated on a contract basis
323121	Postpress services (e.g., beveling, bronzing, edging, foil stamping, gilding, tradebinding) on printed materials
327390	Posts, concrete, manufacturing
321114	Posts, round wood, cutting and treating
321114	Posts, wood, treating
311412	Pot pies, frozen, manufacturing
212391	Potash mining and/or beneficiating
325314	Potassic fertilizers made by mixing purchased materials
325181	Potassium carbonate manufacturing
212391	Potassium compounds prepared at beneficiating plants
212391	Potassium compounds, natural, mining and/or beneficiating
325181	Potassium hydroxide manufacturing
325188	Potassium inorganic compounds, not specified elsewhere by process, manufacturing
325199	Potassium organic compounds, not specified elsewhere by process, manufacturing
325188	Potassium salts manufacturing
422450	Potato chips and related snacks wholesaling
311919	Potato chips manufacturing
111211	Potato farming, field and seed potato production
311211	Potato flour manufacturing
311999	Potato mixes made from purchased dry ingredients
311423	Potato products (e.g., flakes, granules) dehydrating
311221	Potato starches manufacturing
311919	Potato sticks manufacturing
311991	Potatoes, peeled or cut, manufacturing
339999	Potpourri manufacturing
332214	Pots and pans, fabricated metal, manufacturing

http://www.ntis.gov/naics

327112 Pottery products (except plumbing fixtures and porcelain) manufacturing

325314 Potting soil manufacturing

311615 Poultry (e.g., canned, cooked, fresh, frozen) manufacturing

311615 Poultry (e.g., canned, cooked, fresh, frozen) processing

422440 Poultry and poultry products (except canned, packaged frozen) wholesaling

333111 Poultry brooders, feeders, and waterers manufacturing

311615 Poultry canning (except baby, pet food)

445210 Poultry dealers

311119 Poultry feeds, supplements, and concentrates manufacturing

112340 Poultry hatcheries

311615 Poultry slaughtering, dressing, and packing

422490 Poultry, canned, wholesaling

422440 Poultry, live and dressed, wholesaling

422420 Poultry, packaged frozen, wholesaling

332812 Powder coating metals and metal products for the trade

331314 Powder made from purchased aluminum

331423 Powder made from purchased copper

331221 Powder made from purchased iron or steel

333513 Powder metal forming presses manufacturing

332117 Powder metallurgy products manufactured on a job or order basis

314999 Powder puffs and mitts manufacturing

331111 Powder, iron or steel, made in steel mills

311999 Powdered drink mixes (except chocolate, coffee, tea, milk based) manufacturing

311514 Powdered milk manufacturing

325620 Powders (e.g., baby, body, face, talcum, toilet) manufacturing

311999 Powders, baking, manufacturing

333912 Power (i.e., pressure) washer units manufacturing

332410 Power boilers manufacturing

335313 Power circuit breakers manufacturing

335313 Power connectors manufacturing

335999 Power converter units (i.e., AC to DC), static, manufacturing

444210 Power equipment stores, outdoor

235950 Power generating equipment construction contractors

221119 Power generation, electric (except fossil fuel, hydroelectric, nonhazardous solid waste, nuclear)

221112 Power generation, fossil fuel (e.g., coal, gas, oil), electric

221111 Power generation, hydroelectric

562213 Power generation, nonhazardous solid waste combustor or incinerator electric

221113 Power generation, nuclear electric

221119 Power generation, solar electric

221119 Power generation, tidal electric

221119 Power generation, wind electric

421710 Power handtools (e.g., drills, sanders, saws) wholesaling

234920 Power line construction

541990 Power line inspection (i.e., visual) services

334515 Power measuring equipment, electrical, manufacturing

234930 Power plant (except hydroelectric) construction

234990 Power plant, hydroelectric, construction

336330 Power steering hose assemblies manufacturing

336330 Power steering pumps manufacturing

335999 Power supplies, regulated and unregulated, manufacturing

335313 Power switching equipment manufacturing

335311 Power transformers, electric, manufacturing

421610 Power transmission equipment, electrical, wholesaling

421840	Power transmission supplies (e.g., gears, pulleys, sprockets), mechanical, wholesaling
333319	Power washer cleaning equipment manufacturing
561790	Power washing building exteriors
336322	Power window and door lock systems, automotive, truck, and bus, manufacturing
333991	Power-driven handtools manufacturing
621399	Practical nurses' offices (e.g., centers, clinics), licensed
334612	Pre-recorded magnetic audio tapes and cassettes mass reproducing
327331	Precast concrete block and brick manufacturing
327332	Precast concrete pipe manufacturing
327390	Precast concrete products (except brick, block, pipe) manufacturing
421940	Precious metals wholesaling
212399	Precious stones mining and/or beneficiating
421940	Precious stones wholesaling
811219	Precision equipment calibration
332212	Precision tools, machinist's (except optical), manufacturing
332721	Precision turned products manufacturers (i.e., known as)
233220	Prefabricated apartment erection
233220	Prefabricated building (except house) erection, residential
444190	Prefabricated building dealers
233310	Prefabricated building erection, industrial
421390	Prefabricated buildings (except wood) wholesaling
332311	Prefabricated buildings, metal, manufacturing
421310	Prefabricated buildings, wood, wholesaling
321992	Prefabricated homes (except mobile homes), wood, manufacturing
332311	Prefabricated homes, metal, manufacturing
233210	Prefabricated house erection
321992	Prefabricated wood buildings manufacturing
621410	Pregnancy counseling centers
325413	Pregnancy test kits manufacturing
334611	Prepackaged software, mass reproducing
311822	Prepared flour mixes made from purchased flour
311211	Prepared flour mixes made in flour mills
422490	Prepared foods (except frozen) wholesaling
422420	Prepared foods, frozen (except dairy products), wholesaling
422430	Prepared foods, frozen dairy, wholesaling
311991	Prepared meals, perishable, packaged for individual resale
311941	Prepared sauces (except gravy, tomato based) manufacturing
323122	Prepress printing services (e.g., color separation, imagesetting, photocomposition, typesetting)
421990	Prerecorded audio and video tapes and discs wholesaling
512220	Prerecorded audio tapes and compact discs integrated manufacture, release, and distribution
454110	Prerecorded tape, compact disc, and record mail-order houses
624410	Preschool centers
422210	Prescription drugs wholesaling
311421	Preserves (e.g., imitation) canning
321114	Preserving purchased wood and wood products
313311	Preshrinking broadwoven fabrics
313312	Preshrinking textile products and fabrics (except broadwoven)
332111	Press forgings made from purchased iron or steel, unfinished
332112	Press forgings made from purchased nonferrous metals, unfinished
422130	Pressed and molded pulp goods (e.g., egg cartons, shipping supplies) wholesaling
321999	Pressed logs of sawdust and other wood particles, nonpetroleum binder, manufacturing

333513	Presses (e.g., bending, punching, shearing, stamping), metal forming, manufacturing
333294	Presses (i.e., food manufacturing-type) manufacturing
333210	Presses for making composite woods (e.g., hardboard, medium density fiberboard (MDF), particleboard, plywood) manufacturing
333293	Presses, printing (except textile), manufacturing
332911	Pressure control valves (except fluid power), industrial-type, manufacturing
332912	Pressure control valves, fluid power, manufacturing
332214	Pressure cookers, household-type, manufacturing
334513	Pressure instruments, industrial process-type, manufacturing
322222	Pressure sensitive paper and tape (except medical) made from purchased materials
321113	Pressure treated lumber made from logs or bolts and treated
321114	Pressure treated lumber made from purchased lumber
334512	Pressurestats manufacturing
327331	Prestressed concrete blocks or bricks manufacturing
327332	Prestressed concrete pipes manufacturing
327390	Prestressed concrete products (except blocks, bricks, pipes) manufacturing
722213	Pretzel shops, on premise baking and carryout service
422490	Pretzels (except frozen) wholesaling
311919	Pretzels (except soft) manufacturing
422420	Pretzels, frozen, wholesaling
311812	Pretzels, soft, manufacturing
335129	Prewired poles, brackets, and accessories for electric lighting, manufacturing
331312	Primary aluminum production and manufacturing aluminum alloys
331312	Primary aluminum production and manufacturing aluminum shapes (e.g., bar, ingot, rod, sheet)
335912	Primary batteries manufacturing
331312	Primary refining of aluminum
331411	Primary refining of copper
331419	Primary refining of nonferrous metals (except aluminum, copper)
611110	Primary schools
331312	Primary smelting of aluminum
331411	Primary smelting of copper
331419	Primary smelting of nonferrous metals (except aluminum, copper)
335312	Prime mover generator sets (except turbine generator sets) manufacturing
332993	Primers (i.e., more than 30 mm., more than 1.18 inch), ammunition, manufacturing
334418	Printed circuit assemblies manufacturing
334418	Printed circuit boards loading
421690	Printed circuit boards wholesaling
334412	Printed circuit boards, bare, manufacturing
334419	Printed circuit laminates manufacturing
334119	Printers, computer, manufacturing
421430	Printers, computer, wholesaling
323117	Printing books without publishing
313311	Printing broadwoven fabrics grey goods
313312	Printing fabric grey goods (except broadwoven)
325910	Printing inks manufacturing
421840	Printing inks wholesaling
333292	Printing machinery for textiles manufacturing
323116	Printing manifold business forms
422120	Printing paper (except bulk) wholesaling
422110	Printing paper, bulk, wholesaling
333293	Printing plate engraving machinery manufacturing
323122	Printing plate preparation services
333293	Printing plates, blank (except photosensative), manufacturing

http://www.ntis.gov/naics

323121	Printing postpress services (e.g., beveling, bronzing, edging, foil stamping) to printed products (e.g., books, cards, paper)
323122	Printing prepress services (e.g., color separation, imagesetting, photocomposition, typesetting)
333293	Printing presses (except textile) manufacturing
313312	Printing textile products (except apparel)
421830	Printing trade machinery, equipment, and supplies wholesaling
323115	Printing, digital (e.g., billboards, other large format graphical materials)
323115	Printing, digital (e.g., graphics, high resolution)
323119	Printing, engraving, on paper products
323112	Printing, flexographic (except books, grey goods, manifold business forms)
323111	Printing, gravure (except books, grey goods, manifold business forms)
323119	Printing, letterpress (except books, grey goods, manifold business forms)
323110	Printing, lithographic (except books, grey goods, manifold business forms, quick printing)
323110	Printing, photo-offset (except books, grey goods, manifold business forms, printing books)
323114	Printing, quick
323113	Printing, screen (except books, manifold business forms, printing grey goods)
233310	Printing/publishing plant construction
333314	Prisms, optical, manufacturing
233320	Prison construction
922140	Prisons
522190	Private banks (i.e., unincorporated)
334210	Private branch exchange (PBX) equipment manufacturing

561611	Private detective services
525920	Private estates (i.e., administering on behalf of beneficiaries)
814110	Private households with employees
561611	Private investigation services (except credit)
561431	Private mail centers
561431	Private mailbox rental centers
493190	Private warehousing and storage (except farm products, general merchandise, refrigerated)
493130	Private warehousing and storage, farm products (except refrigerated)
493110	Private warehousing and storage, general merchandise
493120	Private warehousing and storage, refrigerated
922150	Probation offices
334513	Process control instruments, industrial, manufacturing
541199	Process serving services
314999	Processing of textile mill waste and recovering fibers
422910	Produce containers wholesaling
445230	Produce markets
445230	Produce stands, permanent
454390	Produce stands, temporary
422480	Produce, fresh, wholesaling
813910	Producers' associations
711510	Producers, independent
561910	Product sterilization and packaging services
541380	Product testing laboratories or services
524128	Product warranty insurance carriers, direct
541614	Production planning and control consulting services
541614	Productivity improvement consulting services
813920	Professional associations
711219	Professional athletes, independent (i.e., participating in sports events)
323121	Professional book binding without printing
511130	Professional book publishers
511130	Professional book publishers and printing combined

http://www.ntis.gov/naics

511130 Professional book publishing (i.e., establishments known as publishers)

611430 Professional development training

561330 Professional employer organizations (PEO)

421490 Professional equipment and supplies (except dental, medical, ophthalmic) wholesaling

611691 Professional examination review instructions

421490 Professional instruments wholesaling

511120 Professional magazine and periodical publishers

511120 Professional magazine and periodical publishers and printing combined

813920 Professional membership associations

611310 Professional schools (e.g., business administration, dental, law, medical)

711211 Professional sports clubs

813920 Professional standards review boards

326130 Profile shapes (e.g., plate, rod, sheet), laminated plastics, manufacturing

326121 Profile shapes (e.g., rod, tube), nonrigid plastics, manufacturing

525990 Profit-sharing funds

512110 Program producing, television

541511 Programming services, custom computer

333315 Projection equipment (e.g., motion picture, slide), photographic, manufacturing

421410 Projection equipment (e.g., motion picture, slide), photographic, wholesaling

333315 Projection screens (i.e., motion picture, overhead, slide) manufacturing

334310 Projection television manufacturing

332995 Projectors (e.g., antisub, depth charge release, grenade, livens, rocket), ordnance, manufacturing

711310 Promoters of agricultural fairs with facilities

711320 Promoters of agricultural fairs without facilities

711310 Promoters of arts events with facilities

711320 Promoters of arts events without facilities

561920 Promoters of conventions with or without facilities

711310 Promoters of festivals with facilities

711320 Promoters of festivals without facilities

711310 Promoters of live performing arts productions (e.g., concerts) with facilities

711320 Promoters of live performing arts productions (e.g., concerts) without facilities

711310 Promoters of sports events with facilities

711320 Promoters of sports events without facilities

561920 Promoters of trade fairs or shows with or without facilities

561410 Proofreading services

422710 Propane bulk stations and terminals

324110 Propane gases made in petroleum refineries

332999 Propellers, ship and boat, made from purchased metal

524126 Property and casualty insurance carriers, direct

524130 Property and casualty reinsurance carriers

531312 Property managers' offices, nonresidential real estate

531311 Property managers' offices, residential real estate

813990 Property owners' associations

326299 Prophylactics manufacturing

112910 Propolis production, bees

336415 Propulsion units and parts, guided missile and space vehicle, manufacturing

324110 Propylene (i.e., propene) made in petroleum refineries

325110 Propylene made from refined petroleum or liquid hydrocarbons

325211	Propylene resins manufacturing
339113	Prosthetic appliances and supplies manufacturing
421450	Prosthetic appliances and supplies wholesaling
446199	Prosthetic stores
316211	Protective footwear, plastics or plastics-soled fabric upper, manufacturing
316211	Protective footwear, rubber or rubber-soled fabric upper, manufacturing
561612	Protective guard services
334516	Protein analyzers, laboratory-type, manufacturing
325222	Protein fibers and filaments manufacturing
325211	Protein plastics manufacturing
334511	Proximity warning (i.e., collision avoidance) equipment manufacturing
111339	Prune farming
115112	Pruning of orchard trees and vines
561730	Pruning services, ornamental tree and shrub
332212	Pry (i.e., crow) bars manufacturing
621420	Psychiatric centers and clinics (except hospitals), outpatient
623220	Psychiatric convalescent homes or hospitals
622210	Psychiatric hospitals (except convalescent)
621112	Psychiatrists' offices (e.g., centers, clinics)
812990	Psychic services
621112	Psychoanalysts' (MDs or DOs) offices (e.g., centers, clinics)
621330	Psychoanalysts' (except MDs or DOs) offices (e.g., centers, clinics)
813920	Psychologists' associations
621330	Psychologists' offices (e.g., centers, clinics), clinical
541720	Psychology research and development services
621112	Psychotherapists' (MDs or DOs) offices (e.g., centers, clinics)
621330	Psychotherapists' (except MDs or DOs) offices (e.g., centers, clinics)
541211	Public accountants' (CPAs) offices, certified
541219	Public accountants' (except CPAs) offices
811213	Public address system repair and maintenance services
334310	Public address systems and equipment manufacturing
421690	Public address systems and equipment wholesaling
421210	Public building furniture wholesaling
922130	Public defenders' offices
711410	Public figures' agents or managers
923120	Public health program administration, nonoperating
541910	Public opinion polling services
541910	Public opinion research services
922130	Public prosecutors' offices
541820	Public relations agencies
541820	Public relations services
813319	Public safety advocacy organizations
922190	Public safety bureaus and statistics centers, government
813410	Public speaking improvement clubs
611699	Public speaking training
561492	Public stenography services
926130	Public utility (except transportation) commissions, nonoperating
813910	Public utility associations
551112	Public utility holding companies
233320	Public warehouse construction
493190	Public warehousing and storage (except farm products, general merchandise, refrigerated, self storage)
493110	Public warehousing and storage (except self storage), general merchandise
493130	Public warehousing and storage, farm products (except refrigerated)
493120	Public warehousing and storage, refrigerated
51	Publishers (see specific type)
51	Publishers and printing combined (see specific type of publisher)
51	Publishers or publishing (see specific type)
541840	Publishers' advertising representatives (i.e., independent of media owners)

511130 Publishers, book
511130 Publishers, book, combined with printing
511140 Publishers, database
511140 Publishers, directory
511191 Publishers, greeting card
511191 Publishers, greeting card, combined with printing
511120 Publishers, magazine
511120 Publishers, magazine, combined with printing
511199 Publishers, map
512230 Publishers, music
511110 Publishers, newspaper
511110 Publishers, newspaper, combined with printing
511210 Publishers, packaged computer software
511120 Publishers, periodical
511120 Publishers, periodical, combined with printing
511199 Publishers, racing form
311520 Pudding pops, frozen, manufacturing
311999 Puddings, dessert, manufacturing
333923 Pulleys (except power transmission), metal, manufacturing
333613 Pulleys, power transmission, manufacturing
322122 Pulp and newsprint combined manufacturing
322121 Pulp and paper (except groundwood, newsprint) combined manufacturing
322130 Pulp and paperboard combined manufacturing
333291 Pulp making machinery manufacturing
322110 Pulp manufacturing (i.e., chemical, mechanical, or semichemical processes) without making paper
322110 Pulp manufacturing (made from bagasse, linters, rags, straw, wastepaper, or wood) without making paper
322122 Pulp mills and groundwood paper, uncoated and untreated, manufacturing

322110 Pulp mills not making paper or paperboard
322130 Pulp mills producing paperboard
322299 Pulp products, molded, manufacturing
113310 Pulpwood logging camps
421990 Pulpwood wholesaling
327992 Pumice (except abrasives) processing beyond beneficiation
327910 Pumice and pumicite abrasives manufacturing
562991 Pumping (i.e., cleaning) cesspools and septic tanks
562991 Pumping (i.e., cleaning) portable toilets
111219 Pumpkin farming, field and seed production
336312 Pumps (e.g., fuel, oil, water), mechanical, automotive and truck gasoline engine (except power steering), manufacturing
333911 Pumps (except fluid power), general purpose, manufacturing
421830 Pumps and pumping equipment, industrial-type, wholesaling
333996 Pumps, fluid power, manufacturing
333911 Pumps, industrial and commercial-type, general purpose, manufacturing
333913 Pumps, measuring and dispensing (e.g., gasoline), manufacturing
333911 Pumps, oil field or well, manufacturing
333911 Pumps, sump or water, residential-type, manufacturing
332212 Punches (except paper), nonpowered handtool, manufacturing
333513 Punching machines, metalworking, manufacturing
711110 Puppet theaters
339999 Puppets manufacturing
522298 Purchasing of accounts receivable
316993 Purses (except precious metal), men's, manufacturing
316992 Purses (except precious metal), women's, manufacturing
339911 Purses, precious metal or clad with precious metal, manufacturing

332212	Putty knives manufacturing
212393	Pyrite mining and/or beneficiating
325191	Pyroligneous acids manufacturing
327112	Pyrometer tubes manufacturing
327112	Pyrometric cones, earthenware, manufacturing
212399	Pyrophyllite mining and/or beneficiating
327992	Pyrophyllite processing beyond beneficiation
325998	Pyrotechnics (e.g., flares, flashlight bombs, signals) manufacturing
112390	Quail production
333131	Quarrying machinery and equipment manufacturing
421810	Quarrying machinery and equipment wholesaling
334419	Quartz crystals, electronic application, manufacturing
323114	Quick printing
327410	Quicklime (i.e., calcium oxide) manufacturing
314999	Quilting of textiles
314129	Quilts made from purchased materials
523999	Quotation services, stock
525930	REITs (real estate investment trusts)
525990	REMICs (real estate mortgage investment conduits)
522294	REMICs (real estate mortgage investment conduits) issuing, private
621399	RNs' (registered nurses) offices (e.g., centers, clinics)
721211	RV (recreational vehicle) parks
532120	RV (recreational vehicle) rental or leasing
441210	RV dealers
311119	Rabbit food manufacturing
112930	Rabbit production
711219	Race car drivers
711219	Race car owners (i.e., racing cars)
336999	Race cars manufacturing
711219	Race dog owners (i.e., racing dogs)
711219	Racehorse owners (i.e., racing horses)
711219	Racehorse training
511199	Racetrack program publishers
511199	Racetrack program publishers and printing combined
323112	Racetrack programs flexographic printing without publishing
323111	Racetrack programs gravure printing without publishing
323110	Racetrack programs lithographic (offset) printing without publishing
323119	Racetrack programs printing (except flexographic, gravure, lithographic, screen) without publishing
323113	Racetrack programs screen printing without publishing
711212	Racetracks (e.g., automobile, dog, horse)
332212	Ratchets, nonpowered, manufacturing
511199	Racing form publishers
511199	Racing form publishers and printing combined
323112	Racing forms flexographic printing without publishing
323111	Racing forms gravure printing without publishing
323110	Racing forms lithographic (offset) printing without publishing
323119	Racing forms printing (except flexographic, gravure, lithographic, screen) without publishing
323113	Racing forms screen printing without publishing
711219	Racing stables, horse
711219	Racing teams (e.g., automobile, motorcycle, snowmobile)
334417	Rack and panel connectors manufacturing
336330	Rack and pinion steering assemblies manufacturing
336399	Racks (e.g., bicycle, luggage, ski, tire), automotive, truck, and bus, manufacturing
332618	Racks, household-type, made from purchased wire
713940	Racquetball club facilities
334511	Radar detectors manufacturing
421690	Radar equipment wholesaling
334511	Radar systems and equipment manufacturing
334519	Radiation detection and monitoring instruments manufacturing

339113	Radiation shielding aprons, gloves, and sheeting manufacturing
541380	Radiation testing laboratories or services
325998	Radiator additive preparations manufacturing
811118	Radiator repair shops, automotive
333414	Radiators (except motor vehicle, portable electric) manufacturing
336399	Radiators and cores, manufacturing
335211	Radiators, portable electric, manufacturing
541840	Radio advertising representatives (i.e., independent of media owners)
443112	Radio and television stores
488330	Radio beacon (i.e., ship navigation) services
513111	Radio broadcasting networks
513112	Radio broadcasting stations (e.g., AM, FM, shortwave)
513111	Radio broadcasting syndicates
711510	Radio commentators, independent
541690	Radio consulting services
511120	Radio guide publishers
511120	Radio guide publishers and printing combined
323112	Radio guides flexographic printing without publishing
323111	Radio guides gravure printing without publishing
323110	Radio guides lithographic (offset) printing without publishing
323119	Radio guides printing (except flexographic, gravure, lithographic, screen) without publishing
323113	Radio guides screen printing without publishing
334551	Radio headphones manufacturing
513321	Radio paging services communication carriers
512290	Radio program tape production (except independent producers)
334310	Radio receiving sets manufacturing
811211	Radio repair and maintenance services without retailing new radios
511120	Radio schedule publishers
513112	Radio stations (e.g., AM, FM, shortwave)

334220	Radio transmitting antennas and ground equipment manufacturing
325188	Radioactive elements manufacturing
541360	Radioactive geophysical surveying services
325412	Radioactive in-vivo diagnostic substances manufacturing
325188	Radioactive isotopes manufacturing
562112	Radioactive waste collecting and/or local hauling
562211	Radioactive waste collecting and/or local hauling in combination with disposal and/or treatment facilities
562211	Radioactive waste disposal facilities
484230	Radioactive waste hauling, long-distance
562211	Radioactive waste treatment facilities
541380	Radiographic testing laboratories or services
541380	Radiographing welded joints on pipes and fittings
541380	Radiography inspection services
621512	Radiological laboratories, medical
421690	Radios (except household-type) wholesaling
421620	Radios, household-type, wholesaling
111219	Radish farming, field and seed production
212291	Radium ores mining and/or beneficiating
235990	Radon remediation construction contractors
541380	Radon testing laboratories or services
326299	Rafts, rubber inflatable, manufacturing
421930	Rags wholesaling
336510	Rail laying and tamping equipment manufacturing
332323	Railings, metal, manufacturing
926120	Railroad and warehouse commissions, nonoperating
532411	Railroad car rental and leasing
336510	Railroad cars and car equipment manufacturing
421860	Railroad cars wholesaling
421860	Railroad equipment and supplies wholesaling

336510	Railroad locomotives and parts (except diesel engines) manufacturing
336510	Railroad rolling stock manufacturing
336360	Railroad seating manufacturing
334290	Railroad signaling equipment manufacturing
488210	Railroad switching services
488210	Railroad terminals, independent operation
561599	Railroad ticket offices
321114	Railroad ties (i.e., bridge, cross, switch) treating
487110	Railroad, scenic and sightseeing, operation
482111	Railroads, line-haul
482112	Railroads, short-line or beltline
421510	Rails and accessories, metal, wholesaling
331319	Rails made by rolling or drawing purchased aluminum
331319	Rails, aluminum, made in integrated secondary smelting and drawing plants
331319	Rails, aluminum, made in integrated secondary smelting and rolling mills
234990	Railway roadbed construction
485112	Railway systems (except mixed mode), commuter
315211	Raincoats water resistant, men's and boys', cut and sew apparel contractors
313320	Raincoats waterproofing (i.e., oiling)
315291	Raincoats, water resistant, infants', cut and sewn from purchased fabric (except apparel contractors)
315228	Raincoats, water resistant, nontailored, men's and boys', cut and sewn from purchased fabric (except apparel contractors)
315239	Raincoats, water resistant, nontailored, women's, misses', and girls', cut and sewn from purchased fabric (except apparel contractors)
315222	Raincoats, water resistant, tailored, men's and boys', cut and sewn from purchased fabric (except apparel contractors)
315234	Raincoats, water resistant, tailored, women's, misses', and girls', cut and sewn from purchased fabric (except apparel contractors)
315212	Raincoats, water resistant, women's, girls', and infants', cut and sew apparel contractors
315291	Raincoats, water-repellent, infants', cut and sewn from purchased fabric (except apparel contractors)
315211	Raincoats, water-repellent, men's and boys', cut and sew apparel contractors
315228	Raincoats, water-repellent, nontailored, men's and boys', cut and sewn from purchased fabric (except apparel contractors)
315239	Raincoats, water-repellent, nontailored, women's, misses', and girls', cut and sewn from purchased fabric (except apparel contractors)
315222	Raincoats, water-repellent, tailored, men's and boys', cut and sewn from purchased fabric (except apparel contractors)
315234	Raincoats, water-repellent, tailored, women's, misses', and girls', cut and sewn from purchased fabric (except apparel contractors)
315212	Raincoats, water-repellent, women's, girls', and infants', cut and sew apparel contractors
315299	Raincoats, waterproof (except infants'), cut and sewn from purchased fabric (except apparel contractors)
315299	Raincoats, waterproof, infants', cut and sewn from purchased fabric (except apparel contractors)
315211	Raincoats, waterproof, men's and boys', cut and sew apparel contractors
315212	Raincoats, waterproof, women's, girls', and infants', cut and sew apparel contractors

111332	Raisin farming
112990	Raising swans, peacocks, flamingos, or other adornment birds
311423	Raisins made in dehydration plants
332212	Rakes, nonpowered handtool, manufacturing
333315	Range finders, photographic, manufacturing
335211	Range hoods, household-type, manufacturing
333319	Ranges, commercial-type, manufacturing
335221	Ranges, household-type cooking, manufacturing
624190	Rape crisis centers
311225	Rapeseed (i.e., canola) oil made from purchased oils
311223	Rapeseed (i.e., canola) oil made in crushing mills
111120	Rapeseed farming, field and seed production
336510	Rapid transit cars and equipment manufacturing
325188	Rare earth compounds, not specified elsewhere by process, manufacturing
212299	Rare earth metal ores mining and/or beneficiating
453310	Rare manuscript stores
111334	Raspberry farming
332212	Rasps, handheld, manufacturing
112390	Ratite production
337125	Rattan furniture, household-type, manufacturing
311313	Raw beet sugar manufacturing
422590	Raw farm products (e.g., field beans, grains) wholesaling
316110	Rawhide manufacturing
325221	Rayon fibers and filaments manufacturing
332211	Razor blades manufacturing
422210	Razor blades wholesaling
332211	Razors (except electric) manufacturing
422210	Razors (except electric) wholesaling
335211	Razors, electric, manufacturing
421620	Razors, electric, wholesaling
324191	Re-refining used petroleum lubricating oils
332410	Reactors, nuclear, manufacturing
336211	Ready-mix concrete trucks assembling on purchased chassis
327320	Ready-mixed concrete manufacturing and distributing
531190	Real estate (except building) rental or leasing
531210	Real estate agencies
531210	Real estate agents' offices
531320	Real estate appraisers' offices
813910	Real estate boards
531210	Real estate brokerages
531210	Real estate brokers' offices
531390	Real estate consultants' (except agents, appraisers) offices
531390	Real estate escrow agencies
531390	Real estate escrow agents' offices
531390	Real estate fiduciaries' offices
525930	Real estate investment trusts (REITs)
541110	Real estate law offices
525990	Real estate mortgage investment conduits (REMICs)
522294	Real estate mortgage investment conduits (REMICs) issuing, private
531312	Real estate property managers' offices, commercial
531311	Real estate property managers' offices, residential
531130	Real estate rental or leasing of miniwarehouses and self-storage units
531120	Real estate rental or leasing of nonresidential building (except miniwarehouse)
531110	Real estate rental or leasing of residential building
611519	Real estate schools
524127	Real estate title insurance carriers, direct
561492	Real-time (i.e., simultaneous) closed captioning of live television performances, meetings, conferences, and so forth
336312	Rebuilding automotive and truck gasoline engines

326212	Rebuilding tires		621340	Recreational (e.g., art, dance, music) therapists' offices (e.g., centers, clinics)
422120	Receipt books wholesaling			
334220	Receiver-transmitter units (i.e., transceivers) manufacturing		721214	Recreational camps with accommodation facilities (except campgrounds)
335931	Receptacles (i.e., outlets), electrical, manufacturing			
421610	Receptacles, electrical, wholesaling		713990	Recreational camps without accommodations
335911	Rechargeable nickel cadmium (NICAD) batteries manufacturing		713990	Recreational day camps (except instructional)
314999	Reclaimed wool processing		421910	Recreational equipment and supplies (except vehicles) wholesaling
326299	Reclaiming rubber from waste or scrap			
332995	Recoilless rifles manufacturing		532292	Recreational goods rental
421840	Reconditioned barrels and drums wholesaling		924120	Recreational programs administration, government
811310	Reconditioning shipping barrels and drums		713940	Recreational sports club facilities
321219	Reconstituted wood sheets and boards manufacturing		713990	Recreational sports clubs (i.e., sports teams) not operating sports facilities
312229	Reconstituting tobacco			
512210	Record production (except independent record producers) without duplication or distribution		713990	Recreational sports teams and leagues
			441210	Recreational vehicle (RV) dealers
512220	Record releasing, promoting, and distributing combined with mass duplication		532120	Recreational vehicle (RV) rental or leasing
			721211	Recreational vehicle parks
451220	Record stores, new		441210	Recreational vehicle parts and accessories stores
453310	Record stores, used			
421620	Recorders (e.g., tape, video), household-type, wholesaling		421110	Recreational vehicles wholesaling
			335999	Rectifiers (except electronic component type, semiconductor) manufacturing
334513	Recorders, industrial process control-type, manufacturing			
334515	Recorders, oscillographic, manufacturing		334419	Rectifiers, electronic component-type (except semiconductor), manufacturing
512290	Recording books on tape or disc (except publishers)		421690	Rectifiers, electronic, wholesaling
512290	Recording seminars and conferences, audio		334413	Rectifiers, semiconductor, manufacturing
512240	Recording studios, sound, operating on a contract or fee basis		562111	Recyclable material collection services
711510	Recording technicians, independent		562111	Recyclable material hauling, local
541611	Records management consulting services		484230	Recyclable material hauling, long-distance
314999	Recovered fibers processing		421930	Recyclable materials (e.g., glass, metal, paper) wholesaling
331492	Recovering and refining of nonferrous metals (except aluminum, copper) from scrap		325612	Recycling drycleaning fluids
			811212	Recycling inkjet cartridges
331492	Recovering silver from used photographic film or X-ray plates		325998	Recycling services for degreasing solvents (e.g., engine, machinery) manufacturing

325199 Red oil (i.e., oleic acid) manufacturing

925120 Redevelopment land agencies, government

333612 Reducers, speed, manufacturing

337125 Reed furniture (except upholstered), household-type, manufacturing

339920 Reels, fishing, manufacturing

332999 Reels, metal, manufacturing

321999 Reels, wood, manufacturing

561310 Referral agencies or services, employment

624190 Referral services for personal and social problems

486910 Refined petroleum products pipeline transportation

324110 Refineries, petroleum

324110 Refinery gases made in petroleum refineries

421830 Refinery machinery and equipment wholesaling

331312 Refining aluminum, primary

331314 Refining aluminum, secondary

331411 Refining copper, primary

331423 Refining copper, secondary

331419 Refining nonferrous metals and alloys (except aluminum, copper), primary

331492 Refining nonferrous metals and alloys (except aluminum, copper), secondary

115310 Reforestation

325991 Reformulating plastics resins from recycled plastics products

421840 Refractories (e.g., block, brick, mortar, tile) wholesaling

327124 Refractories (e.g., block, brick, mortar, tile), clay, manufacturing

327125 Refractories (e.g., block, brick, mortar, tile), nonclay, manufacturing

212325 Refractory minerals mining and/or beneficiating

722330 Refreshment stands, mobile

311822 Refrigerated doughs made from purchased flour

484220 Refrigerated products trucking, local

484230 Refrigerated products trucking, long-distance

493120 Refrigerated warehousing

333415 Refrigeration compressors manufacturing

334512 Refrigeration controls, residential and commercial-type, manufacturing

421740 Refrigeration equipment and supplies, commercial-type, wholesaling

811310 Refrigeration equipment repair and maintenance services, industrial and commercial-type

333415 Refrigeration equipment, industrial and commercial-type, manufacturing

333415 Refrigeration units, truck-type, manufacturing

335222 Refrigerator/freezer combinations, household-type, manufacturing

421740 Refrigerators (e.g., reach-in, walk-in), commercial-type, wholesaling

421620 Refrigerators, household-type, wholesaling

624230 Refugee settlement services

562212 Refuse collecting and operating solid waste landfills

562111 Refuse collection services

562213 Refuse disposal combustors or incinerators

562212 Refuse disposal landfills

562111 Refuse hauling, local

484230 Refuse hauling, long-distance

925120 Regional planning and development program administration

621399 Registered nurses' (RNs) offices (e.g., centers, clinics)

332323 Registers, metal air, manufacturing

561310 Registries, employment

335311 Regulating transformers, power system-type, manufacturing

926140 Regulation and inspection of agricultural products

336322 Regulators, motor vehicle voltage for internal combustion engines manufacturing

421610 Regulators, voltage (except motor vehicle), wholesaling

624190 Rehabilitation agencies for offenders

622310	Rehabilitation hospitals (except alcoholism, drug addiction)
622210	Rehabilitation hospitals, alcoholism and drug addiction
332618	Reinforcing mesh, concrete, made from purchased wire
524130	Reinsurance carriers
421610	Relays wholesaling
335314	Relays, electrical and electronic, manufacturing
624230	Relief services, disaster
624230	Relief services, emergency
323121	Religious book binding without printing
511130	Religious book publishers
511130	Religious book publishers and printing combined
451211	Religious book stores
453998	Religious goods (except books) stores
813110	Religious organizations
421490	Religious supplies wholesaling
311421	Relishes canning
562910	Remediation and clean up of contaminated buildings, mine sites, soil, or ground water
562910	Remediation services, environmental
422310	Remnants, piece goods, wholesaling
334290	Remote control units (e.g., garage door, television) manufacturing
541360	Remote sensing geophysical surveying services
621492	Renal dialysis centers and clinics
311613	Rendering fats
311613	Rendering plants
422990	Rennets wholesaling
532310	Rent-all centers
******	Rental—see type of article or property being rented
531210	Renting real estate for others (i.e. agents, brokers)
541611	Reorganizational consulting services
522294	Repackaging loans for sale to others (i.e., private conduits)
******	Repair—see type of article being repaired
323121	Repairing books
334210	Repeater and transceiver equipment, carrier line, manufacturing
711110	Repertory companies, theatrical
711510	Reporters, independent (freelance)
561491	Repossession services
512199	Reproduction of motion picture films for theatrical distribution
561439	Reprographic services
712130	Reptile exhibits, live
321912	Resawing purchased lumber
621910	Rescue services, medical
513340	Resellers, satellite telecommunication
513330	Resellers, telecommunication (except satellite)
561599	Reservation (e.g., airline, car rental, hotel, restaurant) services
522320	Reserve and liquidity services (except central bank)
234990	Reservoir construction
561720	Residential cleaning services
721310	Residential clubs
623220	Residential group homes for the emotionally disturbed
531110	Residential hotel rental or leasing
531311	Residential real estate property managers' offices
531190	Residential trailer parks
326192	Resilient floor coverings (e.g., sheet, tile) manufacturing
325211	Resins, plastics (except custom compounding purchased resins), manufacturing
422610	Resins, plastics, wholesaling
422690	Resins, synthetic rubber, wholesaling
333992	Resistance welding equipment manufacturing
334415	Resistors, electronic, manufacturing
421690	Resistors, electronic, wholesaling
334419	Resonant reed devices, electronic, manufacturing
721120	Resort hotels with casinos
721110	Resort hotels without casinos
621399	Respiratory therapists' offices (e.g., centers, clinics)

http://www.ntis.gov/naics

623110	Rest homes with nursing care
623312	Rest homes without nursing care
561720	Rest room cleaning services
812990	Rest room operation
813910	Restaurant associations
233320	Restaurant construction
421440	Restaurant equipment (except furniture) wholesaling
337127	Restaurant furniture (e.g., carts, chairs, foodwagons, tables) manufacturing
421210	Restaurant furniture wholesaling
561720	Restaurant kitchen cleaning services
492210	Restaurant meals delivery services (i.e., independent delivery services)
722211	Restaurants, carryout
722211	Restaurants, fast food
722110	Restaurants, full service
811420	Restoration and repair of antique furniture
811121	Restoration shops, antique and classic automotive
561410	Resume writing services
******	Retail —see type of dealer, shop, or store
333997	Retail scales (e.g., butcher, delicatessen, produce) manufacturing
813910	Retailers' associations
325998	Retarders (e.g., flameproofing agents, mildewproofing agents) manufacturing
813410	Retirement associations, social
623311	Retirement communities, continuing care
623110	Retirement homes with nursing care
623312	Retirement homes without nursing care
525110	Retirement pension plans
326211	Retreading materials, tire, manufacturing
326212	Retreading tires
813110	Retreat houses, religious
811420	Reupholstery shops, furniture
332994	Revolvers manufacturing
335931	Rheostats (i.e., dimmer switches), current carrying wiring device, manufacturing
334419	Rheostats, electronic, manufacturing
335314	Rheostats, industrial control, manufacturing
339944	Ribbons (e.g., cash register, printer, typewriter), inked, manufacturing
314999	Ribbons made from purchased fabrics
313221	Ribbons made in narrow woven fabric mills
313230	Ribbons made in nonwoven fabric mills
339944	Ribbons, inked, manufacturing
422120	Ribbons, inked, wholesaling
422310	Ribbons, textile, wholesaling
111160	Rice (except wild rice) farming, field and seed production
311212	Rice bran, flour, and meals, manufacturing
311230	Rice breakfast foods manufacturing
311212	Rice cleaning and polishing
311213	Rice malt manufacturing
311212	Rice meal manufacturing
311212	Rice milling
311999	Rice mixes (i.e., uncooked and packaged with other ingredients) made from purchased rice and dry ingredients
311423	Rice mixes (i.e., uncooked and packaged with other ingredients) made in dehydration plants
311212	Rice mixes (i.e., uncooked and packaged with other ingredients) made in rice mills
311221	Rice starches manufacturing
311212	Rice, brewer's, manufacturing
422490	Rice, polished, wholesaling
422510	Rice, unpolished, wholesaling
713990	Riding clubs, recreational
611620	Riding instruction academies or schools
713990	Riding stables
713990	Rifle clubs, recreational
332994	Rifles (except recoilless, toy) manufacturing
332995	Rifles, recoilless, manufacturing
339932	Rifles, toy, manufacturing
336399	Rims, automotive, truck, and bus wheel, manufacturing

336311	Rings, piston, manufacturing
713940	Rinks, ice or roller skating
483211	River freight transportation
483212	River passenger transportation
713990	River rafting, recreational
713210	Riverboat casinos
332722	Rivets, metal, manufacturing
234110	Road (except elevated) construction
711110	Road companies, theatrical
421810	Road construction and maintenance machinery wholesaling
234120	Road elevated (e.g., bridges) construction
311911	Roasted nuts and seeds manufacturing
112320	Roaster chicken production
311920	Roasting coffee
315291	Robes, lounging, infants', cut and sewn from purchased fabric (except apparel contractors)
315192	Robes, lounging, made in apparel knitting mills
315211	Robes, lounging, men's and boys', cut and sew apparel contractors
315221	Robes, lounging, men's and boys', cut and sewn from purchased fabric (except apparel contractors)
333120	Rock crushing machinery, portable, manufacturing
333131	Rock crushing machinery, stationary, manufacturing
333132	Rock drill bits, oil and gas field-type, manufacturing
333120	Rock drills, construction and surface mining-type, manufacturing
333131	Rock drills, underground mining-type, manufacturing
212393	Rock salt mining and/or beneficiating
336312	Rocker arms and parts, automotive and truck gasoline engine, manufacturing
336412	Rocket engines, aircraft, manufacturing
336415	Rocket engines, guided missile, manufacturing
332995	Rocket launchers manufacturing
336414	Rockets (guided missiles), space and military, complete, manufacturing
332993	Rockets, ammunition (except guided missiles, pyrotechnic), manufacturing
331316	Rod made by extruding purchased aluminum
331319	Rod made by rolling purchased aluminum
331316	Rod, aluminum, made in integrated secondary smelting and extruding mills
331319	Rod, aluminum, made in integrated secondary smelting and rolling mills
325320	Rodenticides manufacturing
711310	Rodeo managers with facilities
711320	Rodeo managers without facilities
711310	Rodeo organizers with facilities
711320	Rodeo organizers without facilities
711310	Rodeo promoters with facilities
711320	Rodeo promoters without facilities
326299	Rods, hard rubber, manufacturing
331111	Rods, iron or steel, made in steel mills
421510	Rods, metal (except precious), wholesaling
332991	Roller bearings manufacturing
713940	Roller skating rinks
333516	Rolling mill machinery and equipment, metalworking, manufacturing
333516	Rolling mill roll machines manufacturing
331511	Rolling mill rolls, iron, manufacturing
331513	Rolling mill rolls, steel, manufacturing
336510	Rolling stock, railroad, rebuilding
311812	Rolls and buns (including frozen) made in commercial bakeries
326299	Rolls and roll coverings, rubber (e.g., industrial, papermill, painters', steelmill) manufacturing
111219	Romaine lettuce farming, field and seed production

321214 Roof trusses, wood, manufacturing
326299 Roofing (i.e., single ply rubber membrane) manufacturing
324122 Roofing cements, asphalt, made from purchased asphaltic materials
324122 Roofing coatings made from purchased asphaltic materials
235610 Roofing construction contractors
324122 Roofing felts made from purchased asphaltic materials
444190 Roofing material dealers
421330 Roofing materials (except wood) wholesaling
421310 Roofing materials, wood, wholesaling
327123 Roofing tile, clay, manufacturing
327390 Roofing tile, concrete, manufacturing
332322 Roofing, sheet metal, manufacturing
333415 Room air-conditioners manufacturing
421620 Room air-conditioners wholesaling
335211 Room heaters, portable electric, manufacturing
721310 Rooming and boarding houses
311221 Root starches manufacturing
332618 Rope, wire, made from purchased wire
314991 Ropes (except wire rope) manufacturing
421840 Ropes (except wire rope) wholesaling
313111 Ropes, hemp, made from purchased fiber
421510 Ropes, wire (except insulated), wholesaling
111421 Rose bush growing
325211 Rosin (i.e., modified resins) manufacturing
325191 Rosin made by distillation of pine gum or pine wood
422690 Rosins wholesaling
421990 Roundwood wholesaling
333991 Routers, handheld power-driven, manufacturing
233210 Row house single family construction

532292 Rowboat rental
336612 Rowboats manufacturing
713990 Rowing clubs, recreational
112910 Royal jelly production, bees
326220 Rubber and plastics belts and hoses (without fittings) manufacturing
326299 Rubber bands manufacturing
325520 Rubber cements manufacturing
326192 Rubber floor coverings manufacturing
326291 Rubber goods, mechanical (i.e., extruded, lathe-cut, molded), manufacturing
421840 Rubber goods, mechanical (i.e., extruded, lathe-cut, molded), wholesaling
422210 Rubber goods, medical, wholesaling
325998 Rubber processing preparations (e.g., accelerators, stabilizers) manufacturing
421930 Rubber scrap and scrap tires wholesaling
339943 Rubber stamps manufacturing
313221 Rubber thread and yarns, fabric covered, manufacturing
333220 Rubber working machinery manufacturing
422990 Rubber, crude, wholesaling
325212 Rubber, synthetic, manufacturing
313320 Rubberizing purchased textiles and apparel
562111 Rubbish (i.e., nonhazardous solid waste) hauling, local
562111 Rubbish collection services
562213 Rubbish disposal combustors or incinerators
562212 Rubbish disposal landfills
484220 Rubbish hauling without collection or disposal, truck, local
484230 Rubbish hauling without collection or disposal, truck, long-distance
562119 Rubble removal services
325612 Rug cleaning preparations manufacturing
561740 Rug cleaning services
442210 Rug stores
314110 Rugs and carpets made from textile materials

421220	Rugs wholesaling
321999	Rulers and rules (except slide), wood, manufacturing
332212	Rulers, metal, manufacturing
326199	Rulers, plastics, manufacturing
334519	Rules, slide, manufacturing
488119	Runway maintenance services
325998	Rust preventive preparations manufacturing
332812	Rustproofing metals and metal products for the trade
811198	Rustproofing shops, automotive
212299	Ruthenium ore mining and/or beneficiating
111199	Rye farming, field and seed production
311211	Rye flour manufacturing
311213	Rye malt manufacturing
522294	SLMA (Student Loan Marketing Association)
322224	Sacks, multiwall, made from purchased uncoated paper
422130	Sacks, paper, wholesaling
713990	Saddle horse rental services, recreational
316110	Saddlery leather manufacturing
811430	Saddlery repair shops without retailing new saddlery
451110	Saddlery stores
422910	Saddlery wholesaling
316999	Saddles and parts, leather, manufacturing
332999	Safe deposit boxes and chests, metal, manufacturing
332999	Safes, metal, manufacturing
421420	Safes, security, wholesaling
332911	Safety (i.e., pop-off) valves, industrial-type, manufacturing
316999	Safety belts, leather, manufacturing
541690	Safety consulting services
327215	Safety glass (including motor vehicle) made from purchased glass
311225	Safflower oil made from purchased oils
311223	Safflower oil made in crushing mills
336612	Sailboat building, not done in shipyards
532292	Sailboat rental
713930	Sailing clubs with marinas
713990	Sailing clubs without marinas
336611	Sailing ships, commercial, manufacturing
314912	Sails made from purchased fabrics
311423	Salad dressing mixes, dry, made in a dehydration plant
311942	Salad dressing mixes, dry, manufacturing
311941	Salad dressings manufacturing
422490	Salad dressings wholesaling
422490	Salad oils wholesaling
311991	Salads, fresh or refrigerated, manufacturing
422120	Sales books wholesaling
323116	Sales books, manifold, printing
522220	Sales financing
541613	Sales management consulting services
325199	Salicylic acid (except medicinal) manufacturing
325411	Salicylic acid, medicinal, uncompounded, manufacturing
114111	Salmon fishing
233320	Salon construction
311421	Salsa canning
325998	Salt (except table) manufacturing
311942	Salt substitute manufacturing
212393	Salt, common, mining and/or beneficiating
311942	Salt, table, manufacturing
422490	Salt, table, wholesaling
311821	Saltines manufacturing
422210	Salts, bath, wholesaling
422690	Salts, industrial, wholesaling
334516	Sample analysis instruments (except medical) manufacturing
541870	Sample direct distribution services
323121	Samples and displays mounting
541910	Sampling services, statistical
421320	Sand (except industrial) wholesaling
212321	Sand and gravel quarrying (i.e., construction grade) and/or beneficiating
212321	Sand, construction grade, quarrying and/or beneficiating

212322	Sand, industrial (e.g., engine, filtration, glass grinding), quarrying and/or beneficiating
421840	Sand, industrial, wholesaling
316219	Sandals, children's (except rubber, plastics), manufacturing
316213	Sandals, men's footwear (except rubber, plastics), manufacturing
316211	Sandals, plastics or plastics soled fabric upper, manufacturing
316211	Sandals, rubber or rubber soled fabric upper, manufacturing
316214	Sandals, women's footwear (except rubber, plastics), manufacturing
332813	Sandblasting metals and metal products for the trade
235990	Sandblasting of building exteriors construction contractors
333991	Sanders, handheld power-driven, manufacturing
333210	Sanding machines, woodworking-type, stationary, manufacturing
327910	Sandpaper manufacturing
212319	Sandstone crushed and broken stone mining
722211	Sandwich shops, limited service
311941	Sandwich spreads, salad dressing based, manufacturing
422490	Sandwiches wholesaling
311991	Sandwiches, fresh (i.e., assembled and packaged for wholesale market), manufacturing
322212	Sanitary food container, folding, made from purchased paperboard
422130	Sanitary food containers (e.g., disposable plastics, paper, paperboard) wholesaling
322215	Sanitary food containers (except folding) made from purchased paper or paperboard
562212	Sanitary landfills
322291	Sanitary napkins and tampons made from purchased paper or textile fiber
322121	Sanitary napkins and tampons made in paper mills
322121	Sanitary paper products (except newsprint, uncoated groundwood) made in paper mills
422130	Sanitary paper products wholesaling
322121	Sanitary paper stock manufacturing
322291	Sanitary products made from purchased sanitary paper stock
322121	Sanitary products made in paper mills
332998	Sanitary ware (e.g., bathtubs, lavatories, sinks), metal, manufacturing
421720	Sanitary ware, china or enameled iron, wholesaling
541620	Sanitation consulting services
926130	Sanitation districts, nonoperating
332321	Sash, door and window, metal, manufacturing
321911	Sash, door and window, wood and covered wood, manufacturing
334220	Satellite antennas manufacturing
334220	Satellite communications equipment manufacturing
513220	Satellite master antenna television service (SMATV)
513111	Satellite radio networks
513340	Satellite telecommunication carriers
513340	Satellite telecommunication resellers
513220	Satellite television distribution systems
513210	Satellite television networks
513390	Satellite tracking stations on a contract or fee basis
311423	Sauce mixes, dry, made in dehydration plants
311942	Sauce mixes, dry, manufacturing
311941	Sauces (except tomato based) manufacturing
311421	Sauces, tomato-based, canning
311421	Sauerkraut manufacturing
812199	Saunas
311612	Sausage and similar cased products made from purchased carcasses
422490	Sausage casings wholesaling
311612	Sausage casings, collagen, made from purchased hides
311611	Sausage casings, natural, produced in slaughtering plant
326121	Sausage casings, plastics, manufacturing
522120	Savings and loan associations (S&L)

522120	Savings banks
332213	Saw blades, all types, manufacturing
321113	Sawdust and shavings (i.e., sawmill byproducts) manufacturing
422990	Sawdust wholesaling
333210	Sawmill equipment manufacturing
532490	Sawmill machinery rental or leasing
421830	Sawmill machinery, equipment, and supplies wholesaling
321113	Sawmills
333210	Saws, bench and table, power-driven, woodworking-type, manufacturing
332213	Saws, hand, nonpowered, manufacturing
333991	Saws, handheld power-driven, manufacturing
339112	Saws, surgical, manufacturing
235990	Scaffolding construction contractors
532490	Scaffolding rental or leasing
421810	Scaffolding wholesaling
332323	Scaffolds, metal, manufacturing
333997	Scales (except laboratory-type) manufacturing
339111	Scales and balances, laboratory-type, manufacturing
339111	Scales, laboratory, manufacturing
114112	Scallop fishing
812199	Scalp treating services
315191	Scarves made in apparel knitting mills
315211	Scarves, men's and boys', cut and sew apparel contractors
315993	Scarves, men's and boys', cut and sewn from purchased fabric (except apparel contractors)
315212	Scarves, women's, girls', and infants', cut and sew apparel contractors
315999	Scarves, women's, misses', and girls', cut and sewn from purchased fabric (except apparel contractors)
336350	Scattershield, engine, manufacturing
711510	Scenery designers, independent theatrical
532490	Scenery, theatrical, rental or leasing
487990	Scenic and sightseeing excursions, aerial
487110	Scenic and sightseeing excursions, land
487210	Scenic and sightseeing excursions, water
481112	Scheduled air freight carriers
481111	Scheduled air passenger carriers
313222	Schiffli machine embroideries manufacturing
333292	Schiffli machinery manufacturing
511120	Scholarly journal publishers
511120	Scholarly journal publishers and printing combined
323112	Scholarly journals flexographic printing without publishing
323111	Scholarly journals gravure printing without publishing
323110	Scholarly journals lithographic (offset) printing without publishing
323119	Scholarly journals printing (except flexographic, gravure, lithographic, screen) without publishing
323113	Scholarly journals screen printing without publishing
813211	Scholarship trusts (i.e., grantmaking, charitable trust foundations)
511120	Scholastic magazine and periodical publishers
511120	Scholastic magazine and periodical publishers and printing combined
323111	Scholastic magazines and periodicals gravure printing without publishing
323112	Scholastic magazines and periodicals flexographic printing without publishing
323110	Scholastic magazines and periodicals lithographic (offset) printing without publishing
323119	Scholastic magazines and periodicals printing (except flexographic, gravure, lithographic, screen) without publishing
323113	Scholastic magazines and periodicals screen printing without publishing

611110 School boards, elementary and secondary
233320 School building construction
485410 School bus services
336211 School buses assembling on purchased chassis
421110 School buses wholesaling
611110 School districts, elementary or secondary
421490 School equipment and supplies (except books, furniture) wholesaling
337127 School furniture manufacturing
421210 School furniture wholesaling
541921 School photography (i.e., portrait photography) services
453210 School supply stores
323121 School text books binding without printing
511130 School textbook publishers
511130 School textbook publishers and printing combined
611110 Schools for the handicapped, elementary or secondary
611110 Schools for the mentally retarded (except preschool, job training, vocational rehabilitation)
611110 Schools for the physically disabled, elementary or secondary
611512 Schools, aviation
611511 Schools, barber
611511 Schools, beauty
611410 Schools, business, not offering academic degrees
611310 Schools, correspondence, college level
611511 Schools, cosmetology
611610 Schools, drama (except academic)
611110 Schools, elementary
611210 Schools, junior college
611630 Schools, language
611610 Schools, music (except academic)
611110 Schools, secondary
611620 Schools, sports instruction
712110 Science and technology museums
339932 Science kits (e.g., chemistry sets, microscopes, natural science sets), manufacturing

813920 Scientific associations
327215 Scientific glassware made from purchased glass
327212 Scientific glassware, pressed or blown, made in glass making plants
421490 Scientific instruments wholesaling
421490 Scientific laboratory equipment wholesaling
335211 Scissors, electric, manufacturing
332211 Scissors, nonelectric, manufacturing
339950 Scoreboards manufacturing
313312 Scouring and combing textile fibers
325611 Scouring cleansers (e.g., pastes, powders) manufacturing
332999 Scouring pads, soap impregnated, manufacturing
813410 Scouting organizations
421930 Scrap materials wholesaling
323118 Scrapbooks and refills manufacturing
422120 Scrapbooks wholesaling
332321 Screen doors, metal frame, manufacturing
323122 Screen for printing, preparation services
323113 Screen printing (except manifold business forms, printing grey goods, printing books)
323113 Screen printing apparel and textile products (e.g. caps, napkins, placemats, T-shirts, towels)
333120 Screening machinery, portable, manufacturing
333131 Screening machinery, stationary, manufacturing
334419 Screens for liquid crystal display (LCD) manufacturing
332321 Screens, door and window, metal frame, manufacturing
321911 Screens, door and window, wood framed, manufacturing
333315 Screens, projection (i.e., motion picture, overhead, slide), manufacturing
421310 Screens, window and door, wholesaling
332212 Screw drivers, nonelectric, manufacturing

333991	Screwdrivers and nut drivers, handheld power-driven, manufacturing
332722	Screws, metal, manufacturing
339920	Scuba diving equipment manufacturing
711510	Sculptors, independent
327420	Sculptures (e.g., gypsum, plaster of paris) manufacturing
327112	Sculptures, architectural, clay, manufacturing
114112	Sea urchin fishing
422460	Seafood (except canned, packaged frozen) wholesaling
311711	Seafood and seafood products canning
311711	Seafood and seafood products curing
311712	Seafood dinners, frozen, manufacturing
445220	Seafood markets
311712	Seafood products, fresh prepared, manufacturing
311712	Seafood products, frozen, manufacturing
422490	Seafood, canned, wholesaling
311712	Seafood, fresh prepared, manufacturing
311712	Seafood, frozen, manufacturing
422420	Seafoods, packaged frozen, wholesaling
422690	Sealants wholesaling
335110	Sealed beam automotive light bulbs manufacturing
325520	Sealing compounds for pipe threads and joints manufacturing
421840	Seals wholesaling
339991	Seals, grease or oil, manufacturing
334511	Search and detection systems and instruments manufacturing
514199	Search services, information, on a contract or fee basis
453220	Seasonal and holiday decoration stores
561730	Seasonal property maintenance services (i.e., snow plowing in winter, landscaping during other seasons)

311942	Seasoning salt manufacturing
336360	Seat belts, motor vehicle and aircraft, manufacturing
326150	Seat cushions, foam plastics (except polystyrene), manufacturing
336360	Seats for public conveyances, manufacturing
336360	Seats, railroad, manufacturing
321999	Seats, toilet, wood, manufacturing
488310	Seaway operation
114119	Seaweed gathering
311711	Seaweed processing (e.g., dulse)
522294	Secondary market financing (i.e., buying, pooling, repackaging loans for sale to others)
331492	Secondary refining of nonferrous metals (except aluminum, copper)
331492	Secondary smelting of nonferrous metals (except aluminum, copper)
611410	Secretarial schools
561410	Secretarial services
332311	Sections for prefabricated metal buildings manufacturing
321992	Sections, prefabricated wood building, manufacturing
523120	Securities brokerages
523110	Securities dealing (i.e., acting as a principal in dealing securities to investors)
523110	Securities distributing (i.e., acting as a principal in dealing securities to investors)
523210	Securities exchanges
523120	Securities floor brokers
523110	Securities floor traders (i.e., acting as a principal in dealing securities to investors)
523999	Securities holders' protective services
523110	Securities originating (i.e., acting as a principal in dealing securities to investors)
926150	Securities regulation commissions
523110	Securities trading (i.e., acting as a principal in dealing securities to investors)

523999	Securities transfer agencies
523110	Securities underwriting
561621	Security alarm systems sales combined with installation, maintenance, or monitoring services
541690	Security consulting services
561612	Security guard services
561612	Security patrol services
421420	Security safes wholesaling
561621	Security system monitoring services
421610	Security systems wholesaling
325412	Sedative preparations manufacturing
314911	Seed bags made from purchased woven or knitted materials
115112	Seed bed preparing
115114	Seed cleaning
541380	Seed testing laboratories or services
115112	Seeding crops
561730	Seeding lawns
422450	Seeds (e.g., canned, roasted, salted) wholesaling
422910	Seeds (e.g., field, flower, garden) wholesaling
311911	Seeds, snack (e.g., canned, cooked, roasted, salted) manufacturing
541360	Seismic geophysical surveying services
334519	Seismographs manufacturing
325188	Selenium compounds, not specified elsewhere by process, manufacturing
531130	Self-storage unit rental or leasing
624190	Self-help organizations (except for disabled persons, the elderly, persons diagnosed with mental retardation)
624120	Self-help organizations for disabled persons, the elderly, and persons diagnosed with mental retardation
624110	Self-help organizations, youth
525190	Self-insurance funds (except employee benefit funds)
811192	Self-service carwash
812310	Self-service drycleaners and laundries
531130	Self-storage warehousing
531210	Selling real estate for others (i.e., agents, brokers)

422590	Semen, bovine, wholesaling
421510	Semi-finished metal products wholesaling
336212	Semi-trailer manufacturing
532120	Semi-trailer rental or leasing
333295	Semiconductor assembly and packaging machinery manufacturing
334413	Semiconductor circuit networks (i.e., solid-state integrated circuits) manufacturing
334413	Semiconductor devices manufacturing
421690	Semiconductor devices wholesaling
334413	Semiconductor dice and wafers manufacturing
333295	Semiconductor making machinery manufacturing
334413	Semiconductor memory chips manufacturing
334515	Semiconductor test equipment manufacturing
333618	Semidiesel engines manufacturing
611310	Seminaries, theological, offering baccalaureate or graduate degrees
711211	Semiprofessional sports clubs
331511	Semisteel foundries
485991	Senior citizens transportation services
813311	Senior citizens advocacy organizations
624120	Senior citizens centers
562991	Septic tank cleaning services
562991	Septic tank pumping (i.e., cleaning) services
421390	Septic tanks (except concrete) wholesaling
421320	Septic tanks, concrete, wholesaling
332420	Septic tanks, heavy gauge metal, manufacturing
326199	Septic tanks, plastics or fiberglass, manufacturing
334512	Sequencing controls for electric heating equipment manufacturing
325414	Serums (except diagnostic substances) manufacturing
315211	Service apparel, washable, men's and boys', cut and sew apparel contractors

315225	Service apparel, washable, men's and boys', cut and sewn from purchased fabric (except apparel contractors)
315212	Service apparel, washable, women's, cut and sew apparel contractors
315239	Service apparel, washable, women's, misses' and girls', cut and sewn from purchased fabric (except apparel contractors)
421850	Service establishment equipment and supplies wholesaling
813910	Service industries associations
811310	Service machinery and equipment repair and maintenance services
561720	Service station cleaning and degreasing services
233320	Service station construction
447190	Service stations, gasoline
711510	Set designers, independent theatrical
541191	Settlement offices, real estate
322213	Setup (i.e., not shipped flat) boxes made from purchased paperboard
221320	Sewage disposal plants
333319	Sewage treatment equipment manufacturing
234990	Sewage treatment plant construction
221320	Sewage treatment plants or facilities
562998	Sewer cleaning and rodding services
562998	Sewer cleanout services
234910	Sewer construction
327123	Sewer pipe and fittings, clay, manufacturing
327332	Sewer pipe, concrete, manufacturing
221320	Sewer systems
422310	Sewing accessories wholesaling
315211	Sewing fabric owned by others for men's and boys' apparel
315212	Sewing fabric owned by others for women's, girls' and infants' apparel
337129	Sewing machine cabinets, wood, manufacturing
443111	Sewing machine stores, household-type
811412	Sewing machine, household-type, repair shops without retailing new sewing machines
333298	Sewing machines (including household-type) manufacturing
421620	Sewing machines, household-type, wholesaling
421830	Sewing machines, industrial, wholesaling
451130	Sewing supply stores
313113	Sewing threads manufacturing
335121	Shades, lamp (except glass, plastics), residential-type, manufacturing
337920	Shades, window (except outdoor canvas awnings), manufacturing
321113	Shakes (i.e., hand split shingles) manufacturing
212325	Shale (except oil shale) mining and/or beneficiating
327992	Shale, expanded, manufacturing
211111	Shale, oil, mining and/or beneficiating
325620	Shampoos and conditioners, hair, manufacturing
333210	Shapers, woodworking-type, manufacturing
114111	Shark fishing
325620	Shaving preparations (e.g., creams, gels, lotions, powders) manufacturing
422210	Shaving preparations wholesaling
333513	Shearing machines, metal forming, manufacturing
332211	Shears, nonelectric, household-type (e.g., kitchen, barber, tailor) manufacturing
332212	Shears, nonelectric, tool-type (e.g., garden, pruners, tinsnip), manufacturing
333111	Shears, powered, for use on animals, manufacturing
115210	Sheep dipping and shearing
112410	Sheep farming (e.g., meat, milk, wool production)
422520	Sheep wholesaling
326140	Sheet (i.e., board), polystyrene foam insulation, manufacturing
235610	Sheet metal work (except plumbing, heating, air-conditioning) construction contractors

332322 Sheet metal work (except stamped) manufacturing
323112 Sheet music flexographic printing without publishing
323111 Sheet music gravure printing without publishing
323110 Sheet music lithographic (offset) printing without publishing
323119 Sheet music printing (except flexographic, gravure, lithographic, screen) without publishing
512230 Sheet music publishers
512230 Sheet music publishers and printing combined
323113 Sheet music screen printing without publishing
451140 Sheet music stores
422990 Sheet music wholesaling
331315 Sheet, aluminum, made by flat rolling purchased aluminum
331315 Sheet, aluminum, made in integrated secondary smelting and flat rolling mills
326130 Sheet, laminated plastics (except flexible packaging), manufacturing
326113 Sheet, plastics, unlaminated (except packaging), manufacturing
326299 Sheeting, rubber, manufacturing
314129 Sheets and pillowcases made from purchased fabrics
313210 Sheets and pillowcases made in broadwoven fabric mills
331111 Sheets, steel, made in steel mills
311119 Shell crushing and grinding for animal feed
332993 Shell loading and assembly plants
212399 Shell mining and/or beneficiating
339999 Shell novelties
325510 Shellac manufacturing
422950 Shellac wholesaling
311711 Shellfish and shellfish products canning
311711 Shellfish curing
114112 Shellfish fishing (e.g., clam, crab, oyster, shrimp)
112512 Shellfish hatcheries
311712 Shellfish products, fresh prepared, manufacturing

311712 Shellfish products, frozen, manufacturing
311712 Shellfish, fresh prepared, manufacturing
311712 Shellfish, frozen, manufacturing
332993 Shells, artillery, manufacturing
332992 Shells, small arms (i.e., 30 mm. or less, 1.18 inch or less), manufacturing
624310 Sheltered workshops (i.e., work experience centers)
624221 Shelters (except for victims of domestic or international disasters or conflicts), emergency
624230 Shelters for victims of domestic or international disasters or conflicts, emergency
624221 Shelters, temporary (e.g., battered women's, homeless, runaway youth)
337215 Shelving (except wire) manufacturing
421440 Shelving, commercial, wholesaling
332618 Shelving, wire, made from purchased wire
311520 Sherbets manufacturing
922120 Sheriffs' offices (except court functions only)
922110 Sheriffs' offices, court functions only
321113 Shingle mills, wood
421330 Shingles (except wood) wholesaling
324122 Shingles made from purchased asphaltic materials
321113 Shingles, wood, sawed or hand split, manufacturing
421310 Shingles, wood, wholesaling
422990 Ship chandler wholesaling
483113 Ship chartering with crew, coastal or Great Lakes freight transportation
483114 Ship chartering with crew, coastal or Great Lakes passenger transportation
483111 Ship chartering with crew, deep sea freight transportation to or from foreign ports

http://www.ntis.gov/naics

483112	Ship chartering with crew, deep sea passenger transportation to or from foreign ports
483211	Ship chartering with crew, freight transportation, inland waters (except on Great Lakes system)
483212	Ship chartering with crew, passenger transportation, inland waters (except on Great Lakes system)
561310	Ship crew employment agencies
561310	Ship crew registries
488320	Ship hold cleaning services
532411	Ship rental or leasing
336611	Ship repair done in a shipyard
336611	Ship scaling services done at a shipyard
488390	Ship scaling services not done at a shipyard
332312	Ship sections, prefabricated metal, manufacturing
513322	Ship-to-shore broadcasting communication carriers (except satellite)
488510	Shipping agents (freight forwarding)
314911	Shipping bags made from purchased woven or knitted materials
813910	Shipping companies' associations
322211	Shipping containers made from purchased paperboard
322211	Shipping containers, corrugated, made from purchased paper or paperboard
321920	Shipping crates, wood, manufacturing
483113	Shipping freight to and from domestic ports (i.e., coastal, deep sea, Great Lakes system)
483111	Shipping freight to or from foreign ports, deep sea
483211	Shipping freight, inland waters (except on Great Lakes system)
326150	Shipping pads and shaped cushioning, foam plastics (except polystyrene), manufacturing
326140	Shipping pads and shaped cushioning, polystyrene foam, manufacturing

511140	Shipping register publishers
511140	Shipping register publishers and printing combined
323112	Shipping registers flexographic printing without publishing
323111	Shipping registers gravure printing without publishing
323110	Shipping registers lithographic (offset) printing without publishing
323119	Shipping registers printing (except flexographic, gravure, lithographic, screen) without publishing
323113	Shipping registers screen printing without publishing
422130	Shipping supplies, paper and disposable plastics, wholesaling
336611	Ships (i.e., not suitable or intended for personal use) manufacturing
421860	Ships wholesaling
336611	Shipyard (i.e., facility capable of building ships)
315223	Shirts, outerwear (except work shirts), men's and boys', cut and sewn from purchased fabric (except apparel contractors)
315225	Shirts, outerwear work, men's and boys', cut and sewn from purchased fabric (except apparel contractors)
315291	Shirts, outerwear, infants', cut and sewn from purchased fabric (except apparel contractors)
315191	Shirts, outerwear, made in apparel knitting mills
315211	Shirts, outerwear, men's and boys', cut and sew apparel contractors
315223	Shirts, outerwear, unisex (i.e., sized without regard to gender), cut and sewn from purchased fabric (except apparel contractors)
315212	Shirts, outerwear, women's, girls', and infants', cut and sew apparel contractors
315232	Shirts, outerwear, women's, misses', and girls', cut and sewn from purchased fabric (except apparel contractors)

315291	Shirts, underwear, infants', cut and sewn from purchased fabric (except apparel contractors)
315192	Shirts, underwear, made in apparel knitting mills
315211	Shirts, underwear, men's and boys', cut and sew apparel contractors
315221	Shirts, underwear, men's and boys', cut and sewn from purchased fabric (except apparel contractors)
315212	Shirts, underwear, women's, girls', and infants', cut and sew apparel contractors
315231	Shirts, underwear, women's, misses', and girls', cut and sewn from purchased fabric (except apparel contractors)
336330	Shock absorbers, automotive, truck, and bus, manufacturing
448210	Shoe (except bowling, golf, spiked) stores
326299	Shoe and boot parts (e.g., heels, soles, soling strips), rubber, manufacturing
322212	Shoe boxes, folding, made from purchased paperboard
322213	Shoe boxes, setup, made from purchased paperboard
541490	Shoe design services
333298	Shoe making and repairing machinery manufacturing
421830	Shoe manufacturing and repairing machinery wholesaling
326199	Shoe parts (e.g., heels, soles), plastics, manufacturing
325612	Shoe polishes and cleaners manufacturing
421850	Shoe repair materials wholesaling
811430	Shoe repair shops without retailing new shoes
316999	Shoe soles, leather, manufacturing
448210	Shoe stores, orthopedic
451110	Shoe stores, specialty sports footwear (e.g., bowling, golf, spiked)
321999	Shoe stretchers manufacturing
321999	Shoe trees manufacturing
422340	Shoes wholesaling
316219	Shoes, athletic (except rubber or plastics soled with fabric upper), manufacturing
316219	Shoes, children's and infant's (except house slippers, orthopedic extension, plastics, rubber), manufacturing
316219	Shoes, cleated or spiked, all materials, manufacturing
316213	Shoes, men's (except house slippers, athletic, rubber, extension shoes), manufacturing
339113	Shoes, orthopedic extension, manufacturing
316211	Shoes, plastics or plastics soled fabric upper (except cleated athletic shoes), manufacturing
316211	Shoes, rubber or rubber soled fabric upper (except cleated athletic), manufacturing
316214	Shoes, women's (except house slippers, athletic, orthopedic extension, plastic, rubber), manufacturing
812990	Shoeshine parlors
812990	Shoeshine services
321920	Shook, box, manufacturing
713990	Shooting clubs, recreational
713990	Shooting galleries
713990	Shooting ranges
233320	Shop construction
421120	Shop equipment, service station, wholesaling
422130	Shopping bags, paper and plastics, wholesaling
233320	Shopping center or mall construction
812990	Shopping services, personal
******	Shops—see type
235990	Shoring and underpinning construction contractors
111421	Short rotation woody tree growing (i.e., growing and harvesting cycle ten years or less)
482112	Short-line railroads
522298	Short-term inventory credit lending
311223	Shortening (except soybean) made in crushing mills

http://www.ntis.gov/naics

311222	Shortening , soybean, made in crushing mills
311225	Shortening made from purchased fats and oils
422490	Shortening, vegetable, wholesaling
315291	Shorts, outerwear, infants', cut and sewn from purchased fabric (except apparel contractors)
315191	Shorts, outerwear, made in apparel knitting mills
315211	Shorts, outerwear, men's and boys', cut and sew apparel contractors
315228	Shorts, outerwear, men's and boys', cut and sewn from purchased fabric (except apparel contractors)
315212	Shorts, outerwear, women's, girls', and infants', cut and sew apparel contractors
315239	Shorts, outerwear, women's, misses', and girls', cut and sewn from purchased fabric (except apparel contractors)
315192	Shorts, underwear, made in apparel knitting mills
315211	Shorts, underwear, men's and boys', cut and sew apparel contractors
315221	Shorts, underwear, men's and boys', cut and sewn from purchased fabric (except apparel contractors)
332992	Shot, BB, manufacturing
332992	Shot, pellet, manufacturing
332992	Shotgun shells manufacturing
332994	Shotguns manufacturing
333120	Shovel loaders manufacturing
332212	Shovels, handheld, manufacturing
337215	Showcases (except refrigerated) manufacturing
421440	Showcases (except refrigerated) wholesaling
333415	Showcases, refrigerated, manufacturing
314129	Shower and bath curtains, all materials, made from purchased fabric or sheet goods
332913	Shower heads, plumbing, manufacturing
332999	Shower rods, metal, manufacturing
332998	Shower stalls, metal, manufacturing
326191	Shower stalls, plastics or fiberglass, manufacturing
115210	Showing of cattle, hogs, sheep, goats, and poultry
333111	Shredders, farm-type, manufacturing
114112	Shrimp fishing
112512	Shrimp production, farm raising
813110	Shrines, religious
561910	Shrink wrapping services
313311	Shrinking broadwoven fabrics
313312	Shrinking textile products and fabrics (except broadwoven)
561730	Shrub services (e.g., bracing, planting, pruning, removal, spraying, surgery, trimming)
111421	Shrubbery farming
311712	Shucking and packing fresh shellfish
332321	Shutters, door and window, metal, manufacturing
326199	Shutters, plastics, manufacturing
321918	Shutters, wood, manufacturing
485999	Shuttle services (except employee bus)
446199	Sick room supply stores
332212	Sickles manufacturing
421330	Siding (except wood) wholesaling
235610	Siding construction contractors
444190	Siding dealers
324122	Siding made from purchased asphaltic materials
321113	Siding mills, wood
326199	Siding, plastics, manufacturing
332322	Siding, sheet metal, manufacturing
421310	Siding, wood, wholesaling
333294	Sieves and screening equipment (i.e., food manufacturing-type) manufacturing
333298	Sieves and screening equipment, chemical preparation-type, manufacturing
333999	Sieves and screening equipment, general purpose-type, manufacturing
487110	Sightseeing bus operation
235990	Sign contractors, installation (on buildings)

234110	Sign erection (i.e., highway, street) contractors
611630	Sign language instruction
541930	Sign language services
541890	Sign lettering and painting services
421610	Signal systems and devices wholesaling
334290	Signals (e.g., highway, pedestrian, railway, traffic) manufacturing
421990	Signs (except electrical) wholesaling
339950	Signs and signboards (except paper, paperboard) manufacturing
421440	Signs, electrical, wholesaling
327910	Silicon carbide abrasives manufacturing
334413	Silicon wafers, chemically doped, manufacturing
327992	Silicon, ultra high purity, manufacturing
325199	Silicone (except resins) manufacturing
325211	Silicone resins manufacturing
325212	Silicone rubber manufacturing
541430	Silk screen design services
333292	Silk screens for textile fabrics manufacturing
422590	Silk, raw, wholesaling
327390	Sills, concrete, manufacturing
327390	Silos, prefabricated concrete, manufacturing
331419	Silver bullion or dore bar produced at primary metal refineries
325188	Silver compounds, not specified elsewhere by process, manufacturing
332999	Silver foil and leaf not made in rolling mills
331491	Silver foil made by rolling purchased metals or scrap
212222	Silver ores mining and/or beneficiating
331492	Silver recovering from used photographic film or X-ray plates
331419	Silver refining, primary
421940	Silverware, precious and plated, wholesaling

711130	Singers, independent
813410	Singing societies
812990	Singing telegram services
332998	Sinks, metal, manufacturing
326191	Sinks, plastics, manufacturing
327111	Sinks, vitreous china, manufacturing
212210	Sintered iron ore produced at the mine
334290	Sirens (e.g., air raid, industrial, marine, vehicle) manufacturing
541620	Site remediation consulting services
562910	Site remediation services
541611	Site selection consulting services
812990	Sitting services, house
812910	Sitting services, pet
313311	Sizing of broadwoven fabrics
313312	Sizing of fabric (except broadwoven)
713990	Skeet shooting facilities
541320	Ski area design services
541320	Ski area planning services
532292	Ski equipment rental
713920	Ski lift and tow operators
721110	Ski lodges and resorts with accommodations
315191	Ski pants made in apparel knitting mills
315291	Ski pants, infants', cut and sewn from purchased fabric (except apparel contractors)
315211	Ski pants, men's and boys', cut and sew apparel contractors
315228	Ski pants, men's and boys', cut and sewn from purchased fabric (except apparel contractors)
315212	Ski pants, women's, girls', and infants', cut and sew apparel contractors
315239	Ski pants, women's, misses', and girls', cut and sewn from purchased fabric (except apparel contractors)
713920	Ski resorts without accommodations
321920	Skids and pallets, wood or wood and metal combination, manufacturing
332999	Skids, metal, manufacturing
711219	Skiers, independent (i.e., participating in sports events)

713920	Skiing facilities, cross country, without accommodations
713920	Skiing facilities, downhill, without accommodations
611620	Skiing instruction, camps, or schools
422990	Skins, dressed, wholesaling
422590	Skins, raw, wholesaling
316110	Skins, tanning, currying and finishing
561611	Skip tracing services
315234	Skirts (except tennis skirts), women's, misses', and girls', cut and sewn from purchased fabric (except apparel contractors)
315191	Skirts made in apparel knitting mills
315291	Skirts, infants', cut and sewn from purchased fabric (except apparel contractors)
315239	Skirts, tennis, women's, misses', and girls', cut and sewn from purchased fabric (except apparel contractors)
315212	Skirts, women's, misses', girls', and infants', cut and sew apparel contractors
235610	Skylight construction contractors
332322	Skylights, sheet metal, manufacturing
315191	Slacks made in apparel knitting mills
315291	Slacks, infants', cut and sewn from purchased fabric (except apparel contractors)
315291	Slacks, jean-cut casual, infants', cut and sewn from purchased fabric (except apparel contractors)
315191	Slacks, jean-cut casual, made in apparel knitting mills
315211	Slacks, jean-cut casual, men's and boys', cut and sew apparel contractors
315224	Slacks, jean-cut casual, men's and boys', cut and sewn from purchased fabric (except apparel contractors)
315212	Slacks, jean-cut casual, women's, girls', and infants', cut and sew apparel contractors

315239	Slacks, jean-cut casual, women's, misses', and girls', cut and sewn from purchased fabric (except apparel contractors)
315211	Slacks, men's and boys', cut and sew apparel contractors
315224	Slacks, men's and boys', cut and sewn from purchased fabric (except apparel contractors)
315212	Slacks, women's, girls', and infants', cut and sew apparel contractors
315239	Slacks, women's, misses', and girls', cut and sewn from purchased fabric (except apparel contractors)
212319	Slate crushed and broken stone mining and/or beneficiating
212311	Slate mining or quarrying
327991	Slate products manufacturing
311611	Slaughtering, custom
311991	Slaw, cole, fresh, manufacturing
332212	Sledgehammers manufacturing
339932	Sleds, children's, manufacturing
621498	Sleep disorder centers and clinics, outpatient
337215	Sleeper mechanisms, convertible bed, manufacturing
314999	Sleeping bags manufacturing
316999	Sleeves, welder's, leather, manufacturing
333294	Slicing machinery (i.e., food manufacturing-type) manufacturing
339993	Slide fasteners (i.e., zippers) manufacturing
335312	Slip rings for motors and generators manufacturing
314129	Slipcovers, all materials, made from purchased materials
316212	Slipper socks made from purchased socks
315119	Slipper socks made in sock mills
422340	Slippers wholesaling
316219	Slippers, ballet, manufacturing
316212	Slippers, house, manufacturing
315192	Slips made in apparel knitting mills
315212	Slips, women's and girls', cut and sew apparel contractors

315231	Slips, women's, misses', and girls', cut and sewn from purchased fabric (except apparel contractors)
713290	Slot machine concession operators (i.e., supplying and servicing in others' facilities)
713290	Slot machine parlors
339999	Slot machines manufacturing
562212	Sludge disposal sites
327331	Slumped brick manufacturing
486990	Slurry pipeline transportation
332992	Small arms ammunition (i.e., 30 mm. or less, 1.18 inch or less) manufacturing
926110	Small business development agencies
811411	Small engine repair and maintenance shops
311615	Small game, processing, fresh, frozen, canned or cooked
311615	Small game, slaughtering, dressing and packing
421830	Smelting machinery and equipment wholesaling
331492	Smelting nonferrous metals (except aluminum, copper), secondary
331419	Smelting of nonferrous metals (except aluminum, copper), primary
333994	Smelting ovens manufacturing
334290	Smoke detectors manufacturing
421620	Smoke detectors, household-type, wholesaling
332995	Smoke generators manufacturing
311612	Smoked meats made from purchased carcasses
422990	Smokers' supplies wholesaling
453991	Smokers' supply stores
621999	Smoking cessation programs
312229	Smoking tobacco (e.g., cigarette, pipe) manufacturing
333311	Snack and confection vending machines manufacturing
722213	Snack bars (e.g., cookies, popcorn, pretzels), fixed location
722330	Snack stands, mobile
111219	Snap bean farming (i.e., bush and pole), field and seed production
333415	Snow making machinery manufacturing
333120	Snow plow attachments (except lawn, garden-type) manufacturing
333112	Snow plow attachments, lawn and garden-type, manufacturing
561790	Snow plowing driveways and parking lots (i.e., not combined with any other service)
561730	Snow plowing services combined with landscaping services (i.e., seasonal property maintenance services)
421810	Snow plows wholesaling
421810	Snowblowers (except household-type) wholesaling
333112	Snowblowers and throwers, residential-type, manufacturing
421820	Snowblowers, household-type, wholesaling
441229	Snowmobile dealers
711212	Snowmobile racetracks
711219	Snowmobile racing teams
336999	Snowmobiles and parts manufacturing
421110	Snowmobiles wholesaling
713990	Snowmobiling, recreational
312229	Snuff manufacturing
422940	Snuff wholesaling
327111	Soap dishes, vitreous china and earthenware, manufacturing
325611	Soaps (e.g., bar, chip, powder) manufacturing
212399	Soapstone mining and/or beneficiating
711211	Soccer clubs, professional or semiprofessional
713990	Soccer clubs, recreational
923130	Social Security Administration, federal
813319	Social change advocacy organizations
813410	Social clubs
813410	Social organizations, civic and fraternal
541720	Social science research and development services
813319	Social service advocacy organizations

624190	Social service agencies, family
624190	Social service centers, multipurpose
422120	Social stationery wholesaling
813920	Social workers' associations
541720	Sociological research and development services
541720	Sociology research and development services
332212	Sockets and socket sets manufacturing
315119	Socks knitting or knitting and finishing
315119	Socks, men's and boy's, manufacturing
316212	Socks, slipper, made from purchased socks
315119	Socks, slipper, made in sock mills
111421	Sod farming
561730	Sod laying services
325181	Soda ash manufacturing
212391	Soda ash mining and/or beneficiating
312111	Soda carbonated, manufacturing
311821	Soda crackers manufacturing
333415	Soda fountain cooling and dispensing equipment manufacturing
421440	Soda fountain fixtures (except refrigerated) wholesaling
311930	Soda fountain syrups manufacturing
312111	Soda pop manufacturing
325181	Sodium bicarbonate manufacturing
325181	Sodium carbonate (i.e., soda ash) manufacturing
212391	Sodium compounds prepared at beneficiating plants
212391	Sodium compounds, natural (except common salt), mining and/or beneficiating
325181	Sodium hydroxide (i.e., caustic soda) manufacturing
325188	Sodium hypochlorite manufacturing
325188	Sodium inorganic compounds, not specified elsewhere by process, manufacturing
325199	Sodium organic compounds, not specified elsewhere by process, manufacturing
325188	Sodium silicate (i.e., water glass) manufacturing
325188	Sodium sulfate manufacturing
337121	Sofa beds and chair beds, upholstered, manufacturing
337121	Sofas, convertible (except futons), manufacturing
337121	Sofas, upholstered, manufacturing
722213	Soft drink beverage bars, nonalcoholic, fixed location
311930	Soft drink concentrates (i.e., syrup) manufacturing
445299	Soft drink stores, bottled
333311	Soft drink vending machines manufacturing
312111	Soft drinks manufacturing
422490	Soft drinks wholesaling
311812	Soft pretzels made in a commercial bakery
325613	Softeners, leather or textile, manufacturing
541511	Software analysis and design services, custom computer
611420	Software application training
511210	Software computer, packaged, publishers
541519	Software installation services, computer
541511	Software programming services, custom computer
511210	Software publishers
511210	Software publishers, packaged
443120	Software stores, computer
421430	Software, computer, packaged, wholesaling
334611	Software, packaged, mass reproducing
321912	Softwood dimension lumber and stock, resawing purchased lumber
325191	Softwood distillates manufacturing
321212	Softwood veneer or plywood, manufacturing
562910	Soil remediation services
325998	Soil testing kits manufacturing
541380	Soil testing laboratories or services
334413	Solar cells manufacturing
421690	Solar cells wholesaling
333414	Solar energy heating equipment manufacturing

421720	Solar heating panels and equipment wholesaling
333414	Solar heating systems manufacturing
421330	Solar reflective film wholesaling
333992	Soldering equipment (except hand held) manufacturing
332212	Soldering guns and irons, handheld (including electric), manufacturing
335931	Solderless connectors (electric wiring devices) manufacturing
332911	Solenoid valves (except fluid power), industrial-type, manufacturing
332912	Solenoid valves, fluid power, manufacturing
334419	Solenoids for electronic applications manufacturing
541110	Solicitors' offices
922130	Solicitors' offices, government
562213	Solid waste combustors or incinerators, nonhazardous
562212	Solid waste landfills combined with collection and/or local hauling of nonhazardous waste materials
562212	Solid waste landfills, nonhazardous
711130	Soloists, independent musical
334511	Sonabuoys manufacturing
421690	Sonar equipment wholesaling
334511	Sonar fish finders manufacturing
334511	Sonar systems and equipment manufacturing
512230	Song publishers
512230	Song publishers and printing combined
711510	Song writers, independent
111199	Sorghum farming, field and seed production
311999	Sorghum syrup manufacturing
813410	Sororities (except residential)
721310	Sorority houses
115114	Sorting, grading, cleaning, and packing of fruits and vegetables
512191	Sound dubbing services, motion picture
421330	Sound insulation wholesaling
235420	Sound proofing construction contractors
512240	Sound recording studios (except integrated record companies)
512220	Sound recording, integrated production, reproduction, release, and distribution
512220	Sound recording, releasing, promoting, and distributing
624210	Soup kitchens
311423	Soup mixes made in a dehydration plant
311999	Soup mixes, dry, made from purchased dry ingredients
422490	Soups (except frozen) wholesaling
311422	Soups (except seafood) canning
311711	Soups, fish and seafood, canning
311412	Soups, frozen (except seafood), manufacturing
311712	Soups, frozen fish and shellfish, manufacturing
422420	Soups, frozen, wholesaling
311511	Sour cream manufacturing
453220	Souvenir shops
311941	Soy sauce manufacturing
311225	Soybean cooking oil made from purchased oils
111110	Soybean farming, field and seed production
311222	Soybean oil, cake, and meal, made in crushing mills
311222	Soybean oil, crude, manufacturing
311222	Soybean oil, deodorized, made in oil mills
311222	Soybean oil, refined, made in crushing mills
311222	Soybean protein isolates made in crushing mills
422510	Soybeans wholesaling
336419	Space capsules manufacturing
927110	Space flight operations, government
333414	Space heaters (except portable electric) manufacturing
927110	Space research and development
334220	Space satellites, communications, manufacturing
339113	Space suits manufacturing
481212	Space transportation, freight, nonscheduled
334511	Space vehicle guidance systems and equipment manufacturing

336414	Space vehicles, complete, manufacturing
311422	Spaghetti canning
311421	Spaghetti sauce canning
422490	Spaghetti wholesaling
311823	Spaghetti, dry, manufacturing
327113	Spark plug insulators, porcelain, manufacturing
336322	Spark plugs for internal combustion engines manufacturing
312130	Sparkling wine manufacturing
713940	Spas without accommodations, fitness
337129	Speaker cabinets (i.e., housings), wood, manufacturing
813410	Speaker clubs
334310	Speaker systems manufacturing
711410	Speakers' bureaus
711510	Speakers, independent
711510	Special effect technicians, independent
512191	Special effects for motion picture production, post-production
485991	Special needs passenger transportation services
336211	Special purpose highway vehicle (e.g., firefighting vehicles) assembling on purchased chassis
336120	Special purpose highway vehicles (e.g., firefighting vehicles) assembling on heavy chassis of own manufacture
336211	Special purpose highway vehicle (e.g., firefighting vehicles) bodies manufacturing
421830	Special purpose industrial machinery and equipment wholesaling
525990	Special purpose vehicles
445299	Specialty food stores
335311	Specialty transformers, electric, manufacturing
422210	Specialty-line pharmaceuticals wholesaling
334516	Spectrometers (e.g., electron diffraction, mass, NMR, Raman) manufacturing
541930	Speech (i.e., language) interpretation services
621340	Speech defect clinics
621340	Speech pathologists' offices (e.g., centers, clinics)
621340	Speech therapists' offices (e.g., centers, clinics)
333612	Speed changers (i.e., power transmission equipment) manufacturing
611699	Speed reading instruction
333612	Speed reducers (i.e., power transmission equipment) manufacturing
441310	Speed shops
711212	Speedways
621991	Sperm banks, human
111998	Spice farming
111419	Spice farming, grown under cover
311942	Spice grinding and blending
311942	Spice mixtures manufacturing
445299	Spice stores
311942	Spices and spice mix manufacturing
422490	Spices wholesaling
332913	Spigots, plumbing fixture fitting, manufacturing
321999	Spigots, wood, manufacturing
332618	Spikes made from purchased wire
331222	Spikes, iron or steel, made in wire drawing plants
421510	Spikes, metal, wholesaling
111219	Spinach farming, field, bedding plant and seed production
333292	Spindles for textile machinery manufacturing
313111	Spinning carpet and rug yarn from purchased fiber
333292	Spinning machinery for textiles manufacturing
333513	Spinning machines, metalworking, manufacturing
332116	Spinning unfinished metal products
313111	Spinning yarn from purchased fiber
312140	Spirits, distilled (except brandy), manufacturing
422820	Spirits, distilled, wholesaling
339113	Splints manufacturing
114119	Sponge gathering
422990	Sponges wholesaling
332999	Sponges, metal scouring, manufacturing

326199 Sponges, plastics, manufacturing
326299 Sponges, rubber, manufacturing
313311 Sponging broadwoven fabrics
313312 Sponging textile products and fabrics (except broadwoven)
313112 Spooling of yarn
313112 Spooling of yarns for the trade
321999 Spools (except for textile machinery), wood, manufacturing
333292 Spools for textile machinery manufacturing
315222 Sport coats (except fur, leather), men's and boys', cut and sewn from purchased fabric (except apparel contractors)
315292 Sport coats, fur (except apparel contractors), manufacturing
315211 Sport coats, fur, men's and boys', cut and sew apparel contractors
315292 Sport coats, leather (including artificial and tailored) (except apparel contractors), manufacturing
315211 Sport coats, leather (including artificial and tailored), men's and boys', cut and sew apparel contractors
315211 Sport coats, men's and boys', cut and sew apparel contractors
336112 Sport utility vehicles assembling on chassis of own manufacture
421110 Sport utility vehicles wholesaling
811490 Sporting equipment repair and maintenance without retailing new sports equipment
421910 Sporting firearms and ammunition wholesaling
339920 Sporting goods (except ammunition, clothing, footwear, small arms) manufacturing
421910 Sporting goods and supplies wholesaling
532292 Sporting goods rental
451110 Sporting goods stores
453310 Sporting goods stores, used
711310 Sports arena operators
611620 Sports camps (e.g., baseball, basketball, football), instructional

315228 Sports clothing (except team uniforms), men's and boys', cut and sewn from purchased fabric (except apparel contractors)
315239 Sports clothing (except team uniforms), women's, misses', and girls', cut and sewn from purchased fabric (except apparel contractors)
315191 Sports clothing made in apparel knitting mills
315211 Sports clothing, men's and boys', cut and sew apparel contractors
315299 Sports clothing, team uniforms, cut and sewn from purchased fabric (except apparel contractors)
315212 Sports clothing, women's and girls', cut and sew apparel contractors
713940 Sports club facilities, physical fitness
713990 Sports clubs (i.e., sports teams) not operating sports facilities, recreational
711211 Sports clubs, professional or semiprofessional
421910 Sports equipment and supplies wholesaling
532292 Sports equipment rental
711310 Sports event managers with facilities
711320 Sports event managers without facilities
711310 Sports event organizers with facilities
711320 Sports event organizers without facilities
711310 Sports event promoters with facilities
711320 Sports event promoters without facilities
711410 Sports figures' agents or managers
451110 Sports gear stores (e.g., outdoors, scuba, skiing)
712110 Sports halls of fame
611620 Sports instruction, camps, or schools
611620 Sports instructors, independent (i.e., not participating in sporting events)

711219	Sports professionals, independent (i.e., participating in sports events)
711310	Sports stadium operators
713990	Sports teams and leagues, recreational or youth
711211	Sports teams, professional or semiprofessional
621340	Sports therapists' offices (e.g., centers, clinics)
561599	Sports ticket offices
711219	Sports trainers, independent
422320	Sportswear, men's and boys', wholesaling
325612	Spot removers (except laundry presoaks) manufacturing
335129	Spotlights (except vehicular) manufacturing
336321	Spotlights, vehicular, manufacturing
422950	Spray painting equipment (except industrial-type) wholesaling
421830	Spray painting equipment, industrial-type, wholesaling
333111	Sprayers and dusters, farm-type, manufacturing
421820	Sprayers, farm, wholesaling
333912	Sprayers, manual pump, general purpose-type, manufacturing
115112	Spraying crops
561730	Spraying lawns
333111	Spreaders, farm-type, manufacturing
421820	Spreaders, fertilizer, wholesaling
333112	Spreaders, lawn and garden-type, manufacturing
311513	Spreads, cheese, manufacturing
312112	Spring waters, purifying and bottling
333513	Spring winding and forming machines, metalworking, manufacturing
332612	Springs and spring units for seats made from purchased wire
337910	Springs, assembled bed and box, made from purchased spring
334518	Springs, clock and watch, made from purchased wire
332611	Springs, heavy gauge, manufacturing
332612	Springs, light gauge (except clock, watch), made from purchased wire

332612	Springs, precision (except clock, watch), manufacturing
421510	Springs, steel, wholesaling
235110	Sprinkler system construction contractors
333999	Sprinkler systems, automatic fire, manufacturing
421850	Sprinkler systems, fire, wholesaling
421820	Sprinklers, agricultural, wholesaling
332919	Sprinklers, lawn, manufacturing
333613	Sprockets, power transmission equipment, manufacturing
332212	Squares, carpenters', metal, manufacturing
713940	Squash club facilities
339920	Squash equipment (except apparel) manufacturing
111219	Squash farming, field, bedding plant and seed production
711219	Stables, horse racing
713990	Stables, riding
333924	Stackers, industrial, truck-type, manufacturing
421830	Stackers, industrial, wholesaling
333924	Stackers, portable (except farm), manufacturing
233320	Stadium and arena construction
711310	Stadium operators
337127	Stadium seating manufacturing
531120	Stadium, no promotion of events, rental or leasing
561330	Staff leasing services
327211	Stained glass and stained glass products made in glass making plants
327215	Stained glass products made from purchased glass
331513	Stainless steel castings (except investment), unfinished, manufacturing
331111	Stainless steel made in steel mills
325510	Stains (except biological) manufacturing
422950	Stains wholesaling
325132	Stains, biological, manufacturing
332323	Stair railings, metal, manufacturing
321918	Stair railings, wood, manufacturing
332323	Stair treads, metal, manufacturing

326299 Stair treads, rubber, manufacturing
332323 Staircases, metal, manufacturing
332323 Stairs, metal, manufacturing
333921 Stairways, moving, manufacturing
321918 Stairwork (e.g., newel posts, railings, staircases, stairs), wood, manufacturing
332323 Stalls, metal, manufacturing
325998 Stamp pad ink manufacturing
339943 Stamp pads manufacturing
339911 Stamping coins
339943 Stamping devices, hand operated, manufacturing
333513 Stamping machines, metalworking, manufacturing
336370 Stamping metal motor vehicle body parts
336370 Stamping metal motor vehicle moldings and trims
332116 Stampings (except automotive, cans, cooking, closures, crowns), metal, unfinished, manufacturing
813920 Standards review committees, professional
926150 Standards, setting and management, agencies, government
337215 Stands (except wire), merchandise display, manufacturing
333991 Staplers and nailers, handheld power-driven, manufacturing
339942 Staplers manufacturing
332618 Staples made from purchased wire
421710 Staples wholesaling
331222 Staples, iron or steel, made in wire drawing plants
325520 Starch glues manufacturing
311221 Starches (except laundry) manufacturing
325612 Starches, laundry, manufacturing
336322 Starter and starter parts for internal combustion engines manufacturing
928120 State Department
522110 State commercial banks
522130 State credit unions
923110 State education departments
922120 State police
522120 State savings banks
921130 State tax commissions

334413 Static converters, integrated circuits, manufacturing
332410 Stationary power boilers manufacturing
327112 Stationery articles, pottery, manufacturing
323110 Stationery lithographic (offset) printing on a job-order basis
322233 Stationery made from purchased paper
453210 Stationery stores
422120 Stationery supplies wholesaling
327420 Statuary (e.g., gypsum, plaster of paris) manufacturing
422990 Statuary (except religious) wholesaling
327112 Statuary, clay and ceramic, manufacturing
327991 Statuary, marble, manufacturing
722110 Steak houses, full service
722211 Steak houses, limited service
812199 Steam baths
561790 Steam cleaning building exteriors
332410 Steam condensers manufacturing
611513 Steam fitters' apprenticeship training
235110 Steam fitting construction contractors
332919 Steam fittings, metal, manufacturing
333414 Steam heating equipment manufacturing
221330 Steam heating systems (i.e., suppliers of heat)
334512 Steam pressure controls, residential and commercial heating-type, manufacturing
221330 Steam production and distribution
333999 Steam separating machinery manufacturing
333319 Steam tables manufacturing
487110 Steam train excursions
332911 Steam traps, industrial-type, manufacturing
333611 Steam turbine generator set units manufacturing
333611 Steam turbines manufacturing
532411 Steamship rental or leasing
311613 Stearin, animal, rendering
332431 Steel cans manufacturing

http://www.ntis.gov/naics

331513	Steel castings (except investment), unfinished, manufacturing
332111	Steel forgings made from purchased steel, unfinished
331513	Steel foundries (except investment)
331512	Steel investment castings, unfinished, manufacturing
331512	Steel investment foundries
332312	Steel joists manufacturing
331111	Steel manufacturing
331111	Steel mill products (e.g., bar, plate, rod, sheet, structural shapes) manufacturing
331111	Steel mills
327910	Steel shot abrasives manufacturing
421510	Steel wholesaling
332999	Steel wool manufacturing
421510	Steel wool wholesaling
235910	Steel work structural, construction contractors
336330	Steering boxes, manual and power assist, manufacturing
336330	Steering columns, automotive, truck, and bus, manufacturing
336330	Steering wheels, automotive, truck, and bus, manufacturing
327215	Stemware made from purchased glass
327212	Stemware, glass, made in glass making plants
325910	Stencil inks manufacturing
339944	Stencil paper manufacturing
339943	Stencils for painting and marking (e.g., cardboard, metal) manufacturing
561410	Stenographic services (except court or stenographic reporting)
333313	Stenography machinery manufacturing
561492	Stenography services, public
561492	Stenotype recording services
332999	Stepladders, metal, manufacturing
321999	Stepladders, wood, manufacturing
337129	Stereo cabinets (i.e., housings), wood, manufacturing
532210	Stereo equipment rental
811211	Stereo equipment repair shops without retailing new stereo equipment
421620	Stereo equipment wholesaling
443112	Stereo stores (except automotive)
441310	Stereo stores, automotive
325212	Stereorubber manufacturing
339114	Sterilizers, dental, manufacturing
339113	Sterilizers, hospital and surgical, manufacturing
339111	Sterilizers, laboratory-type (except dental), manufacturing
325411	Steriods, uncompounded, manufacturing
339112	Stethoscopes manufacturing
488320	Stevedoring services
315211	Stitching, decorative and novelty, contractors on men's and boys' apparel
315212	Stitching, decorative and novelty, contractors on women's, girls', and infants' apparel
523120	Stock brokerages
711212	Stock car racetracks
711219	Stock car racing teams
711110	Stock companies, theatrical
523210	Stock exchanges
512199	Stock footage film libraries
523110	Stock options dealing (i.e., acting as a principal in dealing securities to investors)
514199	Stock photo agencies
523999	Stock quotation services
315111	Stockings, sheer, women's, misses', and girls', full-length and knee-length, knitting or knitting and finishing
488999	Stockyards (i.e., not for fattening or selling livestock), transportation
212319	Stone (except limestone and granite) beneficiating plants (e.g., grinding)
212311	Stone (except limestone and granite) mining or quarrying
332213	Stone cutting saw blades manufacturing
235410	Stone setting construction contractors
313311	Stone washing broadwoven fabrics
313312	Stone washing textile products, apparel, and fabrics (except broadwoven)

333298	Stone working machinery manufacturing
421320	Stone, building or crushed, wholesaling
212319	Stone, crushed and broken (except granite or limestone), mining and/or beneficiating
332212	Stonecutters' handtools, nonpowered, manufacturing
212399	Stones, abrasive (e.g., emery, grindstones, hones, pumice), mining and/or beneficiating
421940	Stones, precious and semiprecious, wholesaling
327999	Stones, synthetic, for gem stones and industrial use, manufacturing
327112	Stoneware (i.e., pottery products) manufacturing
212325	Stoneware clay mining and/or beneficiating
235410	Stonework construction contractors
332911	Stop valves, industrial-type, manufacturing
332913	Stopcock drains, plumbing, manufacturing
421610	Storage batteries (except automotive) wholesaling
335911	Storage batteries manufacturing
421390	Storage bins wholesaling
334112	Storage devices, computer, manufacturing
486210	Storage of natural gas
235910	Storage tanks metal, construction contractors
332420	Storage tanks, heavy gauge metal, manufacturing
421510	Storage tanks, metal, wholesaling
233320	Store construction
541850	Store display advertising services
337215	Store display fixtures manufacturing
421440	Store equipment (except furniture) wholesaling
235510	Store fixture construction contractors (i.e., built-in, on site)
421440	Store fixtures (except refrigerated) wholesaling
421210	Store furniture wholesaling
******	Stores—see type
562998	Storm basin cleanout services
332321	Storm doors and windows, metal, manufacturing
321911	Storm doors and windows, wood framed, manufacturing
711510	Storytellers, independent
312120	Stout brewing
332322	Stove boards, sheet metal, manufacturing
327123	Stove lining, clay, manufacturing
332322	Stove pipes and flues, sheet metal, manufacturing
421720	Stoves, cooking and heating (except electric), household-type, wholesaling
335221	Stoves, household-type cooking, manufacturing
333924	Straddle carriers, mobile, manufacturing
332211	Straight razors manufacturing
332911	Straightway (i.e., Y-type) valves, industrial-type, manufacturing
332618	Stranded wire, uninsulated, made from purchased wire
332999	Strappings, metal, manufacturing
316999	Straps (except watch), leather, manufacturing
316993	Straps, watch (except metal), manufacturing
339911	Straps, watch, precious metal, manufacturing
541611	Strategic planning consulting services
111333	Strawberry farming
234110	Street construction
335129	Street lighting fixtures (except traffic signals) manufacturing
511199	Street map guide publishers
485119	Street railway systems (except mixed mode), commuter
421810	Street sweeping and cleaning equipment wholesaling
454390	Street vendors (except food)
722330	Street vendors, food
234990	Streetcar line construction
336510	Streetcars and car equipment, urban transit, manufacturing

336211	Stretch limousines assembling on purchased chassis
314991	Strings manufacturing
339992	Strings, musical instrument, manufacturing
212113	Strip mining, anthracite, on own account
212111	Strip mining, bituminous coal or lignite, on own account
331421	Strip, copper and copper alloy, made from purchased copper or in integrated secondary smelting and rolling, drawing or extruding plants
331111	Strip, iron or steel, made in steel mills
211111	Stripper well production
325188	Strontium compounds, not specified elsewhere by process, manufacturing
212393	Strontium mineral mining and/or beneficiating
421510	Structural assemblies, metal, wholesaling
421390	Structural assemblies, prefabricated (except wood), wholesaling
421310	Structural assemblies, prefabricated wood, wholesaling
421320	Structural clay tile (except refractory) wholesaling
327121	Structural clay tile manufacturing
321213	Structural members, glue laminated or pre-engineered wood, manufacturing
331319	Structural shapes made by rolling purchased aluminum
331319	Structural shapes, aluminum, made in integrated secondary smelting and rolling mills
332312	Structural steel, fabricated, manufacturing
321213	Structural wood members (except trusses), fabricated, manufacturing
336330	Struts, automotive, truck, and bus, manufacturing
327999	Stucco and stucco products manufacturing

235420	Stucco construction contractors
321113	Stud mills
522294	Student Loan Marketing Association (SLMA)
813410	Student clubs
611710	Student exchange programs
522291	Student loan companies
813410	Students' associations
813410	Students' unions
233320	Studio construction
334220	Studio equipment, radio and television broadcasting, manufacturing
541430	Studios, commercial art
332322	Studs, sheet metal, manufacturing
339931	Stuffed toys (including animals) manufacturing
113310	Stump removing in the field
325110	Styrene made from refined petroleum or liquid hydrocarbons
324110	Styrene made in petroleum refineries
325211	Styrene resins manufacturing
332994	Submachine guns manufacturing
336611	Submarine building
334210	Subscriber loop equipment, telephone, manufacturing
513210	Subscription television networks
551114	Subsidiary management offices
623220	Substance abuse (i.e., alcoholism, drug addiction) halfway houses
623220	Substance abuse facilities, residential
813319	Substance abuse prevention advocacy organizations
621420	Substance abuse treatment centers and clinics (except hospitals), outpatient
335311	Substation transformers, electric power distribution, manufacturing
512191	Subtitling of motion picture film or video
485113	Suburban bus line services (except mixed mode)
485112	Suburban commuter rail systems (except mixed mode)
485111	Suburban transit systems, mixed mode (e.g., bus, commuter rail, subway combinations)

541850	Subway card display advertising services
336510	Subway cars manufacturing
421860	Subway cars wholesaling
234990	Subway construction
485119	Subway systems (except mixed mode), commuter
812320	Suede garment cleaning services
313311	Sueding broadwoven fabrics
313312	Sueding textile products and fabrics (except broadwoven)
111991	Sugar beet farming
115113	Sugar beets, machine harvesting
311221	Sugar made by wet milling corn
333294	Sugar refining machinery manufacturing
325998	Sugar substitutes (i.e., synthetic sweeteners blended with other ingredients) made from purchased synthetic sweeteners
325199	Sugar substitutes (i.e., synthetic sweeteners blended with other ingredients) made in synthetic sweetener establishments
311312	Sugar, cane, made from purchased raw cane sugar
311311	Sugar, clarified, granulated, and raw, made in sugarcane mill
311312	Sugar, confectionery, made from purchased raw cane sugar
311313	Sugar, confectionery, made from sugar beets
311311	Sugar, confectionery, made in sugarcane mill
311312	Sugar, granulated, made from purchased raw cane sugar
311313	Sugar, granulated, made from sugar beets
311311	Sugar, granulated, made in sugarcane mill
311312	Sugar, invert, made from purchased raw cane sugar
311313	Sugar, invert, made from sugar beets
311311	Sugar, invert, made in sugarcane mill
311313	Sugar, liquid, made from sugar beets
311311	Sugar, raw, made in sugarcane mill
422590	Sugar, raw, wholesaling
311312	Sugar, refined, made from purchased raw cane sugar
422490	Sugar, refined, wholesaling
111930	Sugarcane farming, field production
311311	Sugarcane mills
311311	Sugarcane refining
115113	Sugarcane, machine harvesting
624190	Suicide crisis centers
316991	Suitcases, all materials, manufacturing
315211	Suits (i.e., nontailored, tailored, work), men's and boys', cut and sew apparel contractors
315212	Suits (i.e., nontailored, tailored, work), women's, misses', girls', and infants', cut and sew apparel contractors
315191	Suits made in apparel knitting mills
339113	Suits, firefighting, manufacturing
315291	Suits, infants' (e.g., warm-up, jogging, snowsuits), cut and sewn from purchased fabric (except apparel contractors)
422320	Suits, men's and boys', wholesaling
315239	Suits, nontailored (e.g., jogging, snow suit, warm-up), women's, misses', and girls', cut and sewn from purchased fabric (except apparel contractors)
315228	Suits, nontailored (e.g., jogging, snow, ski, warm-up), men's and boys', cut and sewn from purchased fabric (except apparel contractors)
339113	Suits, space, manufacturing
315222	Suits, tailored, men's and boys', cut and sewn from purchased fabric (except apparel contractors)
315234	Suits, tailored, women's, misses', and girls', cut and sewn from purchased fabric (except apparel contractors)
325411	Sulfa drugs, uncompounded, manufacturing

http://www.ntis.gov/naics

325188	Sulfides and sulfites manufacturing
325188	Sulfur and sulfur compounds, not specified elsewhere by process, manufacturing
212393	Sulfur mining and/or beneficiating
211112	Sulfur recovered from natural gas
325188	Sulfur recovering or refining (except from sour natural gas)
325188	Sulfuric acid manufacturing
422690	Sulfuric acid wholesaling
325192	Sulphonated derivatives manufacturing
311423	Sulphured fruit and vegetables manufacturing
721214	Summer camps (except day instructional)
713990	Summer day camps (except instructional)
711110	Summer theaters
235110	Sump pump construction contractors
333911	Sump pumps, residential-type, manufacturing
115114	Sun drying of fruits and vegetables
111120	Sunflower farming, field and seed production
311223	Sunflower seed oil, cake and meal, made in crushing mills
446130	Sunglass stores
339115	Sunglasses and goggles manufacturing
421460	Sunglasses wholesaling
336399	Sunroofs and parts, automotive, truck, and bus, manufacturing
325620	Sunscreen lotions and oils manufacturing
315291	Sunsuits, infants', cut and sewn from purchased fabric (except apparel contractors)
325620	Suntan lotions and oils manufacturing
331111	Superalloys, iron or steel, manufacturing
331492	Superalloys, nonferrous based, made from purchased metals or scrap
445110	Supermarkets
325312	Superphosphates manufacturing
452910	Superstores (i.e., food and general merchandise)

921190	Supply agencies, government
332913	Supply line assemblies, plumbing (i.e., flexible hose with fittings), manufacturing
339113	Supports, orthopedic (e.g., abdominal, ankle, arch, kneecap), manufacturing
524126	Surety insurance carriers, direct
325613	Surface active agents manufacturing
422690	Surface active agents wholesaling
322226	Surface coating purchased paperboard
333120	Surface mining machinery (except drilling) manufacturing
335999	Surge suppressors manufacturing
621111	Surgeons' (except dental) offices (e.g., centers, clinics)
541940	Surgeons' offices, veterinary
621210	Surgeons', dental, offices (e.g., centers, clinics)
115112	Surgery on trees and vines
541940	Surgery services, veterinary
421450	Surgical appliances wholesaling
339112	Surgical clamps manufacturing
339113	Surgical dressings manufacturing
339113	Surgical implants manufacturing
811219	Surgical instrument repair and maintenance services
421450	Surgical instruments and apparatus wholesaling
339112	Surgical knife blades and handles manufacturing
339112	Surgical stapling devices manufacturing
339113	Surgical supplies (except medical instruments) manufacturing
421450	Surgical supplies wholesaling
334510	Surgical support systems (e.g., heart-lung machines) (except iron lungs) manufacturing
421450	Surgical towels wholesaling
311711	Surimi canning
311712	Surimi, fresh and frozen, manufacturing
541370	Surveying and mapping services (except geophysical)
421490	Surveying equipment and supplies wholesaling

334519 Surveying instruments manufacturing

541360 Surveying services, geophysical

611699 Survival training instruction

315999 Suspenders cut and sewn from purchased fabric (except apparel contractors)

315211 Suspenders, men's and boys', cut and sew apparel contractors

315212 Suspenders, women's, girls', and infants', cut and sew apparel contractors

339113 Sutures, surgical, manufacturing

487210 Swamp buggy operation

315299 Sweat bands cut and sewn from purchased fabric (except apparel contractors)

315191 Sweat bands made in apparel knitting mills

315211 Sweat bands, men's and boys', cut and sew apparel contractors

315212 Sweat bands, women's, girls', and infants', cut and sew apparel contractors

315191 Sweat pants made in apparel knitting mills

315291 Sweat pants, infants', cut and sewn from purchased fabric (except apparel contractors)

315228 Sweat pants, men's, boys', and unisex (i.e., sized without regard to gender), cut and sewn from purchased fabric (except apparel contractors)

315211 Sweat pants, men's, boys', and unisex, cut and sew apparel contractors

315212 Sweat pants, women's, girls', and infants', cut and sew apparel contractors

315239 Sweat pants, women's, misses', and girls', cut and sewn from purchased fabric (except apparel contractors)

315191 Sweat suits made in apparel knitting mills

315291 Sweat suits, infants', cut and sewn from purchased fabric (except apparel contractors)

315211 Sweat suits, men's and boys', cut and sew apparel contractors

315228 Sweat suits, men's and boys', cut and sewn from purchased fabric (except apparel contractors)

315212 Sweat suits, women's, girls', and infants', cut and sew apparel contractors

315239 Sweat suits, women's, misses', and girls', cut and sewn from purchased fabric (except apparel contractors)

315191 Sweaters made in apparel knitting mills

315291 Sweaters, infants', cut and sewn from purchased fabric (except apparel contractors)

315211 Sweaters, men's and boys', cut and sew apparel contractors

315228 Sweaters, men's and boys', cut and sewn from purchased fabric (except apparel contractors)

315212 Sweaters, women's, and girls', and infants', cut and sew apparel contractors

315239 Sweaters, women's, misses', and girls', cut and sewn from purchased fabric (except apparel contractors)

315191 Sweatshirts made in apparel knitting mills

315291 Sweatshirts, infants', cut and sewn from purchased fabric (except apparel contractors)

315211 Sweatshirts, men's and boys', cut and sew apparel contractors

315223 Sweatshirts, men's and boys', cut and sewn from purchased fabric (except apparel contractors)

315223 Sweatshirts, outerwear, unisex (sized without regard to gender), cut and sewn from purchased fabric (except apparel contractors)

315212 Sweatshirts, women's, girls', and infants', cut and sew apparel contractors

315232 Sweatshirts, women's, misses', and girls', cut and sewn from purchased fabric (except apparel contractors)

111219	Sweet corn farming, field and seed production
111219	Sweet potato farming, field and seed potato production
311999	Sweetening syrups (except pure maple) manufacturing
611620	Swimming instruction
325998	Swimming pool chemical preparations manufacturing
561790	Swimming pool cleaning and maintenance services
235990	Swimming pool construction contractors
326199	Swimming pool covers and liners, plastics, manufacturing
333319	Swimming pool filter systems manufacturing
333414	Swimming pool heaters manufacturing
453998	Swimming pool supply stores
713940	Swimming pools
421910	Swimming pools and equipment wholesaling
339920	Swimming pools, above ground, manufacturing
315191	Swimsuits made in apparel knitting mills
315291	Swimsuits, infants', cut and sewn from purchased fabric (except apparel contractors)
315211	Swimsuits, men's and boys', cut and sew apparel contractors
315228	Swimsuits, men's and boys', cut and sewn from purchased fabric (except apparel contractors)
315212	Swimsuits, women's, girls', and infants', cut and sew apparel contractors
315239	Swimsuits, women's, misses', and girls', cut and sewn from purchased fabric (except apparel contractors)
448190	Swimwear stores
422320	Swimwear, men's and boys', wholesaling
422330	Swimwear, women's, children's, and infants', wholesaling
311119	Swine feed, supplements, concentrates, and premixes, manufacturing
335932	Switch boxes, electrical wiring, manufacturing
335313	Switchboards and parts, power, manufacturing
421610	Switchboards, electrical distribution, wholesaling
335931	Switches for electrical wiring (e.g., pressure, pushbotton, snap, tumbler) manufacturing
334419	Switches for electronic applications manufacturing
335313	Switches, electric power (except pushbutton, snap, solenoid, tumbler), manufacturing
421610	Switches, electrical, wholesaling
421690	Switches, electronic, wholesaling
335931	Switches, outlet box mounting-type, manufacturing
334512	Switches, pneumatic positioning remote, manufacturing
335313	Switchgear and switchgear accessories, manufacturing
334210	Switching equipment, telephone, manufacturing
488210	Switching services, railroad
114111	Swordfish fishing
332211	Swords, nonprecious and precious plated metal, manufacturing
212313	Syenite (except nepheline) crushed and broken stone mining and/or beneficiating
212311	Syenite (except nepheline) mining or quarrying
212325	Syenite, nepheline, mining and/or beneficiating
711130	Symphony orchestras
813110	Synagogues
514110	Syndicates, news
339992	Synthesizers, music, manufacturing
311340	Synthetic chocolate manufacturing
325212	Synthetic rubber (i.e., vulcanizable elastomers) manufacturing
422690	Synthetic rubber wholesaling
327999	Synthetic stones, for gem stones and industrial use, manufacturing

325199 Synthetic sweeteners (i.e., sweetening agents) manufacturing

339112 Syringes, hypodermic, manufacturing

422490 Syrup (except fountain) wholesaling

311313 Syrup made from sugar beets

311930 Syrup, beverage, manufacturing

311312 Syrup, cane, made from purchased raw cane sugar

311311 Syrup, cane, made in sugarcane mill

311320 Syrup, chocolate, made from cacao beans

311330 Syrup, chocolate, made from purchased chocolate

311999 Syrup, corn (except wet milled), manufacturing

311221 Syrup, corn, made by wet milling

311930 Syrup, flavoring (except coffee based), manufacturing

311920 Syrup, flavoring, coffee based, manufacturing

422450 Syrup, fountain, wholesaling

111998 Syrup, pure maple (i.e., maple syrup reducing)

311999 Syrup, sweetening (except pure maple), manufacturing

311999 Syrup, table, artificially flavored, manufacturing

541512 Systems integration design consulting services, computer

541512 Systems integration design services, computer

448190 T-shirt shops, custom printed

315291 T-shirts, outerwear, infants', cut and sewn from purchased fabric (except apparel contractors)

315191 T-shirts, outerwear, made in apparel knitting mills

315223 T-shirts, outerwear, men's and boys', cut and sewn from purchased fabric (except apparel contractors)

315211 T-shirts, outerwear, men's, boys' and unisex, cut and sew apparel contractors

315223 T-shirts, outerwear, unisex (i.e., sized without regard to gender), cut and sewn from purchased fabric (except apparel contractors)

315212 T-shirts, outerwear, women's, girls', and infants', cut and sew apparel contractors

315232 T-shirts, outerwear, women's, misses', and girls', cut and sewn from purchased fabric (except apparel contractors)

315291 T-shirts, underwear, infants', cut and sewn from purchased fabric (except apparel contractors)

315192 T-shirts, underwear, made in apparel knitting mills

315211 T-shirts, underwear, men's and boys', cut and sew apparel contractors

315221 T-shirts, underwear, men's and boys', cut and sewn from purchased fabric (except apparel contractors)

315231 T-shirts, underwear, women's, misses', and girls', cut and sewn from purchased fabric (except apparel contractors)

315212 T-shirts, underwear, women's, misses', girls', and infants', cut and sew apparel contractors

334510 TENS (transcutaneous electrical nerve stimulator) manufacturing

325920 TNT (trinitrotoluene) manufacturing

334310 TV (television) sets manufacturing

532490 TV broadcasting and studio equipment rental or leasing

337124 TV stands and similar stands for consumer electronics, metal, manufacturing

337125 TV stands and similar stands for consumer electronics, plastics, manufacturing

337122 TV stands and similar stands for consumer electronics, wood, manufacturing

532299 Table and banquet accessory rental

327112 Table articles, earthenware, manufacturing

327112 Table articles, vitreous china, manufacturing

332211 Table cutlery, nonprecious and precious plated metal, manufacturing

339912	Table cutlery, precious metal, manufacturing
335121	Table lamps (i.e., lighting fixtures) manufacturing
311225	Table oil made from purchased oils
311221	Table oil, corn, made by wet milling
311942	Table salt manufacturing
327991	Table tops, marble, manufacturing
314129	Tablecloths (except paper) made from purchased materials
313249	Tablecloths made in a lace mills
313249	Tablecloths made in a warp knitting mills
313210	Tablecloths made in broadwoven fabric mills
313241	Tablecloths made in weft knitting mills
322291	Tablecloths, paper, made from purchased paper
337214	Tables (except wood), office-type, manufacturing
337124	Tables, metal household-type, manufacturing
337122	Tables, wood household-type, manufacturing
337211	Tables, wood, office-type, manufacturing
322233	Tablets (e.g., memo, note, writing) made from purchased paper
322121	Tablets (e.g., memo, note, writing) made in paper mills
421220	Tableware (except disposable, plated, precious) wholesaling
327215	Tableware made from purchased glass
327212	Tableware made in glass making plants
422130	Tableware, disposable, wholesaling
421940	Tableware, precious and plated, wholesaling
327112	Tableware, vitreous china, manufacturing
451110	Tack shops
451110	Tackle shops (i.e., fishing)
421710	Tacks wholesaling
332618	Tacks, metal, made from purchased wire
811490	Tailor shops, alterations only
332211	Tailor's scissors, nonelectric, manufacturing
421850	Tailors' supplies wholesaling
722211	Take out eating places
327992	Talc processing beyond beneficiation
325620	Talcum powders manufacturing
711410	Talent agencies
711410	Talent agents
541214	Talent payment services
325191	Tall oil (except skimmings) manufacturing
311611	Tallow produced in a slaughtering plant
311613	Tallow produced in rendering plant
334514	Tallying meters (except clocks, electrical instruments, watches) manufacturing
111320	Tangelo groves
111320	Tangerine groves
332995	Tank artillery manufacturing
336211	Tank bodies for trucks manufacturing
562998	Tank cleaning and disposal services, commercial or industrial
562991	Tank cleaning services, septic
315291	Tank tops, infants', cut and sewn from purchased fabric (except apparel contractors)
315211	Tank tops, men's and boys', cut and sew apparel contractors
315191	Tank tops, outerwear, made in apparel knitting mills
315223	Tank tops, outerwear, men's and boys', cut and sewn from purchased fabric (except apparel contractors)
315232	Tank tops, outerwear, women's, misses', and girls', cut and sewn from purchased fabric (except apparel contractors)
315192	Tank tops, underwear, made in apparel knitting mills
315221	Tank tops, underwear, men's and boys', cut and sewn from purchased fabric (except apparel contractors)

315231	Tank tops, underwear, women's, misses', and girls', cut and sewn from purchased fabric (except apparel contractors)
315212	Tank tops, women's, girls', and infants', cut and sew apparel contractors
336212	Tank trailer, liquid and dry bulk, manufacturing
336211	Tank trucks (e.g., fuel oil, milk, water) assembling on purchased chassis
484220	Tanker trucking (e.g., chemical, juice, milk, petroleum), local
484230	Tanker trucking (e.g., chemical, juice, milk, petroleum), long-distance
327390	Tanks, concrete, manufacturing
327111	Tanks, flush, vitreous china, manufacturing
332420	Tanks, heavy gauge metal, manufacturing
336992	Tanks, military (including factory rebuilding), manufacturing
421510	Tanks, storage metal, wholesaling
326199	Tanks, storage, plastics or fiberglass, manufacturing
316110	Tannery leather manufacturing
333298	Tannery machinery manufacturing
325191	Tannic acid (i.e., tannins) manufacturing
316110	Tanning and currying furs
325191	Tanning extracts and materials, natural, manufacturing
812199	Tanning salons
212299	Tantalite mining and/or beneficiating
212299	Tantalum ores mining and/or beneficiating
512120	Tape distribution for television
332212	Tape measures, metal, manufacturing
334310	Tape players and recorders, household-type, manufacturing
421620	Tape players and recorders, household-type, wholesaling
334112	Tape storage units (e.g., drive backups), computer peripheral equipment, manufacturing
512191	Tape transfer service
332991	Tapered roller bearings manufacturing
322231	Tapes (e.g., adding machine, calculator, cash register) made from purchased paper
322222	Tapes (e.g., cellophane, masking, pressure sensitive), gummed, made from purchased paper or other materials
313221	Tapes weaving
421690	Tapes, blank, audio and video, wholesaling
422120	Tapes, cellophane, wholesaling
334613	Tapes, magnetic recording (i.e., audio, data, video), blank, manufacturing
339113	Tapes, medical adhesive, manufacturing
421450	Tapes, medical and surgical, wholesaling
313230	Tapes, nonwoven fabric, manufacturing
421990	Tapes, prerecorded, audio or video, wholesaling
422310	Tapes, textile, wholesaling
313320	Tapes, varnished and coated (except magnetic), made from purchased fabric
333515	Taps and dies (i.e., a machine tool accessory) manufacturing
324121	Tar and asphalt paving mixtures made from purchased asphaltic materials
325191	Tar and tar oils made by distillation of wood
325192	Tar made by distillation of coal tar
324122	Tar paper made from purchased asphaltic materials and paper
324122	Tar roofing cements and coatings made from purchased asphaltic materials
336411	Target drones, aircraft, manufacturing
336413	Targets, trailer type, aircraft, manufacturing
541614	Tariff rate consulting services
314912	Tarpaulins made from purchased fabrics

311941	Tartar sauce manufacturing
812199	Tattoo parlors
722410	Taverns (i.e., drinking places)
561440	Tax collection services on a contract or fee basis
541110	Tax law attorneys' offices
523910	Tax liens dealing (i.e., acting as a principal in dealing tax liens to investors)
541213	Tax return preparation services
921130	Taxation departments
541850	Taxicab card advertising services
485310	Taxicab dispatch services
485310	Taxicab fleet operators
485310	Taxicab organizations
485310	Taxicab owner-operators
485310	Taxicab services
421110	Taxicabs wholesaling
711510	Taxidermists, independent
421850	Taxidermy supplies wholesaling
334514	Taximeters manufacturing
813319	Taxpayers' advocacy organizations
311920	Tea (except herbal) manufacturing
445299	Tea and coffee (i.e., packaged) stores
311920	Tea blending
111998	Tea farming
422490	Tea wholesaling
311920	Tea, herbal, manufacturing
312111	Tea, iced, manufacturing
311920	Tea, instant, manufacturing
561310	Teacher registries
333319	Teaching machines (e.g., flight simulators) manufacturing
421490	Teaching machines (except computers), electronic, wholesaling
315299	Team athletic uniforms cut and sewn from purchased fabric (except apparel contractors)
315211	Team athletic uniforms, men's and boys', cut and sew apparel contractors
315212	Team athletic uniforms, women's and girls', cut and sew apparel contractors
511120	Technical magazine and periodical publishers
511120	Technical magazine and periodical publishers and printing combined
323112	Technical magazines and periodicals flexographic printing without publishing
323111	Technical magazines and periodicals gravure printing without publishing
323110	Technical magazines and periodicals lithographic (offset) printing without publishing
323119	Technical magazines and periodicals printing (except flexographic, gravure, lithographic, screen) without publishing
323113	Technical magazines and periodicals screen printing without publishing
511130	Technical manual and paperback book publishers
511130	Technical manual and paperback book publishers and printing combined
323121	Technical manual paper (books) binding without printing
511130	Technical manual publishers
323117	Technical manuals and papers (books) printing and binding without publishing
323117	Technical manuals and papers (books) printing without publishing
421450	Teeth, dental, wholesaling
513322	Telecommunications carriers, cellular telephone
513310	Telecommunications carriers, wired
513310	Telecommunications networks, wired
513330	Telecommunications resellers
532490	Telecommunications equipment rental or leasing
234920	Telecommunications line (e.g., telephone, telegraph) construction
541618	Telecommunications management consulting services
235310	Telecommunications wiring installation contractors
513310	Telegram services
812990	Telegram services, singing
421690	Telegraph equipment wholesaling
561422	Telemarketing bureaus
561422	Telemarketing services on a contract or fee basis

513390	Telemetry and tracking system operations on a contract or fee basis
334416	Telephone and telegraph transformers, electronic component-type, manufacturing
334210	Telephone answering machines manufacturing
421620	Telephone answering machines wholesaling
561421	Telephone answering services
561422	Telephone call centers
334210	Telephone carrier line equipment manufacturing
334210	Telephone carrier switching equipment manufacturing
513310	Telephone carriers, facilities-based (except wireless)
513340	Telephone communications carriers, satellite
513330	Telephone communications resellers (except satellite)
513322	Telephone communications carriers, wireless (except satellite)
624190	Telephone counseling services
323112	Telephone directories flexographic printing without publishing
323111	Telephone directories gravure printing without publishing
323110	Telephone directories lithographic (offset) printing without publishing
323119	Telephone directories printing (except flexographic, gravure, lithographic, screen) without publishing
323113	Telephone directories screen printing without publishing
541870	Telephone directory distribution services, door-to-door
511140	Telephone directory publishers
511140	Telephone directory publishers and printing combined
811213	Telephone equipment repair and maintenance services without retailing new telephone equipment
421690	Telephone equipment wholesaling
561422	Telephone solicitation services on a contract or fee basis

443112	Telephone stores (including cellular)
514199	Telephone-based recorded information services
334210	Telephones (except cellular telephone) manufacturing
421690	Telephones wholesaling
334220	Telephones, cellular, manufacturing
334210	Telephones, coin operated, manufacturing
334113	Teleprinters (i.e., computer terminals) manufacturing
512191	Teleproduction services
333314	Telescopes manufacturing
334310	Television (TV) sets manufacturing
541840	Television advertising representatives (i.e., independent of media owners)
443112	Television and radio stores
513120	Television broadcasting networks
513120	Television broadcasting stations
337129	Television cabinets (i.e., housings), wood, manufacturing
421410	Television cameras wholesaling
512110	Television commercial production
511120	Television guide publishers
511120	Television guide publishers and printing combined
323112	Television guides flexographic printing without publishing
323111	Television guides gravure printing without publishing
323110	Television guides lithographic (offset) printing without publishing
323119	Television guides printing (except flexographic, gravure, lithographic, screen) without publishing
323113	Television guides screen printing without publishing
513220	Television operations multichannel multipoint distribution services (MMDS)
513220	Television operations, closed circuit
513220	Television operations, multipoint distribution system
454110	Television order, home shopping
334411	Television picture tubes manufacturing

711510	Television producers, independent
811211	Television repair services without retailing new televisions
421620	Television sets wholesaling
512110	Television show production
512120	Television show syndicators
513210	Television subscription services
334220	Television transmitting antennas and ground equipment manufacturing
334220	Television, closed-circuit equipment, manufacturing
813319	Temperance organizations
334512	Temperature controls, automatic, residential and commercial-types, manufacturing
334513	Temperature instruments, industrial process-type (except glass and bimetal thermometers), manufacturing
332811	Tempering metals and metal products for the trade
339115	Temples and fronts (i.e., eyeglass frames), ophthalmic, manufacturing
813110	Temples, religious
561320	Temporary employment services
561320	Temporary help services
624221	Temporary shelters (e.g., battered women's, homeless, runaway youth)
561320	Temporary staffing services
813990	Tenants' associations (except advocacy)
813319	Tenants' advocacy associations
813319	Tenants' associations, advocacy
713940	Tennis club facilities
713940	Tennis courts
711219	Tennis professionals, independent (i.e., participating in sports events)
315191	Tennis skirts made in apparel knitting mills
315212	Tennis skirts, women's and girls', cut and sew apparel contractors
315239	Tennis skirts, women's, misses', and girls', cut and sewn from purchased fabric (except apparel contractors)
336214	Tent trailers (hard top and soft top) manufacturing
314912	Tents made from purchased fabrics
334113	Terminals, computer, manufacturing
422710	Terminals, petroleum
561710	Termite control services
421510	Terneplate wholesaling
114119	Terrapin fishing
235430	Terrazzo construction contractors
327390	Terrazzo products, precast (except brick, block and pipe), manufacturing
611710	Test development and evaluation services, educational
525920	Testamentary trusts
421830	Testing and measuring equipment, electrical (except automotive), wholesaling
334519	Testing equipment (e.g., abrasion, shearing strength, tensile strength, torsion) manufacturing
541380	Testing laboratories (except medical, veterinary)
621511	Testing laboratories, medical
541940	Testing laboratories, veterinary
541940	Testing services for veterinarians
488190	Testing services, aircraft
611710	Testing services, educational
333993	Testing, weighing, inspecting, packaging machinery manufacturing
325411	Tetracycline, uncompounded, manufacturing
314911	Textile bags made from purchased woven or knitted materials
422990	Textile bags wholesaling
561990	Textile cutting services
541490	Textile design services
325613	Textile finishing assistants manufacturing
333292	Textile finishing machinery (e.g., bleaching, dyeing, mercerizing, printing) manufacturing
314999	Textile fire hose made from purchased material
561910	Textile folding and packaging services
327212	Textile glass fibers made in glass making plants
327112	Textile guides, porcelain, manufacturing

421830	Textile machinery and equipment wholesaling
333292	Textile making machinery (except sewing machines) manufacturing
233310	Textile mill construction
333292	Textile printing machinery manufacturing
313210	Textile products (except apparel) made in broadwoven fabric mills
313249	Textile products (except apparel) made in lace mills
313221	Textile products (except apparel) made in narrow woven fabric mills
313249	Textile products (except apparel) made in warp knitting mills
313241	Textile products (except apparel) made in weft knitting mills
313312	Textile products finishing
325613	Textile scouring agents manufacturing
313320	Textile waterproofing
422310	Textiles (except burlap, felt) wholesaling
325221	Texturizing cellulosic yarn made in the same establishment
333292	Texturizing machinery for textiles manufacturing
325222	Texturizing noncellulosic yarn made in the same establishment
313112	Texturizing purchased yarn
711110	Theater companies (except dance)
711120	Theater companies, dance
421410	Theater equipment (except seats) wholesaling
711310	Theater operators
337127	Theater seating manufacturing
531120	Theater, property operation, rental or leasing
711120	Theaters, dance
711110	Theaters, dinner
711110	Theaters, live theatrical production (except dance)
512131	Theaters, motion picture (except drive-in)
512132	Theaters, motion picture, drive-in
512131	Theaters, motion picture, indoor
512132	Theaters, outdoor motion picture
711320	Theatrical booking agencies (except motion picture)
711120	Theatrical dance productions, live
561310	Theatrical employment agencies
532490	Theatrical equipment (except costumes) rental or leasing
711310	Theatrical production managers with facilities
711320	Theatrical production managers without facilities
711310	Theatrical production organizers with facilities
711320	Theatrical production organizers without facilities
711310	Theatrical production promoters with facilities
711320	Theatrical production promoters without facilities
711110	Theatrical repertory companies
711110	Theatrical road companies
711110	Theatrical stock companies
711410	Theatrical talent agents
561599	Theatrical ticket offices
532220	Theatrical wardrobe and costume rental
713110	Theme parks, amusement
611310	Theological seminaries offering baccalaureate or graduate degrees
******	Therapists' offices—see type
421450	Therapy equipment wholesaling
326140	Thermal insulation, polystyrene foam, manufacturing
541380	Thermal testing laboratories or services
334415	Thermistors (except industrial process-type) manufacturing
333993	Thermoform, blister, and skin packaging machinery manufacturing
333220	Thermoforming machinery for plastics manufacturing
334519	Thermometer, liquid-in-glass and bimetal types (except medical), manufacturing
421450	Thermometers wholesaling
339112	Thermometers, medical, manufacturing
325211	Thermoplastic resins and plastics materials manufacturing
325211	Thermosetting plastics resins manufacturing

325212	Thermosetting vulcanizable elastomers manufacturing
334512	Thermostats (e.g., air-conditioning, appliance, comfort heating, refrigeration) manufacturing
336399	Thermostats, automotive, truck, and buses manufacturing
334413	Thin film integrated circuits manufacturing
115112	Thinning of crops, mechanical and chemical
711212	Thoroughbred racetracks
422310	Thread (except industrial) wholesaling
313312	Thread finishing
333292	Thread making machinery manufacturing
313113	Thread mills
313113	Thread, all fibers, manufacturing
421840	Thread, industrial, wholesaling
326299	Thread, rubber (except fabric covered), manufacturing
115113	Threshing service
453310	Thrift shops, used merchandise
325221	Throwing cellulosic yarn made in the same establishment
325222	Throwing noncellulosic yarn made in the same establishment
313112	Throwing purchased yarn
332991	Thrust roller bearings manufacturing
334413	Thyristors manufacturing
325412	Thyroid preparations manufacturing
325320	Tick powders or sprays manufacturing
561599	Ticket (e.g., airline, bus, cruise ship, sports, theatrical) offices
561599	Ticket (e.g., amusement, sports, theatrical) agencies
561599	Ticket (e.g., amusement, sports, theatrical) sales agencies
448150	Tie shops
327390	Ties, concrete, railroad, manufacturing
321113	Ties, wood, made from logs or bolts
421990	Ties, wood, wholesaling
235430	Tile construction contractors
333298	Tile making machinery (except kilns) manufacturing
444190	Tile stores, ceramic
327122	Tile, ceramic wall and floor, manufacturing
327121	Tile, clay, structural, manufacturing
327123	Tile, roofing and drain, clay, manufacturing
327123	Tile, sewer, clay, manufacturing
421320	Tile, structural clay (except refractory), wholesaling
333994	Tilemaking kilns manufacturing
326192	Tiles, floor (i.e., linoleum, rubber, vinyl), manufacturing
333112	Tillers, lawn and garden-type, manufacturing
421990	Timber and timber products (except lumber) wholesaling
113310	Timber piling
113310	Timber pole cutting
113110	Timber tracts operations
115310	Timber valuation
321113	Timbers, made from logs or bolts
321213	Timbers, structural, glue laminated or pre-engineered wood, manufacturing
334518	Time clocks and time recording devices manufacturing
334518	Time locks manufacturing
323118	Time planners/organizers and refills manufacturing
421420	Time recording machines wholesaling
561599	Time share exchange services, condominium
336312	Timing gears and chains, automotive and truck gasoline engine, manufacturing
325188	Tin compounds, not specified elsewhere by process, manufacturing
332999	Tin foil not made in rolling mills
421510	Tin plate wholesaling
331419	Tin refining, primary
325998	Tint and dye preparations, household-type (except hair), manufacturing
325620	Tints, dyes, and rinses, hair, manufacturing
421130	Tire and tube repair materials wholesaling

332618	Tire chains made from purchased wire
314992	Tire cord and fabric, all materials, manufacturing
336360	Tire covers made from purchased fabric
441320	Tire dealers, automotive
333220	Tire making machinery manufacturing
333220	Tire recapping machinery manufacturing
421830	Tire recapping machinery wholesaling
326211	Tire repair materials manufacturing
811198	Tire repair shops (except retreading), automotive
326212	Tire retreading, recapping or rebuilding
333220	Tire shredding machinery manufacturing
421130	Tire tubes, motor vehicle, wholesaling
326211	Tires (e.g., pneumatic, semi-pneumatic, solid rubber) manufacturing
421130	Tires, motor vehicle, wholesaling
326199	Tires, plastics, manufacturing
421930	Tires, scrap, wholesaling
421130	Tires, used (except scrap), wholesaling
111421	Tissue culture farming
322121	Tissue paper stock manufacturing
422130	Tissue paper, toilet and facial, wholesaling
325131	Titanium based pigments manufacturing
332112	Titanium forgings made from purchased metals, unfinished
212299	Titanium ores mining and/or beneficiating
331419	Titanium refining, primary
541191	Title abstract companies, real estate
541191	Title companies, real estate
524127	Title insurance carriers, real estate, direct
541191	Title search companies, real estate
512191	Titling of motion picture film or video
335211	Toaster ovens, household-type electric, manufacturing
421620	Toasters, electric, wholesaling
335211	Toasters, household-type electric, manufacturing
422940	Tobacco (except leaf) wholesaling
422590	Tobacco auction markets
111910	Tobacco farming, field and seed production
115114	Tobacco grading
312210	Tobacco leaf processing and aging
339999	Tobacco pipes manufacturing
333298	Tobacco processing machinery (except farm-type) manufacturing
312229	Tobacco products (e.g., chewing, smoking, snuff) manufacturing
422940	Tobacco products wholesaling
312229	Tobacco products, imitation (except cigarettes) manufacturing
312210	Tobacco stemming and redrying
453991	Tobacco stores
422590	Tobacco, leaf, wholesaling
311340	Toffee manufacturing
311991	Tofu (i.e., bean curd) (except frozen desserts) manufacturing
311520	Tofu frozen desserts manufacturing
332722	Toggle bolts, metal, manufacturing
325612	Toilet bowl cleaners manufacturing
332998	Toilet fixtures manufacturing
326191	Toilet fixtures, plastics, manufacturing
327111	Toilet fixtures, vitreous china, manufacturing
316993	Toilet kits and cases (except metal) manufacturing
339911	Toilet kits and cases, precious metal, manufacturing
322291	Toilet paper made from purchased paper
322121	Toilet paper made in paper mills
325620	Toilet preparations (e.g., cosmetics, deodorants, perfumes) manufacturing
422210	Toilet preparations wholesaling
562991	Toilet renting and/or servicing, portable

321999	Toilet seats, wood, manufacturing
422210	Toilet soaps wholesaling
422130	Toilet tissue wholesaling
422210	Toiletries wholesaling
334210	Toll switching equipment, telephone, manufacturing
325110	Toluene made from refined petroleum or liquid hydrocarbons
324110	Toluene made in petroleum refineries
325192	Toluidines manufacturing
111219	Tomato farming (except under cover), field, bedding plant and seed production
325992	Toner cartridges manufacturing
325992	Toner cartridges rebuilding
422120	Toner cartridges wholesaling
325132	Toners (except electrostatic, photographic) manufacturing
325992	Toners, electrostatic and photographic, manufacturing
339113	Tongue depressors manufacturing
332439	Tool boxes, light gauge metal, manufacturing
321999	Tool handles, wood, turned and shaped, manufacturing
541420	Tool industrial design services
444130	Tool stores, power and hand (except outdoor)
333515	Tools and accessories for machine tools manufacturing
421120	Tools and equipment, motor vehicle, wholesaling
421710	Tools, hand (except motor vehicle, machinists' precision tools), wholesaling
332212	Tools, hand, metal blade (e.g., putty knives, scrapers, screw drivers)
333991	Tools, handheld power-driven, manufacturing
332212	Tools, handheld, nonpowered (except kitchen-type), manufacturing
421830	Tools, machinists' precision, wholesaling
332212	Tools, woodworking edge (e.g., augers, bits, countersinks), manufacturing

339994	Toothbrushes (except electric) manufacturing
422210	Toothbrushes (except electric) wholesaling
335211	Toothbrushes, electric, manufacturing
421620	Toothbrushes, electric, wholesaling
325611	Toothpastes, gels, and tooth powders manufacturing
321999	Toothpicks, wood, manufacturing
541370	Topographic mapping services
541370	Topographic surveying services
422490	Toppings (except fountain) wholesaling
336399	Tops, convertible automotive, manufacturing
332995	Torpedo tubes manufacturing
332993	Torpedoes manufacturing
336350	Torque converters, automotive, truck, and bus, manufacturing
332611	Torsion bar manufacturing
311919	Tortilla chips manufacturing
311830	Tortillas manufacturing
334514	Totalizing fluid meters manufacturing
334514	Totalizing meters (except aircraft), consumption registering, manufacturing
422990	Toupees wholesaling
487110	Tour bus, scenic and sightseeing, operation
561520	Tour operators (i.e., arranging and assembling tours)
561591	Tourism bureaus
713990	Tourist guide services
721199	Tourist homes
561591	Tourist information bureaus
336413	Tow targets, aircraft, manufacturing
336211	Tow trucks (including tilt and load) assembling on purchased chassis
336611	Towboat building and repairing
327111	Towel bar holders, vitreous china and earthenware, manufacturing
325620	Towelettes, premoistened, manufacturing
313210	Towels and washcloths made in broadwoven fabric mills
313249	Towels and washcloths made in warp knitting mills

313241	Towels and washcloths made in weft knitting mills
314129	Towels or washcloths made from purchased fabrics
421840	Towels, industrial, wholesaling
322291	Towels, paper, made from purchased paper
322121	Towels, paper, made in paper mills
421450	Towels, surgical, wholesaling
234920	Tower construction, radio and television transmitting/receiving
336399	Towing bars and systems manufacturing
483211	Towing service, inland waters (except on Great Lakes system)
488410	Towing services, motor vehicle
233210	Town house construction
531110	Town house rental or leasing
233220	Town house-type apartment construction
541320	Town planning services
562910	Toxic material abatement services
562910	Toxic material removal contractors
325414	Toxoids (e.g., diphtheria, tetanus) manufacturing
451120	Toy stores
339932	Toys (except dolls, stuffed toys) manufacturing
421920	Toys (including electronic) wholesaling
339931	Toys, stuffed, manufacturing
335121	Track lighting fixtures and equipment, residential, electric, manufacturing
532490	Tractor, farm, rental or leasing
532490	Tractor, garden, rental or leasing
333120	Tractors and attachments, construction-type, manufacturing
333111	Tractors and attachments, farm-type, manufacturing
333112	Tractors and attachments, lawn and garden-type, manufacturing
333120	Tractors, crawler, manufacturing
421820	Tractors, farm and garden, wholesaling
421110	Tractors, highway, wholesaling
333924	Tractors, industrial, manufacturing
421830	Tractors, industrial, wholesaling
336120	Tractors, truck for highway use, assembled on chassis of own manufacture
813910	Trade associations
522293	Trade banks (i.e., international trade financing)
323121	Trade binding services
926110	Trade commissions, government
561920	Trade fair managers
561920	Trade fair organizers
561920	Trade fair promoters
511120	Trade journal publishers
511120	Trade journal publishers and printing combined
323112	Trade journals flexographic printing without publishing
323111	Trade journals gravure printing without publishing
323110	Trade journals lithographic (offset) printing without publishing
323119	Trade journals printing (except flexographic, gravure, lithographic, screen) without publishing
323113	Trade journals screen printing without publishing
511120	Trade magazine and periodical publishers
511120	Trade magazine and periodical publishers and printing combined
323112	Trade magazines and periodicals flexographic printing without publishing
323111	Trade magazines and periodicals gravure printing without publishing
323110	Trade magazines and periodicals lithographic (offset) printing without publishing
323119	Trade magazines and periodicals printing (except flexographic, gravure, lithographic, screen) without publishing
323113	Trade magazines and periodicals screen printing without publishing

http://www.ntis.gov/naics

561920	Trade show managers
561920	Trade show organizers
561920	Trade show promoters
611513	Trade union apprenticeship training programs
813930	Trade unions (except apprenticeship programs)
533110	Trademark licensing
452990	Trading posts, general merchandise
334290	Traffic advisory and signalling systems manufacturing
541330	Traffic engineering consulting services
235210	Traffic lane painting construction contractors
514110	Traffic reporting services
334290	Traffic signals manufacturing
713990	Trail riding, recreational
234990	Trailer camp construction
336399	Trailer hitches, motor vehicle, manufacturing
421120	Trailer parts, new, wholesaling
336214	Trailers for transporting horses (except fifth-wheel type) manufacturing
336214	Trailers, camping, manufacturing
336212	Trailers, fifth-wheel type, for transporting horses, manufacturing
421830	Trailers, industrial, wholesaling
421110	Trailers, motor vehicle, wholesaling
115210	Training horses (except racehorses)
711219	Training race dogs
711219	Training racehorses
713990	Trampoline facilities, recreational
485119	Tramway systems (except mixed mode), commuter
325412	Tranquilizer preparations manufacturing
336350	Transaxles, automotive, truck, and bus, manufacturing
334220	Transceivers (i.e., transmitter-receiver units) manufacturing
561410	Transcription services
334510	Transcutaneous electrical nerve stimulators (TENS) manufacturing
334419	Transducers (except pressure) manufacturing

523999	Transfer agencies, securities
421610	Transformers (except electronic) wholesaling
334416	Transformers, electronic component-types, manufacturing
421690	Transformers, electronic, wholesaling
335311	Transformers, separate solid-state arc-welding, manufacturing
334413	Transistors manufacturing
421690	Transistors wholesaling
541850	Transit advertising services
922120	Transit police
926120	Transit systems and authorities, nonoperating
485111	Transit systems, mixed mode (e.g., bus, commuter rail, subway combinations)
327320	Transit-mixed concrete manufacturing
624229	Transitional housing agencies
541930	Translation services, language
335311	Transmission and distribution voltage regulators manufacturing
336399	Transmission coolers manufacturing
421610	Transmission equipment, electrical, wholesaling
325998	Transmission fluids, synthetic, manufacturing
221121	Transmission of electric power
335932	Transmission pole and line hardware manufacturing
811113	Transmission repair shops, automotive
332312	Transmission tower sections, fabricated structural metal, manufacturing
336350	Transmissions and parts, automotive, truck, and bus, manufacturing
334513	Transmitters, industrial process control-type, manufacturing
115112	Transplanting services
******	Transportation—see mode
926120	Transportation departments, nonoperating
421860	Transportation equipment and supplies (except marine pleasure craft, motor vehicles) wholesaling

336360 Transportation equipment seating manufacturing

541614 Transportation management consulting services

212319 Trap rock crushed and broken stone mining and/or beneficiating

332913 Traps, water, manufacturing

713990 Trapshooting facilities, recreational

333319 Trash and garbage compactors, commercial-type, manufacturing

335228 Trash and garbage compactors, household-type, manufacturing

562111 Trash collection services

326199 Trash containers, plastics, manufacturing

562213 Trash disposal combustors or incinerators

562212 Trash disposal landfills

562111 Trash hauling, local

484230 Trash hauling, long-distance

621493 Trauma centers (except hospitals), freestanding

561510 Travel agencies

511130 Travel guide book publishers

511130 Travel guide book publishers and printing combined

323117 Travel guide books printing and binding without publishing

323117 Travel guide books printing without publishing

561520 Travel tour operators

721211 Travel trailer campsites

441210 Travel trailer dealers

421110 Travel trailers (e.g., tent trailers) wholesaling

336214 Travel trailers, recreational, manufacturing

522390 Travelers' check issuance services

711190 Traveling shows, carnival

334411 Traveling wave tubes manufacturing

212312 Travertine crushed and broken stone mining and/or beneficiating

322299 Trays, food, molded pulp, manufacturing

332618 Trays, wire, made from purchased wire

921130 Treasurers offices', government

321114 Treating purchased wood and wood products

111335 Tree nut farming

311225 Tree nut oils (e.g., tung, walnut) made from purchased oils

311223 Tree nut oils (e.g., tung, walnut) made in crushing mill

113210 Tree seed extracting

113210 Tree seed gathering

113210 Tree seed growing for reforestation

561730 Tree services (e.g., bracing, planting, pruning, removal, spraying, surgery, trimming)

339999 Trees and plants, artificial, manufacturing

422930 Trees wholesaling

921150 Tribal councils, American Indian or Alaska Native

921150 Tribal courts, American Indian or Alaska Native

339932 Tricycles (except metal) manufacturing

336991 Tricycles, metal, adult and children's, manufacturing

332321 Trim and molding (except motor vehicle), metal, manufacturing

332321 Trim, metal, manufacturing

333112 Trimmers, hedge, electric, manufacturing

332212 Trimmers, hedge, nonelectric, manufacturing

333112 Trimmers, string, lawn and garden-type, manufacturing

325920 Trinitrotoluene (TNT) manufacturing

333315 Tripods, camera and projector, manufacturing

485119 Trolley systems (except mixed mode), commuter

487110 Trolley, scenic and sightseeing, operation

421940 Trophies wholesaling

332999 Trophies, nonprecious and precious plated metal, manufacturing

339912 Trophies, precious (except precious plated) metal, manufacturing

453998 Trophy (including awards and plaques) shops

112511 Tropical fish production, farm raising

http://www.ntis.gov/naics

422990	Tropical fish wholesaling
315191	Trousers made in apparel knitting mills
315211	Trousers, men's and boys', cut and sew apparel contractors
315224	Trousers, men's and boys', cut and sewn from purchased fabric (except apparel contractors)
114111	Trout fishing
112511	Trout production, farm raising
332212	Trowels manufacturing
532120	Truck (except industrial) rental or leasing
233310	Truck and automobile assembly plant construction
811192	Truck and bus washes
336211	Truck bodies and cabs manufacturing
336211	Truck bodies assembling on purchased chassis
336214	Truck campers (i.e., slide-in campers) manufacturing
441310	Truck cap stores
611519	Truck driving schools
111219	Truck farming, field, bedding plant and seed production
421120	Truck parts, new, wholesaling
811111	Truck repair shops, general
447190	Truck stops
532120	Truck tractor rental or leasing
336120	Truck tractors for highway use, assembling on chassis of own manufacture
336211	Truck tractors for highway use, assembling on purchased chassis
421110	Truck tractors, road, wholesaling
421110	Truck trailers wholesaling
488490	Truck weighing station operation
532490	Truck, industrial, rental or leasing
327320	Truck-mixed concrete manufacturing
488490	Trucking terminals, independently operated
484210	Trucking used household, office, or institutional furniture and equipment
484110	Trucking, general freight, local
484122	Trucking, general freight, long-distance, less-than-truckload (LTL)
484121	Trucking, general freight, long-distance, truckload
484220	Trucking, specialized freight (except used goods), local
484230	Trucking, specialized freight (except used goods), long-distance
336120	Trucks, heavy, assembling on chassis of own manufacture
333924	Trucks, industrial, manufacturing
421830	Trucks, industrial, wholesaling
336112	Trucks, light duty, assembling on chassis of own manufacture
333120	Trucks, off-highway, manufacturing
421110	Trucks, road, wholesaling
316991	Trunks (i.e., luggage), all materials, manufacturing
332313	Truss plates, metal, manufacturing
321214	Trusses, wood, glue laminated or metal connected, manufacturing
523991	Trust administration, personal investment
813211	Trusts, charitable, awarding grants
813211	Trusts, educational, awarding grants
813211	Trusts, religious, awarding grants
325612	Tub and tile cleaning preparations manufacturing
331210	Tube (e.g., heavy riveted, lock joint, seamless, welded) made from purchased iron or steel
331316	Tube blooms made by extruding purchased aluminum
331316	Tube blooms, aluminum, made in integrated secondary smelting and extruding mills
331316	Tube made by drawing or extruding purchased aluminum
333516	Tube rolling mill machinery, metalworking, manufacturing
331111	Tube rounds, iron or steel, made in steel mills
331316	Tube, aluminum, made in integrated secondary smelting and drawing plants
331316	Tube, aluminum, made in integrated secondary smelting and extruding mills
331111	Tube, iron or steel, made in steel mills

331315 Tube, welded, aluminum, made by flat rolling purchased aluminum

331315 Tube, welded, aluminum, made in integrated secondary smelting and flat rolling mills

332996 Tubes made from purchased metal pipe

334517 Tubes, X-ray, manufacturing

334411 Tubes, cathode ray, manufacturing

334411 Tubes, electron, manufacturing

421690 Tubes, electronic (e.g., industrial, receiving, transmitting), wholesaling

334411 Tubes, klystron, manufacturing

332999 Tubing, flexible metal, manufacturing

421510 Tubing, metal, wholesaling

326299 Tubing, rubber (except extruded, molded, lathe-cut), manufacturing

332998 Tubs, laundry and bath, metal, manufacturing

333292 Tufting machinery for textiles manufacturing

336611 Tugboat building

532411 Tugboat rental or leasing

488330 Tugboat services, harbor operation

114111 Tuna fishing

811118 Tune-up shops, automotive

325188 Tungsten compounds, not specified elsewhere by process, manufacturing

212299 Tungsten ores mining and/or beneficiating

234120 Tunnel construction

333611 Turbine generator set units manufacturing

333611 Turbines (except aircraft) manufacturing

421830 Turbines (except transportation) wholesaling

421860 Turbines, transportation, wholesaling

561730 Turf (except artificial) installation services

112330 Turkey egg production

311119 Turkey feeds, prepared, manufacturing

112340 Turkey hatcheries

112330 Turkey production

812199 Turkish baths

333512 Turning machines (i.e., lathes), metalworking, manufacturing

325191 Turpentine made by distillation of pine gum or pine wood

422690 Turpentine wholesaling

332995 Turrets, gun, manufacturing

114119 Turtle fishing

112519 Turtle production, farm raising

611691 Tutoring, academic

532220 Tuxedo rental

315211 Tuxedos cut and sew apparel contractors

315222 Tuxedos cut and sewn from purchased fabric (except apparel contractors)

421840 Twine wholesaling

314991 Twines manufacturing

421830 Twist drills wholesaling

323122 Typesetting (i.e., computer controlled, hand, machine)

333293 Typesetting machinery manufacturing

422120 Typewriter paper wholesaling

333313 Typewriters manufacturing

421420 Typewriters wholesaling

561410 Typing services

531130 U-lock storage

311514 UHT (ultra high temperature) milk manufacturing

335999 UPS (uninterruptible power supplies) manufacturing

336411 Ultra light aircraft manufacturing

335999 Ultrasonic cleaning equipment (except dental, medical) manufacturing

339114 Ultrasonic dental equipment manufacturing

339113 Ultrasonic medical cleaning equipment manufacturing

334510 Ultrasonic medical equipment manufacturing

333992 Ultrasonic welding equipment manufacturing

621512	Ultrasound imaging centers
339999	Umbrellas manufacturing
322122	Uncoated groundwood paper mills
811198	Undercoating shops, automotive
333131	Underground mining machinery manufacturing
812210	Undertaker services
421850	Undertakers' equipment and supplies wholesaling
315192	Underwear made in apparel knitting mills
315192	Underwear shirts made in apparel knitting mills
315291	Underwear shirts, infants', cut and sewn from purchased fabric (except apparel contractors)
315211	Underwear shirts, men's and boys', cut and sew apparel contractors
315221	Underwear shirts, men's and boys', cut and sewn from purchased fabric (except apparel contractors)
315212	Underwear shirts, women's, girls', and infants', cut and sew apparel contractors
315231	Underwear shirts, women's, misses', and girls', cut and sewn from purchased fabric (except apparel contractors)
315192	Underwear shorts made in apparel knitting mills
315291	Underwear shorts, infants', cut and sewn from purchased fabric (except apparel contractors)
315211	Underwear shorts, men's and boys', cut and sew apparel contractors
315221	Underwear shorts, men's and boys', cut and sewn from purchased fabric (except apparel contractors)
315212	Underwear shorts, women's, girls', and infants', cut and sew apparel contractors
315231	Underwear shorts, women's, misses', and girls', cut and sewn from purchased fabric (except apparel contractors)
315291	Underwear, infants', cut and sewn from purchased fabric (except apparel contractors)
315211	Underwear, men's and boys', cut and sew apparel contractors
315221	Underwear, men's and boys', cut and sewn from purchased fabric (except apparel contractors)
422320	Underwear, men's and boys', wholesaling
422330	Underwear, women's, children's, and infants', wholesaling
315231	Underwear, women's, misses', and girls', cut and sewn from purchased fabric (except apparel contractors)
315212	Underwear, women's, misses', girls', and infants', cut and sew apparel contractors
923130	Unemployment insurance program administration
812331	Uniform (except industrial) supply services
448190	Uniform stores (except athletic)
451110	Uniform stores, athletic
812332	Uniform supply services, industrial
315299	Uniforms, band, cut and sewn from purchased fabric (except apparel contractors)
315211	Uniforms, band, men's and boys', cut and sew apparel contractors
315212	Uniforms, band, women's, girls', and infants', cut and sew apparel contractors
315211	Uniforms, dress (e.g., fire fighter, military, police), men's, cut and sew apparel contractors
315222	Uniforms, dress (e.g., fire fighter, military, police), men's, cut and sewn from purchased fabric (except apparel contractors)
315212	Uniforms, dress (e.g., military, police, fire fighter), women's, cut and sew apparel contractors
315234	Uniforms, dress, tailored (e.g., fire fighter, military, police), women's, misses', and girls', cut and sewn from purchased fabric (except apparel contractors)
315299	Uniforms, team athletic, cut and sewn from purchased fabric (except apparel contractors)

315211	Uniforms, team athletic, men's and boys', cut and sew apparel contractors
315212	Uniforms, team athletic, women's and girls', cut and sew apparel contractors
335999	Uninterruptible power supplies (UPS) manufacturing
525110	Union pension funds
813930	Unions (except apprenticeship programs), labor
813930	Unions (except apprenticeship programs), labor
332919	Unions, pipe, metal (except made from purchased pipe), manufacturing
448140	Unisex clothing stores
422330	Unisex clothing wholesaling
812112	Unisex hair stylist shops
525990	Unit investment trust funds
323116	Unit set forms (e.g., manifold credit card slips) printing
928120	United Nations
813219	United fund councils
813219	United funds for colleges
333613	Universal joints (except aircraft, motor vehicle) manufacturing
336413	Universal joints, aircraft, manufacturing
336350	Universal joints, automotive, truck, and bus, manufacturing
611310	Universities
813410	University clubs
923110	University regents or boards, government
311812	Unleavened bread made in commercial bakeries
337121	Upholstered furniture, household-type, custom, manufacturing
337121	Upholstered furniture, household-type, on frames of any material, manufacturing
421850	Upholsterers' equipment and supplies (except fabrics) wholesaling
314999	Upholstering filling (except nonwoven fabric) manufacturing
811420	Upholstery (except motor vehicle) repair services
561740	Upholstery cleaning services
451130	Upholstery materials stores
811121	Upholstery shops, automotive
332612	Upholstery springs and spring units made from purchased wire
332111	Upset forgings made from purchased iron or steel, unfinished
332112	Upset forgings made from purchased nonferrous metals, unfinished
325188	Uranium compounds, not specified elsewhere by process, manufacturing
212291	Uranium ores mining and/or beneficiating
325188	Uranium, enriched, manufacturing
212291	Uranium-radium-vanadium ore mine site development for own account
212291	Uranium-radium-vanadium ores mining and/or beneficiating
485113	Urban bus line services (except mixed mode)
485112	Urban commuter rail systems (except mixed mode)
925120	Urban planning commissions, government
541320	Urban planning services
485111	Urban transit systems, mixed mode (e.g., bus, commuter rail, subway combinations)
325311	Urea manufacturing
325211	Urea resins manufacturing
326150	Urethane foam products manufacturing
325212	Urethane rubber manufacturing
621493	Urgent medical care centers and clinics (except hospitals), freestanding
332998	Urinals, metal, manufacturing
326191	Urinals, plastics, manufacturing
327111	Urinals, vitreous china, manufacturing
327420	Urns (e.g., gypsum, plaster of paris) manufacturing
441229	Used aircraft dealers
441310	Used automotive parts stores
441320	Used automotive tire dealers
453310	Used bicycle (except motorized) shops

http://www.ntis.gov/naics

441222	Used boat dealers
441120	Used car dealers
421110	Used cars wholesaling
484210	Used household and office goods moving
453930	Used manufactured (mobile) home dealers
453310	Used merchandise stores
441221	Used motorcycle dealers
421140	Used parts, motor vehicle, wholesaling
441210	Used recreational vehicle (RV) dealers
441320	Used tire dealers
421130	Used tires, motor vehicle, wholesaling
441229	Used utility trailer dealers
541618	Utilities management consulting services
332311	Utility buildings, prefabricated metal, manufacturing
326199	Utility containers (e.g., baskets, bins, boxes, buckets, dishpans, pails), plastics (except foam), manufacturing
441229	Utility trailer dealers
532120	Utility trailer rental or leasing
336214	Utility trailers manufacturing
421110	Utility trailers wholesaling
334310	VCR (video cassette recorder) manufacturing
721214	Vacation camps (except campgrounds, day instructional)
115210	Vaccinating livestock (except by veterinarians)
541940	Vaccination services, veterinary
422210	Vaccines wholesaling
332439	Vacuum bottles and jugs manufacturing
336340	Vacuum brake booster, automotive, truck, and bus, manufacturing
443111	Vacuum cleaner stores, household-type
335212	Vacuum cleaners (e.g., canister, handheld, upright) household-type electric, manufacturing
421620	Vacuum cleaners, household-type, wholesaling

333319	Vacuum cleaners, industrial and commercial-type, manufacturing
235950	Vacuum cleaning systems, built-in, construction contractors
333912	Vacuum pumps (except laboratory) manufacturing
339111	Vacuum pumps, laboratory-type, manufacturing
332420	Vacuum tanks, heavy gauge metal, manufacturing
327215	Vacuum tube blanks, glass, made from purchased glass
327212	Vacuum tube blanks, glass, made in glass making plants
334411	Vacuum tubes manufacturing
812930	Valet parking services
421840	Valves (except hydraulic, plumbing, pneumatic) wholesaling
332911	Valves for nuclear applications manufacturing
332911	Valves for water works and municipal water systems manufacturing
336311	Valves, engine, intake and exhaust, manufacturing
332912	Valves, hydraulic and pneumatic, fluid power, manufacturing
421830	Valves, hydraulic and pneumatic, wholesaling
332911	Valves, industrial-type (e.g., check, gate, globe, relief, safety), manufacturing
332919	Valves, inline plumbing and heating (e.g., cutoffs, stop), manufacturing
421720	Valves, plumbing and heating, wholesaling
336213	Van and minivan conversions on purchased chassis
811121	Van conversion shops (except on assembly line or factory basis)
484210	Van lines, moving and storage services
212291	Vanadium ores mining and/or beneficiating
337110	Vanities (except freestanding), stock or custom wood, manufacturing
337110	Vanity tops, wood or plastics laminated on wood, manufacturing

http://www.ntis.gov/naics

485999	Vanpool operation
488999	Vanpools, arrangement of
336112	Vans, commercial and passenger light duty, assembling on chassis of own manufacture
311612	Variety meats, edible organs, made from purchased meats
311611	Variety meats, edible organs, made in slaughtering plants
452990	Variety stores
334415	Varistors manufacturing
325510	Varnishes manufacturing
422950	Varnishes wholesaling
332812	Varnishing metals and metal products for the trade
313320	Varnishing purchased textiles and apparel
327420	Vases (e.g., gypsum, plaster of paris) manufacturing
327215	Vases, glass, made from purchased glass
327212	Vases, glass, made in glass making plants
327112	Vases, pottery (e.g., china, earthenware, stoneware), manufacturing
332420	Vats, heavy gauge metal, manufacturing
332439	Vats, light gauge metal, manufacturing
711110	Vaudeville companies
332999	Vaults (except burial), metal, manufacturing
339995	Vaults (except concrete) manufacturing
311611	Veal carcasses, half carcasses, primal and sub-primal cuts, produced in slaughtering plants
311612	Veal, primal and sub-primal cuts, made from purchased carcasses
325411	Vegetable alkaloids (i.e., basic chemicals) (e.g., caffeine, codeine, morphine, nicotine), manufacturing
111211	Vegetable and melon farming, potato dominant crop, field and seed production

111219	Vegetable and melon farming, vegetable (except potato) and melon dominant crops, field, bedding plants and seed production
111211	Vegetable and potato farming, potato dominant crop, field and seed potato production
111219	Vegetable and potato farming, vegetable (except potato) dominant crops, field, bedding plants and seed production
311421	Vegetable brining
422990	Vegetable cake and meal wholesaling
311421	Vegetable canning
422910	Vegetable dusts and sprays wholesaling
111419	Vegetable farming, grown under cover
311211	Vegetable flour, meal, and powders, made in flour mills
311411	Vegetable juice concentrates, frozen, manufacturing
311421	Vegetable juices canning
311421	Vegetable juices, fresh, manufacturing
445230	Vegetable markets
311223	Vegetable oils (except soybean) made in crushing mills
311225	Vegetable oils made from purchased oils
115114	Vegetable precooling
311221	Vegetable starches manufacturing
311423	Vegetables dehydrating
311421	Vegetables pickling
422490	Vegetables, canned, wholesaling
311991	Vegetables, cut or peeled, fresh, manufacturing
422480	Vegetables, fresh, wholesaling
311411	Vegetables, frozen, manufacturing
422420	Vegetables, frozen, wholesaling
115113	Vegetables, machine harvesting
336991	Vehicle, children's, metal manufacturing
339932	Vehicles, children's (except bicycles and metal tricycles), manufacturing
421920	Vehicles, children's (except bicycles), wholesaling

http://www.ntis.gov/naics

421110	Vehicles, recreational, wholesaling
336321	Vehicular lighting fixtures manufacturing
454210	Vending machine merchandisers, sale of products
333311	Vending machines manufacturing
421440	Vending machines wholesaling
321211	Veneer mills, hardwood
321212	Veneer mills, softwood
421730	Ventilating equipment and supplies (except household-type fans) wholesaling
333412	Ventilating fans, industrial and commercial-type, manufacturing
335211	Ventilation and exhaust fans (except attic fans), household-type, manufacturing
561790	Ventilation duct cleaning services
523910	Venture capital companies
212399	Vermiculite mining and/or beneficiating
327992	Vermiculite, exfoliated, manufacturing
312130	Vermouth manufacturing
332420	Vessels, heavy gauge metal, manufacturing
315299	Vestments, academic and clerical, cut and sewn from purchased fabric (except apparel contractors)
315211	Vestments, academic and clerical, men's and boys', cut and sew apparel contractors
315212	Vestments, academic and clerical, women's and girls', cut and sew apparel contractors
315211	Vests, men's and boys', cut and sew apparel contractors
813410	Veterans' membership organizations
923140	Veterans' affairs offices
813311	Veterans' rights organizations
339112	Veterinarians' instruments and apparatus manufacturing
422210	Veterinarians' medicines wholesaling
421490	Veterinarians' equipment and supplies wholesaling
541940	Veterinarians' offices
541940	Veterinary clinics
325412	Veterinary medicinal preparations manufacturing
541710	Veterinary research and development laboratories or services
541940	Veterinary services
541940	Veterinary testing laboratories
541380	Vibration testing laboratories or services
421410	Video cameras (except household-type) wholesaling
334310	Video cameras, household-type, manufacturing
421620	Video cameras, household-type, wholesaling
334310	Video cassette recorders (VCR) manufacturing
334613	Video cassettes, blank, manufacturing
334612	Video cassettes, pre-recorded, mass reproducing
512191	Video conversion services (i.e., between formats)
532230	Video disc rental for home electronic equipment (e.g., VCR)
713290	Video gambling device concession operators (i.e., supplying and servicing in others' facilities)
713120	Video game arcades (except gambling)
339932	Video game machines (except coin-operated) manufacturing
541921	Video photography services, portrait
512191	Video post-production services
512110	Video production
512110	Video production and distribution
512120	Video productions, distributing
334612	Video tape or disk mass reproducing
532230	Video tape rental for home electronic equipment (e.g., VCR)
532230	Video tape rental stores
451220	Video tape stores
334613	Video tapes, blank, manufacturing
421690	Video tapes, blank, wholesaling
421990	Video tapes, prerecorded, wholesaling

http://www.ntis.gov/naics

541921 Video taping services, special events (e.g., birthdays, weddings)

512199 Videotape libraries, stock footage

311941 Vinegar manufacturing

115112 Vineyard cultivation services

325199 Vinyl acetate (except resins) manufacturing

313320 Vinyl coated fabrics manufacturing

325222 Vinyl fibers and filaments manufacturing

326192 Vinyl floor coverings manufacturing

325211 Vinyl resins manufacturing

421330 Vinyl siding wholesaling

316219 Vinyl upper athletic footwear manufacturing

325211 Vinylidene resins manufacturing

325414 Virus vaccines manufacturing

332212 Vises (except machine tool attachments) manufacturing

621610 Visiting nurse associations

561591 Visitors bureaus

325412 Vitamin preparations manufacturing

446191 Vitamin stores

422210 Vitamins wholesaling

325411 Vitamins, uncompounded, manufacturing

711130 Vocalists, independent

611513 Vocational apprenticeship training

624310 Vocational rehabilitation agencies

624310 Vocational rehabilitation job training facilities (except schools)

624310 Vocational rehabilitation or habilitation services (e.g., job counseling, job training, work experience)

561421 Voice mailbox services

621340 Voice pathologists' offices (e.g., centers, clinics)

212399 Volcanic ash mining and/or beneficiating

421610 Voltage regulators (except motor vehicle) wholesaling

336322 Voltage regulators for internal combustion engines manufacturing

334413 Voltage regulators, integrated circuits, manufacturing

334515 Voltmeters manufacturing

813212 Voluntary health organizations

624229 Volunteer housing repair organizations

333313 Voting machines manufacturing

421850 Voting machines wholesaling

333220 Vulcanizing machinery manufacturing

541511 WEB (i.e., internet) page design services, custom

333295 Wafer processing equipment, semiconductor, manufacturing

321219 Waferboard manufacturing

334413 Wafers (semiconductor devices) manufacturing

311412 Waffles, frozen, manufacturing

561421 Wakeup call services

333921 Walkways, moving, manufacturing

235210 Wall covering or removal construction contractors

422950 Wall coverings (e.g., fabric, plastic) wholesaling

327122 Wall tile, ceramic, manufacturing

421310 Wallboard wholesaling

327420 Wallboard, gypsum, manufacturing

316993 Wallets (except metal) manufacturing

339911 Wallets, precious metal, manufacturing

444120 Wallpaper and wall coverings stores

322222 Wallpaper made from purchased papers or other materials

422950 Wallpaper wholesaling

111335 Walnut farming

452910 Warehouse clubs (i.e., food and general merchandise)

332311 Warehouses, prefabricated metal, manufacturing

493190 Warehousing (except farm products, general merchandise, refrigerated)

493110 Warehousing (including foreign trade zones), general merchandise

493110 Warehousing and storage, general merchandise

813910 Warehousing associations

493130 Warehousing, farm products (except refrigerated)

493120	Warehousing, refrigerated
531130	Warehousing, self storage
421730	Warm air heating equipment wholesaling
315228	Warmup suits, men's and boys', cut and sewn from purchased fabric (except apparel contractors)
315239	Warmup suits, women's, misses', and girls', cut and sewn from purchased fabric (except apparel contractors)
313249	Warp fabrics knitting
333292	Warping machinery manufacturing
524128	Warranty insurance carriers (e.g., appliance, automobile, homeowners, product), direct
315211	Washable service apparel (e.g., barbers', hospital, professional), men's and boys', cut and sew apparel contractors
315225	Washable service apparel (e.g., barbers', hospital, professional), men's and boys', cut and sewn from purchased fabric (except apparel contractors)
315212	Washable service apparel, women's and girls', cut and sew apparel contractors
315239	Washable service apparel, women's, misses', and girls', cut and sewn from purchased fabric (except apparel contractors)
332722	Washers, metal, manufacturing
335224	Washing machines, household-type, manufacturing
333312	Washing machines, laundry (except household-type), manufacturing
561720	Washroom sanitation services
562213	Waste (except sewage) treatment facilities, nonhazardous
562119	Waste (except solid and hazardous) collection services
562119	Waste (except solid and hazardous) hauling, local
562112	Waste collection services, hazardous
562111	Waste collection services, nonhazardous solid
221320	Waste collection, treatment, and disposal through a sewer system
562213	Waste disposal combustors or incinerators, nonhazardous solid
562211	Waste disposal facilities, hazardous
562212	Waste disposal landfills, nonhazardous solid
234990	Waste disposal plant construction
484220	Waste hauling, hazardous, local
484230	Waste hauling, hazardous, long-distance
562112	Waste hauling, local, hazardous
562111	Waste hauling, local, nonhazardous solid
484220	Waste hauling, nonhazardous, local
484230	Waste hauling, nonhazardous, long-distance
924110	Waste management program administration
421930	Waste materials wholesaling
562920	Waste recovery facilities
562112	Waste transfer stations, hazardous
562111	Waste transfer stations, nonhazardous solid
562211	Waste treatment facilities, hazardous
562211	Waste treatment plants, hazardous
322214	Wastebaskets, fiber made from purchased paperboard
316993	Watch bands (except metal) manufacturing
339914	Watch bands, metal (except precious), manufacturing
339911	Watch bands, precious metal, manufacturing
335912	Watch batteries manufacturing
327215	Watch crystals made from purchased glass
326199	Watch crystals, plastics, manufacturing
334518	Watch jewels manufacturing
811490	Watch repair shops without retailing new watches
448310	Watch shops
334518	Watches and parts (except crystals) manufacturing
421940	Watches and parts wholesaling
333415	Water (i.e., drinking) coolers, mechanical, manufacturing
325412	Water (i.e., drinking) decontamination or purification tablets manufacturing

337910	Water bed mattresses manufacturing
339942	Water colors, artist's, manufacturing
561990	Water conditioning services
924110	Water control and quality program administration
421740	Water coolers, mechanical, wholesaling
221310	Water distribution for irrigation
333319	Water heaters (except boilers), commercial-type, manufacturing
421720	Water heaters (except electric) wholesaling
335228	Water heaters (including nonelectric), household-type, manufacturing
421620	Water heaters, electric, wholesaling
326220	Water hoses, rubber or plastics, manufacturing
234910	Water main and line construction
713110	Water parks, amusement
333319	Water purification equipment manufacturing
334513	Water quality monitoring and control systems manufacturing
325510	Water repellant coatings for wood, concrete and masonry manufacturing
315228	Water resistant jackets and windbreakers, nontailored, men's and boys', cut and sewn from purchased fabric (except apparel contractors)
315228	Water resistant outerwear (except overcoats), men's and boys', cut and sewn from purchased fabric (except apparel contractors)
315239	Water resistant outerwear (except overcoats), women's, misses', and girls', cut and sewn from purchased fabric (except apparel contractors)
315291	Water resistant outerwear infants', cut and sewn from purchased fabric (except apparel contractors)
315212	Water resistant outerwear, women's, girls', and infants', cut and sew apparel contractors
315222	Water resistant overcoats, men's and boys', cut and sewn from purchased fabric (except apparel contractors)
315234	Water resistant overcoats, women's, misses', and girls', cut and sewn from purchased fabric (except apparel contractors)
315211	Water resistant, men's and boys', cut and sew apparel contractors
454390	Water softener service providers, direct selling
421720	Water softening and conditioning equipment wholesaling
422690	Water softening compounds wholesaling
561990	Water softening services
445299	Water stores, bottled
221310	Water supply systems
332420	Water tanks, heavy gauge metal, manufacturing
483212	Water taxi services
332913	Water traps manufacturing
221310	Water treatment and distribution
333319	Water treatment equipment manufacturing
421830	Water treatment equipment, industrial, wholesaling
421850	Water treatment equipment, municipal, wholesaling
234990	Water treatment plant construction
221310	Water treatment plants
235810	Water well drilling (except oil or gas field water intake) construction contractors
333132	Water well drilling machinery manufacturing
312111	Water, artificially carbonated, manufacturing
422490	Water, bottled (except water treating), wholesaling
325998	Water, distilled, manufacturing
312111	Water, flavored, manufacturing
312112	Water, naturally carbonated, purifying and bottling
315228	Water-repellent outerwear (except overcoats), men's and boys', cut and sewn from purchased fabric (except apparel contractors)

315239	Water-repellent outerwear (except overcoats), women's, misses', and girls', cut and sewn from purchased fabric (except apparel contractors)
315291	Water-repellent outerwear, infants', cut and sewn from purchased fabric (except apparel contractors)
315211	Water-repellent outerwear, men's and boys', cut and sew apparel contractors
315212	Water-repellent outerwear, women's, girls', and infants', cut and sew apparel contractors
315222	Water-repellent overcoats, men's and boys', cut and sewn from purchased fabric (except apparel contractors
315234	Water-repellent overcoats, women's, misses', and girls', cut and sewn from purchased fabric (except apparel contractors)
712190	Waterfalls (i.e., natural wonder tourist attractions)
488310	Waterfront terminal operation (e.g., docks, piers, wharves)
111219	Watermelon farming, field, bedding plant and seed production
334514	Watermeters, consumption registering, manufacturing
315999	Waterproof outerwear cut and sewn from purchased fabric (except apparel contractors)
315211	Waterproof outerwear, men's and boys', cut and sew apparel contractors
315999	Waterproof outerwear, rubberizing fabric and manufacturing outerwear
315212	Waterproof outerwear, women's, girls', and infants', cut and sew apparel contractors
313320	Waterproofing apparel, fabrics and textile products (e.g., oiling, rubberizing, waxing, varnishing)
713990	Waterslides (i.e., amusement rides)
332911	Waterworks and municipal water system valves manufacturing

334515	Watt-hour meters, electric, manufacturing
334515	Wattmeters manufacturing
713940	Wave pools
712110	Wax museums
322222	Waxed paper for nonpackaging applications made from purchased paper
322221	Waxed paper for packaging applications made from purchased paper
422690	Waxes (except petroleum) wholesaling
324199	Waxes, petroleum, made from refined petroleum
324110	Waxes, petroleum, made in petroleum refineries
325612	Waxes, polishing (e.g., floor, furniture), manufacturing
313320	Waxing purchased textiles and apparel
115114	Waxing, fruits or vegetables
112210	Weaning pig operations
336992	Weapons, self-propelled, manufacturing
541990	Weather forecasting services
924120	Weather research program administration
332321	Weatherstrip, metal, manufacturing
314999	Weatherstripping made from purchased textiles
313221	Weaving and finishing narrow fabrics
313210	Weaving and finishing of broadwoven fabrics (except rugs, tire fabric)
313210	Weaving broadwoven fabrics (except rugs, tire fabrics)
313210	Weaving broadwoven felts
333292	Weaving machinery manufacturing
313221	Weaving narrow fabrics
314110	Weaving rugs, carpets, and mats
313221	Webbing weaving
812990	Wedding chapels (except churches)
315212	Wedding dresses, women's, cut and sew apparel contractors

721214	Wilderness camps
813312	Wildlife preservation organizations
712190	Wildlife sanctuaries
337125	Willow furniture (except upholstered), household-type, manufacturing
333923	Winches manufacturing
421830	Winches wholesaling
313112	Winding purchased yarn
313112	Winding, spooling, beaming and rewinding of purchased yarn
333611	Windmills, electric power, generation-type, manufacturing
333111	Windmills, farm-type, manufacturing
235510	Window and door construction contractors
325612	Window cleaning preparations manufacturing
561720	Window cleaning services
541890	Window dressing or trimming services, store
332321	Window frames and sash, metal, manufacturing
321911	Window frames and sash, wood and covered wood, manufacturing
332618	Window screening, woven, made from purchased wire
332321	Window screens, metal frame, manufacturing
337920	Window shades (except awnings) manufacturing
421220	Window shades and blinds wholesaling
811122	Window tinting, automotive
442291	Window treatment stores
321911	Window units, wood and covered wood, manufacturing
421310	Windows and window frames wholesaling
326199	Windows and window frames, plastics, manufacturing
332321	Windows, metal, manufacturing
321911	Windows, wood and covered wood, manufacturing
336322	Windshield washer pumps, automotive, truck, and bus, manufacturing

336399	Windshield wiper blades and refills manufacturing
336322	Windshield wiper systems, automotive, truck, and bus, manufacturing
326199	Windshields, plastics, manufacturing
312130	Wine coolers manufacturing
422820	Wine coolers, alcoholic, wholesaling
445310	Wine shops, packaged
312130	Wineries
312130	Wines manufacturing
422820	Wines wholesaling
312130	Wines, cooking, manufacturing
336399	Wipers, windshield, automotive, truck, and bus, manufacturing
421510	Wire (except insulated) wholesaling
421510	Wire and cable (except electrical) wholesaling
333298	Wire and cable insulating machinery manufacturing
331422	Wire cloth made from purchased copper in wire drawing plants
331422	Wire cloth, copper, made in integrated secondary smelting and drawing plants
514110	Wire photo services
331111	Wire products, iron or steel, made in steel mills
331222	Wire products, iron or steel, made in wire drawing plants
421510	Wire rope (except insulated) wholesaling
421510	Wire screening wholesaling
331319	Wire screening, aluminum, made in integrated secondary smelting and drawing plants
561422	Wire services (i.e., telemarketing services), floral
514110	Wire services, news
331319	Wire, armored, made in aluminum wire drawing plants
331319	Wire, bare, made in aluminum wire drawing plants
331422	Wire, copper (except mechanical) (e.g., armored, bare, insulated), made from purchased copper in wire drawing plants

331422	Wire, copper (except mechanical) (e.g., armored, bare, insulated), made in integrated secondary smelting and drawing plants
331319	Wire, insulated, made in aluminum wire drawing plants
421610	Wire, insulated, wholesaling
331222	Wire, iron or steel (e.g., armored, bare, insulated), made in wire drawing plants
331421	Wire, mechanical, copper and copper alloy, made from purchased copper or in integrated secondary smelting and rolling, drawing or extruding plants
331491	Wire, nonferrous metals (except aluminum, copper), made from purchased nonferrous metals (except aluminum, copper) in wire drawing plants
331491	Wire, nonferrous metals (except aluminum, copper), made in integrated secondary smelting mills and wire drawing plants
513330	Wired telecommunication resellers
333518	Wiredrawing and fabricating machinery and equipment (except dies) manufacturing
513330	Wireless telecommunication resellers (except satellite)
513322	Wireless telephone communications carriers (except satellite)
336322	Wiring harness and ignition sets for internal combustion engines manufacturing
421610	Wiring supplies wholesaling
422330	Women's and children's clothing accessories wholesaling
422330	Women's clothing wholesaling
813410	Women's auxiliaries
813410	Women's clubs
321213	Wood I-joists manufacturing
113310	Wood chipping in the field
332213	Wood cutting saw blades manufacturing
325191	Wood distillates manufacturing
321911	Wood door frames and sash manufacturing

421310	Wood fencing wholesaling
325510	Wood fillers manufacturing
235520	Wood flooring construction contractors
321918	Wood flooring manufacturing
421310	Wood flooring wholesaling
337121	Wood framed furniture, upholstered, household-type, manufacturing
321918	Wood moldings (e.g., pre-finished, unfinished), clear and finger joint, manufacturing
325191	Wood oils manufacturing
421990	Wood products (e.g., chips, posts, shavings, ties) wholesaling
322110	Wood pulp manufacturing
422990	Wood pulp wholesaling
421310	Wood shingles wholesaling
321918	Wood shutters manufacturing
421310	Wood siding wholesaling
333414	Wood stoves manufacturing
422690	Wood treating preparations wholesaling
321911	Wood window frames and sash manufacturing
442299	Wood-burning stove stores
321999	Woodenware, kitchen and household, manufacturing
421830	Woodworking machinery wholesaling
333210	Woodworking machines (except handheld) manufacturing
313210	Wool fabrics, broadwoven, weaving
313312	Wool tops and noils manufacturing
422590	Wool tops and noils wholesaling
314999	Wool waste processing
422590	Wool, raw, wholesaling
311941	Worcestershire sauce manufacturing
333313	Word processing equipment, dedicated, manufacturing
561410	Word processing services
624229	Work (sweat) equity home construction organizations
337127	Work benches manufacturing
422320	Work clothing, men's and boys', wholesaling
624310	Work experience centers (i.e., sheltered workshops)
315191	Work gloves and mittens, knit, made in apparel knitting mills

315992	Work gloves, leather (except apparel contractors), manufacturing
315211	Work gloves, leather, men's and boys', cut and sew apparel contractors
315212	Work gloves, leather, women's and girls', cut and sew apparel contractors
315225	Work pants (except dungarees, jeans), men's and boys', cut and sewn from purchased fabric (except apparel contractors)
315211	Work pants, men's and boys', cut and sew apparel contractors
315211	Work shirts, men's and boys', cut and sew apparel contractors
315225	Work shirts, men's and boys', cut and sewn from purchased fabric (except apparel contractors)
923130	Workers' compensation program administration
721310	Workers' camps
525190	Workers' compensation insurance funds
721310	Workers' dormitories
624310	Workshops for persons with disabilities
334111	Workstations, computer, manufacturing
928120	World Bank
813319	World peace and understanding advocacy organizations
112990	Worm production
333993	Wrapping (i.e., packaging) machinery manufacturing
422130	Wrapping paper (except giftwrap) wholesaling
488410	Wrecker services (i.e., towing services), motor vehicle
332212	Wrenches, handtools, nonpowered, manufacturing
333991	Wrenches, impact, handheld power-driven, manufacturing
711219	Wrestlers, independent professional
711510	Writers, independent (freelance)
813410	Writing clubs
325998	Writing inks manufacturing
325992	X-ray film and plates, sensitized, manufacturing

334517	X-ray generators manufacturing
541380	X-ray inspection services
334517	X-ray irradiation equipment manufacturing
621512	X-ray laboratories, medical or dental
421450	X-ray machines and parts, medical and dental, wholesaling
334517	X-ray tubes manufacturing
324110	Xylene made in petroleum refineries
325110	Xylene made from refined petroleum or liquid hydrocarbons
336612	Yacht building, not done in shipyards
713930	Yacht clubs with marinas
713990	Yacht clubs without marinas
336611	Yachts built in shipyards
422310	Yard goods, textile (except burlap, felt), wholesaling
321999	Yardsticks, wood, manufacturing
313111	Yarn spinning mills
313111	Yarn spun from purchased fiber
333292	Yarn texturizing machines manufacturing
313112	Yarn throwing, twisting, and winding of purchased yarn
313111	Yarn, carpet and rug, spun from purchased fiber
325221	Yarn, cellulosic filament, manufacturing
325221	Yarn, cellulosic filament, manufacturing and texturizing
327212	Yarn, fiberglass, made in glass making plants
325222	Yarn, noncellulosic fiber and filament, manufacturing
325222	Yarn, noncellulosic fiber and filament, manufacturing and texturizing
422990	Yarns wholesaling
511199	Yearbook publishers
511199	Yearbook publishers and printing combined
323112	Yearbooks flexographic printing without publishing
323111	Yearbooks gravure printing without publishing
323110	Yearbooks lithographic (offset) printing without publishing

http://www.ntis.gov/naics

323119 Yearbooks printing (except flexographic, gravure, lithographic, screen) without publishing
323113 Yearbooks screen printing without publishing
311999 Yeast manufacturing
422490 Yeast wholesaling
311511 Yogurt (except frozen) manufacturing
311514 Yogurt mix manufacturing
422430 Yogurt wholesaling
311520 Yogurt, frozen, manufacturing
624110 Youth centers (except recreational only)
813410 Youth civic clubs
813410 Youth farming organizations
624110 Youth guidance organizations
721199 Youth hotels
813410 Youth scouting organizations
624110 Youth self-help organizations
813410 Youth social clubs
713990 Youth sports leagues or teams

325131 Zinc based pigments manufacturing
325188 Zinc compounds, not specified elsewhere by process, manufacturing
332999 Zinc foil and leaf not made in rolling mills
212231 Zinc ore mine site development for own account
212231 Zinc ores mining and/or beneficiating
325188 Zinc oxide (except pigments) manufacturing
331419 Zinc refining, primary
339993 Zippers (i.e., slide fasteners) manufacturing
422310 Zippers wholesaling
212299 Zirconium ores mining and/or beneficiating
331419 Zirconium refining, primary
925120 Zoning boards and commissions
712130 Zoological gardens
712130 Zoos